Classics Edition

Algebra
AND **Trigonometry**

Functions and Applications

Paul A. Foerster

PEARSON

Prentice
Hall

Boston, Massachusetts
Upper Saddle River, New Jersey

Paul A. Foerster has taught mathematics at Alamo Heights High School in San Antonio, Texas since 1961. In that same year he received his teaching certificate from Texas A&M University. His B.S. degree in Chemical Engineering and M.A. degree in Mathematics are from the University of Texas. Among many honors, he was awarded the Presidential Award for Excellence in Mathematics Teaching in 1983.

To A.W. Foerster, who helped me to understand the real world, to Admiral Rickover, who taught me how to write about it, and to my wife, who helps me to live in it.

ISBN 0-13-165710-0

12 13 14 15 V031 15 14

Foreword

Algebra and Trigonometry—Functions and Applications is designed for a course in intermediate algebra, advanced algebra, and trigonometry. The book can be used in two different ways:

1. As an algebra and trigonometry book, with applications,
2. As an applications book, with supporting algebra and trigonometry.

In either case, there are two possible sequences of presentation:

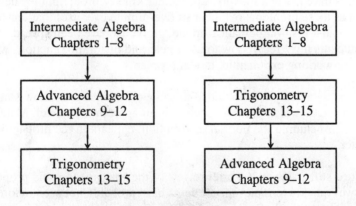

Applications are handled by creating mathematical models of phenomena in the real world. Students must select a kind of function that fits a given situation, and derive an equation that suits the information in the problem. The equation is then used to predict values of y when x is given or values of x when y is given. Sometimes students must use the results of their work to make interpretations about the real world, such as what "slope" means, or why there cannot be people as small as in *Gulliver's Travels*. The problems require the students to use *many* mathematical concepts in the *same* problem. This is in contrast to the traditional "word problems"

of elementary algebra, in which the same one concept is used in many problems.

The computer is assumed to be a normal part of students' classroom experience rather than simply a novelty. For the most part, students are expected to use existing computer programs, notably computer graphic programs, rather than write their own. A disk accompanying the Teacher's Resource Book contains programs written by the author that are sufficient for the purposes of this text. You are, however, urged to seek out commercially-available software that is faster and more user-friendly.

Ideas for using calculators have caused substantial differences in presentation of certain topics. For instance, exponential equations are solved at the beginning of Chapter 6 by iterative methods on the calculators. Logarithms then arise naturally as a quicker way to get the unknown exponent. Presented this way, there is no doubt in the students' minds that a logarithm is an exponent! The calculator thus leads to a better understanding of theoretical concepts and is not simply a way to work old problems quicker.

Pedagogically, there are many opportunities for review of previous concepts. One major way this review is accomplished is through the "Do These Quickly" problems at the beginning of each problem set. Once the students have learned to work a particular kind of problem, they develop speed as these problems reappear in five-minute exercises that concentrate only on answers. Mathematical-model problems have been spread out so the students must recall how to use linear and quadratic functions while they are working exponential model problems.

Work on data analysis is included in some problem sets to show students how to decide which kind of function is an appropriate model. Material on statistics, including the normal distribution, appears in the probability chapter.

The text still starts with a brief review of the basic axioms and properties. It moves quickly to topics the students have probably not seen before, at least in the method of presentation. The purpose is two-fold. First, students should not feel as if most of the course is spent reviewing elementary algebra. Second, the presentation emphasizes the role of algebra and trigonometry as the foundation for calculus, rather than as the completion of elementary algebra. By presenting both algebra and trigonometry as the study of classes of functions, students learn the essential unity of the two subjects.

Henry Pollack of Bell Telephone Labs claims that there are just two kinds of numbers: "real" numbers such as encountered in everyday life, and "fake" numbers such as encountered in most mathematics classes! Since this book has many problems involving untidy decimals ("real" numbers), a calculator or computer are called for where appropriate. There are also problems that have small-integer answers ("fake" numbers) so that students may gain confidence in their work when they are just learning a new technique.

Since all educators share the responsibility of teaching students to read and write, there are discovery exercises so that students may wrestle with a new concept before it is reinforced by classroom discussion. The students are helped with this reading by the fact that much of the wording came from the mouths of my own students. Special thanks go to Susan Cook, Brad Foster, and Nancy Carnes, whose good class notes supplied input for certain sections. Students Lewis Donzis and David Fey wrote computer programs for some of the problems.

Thanks go to instructors in Florida, Illinois, Pennsylvania, South Dakota, Texas, and Virginia for pilot testing the original materials. Special thanks go to Bob Enenstein and his instructors in California for pilot testing the second edition. The text reflects comments from review and classroom testing by Charley Brown, Sharon Sasch Button, Pat Causey, Loyce Collenback, Bob Davies, Walter DeBill, Rich Dubsky, Michelle Edge, Sandra Frasier, Byron Gill, Pat Johnson, Michael Keeton, Carol Kipps, Bill McNabb, Shirley Scheiner, Ann Singleton, Chuck Straley, Rhetta Tatsch, Joel Teller, Susan Thomas, Kay Thompson, Zalman Usiskin, Jim Wieboldt, Marv Wielard, Mercille Wisakowsky, Martha Zelinka, and Isabel Zsohar. Calvin Butterball and Phoebe Small appear with the kind permission of their parents, Richard and Josephine Andree.

Paul A. Foerster

Contents

number line

dependent and
independent variables

linear functions with
positive and negative
slopes

intersection of linear
functions

direct power variation

ellipse and hyperbola

cubic function

linear and geometric
series

bell-shaped curve

cosine, tangent, and
secant

secant, cosine, and tangent

14 PROPERTIES OF TRIGONOMETRIC AND CIRCULAR FUNCTIONS 799

15 TRIANGLE PROBLEMS 862

vector addition

A resource for problem solving strategies and other skills
you may want to review during this course.

Photograph Acknowledgements

Australian Information Service: 304
Joe Baraban: 322
The Bettmann Archive: 402
Daniel S. Brody Stock, Boston: 709
John Colwell/Grant Heilman Photography: 110, 219, 631
José Cuervo: 72
E. R. Degginger/Bruce Coleman Inc.: 433
Diamond Information Center, N.W. Ayer ABH International: 398
Richard H. Dohrmann*: 228; 559 left; 559 right, courtesy Fidelity Savings &
Loan Association
Howard Hall/Tom Stack & Associates: 401
Grant Heilman: 307, 394, 437
Ira Kirschenbaum/Stock, Boston: 306
Keith Murakami/Tom Stack & Associates: 669
© Bill Pierce/Rainbow: 666
Bil Plummer*: 799
F. Roe/Camera 5: 513
Joe Scherschel, *Life* Magazine, © 1957 Time Inc.: 413
Peter Southwick/Stock, Boston: 50
U.S. Department of the Interior, Bureau of Reclamation: 173
Yerkes Observatory: 460

*Photographs provided expressly for the publisher. All other photographs by
Addison-Wesley staff.

Contrary to former views of mathematics, numbers were **invented** by people, rather than simply being discovered. In this book you will see how things invented mainly to form a complete mathematical system can be used to describe things that happen in the real world. First, however, you must be sure that you and your instructor are speaking the same language! The first chapter is designed with this purpose in mind.

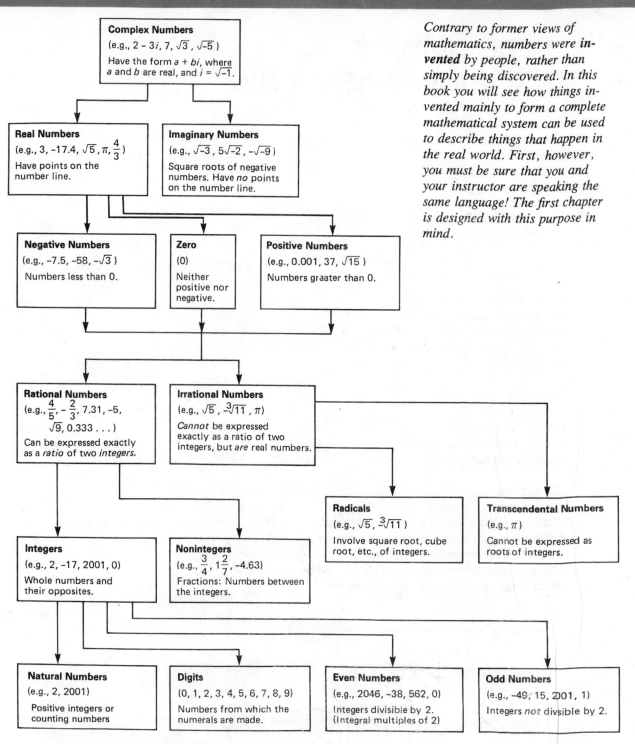

Complex Numbers

(e.g., $2 - 3i$, 7, $\sqrt{3}$, $\sqrt{-5}$)

Have the form $a + bi$, where a and b are real, and $i = \sqrt{-1}$.

Real Numbers

(e.g., 3, -17.4, $\sqrt{5}$, π, $\frac{4}{3}$)

Have points on the number line.

Imaginary Numbers

(e.g., $\sqrt{-3}$, $5\sqrt{-2}$, $-\sqrt{-9}$)

Square roots of negative numbers. Have *no* points on the number line.

Negative Numbers

(e.g., -7.5, -58, $-\sqrt{3}$)

Numbers less than 0.

Zero

(0)

Neither positive nor negative.

Positive Numbers

(e.g., 0.001, 37, $\sqrt{15}$)

Numbers greater than 0.

Rational Numbers

(e.g., $\frac{4}{5}$, $-\frac{2}{3}$, 7.31, -5, $\sqrt{9}$, $0.333\ldots$)

Can be expressed exactly as a *ratio* of two *integers*.

Irrational Numbers

(e.g., $\sqrt{5}$, $-\sqrt[3]{11}$, π)

Cannot be expressed exactly as a ratio of two integers, but *are* real numbers.

Radicals

(e.g., $\sqrt{5}$, $\sqrt[3]{11}$)

Involve square root, cube root, etc., of integers.

Transcendental Numbers

(e.g., π)

Cannot be expressed as roots of integers.

Integers

(e.g., 2, -17, 2001, 0)

Whole numbers and their opposites.

Nonintegers

(e.g., $\frac{3}{4}$, $1\frac{2}{7}$, -4.63)

Fractions: Numbers between the integers.

Natural Numbers

(e.g., 2, 2001)

Positive integers or counting numbers

Digits

(0, 1, 2, 3, 4, 5, 6, 7, 8, 9)

Numbers from which the numerals are made.

Even Numbers

(e.g., 2046, -38, 562, 0)

Integers divisible by 2. (Integral multiples of 2)

Odd Numbers

(e.g., -49, 15, 2001, 1)

Integers *not* divisible by 2.

From previous work in mathematics you should recall the names of different kinds of numbers (positive, even, irrational, etc.). In this section you will refresh your memory so that you will know the exact meaning of these names.

Objective:
Given the name of a set of numbers, provide an example; or given a number, name the sets to which it belongs.

There are two major sets of numbers you will deal with in this course, the *real* numbers and the *imaginary* numbers. The real numbers are given this name because they are used for "real" things such as measuring and counting. The imaginary numbers are square roots of negative numbers. They are useful, too, but you must learn more mathematics to see why.

The real numbers are all numbers which you can plot on a number line (see Figure 1-1). They can be broken into subsets in several ways. For instance, there are positive and negative real numbers, integers and non-integers, rational and irrational real numbers, and so forth. The diagram facing this page shows some subsets of the set of real numbers.

The numbers in the diagram were invented in *reverse* order. The natural (or "counting") numbers came first because mathematics was first used for counting. The negative numbers (those less than zero) were invented so that there would always be answers to subtraction problems. The rational numbers were invented to provide answers to division problems, and the irrational ones came when it was shown that numbers such as $\sqrt{2}$ could not be expressed as a ratio of two integers.

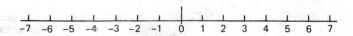

The real number line

Figure 1-1

Other operations you will invent, such as taking logarithms and cosines, lead to irrational numbers which go beyond even extracting roots. These are called "transcendental" numbers, meaning "going beyond." When all of these various kinds of numbers are put together, you get the set of *real* numbers. The imaginary numbers were invented because no real number squared equals a negative number. Later, you will see that the real and imaginary numbers are themselves simply subsets of a larger set, called the "complex numbers."

The following exercise is designed to help you accomplish the objectives of this section.

EXERCISE 1-1

1. Write a definition for each of the following sets of numbers. Try to do this *without* referring to the diagram opposite page 1. Then look to make sure you are correct.
    a. {integers}   b. {digits}
    c. {even numbers}   d. {positive numbers}
    e. {negative numbers} f. {rational numbers}
    g. {irrational numbers} h. {imaginary numbers}
    i. {real numbers}   j. {natural numbers}
    k. {counting numbers} l. {transcendental nos.}

2. Write an example of each type of number mentioned in Problem 1.

3. Copy the chart at right. Put a check mark in each box for which the number on the left of the chart belongs to the set across the top.

4. Write another name for {natural numbers}.

5. Which of the sets of numbers in Problem 1 do you suppose was the *first* to be invented? Why?

6. One of the sets of numbers in Problem 1 contains all but one of the others as subsets.
    a. Which one *contains* the others?
    b. Which one is left out?

7. Do decimals such as 2.718 represent *rational* numbers or *irrational* numbers? Explain.

8. Do repeating decimals such as 2.3333 . . . represent *rational* numbers or *irrational* numbers? Explain.

    ·t real number is neither positive nor negative?

	Integers	Digits	Even Numbers	Positive Numbers	Negative Numbers	Rational Numbers	Irrational Numbers	Imaginary Numbers	Real Numbers	Natural Numbers	Counting Numbers	Transcendental Numbers
a. 5												
b. 2/3												
c. −7												
d. $\sqrt{3}$												
e. $\sqrt{16}$												
f. $\sqrt{-16}$												
g. $\sqrt{-15}$												
h. 44												
i. π												
j. 1.765												
k. −10000												
l. $-1\frac{1}{2}$												
m. $-\sqrt{6}$												
n. 0												
o. 1												
p. 1/9												

1-2 | THE FIELD AXIOMS

From previous mathematics courses you probably remember names such as "Distributive Property," "Reflexive Property," and "Multiplication Property of Zero." Some of these properties, called *axioms*, are accepted without proof and are used as starting points for working with numbers.

From a small number of rather obvious axioms, you will derive all the other properties you will need. In this section you will concentrate on the axioms that apply to the *operations* with numbers such as $+$ and $\times$. In Section 1-7 you will find the axioms that apply to the *relationships* between numbers, such as $=$ and $<$.

Objective:

Given the name of an axiom that applies to $+$ or $\times$, give an example that shows you understand the meaning of the axiom; and vice versa.

There are eleven axioms that apply to adding and multiplying real numbers. These are called the *Field Axioms,* and are listed in the following table. If you already feel familiar with these axioms, you may go right to the problems in Exercise 1-2. If not, then read on!

THE FIELD AXIOMS

CLOSURE

{real numbers} is *closed* under addition and under multiplication. That is, if x and y are real numbers, then

$x + y$ is a *unique, real* number,
xy is a *unique, real* number.

COMMUTATIVITY

Addition and multiplication of real numbers are *commutative* operations. That is, if x and y are real numbers, then

$x + y$ and $y + x$ are *equal* to each other,
xy and yx are equal to each other.

ASSOCIATIVITY

Addition and multiplication of real numbers are *associative* operations. That is, if x, y, and z are real numbers, then

$(x + y) + z$ and $x + (y + z)$ are *equal* to each other.
$(xy)z$ and $x(yz)$ are *equal* to each other.

DISTRIBUTIVITY

Multiplication *distributes* over addition. That is, if x, y, and z are real numbers, then

$x(y + z)$ and $xy + xz$ are *equal* to each other.

IDENTITY ELEMENTS

{real numbers} contains:

A *unique* identity element for *addition,* namely 0. (Because $x + 0 = x$ for any real number x.)

A *unique* identity element for *multiplication,* namely 1. (Because $x \cdot 1 = x$ for any real number x.)

INVERSES

{real numbers} contains:

A *unique additive* inverse for every real number x. (Meaning that every real number x has a real number $-x$ such that $x + (-x) = 0$.)

A *unique multiplicative* inverse for every real number x except zero.

(Meaning that every non-zero number x has a real number $\frac{1}{x}$ such that $x \cdot \frac{1}{x} = 1$.)

Notes:

1. Any set that obeys all eleven of these axioms is a *field*.
2. The eleven Field Axioms come in 5 pairs, one of each pair being for addition and the other for multiplication. The Distributive Axiom expresses a relationship between these two operations.
3. The properties $x + 0 = x$ and $x \cdot 1 = x$ are sometimes called the "Addition Property of 0" and the "Multiplication Property of 1," respectively, for obvious reasons.
4. The number $-x$ is called, "the *opposite* of x," "the *additive inverse* of x," or "negative x."
5. The number $\frac{1}{x}$ is called the "multiplicative inverse of x," or the "reciprocal of x."

Closure —By saying that a set is "closed" under an operation, you mean that you cannot get an answer that is *out* of the set by performing that operation on numbers *in* the set. For example, {0, 1} is closed under multiplication because $0 \times 0 = 0$, $0 \times 1 = 0$, $1 \times 0 = 0$, and $1 \times 1 = 1$. All the answers are *unique,* and are *in* the given set. This set is *not* closed under addition because $1 + 1 = 2$, and 2 is *not* in the set. It is not closed under the operation "taking the square root" since there are *two* different square roots of 1: $+1$ and -1.

Commutativity—The word "commute" comes from the Latin word "commutare," which means "to exchange." People who travel back and forth between home and work are called "commuters" because they regularly exchange positions. The fact that addition and multiplication are commutative operations is somewhat unusual. Many operations such as subtraction and exponentiation (raising to powers) are *not* commutative. For example,

$$2 - 5 \text{ does } not \text{ equal } 5 - 2,$$

and

$$2^3 \text{ does } not \text{ equal } 3^2.$$

Indeed, most operations in the real world are not commutative. Putting on your shoes and socks (in that order) produces a far different result from putting on your socks and shoes!

Associativity—You can remember what this axiom states by remembering that to "associate" means to "group." Addition and multiplication are associative, as shown by

$$(2 + 3) + 4 = 9 \quad \text{and} \quad 2 + (3 + 4) = 9.$$

But subtraction is *not* associative. For example,

$$(2 - 3) - 4 = -5 \quad \text{and} \quad 2 - (3 - 4) = 3.$$

Distributivity—Parentheses in an expression such as $2 \times (3 + 4)$ mean, "Do what is inside *first*." But you don't *have* to do $3 + 4$ first. You could "distribute" a 2 to each term inside the parentheses, getting $2 \times 3 + 2 \times 4$. The Distributive Axiom expresses the fact that you get the same answer either way. That is,

$$2 \times (3 + 4) = 14 \quad \text{and} \quad 2 \times 3 + 2 \times 4 = 14.$$

Note that multiplication does *not* distribute over multiplication. For example,

$$2 \times (3 \times 4) \quad \text{does } not \text{ equal} \quad 2 \times 3 \times 2 \times 4,$$

as you can easily check by doing the arithmetic.

Identity Elements—The numbers 0 and 1 are called "identity elements" for adding and multiplying, respectively, since a number comes out "identical" if you add 0 or multiply by 1. For example,

$$5 + 0 = 5 \quad \text{and} \quad 5 \times 1 = 5.$$

Inverses—A number is said to be an *inverse* of another number for a certain operation if it "undoes" (or inverts) what the other number did. For example, $\frac{1}{3}$ is the multiplicative inverse of 3. If you start with 5 and multiply by 3 you get

$$5 \times 3 = 15.$$

Multiplying the answer, 15, by $\frac{1}{3}$ gives

$$15 \times \frac{1}{3} = 5,$$

which "undoes" or "inverts" the multiplication by 3. It is easy to tell if two numbers are *multiplicative inverses* of each other because their product is always equal to 1, the multiplicative identity element. For example,

$$3 \times \frac{1}{3} = 1.$$

Similarly, two numbers are *additive inverses* of each other if adding them to each other gives 0, the additive identity element. For example, $\frac{5}{7}$ and $-\frac{5}{7}$ are additive inverses of each other because

$$\tfrac{5}{7} + (-\tfrac{5}{7}) = 0.$$

The following exercise is designed to familiarize you with the names and meanings of the Field Axioms.

EXERCISE 1-2

Do These Quickly

The following problems are intended to refresh your skills. Some problems come from the last section, and others probe your general knowledge of mathematics. You should be able to do all 10 in less than 5 minutes.

Q1. Simplify: $11 - 3 + 5$

Q2. Multiply and simplify: $\left(\dfrac{2}{3}\right)\left(\dfrac{6}{7}\right)$

Q3. Add: $3.74 + 5$

Q4. If $x + 7$ is 42, what does x equal?

Q5. Is -13 an integer?

Q6. Multiply: $(9x)(6x)$

Q7. Square 7.

Q8. Is 1.3 a rational number?

Q9. Multiply: $5(3x - 8)$

Q10. Simplify: $(-3)(0.7)(-5)(-1)$

Work the following problems.

1. Tell what is meant by
   a. additive identity element,
   b. multiplicative identity element.

2. What is
   a. the *additive* inverse of $\frac{2}{3}$?
   b. the *multiplicative* inverse of $\frac{2}{3}$?

3. Using variables (x, y, z, etc.) to stand for numbers, write an example of each of the eleven field axioms. Try to do this by writing all eleven

examples first, then checking to be sure you are right. Correct any
which you left out or got wrong.

4. Explain why 0 has *no* multiplicative inverse.

5. The Closure Axiom states that you get a *unique* answer when you add
    two real numbers. What is meant by a "unique" answer?

6. You get the same answer when you add a column of numbers "up" as
    you do when you add it "down." What axiom(s) show that this is
    true?

7. Calvin Butterball and Phoebe Small use the distributive property as
    follows:

    Calvin: $3(x + 4)(x + 7) = (3x + 12)(x + 7)$.
    Phoebe: $3(x + 4)(x + 7) = (3x + 12)(3x + 21)$.

    Who is right? What mistake did the other one make?

8. Write an example which shows that:
    a. Subtraction is *not* a commutative operation.
    b. {negative numbers} is *not* closed under multiplication.
    c. {digits} is *not* closed under addition.
    d. {real numbers} is *not* closed under the $\sqrt{}$ operation (taking the
        square root).
    e. Exponentiation ("raising to powers") is *not* an associative opera-
        tion. (Try 4^{2^3}.)

9. For each of the following, tell which of the Field Axioms was used,
    and whether it was an axiom for *addition* or for *multiplication*. As-
    sume that x, y, and z stand for real numbers.
    a. $x + (y + z) = (x + y) + z$
    b. $x \cdot (y + z)$ is a real number
    c. $x \cdot (y + z) = x \cdot (z + y)$
    d. $x \cdot (y + z) = (y + z) \cdot x$
    e. $x \cdot (y + z) = xy + xz$
    f. $x \cdot (y + z) = x \cdot (y + z) + 0$
    g. $x \cdot (y + z) + (-[x \cdot (y + z)]) = 0$
    h. $x \cdot (y + z) = x \cdot (y + z) \cdot 1$
    i. $x \cdot (y + z) \cdot \dfrac{1}{x \cdot (y + z)} = 1$

10. Tell whether or not the following sets are *fields* under the opera-
    tions + and ×. If the set is not a field, tell which one(s) of the Field
    Axioms do not apply.
    a. {rational numbers}
    b. {integers}
    c. {positive numbers}
    d. {non-negative numbers}

1-3 | VARIABLES AND EXPRESSIONS

In previous mathematics courses you have seen *expressions,* such as

$$3x^2 + 5x - 7,$$

that stand for numbers. Just *what* number an expression stands for depends on what value you pick for the *variable* (x in this case). The name "variable" is picked because x can stand for various different numbers at different times. The numbers 3, 5, -7, $\frac{9}{10}$, $\sqrt{11}$ etc., are called *constants* because they stand for the *same* number *all* the time.

In this section you will *evaluate* expressions by substituting values for the variable. In order to do this more easily, you can *simplify* the expression using the axioms of the previous section.

Objective:
Given an expression containing a variable,

a. *evaluate* it by substituting a given number for the variable, and finding the value of the expression,
b. *simplify* it by using the Field Axioms to transform it to an equivalent expression that is easier to evaluate.

DEFINITION

> **VARIABLE**
> A **variable** is a letter which stands for an *unspecified* number from a *given* set.

For example, if the set you have in mind is {digits}, and x is the variable, then x could stand for any one of the numbers 0, 1, 2, 3, 4, 5, 6, 7, 8, or 9. In this case, {digits} is called the *domain* of x. The word comes from the Latin "domus," meaning "house." So the domain of a variable is "where it lives." Since the domain of most variables in this course will be {real numbers}, you make the following agreement:

AGREEMENT

> Unless otherwise specified, the domain of a variable will be assumed to be the set of all real numbers.

DEFINITION

> **EXPRESSION**
> An **expression** is a collection of variables and constants connected by operation signs ($+$, $-$, $\times$, $\div$, etc.) which stands for a *number*.

To find out *what* number an expression stands for, you must substitute a value for each variable, then do the indicated operations.

EXAMPLE 1

Evaluate $3x^2 + 5x - 7$ if $x = 4$.

Solution:

$$
\begin{array}{ll}
\quad 3x^2 + 5x - 7 & \text{Write the given expression.} \\
= 3 \cdot 4^2 + 5 \cdot 4 - 7 & \text{Substitute 4 for } x. \\
= 3 \cdot 16 + 5 \cdot 4 - 7 & \text{Square the 4.} \\
= 48 + 20 - 7 & \text{Do the multiplication.} \\
= \underline{61} & \text{Add and subtract from left to right.}
\end{array}
$$

There are several things you should realize about the preceding calculations. First, you must substitute the *same* value of *x everywhere* it appears in the expression. Although a variable can take on different values at different times, it stands for the *same* number at any *one* time. This fact is expressed in the Reflexive Axiom, which states, "$x = x$."

The second thing you should realize is that this expression involves *subtraction* and *exponentiation* (raising to powers). These operations, as well as *division*, can be defined in terms of addition and multiplication.

DEFINITIONS

> **Subtraction:** $x - y$ means $x + (-y)$.
>
> **Division:** $x \div y$ means $x \cdot \frac{1}{y}$. (The symbols $\frac{x}{y}$ and x/y are also used for $x \div y$.)
>
> **Exponentiation:** x^n means n, x's *multiplied* together. For example,
> $$x^3 \text{ means } x \cdot x \cdot x.$$

The third thing you should realize is that the answer you get depends on the *order* in which you do the operations. So that there will be no doubt about what an expression such as $3x^2 + 5x - 7$ means, you make the following agreement:

AGREEMENT

> **ORDER OF OPERATIONS**
>
> 1. Do any operations inside parentheses *first*.
> 2. Do any exponentiating next.
> 3. Do multiplication and division in the order in which they occur, from left to right.
> 4. Do addition and subtraction last, in the order in which they occur, from left to right.

EXAMPLE 2

Carry out the following operations:

a. $3 + 4 \times 5$ Multiply *first*.

    $= 3 + 20$

    $= \underline{\underline{23}}$ Add *last*.

b. $3 + 4 \times 5 \div 2$

    $= 3 + 20 \div 2$ Multiply and divide from left to right.

    $= 3 + 10$ Divide *before* adding.

    $= \underline{\underline{13}}$ Add *last*.

c. $3 - 4 \times 5 \div 2 + 9$

    $= 3 - 20 \div 2 + 9$ Multiply and divide from left to right.

    $= 3 - 10 + 9$ Divide *before* + and −.

    $= -7 + 9$ Add and subtract from left to right.

    $= \underline{\underline{2}}$ Add and subtract last.   ■

An expression might contain the *absolute value* operation. The symbol $|x|$ means the *distance* between the number x and the origin of the number line. For example, $|-3|$ and $|3|$ are both equal to 3, since both 3 and -3 are located 3 units from the origin (Figure 1-3).

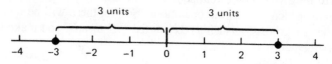

Figure 1-3 _____

Similarly,

$$|5| = 5$$
$$|-7| = 7$$
$$|0| = 0,$$

and so forth.

The absolute value of a *variable* presents a problem. If x is a *positive* number, then $|x|$ is equal to x. But if x is a *negative* number, then $|x|$ is equal to the *opposite* of x. For instance, if $x = -9$, then

$$|x| = |-9| = -(-9) = 9.$$

A precise definition of absolute value can be written as follows:

DEFINITION

$$|x| = x \text{ if } x \text{ is } positive \text{ (or 0)}$$
$$|x| = -x \text{ if } x \text{ is } negative$$

EXAMPLE 3

Evaluate $|17 - 4x| - 2$ if

a. $x = 5$
b. $x = -3$.

a. $|17 - 4x| - 2$

  $= |17 - 20| - 2$ Substitute 5 for x.

  $= |-3| - 2$ Arithmetic

  $= 3 - 2$ Definition of absolute value

  $= \underline{\underline{1}}$ Arithmetic

b. $|17 - 4x| - 2$

  $= |17 + 12| - 2$ Substitute -3 for x.

$$= |29| - 2 \qquad \text{Arithmetic}$$

$$= 29 - 2 \qquad \text{Definition of absolute value}$$

$$= \underline{\underline{27}} \qquad \text{Arithmetic} \qquad \blacksquare$$

Two expressions are equivalent if they *equal* each other for *all* values of the variable. For example, $3x + 8x$ and $11x$ are equivalent expressions. *Simplifying* an expression means transforming it to an equivalent expression that is in some way simpler to work with. The expression $11x$ is considered to be simpler than $3x + 8x$ because it is easier to evaluate when you pick a value of x. Adding the $3x$ and $8x$ is called "collecting like terms." It is justified by using the Distributive Axiom *backwards*.

$$3x + 8x = (3 + 8)x \qquad \text{Distributivity}$$

$$= 11x \qquad \text{Arithmetic}$$

EXAMPLE 4

Simplify $7x \cdot 2 \div x$.

Since the Field Axioms apply to multiplication rather than division, you would treat "$\div x$" as "$\cdot \frac{1}{x}$", commute the multiplication, and get

$$7x \cdot 2 \div x$$

$$= 7x \cdot 2 \cdot \frac{1}{x} \qquad \text{Definition of division}$$

$$= \left(7x \cdot \frac{1}{x}\right) \cdot 2 \qquad \text{Commutativity and associativity}$$

$$= 7 \cdot 2 \qquad \text{Associativity and multiplicative inverses}$$

$$= \underline{\underline{14}} \qquad \text{Arithmetic} \qquad \blacksquare$$

EXAMPLE 5

Simplify $2 - 3[x - 2 - 5(x - 1)]$.

Here you must observe the agreed-upon sequence of operations. The first thing to do is *start inside the innermost parentheses* and work your way out (like a termite!).

$$2 - 3[x - 2 - 5(x - 1)]$$

$$= 2 - 3[x - 2 - 5x + 5] \qquad \text{Distributivity}$$

$$= 2 - 3[-4x + 3] \qquad \text{Collecting like terms}$$

$$= 2 + 12x - 9 \qquad \text{Distributivity}$$

$$= \underline{\underline{12x - 7}} \qquad \text{Commutativity and associativity} \qquad \blacksquare$$

Notes:

1. You must remember some things from previous mathematics courses. For example, a negative number times a negative number is a *positive* number. This sort of thing can be proved using the Field Axioms, as you will see in Section 1-7.
2. There are several kinds of symbols of inclusion.
   ( ) Parentheses.
   [ ] Brackets.
   { } Braces (also used for *set* symbols).
   ‾ Vinculum (an overhead line, used in fractions and elsewhere, such as in $\frac{x-3}{x+7}$).

To avoid so many different symbols, sometimes "nested" parentheses are used. For example, the expression

$$2 - (3 + 4(5 - 6(7 + x)))$$

would be simplified by starting with the *innermost* parentheses.

In the following exercise, you will practice simplifying and evaluating expressions. If the going gets difficult, just tell yourself that no matter how complicated an expression looks, it just stands for a *number*. And people *invented* numbers!

EXERCISE 1-3

Do These Quickly

The following problems are intended to refresh your skills. Some are from the first two sections of this chapter, and others probe your general knowledge of mathematics. You should be able to do all 10 in less than 5 minutes.

Q1. Is $\sqrt{9}$ an integer?

Q2. Is $-\frac{4}{7}$ a real number?

Q3. Commute the 3 and the x: $2y + 3 + x$

Q4. Associate the $4a$ and the $2c$: $4a + 2c + 5d$

Q5. Distribute the 5: $5(3x - 7)$

Q6. Write the additive inverse of $\frac{5}{8}$.

Q7.   Write the multiplicative identity element.

Q8.   If $3x$ equals 42, what does x equal?

Q9.   Multiply: $(2.3)(4)$

Q10.   Divide and simplify: $(\frac{2}{3}) \div (\frac{6}{7})$

For Problems 1 through 10, carry out the indicated operations in the agreed-upon order.

1. $5 + 6 \times 7$

2. $3 + 8 \times 7$

3. $9 - 4 + 5$

4. $11 - 6 + 4$

5. $12 \div 3 \times 2$

6. $18 \div 9 \times 2$

7. $7 - 8 \div 2 + 4$

8. $24 - 12 \times 2 + 4$

9. $16 - 4 + 12 \div 6 \times 2$

10. $50 - 30 \times 2 + 8 \div 2$

For Problems 11 through 24, evaluate the given expression

(a) for $x = 2$
(b) for $x = -3$.

11. $4x - 1$

12. $3x - 5$

13. $|3x - 5|$

14. $|4x - 1|$

15. $5 - 7x - 8$

16. $8 - 5x - 2$

17. $|8 - 5x| - 2$

18. $|5 - 7x| - 8$

19. $x^2 - 4x + 6$

20. $x^2 + 6x - 9$

21. $4x^2 - 5x - 11$

22. $5x^2 - 7x + 1$

23. $5 - 2 \cdot x$

24. $3 + 4 \cdot x$

For Problems 25 through 40, simplify the given expression.

25. $6 - [5 - (3 - x)]$

26. $2x - [3x + (x - 2)]$

27. $7(x - 2(3 - x))$

28. $3(6x - 5(x - 1))$

29. $7 - 2[3 - 2(x + 4)]$

30. $8 + 4[5 - 6(x - 2)]$

31. $3x - [2x + (x - 5)]$

32. $4x - [3x - (2x - x)]$

33. $6 - 2[x - 3 - (x + 4) + 3(x - 2)]$

34. $7[2 - 3(x - 4) + 4(x - 6)]$

35. $6[x - \frac{1}{2}(x - 1)]$

36. $8[2x - \frac{1}{4}(6x + 5)]$

37. $x^2 + y^2 - [x(x + y) - y(y - x)]$

38. $4x^2 - 2x(x - 2y) + 2y(2y + x) - 2x^2$

39. $-(-(-(-x)))$ 40. $x - [x - (x - \overline{x - y})]$

41. Calvin Butterball and Phoebe Small evaluate the expression $|x - 3|$ for $x = 7$, getting:

$$\text{Calvin: } |x - 3| = |7 - 3| = 7 + 3 = \underline{\underline{10}}$$

$$\text{Phoebe: } |x - 3| = |7 - 3| = |4| = \underline{\underline{4}}$$

Who is right? What mistake did the other one make?

42. Kay Oss evaluates the expression $|x + 2| - 5x$ by substituting 7 for the first x and 3 for the second x. What axiom did Kay violate?

1-4 | POLYNOMIALS

Polynomials are algebraic expressions that involve only the operations of *addition, subtraction,* and *multiplication* of variables. For example,

$$3x^2 + 5x - 7, \quad x + 2, \quad \text{and} \quad xy^3z^2$$

are polynomials. They involve no non-algebraic operations such as absolute value, and no operations under which the set of real numbers is not closed, such as division and square root. Thus, polynomials stand for *real* numbers no matter what real values you substitute for the variables.

Objectives:

1. Given an expression, tell whether or not it is a polynomial. If it is, then *name* it by "degree" and by number of terms.
2. Given two binomials, multiply them together.

Notes:

1. The expression $\frac{3}{x - 5}$ is *not* a polynomial since it involves *division* by a *variable*. If x were 5, the expression would have the form $\frac{3}{0}$, which is *not* a real number.
2. The expression $\sqrt{x}$ is *not* a polynomial since it involves the *square root* of a *variable*. If x were less than 0, the expression would stand for an imaginary number rather than a real number.

3. The expression $|x - 7|$ is *not* a polynomial since it involves the *non-algebraic operation* "absolute value."
4. Expressions such as $\sqrt{3}x$ and $\frac{x}{3}$ (which equals $\frac{1}{3} \cdot x$) *are* considered to be polynomials since the operations $\div$ and $\sqrt{}$ are performed on *constants* rather than variables.
5. The operation exponentiation ("raising to powers") is *not* listed among the polynomial operations. If the exponent is an integer, such as in x^4, then exponentiation is just repeated multiplication. So expressions with only *integer* exponents *are* polynomials. In Chapter 6 you will learn what happens when the exponent is not an integer.

"Terms" in an expression are parts of the expression that are *added* or *subtracted*. For example, the expression

$$3x^2 + 5x - 7$$

has three terms, namely, $3x^2$, $5x$, and 7. Special names are used for expressions that have 1, 2, or 3 terms.

NAMES

No. of Terms	Name	Example
1	monomial	$3x^2y^5$
2	binomial	$3x^2 + y^5$
3	trinomial	$3 - x^2 + y^5$
4 or more	(no special name)	$3x^5 - 2x^4 + 5x^3 - 6x^2 + 2x$

The word "polynomial" originally meant "many terms." However, it is possible to get a *monomial* by adding two polynomials. For example,

$$(3x^2 + 5x - 7) + (8x^2 - 5x + 7) = 11x^2,$$

a *monomial*. By calling monomials, binomials, and trinomials "polynomials," too, the set of polynomials has the desirable property of being *closed* under addition. It is also closed under multiplication.

"Factors" in an expression are parts of the expression that are *multiplied* together. For example, $5x^2$ has *three* factors, 5, x, and x. Special names are given to polynomials depending on how many *variables* are *multiplied* together.

For example, $3x^2y^5$ is *seventh* degree because seven variables are multiplied together $(x \cdot x \cdot y \cdot y \cdot y \cdot y \cdot y)$. But $3x^2 + y^5$ is only *fifth* degree because at most five variables are multiplied together $(y \cdot y \cdot y \cdot y \cdot y)$. An expression such as $17x$ that has only *one* variable is called *first* degree, and a constant such as 17 which has *no* variable is called *zero* degree.

DEFINITION

> ### DEGREE OF A POLYNOMIAL
> The **degree** of a polynomial is the maximum number of variables that appear as factors in any one term.

Various degrees are given special names, as follows:

NAMES

Degree	Name	Example	Memory Aid
0	constant	13	Constants do not vary.
1st	linear	$5x$	A line has *one* dimension.
2nd	quadratic	$7x^2$	A square is a quadrangle.
3rd	cubic	$4x^3$	A cube has *three* dimensions.
4th	quartic	x^4	A *quart* is a *fourth* of a gallon.
5th	quintic	$9x^5$	Quintuplets are *five* children.
6th or more	(no special name)	$3x^{17}$	(Make up your *own* names, Hectic, Septic, etc.)

Notes:

1. Various parts of a monomial such as $3x^2$ have special names.

    3 is the *numerical coefficient*.
    x is the *base*.
    2 is the *exponent*.
    x^2 is a *power* (the second power of x).

2. "Zero" could have *any* degree, because 0 equals $0x^3$, $0x^{15}$, $0x^{1066}$, etc. To avoid this difficulty, 0 is usually called a polynomial with *no* degree.

Multiplying Binomials: Multiplying binomials requires a *double* use of the distributive property.

For example,

$$(x - 3)(2x + 5)$$

can be thought of as

$$\text{number} \times (2x + 5).$$

Distributing the "number," you get

$$\text{number} \times 2x + \text{number} \times 5.$$

Recalling that "number" is actually $(x - 3)$, you get

$$(x - 3) \times 2x + (x - 3) \times 5.$$

Distributing the $2x$ and the 5 gives

$$2x^2 - 6x + 5x - 15,$$

which can be simplified by combining like terms to give

$$2x^2 - x - 15.$$

Once you understand the procedure, you can multiply two binomials *quickly,* in your head. Just multiply each term of one binomial by each term of the other, and write down the answer.

The following exercise is designed to give you practice identifying and naming polynomials, and multiplying binomials.

EXERCISE 1-4

Do These Quickly

The following problems are intended to refresh your skills. You should be able to do all 10 in less than 5 minutes.

Q1.   Evaluate: $23 - 3 \cdot 7$

Q2.   Evaluate $|12x - 4|$ if x is -2.

Q3.   Distribute the 0.5: $0.5(8x - 9t)$

Q4.   Find 70% of 700.

Q5.   Subtract and simplify: $\frac{2}{9} - \frac{8}{9}$

Q6.   What axiom was used? $(3 + x) + 4 = (x + 3) + 4$

Q7.   What axiom tells that 2 times 3 is a unique real number?

Q8.   Is $\sqrt{48}$ a rational number?

Q9.   Square 7.

Q10.   Write an expression representing 17 more than x.

For Problems 1 through 24, tell whether or not the given expression is a polynomial. If it *is,* then name it according to its *degree* and number of *terms* (e.g., "quadratic trinomial"). If it is *not* a polynomial, then tell *why* not.

1. $3x^4 - 2x + 51$ 2. $3^2x^3 + 5y^4$

3. $9xy + 2z$

4. $9xyz + 2$

5. $3x^2y - \dfrac{57}{x}$

6. $3x^2y - \sqrt{57x}$

7. $\dfrac{x}{2} - 1$

8. $\sqrt{x} \times 5$

9. $\dfrac{2}{x} - 1$

10. $x + \sqrt{5}$

11. -13

12. 19

13. $8x^3 + 5x^2 - 2x + 11$

14. $3x^2 + 5x - 7$

15. $x^3y^2 - \pi$

16. $xy^5 - \pi^7$

17. $\sqrt{x} + 11$

18. $\dfrac{x}{4} - 17$

19. $x + \sqrt{11}$

20. $\dfrac{4}{x} - 17$

21. $5^2x^3y^7 + 8z^9$

22. $6^3x^5y^2 - 3z^6$

23. 0

24. $0x^5$

For Problems 25 through 34, multiply the two binomials.

25. $(x - 3)(x + 7)$

26. $(x - 6)(x + 5)$

27. $(x + 4)(2x - 1)$

28. $(3x + 1)(x - 2)$

29. $(3x - 8)(2x - 7)$

30. $(4x - 3)(7x - 5)$

31. $(2x - 5)(2x - 5)$

32. $(3x - 10)(3x - 10)$

33. $(2x - 5)^2$

34. $(3x - 10)^2$

1-5 EQUATIONS

Evaluating an expression may be thought of as finding out what number the expression equals when you know the value of the variable. You are ready to *reverse* the process, and find out the value of the *variable* when you know what number the *expression* equals. For example, if

$$3x - 5 = 16,$$

then x must equal 7, since $3 \times 7 - 5$ equals 16. The statement "$3x - 5 = 16$" is an equation, and the process of writing down what x

must equal is called *solving* the equation. Since there may be more than one solution, it is customary to write the solutions in a *solution set*. For the above equation,

$$S = \{7\}.$$

AGREEMENT

Solving an equation means writing its solution set.

Most of the equations you will encounter are too complicated to solve by inspection. So the procedure is to transform them to one or more equations of the form

$$x = \text{a constant.}$$

Then the solution set *can* be written by inspection.

EXAMPLE 1

Solve $3x - 5 = 16$.

Solution:
The technique is to transform the equation to $x = $ constant by getting rid of the unwanted numbers around the x in the left member.

$3x - 5 = 16$ Write the given equation.

$3x = 21$ Add 5 to each member.

$x = 7$ Multiply each member by $\dfrac{1}{3}$.

This equation is *equivalent* to the original one, meaning it has the *same* solution set. By inspection, you can write

$$S = \{7\}. \qquad \blacksquare$$

Notes:

1. Before writing the solution set, you should substitute the value(s) of x back into the original equation to be sure you have made no mistakes.
2. You should not stop at the step "$x = 7$." Since you have agreed that solving an equation means writing the solution set, the equation is not solved until you write "$S = \{7\}$."
3. Adding (or subtracting) and multiplying (or dividing) both members of an equation by the same number are justified by the *Addition Property of Equality* and the *Multiplication Property of Equality,* respectively.

These properties can be proved from the axioms, as you will see in Section 1-7.

EXAMPLE 2

Solve $x + 3 = x$.

Solution:
This equation has no solutions at all, since no number comes out the same when 3 is added to it. The solution set is *empty,* and you would write

$$S = \emptyset \text{ or } S = \{\ \}.$$ ■

EXAMPLE 3

Solve $(3x - 4)(x + 5) = 0$.

Solution:
This equation contains a *product* which equals *zero.* The only way a product of two real numbers can equal zero is for one of the factors to equal zero. This fact is expressed in the converse of the *Multiplication Property of Zero,* which can be proved from the axioms as in Section 1-7.

Because of this fact, you can transform the equation to

$$3x - 4 = 0 \text{ or } x + 5 = 0.$$

Further transformations give

$$3x = 4 \text{ or } x = -5 \qquad \text{Adding 4 or subtracting 5.}$$
$$x = \tfrac{4}{3} \text{ or } x = -5 \qquad \text{Dividing by 3.}$$
$$\therefore S = \{\tfrac{4}{3}, -5\}. \qquad \text{Solving the transformed equation.} \quad ■$$

Note: In order for a number to be a solution, it must be in the *domain* of the variable. If the domain of x were

$$x \in \{\text{positive numbers}\},$$

then $S = \{\tfrac{4}{3}\}$. If the domain is

$$x \in \{\text{integers}\},$$

then $S = \{-5\}$. If the domain is

$$x \in \{\text{natural numbers}\},$$

then $S = \emptyset$, since neither of the possible solutions is a positive integer.

EXAMPLE 4

Solve $|x - 2| = 3$.

Solution:
By inspection you might see that x could equal 5. But x could also equal -1. To make sure you do not overlook any solutions, you try to transform the equation to equivalent equations of the form $x =$ a constant. You can

do this by realizing that there are just *two* numbers whose absolute value is 3, namely 3 and -3. So the expression inside the absolute value sign, $x - 2$, must equal one of these two numbers. You would write

$$x - 2 = 3 \text{ or } x - 2 = -3.$$

Adding 2 to each member of each equation gives

$$x = 5 \text{ or } x = -1,$$

so that

$$S = \{5, -1\}. \qquad \blacksquare$$

Extraneous Solutions and Irreversible Steps — Two equations are *equivalent* if they have the *same* solution set. Unfortunately, there are transformations which you can perform on an equation which seem perfectly correct, but which *change* the solution set. Since it is the *original* equation you are trying to solve, you must be aware of the types of transformations which might *not* produce an equivalent equation.

1. *Multiply by an expression which can equal zero* — For example, the equation

    $$x = 5$$

    has $S = \{5\}$. But if you multiply both members by $x - 2$ you get

    $$x(x - 2) = 5(x - 2).$$

    This transformed equation is still true when $x = 5$, as the Multiplication Property of Equality tells you it must be. But it is also true when $x = 2$ because

    $$2(2 - 2) = 5(2 - 2) \quad \text{or} \quad 2 \times 0 = 5 \times 0$$

    is also a true statement. So 2 is a solution of the transformed equation which *does not* satisfy the original equation. Such a solution is called an *extraneous* solution, "extra-" meaning "added," and "-neouis" meaning "new."

DEFINITION

> An **extraneous** solution is a number which satisfies a transformed equation, but not the original equation.

Mutiplying both members of an equation by an expression which can equal zero is called an *irreversible step*. You cannot go backwards and divide both members by that expression since division by zero is undefined. Irreversible steps sometimes produce extraneous solutions.

2. *Divide by an expression that can equal zero* — For example, the equation

$$x^2 = 4x$$

has the solution set $S = \{4, 0\}$, as you can see by substituting these numbers. But if you divide both members by x you get

$$x = 4,$$

which has only $S = \{4\}$. So dividing by a variable can *lose* a valid solution.

The following exercise is designed to give you practice solving equations of the type you should recall from previous mathematics courses. You will also demonstrate that you understand about transformations that do *not* produce equivalent equations.

EXERCISE 1-5

Do These Quickly

The following problems are intended to refresh your skills. You should be able to do all 10 in less than 5 minutes.

Q1.   Find 40% of 700.

Q2.   What axiom expresses the fact that $0 + 1776$ equals 1776?

Q3.   What degree is $5^2 x^7 y$?

Q4. $x^2 + 7x - 2$ is a ____nomial. What goes in the blank?

Q5.   Is π an irrational number?

Q6.   Add and simplify: $\dfrac{2}{3} + \dfrac{6}{7}$

Q7.   Square -5.

Q8.   Distribute: $3(x^2 - 5x + 11)$

Q9.   Is $\dfrac{5x}{13}$ a polynomial?

Q10.   Is 0.666666… (repeating) a rational number?

For Problems 1 through 22, solve the equation in the indicated domain.

1. $3x + 7 = -8$ {real numbers}

2. $4x - 6 = 10$ {real numbers}

3. $2x + 3 = x - 1$ {positive numbers}

4. $5x - 1 = 2x + 5$ {negative numbers}

5. $5x + 3 = 2x + 3$ {real numbers}

6. $5x + 3 = 5x - 4$ {real numbers}

7.   a. $4x + 3 = x - 8$ {rational numbers}

    b. $4x + 3 = x - 8$ {integers}

8.   a. $7x - 4 = 2x - 19$ {rational numbers}

    b. $7x - 4 = 2x - 19$ {integers}

9.   a. $x^2 = 16$ {negative numbers}

    b. $x^2 = 16$ {real numbers}

10. a. $x^2 = 36$ {positive numbers}

    b. $x^2 = 36$ {real numbers}

11. a. $x^2 = 1/9$ {rational numbers}

    b. $x^2 = 1/9$ {integers}

12. a. $x^2 = 7$ {rational numbers}

    b. $x^2 = 7$ {irrational numbers}

13. $(x + 3)(3x - 2) = 0$ {real numbers}

14. $(2x - 5)(x + 1) = 0$ {real numbers}

15. $(2x - 5)(x + 1) = 0$ {integers}

16. $(x + 3)(3x - 2) = 0$ {integers}

17. $(x + 3)(3x - 2) = 0$ {positive numbers}

18. $(2x - 5)(x + 1) = 0$ {positive numbers}

19. $(2x + 3)(x - 5)(x + 1) = 0$ {real numbers}

20. $(4x - 3)(x + 2)(x - 6) = 0$ {real numbers}

21. $x(2x - 1)(x + 4) = 0$ {real numbers}

22. $x(5x - 3)(x - 6) = 0$ {real numbers}

For Problems 23 through 32, solve the equation assuming that the domain is $x \in$ {real numbers}.

23. $|x| = 7$ 24. $|x| = 5$

25. $|x| = -6$ 26. $|x| = -9$

27. $|x + 3| = 5$ 28. $|x - 2| = 14$

29. $|4x - 1| = 11$ 30. $|5x + 3| = 7$

31. $|9x - 17| = 1$ 32. $|7x - 2| = 4$

33. Although they do not look much alike, there *is* a relationship between the equations $(x + 7)(3x - 5) = 0$ and $|3x + 8| = 13$.
    a. Find the solution set of each equation.
    b. What word best describes the relationship between the two equations?

34. Given the equation $(x - 3)(x - 7) = 0$:
    a. Write the solution set.
    b. Divide both members of the equation by $(x - 3)$, and write the solution set of the transformed equation.
    c. Is the transformed equation *equivalent* to the original one? Explain.
    d. Multiply both members of the original equation by $(x - 2)$. What number is a solution of the transformed equation which was *not* a solution of the original one?
    e. What name is given to the solution in part d?
    f. What name is given to the operation of multiplying both members of an equation by an expression which can equal 0?

35. ***Introduction to Inequalities*** — The statement $5 < 7$ is an *inequality*. It is *true* because 5 *is less* than 7.
    a. Add the positive number 3 to both members. Is the resulting inequality true?
    b. Add the negative number -8 to both members of the original inequality. Is the resulting inequality true?
    c. Use variables to write a statement of the *Addition Property of Order*, which states that you may add the same number to both members of an inequality *without* changing the order (from $<$ to $>$, for example).

36. ***More about Inequalites*** — Given the true inequality $5 < 7$:
    a. Multiply both members of the inequality by the positive number 3. Is the resulting inequality true?
    b. Multiply both members of the original inequality by the negative number $- 8$. Is the resulting inequality true?
    c. Multiply both members of the original inequality by 0. Is the resulting inequality true?
    d. Write a statement of the *Multiplication Property of Order* which takes into account what you have observed in parts a, b, and c.
    e. In your own words, tell what happens to the order in an inequality when you multiply both members by a *negative* number. Tell also what *you* must do to make a true statement out of the resulting inequality.

1-6 | INEQUALITIES

If the "=" sign in an equation is replaced by one of the order signs, $<$, $>$, $\leq$, or $\geq$, the resulting sentence is called an *inequality*. For example,

$$3x - 5 < 16.$$

The solution set of an inequality contains all values of the variable that make the sentence true. Since the solution set usually contains an *infinite* number of solutions, it is customary to draw a graph rather than write the set.

Objective:
Given an inequality, transform it to a simpler, equivalent inequality so that you can draw a graph of its solution set.

If you cannot see the solution set by inspection, you can transform the inequality by

1. adding the same number to both members, or
2. multiplying both members by the same number. (This is tricky! See Example 2.)

EXAMPLE 1

Graph the solution set of $3x - 5 < 16$.

Solution:
Starting with

$$3x - 5 < 16,$$

you would add 5 to each member, getting

$$3x < 21.$$

Then you would multiply each member by $\frac{1}{3}$, getting

$$x < 7.$$

The graph would be plotted on a number line, looking like this:

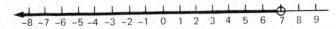

The open circle at 7 indicates that the endpoint of the ray is *not* included. A *closed* circle would be used for inequalities with $\leq$ or $\geq$, where the endpoint *is* included. ■

Suppose you were asked to graph the solution set of

$$-2x \geq 18.$$

To get rid of the "-2" on the left, you must multiply each member of the inequality by $-\frac{1}{2}$. But multiplying each member of an inequality by a *negative* number makes the order *reverse*. You can see why, by multiplying both members of an inequality like $5 < 7$ by a negative number such as -8. The result will be that -40 is *greater* than -56. So *you* must reverse the order sign whenever you multiply both members of an inequality by a negative number. This fact is summarized in the Multiplication Property of Order.

PROPERTY

Multiplication Property of Order

If $x < y$, then

$$xz < yz, \text{ if } z \text{ is } positive,$$
$$xz > yz, \text{ if } z \text{ is } negative,$$
$$xz = yz, \text{ if } z \text{ is } zero.$$

A similar property applies to the relationship $>$.

EXAMPLE 2

Graph the solution set of $-2x \geq 18$.

Solution:
The steps in solving the inequality would be:

$-2x \geq 18$ Write the given inequality.

$-\frac{1}{2}(-2x) \leq -\frac{1}{2}(18)$ Multiply by $-\frac{1}{2}$ and reverse the order sign.

$x \leq -9$ Associate and do the arithmetic.

The graph would be

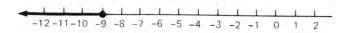

EXAMPLE 3

Graph the solution set of $3 \leq 2x + 5 < 11$.

Solution:
This inequality has *three* members. Starting with

$$3 \le 2x + 5 < 11,$$

you would add -5 to *all three* members, getting

$$-2 \le 2x < 6.$$

Multiplying all three members by $\frac{1}{2}$ gives

$$-1 \le x < 3.$$

The graph is all numbers between -1 and 3, including the -1 but not including the 3.

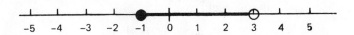

EXAMPLE 4

Graph the solution set of $|x| > 29$.

Solution:
$|x|$ means, "the distance between the origin and x." So the inequality really says, "x is a number that is *more than* 29 units from the origin." Therefore, one part of the graph will start at 29 and go "upward," and the other part will start at -29 and go "downward." The graph is

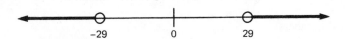

From the graph you should be able to tell that the inequality $|x| > 29$ is equivalent to the *combined* inequalities,

$$x > 29 \text{ or } x < -29$$

EXAMPLE 5

Graph the solution set of $|x| < 29$.

The solution set will contain all numbers that are *closer* to the origin than 29 units. So the graph will be all those points *between* -29 and 29. The graph is

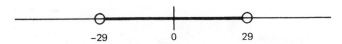

From this graph, you should be able to tell that $|x| < 29$ is equivalent to

$$x < 29 \text{ and } x > -29,$$

which is equivalent to

$$-29 < x < 29.$$ ∎

From Examples 4 and 5, you can figure out a way to transform inequalities to eliminate the absolute value sign.

CONCLUSION

If c is a non-negative constant, then
$|\text{expression}| > c$ is equivalent to:

$$\text{expression} > c \; or \; \text{expression} < -c.$$

$|\text{expression}| < c$ is equivalent to:

$$\text{expression} < c \; and \; \text{expression} > -c.$$
$$(\text{or to } -c < \text{expression} < c).$$

If you ever forget these transformations, you can think them up easily by recalling that the absolute value of a number is its distance from the origin.

EXAMPLE 6

Graph the solution set of $|3x - 5| \le 13$ if the domain of x is

a. {real numbers},
b. {positive numbers},
c. {integers}.

Starting with

$$|3x - 5| \le 13,$$

you use the appropriate transformation, above, to write

$$-13 \le 3x - 5 \le 13.$$

Adding 5 to all three members,

$$-8 \le 3x \le 18.$$

Dividing all three members by 3 gives

$$-\tfrac{8}{3} \le x \le 6.$$

The graphs are as follows.

a. {real numbers}

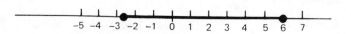

b. {positive numbers}

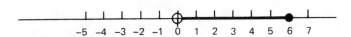

c. {integers}

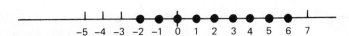

The following exercise is designed to give you practice in graphing the solution sets of inequalities.

EXERCISE 1-6

Do These Quickly

The following problems are intended to refresh your skills. You should be able to do all 10 in less than 5 minutes.

Q1.   Solve: $4x + 8 = 28$

Q2.   Simplify: $4x + 8 - 28$

Q3.   Simplify: $4(x + 8) - 28$

Q4.   Find 10% of 1234.

Q5.   Multiply and simplify: $(\frac{5}{3})(\frac{3}{5})$

Q6.   What axiom is illustrated? $3(x + 4) \cdot 1 = 3(x + 4)$

Q7.   Is $\dfrac{3}{5}$ an integer?

Q8.   Name by degree and number of terms: $x^3 - 17^4$

Q9.   Solve: $|x - 2| = 7$

Q10. Evaluate if x is 14: $|13 - x|$

For Problems 1 through 14, graph the *solution* set of the inequality, observing the given domain.

1. $3x - 5 < 4$ {real numbers}

2. $4x - 7 > 1$ {real numbers}

3. $2 - 6x \le 8$ {real numbers}

4. $5 - 3x \geq -4$ {real numbers}

5. $2x + 3 > 10$ {integers}

6. $3x - 5 < 2$ {integers}

7. $-6 < x - 5 \leq 2$ {real numbers}

8. $4 \leq x - 1 < 7$ {real numbers}

9. $x + 3 \geq 2$ or $x + 3 < -7$ {real numbers}

10. $x - 4 > -1$ or $x - 4 \leq -6$ {real numbers}

11. $x + 2 < 5$ or $x + 2 \geq 7$ {positive numbers}

12. $3 \leq x + 4 < 5$ {negative numbers}

13. $3 - 2x > 5$ {positive numbers}

14. $4 - 3x < -2$ {negative numbers}

For Problems 15 through 32, graph the solution set assuming that the domain is:

a. $x \in$ {real numbers}
b. $x \in$ {integers}
c. $x \in$ {positive numbers}

15. $|x| < 5$ 16. $|x| \leq 7$

17. $|x| \geq 2$ 18. $|x| > 3$

19. $|x + 2| \leq 3$ 20. $|x - 1| < 4$

21. $|2x + 5| > 9$ 22. $|3x + 7| \geq 7$

23. $|5x - 6| \leq 16$ 24. $|4x - 3| < 7$

25. $|2x - 7| \geq 21$ 26. $|5x - 3| > 22$

27. $|4x + 2| < 9$ 28. $|2x + 4| \leq 9$

29. $|x - 1| < -3$ 30. $|x + 3| > -6$

31. $3 \leq |x - 2| < 5$ 32. $4 < |x - 3| \leq 7$

1-7   PROPERTIES PROVABLE FROM THE AXIOMS

The Field Axioms you studied in Section 1-2 express properties of addition and multiplication which should be obvious to you. However, there are some true properties which are *not* obvious, and some things which seem obvious, but are *not true*. Therefore, mathematicians seek ways of proving new properties from a small handful of axioms.

The properties you will be proving in this section form the basis for the mathematics you will study for the rest of the course. Some you already know. The others you can either prove *now*, or you can go on to Chapter 2 and return to these proofs as you need the properties.

Objectives:

1. Given the steps in the proof of a new property, name a property justifying each step.
2. Given the name or statement of a new property and some clues about how to prove it, prove the property giving reasons for each step.

You must first recall the axioms which apply to the relationships $=$, $<$, and $>$. These are as follows.

AXIOM

REFLEXIVE PROPERTY

If x is a real number, then $x = x$.

Equality is said to be a *reflexive* relationship. The name is picked because a number can "look into the '$=$' sign" and see its own "reflection" on the other side. It is this axiom which expresses the fact that a variable stands for the *same* number, wherever it appears in an expression. Note that order is *not* reflexive since statements like $5 < 5$ or $5 > 5$ are *false*.

AXIOM

SYMMETRY

If $x = y$, then $y = x$.

Equality is said to be a *symmetric* relationship. The "$=$" sign looks the same when viewed from either direction. So it does not matter on which side of the "$=$" sign a number appears. The order relationships are *not* symmetrical. For example, the statement $4 < 5$ *cannot* have the numbers reversed. The statement $5 < 4$ is *false*.

AXIOM

> **TRANSITIVITY**
>
> For Equality: If $x = y$ and $y = z$, then $x = z$.
>
> For Order: If $x < y$ and $y < z$, then $x < z$.
>   If $x > y$ and $y > z$, then $x > z$.

The prefix "trans-" means, "across," "beyond," or "through." For example, a rapid *transit* system carries you *through* a city. The name is used here because the equality or order carries through from the first number to the last one. The property, extended, can be used when you are simplifying an expression to connect the original form to the final form. For example:

$$(x + 3)(x + 4)$$
$$= x(x + 4) + 3(x + 4)$$
$$= x^2 + 4x + 3x + 12$$
$$= x^2 + 7x + 12$$
$$\therefore (x + 3)(x + 4) = x^2 + 7x + 12 \leftarrow \text{Transitivity used } here.$$

Note that the "=" signs on the second and third lines connect the expression to the one *just above* it, not to the original expression. This is why the transitive step is needed at the end. See Appendix B for a proof of this "extended" transitive property.

AXIOM

> **TRICHOTOMY**
>
> If x and y are two real numbers, then *exactly one* of the following must be true:
>
> $$y < x$$
> $$y > x$$
> $$y = x.$$

This axiom tells you how any two given numbers must *compare* to each other. The words, "exactly one" mean two things. *One* of the statements *must* be true, and *only one* of the statements can be true. The word "trichotomy," meaning "cut in three," is used because placing a number x on the number line *cuts* it into *three* pieces.

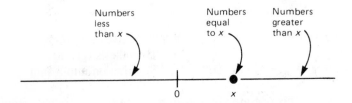

Any other number, y, must be on one of these three pieces.

These axioms help you with the mechanics of going from one step to the next in a proof. You are now armed with the tools you need to do some proving.

EXAMPLE 1

Substitution into Sums and Products (*not* an axiom)

Prove that if $z = x$, then

> $x + y$ and $z + y$ stand for *equal* numbers,
> xy and zy stand for *equal* numbers.

(In plain English, this property says that equals can be substituted for equals in sums or products.)

Proof:

The Closure Axiom states that a sum such as $x + y$ or a product such as xy stands for a *unique* real number. For this reason, it does not matter what other symbol you use for the number x. Therefore, $x + y = z + y$, and $xy = zy$, Q.E.D.   ■

This is called a *paragraph proof*. You have written a paragraph explaining why a certain property is true. The letters "Q.E.D." at the end stand for the Latin words, "quod erat demonstrandum," meaning, "which was to be proved."

EXAMPLE 2

Addition Property of Equality (not an axiom)

Prove that if $x = y$, then $x + z = y + z$.

(In plain English, prove that you can add the same number to each member of an equation.)

Proof:

a. $x + z = x + z$ a. Reflexive Axiom.
b. $x = y$ b. Hypothesis (given).
c. $\therefore x + z = y + z$, Q.E.D.   c. Substitution into a sum. ∎

Proofs such as this one are not easy to think up from "scratch." However, there is usually a "key step" that forms the heart of the proof. In this case, the thought process is, "I want an equation that has $x + z$ on the left side, so I'll *write* an equation like that and *transform* it to the one I want." The substitution property gives you a way to do the transformation.

The "if" part of a property is called the "hypothesis." The word comes from "hypo-" (as in hypodermic), meaning "under," and "thesis," (as in thesis sentence), meaning "main idea." The property you get by *reversing* the hypothesis and the conclusion is called the *converse* of the property. The converse of a true statement may or may not be true. For example,

"If you play varsity football, then you are male,"

is (probably!) a true statement. But its converse,

"If you are a male, then you play varsity football,"

is *not* true. In the next example is a proof of the converse of the Addition Property of Equality.

EXAMPLE 3

Converse of the Addition Property of Equality

Prove that if $x + z = y + z$, then $x = y$.

Proof:

a. $x + z = y + z$ a. Given ("hypothesis")
b. $(x + z) + (-z) = (y + z) + (-z)$ b. Addition property of equality.
c. $x + (z + (-z)) = y + (z + (-z))$ c. Associativity for addition.
d. $x + 0 = y + 0$ d. Additive inverses.
e. $x = y$, Q.E.D.   e. Additive identity. ∎

In this proof it was helpful to start with the hypothesis and work toward the conclusion. Note that you can *never* start with the conclusion, nor can you use the conclusion as a reason in the proof. Doing so is called "circular reasoning," for which your instructor will probably give you circular grades!

The heart of this proof is doing something to "cancel out" the unwanted z's. Adding $-z$ to both members in step b does this job. The remainder of the proof consists of tidying up the resulting equation. This property is sometimes called the *Cancellation Property of Equality for Addition*.

A theorem used to make the proof of a subsequent theorem easier is called a *lemma* for that theorem. A theorem which follows directly from a previous theorem is called a *corollary* of that theorem. Thus, the addition property of equality is used as a lemma for proving its converse.

If both the theorem and its converse are true, you may write both as a *single* statement. You use the words "if and only if":

$$x + z = y + z \text{ if and only if } x = y.$$

EXAMPLE 4

Adding Like Terms

Prove, for example, that $2x + 3x = 5x$.

Proof:

a. $2x + 3x$
    $= (2 + 3)x$ Distributivity
b. $= 5x$ Arithmetic
c. $\therefore 2x + 3x = 5x$ Transitivity   ■

In this proof you started with *one member* of the equation in the conclusion, and transformed it to the *other* member. The transitive step at the end connects the original expression with the final one, thus expressing the desired conclusion.

These four examples illustrate three slightly different techniques for proving theorems.

THEOREM-PROVING TECHNIQUES

1. Start with one member of the desired equation and transform it to the other member (Example 4).
2. Start with a given equation and transform it to the desired equation (Example 3).
3. Start somewhere else and use a clever series of transformations or a clever argument (Examples 1 and 2).

The following exercise contains most of the basic properties you learned in previous mathematics courses. Your main purpose in proving these properties is so that you will realize that they are all based on the *axioms*. You must also, of course, remember *what* they say so that you will be able to use them later on.

EXERCISE 1-7

Do These Quickly

The following problems are intended to refresh your skills. You should be able to do all 10 in les than 5 minutes.

Q1. Solve: $(x - 3) = 9$

Q2. Simplify: $(x - 3) - 9$

Q3. Commute the two factors: $(x + 4)(x - 7)$

Q4. Distribute: $4x(x + 13)$

Q5. Write the additive identity element.

Q6. Find 7% of 700.

Q7. Evaluate $|3x - 29|$ if x is 4.

Q8. Is -3000 an even number?

Q9. Is $\sqrt{-9}$ a real number?

Q10. Add: $4.7 + 3$

Work the following problems.

1. Write an example of each of the following axioms:
    a. Transitivity for equality.
    b. Transitivity for order.
    c. Symmetry for equality.
    d. Reflexive axiom for equality.
    e. Trichotomy.

2. Explain why the order relationship "$<$" is *not* symmetric and *not* reflexive.

3. What is the difference between an axiom and any other property?

4. Calvin Butterball sees the expression $x^2 + 3x - 5$. He decides to substitute 7 for the first x and 2 for the second x. What axiom has he violated?

5. What axiom tells you that a variable such as x can stand for only *one* number at a time?

6. State, without proof,
    a. the Addition Property of Order, and
    b. the Multiplication Property of Order.

For Problems 7 through 32, prove the property either from scratch or by supplying names of the properties justifying the given steps. As reasons for steps, you may use any axiom or definition, or any other property whose proof appears *before* the one you are doing.

7. Prove the *Multiplication Property of Equality* which states that you can multiply both members of an equation by the same number.

8. Prove the *converse* of the Multiplication Property of Equality.

9. If you proved the property in Problem 8, you proved a *false* theorem! For example, $3 \times 0 = 5 \times 0$, but 3 does *not* equal 5. Fix the hypothesis in Problem 8 so that the theorem *is* true. Then think up a good name for this property.

10. Can the Multiplication Property of Equality and its converse be written as a single statement using "if and only if"? Explain.

11. The symbol $-(-x)$ means the additive inverse of $-x$. Use this fact to prove that $-(-x) = x$.

12. The symbol $\frac{1}{\frac{1}{x}}$ means the multiplicative inverse (reciprocal) of $\frac{1}{x}$. Use this fact to prove that $\frac{1}{\frac{1}{x}} = x$. For what value of x is the theorem *false*?

13. *Property of the Reciprocal of a Product*

    Prove that $\frac{1}{xy} = \frac{1}{x} \cdot \frac{1}{y}$.

    Proof:

    a. $\left(\dfrac{1}{xy}\right)(xy) = 1$

    b. $\left[\left(\dfrac{1}{xy}\right)(xy)\right] \cdot \dfrac{1}{y} = 1 \cdot \dfrac{1}{y}$

    c. $\left[\left(\dfrac{1}{xy}\right)(x)\right]\left(y \cdot \dfrac{1}{y}\right) = 1 \cdot \dfrac{1}{y}$

d. $\left[\left(\dfrac{1}{xy}\right)(x)\right] \cdot 1 = 1 \cdot \dfrac{1}{y}$

e. $\left(\dfrac{1}{xy}\right)(x) = \dfrac{1}{y}$

f. $\left[\left(\dfrac{1}{xy}\right)(x)\right] \cdot \dfrac{1}{x} = \dfrac{1}{y} \cdot \dfrac{1}{x}$

g. $\dfrac{1}{xy}\left(x \cdot \dfrac{1}{x}\right) = \dfrac{1}{y} \cdot \dfrac{1}{x}$

h. $\dfrac{1}{xy} \cdot 1 = \dfrac{1}{y} \cdot \dfrac{1}{x}$

i. $\dfrac{1}{xy} = \dfrac{1}{y} \cdot \dfrac{1}{x}$

j. $\therefore \dfrac{1}{xy} = \dfrac{1}{x} \cdot \dfrac{1}{y}$, Q.E.D.

Multiplication Property of Zero

Prove that for any real number x, $x \cdot 0 = 0$.

Proof:
a. $0 = 0$
b. $0 + 0 = 0$
c. $x(0 + 0) = x \cdot 0$
d. $x(0 + 0) = 0 + x \cdot 0$
e. $x \cdot 0 + x \cdot 0 = 0 + x \cdot 0$
f. $\therefore x \cdot 0 = 0$, Q.E.D.

Converse of the Multiplication Property of Zero

Prove that if $xy = 0$, then $x = 0$ or $y = 0$.

Proof:
a.   Either $y = 0$ or $y \neq 0$

b.   If $y = 0$, the conclusion is true.
      (Only *one* clause of an "or" statement needs to be true.)

c.   If $y \neq 0$, then $\frac{1}{y}$ is a real number.

d. $xy = 0$

e. $(xy) \cdot \dfrac{1}{y} = 0 \cdot \dfrac{1}{y}$

f. $(xy) \cdot \dfrac{1}{y} = 0$

g. $x\left(y \cdot \dfrac{1}{y}\right) = 0$

h. $x \cdot 1 = 0$

i. $x = 0$

j. $\therefore x = 0$ or $y = 0$, Q.E.D.
(From Steps b and i.)

16. The Multiplication Property of Zero can be stated, "If $x = 0$ or $y = 0$, then $xy = 0$." Write this property and its converse as a *single* statement using "if and only if" terminology.

17. *Lemma—Multiplication Property of Negative One*

Prove that $-1 \cdot x = -x$.

Proof:

$$-1 \cdot x + x$$
a. $\quad = -1 \cdot x + 1 \cdot x$
b. $\quad = (-1 + 1)(x)$
c. $\quad = 0 \cdot x$
d. $\quad = 0$
e. $\quad = -x + x$
f. $\quad \therefore -1 \cdot x + x = -x + x$
g. $\quad \therefore -1 \cdot x = -x$, Q.E.D.

Theorem—The Product of Two Negatives is Positive.

Prove that $(-x)(-y) = xy$.

Proof:

$$(-x)(-y)$$
a. $\quad = (-1 \cdot x)(-1 \cdot y)$
b. $\quad = (-1)[x \cdot (-1)](y)$
c. $\quad = (-1)[-1 \cdot x](y)$
d. $\quad = [-1 \cdot (-1)](xy)$
e. $\quad = 1 \cdot xy$
f. $\quad = xy$
g. $\quad \therefore (-x)(-y) = xy$, Q.E.D.

Note that there *is* a reason why $-1 \cdot (-1) = 1$ in Step e which does not involve circular reasoning. You must treat each of the -1's *differently* to see how the reasoning works. This property tells you the *real* reason why the product of two negatives is positive. If it came out any other way, it would contradict the Field Axioms. This is an example of a not-so-obvious property which turns out to be *true*.

19. *If Two Real Numbers are Equal, then their Additive Inverses are Equal.*
    a. *State* this property using letters to stand for the numbers.
    b. *Prove* this property. You may find that the Multiplication Property of -1 is useful as a lemma.

20. *If Two Real Numbers are Equal, then their Multiplicative Inverses are Equal.*
    a. *State* this property using letters to stand for the numbers. Be sure that the hypothesis *excludes* the one number for which the property is false.
    b. *Prove* the property.

21. Prove that *the square of a real number is never negative.* Do this by showing that whatever value you pick for x,

    $$x^2 \geq 0.$$

    The axiom of trichotomy and the Multiplication Property of Order should be helpful as lemmas.

22. *Multiplication Distributes over Subtraction.*

    Prove that $x(y - z) = xy - xz$.

    Proof:

           $x(y - z)$
    a. $= x[y + (-z)]$
    b. $= xy + x(-z)$
    c. $= xy + x[(-1)(z)]$
    d. $= xy + [(x)(-1)]z$
    e. $= xy + [(-1)(x)]z$
    f. $= xy + (-1)(xz)$
    g. $= xy + (-xz)$
    h. $= xy - xz$
    i. $\therefore x(y - z) = xy - xz$, Q.E.D.

23. Prove that *division distributes over addition.* That is, prove that

    $$\frac{x + y}{z} = \frac{x}{z} + \frac{y}{z}.$$

    Do this by first transforming the division to multiplication using the Definition of Division. Then distribute the multiplication over the addition.

    Note that this property when read backwards says that you can add two fractions when they have a *common* denominator. This explains

why you must *find* a common denominator before you *can* add two
fractions. Adding fractions any other way (such as adding the numerators and adding the denominators) would violate the field axioms.

24. *Multiplication Property of Fractions*

Prove that $\dfrac{xy}{ab} = \dfrac{x}{a} \cdot \dfrac{y}{b}$.

Proof:

a. $\qquad \dfrac{xy}{ab} = (xy) \cdot \dfrac{1}{ab}$

b. $\qquad = (xy)\left(\dfrac{1}{a} \cdot \dfrac{1}{b}\right)$

c. $\qquad = x\left(y \cdot \dfrac{1}{a}\right) \cdot \dfrac{1}{b}$

d. $\qquad = x\left(\dfrac{1}{a} \cdot y\right) \cdot \dfrac{1}{b}$

e. $\qquad = \left(x \cdot \dfrac{1}{a}\right)\left(y \cdot \dfrac{1}{b}\right)$

f. $\qquad = \dfrac{x}{a} \cdot \dfrac{y}{b}$

g. $\therefore \dfrac{xy}{ab} = \dfrac{x}{a} \cdot \dfrac{y}{b}$, Q.E.D.

Note that this property when read backwards says that the way to
multiply two fractions is to multiply their denominators together and
multiply their numerators together. Again, the reason you do not
multiply fractions in other ways is because to do so would violate the
field axioms.

25. Prove that *division distributes over subtraction.*

26. Prove that a *non-zero number divided by itself equals 1*, i.e., $\frac{n}{n} = 1$.

27. Prove that *1 is its own reciprocal.* That is, $\frac{1}{1} = 1$.

28. Prove that a *number divided by 1 is that number,* i.e., $\frac{n}{1} = n$.

29. Prove that a *negative number divided by a positive number is negative,* $\frac{-x}{y} = -\frac{x}{y}$.

30. Prove that a *positive number divided by a negative number is negative*, $\frac{x}{-y} = -\frac{x}{y}$.

31. Prove that *the negative of a sum equals the sum of the negatives*. That is, prove that $-(x + y) = -x + (-y)$.

32. Prove that $x - y$ *and* $y - x$ *are additive inverses of each other*. That is, prove that $-(x - y) = y - x$.

1-8 | CHAPTER REVIEW AND TEST

The purpose of this chapter has been to refresh your memory about some of the words and techniques of mathematics so that you and your instructor will be speaking the same language. The objectives of the chapter can be summarized as follows:

1. *Name various kinds of numbers.*
2. *State and prove properties.*
3. a. *Recognize and name polynomials.*
   b. *Simplify expressions.*
   c. *Evaluate expressions.*
4. *Solve equations and inequalities.*

The Review Problems below give you a relatively straightforward test of these objectives. The problem numbers correspond to the objectives so that you will have no doubt about what is expected of you. The Concepts Test, on the other hand, has problems that may require you to use *several* of the objectives. In some cases, you will have the chance to *extend* your knowledge by applying what you know to *new* situations. For this reason, the Concepts Test may be longer and more difficult than a test your instructor might give you.

REVIEW PROBLEMS

The following problems are numbered according to the four objectives listed above.

R1. a. Give an example of
   i.   a rational number that is not an integer,
   ii. an irrational number that is not positive,
   iii. an imaginary number,
   iv. a transcendental number,

     v. a negative even number,
    vi. a positive integer that is not a digit,
   vii. a natural number,
  viii. a real number that is not a natural number,
    ix. a real number that is neither positive nor negative,
    x. an irrational number that is not a real number.

b. Name all the sets of numbers to which each of the following belongs.
     i. 2
    ii. -3
   iii. $\sqrt{3}$
   iv. $\sqrt{-3}$
    v. 2.3

R2. a. What is meant by
     i. an axiom?
    ii. a lemma?
   iii. a corollary?
   iv. a hypothesis?

    b. State each of the following, and tell whether or not it is an axiom. If so, is it a *Field* Axiom?
     i. Definition of Subtraction.
    ii. Multiplicative Inverses Property.
   iii. Trichotomy.
   iv. Closure of {real numbers} under addition.
    v. Additive Identity Property.
   vi. Multiplication Property of Order.

    c. *Positive Divided by Negative* — Justify each step of the following proof.

Prove that $\frac{x}{-y} = -\frac{x}{y}$.

Proof:
$$\frac{x}{-y}$$

i. $= x \cdot \dfrac{1}{-y}$

ii. $= x \cdot \dfrac{1}{-1 \cdot y}$

iii. $= x \cdot \left(\dfrac{1}{-1} \cdot \dfrac{1}{y} \right)$

iv. $= x \cdot \left(-1 \cdot \dfrac{1}{y} \right)$

v. $= [x \cdot (-1)] \cdot \dfrac{1}{y}$

vi. $= [-1 \cdot x] \cdot \dfrac{1}{y}$

vii. $= -1 \cdot \left(x \cdot \dfrac{1}{y} \right)$

viii. $= -1 \cdot \dfrac{x}{y}$

ix. $= -\dfrac{x}{y}$

x. $\therefore \dfrac{x}{-y} = -\dfrac{x}{y}$, Q.E.D.

d. The Distributive Axiom states that multiplication distributes over a sum of *two* terms. That is, $a(b + c) = ab + ac$. Prove that multiplication also distributes over a sum of *three* terms. Starting with $a(b + c + d)$, you can use the Associative Property to write the expression inside the parentheses as *two* terms. Then you can use the Distributive Axiom *twice* to get the desired result.

R3. a. Name each polynomial by degree and by number of terms. If it is *not* a polynomial, tell *why* not.
   i. $x^2y - 5$
   ii. $\dfrac{x^2}{y} - 5$
   iii. $x^2\sqrt{y} - 5$
   iv. $x^2y^2 - \sqrt{5}$
   v. $4^2r^2s^3$
   vi. $6x^2 + 7x - 5$

b. Carry out the indicated operations and simplify.
   i. $13 - 5 + 1$
   ii. $40 \div 10 \times 2$
   iii. $24 - 12 \div 3 + 1$
   iv. $(3x + 7)(x - 8)$
   v. $5 - 3[x - 7(2x - 6)]$

c. Evaluate the following expressions for $x = 5$ and $x = -4$.
   i. $3x - 8$
   ii. $|2x - 10|$
   iii. $3x^2 - 2x + 11$

R4. a. Write the solution set.
   i. $2x + 7 = -5$, $x \in \{\text{integers}\}$
   ii. $5x - 3 = 8$, $x \in \{\text{integers}\}$
   iii. $(2x + 6)(3x - 2) = 0$, $x \in \{\text{rational numbers}\}$
   iv. $|4x + 3| = 9$, $x \in \{\text{positive numbers}\}$
   v. $x^2 = 81$, $x \in \{\text{real numbers}\}$

b. Graph the solution set.
  i. $4x - 3 < 7,$ $x \in$ {real numbers}
  ii. $2 - 5x \leq 17,$ $x \in$ {real numbers}
  iii. $|x - 2| > 5,$ $x \in$ {integers}
  iv. $|3 - 4x| \leq 9,$ $x \in$ {integers}

CONCEPTS TEST

Work each of the problems below. For each part of each problem, tell by number and letter which one or ones of the above objectives you used in that problem. Also, if the problem involves a new concept, write, "new concept."

T1. Give an example of
  a. a cubic binomial with three variables,
  b. a quintic monomial with two variables,
  c. a quadratic trinomial,
  d. an expression that is not a polynomial,
  e. a rational number between -12 and -13,
  f. a radical that represents a rational number,
  g. the Multiplicative Identity Axiom,
  h. the Additive Inverse Axiom.

T2. Write an example that shows why,
  a. subtraction is *not* associative,
  b. exponentiation is *not* commutative,
  c. {real numbers} is *not* closed under the operation "square root,"
  d. multiplication *does* distribute over subtraction.

T3. Given the expression $3x - 4[2x - (5x - 9)],$
  a. *evaluate* it by substituting 7 for x, and then doing the indicated operations,
  b. *simplify* it, *without* substituting a value for x,
  c. substitute 7 for x in the simplified expression of part b and show that you get the same value as in part a.

T4. Given the expression $(x + 7)(2x - 3),$
  a. carry out the indicated multiplication and simplify,
  b. find the value(s) of x that make the expression equal to 0.

T5. Transform the following to equivalent inequalities that have *no* absolute value signs. Then graph the solution sets.
  a. $|x - 3| < 7,$ $x \in$ {integers}
  b. $|7 - 2x| \leq 1,$ $x \in$ {real numbers}

T6. What extraneous solution is created if you multiply both members of the equation $x = 17$ by the expression $(x - 23)$?

T7. There is a set of numbers that contains both the real numbers *and* the imaginary numbers. What is the name of this set?

T8. Write the Multiplication Property of Zero and its converse, as a *single* statement, using "if and only if."

T9. a. If the converse of the Multiplication Property of Equality were true, what would it say?
     b. Explain why this converse is *false*.

T10. Professor Snarff gives an algebra test on which students must add

$$\frac{5}{7} + \frac{6}{7}.$$

Calvin Butterball gets $\frac{11}{14}$ and Phoebe Small gets $\frac{11}{7}$.
     a. Who is right?
     b. Name the property that explains *why* he or she is right.

T11. You have learned what it means to say that equality is "reflexive," "symmetric," and "transitive." Answer the following questions about the relationship " $\neq$," which means, "is *not* equal to."
     a. Is $\neq$ reflexive?   Justify your answer.
     b. Is $\neq$ symmetric?   Justify your answer.
     c. Write an example that shows why $\neq$ is *not* transitive.

T12. In Section 1-7 it was stated that the Transitive Property of Order is an *axiom*. By making precise definitions of $>$ and $<$, you can use other axioms to *prove* that order is transitive.

DEFINITION

> **$>$ AND $<$**
>
> $a > b$ if and only if $a - b$ is *positive*.
> $a < b$ if and only if $b > a$.

The only other fact you need to know is that {positive numbers} is *closed* under $+$ and $\times$. Supply reasons for the following proof.

Prove that if $x > y$ and $y > z$, then $x > z$.

Proof:

a. $x > y$ and $y > z$.
b. $x - y$ is positive and $y - z$ is positive.

c. $(x - y) + (y - z)$ is positive.
d. $x + (-y + y) - z$ is positive.
e. $x + 0 - z$ is positive.
f. $x - z$ is positive.
g. $x > z$,   Q.E.D.

T13.   Prove that if you multiply both members of an inequality by a *positive* number, the order does *not* change. That is, prove that if $x > y$ and z is positive, then $xz > yz$.

T14.   Supply reasons that the order *reverses* in the steps in the following proof when you multiply both members of an inequality by a *negative* number.

Prove that if $x > y$ and z is negative, then $xz < yz$.

Proof:

a. z is negative.
b. $\therefore (-1)(z)$ is positive.
c. $\therefore -z$ is positive.
d. $x > y$
e. $\therefore x - y$ is positive.
f. $\therefore (x - y)(-z)$ is positive.
g. $\therefore -xz + yz$ is positive.
h. $\therefore yz + (-xz)$ is positive.
i. $\therefore yz - xz$ is positive.
j. $\therefore yz > xz$.
k. $\therefore xz < yz$,   Q.E.D.

T15.   Use the result of Problem Concepts Test 14 as a lemma to prove that if $x < y$ and z is negative, then $xz > yz$.

2

Functions and Relations

In Chapter 1 you refreshed your memory about properties of numbers, and how the properties are used to evaluate expressions and solve equations. Now you will concentrate on equations that have **two** variables. These equations tell how one variable is **related** to the other. In Exercise 2-3 you will draw graphs showing the relationship betwen variables such as the altitude of a football and the time since it was kicked, or the temperature of the water and the time since the "hot" faucet was turned on.

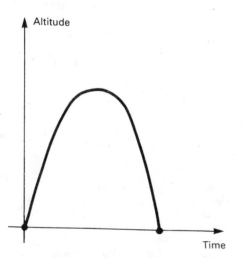

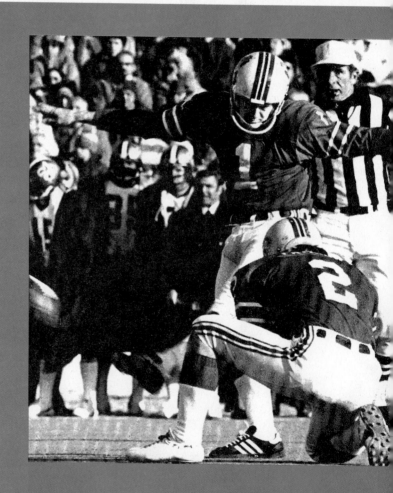

<table>
<tr><td>2-1</td><td>GRAPHS OF EQUATIONS WITH TWO VARIABLES</td></tr>
</table>

You have learned how to plot number-line graphs of equations with *one* variable. In this section you will plot a graph of an equation with *two* variables.

Objective:
Use what you recall from previous mathematics courses to draw the graph of an equation with two variables.

In order to satisfy the equation

$$2x - 3y = 15,$$

it is necessary to specify values for both x and y. For instance, if $x = 9$, then

$$2 \cdot 9 - 3y = 15 \quad \text{Substituting 9 for } x.$$

$$- 3y = -3 \quad \text{Subtracting 18.}$$

$$y = 1. \quad \text{Dividing by } -3.$$

So $x = 9$ and $y = 1$ is a solution of $2x - 3y = 15$.

It is customary to write the values of the two variables as *ordered pairs*, such as (9, 1), where the first number stands for a value of x and the second for a value of y.

The solution set of an equation with two variables contains all the ordered pairs that make the equation true. Since there are *two* numbers in each ordered pair, the graph will consist of points in a *two*-dimensional plane, as in Figure 2-1, rather than a one-dimensional number line. The first coordinate ("abscissa") in the ordered pair is plotted horizontally and the second

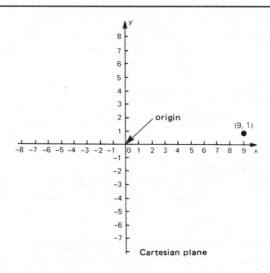

Figure 2-1 _____

coordinate ("ordinate") is plotted vertically. You may recall from previous mathematics courses that this plane is called a Cartesian coordinate system, after the French mathematician Rene Descartes who lived from 1596 to 1650.

In the following exercise you will plot more solutions of the equation $2x - 3y = 15$, and try to see what pattern the points follow.

EXERCISE 2-1

1. Show that the ordered pair (9, 1) satisfies the equation $2x - 3y = 15$. Do this by substituting 9 for x and 1 for y, and showing that you get a *true* statement.

2. Show that the ordered pair (1, 9) does *not* satisfy the equation $2x - 3y = 15$.

3. Substitute 6 for x in $2x - 3y = 15$, and solve for y. Then draw a Cartesian coordinate system as in Figure 2-1, and plot this point on it.

4. Repeat Problem 3 for $x = 3$, 0, and -3. Use the same Cartesian coordinate system.

5. Connect the points you have drawn on the Cartesian coordinate system of Problem 3. If they do not all lie on the same straight line, go back and check your work!

2-2 | GRAPHS OF FUNCTIONS

In Exercise 2-1 you plotted the graph of the solution set of $2x - 3y = 15$. The graph should look like Figure 2-2a.

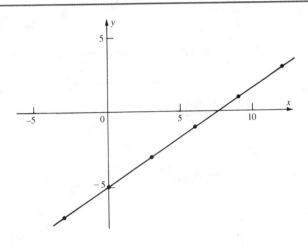

Figure 2-2a

The graph can be more easily plotted if you first transform the equation so that y is by itself on one side.

$$2x - 3y = 15 \qquad \text{Write the given equation.}$$
$$-3y = -2x + 15 \qquad \text{Subtract } 2x \text{ from each member.}$$
$$y = \tfrac{2}{3}x - 5 \qquad \text{Divide each member by } -3.$$

All you need to do to find many ordered pairs is pick values of x (preferably multiples of 3 in this case), substitute them, and calculate y. The dots in Figure 2-2a show some of these ordered pairs.

Whenever a unique value of y can be found for each value of x, y is said to be a *function* of x. The formal definition of function is in Section 2-4. The variable that appears by itself on one side of the equation is called the *dependent variable* because the value you get for it depends on what you picked for the other variable. The other variable is called the *independent variable*. The dependent variable is usually plotted on the vertical axis.

Objective:
Given the equation of a function, plot the graph.

The graph in Figure 2-2a is a straight line. Many functions have graphs that are curved. In order to plot such graphs you should evaluate y for enough values of x to find a pattern. Then connect the points with a smooth curve.

EXAMPLE 1

Plot the graph of $y = 0.2x^2$.

Solution:
Make a table of values, then plot these as shown in Figure 2-2b.

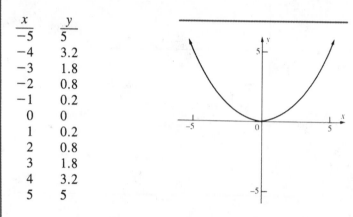

x	y
-5	5
-4	3.2
-3	1.8
-2	0.8
-1	0.2
0	0
1	0.2
2	0.8
3	1.8
4	3.2
5	5

Figure 2-2b ⬛

Sometimes not all values of x are permitted. For instance, in the function $y = \frac{1}{(x-2)}$, x cannot be 2 or you would wind up dividing by zero. At other times you are simply told that the function applies only for certain values of x. The values of x that you are allowed to substitute is called the domain of the function.

DEFINITION

> **DOMAIN**
> The **domain** of a function is the set of values of the *independent variable*.

As was pointed out in Section 1-3, the word "domain" comes from the Latin word "domus," meaning "house." So the domain of a function is where the independent variable "lives."

The set of values you would get for y by substituting all permissible values of x is called the range of the function.

DEFINITION

> **RANGE**
> The *range* of a function is the set of values of the *dependent* variable corresponding to all values of the independent variable in the domain.

The graph in Figure 2-2c is intended to help you keep in mind the definitions of domain and range.

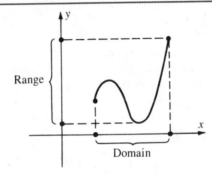

Figure 2-2c

EXAMPLE 2

Plot the graph of $y = \frac{10}{x}$ if the domain is {integers between 1 and 6, inclusive}. Tell the range.

Solution:

x	y
1	10
2	5
3	$3\frac{1}{3}$
4	$2\frac{1}{2}$
5	2
6	$1\frac{2}{3}$

Range $= \{10, 5, 3\frac{1}{3}, 2\frac{1}{2}, 2, 1\frac{2}{3}\}$

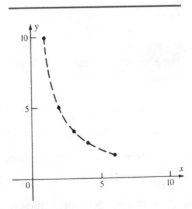

Figure 2-2d

The graph is shown in Figure 2-2d. Note that the graph is a set of discrete points. The dotted line connecting the points just shows the pattern they follow, and is not part of the graph itself.   ■

In the following exercise you will plot graphs of functions.

EXERCISE 2-2

Do These Quickly

The following are 10 miscellaneous problems. They are intended to refresh your skills from the first chapter and from previous courses. You should be able to do all 10 in less than 5 minutes.

Q1.   Tell what axiom was used: $4(3 + x) = 4(x + 3)$

Q2.   Solve: $8x + 3 = 39$

Q3.   Simplify: $5x - 2 + 6x$

Q4.   Distribute: $7x(x^3 - 2)$

Q5.   Find 70% of 42.

Q6.   Write $\frac{3}{8}$ as a decimal.

Q7.   Solve: $|x - 2| = 8$

Q8.   Isolate x: $-5x > 34$

Q9.   Write a negative rational number that is not an integer.

Q10.   Tell the degree: $5^3x^9 - y^4z^6$

For Problems 1 through 12, plot the graph of the function and tell the range.

1. $y = 0.3x^2$, domain = {real numbers}

2. $y = -0.5x^2$, domain = {real numbers}

3. $y = x + 3$, domain = {non-negative integers}

4. $y = x - 5$, domain = {positive integers}

5. $y = \frac{-12}{x}$, domain = {positive real numbers}

6. $y = \frac{5}{x}$, domain $= \{x: 0.4 \le x \le 10\}$

7. $y = \frac{2}{3}x + 4$, domain $= \{x: -3 < x < 9\}$

8. $y = -0.4x + 5$, domain $= \{x: -2 \le x \le 6\}$

9. $y = |x - 3|$, domain $= \{x: 0 \le x \le 7\}$

10. $y = |x + 2|$, domain $= \{$real numbers$\}$

11. $y = x^2 - 5x + 7$, domain $= \{0, 1, 2, 3, 4, 5, 6\}$

12. $y = -x^2 + 5.4x + 1$, domain $= \{$positive numbers$\}$

For Problems 13 through 16, tell the domain and range of the function.

13.
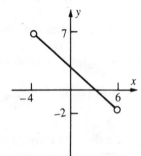

14.
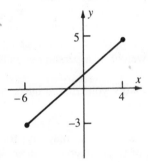

15.
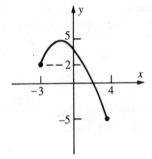

16.
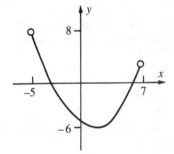

For Problems 17 through 20, sketch a graph of a function with the given domain and range.

17. domain: $\{x: 3 \le x \le 7\}$, range: $\{y: 1 \le y \le 10\}$

18. domain: $\{x: 1 \le x \le 4\}$, range: $\{y: -3 \le y \le 5\}$

19. domain: $\{x: 2 < x < 3\}$, range: $\{y: 5 < y < 7\}$

20. domain: $\{x: 0 < x < 5\}$, range: $\{y: 2 < y \le 7\}$ (Be clever!)

2·3 | FUNCTIONS IN THE REAL WORLD

In the last section you plotted graphs of functions that had equations such as

$$y = \frac{10}{x}.$$

In situations from the real world there are often two variable quantities that are related in such a way that the value of one variable depends on the value of the other. For example:

1. The position of a speedometer needle depends on how fast the car is going.
2. The distance you travel depends on how long you have been traveling (and on how fast you are going, also!).
3. The weight of a person depends on his or her height (and on other variables).
4. How badly your thumb hurts depends on how hard you hit it with a hammer.

In cases like this you may say, for example, that the distance traveled is a *function* of time. If you know something about the relationship between distance and time, you may be able to write an equation relating the variables. Even if you don't know enough to write an equation, you can still draw a reasonable graph representing the relationship. In this section you will sketch this kind of graph.

Objective:
Given a situation from the real world in which the value of one variable depends on the value of the other, sketch a reasonable graph showing this relationship.

EXAMPLE 1

The time it takes you to get home from the football game and the speed you drive are related to each other. Sketch a reasonable graph showing this relationship.

Solution:
Since you are not told which variable depends on the other, your first job is to make this decision. You should ask yourself which of the following sounds more reasonable:

"How long it takes depends on how fast I go." "How fast I go depends on how long it takes."

Most people feel that the first sentence is more reasonable, and pick *time* as the dependent variable. So speed is the independent variable. Since you have already agreed to plot the dependent variable on the vertical axis, you draw and label axes as in Figure 2-3a.

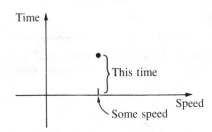

Figure 2-3a

To figure out what the graph looks like, pick some moderate speed and plot a point at a moderate length of time, as in Figure 2-3a. Then think about what happens to the time as your speed varies. When speed is *lower*, time is *longer*. When speed is *higher*, time is *shorter*. Put a point to the left and above the first one, and another to the right and below the first one, as in Figure 2-3b.

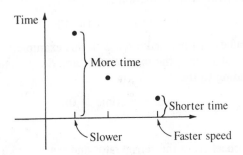

Figure 2-3b

When you have enough points to tell what the graph looks like, connect them with a line or curve. Figure 2-3c shows the completed graph. Since it always takes you *some* amount of time no matter how fast you drive, the graph never touches the horizontal axis. Similarly, since you would *never* get home if speed were zero, the graph never touches the vertical axis.

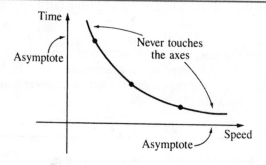

Figure 2-3c _____

A line the graph approaches as it does the horizontal or vertical axis in Figure 2-3 is called an *asymptote*. The word comes from Greek, and means, "not coming together."

DEFINITION

> **ASYMPTOTE**
> An **asymptote** is a line which a graph gets arbitrarily close to, but never touches, as the independent or dependent variable gets very large (in the positive or the negative direction).

In Example 1, the speed should always be positive. Negative speeds have no meaning in this case since going "backwards" would not take you home. So the domain of this function is

$$\text{Domain} = \{\text{speed} > 0\}.$$

Only positive values of time make sense in this example. You cannot get home *before* you start or at the *instant* you start. So the range of the functioin, corresponding to the domain, is

$$\text{Range} = \{\text{time} > 0\}.$$

EXAMPLE 2

You take a roast beef from the refrigerator and put it into a hot oven. The temperature of the beef depends on how long it has been in the oven. Sketch a reasonable graph.

Solution:

Figure 2-3d shows a reasonable graph. When time < 0, the beef is still in the refrigerator, so its temperature is the same as that of the refrigerator. For time > 0, the beef warms up rapidly at first, then more slowly, and finally approaches the oven temperature very gradually. It is debatable whether the beef ever actually *reaches* oven temperature, or just gets so close that nobody can tell the difference. Thus, the dotted line at oven

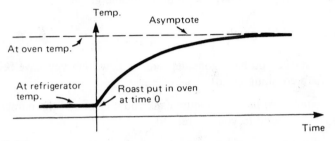

Figure 2-3d _____

temperature is an *asymptote*. The domain in this case includes both positive and negative values of time. The range is the set of temperatures between refrigerator temperature and oven temperature. The temperatures *could* be *negative* if the beef had been in the freezer. You might be able to think of ways to make the graph even more reasonable in that case! ■

In the exercise which follows, you will obtain practice sketching reasonable graphs of real-world situations in accordance with the objective of this section. Many of these real-world situations will appear in later chapters when you study about relations which have graphs like these.

EXERCISE 2-3

Do These Quickly

The following problems are intended to refresh your skills. You should be able to do all 10 in less than 5 minutes.

Q1.   On which axis is the independent variable plotted?

Q2.   Draw an isosceles triangle.

Q3.   Find 3% of 800.

Q4.   Multiply: $(2x + 7)(3x - 4)$

Q5.   If j is a function of p, which variable *depends*?

Q6.   Multiply: $(0.3)(0.2)$

Q7.   Add and simplify: $\frac{2}{3} + \frac{3}{4}$

Q8.   Associate the 7 and the y: $4 + 7 + y$

Q9.   Solve: $|x - 4| = 13$

Q10.   Draw a number-line graph: $-x < 5$

For Problems 1 through 44, sketch a reasonable graph.

Sketch a reasonable graph.

1. The distance you have gone depends on how long you have been going (at a constant speed).

2. The number of used aluminum cans you collect and the number of dollars refunded to you are related.

3. The distance required to stop your car depends on how fast you are going when you apply the brakes.

4. The mass of a person of average build depends on his or her height.

5. Your car is standing on a long, level highway. You start the motor and floorboard the gas pedal. The speed you are going depends on the number of seconds that have passed since you stepped on the gas pedal.

6. The altitude of a punted football depends on the number of seconds since it was kicked.

7. The maximum speed your car will go depends on how steep a hill you are going up or down.

8. Dan Druff's age and the number of hairs he has growing on his head are related.

9. The distance you are from the band and how loud it sounds to you are related.

10. You fill up your car's gas tank and start driving. The amount of gas you have left in the tank depends on how far you have driven.

11. Your age and your height are related to one another.

12. You pull the plug out of the bathtub. The amount of water remaining in the tub and the number of seconds since you pulled the plug are related to each other.

13. The price you pay for a carton of milk depends on how much milk the carton holds.

14. Calvin Butterball desires to lose some weight, so he reduces his food intake from 8000 calories per day to 2000 calories per day. His weight depends on the number of days that have elapsed since he reduced his food intake.

15. The price you pay for a pizza depends on the diameter of the pizza.

16. The distance you are from the reading lamp and the amount of light it shines on your book are related.

17. You climb to the top of the 190-meter tall Tower of the Americas and drop your algebra book off. The distance the book is above the

ground depends on the number of seconds that have passed since you dropped it.

18. As you blow up a balloon, its diameter and the number of breaths you have blown into it are related.

19. The temperature of your cup of coffee is related to how long it has been cooling.

20. You turn on the hot water faucet. As the water runs, its temperature depends on the number of seconds it has been since you turned on the faucet.

21. The time of sunrise depends on the day of the year.

22. As you breathe, the volume of air in your lungs depends upon time.

23. You start running, and go as fast as you can for a long period of time. The number of minutes you have been running and the speed you are going are related to each other.

24. As you play with a yo-yo, the number of seconds that have passed and the yo-yo's distance from the floor are related.

25. You run the mile once each day. The length of time it takes you to run it depends on the number of times you have run it in practice.

26. When you dive off the 3-meter diving board, time, and your position in relation to the water's surface, are related to each other.

27. The rate at which you are breathing depends on how long it has been since you finished running a race.

28. Taryn Feathers catches the bus to work each morning. Busses depart every 10 minutes. The time she gets to work depends on the time she leaves home.

29. Milt Famey pitches his famous fast ball to Stan Dupp, who hits it for a home run. The number of seconds that have elapsed since Milt released the ball and its distance from the ground are related.

30. The amount of postage you must put on a first-class letter depends on the weight of the letter.

31. The amount of water you have put on your lawn depends on how long the sprinkler has been running.

32. You plant an acorn. The height of the resulting oak tree depends on the number of years that have elapsed since the planting.

33. A leading soft drink company comes out with a new product, Ms. Phizz. They figure that there is a relationship between how much of the stuff they sell and how many dollars they spend on advertising.

34. Your car stalls, so you get out and push. The speed at which the car goes depends on how hard you push.

35. The number of letters in the corner mailbox depends upon the time of day.

36. The diameter of a plate and the amount of food you can put on it are related to each other.

37. The number of cents you pay for a long distance telephone call depends on how long you talk.

38. The grade you could make on a particular test depends upon how long you study for it.

39. You go from the sunlight into a dark room. The diameter of your pupils and the length of time you have been in the room are related.

40. The grade you could make on a particular test depends on how much time elapses between the time you study for it and the time you take the test.

41. You pour some cold water from the refrigerator into a glass, but forget to drink it. As the water sits there, its temperature depends on the number of minutes that have passed since you poured it.

42. Your efficiency at studying algebra depends on how late at night it is.

43. You pour some popcorn into a popper and turn it on. The number of pops per second depends on how long the popper has been turned on.

44. How well you can concentrate on algebra homework and how late at night it is are related.

2-4 | GRAPHS OF FUNCTIONS AND RELATIONS

So far the functions you have graphed have had a common feature. For any value of x you picked, there is only *one* value of y. Sometimes two variables are related by an equation that produces more than one value of y for a given value of x. For instance, if

$$y^2 = x,$$

then substituting a value such as 9 for x leads to

$$y^2 = 9$$

$$y = 3 \text{ or } -3.$$

Substituting a negative value for x produces no real value of y at all!

$$y^2 = -25$$

$$y = \text{no real number.}$$

Substituting other convenient values of x produces the following table.

x	y
0	0
1	1 or -1
4	2 or -2
9	3 or -3
-1	no real value
-4	no real value

The graph is shown in Figure 2-4a.

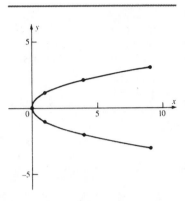

Figure 2-4a _____

If substituting a value of x ever produces more than one value for y, then y is not said to be a function of x. However, x and y are still related. Any set of ordered pairs relating two variables is called a *relation*. The name "function" is used only if each value of x has a unique value of y. This fact leads to the following formal definitions of relation and function.

DEFINITIONS

RELATION
A *relation* is a set of ordered pairs.

FUNCTION
A *function* is a relation for which there is *exactly one* value of the dependent variable for each value of the independent variable.

Objective:
Given the equation of a relation, draw its graph and tell whether or not the relation is a function.

EXAMPLE 1

Graph $|y| = x$. Tell whether or not the relation is a function.

Solution:
Substituting a positive value for x produces two values for y. For instance, if x is 4, then $|y| = 4$, and y is 4 or -4. Substituting a negative value for x produces no value for y. The equation $|y| = -3$ has no solutions. The graph is shown in Figure 2-4b.

x	y
-1	no value
0	0
1	1 or -1
2	2 or -2
3	3 or -3
4	4 or -4

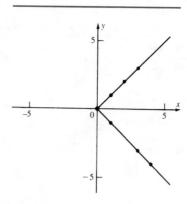

Figure 2-4b _____

Not a function.

If you already know what the graph of a relation looks like, you can tell quickly whether or not it is a function by using the *vertical line test*. Pick a value of x and draw a vertical line. If the graph ever crosses a vertical line more than once, then the relation is not a function. The result is shown in Figure 2-4c.

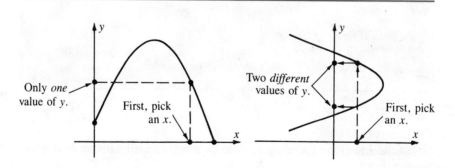

Figure 2-4c _____

The words "domain" and "range" are used for all relations, not just for those that are functions.

In the following exercise you will graph relations some of which are functions, and others of which are not.

EXERCISE 2-4

Do These Quickly

The following are 10 miscellaneous problems. They are intended to refresh your skills. You should be able to do all 10 in less than 5 minutes.

Q1.   Tell what axioms are used: $4(3 + x) = 4x + 12$

Q2.   Solve: $2x - 6x = 14$

Q3.   Simplify: $2x - 6x - 14$

Q4.   Multiply: $(2x + 5)(3x - 1)$

Q5.   50 is 40% of what number?

Q6.   Write $\frac{5}{8}$ as a decimal.

Q7.   Draw a parallelogram.

Q8.   Isolate x: $5x > -34$

Q9.   Write an expression for 3 less than twice x.

Q10.   Find $|13|$.

For Problems 1 through 10, plot the graph and tell whether or not the relation is a function. Assume that the domain is the set of all values of x for
which there are real-number values of y.

1. $y^2 = 9x$ 2. $9y = x^2$

3. $y = |x - 3|$ 4. $|y| = x + 2$

5. $2x + 3y = 12$ 6. $5x - 2y = 10$

7. $|y| = 0.5x$ 8. $y^2 = 4x$

9. $|y| = |x|$ 10. $2y = x + |x|$

For Problems 11 through 26, tell whether or not the relation graphed is a
function.

11.   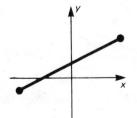   12.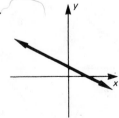

13.
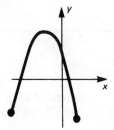

14.
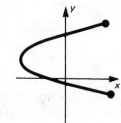

15.
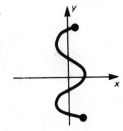

16.
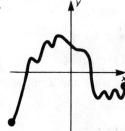

17.
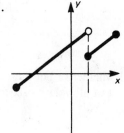

18.
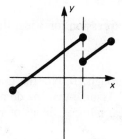

19.
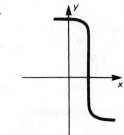

20.
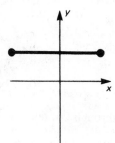

21.
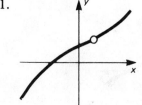

22.
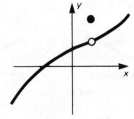

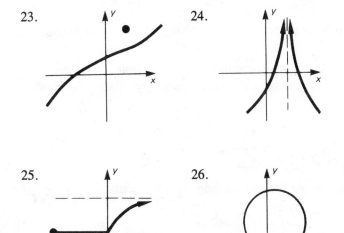

23.   24.

25.   26.

| 2-5 | CHAPTER REVIEW AND TEST |

In this chapter you have been introduced to the concept of a mathematical *function*. A function is a special kind of *relation*, or set of ordered pairs. A relation can be specified by an equation that tells how the two variables are related. The graph of such an equation can be plotted by calculating enough points to discover a pattern. Once you have plotted the graph, you can tell whether or not the relation is a function by seeing whether there are any values of x that have more than one value of y. Functions are important because they can be used to describe the relationship between two variable quantities in the real world.

The objectives of this chapter may be summarized as follows:

1. *Plot the graph of a given equation.*
2. *Tell whether or not a given graph is a function graph.*
3. *Draw reasonable graphs of real-world situations.*

Following are two sets of problems. The Review Problems are similar to those you have worked in this chapter. They are numbered according to the three objectives above. The Concepts Test requires you to put together two or more of these techniques (or to use concepts learned before), to work problems that are somewhat different. One of the most important things you should learn during your education is how to apply your knowledge to new situations!

REVIEW PROBLEMS

The following problems are numbered according to the three objectives listed above.

R1.   Plot the graph of the given equation in the indicated domain. Tell the corresponding range and whether or not the relation is a function.
    a. $x + y = 2,$ $-1 \leq x \leq 3$
    b. $x^2 + y = 2,$ $x \in \{-2, -1, 0, 1, 2\}$
    c. $x + y^2 = 2,$ $x \in \{-2, 1, 2\}$
    d. $x + |y| = 2,$ $-2 \leq x \leq 2$

R2.   Tell whether or not the relation graphed is a function.
    a.   b.

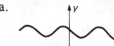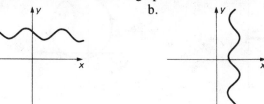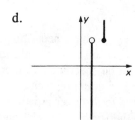

    c.   d.

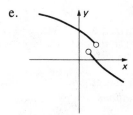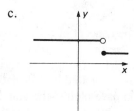

    e.   f.

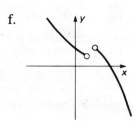

R3.   For each of the following, sketch a reasonable graph showing how the *dependent* variable is related to the *independent* variable.
    a. Your car stalls, and you roll to a stop without putting on the brakes. The car's speed depends on how long it has been since it stalled.

b.   The length of time an oven has been turned on and the oven's temperature are related.

c.   The angle at which you have to look up to see the Sun depends on the time of day. Make the domain extend for *several* days.

d.   The number of cars in the student parking lot and the time of day are related.

CONCEPTS TEST

The following problems combine all of the objectives of this chapter. For each part of each problem, do what is asked, then identify by number which one or ones of the objectives you used in working that part.

T1.   Consider the relation whose equation is

$$y = 1 + 4x - x^2.$$

a.   Plot the graph of this relation, assuming that the domain is the set of non-negative numbers, and that the range must also contain only non-negative numbers.

b.   What is the range of this relation?

c.   Is the relation a function? Justify your answer.

d.   At what value of y does the graph touch the y-axis?

e.   At approximately what value of x does the graph touch the x-axis?

f.   Tell *two* different real-world situations having graphs looking like this one.

T2.   *Introduction to Polynomial Functions* A function is called a "polynomial function" if it has an equation of the form

$$y = \text{a polynomial involving } x.$$

a.   Which of the relations in Problems 1–12 of Exercise 2-2 are polynomial functions?

b.   Explain how closure insures that the domain of a polynomial function can be the set of *all* real numbers.

c.   Explain how closure insures that a polynomial function really *is* a function.

3

Linear Functions

In Chapter 2 you learned that a **function** relates two variables. In this chapter you will study a special kind of function, the **linear** function. Your ultimate objective is to be able to write the **equation** for a linear function from given information about its graph. In Exercise 3-5 you will use this kind of equation to predict such things as how high a sky diver is.

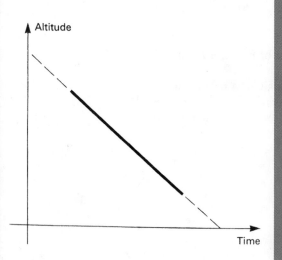

3-1 | INTRODUCTION TO LINEAR FUNCTIONS

A function is named according to its equation. For instance, if the equations is

$$y = 3x + 7,$$

then the function is called a *linear* function. This name is picked because y equals a linear polynomial in the variable x.

DEFINITION

> **LINEAR FUNCTION**
> A **linear function** is a function whose general equation is
> $$y = mx + b,$$
> where m and b stand for constants, and $m \neq 0$.

The equation $y = mx + b$ is called a *general equation*. If particular values are chosen for m and b, such as in $y = 3x + 7$, the equation is called a *particular equation*. If a particular equation had $m = 0$, such as $y = 7$, then y would equal a zero-degree polynomial. Thus, the function would be called a constant function, not a linear function.

Objective:
Discover what the graph of a linear function looks like, and what effects the values of m and b have.

In the following exercise you will accomplish this objective.

EXERCISE 3-1

1. Plot the graphs of the following functions by selecting values of x, calculating the corresponding values of y, and plotting the points.

   a. $y = x + 5$
   b. $y = 2x + 5$
   c. $y = 3x + 5$
   d. $y = -2x + 5$
   e. $y = 2x - 5$
   f. $y = 0x + 5$

2. From the graphs in Problem 1, answer the following questions.
   a. Why are first-degree functions called *linear* functions?
   b. What is the effect on the graph of changing the x-coefficient?
   c. What is the effect on the graph of changing the constant term?
   d. From what you have learned in previous mathematics courses, tell the special names given to the constants m and b in $y = mx + b$.

3. If m equals zero as in part (f) of Problem 1, the graph is a horizontal straight line. Yet the function is *not* called "linear." Why not?

3-2 | PROPERTIES OF LINEAR FUNCTION GRAPHS

In Exercise 3-1 you plotted the graphs of some linear functions. Figure 3-2a shows what some of these graphs look like.

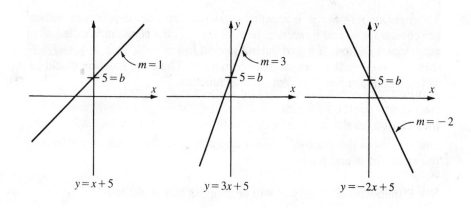

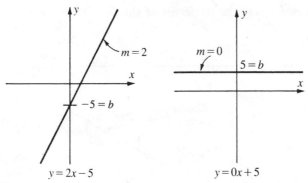

Figure 3-2a

From the graphs you should be able to see the following properties:

1. The graphs are *straight lines*.
2. The value of m determines how "tilted" the graph is:
   If m is positive: Graph slopes *up* as x increases.
   If m is negative: Graph slopes *down* as x increases.
   If m is zero: Graph is horizontal (constant function).
3. The value of b tells where the graph crosses the y-axis.

If you let x equal zero in an equation like $y = 3x + 7$, you get $y = 7$. So the value of y when $x = 0$ is the same as the constant term in the equation. Since this is the value of y where the graph "intercepts" the y-axis, it is called the y-intercept. Similarly, the x-intercept is the value of x when $y = 0$.

DEFINITION

> **INTERCEPTS**
> The **y-intercept** of a function is the value of y when $x = 0$.
> An **x-intercept** of a function is a value of x when $y = 0$.

A property of linear function graphs is illustrated in Figure 3-2b. If you start at any point on the graph and run along in the positive direction, then rise up (or down) to another point on the graph, then the ratio

$$\frac{\text{rise}}{\text{run}}$$

will be *constant*, no matter what two points you pick. This property is a direct consequence of the properties of similar triangles that you learned in geometry.

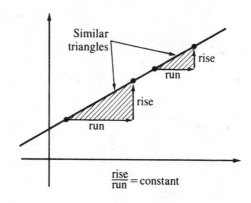

Figure 3-2b

The ratio rise/run is defined to be the *slope* of a linear function.

DEFINITION

> **SLOPE**
> The **slope** of a linear function is the ratio
>
> $$\frac{\text{rise}}{\text{run}}$$
>
> where the run is the horizontal distance between two points on the graph and the rise is vertical distance between the same two points.

If (x_1, y_1) and (x_2, y_2) are two points on the graph, then the rise and run can be found by subtracting the coordinates. Figure 3-2c shows why.

$$\text{rise} = y_2 - y_1 = \Delta y$$

$$\text{run} = x_2 - x_1 = \Delta x$$

The symbols Δy and Δx are pronounced "delta y" and "delta x." The Greek letter Δ is used because the rise and run are *differences* between y or x values.

Substituting these values into the definition of slope gives an equation that is called the *slope formula*.

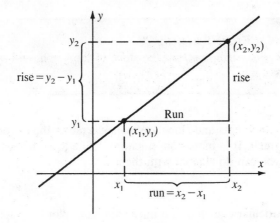

Figure 3-2c

PROPERTY

THE SLOPE FORMULA
If (x_1, y_1) and (x_2, y_2) are two points on the graph of a linear function, then

$$\text{slope} = \frac{y_2 - y_1}{x_2 - x_1} = \frac{\Delta y}{\Delta x}$$

It turns out that the constant m in the equation is also equal to the slope. To see why, follow the steps in the proof below. You should supply reasons for the steps, as you did in Section 1-7.

THEOREM

If $y = mx + b$, then m is the slope.

Proof:
Let (x_1, y_1) and (x_2, y_2) be two points on the graph.
Then $y_2 = mx_2 + b$,   and
        $y_1 = mx_1 + b$.
Subtracting the bottom equation from the top one gives

$$y_2 - y_1 = mx_2 - mx_1$$

$$\therefore y_2 - y_1 = m(x_2 - x_1)$$

$$\therefore \frac{y_2 - y_1}{x_2 - x_1} = m$$

$$\therefore m \text{ is the slope,}\quad \text{Q.E.D.}$$

PROPERTY

> **SLOPE-INTERCEPT FORM**
> If $y = mx + b$, then m equals the slope of the graph, and b equals the y-intercept.

Note that the intercepts and slope are *numbers* rather than geometrical features of the graph. It is more convenient to define these features as numbers so that you can do algebra with them.

Objective:
Given the particular equation of a linear function, plot its graph quickly, using slope and y-intercept.

EXAMPLE 1

Plot the graph of $y = \frac{2}{3}x + 4$ quickly.

Solution:
Your thought process should be:

1. The y-intercept is 4, because $y = 4$ when $x = 0$. Put your pencil on the y-axis, 4 units up.
2. The slope is $\frac{2}{3}$. Run across 3 units to the right, then rise up 2 units. Mark another point on the graph. Repeat the process, if necessary, to get more points.
3. Connect the points with a straight line.

Figure 3-2d shows these three steps.   ■

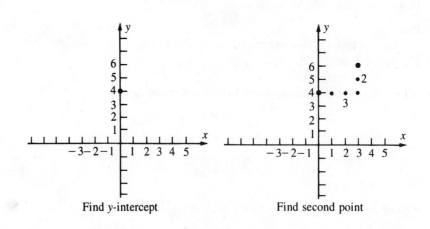

Find y-intercept   Find second point

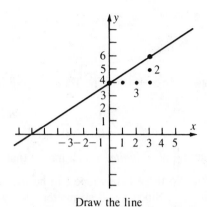

Draw the line

Figure 3-2d _____ ■

EXAMPLE 2

Plot the graph of $5x + 7y = 14$ quickly.

Solution:
You can change this new problem into an "old" problem by transforming the equation to the form $y = mx + b$. You would write:

$$5x + 7y = 14$$
$$7y = -5x + 14$$
$$y = -\tfrac{5}{7}x + 2$$

So $m = -\tfrac{5}{7}$ and $b = 2$. Since the slope is a negative number, either the rise or the run must be negative (and the other must be positive). Starting at $(0, 2)$ on the graph, you can either run forward 7 and down 5, or run backward 7 and up 5 to find another point. The graph is shown in Figure 3-2e.

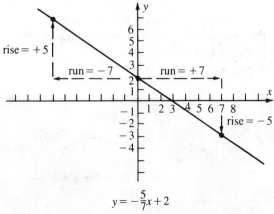

$$y = -\tfrac{5}{7}x + 2$$

Figure 3-2e _____ ■

EXAMPLE 3

Plot the graph of $x = 6$.

Solution:

This equation has the form $x + 0y = 6$. Transforming it to $y = mx + b$ form would give

$$y = -\frac{1}{0}x + \frac{6}{0}$$

The quantities $-\frac{1}{0}$ and $\frac{6}{0}$ are *infinite,* which means that they are larger than any real number. So there is no slope and no y-intercept. But drawing the graph is easy. Since x is 6 no matter what y is, the graph is a vertical line (Figure 3-2f). The relation is *not* a function, since there is more than one value of y when x is 6.

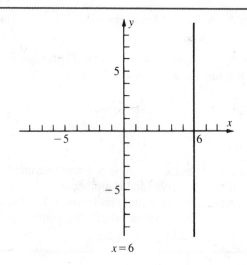

$x = 6$

Figure 3-2f ▬

If the equation in Example 3 had been $y = 7$, the graph would be a *horizontal* straight line. No matter what x is, y would always be 7. From this observation, a property can be concluded.

PROPERTY

HORIZONTAL AND VERTICAL LINES
If y = constant, then the graph is a horizontal straight line. The slope is 0.

If x = constant, then the graph is a vertical straight line. There is no number for the slope. The slope is infinitely large.

In the following exercise you will practice drawing linear graphs.

EXERCISE 3-2

Do These Quickly

The following problems are intended to refresh your skills from the first two chapters and from previous courses. You should be able to do all 10 in less than 5 minutes.

Q1.   Write a rational number that is not an integer.

Q2.   Write an integer that is not positive.

Q3.   Write an odd prime number.

Q4.   Solve: $3x + 7 = 31$

Q5.   Evaluate $5x - 2$ if x is 3.

Q6.   Find 20% of 63.

Q7.   What axiom is illustrated: "If $x = y$, then $y = x$."

Q8.   Evaluate $|2 - 5x|$ if x is 3.

Q9.   Sketch the graph of a relation that is not a function.

Q10.   Add $\frac{2}{3}$ and $\frac{3}{4}$.

Work these problems.

For Problems 1 through 20, plot the graph neatly on graph paper. Use the slope and y-intercept, where possible.

1. $y = \frac{3}{5}x + 3$

2. $y = \frac{5}{2}x - 1$

3. $y = -\frac{3}{2}x - 4$

4. $y = -\frac{1}{4}x + 3$

5. $y = 2x - 5$

6. $y = 3x - 2$

7. $y = -3x + 1$

8. $y = -2x + 6$

9. $7x + 2y = 10$

10. $3x + 5y = 10$

11. $x - 4y = 12$

12. $2x - 5y = 15$

13. $y = 3x$

14. $y = -2x$

15. $y = 3$

16. $y = -5$

17. $x = -4$ 18. $x = 2$

19. $y = 0$ 20. $x = 0$

21.   Relations such as in Problems 15 through 20 where

$$x = \text{constant} \quad \text{or} \quad y = \text{constant}$$

are not called linear functions, even though their graphs are straight lines. However, the reason is different in each case. Explain why such relations are not called linear functions.

22.   *Intercepts Problem*   In the definition of intercepts, it says *the y*-intercept, but *an x*-intercept. Sketch a graph which shows that a function could have more than one *x*-intercept. Explain why a function could not have more than one *y*-intercept.

23.   *Division by Zero Problem*   Evaluate $\frac{1}{0.1}$, $\frac{1}{0.01}$, $\frac{1}{0.001}$, and $\frac{1}{0.0001}$. What happens to the size of a fraction as its denominator gets very close to zero? Why would $\frac{1}{0}$ be larger than any real number? What name is used for a quantity that is larger than any real number?

24.   *Slope Proof Problem*   Prove that if $y = mx + b$, where m and b are constants, then m is the slope. Write a reason to justify each step in the proof.

25.   *Another Form of the Linear Function Equation*
      a.   Show that the relation

$$y - 4 = 2(x - 5)$$

is a *linear* function by transforming to $y = mx + b$. $y = 2x - 6$
      b.   Plot the graph of the function.   Check student work.
      c.   What does the number 2 in the original equation tell you about the graph?   The slope is 2; the graph slopes up.
      d.   The coordinates of a point on the graph are concealed in the original equation! What point?   (5, 4)

3-3	**OTHER FORMS OF THE LINEAR FUNCTION EQUATION**

Suppose that a relation has the equation

$$y - 4 = 2(x - 5).$$

If you substitute (5, 4) for (x, y), both members of the equation are zero. So (5, 4) is a point on the graph because it makes the equation a *true* statement. By distributing the 2, then adding 4 to each member, the equation becomes

$$y = 2x - 6.$$

So the relation is a *linear function* with slope 2. You may already have discovered this if you worked Problem 25 in Exercise 3-2.

An equation such as $y - 4 = 2(x - 5)$ is said to be in *point-slope* form because the coordinates of a point and the slope of the line appear in the equation. The familiar $y = mx + b$ form of the linear function equation is called *slope-intercept* form.

A linear function equation can be written as $3x + 4y = 13$. In this text, the name "$Ax + By = C$ form" is used if both variables are on one side, and the constant is on the other.

FORMS OF THE LINEAR FUNCTION GENERAL EQUATION

$y = mx + b$	Slope-intercept form.
$y - y_1 = m(x - x_1)$	Point-slope form.
	(x_1, y_1) is a point on the graph.
$Ax + By = C$	"$Ax + By = C$" form.
	$A, B,$ and C stand for constants.

Objective:
Given an equation in point-slope form, plot the graph quickly, and transform it to the other two forms.

EXAMPLE

If $y - 5 = -\dfrac{3}{2}(x + 1)$,

a. Plot the graph quickly.
b. Transform the equation to slope-intercept form.
c. Transform the equation to $Ax + By = C$ form, where $A, B,$ and C stand for *integer* constants.

Solution
a. From the equation, the slope is $-\frac{3}{2}$. A point on the graph is $(-1, 5)$ because substituting 5 for y makes the left member 0 and substituting -1 for x makes the right member 0. The graph is shown in Figure 3-3.

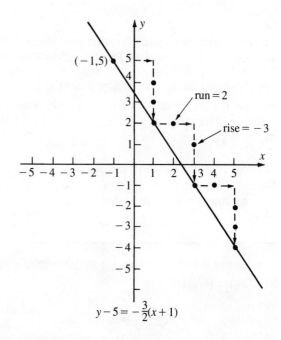

$$y - 5 = -\frac{3}{2}(x + 1)$$

Figure 3-3 _____

b. The equation can be transformed to slope-intercept form by distributing
   the $-\frac{3}{2}$, then adding 5 to each member.

$$y - 5 = -\frac{3}{2}(x + 1),$$

$$y - 5 = -1.5x - 1.5$$

$$\underline{y = -1.5x + 3.5}$$

c. Starting with the answer in part (b), you can add $1.5x$ to each member,
   then multiply by 2 to make each coefficient an integer.

$$1.5x + y = 3.5$$

$$\underline{3x + 2y = 7}$$

The following exercise gives you practice using the point-slope form to
plot graphs, and transforming from point-slope form to the other forms.

EXERCISE 3-3

Do These Quickly

The following problems are intended to refresh your skills. You should be able to do all 10 in less than 5 minutes.

Q1. Sketch a graph in which y increases as x increases.

Q2. Simplify: $3 + 2(x - 5)$

Q3. Multiply: $(2x - 7)(x + 3)$

Q4. Solve: $2x - 7 = 31$

Q5. Evaluate $5x^2$ if x is 3.

Q6. What percent of 40 is 12?

Q7. What axiom is illustrated: "$x = x$."

Q8. Evaluate: $\sqrt{49}$

Q9. Multiply $\frac{2}{3}$ by $\frac{3}{4}$.

Q10. Factor: $x^2 + 4x - 5$

Work these problems.

For Problems 1 through 10,

a. Plot the graph, showing clearly the point and slope that appear in the equation.
b. Transform the equation to slope-intercept form.
c. Transform the equation to $Ax + By = C$ form, where A, B, and C are all integers.

1. $y - 2 = \dfrac{3}{5}(x - 1)$

2. $y - 3 = \dfrac{2}{5}(x - 6)$

3. $y + 4 = \dfrac{7}{2}(x - 3)$

4. $y + 1 = \dfrac{7}{3}(x - 4)$

5. $y - 6 = -\dfrac{1}{4}(x + 2)$

6. $y - 2 = -\dfrac{1}{2}(x + 5)$

7. $y + 1 = -2(x + 4)$

8. $y + 6 = -3(x + 2)$

9. $y = \dfrac{1}{3}(x - 12)$

10. $y - 5 = \dfrac{2}{5}x$

If you really understand a concept, you should be able to use it *backward* as well as forward. For Problems 11 through 14, write an equation in point-slope form for the linear function described.

11.   Contains the point (5, 7), and has slope -3.

12.   Contains the point (6, 3), and has slope 5.

13.   Contains the point $(-2, 5)$, and has slope $\frac{9}{13}$.

14.   Contains the point $(7, -9)$, and has slope $-\frac{22}{7}$.

3-4 | EQUATIONS OF LINEAR FUNCTIONS FROM THEIR GRAPHS

Suppose someone says, "If the equation is $y = 3x - 8$, what are the slope and y-intercept?" You would say, "That's easy! They are 3 and -8." It is just as easy for you to answer the question, "If the slope and y-intercept are -5 and 13, what is the equation?" The answer is

$$y = -5x + 13.$$

In this section you will use information about the graph to write equations of particular linear functions.

Objective:
Given information about the graph of a linear function, write its particular equation.

EXAMPLE 1

Find the particular equation of the linear function with slope $-\frac{3}{2}$, containing the point $(7, -5)$.

Solution:
Since a point and the slope are given, the easiest form to use is the point-slope form. You would write

$$y + 5 = -\frac{3}{2}(x - 7)$$

The "+" is used on the left since the left member must be 0 when y is -5. The "−" is used on the right for similar reasons. It is not necessary to transform to any other form unless you are asked to do so.   ■

EXAMPLE 2

Find the particular equation of the linear function containing the points $(-4, 5)$ and $(6, 10)$.

Solution:

This new problem can be turned into an old problem by first using the slope formula to find the slope, m.

$$m = \frac{10 - 5}{6 - (-4)} = \frac{5}{10} = 0.5$$

You can use either of the given points in the point-slope form.

$$y - 5 = 0.5(x + 4) \quad \text{or} \quad y - 10 = 0.5(x - 6)$$

These two equations are equivalent, as you can see by transforming each to slope-intercept form or $Ax + By = C$ form.

$$y = 0.5x + 7 \quad \text{or} \quad x - 2y = -14 \qquad \blacksquare$$

Two lines are *parallel* to each other if their slopes are equal. Figure 3-4a illustrates this fact. If the lines are perpendicular to each other, the slope of one is the *opposite* of the *reciprocal* of the other. For instance, the slope of Line (2) in Figure 3-4a is $\frac{2}{3}$. The slope of Line (3), perpendicular to Line (2), is $-\frac{3}{2}$. These facts can be used to find particular equations.

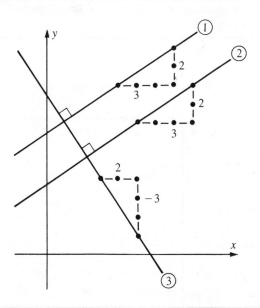

Figure 3-4a

PROPERTY

PARALLEL AND PERPENDICULAR LINES
If the equation of a line is $y = mx + b$, then:

A **parallel** line also has slope m.

A **perpendicular** line has slope $\dfrac{-1}{m}$.

EXAMPLE 3

Find the particular equation of the linear function containing $(-2, 7)$ if its graph is perpendicular to the graph of $3x + 4y = 72$.

Solution:
Transforming $3x + 4y = 72$ to $y = mx + b$ gives

$$y = -\frac{3}{4}x + 18$$

The slope of the given line is $-\frac{3}{4}$. So the slope of the desired line must be $\frac{4}{3}$, the opposite of the reciprocal of $-\frac{3}{4}$. The particular equation is thus

$$y - 7 = \frac{4}{3}(x + 2)$$

■

EXAMPLE 4

Find the particular equation of the horizontal line through $(7, 8)$.

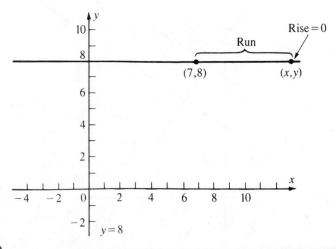

Figure 3-4b

Solution:
The easiest way to work this problem is to realize that horizontal lines
have equations of the form y = constant. So you just write

$$y = 8.$$

The graph is shown in Figure 3-4b.

The problem can also be worked by realizing that the slope of a horizontal
line is 0. Using the point-slope form gives

$$y - 8 = 0(x - 7),$$

which can be transformed to $y = 8$.   ■

EXAMPLE 5

Write the particular equation of the vertical line through (7, 8).

Solution:
The only way you can answer this question is to be brilliant, and just write
down

$$x = 7.$$

Since the slope of a vertical line does not equal a real number, neither the
point-slope nor the slope-intercept form can be used. The graph is shown
in Figure 3-4c.

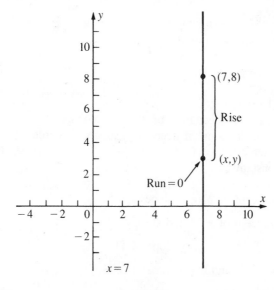

Figure 3-4c _____   ■

In the following exercise you will get practice writing equations if information about the graph is given. It is this technique that will let you use linear functions in the next section to represent situations from the real world.

EXERCISE 3-4

Do These Quickly

The following problems are intended to refresh your skills. You should be able to do all 10 in less than 5 minutes.

Q1.   Write the general equation for slope-intercept form.

Q2.   Find the *x*-intercept: $3x + 4y = 36$

Q3.   Factor: $x^2 - x - 72$

Q4.   Solve: $2x - 3 = 2(x + 4)$

Q5.   30 is 40% of what number?

Q6.   Write the equation in the commutative axiom for addition.

Q7.   Find the slope: $y = \frac{4}{7} + 3x$

Q8.   Evaluate 5^3.

Q9.   Divide $\frac{2}{3}$ by $\frac{3}{4}$.

Q10.   Do the squaring: $(x - 3)^2$

Work these problems.

For Problems 1 through 26,
a.   Write the particular equation of the line described.
b.   Transform the equation (if necessary) to slope-intercept form.
c.   Transform the equation to $Ax + By = C$ form, where A, B, and C are *integer* constants.

1.   Has *y*-intercept of 21 and slope of -5.

2.   Has *y*-intercept of -13 and slope of 7.

3.   Contains $(3, 7)$ and has a slope of 11.

4.   Contains $(4, 9)$ and has a slope of 5.73.

5.   Contains $(4, -5)$ and has a slope of -6.

6. Contains $(-3, 7)$ and has a slope of $-\frac{8}{5}$.

7. Contains $(1, 7)$ and $(3, 10)$.

8. Contains $(5, 2)$ and $(8, 11)$.

9. Contains $(2, -4)$ and $(-5, -10)$.

10. Contains $(-1, 4)$ and $(-5, -4)$.

11. Contains $(5, 8)$ and is parallel to the graph of $y = 7x - 6$.

12. Contains $(7, 2)$ and is parallel to the graph of $y = -4x + 3$.

13. Contains $(-4, 6)$ and is perpendicular to the graph of $y = 0.4x + 7$.

14. Contains $(3, -5)$ and is perpendicular to the graph of $y = -8x + 6$.

15. Contains $(5, 8)$ and is parallel to the graph of $2x + 3y = 9$.

16. Contains $(7, 2)$ and is parallel to the graph of $5x - 3y = 6$.

17. Contains $(4, 1)$ and is perpendicular to the graph of $5x - 7y = 44$.

18. Contains $(0, 6)$ and is perpendicular to the graph of $3x + 4y = 120$.

19. Has x-intercept of 5 and slope of $-\frac{2}{3}$.

20. Has x-intercept of 7 and y-intercept of 5.

21. Contains the origin, and has slope of 0.315.

22. Contains the origin, and has slope of 2.

23. Is horizontal, and contains $(-8, 9)$.

24. Is horizontal, and contains $(11, -13)$.

25. Is vertical, and contains $(-8, 9)$.

26. Is vertical, and contains $(11, -13)$.

For Problems 27 through 30, tell whether or not there is a linear function that contains *all* the points listed. If there is, find its particular equation.

27. $(6, 2), (5, 3), (1, 7)$

28. $(-3, 16), (1, 10), (9, -3)$

29. $(1, 4), (3, 7), (5, 10), (7, 13)$

30. $(4, 9), (20, 23), (13, 17), (29, 31)$

31. ***Intercept Form Problem***   Another form of the linear function equation is

$$\frac{x}{a} + \frac{y}{b} = 1,$$

where a and b stand for constants. Do the following.

a. Show that a and b are the x- and y-intercepts, respectively.

b. Transform the equation $\frac{x}{3} + \frac{y}{5} = 1$ to the following forms:

    i.　$Ax + By = C$, where A, B, and C are integer constants.

    ii.　$y = mx + b$.

c. Transform the equation $y = 4x - 12$ to the intercept form. Then tell what the two intercepts equal.

d. Why do you suppose the letter "b" is used in the slope-intercept form instead of some other letter?

32. *Computer Program for Linear Function Equations*

a. Write a computer program for finding the particular equation of a line from two given points. The input should be the two coordinates of the two points. The normal output should be an equation in slope-intercept form. The program should be able to do the proper thing when the slope is either zero or infinite.

b. Test your program on the following pairs of points:

    i.　$(1, 7)$ and $(3, 10)$.

    ii.　$(-1, -4)$ and $(-5, 4)$.

    iii.　$(3, 8)$ and $(6, 8)$.

    iv.　$(-2, 13), (-2, 4)$.

c. Run your program with the ordered pairs $(0, 3)$ and $(2, 7)$. If it does not work, modify the program to get around the difficulty.

33. *Computer Graphics Problem*　In this problem you will make some predictions about the graphs of various linear functions, then confirm (or refute!) your predictions by plotting the graphs on the computer. You may use the program PLOT LINEAR on the accompanying disk, or any other available plotting program.

a. Without drawing the graph, how could you tell whether the graph of $3x + 5y = 30$ will go *up* or *down* as you go from left to right? Which way do you predict that it will go?

b. Plot the graph of $3x + 5y = 30$ on the computer screen. Did the graph confirm your prediction in part (a)?

c. How do you expect the graph of $3x + 5y = -20$ to be related to the graph in part (a)?

d. Plot the graph of $3x + 5y = -20$ on the computer screen. Did the graph confirm your prediction in part (c)?

e. What will be the slope of a graph perpendicular to the line in part (a)? What will be the equation of this perpendicular line if it has the same y-intercept as the line in part (c)?

f. Plot the graph of the equation in part (e) on the screen. Is it really perpendicular to the other two? (You may have to adjust the vertical size on your monitor to make the scales on the axes the same before the lines will actually look perpendicular.)

34. *Introduction to Linear Models*　Calvin Butterball drives from his home on the farm to the nearby town of Scorpion Gulch. As he

drives, his distance from Scorpion Gulch depends on the number of minutes he has been driving. When he has been driving for 6 minutes, he is 17 km away; when he has been driving for 15 minutes, he is 11 km away.

Let y be the number of kilometers Calvin is from Scorpion Gulch. Let x be the number of minutes Calvin has been driving.

a. Write the information about distances and times as two ordered pairs.
b. Plot the two ordered pairs on a Cartesian coordinate system.
c. Assume that the distance, time relation is a *linear* function. Draw the graph on the Cartesian coordinate system in part (b).
d. Write the particular equation for this function. Transform it, if necessary, so that y is by itself on one side of the equation.
e. Use the equation to predict Calvin's distance from Scorpion Gulch when he has been driving for 24 minutes.
f. Use the equation to predict the time when Calvin arrives at Scorpion Gulch.
g. In this problem, you have used a linear function as a "mathematical model." Why do you suppose these words are used?

3-5 LINEAR FUNCTIONS AS MATHEMATICAL MODELS

In Section 2-3 you drew "reasonable" graphs relating two real-world variables. Sometimes the graph was a straight line. You know how to find an equation for a linear function if information about the graph is given. This equation could be used to calculate values of one variable if values of the other variable are known. In this way the function can be used to predict things about the real world. A function used in this way is called a *mathematical model*.

Objective:
Given a situation in which two real-world variables are related by a straight-line graph, be able to:

a. Sketch the graph.
b. Find the particular equation.
c. Use the equation to predict values of either variable.
d. Figure out what the slope and intercepts tell you about the real world.

EXAMPLE 1

Driving Home Problem   As you drive home from the football game, the number of kilometers you are away from home depends on the number of minutes you have been driving. Assume that distance varies linearly with time. Suppose that you are 11 km from home when you have been driving for 10 minutes, and 8 km from home when you have been driving for 15 minutes.

a. Define variables for distance and time, and sketch the graph.
b. Find the particular equation expressing distance in terms of time.
c. Predict your distance from home when you have been driving for 20, 25, and 30 minutes.
d. When were you 7 km from home?
e. What does the distance-intercept equal, and what does it represent in the real world?
f. What does the time-intercept equal, and what does it represent in the real world?
g. In what domain does this linear function give you reasonable answers?
h. What are the units of the slope? Based on these units, what do you suppose the slope represents in the real world? What is the significance of the fact that the slope is negative?

Solution:

a. Let d = no. of kilometers from home.
   Let t = no. of minutes you have been driving.
   The graph is shown in Figure 3-5a. All that is needed here is a reasonable sketch such as you drew in Section 2-3. Since you are assuming a linear function, the graph should be a straight line. It starts high and slopes downward since your distance from home decreases as you drive.

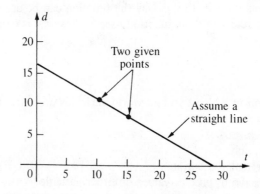

Figure 3-5a

b. To make this problem more familiar you can write the two given pieces of information as ordered pairs. Since d depends on t, you would write

(10, 11), (15, 8)

$$m = \frac{8 - 11}{15 - 10} = -\frac{3}{5}$$

Substituting the slope and the first ordered pair in the point-slope form gives

$$d - 11 = -\frac{3}{5}(t - 10)$$

The question calls for d to be expressed in terms of t. So you would transform it to slope-intercept form.

$$d = -\frac{3}{5}t + 17$$

c. To predict the distance when the time is given, all you need to do is substitute the given values for t and calculate d.

$$t = 20: d = -\frac{3}{5}(20) + 17 = 5 \text{ km}$$

$$t = 25: d = -\frac{3}{5}(25) + 17 = 2 \text{ km}$$

$$t = 30: d = -\frac{3}{5}(30) + 17 = -1 \text{ km}$$

Note that substituting 30 for t gives a negative value of distance. Since you would probably not drive past home, the domain of the function should stop before t reaches 30.

d. To predict the time when you are 7 km from home, you would substitute 7 for d and solve the equation.

$$7 = -\frac{3}{5}t + 17 \quad \text{Substitute 7 for } d.$$

$$\frac{3}{5}t = 10 \qquad\qquad \text{Add } \frac{3}{5}t \text{ and subtract 7.}$$

$$t = \frac{50}{3} \qquad\qquad \text{Multiply by } \frac{5}{3}.$$

about $16\frac{2}{3}$ *minutes*

e. The d-intercept is *17*, the value of d when $t = 0$. When $t = 0$ you are just starting for home. Therefore, it must be *17 km between the sta-dium and home*.

f. The t-intercept is the value of t when $d = 0$. Setting $d = 0$ in the equation gives

$$0 = -\frac{3}{5}t + 17$$

$$\frac{3}{5}t = 17$$

$$t = 28\frac{1}{3}$$

When $d = 0$ you are at home. So *it takes you about $28\frac{1}{3}$ minutes to get home.*

g. The domain should be $\{t: 0 \le t \le 28\frac{1}{3}\}$, the values of t for which you are actually driving home.

h. The slope is rise/run. The rise is in kilometers and the run is in minutes. Since "per" is a word used for "divided by," the slope has the units *km per min*. This means that your *speed is $\frac{3}{5}$ km/min*. The negative sign tells you that the distance from home is *decreasing* at $\frac{3}{5}$ km/min.   ■

You should realize that the predictions you make with a mathematical model are no better than the assumptions you make in setting up the model. For the example above you assumed a *linear* function, that has a constant slope. If the speed varies, the graph would actually have different slopes at different places. Figure 3-5b shows what the actual graph might look like, and that the linear model may fit only approximately.

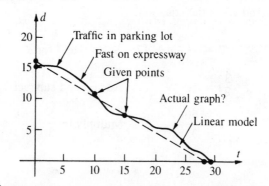

Figure 3-5b

Sometimes you are told a relationship between two variables which lets you conclude that a linear function relates them. In Example 2 you will see such a problem.

EXAMPLE 2

Donuts Problem

A local donut establishment charges 20 cents each for a donut, plus a one-time charge of 15 cents for the box, the service, etc.

a. Write an equation expressing the amount charged as a function of the number of donuts bought.
b. Explain why the function in part (a) is a *linear* function.
c. Predict the price of a box with a dozen donuts.
d. How many donuts would be in a box priced at $3.55?
e. Plot a graph of the function, using a reasonable domain.

Solution:

a. Let d = number of donuts in the box.
   Let p = number of cents you pay.
   The equation is $\underline{p = 20d + 15}$.
b. The function is linear because the equation has the form p equals a linear (first degree) expression in the variable d.
c. $d = 12$: $p = 20(12) + 15 = 255$

   Answer: $\underline{\underline{\$2.55}}$

   Note that 255 is the answer to the *algebra* problem. But the answer to the question that was asked is better written in the form of dollars, $2.55.
d. $p = 355$: $355 = 20d + 15$

   $$340 = 20d$$
   $$17 = d$$

   Answer: $\underline{17 \text{ donuts}}$

e. The graph is shown in Figure 3-5c. Since you are asked to *plot* the graph, you must use graph paper, show scales, use a ruler, and so forth. The domain is just the non-negative integers since you seldom

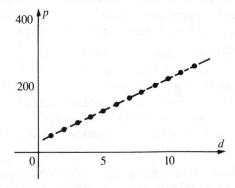

Figure 3-5c

buy fractions of donuts. The domain might stop at 12 if the store sells only boxes of up to a dozen. The p-intercept, 15, is excluded since you probably would not buy a box if you bought no donuts.

The following exercises will give you experience in using linear functions as mathematical models.

EXERCISE 3-5

Do These Quickly

The following problems are intended to refresh your skills. You should be able to do all 10 in less than 5 minutes.

Q1.   Tell what axiom was used: $4(3 + x) = 4(x + 3)$

Q2.   Find the slope: $3x + 5y = 30$

Q3.   Simplify: $33 - 3(x + 7)$

Q4.   Do the squaring: $(3x - 5)^2$

Q5.   35 is what percent of 50?

Q6.   Write 0.375 as a fraction in lowest terms.

Q7.   Draw the graph of a linear function with negative slope.

Q8.   Draw the graph of a relation that is not a function.

Q9.   Draw an isosceles triangle.

Q10.   How many weeks are there in a year?

Work the following problems.

1.   *Computer Diskette Problem*   A computer store sells 10 floppy diskettes for $15, and 30 diskettes for $40. Assume that the number of dollars varies linearly with the number of diskettes. Write the particular equation expressing dollars in terms of diskettes, and use it to predict the price for a box of 100 diskettes. Sketch the graph.

2.   *Reading Problem*   Phoebe Small still has 35 pages of history to be read after she has been reading for 10 minutes, and 5 pages left after she has been reading for 50 minutes. Assume that the number of pages left to read varies linearly with the number of minutes she has been reading. Write the particular equation expressing pages in terms of minutes, and use it to predict the time when she has finished reading. Sketch the graph.

3.   *Milk Problem*   Handy Andy sells one-gallon cartons of milk (4 quarts) for $3.09 each and half-gallon cartons for $1.65 each. As-

sume that the number of cents you pay for a carton of milk varies linearly with the number of quarts the carton holds.

a. Write the particular equation expressing price in terms of quarts.

b. If Handy Andy sold 3-gallon cartons, what would your equation predict the price to be?

c. The actual prices for pint cartons ($\frac{1}{2}$ quart) and one-quart cartons are $.57 and $.99, respectively. Do these prices fit your mathematical model? If not, are they higher than predicted, or lower?

d. Suppose that you found cartons of milk marked at $3.45, but that there was nothing on the carton to tell what size it is. According to your model, how much would such a carton hold?

e. Sketch the graph of the function, consistent with the slope and intercept in your equation.

f. What does the price-intercept represent in the real world?

g. What are the units of the slope? What real-world quantity does this number represent?

4. **Reaction Time Problem** When you are pricked with a pin, there is a short time delay before you say, "Ouch!" This reaction time varies linearly with the distance between your brain and the place you are pricked. Dr. Hollers pricks Leslie Morley's finger and toe, and measures reaction times of 15.2 and 22.9 milliseconds, respectively. (A millisecond is $\frac{1}{1000}$ of a second.) Leslie's finger is 100 cm from the brain, and her toe is 170 cm from the brain.

a. Write the particular equation expressing time delay in terms of distance.

b. How long would it take Leslie to say "Ouch!" if pricked in the neck, 10 cm from the brain?

c. What does the time-intercept equal, and what does it represent in the real world?

d. Sketch the graph of this function.

e. Since the slope is in milliseconds per centimeter, its reciprocal is the speed which nerve impulses travel in centimeters per millisecond. How fast do the impulses travel in cm/sec?

5. **Cricket Problem** Based on information in *Deep River Jim's Wilderness Trailbook*, the rate at which crickets chirp is a linear function of temperature. At 59°F they make 76 chirps per minute, and at 65°F they make 100 chirps per minute.

a. Write the particular equation expressing chirping rate in terms of temperature.

b. Predict the chirping rate for 90°F.

c. How warm is it if you count 120 chirps per minute?

d. Calculate the temperature-intercept. What does this number tell you about the real world?

e. Sketch the graph of this function in a reasonable domain.

f. What does the chirping-rate-intercept tell you about the real world?

6. *Cost of Owning a Car Problem*   The number of dollars per month it costs you to own a car is a function of the number of kilometers per month you drive it. Based on information in an issue of *Time* magazine, the cost varies linearly with the distance, and is $366 per month for 300 km per month, and $510 per month for 1500 km per month.
   a.   Write the particular equation expressing cost in terms of distance.
   b.   Sketch the graph of this function.
   c.   Predict your monthly cost if you drive 500, 1000, and 2000 km/month.
   d.   About how far could you drive in a month without exceeding a monthly cost of $600?
   e.   What does the slope represent?
   f.   List all the reasons you can think of to explain why the dollars per month intercept is greater than zero.

7. *Speed On a Hill Problem*   Assume that the maximum speed your car will go is a linear function of the steepness of the hill it is going up or down. Suppose that the car can go a maximum of 55 mph up a 5° hill, and a maximum of 104 mph down a 2° hill. (Going downhill can be thought of as going up a hill of −2°.)
   a.   Write the particular equation expressing maximum speed in terms of steepness.
   b.   How fast could you go down a 7° hill?
   c.   If your top speed is 83 mph, how steep is the hill? Is it up or down? Justify your answer.
   d.   What does the speed-intercept equal, and what does it represent?
   e.   What does the steepness-intercept equal, and what does it represent?
   f.   Sketch the graph of this function, using a reasonable domain.

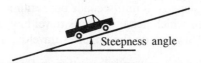

Steepness angle

8. *Thermal Expansion Problem*   Bridges on expressways often have expansion joints, which are small gaps in the roadway between one bridge section and the next. The gaps are put there so that the bridge will have room to expand when the weather gets hot. (See sketch.) Suppose that a bridge has a gap of 1.3 cm when the temperature is 22°C, and that the gap narrows to 0.9 cm when the temperature warms to 30°C. Assume that the gap width varies linearly with the temperature.
   a.   Write the particular equation for gap width as a function of temperature.
   b.   How wide would the gap be at 35°C? At −10°C?

c. At what temperature would the gap close completely? What mathematical name is given to this temperature?
d. Would the temperature ever be likely to get hot enough to close the gap? Justify your answer.
e. Sketch the graph of this linear function. Use an appropriate domain.

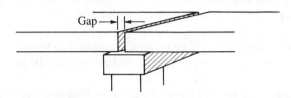

9. *Calorie Consumption Problem*   H. E. Lansburg's *Weather and Health* reports data gathered during World War II which shows that people use about 30 more calories per day for each 1° drop in the Celsius temperature. At 21°C, a working person uses about 3000 calories per day.
a. Explain how you know that the calorie consumption varies *linearly* with temperature. What is the slope? Write the particular equation.
b. How many calories per day would a working person use
    i.   in the Sahara Desert, when the temperature is 50°C?
    ii. in Antarctica in August, when the temperature is −50°C?
c. At what temperature does your model predict that a working person would use no calories at all? Do you think the linear function gives meaningful answers for temperatures this hot? Explain.
d. Sketch the graph of this function in a reasonable domain.

10. *Gas Tank Problem*   Suppose that you get your car's gas tank filled up, then drive off down the highway. As you drive, the number of minutes, t, since you had the tank filled, and the number of liters, g, remaining in the tank are related by a linear function.
a. Which variable should be independent, and which should be dependent?
b. After 40 minutes you have 52 liters left. An hour after the fill-up you have 40 liters left. Write the particular equation for this function.
c. Use the equation to predict the time when you will run out of gas.
d. Find the g-intercept, and tell what it represents in the real world.
e. Sketch the graph of this linear function.
f. Tell what the slope represents in the real world, and tell the significance of the fact that the slope is negative.

11. *Terminal Velocity Problem*   If you jump out of an airplane at high
     altitude, but do not open your parachute, you will soon be falling at a
     constant velocity called your "terminal velocity." Suppose that at
     time $t = 0$ you jump. When $t = 15$ seconds, your wrist altimeter
     shows that your distance from the ground, d, is 3600 meters. When
     $t = 35$, you have dropped to $d = 2400$ meters. Assume that you
     have already reached your terminal velocity by the time $t = 15$.
     a. Explain why d varies *linearly* with t after you have reached your
         terminal velocity.
     b. Write the particular equation expressing d in terms of t.
     c. If you neglect to open your parachute, when will you hit the
         ground?
     d. According to your linear model, how high was the airplane when
         you jumped?
     e. The airplane was actually at 4200 meters when you jumped.
         How do you reconcile this fact with your answer to part (d)?
     f. Sketch a reasonable graph of d versus t, showing the linear part,
         the part before you reached terminal velocity, and the part after
         you open your parachute.
     g. What was your terminal velocity in meters per second? In kilo-
         meters per hour?

12. *Linear Depreciation Problem*   Suppose you own a car that is
     presently 40 months old. From an automobile dealer's "Blue Book"
     you find that its present trade-in value is $3300. From an old Blue
     Book you find that its trade-in value 10 months ago was $4700. As-
     sume that its trade-in value decreases linearly with time.
     a. Write the particular equation expressing trade-in value of your
         car as a function of its age in months.
     b. You plan to get rid of the car when its trade-in value drops to
         $1000. How much longer can you keep the car?
     c. By how many dollars does the car "depreciate" (decrease in
         value) each month? What part of the mathematical model tells
         you this?
     d. When do you predict that the car will be worthless? What part
         of the mathematical model tells you this?
     e. According to your linear model, what was the trade-in value of
         your car when it was new?
     f. The car actually cost $10,560 when it was new. How do you ex-
         plain the difference between this number and the answer to part
         (e)?
     g. Sketch the graph of this function.

13. *Shoe Size Problem*   The size of shoe a person needs varies linearly
     with the length of his or her foot. The smallest adult shoe is Size 5,
     and fits a 9-inch long foot. An 11-inch long foot takes a Size 11
     shoe.

a. Write the particular equation expressing shoe size in terms of foot length.
b. If your foot is a foot long, what size shoe do you need?
c. Bob Lanier, who once played basketball for the Detroit Pistons, wears a Size 22 shoe. How long is his foot?
d. Plot the graph of adult shoe size versus foot length. Be sure to observe the domain implied at the beginning of this problem.

14. *Hippopotamus Problem*   In order to hunt hippopotami, a hunter must have a hippopotamus hunting license. Since the hunter can sell the hippos he catches, he can use the proceeds to pay for part or all of the cost of the license. If he catches only 3 hippos, he is still in debt by $2050. If he catches 7 hippos, he makes a profit of $1550. The African Game and Wildlife Commission allows a limit of 10 hippos per hunter. Let h be the number of hippos caught, and let d be the number of dollars profit made. Assume that h and d are related by a linear function.
a. Which variable should be dependent, and which should be independent?
b. Write a suitable domain for the independent variable.
c. Write the particular equation expressing dependent variable in terms of independent variable.
d. Plot the graph of this function, observing the domain in part (b).
e. Calculate the d- and h-intercepts. Tell what each means in the real world.
f. State what real-world quantity the slope represents.
g. What is the origin of the word "hippopotamus?"

15. *Celsius-to-Fahrenheit Temperature Conversion*   The Fahrenheit temperature, "F," and the Celsius temperature, "C," of an object are related by a linear function. Water boils at 100°C or 212°F, and freezes at 0°C or 32°F.
a. Write an equation expressing F in terms of C.
b. Transform the equation so that C is in terms of F.
c. Lead boils at 1620°C. What Fahrenheit temperature is this? Which form of the equation is more appropriate to use in answering this question?
d. Normal body temperature is 98.6°F. What Celsius temperature is this?
e. If the weather forecaster says it will be 40°C today, will it be hot, cold, or medium? Explain.
f. The coldest possible temperature is absolute zero, −273°C, where molecules stop moving. What Fahrenheit temperature is this?
g. For what temperature is the number of Fahrenheit degrees equal to the number of Celsius degrees?
h. Sketch the graph of F as a function of C, showing clearly the domain implied by part (f), and the F-intercept.

16.   *Charles's Gas Law*   In 1787 the French scientist Jacques Charles
       observed that when he plotted the graph of volume of a fixed amount
       of air versus the temperature of the air, the points lay along a
       straight line. Therefore, he concluded that volume of a gas varies lin-
       early with temperature. Suppose that at 27°C a certain amount of air
       occupies a volume of 500 cm³. When it is warmed to 90°C it occu-
       pies 605 cm³.
       a.   Write the particular equation expressing volume in terms of tem-
            perature.
       b.   Predict the volume at 60°C.
       c.   The process of predicting a value *between* two given data points
            is called "interpolation." What is the origin of this word?
       d.   Predict the volume at 300°C.
       e.   The process of predicting a value *beyond* any given data points
            is called "extrapolation." What is the origin of this word?
       f.   Extrapolate your mathematical model back to the point where
            the volume is zero. That is, find the temperature-intercept.
       g.   Find out what special name is given to the temperature in part
            (f). Absolute Zero
       h.   Sketch the graph of volume versus temperature. Check work.

17.   *Elevator Problem*   The number of feet of cable needed for an eleva-
       tor depends on the number of stories in the building it serves. Sup-
       pose that $c = 20s + 35$, where c is the number of feet of elevator
       cable and s is the number of stories.
       a.   How do you know that c varies *linearly* with s?
       b.   How much cable is needed for a 29-story building?
       c.   How tall a building needs 375 feet of cable?
       d.   What does the slope represent in the real world?
       e.   What does the c-intercept equal? Why do you suppose that it is
            greater than zero?
       f.   Write a suitable domain for the linear function.
       g.   On graph paper, plot the graph of this function, observing the
            domain you wrote in part (f).

18.   *Speeding Bullet Problem*   The speed a bullet is traveling depends
       on the number of feet the bullet has traveled since it left the gun.
       Assume that $s = -4d + 3600$, where s is the number of feet per
       second and d is the number of feet.
       a.   How do you know that s varies *linearly* with d?
       b.   How fast is the bullet going when it has traveled 300 feet?
       c.   How far has the bullet gone when it has slowed to 500 feet per
            second?
       d.   What does the slope represent in the real world?
       e.   What does the d-intercept equal? What does it tell you about the
            bullet?
       f.   Write a suitable domain for the linear function.

g.   On graph paper, plot the graph of this function, observing the domain you wrote in part (f).

19.   ***Income Tax Problem***   Starting in 1988, the Internal Revenue Service's formula for finding income tax was $9,761 plus 33% of the quantity (Taxable Income minus $43,150). This formula applied for taxable incomes between $43,150 and $89,560. Let x be number of dollars of taxable income.

a.   Write the particular equation expressing tax in terms of taxable income.

b.   Find the tax for a person making $43,150, and for another person making $89,560.

c.   Show that the tax for a person making $89,560 is exactly 28% of his or her taxable income.

d.   Plot the graph of this function in the domain for which it applies.

e.   For taxable incomes above $89,560, the formula for tax due is simply 28% of the taxable income. Calculate the tax on a taxable income of $120,000.

f.   Plot the graph of the tax for incomes above $89,560 on your graph in part (d). If your work is right, the two graphs should connect.

20.   ***Direct Variation, Pancake Problem***   If the constant b in $y = mx + b$ equals zero, then y is said to vary *directly* with x. The amount of pancake batter you must mix up varies directly with the number of people who come to breakfast. Suppose that it takes 7 cups of batter to serve 10 people.

a.   Write the particular equation expressing number of cups in terms of number of people.

b.   How many cups must you prepare for 50 people?

c.   About how many people can you serve with 12 cups of batter?

d.   Sketch the graph of this function. Through what special point does the graph of a direct variation function go?

3-6 | CHAPTER REVIEW AND TEST

In this chapter you have studied one kind of function, the linear function. You defined it by the general equation $y = mx + b$. You graphed it, first by pointwise plotting. Then you learned properties that allowed you to plot the graph quickly. Finally, you learned how to find the particular equation from given points so that you could use a linear function as a mathematical model.

The Review Problems below parallel the sections in this chapter. The Concepts Problems let you try your hand at applying what you know to analyze a new situation. The Chapter Test is similar to one your instructor might give to see how well you understand linear functions.

REVIEW PROBLEMS

R1. Given the equation $y = 3x - 7$:
   a. Evaluate y if $x = -1$, $x = 2$, and $x = 5$.
   b. Show by graphing that the points lie in a straight line.

R2. Plot quickly the graphs of the following:
   a. $y = \frac{2}{5}x - 3$
   b. $7x + 3y = 21$
   c. $x = 3$
   d. $y = -4$

R3. For the linear function $y + 3 = -\frac{5}{2}(x - 4)$
   a. Name the form of the equation.
   b. Write the coordinates of the point that appears in the equation.
   c. Plot the graph.
   d. Transform the equation to slope-intercept form.
   e. Transform the equation to $Ax + By = C$ form, where A, B, and C are integers.

R4. Find the particular equation of the line described.
   a. Contains $(2, -7)$ and $(5, 3)$.
   b. Contains $(-4, 1)$ and is parallel to the graph of $2x - 9y = 47$.
   c. Contains $(3, -8)$ and is perpendicular to the graph of $y = 0.2x + 11$
   d. Has x-intercept of 5 and y-intercept of -6.
   e. Is vertical, and contains $(-13, 8)$.
   f. Is horizontal, and contains $(22, \pi)$.
   g. Has the x-axis as its graph.
   h. Has a slope that is infinitely large, and contains $(5, 7)$.

R5. *Computer Time Problem* If a computer program has a loop in it, the length of time it takes the computer to run the program varies linearly with the number of times it must go through the loop. Suppose a computer takes 8 seconds to run a given program when it goes through the loop 100 times, and 62 seconds when it loops 1000 times.
   a. Write the particular equation expressing seconds in terms of loops.
   b. Predict the length of time needed to loop 30 times; 10,000 times.

c.   Suppose the computer takes 23 seconds to run the program. How many times does it go through the loop?

d.   How long does it take the computer to run the rest of the program, excluding the loop? What part of the mathematical model tells you this?

e.   How long does it take the computer to go through the loop once? What part of the mathematical model tells you this?

f.   Plot the graph of this function.

CONCEPTS PROBLEM

Income Tax Problem   The amount of income tax you pay to the Federal Government varies linearly with the amount of taxable income you have. However, the percent of your income that you pay in tax is different in different parts of the domain. For 1988 the rates for single taxpayers were specified the following way by the Internal Revenue Service:

Taxable Income (TI) Tax Payable

$0 to $17,850 .... 15% of TI
$17,850 to $43,150... $2,677.50 plus 28% of (TI − $17,850)
$43,150 to $89,560... $9,761.50 plus 33% of (TI − $43,150)
$89,560, up .... 28% of TI.

a.   Write four particular equations expressing tax payable in terms of taxable income, one for each part of the domain.

b.   What will be the tax for $10,000? $30,000? $50,000? $100,000?

c.   You overhear somebody say they paid $20,000 in taxes. What was their taxable income?

d.   Show that there are no discontinuities at the three places where the tax rate changes. You must figure out what "discontinuities" means, and how to answer this question.

e.   Draw the graph of tax payable versus taxable income for incomes from $0 through $100,000.

f.   A $2 change in income, from $17,849 to $17,851, would put a person in a higher "tax bracket." That is, one would be paying 28% instead of 15%. Many people think that the extra $2 earned would cause them to pay hundreds of dollars more in taxes. Is their thinking correct? Explain.

g.   Faye Doubt makes $60,000 taxable income. She is upset because she is in a 33% tax bracket, while people who make $100,000 are in only a 28% tax bracket. Convince Faye that she would pay *more* tax on her $60,000 using the equation for the higher-income person.

h.   The Internal Revenue Service rules for the two middle-income tax brackets look a lot like one of the forms of the linear function equation. Which form?

CHAPTER TEST

Algebra II is a study of functions. The first kind of function you have studied is the *linear* function.

T1. Write the general equation for a linear function.

For Problems T2 and T3, transform to slope-intercept form.

T2. $3x - 7y = 42$ T3. $y - 5 = -\frac{1}{2}(x - 3)$

T4. Write the definition of x-intercept. Use this definition to find the x-intercept for the function whose equation is $y = 5x - 7$.

T5. *Beans Problem*   Handy Andy sells 23 oz cans of ranch style beans for 63 cents and 15 oz cans for 45 cents. Assume that the price varies linearly with the number of ounces.
 a. Write the particluar equation expressing number of cents in terms of number of ounces.
 b. Sketch the graph.
 c. A 52 oz can costs $1.39. According to your model, is this can over-priced or under-priced? By how much?
 d. Suppose that an "individual serving" can was priced at $0.21. About how many ounces of beans would you expect to get?

It is important for you to remember old techniques.

T6. Tell the range and domain of the relation in Figure 3-6a, and whether or not it is a function.

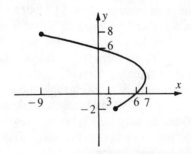

Figure 3-6a

T7. The length of your thumbnail depends on how long it has been since you cut the nail. Sketch a reasonable graph.

For Problems T8 through T11, plot the graph.

T8. $y = -\dfrac{3}{5}x - 2$ T9. $y = 3x$

T10. $x - 4y = 12$ T11. $x = 2$

Some functions are not linear, and some relations are not functions.

T12. Plot the graph of the relation $|y| = x - 3$. Tell what the domain of the relation must be so that the value of y will be a real number. Tell whether or not the relation is a function.

4

Systems of Linear Equations and Inequalities

Linear functions may be used as mathematical models of the real world. **Two** *or more linear functions with the* **same** *variables form what is called a* **system** *of equations. In this chapter you will learn how to find the intersection of the graphs, and how to tell what this intersection can represent. The techniques you develop can be used to find the "best" way to operate a business, such as raising race horses.*

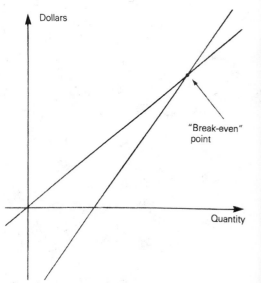

Dollars

"Break-even" point

Quantity

4-1	INTRODUCTION TO LINEAR SYSTEMS

Two or more equations that have the same variables, such as

$$2x - y = 10$$
$$x + 3y = -9$$

form what is called a *system of equations*. A solution of such a system is an ordered pair that satisfies both of the equations at the same time. For this reason, the equations in a system are often called *simultaneous equations*. "Simultaneous" means "at the same time." Finding the solution is called "solving the system." By working the following exercise you will refresh your memory about how you solved systems in previous mathematics courses.

DEFINITIONS

SYSTEM
A **system** of equations or inequalities is a set of open sentences each of which contains the same variables.

SOLUTION SET
The **solution set** of a system with two variables is the set of all ordered pairs that satisfy all the open sentences in the system.

EXERCISE 4-1

These questions concern calculating the solution of the system

$$2x - y = 10 \ \text{----} \ (1)$$
$$x + 3y = -9 \ \text{----} \ (2)$$

1. Multiply each member of Equation (1) by 3. Label the answer
---- (3), as the given equations are labeled.

2. Add -9 to both sides of Equation (3). Do this by adding -9 to the
right side, and $x + 3y$ (which equals -9) to the left side. The resulting equation should have only x as the variable. The y should have
been eliminated.

3. Solve the equation from Problem 2 to find the value of x. This number will be the x-coordinate of the point where the two graphs cross
each other.

4. To find the value of y at the point where the graphs cross, substitute
the value of x you found in Problem 3 into either Equation (1) or
Equation (2). Solve the resulting equation for y.

5. Write the ordered pair for the point where the graphs cross.

6. Plot the graphs of both equations on the same Cartesian coordinate
system. Verify that the graphs really do cross at the point you wrote
in Problem 5.

4-2 | SOLUTION OF SYSTEMS OF LINEAR EQUATIONS

In Exercise 4-1 you solved the system

$$2x - y = 10 \text{ ---- (1)}$$
$$x + 3y = -9 \text{ ---- (2)}$$

Multiplying each member of Equation (1) by 3 makes the y-coefficients
opposites of each other.

$$6x - 3y = 30 \text{ ---- (1) multiplied by 3}$$
$$x + 3y = -9 \text{ ---- (2)}$$

Adding the two equations, left member to left member, and right to right,
eliminates y, leaving an equation with only x as the variable.

$$7x \quad = 21$$

Dividing each member by 7 gives

$$x = 3.$$

Substituting 3 for x in either Equation (1) or (2) gives an equation with
only y as the variable.

$$2(3) - y = 10 \qquad \text{Substitute 3 for } x \text{ in Eqn. (1).}$$
$$-y = 4$$
$$y = -4$$

The two equations

$$x = 3$$
$$y = -4$$

form another system. Neither equation is equivalent to Equations (1) or (2). But the *systems* of equations *are* equivalent. As you can see from Figure 4-2a, both pairs of equations intersect at the same point, (3, −4). Obviously, the second system is simple enough to solve by inspection! You would write

$$S = \{(3, -4)\}$$

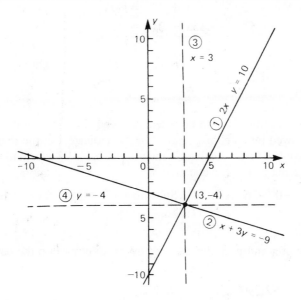

Figure 4-2a

Objective:
Given a system of two linear equations in two variables, solve it by transforming it to an equivalent system of the form

$$x = \text{constant},$$
$$y = \text{constant}.$$

The secret to eliminating a variable is making the x- or y-coefficients in the two equations either equal to each other or opposites of each other. The elimination can then be accomplished by subtracting the equations or by adding the equations.

EXAMPLE 1

Solve the system

$$3x + 4y = 6$$
$$5x - 7y = 14$$

Solution:

Decide on which variable to eliminate. To eliminate x you could multiply the first equation by 5 and the second equation by 3, then subtract. A convenient way to keep track of what you do is to draw arrows to the right of the equations, and write messages such as "m5" over them to indicate multiplication by 5.

$$3x + 4y = 6 \xrightarrow{\text{m5}} 15x + 20y = 30$$
$$5x - 7y = 14 \xrightarrow{\text{m3}} \underline{15x - 21y = 42}$$
$$41y = -12 \qquad \text{Subtract.}$$
$$y = -0.2926\ldots \quad \text{Divide by 41.} \quad ■$$

If the value of y turns out to be a decimal, you should write the first few digits, followed by an ellipsis mark, ... , to indicate that the more precise value is saved in your calculator's memory. Find x by substituting $-0.2926\ldots$ for y in either equation.

$$5x - 7(-0.2926\ldots) = 14 \quad \text{Substitute } -0.2926\ldots \text{ for } y \text{ in Eqn. (2).}$$
$$5x = 11.95\ldots$$
$$x = 2.3902\ldots$$

The values of x and y can be checked by substituting into the *other* equation.

$$3(2.3902\ldots) + 4(-0.2926\ldots) = 6$$
$$6 = 6, \text{ which checks.}$$

The final answers may be rounded off to a reasonable number of places.

$$\underline{\underline{S = \{(2.39, -0.29)\}}}$$

Note that the answer is a solution set. The set contains the one ordered pair, (2.39, -0.29). So both the parentheses and the set symbols must be used.

The process of multiplying two variables by constants and adding the results is called "linearly combining" them. For example, $3r + 7s$ is a linear combination of r and s. This is why the name *linear combination method* is used for the process of solving a system of equations by multiplying each by a constant then adding or subtracting. The words *addition-subtraction method* are also used. In previous courses you have probably used the *substitution method* and the *graphing method*. Problems 41 through 50 in the following exercise will refresh your memory about those techniques.

EXAMPLE 2

Solve the system, and graph.

$$5x + 2y = 10$$
$$5x + 2y = 20$$

Solution:
Subtracting the equations gives

$$0 = -10.$$

This statement is never true, no matter what x or y may happen to be. As shown in Figure 4-2b, the graphs are parallel to each other, and thus do not intersect. So the solution set is empty and you would write

$$\underline{\underline{S = \emptyset. \quad \text{Equations are inconsistent.}}}$$

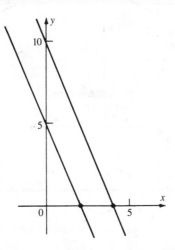

Figure 4-2b ⬛

The words *inconsistent equations* are used for any equations that have no common solutions. If the two equations in the system have the same graph, then they are called *dependent equations*. Such systems have an infinite number of solutions. Linear equations whose graphs intersect at just one point are called *independent equations*. Figure 4-2c illustrates the three possibilities.

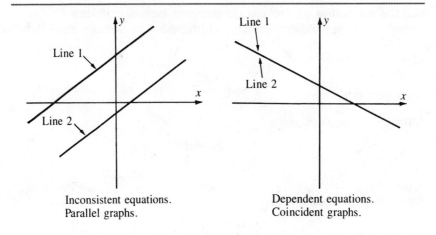

Inconsistent equations.   Dependent equations.
Parallel graphs.   Coincident graphs.

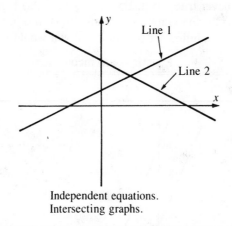

Independent equations.
Intersecting graphs.

Figure 4-2c _____

EXERCISE 4-2

Do These Quickly

The following are 10 miscellaneous problems. They are intended to refresh your skills. You should be able to do all 10 in less than 5 minutes.

Q1. Find 30% of 90.

Q2. Subtract: $13.7 - 5$

Q3. Find the probability of drawing a black marble from a bag contain-
     ing 7 black marbles and 13 red ones.

Q4.   Find the slope of the line connecting $(2, -4)$ and $(-3, 7)$.

Q5.   Find the x-intercept: $y = 3x - 4$

Q6.   Draw two parallel lines cut by a transversal, and indicate a pair of alternate interior angles.

Q7.   Simplify: $32 - 2(3 + 4x)$

Q8.   Write an imaginary number.

Q9.   Write the equation that appears in the Associative Axiom for Addition.

Q10.   Sketch the graph of a relation that is not a function.

For Problems 1 through 30, solve the system. Some of the later problems have additional instructions or suggestions.

1. $\begin{aligned} 5x + 2y &= 11 \\ x + y &= 4 \end{aligned}$ 2. $\begin{aligned} x - y &= -11 \\ 7x + 4y &= -22 \end{aligned}$

3. $\begin{aligned} 6x - 7y &= 47 \\ 2x + 5y &= -21 \end{aligned}$ 4. $\begin{aligned} 8x + 3y &= 41 \\ 6x + 5y &= 39 \end{aligned}$

5. $\begin{aligned} 5x + 7y &= -15 \\ 2x + 9y &= -6 \end{aligned}$ 6. $\begin{aligned} 9x - 5y &= 26 \\ 4x - 3y &= 17 \end{aligned}$

7. $\begin{aligned} 2x + 3y &= 2 \\ 4x - 9y &= -1 \end{aligned}$ 8. $\begin{aligned} 3x + 10y &= -24 \\ 6x + 7y &= -9 \end{aligned}$

9. $\begin{aligned} 9x - 7y &= 5 \\ 10x + 3y &= -16 \end{aligned}$ 10. $\begin{aligned} 11x - 5y &= -38 \\ 9x + 2y &= -25 \end{aligned}$

For Problems 11 through 20, there is an *easy* multiplication that will work. In Problem 11, for example, x can be eliminated by multiplying the first equation by 3 and the second one by -2.

11. $\begin{aligned} 14x + 31y &= -6 \\ 21x + 17y &= 50 \end{aligned}$ 12. $\begin{aligned} 12x - 7y &= 59 \\ 8x + 11y &= -39 \end{aligned}$

13. $\begin{aligned} 13x + 10y &= -7 \\ 17x - 15y &= 47 \end{aligned}$ 14. $\begin{aligned} 13x + 20y &= -1 \\ 19x - 15y &= 87 \end{aligned}$

15. $\begin{aligned} 22x - 19y &= 28 \\ 55x - 29y &= 107 \end{aligned}$ 16. $\begin{aligned} 37x - 36y &= 180 \\ 41x - 24y &= 120 \end{aligned}$

17. $\begin{aligned} -37x - 24y &= 35 \\ 15x - 18y &= 69 \end{aligned}$ 18. $\begin{aligned} 18x - 19y &= 161 \\ 54x + 25y &= 565 \end{aligned}$

19. $\begin{aligned} 23x - 34y &= -46 \\ 13x + 51y &= -26 \end{aligned}$ 20. $\begin{aligned} 33x + 16y &= -2 \\ -29x + 20y &= 138 \end{aligned}$

Problems 21 through 26 have "untidy" fractions for answers. You may
want to use the linear combination to find *both* variables, rather than substituting a fraction back into one of the equations.

21. $4x - 3y = 11$ 22. $3x + 4y = 18$
      $5x - 6y = 9$ $9x + 6y = 17$

23. $3x + 4y = 8$ 24. $5x - 3y = 22$
      $2x - 2y = 7$ $6x - 7y = 41$

25. $-x + 5y = 22$ 26. $8x + 5y = 23$
      $7x - 2y = 19$ $3x - 2y = 37$

For Problems 27 through 30, you can write $\dfrac{2}{x}$ as $2\left(\dfrac{1}{x}\right)$, $\dfrac{-5}{y}$ as $-5\left(\dfrac{1}{y}\right)$,
and so forth. Then you can solve for $\dfrac{1}{x}$ and $\dfrac{1}{y}$. To find x and y, recall that
if two numbers are equal, then their reciprocals are equal.

27. $\dfrac{2}{x} - \dfrac{5}{y} = 5$ 28. $\dfrac{3}{x} + \dfrac{6}{y} = 1$

      $\dfrac{3}{x} + \dfrac{10}{y} = 18$ $\dfrac{3}{x} + \dfrac{7}{y} = 2$

29. $\dfrac{12}{x} + \dfrac{5}{y} = 25$ 30. $\dfrac{6}{x} - \dfrac{7}{y} = 8$

      $\dfrac{2}{x} - \dfrac{15}{y} = -18$ $\dfrac{15}{x} - \dfrac{14}{y} = 21$

For Problems 31 through 38, determine whether the equations in the system are independent, dependent, or inconsistent.

31. $15x + 12y = 8$ 32. $24x - 56y = 72$
      $10x + 8y = 13$ $-15x + 35y = -45$

33. $15x - 12y = 8$ 34. $24x - 56y = 72$
      $10x + 8y = 13$ $15x - 35y = -45$

35. $15x - 12y = 18$ 36. $24x + 56y = 72$
      $10x - 8y = 12$ $15x - 35y = -45$

37. $15x - 12y = 18$ 38. $24x - 56y = 72$
      $10x - 8y = 14$ $15x - 35y = 54$

For Problems 39 and 40, plot the three graphs on the same Cartesian coordinate system. They should cross at or near the same point. Then either

find an ordered pair that satisfies all three equations, or demonstrate that there is no such ordered pair.

39. $5x + 3y = 19$
     $2x - y = 9$
     $4x - 3y = 19$

40. $3x - y = 5$
     $2x + 3y = 7$
     $x - 4y = 9$

Graphical Solution Method: For Problems 41 and 42, plot the graphs accurately by finding the x- and y-intercepts of each line. Read the coordinates of the intersection point to the nearest 0.1 unit. Then solve the system by linear combination and verify that your graphical solution is correct.

41. $2x + 3y = -12$
     $8x - 5y = 40$

42. $5x + 2y = 20$
     $3x - 7y = 21$

Substitution Method: It is possible to eliminate a variable by solving one equation for x in terms of y (or y in terms of x), and substituting the result into the other equation. For instance, in the Problem 43, below, the first equation can be transformed to $x = 2 - 2y$. Substituting $2 - 2y$ for x in the second equation eliminates x, giving $5(2 - 2y) - 3y = -29$. This equation can then be solved for y. For Problems 43 through 50, solve the system using this substitution method.

43. $x + 2y = 2$
     $5x - 3y = -29$

44. $3x + y = 13$
     $2x - 4y = 18$

45. $2x - 9y = 14$
     $6x - y = 42$

46. $7x - 6y = -30$
     $x - 4y = -20$

47. $x - 3y = 13$
     $5x + 3y = 2$

48. $7x - 3y = -23$
     $x - 5y = 32$

49. $x = 0.6(300 + y)$
     $y = 0.2(300 + x)$

50. $x = 0.3(200 - y)$
     $y = 0.2(200 - x)$

51. *Addition of Equations. Theory Problem:*
     a. For the system

$$3x + 5y = 17$$
$$4x - 5y = 23$$

you could add the equations and eliminate y. The addition property of equality allows you to add the same number to each member of the first equation. Explain how this property and certain others let you add the two equations, left member to left member, and right member to right.

b. Do a formal proof of the theorem which states, "If $p = q$ and $r = s$, then $p + r = q + s$."

Solving a system of equations is fairly tedious, especially if the coefficients are large numbers. If you solve a *general* system of linear equations, a pattern appears that is easy to remember. With the pattern, you can solve a system mentally, writing only the answer, if the coefficients are small enough, and by calculator otherwise.

The general system of linear equations with two variables is

$$ax + by = c$$
$$dx + ey = f,$$

where a, b, c, d, e, and f stand for constant coefficients. To eliminate y, you would multiply the first equation by e and the second by b, then subtract.

$$
\begin{array}{ll}
ax + by = c \xrightarrow{\ me\ } & aex + bey = ce \\
dx + ey = f \xrightarrow{\ mb\ } & bdx + bey = bf \\
\hline
& aex - bdx = ce - bf \quad \text{Subtract.}
\end{array}
$$

The x can be factored from the left member, giving

$$(ae - bd)x = ce - bf$$

The result is an equation whose form is as simple as $3x = 7$. You merely divide each member by $(ae - bd)$, the coefficient of x.

$$x = \frac{ce - bf}{ae - bd}$$

This is a formula that can be used to evaluate x. Eliminating x and solving the original system for y gives

$$y = \frac{af - cd}{ae - bd}$$

Three things appear when you compare these formulas with the original system,

$$ax + by = c$$
$$dx + ey = f.$$

1. Both denominators are the *same,* and contain only the coefficients of the *left* members of the equations.
2. The numerator for x does *not* contain the x-coefficients, a and d.
3. The numerator for y does *not* contain the y-coefficients, b and e.

There is a way to remember how to get the denominators. You write the four coefficients of x and y this way:

$$\begin{vmatrix} a & b \\ d & e \end{vmatrix}.$$

The value is found by a diagonal multiplication scheme. Multiply *top left* by *bottom right*. Subtract *top right* times *bottom left*.

$$D = \begin{vmatrix} a & b \\ d & e \end{vmatrix} = ae - bd$$

Looking back at the formulas for x and y, you can see that this is actually the correct denominator.

The four-number symbol with vertical bars is called a *second-order determinant*.

DEFINITION

> **SECOND-ORDER DETERMINANT**
> A **second-order determinant** is a square array of numbers that is expanded (evaluated) according to the rule
> $$\begin{vmatrix} r & s \\ t & u \end{vmatrix} = ru - st$$

The letter D is used for *Denominator* determinant. The numerators in the formulas can also be written as determinants. Recalling that the x-numerator does not have the coefficients of x, you simply replace the x-coefficients in the left members of the equations with the constants c and f from the right members.

Delete a and d.

$$a\,x + by = c$$
$$d\,x + ey = f$$

Replace with c and f.

You get a new determinant with c and f in the x-column (and b and e still in the y-column).

$$N_x = \begin{vmatrix} c & b \\ f & e \end{vmatrix}$$

The symbol N_x stands for "x-numerator." Expanding this determinant by the diagonal multiplication pattern gives

$$N_x = \begin{vmatrix} c & b \\ f & e \end{vmatrix} = ce - bf,$$

which is the correct value. The y-numerator, N_y, is found by replacing the y-coefficients, b and e, with the constant terms c and f.

Delete b and e.

$$ax + b\,y = c$$
$$dx + e\,y = f$$

Replace with c and f.

$$N_y = \begin{vmatrix} a & c \\ d & f \end{vmatrix} = af - cd,$$

which is the correct y-numerator. The solutions are N_x/D and N_y/D

Objective:
Given a system of two linear equations with two variables, solve the system using second-order determinants.

Solving by determinants is often called *Cramer's Rule*.

EXAMPLE
Solve by determinants (Cramer's Rule):

$$3x + 4y = 2$$
$$5x - 7y = 17$$

Solution:
The first step is to write the denominator for x.

$$x = \cfrac{}{\begin{vmatrix} 3 & 4 \\ 5 & -7 \end{vmatrix}}$$

Next, you write the numerator determinant by replacing the numbers in the x-column with the 2 and 17 from the right members of the equations.

$$x = \cfrac{\begin{vmatrix} 2 & 4 \\ 17 & -7 \end{vmatrix}}{\begin{vmatrix} 3 & 4 \\ 5 & -7 \end{vmatrix}}$$

Then you expand the two determinants.

$$x = \frac{\begin{vmatrix} 2 & 4 \\ 17 & -7 \end{vmatrix}}{\begin{vmatrix} 3 & 4 \\ 5 & -7 \end{vmatrix}} = \frac{-14 - 68}{-21 - 20} = \frac{-82}{-41} = 2,$$

For y, you write the numerator determinant by replacing the numbers in the y-column of the *denominator* determinant with the 2 and 17 from the right members of the equations. You already know that the denominator is -41, so you write

$$y = \frac{\begin{vmatrix} 3 & 2 \\ 5 & 17 \end{vmatrix}}{-41} = \frac{51 - 10}{-41} = \frac{41}{-41} = -1.$$

$$\therefore S = \{(2, -1)\}. \qquad \blacksquare$$

In the following exercise you will solve systems by Cramer's rule.

EXERCISE 4-3

Do These Quickly

The following are 10 miscellaneous problems. They are intended to refresh your skills. You should be able to do all 10 in less than 5 minutes.

Q1. Solve by linear combination: $3x + y = 11$ and $x + y = 5$

Q2. Subtract: $\frac{2}{3} - \frac{1}{6}$

Q3. What is the probability of getting a 3 or larger in one roll of a die?

Q4. Sketch the graph of a line with infinite slope.

Q5. Evaluate 2^5.

Q6. Draw a rhombus.

Q7. Simplify: $37 - 7(3 - 4x)$

Q8. Write a transcendental number.

Q9. Write the equation that appears in the Reflexive Axiom.

Q10.   If 40% of a class of 30 students are male, how many are female?

For Problems 1 through 16, solve the system using second-order determinants. Problems 1 through 10 are the same as Problems 1 through 10 in Exercise 4-2. Problems 11 through 16 are the same as Problems 21 through 26 in Exercise 4-2.

1. $5x + 2y = 11$
    $x + y = 4$

2. $x - y = -11$
    $7x + 4y = -22$

3. $6x - 7y = 47$
    $2x + 5y = -21$

4. $8x + 3y = 41$
    $6x + 5y = 39$

5. $5x + 7y = -15$
    $2x + 9y = -6$

6. $9x - 5y = 26$
    $4x - 3y = 17$

7. $2x + 3y = 2$
    $4x - 9y = -1$

8. $3x + 10y = -24$
    $6x + 7y = -9$

9. $9x - 7y = 5$
    $10x + 3y = -16$

10. $11x - 5y = -38$
    $9x + 2y = -25$

11. $4x - 3y = 11$
    $5x - 6y = 9$

12. $3x + 4y = 18$
    $9x + 6y = 17$

13. $3x + 4y = 8$
    $2x - 2y = 7$

14. $5x - 3y = 22$
    $6x - 7y = 41$

15. $-x + 5y = 22$
    $7x - 2y = 19$

16. $8x + 5y = 23$
    $3x - 2y = 37$

17. a. Graph the following system of equations and write the ordered pair at which they seem to intersect.

$$5x - 2y = 4$$
$$3x + 7y = 26$$

   b. Solve the above system using determinants and express the answers as mixed numbers.
   c. Based on the answers to parts a and b, why do you suppose that it is safer to get answers by *calculation* than it is by graphing?

18. a. Plot the graph of each of the following equations on the *same* Cartesian coordinate system:

$$x + y = 5 \quad \text{———} \quad ①$$
$$3x - 2y = 8 \quad \text{———} \quad ②$$
$$x + 3y = 8 \quad \text{———} \quad ③$$

If you have done the work correctly, the graphs will all intersect at (or near) the *same* point.

b.   Solve the systems formed by equation ① and ②, by ② and ③, and by ① and ③ using determinants. Write the answers as mixed numbers and by comparing the three answers, tell whether or not all three *really* intersect at the same point.

19.   *Inconsistent Equations, Dependent Equations, and Determinants*

a. On *separate* sets of axes, plot the graphs of the following two systems:

i. $3x + 2y = 7$
$6x + 4y = 8$

ii. $3x + 2y = 7$
$6x + 4y = 14$

b.   From your graphs, tell which pair of equations is *inconsistent* (graphs are parallel), and which pair of equations is *dependent* (graphs coincide).

c.   Show that the denominator determinant for each system equals zero.

d.   Find the numerator determinant, N_x, for each system. How can you tell from the value of this determinant whether the equations are inconsistent or dependent?

e.   Solve the following systems by determinants. If the denominator determinant equals zero, tell whether the equations are inconsistent or dependent.

i. $15x + 12y = 8$
$10x + 8y = 13$

ii. $15x - 12y = 8$
$10x + 8y = 13$

iii. $15x - 12y = 18$
$10x - 8y = 12$

iv. $15x - 12y = 18$
$10x - 8y = 14$

20.   *Computer Solution of Linear Systems*   Write a computer program that will solve a system of two linear equations with two variables. The input should be the six coefficients, three for one equation and three for the other. The computer should evaluate the denominator and the two numerators, and print these values, along with messages to tell which is which. If the denominator is zero, the program should print the message "INCONSISTENT" or "DEPENDENT," whichever is correct. Otherwise, the computer should do the dividing and print the answer as an ordered pair. Debug your program by solving all four systems in Problem 19, part (e), above.

21.   *Computer Graphics for Linear Systems*   The solution of a system of linear equations is the ordered pair where the graphs cross each other. This ordered pair can be found by actually graphing the two equations and reading the ordered pair. An efficient way to do the graphing is by computer. For each of the systems below, use the program PLOT LINEAR on the accompanying disk, or similar plotting program, to draw the two graphs. You may need to change scales or axis locations to make the intersection appear on the screen. Then estimate the coordinates of the intersection point to one decimal place. The GRID and POINT options will help. In each case, show

by calculation that the ordered pair you get really does satisfy both equations in the system.

a. $9x - 7y = 5$ b. $8x + 5y = 23$
    $10x + 3y = -16$ $3x - 2y = 37$

22. *Mental Solution of Systems*   With practice, you can solve simple systems of linears in your head, writing down only the answer. The secret is being able to visualize the diagonal multiplication scheme, without actually writing the determinants. Solve the following systems mentally. Then check the answers in the back of the book to make sure you are right. If not, try the problem again, mentally, till you get it right. The solutions are not necessarily integers.

a. $2x + 3y = 8$ b. $4x - 3y = 1$
    $5x + y = 6$ $6x + 2y = -5$

23. *Formula Derivation Problem*   Given the general system

$$ax + by = c$$
$$dx + ey = f,$$

solve for y by linear combination, eliminating y. Show that your answer is equivalent to the formula in the text.

4-4 | $f(x)$ TERMINOLOGY, AND SYSTEMS AS MODELS

In the preceding sections you have studied systems of equations such as

$$3x - 4y = -12$$
$$5x - 2y = 10.$$

For graphing purposes, each equation could be transformed to point-slope form, $y = mx + b$, giving

$$y = \frac{3}{4}x + 3$$

$$y = \frac{5}{2}x - 5.$$

The graphs are shown in Figure 4-4a.

The equations can be thought of as representing two different functions with the same independent variable, x. For example, a newspaper carrier's expenses and income both depend on the number of papers he or she delivers. The intersection point of the two graphs would represent the number of papers for which the income equals the expenses (the "break-even" point).

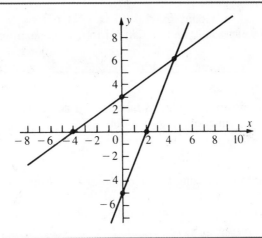

Figure 4-4a _____

Suppose someone asks, "What does y equal when x is 4?" You cannot answer this question since there are two different functions. Fortunately, mathematicians use terminology that allows you to distinguish between functions with the same independent variable. They write

$$f(x) = \frac{3}{4}x + 3$$

$$g(x) = \frac{5}{2}x - 5.$$

The symbol $f(x)$ is pronounced "f of x." It means "the value of y in function f, where the independent variable is x." Similarly, $g(x)$ means the value of y in another function, g, with independent variable x. Any letter may be used for the name of a function. The letters f and g are often used because f is the first letter of the "function," and g comes next to f in the alphabet.

This "$f(x)$ terminology" allows you to show what value is being substituted for x. For instance, the symbol $f(4)$ would mean the value of y in function f when 4 is substituted for x. The symbol $g(4)$ would have the same meaning for function g.

$$f(4) = \frac{3}{4} \cdot 4 + 3 = 3 + 3 = 6,$$

$$g(4) = \frac{5}{2} \cdot 4 - 5 = 10 - 5 = 5.$$

DEFINITION

$f(x)$
The symbol $f(x)$, pronounced "f of x," or "f at x," means the value of the dependent variable in function f if the independent variable is x.

Beware! Do not misinterpret $f(x)$ as meaning f times x. The letter f is simply the *name* of the function, not a variable.

Objectives:

1. Become comfortable using $f(x)$ terminology by using it to evaluate functions.
2. Use systems of linear functions as mathematical models.

EXAMPLE 1

Given $f(x) = 3x^2$ and $g(x) = 4x + 1$, find

a. f(5)   b. $g(5)$ c. $\dfrac{f(2)}{g(2)}$ d. $f(g(6))$

Solutions:

a. $f(5) = 3 \cdot 5^2 = 3 \cdot 25 = \underline{\underline{75}}$
b. $g(5) = 4 \cdot 5 + 1 = \underline{\underline{21}}$

c. $\dfrac{f(2)}{g(2)} = \dfrac{3 \cdot 2^2}{4 \cdot 2 + 1} = \underline{\underline{\dfrac{12}{9}}}$

Note that you can *not* cancel the 2's in $\dfrac{f(2)}{g(2)}$ because $f(2)$ and $g(2)$ are simply *names* for the y-values in the functions.

d. $f(g(6)) = f(4 \cdot 6 + 1) = f(25) = 3 \cdot 25^2 = \underline{\underline{1875}}$

The symbol $f(g(6))$ is pronounced, "f of g of 6." As is usual in algebra, you work what is inside the parentheses first.   ■

EXAMPLE 2

Air Conditioner Problem   Suppose that your family is going to buy a new air conditioning unit. One brand costs $1800 to buy, and $60 a month to operate. A more expensive band costs $2600 to buy. But it is more efficient, and costs only $50 a month to operate.

Let x = number of months since you purchased the unit.

Let $f(x)$ = total number of dollars spent in x months if you buy the cheaper unit.

Let $g(x)$ = total number of dollars spent in x months if you buy the more expensive unit.

a. Write the particular equations expressing $f(x)$ and $g(x)$ in terms of x.
b. Find $f(100)$ and $g(100)$. What do these numbers tell you about the relative costs of the two units after 100 months?
c. Plot the graphs of functions f and g on the same set of axes.
d. Solve the system of equations in part (a) to find the "break-even" point. That is, find the number of months for which the total cost of either unit would be the same.

Solution:

a. Since it costs \$60 a month to run the cheaper unit, it will cost $60x$ dollars to run it for x months. So the total cost is

$$f(x) = 60x + 1800.$$

Similarly, the cost of the more expensive unit is

$$g(x) = 50x + 2600.$$

b. $f(100) = 60 \cdot 100 + 1800 = \underline{\underline{7800}}$
   $g(100) = 50 \cdot 100 + 2600 = \underline{\underline{7600}}$

So it costs *less* to own the *expensive* (efficient) unit if you keep it as long as 100 months!

c. The "y"-intercepts are $f(0) = 1800$ and $g(0) = 2600$. Since $f(100) = 7800$, the point $(100, 7800)$ is on the f graph. Similarly, $(100, 7600)$ is on the g graph. The result is as in Figure 4-4b.

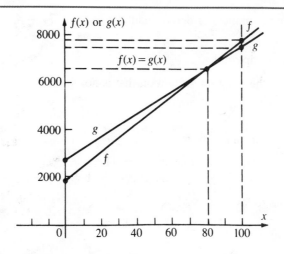

Figure 4-4b

d. The easiest way to solve the system in part (a) is to realize that where
   the graphs cross, $f(x) = g(x)$.

$$60x + 1800 = 50x + 2600 \quad \text{Equate } f(x) \text{ and } g(x).$$
$$10x = 800$$
$$x = 80$$

So you break even after <u>80 months</u>.   ■

The following exercise gives you some practice using $f(x)$ terminology.

EXERCISE 4-4

Do These Quickly

The following problems are intended to refresh your skills. You should be
able to do all 10 in less than 5 minutes.

Q1. Find 40% of 2.7.

Q2. Find the slope of the line from $(-3, 5)$ to $(4, 8)$.

Q3. Solve for p: $\dfrac{3}{p} = \dfrac{5}{7}$

Q4. Solve for j: $|j - 2| = 5$

Q5. Commute the 2 and the $3x$: $5 + 3x + 2$

Q6. Evaluate the determinant: $\begin{vmatrix} 4 & 7 \\ 2 & 9 \end{vmatrix}$

Q7. Write the numerator determinant for y: $3x + 7y = 4$
                                              $5x - 6y = 8$

Q8. Draw a trapezoid.

Q9. Sketch the graph of a function that is not linear.

Q10. Solve for x: $-5x > 20$

For Problems 1 through 26, let

$$f(x) = 3x + 11$$
$$g(x) = x^2 + x + 1$$

Evaluating the following:

1. $f(7)$ 2. $g(5)$
3. $g(-3)$ 4. $f(-4)$

5. $f(0)$ 6. $g(0)$

7. $g\left(\dfrac{1}{3}\right)$ 8. $f(0.5)$

9. $\dfrac{f(5)}{g(5)}$ 10. $\dfrac{g(2)}{f(2)}$

11. $\dfrac{g(1)}{g(0)}$ 12. $\dfrac{f(6)}{g(3)}$

13. $f(g(2))$ 14. $g(f(-5))$

15. $g(g(0))$ 16. $f(f(-2))$

For Problems 17 through 26, you should realize that f ("expression") means substitute "expression" for x. Evaluate, and simplify if possible.

17. $f(r)$ 18. $g(n)$

19. $g(k)$ 20. $f(j)$

21. $f(s + t)$ 22. $g(4 - a)$

23. $g(f(x))$ 24. $f(g(x))$

25. $f(f(x))$ 26. $g(g(x))$

27. **Cops and Robbers Problem** Robin Banks robs a bank and drives off. A short time later he passes a truck stop at which police officer Willie Katchup is dining. Willie receives a call from his dispatcher, and takes off in pursuit of Robin.

> Let t = number of minutes that have elapsed since Robin passed the truck stop.
> Let $f(t)$ = number of kilometers Robin has gone past the truck stop.
> Let $g(t)$ = number of kilometers Willie has gone from the truck stop.

a. Robin's equation is $f(t) = 0.75t$. Find $f(12)$, $f(4)$, and $f(-8)$.
b. Willie's equation is $g(t) = 2(t - 5)$. Find $g(7)$ and $g(15)$.
c. By calculation, find the time and place Willie Katchup catches up with Robin Banks.
d. When did Willie leave the truck stop?
e. Sketch the graphs of functions f and g on the same set of axes, showing the point where they cross.
f. How fast were Robin and Willie going?

28. **Pedalboat Problem** Eb and Flo go pedalboating on the San Antonio River. They check out a boat, head out along the river for awhile, then turn around and come back to the boatdock.

Let t = number of minutes that have elapsed since they left the boatdock.

Let $f(t)$ = number of meters they are from the boatdock on the way out.

Let $g(t)$ = number of meters they are from the boatdock on the way back in.

a. They find that the equation for function f is $f(t) = 32t$. Find $f(3), f(7)$, and $f(10)$.

b. The equation for function g is $g(t) = -17t + 510$. Find $g(18)$ and $g(23)$.

c. Sketch the graphs of f and g on the same set of axes. Use dotted lines for the graphs in parts of the domain where the equations do not apply.

d. Calculate the point where the graphs intersect.

e. What was happening in the real world at the time in part (d)?

f. When did they arrive back at the boatdock?

g. Assuming that they were going the same speed through the water for both parts of the trip, did they start out going upstream or downstream? Justify your answer.

h. Just for fun, see if you can figure out the speed of the current in the San Antonio River.

29. *Efficient Car Problem*   A particular brand of car with the normal engine costs $11,000 to purchase, and 22 cents a mile to drive. The same car with a fuel-injection engine costs $11,300 to purchase, but only 20 cents a mile to operate.

a. Let d be a variable equal to the number of miles you have driven the car, and $f(d)$ be the total number of dollars it costs to own the $11,000 car. Write the particular equation for function f.

b. Calculate $f(1,000), f(10,000)$, and $f(100,000)$.

c. Let $g(d)$ be the total number of dollars it costs to drive the $11,300 car for d miles. Write the particular equation for function g.

d. Calculate $g(1,000), g(10,000)$, and $g(100,000)$.

e. How many miles would you have to drive to "break even?" That is, when does the total cost of owning the car with the normal engine equal the cost of owning the car with the fuel-injected engine?

30. *Hamburger Problem*   Sue Flay and Cassa Roll obtain a franchise to operate a hamburger stand for a well-known national hamburger chain. They pay $20,000 for the franchise, and have additional expenses of $250 per thousand hamburgers they sell. They sell the hamburgers for $.75 each, so they take in a revenue of $750 per thousand burgers.

a. Let $r(x)$ be the number of dollars revenue they take in by selling x thousand burgers. Write the particular equation for function r.

b. Find $r(20)$, $r(50)$, and $r(0)$.
c. Let $c(x)$ be the total cost of owning the hamburger stand, in-
    cluding the $20,000 franchise fee. Write the particular equation
    for function c.
d. Find $c(20)$, $c(50)$, and $c(0)$.
e. Sketch the graphs of r and c on the same set of axes. Have they
    crossed by the time x is 50?
f. How many burgers must Sue and Cassa sell in order to break
    even?

4-5   LINEAR EQUATIONS WITH THREE OR MORE VARIABLES

In Section 4-4 you studied situations in which there were *three* variables.
Two dependent variables such as distance were related to one independent
variable such as time. In this section you will study linear equations with
three variables *without* being concerned with which are dependent and
which are independent.

Objective:
Determine what the graph of a linear equation with three variables looks
like, and be able to sketch the graph.

Since you are not concerned with whether the variables are dependent or
independent, you usually write equations with the variables on one side
and the constant on the other. For example,

$$2x + 3y + 4z = 12.$$

A solution to such an equation must contain *three* numbers, one for each
of the three variables. It is customary to write the solutions as ordered
triples; for example $(4, 0, 1)$. The order in which the numbers appear tells
which variable they stand for. If the equation contained four variables, the
solutions would be called ordered *quadruples;* for five variables, ordered
quintuples; for n variables, ordered *n-tuples*.

Agreement: Unless otherwise specified, variables in ordered n-tuples will
come in alphabetical order.

Equations with three variables can be graphed on a three-dimensional
Cartesian coordinate system. In addition to the normal x- and y-axes,
there is a z-axis perpendicular to the xy-plane, passing through the origin.
The positive portions of the three axes are shown in Figure 4-5a.

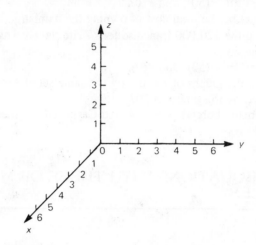

Figure 4-5a ——————————————————————

Plotting an equation such as

$$2x + 3y + 4z = 12,$$

can be accomplished by picking values of *one* variable, and seeing what you get for the others.

$$\textit{If } z = 0, \text{ then } 2x + 3y = 12 \quad \underline{\quad}. \quad ①$$

$$\text{If } z = 1, \text{ then } 2x + 3y + 4 = 12$$
$$2x + 3y = 8 \quad \underline{\quad}. \quad ②$$

$$\text{If } z = 2, \text{ then } 2x + 3y + 8 = 12$$
$$2x + 3y = 4 \quad \underline{\quad}. \quad ③$$

Graphs of Equations ①, ②, and ③ are shown in Figure 4-5b.

The three lines in Figure 4-5b are the parts of the graph at $z = 0$, at $z = 1$, and at $z = 2$. By stacking theses three planes on top of each other (Figure 4-5c), you can see that the whole graph is a *plane* in *space*, containing these three lines.

Conclusion: The graph of a linear equation with three variables is a *plane* in *space*.

Once you realize what the graph looks like, you can draw it more quickly. The line where the graph cuts the *xy*-plane is called the graph of the *xy*-*trace*. It is obtained by setting $z = 0$. Similarly, the *yz*-trace and *xz*-trace are found by letting *x* and *y* equal zero, respectively. By drawing these three traces, you get a reasonable picture of the plane (Figure 4-5d).

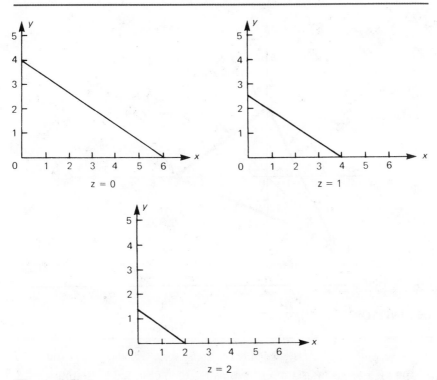

Figure 4-5b

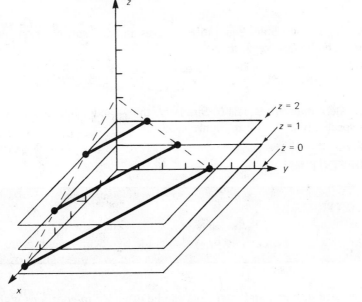

Figure 4-5c

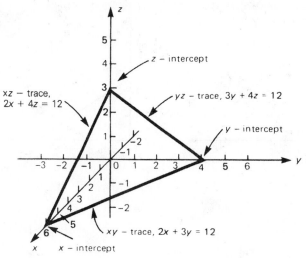

Figure 4-5d

DEFINITION

> **TRACE**
> The **xy-trace** is the set of ordered pairs (x, y) obtained by setting $z = 0$. The other traces are similarly defined.

Setting *two* variables equal to zero gives an *intercept*. For example, if y and z both equal zero, then

$$2x + 0 + 0 = 12,$$
$$x = 6.$$

So the x-intercept equals 6. Similarly, the y- and z-intercepts are 4 and 3, respectively as shown in Figure 4-5d.

DEFINITION

> **INTERCEPT**
> The **x-intercept** is the value of x when y and z are both zero. The other intercepts are similarly defined.

The idea of traces and intercepts can be extended to equations with more than three variables. Since you have used an *algebraic* definition of these

quantities, the fact that there can be no four or five dimensional graphs becomes insignificant. A trace is obtained simply by letting *one* variable
equal zero, while an intercept is obtained by setting *all but one* variable
equal to zero.

EXERCISE 4-5

Do These Quickly

The following problems are intended to refresh your skills. You should be
able to do all 10 in less than 5 minutes.

Q1.   Write the particular equation of the linear function containing
      (3, 7) and (5, 12).

Q2.   Sketch the graph of a relation that is not a function.

Q3.   Multiply 37.4925 by 1000 *without* a calculator!

Q4.   Find 3% of 33.

Q5.   Divide 50 by one-half, and add three.

Q6.   Solve: $|x - 2| = -7$

Q7.   Is $\sqrt{-25}$ a real number?

Q8.   Name by degree and number of terms: $5y^2 - 4y + 7$

Q9.   Factor: $x^2 + 2x - 35$

Q10. Draw a triangle inscribed in a circle.

Work the following problems.

1. Sketch a graph of each of the following equations by drawing its
    three traces as in Figure 4-5d.
    a. $6x + 4y + 3z = 24$
    b. $2x - 3y + z = 12$
    c. $3x + 5y - 3z = 15$
    d. $4x - 2y - z = 8$
    e. $x + y + z = -7$

2. There are some interesting special cases in which the graphs turn out
    to be parallel, perpendicular, or coincident with the coordinate
    planes or axes. Sketch a graph of each of the following equations by
    drawing their traces as in Problem 1. Then tell what the graph is par-
    allel to, or coincident with.

a. $x + y = 7$
b. $y + z = 4$
c. $x + y = 0$
d. $y - z = 0$
e. $x = 5$
f. $y = -6$

3. For the equation $7w + 3x - 4y + 6z = 42$,
    a. find the four intercepts, and
    b. find the equation of the xyz-trace.

4. Explain why a trace is the same as an intercept for an equation with two variables.

5. Obtain three pieces of cardboard; playing cards or index cards will do. These will represent graphs of equations with three variables.
    a. Hold two of the cardboards together so that they meet along an edge. What do the points of intersection represent with regard to a system of two equations in three variables? How many ordered triples normally satisfy a system of two equations in three variables?
    b. Hold the third cardboard so that its corner touches the line of intersection of the other two. Why do you suppose that a system of *three* linear equations in three variables has a *unique* solution, whereas a system with only two does *not*?
    c. Hold the three cardboards in such a way that they intersect at an *infinite* number of points. There are at least two ways to do this. If this happens, the three equations are said to be "dependent."
    d. Hold the three cardboards in such a way that there are *no* points common to all three. There are at least three ways of doing this besides the obvious way of three parallel planes. If this happens, the three equations are said to be "inconsistent."
    e. From what you observed above, can you conclude that a system of three linear equations in three variables *always* has a unique solution? Explain.

4-6 | SYSTEMS OF LINEAR EQUATIONS WITH THREE OR MORE VARIABLES

The graph of a linear equation with three variables is a plane in space. If you hold three index cards as shown in Figure 4-6, you can see that *three* such planes usually intersect at a *single* point. So a system of three linear equations with three variables will usually have a *single* ordered triple in its solution set.

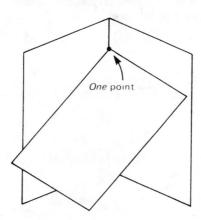

One point

Three intersecting planes

Figure 4-6 _____

Objective:

Be able to find the single ordered triple that satisfies a system of three linear equations with three variables.

EXAMPLE

Solve the system $2x + 3y - z = -1$
$-x + 5y + 3z = -10$
$3x - y - 6z = 5$

Solution:

The technique is to *eliminate* a variable, and get a system of two equations with two variables. Suppose you choose to eliminate x by linearly combining the first and second equations. The work would look like this:

$2x + 3y - z = -1 \xrightarrow{\text{m1}} 2x + 3y - z = -1$

$13y + 5z = -21$

$-x + 5y + 3z = -10 \xrightarrow{\text{m2}} -2x + 10y + 6z = -20$

The equation $13y + 5z = -21$ has only y and z. To get another equation with y and z you can eliminate x by linearly combining a different pair of equations. Using the second and third gives

$-x + 5y + 3z = -10 \xrightarrow{\text{m3}} -3x + 15y + 9z = -30$

$14y + 3z = -25$

$3x - y - 6z = 5 \xrightarrow{\text{m1}} 3x - y - 6z = 5$

From here on it is an old problem. These two equations can be linearly combined to eliminate z as follows:

$$13y + 5z = -21 \xrightarrow{\text{m3}} 39y + 15z = -63$$

$$31y = -62$$

$$14y + 3z = -25 \xrightarrow{\text{m5}} 70y + 15z = -125$$

Dividing by 31 gives

$$y = -2.$$

Substituting -2 for y in one of the two-variable equations gives

$$-26 + 5z = -21$$
$$5z = 5$$
$$z = 1.$$

Substituting -2 for y and 1 for z in one of the original equations gives

$$2x - 7 = -1$$
$$2x = 6$$
$$x = 3$$
$$\therefore S = ((3, -2, 1)) \qquad \blacksquare$$

There is quite a bit of work involved in solving a three-variable system. The horizontal format, shown above, seems to make the work as easy as is possible.

In the following exercise you will practice solving systems with three variables. You will also apply what you have learned to systems with more than three variables.

EXERCISE 4-6

Do These Quickly

The following problems are intended to refresh your skills. You should be able to do all 10 in less than 5 minutes.

Q1.   Sketch the plane with intercepts $x = 5$, $y = 3$, and $z = 8$.

Q2.   Find the slope of $3x - 7y = 42$.

Q3.   If $f(x) = 3x^2$, find $f(-4)$.

Q4.   Show two corresponding angles if two parallel lines are cut by a transversal.

Q5.   Write the hypothesis of the addition property of equality.

Q6.   Solve: $5x + 11 = -24$

Q7.   Draw a number-line graph: $|p| > 3$

Q8.   Find 20% of 600.

Q9.   Does (3, 1) satisfy $4x + 5y = 19$?

Q10.   Evaluate: $17 - 7 \cdot 4$

Solve the following systems.

1. $\begin{aligned} x - 2y + 3z &= 3 \\ 2x + y + 5z &= 8 \\ 3x - y - 3z &= -22 \end{aligned}$ 2. $\begin{aligned} 2x - y - z &= 7 \\ 3x + 5y + z &= -10 \\ 4x - 3y + 2z &= 4 \end{aligned}$

3. $\begin{aligned} 3x + 2y - z &= 10 \\ x + 4y + 2z &= 3 \\ 2x + 3y - 5z &= 23 \end{aligned}$ 4. $\begin{aligned} 3x + 4y + 2z &= 6 \\ x + 3y - 5z &= -7 \\ 5x + 7y - 3z &= 3 \end{aligned}$

5. $\begin{aligned} 5x - 4y + 3z &= 15 \\ 6x + 2y + 9z &= 13 \\ 7x + 6y - 6z &= 6 \end{aligned}$ 6. $\begin{aligned} 3x - 2y + 5z &= -17 \\ 2x + 4y - 3z &= 29 \\ 5x - 6y - 7z &= 7 \end{aligned}$

7. $\begin{aligned} 5x - 4y - 6z &= 21 \\ -2x + 3y + 4z &= -15 \\ 3x - 7y - 5z &= 15 \end{aligned}$ 8. $\begin{aligned} 2x + 2y + 3z &= -1 \\ 3x - 5y - 2z &= 21 \\ 7x + 3y + 5z &= 10 \end{aligned}$

Problems 9 and 10 have some variables "missing." This makes the systems *easier*, if you are clever enough to figure out *why*.

9. $\begin{aligned} 3x + 4y &= 19 \\ 2y + 3z &= 8 \\ 4x \quad\; - 5z &= 7 \end{aligned}$ 10. $\begin{aligned} 2x - 3y &= 5 \\ 4y + 2z &= -6 \\ 5x \quad\; + 7z &= -15 \end{aligned}$

The equations in Problems 11 and 12 are either *inconsistent* (*no* common solution), or *dependent* (an *infinite* number of common solutions). By solving the two systems, tell which is which.

11. $\begin{aligned} 6x + 9y - 12z &= 14 \\ 2x + 3y - 4z &= -11 \\ x + y + z &= 1 \end{aligned}$ 12. $\begin{aligned} 3x + 2y - z &= 4 \\ 5x - 3y + 2z &= 1 \\ 9x - 13y + 8z &= -5 \end{aligned}$

Problems 13 and 14 are systems with *four* variables.

13. $\begin{aligned} 4w + x + 2y - 3z &= -16 \\ -3w + 3x - y + 4z &= 20 \\ -w + 2x + 5y + z &= -4 \\ 5w + 4x + 3y - z &= -10 \end{aligned}$

14. $w - 5x + 2y - z = -18$
$3w + x - 3y + 2z = 17$
$4w - 2x + y - z = -1$
$-2w + 3x - y + 4z = 11$

Problems 15 and 16 involve fractions. With *constants* in the denominators, as in Problem 15, you may simply *multiply* both members by some number that will get rid of the fractions. With *variables* in the denominators, as in Problem 16, you may first solve for $\frac{1}{x}, \frac{1}{y}$, and $\frac{1}{z}$, recognizing that $\frac{4}{x}$ is the same as $4(\frac{1}{x})$, etc.

15. $\dfrac{x}{2} + \dfrac{y}{4} + \dfrac{z}{3} = 24$

$\dfrac{x}{4} + \dfrac{y}{3} + \dfrac{z}{2} = 29$

$\dfrac{x}{3} + \dfrac{y}{2} + \dfrac{z}{4} = 25$

16. $\dfrac{4}{x} - \dfrac{2}{y} + \dfrac{6}{z} = -5$

$-\dfrac{3}{x} - \dfrac{5}{y} + \dfrac{4}{z} = -3$

$\dfrac{2}{x} + \dfrac{7}{y} - \dfrac{10}{z} = 2$

Problems 17 and 18 require you to *find* a system of three equations in three variables. Then you must *solve* the system so that you can answer the problem.

17.   Three robot prototypes—a Wat1000, a UB41, and a Pi314—agreed to race. The sum of their speeds was 30 miles per hour. The Pi314's speed plus one third of the Wat1000's speed was 22 miles per hour more than the UB41's speed. Four times the Wat1000's speed plus three times the UB41's speed minus twice the Pi314's speed was 12 miles per hour. Find out how fast each robot ran. Then tell what was unfortunate about the UB41.

18.   The road from Tedium to Ennui is uphill for 5 miles, level for 4 miles, then downhill for 6 miles. John Garfinkle walks from Ennui to Tedium in 4 hours; later he walks halfway from Tedium to Ennui and back again in 3 hours and 55 minutes. Still later he walks from Tedium all the way to Ennui in 3 hours and 52 minutes. What are his rates of walking uphill, downhill, and on level ground, if these rates remain constant?

4-7   SOLUTION OF SECOND-ORDER SYSTEMS BY AUGMENTED MATRICES

There is a methodical way to solve a systems of equations by linear combination. The procedure, called "augmented matrices," may seem to be more tedious at first. But it has the advantage that it can be done by computer. In this section you will learn how to solve two-variable systems this way, and practice using the computer so that you will be prepared to solve systems with three or more variables in the next section.

Suppose that you are to solve the system

$$2x + 3y = 32$$
$$5x + 4y = 59$$

The coefficient of x can be made zero by multiplying the second equation by 2 and adding -5 times the first equation.

$$0x - 7y = -42$$

The $0x$ term has been left in deliberately so that you can better understand what follows. Dividing each member by -7 gives

$$0x + y = 6$$

So y must equal 6.

The system can be written as follows:

$$\begin{bmatrix} 2 & 3 & | & 32 \\ 5 & 4 & | & 59 \end{bmatrix}$$

The whole thing is called an *augmented matrix*. The coefficients and constants are written in exactly the order they appear in the two equations. The matrix is the square array of numbers to the left of the vertical bar. It has the same pattern as the denominator determinant for the system. The matrix has been "augmented" (added to) by attaching the constants to the right of the vertical bar.

Operations can be performed on the rows of this augmented matrix exactly as they were for the system itself. Multiplying the second row by 2 and subtracting 5 times the first row produces

$$\begin{bmatrix} 2 & 3 & | & 32 \\ 5 & 4 & | & 59 \end{bmatrix} \xrightarrow[+(-5) \times 1]{m2} \begin{bmatrix} 2 & 3 & | & 32 \\ 0 & -7 & | & -42 \end{bmatrix}$$

The arrow indicates that the second row is being changed. The symbol "m2" above the arrow stands for "multiply each number by 2." The "$+(-5) \times 1$" below the line stands for "add -5 times row 1."

The second row can now be divided by -7. Continuing across the page, you would write

$$\begin{bmatrix} 2 & 3 & | & 32 \\ 5 & 4 & | & 59 \end{bmatrix} \xrightarrow[+(-5) \times 1]{m2} \begin{bmatrix} 2 & 3 & | & 32 \\ 0 & -7 & | & -42 \end{bmatrix} \xrightarrow{\div (-7)} \begin{bmatrix} 2 & 3 & | & 32 \\ 0 & 1 & | & 6 \end{bmatrix}$$

The second row now says $0x + 1y = 6$, which is equivalent to the solution $y = 6$ found above.

To find x, you make the coefficient of y in the *first* row equal to zero. This can be done by multiplying the first row by 1 and adding -3 times the second row. When you run out of room at the side of the page, just write the instructions at the end of the line, and the result on the lines below.

$$\begin{bmatrix} 2 & 3 & | & 32 \\ 5 & 4 & | & 59 \end{bmatrix} \xrightarrow[+(-5) \times 1]{m2} \begin{bmatrix} 2 & 3 & | & 32 \\ 0 & -7 & | & -42 \end{bmatrix} \xrightarrow{\div(-7)} \begin{bmatrix} 2 & 3 & | & 32 \\ 0 & 1 & | & 6 \end{bmatrix} \xrightarrow[+(-3) \times 2]{m1}$$

$$\begin{bmatrix} 2 & 0 & | & 14 \\ 0 & 1 & | & 6 \end{bmatrix} \xrightarrow{\div 2} \begin{bmatrix} 1 & 0 & | & 7 \\ 0 & 1 & | & 6 \end{bmatrix}$$

$S = \{(7, 6)\}$

The completed transformation looks as shown above. The final form of the augmented matrix is equivalent to the system

$$1x + 0y = 7$$
$$0x + 1y = 6$$

When there are 1's on the diagonal from the upper left of the matrix to the lower right, and 0's everywhere else, then the solutions appear in the augmented part of the matrix.

In the following exercise you will get practice "diagonalizing" augmented matrices. ("Matrices" is the plural of "matrix.") Remember as you work these problems that although the method may seem more tedious at first, you are learning it to be able to understand what a computer does in the next section.

EXERCISE 4-7

Do These Quickly

The following problems are intended to refresh your skills. You should be able to do all 10 in less than 5 minutes.

Q1.   40 is 20% of what number?

Q2.   Solve for p: $rs = pv$

Q3.   Associate the 3 and the 5: $4 + 3 + 5$

Q4.   Find the slope: $5x + 3y = 30$

Q5.   Sketch the graph of a linear function with positive y-intercept and negative slope.

Q6.   Sketch a trapezoid.

Q7.   Find $f(4)$: $f(x) = 7x - 3$

Q8.   Solve: $3x + 5 = 17$

Q9.   Simplify: $3x + 5 - 17$

Q10.   Multiply: $\left(\dfrac{2}{3}\right)\left(\dfrac{5}{7}\right)$

For Problems 1 through 10, solve the system by augmented matrices.

1. $3x + 8y = 54$
    $4x + 5y = 38$

2. $4x + 7y = 68$
    $2x + 5y = 46$

3. $4x + 3y = 29$
    $6x + 7y = 41$

4. $9x + 2y = -16$
    $4x + 3y = -5$

5. $5x - 3y = -7$
    $2x + 5y = 22$

6. $7x + 2y = 13$
    $4x - 5y = -11$

7. $4x - y = -21$
    $3x - 7y = -22$

8. $10x - 3y = 46$
    $x - 7y = 18$

9. $-3x + 2y = 6$
    $-5x - 8y = 10$

10. $-2x - 3y = 15$
    $6x - y = 5$

Problems 11 through 14 are systems whose solutions are not integers. Solve by augmented matrices.

11. $5x + 2y = 43$
    $3x - y = 71$

12. $x - 8y = 31$
    $2x + 5y = -17$

13. $83x + 51y = 463$
    $22x + 19y = 291$

14. $38x + 57y = 1066$
    $92x + 29y = 1492$

Problems 15 through 18 are systems whose equations are either dependent or inconsistent. Try to solve by augmented matrices. Then write a conclusion about how augmented matrices tell you when you have this kind of system, and how they allow you to distinguish between dependent equations and inconsistent equations.

15. $10x + 15y = 21$
    $12x + 18y = 35$

16. $30x + 48y = 126$
    $20x + 32y = 84$

17. $24x + 18y = 66$
    $28x + 21y = 77$

18. $25x + 10y = 37$
    $20x + 8y = 51$

For Problems 19 through 26, solve the system by the interactive computer program MATRIX ROWS on the disk accompanying this text, or similar program.

19.   Problem 1, above

20.   Problem 2, above

21.   Problem 7, above

22.   Problem 8, above

23.   Problem 13, above   24.   Problem 14, above

25.   Problem 15, above   26.   Problem 16, above

4-8 | SOLUTION OF HIGHER-ORDER SYSTEMS BY AUGMENTED MATRICES

Once you understand the augmented matrix procedure in Section 4-7, you can apply it to systems with more than three variables, such as

$$3x - 2y + 5z = -17 \ ..... \ (1)$$
$$2x + 4y - 3z = \ \ 29 \ ..... \ (2)$$
$$5x - 6y - 7z = \ \ \ \ 7 \ ..... \ (3)$$

The matrix contains the coefficients and constants as it did for systems with two variables.

$$\begin{bmatrix} 3 & -2 & 5 & -17 \\ 2 & 4 & -3 & 29 \\ 5 & -6 & -7 & 7 \end{bmatrix}$$

If you "eliminate" a variable by linearly combining two equations, you are really just making that variable's coefficient equal to *zero*. For instance, eliminating x using Equations (1) and (2) gives

$$\begin{array}{rl} (1)m2: & 6x - \ \ 4y + 10z = \ \ -34 \\ (2)m-3: & \underline{-6x - 12y + \ \ 9z = \ \ -87} \\ & 0x - 16y + 19z = -121 \end{array}$$

The instructions to the left say, "Equation (1) multiplied by 2," for example. Replacing the second equation with $0x - 16y + 19z = -121$ gives a different, but equivalent, system, and a new matrix.

$$\begin{array}{r} 3x - \ \ 2y + \ \ 5z = \ \ -17 \\ 0x - 16y + 19z = -121 \\ 5x - \ \ 6y - \ \ 7z = \ \ \ \ 7 \end{array} \qquad \begin{bmatrix} 3 & -2 & 5 & -17 \\ 0 & -16 & 19 & -121 \\ 5 & -6 & -7 & 7 \end{bmatrix}$$

So eliminating a variable by linear combination corresponds to *putting a zero* in the appropriate place in the matrix. The operations you can do on the rows of a matrix are the same as the operations you do in linear combination of two equations.

By performing these *row operations* in an appropriate order, you can transform the matrix so that there are zeros everywhere except along the *main diagonal,* and ones there. The above matrix would become

$$\begin{bmatrix} 1 & 0 & 0 & 2 \\ 0 & 1 & 0 & 4 \\ 0 & 0 & 1 & -3 \end{bmatrix}$$

The top row of the matrix really says,

$$1x + 0y + 0z = 2,$$

from which you can tell instantly that $x = 2$. Similarly, $y = 4$ and $z = -3$.

The transformed matrix above is said to have been *diagonalized*. The example below shows how you can do the diagonalizing with pencil, paper, and a calculator. Once you understand the process, you can do the operations on a computer so that you won't have to write the entire matrix over again at each step.

Objective:

Given a system of three linear equations with three variables, solve the system by writing it as an augmented matrix and performing the row operations necessary to diagonalize the matrix.

EXAMPLE

Diagonalize the augmented matrix and write the solution set:

$$\begin{bmatrix} 3 & -2 & 5 & | & -17 \\ 2 & 4 & -3 & | & 29 \\ 5 & -6 & -7 & | & 7 \end{bmatrix}$$

Solution:

The following steps show what you should write. An instruction such as

$$\xrightarrow[+\text{(1)m2}]{\text{(2)m}-3}$$

indicates that row (2) is to be multiplied by -3, and the result is to be added to row (1) multiplied by 2. If you write this sort of instruction, you can do the operations on a calculator, one entry at a time, without having to write down any intermediate steps. The word *pivot* is used for the row that does *not* change as you do the row operations.

$$\begin{bmatrix} 3 & -2 & 5 & | & -17 \\ 2 & 4 & -3 & | & 29 \\ 5 & -6 & -7 & | & 7 \end{bmatrix} \begin{array}{c} \\ \xrightarrow[+①m2]{②m-3} \\ \xrightarrow[+①m5]{③m-3} \end{array} \begin{bmatrix} 3 & -2 & 5 & | & -17 \\ 0 & -16 & 19 & | & -121 \\ 0 & 8 & 46 & | & -106 \end{bmatrix} \xrightarrow[+②m1]{③m2} \begin{bmatrix} 3 & -2 & 5 & | & -17 \\ 0 & -16 & 19 & | & -121 \\ 0 & 0 & 111 & | & -333 \end{bmatrix} \xrightarrow{③d\,111}$$

$$\begin{bmatrix} 3 & -2 & 5 & | & -17 \\ 0 & -16 & 19 & | & -121 \\ 0 & 0 & 1 & | & -3 \end{bmatrix} \begin{array}{c} \xrightarrow[+③m-5]{①m1} \\ \xrightarrow[+③m-19]{②m1} \end{array} \begin{bmatrix} 3 & -2 & 0 & | & -2 \\ 0 & -16 & 0 & | & -64 \\ 0 & 0 & 1 & | & -3 \end{bmatrix} \xrightarrow{②d-16}$$

$$\begin{bmatrix} 3 & -2 & 0 & | & -2 \\ 0 & 1 & 0 & | & 4 \\ 0 & 0 & 1 & | & -3 \end{bmatrix} \xrightarrow[+②m2]{①m1} \begin{bmatrix} 3 & 0 & 0 & | & 6 \\ 0 & 1 & 0 & | & 4 \\ 0 & 0 & 1 & | & -3 \end{bmatrix} \xrightarrow{①d\,3} \begin{bmatrix} 1 & 0 & 0 & | & 2 \\ 0 & 1 & 0 & | & 4 \\ 0 & 0 & 1 & | & -3 \end{bmatrix}$$

$S = \{(2, 4, -3)\}$. ■

In the following exercise you will solve one or two systems with pencil and paper to make sure you understand the concepts. If computers are available, you can solve the other systems by simply instructing the computer what row operation to do, and having it do the work and rewrite the matrix.

EXERCISE 4-8

Do These Quickly

The following problems are intended to refresh your skills. You should be able to do all 10 in less than 5 minutes.

Q1.   Expand the determinant: $\begin{vmatrix} 7 & -3 \\ 5 & 8 \end{vmatrix}$

Q2.   Find the x-intercept: $3x - 7y = 42$

Q3.   If $y = -3x + 51$, then y varies _____ with x. What word goes in the blank?

Q4.   Commute the $8x$ and the $3x$: $5 + 8x + 3x$

Q5.   Is $\sqrt{-17}$ an irrational number?

Q6.   Find $f(-4)$ if $f(x) = |15 - 3x|$.

Q7.   Draw a pair of vertical angles.

Q8.   Solve for x: $3x + y = 17$
                     $2x - y = 6$

Q9.   Sketch the graph of a linear function with negative slope and positive y-intercept.

Q10. Find 90% of 900.

Problems 1 through 14 are the same as in Exercise 4-6. For Problems 1 and 2, solve the system by pencil, paper, and calculator using augmented matrices.

1. $\begin{aligned} x - 2y + 3z &= 3 \\ 2x + y + 5z &= 8 \\ 3x - y - 3z &= -22 \end{aligned}$

2. $\begin{aligned} 2x - y - z &= 7 \\ 3x + 5y + z &= -10 \\ 4x - 3y + 2z &= 4 \end{aligned}$

For Problems 3 through 17, solve the system by augmented matrices using the program MATRIX ROWS on the accompanying disk (or similar interactive program). Problems 13, 14, and 17 have systems with more than three variables.

3. $\begin{aligned} 3x + 2y - z &= 10 \\ x + 4y + 2z &= 3 \\ 2x + 3y - 5z &= 23 \end{aligned}$

4. $\begin{aligned} 3x + 4y + 2z &= 6 \\ x + 3y - 5z &= -7 \\ 5x + 7y - 3z &= 3 \end{aligned}$

5. $\begin{aligned} 5x - 4y + 3z &= 15 \\ 6x + 2y + 9z &= 13 \\ 7x + 6y - 6z &= 6 \end{aligned}$

6. $\begin{aligned} 3x - 2y + 5z &= -17 \\ 2x + 4y - 3z &= 29 \\ 5x - 6y - 7z &= 7 \end{aligned}$

7. $\begin{aligned} 5x - 4y - 6z &= 21 \\ -2x + 3y + 4z &= -15 \\ 3x - 7y - 5z &= 15 \end{aligned}$

8. $\begin{aligned} 2x + 2y + 3z &= -1 \\ 3x - 5y - 2z &= 21 \\ 7x + 3y + 5z &= 10 \end{aligned}$

9. $\begin{aligned} 3x + 4y &= 19 \\ 2y + 3z &= 8 \\ 4x - 5z &= 7 \end{aligned}$

10. $\begin{aligned} 2x - 3y &= 5 \\ 4y + 2z &= -6 \\ 5x + 7z &= -15 \end{aligned}$

11. $\begin{aligned} 6x + 9y - 12z &= 14 \\ 2x + 3y - 4z &= -11 \\ x + y + z &= 1 \end{aligned}$

12. $\begin{aligned} 3x + 2y - z &= 4 \\ 5x - 3y + 2z &= 1 \\ 9x - 13y + 8z &= -5 \end{aligned}$

13. $\begin{aligned} 4w + x + 2y - 3z &= -16 \\ -3w + 3x - y + 4z &= 20 \\ -w + 2x + 5y + z &= -4 \\ 5w + 4x + 3y - z &= -10 \end{aligned}$

14. $\begin{aligned} w - 5x + 2y - z &= -18 \\ 3w + x - 3y + 2z &= 17 \\ 4w - 2x + y - z &= -1 \\ -2w + 3x - y + 4z &= 11 \end{aligned}$

15. $\begin{aligned} 2x + 4y - 3z &= 7 \\ 7x - 3y + 2z &= 8 \\ 5x - 5y + 7z &= -1 \end{aligned}$

16. $\begin{aligned} 3x - 7y + 2z &= 11 \\ 8x + 2y - 5z &= -3 \\ 5x - 3y - 3z &= 4 \end{aligned}$

17. $\begin{aligned} 3v - 5w + 2x + 4y + z &= 35 \\ 2v + 4w - x - 3y + 6z &= -16 \\ 4v - 2w - 3x + y + 2z &= 18 \\ -5v + w + 4x - y - 3z &= -18 \\ -2v + 5w + 6x - 2y + z &= -19 \end{aligned}$

4-9 | HIGHER-ORDER DETERMINANTS

In Section 4-3 you learned how to use determinants to solve a system of
two linear equations in two variables. It is possible to solve a system of
any number of linear equations in that same number of variables using
higher-order determinants. Although the technique becomes unwieldy for
more than three variables, it is interesting to see how what you learned
about determinants generalizes to higher order systems.

Objective:
Be able to use determinants to solve a system of three (or more) linear
equations with three (or more) variables.

You recall that the system

$$3x + 4y = -7$$
$$2x - 5y = 8$$

has x and y values as follows:

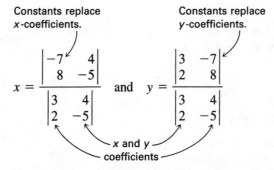

The denominator determinant contains the x- and y-coefficients from the
equations. The x-numerator is obtained by replacing the x-coefficients with
the constants -7 and 8 from the right members of the equations. The y-
numerator is obtained by replacing the y-coefficients with these constants.

The solutions of a system of three or more linear equations in three or
more variables can be written the same way. For instance, the system in
the example of Section 4-6 has the following value for y:

System:

$$2x + 3y - z = -1$$
$$-x + 5y + 3z = -10$$
$$3x - y - 6z = 5$$

y-value:

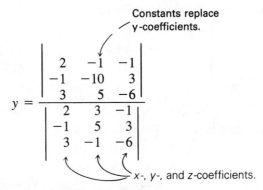

Constants replace
y-coefficients.

$$y = \frac{\begin{vmatrix} 2 & -1 & -1 \\ -1 & -10 & 3 \\ 3 & 5 & -6 \end{vmatrix}}{\begin{vmatrix} 2 & 3 & -1 \\ -1 & 5 & 3 \\ 3 & -1 & -6 \end{vmatrix}}$$

x-, y-, and z-coefficients.

There is another way to evaluate a second-order determinant that carries over to higher-order ones. For example, to evaluate

$$\begin{vmatrix} 3 & 4 \\ 2 & -5 \end{vmatrix}$$

you first write down the *top left* number, 3. Then you cross out its row and its column, and multiply by whatever is left, in this case, -5.

$$\begin{vmatrix} 3 & 4 \\ 2 & -5 \end{vmatrix} = 3(-5) \ldots$$

Next, you write the 4 from the *top right* position, cross out its row and its column, and multiply by what is left, 2. This is *subtracted* from the first term.

$$\begin{vmatrix} 3 & 4 \\ 2 & -5 \end{vmatrix} = 3(-5) - 4(2).$$

Completing the arithmetic, the determinant equals -23.

Third-order determinants are evaluated exactly the same way. First, write down the *top left* number, cross out its row and its column, and multiply by what is left. For example,

$$\begin{vmatrix} 2 & 3 & -1 \\ -1 & 5 & 3 \\ 3 & -1 & -6 \end{vmatrix} = 2 \begin{vmatrix} 5 & 3 \\ -1 & -6 \end{vmatrix} \ldots$$

Note that "what is left" is simply a *second*-order determinant. This is called a *minor* determinant. Proceeding across the top row, the next number is 3. Crossing out its row and column and multiplying by the minor determinant remaining,

$$\begin{vmatrix} 2 & 3 & -1 \\ -1 & 5 & 3 \\ 3 & -1 & -6 \end{vmatrix} = 2 \begin{vmatrix} 5 & 3 \\ -1 & -6 \end{vmatrix} - 3 \begin{vmatrix} -1 & 3 \\ 3 & -6 \end{vmatrix} \ldots$$

Note that this minor determinant is *subtracted* from the first one. Finally the -1 at the end of the top row is multiplied by its minor determinant, found by crossing out its row and column, and the result is *added* to the other terms. The final answer is:

$$\begin{vmatrix} 2 & 3 & -1 \\ -1 & 5 & 3 \\ 3 & -1 & -6 \end{vmatrix} = 2 \begin{vmatrix} 5 & 3 \\ -1 & -6 \end{vmatrix} - 3 \begin{vmatrix} -1 & 3 \\ 3 & -6 \end{vmatrix}$$
$$+ (-1) \begin{vmatrix} -1 & 5 \\ 3 & -1 \end{vmatrix}.$$

Expanding the minor determinants gives

$$2(-30 - (-3)) - 3(6 - 9) + (-1)(1 - 15)$$
$$= -54 + 9 + 14$$
$$= -31.$$

The denominators for x, y, and z are all the *same*. In this case, they equal -31. The numerator for y, shown above, equals 62. The numerators for x and z are found by replacing the x- and z-coefficients, respectively, with the constants on the right of the equations. Expanding these determinants by minors gives

$$x = \frac{-93}{-31} = 3, \quad y = \frac{62}{-31} = -2, \quad \text{and} \quad z = \frac{-31}{-31} = 1.$$

From these, the solution set is $S = \{(3, -2, 1)\}$.

The procedure is easier than linear combination from the standpoint that you immediately know the answers. A lot of arithmetic must be done to simplify the answer, though. The "payoff" comes when you must solve equations that have "untidy" fractions for answers. Determinants work just as easily on these systems as on systems that have integer answers!

Systems with four, five, and more variables can be solved by determinants. A fourth order determinant can be expanded into four third-order minors, which, in turn, give 12 second-order minors. A tenth-order determinant would have almost two *million* second-order minors!

In the following exercise you will solve four of the systems in Exercise 4-6 using determinants (sometimes called using **Cramer's Rule**).

EXERCISE 4-9

Solve the following systems by determinants (Cramer's Rule). These are the same as Problems 1 through 4 in Exercise 4-6.

1. $x - 2y + 3z = 3$
    $2x + y + 5z = 8$
    $3x - y - 3z = -22$

2. $2x - y - z = 7$
    $3x + 5y + z = -10$
    $4x - 3y + 2z = 4$

3. $3x + 2y - z = 10$
    $x + 4y + 2z = 3$
    $2x + 3y - 5z = 23$

4. $3x + 4y + 2z = 6$
    $x + 3y - 5z = -7$
    $5x + 7y - 3z = 3$

4-10 | SYSTEMS OF LINEAR INEQUALITIES

You have extended the concept of a system to more than two equations and to more than two variables. Now you are ready to extend the concept to linear *inequalities*.

The line in Figure 4-10a is the graph of the equation

$$y = 2x - 5.$$

The equation really says, "The points are *on* the line." Similarly, the *inequality*

$$y > 2x - 5$$

says that the points are *above* the line. The inequality

$$y < 2x - 5$$

says that the points are *below* the line.

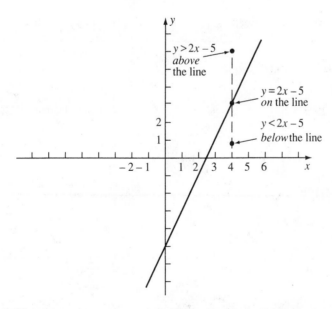

Figure 4-10a _____

The line plays a part in all three open sentences. For the equation $y = 2x - 5$, the line *is* the graph. For the two inequalities, the line is the *boundary* of a region. For $y > \ldots$, the points are above the boundary line, and for $y < \ldots$, the points are below.

With this knowledge you can graph one or more inequalities fairly quickly.

Objective:

Be able to draw the graph of a system of linear inequalities with two variables *quickly*.

EXAMPLE 1

Graph $y > 2x - 5$.

Solution:

First, draw the boundary line, $y = 2x - 5$. Make it *dotted*, because y is not allowed to *equal* $2x - 5$. Then shade the region *above* the line because y is *greater* than $2x - 5$. The finished graph is shown in Figure 4-10b.

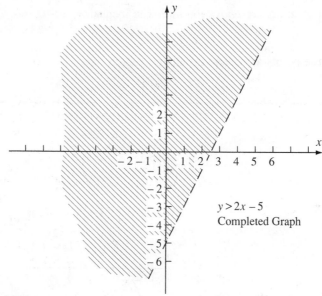

$$y > 2x - 5$$
Completed Graph

Figure 4-10b

EXAMPLE 2

Graph the system

$$y > 2x - 5 \qquad\qquad y \le -\frac{1}{3}x + 3.$$

Solution:

For a system of inequalities, you first plot the boundary line for each inequality. The first inequality is the same as in Example 1. The second says greater than *or equal to* … . So its boundary will be solid, not dotted.

Rather than shading each region as you go, it is tidier to draw small arrows on each boundary line to indicate which side the region will be on. See Figure 4-10c. The solution set of the system is the set of ordered pairs

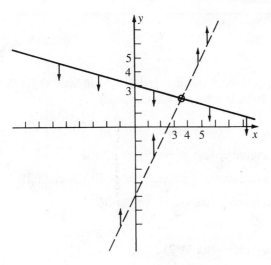

Figure 4-10c _____

that satisfy *all* the inequalities. So you shade the region where arrows from *all* boundary lines point. Figure 4-10d shows the completed graph.

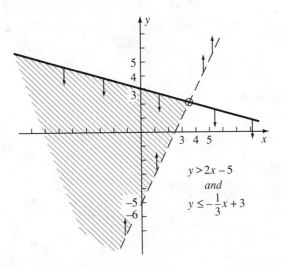

$$y > 2x - 5$$
$$and$$
$$y \leq -\frac{1}{3}x + 3$$

Figure 4-10d _____ ■

The following exercise is designed to give you practice plotting graphs of linear systems in preparation for the real-world problems in the next section.

EXERCISE 4-10

Do These Quickly

The following problems are intended to refresh your skills. You should be able to do all 10 in less than 5 minutes.

Q1.   Draw a number-line graph: $x > -5$

Q2.   Draw a number-line graph: $3x \leq 12$

Q3.   Draw a number-line graph: $-5x > 30$ (Be careful!)

Q4.   Draw a number-line graph: $|x| \geq 7$

Q5.   Solve: $8x + 11 = 67$

Q6.   Multiply: $(x - 9)(x + 7)$

Q7.   If $f(x) = 5x^2$, find $f(3)$.

Q8.   What is 4% of 300?

Q9.   Draw two internally tangent circles.

Q10.   Sketch the graph of the function $f(x) = 7$.

For Problems 1 through 16, plot the graph of the inequality or system of inequalities.

1. $y < 3x + 1$

2. $y \leq -x + 4$

3. $2x + 3y \geq 6$
     $2x - y < 7$

4. $3x + 4y > 12$
     $x - 4y \geq -8$

5. $5x - 2y < 10$
     $x + y < 4$

6. $5x + 2y > -12$
     $7x + 2y < -18$

7. $5x + 3y \geq -15$
     $2x + 6y < -9$

8. $3x + 4y \leq 24$
     $x - y > 5$

9. $y < 3x - 4$
     $2x - 3y > 6$
     $y - 2 \leq -\dfrac{3}{5}(x - 4)$

10. $3x + 2y \leq 12$
      $-2x + 5y > -10$
      $x - y \geq -1$

11. $x > 2$
      $y \leq 3$
      $x + y \geq -4$
      $x + y < -1$

12. $2 \leq x \leq 6$
      $y > -1$
      $x - 2y \geq -6$
      $y - 5 \leq -\dfrac{1}{2}(x - 4)$

13. $y \leq 3x$
     $x + 4y > 12$

14. $y > x$
     $2x - 5y \geq 10$

15. $x + y \leq 4$ (Watch out for a surprise!)
     $2x - y > 6$
     $x - 2y = 8$

16. $x + y \geq 3$ (Watch out for a different surprise!)
     $3x - 2y > 6$
     $y \geq 4x + 1$

17. ***Computer Graphics Problem***   Use the program PLOT LINEAR on
     the accompanying disk, or similar graphing program, to graph the
     boundary lines for syster
     a.   Problem 5, above.
     b.   Problem 6, above.
     c.   Problem 9, above.
     d.   Problem 12, above.

4-11 | LINEAR PROGRAMMING

In previous sections you have studied equations with three or more variables, and systems of linear inequalities. You are now equipped with the
tools you need to work some rather significant problems from the real
world. The following example leads you stepwise through the solution of
such a problem. The objective for this section will be clearer to you after
you have studied the example.

EXAMPLE

A School Board is investigating various ways of composing the faculty for
a proposed new elementary school. They can hire teachers and aides. The
amount of money the school district will have to spend on salaries each
year depends on how many teachers and on how many aides are hired.

> Let t = number of teachers hired.
> Let a = number of aides hired.
> Let d = number of *thousands* of dollars spent
>   annually on faculty salaries.

The Board finds that the average teacher's annual salary is \$15,000, and
the average aide's annual salary is \$10,000. Since there are t teachers and
a aides,

$$d = 15t + 10a.$$

So d is a function of *two* independent variables, t, and a. The domain of
this function will be the set of all permissible *ordered pairs*, (t, a).

Suppose that the Board finds the following requirements concerning the permissible numbers of teachers and aides:

i.   The building can accommodate no more than 50 faculty members, total. Since the total number of faculty members is $t + a$, this means that

$$t + a \leq 50.$$

ii. A minimum of 20 faculty members is needed to staff the school. This means that

$$t + a \geq 20.$$

iii. The school cannot be run entirely by aides, so there must be at least 12 teachers. Since "at least" means "greater than or equal to," you can write

$$t \geq 12.$$

iv. For a proper teacher-to-aide ratio, the number of teachers must be at least half the number of aides. Therefore,

$$t \geq \frac{1}{2}a.$$

v.   It is impossible (obviously!) to hire a *negative* number of teachers or aides. Therefore,

$$t \geq 0 \quad \text{and} \quad a \geq 0.$$ ∎

The six inequalities, above, form a *system* that can be plotted using the techniques of Section 4-10. The graph is shown in Figure 4-11a. Ordered pairs (t, a) in this region are possible, or "feasible." So this region is called the *feasible* region. You may now use the equation

$$d = 15t + 10a$$

to find out *which* of the feasible ordered pairs gives the *minimum* cost.

Since d is a third variable, the d-axis should come up vertically out of the page! However, there is a clever way to reduce this three-dimensional problem to a two-dimensional one. Suppose that you wish to find the portion of the feasible region in which the cost is less than or equal to some fixed amount, say \$600,000. That is, you want to find out where $d \leq 600$. Since $15t + 10a$ is equal to d, you can write

$$15t + 10a \leq 600.$$

Solving for a in terms of t,

$$10a \leq -15t + 600.$$

$$a \leq -\frac{3}{2}t + 60.$$

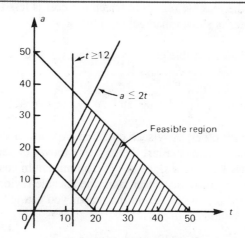

Figure 4-11a _____

This inequality can be graphed on the feasible region, as shown in Figure 4-11b. The darkly-shaded region represents the values of t and a that make the feasible cost less than or equal to $600,000 per year.

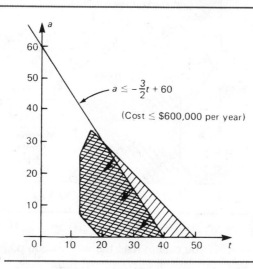

Figure 4-11b _____

Picking another fixed value of the cost, say $400,000, you can find the values of t and a that lead to a cost no more than this:

$$15t + 10a \leq 400.$$

This can be transformed to

$$10a \leq -15t + 400$$

$$a \leq -\frac{3}{2}t + 40.$$

The portion of the feasible region in which the cost is less than or equal to $400,000 per year is shown in Figure 4-11c.

To find the *minimum* feasible cost, observe that the two "cost boundary lines,"

$$a = -\frac{3}{2}t + 60 \quad \text{and} \quad a = -\frac{3}{2}t + 40,$$

are *parallel* to each other. Any such cost line will have a slope of $\frac{-3}{2}$. As the cost gets smaller and smaller, the cost line moves closer and closer to the origin, always keeping a slope of $\frac{-3}{2}$. The minimum cost, therefore, occurs at the *last* point to disappear from the feasible region as the cost line moves toward the origin. From the graph, you can tell that this is the point where the boundary lines

$$t = 12 \quad \text{and} \quad t + a = 20$$

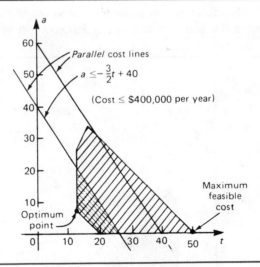

Figure 4-11c

intersect each other. If you cannot read the intersection point from the graph, you can solve this *system* of equations. Either way, the point is

$$(t, a) = (12, 8).$$

The cost can be found by substituting $(12, 8)$ into the cost equation, $d = 15t + 10a$, getting

$$d = 15(12) + 10(8)$$

$$= 260.$$

So, the minimum feasible cost is $\underline{\$260,000 \text{ per year}}$.

The maximum feasible cost could be found by sliding the cost line in the *opposite* direction, always keeping a slope of $\frac{-3}{2}$. From Figure 4-11c you can tell that the point would be (50, 0), for which *d* would equal 750.

The point (12, 8), at which the minimum cost occurs is called the *optimum* point, from the Latin word for "best." The lowest cost is the "best" from the point of view of the School Board. [The point (50, 0) might be considered to be "optimum" by the teachers since more money would go to teachers!] The process of finding the optimum point for a linear function such as $d = 15t + 10a$ is called *linear programming*. Your objective is to be able to work linear programming problems.

Objective:
Given information about permissible values of two independent variables, find the pair of values that either *maximizes* or *minimizes* a third, dependent variable.

In the exercise that follows, you will solve some linear programming problems. The first problem has the steps spelled out in great detail, but in later problems you will be expected to know what to do with progressively less instruction.

EXERCISE 4-11

Do These Quickly

The following problems are intended to refresh your skills. You should be able to do all 10 in less than 5 minutes.

Q1.   Solve: $x + 5 > 3$

Q2.   Solve: $x - 7 \leq 11$

Q3.   Solve: $4x \geq 19$

Q4.   Solve: $-2x < 15$

Q5.   Solve: $10x > -29$

Q6.   Write an expression meaning 3 less than x.

Q7.   Write an inequality saying 3 is less than x.

Q8.   Write an inequality saying x is at least 3.

Q9.   Write an inequality saying x is between 4 and 7.

Q10.   Sketch the graphs of two inconsistent linear equations.

Work the following problems.

1. *Music Shop Problem*   Jake Garcia opens a music shop in which he
    will sell guitars and basses. He wants to find out the maximum
    amount of money he may have to borrow to purchase the instru-
    ments.

    a.   Each bass will cost him $900 and each guitar will cost him
         $750. He buys B basses and G guitars. Write an equation for the
         total number of dollars, C, he will have to spend.

    b.   Jake has certain restrictions on the numbers of each kind of in-
         strument he can stock.

         i.   His store is small, so he can buy no more than 50 instru-
               ments, total.
         ii.   Because guitars are more popular than basses, the number of
               guitars must be at least twice the number of basses.
         iii. To get started, he must buy at least 17 guitars and at least 5
               basses.

         Write a system of inequalities expressing these restrictions.

    c.   Plot the graph of the system in part (b).

    d.   Write an inequality stating that Jake spends at least $36,000 on
         instruments. Darken the part of the feasible region in part (c) for
         which Jake spends at least $36,000.

    e.   What number of basses and what number of guitars would give
         the maximum feasible cost? What would this cost be?

2. *Oil Refinery Problem*   Sabrina Burmeister is Chief Mathematician
    for Pedro Leum's Oil Refinery. Pedro can buy Texas oil, priced at
    $30 per barrel, and California oil, priced at $15 per barrel. He con-
    sults Sabrina to find out what is the most he might have to pay in a
    month for the oil the refinery uses.

    a.   Define variables for the number of barrels of Texas oil and the
         number of barrels of California oil purchased in a month. Then
         write an equation expressing the total cost of the oil in terms of
         these two variables.

    b.   Sabrina finds the following restrictions on the amounts of oil
         that can be purchased in a month.

         i.   The refinery can handle as much as 40,000 barrels per
               month.
         ii.   To stay in business, the refinery must process at least 18,000
               barrels a month.
         iii. California oil has 6 pounds of impurities per barrel. Texas
               oil has only 2 pounds of impurities per barrel. The most
               the refinery can handle is 120,000 pounds of impurities a
               month.

         Write a system of inequalities representing this information.

    c.   Plot the graph of the system in part (b).

d.   Write an inequality saying that Pedro spends at least $660,000 per month buying oil. Darken the part of the feasible region in part (c) which satisfies this inequality.

e.   What is the maximum feasible amount Pedro might have to spend in a month? How much of each kind of oil would give this maximum cost?

3.   *Park Clean-Up Problem*   Your mathematics club has arranged to earn some extra money by cleaning up Carr Park. The City Recreation Department agrees to pay each old member $10 and each new member $8 for their services. (The club did the same thing last year, so the old members are experienced.)

a.   Define variables, then write an equation expressing the dollars the club earns in terms of the numbers of old and new members who work.

b.   The following facts restrict the numbers of students who can work:

   i.   The number of old members is non-negative, and so is the number of new members.

   ii.   The club has at most 9 old members and at most 8 new members who can work.

   iii. The Department will hire at least 6 students, but no more than 15.

   iv.   There must be at least 3 new members.

   v.   The number of new members must be at least 1/2 the number of old members, but less than 3 times the number of old members.

   Write inequalities for each of the above requirements.

c.   Draw a graph of the solution set of this system of inequalities. Remember that club members come only in *integer* quantities!

d.   Based on your graph, is it feasible to do without any old members at all? Explain.

e.   Shade the portion of the feasible region in which the club would make *at least* $100.

f.   Draw a line on the graph showing the number of old and new members needed to make $160. Is it feasible to make $160? Explain.

g.   What numbers of old and new members would earn the *maximum* feasible amount? What would this amount be?

h.   What is the *minimum* feasible amount the club could earn?

i.   Suppose tradition was broken and the new members were paid more than the old members. What would be the maximum feasible earnings if new members get $12 and old members get $10?

4.   *Vitamin Problem*   Suppose that you are Chief Mathematician for the Government's million dollar Vitamin Research Project. Your scientists have been studying the combined effects of vitamins A and B

on the human system, and have turned to *you* for analysis of their findings:

  i. The body can tolerate no more than 600 units per day of vitamin A, and no more than 500 units per day of vitamin B.
  ii. The total number of units per day of the two vitamins must be between 400 and 1000, inclusive.
 iii. Due to the combined effects of the two vitamins, the number of units per day of vitamin B must be more than 1/2 the number of units per day of vitamin A, but less than or equal to three times the number of units per day of vitamin A.

Let x and y be the numbers of units per day of vitamins A and B, respectively. Answer the following questions:

  a. Let c be the number of cents per day it costs you for vitamins. Write an equation expressing c in terms of x and y if vitamin A cost 0.06 cents per unit (*not* $0.06!), and vitamin B costs 0.05 cents per unit.
  b. Write inequalities to represent each of the above requirements, and plot a graph of the solution set of the system.
  c. What does a point lying in this solution set represent in the real world?
  d. Plot lines on your graph showing where the cost per day is
    i. 60 cents,
    ii. 30 cents,
   iii. 15 cents.
    You might use a different colored pencil to make these lines show up more distinctly.
  e. Is it feasible to spend 60 cents per day on vitamins? 30 cents per day? 15 cents per day? Explain why or why not.
  f. What word describes the point at which the feasible cost is a *minimum*? Write the coordinates of this point, and find the minimum cost.

5. *Aircraft Problem*   Calvin Butterball is Chief mathematician for Fly-By-Night Aircraft Corp. He is responsible for mathematical analysis of the manufacturing of the Company's two models of planes, the Sopwith Camel and the larger Sopwith Hippopotamus. Each Department at Fly-By-Night has certain restrictions concerning the number of planes which can be manufactured per day.

  i. Production: No more than 7 Hippopotami and no more than 11 Camels can be manufactured per day.
  ii. Shipping: No more than 12 planes, total, can be manufactured per day.
 iii. Sales: the number of Hippopotami manufactured per day must be no more than twice the number of Camels.
  iv. Labor: You must use more than 1000 man-hours of labor per day. (It takes 100 man-hours to manufacture each Camel and 200 man-hours to manufacture each Hippo.)

a.   Select variables to represent the number of Camels and Hippo-potami manufactured per day, write inequalities expressing each of the above restrictions, and draw a graph of the feasible region (the solution set of the system).

b.   If Fly-by-Night makes a profit of $300 per Camel and $200 per Hippo, show the region on your graph in which the daily profit would be at least $3000.

c.   How many Hippos and how many Camels should be produced per day to give the *greatest* feasible profit? What would this profit be?

6.   *CB Radio Manufacturing Problem*   Suppose that you work for a small company that makes high-quality CB radios. They wish to optimize the numbers of the two models they produce, "Breakers" and "Good Buddies." Since you are an expert at linear programming, your Boss assigns you the job. You find the following information:

  i.   The assembly lines can produce no more than 25 Breakers and 16 Good Buddies per day.

  ii.   No more than 32 radios, total, can be produced per day.

  iii. They can spend a total of no more than 189 man-hours a day assembling radios. It takes 7 man-hours to assemble a Breaker and 3 man-hours to assemble a Good Buddy.

  iv.   They can spend at most 68 man-hours per day, total, testing radios. It takes 1 man-hour to test a Breaker and 4 man-hours to test a Good Buddy.

  v.   The number of Breakers produced per day must be more than half the number of Good Buddies.

Using this information, answer the following questions:

a.   Define variables, write inequalities for each of the above requirements, and plot the graph of the feasible region. (It may be easier if you plot Breakers on the vertical axis.)

b.   The company makes a profit of $40 on each Breaker and $20 on each Good Buddy. Write an equation expressing dollars profit earned per day in terms of the numbers of Breakers and Good Buddies produced each day.

c.   Shade the portion of the feasible region in which the daily profit is at least $960.

d.   Find the optimum point at which the daily profit is a maximum, and the number of dollars they would earn per day by operating at this point.

7.   *Feedlot Problem*   Butch Err owns a feedlot on which he fattens up cattle for market by feeding them a mixture of corn and pellets. He wants to find what mixture of corn and pellets will give the minimum feasible cost.

The pellets and corn contain the following ingredients per 100 pound (lb) sack:

| Pounds per 100 lb. sack | | | |
	Protein	Minerals	Starch	Bulk
Pellets*	25	12	20	12
Corn	10	10	32	48

*Pellets contain a "secret ingredient," not shown here.

For the number of cattle Mr. Err owns, the daily needs are

    i.   total protein: at least 250 lb/day,

    ii. total minerals: at least 200 lb/day,

    iii. total starch: at least 512 lb/day,

    iv. total bulk: at least 480 lb/day,

    v.   total food: no more than 3000 lb/day.

a.   Let x and y be the numbers of 100 lb sacks of pellets and corn, respectively, used per day. Since each sack of pellets has 25 lb of protein and each sack of corn has 10 lb of protein, the total amount of protein is $25x + 10y$. Write a system of inequalities expressing the five requirements above, and draw the graph of the feasible region.

b.   Is it feasible to feed only corn? Only pellets? Explain.

c.   Pellets cost $16 per 100 lb sack and corn costs $8 per 100 lb sack. Write an equation expressing the number of dollars, d, spent per day in terms of x and y.

d.   Show the portion of the feasible region in which the daily cost is

    i.   no more than $240,

    ii. no more than $200.

e.   Show that there are four optimum points with integer coordinates, each of which gives the *same* minimum feasible cost.

f.   How much would Mr. Err save by feeding at one of the optimum points of part e rather than by feeding the minimum feasible "all-corn" diet?

g.   Find the exact point of intersection of the two boundary lines that meet at the *actual* (non-integer) optimum point. How much could Mr. Err save per day by feeding at this optimum point rather than one of the integer points of part e?

8.   *Thoroughbred and Quarter Horses Problem*   Suppose that you go into business raising Thoroughbreds and quarter horses. Having studied linear programming, you decide to maximize the feasible profit you can make. Let x be the number of Thoroughbreds, and let y be the number of quarter horses you raise each year.

a.   Write inequalities expressing each of the following requirements:

    i.   Your supplier can get you at most 20 Thoroughbreds and at most 15 quarter horses to raise each year.

    ii.   You must raise at least 12 horses, total, each year to make the business worthwhile.

    iii.   A Thoroughbred eats 2 tons of food per year, but a quarter horse eats 6 tons per year. You can handle no more than 96 tons of food per year.

    iv.   A Thoroughbred requires 1000 hours of training per year, and a quarter horse only 250 hours per year. You have enough personnel to do at most 10,000 hours of training per year.

b.   Draw a graph of the feasible region.

c.   One of the inequalities has no effect on the feasible region. Which one? Tell what this means in the real world.

d.   What is the minimum feasible number of quarter horses?

e.   What is the maximum feasible number of Thoroughbreds?

f.   Is it feasible to raise *no* Thoroughbreds? Explain.

g.   You can make a profit of $500 for each Thoroughbred and $200 for each quarter horse. Shade the portion of the feasible region in which the profit would be at least $5000 per year.

h.   What is the maximum feasible profit you could make per year, and how would you operate in order to attain that profit?

i.   How much more profit do you make per year by operating at the optimum point of part h rather than by operating at the *worst* feasible point?

9.   *Cookie Problem*   Craig Browning bakes cookies for the elementary school cookie sale. His chocolate chip cookies sell for $1.00 a dozen, and his oatmeal brownie cookies sell for $1.50 a dozen. He will bake up to 20 dozen chocolate chip cookies, and up to 40 dozen oatmeal brownie cookies, but no more than 50 dozen cookies, total. Also, the number of oatmeal brownie cookies will be no more than three times the number of chocolate chip cookies. How many of each kind should Craig make in order for the elementary school to make the most money? How much money will this be?

10.   *Christmas Tree Problem*   Monica Pety runs a gift shop in which she sells expensive trees at Christmas time. Her supplier, Connie Furr, charges her $80 for each real tree, and $160 for each artificial tree. She can buy between 20 and 90 real trees, inclusive, but up to 100 artificial trees. Connie can supply anywhere between 50 and 120 trees, total, but requires that the number of artificial trees ordered be at least half the number of real trees. Monica is hard-up for cash this year, and wants to invest the minimum feasible amount in trees. How many of each kind should she buy? What is her minimum feasible investment?

11.   *Coal Problem*   Skinflint Coal Company has a stock of 16 tons of Number Nine Coal. Ten tons of this is located at Warehourse No. 1

and the remaining 6 tons is located at Warehouse No. 2. Mr. Skinflint has orders from Weedies Cereal Co. for 5 tons, from Pikkitt Lock Co. for 7 tons, and from Treadwell Tire Co. for 4 tons. He wants to minimize the cost of shipping the coal.

Let x, y, and z represent the number of tons sent from Warehouse 1 to Pikkitt, Weedies, and Treadwell, respectively.

a. The remainder of each order must come from Warehouse 2. Write expressions in terms of x, y, and z representing how much must be shipped from Warehouse 2 to each customer.

b. Write an equation stating that all 10 tons of coal from Warehouse 1 must be shipped. Then transform the equation so that z is expressed in terms of x and y.

c. Substitute the value of z from part b into the appropriate expression from part (a) so that all three of these expressions are in terms of x and y alone.

d. Write inequalities representing each of the following conditions:
   i. x is non-negative.
   ii. y is non-negative.
   iii.   Pikkitt gets no more than 7 tons from Warehouse 1.
   iv.   Weedies gets no more than 5 tons from Warehouse 1.
   v.   Treadwell gets no more than 4 tons from Warehouse 1.
   vi.   The total shipped from Warehouse 1 to Weedies and Pikkitt is no more than 10 tons (the total contents of Warehouse 1).

e. Plot a graph of the system of inequalities in part d.

f. The distances from the warehouses to the customers are shown in Figure 4-11d. Let d be the number of dollars it costs to ship

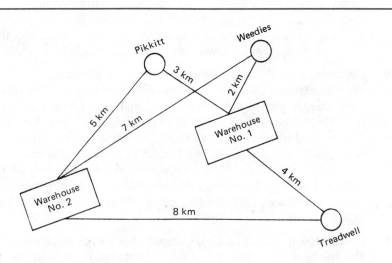

Figure 4-11d

all the coal. Write an equation expressing d in terms of x and y if it costs \$3.00 to ship one ton one kilometer.

g.   Mr. Skinflint desires to keep the total shipping cost below \$192. Write an inequality expressing this requirement, plot it on your graph, and indicate its intersection with your present feasible region.

h.   What values of x and y would result in a *minimum* shipping cost? A *maximum* shipping cost? What would these maximum and minimum costs be?

4-12   CHAPTER REVIEW AND TEST

In this chapter you have studied relations that involve more than one linear equation or inequality. The objectives for the chapter are summarized below.

1.   *Solve systems of two linear equations with two variables.*

2.   *Find intersections of real-world graphs, and use f(x) terminology.*

3.   *Solve systems of three (or more) linear equations with three (or more) variables.*

4.   *Graph systems of linear inequalities.*

5.   *Use linear programming techniques to find optimum values of* **two** *independent variables.*

By working the Review Problems below, you will see how well you can accomplish these objectives one at a time. In the Concepts Test you will have to put together several concepts. Some parts of the problems allow you to extend your knowledge to concepts you have never seen before!

REVIEW PROBLEMS

The following problems are numbered according to the five objectives listed above.

R1.   a.   Solve the system by linear combination:

$$5x - 8y = 47$$
$$2x + 7y = -22.$$

b.   Solve the system by determinants:

$$4x - 3y = 5$$
$$7x + 2y = -1.$$

R2.   At Annie Moore's Coffee Shop, the waiteress earns $16 and the cook earns $24 in a normal shift. In addition, the waitress gets 70% of the tip money received, and the cook gets 30%.

Let t = total dollars in tips received in a shift.
Let $w(t)$ = total dollars the waitress gets in a shift.
Let $c(t)$ = total dollars the cook gets in a shift.

a.   Write equations expressing $w(t)$ and $c(t)$ in terms of t.
b.   Calculate $w(5)$ and $c(5)$.
c.   How much would have to be received in tips for the waitress and the cook to break even?
d.   Plot graphs of functions w and c, and thus show that your answer to part c is correct.

R3.   Solve the system:

$$3x - 2y + 5z = -1$$
$$4x + 3y - 2z = -13$$
$$2x + 5y - 4z = -9.$$

R4.   Graph the solution set of the system:

$$y \geq 3x + 2$$
$$2x - 3y > -15$$
$$y + 2 \geq -\frac{2}{5}(x + 3)$$
$$y > -1.$$

R5.   *Achievement Test*   You are to take a mathematics achievement test. Two days before the test you receive the following instructions concerning the point values of the two kinds of questions, and how many of each you must answer.
    i.   There are 10 questions worth 7 points each, and 16 questions worth 5 points each.
    ii.   You can receive credit for a maximum of 20 questions. Any others you answer will not be scored.
    iii.   To receive any credit at all, you must answer at least 5 questions.
    iv.   The number of 5-point questions you answer must be no more than twice the number of 7-point questions.
    v.   The number of 5-point questions you answer must be more than $\frac{1}{2}$ the quantity (number of 7-point questions minus 5).
a.   What are the optimum numbers of 5- and 7-point questions to answer in order to maximize your score?

b.   What is the maximum feasible score?
c.   What is the minimum feasible score, assuming that you satisfy all of the above requirements, and answer each question correctly?

CONCEPTS TEST

Answer the following two questions. For each part of each question, tell which one(s) of the five objectives you used. If the part of the problem involves a new concept, write "new concept."

T1.   *Camping Trip Problem*   Suppose that you are going on a prolonged camping trip. There are two types of condensed food you can take along, X-rations and Yummies. You wish to minimize the amount of money you spend on food for the trip while still meeting all your nutritional requirements.
a.   Define variables for the numbers of pounds of X-rations and Yummies, and for the number of dollars spent on food.
b.   Each pound of X-rations and Yummies contains the following:

	Vitamins	Calories	Protein	Carbohydrates
X-rations	400 units	800	1 ounce	4 ounces
Yummies	100 units	700	4 ounces	5 ounces

Your total needs for the trip are:
i.   Vitamins, at least 4000 units.
ii.   Calories, no less than 16,800.
iii.   Protein, more than or equal to 28 ounces.
iv.   Carbohydrates, 100 ounces or more.
Write inequalities for each of these requirements.
c.   Write an inequality expressing the fact that the total weight of X-rations and Yummies must be less than 30 pounds.
d.   Plot a graph of the feasible region formed by the inequalities of parts b and c.
e.   If you took only X-rations, what is the smallest feasible number of pounds you could take?
f.   If you took only Yummies, what is the smallest feasible number of pounds you could take?

g.   X-rations cost $3 per pound and Yummies cost $2 per pound. Write an equation expressing the number of dollars spent for food in terms of the numbers of pounds of X-rations and Yummies.
h.   Shade the portion of the feasible region in which your total cost would be at most $60.

i.   Mark the optimum point on your graph.

    j.   The optimum point of part i does *not* have integer coordinates. Write *equations* for the two boundary lines that cross at the optimum point (replace the "≥" signs with "=" signs). Then solve this system of equations to find the *exact* coordinates of the optimum point.

    k.   What is the minimum feasible cost?

    l.   What point with *integer* coordinates gives the minimum feasible cost? (Your graphs must be *very* carefully drawn because the answer is somewhat surprising!)

T2.   So far you have studied *linear* functions and relations. In a *quadratic* function, *y* equals a *quadratic trinomial*. That is, the general equation of a quadratic function is

$$f(x) = ax^2 + bx + c,$$

where *a*, *b*, and *c* stand for *constants* (just like *m* and *b* stand for constants in a linear function).

    a.   Suppose that for a particular quadratic function, $f(3) = 7$. Explain why the following equation involving *a*, *b*, and *c* must be true:

$$9a + 3b + c = 7.$$

    b.   If this particular function also has $f(2) = 6$, and $f(1) = 3$, write two other equations involving *a*, *b*, and *c*, as in part a.

    c.   The three equations in parts a and b, above, form a system of three linear equations in the three "variables" *a*, *b*, and *c*. Solve this system to find the values of *a*, *b*, and *c*.

    d.   Write the particular equation for $f(x)$.

    e.   Find $f(6)$.

5

Quadratic Functions and Complex Numbers

12 to 20 days

The linear functions in Chapters 3 and 4 had straight-line graphs. In this chapter you will encounter **quadratic** functions whose graphs are **curved** lines. Along the way you will learn something about imaginary and complex numbers. Again, your ultimate objective will be to find the particular equation of a quadratic function from information about its graph. In Exercise 5-7 you will use such equations in problems ranging from bridge design to predicting the price of pizza!

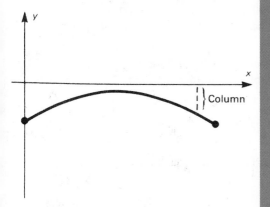

| 5-1 | INTRODUCTION TO QUADRATIC FUNCTIONS |

You recall from Chapter 3 that a function with an equation such as
$y = 8x + 13$ is called a linear function. Functions are named by the kind
of expression that y equals. So if

$$y = 3x^2 - 7x + 11,$$

the function is called a quadratic function.

DEFINITION

> **QUADRATIC FUNCTION**
> A **quadratic** function is a function whose general equation is
>
> $$y = ax^2 + bx + c,$$
>
> where a, b, and c stand for constants, and $a \neq 0$. (If a were equal to
> 0, the function would be linear, not quadratic.)

After a new function has been defined, your first task is to explore its
graph. In this section you will discover by pointwise plotting what the
graph of one quadratic function looks like.

Objective:
Discover by pointwise plotting what the major features of a quadratic function graph are.

The following exercise is designed to help you accomplish this objective.

EXERCISE 5-1

This exercise concerns the graph of $y = x^2 - 6x + 2$.

1. Make a table of values of y for each integer value of x from -2 through 8. Then plot the points on graph paper. If your work is correct, the points should lie along a smooth U-shaped figure called a *parabola*.

2. The low point of the graph is called the *vertex*. Write the coordinates of the vertex as an ordered pair.

3. The graph is symmetrical to a vertical line through the vertex. Draw a dotted line on your graph representing this *axis of symmetry*.

4. What does the y-intercept equal? Where does this number appear in the original equation?

5. There are *two* x-intercepts. What, approximately, do they equal?

6. Why is this function called a *quadratic* function?

7. Explain how the Closure Axioms insure that a quadratic function really is a *function*.

5-2 | GRAPHS OF QUADRATIC FUNCTIONS

In Exercise 5-1 you plotted the graph of $y = x^2 - 6x + 2$. The graph is a U-shaped curve called a *parabola*. As shown in Figure 5-2a, this parabola has a low point called the *vertex* at $(3, -7)$. The vertex could also be a high point, as you will soon learn. The vertical line through the vertex is called the *axis of symmetry*. If you fold the graph paper along this line, the two parts will fit on top of each other. In the table of values you can see that the values of y repeat themselves on either side of $x = 3$.

In this section you will learn how to sketch the graph quickly by first calculating the location of the vertex.

Objective:
Given the equation of a quadratic function, calculate the location of the vertex, and use this information to sketch the graph.

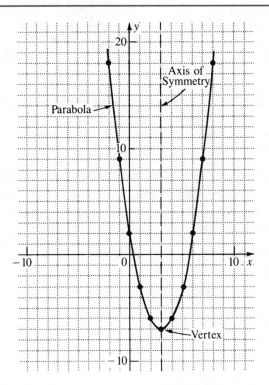

Figure 5-2a _____

Background: Completing the Square

From previous mathematics courses you should recall how to square a binomial. For example, to square $(x - 5)$, you could write

$(x - 5)^2$

$= (x - 5)(x - 5)$ Definition of squaring

$= x^2 - 5x - 5x + 25$ Multiply each term of one binomial by each term of the other.

$= x^2 - 10x + 25.$ Combine like terms.

Observe that the "-10" in the answer is twice the "-5" in the original binomial. In general, if the x-coefficient in the binomial you are squaring is equal to 1, then the middle term's coefficient in the answer is *twice* the *constant* term in the binomial.

Suppose that you must find the constant term to add to an expression such as $x^2 + 7x$ in order to make the expression the square of a binomial. Reversing the above observation, the constant in the binomial must be *half* the coefficient of x. So the binomial will be $(x + 3.5)$. The constant to add to $x^2 + 7x$ is thus $(3.5)^2$, or 12.25. So

$$x^2 + 7x + 12.25 = (x + 3.5)^2.$$

The process of adding 12.25 to $x^2 + 7x$ is called *completing the square*.

PROCEDURE

> **COMPLETING THE SQUARE**
> If the coefficient of the quadratic term equals 1, as in $x^2 + bx$, then the number that **completes the square** is found by taking *half* of the linear coefficient, b, and *squaring* it. The result is $x^2 + bx + \left(\dfrac{b}{2}\right)^2$.

To accomplish the above objective, you can transform the given equation by completing the square. For instance, if $y = x^2 - 6x + 2$, you would write

$y = x^2 - 6x + 2$

$y - 2 = x^2 - 6x$ Subtract 2 from each member to make room to complete the square.

$y - 2 + 9 = x^2 - 6x + 9$ Add 9 to the right member to complete the square. Add 9 to the left member to balance the equation.

$y + 7 = (x - 3)^2$ Simplify and factor.

The coordinates of the vertex, $(3, -7)$, can now be picked out of the equation. The 3 is the value of x that makes the right member of the equation equal zero. The -7 is the value of y that makes the left member equal zero. The equation $y + 7 = (x - 3)^2$ is said to be in *vertex form* because the coordinates of the vertex can be found from it.

CONCLUSION

> **VERTEX FORM**
> If the equation of a quadratic function is in the form
>
> $$\boxed{y - k = a(x - h)^2}$$
>
> where a, h, and k are constants, then the vertex is at the point (h, k).

Armed with this conclusion, you can calculate the vertex of any quadratic function graph.

EXAMPLE 1

For $y = -3x^2 - 24x + 11$, transform to vertex form, write the coordinates of the vertex and two other points, and use these to sketch the graph.

Solution:

$y = -3x^2 - 24x + 11$

$y - 11 = -3x^2 - 24x$ Subtract 11 to make room to complete the square.

$y - 11 = -3(x^2 + 8x)$ Factor out -3 so that the x^2-coefficient will equal 1.

$y - 11 + (-3)(16) = -3(x^2 + 8x + 16)$
         Add 16 on the right to complete the square. Add $(-3)(16)$ on the left to balance the equation.

$y - 59 = -3(x + 4)^2$ Simplify and factor. This is vertex form.

Vertex: $(-4, 59)$ These values make the right and left members equal zero.

y-intercept $= 11$ Set $x = 0$.

Another point is $(-8, 11)$.   This point is directly across the axis of symmetry from the y-intercept.

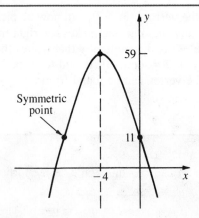

Figure 5-2b

Notes:

1. The parabola in Example 1 opens *downward*. This is what happens if the x^2-coefficient is *negative*.

2. In this section, the point across the axis of symmetry from another point will be called the *symmetric point*.
3. Since only a *sketch* was asked for, you don't need to show scales on the axes. You need show only the coordinates of the vertex, the y-intercept, and the symmetric point.
4. Different scales can be used for the two axes, if necessary, so that the graph will not be too long and skinny.   ■

In the following exercise you will plot several parabolas accurately to be sure you know the shape. Then you will sketch parabolas quickly by first finding the vertex.

EXERCISE 5-2

Do These Quickly

The following problems are intended to refresh your skills. You should be able to do all 10 in less than 5 minutes.

Q1.   Write an equation saying that y is 37% of x.

Q2.   Evaluate $7x^2$ if x is -3.

Q3.   Simplify: $17 - 7(x - 8)$

Q4.   Write the general equation of a linear function.

Q5.   Find the area of a triangle with base 10 cm and altitude 9 cm.

Q6.   Square 11.

Q7.   Sketch the graph of a linear function with negative slope.

Q8.   Write $\dfrac{47}{8}$ as a mixed number.

Q9.   State the Associative Axiom for Multiplication.

Q10.   Solve: $8x - 13 = 47$

Work the following problems.

For Problems 1 through 4, do the squaring.

1. $(x - 8)^2$ 2. $(x + 7)^2$

3. $(5x + 6)^2$ 4. $(3x - 9)^2$

For Problems 5 through 8, tell what number must be added to complete the square.

5. $x^2 + 20x + \underline{\quad}$ 6. $x^2 - 24x + \underline{\quad}$

7. $x^2 - 13x + \underline{\quad}$ 8. $x^2 + 11x + \underline{\quad}$

For Problems 9 through 12, plot the graph accurately by making a table of values of x and y. You may use different scales on the two axes, if necessary, to make the graphs have reasonable proportions.

9. $y = x^2 - 3x + 5$ 10. $y = -x^2 + 5x + 11$

11. $y = -3x^2 + 5x - 10$ 12. $y = 5x^2 + 12x - 13$

For Problems 13 through 18, sketch the graph of the quadratic function with the given vertex and intercept.

13. Vertex: $(2, 3)$, y-intercept: 7

14. Vertex: $(-3, 2)$, y-intercept: -4

15. Vertex: $(3, -1)$, y-intercept: -6

16. Vertex: $(-3, -6)$, y-intercept: -4

17. Vertex: $(-3, -4)$, x-intercept: 2

18. Vertex: $(3, 4)$, x-intercept: 1

For Problems 19 through 30, find the vertex, the y-intercept, and symmetric point, and use these to sketch the graph.

19. $y = x^2 + 6x + 11$ 20. $y = x^2 + 8x + 21$

21. $y = 3x^2 - 24x + 17$ 22. $y = 5x^2 - 30x + 31$

23. $y = 4x^2 + 12x - 11$ 24. $y = 8x^2 + 40x + 37$

25. $y = 2x^2 - 11x - 12$ 26. $y = 2x^2 - 7x + 12$

27. $y = -5x^2 - 30x + 51$ 28. $y = -3x^2 - 24x - 41$

29. $y = -x^2 + x + 1$ 30. $y = -x^2 - x + 3$

31. *Parabola Proportions Problem* Use the computer program PLOT QUADRATIC on the disk accompanying this text, or a similar function plotter, to plot the following graphs and answer the questions.
    a. Plot $y = x^2$. Which direction does the graph open, up or down?
    b. Plot $y = 0.1x^2$. Does decreasing the x^2-coefficient from 1 to 0.1 make the graph open wider or narrower?
    c. Plot $y = -0.1x^2$. What seems to be true about the graph if the x^2-coefficient is negative? Does the graph seem to have the same proportions as that of $y = 0.1x^2$ from part (b)?

d.   Plot $y = 0.1x^2 - 3$. What effect does subtracting 3 have on the proportions and the placement of the graph?

e.   Plot $y = 0.1x^2 + 0.6x - 3$. Does adding an x-term affect the proportions of the graph, or just its location on the xy-plane?

f.   Suppose that the graph of $y = -0.3x^2 + 2x - 4$ is to be plotted. Make the following predictions about what the graph will look like:

 i.   Will it open upward or downward? How do you tell?

 ii.   Will it open wide or narrow? How do you tell?

 iii.   Will the vertex be on the y-axis or somewhere else? How do you tell?

 iv.   Will the graph cross the y-axis above the origin or below? How do you tell?

g.   After you have made the predictions in part (f), plot the graph to confirm (or refute!) them.

32.   *Squaring Binomials Problem* The following sequence of steps shows why you can square a binomial the short way. Copy the steps on your paper. For each step, name the definition or property that justifies the step.

$$(a + b)^2$$

a. $= (a + b)(a + b)$

b. $= (a + b)(a) + (a + b)(b)$

c. $= a^2 + ba + ab + b^2$

d. $= a^2 + 2ab + b^2$

33.   *General Vertex Form Problem*

a.   Transform the general equation $y = ax^2 + bx + c$ to vertex form.

b.   Write a formula for h, the x-coordinate of the vertex.

c.   Write a formula for k, the y-coordinate of the vertex.

d.   Show that the constant a in vertex form is the same number as the coefficient of x^2 in $y = ax^2 + bx + c$ form.

5-3   *X*-INTERCEPTS, AND THE QUADRATIC FORMULA

Finding the y-intercept of a quadratic function such as $y = 3x^2 + 13x + 7$ is easy. You just substitute 0 for x and get $y = 7$. Finding x-intercepts is harder. Substituting 0 for y gives a quadratic equation such as

$$0 = 3x^2 + 13x + 7.$$

Solving this kind of equation is most easily done using the quadratic formula, which you should have encountered in earlier mathematics courses.

THE QUADRATIC FORMULA

If a quadratic equation has the form $ax^2 + bx + c = 0$, then the solutions are

$$x = \frac{-b \pm \sqrt{b^2 - 4ac}}{2a}$$

The formula is pronounced, "x equals the opposite of b, plus or minus the square root of the quantity b^2 minus $4ac$, all divided by $2a$."

In case you need a refresher, the formula is derived at the end of this section. The technique used there is completing the square.

For the equation $0 = 3x^2 + 13x + 7$, above, you would simply substitute 3 for a, 13 for b, and 7 for c in the formula, getting

$$x = \frac{-13 \pm \sqrt{169 - 4(3)(7)}}{2(3)}$$

$$x = \frac{-13 \pm \sqrt{85}}{6}$$

$$x = -0.63007\ldots \quad \text{or} \quad -3.70325\ldots$$

In doing the calculation you should be sure to press the ⊟ key before you divide by 6. Otherwise, the calculator will just divide $\sqrt{85}$ by 6. You know, of course, that there are two separate calculations to do, and that the "$\pm$" in the quadratic formula is not the same as the "sign change" key, marked ⟨ +/− ⟩, on your calculator.

Objective:

Given a quadratic equation, solve it using the quadratic formula, and use the results to find the x-intercepts of a quadratic function.

EXAMPLE 1

Solve $6x^2 - 11x - 5 = 0$.

Solution:

This problem involves a straightforward application of the quadratic formula. Here, $a = 6$, $b = -11$, and $c = -5$.

$$6x^2 - 11x - 5 = 0$$

$$x = \frac{11 \pm \sqrt{121 - 4(6)(-5)}}{2(6)}$$

$$x = \frac{11 \pm \sqrt{241}}{12}$$

$$x = 2.2103. \ldots \quad \text{or} \quad x = -0.3770. \ldots$$

$$\therefore S = \{2.2103. \ldots, -0.3770. \ldots\}$$

EXAMPLE 2

Solve $x^2 - 3x + 15 = 0$.

Solution:
The technique again is to apply the quadratic formula, this time with $a = 1$, $b = -3$, and $c = 15$. But there is a surprise!

$$x^2 - 3x + 15 = 0$$

$$x = \frac{3 \pm \sqrt{9 - 4(1)(15)}}{2(1)}$$

$$x = \frac{3 \pm \sqrt{-51}}{2}$$

Since $\sqrt{-51}$ is not a real number, there are *no real solutions*. The solutions involve *imaginary* numbers, which, as you recall, are square roots of negative numbers. In the next section you will study these numbers in more detail.

The quantity $b^2 - 4ac$ that appears under the radical sign in the quadratic formula is called the *discriminant*. The name is used because this number "discriminates" between quadratic equations that have real solutions, and those that do not. If all you want to know about a quadratic equation is whether or not it has real solutions, just evaluate the discriminant. If it is negative, there are no real solutions!

DEFINITION

THE DISCRIMINANT
If $ax^2 + bx + c = 0$, then the quantity $b^2 - 4ac$ is called the **discriminant**.

CONCLUSION

> **NATURE OF THE SOLUTIONS OF A QUADRATIC EQUATION**
>
> Given: $ax^2 + bx + c = 0$, where a, b, and c are real numbers.
>
> If $b^2 - 4ac$ is negative, the equation has solutions with *imaginary* numbers.
>
> If $b^2 - 4ac$ is positive, the equation has *real-number* solutions.
>
> If $b^2 - 4ac$ is a perfect square, and a, b and c are rational numbers, then the solutions are rational numbers.

The second part of the objective is using the quadratic formula to find x-intercepts.

EXAMPLE 3

For $y = x^2 - 5x + 3$, find the vertex, the x-intercepts, and the y-intercept and its symmetric point. Use this information to sketch the graph.

Solution:
Transforming to vertex form gives

$$y + 3.25 = (x - 2.5)^2.$$

So the vertex is at $(2.5, -3.25)$.

Substituting 0 for y in the original equation gives

$$0 = x^2 - 5x + 3.$$

By the quadratic formula,

$$x = \frac{5 \pm \sqrt{25 - 4(1)(3)}}{2(1)}$$

$$x = \frac{5 \pm \sqrt{13}}{2}$$

$$x = 4.3027\ldots \quad \text{or} \quad 0.6972\ldots$$

The y-intercept is 3, and the symmetric point is $(5, 3)$. The graph is shown in Figure 5-3a. ∎

There is a way to locate the vertex more quickly than transforming to vertex form. In Figure 5-3a you should be able to notice that the axis of symmetry is halfway between the two x-intercepts. Thus, the x-coordinate of the vertex is the *average* of the x-intercepts.

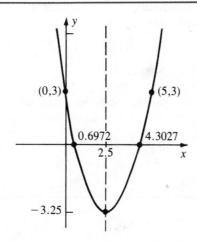

Figure 5-3a

If $y = ax^2 + bx + c$, the x-intercepts are the two values given by the quadratic formula

$$x = \frac{-b + \sqrt{b^2 - 4ac}}{2a} \quad \text{and} \quad x = \frac{-b - \sqrt{b^2 - 4ac}}{2a}.$$

If you add these two values of x, the radicals add up to zero. All that is left is $\frac{-b}{2a} - \frac{b}{2a}$, which equals $\frac{-b}{a}$. Dividing by 2 to get the average produces $x = -\frac{b}{2a}$. This number is h, the x-coordinate of the vertex.

CONCLUSION

VERTEX OF A PARABOLA
If $y = ax^2 + bx + c$, then the x-coordinate of the vertex is

$$h = -\frac{b}{2a}$$

EXAMPLE 4

Find the vertex of $y = 7x^2 - 29x + 37$ using the short cut.

Solution:

$$h = -\frac{b}{2a} = -\frac{-29}{2(7)} = 2.071428. . .$$

Store this value of x in memory. Then substitute it into the original equation to find the y-coordinate, k.

$$k = 7(2.07. . .)^2 - 29(2.07. . .) + 37 = 6.964285. . .$$

∴ vertex is at *(2.07. . . , 6.96. . .)*   ■

In the following exercise you will solve quadratic equations, transform quadratic function equations to vertex form, find the vertex and intercepts, and sketch the graph.

EXERCISE 5-3

Do These Quickly

The following problems are intended to refresh your skills. You should be able to do all 10 in less than 5 minutes.

Q1.   Evaluate $\sqrt{49}$.

Q2.   Factor: $x^2 - 10x + 25$

Q3.   Multiply: $(2x - 7)(5x + 3)$

Q4.   Name by degree and number of terms: $xy^2 + z$

Q5.   Find the perimeter of a triangle with sides 3, 4, and 5 inches.

Q6.   Find 20% of 600.

Q7.   Sketch the graph of a pair of inconsistent linear equations.

Q8.   Multiply and simplify: $\left(\dfrac{6}{7}\right)\left(\dfrac{3}{14}\right)$

Q9.   What property says that x stands for the same number anywhere it appears in an expression?

Q10.   Solve: $8x - 10 = 3x$

Work the following problems.

For Problems 1 through 20, solve the equation.

1. $x^2 - 3x + 2 = 0$ 2. $x^2 - 5x + 6 = 0$

3. $x^2 + 7x + 12 = 0$ 4. $x^2 + 8x + 15 = 0$

5. $x^2 - 2x - 8 = 0$ 6. $x^2 - x - 12 = 0$

7. $x^2 + 4x - 3 = 0$ 8. $x^2 - 6x + 4 = 0$

9. $2x^2 + 9x - 5 = 0$
10. $3x^2 + 7x + 2 = 0$

11. $3x^2 - 7x = 0$
12. $2x^2 - 15x = 0$

13. $4x^2 - 12x + 9 = 0$
14. $9x^2 + 30x + 25 = 0$

15. $x^2 + 2x + 13 = 0$
16. $x^2 - 10x + 26 = 0$

17. $2x^2 + 2x - 2 = x - x^2$
18. $4x^2 - 8x + 5 = x + 3$

19. $x^2 - 2x + 2 = 2x$
20. $2x^2 - 2x - 2 = x^2$

For Problems 21 through 30, find the discriminant. Then, without actually solving the equation, tell what kind of numbers the solutions will be, real or imaginary. If the solutions are real numbers, tell whether they will be rational or irrational.

21. $3x^2 - 5x + 6 = 0$
22. $5x^2 + 7x - 3 = 0$

23. $2x^2 - 13x + 15 = 0$
24. $9x^2 + 6x + 1 = 0$

25. $10x^2 + 19x + 7 = 0$
26. $x^2 - 6x + 3 = 0$

27. $-3x^2 + 5x - 2 = 0$
28. $x^2 + x + 1 = 0$

29. $-x^2 + 4x - 4 = 0$
30. $x^2 + 6x + 10 = 0$

For Problems 31 through 44, find the vertex, the x- and y-intercepts, and the symmetric point, and sketch the graph.

31. $y = x^2 - 6x + 8$
32. $y = x^2 + 4x + 3$

33. $y = x^2 - 2x - 15$
34. $y = x^2 + 2x - 8$

35. $y = -x^2 - 2x + 3$
36. $y = -x^2 + 4x + 5$

37. $y = 2x^2 + 7x + 3$
38. $y = 3x^2 - 7x + 2$

39. $y = -4x^2 + 4x - 1$
40. $y = x^2 + 6x + 9$

41. $y = x^2 + 2x + 5$
42. $y = -2x^2 + 4x - 3$

43. $y = x^2 + 2x - 5$
44. $y = -x^2 + 4x - 1$

45. **Solving Quadratics by Completing the Square** If you did not know the quadratic formula, you could still solve a quadratic equation. All you have to know is how to complete the square. The following example shows you the way.

$5x^2 + 30x + 7 = 0$	The equation to be solved
$5x^2 + 30x \quad = -7$	Clear off space to complete the square.
$x^2 + 6x \quad = -1.4$	Divide by 5 to make the x^2-coefficient equal 1.

$$x^2 + 6x + 9 = -1.4 + 9 \qquad \text{(Half of 6)}^2 \text{ is 9.}$$

$$(x + 3)^2 = 7.6 \qquad \text{Factor the left member.}$$
Simplify the right member.

$$x + 3 = \pm\sqrt{7.6} \qquad \text{Take the square root of each}$$
member.

$$x = -3 \pm \sqrt{7.6} \qquad \text{Subtract 3.}$$

$$x = -0.243\ldots \quad \text{or} \quad -5.756\ldots \quad \text{Arithmetic}$$

Solve the following equations by completing the square.

a. $x^2 + 6x + 4 = 0$ b. $x^2 - 10x + 21 = 0$
c. $7x^2 + 14x + 3 = 0$ d. $x^2 - 7x - 4 = 0$
e. $2x^2 - 10x + 11 = 0$

46. ***Derivation of the Quadratic Formula, Part I*** Solve

$$7x^2 + 13x + 5 = 0$$

by completing the square. Do *not* simplify any of the numbers along the way! For instance, when you divide each member by 7, leave the answer as

$$x^2 + \frac{13}{7}x = -\frac{5}{7}.$$

Your objective is to have the 7, 13, and 5 show up in the answer.

47. ***Derivation of the Quadratic Formula, Part II*** Let a, b, and c be constants, with $a \neq 0$. Solve the equation

$$ax^2 + bx + c = 0$$

by completing the square. Show that the result is equivalent to the quadratic formula.

5-4 | IMAGINARY AND COMPLEX NUMBERS

If you solve a quadratic equation such as

$$x^2 - 10x + 34 = 0$$

using the quadratic formula, a negative number appears under the radical sign.

$$x = \frac{10 \pm \sqrt{100 - 4(1)(34)}}{2}$$

$$x = \frac{10 \pm \sqrt{-36}}{2}$$

The symbol $\sqrt{-36}$ means, "a number which, when squared, gives -36 for the answer." Since the square of any real number is *non*-negative, $\sqrt{-36}$ is not a real number. Instead of just giving up, and saying, "The equation has no solutions," mathematicians choose to invent a new kind of number. As you recall from Chapter 1, square roots of negative numbers are called *imaginary numbers*.

To make sense out of imaginary numbers, the first step is to define a number whose square root is -1. This number is called i (for "imaginary").

DEFINITION

UNIT IMAGINARY NUMBER
i is a number whose square is -1. That is,

$$i^2 = -1$$

Notes:

1. Since $i^2 = -1$, it is customary to write

$$i = \sqrt{-1}$$

2. The reason for the name "imaginary" number is that when they were proposed several hundred years ago, people could not "imagine" such a number. However, they are no less real than "real" numbers since both kinds of number are inventions of *people*.
3. The number i is called the *unit* imaginary number, just as 1 (or $\sqrt{+1}$) is called the unit *real* number.

A number such as $\sqrt{-36}$ can now be defined in terms of i. It can be written this way:

$$\sqrt{-36}$$
$$= \sqrt{(-1)(36)}$$
$$= \sqrt{-1}\,\sqrt{36}$$
$$= i\sqrt{36}, \quad \text{or more simply, } 6i.$$

From this example, the definition follows.

DEFINITION

> **IMAGINARY NUMBERS IN TERMS OF *i***
> If *x* is a non-negative real number, then
>
> $$\sqrt{-x} = i\sqrt{x}$$

So any imaginary number is the product of a *real* number and the unit imaginary number *i*.

With the aid of the above definition, you can now write the solution to the above equation in terms of *i*.

$$x = \frac{10 \pm \sqrt{-36}}{2}$$

$$x = \frac{10 \pm 6i}{2}$$

$$x = 5 \pm 3i$$

The sum of a real number and an imaginary number, such as $5 + 3i$, is called a *complex* number. The 5 is called the *real* part of $5 + 3i$ and the coefficient 3 is called the *imaginary part* of $5 + 3i$.

DEFINITION

> **COMPLEX NUMBERS**
> A **complex number** is a number of the form $a + bi$, where the real number *a* is called the *real part* of $a + bi$, the real number *b* is called the *imaginary part* of $a + bi$, and *i* is $\sqrt{-1}$.

The two numbers $5 + 3i$ and $5 - 3i$, which are the solutions of the equation at the beginning of this section, are called *complex conjugates* of each other. If a quadratic equation has real numbers for its coefficients, then its solutions will always be complex conjugates.

DEFINITION

> **COMPLEX CONJUGATES**
> The complex numbers $a + bi$ and $a - bi$ are called **complex conjugates** of each other.

The next thing to do is see how complex numbers fit in with the real numbers you have always used. Imaginary numbers can be plotted on their own number line. The scale is marked off in multiples of i, like this:

Imaginary Number Line

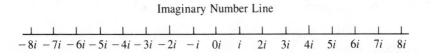

If you consider $0i$ and 0 to be the same number, the imaginary-number line and real-number line can be crossed at their origins. The result is a Cartesian coordinate system, shown in Figure 5-4a.

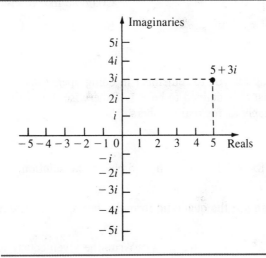

Figure 5-4a

To graph a complex number like $5 + 3i$, you go across 5 in the "real" direction, then up 3 in the "imaginary" direction. This number is plotted in Figure 5-4a.

The coordinate system is called the *complex-number plane*. If you will back off and look at it from a distance, you should be able to see that the real numbers are just a subset of the complex numbers. The imaginary and complex numbers fill in the space above and below the old, familiar number line. All along you have been operating in the set of complex numbers, but perhaps had never thought to look *above* and *below* the real-number line to see what was there!

Objective:
Given a quadratic equation whose solutions are complex numbers, write the solutions in terms of i, and check them by substitution.

EXAMPLE 1

Solve $x^2 - 10x + 34 = 0$ and check one of the solutions.

Solution:

From the work above, the solutions are $5 + 3i$ and $5 - 3i$.

$\therefore S = \{5 + 3i, 5 - 3i\}$

Check of $5 - 3i$:

$\quad (5 - 3i)^2 - 10(5 - 3i) + 34$

$= 25 - 30i + 9i^2 - 50 + 30i + 34$ Square the binomial and distribute the -10.

$= 9 + 9i^2$ Combine like terms.

$= 9 - 9$ Because $i^2 = -1$

$= 0$, which checks.   ■

The main thing for you to remember in doing operations with complex numbers is that i^2 is defined to be -1. Otherwise, all of the properties and axioms apply as for real numbers.

EXAMPLE 2

Solve $7x^2 + 8x + 25 = 5x + 6$, and check one solution.

Solution:

Before you can use the quadratic formula, one side of the equation must equal zero.

$7x^2 + 8x + 25 = 5x + 6$ Write the given equation.

$7x^2 + 3x + 19 = 0$ Subtract $5x$ and subtract 6.

$x = \dfrac{-3 \pm \sqrt{9 - 4(7)(19)}}{14}$ Use the quadratic formula.

$x = \dfrac{-3 \pm \sqrt{-523}}{14}$ Simplify the radical.

$x = \dfrac{-3 \pm i\sqrt{523}}{14}$ Definition of imaginary numbers

$x = -0.2142... \pm 1.6335...i$ By calculator

$\therefore S = \{-0.2142... + 1.6335...i, -0.2142... - 1.6335...i\}$

Check: (Use $-0.2142... \pm 1.6335...i$.)

If your calculator has a complex number mode, you can do the check directly. If not, and your calculator has two memories, store the real part in one memory and the imaginary part in the other. Remember, $i^2 = -1$.

$7(-0.2142... + 1.6335...i)^2 + 8(-0.2142... + 1.6335...i) + 25$

$$\overset{?}{=} 5(-0.2142... + 1.6335...i) + 6$$

$7(0.0459... - 0.70007...i - 2.6683...) - 1.7142...$

$$+ 13.0681...i + 25 \overset{?}{=} -1.0714... + 8.1675...i + 6$$

$0.3214... - 4.90054...i - 18.6785... - 1.7142...$

$$+ 13.0681...i + 25 \overset{?}{=} 4.9285... + 8.1675...i$$

$4.9285... + 8.1675...i = 4.9285... + 8.1675...i$, which checks. ∎

In the following exercise you will solve and check some quadratic equations, and gain a bit more insight into the nature of complex numbers.

EXERCISE 5-4

Do These Quickly

The following problems are intended to refresh your skills. You should be able to do all 10 in less than 5 minutes.

Q1. Do the squaring: $(p + 5)^2$

Q2. Do the squaring: $(y - 7)^2$

Q3. Do the squaring: $(3x + 8)^2$

Q4. Do the squaring: 13^2

Q5. Sketch the graph of a quadratic function opening downward.

Q6. Sketch the graph of a linear function with negative slope.

Q7. Find the discriminant of $x^2 + 7x + 20 = 0$.

Q8. Evaluate the determinant: $\begin{vmatrix} 3 & 7 \\ 4 & 9 \end{vmatrix}$

Q9. Find 2% of 700.

Q10. Add: $\dfrac{2}{3} + \dfrac{3}{4}$

For Problems 1 through 12,
a. Solve the equation.
b. Check one of the solutions.

1. $x^2 - 14x + 58 = 0$　　　　　2. $x^2 - 6x + 73 = 0$

3. $x^2 - 10x + 26 = 0$ 4. $x^2 - 14x + 50 = 0$

5. $9x^2 + 12x + 68 = 0$ 6. $9x^2 + 90x + 226 = 0$

7. $2x^2 - 3x - 5 = 0$ 8. $4x^2 - 21x - 18 = 0$

9. $x^2 - 3x + 41 = x + 12$ 10. $x^2 + 5x + 50 = 3x - 15$

11. $3x(x + 5) + 2x^2 = 8x - 11$ 12. $8(x - 1)^2 = 7x - 32$

For Problems 13 through 20, plot the complex number on a complex-number plane.

13. $4 + 9i$ 14. $6 + 2i$

15. $-3 + 5i$ 16. $5 - 7i$

17. $7 - 10i$ 18. $-6 + i$

19. $-1 - 2.6i$ 20. $-3.2 - 4i$

21. ***Quadratic Function Intercepts Problem*** The following quadratic functions differ only in the constant term.

$$f(x) = x^2 - 6x + 5$$
$$g(x) = x^2 - 6x + 9$$
$$h(x) = x^2 - 6x + 13$$

    a. Find the x-intercepts of each function.
    b. Draw the graph of each function. You may make a sketch using information you have already found, or use a computer graphics program such as PLOT QUADRATIC on the accompanying disk.
    c. What is true about the graph of a quadratic function if the x-intercepts are both *real* numbers? both non-real *complex* numbers? both *equal* to each other?

22. Why do you suppose part (c) of Problem 21, above, says *non-real* complex numbers, not just complex numbers?

23. ***Complex Conjugates Problem***
    a. Write the complex conjugate of $4 + 7i$.
    b. Write the complex conjugate of $3 - 8i$.
    c. Do the multiplying: $(7 + 3i)(7 - 3i)$. What do you notice about the answer?
    d. Do the addition: $(11 + 5i) + (11 - 5i)$. What do you notice about the answer?
    e. Do the subtraction: $(6 + 10i) - (6 - 10i)$. What do you notice about the answer?
    f. Prove that the sum and the product of two complex conjugates is always a *real* number, and the difference between a complex number and its conjugate is always a pure imaginary number.

24. ***Complex Conjugates and Quadratic Equations Problem*** Prove that if $ax^2 + bx + c = 0$, where a, b, and c are real numbers, and the discriminant is negative, then the two solutions are complex conjugates of each other.

25. ***Powers of*** i ***Problem*** The definition of i makes i^2 equal to -1. Since $i^3 = i^2 \cdot i$, it follows that $i^3 = -i$.
   a. Evaluate each positive integer power of i from i^4 through i^{10}.
   b. Describe the pattern that shows up in the powers of i.
   c. Show that i and i^0 both fit the pattern in part (a).
   d. Quick! Tell what i^{100} will equal.
   e. What will i^{2001} equal? What will i^{137} equal? What will i^{50} equal?

5-5	EVALUATING QUADRATIC FUNCTIONS

When you use a function as a mathematical model, you must be able to calculate y when x is known, and be able to calculate x when y is known. In this section you will practice these things so that you will be comfortable doing them in the problems of the next section.

Objective:
Given the equation of a quadratic function, be able to calculate the value of y for a known value of x, and the value(s) of x for a known value of y.

EXAMPLE 1

If $f(x) = 3x^2 + 2x - 11$, find
a. $f(-4)$
b. x, if $f(x) = -6$, and
c. the x-intercepts.

Solution:
a. If you wish, you may do the whole calculation on your calculator without writing down intermediate results. Otherwise, the steps are:

$$f(-4) = 3(-4)^2 + 2(-4) - 11$$
$$= 3(16) + 2(-4) - 11$$
$$= 48 - 8 - 11$$
$$= \underline{\underline{29}}$$

b. Substituting -6 for $f(x)$ leads to a quadratic equation. Before you use the quadratic formula you must transform the equation so that one member equals zero.

$$-6 = 3x^2 + 2x - 11$$

$$3x^2 + 2x - 5 = 0$$

$$x = \frac{-2 \pm \sqrt{4 - 4(3)(-5)}}{2(3)}$$

$$x = \frac{-2 \pm \sqrt{64}}{6}$$

$$x = 1 \quad \text{or} \quad x = \frac{-5}{3}$$

Note that since the equation said, "Find the values of x. . . ," not "Solve the equation. . . ," it is not necessary to write the answer as a solution set.

c. As you recall, an x-intercept is a value of x when $y = 0$. Setting $f(x) = 0$ gives

$$0 = 3x^2 + 2x - 11$$

$$x = \frac{-2 \pm \sqrt{4 - 4(3)(-11)}}{2(3)}$$

$$x = \frac{-2 \pm \sqrt{136}}{6}$$

$$x = 1.6103\ldots \quad \text{or} \quad x = -2.2769\ldots \qquad \blacksquare$$

Sometimes all you are interested in knowing about a function is whether or not y ever equals a particular given value. As shown in Figure 5-5a, the parabola might not get high enough or low enough to reach the given y-value. One way to find out is to set y equal to the given value and solve

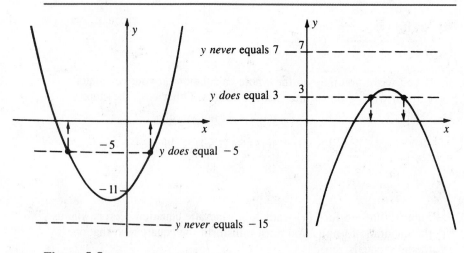

Figure 5-5a

the equation for x. If there are *real* values of x, then y *does* reach the given value. If the values of x are non-real complex numbers, then y does *not* reach the given value.

EXAMPLE 2

If $f(x) = 3x^2 + 2x - 11$, does $f(x)$ ever equal:
a. -5?
b. -15?

Solution:

a. Setting $f(x) = -5$ gives:

   $-5 = 3x^2 + 2x - 11$

   $3x^2 + 2x - 6 = 0$

   $b^2 - 4ac = 4 - 4(3)(-6)$ Definition of discriminant

   $\qquad\quad = 76.$

   Since the discriminant is positive, there are *real* values of x for which $f(x) = -5$.

b. Setting $f(x) = -15$ gives:

   $-15 = 3x^2 + 2x - 11$

   $3x^2 + 2x + 4 = 0$

   $b^2 - 4ac = 4 - 4(3)(4)$

   $\qquad\quad = -44.$

   Since the discriminant is negative, the solutions of the equation will be (non-real) complex numbers. So $\underline{f(x)\text{ never reaches} -15}$. ■

EXERCISE 5-5

Do These Quickly

The following problems are intended to refresh your skills. You should be able to do all 10 in less than 5 minutes.

Q1. Square -3.

Q2. Square $5i$.

Q3. Square $x - 7$.

Q4. Factor: $x^2 + 3x - 40$

Q5.   Find the slope: $3x + 7y = 42$

Q6.   Find the x-coordinate of the vertex: $f(x) = 5x^2 - 30x + 17.9$

Q7.   30 is 60% of what number?

Q8.   Multiply: $\left(\dfrac{3}{7}\right)\left(\dfrac{2}{3}\right)$

Q9.   Solve for y: $x + y = 5$
$x - y = 2$

Q10. Sketch the graph of a quadratic function with vertex below the x-axis and no real x-intercepts.

Work the following problems.

1.   Suppose that $f(x) = 5x^2 + 8x - 7$.
a.   Find $f(-3)$.
b.   Find x when $f(x) = -3$.
c.   Find the x-intercepts.

2.   Suppose that $g(x) = 2x^2 - 5x - 11$.
a.   Find $g(-4)$.
b.   Find x when $g(x) = -4$.
c.   Find the x-intercepts.

3.   Suppose that $h(x) = -2x^2 + 3x - 10$.
a.   Find $h(-9)$.
b.   Find x when $h(x) = -9$.
c.   Find the x-intercepts.

4.   Suppose that $f(x) = -4x^2 + 4x + 15$.
a.   Find $f(-3)$.
b.   Find x when $f(x) = 20$.
c.   Find the x-intercepts.

5.   Suppose that $y = x^2 + 8x + 15$. Find the value(s) of x for which
a. $y = 3$,   b. $y = 2$,   c. $y = 0$,
d. $y = -1$,   e. $y = -3$,   f. $y = 15$.

6.   Suppose that $y = -x^2 - 6x - 5$. Find the value(s) of x for which
a. $y = 5$,   b. $y = 4$,   c. $y = 3$,
d. $y = 2$,   e. $y = 0$,   f. $y = -5$.

For Problems 7 through 14, use the discriminant to tell whether or not the indicated function ever has the given values of y (for *real* values of x).

7. $y = 4x^2 - 7x + 2$; $y = 5$, $y = -3$.

8. $y = 3x^2 + 10x - 1$; $y = 6$, $y = -4$.

9. $y = 2x^2 + 3x + 6;$ $y = 1,$ $y = -5.$

10. $y = 5x^2 - 8x + 6;$ $y = 3,$ $y = -4.$

11. $y = -3x^2 + 5x + 1;$ $y = 4,$ $y = -3.$

12. $y = -2x^2 + 6x - 7;$ $y = 10,$ $y = -10.$

13. $y = -x^2 + 10x - 8;$ $y = 7,$ $y = 0.$

14. $y = -x^2 - 6x - 9;$ $y = 1,$ $y = 0.$

15.   ***Graphs of Complex Solutions Problem*** The graph of

$$f(x) = x^2 - 6x + 34$$

opens upward, and has a vertex above the x-axis. So the x-intercepts turn out to be complex numbers. If you stretch out the x-axis into a complex-number plane, you get the three-dimensional graph shown in Figure 5-5b. The parabola is in the plane of the x-axis and $f(x)$-axis. Below the vertex, there is another parabola. It is in a plane perpendicular to the real x-axis. The two intercepts lie at the points where this second parabola pierces the complex x-plane. Answer the following questions.

a.   Set $f(x)$ equal to zero, and thus show that the x-intercepts really are $3 + 5i$ and $3 - 5i$.

b.   Show that $f(3 + 5i)$ really does equal zero.

c.   Show that $f(3 + 2i)$ is a real number.

d.   Show that $f(7 + 4i)$ is *not* a real number.

e.   Make a conjecture about values of a and b for which $f(a + bi)$ is a real number. Explain how you arrived at your conjecture.

f.   Prove that your conjecture in part (e) is true.

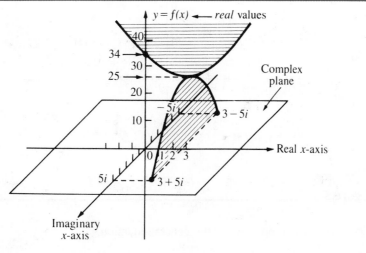

Figure 5-5b _____

| # EQUATIONS OF QUADRATIC FUNCTIONS FROM THEIR GRAPHS

In order to use a quadratic function as a mathematical model of something in the real world, you must be able to find the particular equation from information about the graph. For linear functions, you needed only two ordered pairs. For quadratic functions, it takes three ordered pairs.

Objective:
Given three points on the graph of a quadratic function, or the vertex and one other point, find the particular equation of the function.

EXAMPLE 1

Find the particular equation of the quadratic function containing $(-2, -11)$, $(4, 13)$, and $(6, 29)$.

Solution:
The graphs of the three given points are shown in Figure 5-6a. Since they do not lie in a straight line, there is a quadratic function whose graph contains the three points.

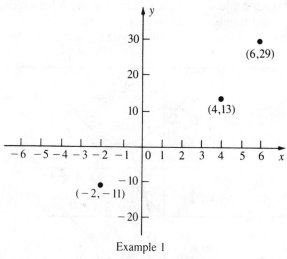

Example 1

Figure 5-6a

The first thing to do is write the general equation.

$$y = ax^2 + bx + c$$

Substituting the first ordered pair, $(-2, -11)$ for (x, y) gives

$$-11 = a(-2)^2 + b(-2) + c,$$

which can be transformed to

$$4a - 2b + c = -11 \quad \ldots \ldots \quad (1)$$

This is a linear equation in the "variables" a, b, and c. Substituting the other two ordered pairs, $(4, 13)$ and $(6, 29)$, gives two more equations.

$$16a + 4b + c = 13 \quad \ldots \ldots (2)$$

$$36a + 6b + c = 29 \quad \ldots \ldots (3)$$

The system formed by Equations (1), (2), and (3), can be solved by linear combinations.

$$4a - 2b + c = -11$$
$$16a + 4b + c = 13$$
$$36a + 6b + c = 29$$

$12a + 6b = 24 \longrightarrow 2a + b = 4$

$20a + 2b = 16 \longrightarrow 10a + b = 8$

$8a = 4$

$\therefore a = 0.5$

Substituting 0.5 for a in a two-variable equation gives

$$1 + b = 4$$
$$b = 3.$$

Substituting 0.5 for a and 3 for b in the first equation gives

$$2 - 6 + c = -11$$
$$c = -7$$

So the desired equation is $y = 0.5x^2 + 3x - 7$.
Note that the answer is an *equation*, not a solution set.   ■

EXAMPLE 2

Find the particular equation of the quadratic function containing $(0, 5)$, $(2, 13)$, and $(3, 26)$.

Solution:
The job of finding this equation is easier because you know the y-intercept. Substituting $(0, 5)$ for (x, y) in $y = ax^2 + bx + c$ gives

$$5 = a \cdot 0^2 + b \cdot 0 + c,$$

from which $c = 5$. Using this value of c when you substitute the other two ordered pairs gives *two* equations in a and b:

$13 = 4a + 2b + 5$ Substitute $(x, y) = (2, 13)$ and $c = 5$.

$26 = 9a + 3b + 5$ Substitute $(x, y) = (3, 26)$ and $c = 5$.

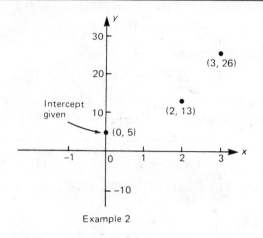

Example 2

Figure 5-6b _____

which can be transformed to

$$2a + b = 4 \quad \underline{\quad} \quad \text{①}$$

$$3a + b = 7 \quad \underline{\quad} \quad \text{②.}$$

Multiplying ① by -1 and adding it to ② gives

$$a = 3.$$

Substituting 3 for a in ① gives

$$6 + b = 4,$$

$$b = -2.$$

So the desired equation is

$$\underline{y = 3x^2 - 2x + 5.}$$

EXAMPLE 3

Find the particular equation of the quadratic function with vertex at
$(2, -5)$ and containing $(3, 1)$.

Solution:
If you know that one of the given points is the *vertex*, then it would be
easier to use the *vertex* form, $y - k = a(x - h)^2$. Substituting $(2, -5)$ for
the vertex (h, k) gives

$$y - (-5) = a(x - 2)^2.$$

The only constant left to be evaluated is a. This is why you need only *one*
other ordered pair. Substituting $(3, 1)$ for (x, y) gives

$$1 - (-5) = a(3 - 2)^2$$

$$6 = a.$$

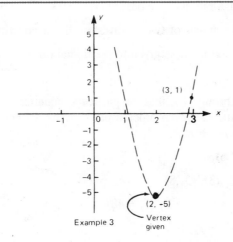

Figure 5-6c ———————————————————

Therefore, the equation is

$$y + 5 = 6(x - 2)^2.$$

If desired, this equation can be transformed to

$$y = 6x^2 - 24x + 19.$$

The exercise which follows is designed to give you practice in finding the equation of a quadratic function from information about its graph. This is the fundamental technique which you will use in Section 5-8 for making quadratic mathematical models of situations in the real world. ■

EXERCISE 5-6

Do These Quickly

The following problems are intended to refresh your skills. You should be able to do all 10 in less than 5 minutes.

Q1.   Does $7x^2 + 3x + 5 = 0$ have real-number solutions?

Q2.   Find the vertex: $y = x^2 - 6x + 2$

Q3.   Find the x-intercept: $3x + 4y = 24$

Q4.   Sketch the graph of a quadratic function opening downward.

Q5.   Find $f(2)$ if $f(x) = x^3$.

Q6.   Add: $\dfrac{4}{9} + \dfrac{1}{2}$

Q7.   Find 20% of 3.

Q8.   Is $-\sqrt{81}$ a rational number?

Q9.   Sketch the graphs of two inconsistent linear equations.

Q10. What special name is given to the domain in a linear programming problem?

For Problems 1 through 14, find the particular equation of the quadratic function containing the given ordered pairs. Write the equation in the form $y = ax^2 + bx + c$.

1. $(1, 6), (3, 26), (-2, 21)$

2. $(1, 2), (-2, 23), (3, 8)$

3. $(-2, -41), (-3, -72), (5, -48)$

4. $(-3, 18), (6, -9), (12, -57)$

5. $(4, 7.3), (6, 12.7), (-3, 1.0)$

6. $(10, 1), (20, 22), (-30, -3)$

7. $(10, 40), (-20, 160), (-5, 10)$

8. $(2, -2.8), (-3, -6.3), (5, -17.5)$

9. $(-4, -37), (2, 11), (0, -1)$

10. $(0, 5), (4, 1), (-3, -13)$

11. $(0, 0), (-1, 7), (6, 42)$

12. $(0, 0), (-1, 4), (3, -48)$

13. Vertex at $(-4, 3)$, also containing $(-6, 11)$

14. Vertex at $(-2, 3)$, also containing $(4, 12)$

15. Show that there is *no* quadratic function which contains the points $(5, 2), (6, -4)$, and $(5, -7)$. Explain what it is about these three points that prevents there being a quadratic function containing all of them.

16. Show that there is *no* quadratic function which contains the points $(-2, -1), (1, 8)$, and $(3, 14)$. Explain what it is about these three points that prevents there being a quadratic function containing all of them.

5-7   QUADRATIC AND LINEAR FUNCTIONS AS MATHEMATICAL MODELS

Now that you know how to find the particular equation of a quadratic function from points on its graph, you can use this kind of function as a mathematical model of the relationship between two real-world variables. Quadratic functions are reasonable models where the graph is curved rather than straight. They are especially appropriate if the graph has a high point or a low point. As you recall from Chapter 3, linear functions are more appropriate where the graph is a straight line.

Objective:

Be able to use a quadratic function or a linear function as a mathematical model for a real-world situation, depending on which one is called for.

EXAMPLE 1

An old Pizza Inn menu from the 1960's lists the following prices for plain cheeze pizzas:

> Small (8″ diameter) $0.85
> Medium (10″ diameter) $1.15
> Large (13″ diameter)........ $1.75

a. Assume that the price is a quadratic function of the diameter. Write the particular equation expressing price in terms of diameter.
b. If Pizza Inn had made 20″ pizzas, what do you predict the price would have been?
c. Suppose that the menu had listed a "Colossal" pizza costing $6.00. What do you predict its diameter would have been?
d. The price-intercept is the price when the diameter is zero. What does the price-intercept equal in this mathematical model? Why do you suppose that it is greater than zero?
e. Use the discriminant to show that there are no diameters for which the price is zero.
f. Show that a linear function does *not* fit the original data.
g. Find the vertex. Use it and other points that are given or that have been calculated to sketch the graph.

Solutions:

a. Let p = number of *cents* for a pizza.
   Let d = number of inches diameter.
   General equation: $p = ad^2 + bd + c$
   Ordered pairs: (8, 85), (10, 115), (13, 175)

(Note: Once you get to this point, you are out of the real world and into the mathematical world. The rest of the problem involves using mathematical techniques with which you should now be familiar, and interpreting answers you get in the mathematical world apply to the real world.)

Substituting the three ordered pairs gives

$$64a + 8b + c = 85$$
$$100a + 10b + c = 115$$
$$169a + 13b + c = 175$$

Solving this system, as in the previous section, gives

$$a = 1, \quad b = -3, \quad c = 45.$$

Equation is: $p = d^2 - 3d + 45$

b. Substitute 20 for d.

$$p = 20^2 - 3(20) + 45$$
$$= 385$$

<u>20-inch pizza would have cost about $3.85</u>

c. Substitute 600 for p.

$$d^2 - 3d + 45 = 600$$
$$d^2 - 3d - 555 = 0$$
$$d = \frac{3 \pm \sqrt{9 - 4(1)(-555)}}{2(1)}$$
$$= \frac{3 \pm \sqrt{2229}}{2}$$
$$= 25.106\ldots \text{ or } -22.106\ldots$$

<u>Diameter would have been about 25″.</u>

(Note that the negative solution is meaningless this time. The precise answer 25.106... from the mathematical world should be rounded off to something that is appropriate for the real world.)

d. Let $d = 0$.
Price-intercept is <u>45</u>.
It is greater than zero because there are fixed charges, such as cooking, serving, and washing dishes, which do not depend on the size of the pizza, just on the fact that you ordered a pizza.

e. Let $p = 0$.
$d^2 - 3d + 45 = 0$
Discriminant $= (-3)^2 - 4(1)(45) = -171$
No real solutions. Therefore, there are no diameters for which the price is zero.

f. From (8, 85) to (10, 115), the slope of the line would be $\frac{30}{2} = 15$.

From (10, 115) to (13, 175), the slope would be $\frac{60}{3} = 20$. So a linear function does not fit because the slopes are not equal.

g. The horizontal coordinate of the vertex is

$$d = \frac{-b}{2a} = -\frac{-3}{2} = 1.5.$$

Substituting 1.5 for d gives

$$p = (1.5)^2 - 3(1.5) + 45 = 42.75.$$

Vertex is at $\underline{(1.5, 42.75)}$.

The graph is shown in Figure 5-7a.

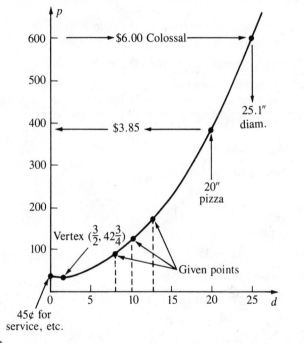

Figure 5-7a

EXAMPLE 2 *Rectangular Walkway Problem*

A rectangular pond 5 meters by 7 meters is to be surrounded by a walkway of width x meters (see Figure 5-7b). This problem concerns the rectangular region taken up by the pond and walkway.

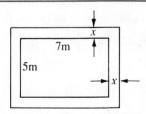

Figure 5-7b

a. Write the length and width of the region as functions of x. What kind of functions are these?
b. Write the area of the region as a function of x. What kind of function is this?
c. Predict the area of the region if $x = 1, 2$, and 3.
d. Find the value of x which makes the region have an area of 150 square meters.
e. Sketch the graph in a reasonable domain.
f. Find the value of x which makes the walkway have an area equal to the area of the pond.

Solutions:

a. x = number of meters wide the strip is.
    $\underline{\underline{7 + 2x}}$ = number of meters long the rectangle is.

    $\underline{\underline{5 + 2x}}$ = number of meters wide the rectangle is.

    These are *linear functions* of x.

b. Let A = number of square meters in the area of the rectangle.

   $. . A = (7 + 2x)(5 + 2x)$

   $A = 4x^2 + 24x + 35$

   This is a *quadratic function*.

c.

x	Area
1	63
2	99
3	143

d. $150 = 4x^2 + 24x + 35$

   $4x^2 + 24x - 115 = 0$

   $x = \dfrac{-24 \pm \sqrt{576 - 4(4)(-115)}}{8}$

   $x = \dfrac{-24 \pm \sqrt{2416}}{8}$

                                        Out of domain

   $x = 3.144...$ or $\cancel{-9.144...}$

   $\underline{\underline{\text{About } 3.14 \text{ m}}}$

e. See Figure 5-7c.
f. If the area of the walkway equals the area of the pond, then the area of the total rectangle is twice the area of the pond, or 70 square meters.

   $70 = 4x^2 + 24x + 35$

   $4x^2 + 24x - 35 = 0$

   $x = \dfrac{-24 \pm \sqrt{576 - 4(4)(-35)}}{8}$

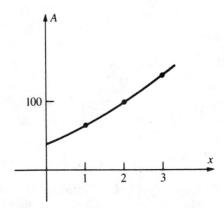

Figure 5-7c _____

$$x = \frac{-24 \pm \sqrt{1136}}{8}$$

Out of domain

$x = 1.213\ldots$ or $=7.213\ldots$.

<u>About 1.21 m</u>

In the following exercise you are to construct and use mathematical models. Remember that the most important thing is getting the particular equation correct. With an incorrect equation, other parts of the problem may turn out to be senseless. Be alert to the fact that some of the problems call for a *linear* function, not a quadratic function!

EXERCISE 5-7

Do These Quickly

The following problems are intended to refresh your skills. You should be able to do all 10 in less than 5 minutes.

Q1.   Write the general equation for a linear function.

Q2.   Write the general equation for a quadratic function.

Q3.   Does the graph of $y = 15 + 7x - 5x^2$ open upward or downward?

Q4.   Does the graph of $y = 3x - 5$ have positive slope or negative slope?

Q5.   Find the discriminant: $x^2 + 3x + 12 = 2$ (Beware!)

Q6.   Solve for a: $3a + b = 17$
$$5a + b = 10$$

Q7.   Do the squaring: $(x + 7)^2$

Q8.   Factor: $x^2 + 12x + 20$

Q9.   Draw a rhombus.

Q10.   Multiply: $\left(\dfrac{3}{11}\right)\left(\dfrac{22}{7}\right)$

Work the following problems.

1.   *Phoebe Small's Rocket Problem*   Phoebe Small is out Sunday driving in her spaceship. As she approaches Mars, she changes her
mind, decides that she does not wish to visit that planet, and fires
her retro-rocket. The spaceship slows down, and if all goes well,
stops for an instant then starts pulling away. While the rocket motor
is firing, Phoebe's distance, d, from the surface of Mars depends by
a quadratic function on the number of minutes, t, since she started
firing the rocket.

    a.   Phoebe finds that at times $t = 1$, 2, and 3 minutes, her distances
are $d = 425$, 356, and 293 kilometers, respectively. Find the
particular equation expressing d in terms of t.

    b.   Find the d-intercept and tell what this number represents in the
real world.

    c.   According to the equation, where will Phoebe be when $t = 15$?
When $t = 16$? Does this tell you she is pulling away from Mars
when $t = 16$, or still approaching?

    d.   Does your model tell you that Phoebe crashed into the surface of
Mars, just touches the surface, or pulls away before reaching the
surface? Explain.

    e.   Draw the graph of this quadratic function. Show the vertex.

    f.   Based on your answers to the above questions, in what domain
do you think this quadratic function will give reasonable values
for d? Modify your graph in part e, if necessary, by using a *dotted* line for those parts of the graph that are out of this domain.

2.   *Bathtub Problem*   Assume that the number of liters of water remaining in the bathtub varies quadratically with the number of minutes
which have elapsed since you pulled the plug.

    a.   If the tub has 38.4, 21.6, and 9.6 liters remaining at 1, 2, and 3
minutes respectively, since you pulled the plug, write an equation expressing liters in terms of time.

    b.   How much water was in the tub when you pulled the plug?

    c.   When will the tub be empty?

    d.   In the real world, the number of liters would never be negative.
What is the lowest number of liters the *model* predicts? Is this
number reasonable?

e.   Draw a graph of the function in the appropriate domain.
f.   Why is a quadratic function more reasonable for this problem than a linear function would be?

3.   *Car Insurance Problem*   Suppose that you are an actuary for F. Bender's Insurance Agency. Your company plans to offer a senior citizen's accident policy, and you must predict the likelihood of an accident as a function of the driver's age. From previous accident records, you find the following information:

Age (years)	Accidents per 100 Million Kilometers Driven
20	440
30	280
40	200

You know that the number of accidents per 100 million kilometers driven should reach a minimum then go up again for very old drivers. Therefore, you assume that a *quadratic* function is a reasonable model.
a.   Write the particular equation expressing accidents per 100 million kilometers in terms of age.
b.   How many accidents per 100 million kilometers would you expect for an 80-year-old driver?
c.   Based on your model, who is safer; a 16-year-old driver or a 70-year-old driver?
d.   What age driver appears to be the safest?
e.   Your company decides to insure licensed drivers up to the age where the accident rate reaches 830 per million kilometers. What, then, is the domain of this quadratic function?

4.   *Cost of Operating a Car Problem*   The number of cents per kilometer it costs to drive a car depends on how fast you drive it. At low speeds the cost is high because the engine operates inefficiently, while at high speeds the cost is high because the engine must overcome high wind resistance. At moderate speeds the cost reaches a minimum. Assume, therefore, that the number of cents per kilometer varies *quadratically* with the number of kilometers per hours (kph).
a.   Suppose that it costs 28, 21, and 16 cents per kilometer to drive at 10, 20, and 30 kph, respectively. Write the particular equation for this function.
b.   How much would you spend to drive at 150 kph?
c.   Between what two speeds must you drive to keep your cost no more than 13 cents per kilometer?
d.   Is it possible to spend only 10 cents per kilometer? Justify your answer.
e.   The *least* number of cents per kilometer occurs when you get the *most* kilometers per liter of gas. If your tank were nearly empty, at what speed should you drive to have the best chance of making it to a gas station before you run out?

5. *Artillery Problem*   Artillerymen on a hillside are trying to hit a
    target behind a mountain on the other side of the river (see Figure
    5-7c). Their cannon is at $(x, y) = (3, 250)$, where x is in kilometers
    and y is in meters. The target is at $(x, y) = (-2, 50)$. In order to
    avoid hitting the mountain on the other side of the river, the projec-
    tile from the cannon must go through the point $(x, y) = (-1, 410)$.

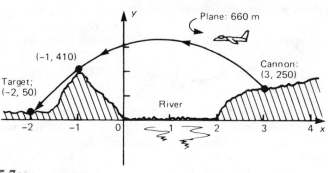

Figure 5-7c

   a. Write the particular equation of the parabolic path of the projec-
       tile.
   b. How high above the river will the projectile be where it crosses
       i.   the right riverbank, $x = 2$?
       ii. the left riverbank, $x = 0$?
   c. Approximately where will the projectile be when $y = 130$?
   d. A reconnaissance plane is flying at 660 meters above the river.
       Is it in danger of being hit by projectiles fired along this
       parabolic path? Justify your answer.

6. *Football Problem*   When a football is punted, it goes up into the
    air, reaches a maximum altitude, then comes back down. Assume,
    therefore, that a quadratic function is a reasonable mathematical
    model for this real-world situation.

    Let t = number of seconds that have elapsed since the ball was
             punted.
    Let d = number of feet the ball is above the ground.

   a. When the ball was kicked it was 4 feet above the ground. One
       second later, it was 28 feet above the ground. Two seconds after
       it was kicked, it was 20 feet up. Write the particular equation
       expressing d in terms of t.
   b. Find the d and t coordinates of the vertex, and tell what each
       represents in the real world.
   c. Find the t-intercepts and tell what each represents in the real
       world. Use square root tables or an educated guess to find a dec-
       imal approximation for any square roots you may encounter.

  d.   Draw a graph of the function. Select scales which make the
       graph fill up most of the sheet of graph paper. You should have
       enough points with the vertex, intercepts, given points, and
       points obtainable easily from symmetry.
  e.   By looking at your graph and thinking about what it represents,
       figure out a *domain* for this function. Why would your model
       not give reasonable answers for *d* when the value of *t* is
       i.   below the lower bound of the domain?
       ii.   above the upper bound of the domain?
       Modify your graph, if necessary, to agree with this domain.
  f.   What influences in the real world might make your model
       slightly inaccurate *within* the domain?
  g.   From your graph and your calculations, tell what the *range* of
       this function is.

7. *Rectangular Field Problem*   A rectangular field is 300 yards by 500
    yards. A roadway of width *x* yards is to be built inside the field (see
    Figure 5-7d). This problem concerns the region inside the roadway.

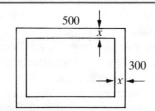

Figure 5-7d

  a.   Write the length and width of the region as functions of *x*. What
       kind of functions are these?
  b.   Write the area of the region as a function of *x*. What kind of
       function is this?
  c.   Predict the area of the region if $x = 5$, 10, and 15.
  d.   What is the widest the roadway can be and still leave 100,000
       square yards in the region?
  e.   Sketch the graph of area versus *x* in a reasonable domain.
  f.   Find the value of *x* which makes the roadway have an area equal
       to the area of the field.

8. *Corral Problem*   A rectangular corral is to be built by stringing an
    electric fence as shown with *y* feet for the side parallel to the river
    and *x* feet for each of the two sides perpendicular to the river (Figure
    5-7f). The total length of the fence is to be 900 feet.
  a.   Write an equation expressing *y* in terms of *x*. What kind of func-
       tion is this?
  b.   Let $A(x)$ be the number of square feet area taken up by the cor-
       ral. Write the particular equation for $A(x)$. What kind of func-
       tion is this?

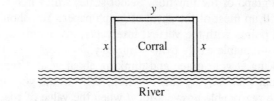

Figure 5-7e _____

c. Find $A(100)$ and $A(300)$.
d. What value of x makes $A(x)$ a maximum? What is this maximum area?
e. What values of x make $A(x)$ equal 0?
f. Sketch the graph of function A in a reasonable domain.

9. *Loan Problem*   You borrow some money from your parents to buy a used motorcycle, and agree to pay it off at $17 a week. After 13 weeks you still owe them $544. Answer the following questions:
   a. Write the particular equation expressing the amount you still owe in terms of the number of weeks.
   b. Explain why the amount you still owe is a *linear* function of the number of weeks.
   c. How much will you still owe after 20 weeks?
   d. When will the amount you owe first drop below $100?
   e. Find the dollars intercept. What does this represent?
   f. Find the weeks intercept. What does this represent?
   g. Sketch the graph, using a suitable domain.

10. *Breathing Problem*   Your nose, windpipe, and so forth, hold about a pint of air. So when you breathe in, the first pint of air to reach your lungs is air you have breathed before. If you breathe more than a pint, the rest of the air reaching your lungs is fresh air. The maximum amount you can inhale on any one breath is about 4 pints.
    a. Sketch a graph of f, the pints of fresh air reaching the lungs, as a function of a, the total pints of air breathed in. Explain why the function is linear, and tell its slope and a-intercept.
    b. Write the particular equation expressing f in terms of a.
    c. What percent of the air reaching your lungs is fresh air if you inhale 1 pint? 2 pints? 3 pints? 4 pints?
    d. Plot the graph of percent of fresh air reaching the lungs as a function of pints of air breathed in. Is the function linear? Justify your answer.
    e. What would happen to you if you breathed very shallow breaths, less than a pint, for a long period of time?

11. *Dee Side's Pig Problem*   Dee Side has a pig that presently weighs 200 pounds. She could sell it now for a price of $1.40 a pound.
    a. What is the worth of the pig now?

b. The pig is gaining 5 pounds a week. Write an equation for its weight as a function of weeks. What kind of function is this?

c. The price per pound is dropping 2 cents a week. Write an equation for price per pound as a function of weeks. What kind of function is this?

d. Write an equation for the total worth of the pig as a function of weeks. What kind of function is this?

e. Predict the worth of the pig after 8 weeks, 16 weeks, and 24 weeks.

f. When should Dee sell the pig to get the maximum amount of money for it?

g. Sketch the graph of worth versus time in a reasonable domain.

12. *Luke and Leia Problem*   Luke and Leia are trapped in a room on a space station. The room is 20 meters long and 15 meters wide. But the length is decreasing linearly with time at a rate of 2 meters per minute, and the width is increasing linearly with time at a rate of 3 meters per minute.

a. Let $L(t)$ and $W(t)$ be the length and width of the room, respectively, in meters. Let t be the number of minutes since the room was 20 by 15. Write particular equations for functions L and W.

b. Let $A(t)$ be the number of square meters of floor area in the room. Write the particular equation for function A.

c. Does the area of the room reach a maximum for a positive value of t? If so, what value of t? If not, how do you tell?

d. When will the area of the room be zero?

e. Sketch the graph of area versus time.

13. *Quadratic or Linear Problem Number 1*   In science lab, Wanda Ngo measures the following values of x and y:

x	y
11	341
18	411
23	471

Wanda wants to know whether the function could be linear. Tell her the answer, and how you decided. If it is linear, find the particular equation. If it is not linear, assume it is quadratic and find the particular equation.

14. *Quadratic or Linear Problem Number 2*   In science lab, Ida Ngo measures the following values of x and y:

x	y
11	394
18	807
23	1162

Ida wants to know whether the function could be linear. Tell her the answer, and how you decided. If it is linear, find the particular equation. If it is not linear, assume it is quadratic and find the particular equation.

15. **Color TV Problem**   The following are prices of a popular brand of color TV:

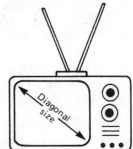

Size (in.)	Price
5″	$450
9″	$430
12″	$400
15″	$450
17″	$510
19″	$570
21″	$700

a. Plot these ordered pairs (size, price) on a Cartesian coordinate system. Connect the dots with a smooth curve.

b. Assume that the price varies quadratically with screen size. Use the ordered pairs of 9″, 15″, and 19″ screens to derive the particular equation for this function.

c. If the manufacturer produced a 24″ TV set, how much would you expect to pay for one?

d. Use the equation to calculate the prices of 5″, 12″, 17″, and 21″ diagonal sets.

e. Plot the predicted points from part d on the Cartesian coordinate system of part a. Connect these points with a smooth curve. Use means such as a colored pencil to distinguish clearly between the two graphs.

f. Based on the two graphs, would you describe the quadratic model as *accurate*, *reasonable*, or *inaccuate*?

g. Why do you suppose the price goes *up* as the size gets very small?

16. **Calvin Butterball's Gasoline Problem**   Calvin Butterball is driving along the highway. He starts up a long, straight hill (see Figure 5-7f). 114 meters from the bottom of the hill Calvin's car runs out of gas. He doesn't put on the brakes, so the car keeps rolling for awhile, coasts to a stop, then starts rolling backwards. He finds that his distances from the bottom of the hill 4 and 6 seconds after he runs out of gas are 198 and 234 meters, respectively.

a. There are *three* ordered pairs of time and distance in the information given above. What are they?

b. Write an equation expressing Calvin's distance from the bottom of the hill in terms of the number of seconds which have elapsed since he ran out of gas. Assume that a quadratic function is a reasonable mathematical model.

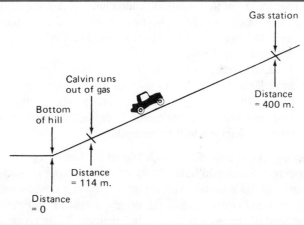

Figure 5-7f

    c. Use the model to predict Calvin's distance from the bottom of the hill 10 and 30 seconds after he ran out of gas.

    d. Draw a graph of this function. Use the given points, the calculated points from part c, and any other points you find useful.

    e. Last Chance Texaco Station is located 400 meters from the bottom of the hill. Based on your model, will Calvin's car reach the station before it stops and starts rolling backwards? Justify your answer.

17. *Spaceship Problem*   When a spaceship is sent to the Moon, it is first put into orbit around the Earth. Then just at the right time, the rocket motor is fired to start it on its parabolic path to the Moon (see Figure 5-7g). Let x and y be coordinates measuring the position of

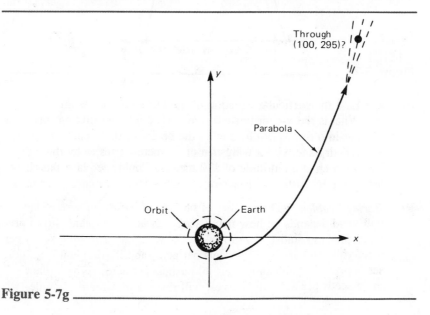

Figure 5-7g

the spacecraft (in thousands of kilometers) as it goes moonward.
When the rocket is fired, $x = 0$ and $y = -7$. The tracking station
measures the position at two later times, and finds that $y = -4$ when
$x = 10$, and $y = 5$ when $x = 20$.

a.   Find an equation of the parabolic path in Figure 5-7g.
b.   In order to hit the Moon without a mid-course maneuver, the
path of the spaceship must pass through the point (100, 295).
Use your mathematical model to predict whether or not a mid-
course maneuver will be necessary.

18.   *Gateway Arch Problem*   On a trip to St. Louis you visit the Gateway Arch. Since you have plenty of time on your hands, you decide
to estimate its altitude. You set up a Cartesian coordinate system
with one end of the arch at the origin, as shown in Figure 5-7h. The
other end of the arch is at $x = 162$ meters. To find a third point on
the arch, you measure a value of $y = 4.55$ meters when $x = 1$ meter. You assume that the arch is parabolic.

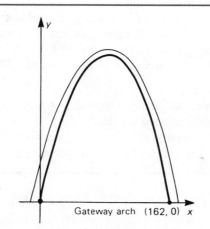

Gateway arch   (162, 0) x

Figure 5-7h

a.   Find the particular equation of the underside of the arch.
b.   What is the x-coordinate of the vertex? By substituting this number into the equation, predict the height of the arch.
c.   An airplane with a wingspan of 40 meters tries to fly through
the arch at an altitude of 170 meters. Could the plane possibly
make it? Justify your answer.

19.   *Barley Problem*   The number of bushels of barley an acre of land
will yield depends on how many seeds per acre you plant. From previous planting statistics you find that if you plant 2 million seeds per
acre, you can harvest 22 bushels per acre, and if you plant 4 million
seeds per acre you can harvest 40 bushels per acre. As you plant
more seeds per acre, the harvest will reach a maximum, then de-

crease. This happens because the young plants crowd each other out and compete for food and sunlight. Assume, therefore, that the number of bushels per acre you can harvest varies *quadratically* with the number of millions of seeds per acre you plant.

a.   Write *three* ordered pairs of (millions of seeds per acre, bushels per acre). The third ordered pair is not given above, but should be obvious.

b.   Write the particular equation for this function.

c.   How many bushels per acre would you expect to get if you plant 16 million seeds per acre?

d.   Based on your model, would it be possible to get a harvest of 70 bushels per acre? Justify your answer.

e.   How much should you plant to get the *maximum* number of bushels per acre?

f.   According to your model, is it possible to plant so many seeds that you harvest no barley at all?

g.   Plot the graph of this quadratic function in a suitable domain.

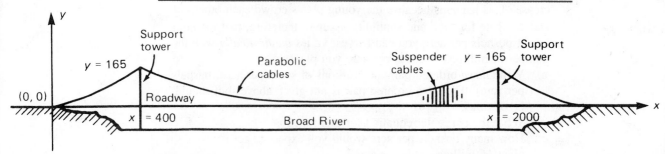

Figure 5-7i

20. *Suspension Bridge Problem*   In a suspension bridge such as the
Golden Gate Bridge in California or the Verrazano-Narrows Bridge
in New York, the roadway is supported by parabolic cables hanging
from support towers, as shown in Figure 5-7i. Vertical suspender cables connect the parabolic cables to the roadway.

Suppose that you work for Ornery & Sly Construction Company.
Your job is to procure the vertical suspender cables for the center
span of the new bridge to be built across Broad River. From the Design Department, you find the following information:
  i.   The support towers are located at $x = 400$ meters and
       $x = 2000$ meters (making this span slightly longer than the
       Verrazano-Narrows Bridge). The tops of the towers are 165
       meters above the roadway, at $y = 165$.
  ii. There are four parallel parabolic cables that go from tower
       top to tower top. They are 5 meters above the roadway at
       their lowest points, halfway between the two towers.
  iii. The vertical suspender cables are spaced every 20 meters,
       starting at $x = 420$ and ending at $x = 1980$. Each of the
       four parabolic cables has *two* suspender cables at each value
       of x.
  a. Demonstrate that you understand the above information by writ-
     ing *three* ordered pairs for points on the parabolic cables.
  b. Find the particular equation of the parabolic cables. You may
     use the vertex form or the $y = ax^2 + bx + c$ form, whichever
     seems more convenient.
  c. The success of the $700,000,000 project (and whether or not
     you keep your job!) depends on the correctness of your calcula-
     tions. Demonstrate that your equation gives correct values of y
     by substituting the three values of x from the given ordered pairs
     in part a.
  d. As a further check on the correctness of your equation, substi-
     tute 0 for y, and show that the resulting values of x are consis-
     tent with the given information.

e. Write a computer program to calculate and print the length of each vertical suspender cable and its corresponding value of x. As each value is calculated, the computer should add it to the sum of the previous values of y. When all values are printed, the computer should print the total length of suspender cable that will be used for the center span so that the Purchasing Department may buy the correct amount of cable.

f. Remember, you will be *fired* if you present your boss with an incorrect answer. Perform a *quick* calculation to show that the total computed cable length is *reasonable*.

5-8	CHAPTER REVIEW AND TEST

In this chapter you have studied the second major kind of function, the quadratic function. You have learned that the graphs are curved, and are called parabolas. While solving quadratic equations to find x for given values of y, you ran across imaginary and complex numbers. Finding the particular equation for mathematical models problems required that you solve a system of linear equations, as you did in Chapter 4. You also made progress in distinguishing between linear and quadratic model problems.

The Review Problems below parallel the sections in this chapter. The Concepts Problems let you try your hand at applying what you know to analyze a new situation. The Chapter Test is similar to one your instructor might give to see how well you understand quadratic functions.

REVIEW PROBLEMS

R1. If $f(x) = 3x^2 - 7x + 11$, find $f(-5)$. Tell what kind of function f is.

R2. a. Do the squaring: $(3x - 4)^2$
  b. Transform to vertex form: $y = 5x^2 + 14x - 3$
  c. Sketch a parabola with vertex at (5, 11) and y-intercept 3.
  d. Find the x-intercepts: $y = -6x^2 + 10x + 7$

R3. a. Solve: $8x^2 - 5x - 30 = 4$ (Watch out!)
  b. Find the discriminant: $9x^2 + 11x + 13 = 0$
  c. Describe the solutions of the quadratic equation with rational coefficients if the discriminant equals:
    i.   121
    ii. 50
    iii. 0
    iv. −9

d. Find the vertex *without* transforming to vertex form:
$y = 5x^2 + 17x + 91$

R4. a. Write in terms of i: $\sqrt{-64}$
     b. Plot $-3 + 2i$ on the complex plane.
     c. Solve: $3x^2 - 8x + 50 = 2x(x - 3)$

R5. If $g(x) = x^2 - 7x + 4$,
     a. find $g(9)$,
     b. find x if $g(x) = 42$,
     c. tell whether or not $g(x)$ ever equals -10.

R6. a. Find the particular equation of the quadratic function containing $(2, 1)$, $(5, 31)$, and $(-1, 7)$.
     b. Find the particular equation of the linear function containing $(7, 4)$ and $(10, 19)$.

R7. ***Diving Board Problem*** Jack Potts dives off the high diving board. His distance from the surface of the water varies *quadratically* with the number of seconds that have passed since he left the board.
     a. His distances at times of 1, 2 and 3 seconds since he left the board are 24, 18, and 2 meters above the water, respectively. Write the particular equation expressing distance in terms of time.
     b. How high is the diving board? Justify your answer.
     c. What is the highest Jack gets above the water?
     d. When does he hit the water?
     e. Draw the graph of the quadratic function using a suitable domain.

CONCEPTS PROBLEM

Office Building Problem Suppose that you work for a company that is planning to operate a new office building. You find that the monthly payments the company must make vary directly with the *square* of the number of stories in the building. That is, the general equation is payment = (constant)(stories)^2. The amount of money the company will take in each month from people renting office space will vary *linearly* with the number of stories. The *profit* the company will make each month equals the rent payments it takes in minus the monthly payments it pays out.
     a. Write general equations expressing in terms of number of stories
        i. the monthly payments you pay out,
       ii. the rent payments you take in, and
      iii. the monthly profit.
     b. Tell in words how the monthly profit varies with the number of stories.
     c. You predict monthly profits of 4, 9, and 12 thousand dollars

for buildings of 2, 3, and 4 stories, respectively. Find the particular equation expressing monthly profit as a function of the number of stories.

d.   Will the profit ever equal $15 thousand per month? Justify your answer.

e.   What number of stories gives the *maximum* monthly profit?

f.   Between what two numbers of stories will your monthly profit be positive?

g.   If the building is 7 stories high, how much would you *receive* per month in rent, and how much would you *pay* out per month in monthly payments?

h.   Plot a graph of this function, using a suitable domain.

CHAPTER TEST

Algebra II is a study of functions. You have been studying quadratic functions.

T1.   Write the general equation for a quadratic function.

T2.   For $y = 8x^2 - 80x + 207$, transform to vertex form and write the coordinates of the vertex.

T3.   If $z = p^2 + 7p + 5$, find the p-intercepts.

T4.   Given $f(x) = 3x^2 - 7x + 11$,
   a.   Find $f(-9)$.
   b.   Find the values of x for which $f(x) = 5$.

T5.   Suppose that $y = 7x^2 - 19x + 23$. Use the discriminant in an appropriate manner to show that there *are* real values of x for which $y = 14$. Are these values *rational* numbers or *irrational* numbers? Justify your answer.

T6.   Given that the vertex of a parabola is at $(-4, 11)$, and that the y-intercept is 3, sketch the parabola.

T7.   Solve $x^2 + 4x + 104 = 0$ if the domain of x is the complex numbers.

T8.   *Motel Problem*   A small motel is to be built as shown in the sketch with two long walls y feet long each and 6 short walls x feet long each. The total length of the walls is to be 300 feet.

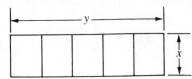

a. Write an equation expressing y in terms of x. What kind of function is this?
b. Let $A(x)$ be the number of square feet area taken up by the motel. Write the particular equation for $A(x)$. What kind of function is this?
c. Find $A(10)$ and $A(30)$.
d. What value of x makes $A(x)$ a maximum? What is this maximum area?
e. What values of x make $A(x)$ equal 0?
f. Sketch the graph of function A in a reasonable domain.

5-9 | CUMULATIVE REVIEW: CHAPTERS 1 THROUGH 5

The following exercise may be considered to be a "final exam" covering the materials on linear and quadratic functions, and the properties leading up to these. If you are thoroughly familiar with the material in Chapters 1 through 5, you should be able to work all of these problems in about 2 to 3 hours.

EXERCISE 5-9

1. Calvin Butterball and Phoebe Small are studying for their algebra examination. In the table on the following page they give the answers indicated to the questions on the left. Tell which, if either, of them is right. Use "Calvin," "Phoebe," "Both," or "Neither "

2. Given the statement, "If R is a relation, then R is a function:"
    a. Draw a graph which shows clearly why the statement is *false*.
    b. Write the *converse* of the statement.
    c. Is the converse true or false? Explain.

3. You have learned that graphs of two linear functions are parallel if their slopes are equal. It is also true that the graphs of two linear functions are *perpendicular* if the slope of one is equal to the *negative* of the *reciprocal* of the other slope. Given the equations

$$y = \frac{2}{3}x - 4 \quad \text{(A)}, \qquad 3y - 2x = 6 \quad \text{(C)},$$

$$2x + 3y = 12 \quad \text{(B)}, \qquad y - 5 = -\frac{3}{2}(x + 1) \quad \text{(D)}.$$

	Problem	Calvin	Phoebe
a.	$17ax + 34a^2 = 17a(x + 2a)$	distributivity	associativity
b.	$(xy + z) + w = xy + (z + w)$	commutativity	associativity
c.	$2 + ab = 2 + ba$	commutativity	reflexive property
d.	Either $x > 0$, $x < 0$, or $x = 0$	comparison	trichotomy
e.	$xy \in$ {real numbers}	closure	agreement
f.	$\dfrac{xy}{ab} = xy \cdot \dfrac{1}{ab}$	reciprocal of a product	definition of division
g.	$xy + (-xy) = 0$	additive inverses	multiplicative inverses
h.	A field axiom	reflexive	symmetric
i.	An axiom which is *not* a field axiom	transitive	closure
j.	Name for 4th degree	quadratic	quintic
k.	Degree of $3^5 x^4 y^3 + z^6$	6	12
l.	$\sqrt{x^2} =$	x	$|x|$
m.	Set containing $\sqrt{-7}$	{irrational numbers}	{imaginary numbers}
n.	If $-2x < 6$, then	$x > -3$	$x < -3$

a.   Find the slope of each graph.
b.   From the slopes, tell which (if any) of the graphs are parallel, and which (if any) are perpendicular. Use symbols such as $A \| B$, or $A \perp B$.
c.   Plot a graph of each equation on the *same* coordinate system.

4.   The following sketch shows the feasible region for a problem involving the manufacture of two products. This is similar to a linear programming problem, but the boundaries of the region are not linear. If the profit for this process is given by

$$P = 30x - 50y + 500,$$

a.   Trace or copy the graph. Then shade the portion of the feasible region in which the profit is more than 300.
b.   Find the point with integer coordinates that gives the maximum profit, and tell what this profit equals.

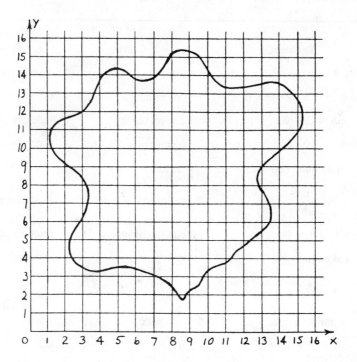

5. The following is a proof that a number divided by itself equals 1.
    Supply a reason for each step. Tell whether or not the reason is an
    axiom, and if so, whether it is a field axiom.

    Prove that

    $$\frac{n}{n} = 1.$$

    Proof:

    $$\frac{n}{n} = n \cdot \frac{1}{n}$$

    $$= 1$$

    $$\therefore \frac{n}{n} = 1.$$

6. The grade you could make on an algebra final exam is related to the
    number of days which elapse after the last day of classes if you don't
    study until you take the exam. Draw a reasonable graph showing
    how these two variables are related.

7. Assume that your height and your age are related by a *linear* func-
    tion. Consulting your health records, you find that at age $A = 5$ your
    height was $H = 39$ inches, and when $A = 9$, $H = 55$ inches.

a.   Write an equation expressing the dependent variable in terms of the independent variable.
b.   Predict your height at age 16.
c.   What does the H-intercept equal, and what does it represent in the real world?
d.   Since you are using a linear function as a model, what are you assuming about the rate at which you grow?
e.   What fact in the real world sets an upper bound on the domain in which this linear model gives reasonable answers?

8.   For the quadratic function $y = -2x^2 - 12x - 10$,
a.   Transform the equation to the form $y - k = a(x - h)^2$.
b.   Find the vertex.
c.   Find the x and y-intercepts.
d.   Sketch the graph.
e.   By using what you have learned about graphing linear inequalities, shade the region on your graph paper corresponding to the solution set of the *quadratic* inequality

$$y \geq -2x^2 - 12x - 10.$$

9.   S. Bones is the doctor in Deathly, Ill., a suburb of Chicago. One day, John Garfinkle comes in with a high fever. Dr. Bones takes a blood sample and finds that it contains 1300 flu viruses per cubic millimeter and is *increasing*. John immediately gets a shot of penicillin. The virus count should continue to increase for awhile, then (hopefully!) level off and go back down. After 5 minutes the virus count is up to 1875, and after 5 more minutes, it is 2400. Assume that the virus count varies quadratically with the number of minutes since the shot.
a.   Write an equation expressing the number of viruses per cubic millimeter in terms of the number of minutes since the shot.
b.   Dr. Bones realizes that if the virus count ever reaches 4500, John must go to the hospital. Must he go? Explain.
c.   According to your model, when will his flu be completely cured?
d.   Draw a graph of this quadratic function.
e.   Tell the range and domain of this quadratic function.

10. For each of the following equations, calculate the discriminant. Then, without actually solving the equation, tell what *kind* of numbers (rational, irrational, imaginary) will be in the solution set.
a. $3x^2 - 2x - 8 = 0$
b. $3x^2 - 2x + 8 = 0$
c. $x^2 - 6x + 2 = 0$
d. $x^2 - 6x + 9 = 0$

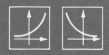

6

Exponential and Logarithmic Functions

*The polynomial functions you have studied so far have had variables raised to constant powers. In this chapter you will encounter exponential functions that have **constants** raised to **variable** powers. Since variables can be negative numbers or fractions, you must invent meanings for these kinds of exponents. The tool that allows you to operate with such powers is called the "logarithm." The resulting exponential functions are reasonable mathematical models for things from figuring out compound interest to predicting the temperature of a cup of coffee.*

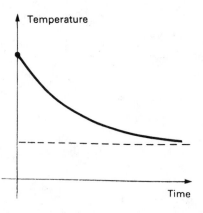

6-1	INTRODUCTION TO EXPONENTIAL FUNCTIONS

A quadratic function might have an equation of the form $y = ax^2$. If the x and the 2 are reversed, you get a completely different kind of function.

$$y = a \cdot 2^x$$

Since the variable is an exponent, this is called an *exponential* function.

DEFINITION

> **EXPONENTIAL FUNCTION**
> An **exponential function** is a function whose general equation is
>
> $$y = a \cdot b^x$$
>
> where a and b stand for constants, b is positive, and x and y are independent and dependent variables, respectively.

To describe such a function verbally you may say, "y varies exponentially with x." The effects of a and b on the graph, and the reason b must be positive will become clear later in the chapter.

Objective:
Discover by pointwise plotting what the graph of an exponential function looks like.

In the exercise that follows, you will accomplish this objective.

EXERCISE 6-1

1. Let $f(x) = 2^x$. Calculate $f(4), f(3), f(2)$, and $f(1)$. Plot the corresponding points on graph paper and connect them with a smooth curve.

2. Write the results of Problem 1 in table form, like this:

$$
\begin{array}{c|c}
x & f(x) \\
\hline
4 & \underline{\quad} \\
3 & \underline{\quad} \times \frac{1}{2} \\
2 & \underline{\quad} \times \frac{1}{2} \\
1 & \underline{\quad} \times \frac{1}{2}
\end{array}
$$

   Observe that $f(3)$ is *half* of $f(4)$, $f(2)$ is *half* of $f(3)$, and so forth. By continuing this pattern, find values of $f(0), f(-1), f(-2)$, and $f(-3)$. Plot these points on your graph and extend the smooth curve through the points.

3. How does the negative part of the x-axis seem to be related to the graph?

4. Although you know no definition of powers with fractional exponents, you can estimate them from the graph. Find an approximation (1 decimal place) for $2^{2.5}$ by reading the value of $f(2.5)$ from your graph.

5. Confirm that your answers to Problems 2 and 4 are correct by evaluating 2^0, 2^{-1}, 2^{-2}, 2^{-3} and $2^{2.5}$ with a calculator. The sequence of keystrokes for 2^{-3}, for example, is

$$2 \;\boxed{y^x}\; 3 \;\boxed{+/-}\; \boxed{=}$$

6-2 | ## EXPONENTIATION FOR POSITIVE INTEGER EXPONENTS

If you did Exercise 6-1 correctly you should have gotten a graph such as in Figure 6-2 for $f(x) = 2^x$. The points for 0 and negative values of x you got by crossing your fingers and following a pattern. The points for fractional values you got by connecting the integer points with a smooth curve and reading the graph.

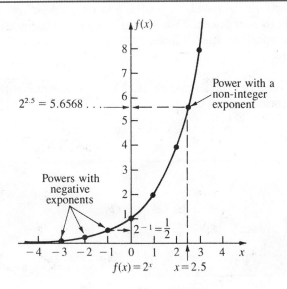

Figure 6-2 _____

Then by calculator you found that 2^{-3} equals 0.125, which agrees with the value of $\frac{1}{8}$ you found by the pattern. Also, the calculator value of $2^{2.5}$, namely 5.656. . . , fits the smooth curve you got by connecting the points.

In this section and the next you will lay the foundation for precise definitions of powers with exponents that are not positive integers.
The operation of raising a number to a power is called **exponentiation.**
The word is pronounced "ex-po-nen-chee-ā'-shun." From your previous work in mathematics, you should know that

$$x^3 = x \cdot x \cdot x,$$

$$x^7 = x \cdot x \cdot x \cdot x \cdot x \cdot x \cdot x,$$

$$x^1 = x,$$

and so forth. These examples lead to the following definition.

DEFINITION

EXPONENTIATION FOR POSITIVE INTEGER EXPONENTS

x^n means the product of n x's.

This definition can be stated, "x used as a factor n times," or "take n x's and multiply them together." You should avoid such statements as "x^3 means x multiplied by itself 3 times," because $x \cdot x \cdot x$ has only *two* "times" signs.

Various parts of an expression such as x^n have precise names that you should get accustomed to using.

NAMES

> In the expression x^n,
>
> x is called the *base*,
>
> n is called the *exponent*,
>
> x^n (the whole thing) is called a *power*.

When you combine exponentiation with other operations, you must recall the order of operations. Expressions without parentheses have definite and often surprising meanings. Since exponentiation is done before multiplication, in $4x^3$ only x is the base, not $4x$. If you want to cube $4x$, you must use parentheses.

$$4x^3 \text{ means } 4 \cdot x \cdot x \cdot x$$

$$(4x)^3 \text{ means } (4x)(4x)(4x)$$

Similarly, exponentiation is done before taking opposites. Thus, in $-x^4$, only x is the base, not $-x$. If you want to raise $-x$ to the fourth, you must use parentheses.

$$-x^4 \text{ means } -(x \cdot x \cdot x \cdot x)$$

$$(-x)^4 \text{ means } (-x)(-x)(-x)(-x)$$

As a "rule of thumb," you can use the following agreement.

AGREEMENT

> If the base of a power consists of more than one symbol, then it must be placed in parentheses. For example,
>
> $$(xy)^5, \quad (x - y)^5, \quad (-x)^5.$$
>
> Otherwise, the exponent applies only to *one* symbol. For example,
>
> $$xy^5 = x(y^5), \quad x - y^5 = x - (y^5), \quad -x^5 = -(x^5)$$

Objective:

Use the definition of exponentiation to evaluate expressions that have powers with positive integer exponents, in preparation for learning the properties in the next section.

EXAMPLE 1

Evaluate $2 \cdot 3^4$.

Solution:

This is a "head" problem that you should be able to do without a calculator. The 3 is raised to the fourth first. 3 times 3 is 9, 9 times 3 is 27, and 27 times 3 is 81. Then 81 times 2 is <u>162</u>. ∎

EXAMPLE 2

Evaluate $(-2)^4$.

Solution:

The parentheses indicate that -2 is being raised to the fourth, not just 2. In your head you should think, "Since there is an *even* number of negative factors, the answer will be *positive*. 2 times 2 times 2 times 2 is <u>16</u>." ∎

EXAMPLE 3

Evaluate 7^5 by multiplication, then confirm the result using the $\boxed{y^x}$ key on your calculator.

Solution:

By multiplication, $7^5 = 7 \cdot 7 \cdot 7 \cdot 7 \cdot 7 = \underline{16807}$.

By calculator, press 7 $\boxed{y^x}$ 5 $\boxed{=}$.   The answer is <u>16807</u>. ∎

In the following exercise you will first "warm up" by evaluating powers using the definition. You *must* work all five of Problems 15 through 19 in preparation for the next section.

EXERCISE 6-2

Do These Quickly

The following problems are intended to be done mentally. You should be able to do all 10 in about 1 minute!

Q1.   Evaluate: 2^3

Q2.   Evaluate: 3^2

Q3.   Evaluate: 3^3

Q4.   Evaluate: $3 \cdot 2$

Q5.   Evaluate: $3 + 2$

Q6.   Evaluate: $(0.3)(2)$

Q7.   Evalute: $(0.3)(0.2)$

Q8.   Evaluate: -3^2

Q9.   Evaluate: -2^3

Q10.   Evaluate: $(-3)^2$

Work the following problems.

For Problems 1 through 10, evaluate the expression.

1.   a. $(2 \cdot 3)^4$ b. $2 \cdot (3^4)$ c. $2 \cdot 3^4$

2.   a. $(3 \div 2)^4$ b. $3 \div (2^4)$ c. $3 \div 2^4$

3.   a. $(3 + 2)^4$ b. $3 + (2^4)$ c. $3 + 2^4$

4.   a. $(3 - 7)^2$ b. $3 - (7^2)$ c. $3 - 7^2$

5.   a. $(4 - 7)^3$ b. $4 - (7^3)$ c. $4 - 7^3$

6.   a. $(-6)^2$ b. $-(6^2)$ c. -6^2

7.   a. $-2 \cdot 3^4$ b. $(-2 \cdot 3)^4$
     c. $-(2 \cdot 3^4)$ d. $-2 \cdot (3^4)$

8. $3 \cdot 4 + 5 \cdot 6^2$

9. $64/2^3 \cdot 4$

10. $4 + 8^2 - 2 \cdot 3^5 + 6(-4)^2$

For Problems 11 through 14, evaluate the power by multiplication and also by using the $\boxed{y^x}$ key. Show that the answers are the same.

11. 3^7 12. 4^6

13. 8^5 14. 11^4

For Problems 15 through 19 you will learn some ways to operate on the *exponents* in powers. These problems lay the foundation for what you will learn in the next section.

15. *Product of Two Powers Problem*
    a.   Evaluate $x^3 \cdot x^5$ by writing out all the x's and counting them up.

   b.   What operation could you perform on the exponents to get the
        answer in part (a) without writing out all the x's?

16.   *Quotient of Two Powers Problem*
      a.   Evaluate $\frac{x^5}{x^3}$ by writing out the x's and canceling.
      b.   What operation could you perform on the exponents to get the
           answer in part (a) without writing out all the x's?

17.   *Power of a Power Problem*
      a.   Evaluate $(x^5)^3$ by writing out the three x^5's and then doing
           something appropriate.
      b.   What operation could you perform on the exponents to get the
           answer in part (a) in *one* step?

18.   *Power of a Product Problem*
      a.   Evaluate $(xy)^4$ by writing out the four xy's, then commuting and
           associating so that the x's are together and the y's are together.
           Write the answer as simply as possible.
      b.   The operation inside the parentheses is multiplication. The oper-
           ation outside is exponentiation. What does exponentiation seem
           to do to multiplication?

19.   *Power of a Quotient Problem*
      a.   Evaluate $(\frac{x}{y})^4$ by writing out all the $\frac{x}{y}$'s. Recall that you multiply
           fractions by multiplying their numerators and multiplying their
           denominators.
      b.   The operation inside the parentheses is division. The operation
           outside is exponentiation. What does exponentiation seem to do
           to division?

20.   *Exponential Function Graph Problem*   Given $f(x) = 3^x$:
      a.   Evaluate $f(3), f(2)$, and $f(1)$.
      b.   You should be able to see that $f(2)$ is $\frac{1}{3}$ of $f(3)$, and $f(1)$ is $\frac{1}{3}$ of
           $f(2)$. By following this pattern, find $f(0), f(-1), f(-2)$, and
           $f(-3)$.
      c.   Plot the graph of function f in the domain $-3 \leq x \leq 2$.
      d.   If your graph is correct there is an asymptote. Is the asymptote
           the *graph itself* or the *x-axis*?

21.   *Computer Graphics Problem*   Given the two functions:

$$f(x) = 1.7^x \quad \text{and} \quad g(x) = 0.6^x$$

      a.   What do you expect $f(0)$ to be? $g(0)$?
      b.   As x gets very large, what do you expect the graph of function f
           to look like? What do you expect the graph of g to look like?

c. Use the computer program PLOT EXPONENTIAL from the
accompanying disk, or a similar plotting program, to plot the
graphs of functions f and g on the screen at the same time. Did
the actual graphs confirm your predictions in parts (a) and (b),
or refute them?

22. **Exponents by Trial and Error**   Suppose that $f(x) = 1.005^x$.
a. Find $f(100)$ by calculator. The sequence of keystrokes is

$$1.005 \boxed{y^x} \; 100 \; \boxed{=} \quad \text{(for algebraic logic calculators)}$$

$$1.005 \boxed{\text{enter}} \; 100 \; \boxed{y^x} \quad \text{(for RPN calculators)}$$

b. Find the smallest integer value of x for which $f(x)$ first exceeds
2.
c. Find the smallest integer value of x for which $f(x)$ first exceeds
10.
d. True or false: "Since 10 is five times 2, the answer to part (c) is
five times the answer to part (b)." Justify your answer.

6-3 | PROPERTIES OF EXPONENTIATION

It is possible to simplify expressions involving powers by operating with
their exponents. There are five possible cases, as you may have seen in
Problems 15 through 19 of Exercise 6-2.

Case 1: If you multiply two powers that have equal bases, such as $x^3 \cdot x^5$,
you can write

$$x^3 \cdot x^5$$

$$= (x \cdot x \cdot x)(x \cdot x \cdot x \cdot x \cdot x) \quad \text{Definition of exponentiation}$$

$$= x \cdot x \cdot x \cdot x \cdot x \cdot x \cdot x \cdot x \quad \text{Associativity}$$

$$= x^8 \quad \text{Definition of exponentiation}$$

You can eliminate the steps in the middle and simply write down the answer by *adding* the exponents. In words, you can say, "When multiplying
two powers that have equal bases, *add* the exponents and use the *same*
base."

The other four cases are as follows. You should think of reasons for each
step. But most important, you should remember how to get the answer
quickly, just by operating with the exponents.

Case 2: $\dfrac{x^5}{x^3} = \dfrac{x \cdot x \cdot x \cdot x \cdot x}{x \cdot x \cdot x} = x^2$

Words: "When you divide two powers that have equal bases, you can *subtract* the exponents (numerator exponent minus denominator exponent) and use the *same* base."

Case 3: $(x^5)^3 = (x^5)(x^5)(x^5) = x^{5 \cdot 3} = x^{15}$

Words: "When you raise a power to a power, you can *multiply* the exponents and use the *same* base.

Case 4: $(xy)^4 = (xy)(xy)(xy)(xy) = (x \cdot x \cdot x \cdot x)(y \cdot y \cdot y \cdot y) = x^4 y^4$

Words: "When you raise a product to a power, you can *distribute* the exponent to each factor," or more simply, "Exponentiation distributes over multiplication."

Case 5: $\left(\dfrac{x}{y}\right)^4 = \left(\dfrac{x}{y}\right)\left(\dfrac{x}{y}\right)\left(\dfrac{x}{y}\right)\left(\dfrac{x}{y}\right) = \dfrac{x \cdot x \cdot x \cdot x}{y \cdot y \cdot y \cdot y} = \dfrac{x^4}{y^4}$

Words: "When you raise a quotient to a power, you can *distribute* the exponent to the numerator and denominator," or, "Exponentiation distributes over division."

These five examples illustrate the five properties of exponentiation.

PROPERTIES

PROPERTIES OF EXPONENTIATION:
In these properties, a and b stand for positive integers.

1. *Product of two powers with equal bases:*
$$x^a \cdot x^b = x^{a+b}$$

2. *Quotient of two powers with equal bases:*
$$\frac{x^a}{x^b} = x^{a-b}$$

3. *Power of a power:*
$$(x^a)^b = x^{ab}$$

4. *Power of a product:*
(Distributive property of exponentiation over multiplication)
$$(xy)^a = x^a y^a$$

5. *Power of a quotient:*
(Distributive property of exponentiation over division)
$$\left(\frac{x}{y}\right)^a = \frac{x^a}{y^a}$$

The formal proofs of these properties for *any* positive integer exponents
are done by mathematical induction, as shown in Appendix B. For your
purposes now, it is sufficient to remember how to derive the properties by
example, and be able to use them to simplify expressions.

Objective:

Be able to explain by example why the properties of exponentiation are
correct, verify them by calculator, and use them to transform expressions.

The examples above illustrate the first part of the objective. The examples
below illustrate the other parts.

EXAMPLE 1

Simplify: $(5x^2y^7)^3(4y^8)$

Solution:

$(5x^2y^7)^3(4y^8)$

$= (125x^6y^{21})(4y^8)$ Distribute the exponent 3 to *each* factor in
                            the product.

$= 500x^6y^{29}$ Commute and associate the 125 and 4,
                            and the two powers of y.   ■

EXAMPLE 2

Demonstrate that $\dfrac{3^{16}}{3^7} = 3^9$.

Solution:

$$\frac{3^{16}}{3^7} = 43046721/2187 = \underline{\underline{19683}} \longleftarrow$$

$$3^9 = \underline{\underline{19683}} \longleftarrow$$

the same

The sequence of keystrokes for the first line using a calculator with algebraic logic is

$$3 \quad \boxed{y^x} \quad 16 \quad \boxed{\div} \quad 3 \quad \boxed{y^x} \quad 7 \quad \boxed{=}.$$

For reverse Polish notation (RPN) calculators the keystrokes are

$$3 \quad \boxed{\text{enter}} \quad 16 \quad \boxed{y^x} \quad 3 \quad \boxed{\text{enter}} \quad 7 \quad \boxed{y^x} \quad \boxed{\div}.$$

It is not necessary to write down any intermediate steps. You can just say,
"Both are equal to 19,683."   ■

In the following exercise you will simplify powers and verify and justify properties of exponentiation.

EXERCISE 6-3

Do These Quickly

The following problems are intended to refresh your skills. You should be able to do all 10 in less than 5 minutes.

Q1. Write the general equation for a quadratic function.

Q2. Evaluate $3x^2$ if x is -5.

Q3. Evaluate $4x^3$ if x is -2.

Q4. Evaluate -3^4.

Q5. If a \$20 item is on sale for 30% off, what is the sale price?

Q6. Sketch the graph of an exponential function.

Q7. Solve for p in terms of the other variables: $\dfrac{v}{p} = 4x$

Q8. Solve for x: $3 - x > 7$

Q9. Multiply: $(3x - 5)(2x + 8)$

Q10. Tell the axiom used: $3(x + y) = 3(y + x)$

Work the following problems.

For Problems 1 through 10, evaluate the expression.

1. $4 \cdot 3^2$ 2. $3 \cdot 5^2$

3. $5(-4)^2$ 4. $7(-3^2)$

5. $6(-5^2)$ 6. $8(-6)^2$

7. $-(-3)^4$ 8. $-(-5)^3$

9. $-(-4)^3$ 10. $-(-3)^2$

For Problems 11 through 20, simplify the expression.

11. $(5x^7)^4$ 12. $(3x^9)^4$

13. $(8y)(7y)^2$ 14. $(17z)(3z)^2$

15. $\dfrac{(3x^2)^3}{6x^5}$

16. $\dfrac{(5x^2)^3}{100x^5}$

17. $\left(\dfrac{x^7}{y^4}\right)^8 \left(\dfrac{y^{10}}{x^{10}}\right)^3$

18. $\left(\dfrac{a^{11}}{b^{11}}\right)^5 \left(\dfrac{b^9}{a^7}\right)^7$

19. $\left(\dfrac{3k^5m^8}{2k^3m^7}\right)^5$

20. $\left(\dfrac{10p^{12}n^7}{5p^3n^5}\right)^6$

For Problems 21 through 26, verify that the property of exponentiation works by evaluating the expression on the left and on the right, and showing that they are really equal.

21. $(3 \cdot 7)^5 = 3^5 \cdot 7^5$

22. $(2^3)^4 = 2^{12}$

23. $(3^2)^{10} = 3^{20}$

24. $5^7 \cdot 5^4 = 5^{11}$

25. $\dfrac{2^{25}}{2^5} = 2^{20}$

26. $\left(\dfrac{12}{4}\right)^5 = \dfrac{12^5}{4^5}$

For Problems 27 through 32, evaluate the expression. You may find that your calculator "overflows" if you try to evaluate the expressions without first simplifying them!

27. $\dfrac{3^{723}}{3^{721}}$

28. $\dfrac{7^{200}}{7^{198}}$

29. $\dfrac{7 \cdot 4^{2001}}{2 \cdot 4^{1997}}$

30. $\dfrac{8 \cdot 6^{1776}}{3 \cdot 6^{1773}}$

31. $\dfrac{(9^{54})^{10}}{(9^{49})^{11}}$

32. $\dfrac{(2^{1066})^{10}}{(2^{1184})^9}$

For Problems 33 through 38, give an example using the definition of exponentiation to show why the property works.

33. Power of a power

34. Power of a product

35. Product of two powers that have equal bases

36. Quotient of two powers that have equal bases

37. Exponentiation distributes over division

38. Exponentiation distributes over multiplication

39. Prove by counter-example that exponentiation does *not* distribute over addition.

40. Mae Danerror sees the equation $3^5 \cdot 3^8 = 3^{13}$, and asks, "Where did the other 3 go?" Convince Mae that there are just as many 3's on the right side of the equation as there are on the left.

41. ***Exponential Function Graphing Problem***   Given $f(x) = 1.5^x$.
   a.   Evaluate $f(4), f(3), f(2)$, and $f(1)$.
   b.   Evaluate $f(0), f(-1), f(-2)$, and $f(-3)$ by observing the pattern that each value equals the previous one divided by 1.5.
   c.   Verify that the *calculator gives the same answer* for $f(-3)$ as you got in part (b). The sequence of keystrokes is

   1.5 $\boxed{y^x}$ 3 $\boxed{+/-}$ $\boxed{=}$ (for algebraic logic)

   1.5 $\boxed{\text{enter}}$ 3 $\boxed{\text{chs}}$ $\boxed{y^x}$ (for RPN)

   d.   Plot the graph of f in the domain $-3 \le x \le 4$. If your work is correct, the graph should be a smooth curve. You may plot the graph by computer using PLOT EXPONENTIAL from the accompanying disk, or similar plotting program. If you do this, use the POINT option after you have plotted the graph to show that the points in parts (a) and (b) really are on the graph.
   e.   From your graph, estimate to one decimal place the value of x for which $f(x) = 2$. Show by calculator that this value of x really does give a value of $f(x)$ close to 2.

42. ***Fractional Exponents by Trial and Error***   Suppose that $f(x) = 3^x$, and you are to find the value of x that makes $f(x)$ equal to 17.
   a.   Explain how you know that the answer must be between 2 and 3.
   b.   By trial and error, find the two decimal place value of x that makes $f(x)$ closest to 17.

43. ***Ancestors Problem***   You have two first-generation ancestors, your (natural) parents. You have four second-generation ancestors, eight third-generation ancestors, and so on. Write an equation expressing the number of ancestors as a function of generation number. What kind of function is it? How many 20th-generation ancestors did you have?

44. If you have studied mathematical induction (Appendix B), prove that
   a. $x^a x^b = x^{a+b}$ for all integer values of $b \ge 1$.
   b. $(x^a)^b = x^{ab}$ for all integer values of $b \ge 1$.
   c. $(xy)^a = x^a y^a$ for all integer values of $a \ge 1$.

6-4 | EXPONENTIATION FOR RATIONAL EXPONENTS
_____

In the last two sections you have refreshed your memory about the definition and properties of exponentiation for positive integer exponents.

You have also seen that the calculator gives values for powers with *negative* exponents or *non-integer* exponents. For instance,

$$2^{-3} = 0.125, \qquad 2^{2 \cdot 5} = 5.656854. \ldots$$

You are now prepared to understand why calculators have been programmed to give the answers they do for such powers.

The property of the quotient of two powers with equal bases states that

$$\frac{x^a}{x^b} = x^{a-b}.$$

If *a* is *less* than *b*, the property leads to negative exponents. For example,

$$\frac{x^3}{x^5} = x^{3-5} = x^{-2}.$$

The actual answer can be found in writing out the *x*'s and canceling, as you did in Section 6-3.

$$\frac{x^3}{x^5} = \frac{x \cdot x \cdot x}{x \cdot x \cdot x \cdot x \cdot x} = \frac{1}{x^2}$$

So x^{-2} seems to equal the *reciprocal* of x^2. In order for the property to work with negative exponents, it is necessary to *define* negative exponents in terms of reciprocals.

DEFINITION

EXPONENTIATION FOR NEGATIVE EXPONENTS
The expression x^{-n} is defined to be

$$x^{-n} = \frac{1}{x^n}$$

Similarly, if *a* is *equal* to *b*, the property leads to a zero exponent. For example,

$$\frac{x^3}{x^3} = x^{3-3} = x^0.$$

The actual answer is 1, since any number (except 0) divided by itself gives 1. Again, to make the quotient of two powers property applicable for all exponents, it is necessary to define x^0 to be 1.

DEFINITION

> **EXPONENTIATION FOR 0 EXPONENT**
>
> $$\boxed{x^0 = 1}\ ,\ \text{provided } x \neq 0.$$

Fractional exponents have a surprising meaning! If the property of a power raised to a power is to work for all kinds of exponents, then the following must be true:

$$(x^{\frac{1}{3}})^3 = x^{(\frac{1}{3})(3)} = x^1 = x$$

So $x^{\frac{1}{3}}$ is a number that when *cubed* gives x for the answer. But this is just the meaning of *cube root*. In general, an nth *root of* x is a number that when raised to the n power gives x for the answer. The definition of reciprocal exponents follows from this meaning.

DEFINITION

> **EXPONENTIATION FOR RECIPROCAL EXPONENTS**
>
> $$\boxed{x^{\frac{1}{n}} = \sqrt[n]{x}}$$

The expression $\sqrt[n]{x}$ is called a *radical*. It is pronounced, "the nth root of x." The word "radical" comes from the same word as "radish," which is, as you well know, a kind of root! The parts of $\sqrt[n]{x}$ have names that you should learn and use.

n . . . *root index*   (It *points out* what root to take.)

x . . . *radicand*

$\sqrt{}$ . . . *radical sign*

— . . . a symbol of incluson (like parentheses) called a *vinculum*.

If the exponent is a fraction such as $\frac{3}{4}$, and the properties of exponentiation are still to be true, then

$$x^{\frac{3}{4}} = x^{(\frac{1}{4})(3)} = (x^{\frac{1}{4}})^3 = (\sqrt[4]{x})^3.$$

This leads to a general definition of fractional exponents.

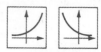

DEFINITION

EXPONENTIATION FOR FRACTIONAL EXPONENTS

$$x^{\frac{a}{b}} = (\sqrt[b]{x})^a$$

where a and b stand for integers.

With these definitions you have a precise meaning for a power with any
rational number for its exponent. Since an irrational number cannot be expressed as a ratio of integers, you still have no definition of exponentiation
for irrational exponents. However, you can evaluate expressions like 2^π or
$7^{\sqrt{5}}$ by using calculator approximations for the irrational exponents.

Objective:
Learn the definitions of exponentiation for rational exponents by evaluating
powers and by simplifying expressions involving rational exponents.

EXAMPLE 1

Evaluate $136^{\frac{3}{4}}$ two ways, first as $(136^{\frac{1}{4}})(136^{\frac{1}{4}})(136^{\frac{1}{4}})$, then directly as
$136^{0.75}$. Show that the two answers are equal. Explain how what you have
done confirms the definition of exponentiation for fractional exponents.

Solution:
Press 136 $\boxed{y^x}$ 4 $\boxed{1/x}$ $\boxed{=}$. The result is 3.41495. . . .
Store the answer in the calculator's memory. Then press
$\boxed{RCL}$ $\boxed{\times}$ $\boxed{RCL}$ $\boxed{\times}$ $\boxed{RCL}$ $\boxed{=}$. The result is *39.82485*. . . . Next,
press 136 $\boxed{y^x}$ 0.75 $\boxed{=}$. The result is *39.82485*. . . The two answers are
the *same*. This confirms that $136^{\frac{3}{4}}$ equals $\left(136^{\frac{1}{4}}\right)^3$, or $(\sqrt[4]{136})^3$. The sequence of keystrokes for an RPN calculator is

136 $\boxed{enter}$ 4 $\boxed{1/x}$ $\boxed{y^x}$
$\boxed{enter}$ $\boxed{enter}$ $\boxed{\times}$ $\boxed{\times}$ ■

EXAMPLE 2

Evaluate $\sqrt[6]{85.766121}$ using the definition of fractional exponents. Confirm
that your answer is right by multiplication.

Solution:

$$\sqrt[6]{85.766121} = 85.766121^{\frac{1}{6}}$$

The sequence of keystrokes is

85.766121 $\boxed{y^x}$ 6 $\boxed{1/x}$ $\boxed{=}$. The answer is <u>2.1.</u>

For an RPN calculator, press 85.766121 $\boxed{\text{enter}}$ 6 $\boxed{1/x}$ $\boxed{y^x}$.

To verify the answer, multiply $(2.1)(2.1)(2.1)(2.1)(2.1)(2.1)$. The answer is *85.766121*. ∎

EXAMPLE 3

Simplify: $\dfrac{(6x^{\frac{2}{7}}y^{-4}z^0)^3}{9x^2y^5z^{-8}}$

Solution:

$\dfrac{(6x^{\frac{2}{7}}y^{-4}z^0)^3}{9x^2y^5z^{-8}}$

$= \dfrac{216x^{\frac{6}{7}}y^{-12}z^0}{9x^2y^5z^{-8}}$ Distribute the exponent 3 to *all* numerator factors.

$= 24x^{-\frac{8}{7}}y^{-17}z^8$ Divide the constants and the powers with equal bases. ∎

EXERCISE 6-4

Do These Quickly

The following problems are intended to refresh your skills. You should be able to do all 10 in less than 5 minutes.

Q1.   Write as a power: $x \cdot x \cdot x \cdot x \cdot x \cdot x$

Q2.   Write 81 as a power that has 3 as its base.

Q3.   Write 64 as a power that has 3 as its exponent.

Q4.   Evaluate $(-3)^4$.

Q5.   Find 3% of 300.

Q6.   Sketch the graph of a quadratic function whose equation has a negative x^2 term.

Q7.   Solve: $x^2 = 9$

Q8.   Factor: $2x^2 - 3x + 1$

Q9.   Evaluate the determinant: $\begin{vmatrix} 5 & 7 \\ 4 & 9 \end{vmatrix}$

Q10.   Tell the axiom used: $(3)(x + y) = (x + y)(3)$

Work the following problems.

1. Evaluate 3^{-2} mentally, using the definition of negative exponents. Then evaluate 3^{-2} by calculator. Show that the two answers are equal.

2. Evaluate 5^0 mentally, using the definition of zero exponent. Then evaluate 5^0 by calculator and show that you get the same answer.

3. Evaluate $57^{\frac{1}{3}}$ by calculator. Store the answer in memory. Tell why the answer is reasonable. Then cube the answer by multiplying (answer)(answer)(answer). Tell in words why what you have done confirms the definition of powers with reciprocal exponents.

4. Evaluate $70^{\frac{1}{5}}$ by calculator and save it in memory. Next, cube the answer by multiplying (answer)(answer)(answer), and save that result in memory. Finally, evaluate $70^{\frac{3}{5}}$ directly by calculator. Tell in words why what you have done confirms the definition of powers with fractional exponents.

5. Evaluate $64^{\frac{1}{3}}$ by first writing 64 as a power of 2 and operating with the exponents. Then evaluate $64^{\frac{1}{3}}$ directly by calculator. Tell in words how what you have just done explains *why* powers with fractional exponents are defined the way they are.

6. Evaluate $(\frac{1}{4})^{-3}$ by first using the definition of negative exponents, then cubing. Simplify the answer as much as possible. Then evaluate $(\frac{1}{4})^{-3}$ directly by calculator. Tell in words how what you have just done explains *why* powers with negative exponents are defined the way they are.

7. Evaluate $\frac{7^3}{7^3}$ by first subtracting the exponents. Then evaluate $\frac{7^3}{7^3}$ by multiplying out the numerator and denominator, then canceling. Tell in words how what you have just done explains the reason *why* a power with exponent zero is defined the way it is.

8. Evaluate $\sqrt{789}$ by writing it as a power with a fractional exponent. Then evaluate $\sqrt{789}$ directly with the square root key on your calculator. Show that the answers are the same. Also, show that when you square either answer you get 789.

9. Hy Pertension loses points on a test for saying that $8^{-\frac{1}{3}}$ equals $\frac{1}{(8^3)}$. Tell Hy what error he made, and how to avoid it in the future.

10. *Powers of Zero Problem*
    a. Evaluate 0^5.
    b. Evaluate 5^0.

c. Wanda Ngo thinks that any number to the 0 power is 1, and 0 to any power is 0. She wants to know whether 0^0 equals 1 or 0. Tell her the correct answer.

d. Ira Member presses 0^{-3} on his calculator and gets an "error" message. What should he remember to explain this result?

For Problems 11 through 18, evaluate the radical using the definition of reciprocal exponents. Check your answer by multiplication.

11. $\sqrt[5]{437}$

12. $\sqrt[8]{58713}$

13. $\sqrt[4]{99735}$

14. $\sqrt[10]{1020301}$

15. $\sqrt[7]{279936}$

16. $\sqrt[9]{40353607}$

17. $\sqrt{73157}$

18. $\sqrt{55696}$

For Problems 19 through 46, use the properties of exponentiation to simplify the expression. Write the answers as products of powers, with no variables in denominators.

19. $6x^5 \cdot 3x^{-2}$

20. $7x^{-3} \cdot 8x^9$

21. $5x^{-4} \cdot 2x^{-3}$

22. $9x^{-2} \cdot 6x^{-5}$

23. $3a^{-11} \cdot 17a^5$

24. $11p^7 \cdot 4p^{-12}$

25. $(-2x^2)^3(3x^{-1}y^2)^4$

26. $(4x^3)^2(-2x^{-3}y^{-1})^3$

27. $(3x^2y^{-3})^4(2x^{-4}y^5)^3$

28. $(5a^3b^{-2})^4(5a^{-4}b^{-5})^{-2}$

29. $(7a^{-5}b^6) \div (21a^4b^{-2})$

30. $(1001x^{-4}y^{-3}) \div (77x^6y^{-7})$

31. $\dfrac{5}{a^{-2}} - \dfrac{3}{a^{-1}}$

32. $\dfrac{7}{x^{-5}} - \dfrac{4}{x^{-1}}$

33. $\dfrac{x^{-1}y^{-4}z}{x^{-2}yz^{-3}}$

34. $\dfrac{r^{-5}st^{-3}}{r^{-1}s^{-5}t}$

35. $\dfrac{13x^5y^{-2}z^0}{39xy^{-3}z^2}$

36. $\dfrac{3^4a^{-7}b^3d^{-4}}{43^0a^{-4}b^{-5}c^6}$

37. $(3758x^{89})^{-53}(3758x^{89})^{53}$

38. $(490x^{17}y^{23})^0$

39. $3x^{-\frac{1}{2}} \cdot 4x^{\frac{2}{3}}$

40. $5x^{-\frac{1}{2}} \cdot 6x^{\frac{1}{8}}$

41. $(4x^{-\frac{1}{2}})^3 \div (9x^{\frac{1}{3}})^{-\frac{3}{2}}$

42. $(64x^2)^{-\frac{1}{6}}(32x^5)^{-\frac{2}{5}}$

43. $\dfrac{u^{3.7}p^{4.8}}{u^{-2.9}p^{1.8}}$

44. $\dfrac{d^{-4.3}v^{1.5}}{d^{-3.7}v^{-2}}$

45. $\sqrt[4]{x^{12}y^7}$

46. $\sqrt[5]{m^{30}k^{32}}$

47. *Increasing and Decreasing Exponential Functions Problem*
     $f(x) = 1.5^x$ and let $g(x) = 0.3^x$.
     a. Plot accurate graphs of functions f and g in the domain
         $0 \le x \le 2$. You may use a computer graphics program such as
         PLOT EXPONENTIAL on the accompanying disk. If you plot
         the graphs on paper, pick enough values of x, both integer and
         decimal, to get smooth curves.
     b. In what way do the two graphs differ? In what way are they the
         same?
     c. A function h is defined to be *increasing* on its domain if
         $h(x_2) > h(x_1)$ whenever $x_2 > x_1$ (and, of course, the x's are in
         the domain). Which function, f or g, above, is increasing on
         $0 \le x \le 2$?
     d. For an exponential function $e(x) = b^x$, how do you tell just by
         looking at the particular equation whether it will be increasing
         or decreasing?

48. *Money Doubling Problem*   Suppose your parents agree to pay you
     one cent today, two cents tomorrow (the first day after today), four
     cents the next day (second day after today), and so forth. Each time
     they double the amount they pay you. Write an equation expressing
     amount paid in terms of number of days after today. What kind of
     function is this? How much will they pay you the 30th day? Surpris-
     ing?! Show that the amount paid today (0 days after today) agrees
     with the definition of zero exponents.

6-5 | POWERS AND RADICALS WITHOUT CALCULATORS

You have learned how to raise numbers to powers where the exponent is
any rational number, positive or negative. It is important for you to develop your ability to do such operations quickly, in your head, when the
numbers are relatively small and "come out even." In this section you will
learn ways to do this.

Objective:
Given an expression containing radicals or fractional exponents, evaluate it
quickly in your head, using a calculator only to check your answer.

EXAMPLE 1

Evaluate $8^{\frac{2}{3}}$.

Solution:
Your thought process should be something like this: "Cube-root the 8, getting 2. Square the 2, getting 4." ∎

In order to work such a problem mentally, you must recognize that 8 is 2^3, so that the cube root of 8 is 2. If you don't recognize this fact, you can figure it out by multiplying enough 2's to get 8 for the answer.

EXAMPLE 2

Evaluate $216^{\frac{4}{3}}$.

Solution:

Since the base, 216, is relatively large, you may have to factor it first to express it as powers. A clever scheme for doing this is shown at the right. The procedure might best be described as "upside-down short division." 2 into 216 is 108. The 108 is written below the 216, as shown in the first step. The process is continued, always dividing by the *smallest prime* that divides the current quotient. The prime factors of 216 appear on the left, outside the division signs. So

First Step:

$$\begin{array}{r} 2)\underline{\ 216\ } \\ 108 \end{array}$$

All Steps:

$$\begin{array}{r} 2)\underline{\ 216\ } \\ 2)\underline{\ 108\ } \\ 2)\underline{\ 54\ } \\ 3)\underline{27} \\ 3)\underline{9} \\ 3 \end{array}$$

$$216 = 2 \cdot 2 \cdot 2 \cdot 3 \cdot 3 \cdot 3 = 2^3 \cdot 3^3.$$

To evaluate $216^{\frac{4}{3}}$, you would write

$$216^{\frac{4}{3}}$$

$$= (2^3 \cdot 3^3)^{\frac{4}{3}} \quad \text{Factor the base.}$$

$$= 2^4 \cdot 3^4 \quad \text{Distribute the } \frac{4}{3}.$$

$$= 16 \cdot 81$$

$$= 1296 \quad \blacksquare$$

Radical expressions can sometimes be simplified without getting a decimal approximation. The procedure is to transform the radicals to powers with fractional exponents. Then you can use the properties of exponents to do the simplification.

EXAMPLE 3

Simplify $\sqrt[6]{256} \div \sqrt[4]{64}$.

Solution:

$$\sqrt[6]{256} \div \sqrt[4]{64}$$

$$= 256^{\frac{1}{6}} \div 64^{\frac{1}{4}} \quad \text{Transform to exponential form.}$$

$$= (2^8)^{\frac{1}{6}} \div (2^6)^{\frac{1}{4}} \quad 256 = 2^8 \text{ and } 64 = 2^6$$

$$= 2^{\frac{4}{3}} \div 2^{\frac{3}{2}}$$ Multiply the exponents and simplify.

$$= 2^{-\frac{1}{6}}$$ Subtract the exponents.

The answer may also be written in radical form, $\dfrac{1}{\sqrt[6]{2}}$.

EXAMPLE 4

256 equals 4^4 and also 16^2. Explain *why*.

Solution:
4^4 equals $(2^2)^4$, which equals 2^8.
16^2 equals $(2^4)^2$, which also equals 2^8.
Since 2^8 equals 256, both 4^4 and 16^2 equal 256.

In the following exercise you will get practice evaluating radicals and powers mentally.

EXERCISE 6-5

Do These Quickly

The following problems are intended to refresh your skills. You should be able to do all 10 in less than 5 minutes.

Q1.   Evaluate: $\sqrt{25}$

Q2.   Evaluate: $\sqrt[3]{8}$

Q3.   Write 81 as a power that has 3 as its base.

Q4.   Write in terms of i: $\sqrt{-81}$

Q5.   What percent of 500 is 20?

Q6.   Sketch the graph of a linear function with a negative slope and a positive y-intercept.

Q7.   Solve: $2^x = 8$

Q8.   Simplify: $\dfrac{36}{24}$

Q9.   Solve for n: $\dfrac{u}{p} = \dfrac{i}{n}$

Q10.   Tell the axiom used: $(3)(x + y) = 3x + 3y$

Work the following problems.

1. *Table of Powers Problem*   Use a calculator, where necessary, to make a short table of powers of integers. Your table should include 2^2 through 2^{10}, 3^2 through 3^6, 4^2 through 4^5, 5^2 through 5^4, and the squares and cubes of 6, 7, 8, 9, 10, 11, and 12. It is not necessary for you to memorize these numbers, but recognizing them should be part of your repertoire as a literate (or numerate?) mathematics student.

2. Certain numbers in the table of Problem 1 appear more than once. Which ones? For each number, explain *why* it appears more than once.

For Problems 3–12, evaluate the radical mentally.

3. $\sqrt[3]{64}$

4. $\sqrt[4]{81}$

5. $\sqrt[4]{625}$

6. $\sqrt[5]{1024}$

7. $\sqrt[3]{216}$

8. $\sqrt[3]{343}$

9. $\sqrt[5]{32}$

10. $\sqrt[3]{512}$

11. $\sqrt{1024}$

12. $\sqrt{625}$

For Problems 13 through 38, evaluate the power mentally. Write the answer in *exact* form, as a fraction if necessary. You may check your answer by calculator.

13. $64^{\frac{2}{3}}$

14. $64^{\frac{3}{2}}$

15. $64^{\frac{5}{6}}$

16. $64^{\frac{7}{6}}$

17. $64^{-\frac{3}{2}}$

18. $64^{-\frac{2}{3}}$

19. $(-64)^{\frac{2}{3}}$

20. $(-64)^{\frac{3}{2}}$

21. $-64^{\frac{2}{3}}$

22. $-64^{\frac{3}{2}}$

23. $32^{-\frac{6}{5}}$

24. $-32^{-\frac{6}{5}}$

25. $128^{\frac{2}{7}}$

26. $256^{\frac{3}{4}}$

27. $81^{-\frac{3}{2}}$

28. $243^{-\frac{4}{5}}$

29. $343^{\frac{2}{3}}$

30. $36^{\frac{3}{2}}$

31. $-100^{-\frac{3}{2}}$

32. $-1000^{-\frac{2}{3}}$

33. $\left(\dfrac{9}{49}\right)^{-\frac{3}{2}}$

34. $\left(\dfrac{256}{625}\right)^{-\frac{3}{4}}$

35. $\left(-\dfrac{729}{64}\right)^{-\frac{2}{3}}$

36. $\left(-\dfrac{125}{27}\right)^{-\frac{4}{3}}$

37. $1728^{\frac{1}{3}}$

38. $121^{\frac{1}{2}}$

For Problems 39 through 52, simplify the expression by first transforming the radicals to exponential form. Leave the answer in *exact* form as a radical or a power, not as a decimal approximation. You may check your answer using a calculator.

39. $\sqrt{6} \div \sqrt{2}$

40. $\sqrt[3]{88} \div \sqrt[3]{11}$

41. $\sqrt{8} \div \sqrt[4]{32}$

42. $\sqrt[3]{81} \div \sqrt[5]{729}$

43. $\sqrt[3]{128} \cdot \sqrt{32}$

44. $\sqrt[3]{81} \cdot \sqrt[3]{9}$

45. $\sqrt[3]{2^{3.1}} \div 2^{0.7}$

46. $\sqrt[5]{7^{9.8}} \div 7^{1.6}$

47. $\sqrt[5]{10^{4.4} \times 10^{-6.3} \div 10^{-8.1}}$

48. $\sqrt{10^{2.6} \times 10^{0.5} \div 10^{1.5}}$

49. $\sqrt[4]{\sqrt[3]{16}}$

50. $\sqrt{\sqrt[3]{64}}$

51. $\sqrt{\sqrt[3]{36}}$

52. $\sqrt[3]{\sqrt[4]{\sqrt[5]{7}}}$

For Problems 53 through 60, find the value of x. You must be clever to do this, since no example is given!

53. $64^x = 4$

54. $64^x = 8$

55. $49^x = 343$

56. $144^x = 1728$

57. $2^x = 1024$

58. $512^x = 4$

59. $625^x = 1$

60. $36^x = 0$

61. *Areas and Volumes Problem*   Quick! Answer the following.
    a.   How many cubic inches in a cubic foot?
    b.   How many cubic feet in a cubic yard?
    c.   How many square inches in a square foot?
    d.   How many square feet in a square yard?
    e.   How many square centimeters in a square meter?
    f.   How many cubic centimeters in a cubic meter?
    g.   How many cubic meters in a cubic kilometer?

62. *Exponential Function Graphing Problem*   Given $f(x) = 32^x$,
    a.   Evaluate $f(0), f(0.2), f(0.4), f(0.6), f(0.8)$, and $f(1)$ mentally, without the use of a calculator.
    b.   Plot the graph of function f in the domain $0 \le x \le 1$. Use a large enough scale for the x-axis so that the graph has reasonable proportions.
    c.   The value of $f(0.5)$ is between $f(0.4)$ and $f(0.6)$. From your graph, does it seem to be closer to $f(0.4)$, closer to $f(0.6)$, or exactly halfway between?

63. *Negative Bases Problem*   Raising negative bases to non-integer powers can produce awkward and contradictory results.
    a.   Evaluate $(-8)^{\frac{1}{3}}$.

b.   Evaluate $(-8)^{\frac{2}{6}}$ by squaring first, then taking the sixth root.

c.   Explain why evaluating $(-8)^{\frac{2}{6}}$ by taking the sixth root first takes you out of the set of real numbers.

d. $\frac{1}{3}$ equals $\frac{2}{6}$. Can equals be substituted for equals in an expression such as $(-8)^{\frac{1}{3}}$? Later in your mathematical career you will learn De Moivre's Theorem. That theorem allows you to conclude that there are 3 cube roots of a number and 6 sixth roots. You get the roots in a different order, depending on which operation you do first.

6-6 | SCIENTIFIC NOTATION

"Quick!" somebody says. "About how big is 32418 times 1934?" You think for a moment, then reply, "About 60 million." The secret to such quick mental computation is converting the numbers to *scientific notation*. In this section you will learn how.

Try to evaluate 365^6 on your calculator. Most calculators will display something like this:

$$2.3645973 \ \ 15$$

It means

$$2.3645973 \times 10^{15},$$

which is a rounded-off version of the exact answer,

$$2{,}364{,}597{,}285{,}765{,}625.$$

In 2.3645973×10^{15} the decimal point has been moved 15 places to the left so that it is between the first two digits of the number. Multiplying by 10^{15} compensates for this move. The calculator rounds off the decimal number to 2.3645973, or to whatever number is short enough to fit in its display. A number in this form is said to be in scientific notation.

The two parts of a number in scientific notation have special names. The factor on the left has the decimal point behind the first (non-zero) digit. It is called the *mantissa*. The factor to the right is a power of 10. Its exponent is called the *characteristic*.

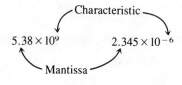

DEFINITION

> **SCIENTIFIC NOTATION**
> A number is in **scientific notation** if and only if it is written in the form
>
> $$\text{mantissa} \times 10^{\text{characteristic}},$$
>
> where the **mantissa** is a number between 1 and 10 (including 1, but not including 10), and the **characteristic** is an integer that tells how many places the decimal point has been moved.

The word "mantissa" comes from a Eutruscan word meaning "make weight." A makeweight is a small slice of meat the butcher puts with what is already on the scale to *make* the *weight* come out right. From its name, you can tell that the mantissa is less significant than the power of 10 that "characterizes" the number.

The number of *significant digits* in a number in scientific notation is the number of digits in the mantissa. For instance,

$$5.38 \times 10^9 \qquad \text{has 3 significant digits,}$$

$$2.345 \times 10^{-6} \qquad \text{has 4 significant digits.}$$

Objectives:

1. Transform numbers to or from scientific notation.
2. Multiply or divide numbers in scientific notation, either mentally to get an approximate answer, or by calculator to get a precise answer.

EXAMPLE 1

Write in scientific notation:
a. 3250000
b. 0.007814

Solution:

a. To get the decimal point in the desired place it must move from the right end of the number (where it is by implication) to the space between the 2 and the 3.

$$3250000.$$

6 places

This requires a move of 6 places, as shown above. Therefore,

$$3250000 = 3.25 \times 10^6$$

b. To get the decimal point in the desired place it must move 3 places to the right, between the 7 and the 8.

$$0.00\underset{\smile}{7}814$$

3 places

Therefore,

$$0.007814 = 7.814 \times 10^{-3}$$ ∎

The tricky part of these transformations is deciding whether the exponent is positive or negative. The most reliable way is to tell yourself, "The $'='$ sign must tell the *truth*." When you multiply the mantissa and the power of 10 back together, you must get the original number.

OBSERVATION

EXPONENT SIGN IN SCIENTIFIC NOTATION
If you make one factor smaller by moving the decimal point, you must make the power of 10 larger (by increasing its exponent), and vice versa, so that the number you get for the answer equals the number you started with.

EXAMPLE 2

Multiply $(3 \times 10^{17})(4 \times 10^{-38})$ mentally. Write the answer in scientific notation.

Solution:

$(3 \times 10^{17})(4 \times 10^{-38})$

$= 12 \times 10^{-21}$ Multiply the mantissas. Add the characteristics.

$= 1.2 \times 10^{-20}$ If you decrease the mantissa, you must increase the characteristic so that the $"="$ sign tells the truth.   ∎

If the numbers are too untidy to multiply or divide in your head, you can either round them to 1 significant digit first and get an approximate answer, or use the scientific notation feature of a calculator. To enter a number such as 5.941×10^{-8}, you use the "enter exponent" key, usually marked $\boxed{\text{exp}}$, $\boxed{\text{eex}}$, or $\boxed{\text{ee}}$. The sequence of keystrokes is

5.941 $\boxed{\text{exp}}$ 8 $\boxed{+/-}$ (for algebraic logic),

5.941 $\boxed{\text{eex}}$ 8 $\boxed{\text{chs}}$ (for RPN)

EXAMPLE 3

Divide $\dfrac{7.41 \times 10^{13}}{5.941 \times 10^{-8}}$

a. approximately, by rounding and dividing mentally,
b. precisely, by calculator, rounding the answer appropriately.

Solution:

a. $\dfrac{7.41 \times 10^{13}}{5.941 \times 10^{-8}} \approx \underline{1 \times 10^{21}}$

The thought process should be, "7.41 is about 7. 5.941 is about 6. 7 divided by 6 is about 1. Subtracting the exponents, $13 - (-8)$ is 21. So the answer is about 1×10^{21}."

b. $\dfrac{7.41 \times 10^{13}}{5.941 \times 10^{-8}}$

$= 1.247264\ldots \times 10^{21}$ By calculator

$\approx \underline{1.25 \times 10^{21}}$ Rounding off   ■

Numbers in scientific notation are usually assumed to be decimal approximations. Therefore, answers to multiplication or division problems can be no more accurate than the *least* accurate of the numbers. This is why the answer in Example 3 was rounded to three significant digits.

AGREEMENT

ROUND-OFF IN MULTIPLICATION OR DIVISION
The answer to a multiplication or division problem involving approximate numbers should be rounded to the number of significant digits in the *least* accurate factor of the numerator and denominator.

Note that the words "*precise*" and "*accurate*" have different meanings. In Example 3, for instance, the 1.247264 is a more *precise* value of the quotient than 1.25. But it is *not* necessarily more accurate. Accuracy refers to how closely an answer fits a *real* world quantity being measured, and depends on how accurately the input numbers are known. Precision refers only to how closely an answer fits for the two numbers that were actually used in the computation.

EXERCISE 6-6

Do These Quickly

The following problems are intended to refresh your skills. You should be able to do all 10 in less than 5 minutes.

Q1.   Write 10,000 as a power that has 10 as its base.

Q2.   Multiply the complex numbers: $(2 + 3i)(5 + 4i)$

Q3.   Factor: $9x^2 - 25y^4$

Q4.   Multiply and simplify: $\left(\dfrac{2}{3}\right)\left(\dfrac{5}{6}\right)$

Q5.   20 is 30% of what number?

Q6.   Sketch the graph of a linear inequality.

Q7.   Solve: $2^x = 32$

Q8.   How far do you drive in 4 hours at 55 miles per hour?

Q9.   Solve for: p: $\dfrac{u}{p} = \dfrac{i}{n}$

Q10. Evaluate: 36^0

Work the following problems.

For Problems 1 through 10, transform to scientific notation.

1.   372000   2.   57260

3.   0.00261   4.   0.0005423

5.   2001   6.   98.6

7.   0.2024   8.   0.9999

9.   24.7 million   10. 468 million

For Problems 11 through 30, do the operations in your *head*, without using a calculator. Write the answer in scientific notation.

11. $(2 \times 10^7)(3 \times 10^8)$ 12. $(2 \times 10^5)(4 \times 10^8)$

13. $(7 \times 10^4)(5 \times 10^{11})$ 14. $(5 \times 10^7)(9 \times 10^8)$

15. $(6 \times 10^3)(7 \times 10^{-8})$

16. $(9 \times 10^6)(7 \times 10^{-13})$

17. $(9 \times 10^{-5})(6 \times 10^5)$

18. $(8 \times 10^{-7})(6 \times 10^7)$

19. $(8 \times 10^{-4})(7 \times 10^{-20})$

20. $(4 \times 10^{-5})(7 \times 10^{-10})$

21. $\dfrac{8 \times 10^{15}}{2 \times 10^4}$

22. $\dfrac{8 \times 10^{17}}{4 \times 10^8}$

23. $\dfrac{6 \times 10^4}{3 \times 10^{11}}$

24. $\dfrac{6 \times 10^5}{2 \times 10^{12}}$

25. $\dfrac{7 \times 10^5}{2 \times 10^{-3}}$

26. $\dfrac{9 \times 10^3}{2 \times 10^{-7}}$

27. $\dfrac{4 \times 10^{-3}}{2 \times 10^{-12}}$

28. $\dfrac{8 \times 10^{-9}}{2 \times 10^{-7}}$

29. $\dfrac{6 \times 10^{-8}}{5 \times 10^8}$

30. $\dfrac{8 \times 10^{-4}}{5 \times 10^4}$

For Problems 31 through 38, use a calculator to evaluate the expression. Write the answer in scientific notation, with the appropriate number of significant digits.

31. $(4.9 \times 10^{17})(1.345 \times 10^{-5})$

32. $(9.06 \times 10^{-9})(5.224 \times 10^3)$

33. $(1.79 \times 10^{-4})(9.7 \times 10^{-9})$

34. $(1.72 \times 10^{-5})(3.6 \times 10^{-11})$

35. $\dfrac{4.976 \times 10^{-8}}{8.2 \times 10^5}$

36. $\dfrac{7.732 \times 10^{-7}}{9.63 \times 10^3}$

37. $\dfrac{6.802 \times 10^{-7}}{5.1996 \times 10^{-11}}$

38. $\dfrac{7.6 \times 10^4}{9.83 \times 10^{-11}}$

For Problems 39 through 60, multiply or divide mentally by first converting to scientific notation (if necessary) and rounding to one significant digit. The answer should also have one significant digit. You may check your answers by calculator, but only after you have done the mental arithmetic.

39. $(2.05 \times 10^6)(3.12 \times 10^7)$

40. $(3.87 \times 10^4)(2.11 \times 10^8)$

41. $(1.3 \times 10^{-5})(4.253 \times 10^{12})$

42. $(8.15 \times 10^3)(2.296 \times 10^{-18})$

43. $(7.9 \times 10^{11})(4.1253 \times 10^5)$

44. $(8.792 \times 10^6)(5.31 \times 10^7)$

45. $(4.83 \times 10^{20})(7.96 \times 10^{-8})$

46. $(3.98 \times 10^{-14})(6.818 \times 10^{19})$

47. $(2.021 \times 10^{-7})(3.95 \times 10^{-8})$

48. $(3.29 \times 10^{-3})(1.9532 \times 10^{-4})$

49. $(8.7 \times 10^{-13})(3.21 \times 10^5)$

50. $(9.032 \times 10^4)(7.91 \times 10^{-17})$

51. $\dfrac{8.043 \times 10^{11}}{2.15 \times 10^4}$

52. $\dfrac{7.76 \times 10^{13}}{3.1 \times 10^5}$

53. $\dfrac{5.97 \times 10^8}{4.31 \times 10^{15}}$

54. $\dfrac{8.92 \times 10^4}{2.6 \times 10^{17}}$

55. $\dfrac{2.11 \times 10^{-9}}{7.94 \times 10^3}$

56. $\dfrac{4.15 \times 10^{-19}}{5.11 \times 10^{-4}}$

57. $(3115)(293)$

58. $(1933)(40556)$

59. $(7811)(41997)$

60. $(58667)(321)$

For Problems 61 through 64, find the reciprocal of the given number.

61. 5.87×10^4

62. 2.93×10^5

63. 1.62×10^{-7}

64. 7.8×10^{-9}

For Problems 65 through 70, raise the number to the indicated power.

65. $(2.34 \times 10^5)^2$

66. $(1.29 \times 10^7)^2$

67. $(4.08 \times 10^{-5})^2$

68. $(6.13 \times 10^{-6})^2$

69. $(8.97 \times 10^4)^3$

70. $(7.21 \times 10^5)^3$

71. **Brain Cell Problem**   The average human brain has about 8 billion neurons. There are about 230 million people in the United States. About how many neurons, total, do these people have? Answer in scientific notation.

72. **Heartbeat Problem**   The average life expectancy of women in the United States is about 76 years. The heart beats about once every 0.9 seconds. About how many times does an average woman's heart beat in a lifetime?

73. **Rainfall Problem**   One day it rains one-tenth of an inch. Disappointed over the small amount of rain, Calvin Butterball seeks to find out how much water fell on his 1 square mile of land. He knows that a cubic foot of water weighs 62.4 pounds. How many pounds of water fell on his land?

74. **Exponential Function Graphing Problem**   Given $f(x) = 10^x$.
    a.   Evaluate $f(0), f(0.2), f(0.4), f(0.6), f(0.8),$ and $f(1)$.
    b.   Plot the graph of function f in the domain $0 \le x \le 1$. Use a large enough scale for the x-axis so that the graph has reasonable proportions. You may use the program PLOT EXPONENTIAL from the accompanying disk.

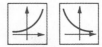

c. Suppose you are told that $f(c)$ is exactly 3. From your graph, estimate the value of c to one decimal place. You can use the
LINE option of PLOT EXPONENTIAL in clever ways to do
this.

d. Confirm that your value of c in part (c) is reasonable by evaluating $f(c)$ and showing that the answer is close to 3.

e. By trial and error, find the value of c correct to *three* decimal
places. See if you can figure out an efficient way to do this.

6-7 | EXPONENTIAL EQUATIONS SOLVED BY BRUTE
     | FORCE

Suppose that $f(x) = 2^x$, and you are asked to find the value of x that
makes $f(x)$ equal 10. As shown in Figure 6-7a, x is somewhere between 3
and 4. To find the exact value, you can set $f(x) = 10$.

$$10 = 2^x$$

This is called an *exponential equation* because the variable is an exponent.
Although the equation looks simple, it cannot be solved explicitly for x using just the operations of algebra you know! In this section you will see
how to find approximate solutions by trial and error.

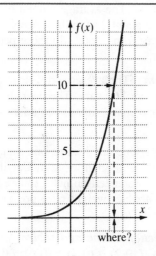

Figure 6-7a

Objective:
Be able to solve an exponential equation by trial and error using either calculator or computer.

EXAMPLE

Given $f(x) = 2^x$, find, correct to 5 decimal places, the value of x that makes $f(x) = 10$.

Solution:
Your thought process should be something like this:

x must be between 3 and 4 because 2^3 is 8 and 2^4 is 16.

$$2^{3.1} = 8.574. . . \qquad \text{(Too small.)}$$
$$2^{3.2} = 9.189. . . \qquad \text{(Too small.)}$$
$$2^{3.3} = 9.849. . . \qquad \text{(Too small.)}$$
$$2^{3.4} = 10.556. . . \qquad \text{(Too big!)}$$

$$2^{3.31} = 9.9588. . . \qquad \text{(Too small.)}$$
$$2^{3.32} = 9.9933. . . \qquad \text{(Too small.)}$$
$$2^{3.33} = 10.0563. . . \qquad \text{(Too big!)}$$

$$2^{3.321} = 9.99356. . . \qquad \text{(Too small.)}$$
(and so forth.)

Continuing this process leads to $x \approx 3.32193$. All you need to write down is the question and the answer, like this:

$$10 = 2^x$$

$$x \approx 3.32193$$

The rest of the work is done on the calculator.   ■

A systematic trial-and-error process such as in the example is called an **iterative** process. The system shown in the example is tedious by calculator, but easy to program on a computer. In the following exercise you will solve exponential equations iteratively, first by calculator, then by computer.

EXERCISE 6-7

Do These Quickly

The following problems are intended to refresh your skills. You should be able to do all 10 in less than 5 minutes.

Q1.   Solve: $3^x = 81$

Q2.   Solve: $10^x = 0.001$

Q3.   Evaluate: 2^3

Q4.   Draw $-4 + i$ on the complex-number plane.

Q5.   What is 15% of 10^3?

Q6.   Draw a parallelogram.

Q7.   Multiply: $(3x + 5)(2x - 7)$

Q8.   If you go 55 miles in 4 hours, what is your average speed?

Q9.   Solve for i: $\dfrac{u}{p} = \dfrac{i}{n}$

Q10.   Evaluate: 0^{36}

Work the following problems.

1.   *Iterative Solution Problem*   Given: $f(x) = 1.7^x$.
   a.   Plot an accurate graph of function f if the domain is
        $-5 \le x \le 5$.
   b.   Calculate $f(3.721)$. Show that this point is on the graph.
   c.   From your graph, approximately what is the value of x if
        $f(x) = 4$? (Answer correct to 1 decimal place.)
   d.   Evaluate $f(x)$ for the value of x you found in part (c). This value
        should be close to, but not quite equal to 4.
   e.   Get a *five* significant digit approximation for the value of x in
        part (c). You may try short-cuts in the iteration process.
   f.   Find a five significant digit approximation for the value of x that
        makes $f(x) = 0.5$.

2.   *Iterative Origin Problem*   Look up the verb "iterate" in a dictionary
     and write down its origin. What do you suppose the word "reiterate"
     really means?

For Problems 3 through 8, solve the exponential equations correct to
3 significant digits.

3. $3^x = 20$ 4. $4^x = 87$

5. $5^x = 0.4$ 6. $6^x = 0.2$

7. $7^x = -15$ 8. $9^x = 0$

9.   *Computer Program for Evaluating Functions*   The program EVAL-
     UATE FUNCTION on the accompanying disk finds function values
     between two specified values of x. Use the program in an appropriate
     manner to find a 5 decimal place approximation for the solution of

$$7^x = 85.$$

10. *Iterative Computer Program*   Write a computer program (or adapt the program EVALUATE FUNCTION) to solve iteratively an equation of the form

$$\text{constant} = f(x).$$

The program should use the iterative technique shown in the example.

For Problems 11 through 16, solve the equation iteratively using the computer program of Problem 10. Get the answers to 6 decimal places.

11. $4^x = 97$ 12. $3^x = 42$

13. $6^x = 0.01$ 14. $5^x = 0.001$

15. $1.03^x = 100$ 16. $0.96^x = 1001$

17. *Compound Interest Problem*   If $1000 is put into a savings account that pays 6% interest per year, compounded once a year, then the amount of money in the account at the end of x years is given by

$$m(x) = 1000 \times 1.06^x.$$

a. How much money is in the account at the end of 10 years? How much of this was interest?

b. How much money is in the account at the end of 30 years? True or false: "The amount of interest earned in 30 years is 3 times the amount earned in 10 years."

c. How much money is in the account at the end of 100 years? Surprising?

d. What is the minimum number of years needed to at least *double* the $1000?

6-8   EXPONENTIAL EQUATIONS SOLVED BY LOGARITHMS

In the last section you solved exponential equations such as

$$10^x = 3$$

by trial and error. In this section you will learn the keys to press in order to solve such equations directly. You should read the following information with calculator at hand so that you can understand what is being said.

The solution of $10^x = 3$ is approximately 0.477122. Confirm that this is correct by raising 10 to the 0.477122. So

$$10^{0.477122} \approx 3.$$

Now find the key on your calculator labeled "log". On some calculators
you may have to press the "second function" key, or the "inverse" key to
use the log function. Press

$$3 \; \boxed{\text{log}} \; .$$

The answer should be 0.4771212547, or whatever your calculator rounds
off to. This is (approximately) the same as the solution of the equation!

The letters "log" on your calculator are short for the word "**logarithm.**"
The word is a combination of "*log*ical" and "*arith*metic." The logarithm of
a number is the exponent in the power of 10 which gives that number as
its value. That is,

$$0.477121. . . = \log 3 \quad \text{because} \quad 10^{0.477121...} = 3.$$

The symbol "log 3" is pronounced "the logarithm of three," or simply "log
three." It is a form of $f(x)$ terminology where the name of the function is
log instead of f; the argument x is 3(in this case) and the parentheses are
not used around the argument unless needed. The symbol log 3 is defined
to mean, "The exponent in the power of 10 that gives 3 for a value." The
formal definition is as follows.

DEFINITION

> **BASE 10 LOGARITHM**
>
> $$y = \log x \quad \text{if and only if} \quad 10^y = x.$$

In this section you will use logarithms to solve exponential equations. The
first ones will have 10 as the base. Later equations will have other numbers as bases.

Objective:
Solve an exponential equation with any positive constant base, using base
10 logarithms.

EXAMPLE 1

Solve and check: $10^x = 457$

Solution:

$$10^x = 457 \qquad \text{Write the given equation.}$$

$$\log 10^x = \log 457 \qquad \text{Take the logarithm of each member.}$$

$$x = 2.659916. \ . \ . \qquad \text{Use the definition of log on the left.}$$
Use a calculator on the right.

You should store this answer, *without round-off,* for use in the check.

$$10^{2.659916...} = 457 \qquad \text{Press } 10 \ \boxed{y^x} \ \boxed{rcl} \ \boxed{=}.$$

$$S = \{2.659916. \ . \ .\} \qquad \text{Write the answer.} \qquad\qquad \blacksquare$$

From the second to the third line in the above example, you should understand how the definition of logarithm has been used on the left member.
The definition would say, "log $(10^x) = x$ if and only if $10^x = 10^x$. Since
the second equation is an identity, the first equation must be true also.
This property is stated formally below.

PROPERTY

LOGARITHM OF A POWER OF 10

$$\log 10^x = x$$

A simple way to remember what this property says is to regard the log as
"canceling out" the 10, leaving only the exponent.

$$\log 10^x = x.$$

EXAMPLE 2

Solve and check: $17 \times 10^{-0.4x} = 29$

Solution:

$$17 \times 10^{-0.4x} = 29$$

$$10^{-0.4x} = \frac{29}{17} \qquad\qquad \text{Divide by 17 first.}$$

$$\log 10^{-0.4x} = \log \frac{29}{17} \qquad\qquad \text{Take a log of each member.}$$

$$-0.4x = \log \frac{29}{17} \qquad\qquad \text{Log of a power of 10}$$

$$x = \frac{\log \dfrac{29}{17}}{-0.4} \qquad\qquad \text{Divide by } -0.4.$$

$$x = -0.579872. \ . \ . \qquad \text{By calculator}$$

You should do all the algebra first, before you evaluate. The sequence of keystrokes for the evaluation is:

29 $\boxed{\div}$ 17 $\boxed{=}$ $\boxed{\text{log}}$ $\boxed{\div}$ 0.4 $\boxed{+/-}$ $\boxed{=}$ (for algebraic)

29 $\boxed{\text{enter}}$ 17 $\boxed{\div}$ $\boxed{\text{log}}$ 0.4 $\boxed{\text{chs}}$ $\boxed{\div}$

(for RPN)

This value should, of course, be stored in memory.

Check: $17 \times 10^{(-0.4 \times -0.579...)} = 29$

$S = \{-0.579872...\}$ ■

The sequence of keystrokes for the check is

17 $\boxed{\times}$ 10 $\boxed{y^x}$ $\boxed{(}$ 0.4 $\boxed{+/-}$ $\boxed{\times}$ $\boxed{\text{rcl}}$ $\boxed{)}$ $\boxed{=}$ (algebraic)

17 $\boxed{\text{enter}}$ 10 $\boxed{\text{enter}}$ 0.4 $\boxed{\text{chs}}$ $\boxed{\text{rcl}}$ $\boxed{\times}$ $\boxed{y^x}$ $\boxed{\times}$ (RPN)

Suppose that the base in the equation is a number other than 10, such as

$$6^x = 152.$$

One way to solve this new problem is to turn it into an *old* problem. Substitute 10 to the appropriate power for 6, then proceed as above.

EXAMPLE 3

Solve and check: $6^x = 152$

Solution:

$$6^x = 152$$

Let $10^k = 6$, so that $k = \log 6$ (by definition of logarithm)

$(10^k)^x = 152$	Substitution
$10^{kx} = 152$	Power of a power
$\log (10^{kx}) = \log 152$	Log each member.
$kx = \log 152$	Log of a power of 10
$x = \dfrac{\log 152}{k}$	Divide by k.
$x = \dfrac{\log 152}{\log 6}$	$k = \log 6$, as shown above.
$x = 2.803881...$	By calculator (Store in memory!)

The sequence of keystrokes is

152 $\boxed{\text{log}}$ $\boxed{\div}$ 6 $\boxed{\text{log}}$ $\boxed{=}$ (algebraic)

152 $\boxed{\text{log}}$ 6 $\boxed{\text{log}}$ $\boxed{\div}$ (RPN)

Check: $6^{2.803...} = 152$ ✔   By calculator

$S = \{2.803881...\}$ Write the answer.   ■

You may be wondering what the calculator does inside to evaluate logarithms. Interestingly, it uses an iterative method similar to the one you used in Section 6-7, only more efficient. Most logarithms are *transcendental* numbers, and thus cannot be expressed exactly using only a finite number of operations of algebra.

In the following exercise you will solve exponential equations, first with 10 as the base, then with other numbers as the base.

EXERCISE 6-8

Do These Quickly

The following problems are intended to refresh your skills. You should be able to do all 10 in less than 5 minutes.

Q1.   Solve: $2^x = 8$

Q2.   Solve: $2^8 = x$

Q3.   Evaluate: $8^{\frac{2}{3}}$

Q4.   Write as a mixed number: $\dfrac{35}{8}$

Q5.   What percent of 80 is 30?

Q6.   Sketch the graph: $y = 0.7^x$

Q7.   Factor: $x^2 + 2x + 5$

Q8.   If you go 20 miles at 30 mph, how many minutes does it take?

Q9.   Solve for u: $\dfrac{u}{p} = \dfrac{i}{n}$

Q10.   Solve for x: $3 - x > 12$

Work the following problems

For Problems 1 through 12, solve the equation. It is advisable to check your answer.

1. $10^x = 397$

2. $10^{-x} = 4.35$

3. $10^{-x} = 0.0247$

4. $10^x = 0.005$

5. $10^x = -2.1$

6. $10^x = 0$

7. $3.5 \times 10^x = 8.53$

8. $47 \times 10^x = 6.7$

9. $10^{3x} = 4.333$ 10. $10^{0.6x} = 2001$

11. $91.2 \times 10^{0.3x} = 438$ 12. $24.2 \times 10^{0.7x} = 6.42$

For Problems 13 through 24, solve the equation by first transforming so
that the base is 10. It is advisable to check your answer.

13. $2^x = 3$ 14. $3^x = 2$

15. $54.3^x = 17.2$ 16. $74.1^x = 2.68$

17. $4.13^{2x} = 987$ 18. $8.09^{5x} = 40800$

19. $7 \times 5^x = 4$ 20. $11 \times 6^x = 12$

21. $13^{5x} = 1000$ 22. $7^{3x} = 10000$

23. $4 \times 23^{0.2x} = 371$ 24. $18 \times 5^{-0.3x} = 0.007$

25. ***Exponential Equation Shortcut Problem***   There is a formula that
     can be used to solve certain exponential equations quickly.
     a. Derive a formula for solving exponential equations by solving
         the *general* equation

$$b^x = c$$

     for x in terms of b and c. You should use the same technique
     used in Example 3.
     b. Use the formula you derived in part (a) to solve $29^x = 0.87$.
     c. Demonstrate that your answer to part (b) is correct.

26. ***Error Problem***   Mae Danerror solves the equation $7^x = 82$ and gets
     11.714236 for her answer. Explain to Mae how she can tell without
     even using a calculator that her answer is unreasonable. What error
     has Mae made?

27. ***Exact Power Problem***   Use the properties and definitions of expo-
     nentiation to show how $81^{-\frac{3}{4}}$ can be evaluated *without* the use of a
     calculator. (You should check your answer *with* a calculator.)

28. ***Logarithmic and Exponential Function Graphs Problem***   Let
     $f(x) = 10^{0.2x}$ and $g(x) = 5(\log x)$.
     a. Plot the graph of functions f and g on the same set of axes. If
         you use computer graphics, such as PLOT FN AND INV on the
         accompanying disk, you will need to divide the function LOG(x)
         by 2.303 since the computer uses logarithms with a different
         base. You will also need to modify the program so that it does
         not try to evaluate $g(x)$ if x is negative or zero. If you plot the
         graphs on paper, pick enough values of x to get smooth curves.
     b. What relationship do you notice between the two graphs?
     c. If you used computer graphics, find $f(2)$ and $g(2)$. Using the
         POINT option of PLOT FN AND INV, show that these values
         are really on the graphs.

   d.   Why do you suppose function *g* is called a *logarithmic* function?
   e.   Why do you suppose a logarithmic function is said to be the *inverse* of an exponential function?

6-9 | LOGARITHMS WITH OTHER BASES

In the last section you solved exponential equations such as

$$2^x = 3$$

by logarithms. You now know enough to start working the exponential models problems in Section 6-14. The information in this section through Section 6-13 is intended to fill out your background on logarithms and introduce you to inverses of functions, specifically logarithmic functions.

The definition of base 10 logarithm is $y = \log x$ if and only if $10^y = x$. The most important thing for you to realize is that a logarithm is an exponent.

A logarithm is an exponent!

For a power such as 2^5, the exponent is called a base 2 logarithm. Since 2^5 equals 32, you can say, "5 is log to the base 2 of 32." This sentence is abbreviated as follows:

$$5 = \log_2 32.$$

From this example, the formal definition of logarithm follows.

DEFINITION

> **BASE *b* LOGARITHM**
>
> $$y = \log_b x \quad \text{if and only if} \quad b^y = x$$
>
> where $x > 0$, $b > 0$, and $b \neq 1$.

In Problem 43 of the following exercise you will find out why there are restrictions on the values of x and b.

The numbers that appear in $y = \log_b x$ have names.

y is the *logarithm*.

b is the *base*.

x is the *argument*.

If the base is a number other than 10, the base is written as a subscript after the letters log. If the base is 10, the 10 may be written as a subscript if you need to emphasize the fact.

$\log x$ and $\log_{10} x$ mean the same thing.

There is a clever way to remember the definition of logarithm that does not rely on sheer memory. Suppose you are to figure out the meaning of

$$r = \log_s t.$$

Your thought process should be:

1. The equation is read, "r equals log *to the base s* of t." So s must be the base.
2. The equation is read "r is a logarithm. . .," and a logarithm is an *exponent*. So r is the exponent.
3. The only number left is t. So that must be the "answer," and you can write

$$s^r = t.$$

Objective:
Learn the definition of logarithm by finding the logarithm, base, or argument, if the other two are given.

EXAMPLE 1

Find x if $\log_3 x = -4$.

Solution:
The key to working this new problem is transforming it to an *old* problem. You would write:

$\log_3 x = -4$

$3^{-4} = x$ 3 is the base, and a logarithm is an exponent.

$x = \dfrac{1}{81}$ Definition of negative exponents   ■

EXAMPLE 2

Find x if $\log_2 8 = x$.

Solution:

$\log_2 8 = x$

$2^x = 8$ 2 is the base, and a logarithm is an exponent.

$2^x = 2^3$ Make the base on the right the same as the base on the left.

$\underline{\underline{x = 3}}$ By inspection   ■

EXAMPLE 3

Find x if $\log_x 4 = \dfrac{2}{3}$.

Solution:

$\log_x 4 = \dfrac{2}{3}$

$x^{\frac{2}{3}} = 4$ x is the base, and a logarithm is an exponent.

$(x^{\frac{2}{3}})^{\frac{3}{2}} = 4^{\frac{3}{2}}$ Raise each member of the $\dfrac{3}{2}$ power, the *reciprocal* of the

                          exponent of x.

$\underline{\underline{x = 8}}$ Multiply the exponents on the left. Evaluate the power
                          on the right   ■

The following exercise will give you practice using the definition of logarithm. Toward the end of the exercise you will be introduced to the properties of logarithms.

EXERCISE 6-9

Do These Quickly

The following problems are intended to refresh your skills. You should be able to do all 10 in less than 5 minutes.

Q1.   Solve: $3^x = 9$

Q2.   Solve: $2^3 = x$

Q3.   Evaluate: $\sqrt[3]{64}$

Q4.   Add: $\dfrac{2}{7} + \dfrac{3}{5}$

Q5.   Find 0.3% of 1000.

Q6.   Sketch the graph of a quadratic function.

Q7.   Do the squaring: $(5x - 11)^2$

Q8.   If you are going 20 mph and someone is approaching you going 30
      mph, what is your relative speed?

Q9.   Solve: $|x - 12| = 25$

Q10. Write the complex conjugate of $-17 + 2i$.

Work the following problems.

For Problems 1 through 12, find the argument, x, of the logarithm:

1. $\log_2 x = 3$ 2. $\log_3 x = 2$

3. $\log_3 x = 3$ 4. $\log_5 x = 2$

5. $\log_{\frac{1}{3}} x = 4$ 6. $\log_3 x = -4$

7. $\log_{\frac{1}{3}} x = -4$ 8. $\log_{\frac{1}{2}} x = 7$

9. $\log_{\frac{1}{2}} x = 4$ 10. $\log_4 x = \dfrac{1}{2}$

11. $\log_4 x = -\dfrac{1}{2}$ 12. $\log_{-4} x = \dfrac{1}{2}$

For Problems 13 through 30, find the logarithm, x:

13. $\log_4 16 = x$ 14. $\log_3 81 = x$

15. $\log_3 \left(\dfrac{1}{9}\right) = x$ 16. $\log_5 \left(\dfrac{1}{625}\right) = x$

17. $\log_2 1024 = x$ 18. $\log_{\frac{1}{2}} 8 = x$

19. $\log_{\frac{1}{3}} 243 = x$ 20. $\log_{\frac{1}{4}} \left(\dfrac{1}{16}\right) = x$

21. $\log_{\frac{1}{5}} \left(\dfrac{1}{125}\right) = x$ 22. $\log_5 0 = x$

23. $\log_3 (-9) = x$ 24. $\log_3 3 = x$

25. $\log_3 1 = x$ 26. $\log_1 3 = x$

27. $\log_{10} 1000000000 = x$ 28. $\log_3 3^5 = x$

29. $\log_7 7^9 = x$ 30. $\log_b b^n = x$

For Problems 31 through 42, find the base, x, of the logarithm:

31. $\log_x 16 = 4$

32. $\log_x 16 = -4$

33. $\log_x 4 = 1$

34. $\log_x \left(\frac{1}{8}\right) = 3$

35. $\log_x \left(\frac{1}{64}\right) = 2$

36. $\log_x 64 = \frac{3}{4}$

37. $\log_x 81 = \frac{4}{3}$

38. $\log_x \left(\frac{1}{25}\right) = \frac{1}{2}$

39. $\log_x \left(\frac{1}{216}\right) = \frac{3}{2}$

40. $\log_x \left(\frac{1}{64}\right) = -6$

41. $\log_x 2 = 0$

42. $\log_x 0 = 2$

43. ***Logarithm Base Restrictions Problem***   The definition of logarithm states that $y = \log_b x$ if and only if $b^y = x$, where $x > 0$, $b > 0$, and $b \neq 1$. In this problem you will see why the restrictions are made on x and b.
   a.   Give an example that shows why x could be an *imaginary* number if b is negative.
   b.   Explain why there are no such numbers as $\log_1 5$ and $\log_0 5$.
   c.   Explain why the argument, x, must be a *positive* number if the base b is positive.
   d.   Try to find log (-5) on your calculator. What happens?

44. ***Logarithm Function Computer Graphing Problem***   Computer languages such as BASIC have a logarithm function. In BASIC the function is written LOG(X).
   a.   Use the program PLOT FUNCTION, or similar plotting program, to draw the graph of Y = LOG(X). If you use PLOT FUNCTION, you must put in an error-trapping line so that the computer does not try to take the log of a non-positive number.
   b.   What is the x-intercept of this logarithm function? Where is there an asymptote?
   c.   Draw a vertical line at $x = 5$. Approximately what is the value of y when $x = 5$?
   d.   Press 5, then the key labeled $\boxed{\ln x}$ on your calculator. What do you notice that is interesting? (The abbreviation ln stands for "natural logarithm," or, more properly, "logarithm natural").
   e.   Draw a horizontal line across the graph at $y = 1$. At approximately what value of x does the line cross the graph?
   f.   Explain how you can conclude that the value of x in part (e) is the *base* of the function LOG on the computer. This number is called e, and is the base of natural logarithms.

45. ***Exponentiation Properties Problem***   In order to make intelligent applications of mathematics you must know the properties. Write the equations that state, in general, the five properties of exponentiation.

46. *Introduction to Properties of Logarithms*   There are three proper-
     ties of logarithms that correspond to three of the properties of expo-
     nentiation you wrote in Problem 45. In this problem you will try to
     discover what these properties are.
  a. *Logarithm of a Product*
       i. Find log 3.
      ii. Find log 5.
     iii. Find log 15.
      iv. True or false: log $(3 \cdot 5)$ = (log 3)(log 5)
       v. Write what log $(3 \cdot 5)$ *really* equals in terms of log 3 and
            log 5.
      vi. Make a conjecture: log (xy) = _____
     vii. Test your conjecture on log $(37 \cdot 89)$ by writing what the
            other side of the equation should equal, then evaluating
            both sides.
    viii. Complete the sentence: "When you take the log of a
            product, you may. . . ."
  b. *Logarithm of a Quotient*
       i. Make a conjecture: log $(\frac{x}{y})$ = _____
      ii. Test your conjecture on log $(\frac{30}{5})$ by writing what the other
            side of the equation should equal, then evaluating both
            sides.
     iii. Test your conjecture on two other numbers. Write down the
            results.
      iv. Complete the sentence: "When you take the log of a quo-
            tient, you may . . . ."
  c. *Logarithm of a Power*   (The *important* property!)
       i. Show that log 2^5 = 5 log 2 by evaluating both sides.
      ii. Make a conjecture: log (x^n) = _____
     iii. Test your conjecture on log (3^4) by writing what the other
            side of the equation should equal, then evaluating both
            sides.
      iv. Complete the sentence: "When you take the log of a power,
            you may . . . ."
       v. Given the equation $7^x = 13$, take the log of both sides.
            Then show how the property in part (c) can be used to
            solve the equation for x.

6-10 | PROPERTIES OF LOGARITHMS

There are three properties of logarithms that come directly from the corresponding properties of exponentiation. You may already have discovered
what these properties are if you worked Problem 46 in the previous section. You should keep your calculator handy as you read the following material so that you can verify what is said.

The log of a composite number such as 15 can be found by adding the logs of the two factors, 5 and 3.

$$\log 5 = 0.698970\ldots$$
$$\log 3 = \underline{0.477121\ldots}$$
$$\log 15 = 1.176091\ldots \quad \longleftarrow \textit{Add} \text{ the two logs.}$$

In other words,

$$\log (5 \cdot 3) = \log 5 + \log 3.$$

This looks almost like a distributive property. But it is not, because the operation changes from multiplication to addition. The property is simply an example of the fact that logarithms are exponents. When you multiply two powers with equal bases, you add their exponents.

A similar property applies to the log of a quotient. For instance, $\frac{30}{5}$ equals 6.

$$\log 30 = 1.477121\ldots$$
$$\log 5 = \underline{0.698970\ldots}$$
$$\log 6 = 0.778151\ldots \quad \longleftarrow \textit{Subtract} \text{ the logs.}$$

In this case,

$$\log \left(\frac{30}{5}\right) = \log 30 - \log 5.$$

Here again the property is a direct result of the fact that logarithms are exponents. When you divide powers with equal bases, you subtract their exponents.

The third property applies to the log of a power. For instance, 32 is equal to 2^5. It is possible to get log 32 by multiplying log 2 by 5.

$$\log 32 = 1.505149\ldots$$
$$5(\log 2) = 5(0.301029\ldots) = 1.505149\ldots$$

In other words,

$$\log (2^5) = 5(\log 2).$$

This property can be explained by repeated use of the log of a product property.

$$\log (2^5)$$
$$= \log (2 \cdot 2 \cdot 2 \cdot 2 \cdot 2)$$
$$= \log 2 + \log 2 + \log 2 + \log 2 + \log 2$$
$$= 5(\log 2)$$

It can also be explained simply by observing that when you raise a power
to a power, you multiply the exponents. Both the 5 and the log 2 are exponents.

The properties work regardless of what permissible number the base is.
They can be stated formally as follows.

PROPERTIES

PROPERTIES OF LOGARITHMS

1. *Logarithm of a Product*
$$\log_b (xy) = \log_b x + \log_b y$$

   Words: "The log of a product equals the sum of the logs of the
   two factors."

2. *Logarithm of a Quotient*
$$\log_b \left(\frac{x}{y}\right) = \log_b x - \log_b y$$

   Words: "The log of a quotient equals the log of the numerator
   minus the log of the denominator."

3. *Logarithm of a Power*
$$\log_b (x^n) = n \log_b x$$

   Words: "The log of a power equals the exponent times the log of
   the base."

Objective:
Learn the properties of logarithms by transforming expressions and solving
equations.

EXAMPLE 1

Given $\log 2 \approx 0.301$ and $\log 3 \approx 0.477$, use the properties of logarithms
to find an approximation for $\log 48$ *without* using the "log" key on the calculator.

Solution:
Your thought process should be to factor 48 into 2's and 3's.

$$\log 48$$

$$= \log (2^4 \cdot 3)$$

$$= \log 2^4 + \log 3 \qquad \text{Log of a product}$$

$$= 4(\log 2) + \log 3 \qquad \text{Log of a power}$$

$$\approx 4(0.301) + 0.477 \qquad \text{Substitute the given values.}$$

$$\approx \underline{1.681} \qquad\qquad\qquad\qquad\qquad \blacksquare$$

If you like, you may check your answer by calculator; log 48 = 1.681241. . . . The answer you get to a problem like this may differ in the third decimal place from the exact answer because you are working with rounded-off numbers.

EXAMPLE 2

Express $\log_7 3 + 2 \log_7 5$ as a *single* logarithm of a *single* argument.

Solution:

$$\log_7 3 + 2 \log_7 5$$

$$= \log_7 3 + \log_7 5^2 \qquad \text{Log of a power (used } backwards!)$$

$$= \log_7 75 \qquad\qquad \text{Log of a product (used backwards!!)} \qquad \blacksquare$$

The properties of logarithms allow you to solve exponential equations without first substituting a power of 10 for the base. You may already have discovered how if you worked Problem 46 in Exercise 6-9.

EXAMPLE 3

Solve $7^x = 83$ by taking the log of each member and using the log of a power property.

Solution:

$$7^x = 83$$

$$\log 7^x = \log 83$$

$$x \log 7 = \log 83 \qquad\qquad \text{Log of a power}$$

$$x = \frac{\log 83}{\log 7} \qquad\qquad \text{Divide by log 7.}$$

$$x = 2.270834. . .$$

The answer is reasonable. $7^2 = 49$, $7^3 = 343$, and 83 is between 49 and 343.

$$S = \{2.270834. . .\} \qquad\qquad\qquad\qquad\qquad\qquad \blacksquare$$

In the following exercise you will work problems like those above. An efficient way is to work a few of these with each assignment as you work the mathematical models problems in Section 6-14.

EXERCISE 6-10

Do These Quickly

The following problems are intended to refresh your skills. You should be able to do all 10 in less than 5 minutes.

Q1.   Write in exponential form: $\log_p k = w$

Q2.   Write in logarithmic form: $c^j = z$

Q3.   Complete the square: $x^2 - 12x +$ _____

Q4.   Multiply mentally: $(3 \times 10^8)(2 \times 10^{-17})$

Q5.   A $12 item is on sale for $9. What percent of the original price do you save?

Q6.   Sketch a pair of alternate interior angles.

Q7.   Multiply and simplify: $\left(\dfrac{2}{3}\right)\left(\dfrac{3}{4}\right)$

Q8.   Evaluate $-x^4$ if x is 3.

Q9.   One solution of $x^2 - 26x + 458 = 0$ is $13 - 17i$. What is the other solution?

Q10.   How far do you travel in 5 hours at 2 miles per minute?

Work the following problems.

For Problems 1 through 6, demonstrate that the property is true by evaluating both members of the equation.

1. $\log (3 \cdot 7) = \log 3 + \log 7$ 2. $\log (9 \cdot 5) = \log 9 + \log 5$

3. $\log (72 \div 8) = \log 72 - \log 8$ 4. $\log (51 \div 3) = \log 51 - \log 3$

5. $\log (7^3) = 3(\log 7)$ 6. $\log (5^4) = 4(\log 5)$

For Problems 7 through 30, find the given logarithm *without* using the log key on your calculator. Assume that $\log 2 \approx 0.301$, $\log 3 \approx 0.477$, and $\log 5 \approx 0.699$.

7. $\log 4$ 8. $\log 6$

9. $\log 8$ 10. $\log 12$

11. $\log \left(\dfrac{2}{3}\right)$ 12. $\log \left(\dfrac{3}{2}\right)$

13. $\log 10$ 14. $\log 5$

15. $\log 15$ 16. $\log 25$

17. $\log 3^6$ 18. $\log 2^{100}$

19. $\log 100$ 20. $\log 1000$

21. $\log 3.000$ 22. $\log 2000$

23. $\log 30.00$ 24. $\log 4000$

25. $\log 300.0$ 26. $\log 6000$

27. $\log 3000$ 28. $\log 8000$

29. $\log (3 \times 10^{12})$ 30. $\log (5 \times 10^3)$

31.   What pattern do you notice in the answers to Problems 21 through 29 odd?

32.   What pattern do you notice in the answers to Problems 22 through 30 even?

For Problems 33 through 44, write the expression as a single logarithm of a single argument.

33. $\log_3 5 + \log_3 7$ 34. $\log_7 3 + \log_7 8$

35. $\log_2 24 - \log_2 8$ 36. $\log_5 12 - \log_5 3$

37. $\log_7 2 + \log_7 5 + \log_7 3$ 38. $\log_{11} 6 + \log_{11} 5 + \log_{11} 4$

39. $\log_5 48 - \log_5 12 + \log_5 4$ 40. $\log_2 225 - \log_2 5 + \log_2 3$

41. $5 \log_{12} 2$ 42. $3 \log_5 4$

43. $3 \log_6 15 - \log_6 25$ 44. $4 \log_8 3 - \log_8 6$

For Problems 45 through 50, solve the equation by taking the log of each member, then using the Log of a Power Property.

45. $17^x = 4.7$ 46. $13^x = 908$

47. $0.8^{2x} = 0.007$ 48. $0.7^{3x} = 21.9$

49. $5.96 \times 10^{-0.2x} = 13.8$ 50. $7.38 \times 10^{0.4x} = 44.1$

51.   ***Log Property Statement Problem***   With your book closed, name and state the three properties of logarithms. Then open your book and find out if you are correct. If you missed *any* of them, close your book and write all three of them over again. Keep doing this until you can get all three correct without looking.

52. *Historical Problem—Products by Logarithms*   Before there were
     calculators (b.c.?!), logarithms provided an efficient way to multiply
     several numbers together, such as

$$(317)(22.4)(7810)(4.9).$$

In the early 1600's, the English mathematician Henry Briggs com-
piled a table of base 10 logs (called *common logs*). With the table, it
was possible to look up the logs of the factors and *add* them. Pencil-
and-paper addition can be done all at once, column-wise, whereas
multiplication must be done just two numbers at a time. The computation looked like this:

Factors:	Logs:
317	2.5011
22.4	1.3502
7810	3.8927
4.9	0.6902
sum	8.4342

The answer equals $10^{8.4342}$. Using the tables backwards, one could
find that $10^{0.4342}$ is about 2.72. So the answer in scientific notation is
approximately 2.72×10^8. (With a calculator, you can easily check
by direct multiplication that the answer is $2.717405. . . \times 10^8$.)

Various parts of the logarithm are given specific names. For instance, in the equation

$$\log 317 \approx 2.5011,$$

the 2 is called the *characteristic* of the logarithm. It is the same as
the characteristic of the number when it is written in scientific notation, 3.17×10^2. The .5011 is called the *mantissa* of the logarithm.
It is the same as the *logarithm* of the mantissa, the 3.17 in scientific
notation. The argument, 317, is called the *antilogarithm* of 2.5011,
or simply the *antilog*.

Briggs' table looked something like Table II at the back of this
book. Part of this table is shown in Figure 6-10a.

The finger is pointing at the entry for 317. Note that only the mantissa appears in the table, and that the decimal point has been omitted for simplicity. People were expected to realize that the characteristic is 2.

Answer the following questions.
a. Look up in Table II the other three logarithms shown above.
    Make sure you know where to find the mantissa, and how to
    figure out what the characteristic will be.

Table II. Four-Place Logarithms of Numbers

n	00	10	20	30	40	50	60	70	80	90
1.0	0000	0043	0086	0128	0170	0212	0253	0294	0334	0374
1.1	0414	0453	0492	0531	0569	0607	0645	0682	0719	0755
1.2	0792	0828	0864	0899	0934	0969	1004	1038	1072	1106
1.3	1139	1173	1206	1239	1271	1303	1335			4298
	4314	4330	4340					4424	4440	4456
2.8	4472	4487	4502	4518	4533	4548	4564	4579	4594	4609
2.9	4624	4639	4654	4669	4683	4698	4713	4728	4742	4757
3.0	4771	4786	4800	4814	4829	4843	4857	4871	4886	4900
3.1	4914	4928	4942	4955	4969	4983	4997	5011	5024	5038

Figure 6-10a

b. Figure out how to use the log table backwards to find that 2.71 is the antilog of .4330.

c. Demonstrate that you understand how to use the log table by using it to approximate (79.2)(37400)(409).

d. The word "logarithm" is a contraction of "*log*ical *arithm*etic." Explain why loarithms *were* a logical way to do multiplication before there were calculators, but are *not* logical for that purpose any more.

e. What seems to be the most important thing that is done with logarithms now?

53. *Powers Too Large for Calculators Problem*   Most calculators cannot give an answer that has an exponent more than 99. However, you can evaluate such powers by calculator if you find the *logarithm* of the answer. Use this clue to do the following.
  a. Evaluate 1776^{53}.
  b. Evaluate 2001^{97}.
  c. Evaluate 0.007^{105}.
  d. If 854^{231} were evaluated exactly, how many digits would the answer have?
  e. If 0.2^{1000} were evaluated exactly, how many zeros would there be between the decimal point and the first non-zero digit?

54. *Earthquake Problem*   The Richter energy number of an earthquake is the base 10 log of the amplitude (i.e., the severity) of the quake vibrations. The Seattle quake of April 29, 1965, measured 7 on the Richter scale. The San Francisco quake of 1906 measured about 8.25 on the Richter scale. To those who know little about logarithms, 8.25 does not sound much more severe than 7. Using what you know about logarithms, tell how many times more severe the San Francisco quake was than the Seattle one.

55. *Decibel Problem* The loudness of sound is measured in decibels. The number of decibels is 10 times the base 10 log of the relative acoustical power of the sound waves. A sound just barely loud enough to be heard is given a relative acoustical power of 1. Calculate to the nearest decibel the loudness of the following sounds:

Sound		*Relative Acoustical Power*
a.	Threshold of audibility	1
b.	Soft recorded music	4000
c.	Loud recorded music	6.8×10^8
d.	Jet aircraft	2.3×10^{12}
e.	Threshold of pain	1×10^{13}

56. *pH Problem* The strength of an acid solution is measured by its pH (for "*power of Hydrogen*"). The pH is the *negative* of the common logarithm of the hydrogen ion concentration (in moles per liter).
    a. Find the pH of the following solutions

Solution:	*Hydrogen Ion Concentration*
Neutral water	1.0×10^{-7}
Human blood	6.3×10^{-8}
Hydrochloric acid	2.5×10^{-2}
Grandma's lye soap suds	9.2×10^{-12}

    b. The pH of ordinary vinegar is 2.8. What is the hydrogen ion concentration?
    c. The pH of tomatoes is about 4.2. Find the hydrogen ion concentration of tomatoes. Are tomatoes more or less acidic than neutral water? That is, do tomatoes have a higher hydrogen ion concentration than water, or a lower one?

6-11   PROOFS OF PROPERTIES OF LOGARITHMS

In the last section you learned three properties of logarithms. In this section you will do formal proofs of these properties. You will also learn other properties, some of which are useful in real-world applications, and others of which will help you succeed on mathematics contests.

Objective:
Derive other properties of logarithms, and prove that they are true.

The first property you will derive comes from the problem of transforming a logarithm with one base to a log with a different base.

EXAMPLE 1

Find a decimal approximation for $\log_2 45$.

Solution:
The way to work this new problem is to turn it into an old problem. Let x equal the logarithm, then solve the equation.

$$x = \log_2 45$$

$2^x = 45$	Definition of logarithm
$\log 2^x = \log 45$	Take the base 10 log of each member.
$x \log 2 = \log 45$	Log of a power
$x = \dfrac{\log 45}{\log 2}$	Divide by log 2.
$\log_2 45 = \dfrac{\log 45}{\log 2}$	Substitute for x.

$$\log_2 45 = 5.491853\ldots$$

Check: $2^{5.491853}\ldots = 45$, by calculator.   ■

The property shows up in the last step before the calculator evaluation. To see what the property says, it helps to display the base 10 in the logs.

$$\log_2 45 = \frac{\log_{10} 45}{\log_{10} 2}$$

A quick way to find the base 2 log of 45 is to find the base 10 log of 45, then divide it by the base 10 log of 2. This is an example of the Change-of-Base Property.

PROPERTY

CHANGE-OF-BASE PROPERTY OF LOGARITHMS

$$\log_b x = \frac{\log_a x}{\log_a b}$$

In Example 2 you will see how to prove one of the three properties from the previous section.

EXAMPLE 2

Prove that $\log_b (xy) = \log_b x + \log_b y$.

Proof:
Let $r = \log_b x$ and $s = \log_b y$.

Then $b^r = x$ and $b^s = y$ by the definition of logarithm.

Multiplying x by y and transforming gives

$$b^r b^s = xy,$$

$$b^{(r+s)} = xy.$$

So $r + s = \log_b (xy)$ by the definition of logarithm.

Therefore, $\log_b (xy) = \log_b x + \log_b y$ by substitution and symmetry, Q.E.D.   ■

In the following exercise you will work problems like those above. It is not necessary for you to master these problems before you start the mathematical models problems of Section 6-14. Rather, you should work on these problems in parallel with later materials.

EXERCISE 6-11

Do These Quickly

The following problems are intended to refresh your skills. You should be able to do all 10 in less than 5 minutes.

Q1.   Evaluate: $\log_7 7$

Q2.   Evaluate: $5.2 - 0.3$

Q3.   Solve for x: $5x + 3y = 17$
                        $2x - 3y = 25$

Q4.   Do the cubing: 7^3

Q5.   Find 120% of 600.

Q6.   Sketch the graph of an exponential function.

Q7.   Solve: $2x = 8$

Q8.   Draw a line that is internally tangent to two circles.

Q9.   Solve for n: $PV = nRT$

Q10.   Multiply the complex numbers and simplify: $(2 + 5i)(3 - i)$

Work the following problems.

For Problems 1 through 10, find a decimal approximation for the logarithm.

1. $\log_7 28$ 2. $\log_4 563$

3. $\log_3 0.58$ 4. $\log_8 0.0039$

5. $\log_5 78125$

6. $\log_7 5764801$

7. $\log_{0.3} 58$

8. $\log_{-2} 13.7$

9. $\log_4 (-22.4)$

10. $\log_{0.6} 0.36$

11. *Log Properties Review Problem*   Name and state the three properties of logarithms from the previous section. Then look them up to make sure you are right.

12. *Special Properties Problem*   Prove the following:

a. $\log_b 1 = 0$ b. $\log_b b = 1$.   c. $\log_b 0$ is undefined.

For Problems 13 through 20, simplify the expression.

13. $\log_{49} 49^8$

14. $\log_{64} 64^{\frac{5}{6}}$

15. $3 \log_{24} 24^{-\frac{2}{3}}$

16. $5 \log_{37} 37^9$

17. $3^{\log_3 7}$

18. $6^{\log_6 13}$

19. $10^{\log_{10} 9}$

20. $10^{\log_{10} 2001}$

21. *Natural Logarithm Problem*   There is a key on your calculator labeled ln . The "l" is for "logarithm," and the "n" is for "natural" or "Naperian" (after the Scottish mathematician John Napier who lived in the 1600's). The two letters are pronounced separately; "ln x" is said, "Ell en of x." (Don't mistake the "l" for an "I" on the calculator key!) In this problem you will investigate natural logs.

a. Find ln 2 and ln 3.

b. One of the special properties of logarithms is that $\log_b b = 1$. So if you can find a number b for which ln $b = 1$, that number is the base of natural logarithms. Find an approximation for this base correct to 3 decimal places.

c. The base of natural logarithms is a transcendental number called e. To find a more precise value of e, enter 1 in your calculator, then press the e^x key. On some calculators this is done by pressing the second-function key, then pressing the ln key. Your answer in part (b) should be close to this value.

22. *Natural Exponential Function Graph Problem*   Let $f(x) = e^x$, where e is the base of natural logarithms, approximately 2.71828.

a. Plot carefully on graph paper the graph of $f(x) = e^x$ in the domain $-2 \le x \le 2$.

b. At the y-intercept, draw a line with a slope of 1. If your work is correct, this line should be *tangent* to the graph at that point.

c. At the point $(1, e)$ on the graph, construct a line with slope e. If your work is correct, this line should also be tangent to the graph.

d. Make a conjecture about the slope of the tangent line at a given point on the graph of function f. Test your conjecture at the point $(-1, e^{-1})$.

23. **Log and Exponential Function Graph Problem**   Given $f(x) = 2^x$
and $g(x) = \log_2 x$.
a. Plot the graph of function f in the domain $-3 \le x \le 3$.
b. On the same set of axes, plot the graph of function g in the domain $0.125 \le x \le 8$.
c. Describe the relationship between the two graphs.

24. **Square and Square Root Function Graph Problem**   Given
$f(x) = x^2$ and $g(x) = \sqrt{x}$.
a. Plot the graph of function f in the domain $0 \le x \le 3$.
b. On the same set of axes, plot the graph of function g in the domain $0 \le x \le 9$.
c. Describe the relationship between the two graphs.

25. **Log Proof Problem 1**   Prove the property of the Logarithm of a
Quotient.

26. **Log Proof Problem 2**   Prove the property of the Logarithm of a
Power.

Problems 27 through 34 present some less-familiar properties of logarithms. These properties are useful in some real-world problems and in
contest mathematics. Prove each property.

27. **Change-of-Base**

$$\log_a x = \frac{\log_b x}{\log_b a}.$$

28. **Direct Proportionality**

$$\log_a x = (c)(\log_b x), \text{ where } c \text{ is a } constant.$$

29. **Reciprocal**

$$\log_a b = \frac{1}{\log_b a}.$$

30. **Product of Two Logs**

$$(\log_a b)(\log_b c) = \log_a c.$$

31. **Product of Three Logs**

$$(\log_a b)(\log_b c)(\log_c d) = \log_a d$$

32. **Log with a Power for its Base**

$$\log_{(b^n)} x = \frac{1}{n} \log_b x.$$

33. **Base and Argument are Like Powers**

$$\log_{(b^n)} (x^n) = \log_b x.$$

34. **Base and Argument are Reciprocals**

$$\log_{\frac{1}{b}} \frac{1}{x} = \log_b x.$$

35. **Base 2 Logs Quickly!**   The Direct Proportionality Property of Problem 28 gives a quick way to find logs to other bases.
    a.   Find the constant you multiply $\log_{10} x$ by to get $\log_2 x$.
    b.   Use the *constant multiplier* feature of your calculator (or store the answer to part (a) in memory) to evaluate
        i. $\log_2 13$
        ii. $\log_2 0.63$
        iii. $\log_2 1776$
        iv. $\log_2 4096$
        v. $\log_2 1000000$

36. **Natural Logs from Base 10 Logs**
    a.   In Problem 21 you learned that $\ln x$ means $\log_e x$, where $e = 2.7182818284. \ldots$ Find the constant that must be multiplied by $\log_{10} x$ to give $\ln x$ for the answer.
    b.   Confirm that your answer to part (a) is right by evaluating $\ln 5$ in two ways; by multiplying $\log 5$ by the constant, and directly with the $\ln$ key on your calculator.
    c.   How could you find $\log 17$ using the fact that $\ln 17 = 2.833213 \ldots$?

37. **Introduction to the Inverse of a Function**   In the next section you will learn what it means to "invert" a function. The following problems are intended to review some of the skills you will need to be successful working with inverse functions.
    a.   If $y = \frac{2}{3}x + 7$, solve for x in terms of y.
    b.   If $y = 3x^2$, solve for x in terms of y.
    c.   If $y = 7^x$, solve for x in terms of y.

38. **Logarithmic Function Computer Graphing Problem**   In this problem you will use the program PLOT FUNCTION, or similar graphing program, to plot graphs of logarithmic functions with various bases.

a. Sketch what you think the graph of $y = \log_2 x$ looks like. Show
    particularly the intercept(s) and asymptote(s).
b. Plot the graph of $y = \log_2 x$. The function LOG(X) in BASIC is
    the base-e logarithm (where $e = 2.718\ldots$). So you must use
    the change of base property in an appropriate way to get base-2
    logs. Also, if you use PLOT FUNCTION, you must add a line
    to prevent the computer from trying to find the log of a non-
    positive number.
c. Did the graph in part (b) confirm your prediction in part (a)? If
    not, where did you go astray?
d. Sketch what you think the graph of $y = \log_{0.2} x$ looks like.
    Show particularly the intercept(s) and asymptote(s).
e. Plot the graph of $y = \log_{0.2} x$ on the computer. Did the actual
    graph confirm your prediction in part (d)? If not, what change
    will you make in your thinking?

Problems 39 through 60 are "tricky" problems involving logarithms of the
type that often appear on mathematics contests. You should find the properties of Problems 27 through 34 helpful in answering these. Also, you
will need to recall the other properties of logarithms, as well as the
definition.

The problems are arranged in *no* special order, so you must decide in each
case just what procedure to use. Find *exact* answers unless a decimal approximation is called for.

39. Evaluate $\log_{12} (\log_9 (\log_5 (\log_2 32)))$.

40. Evaluate $(\log_7 5)(\log_3 7)(\log_2 27)(\log_5 2)$.

41. Given only that $\log_{10} 2 = 0.301$, $\log_{10} 3 = 0.477$, and $\log_{10} 7 =
     0.845$, find $\log_{10} (1 \cdot 2 \cdot 3 \cdot 4 \cdot 5 \cdot 6 \cdot 7 \cdot 8 \cdot 9 \cdot 10)$ *without* using a calcu-
     lator.

42. Solve for y: $(\log_5 x)(\log_x 5x)(\log_{5x} y) = \log_x x^4$.

43. Evaluate $\dfrac{-\log_3 2}{\log_2 (-8)}$.

44. Evaluate $\left(\log_{27} 32 + \log_{27} \dfrac{1}{4}\right)(\log_2 9)$.

45. Solve for $n > 1$: $\log_{10} 2 + \log_{10} 4 + \log_{10} 8 + \ldots + \log_{10} 2^n =
     (\log_{1024} 10)^{-1}$.

46. Simplify: $\log_{1001} 7 + \log_{1001} 11 + \log_{1001} 13$.

47. Solve for x: $(\log_3 x)^2 + \log_3 x^2 + 1 = 0$.

48. Evaluate $\log_7 (7^{\log_7 343})$.

49.   Evaluate $\log_2 (\log_3 (\log_4 64))$.

50.   Evaluate $\log_7 8 \div \log_7 \dfrac{1}{8}$.

51.   Solve the following system for (x, y):

$$\log_9 x + \log_y 8 = 2.$$

$$\log_x 9 + \log_8 y = \frac{8}{3}.$$

52.   Solve for x and y:

$$(\log_3 x)(\log_x 2x)(\log_{2x} y) = \log_x y^2.$$

53.   Evaluate $\log_2 56 - \log_4 49$.

54.   Given $\log_2 3 = 1.58$, find $\log_{16} 81$ *without* using a calculator.

55.   Evaluate $10^{\log_{100} 9}$.

56.   Solve for x: $\log_{10} (x^{\log_{10} x}) = 4$.

57.   Evaluate $\log_4 (2 \sqrt[5]{8}) - \log_8 \sqrt[3]{0.25}$.

58.   Evaluate $4 \log_3 \dfrac{1}{3} + 2 \log_{27} 9$.

59.   Evaluate $4^{\log_2 5}$.

60.   Solve for x:

$$x^2 \log_{10} 8 - x \log_{10} 5 = 2(\log_2 10)^{-1} - x.$$

6-12   INVERSES OF FUNCTIONS—THE LOGARITHMIC FUNCTION

You learned about logarithms for the specific purpose of solving exponential equations. Very often in mathematics, solving a specific problem leads to a whole new concept. In this case, the new concept is that of the *inverse* of a function.

Suppose that $f(x) = 2^x$ and $g(x) = \log_2 x$. The second equation can be solved for x in terms of $g(x)$ using the definition of logarithm:

$$x = 2^{g(x)}.$$

This equation has the same form as $f(x) = 2^x$ except that the independent and dependent variables are *reversed*. The relation you get from reversing the two variables in a function is called the *inverse* of that function.

DEFINITION

INVERSE OF A FUNCTION
If f is a function, then the **inverse** of f, abbreviated f^{-1} and pronounced "f-inverse," is the relation obtained by interchanging the
two variables.

The process of finding the equation of the inverse of a function is called
inverting the function. To invert $f(x) = 2^x$, above, you would write

$$f^{-1}(x) = \log_2 x,$$

which is the same as the function called g earlier.

The graphs of functions f and f^{-1} are shown in Figure 6-12a. The points
for the f graph are found just by substituting values for x and finding $f(x)$.
The points for the f^{-1} graph are most easily found by substituting for
$f^{-1}(x)$ and finding x.

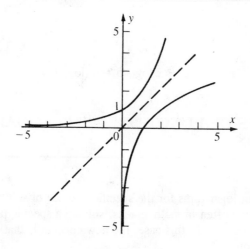

Figure 6-12a

The most striking feature of the two graphs is that they are mirror-images
of each other, where the mirror is placed along the 45° line $y = x$.

In this section you will invert linear and quadratic equations, as well as exponential ones. You will concentrate on how the graphs are related to each
other, and whether or not the inverse is a function.

Objective:
Given the equation of a function, find the equation of its inverse, and draw
graphs of the function and its inverse.

EXAMPLE 1

If $f(x) = 0.2x + 3$, find the equation of f^{-1}, tell whether or not the inverse relation is a function, sketch the two graphs, and show how the
graphs are related to the line $y = x$.

Solution:
The procedure for finding the equation of the inverse is the same as for
finding x in terms of y. For simplicity, use y in place of $f(x)$.

$$y = 0.2x + 3$$
$$y - 3 = 0.2x$$
$$5y - 15 = x$$

To get the equation in the desired form, you reverse the x and y, using the
definition of inverse function, and replace the y with $f^{-1}(x)$. The answer is

$$f^{-1}(x) = 5x - 15$$

The inverse relation *is* a function since its equation is of the form
$y = mx + b$, a linear function. The graphs are shown in Figure 6-12b. As
you can see from the figure, the two graphs are reflections of each other in
the line $y = x$.

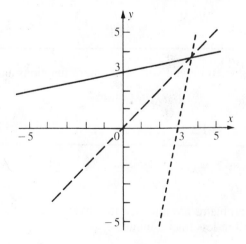

Figure 6-12b

EXAMPLE 2

Invert $f(x) = 0.5x^2$. Tell whether or not the inverse relation is a function. Sketch the two graphs and show how they are related to the line $y = x$.

Solution:
Let $y = 0.5x^2$.

Then $2y = x^2$

  $\pm\sqrt{2y} = x$.

$\therefore f^{-1}(x) = \pm\sqrt{2x}$

The inverse is *not* a function since there are two values of $f^{-1}(x)$ for each positive value of x.

The graphs are shown in Figure 6-12c, along with the line $y = x$.

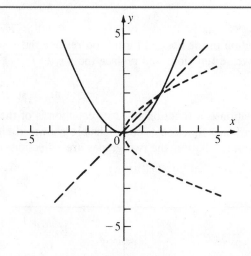

Figure 6-12c —————————————————————— ■

In the following exercise you will invert more functions and draw their graphs.

EXERCISE 6-12

Do These Quickly

The following problems are intended to refresh your skills. You should be able to do all 10 in less than 5 minutes.

Q1. Quick! Find $\log_2 8$.

Q2. Write the general equation for a quadratic function.

Q3. Sketch $-4 - 7i$ in the complex plane.

Q4. Does $x^2 + 7x + 14 = 0$ have *real*-number solutions?

Q5. What word does "log-" in logarithm come from?

Q6. 5 is 20% of what number?

Q7. Find the slope: $3x + 4y = 5$

Q8. Draw a number-line graph: $-2x > 7$

Q9. Factor: $x^2 + 5x - 6$

Q10. Add: $\dfrac{5}{7} + \dfrac{7}{5}$

For Problems 1 through 16,
a. Find an equation for the inverse of the function.
b. Draw the graph of the function and its inverse. You may use a computer graphics program such as PLOT FN AND INV.
c. Tell whether or not the inverse of the given function is a function.

1. $f(x) = 3x + 5$ 　　　　　　　　2. $f(x) = 0.2x - 7$

3. $f(x) = 0.4x - 6$ 　　　　　　　4. $f(x) = 4x + 3$

5. $f(x) = 0.1x^2$ 　　　　　　　　6. $f(x) = \dfrac{x^2}{4}$

7. $f(x) = (x + 2)^3$ 　　　　　　　8. $f(x) = \sqrt[3]{x} + 1$

9. $f(x) = x + 3$ 　　　　　　　　10. $f(x) = -x$

11. $f(x) = \sqrt{x - 4}$ 　　　　　　12. $f(x) = -\sqrt{x + 3}$

13. $f(x) = 1.4^x$ 　　　　　　　　14. $f(x) = \log_2 x$

15. $f(x) = \log_5 (2x)$ 　　　　　　16. $g(x) = 6^{0.5x}$

For Problems 17 through 20, tell whether or not the two functions graphed are inverses of each other.

17.

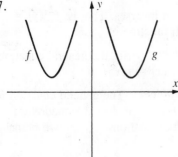

18.

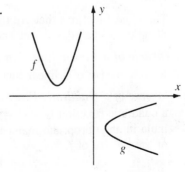

19.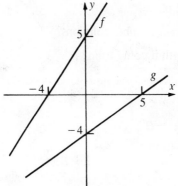

20.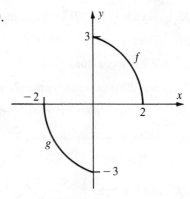

For Problems 21 through 26, find $f(g(x))$. Based on your answer, tell
whether or not two functions are inverses of each other.

21. $f(x) = 2x,\ g(x) = \dfrac{x}{2}$

22. $f(x) = (x + 5),\ g(x) = \dfrac{1}{(x + 5)}$

23. $f(x) = \dfrac{3}{x},\ g(x) = \dfrac{x}{3}$

24. $f(x) = \sqrt{x},\ g(x) = x^2$ (where $x \geq 0$)

25. $f(x) = 3^x$ and $g(x) = \log_3 x$

26. $f(x) = x^5$ and $g(x) = 5x$

27. Show that the inverse of the "multiplying" function, $f(x) = kx$, is
the "dividing" function, $f^{-1}(x) = \dfrac{x}{k}$.

28. Show that the inverse of the "subtracting" function, $f(x) = x - k$, is
the "adding" function, $f(x) = x + k$.

29. Is there an inverse function for the constant function, $f(x) = k$? Explain.

30. There are functions that are their own inverses. That is, $f^{-1}(x) = f(x)$. Write the equation of one such function.

31. *Inverse of a Linear Function Problem*   Write the general equation
for the inverse of a linear function, $f(x) = mx + b$.

32. *Inverse of a Quadratic Function Problem*   The general equation for
a quadratic function is $f(x) = ax^2 + bx + c$. Use the quadratic formula in an appropriate manner to find equations for the two branches
of the inverse of f.

33. *Inverse of an Exponential Function Problem*   The general equation for an exponential function is $f(x) = a \cdot b^x$. Write the general equation for the inverse of an exponential function.

34. *Inverse Functions and Mathematical Models Problem*   In mathematical models problems, one thing you must be able to do is find the value of the independent variable when a value of the dependent is given.
    a. Explain the relationship between this technique and finding the equation of the inverse of a function.
    b. The Fahrenheit temperature of an object is a linear function of its Celsius temperature. You may recall from science or from Chapter 3 that the particular equation is

$$F = 1.8C + 32.$$

Solve this equation for C in terms of F. What word describes how the new function is related to the old one?
    c. Under what conditions might it be more convenient to use the equation for the inverse function in a mathematical model problem, instead of the equation expressing the dependent variable in terms of the independent?

35. *Misconception Problem*   One of the more frequent mistakes students make on standardized tests is thinking that $f^{-1}(x)$ means the *reciprocal* of $f(x)$. Let f be the general linear function, $f(x) = mx + b$. Show that $\frac{1}{f(x)}$ is *not* equal to $f^{-1}(x)$.

36. *Proof Problem*   Prove that if you "f" a number, then "f^{-1}" the answer, you get the original number back again. That is, prove that

$$f^{-1}(f(x)) = x.$$

6-13 | THE ADD-MULTIPLY PROPERTY OF EXPONENTIAL FUNCTIONS

The general equation of an exponential function is

$$f(x) = a \times b^x,$$

where a and b stand for constants. You have learned how to find y when x is given, and how to find x when y is given. In this section you will learn a property of exponential functions that allows you to calculate many values of y, quickly. More important, the property allows you to analyze given data to see if an exponential function fits it.

Suppose that the particular equation of an exponential function is

$$f(x) = 3 \times 2^x.$$

A short table of values is shown below.

x	$f(x)$
0	3
1	6
2	12
3	24
4	48
5	96

Every time 1 is *added* to x, the value of $f(x)$ is *multiplied* by 2. This fact should not be surprising because the exponent, x, tells you how many 2's to multiply together. In general, adding a constant to the value of x in an exponential function has the effect of multiplying $f(x)$ by a (different) constant. For the function above, adding 2 to x multiplies $f(x)$ by 4. This is true no matter where you start in the table.

The following is a general proof of this property.

THEOREM:

If $f(x) = a \times b^x$, then $f(x + c)$ is a constant multiplied by $f(x)$.

PROOF:

The symbol $f(x + c)$ means the value of y when the constant c is added to the value of x.

$f(x + c) = a \times b^{x+c}$ Substitute $x + c$ for x.

$f(x + c) = a \times b^x \times b^c$ Product of powers with equal bases (backwards)

$f(x + c) = f(x) \times b^c$ Substitute $f(x)$ for $a \times b^x$.

$\therefore f(x + c)$ is a constant (namely, b^c) multiplied by $f(x)$, Q.E.D.

PROPERTY

> **ADD-MULTIPLY PROPERTY OF EXPONENTIAL
> FUNCTIONS**
> If $f(x) = a \times b^x$, then $f(x + c) = f(x) \times b^c$.
>
> (Adding a constant to the value of x multiplies $f(x)$ by a (different) constant.)

This property is similar to the slope property of linear functions. In that case, adding a constant to x *adds* a different constant to $f(x)$.

PROPERTY

ADD-ADD PROPERTY OF LINEAR FUNCTIONS
If $f(x) = mx + b$, then $f(x + c) = f(x) + mc$

(Adding a constant to the value of x adds a (different) constant to the value of $f(x)$.)

In the following exercise you will prove this property.

Objective:
Be able to use the add-multiply property of exponential functions to calculate many values quickly and to tell whether or not an exponential function is a suitable mathematical model for a given set of data.

EXAMPLE 1

Suppose that $f(x)$ varies exponentially with x, and $f(3) = 100$ and $f(5) = 80$. Calculate values of $f(x)$ and use the information to draw the graph of f.

Solution:
Observe that the function is exponential, so the add-multiply property can be used. Also, x increases by 2 in going from 3 to 5. To see what factor to multiply by, just ask yourself, "What do you multiply by 100 to get 80?" The answer is $\frac{80}{100}$, or 0.8. For each entry in the table below where x increases by 2, the value of $f(x)$ is found by multiplying the preceding value by 0.8. Where x *decreases* by 2, the value of $f(x)$ is found by *dividing* the previous value by 0.8.

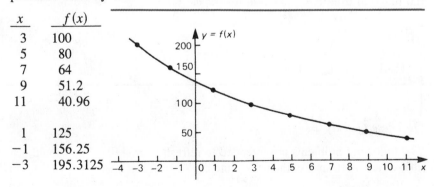

x	$f(x)$
3	100
5	80
7	64
9	51.2
11	40.96
1	125
−1	156.25
−3	195.3125

Figure 6-13a

The repeated multiplications are most easily done by storing the constant 0.8 in memory, or by using the "constant multiplier" feature if your calculator has one. The graph is shown in Figure 6-13a. ∎

EXAMPLE 2

Which of the following functions, f or g, could be an exponential function? Why is the other *not* an exponential function?

x	$f(x)$	$g(x)$
7	1.73	1.73
13	6.40	6.40
19	25.12	23.68
25	82.47	87.63

Solution:
The x-values increase by adding 6 each time. So the add-multiply property can be used. Dividing successive values of successive function values gives the following:

Function f:

$$\frac{6.40}{1.73} = 3.6994\ldots$$

$$\frac{25.12}{6.40} = 3.925$$

$$\frac{82.47}{25.12} = 3.2830\ldots$$

Function g:

$$\frac{6.40}{1.73} = 3.6994\ldots$$

$$\frac{23.68}{6.40} = 3.7$$

$$\frac{87.63}{23.68} = 3.7005\ldots$$

Since the values of $g(x)$ increase by multiplying by about 3.7, g is the exponential function. Since the values of $f(x)$ do not increase by multiplying by a constant, f is *not* an exponential function. ∎

In the following exercise you will practice using the add-multiply property. You will also practice finding the particular equation of an exponential function from two points on its graph.

EXERCISE 6-13

Do These Quickly

The following problems are intended to refresh your skills. You should be able to do all 10 in less than 5 minutes.

Q1. If f is a function, then f^{-1} is defined to be the relation obtained by _____ . What words go in the blank?

Q2. Simplify: $x^3 x^7$

Q3. Simplify: $(x^5)^8$

Q4. Write without negative exponents: 7^{-11}

Q5. Write without fractional exponents: $5^{\frac{1}{3}}$

Q6. Find the discriminant: $3x^2 + 5x - 7 = 0$

Q7. Evaluate the determinant: $\begin{vmatrix} -2 & 4 \\ 3 & 9 \end{vmatrix}$

Q8. Multiply the complex numbers: $(5 + 2i)(5 - 2i)$

Q9. Find 9% of 900.

Q10. Sketch the graph of a quadratic function if the equation has a positive x^2-coefficient.

For Problems 1 through 8, assume that f is an *exponential* function with the two given values. Use the property of exponential functions to calculate values of $f(x)$ for two *larger* values of x and for two *smaller* values of x. Then use the calculated and given points to plot the graph.

1. $f(2) = 36$ and $f(5) = 54$

2. $f(3) = 20$ and $f(7) = 24$

3. $f(4) = 100$ and $f(6) = 70$

4. $f(1) = 50$ and $f(3) = 20$

5. $f(-2) = 1$ and $f(3) = 2$

6. $f(0) = 30$ and $f(10) = 27$

7. $f(8) = 25.7$ and $f(11) = 16.8$

8. $f(-6) = 8.4$ and $f(-1) = 22.7$

For Problems 9 through 14, tell whether or not the function could be an exponential function.

9.

x	$f(x)$
1	12
4	48
7	192
10	768

10.

x	$f(x)$
5	20
10	40
15	60
20	80

11.

x	$f(x)$
2.7	1200
3.1	840
3.5	504
3.9	252

12.

x	$f(x)$
4.6	500
4.8	150
5.0	45
5.2	13.5

13.

x	$f(x)$
400	1.21
500	1.331
600	1.4641
700	1.61051

14.

x	$f(x)$
38	1.68
47	2.10
56	2.625
65	3.28125

15. If $h(x) = 31 \times 2.3^x$, find the factor by which to multiply the value of $h(x)$ to get $h(x + 3)$. Confirm your answer by calculating $h(5)$ and $h(8)$ using the equation, then multiplying $h(5)$ by the factor.

16. If $t(x) = 43 \times 0.71^x$, find the factor by which to multiply the value of $t(x)$ to get $t(x + 2)$. Confirm your answer by calculating $t(3)$ and $t(5)$ using the equation, then multiplying $t(3)$ by the factor.

17. *Particular Equation Problem*   In this problem you will see if you can find the particular equation of a given exponential function from two ordered pairs.
    a.   Suppose that $(0, 7)$ and $(3, 19)$ are two ordered pairs in an exponential function $f(x) = a \times b^x$. Substitute $(0, 7)$ for (x, y). What does this tell you about the constants a and b?
    b.   Substitute $(3, 19)$ for (x, y), and use the information you found in part (a). The resulting equation can be solved for b, but you must be clever to do it!
    c.   Write the particular equation for $f(x)$ in terms of x.
    d.   Use the equation in part (c) to calculate $f(6)$. Show that the answer you get is the same as you would get using the add-multiply property of exponential functions.

18. *The Add-Add Property of Linear Functions*   Prove that for a linear function, $f(x) = mx + b$, each time a constant is added to x, a (different) constant is added to $f(x)$.

6-14 | EXPONENTIAL AND OTHER FUNCTIONS AS
MATHEMATICAL MODELS

Exponential functions make reasonable mathematical models in real-world situations where the graph has a horizontal asymptote, or where you know that the function has the add-multiply property. In this section you will see how to find the particular equation so that you can make the mathematical model. You will also be called upon to use linear and quadratic functions as mathematical models.

Objective:

Given a real-world situation relating two variables, use an exponential, linear, or quadratic function as a mathematical model.

EXAMPLE

Bacteria Problem   Suppose that the number of bacteria per square millimeter in a culture in your biology lab is increasing exponentially with time. On Tuesday there are 2000 bacteria per square millimeter. On Thursday, the number has increased to 4500.

a. Derive the particular equation.
b. Predict the number of bacteria per square millimeter that will be in the culture on Tuesday next week.
c. Predict the time when the number of bacteria per square millimeter reaches 10,000.
d. Draw the graph of the function.

Solutions:

a. Let B be the number of bacteria per square millimeter.
   Let t be the number of days since this Tuesday.

   Since B varies exponentially with t, the general equation is
   $B = a \times b^t$, and the given ordered pairs are (0, 2000) and (2, 4500).
   Substituting (0, 2000) gives:

   $$2000 = a \times b^0$$

   $$2000 = a.$$

   Substituting 2000 for a and (2, 4500) for (t, B) gives:

   $$4500 = 2000 \times b^2.$$

   To isolate the b, first divide by 2000, then raise each member to the $\frac{1}{2}$ power.

   $$2.25 = b^2$$
   $$(2.25)^{\frac{1}{2}} = (b^2)^{\frac{1}{2}}$$
   $$1.5 = b$$

   $$\therefore \text{ Equation is } \underline{B = 2000 \times 1.5^t}$$

   Note that if b turns out to be an untidy decimal, store it, without round-off, in your calculator's memory.

b. On the next Tuesday, t will be 7.

   $$\therefore B = 2000 \times 1.5^7 = 34171.87. . . \approx \underline{34,000 \text{ bacteria/mm}^2.}$$

c. Substitute 10,000 for B. To get the t down out of the exponent you
   must eventually take the log of each member of the resulting equation.
   First, tidy things up a bit!

$$10000 = 2000 \times 1.5^t$$

$$5 = 1.5^t$$

$$\log 5 = \log(1.5^t)$$

$$\log 5 = t \log 1.5$$

$$\frac{\log 5}{\log 1.5} = t$$

$$3.9693\ldots = t$$

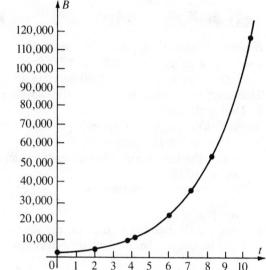

Figure 6-14a

So *almost 4 days later, on Saturday,* the bacteria would number 10,000
per square millimeter.

d. The graph is shown in Figure 6-14a.

In the exercise that follows, you will use exponential functions as mathematical models. You will also get a review of linear and quadratic model
problems. You will get a chance to figure out how to use a *logarithmic*
function as a mathematical model.

EXERCISE 6-14

Do These Quickly

The following problems are intended to refresh your skills. You should be
able to do all 10 in less than 5 minutes.

Q1. Write the general equation for an exponential function.

Q2. Write the general equation for a linear function.

Q3. Write the general equation for a quadratic function.

Q4.   Write in logarithmic form: $w^v = r$

Q5.   Write in exponential form: $k = \log_p j$

Q6.   Multiply: $(x + 5)(x - 11)$

Q7.   Factor: $x^2 - 6x - 55$

Q8.   Simplify: $\dfrac{36}{48}$

Q9.   Find 40% of 9.

Q10.   Find $\log_3 81$.

Problems 1 through 10 are "straightforward" problems similar to the example. From Problem 11 on, you will be required to distinguish among linear, quadratic, and exponential functions, and to use exponential functions in clever ways!

1. *Population Problem*   Assume that the population of the United States is increasing exponentially with time. The 1970 census showed that the population was about 203 million. The 1980 census showed that the population had grown to about 226 million.
   a.   By what factor did the population increase from 1970 to 1980? Use the answer and the properties of exponential functions to predict the outcomes of the 1990, 2000, and 2010 censuses.
   b.   Plot a graph of population versus time from 1970 through 2010.
   c.   Find the particular equation expressing population in terms of the number of years that have elapsed since 1970.
   d.   Use your equation to predict the population *this* year. Plot the value of the graph of part b. If it does not seem to fit with the other points, go back and check your work.
   e.   Predict the year in which the population will reach 400 million.
   f.   According to your mathematical model, what was the population when the Declaration of Independence was signed? Check in an encyclopedia or other source to see how close you came to the *actual* population. Explain any large differences you may observe.

2. *Rabbit Problem*   When rabbits were first brought to Australia last century, they had no natural enemies so their numbers increased rapidly. Assume that there were 60,000 rabbits in 1865, and that by 1867 the number had increased to 2,400,000. Assume that the number of rabbits increased exponentially with the number of years that elapsed since 1865.
   a.   Write the particular equation for this function.
   b.   How many rabbits would you predict in 1870?
   c.   According to your model, when was the *first* pair of rabbits introduced into Australia?

d. Based on the properties of exponential functions, why is it appropriate to say that the rabbits "multiplied?"

e. See *The Alien Animals,* by George Laycock (Ballentine Books, 1966) for the eventual outcome of the rabbit problem.

3. *Car Stopping Problem*   Oliver Sudden is driving along a straight, level highway at 64 kilometers per hour (km/h) when his car runs out of gas. As he slows down, his speed decreases exponentially with the number of seconds since he ran out of gas, dropping to 48 km/h after 10 seconds.

   a. Write the particular equation expressing speed in terms of time.

   b. Predict Oliver's speed after 25 seconds.

   c. At what time will Oliver's speed be 10 km/h?

   d. Draw the graph of the function for speed in the domain from 0 through the time when Oliver reaches 10 km/h.

   e. What would the actual speed-time graph look like for *negative* values of time?

   f. Explain why this mathematical model would not give reasonable answers at very *large* values of time.

4. *Milk Spoiling Problem*   Assume that the number of hours milk stays fresh decreases exponentially with temperature. Suppose that

milk in the refrigerator at 0°C will keep for 192 hours, and milk left
out in the kitchen at 20°C will keep for only 48 hours.

  a.   Let h be the number of hours the milk keeps, and T the Celsius
        temperature. Write the particular equation expressing h in terms
        of T.
  b.   Use the equation to show that milk will keep approximately $\frac{1}{4}$ as
        long at 40°C as it will at 20°C.
  c.   Without any more use of your equation, predict h for tempera-
        tures of 60°C and 80°C.
  d.   Plot the graph of h versus T for values of T from 0 through 80.

5.   *Phoebe's Next Rocket Problem*   Phoebe Small is out Sunday driv-
      ing in her rocket ship. She fills up with fuel at the Scorpion Gulch
      Rocket Fuel Station, and takes off. When she starts the last stage of
      her rocket, she is going 4230 miles per hour (mph). Ten seconds
      later she is going 6850 mph. While the last stage is running, you
      may assume that Phoebe's speed increases exponentially with time.

  a.   In order to go into orbit, Phoebe must be going 17,500 mph.
        She took in enough fuel to last for 30 seconds. Will she orbit?
        Explain.
  b.   What is the minimum length of time the last stage could run and
        still get Phoebe into orbit?
  c.   How long would the last stage have to run to get Phoebe going
        25,000 mph so that she could go off to the Moon?

6.   *Compound Interest Problem*   Banks which compound interest
      "continuously" use an exponential function to calculate the amount
      of money you have at any time. Suppose that you put $1000 into a
      savings account and find that at the end of one year you have $1052.
      Assume that the number of dollars you have in the account increases
      exponentially with time.

  a.   Find the particular equation for this exponential function.
  b.   Predict the amount you will have 10 years after you invested the
        $1000.
  c.   How many years will it take to *double* your investment? That is,
        when will you have $2000?

7.   *Car Trade-In Problem*   A rule-of-thumb used by car dealers is that
      the trade-in value of a car decreases by 30% each year. That is, the
      value at the end of any year is 70% of its value at the beginning of
      that year ("70% of . . ." means "0.7 times . . .").

  a.   Suppose that you own a car whose trade-in value is presently
        $2350. How much will it be worth 1 year from now? 2 years
        from now? 3 years from now?
  b.   Explain how the properties of exponential functions allow you to
        conclude that the trade-in value varies *exponentially* with time.
  c.   Write the particular equation expressing the trade-in value of
        your car as a function of the number of years from the present.

d.   In how many years from now should the trade-in value be $600?

e.   If the car is presently 2.7 years old, what was its trade-in value
     when it was new?

f.   The car cost $7430 when it was new. How do you explain the
     difference between this number and the answer to part e?

8.   *Air Pressure Problem*   The pressure of the air in the Earth's atmo-
     sphere decreases exponentially with altitude above the surface of the
     Earth. The pressure at the Earth's surface (sea level) is about 14.7
     pounds per square inch (psi) and the pressure at 2000 feet is approxi-
     mately 13.5 psi.

a.   Write the particular equation expressing pressure in terms of al-
     titude.

b.   Predict the pressure at
      i.   Mexico City (altitude 7500 feet),
     ii.   Mount Everest (altitude 29,000 feet),
    iii.   where U-2 spy planes fly (80,000 feet),
     iv.   the edge of space (defined by NASA to be 50 miles up).

c.   Human blood at body temperature will boil if the pressure is be-
     low 0.9 psi. At what altitude would your blood start to boil if
     you were in an unpressurized airplane?

d.   Recently it has been discovered that the Mediterranean Sea dried
     up about 6 million years ago, leaving a "valley" 10,000 feet be-

low sea level. What would the air pressure have been at the bottom of this valley?

9.   *Carbon 14 Dating Problem*   Carbon 14 is an isotope of carbon that is formed when radiation from the Sun strikes ordinary carbon dioxide in the atmosphere. Plants such as trees, which get their carbon dioxide from the atmosphere, therefore contain small amounts of carbon 14. Once a particular part of a plant has been formed, no more new carbon 14 is taken in. The carbon 14 in that part of the plant decays slowly, transmuting into nitrogen 14. Let P be the percent of carbon remaining in a part of a tree that grew t years ago.

a.   Write the particular equation expressing P in terms of t. You may assume that the "half-life" of carbon 14 is 5750 years, meaning that of the 100% of carbon 14 present when $t = 0$, only 50% remains when $t = 5750$ years.

b.   Christ was crucified about 2000 years ago. If somebody claimed to have a piece of wood from the cross on which he was crucified, what percent of the carbon 14 would you expect to find remaining in this wood?

c.   The oldest living trees in the World are the bristlecone pines in the White Mountains of California. 4000 "growth rings" have been counted in the trunk of one of these, meaning that the innermost ring is 4000 years old. What percent of the original carbon 14 would you expect to find in the oldest ring of this tree?

d.   A piece of wood believed to have come from Noah's Ark has
48.37% of the carbon 14 remaining. The Great Flood is supposed to have occurred in 4004 B.C. Is this piece of wood *old
enough* to have come from Noah's Ark? Justify your answer.

e.   Coal is supposed to have been formed from trees which lived
100 million years ago. What percent of the original carbon 14
would you expect to find remaining in coal? Why would carbon
14 dating probably *not* be very good for anything as old as coal?

f.   See the article "Carbon 14 and the Prehistory of Europe," by
Colin Renfrew in the October, 1971, issue of *Scientific American* for some surprising results of slight inaccuracies in the carbon 14 technique!

10.   *Biological Half-Life Problem*   You accidentally inhale some mildly
poisonous fumes. Twenty hours later you see a doctor. From a blood
sample, she measures a poison concentration of 0.00372 milligrams
per cubic centimeter (mg/cc), and tells you to come back in 8 hours.
On the second visit, she measures a concentration of 0.00219 mg/cc.
Let t be the number of hours that have elapsed since your first visit
to the doctor, and let C be the concentration of poison in your
blood, in mg/cc. Assume that C varies exponentially with t.

a.   Write the particular equation for this function.

b.   The doctor says you might have had serious body damage if the
poison concentration was ever as high as 0.015 mg/cc. Based on
your mathematical model, was the concentration ever that high?
Justify your answer.

c.   You can resume normal activities when the poison concentration
has dropped to 0.00010 mg/cc. How long after you inhaled the
fumes will you be able to resume normal activities?

d.   The "biological half-life" of the poison is the length of time it
takes for the concentration to drop to *half* of its present value.
Find the biological half-life of this poison.

e.   Plot a graph of C versus t from the time you breathed the fumes
until the time it is safe to resume normal activities. If you are
clever, you can think of a way to get *many* plotting points
quickly.

The problems below require you to distinguish among linear, quadratic,
and exponential functions, and to use exponential functions in ways different from the example. By doing this, you will demonstrate your ingenuity
at applying familiar concepts to unfamiliar problems.

11.   *Corn Flakes Problem*   Handy Andy sells 18 oz boxes of corn flakes
for $1.49 and 12 oz boxes for $1.07. Assume that the price varies
linearly with the number of ounces.

a.   Write the particular equation expressing number of cents in
terms of number of ounces.

b. Sketch the graph.
c. A 24 oz box costs $1.95. According to your model, is this box over-priced or under-priced? By how much?
d. Suppose that "Jumbo" boxes are priced at $3.80. How much corn flakes would you expect the box to contain?

12. *Grade Scaling Problem* Miss Calculate gives a test that is too hard, and decides to let students get half credit for their corrections. That is, students get half the difference between 100 and their original grade added to their original grade. Let x be the original grade and let y be the new grade.
a. Write an equation expressing y in terms of x. Do any obvious simplification.
b. What kind of function is it in part (a)? How do you tell?
c. Plot the graph of the function in an appropriate domain.
d. What would the new grade be if the old grade is 48? Show this on your graph.
e. What was the old grade if the new grade is 83? Show this on your graph.
f. What is the lowest the new grade could be? What part of the mathematical model tells you this?

13. *Studying Problem* Mae Degrade figures that the number of points she will score on her algebra test is a quadratic function of how long she studies the night before. She figures that the particular equation is $p = -5h^2 + 20h + 65$, where p is the number of points, and h is the number of hours.
a. What is the highest grade Mae could make? How long should she study to make that grade?
b. What grade would she make if she doesn't study at all? Write the special name given to this number.
c. According to the mathematical model, is there a number of hours she could study that would give her *zero* for a grade? Explain why your answer is reasonable.
d. Sketch the graph of this quadratic function.

14. *Play Tickets Problem* The senior class is investigating the price they should charge for tickets to the senior play. There were 900 people who attended last year's play when the tickets cost $3.00 each. They figure that at the same price, the same number will attend this year's play, but for each 1 cent increase in price, 2 fewer people will attend.
a. If the price is increased to $3.10, will the total revenue received this year be greater or less than if the price remained $3.00?
b. Let x be the number of dollars by which the price is increased. Let $p(x)$ be the new price and let $n(x)$ be the number who attend. Write particular equations for $p(x)$ and $n(x)$. What kind of functions are these?

c. Let $r(x)$ be the total number of dollars revenue received. Write the particular equation for this function. What kind of function is it?

d. Find $r(.60)$ and $r(1.20)$.

e. For what value of x will the maximum revenue be obtained? What is this maximum revenue?

f. Between what two values of x will the revenue be at least $2800?

g. Attendance can be increased by *lowering* the price. The auditorium holds up to 1100 people. What is the lowest feasible price per ticket?

h. Sketch the graph of function r in a suitable domain.

15. *Coffee Cup Problem*   After you pour a cup of coffee, it cools off in such a way that the *difference* between the coffee temperature and the room temperature decreases exponentially with time. This model is called "Newton's Law of Cooling." Suppose that you pour a cup of coffee. Three minutes later, you measure its temperature and find that it is 85°C. Five minutes after the first reading, you find that it has cooled to 72°C. The room is at 20°C.

Let c = number of degrees of coffee temperature.
Let D = number of degrees *difference* (coffee minus room).
Let t = number of minutes since first temperature reading.

a. Show that you understand the definitions of D and t by writing the given information as two ordered pairs, (t, D).

b. Write the particular equation expressing D in terms of t.

c. What was t when the coffee was first poured? Substitute this value of t into the equation to find D when the coffee was first poured. Based on your answer, what was the temperature, c, of the coffee when it was first poured?

d. Assume that coffee is "drinkable" when its temperature is at least 55°C. For how long *after it was poured* will the coffee be drinkable?

e. Using the properties of exponential functions, predict the temperature, c, of the coffee for every 5 minutes from $t = 10$ through $t = 60$. You may wish to write a short computer program to do the arithmetic. Don't forget to add room temperature to the values of D you calculate!

f. Plot a graph of the coffee temperature, c, from the time the coffee was poured until $t = 60$. Draw a dotted line at the appropriate place to show the asymptote. If you worked Problem 19 in Exercise 2-3, see how well your first thoughts about this real-world situation agree with the exponential model of the present problem.

16. *Calvin's Mass Problem*   Calvin Butterball consumes 8000 calories per day, and has a mass of 150 kg. He reads in a health book that he

could reduce his health risks if he attains a mass of 90 kg. He reduces his consumption to 2000 calories per day. At time $t = 0$ he starts the diet. When $t = 20$ days, he is down to 141 kg. Assume that the *difference* between his mass and 90 kg decreases exponentially with t.

a. Write the particular equation expressing the difference between Calvin's mass and 90 kg in terms of t.
b. Predict the number of kilograms by which Calvin is above 90 kg for times of 40, 60, 80, and 100 days.
c. Calculate Calvin's mass at each of these times.
d. Plot the graph of Calvin's mass versus time. Show what the graph looks like for values of t less than zero.
e. When should Calvin be 100 kg?
f. According to your model, will Calvin ever actually reach 90 kg? Justify your answer. What action must he take to reach 90 kg?

17. *Car Acceleration Problem*   Your car is standing still on a straight, level stretch of highway. At time $t = 0$ seconds, you floorboard the gas pedal. After 5 seconds you are going 40 kilometers per hour (kph). Let D be the *difference* between your car's speed and its top speed of 160 kph. Assume that D decreases exponentially with t.
a. Write the particular equation expressing D in terms of t.
b. How fast will you be going 18 seconds after you floorboarded the gas pedal?
c. How long will it take you to reach 150 kph?
d. Plot the graph of *actual* speed (*not D*) versus t. Draw a dotted line at the appropriate place to show the asymptote.
e. Show that the equation for the actual speed, S, has the form

$$S = a(1 - b^t),$$

where a and b are constants, and S and t are speed and time, respectively.

18. *Advertising Problem*   A well-known soft drink company comes out with a new product, Ms. Phizz. Based upon market analysis, they figure that if all potential users of this product were to buy it, they could sell $300,000 per day worth of the beverage. However, the *actual* sales depend on how much per day they spend on advertising. With *no* advertising, they figure that they will sell *no* Ms. Phizz. With $40,000 per day spent on advertising, they expect sales of $100,000 per day. Assume that the *difference* between $300,000 per day and *actual* sales decreases exponentially with the amount spent per day on advertising.
a. Write the particular equation expressing the *difference* between $300,000 per day and the actual sales in terms of the amount spent per day on advertising. It may be more convenient to express both amounts in *thousands* of dollars.

b. Calculate the difference between $300,000 per day and actual
    sales if 80, 120, 160, and 200 thousand dollars per day are
    spent on advertising. Then use the answers to calculate the ac-
    tual sales for these amounts spent on advertising.
c. Plot the graph of actual sales versus amount spent on advertis-
    ing. Draw a dotted line at the appropriate place to indicate the
    asymptote.
d. The *profit* made on the product is the actual sales *minus* the
    amount spent on advertising. Use the answers from part b to
    predict the profit per day if amounts of 0, 40, 80, 120, 160, and
    200 thousand dollars per day are spent on advertising.
e. Plot a graph of profit versus amount spent on advertising. Use
    the Cartesian coordinate system of part c.
f. What number of dollars per day seems to produce the *maximum*
    profit? (When you study calculus, you will learn how to *calcu-
    late* this maximum value from the equation, *without* having to
    plot the graph!)
g. What do you suppose is meant by, "The Law of Diminishing
    Returns?"
h. Show that the equation for actual sales, part b, has the form

$$S = a(1 - b^A),$$

where a and b are constants, and S and A are the actual sales
and the advertising amounts, respectively.

19. **Sunlight Below the Water Problem**   The intensity of sunlight reach-
    ing points below the surface of the ocean varies exponentially with
    the depth of the point below the surface of the water. Suppose that
    when the intensity at the surface is 1000 units, the intensity at a
    depth of 2 meters is 60 units.
    a. Write the particular equation expressing intensity in terms of
        depth.
    b. Predict the intensity at depths of 4, 6, 8, and 10 meters.
    c. Plants cannot grow beneath the surface if the intensity of sun-
        light is below 0.001 unit. What is the maximum depth at which
        plants will grow?
    d. The intensity of sunlight drops so fast that throughout most of
        the domain, the graph cannot be distinguished from the asymp-
        tote (see Figure 6-14b). Using the given ordered pairs and the
        results of part b, find the *logarithm* of the intensity for each 2
        meters from 0 through 10 meters. Then plot a graph of the *log*
        of intensity versus depth.
    e. What interesting property does the graph from part d seem to
        have? *Prove* that it has this property.

20. **Radio Dial Problem**   You have probably noticed that the distances
    between markings on most radio dials are *not* uniform. For example,

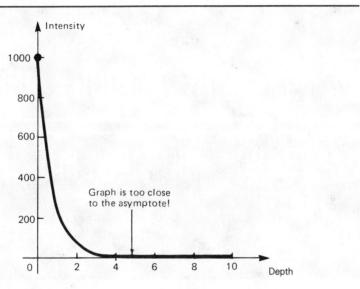

Figure 6-14b

the distance between frequencies of 53 and 60 kilohertz is not much different from the distance between 140 and 160 kilohertz. Assume that the frequency marked on the dial varies exponentially with the distance from the left end of the dial. In this problem you are to figure out how to mark a dial that is to be 12 cm long.

a.   The dial is to be 12 cm long, and the lowest and highest frequencies are to be 53 and 160 kilohertz, respectively. Write these pieces of information as ordered pairs, (distance, frequency).

b.   Write the particular equation expressing frequency in terms of distance.

c.   Transform the equation in part b so that *distance* is expressed in terms of *frequency*. This form of the equation will be more convenient to use when you calculate the distances corresponding to various frequencies.

d.   By looking at your equation in part c, think up some appropriate words to describe how *distance* varies with *frequency*.

e.   Calculate to the nearest tenth of a millimeter the distances for frequencies of 60, 70, 80, 100, 120, and 140 kilohertz, the frequencies that often appear on radio dials. Since a considerable amount of computation is required, you may want to use a calculator or to write a short computer program. If your computer has only base *e* logarithms, you will need to use the change-of-base property.

f.   Use the given points and the results of part e to plot a graph of distance (as the *ordinate*) versus frequency (as the *abscissa*).

g. Use a ruler to make a scale drawing of the radio dial with the
    frequencies marked in. It should look somewhat like that in the
    photograph.

21. ***Deep Oil Well Cost Problem***   Suppose that you are a mathematician
    for Wells Oil Production, Inc. Your company is planning to drill a
    well 50,000 feet deep, deeper than anyone has ever drilled before.
    Your part of the project is to predict the cost of drilling the well.

    From previous well records, you ascertain that the price is $20 per
    foot for drilling at the surface, and $30 per foot for drilling at 10,000
    feet. Assume that the number of dollars per foot for drilling an oil
    well increases exponentially with the depth at which the drill is oper-
    ating.
    a. Write the particular equation expressing price per foot in terms
        of depth. You might find it more convenient to express depth in
        thousands of feet.
    b. Predict the price per foot for drilling at depths of 20, 30, 40,
        and 50 thousand feet.
    c. *Carefully* plot the graph of price per foot versus depth. Choose
        scales that make the graph occupy most of the piece of graph
        paper.
    d. The *area* of the region under the graph (see Figure 6-14c) repre-
        sents the *total* number of dollars it costs to drill the well. You
        can see a reason by considering the *units* of this area. The verti-
        cal distance is $/ft, and the horizontal distance is ft., so the area
        has units

$$\frac{\text{dollars}}{\text{foot}} \times \text{feet,}$$

or simply *dollars*. Count the *number of squares* in this region on *your* graph. Estimate fractional squares to the nearest 0.1 unit (see Figure 6-14c). (When you study calculus, you will learn how to *calculate* such areas from the equation, without having to count squares.)

e.   Calculate the number of dollars corresponding to each square. For example, if the horizontal spacing is 2000 feet, and the vertical spacing is 5 $/ft, as in the right-hand sketch of Figure 6-14c, then each square corresponds to

$$(2000)(5) = 10,000 \text{ dollars.}$$

f.   Calculate the total cost of drilling the well. (Expensive, isn't it!?)

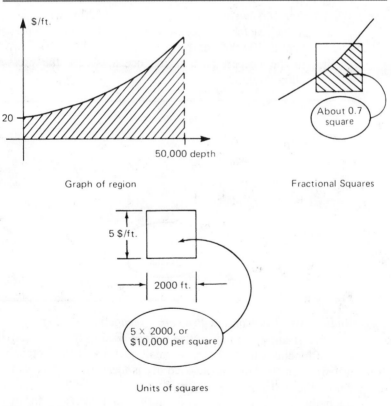

Graph of region   Fractional Squares

Units of squares

Figure 6-14c

22. *Vapor Pressure Problem*   The vapor pressure of water is the pressure that water vapor (i.e., steam) would exert if it, alone, occupied the space above the water in a closed container (Figure 6-14d). About 200 years ago the French scientists Clausius and Clapeyron found that the vapor pressure varies exponentially with the *reciprocal*

of the absolute temperature of the water. That is, if P is the vapor
pressure and T is the absolute temperature, then

$$P = a \times 10^{k\left(\frac{1}{T}\right)}$$

a. Find the particular equation expressing vapor pressure in terms
    of absolute temperature if water at 0°C has a vapor pressure of
    4.6 millimeters of mercury (mm), and at 100°C, has 760 mm.
    (The absolute temperature is 273 plus the Celsius temperature.)
    You must be very clever to figure a way to evaluate the two con-
    stants!
b. Use your equation to predict the vapor pressure of water on a hot
    summer day, 40°C.
c. Water boils when its vapor pressure reaches the pressure of its
    surrounding atmosphere. At what Celsius temperature would wa-
    ter boil
    i.   atop Mt. Everest, where the air is at 220 mm?
    ii. in the reactor of a nuclear power plant, where the pressure is
         kept at 100,000 mm?
    iii. in the deepest part of the ocean, where the pressure is
         800,000 mm?

Closed container

Water Vapor
only (no air)

Water

Figure 6-14d

23. *Radioactive Brain Tracer Problem*   Technetium 99m (pronounced
    "tek-neé-si-um") is a radioactive isotope used to trace the activity of
    certain functions in the brain. A small quantity of the isotope is in-
    jected. Then the level of radioactivity is measured at various times
    during the next few hours to see how much technetium remains in
    the brain. The amount remaining in the brain decreases for two rea-
    sons:

    Physical: Technetium 99m has a half-life of 6 hours, which
    means that at the end of any 6-hour period, the amount remain-
    ing is only half what it was at the beginning of that period, even
    if none is eliminated from the brain.

Biological: The brain eliminates technetium in such a way that even if it were not radioactive, the amount remaining would decrease exponentially with time.

It is the *biological* half-life that doctors seek to measure. As you work the following parts of the problem you will see how this measure can be accomplished.

a.   Let P be the fraction of technetium that would remain after t hours due to physical (radioactive) decay alone, and let B be the fraction that would be left due to biological activity alone. The actual fraction, F, that remains after t hours is

$$F = PB.$$

Prove that if P and B both vary exponentially with time, then F varies exponentially with time also.

b.   A patient is injected with some technetium 99m. Two hours later, only 71.3% ($F = 0.713$) remains. Use this and the fact that $F = 1$ when $t = 0$ to find the particular equation expressing F in terms of t.

c.   Use the 6-hour half-life to find the exponential constant in the equation which expresses P in terms of t. Then use the result in an appropriate manner to find the particular equation for B in terms of t.

d.   Calculate the *biological* half-life of technetium for this particular patient's brain. You can do this by letting $B = 0.5$ and solving for t.

6-15 | CHAPTER REVIEW AND TEST

In this chapter you have studied the third major kind of function, the exponential function. You have learned that the graphs have horizontal asymptotes. Logarithms have been useful for solving exponential equations so that you can find x for given values of y. Logarithms are also an example of the general concept of the inverse of a function. Exponential functions make reasonable mathematical models for variables that are related by the add-multiply property. While working exponential model problems, you had to recall things about linear and quadratic functions.

The Review Problems below parallel the sections in this chapter. The Concepts Problems let you try your hand at applying what you know to analyze a new situation. The Chapter Test is similar to one your instructor might give to see how well you understand exponential functions.

REVIEW PROBLEMS

R1. If $f(x) = 3^x$, find $f(4), f(3), f(2)$, and $f(1)$. Show that $f(3)$ is $\frac{1}{3}$ of

$f(4), f(2)$ is $\frac{1}{3}$ of $f(3)$, and so forth. Show how this pattern leads

to a natural way to define 3^0, 3^{-1}, and 3^{-2}.

R2. Evaluate using the proper order of operations:
   a. $3 \cdot 5^2$ b. $7 - 2^5$ c. $24 - 4^3 - 5 \cdot (-2)^3$

R3. a. Name and state the five properties of exponentiation.
   b. Evaluate: i. -4^2 ii. $(-5)^3$ iii. $(-2)^4$
   c. Simplify: i. $(2x^7)^5$ ii. $4(x^3y^5)^8$

   iii. $\dfrac{6r^{12}p^8}{2r^3p^2}$

   d. Evaluate: $\dfrac{5^{1234}}{5^{1230}}$

   e. Sketch the graph (quickly!): $f(x) = 1.8^x$

R4. a. Write the definition of exponentiation for negative exponents.
   b. Write the definition of exponentiation for zero exponent.
   c. Write the definition of $x^{\frac{1}{i}}$.
   d. Simplify:

   i. $4x^{-3} \cdot (5x^{-4})^2$

   ii. $\left(\dfrac{12x^4y^{-2}}{4x^5y^2}\right)^{-3}$

   iii. $9x^{-\frac{1}{2}} \cdot 16x^{\frac{1}{4}} \cdot 5x^0$

   e. Evaluate:
   i. $128^{\frac{4}{7}}$
   ii. $\sqrt[3]{512}$
   iii. $32^{0.41}$
   iv. $0.41^{3.2}$
   v. $\sqrt[5]{1,924,000,000}$

   f. Sketch the graph (quickly!): $f(x) = 0.7^x$

R5. *a.* Find the exact value:
   i. $64^{\frac{2}{3}}$ ii. $32^{-\frac{2}{5}}$ iii. $\sqrt[5]{248832}$
   b. Simplify. Leave in radical form: $\sqrt[3]{5^{2.7}} \div \sqrt[3]{5^{4.5}}$
   c. Solve: $216^x = 36$
   d. How many cubic millimeters in a cubic centimeter?

R6. a. Evaluate: $(6 \times 10^{17})(9 \times 10^{43})$

   b. Evaluate: $\dfrac{1.2 \times 10^{20}}{5 \times 10^6}$

   c. Evaluate and round: $(2.167 \times 10^{-13})^3$
   d. Sketch the graph (quickly!): $f(x) = 10^{-x}$

R7.   Solve $5^x = 328$ without using logarithms. Get the answer correct to three decimal places.

R8.   a.   Solve: $3.79 \times 0.41^{5x} = 71$
       b.   Sketch the graph (quickly!): $f(x) = \log x$

R9.   a.   Find j: $\log_{27} j = \dfrac{2}{3}$
       b.   Find m: $\log_3 81 = m$
       c.   Find p: $\log_p 343 = 3$

R10.   a.   If $\log 5 \approx 0.699$ and $\log 3 \approx 0.477$, find $\log 45$ without using the log key.
       b.   If $\log 7 \approx 0.845$, find $\log (7^{200})$.
       c.   Write $\log_{13} 300 - \log_{13} 15$ as a single logarithm of a single argument.

R11.   Use the change-of-base property to evaluate $\log_{19} 427$

R12.   a.   If $f(x) = 7x + 42$, find an equation for $f^{-1}(x)$.
       b.   If $g(x) = \log_5 3x$, find an equation for $g^{-1}(x)$.
       c.   If $h(x) = x^2$, and $x \geq 0$, sketch the graphs of h and h^{-1} on the same set of axes.
       d.   If $a(x) = |x + 3|$, is a^{-1} a function? Explain.

R13.   If f is an exponential function with values of $f(1) = 4$ and $f(6) = 7$, find $f(16)$.

R14.   *Fog Problem*   In a fog, the tail lights of the car in front of you seem to appear suddenly. According to Beer's Law of Radiation Absorption, the intensity of the light varies exponentially with the distance between you and the other car. Suppose that the intensity is 128 units when the car is "right at" your car (i.e., the distance is essentially zero). At 43 feet the intensity is only half of that value.
       a.   What is the intensity at 86 feet?
       b.   Write the particular equation expressing intensity as a function of distance.
       c.   If the lights are just visible when the intensity is 3 units, how far away would the car be?
       d.   By what factor does the intensity increase when the car nears from 86 feet away to 43 feet away? From 1043 feet away to 1000 feet away?
       e.   Why do the lights seem to appear so suddenly?

CONCEPTS PROBLEMS

Suppose that $f(x) = 21.6x^n$, where n is a constant, but not necessarily an integer.

C1.   If $n = 0$, write the equation for $f(x)$ in simplest form.

C2. If $n = \dfrac{2}{3}$, write the equation for $f(x)$ in radical form.

C3. If $n = -2$,
   a. Write the equation for $f(x)$ without negative exponents.
   b. Find $f(1), f(2), f(3)$, and $f(10)$.
   c. Find $f(0)$.
   d. Draw the graph of f for positive values of x.
   e. What relationship does the x-axis have to the graph of f?
   f. Does f have the add-multiply property of exponential functions?
       Justify your answer.

C4. If $n = 1.4$,
   a. Find $f(56.17)$,
   b. Find $f(0.007)$,
   c. Find x, if $f(x) = 1776$.

C5. If $n = 2$,
   a. Find an equation for $f^{-1}(x)$.
   b. Find $f^{-1}(2.4)$.

C6. Suppose that f is a mathematical model for the weight of a person as
     a function of his or her height, where x is the number of meters tall
     and $f(x)$ is the number of kilograms.
   a. If a person 1.52m tall is 63 kg, find the particular equation.
   b. Predict the mass of a basketball player 2.34m tall.

CHAPTER TEST

T1. Demonstrate that you understand how logarithms are used to solve
     equations by solving

$$13 \times 8^{0.3x} = 663.$$

T2. There are short cuts that can be used to solve certain exponential
     equations quickly. Solve the *general* equation

$$b^x = c$$

     for x in terms of b and c.

T3. Use the formula you derived in Problem 2 to solve

$$29^x = 0.87.$$

     Demonstrate that your answer is correct.

T4. Cal Q. Later solves the equation $7^x = 82$ and gets 11.714236 for
     his answer. Explain to Cal how he can tell without even using a
     calculator that his answer is unreasonable. What error has Cal
     made?

T5.   In order to make intelligent applications of mathematics you must know the definitions and properties. Write the equations that state, in general, the five properties of exponentiation.

T6.   Use the properties and definitions of exponentiation to show how $81^{-\frac{3}{4}}$ can be evaluated *without* the use of a calculator. (You should check your answer *with* a calculator.)

T7.   On graph paper, plot the part of the graph of $f(x) = 10^{0.2x}$ from $x = -5$ to $x = 5$. Pick enough values of x to get a smooth curve.

T8.   Let $g(x) = 5(\log x)$. Find values of $g(0.1)$, $g(0.5)$, $g(1)$, $g(2)$, $g(5)$, and $g(10)$. Plot the graph of this function on the same set of axes as in Problem 7. What do you notice about the two graphs?

T9.   *Epidemic Problem* During the first stages of an epidemic, the number of sick people increases exponentially with time. Suppose that at time $t = 0$ days there are 40 people sick. By the time $t = 3$, 200 people are sick.
   a.   How many people will be sick by the time $t = 6$?
   b.   Let $s(t)$ be the number of sick people at time t. Find the particular equation expressing $s(t)$ in terms of t.
   c.   Predict the number of sick people at the end of the first week.
   d.   At what time t does the number of sick people reach 7000?

7

Rational Algebraic Functions

In this chapter you will study functions in which there is **division** by the independent variable. The most important mathematical concept is what happens when the variable denominator is close to zero. To investigate this concept, you must refresh your memory about operations with fractions. These operations require you to know various factoring techniques. The mathematical models you will use are called **variation** functions which relate variables such as the force needed to loosen a bolt and the length of the wrench handle.

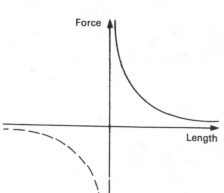

7-1 | INTRODUCTION TO RATIONAL ALGEBRAIC FUNCTIONS

You recall that a rational number is a number that can be written as the ratio of two integers. A **rational algebraic expression** is an expression that can be written as a ratio of two *polynomials*. For instance, these are rational algebraic expressions:

$$\frac{3x - 2}{x^2 - 7x + 11}, \quad x^3 - 7 \quad \left(\text{which equals } \frac{x^3 - 7}{1} \right), \text{ etc.}$$

An expression such as $\dfrac{|x|}{\log x}$ is not called a rational algebraic expression.

Although it is a ratio, it is not a ratio of polynomials. A rational algebraic function is a function in which y equals a rational algebraic expression.

DEFINITION

RATIONAL ALGEBRAIC FUNCTION
A **rational algebraic function** (or simply a "rational function") is a function with the general equation

$$f(x) = \frac{P(x)}{Q(x)},$$

where $P(x)$ and $Q(x)$ stand for polynomials.

The most interesting thing about rational functions is what happens when the value of x you pick makes the denominator equal zero!

Objective:
Discover by pointwise plotting what the graph of a rational function looks like.

EXERCISE 7-1

Given: $f(x) = \dfrac{x + 2}{x^2 - x - 6}$.

1. Find $f(0), f(2), f(4), f(5), f(-1),$ and $f(-3)$.

2. Try to find $f(3)$ and $f(-2)$. What do you notice?

3. What numbers must be *excluded* from the domain of function f?

4. Plot the graph of f. To get a better idea of what happens near $x = 3$ and $x = -2$, try values such as $f(2.9), f(3.1), f(-1.9),$ and $f(-2.1)$.

5. Based on your graph, what *two* different things could happen when the value of x makes the denominator equal zero?

7-2 RATIONAL FUNCTION GRAPHS— DISCONTINUITIES AND ASYMPTOTES

In Exercise 7-1 you plotted the graph of the function

$$f(x) = \frac{x + 2}{x^2 - x - 6}.$$

The job of substituting values for x and evaluating the function can be made much easier if you simplify the fraction first. The denominator will factor, giving

$$f(x) = \frac{x + 2}{(x + 2)(x - 3)}.$$

The numerator and denominator now have $(x + 2)$ as a common factor. As long as x is not -2, this factor can be *canceled* by dividing numerator and denominator by $(x + 2)$.

$$f(x) = \frac{\overset{1}{\cancel{x + 2}}}{\underset{1}{\cancel{(x + 2)}}(x - 3)}.$$

$$f(x) = \frac{1}{x - 3}, \text{ provided } x \neq -2.$$

The canceling could not be done if x were -2 because you would be dividing numerator and denominator by 0. In Problems 5 and 6 of the following exercise you will see that canceling common factors from the numerator and denominator can be justified by the Multiplication Property of Fractions.

Substituting values of x into $\frac{1}{(x-3)}$ is much easier than substituting into the original expression for $f(x)$. Some values are shown in the following table.

x	$f(x)$	x	$f(x)$
-5	$-\frac{1}{8}$	1	$-\frac{1}{2}$
-4	$-\frac{1}{7}$	2	-1
-3	$-\frac{1}{6}$	3	no value
-2	no value	4	1
-1	$-\frac{1}{4}$	5	$\frac{1}{2}$
0	$-\frac{1}{3}$	6	$\frac{1}{3}$
		7	$\frac{1}{4}$

Values of x close to 3 produce interesting results!

$$f(3.1) = \frac{1}{(3.1-3)} = \frac{1}{0.1} = 10$$

$$f(2.9) = \frac{1}{(2.9-3)} = \frac{1}{(-0.1)} = -10$$

$$f(3.01) = 100$$

$$f(2.99) = -100$$

etc.

The closer x gets to 3, the larger $f(x)$ gets in absolute value!! Since x can never *equal* 3, there is a *vertical asymptote* at $x = 3$.

Values of x close to -2 produce less dramatic results.

$$f(-2.1) = \frac{1}{(-2.1-3)} = \frac{1}{(-5.1)} \approx -\frac{1}{5}$$

$$f(-1.9) = \frac{1}{(-1.9-3)} = \frac{1}{(-4.9)} \approx -\frac{1}{5}$$

As x gets closer to -2, $f(x)$ gets closer to $-\frac{1}{5}$. Since x can never *equal*

−2, there is simply a point *missing* from the graph, leaving a "hole" at $(-2, -\frac{1}{5})$. The $-\frac{1}{5}$ is the value you would get by substituting −2 into the *simplified* equation, $f(x) = \frac{1}{(x-3)}$. The graph is shown in Figure 7-2a.

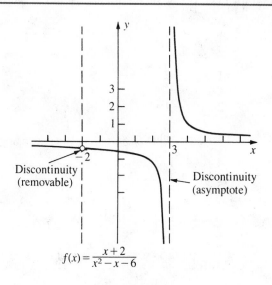

$$f(x) = \frac{x+2}{x^2-x-6}$$

Figure 7-2a _____

A place where the graph of a function stops and starts over again is called a *discontinuity*. If the graph "shoots off to infinity" as it does where $x = 3$, the discontinuity is a *vertical asymptote*. If the graph just stops and starts over again at the same point, as it does where $x = -2$, the discontinuity is called a *removable discontinuity*. The name is appropriate because the discontinuity is *removed* by canceling the $(x + 2)$ in the numerator and denominator, and defining $f(-2)$ to be $-\frac{1}{5}$.

Objective:
Given the equation for a rational algebraic function, simplify it (if necessary), find the discontinuities, and draw the graph.

In the following exercise you will draw a few graphs such as Figure 7-2a. You will also prove that canceling in fractions can be justified by the axioms and properties you have learned.

EXERCISE 7-2

Do These Quickly

The following problems are intended to refresh your skills. You should be able to do all 10 in less than 5 minutes.

Q1.   Multiply: $(x + 3)(x + 5)$

Q2.   Factor: $x^2 + 5x + 4$

Q3.   Multiply: $(x - 2)(x - 7)$

Q4.   Factor: $x^2 - 8x + 15$

Q5.   Multiply: $(x + 3)(x - 2)$

Q6.   Factor: $x^2 + 2x - 8$

Q7.   Multiply: $(x - 5)(x + 2)$

Q8.   Factor: $x^2 - 4x - 5$

Q9.   Find 70% of 300.

Q10.   Write in exponential form: $\log_f p = a$

Work the following problems.

1.   ***Graphing Problem No. 1***   Plot accurately the graph of $f(x) = \frac{1}{x}$ for values of x from 0.1 through 10. Choose enough values such as 0.2, 0.5, etc., to get a smooth curve. Then plot the part of the graph from -10 through -0.1. What feature does the graph have at $x = 0$? What is the relationship of the x-axis to the graph?

2.   ***Graphing Problem No. 2***   Given the function

$$g(x) = \frac{1}{x - 1}$$

    a.   Plot the graph by picking values of x and calculating values of $g(x)$. See how *few* values you have to calculate to find the pattern that the points follow.

    b.   What feature does the graph have at $x = 1$?

    c.   How is the graph of function g related to the graph of function f in Problem 1?

3.   ***Graphing Problem No. 3***   Given the function

$$h(x) = \frac{x - 4}{x^2 - 5x + 4}$$

a. Factor the denominator. Based on the results, find the values of
    x at which there are discontinuities.
b. Simplify the fraction. Based on the simplified fraction, where is
    there a vertical asymptote, and where is there a removable dis-
    continuity?
c. Draw a vertical dotted line at each discontinuity. Then sketch
    the graph of function h. You should be able to do this quickly if
    you have worked Problem 2.

4. *Graphing Problem No. 4*   Sketch the graph of

$$r(x) = \frac{x - 2}{x^2 + 3x - 10}.$$

Show any asymptotes and removable discontinuities.

5. *Canceling Problem*   The following steps form a proof that common
    factors can be canceled from the numerator and denominator of a ra-
    tional algebraic expression. Copy the statement and proof of the the-
    orem. Name the axiom, definition, or other property that justifies
    each step in the proof.

Prove that $\dfrac{cn}{cd} = \dfrac{n}{d}$, provided $c \neq 0$ and $d \neq 0$.

Proof:

$$\frac{cn}{cd}$$

a. $= \dfrac{c}{c} \cdot \dfrac{n}{d}$

b. $= 1 \cdot \dfrac{n}{d}$

c. $= \dfrac{n}{d}$

d. $\therefore \dfrac{cn}{cd} = \dfrac{n}{d}$, Q.E.D.

6. *Another Canceling Problem*   Write a formal proof that

$$\frac{c}{cd} = \frac{1}{d}, \text{ provided } c \neq 0 \text{ and } d \neq 0.$$

7-3 | SPECIAL PRODUCTS AND FACTORING

You have learned that two binomials can be multiplied by distributing each
term in one of them to each term in the other. You have also learned that

a quadratic trinomial can be factored back apart again by searching for the appropriate two binomials. In this section you will learn some shortcuts that will allow you to multiply and factor some special binomials quickly, and multiply any polynomials reasonably quickly.

1. *Product of Conjugate Binomials*
    Suppose two binomials are to be multiplied, and each has exactly the same terms except for the sign between them. For instance,

$$(3x - 5)(3x + 5).$$

Distributing gives

$$9x^2 + 15x - 15x - 25$$
$$= 9x^2 - 25.$$

The result is a *difference* of two *squares*. Binomials of the form $a - b$ and $a + b$ are called **conjugate binomials.** Conjugate binomials can be multiplied quickly if you remember that the middle term always "drops out."

PRODUCT OF CONJUGATE BINOMIALS

$$(a - b)(a + b) = a^2 - b^2$$

Don't confuse multiplying conjugates with *squaring* a binomial!

$$(a - b)^2 = a^2 - 2ab + b^2$$

The square of a binomial *does* have a middle term!!

2. *Products of Any Polynomials*
    Once you understand the distributing pattern for two binomials, you can multiply *any* two polynomials in at most two steps. For instance,

$$(x^3 - 2x^2 + 5x - 7)(x^2 + 4x - 3)$$
$$= x^5 + 4x^4 - 3x^3 - 2x^4 - 8x^3 + 6x^2 + 5x^3 + 20x^2 - 15x$$
$$- 7x^2 - 28x + 21$$
$$= x^5 + 2x^4 - 6x^3 + 19x^2 - 43x + 21.$$

With practice, you can eliminate the middle step by calculating all terms of the same degree and adding them up as you go. Figure 7-3a shows how you can find the x^2-term by moving your fingers toward each other and adding the results in your head.

$$(x^3 - 2x^2 + 5x - 7)\ (x^2 + 4x - 3) = \ldots + 19x^2 + \ldots$$

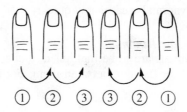

Mental Multiplication of Polynomials

Figure 7-3a ——————————————————————

Objective:

Be able to multiply conjugate binomials, factor a difference of two squares, and multiply polynomials with more than two terms, as well as factor familiar quadratic trinomials.

Examples of the two *multiply* parts of the objective are shown above. The following examples show you application of the concepts to related problems.

EXAMPLE 1

Factor completely: $16x^2 - y^2$

Solution:
You recognize $16x^2 - y^2$ as a difference of two squares. So you just write down the two conjugate binomials that would give this when they are multiplied together.

$$16x^2 - y^2 = \underline{(4x - y)(4x + y)}$$ ∎

EXAMPLE 2

Multiply: $(x + 4)(3x - 2)(x + 5)$

Solution:
Associate the first two factors and multiply them. Then multiply the answer by the third factor by distributing each term of one to each term of the other.

$$(x + 4)(3x - 2)(x + 5)$$
$$= (3x^2 + 10x - 8)(x + 5)$$
$$= 3x^3 + 25x^2 + 42x - 40$$ ∎

EXAMPLE 3

Factor completely: $5x^7 - 405x^3$

Solution:

$$5x^7 - 405x^3$$
$$= 5x^3(x^4 - 81) \qquad\qquad \text{Factor out common factors.}$$
$$= 5x^3(x^2 - 9)(x^2 + 9)$$
$$= \underline{5x^3(x - 3)(x + 3)(x^2 + 9)}$$

There are common factors that can be factored out first. After that, the re-maining factor can be factored *again*! Don't stop till you have factored it *completely*. ■

EXAMPLE 4

Factor completely: $3x^2 - 16x - 12$

Solution:
As you have learned in previous mathematics courses, the most straightfor-ward technique is to write two pairs of parentheses, then try different combinations of terms in each pair.

$$3x^2 - 16x - 12 = (\quad)(\quad)$$

The first terms must multiply to give $3x^2$. The only possible numbers with integer coefficients are $3x$ and x. So you write

$$3x^2 - 16x - 12 = (3x\quad)(x\quad)$$

The second terms must give -12. By trial and error, the combination that gives $-16x$ for the middle term is:

$$3x^2 - 16x - 12 = \underline{(3x + 2)(x - 6)} \qquad ■$$

Examples 3 and 4 say, "Factor completely. . . ." To tell that you have fac-tored completely, the entire expression must be one term with as many factors as possible. The expression $3(x - 5) + 4$ is not factored because it has two terms. The expression $(4x + 6)(3x - 7)$ is not factored com-pletely since 2 can be factored out of the first factor. Although 3 *could* be factored out of the second factor, it would leave an expression with a frac-tion, $(4x + 6)(3)(x - \frac{7}{3})$.

AGREEMENT

COMPLETELY FACTORED FORM

A polynomial is completely factored when it is written as a product of two or more *polynomials* with *integers* for their coefficients.

In the following exercise you will practice multiplying and factoring polynomials. You will also graph some rational functions using what you learned before.

EXERCISE 7-3

Do These Quickly

The following problems are intended to refresh your skills. You should be able to do all 10 in less than 5 minutes.

Q1. Sketch quickly: $y = \dfrac{1}{x}$

Q2. Find the slope of the line through $(2, 7)$ and $(8, 10)$.

Q3. Sketch the graph of a quadratic function with one negative x-intercept and one positive x-intercept.

Q4. Multiply: $(3 \times 10^{40})(2 \times 10^{50})$

Q5. Add: $1\dfrac{1}{2} + \dfrac{3}{4}$

Q6. Find 20% of 400.

Q7. Solve: $17 = 3x - 2$

Q8. Simplify: $3 + 7(8 - 6)$

Q9. Draw an isosceles triangle.

Q10. Complete the square: $x^2 - 20x +$ _____

Work the following problems.

1. *Graphing Problem*   Sketch the graph of

$$f(x) = \frac{x + 3}{x^2 + x - 6}.$$

Show any asymptotes and removable discontinuities. Explain how the discontinuity is *removed* by canceling.

2. *Graph of $f(x) = \dfrac{k}{x}$ Problem*

    a. Draw on graph paper the graph of $f(x) = \frac{1}{x}$ by plotting $f(1)$ and $f(-1)$, then sketching using the asymptotes.

b. On the same set of axes, plot $g(x) = \frac{2}{x}$. In what ways is the graph similar to that of $f(x) = \frac{1}{x}$? In what ways is it different?

c. On the same set of axes, sketch $h(x) = \frac{5}{x}$. You should be able to do this quickly by observing the conclusions in part (b).

For Problems 3 through 42, multiply the polynomials.

3. $(x + 3)(x - 5)$ 4. $(x - 2)(x + 7)$

5. $(x - 4y)(3x - 7y)$ 6. $(x - 6y)(2x - 7y)$

7. $(x - 8)(x + 8)$ 8. $(x - 9)(x + 9)$

9. $(3x + 7)(3x - 7)$ 10. $(5x + 4)(5x - 4)$

11. $(2p - 11f)(2p + 11f)$ 12. $(12c - 7d)(12c + 7d)$

13. $(x^3 + 6)(x^3 - 6)$ 14. $(x^5 + 1)(x^5 - 1)$

15. $(4 - 3x^5)(4 + 3x^5)$ 16. $(11 - 2x^3)(11 + 2x^3)$

17. $(3a + b)(3a + b)$ 18. $(2m - k)(2m - k)$

19. $(6x - 5)^2$ 20. $(100t + k)^2$

21. $(x^2 + 3x - 4)(x + 2)$ 22. $(x^2 - 2x + 5)(x - 3)$

23. $(x - 11)(x^2 - 2x + 8)$ 24. $(x + 12)(x^2 - 3x - 2)$

25. $(x - y)(x^2 + xy + y^2)$ 26. $(x + y)(x^2 - xy + y^2)$

27. $(x^2 - 5x + 7)(2x - 1)$ 28. $(x^2 + 2x - 6)(3x - 1)$

29. $(x^2 - 4x - 7)(x^2 - 2x + 5)$ 30. $(x^2 - 6x + 8)(x^2 - 7x + 1)$

31. $(x^3 + 5x^2 - 3x - 2)(x^2 - 2x + 1)$

32. $(x^3 - 3x^2 - 4x + 6)(x^2 + 2x + 5)$

33. $(x^2 + 3x - 5)(x^3 + 4x^2 - 3x + 2)$

34. $(x^2 - x + 2)(x^3 + 3x^2 - 5x + 4)$

35. $(x + 5)(x - 1)(x + 2)$ 36. $(x - 6)(x - 4)(x + 3)$

37. $(2x - 3)(x + 1)(x - 2)$ 38. $(3x + 2)(x - 1)(x - 4)$

39. $(x - 1)^3$ 40. $(x + 2)^3$

41. $(x + y)^3$ 42. $(x - y)^3$

For Problems 43 through 62, factor the quadratic trinomial completely.

43. $x^2 + 5x - 14$ 44. $x^2 - 9x + 20$

45. $3x^2 + 9x - 30$ 46. $2x^2 - 4x - 70$

47. $8x^2 + 6xy + y^2$ 48. $10x^2 + 3xy - y^2$

49. $3r^2 + rx - 10x^2$ 50. $6p^2 - 11pj - 10j^2$

51. $6x^2 + 11x + 3$ 52. $6x^2 + 7x - 20$

53. $6x^2 + 19x - 20$ 54. $6x^2 + 37x - 20$

55. $10x^2 - 29x + 21$ 56. $4x^2 + 25x - 21$

57. $10x^2 - 29x - 21$ 58. $12x^2 - 7x - 12$

59. $4x^2 - 12x + 9$ 60. $25x^2 + 40x + 16$

61. $x^2 + 16x + 64$ 62. $x^2 - 22x + 121$

For Problems 63 through 86, factor the difference of two squares completely.

63. $x^2 - 9$ 64. $x^2 - 16$

65. $4x^2 - 25$ 66. $25x^2 - 9$

67. $49 - 9x^2$ 68. $4 - 81x^2$

69. $y^2 - 1$ 70. $1 - 36t^2$

71. $36a^2 - 144$ 72. $16c^2 - 64$

73. $80y^2 - 5z^2$ 74. $27 - 3h^2$

75. $x^4 - y^4$ 76. $x^8 - y^8$

77. $x^6 - y^4$ 78. $p^{10} - q^4$

79. $a^5 - a^3$ 80. $k^7 - k^3$

81. $x^4y^2 - x^2y^4$ 82. $x^5y^3 - x^3y^5$

83. $(x + 7)^2 - 9$ 84. $(x - 3)^2 - 25$

85. $36 - (x - 5)^2$ 86. $81 - (2x + 7)^2$

87. *Product of Binomials Proof*   Prove that you can multiply two binomials by distributing each term of one binomial to each term of the other. In other words, prove that for any real numbers, a, b, c, and d,

$$(a + b)(c + d) = ac + ad + bc + bd.$$

You may start by distributing the *quantity* $(a + b)$ to each term in the second factor.

88. *Polynomial Products by Computer*   Write a computer program that will multiply any two given polynomials. When the program is run, the computer should ask you to input the degree and the coefficients

of each polynomial. Then the computer should calculate the coefficients of the product and print the answer. Test your program by
having it multiply

$$(x^3 - 2x^2 + 5x - 7)(x^2 + 4x - 3).$$

The correct answer is at the beginning of this section.

Mental Multiplication of Integers   The Arabic numerals we use for
integers are compact forms of polynomials. For instance, 296 is

$$2(10^2) + 9(10) + 6.$$

So the technique shown in Figure 7-3a can be used to multiply two
integers *mentally*. All you write down is the answer! The only difference is that you start from the *right* instead of from the left so that
you can take care of numbers that are carried. For instance, to multiply 57 by 34 you would think:

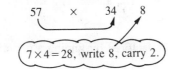

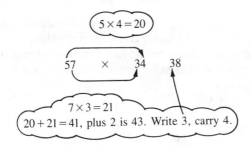

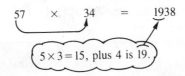

All that appears on your paper is 57 × 34 = 1938. For Problems 89
through 96, multiply the integers mentally. Then check your answers
by calculator.

89. 23 × 87   90. 37 × 48

91. 56 × 91   92. 89 × 67

93. 27 × 518   94. 365 × 24

95. 623 × 451   96. 409 × 489

| 7-4 | MORE FACTORING AND GRAPHING |

In this section you will learn how to factor a sum or difference of two cubes, and apply these techniques to analyzing graphs of rational functions. You will also find a systematic way to factor quadratic trinomials that is simple enough to program into a computer.

1. **Sum or Difference of Two Cubes**
   If you multiply $(x + 5)(x^2 - 5x + 25)$ you get

$$(x + 5)(x^2 - 5x + 25)$$
$$= x^3 - 5x^2 + 25x + 5x^2 - 25x + 125$$
$$= x^3 + 125.$$

The middle terms "drop out." The answer is a *sum of two cubes*,

$$x^3 + 5^3.$$

A sum of two cubes can be factored by finding a pattern in the original product,

$$(x + 5)(x^2 - 5x + 25).$$

The first factor is obvious. It is the binomial without the *cubes*. The first and last terms of the second factor come from dividing the x^3 by x, and the 5^3 by 5. The middle term can be found by multiplying the x by the 5 and taking the *opposite*. The same pattern works for a *difference of two cubes*. For instance,

$$p^3 - f^3$$
$$= (p - f)(p^2 + pf + f^2),$$

as you can verify by multiplying the two factors back together. The $+ pf$ in the second factor is the *opposite* of $(p)(-f)$.

FACTORING A SUM OR DIFFERENCE OF TWO CUBES

$$x^3 + y^3 = (x + y)(x^2 - xy + y^2)$$

$$x^3 - y^3 = (x - y)(x^2 + xy + y^2)$$

---

2. **Factoring Quadratics by Splitting the Middle Term**
   Suppose that you must factor a trinomial such as

$$20x^2 + 39x + 18.$$

The *guess-and-check* technique you have been using is tedious since there are so many possible combinations of factors of 20 and 18 to try. However, if you split the $39x$ into $24x + 15x$, you can factor by grouping.

$$20x^2 + 39x + 18$$
$$= 20x^2 + 24x + 15x + 18$$
$$= 4x(5x + 6) + 3(5x + 6)$$
$$= (5x + 6)(4x + 3)$$

The trick is deciding how to split the middle term. Note that

$$(20)(18) = 360 \text{ from the original trinomial, and}$$

$$(24)(15) = 360 \text{ from the split middle term.}$$

Each one is equal to $(5)(6)(4)(3)$, the product of the coefficients in the two linear factors. To split the middle term, you just multiply the 20 by the 18, get 360, then look for factors of 360 that add up to 39.

Factors of 360		Sum = 39?	
1,	360	361	no
2,	180	182	no
.	.	.	.
.	.	.	.
.	.	.	.
12,	30	42	no
15,	24	39	yes!

The rest of the factoring is done as shown above.

SPLITTING THE MIDDLE TERM
To factor $ax^2 + bx + c$,

1. Multiply a by c.
2. Look for two factors of the answer whose sum is b. (Or start with numbers that add up to b and find two whose product is ac.)
3. Split the middle term into two terms with these numbers as coefficients.

---

3. *Discriminant Test for Prime Quadratics*
   Suppose that you factor a quadratic such as $x^2 + 5x - 14$.

$$x^2 + 5x - 14 = (x - 2)(x + 7)$$

The quadratic *equation* $x^2 + 5x - 14 = 0$ has solutions $x = 2$ and

$x = -7$, the values that make the factors equal zero. Since you are looking only for factors that have *integer* coefficients, you can conclude that a quadratic trinomial will factor if and only if the corresponding quadratic equation has *rational* numbers for its solutions. The solutions will be rational if and only if the discriminant is a perfect square. In the above trinomial,

$$b^2 - 4ac = 5^2 - 4(1)(-14) = 81 = 9^2.$$

So the discriminant is a perfect square. But for

$$3x^2 + 10x + 5,$$

the discriminant is

$$b^2 - 4ac = 100 - 4(3)(5) = 40,$$

which is *not* a perfect square. Therefore, $3x^2 + 10x + 5$ is prime.

> **DISCRIMINANT TEST FOR PRIME QUADRATICS**
> $ax^2 + bx + c$ (where a, b, and c are integers) can be factored into factors with integer coefficients if and only if $b^2 - 4ac$ is a perfect square.

Objectives:

1. Given a sum or difference of two cubes, factor it.
2. Given a quadratic trinomial, determine whether or not it factors, and if so, factor it by inspection or by splitting the middle term.
3. Factor polynomials when you are *not* told which technique to use.
4. Graph rational functions involving sums or differences of two cubes.

EXAMPLE 1

Factor $x^6 - 343$.

Solution:
Each term can be written as a perfect cube. Do this first, either mentally or on your paper.

$$x^6 - 343$$
$$= (x^2)^3 - 7^3$$
$$= (x^2 - 7)(x^4 + 7x^2 + 49) \qquad \blacksquare$$

Examples of parts (2) and (3) of the objective can be found above. Part (4), graphing, is left for you to accomplish in the following exercise.

EXERCISE 7-4

Do These Quickly

The following problems are intended to refresh your skills. You should be able to do all 10 in less than 5 minutes.

Q1. Simplify: $(3x^5)^2$

Q2. Multiply: $(2x + 3)(x - 8)$

Q3. Do the squaring: $(3x + 5)^2$

Q4. Add: $1.73 + 4$

Q5. Draw a quadrilateral that has two pairs of congruent sides, but is *not* a parallelogram.

Q6. Sketch the graph of a decreasing exponential function.

Q7. Write as a single logarithm: $\log 5 + \log 7$

Q8. Solve: $2 - x \le 7$

Q9. Evaluate the determinant: $\begin{vmatrix} 7 & 5 \\ 2 & -8 \end{vmatrix}$

Q10. Evaluate the discriminant: $3x^2 + 5x + 7$

Work the following problems.

1. Sketch the graph of $f(x) = \dfrac{1}{(x - 5)}$.

2. Sketch the graph of $g(x) = \dfrac{1}{(x + 2)}$.

3. Given $h(x) = \dfrac{24x - 48}{x^3 - 8}$
    a. Factor the numerator and denominator and do any canceling.
    b. Show that the denominator of the simplified fraction is *never* equal to zero for any real value of x.
    c. Calculate points and plot the graph, showing all discontinuities.
    d. True or false: "Rational function graphs always have vertical asymptotes."

4. Given $r(x) = \dfrac{x^3 + 8}{x + 2}$
    a. Factor the numerator and denominator and do any canceling.
    b. At what value of x is there a discontinuity?

c.   Except for the fact that there is a discontinuity, what geometrical figure will the graph be?

    d.   Sketch the graph quickly, plotting as few points as possible.

For Problems 5 through 14, factor the polynomial completely.

5. $a^3 - b^3$ 6. $k^3 + n^3$

7. $y^3 + 64$ 8. $c^3 - 729$

9. $d^6 + h^3$ 10. $p^3 - w^{12}$

11. $3c^4 - 81c$ 12. $5j^5 + 5000j^2$

13. $x^3 - x$ 14. $y - y^3$

Problems 15 and 16 can be factored either as a difference of two squares first or as a difference of two cubes first. Factor both ways. Then show that you get more factors by factoring as a difference of two squares first.

15. $x^6 - y^6$ 16. $x^{12} - y^{12}$

For Problems 17 through 26, factor by splitting the middle term, or demonstrate that the polynomial is prime.

17. $12x^2 + 25x + 12$ 18. $18x^2 + 27x + 10$

19. $24x^2 - 121x + 5$ 20. $12x^2 - 179x - 15$

21. $30x^2 + 41x - 6$ 22. $6x^2 - 27x + 20$

23. $35x^2 - 2x - 6$ 24. $9x^2 - 56x + 12$

25. $36x^2 - 63x + 20$ 26. $12x^2 + 27x + 2$

For Problems 27 through 36, calculate the discriminant and use it to tell whether or not the trinomial factors. Factor those that do.

27. $x^2 - 2x + 5$ 28. $x^2 - 2x - 29$

29. $x^2 - 21x + 68$ 30. $x^2 - 10x + 74$

31. $18x^2 - 15x + 2$ 32. $3x^2 - 15x + 14$

33. $18x^2 - 13x + 3$ 34. $3x^2 - 16x + 13$

35. $8x^2 - 79x - 10$ 36. $48x^2 - 22x - 15$

For Problems 37 through 62, factor completely. They are arranged in *no* particular order, so you must decide which technique to use.

37. $4x^2 - 16y^2$ 38. $a^2b^4 - a^4b^2$

39. $4x^2 - 12xy + 9y^2$
40. $x^2 + 11x + 18$
41. $a^2 + 3a - 88$
42. $7a^2x - 6a^2 - 7x + 6$
43. $30x^2 + 95x + 50$
44. $2x^2 + xy - 3y^2$
45. $x^4 + 5x^3 - 2x^2 + 10x$
46. $7x^4 - 28x^2$
47. $x^4 - x^2 - 12$
48. $15x^2 + 8x - 12$
49. $60x^2 - 68x + 8$
50. $x^4 - 26x^2 + 25$
51. $16x^2 - 35x + 6$
52. $7x^3 - 14x^2 - 3x + 6$
53. $5x^3 + 6x^2 - 45x - 54$
54. $81x^2 + 108x + 36$
55. $x^2 + 3x + 4$
56. $(2x + 3y + a)^2 - (x - y + a)^2$
57. $100 - (x - y)^2$
58. $x^2 - 2x - 7$
59. $35a^2 + 47ab + 6b^2$
60. $343 - 7(x + 3)^2$
61. $(a^2 - b^2 - c^2)^2 - 4b^2c^2$
62. $200x^2 + 510x - 1001$

Factoring Harder Differences of Two Squares   For Problems 63 through 70, factor by first grouping the terms 3 and 1 or 1 and 3, whichever gives a difference of two squares.

63. $x^2 + 6x + 9 - y^2$
64. $x^2 - 10x + 25 - y^2$
65. $a^2 - b^2 + 2b - 1$
66. $r^2 - s^2 - 4s - 4$
67. $p^2 - 14p + 49 - 9k^2$
68. $x^2 - 4x + 4 - 100a^2$
69. $x^2 - 4y^2 + 4y - 1$
70. $81 - x^2 + 2xy - y^2$

Factoring by Completing the Square   Some quartics can be factored by adding and subtracting a "middle" term that makes part of the polynomial a perfect square. For instance, for

$$x^4 + 2x^2 + 9,$$

if the middle term were $6x^2$, the trinomial would be a perfect square. So you add and subtract $4x^2$, giving

$$x^4 + 6x^2 + 9 - 4x^2.$$

Associating the first three terms makes this a difference of two squares. For Problems 71 through 80, factor by completing the square.

71. $x^4 - x^2 + 16$
72. $x^4 - 18x^2 + 1$
73. $x^4 + 11x^2 + 36$
74. $x^4 - 19x^2 + 25$

75. $x^4 - 19x^2 + 9$

76. $x^4 - 110x^2 + 25$

77. $x^4 - 26x^2 + 25$

78. $x^4 + 5x^2 + 9$

79. $x^4 + 4$

80. $x^4 - 13x^2 + 36$

81. How are the binomials $x - y$ and $x + y$ related to each other? How are the binomials $x - y$ and $y - x$ related to each other?

82. By selecting appropriate values of x and y, show that $\frac{(x - y)}{(x + y)}$ cannot always be simplified, but $\frac{(x - y)}{(y - x)}$ can.

83. *Factoring Into Radicals Problem*   Factor $x - y$ as a difference of two squares using radicals or fractional exponents. Then factor the result into a product of *three* factors. By continuing the pattern, tell into how many factors it is possible to factor $x - y$. Tell the reason this method of factoring is not in accordance with the agreement about completely-factored form.

84. *Factoring Out a Rabbit Problem*   The binomial $x + y$ can be factored as

$$x + y = x\left(1 + \frac{y}{x}\right).$$

   a. Following this pattern, factor xy out of $x + y$.
   b. Show that n can be factored out of $x + y$, even though it is a common factor that isn't there.
   c. Factor rabbit out of $x + y$.
   d. Explain why factoring out a rabbit is not allowed by the agreement about completely-factored form.

Factoring Constant Integers   The factoring techniques you have learned for variables work just as well for constants. For Problems 85 through 88, factor the number.

85. $2^4 - 1$

86. $3^8 - 1$

87. $2^{16} - 1$

88. $3 \times 2^6 - 2 \times 2^3 - 5$

89. *Factoring Quadratics by Computer*   Write a computer program to factor quadratic trinomials of the form $ax^2 + bx + c$. The computer should first ask you to input values of a, b, and c. Then it should calculate the discriminant to determine whether or not the polynomial factors. If it does, the computer should search for factors using the splitting-the-middle-term technique. The output should be either the two factors, or the message "prime."

90. *LCM, GCF, and Musical Harmony Problem*   The notes A and E around middle C have frequencies of 220 and 330 cycles per second (cps), respectively. Whenever you play or sing a note, you also gen-

erate "overtones" that are notes with multiples of the fundamental frequency. Some overtones of A and E have the following frequencies:

Note	**Overtone**						
	1(fund.)	2	3	4	5	6	. . .
A	220	440	660	880	1100	1320	. . .
E	330	660	990	1320	1650	1980	. . .

A and E harmonize because many of their overtones (660, 1320, 1980, . . .) have the same frequency. The closer the *least* common multiple (LCM) is to the fundamental frequency, the better the harmony. You can calculate the LCM by factoring into primes.

$$220 = 2 \cdot 2 \cdot 5 \cdot 11$$

$$330 = 2 \cdot 3 \cdot 5 \cdot 11$$

The LCM is the *union* of the sets of prime factors:

$$LCM = 2 \cdot 2 \cdot 3 \cdot 5 \cdot 11 = 660.$$

Answer the following questions.

a. A, C, and C sharp have frequencies 220, 264, and 275 cps, respectively. Find the LCM of each *pair* of notes.
b. Which pairs will harmonize well, and which will not?
c. Explain why the relationship "harmonizes with" does *not* have the transitive property.
d. Find the greatest common factor (GCF) of each pair of frequencies in part (a). How could you tell from the GCF whether or not two notes will harmonize well?
e. Show that the product of two numbers equals the product of their LCM and GCF.

7-5 | LONG DIVISION OF POLYNOMIALS

If the denominator of a rational expression is of lower degree than the numerator, as in

$$\frac{3x^3 - 2x^2 - 13x + 14}{x - 2},$$

you can transform to "mixed number" form by long division. The first step is to write

$$x - 2 \overline{)3x^3 - 2x^2 - 13x + 14}$$

Dividing x into $3x^3$ gives $3x^2$. This part of the quotient can be written over the squared term, like this:

$$\begin{array}{r} 3x^2 \\ x - 2 \overline{)3x^3 - 2x^2 - 13x + 14} \end{array}$$

Next, the $3x^2$ is multiplied by the $x - 2$, and the result is subtracted from the original numerator to find out what remains.

$$\begin{array}{r} 3x^2 \\ x - 2 \overline{)3x^3 - 2x^2 - 13x + 14} \\ \underline{3x^3 - 6x^2 } \quad \longleftarrow \text{Subtract} \\ 4x^2 - 13x + 14 \quad \longleftarrow \text{Remainder} \end{array}$$

Then the *remainder* is divided by $x - 2$ using the same sequence of steps. The whole computation looks like this:

$$\begin{array}{r} 3x^2 + 4x - 5 \quad \longleftarrow \text{Quotient} \\ x - 2 \overline{)3x^3 - 2x^2 - 13x + 14} \\ \underline{3x^3 - 6x^2 } \\ 4x^2 - 13x + 14 \\ \underline{4x^2 - 8x } \\ -5x + 14 \\ \underline{-5x + 10} \\ 4 \quad \longleftarrow \text{Final remainder} \end{array}$$

Therefore,

$$\frac{3x^3 - 2x^2 - 13x + 14}{x - 2} = 3x^2 + 4x - 5 + \frac{4}{x - 2}$$

The result is the sum of a quadratic, $3x^2 + 4x - 5$, and a rational expression, $\frac{4}{(x-2)}$. The rational expression can be thought of as a *proper* fraction since its numerator is of *lower* degree than its denominator.

If the remainder had turned out to be *zero*, then the denominator would have been a *factor* of the numerator. In this section you will get experience long-dividing polynomials so that you can use the technique to help with graphing and factoring.

Objective:
Be able to long-divide a polynomial by a polynomial, and use the results to factor and to draw graphs.

One example of long division is shown above. Special care is needed if some terms of the numerator polynomial have zero coefficients. The following example shows you what to do.

EXAMPLE 1

Do the division:

$$\frac{x^3 + 8}{x + 2}$$

Solution:
The numerator should be thought of as $x^3 + 0x^2 + 0x + 8$. Then the division can be done as above. The final result looks like this:

$$
\begin{array}{r}
x^2 - 2x + 4 \\
x + 2 \overline{)x^3 + 0x^2 + 0x + 8} \\
\underline{x^3 + 2x^2} \\
-2x^2 + 0x + 8 \\
\underline{-2x^2 - 4x} \\
4x + 8 \\
\underline{4x + 8} \\
0
\end{array}
$$

Therefore,

$$\frac{x^3 + 8}{x + 2} = x^2 - 2x + 4 \qquad \blacksquare$$

Note that since the remainder in Example 1 is 0, the denominator is a factor of the numerator. You perhaps recognize that this result is the same as that of the factoring technique for a sum of two cubes.

$$x^3 + 8 = (x + 2)(x^2 - 2x + 4)$$

There is a shorter way to do the division, called *synthetic substitution*. If you would like to see how it works, consult the Index to find out where it is, and look it up.

EXERCISE 7-5

Do These Quickly

The following problems are intended to refresh your skills. You should be able to do all 10 in less than 5 minutes.

Q1. Find $\log_2 32$.

Q2.   Reduce: $\dfrac{27}{36}$

Q3.   Find the remainder when 37 is divided by 7.

Q4.   Sketch the graph of $y = \dfrac{1}{x}$.

Q5.   Sketch the graph of $y = x$.

Q6.   Find the slope of the linear function containing $(7, -2)$ and $(3, 1)$.

Q7.   Which way does the graph of $y = x^2 - 17x + 97$ open, upward or downward?

Q8.   Factor: $2x^2 + 15x + 18$

Q9.   Multiply: $(3x - 11)(3x + 11)$

Q10. Factor: $x^3 - 8y^3$

For Problems 1 through 20, do the long division and write the expression in mixed-number form, or in polynomial form if the remainder is zero.

1. $\dfrac{x^3 - 2x^2 - 3x + 12}{x + 2}$

2. $\dfrac{x^3 - 4x^2 - 19x + 9}{x + 3}$

3. $\dfrac{8x^3 + 10x^2 - 13x - 20}{2x + 3}$

4. $\dfrac{12x^3 - 19x^2 - 25x - 10}{4x + 3}$

5. $\dfrac{2x^3 - 3x^2 + 7x - 3}{2x - 1}$

6. $\dfrac{6x^3 + 2x^2 + 11x - 10}{3x - 2}$

7. $\dfrac{x^3 - 7x^2 + 14x - 8}{x - 4}$

8. $\dfrac{x^3 - 9x^2 + 23x - 15}{x - 5}$

9. $\dfrac{x^3 + 7x^2 - 49}{x + 5}$

10. $\dfrac{x^3 + 5x^2 - 20}{x + 3}$

11. $\dfrac{4x^3 - 200x + 28}{x - 7}$

12. $\dfrac{5x^3 + 3x - 8}{x - 1}$

13. $\dfrac{x^3 + 3x^2 + 3x + 1}{x^2 + 2x + 1}$

14. $\dfrac{x^3 - 3x^2 + 3x - 1}{x^2 - 2x + 1}$

15. $\dfrac{x^4 + x^2 + 1}{x^2 + x + 1}$

16. $\dfrac{x^4 + x^2 + 1}{x^2 - x + 1}$

17. $\dfrac{x^4 + 7x^3 + 5x^2 - 8x - 14}{x + 6}$

18. $\dfrac{x^4 + x^3 - 7x^2 - 2x + 8}{x - 2}$

19. $\dfrac{x^4 - 1}{x - 1}$

20. $\dfrac{x^4 - 1}{x + 1}$

21. **Computer Graphics Problem**   For the function

$$f(x) = \frac{x^2 + x - 5}{x - 2}$$

a. Plot the graph using PLOT RATIONAL, on the accompanying disk, or a similar plotting program.

b. Divide the numerator by the denominator, and write the result in mixed-number form.

c. Plot the graph again, this time using the program PLOT COMP GEN or a similar program. The first function should be the quotient, and the second should be the fraction $\frac{(remainder)}{(x - 2)}$. If you use PLOT COMP GEN, you will have to put an error trap in line 415 as follows:

415 IF (U-VA)/HP = 2 THEN 450

d. Was the composed graph in part (c) the same as the graph in part (a)? How do you explain the fact that when x is not close to 2, the graph looks fairly close to a straight line?

7-6   FACTORING HIGHER DEGREE POLYNOMIALS— THE FACTOR THEOREM

In Sections 7-3 and 7-4 you learned how to factor certain special polynomials. For example, the cubic polynomial

$$x^3 - 2x^2 - 3x + 6,$$

can be factored by grouping. You get

$$x^2(x - 2) - 3(x - 2)$$
$$= (x - 2)(x^2 - 3).$$

The technique worked because the $(x - 2)$ was a common factor, and could be factored out.

Unfortunately, this technique will not work with a polynomial such as

$$x^3 - 2x^2 - 5x + 6$$

because there is no way to group and find common binomial factors.

Objective:
Be able to find linear factors for cubic and higher degree polynomials.

One procedure for factoring higher degree polynomials is simply to *guess* a factor, then find out whether you are right by some process such as long division. Obviously, this procedure is extremely tedious. So you seek some systematic procedure for narrowing down the number of factors from which to guess.

Suppose that $P(x) = x^3 - 2x^2 - 5x + 6$, and you wish to find a linear factor. You might guess some of the following:

$$2x - 1, x + 5, x + 1, x - 3.$$

Before you start doing the long division, you can rule out the first two guesses. If $2x - 1$ were a factor, then

$$P(x) = (2x - 1)(\text{some other factor}).$$

The other factor would have to have $\dfrac{1}{2}x^2$ as one of its terms so that $(2x)\left(\dfrac{1}{2}x^2\right)$ would give the x^3 term in $P(x)$. But you have agreed to look only for factors with *integer* coefficients. Similarly, $x + 5$ is impossible. If

$$P(x) = (x + 5)(\text{some other factor}),$$

then the other factor would have to have $\frac{6}{5}$ as its constant term. This is the only way to get the 6 as the constant term of $P(x)$ when you multiply the two factors back together.

The $x + 1$ and $x - 3$ are possible factors because the x-coefficient equals 1, and the 1 and -3 are each *factors* of the *constant* term, 6. Upon doing the long division, you find that $x + 1$ does *not* divide evenly. But $x - 3$ *does*. So

$$P(x) = (x - 3)(x^2 + x - 2).$$

You should try doing the long division on a piece of scratch paper right now so that you can see why this is right.

There is an easy way to test a linear binomial to see if it is a factor *without* doing the long division. If $x = 3$, then $(x - 3) = 0$. So $P(3)$ is a product with a factor equal to 0. By the Multiplication Property of Zero, $P(3)$ must equal zero. But a product equals zero *only* if one of its factors equals 0. So if by some means or other you find that $P(3) = 0$, you can conclude that $P(x)$ has a factor that is zero when $x = 3$. This factor would be $(x - 3)$ because

$$x - 3 = 0 \text{ when } x \text{ is } 3.$$

The Multiplication Property of Zero and its Converse thus form the basis for the following major theorem:

THEOREM

Factor Theorem
$(x - b)$ is a factor of $P(x)$ if and only if $P(b) = 0$.

The problem of searching for linear factors thus reduces to finding all factors of the *constant* term (positive and negative), and substituting them one at a time for x. Whenever you get 0 for an answer, x *minus* whatever you substituted will be a factor.

EXAMPLE 1

Find the factors of

$$P(x) = x^3 + x^2 - 8x - 12.$$

Solution:
The factors of -12 are $\pm 1, \pm 2, \pm 3, \pm 4, \pm 6, \pm 12$.

$P(1) = 1 + 1 - 8 - 12 \neq 0$,   so $(x - 1)$ is not a factor.

$P(-1) = -1 + 1 + 8 - 12 \neq 0$,   so $(x - (-1)) = (x + 1)$ is not a factor.

$P(2) = 8 + 4 - 16 - 12 \neq 0$,   so $(x - 2)$ is not a factor.

$P(-2) = -8 + 4 + 16 - 12 = 0$,   so $(x + 2)$ *is* a factor.

The other factor may be found by long division.

$$
\begin{array}{r}
x^2 - x - 6 \\
x + 2 \overline{\smash{)}\, x^3 + x^2 - 8x - 12} \\
\underline{x^3 + 2x^2} \\
-x^2 - 8x - 12 \\
\underline{-x^2 - 2x} \\
-6x - 12 \\
\underline{-6x - 12} \\
0
\end{array}
$$

$$\therefore P(x) = (x + 2)(x^2 - x - 6).$$

The second factor may or may not factor again. In this case, it does, giving as the final answer

$$P(x) = \underline{(x + 2)(x + 2)(x - 3)}. \qquad \blacksquare$$

EXAMPLE 2

Factor $P(x) = 2x^3 - x^2 - x - 3$.

Solution:
If you want to factor a polynomial like $P(x) = 2x^3 - x^2 - x - 3$, where

the lead coefficient of $P(x)$ is *not* equal to 1, then a linear factor could be $(2x + 3)$, $(2x - 1)$, etc., where the x-coefficient in the linear factor must be a factor of the lead coefficient (2, in this case). In general, the factor would have the form $(ax - b)$, where a must be a factor of the lead coefficient of $P(x)$, and b must be a factor of the constant term of $P(x)$.

If $(ax - b)$ is a factor of $P(x)$, then $P(x)$ will equal zero whenever $(ax - b)$ equals zero. You find out what x must equal by solving the equation

$$ax - b = 0$$

$$\therefore ax = b$$

$$\therefore x = \frac{b}{a}.$$

So it turns out that $(ax - b)$ is a factor of $P(x)$ if and only if $P\left(\dfrac{b}{a}\right) = 0$.

Possible values of $\dfrac{b}{a}$ are $\pm\dfrac{1}{1}$, $\pm\dfrac{3}{1}$, $\pm\dfrac{1}{2}$, and $\pm\dfrac{3}{2}$.

$P(1) = 2 - 1 - 1 - 3 \neq 0,$	so $(x - 1)$ is not a factor.
$P(-1) = -2 - 1 + 1 - 3 \neq 0,$	so $(x + 1)$ is not a factor.
$P(3) = 54 - 9 - 3 - 3 \neq 0,$	so $(x - 3)$ is not a factor.
$P(-3) = -54 - 9 + 3 - 3 \neq 0,$	so $(x + 3)$ is not a factor.
$P\left(\dfrac{1}{2}\right) = \dfrac{1}{4} - \dfrac{1}{4} - \dfrac{1}{2} - 3 \neq 0,$	so $(2x - 1)$ is not a factor.
$P\left(-\dfrac{1}{2}\right) = -\dfrac{1}{4} - \dfrac{1}{4} + \dfrac{1}{2} - 3 \neq 0$	so $(2x + 1)$ is not a factor.
$P\left(\dfrac{3}{2}\right) = \dfrac{27}{4} - \dfrac{9}{4} - \dfrac{3}{2} - 3 = 0,$	so $(2x - 3)$ *is* a factor!!

By division,

$$
\require{enclose}
\begin{array}{r}
x^2 + x + 1 \\[-2pt]
2x - 3 \enclose{longdiv}{2x^3 - x^2 - x - 3} \\[-2pt]
\underline{2x^3 - 3x^2} \\[-2pt]
2x^2 - x - 3 \\[-2pt]
\underline{2x^2 - 3x} \\[-2pt]
2x - 3 \\[-2pt]
\underline{2x - 3} \\[-2pt]
0
\end{array}
$$

$$\therefore P(x) = \underline{(2x - 3)(x^2 + x + 1)}.$$

■

In this case, the second factor does *not* factor again.

THEOREM

> **Rational Root Theorem** $(ax - b)$ is a factor of $P(x)$ if and only if $P\left(\frac{b}{a}\right) = 0$.

The theorem gets its name from the fact that $\frac{b}{a}$ is a solution, or "root," of the equation $P(x) = 0$.

EXAMPLE 3

Factor $P(x) = x^3 - 4x^2 + 3x - 2$.

Solution:
Since the lead coefficient is 1, you need only look for factors of the form $(x - b)$. Possible values of b are ± 1 and ± 2.

$P(1) = 1 - 4 + 3 - 2 \neq 0$ so $(x - 1)$ is not a factor.

$P(-1) = -1 - 4 - 3 - 2 \neq 0$,   so $(x + 1)$ is not a factor.

$P(2) = 8 - 16 + 6 - 2 \neq 0$,   so $(x - 2)$ is not a factor.

$P(-2) = -8 - 16 - 6 - 2 \neq 0$,   so $(x + 2)$ is not a factor.

Since *none* of the factors of the constant term, -2, makes $P(x)$ equal zero, you can conclude that

$$P(x) \text{ has } no \text{ linear factors with integer coefficients.} \quad \blacksquare$$

Sum or Difference of Like Odd Powers   You have learned how to factor a sum or difference of two cubes, such as $x^3 - y^3$. The Factor Theorem can be used to learn how to factor a sum or difference of two *seventh* powers, two *fifth* powers, etc. For example, if

$$P(x) = x^5 + c^5,$$

then

$P(-c) = (-c)^5 + c^5$ Definition of $P(-c)$

$ = -c^5 + c^5$ *Negative* number to an *odd* power

$ = 0$ Additive inverses

$\therefore (x + c)$ is a factor.   Factor Theorem

By long division, you find that

$$P(x) = (x + c)(x^4 - x^3 c + x^2 c^2 - x c^3 + c^4).$$

The pattern is easy enough that you can remember it. The first factor, $(x + c)$, is obvious. In the second factor, the powers of x *decrease*, the powers of c *increase*, and the signs *alternate*. The pattern holds for a sum of any two like, *odd* powers. (In Problem 47, you will prove that it does *not* work for a sum of two *even* powers.) For a *difference* of like, odd powers, you must first transform it into a *sum*.

EXAMPLE 4

Factor $P(x) = x^7 - 128$.

Solution:
The pattern above can be used if you first turn the subtraction into adding the *opposite*. You must also recognize that 128 is equal to 2^7.

$$
\begin{aligned}
x^7 - 128 &= x^7 + (-128) \\
&= x^7 + (-2)^7 \\
&= (x + (-2))(x^6 - x^5(-2) + x^4(-2)^2 \\
&\qquad - x^3(-2)^3 + x^2(-2)^4 - x(-2)^5 + (-2)^6) \\
&= \underline{(x - 2)(x^6 + 2x^5 + 4x^4 + 8x^3 + 16x^2 + 32x + 64)}. \quad \blacksquare
\end{aligned}
$$

Note that for $x^n - c^n$, the first factor is $(x - c)$, and all the signs in the second factor turn out to be *positive*.

Section 10-5 shows ways to shorten the trial-and-error search for factors using Descartes' Rule of Signs and the Upper Bound Theorem.

EXERCISE 7-6

Do These Quickly

The following problems are intended to refresh your skills. You should be able to do all 10 in less than 5 minutes.

Q1.   Factor: $x^2 - 11x + 10$

Q2.   Factor: $x^2 - 64$

Q3.   Factor: $x^3 - 64$

Q4.   Factor: $x^2 + 25$

Q5.   Multiply: $(2c - 7)(c + 8)$

Q6.   Multiply: $\left(\dfrac{2}{7}\right)\left(\dfrac{14}{3}\right)$

Q7.   Find 0.3% of 2000.

Q8.   Sketch the graph of a decreasing exponential function.

Q9.   Write the general equation of a quadratic function.

Q10.   Sketch the graph of $y = \dfrac{1}{(x - 2)}$.

Work the following problems.

In Problems 1 through 22, use the Factor Theorem either to factor the polynomial completely or to prove that it has *no* linear factors with integer coefficients.

1. $x^3 + 3x^2 - 18x - 40$ 2. $x^3 + 9x^2 + 24x + 20$

3. $x^3 - 10x^2 - 17x + 66$ 4. $x^3 + 3x^2 - 6x - 8$

5. $x^3 - x^2 - 5x + 2$ 6. $x^3 - 2x^2 - 14x + 3$

7. $x^3 + 3x^2 - 7x + 2$ 8. $x^3 + 2x^2 - 9x + 3$

9. $x^4 + 2x^3 - 13x^2 - 14x + 24$

10. $x^4 + 4x^3 - 7x^2 - 34x - 24$

11. $x^4 - 2x^3 - 3x^2 + 4x + 4$

12. $x^4 - 7x^3 + 18x^2 - 20x + 8$

13. $x^5 + 5x^4 + 10x^3 + 10x^2 + 5x + 1$

14. $x^6 - 6x^5 + 15x^4 - 20x^3 + 15x^2 - 6x + 1$

15. $2x^3 + 5x^2 + x - 2$ 16. $3x^3 - 2x^2 - 7x - 2$

17. $2x^3 + 3x^2 - x - 1$ 18. $3x^3 + 5x^2 - 5x + 1$

19. $12x^3 + 4x^2 - 3x - 1$ 20. $18x^3 + 9x^2 - 2x - 1$

21. $12x^3 - 20x^2 - 37x + 30$

22. $18x^3 - 9x^2 - 38x + 24$

For Problems 23 through 46, use the pattern for factoring the sum or difference of like, odd powers, and any other techniques you may need, to factor the polynomial completely.

23. $x^7 + y^7$ 24. $x^7 - y^7$ 25. $x^{11} - 1$

26. $x^{11} + 1$ 27. $x^5 + 32$ 28. $x^5 - 32$

29. $a^{13} - b^{13}$ 30. $a^{13} + b^{13}$ 31. $a^5 + 32b^{10}$

32. $32x^5 - b^{10}$ 33. $x^3 - y^3$ 34. $x^3 + y^3$

35. $x^3 + 8$ 36. $x^3 - 27$ 37. $r^3 - s^6$

38. $r^9 + s^6$ 39. $x^6 - y^6$ 40. $x^{12} - y^{12}$

41. $8a^3 - 64b^3$ 42. $27r^3 + 125s^3$

43. $x^4y + xy^4$ 44. $a^2b^5 - a^5b^2$

45. $(a - b)^3 - (a + b)^3$ 46. $(x + y)^3 + (x - y)^3$

47. **Sum of Two Squares** Use the Factor Theorem to prove that a *sum* of two squares, $P(x) = x^2 + c^2$, has *no* linear factors, using only *real* numbers. Then factor it into a product of two *complex* numbers.

48. **Factors of $x^{15} + y^{15}$**
    a. Factor $x^{15} + y^{15}$ by first considering it to be a sum of two *cubes*. You can get 3 factors.
    b. Factor $x^{15} + y^{15}$ by first considering it to be a sum of two *fifth* powers. Again, you can get 3 factors.
    c. Since the sets of factors you get in parts *a* and *b* are *not* identical, one or more of the factors must not be prime. By a clever application of techniques you know, factor $x^{15} + y^{15}$ into *four* polynomials with integer coefficients.

49. **Factor Theorem by Computer** The following is a flow chart for a computer program to search for linear factors of the form $(x - n)$ for cubic polynomials of the form

$$P(x) = Ax^3 + Bx^2 + Cx + D$$

using the Factor Theorem.
    a. Show the simulated computer memory and the output if the input values for A, B, C, and D are:
       i. $1, -1, -5, -3$,
       ii. $1, 1, 1, -2$.
    b. What special name is given to the variable K?
    c. Translate the flow chart into a computer language such as BASIC.
    d. Test your program by finding factors for Problems 1, 3, 5, and 7, above.
    e. When your program is working, use it to find factors of
       $x^3 - 9x^2 - 649x + 2001$.

50. Modify the program of Problem 49 so that it searches for linear factors of the form $(ax - b)$, where a can be an integer greater than 1. Test your modified program by factoring the polynomials you got in Problems 15, 17, 19, and 21, above.

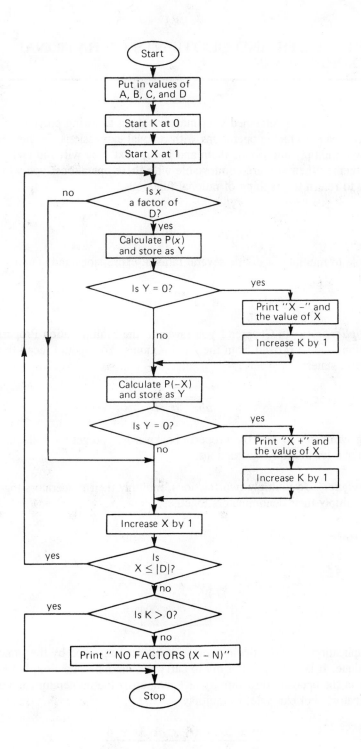

7-7 | PRODUCTS AND QUOTIENTS OF RATIONAL EXPRESSIONS

Now that you have refreshed your memory about factoring polynomials, you are ready to tackle operations with rational expressions. In this section you will multiply and divide them and in the next, you will add and subtract them. When you are comfortable with these operations, you will be ready to return to graphing of rational functions.

Objective:

Be able to multiply or divide several rational expressions and simplify the result.

Multiplication: In Chapter 1 you saw how the Multiplication Property of Fractions can be proved from the Field Axioms. You should recall that this property states:

$$\frac{xy}{ab} = \frac{x}{a} \cdot \frac{y}{b}.$$

Using symmetry to read the property backwards, you get the following technique for multiplying fractions:

Technique: To multiply two fractions, multiply their numerators together and multiply their denominators together.

That is,

$$\boxed{\frac{x}{a} \cdot \frac{y}{b} = \frac{xy}{ab}}$$

Multiplication of two rational expressions is accomplished by the same technique. It is usually better *not* to carry out the multiplication, but rather to go in the opposite direction by factoring apart the numerators and denominators. For example, to multiply

$$\frac{x^2 + 5x + 6}{x^2 - x - 20} \cdot \frac{x^2 + 3x - 4}{x^2 + x - 2},$$

you could first use the multiplication property of fractions to get

$$\frac{(x^2 + 5x + 6)(x^2 + 3x - 4)}{(x^2 - x - 20)(x^2 + x - 2)}.$$

Each trinomial will factor, giving

$$\frac{(x + 2)(x + 3)(x - 1)(x + 4)}{(x + 4)(x - 5)(x - 1)(x + 2)}.$$

The numerator and denominator have several *common* factors. Commuting the *greatest* common factor to the right leads to a considerable simplification:

$$\frac{(x + 3)(x - 1)(x + 2)(x + 4)}{(x - 5)(x - 1)(x + 2)(x + 4)}$$ Commutativity

$$= \frac{x + 3}{x - 5} \cdot \frac{(x - 1)(x + 2)(x + 4)}{(x - 1)(x + 2)(x + 4)}$$ Multiplication property of fractions

$$= \frac{x + 3}{x - 5}.$$ Multiplicative identity

It is clear from the answer that x cannot equal 5. It must be understood that the domain of x also excludes 1, -2, and -4, each of which would make the denominator of the original fraction equal to zero.

Division: Division of fractions is carried out by first applying the definition of division,

$$\boxed{\frac{a}{b} \div \frac{c}{d} = \frac{a}{b} \cdot \frac{d}{c}},$$

then multiplying the resulting expressions as above.

Technique: To divide a fraction by a fraction, use the definition of division, then multiply the resulting fractions.

Simplification: The process of eliminating common factors from the numerator and denominator of a rational expression is called "simplification."

DEFINITION

A rational expression is **simplified** when its numerator and denominator have no common factors other than 1.

The process of simplification can be done by "canceling."

DEFINITION

> **Canceling** in a fraction means *dividing* the numerator and denominator of the fraction by the same common factor.

Canceling may be done rapidly by simply "crossing out" common factors. For example,

$$\frac{\cancel{(x-5)}(x+3)}{(x+2)\cancel{(x-5)}} = \frac{x+3}{x+2}.$$

Note: It is tempting to "cross out the x's," above and get $\frac{3}{2}$. Upper classmen sometimes call this error "freshman canceling." You can easily see that this is wrong by substituting a value for x. For example, if $x = 8$, then

$$\frac{x+3}{x+2} = \frac{8+3}{8+2} = \frac{11}{10},$$

which is *not* equal to $\frac{3}{2}$. The way to avoid such errors is to remember that canceling is a *division* process. "Canceling x" would mean *dividing* the numerator and denominator by x. Since division *distributes* over addition, you would get

$$\frac{x+3}{x+2} = \frac{1 + \dfrac{3x}{x}}{1 + \dfrac{2}{x}},$$

which is more complicated than the original expression!

Special Cases: Specially related binomials such as $x + 3$, $x - 3$, $3 + x$, and $3 - x$ may occur in rational expressions. One case is

$$\frac{x+3}{3+x} = \frac{x+3}{x+3} \qquad \text{Since addition } commutes$$

$$= 1. \qquad \text{Since } \frac{n}{n} = 1$$

A second case is

$$\frac{x-3}{3-x} = \frac{x-3}{-1(x-3)} \qquad \text{Factoring out } -1$$

$$= \frac{1}{-1} \qquad \text{Canceling}$$

$$= \underline{\underline{-1.}} \qquad \text{Positive divided by negative is negative.}$$

An easy way to remember this second case is to realize that $x - 3$ and $3 - x$ are *opposites* of each other and any number divided by its opposite equals -1. For example,

$$\frac{-13}{13} = -1.$$

A third case is

$$\frac{x - 3}{x + 3}.$$

The two binomials are *conjugates* of each other. But *nothing* can be done to simplify the quotient. For example, if x were equal to 8, the expression would be

$$\frac{x - 3}{x + 3} = \frac{8 - 3}{8 + 3}$$

$$= \frac{5}{11}.$$

Clearly, $\frac{5}{11}$ cannot be reduced.

The exercise that follows is designed to allow you to become comfortable with multiplying, dividing, and simplifying rational algebraic expressions. You should work enough problems so that you can do them quickly and correctly.

EXERCISE 7-7

Do These Quickly

The following problems are intended to refresh your skills. You should be able to do all 10 in less than 5 minutes.

Q1.   Multiply: $\left(\frac{4}{9}\right)\left(\frac{2}{3}\right)$

Q2.   Multiply: $(5x - 1)(x - 5)$

Q3.   Factor: $x^2 + 12x + 20$

Q4.   Prove that $x^2 - 7x - 10$ is prime.

Q5.   Factor: $j^3 + 125$

Q6.   Evaluate $-x^2$ if x is 7.

Q7.   Sketch the graph of a quadratic function opening upwards.

Q8.   Sketch the graph of $y = 2^x$.

Q9.   Solve: $|x - 9| = 4$

Q10.   What degree is $3^5 u^7 v^9 + z^{11}$?

1.   *Property of the Reciprocal of a Product*   Using the Field Axioms, prove that the reciprocal of a product of two numbers is equal to the product of their reciprocals. That is, prove that

$$\frac{1}{a \cdot b} = \frac{1}{a} \cdot \frac{1}{b}.$$

What restrictions are there on the values of a and b?

2.   *Multiplication Property of Fractions*   Use the Property of the Reciprocal of a Product (Problem 1, above) as a lemma to prove the Multiplication Property of Fractions. That is, prove that

$$\frac{x}{a} \cdot \frac{y}{b} = \frac{xy}{ab}.$$

3.   Simplify the following as much as possible.

a. $\dfrac{x - 5}{5 - x}$ b. $\dfrac{x + 5}{5 + x}$ c. $\dfrac{x - 5}{x + 5}$ d. $\dfrac{x - 5}{x - 5}$

4.   Simplify the following as much as possible.

a. $\dfrac{r - s}{r + s}$ b. $\dfrac{r - s}{r - s}$ c. $\dfrac{r - s}{s - r}$ d. $\dfrac{r + s}{s + r}$

For Problems 5 through 46, carry out the indicated multiplication and division, and simplify.

5. $\dfrac{2}{x - 2} \cdot \dfrac{x^2 - 4}{4}$

6. $\dfrac{x^2 + 7x + 12}{12} \cdot \dfrac{4}{x + 4}$

7. $\dfrac{x^2 + 4x + 3}{5x} \div \dfrac{x + 1}{x + 5}$

8. $\dfrac{x^2 - 64}{x^2 - 16} \div \dfrac{x + 8}{x + 4}$

9. $\dfrac{x^2 + 6x}{6} \cdot \dfrac{x^2 + 6}{x^3 + 6x^2}$

10. $\dfrac{x^2 - 4}{2x - 4} \cdot \dfrac{2}{x + 2}$

11. $\dfrac{x + y}{x - y} \div \dfrac{y + x}{y - x}$

12. $\dfrac{x^2 - 9}{x^2 + x} \div \dfrac{3 - x}{x^2 - 1}$

13. $\dfrac{x^2 - 49}{49} \cdot \dfrac{7}{7 - x}$

14. $\dfrac{x + 5}{5 - x} \cdot \dfrac{x^2 - 4x - 5}{x^2}$

15. $\dfrac{x^2 + 2xy + y^2}{x^2 - y^2} \div \dfrac{y + x}{y - x}$

16. $\dfrac{(x - y)^2}{y^2 + xy} \div \dfrac{y^2 - x^2}{x^2 + xy}$

17. $\dfrac{x^2 - 3x - 4}{3 + x} \cdot \dfrac{x + 3}{16 - x^2}$

18. $\dfrac{x^2 - x}{1 - x} \cdot \dfrac{x + 2}{x^2 - 2x}$

19. $\dfrac{x^2 - 3xy - 10y^2}{xy} \div \dfrac{x^2 + 7xy + 10y^2}{x - 5y}$

20. $\dfrac{xy}{(x + 2y)(x + 3y)} \div \dfrac{x + 2y}{(x + 3y)(xy)}$

21. $\dfrac{x^2 + x - 2}{x^2 - 4x - 12} \cdot \dfrac{x^2 - 5x - 6}{x^2 - 2x + 1}$

22. $\dfrac{x^2 + 3x - 10}{x^2 - 7x + 6} \cdot \dfrac{x^2 + 2x - 3}{x^2 + x - 6}$

23. $\dfrac{x^2 - 7x + 12}{x^2 - x - 6} \div \dfrac{x^2 - 16}{x^2 + x - 2}$

24. $\dfrac{x^2 - 6x + 8}{x^2 - 5x + 6} \div \dfrac{x^2 - 7x + 12}{x^2 - 4x + 4}$

25. $(x^2 - 5x - 14) \cdot \dfrac{x + 3}{x^2 - 4x - 21}$

26. $\dfrac{x^2 - 81}{x^2 - 18x + 81} \cdot (x^2 - 9x)$

27. $\dfrac{(x + 5)(x + 8)}{5 - x} \div (x + 8)$

28. $(x^2 - x - 72) \div \dfrac{x - 9}{x + 8}$

29. $\dfrac{x^3 - 1}{x + 1} \cdot \dfrac{x^2 + 2x + 1}{x^2 + x + 1}$

30. $\dfrac{x^3 + 8}{x - 2} \cdot \dfrac{x^2 - 4x + 4}{x^2 - 2x + 4}$

31. $\dfrac{x^4 - 27x}{x^2 - 9} \div \dfrac{x^2 + 3x + 9}{x + 3}$

32. $\dfrac{x^3 + y^3}{(x + y)^3} \div \dfrac{x^2 - xy + y^2}{x^2 + 2xy + y^2}$

33. $\dfrac{3x^2 - 2xy + 6x - 4y}{3x^2 + xy - 2y^2} \cdot \dfrac{x - 2}{x^2 - 4}$

34. $\dfrac{x^2 + 3ax - 4x - 12a}{x^2 + 3x} \cdot \dfrac{x + 3}{x^2 - ax - 12a^2}$

Problems 35 through 38 involve higher degree polynomials, so you must use the Factor Theorem.

35. $\dfrac{x^3 - 4x^2 - 3x + 18}{x^2 + x - 6} \cdot \dfrac{x^2 + 7x + 12}{x^2 + x - 12}$

36. $\dfrac{x^3 - 7x + 6}{x^2 + 4x - 5} \cdot \dfrac{x^2 + 9x + 20}{x^3 - 4x^2 + 5x - 2}$

37. $\dfrac{x^3 + x^2 - 4x - 4}{x^2 - 2x - 15} \div \dfrac{x^2 - 4}{x^2 + 8x + 15}$

38. $\dfrac{x^4 + 8x^3 + 24x^2 + 32x + 16}{x^2 - 4} \div \dfrac{x^2 + 4x + 4}{x^2 - x - 2}$

Problems 39 through 46 involve *more* than two fractions to be multiplied or divided. Recall that by the agreed-upon sequence of operations, $\frac{a}{b} \div \frac{c}{d} \cdot \frac{e}{f}$ is equivalent to $\frac{a}{b} \cdot \frac{d}{c} \cdot \frac{e}{f}$. Carry out the indicated operations and simplify:

39. $\dfrac{x + 3}{x - 7} \div \dfrac{x - 7}{x + 5} \cdot \dfrac{x + 5}{x + 3}$

40. $\dfrac{a + 9}{a - 10} \cdot \dfrac{a + 8}{a + 9} \div \dfrac{a - 10}{a + 8}$

41. $\dfrac{25x^2 - 1}{9x^2 - 4y^2} \div \dfrac{5x - 1}{3x - 2y} \div \dfrac{5x + 1}{3x + 2y}$

42. $\dfrac{x + 5}{x - 7} \div \dfrac{x + 3}{7 - x} \div \dfrac{x + 5}{x + 3}$

43. $\dfrac{x + 2}{x - 4} \div \dfrac{x - 4}{x + 3} \div \dfrac{x - 4}{x + 2}$

44. $\dfrac{xy - y^2}{x^2 - x} \cdot \dfrac{x^2 + xy}{xy - y^2} \div \dfrac{xy + y^2}{x^2 - xy}$

45. $\dfrac{x^4 - y^4}{x^3 - y^3} \cdot \dfrac{x^2 - y^2}{x^3 + y^3} \cdot \dfrac{x^6 - y^6}{x^2 + y^2}$

46. $\dfrac{(r^2 + rx)^2}{(r^2 - rx)^2} \div \dfrac{r + x}{r - x} \div \dfrac{r^3 + x^3}{r^3 - x^3}$

Complex Fractions   For Problems 47 through 62 you are asked to simplify fractions that have other fractions in their numerators or denominators. Fractions like this are called *complex fractions*. The simplification can be accomplished by multiplying the fraction by a clever form of 1. For example, to simplify

$$\frac{3 - \dfrac{6}{x + 5}}{1 + \dfrac{7}{x - 4}},$$

you would multiply by 1 in a form that will cancel the minor denominators.

$$\frac{3 - \dfrac{6}{x + 5}}{1 + \dfrac{7}{x - 4}} \cdot \frac{(x + 5)(x - 4)}{(x + 5)(x - 4)}.$$

Multiplying, and associating in the numerator and denominator,

$$\frac{\left[\left(3 - \dfrac{6}{x + 5}\right)(x + 5)\right](x - 4)}{\left[\left(1 + \dfrac{7}{x - 4}\right)(x - 4)\right](x + 5)}.$$

Distributing and simplifying gives

$$\frac{(3x + 15 - 6)(x - 4)}{(x - 4 + 7)(x + 5)} = \frac{3(x + 3)(x - 4)}{(x + 3)(x + 5)}$$

$$= \frac{3x - 12}{x + 5}.$$

Simplify the following complex fractions:

47. $\dfrac{1 - \dfrac{1}{x^2}}{1 + \dfrac{1}{x}}$

48. $\dfrac{12 + \dfrac{6}{x}}{12 - \dfrac{3}{x^2}}$

49. $\dfrac{x + 3 + \dfrac{2}{x}}{1 - \dfrac{4}{x^2}}$

50. $\dfrac{x - 5 + \dfrac{6}{x}}{1 - \dfrac{9}{x^2}}$

51. $\dfrac{\dfrac{1}{x} - \dfrac{2}{x^2} - \dfrac{3}{x^3}}{\dfrac{9}{x} - x}$

52. $\dfrac{1 - \dfrac{y^2}{x^2}}{1 + \dfrac{y}{x}}$

53. $\dfrac{\dfrac{1}{1+x}}{1-\dfrac{1}{1+x}}$

54. $\dfrac{2x+\dfrac{x}{x-2}}{2x-\dfrac{x}{x-2}}$

55. $\dfrac{x-3+\dfrac{12}{x+5}}{x-8+\dfrac{42}{x+5}}$

56. $\dfrac{x+3+\dfrac{5}{x-3}}{x+2+\dfrac{4}{x-3}}$

57. $\dfrac{x^{-2}-y^{-2}}{x^{-1}\,y^{-1}}$

58. $\dfrac{x^{-4}-y^{-4}}{x^{-2}+y^{-2}}$

59. $\dfrac{1-\dfrac{4}{x+1}}{1-\dfrac{2}{x-1}}$

60. $\dfrac{4-\dfrac{12}{x+2}}{2+\dfrac{4}{x-3}}$

61. $\dfrac{x-2-\dfrac{x^2-5x}{x-3}}{x+\dfrac{3x}{x-3}}$

62. $\dfrac{x+y-\dfrac{x^2+y^2}{x+y}}{x+y-\dfrac{2xy}{x+y}}$

7-8 | SUMS AND DIFFERENCES OF RATIONAL EXPRESSIONS

In the previous section you learned how to multiply and divide rational algebraic expressions; in this section you will see how to add and subtract them.

Objective:

Be able to add or subtract several rational expressions and simplify the result.

You   om Chapter 1 that division distributes over addition. That is,

$$\frac{a+b}{c}=\frac{a}{c}+\frac{b}{c}.$$

Using symmetry to read the equation the other way, you can see that two fractions with the same denominator may be added by adding their numerators and using their common denominator.

Subtraction of fractions with the same denominator is done in the same way, because division distributes over subtraction, too.

$$\frac{a}{c} - \frac{b}{c} = \frac{a - b}{c}.$$

Addition or subtraction of fractions with *unlike* denominators may be accomplished by first transforming the fractions so that they have the same denominator. For example, to subtract

$$\frac{7x - 1}{x^2 - 2x - 3} - \frac{6x}{x^2 - x - 2},$$

you would first factor the two denominators, getting

$$\frac{7x - 1}{(x - 3)(x + 1)} - \frac{6x}{(x - 2)(x + 1)}.$$

The LCM of the two denominators is $(x - 3)(x - 2)(x + 1)$. To make the first fraction have this as its denominator, you could multiply it by 1 in the form of $\frac{(x - 2)}{(x - 2)}$. The second fraction could be multiplied by 1 in the form of $\frac{(x - 3)}{(x - 3)}$, giving

$$\frac{7x - 1}{(x - 3)(x + 1)} \cdot \frac{x - 2}{x - 2} - \frac{6x}{(x - 2)(x + 1)} \cdot \frac{x - 3}{x - 3}$$

$$= \frac{7x^2 - 15x + 2}{(x - 3)(x + 1)(x - 2)} - \frac{6x^2 - 18x}{(x - 2)(x + 1)(x - 3)}$$

$$= \frac{7x^2 - 15x + 2 - (6x^2 - 18x)}{(x - 3)(x + 1)(x - 2)}.$$

The fractions have now been subtracted, and all that remains is to tidy up the answer. Associating like terms in the numerator, factoring, and canceling gives

$$\frac{x^2 + 3x + 2}{(x - 3)(x + 1)(x - 2)}$$

$$= \frac{(x + 1)(x + 2)}{(x - 3)(x + 1)(x - 2)}$$

$$= \frac{x + 2}{(x - 3)(x - 2)}.$$

The answer may be left in this form or the factors in the denominator may be multiplied together giving

$$\frac{x + 2}{x^2 - 5x + 6}.$$

There are several ideas to keep in mind when you add or subtract rational expressions:

1. If any of the expressions can be simplified, do the simplifying *before* adding or subtracting. For example,

$$\frac{x + 5}{x^2 + 2x - 15} + \frac{2}{x - 3} = \frac{x + 5}{(x + 5)(x - 3)} + \frac{2}{x - 3}$$

$$= \frac{1}{x - 3} + \frac{2}{x - 3}$$

$$= \frac{3}{x - 3}.$$

2. Make sure that the common denominator is the *least* common multiple of the denominators or you will carry along a lot of excess numbers that would cancel at the end, anyway.

For example, to add

$$\frac{x - 7}{(x + 2)(x - 1)} + \frac{3}{(x + 2)(x + 4)},$$

you would use $(x + 2)(x - 1)(x + 4)$ as the common denominator rather than $(x + 2)(x - 1)(x + 2)(x + 4)$. The factor $(x + 2)$ need appear only *once*.

3. If one denominator has a factor of the form $(a - b)$ and another has a factor of the form $(b - a)$, only *one* of these factors need appear in the common denominator since $a - b$ and $b - a$ are additive inverses of each other. For example, for

$$\frac{3}{x - 2} + \frac{4}{2 - x} + \frac{1}{x}$$

the LCM would be $(x - 2)(x)$ rather than $(x - 2)(2 - x)(x)$. The middle fraction would be multiplied by $\frac{(-x)}{(-x)}$, giving

$$\frac{4}{2 - x} = \frac{4}{2 - x} \cdot \frac{-x}{-x} \quad \text{Multiplication property of 1}$$

$$= \frac{-4x}{(2 - x)(-x)} \quad \text{Multiplication property of fractions}$$

$$= \frac{-4x}{(x - 2)(x)} \quad (-a)(-b) = ab$$

Thus, the middle fraction has $(x - 2)(x)$ as its denominator.

4. Keep the denominator in factored form until the very end so that you will have the best chance of canceling.

The exercise which follows is designed to give you practice in adding and subtracting rational expressions, and combining these operations with multiplication and division.

EXERCISE 7-8

Do These Quickly

The following problems are intended to refresh your skills. You should be able to do all 10 in less than 5 minutes.

Q1.   Multiply: $\dfrac{3}{x + 3} \cdot \dfrac{5}{x - 5}$

Q2.   Divide: $\dfrac{8}{x - 2} \div \dfrac{4}{2 - x}$

Q3.   Multiply: $(3x + 11)(3x - 11)$

Q4.   Do the squaring: $(5x - 2)^2$

Q5.   Sketch the graph of $y = \dfrac{1}{(x + 4)}$.

Q6.   Sketch the graph of $y = x^2$.

Q7.   2% of a certain number is 50. What is the number?

Q8.   Evaluate $\dfrac{56}{x}$ if x is 8.

Q9.   Solve: $4^x = 64$

Q10.   Add: $\dfrac{2}{7} + \dfrac{3}{5}$

1.   ***Distributivity of Division over Addition***   Use the Field Axioms, Equality Axioms, and the Definition of Division to prove that division distributes over addition. That is, prove that
$$\frac{a + b}{c} = \frac{a}{c} + \frac{b}{c}.$$

2.   The expression $ac + bc$ can be transformed to $(a + b)(c)$ by factoring out a common factor. Explain why addition of the two fractions
$$\frac{a}{c} + \frac{b}{c}$$

can be thought of as "factoring out a common *denominator*."

For Problems 3 through 42, carry out the indicated addition and subtraction, and simplify.

3. $\dfrac{x-3}{3} - \dfrac{x-4}{4}$

4. $\dfrac{2x-1}{3} - \dfrac{4x-8}{6}$

5. $\dfrac{1}{x+1} + \dfrac{1}{x-1}$

6. $\dfrac{3}{x-1} + \dfrac{1}{1-x}$

7. $\dfrac{6}{2x-3y} - \dfrac{3}{3y-2x}$

8. $\dfrac{x}{x+y} + \dfrac{y}{x-y}$

9. $\dfrac{2x-1}{x+1} - \dfrac{2x-1}{x-1}$

10. $\dfrac{x+3}{x-3} - \dfrac{x-3}{x+3}$

11. $\dfrac{a-b}{c-d} - \dfrac{b-a}{d-c}$

12. $\dfrac{5}{3(a-b)} + \dfrac{3}{2(b-a)}$

13. $\dfrac{1}{x-y} + \dfrac{2x-y}{x^2-y^2}$

14. $\dfrac{x}{x^2-y^2} + \dfrac{y}{y^2-x^2}$

15. $\dfrac{1}{y-x} + \dfrac{x}{(x-y)^2}$

16. $\dfrac{4x}{(x+y)^2} - \dfrac{4}{x+y}$

17. $\dfrac{1}{1-2x} - \dfrac{2}{1-4x^2}$

18. $\dfrac{3a}{9a^2-4b^2} - \dfrac{1}{3a+2b}$

19. $\dfrac{3}{1-x} + \dfrac{4}{(1-x)^2}$

20. $\dfrac{2y}{(x-2y)^2} + \dfrac{1}{x-2y}$

21. $\dfrac{2}{x-4} - \dfrac{x+12}{x^2-16}$

22. $\dfrac{3}{x+5} - \dfrac{2x-20}{x^2-25}$

23. $\dfrac{x-y}{x^2-y^2} + \dfrac{1}{2x+3y}$

24. $\dfrac{x^2+5x+4}{x+4} - \dfrac{x^2-5x+6}{x-2}$

25. $\dfrac{1}{x-2y} - \dfrac{x^2+4y^2}{x^3-8y^3}$

26. $\dfrac{x+2}{x^3-1} + \dfrac{x+1}{x^2+x+1}$

27. $x+2 - \dfrac{x^2+x-6}{x-3}$

28. $2x+5 - \dfrac{x^2+2x-15}{x-3}$

29. $\dfrac{x+a}{x-a} - \dfrac{x^2+a^2}{ax-a^2}$

30. $\left(\dfrac{x+y}{x-y}\right)^2 - 1$

31. $\dfrac{1}{x+1} - \left(\dfrac{1}{x-1} - \dfrac{1}{x^2-1}\right)$

32. $\dfrac{16x-x^2}{x^2-4} + \dfrac{2x+3}{2-x} + \dfrac{3x-2}{x+2}$

33. $\dfrac{1}{x-1} + \dfrac{2}{x-2} + \dfrac{1}{x-3}$

34. $\dfrac{a}{a^2-b^2} - \dfrac{1}{3(a-b)} - \dfrac{1}{3(a+b)}$

35. $\dfrac{1}{x+y} - \dfrac{1}{x-y} + \dfrac{2x}{x^2-y^2}$

36. $\dfrac{3}{x+6} - \dfrac{4x}{x^2-36} - \dfrac{2}{6-x}$

37. $\dfrac{3}{x^2+x-2} - \dfrac{5}{x^2-x-6}$

38. $\dfrac{5}{x^2-3x-4} - \dfrac{3}{x^2-x-2}$

39. $\dfrac{3x+13}{x^2-3x-10} - \dfrac{16}{x^2-6x+5}$

40. $\dfrac{6}{x^2-7x+12} + \dfrac{5x+9}{x^2-2x-3}$

41. $\dfrac{x-2}{x^2-x-2} + \dfrac{x-4}{x^2-5x+4}$

42. $\dfrac{x+4}{x^2-3x-28} - \dfrac{x-5}{x^2+2x-35}$

Partial Fractions Problems

For Problems 43 through 48 you are asked to *reverse* the process of adding fractions, and split a complicated rational expression apart into a sum of two simpler fractions. For example,

$$\frac{4x+41}{(x-2)(x+5)} = \frac{A}{x-2} + \frac{B}{x+5},$$

where A and B stand for constants. Multiplying both members of this equation by $(x-2)$ gives

$$\frac{4x+41}{x+5} = A + \left(\frac{B}{x+5}\right)(x-2).$$

Substituting 2 for x gives

$$\frac{4 \cdot 2 + 41}{2 + 5} = A + \left(\frac{B}{x+5}\right) \cdot 0$$

$$7 = A.$$

Similarly, multiplying both members of the original equation by $(x + 5)$, then substituting -5 for x, gives $B = -3$. So

$$\frac{4x + 41}{(x - 2)(x + 5)} = \frac{7}{x - 2} - \frac{3}{x + 5}.$$

This process is called "resolving into **partial fractions**." Resolve the following into partial fractions:

43. $\dfrac{5x - 1}{x^2 - x - 2}$ 44. $\dfrac{5x - 10}{x^2 - x - 6}$

45. $\dfrac{3x + 18}{x^2 + 5x + 4}$ 46. $\dfrac{x - 8}{x^2 - 5x + 6}$

47. $\dfrac{4x^2 + 15x - 1}{x^3 + 2x^2 - 5x - 6}$ 48. $\dfrac{-3x^2 + 22x - 31}{x^3 - 8x^2 + 19x - 12}$

49. ***Partial Fractions and Computer Graphics Problem***   For the function $f(x) = \frac{3x + 1}{x^2 - x - 6}$:

   a.   Plot the graph on the computer screen using PLOT RATIONAL, from the accompanying disk, or a similar program. Where does the graph cross the x-axis? Explain why this result is reasonable.
   b.   Resolve the expression for $f(x)$ into partial fractions.
   c.   Use the program PLOT COMP GEN, or a similar program, to plot the graphs of each of the two fractions in part (b) and add the graphs to get a composed graph. If you use PLOT COMP GEN, you will have to add error traps in lines 315 and 415 to protect against division by zero. For instance, if you plot the fraction whose denominator is $(x + 2)$ as FN Y1(X), then line 315 must be:

$$\text{315 IF } (U-VA)/HP = -2 \text{ THEN } 350$$

   d.   Did the composed graph look the same as the graph in part (a)?
   e.   Explain why although neither of the two auxiliary graphs crosses the x-axis, the composed graph *does*.

7-9   GRAPHS OF RATIONAL ALGEBRAIC FUNCTIONS, AGAIN

By now you should be comfortable with simplifying rational expressions. If so, you are ready to return to the problem of plotting rational function graphs.

Objective:

Be able to determine what values of x are excluded from the domain of a given rational function, figure out what happens to the graph at these points, and draw the graph.

In Sections 7-1 and 7-2 you plotted the graph of

$$f(x) = \frac{x + 2}{x^2 - x - 6}.$$

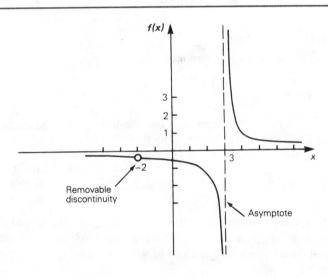

$$f(x) = \frac{x + 2}{(x + 2)(x - 3)}$$

Figure 7-9a

This graph is shown in Figure 7-9a. By factoring the denominator you get

$$f(x) = \frac{x + 2}{(x + 2)(x - 3)}.$$

If $x = -2$ or $x = 3$, $f(x)$ will be *undefined*, since these values of x make the denominator equal *zero*. At $x = 3$, you found a vertical asymptote. At $x = -2$, you found one point deleted from an otherwise "continuous" graph. In this section you will use what you learned in Section 7-2 to sketch rational function graphs.

If you simply substitute 3 for x in the equation for $f(x)$, you get

$$\frac{5}{0}.$$

Expressions such as $\frac{5}{0}$ are said to be *infinitely large*. You can see why by choosing values of the denominator that are close to zero.

$$\frac{5}{0.01} = 500, \frac{5}{-0.0001} = -50{,}000,$$

$$\frac{5}{0.000001} = 5{,}000{,}000$$

The closer the denominator gets to zero, the bigger the fraction becomes (in absolute value).

If you substitute -2 for x in the equation for $f(x)$, you get the form

$$\frac{0}{0}.$$

The form $\frac{0}{0}$ is said to be *indeterminate*. For example,

$$\frac{3x}{x} = 3, \quad \text{if } x \neq 0.$$

When x does equal 0, the expression has the form $\frac{0}{0}$. So you could conclude that $\frac{0}{0}$ is equal to 3! But the same line of reasoning leads to other conclusions, for example,

$$\frac{57x}{x} = 57, \frac{x}{\pi x} = \frac{1}{\pi}, \text{ and } \frac{-13x}{x} = -13.$$

Substituting 0 for x in these expressions would lead to the conclusion that $\frac{0}{0}$ is also equal to 57, $\frac{1}{\pi}$, and -13! The word "indeterminate" is used since you cannot determine what $\frac{0}{0}$ is close to without knowing where the two 0's came from.

These facts allow you to tell how the graph of a rational function behaves when the denominator is 0.

CONCLUSION

Suppose that substituting c for x makes the denominator of $f(x)$ equal 0.

1. If $f(c)$ has the form $\dfrac{\text{non-zero}}{\text{zero}}$, then $f(c)$ is *infinitely large*, and there is a vertical asymptote in the graph at $x = c$.
2. If $f(c)$ has the form $\dfrac{0}{0}$, then $f(c)$ is *indeterminate*.

You must examine the *simplified* fraction to see whether there is a vertical asymptote at $x = c$, or just a removable discontinuity at $x = c$.

Once you have found out what happens to the graph when the denominator equals zero, you need only calculate other points, plot them, and draw the graph.

EXAMPLE

Draw the graph of

$$f(x) = \frac{x^2 - 1}{x^2 + 2x - 3}.$$

Solution:
Factoring the numerator and denominator gives

$$f(x) = \frac{(x + 1)(x - 1)}{(x + 3)(x - 1)}.$$

$f(x)$ is *undefined* when $x = -3$ or $x = 1$. If $x = -3$, then $f(x)$ has the form

$$\frac{8}{0},$$

which is *infinitely large*. So there is a *vertical asymptote* at $x = -3$.

If $x = 1$, $f(x)$ has the form

$$\frac{0}{0},$$

which is *indeterminate*. If the $(x - 1)$ factors are canceled,

$$f(x) = \frac{x + 1}{x + 3}.$$

Substituting $x = 1$ into the simplified fraction gives

$$\frac{1 + 1}{1 + 3} = \frac{2}{4} = \frac{1}{2}.$$

So there is a removable discontinuity in the graph at $(1, \frac{1}{2})$.   ■

Values of $f(x)$ for other values of x can be calculated by constructing a table. Choose values of x from below the smallest value of x that makes the denominator zero, to above the largest such value.

The table is most easily constructed by going *down* the columns. For example, you would find *all* values of $x + 1$ before starting on the values of $x + 3$. The values of $f(x)$ are calculated by simply dividing the numbers in the $x + 1$ column by the numbers in the $x + 3$ column. The graph is shown in Figure 7-9b. Note that as x gets very large, the fraction gets

closer and closer to 1. For example,

$$f(1000) = \frac{1001}{1003} \approx 0.998 \approx 1.$$

x	$x + 1$	$x + 3$	$f(x) = \dfrac{x + 1}{x + 3}$
-6	-5	-3	$\dfrac{-5}{-3} = 1\dfrac{2}{3}$
-5	-4	-2	$\dfrac{-4}{-2} = 2$
-4	-3	-1	$\dfrac{-3}{-1} = 3$
-3	-2	0	$\dfrac{-2}{0}$ (infinite)
-2	-1	1	$\dfrac{-1}{1} = -1$
-1	0	2	$\dfrac{0}{2} = 0$
0	1	3	$\dfrac{1}{3}$
1	2	4	$\dfrac{2}{4}$ (removable discontinuity at $\frac{1}{2}$)
2	3	5	$\dfrac{3}{5}$
3	4	6	$\dfrac{4}{6} = \dfrac{2}{3}$
4	5	7	$\dfrac{5}{7}$

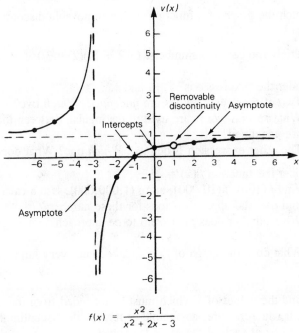

$$f(x) = \frac{x^2 - 1}{x^2 + 2x - 3}$$

Figure 7-9b _____

EXERCISE 7-9

Do These Quickly

The following problems are intended to refresh your skills. You should be able to do all 10 in less than 5 minutes.

Q1.   Multiply: $\dfrac{x + 5}{x + 4} \cdot \dfrac{x + 3}{x + 4}$

Q2.   Add and simplify: $\dfrac{x + 5}{x + 4} + \dfrac{x + 3}{x + 4}$

Q3.   Factor: $x^3 - 8$

Q4.   80 is a certain percent of 400. What percent?

Q5.   Draw a rhombus.

Q6.   Sketch: $y = 0.4x + 3$

Q7.   Find b if $37 = b^{\frac{2}{3}}$.

Q8.   Find the x-coordinate of the vertex: $y = 5x^2 + 3x - 11$

Q9.   Sketch the graph of a function with a removable discontinuity at $x = 3$.

Q10. Multiply the complex numbers: $(-2 + 3i)(2 + 3i)$

1. Consider the "expressions" $\frac{0}{7}$, $\frac{7}{0}$, and $\frac{0}{0}$.
    a. Two of these expressions are *undefined. Which* two?
    b. What special words are used to distinguish between the two that are undefined?
    c. The other expression *is* defined. *Which* one? What does it equal?

2. Consider the function $f(x) = \frac{5x + 7}{2x + 1}$.
    a. Find $f(100)$, $f(10,000)$, and $f(1,000,000)$. Use a calculator to find decimal approximations for these numbers.
    b. What number does $f(x)$ seem to be approaching as x gets very large?
    c. What does the graph of f do as x becomes very large?

For Problems 3 through 30,
    a. find the values of x which must be excluded from the domain,
    b. tell which feature, asymptote or removable discontinuity, there will be at each of the excluded values,
    c. calculate some points and draw the graph,
    d. check by computer graphics using PLOT RATIONAL or a similar program.

3. $f(x) = \dfrac{4}{x - 5}$

4. $f(x) = \dfrac{3}{x + 1}$

5. $f(x) = \dfrac{x^2 - 4x + 3}{x^2 - x - 6}$

6. $f(x) = \dfrac{x^2 - x - 6}{x^2 + 3x + 2}$

7. $f(x) = \dfrac{2}{x^2 + 3x - 10}$

8. $f(x) = \dfrac{5}{x^2 - 2x - 8}$

9. $f(x) = \dfrac{x - 1}{x^2 + 3x - 4}$

10. $f(x) = \dfrac{x - 3}{x^2 - 2x - 3}$

11. $f(x) = \dfrac{x^2 + 2x - 15}{x - 3}$

12. $f(x) = \dfrac{x^2 + 6x - 7}{x - 1}$

For Problems 13 through 16, it will help if you recall how to plot *quadratic* function graphs.

13. $f(x) = \dfrac{x^3 - 8}{x - 2}$

14. $f(x) = \dfrac{x^3 + 1}{x + 1}$

15. $f(x) = \dfrac{x^3 - 2x^2 - 5x + 6}{x + 2}$

16. $f(x) = \dfrac{x^3 + 3x^2 - 18x - 40}{x + 5}$

17. $f(x) = \dfrac{5}{x^2 + 1}$ 18. $f(x) = \dfrac{3x + 3}{x^3 + 1}$

19. $f(x) = \dfrac{x + 5}{x^3 + 9x^2 + 24x + 20}$

20. $f(x) = \dfrac{x + 1}{x^3 + 3x^2 - 6x - 8}$

21. $f(x) = \dfrac{(x - 1)(x - 4)}{(x - 4)(x - 3)(x + 2)}$

22. $f(x) = \dfrac{(x + 2)(x + 3)}{(x + 1)(x - 2)(x + 3)}$

23. $f(x) = \dfrac{(x + 2)(x - 1)}{(x - 2)^2(x - 1)}$

24. $f(x) = \dfrac{(x - 3)(x + 2)}{(x + 3)^2(x + 2)}$

25. $f(x) = \dfrac{(x - 2)(x - 1)}{(x - 2)^2(x - 1)}$

26. $f(x) = \dfrac{(x + 3)(x + 2)}{(x + 3)^2(x + 2)}$

27. $f(x) = \dfrac{8x}{x^2 - 6x + 5} - \dfrac{x - 7}{x^2 + x - 2}$

28. $f(x) = \dfrac{7x + 5}{x^2 + 2x - 3} + \dfrac{3x}{x^2 - 3x + 2}$

29. $f(x) = \dfrac{\dfrac{1}{1 + x}}{1 - \dfrac{1}{1 + x}}$ 30. $f(x) = \dfrac{x - 2 - \dfrac{x^2 - 5x}{x - 3}}{x + \dfrac{3x}{x - 3}}$

31. Plot graphs of the following functions on the *same* set of axes:

a. $f(x) = \dfrac{10}{x^2}$ b. $g(x) = \dfrac{10}{x^2 + 1}$

c. $h(x) = \dfrac{10}{x^2 + 2}$

7-10 | FRACTIONAL EQUATIONS AND EXTRANEOUS SOLUTIONS

A fractional equation is an equation that has a *variable* in a *denominator*. For example,

$$\frac{x}{x - 2} + \frac{2}{x + 3} = \frac{10}{x^2 + x - 6}$$

is a fractional equation. An equation such as $\frac{1}{2}x + 7 = 3$ is *not* called a fractional equation, even though it has a fraction in it, because there are no variables in denominators.

Such equations arise, for example, in finding the value of x for a given value of y in a rational algebraic function. Since fractional equations occur in many other places, it is worth spending some time learning how to solve them.

Objective:
Given a fractional equation, be able to solve it.

The first thing you must recognize is that certain values of x might make a denominator equal *zero*. In the above example, denominators are zero when $x = 2$ and when $x = -3$. These values of x must be excluded from the domain. So you write

$$x \neq 2, \, x \neq -3.$$

Next, you must transform the equation to a familiar form. Multiplying both members by an appropriate expression will eliminate the fractions. To see what this expression would be, it helps to factor any denominators. So you write

$$\frac{x}{x - 2} + \frac{2}{x + 3} = \frac{10}{(x - 2)(x + 3)}.$$

The *least common multiple* (LCM) of the denominators is $(x - 2)(x + 3)$. Multiplying both members of the equation by this expression gives

$$(x - 2)(x + 3)\left(\frac{x}{x - 2} + \frac{2}{x + 3}\right) = \left(\frac{10}{(x - 2)(x + 3)}\right)(x - 2)(x + 3).$$

The denominator on the right cancels immediately. On the left, you must remember to *distribute* the $(x - 2)(x + 3)$ to both terms.

$$(x - 2)(x + 3)\left(\frac{x}{x - 2}\right) + (x - 2)(x + 3)\left(\frac{2}{x + 3}\right) = 10.$$

Canceling and simplifying reduces the equation to

$$(x + 3)(x) + (x - 2)(2) = 10$$
$$x^2 + 5x - 14 = 0.$$

Factoring the left member gives

$$(x - 2)(x + 7) = 0.$$

By the Multiplication Property of Zero and its Converse, you know that the only way this product can be zero is for one of the factors to equal zero. So this equation is equivalent to

$$x - 2 = 0 \quad \text{or} \quad x + 7 = 0,$$
$$x = 2 \quad \text{or} \quad x = -7.$$

Before you write the solution set, you must look back at the excluded values. Since $x \neq 2$, the 2 must be an *extraneous* solution. It satisfies the transformed equation, but not the original one. Such an extraneous solution can occur when you multiply both members of an equation by an expression that can equal zero, as you will demonstrate in Problem 1 of Exercise 7-10. So you write

extraneous

$$x = 2 \quad \text{or} \quad x = -7$$
$$\therefore S = \{-7\}.$$

The following are the steps involved in solving fractional equations.

TECHNIQUE

SOLVING FRACTIONAL EQUATIONS

1. Write the domain,
2. multiply both members of the equation by the smallest expression needed to eliminate all of the fractions,
3. solve the resulting polynomial equation,
4. discard any extraneous solutions, and
5. write the solution set.

The following exercise is designed to give you practice in solving fractional equations. There is also a warm-up on solving polynomial equations by factoring.

EXERCISE 7-10

Do These Quickly

The following problems are intended to refresh your skills. You should be able to do all 10 in less than 5 minutes.

Q1.   Solve: $\frac{2}{3}x = 36$

Q2.   Factor: $3x^2 + 4x + 1$

Q3.   Solve: $(x - 2)(x + 5) = 0$

Q4.   If P is a polynomial and $P(-3) = 0$, then _____ is a factor of $P(x)$. What goes in the blank?

Q5.   If $y = \dfrac{x - 2}{x - 3}$, what is the y-intercept?

Q6.   Solve: $|x - 8| = -3$

Q7.   Sketch the graph of $y = \log_2 x$.

Q8.   Add the complex numbers: $(3 - 7i) + (5 + i)$

Q9.   Write the general equation of a quadratic function.

Q10.   Sketch the graph of a linear function with slope -3.

Work the following problems.

1.   ***Extraneous Solutions Problem***   Starting with the equation $x = 3$, do the following:
    a.   Multiply each member by $(x - 4)$.
    b.   Tell why the transformed equation *is* true when $x = 4$, but the original equation is *not*.
    c.   What name is given to the solution 4?
    d.   Multiplying both members of an equation by an expression which can equal zero, such as $(x - 4)$, is called an *irreversible step*. Why do you suppose that this name is used?

2.   ***Depressed Equation Problem***   Starting with the equation $x^2 = 3x$, do the following:
    a.   Show that the solution set is $S = \{0, 3\}$.
    b.   Divide each member of the equation by x. The transformed equation is called a *depressed* equation. Its degree is lower than that of the original equation. What is the solution set of the depressed equation?

c.   Why is it more dangerous to *divide* both members of an equation by a variable than it is to *multiply*?

For Problems 3 through 20, solve the equation by factoring.

3. $x^2 - 2x - 3 = 0$ 4. $x^2 - x - 20 = 0$

5. $x^2 - 10x - 24 = 0$ 6. $x^2 + 5x - 6 = 0$

7. $2x^2 + 7x + 5 = 0$ 8. $3x^2 - 10x + 8 = 0$

9. $3x^2 - 5x + 2 = 0$ 10. $3x^2 - 7x + 2 = 0$

11. $x^2 + 3x = 0$ 12. $x^2 - 5x = 0$

13. $x^2 = 2x$ 14. $x^2 = -7x$

15. $(x - 2)(x - 3) = 20$ 16. $(x + 3)(x - 1) = 5$

17. $x^3 + 2x^2 - 5x - 6 = 0$

18. $x^3 - 5x^2 - 2x + 24 = 0$

19. $x^3 + x^2 - 6x + 4 = 0$

20. $x^3 + 2x^2 - 6x - 4 = 0$

For Problems 21 through 42, state the domain, then solve the equation. Show the step where you discard any extraneous solutions.

21. $x + \dfrac{x}{x - 2} = \dfrac{2}{x - 2}$ 22. $x + \dfrac{2x}{x - 1} = \dfrac{3 - x}{x - 1}$

23. $\dfrac{x}{x - 3} - \dfrac{7}{x + 5} = \dfrac{24}{x^2 + 2x - 15}$

24. $\dfrac{x}{x + 2} + \dfrac{7}{x - 5} = \dfrac{14}{x^2 - 3x - 10}$

25. $\dfrac{3x}{x + 4} + \dfrac{4x}{x - 3} = \dfrac{84}{x^2 + x - 12}$

26. $\dfrac{4x}{x - 1} - \dfrac{5x}{x - 2} = \dfrac{2}{x^2 - 3x + 2}$

27. $\dfrac{3}{x - 3} + \dfrac{4}{x - 4} = \dfrac{25}{x^2 - 7x + 12}$

28. $\dfrac{11x}{x + 20} + \dfrac{24}{x} = 11 + \dfrac{88}{x(x + 20)}$

29. $\dfrac{x + 2}{x - 3} + \dfrac{x - 2}{x - 6} = 2$ 30. $\dfrac{3x + 2}{x - 1} + \dfrac{2x - 4}{x + 2} = 5$

31. $\dfrac{2}{x + 2} - \dfrac{x}{2 - x} = \dfrac{x^2 + 4}{x^2 - 4}$

32. $\dfrac{x}{x + 4} + \dfrac{4}{x - 4} = \dfrac{x^2 + 16}{x^2 - 16}$

33. $\dfrac{1}{1 - x} = 1 - \dfrac{x}{x - 1}$

34. $\dfrac{x}{x - 1} - \dfrac{2}{1 - x^2} = \dfrac{8}{x + 1}$

35. $\dfrac{x + 3}{2x - 3} = \dfrac{18x}{4x^2 - 9}$

36. $3 - \dfrac{22}{x + 5} = \dfrac{6x - 1}{2x + 7}$

37. $\dfrac{4x}{x^2 - 9} - \dfrac{x - 1}{x^2 - 6x + 9} = \dfrac{2}{x + 3}$

38. $\dfrac{x}{x^2 - 2x + 1} = \dfrac{2}{x + 1} + \dfrac{4}{x^2 - 1}$

39. $\dfrac{3x}{x - 2} + \dfrac{2x}{x + 3} = \dfrac{30}{x^2 + x - 6}$

40. $\dfrac{5}{x - 6} - \dfrac{4}{x + 3} = \dfrac{x + 39}{x^2 - 3x - 18}$

41. $\dfrac{x^3 + 3x - 9}{x(x - 3)} - \dfrac{x + 6}{x - 3} = \dfrac{3}{x}$

42. $\dfrac{5x}{x - 5} + \dfrac{4}{x + 6} = \dfrac{54x + 5}{x^2 + x - 30}$

43. **Continued Fractions**   The following is called a *continued fraction* (for obvious reasons!). It equals an *irrational* number. Find that number.

$$2 + \cfrac{1}{2 + \cfrac{1}{2 + \cfrac{1}{2 + \dots}}}$$

Clue: Let x equal the fraction. Since the pattern continues *forever*, you can write

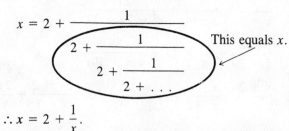

$$\therefore x = 2 + \dfrac{1}{x}.$$

To find the value of this fraction, solve the equation for x. (See Charles G. Moore; *An Introduction to Continued Fractions;* Washington, D.C.; National Council of Teachers of Mathematics; 1964.)

44.   Evaluate:

$$3 + \cfrac{1}{2 + \cfrac{1}{3 + \cfrac{1}{2 + \cfrac{1}{3 + \ldots}}}}$$

7-11   VARIATION FUNCTIONS

A relatively simple type of function that is very useful as a mathematical model has an equation in which y is equal to a constant multiplied or divided by a power of x. Functions with equations such as

$$y = 4x^2, \quad y = \frac{13}{x}, \quad y = \frac{0.732}{x^2}, \quad y = 1.9x,$$

are called *variation* functions. If the constant is *multiplied* by the variable, then y varies *directly* with the power of x. If the constant is *divided* by the variable, then y varies *inversely* with the power of x. The constant, such as 1.9 in $y = 1.9x$, is called the *proportionality constant*. The letter k is often used for this constant, after the German word *Konstante*, meaning "*constant*."

DEFINITION

If k and n are constants, then "y varies directly with the nth power of x" means

$$\boxed{y = kx^n},$$

and "y varies inversely with the nth power of x" means

$$\boxed{y = \frac{k}{x^n}}.$$

Notes:

1. If *n* is a positive integer, then direct variation functions are special cases of *polynomial* functions (linear, quadratic, etc.), and inverse variation functions are special cases of *rational algebraic* functions (such as those in Section 7-9). Variation functions in which *n* is *not* an integer will be explored in Chapter 8.
2. The equation $y = kx^n$ can include both direct and inverse variation functions if *n* is allowed to be *negative*.
3. The words, ". . . varies directly with . . . ," or "varies inversely with . . . ," can be replaced by the words, ". . . is directly proportional to . . . ," or ". . . is inversely proportional to . . . ," respectively.

Some examples of variation function equations and the words that go with them are listed below.

EQUATIONS OF SOME VARIATION FUNCTIONS

General Equation	*Words*
$y = kx$	y varies directly with x.
$y = kx^2$	y varies directly with the square of x.
$y = kx^3$	y varies directly with the cube of x.
$y = \dfrac{k}{x}$	y varies inversely with x.
$y = \dfrac{k}{x^2}$	y varies inversely with the square of x.

Objective:

Given a real-world situation,
a. determine which kind of variation function is a reasonable mathematical model,
b. find the particular equation for the function, and
c. predict values of y or x.

One way to tell whether a certain kind of function is a reasonable mathematical model is to compare its graph with the real-world graph. Figure 7-11a shows several kinds of variation function graphs. For *direct* variation functions, y gets *bigger* as x increases. For *inverse* variation functions, y gets *smaller* as x increases. Inverse variation functions have the x- and y-axes as *asymptotes*.

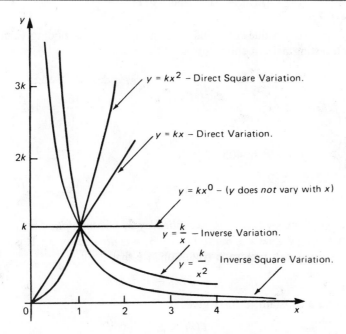

Figure 7-11a _____

There is a property of variation functions that lets you tell *which power* of x to use. For $y = kx$, the graph is a straight line through the origin (Figure 7-11b). By the properties of similar triangles, if x_2 is *three* times x_1, then y_2 will also be *three* times y_1. In general, *multiplying* the value of x by some constant causes the value of y to be *multiplied* by the *same* constant.

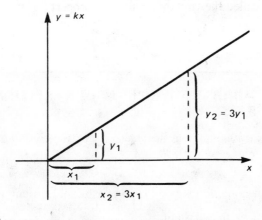

Figure 7-11b _____

A similar property holds for higher degree and for inverse variation functions. Suppose that

$$f(x) = 5x^2 \quad \text{and} \quad g(x) = \frac{162}{x^2}.$$

By picking certain values of x and examining the corresponding values of y, an interesting pattern shows up!

x	$y = f(x)$		x	$y = g(x)$
1	$5 \cdot 1^2 = 5$		1	$\frac{162}{1^2} = 162$
3	$5 \cdot 3^2 = 45$		3	$\frac{162}{3^2} = 18$
9	$5 \cdot 9^2 = 405$		9	$\frac{162}{9^2} = 2$
27	$5 \cdot 27^2 = 3645$			

For function f, every time x is *multiplied* by 3, y is *multiplied* by 3^2. For function g, every time x is *multiplied* by 3, y is *divided* by 3^2. It is not hard to see why this pattern is true. Suppose that

$$y = f(x) = kx^2.$$

Substituting a constant, c for x gives

$$f(c) = kc^2.$$

Substituting $3c$ for x gives

$$\begin{aligned}
f(3c) &= k(3c)^2 && \text{Substitution} \\
&= k(9c^2) && (3c)(3c) = 9c^2 \\
&= 9(kc^2) && \text{Commutativity and associativity} \\
&= 9 \cdot f(c). && \text{Because } kc^2 = f(c)
\end{aligned}$$

This pattern is called the "multiply-multiply" property of variation functions.

PROPERTY

> **MULTIPLY-MULTIPLY PROPERTY OF VARIATION FUNCTIONS**
>
> If $y = kx^n$, then *multiplying* the value of x by the constant c *multiplies* the value of y by the constant c^n.
>
> If $y = \dfrac{k}{x^n}$, then *multiplying* the value of x by the constant c *divides* the value of y by the constant c^n.

Note: This property is similar to the properties of linear and exponential functions.

PROPERTIES

> **ADD-ADD PROPERTY OF LINEAR FUNCTIONS**
> For *linear* functions, *adding* a constant to *x adds* a constant to *y*.
>
> **ADD-MULTIPLY PROPERTY OF EXPONENTIAL FUNCTIONS**
> For *exponential* functions, *adding* a constant to *x multiplies y* by a constant.
>
> **MULTIPLY-MULTIPLY PROPERTY OF VARIATION FUNCTIONS**
> For *variation* functions, *multiplying x* by a constant *multiplies y* by a constant. (Dividing by c^n can be thought of as multiplying by $\frac{1}{c^n}$.)

Once you understand the above properties, you are ready to select the kind of variation function that is appropriate in a given situation.

EXAMPLE 1

The pressure required to force water through a garden hose depends on the number of gallons per minute (gpm) you want to flow. By experiment, you find that for a flow of 3 gpm, a pressure of 10 pounds per square inch (psi) is required. For 6 gpm, a pressure of 40 psi is required. Predict

a. the pressure required for a flow rate of 12 gpm,
b. the pressure required for a flow rate of 4.2 gpm,
c. the number of gpm you would get with a pressure of 5 psi.

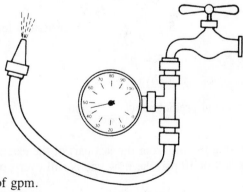

Solutions:
a. Let g = number of gpm.
   Let p = number of psi.

You first observe that *doubling* g (from 3 to 6) makes p get *four* times as big (from 10 to 40). Assuming that this pattern continues, you would expect that doubling g again (from 6 to 12) would make p four times bigger again. So

$$p = 4(40)$$

$$= \underline{160 \text{ psi.}}$$

b. Since 4.2 is not a simple multiple of 3, it is helpful to derive a particular equation expressing p in terms of g. Since *doubling* g makes p *four* times as big, and since 4 is equal to 2^2, you can conclude that p varies directly with the *square* of g. The general equation is thus

$$p = kg^2.$$

Substituting one of the given ordered pairs gives

$$10 = k(3^2) \quad \text{Substitute (3, 10) for (g, p).}$$

$$\frac{10}{9} = k.$$

Thus, the particular equation is $p = \underline{\dfrac{10}{9} g^2}.$

With this equation, you can easily predict p for *any* value of g. Substituting 4.2 for g gives

$$p = \frac{10}{9}(4.2)^2 \quad \text{Substitute 4.2 for g.}$$

$$= \frac{10}{9}(17.64)$$

$$= \underline{19.6 \text{ psi}}$$

c. The particular equation can be used *backwards* to predict g for a known value of p. If $p = 5$, then

$$5 = \frac{10}{9} g^2 \quad \text{Substitute 5 for p.}$$

$$4.5 = g^2$$

$$2.1213 \ldots = g$$

So you would predict about $\underline{2.12 \text{ gpm.}}$ ■

It is interesting to note from the last part of the example that although 5 psi is only *half* of 10 psi, the flow rate is still over $\frac{2}{3}$ of what it was for 10 psi.

EXAMPLE 2

The intensity of light reaching you from a light bulb depends on how far from the bulb you are standing. Suppose that at 3 meters the intensity is 120 units, and at 6 meters it is 30 units.

a. How does intensity vary with distance? Write the general equation.
b. Find the particular equation.
c. Predict the intensity at 10 meters.
d. Predict the intensity at 12 meters.
e. Predict the distance at which the intensity will be 4 units.
f. Draw the graph.
g. Tell the real-world significance of the asymptotes.

Solutions:
a. Let I = number of units of intensity.
    Let d = number of meters distance.

    The two given ordered pairs are (d, I) = (3, 120) and (6, 30). From these, you can see that multiplying d by 2 (from 3 to 6) *divides I by 4* (from 120 to 30). Since $4 = 2^2$, I appears to <u>vary inversely with the <u>square</u> of d.</u>

    Thus, the general equation is <u>$I = \dfrac{k}{d^2}$</u>.

b. To evaluate the proportionality constant, k, you must substitute one of the given ordered pairs. It is usually better to solve the equation for k *before* you substitute.

    $$I = \frac{k}{d^2} \qquad \text{General equation}$$

    $$Id^2 = k \qquad \text{Multiply each member by } d^2.$$

    $$(120)(3^2) = k \quad \text{Substitute (3, 120) for } (d, I).$$

    $$1080 = k$$

    ∴ the particular equation is <u>$I = \dfrac{1080}{d^2}$</u>.

c. The equation is now ready to use for making predictions.

    If $d = 10$, then $I = \dfrac{1080}{10^2} = $ <u>10.8 units</u>.

d. If $d = 12$, you can calculate I *without* using the equation. The thought process is as follows:

    Since 12 is *two* times 6, and the intensity at $d = 6$ is 30 units, the intensity twice as far away will be

$$30 \div (2^2) = 30 \div 4 = \underline{7.5 \text{ units}}.$$

This thought process is easy enough to do in your head. It will work whenever the desired value of x is a simple multiple of a *known* value of x.

e. If $I = 4$, then $4 = \dfrac{1080}{d^2}$.

$$\therefore d^2 = \frac{1080}{4} \qquad \text{Multiply by } d^2 \text{ and divide by 4.}$$

$$d^2 = 270$$

$$d = \sqrt{270}$$

$$d = \underline{16.4 \text{ meters}}$$

f. The graph of this function is shown in Figure 7-11c. You can use the given points, the calculated points, and any other points you feel it is advisable to calculate.

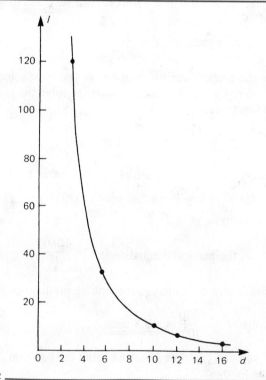

Figure 7-11c

g. From the graph it is clear that the illumination drops off very rapidly as you move away from the bulb. The asymptote at the d-axis can be interpreted as telling you that no matter how far you go from the light, there is still *some* illumination. At great distances, however, the illumination would be so small that it would be zero "for all practical purposes."

The asymptote at the *I*-axis indicates that the intensity at the center of the bulb is *infinite*. This could be true only if all the light came from a single point. Since light comes from the entire bulb, the mathematical model works only in the domain *outside* the bulb. ∎

The multiply-multiply property applies to similarly-shaped geometrical objects. This property helps you to decide upon the proper general equation to use. If two objects are of *similar proportions,* then their linear dimensions, area, and volume vary directly with the first, second, and third power, respectively, of their length. For example, the circumference (a linear dimension), the area, and the volume of a sphere of radius r are given by

$$\text{Circumference} = 2\pi r,$$

$$\text{Area} = 4\pi r^2,$$

$$\text{Volume} = \frac{4}{3}\pi r^3.$$

In these equations, the numbers 2π, 4π, and $(\frac{4}{3})\pi$ are just proportionality constants. For other geometrical figures, the *general* equations are the *same.* Only the proportionality constants are different. For example, similarly shaped *people* have volumes (and thus masses) that are directly proportional to the *cube* of their height.

PROPERTY

MULTIPLY-MULTIPLY PROPERTY OF SIMILAR GEOMETRICAL OBJECTS

For similarly-shaped geometrical objects,
a. A linear dimension is directly proportional to any other linear dimension.
b. An area is directly proportional to the *square* of a linear dimension.
c. The volume is directly proportional to the *cube* of a linear dimension.

In the following exercise you will use variation functions as mathematical models. In some problems you will be expected to use the above properties of similarly shaped figures *without* being told in the problem.

EXERCISE 7-11

Do These Quickly

The following problems are intended to refresh your skills. You should be able to do all 10 in less than 5 minutes.

Write the general equation:

Q1. *y* varies directly with *x*.

Q2. *y* varies linearly with *x*.

Q3. *y* varies inversely with *x*.

Q4. *y* is inversely proportional to *x*.

Q5. *y* is directly proportional to the cube of *x*.

Q6. *y* decreases exponentially with *x*.

Q7. *y* increases exponentially with *x*.

Q8. *y* varies inversely with the square of *x*.

Q9. *y* is a quadratic function of *x*.

Q10. *y* is a constant function.

Work the following problems.

1. ***Kilograms-to-Pounds Problem***   The number of pounds you weigh is directly proportional to the number of kilograms you are. Kay Dense steps onto a scale calibrated in kilograms and finds that she is 50 kilograms. She knows that she weighs 110 pounds.
    a. Write the particular equation expressing pounds in terms of kilograms.
    b. How many pounds would a person weigh if the scale read
        i.   100 kilograms?
        ii.   25 kilograms?
        iii. 150 kilograms?
    c. How many kilograms would Stan Dupp be if he weighed 165 pounds?
    d. How many kilograms are *you*?
    e. Plot the graph of this function.
    f. What quantity does the proportionality constant represent in the real world?

2. ***Water Pressure Problem*** When you swim underwater, the pressure in your ears varies directly with the depth at which you swim. At 10 feet, the pressure is about 4.3 pounds per square inch, (psi).
   a. Write the particular equation expressing pressure in terms of depth.
   b. Predict the pressure at 50 feet.
   c. It is unsafe for amateur divers to swim where the pressure is more than 65 psi. How deep can an amateur diver safely swim?
   d. Plot the graph of pressure versus depth.

3. ***Wrench Problem*** The amount of force you must exert on a wrench handle to loosen a rusty bolt depends on how long the wrench handle is. Suppose that for a particular bolt, a wrench 7 inches long would require a force of 270 pounds, and a wrench 21 inches long would require 90 pounds.

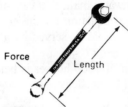

Force   Length

   a. How does force vary with length? Write the general equation.
   b. Write the particular equation.
   c. What are the units of the proportionality constant? (This quantity is called "torque," and is a measure of the amount of "twisting" needed to loosen the bolt.)
   d. Find the force needed for wrenches with handles 3, 10, 15, 30, and 60 inches long.
   e. How long a wrench would be needed by Sarah Sota, who can exert a force of 300 pounds?
   f. How long a wrench would be needed by Sarah's little sister Minnie, who can exert a force of 50 pounds?
   g. Plot a graph of force versus handle length in the domain from 3 through 60 inches. Use the answers to parts d, e, and f, above, the given points, and any others you feel are necessary.

4. ***Multi-Story Building Problem*** The amount of floor space in a building equals the area of each floor multiplied by the number of stories. The area of each floor is equal to the area of land covered by the building. If a building is to contain a *fixed* total floor space, the area of land covered by the building will depend on how many stories high it is.
   a. Show that the number of square meters of land covered by the building *varies inversely* with the number of stories.
   b. Show that the proportionality constant equals the total amount of floor space in the building.

c. A building is to contain 12,000 square meters, total, of floor space. Write the particular equation expressing number of square meters of land covered in terms of number of stories.

d. How much land would be covered if the building were
    i. 3 stories high?   ii. 5 stories high?   iii. 10 stories high?

e. If the building is to cover no more than 1900 square meters, what is the minimum number of stories it can have?

f. Draw a graph of this function in a suitable domain, if city zoning laws prevent buildings from being over 10 stories high.

5. *Water Main Problem*   The number of houses that can be served by a water main is directly proportional to the square of the diameter of the main. This is because the cross-sectional area of the pipe, and thus the number of liters per minute that can flow, varies directly with the square of the diameter. Suppose that the City Waterworks has a 10 cm diameter water main that can supply 50 houses.

a. Write the particular equation for this function.

b. How many houses could be served by a water main of diameter 30 cm? 43 cm? 1 meter?

c. A new subdivision of 1500 houses is being planned. What size water main would be needed?

6. *Boat's Wake Problem*   When a boat is going at high speed, most of the power generated by its engine goes into forming the wake. The amount of power used to generate the wake is directly proportional to the seventh power of the speed of the boat.

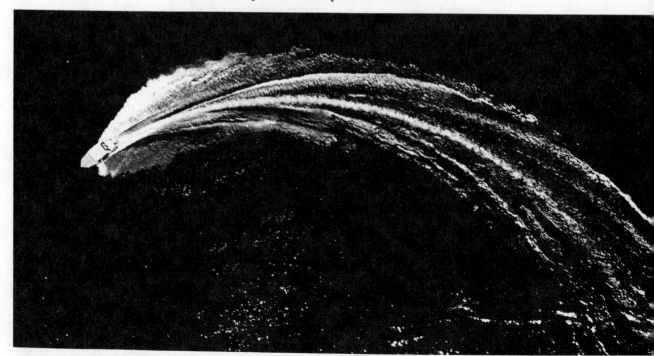

    a. Suppose that a boat going 10 knots (nautical miles per hour) uses 0.1 horsepower for wake generation. Write the particular equation for this function.

    b. How much power goes into wake generation when the boat goes 20 knots? 30 knots?

    c. Why is it so hard for boats to go very fast?

    d. When a boat skims across the water, the proportionality constant in the wake generation function gets much smaller. Why do you suppose that such "hydroplaning" is necessary for a boat that goes 100 knots?

7. *Gas Law Problem* In chemistry you learn Boyle's Law, which states that the volume of a fixed amount of gas (at constant temperature) is inversely proportional to the pressure of the gas.

    a. Write the particular equation expressing volume in terms of pressure if a pressure of 46 pounds per square inch (psi) compresses the gas to a volume of 360 cubic feet.

    b. Plot a graph of volume versus pressure in the domain from 10 to 100 psi.

    c. What pressure would be necessary to compress the gas to a volume of 276 cubic feet?

    d. According to your model, could you compress the gas to *zero* volume? How do you tell?

    e. Prove that the product of the pressure and the volume is constant. (This is the way Boyle's Law is stated in some chemistry books.)

    f. Prove that if (P_1, V_1) and (P_2, V_2) are ordered pairs of pressure and volume, then

$$P_1 V_1 = P_2 V_2 .$$

(This is the way Boyle's Law is stated in other chemistry books.)

8. *Parkinson's Law Problem* In the book *Parkinson's Law* the author, Cyril M. Parkinson, claims (as a joke?) that the amount of time an agency spends discussing an item in its budget is *inversely* proportional to the amount of money involved. Suppose that a university's Board of Regents spent 15 minutes discussing a $1,000,000 item in next year's budget for starting a computer service. According to Parkinson's Law, how much time would they spending discussing

    a. faculty salaries, $30,000,000?

    b. a new bicycle rack, $1,000?

9. *Radio Transmitter Problem* The strength of a radio signal received from the transmitter varies inversely with the square of your distance from the transmitter.

    a. Derive the particular equation expressing strength in terms of distance if the strength is 1000 units at a distance of 2 km.

    b. Predict the strength 10 kilometers from the transmitter.

c. Predict the strength 100 meters from the transmitter.

d. From your answer to part c, tell why when you drive past a transmitting station, the signal from that station can sometimes be heard on your car's radio even though the radio is tuned to another station.

10. *Recycled Can Problem*   The amount of refund you get for returning recyclable aluminum cans varies directly with the number of cans you collect. The price per pound depends on supply and demand, but may be assumed to be about 40 cents a pound (23 cans).

a. Write the particular equation expressing number of cents of refund in terms of number of cans you return.

b. How much refund would you get for 100 cans?

c. If you wanted to earn $100, how many cans would you have to return? Does collecting cans seem to be an easy way to earn a living?

11. *Lightning Problem*   In a lightning storm, the time interval between the flash and the bang is directly proportional to the distance between you and the lightning. Answer the following questions:

a. Define the variables you would like to use for the distance and time intervals. Tell which should be dependent.

b. Write the particular equation for this direct variation function, if the thunder clap from lightning 5 kilometers away takes 15 seconds to reach you.

c. Figure out the units of the constant of proportionality, and from these units figure out what real-world quantity the constant represents.

d. Calculate the times for the thunder sound to reach you from lightning bolts which are 1, 2.5, and 10 kilometers away.

e. Plot a graph of time versus distance.

f. Suppose that you measured a time interval of 29 seconds. Figure out how far away the lightning is.

g. What would be the situation in the real world if you heard the bang at the same instant you see the flash?

12. *Balloon Temperature Problem*   The volume of a fixed amount of gas such as air varies directly with its Kelvin temperature (273° + its Celsius temperature). Suppose that a balloon contains 7.5 liters of air at 300°K (about room temperature).

a. Write the particular equation expressing volume in terms of temperature.

b. Use your mathematical model to predict the volume for temperatures of 400, 600, 900, and 1200 degrees Kelvin.

c. Plot the graph of this function.

d. What things in the real world might set upper and lower bounds on the domain of this direct variation function?

13.   *Friction Problem*   The force needed to overcome friction and drag
      a person across the floor depends on the person's weight. Manuel
      Dexterity can drag Gil O'Teen across the floor by pulling with a
      force of 51 pounds. Gil's brother, Nick, who weighs twice as much,
      can be dragged across the floor by pulling with a force of 102
      pounds.
      a.   How does force vary with the person's weight? Define variables
           and write the general equation.
      b.   Gil weighs 85 pounds. Write the particular equation. (The pro-
           portionality constant is called the "coefficient of friction.")
      c.   Bob Tail weighs 130 pounds. How hard would Manuel have to
           pull to drag him across the floor?
      d.   Manuel can drag Kara Vann across the floor by pulling with a
           force of 65 pounds. How heavy is Kara?
      e.   Plot the graph of this function.

14.   *Radiotherapy Problem*   Tumors are sometimes treated by irradiating
      them with gamma rays from a radioactive source such as cobalt-60.
      The intensity of radiation you receive depends on how far you are
      from the source. Suppose that for a particular source, the intensity is
      80 mr/hr at 2 meters and 5 mr/hr at 8 meters. ("Mr/hr" stands for
      "milliroentgens per hour." The word "roentgen" is pronounced
      "rent'-ken.")
      a.   How does the intensity vary with distance? Write the general
           equation.
      b.   Write the particular equation.
      c.   What would the intensity be if your distance were
             i.   16 meters?
            ii.   12 meters?
           iii.   10 meters?
            iv.   10 centimeters?
      d.   At what distance would the intensity be 0.5 mr/hr?
      e.   Plot the graph of this function.

15.   *Radiant Heat Problem*   The rate at which a hot object radiates heat
      varies directly with some power of its Kelvin temperature. (The
      Kelvin temperature equals the Celsius temperature plus 273°.) By ex-
      periment, you find that an electric heater radiates 5 calories per
      minute when it is at 300°K, and 80 calories per minute when it is at
      600°K.
      a.   At what rate would it radiate heat if the heater were at 1200°K?
      b.   With what power of the Kelvin temperature does the heat radia-
           tion rate vary?
      c.   Write the particular equation expressing radiation rate for this
           heater in terms of temperature.
      d.   Use the equation to predict the radiation rate if the heater is at
             i.   800°K,   ii.   1000°K.

e. Plot a graph of radiation rate as a function of temperature.

16. *Diamond Problem* A discount diamond house ran an ad in a local newspaper which showed a $\frac{3}{4}$ carat diamond for $360 and a 1.5 carat diamond for $1440.

    a. Based on these figures, how would you expect the price of a diamond to vary with its weight (number of carats)?

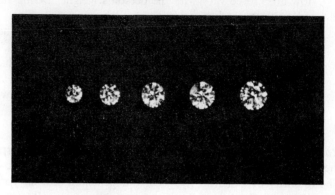

    b. Predict the price of
       i. a 3 carat diamond,
      ii. a $\frac{1}{4}$ carat diamond.

    c. Write the particular equation expressing the number of dollars in terms of the number of carats.

    d. The Hope Diamond weighs 44.5 carats. Based on your model, how much should it be worth?

    e. Approximately how large a diamond could you get for $2000?

    f. The weights of similarly shaped diamonds are directly proportional to the *cubes* of their diameters. Write a general equation expressing this fact.

    g. Substitute the expression for weight from part f into the equation for price in part c, and simplify as much as possible. Then tell how the *price* of a diamond varies with its *diameter*.

    h. If a particular diamond cost $500, how much would you expect to pay for one with *twice* the diameter?

17. *Ruby Problem* Based on a comparison of prices, you find that the price of a ruby varies directly with the fourth power of its weight. Suppose that a particular ruby is worth $200.

    a. How much would you expect to pay for a ruby weighing 10 times as much as the $200 one? What does this tell you about the availability of very large rubies?

    b. How much would you expect to pay for a ruby weighing $\frac{1}{10}$ as much as the $200 one? What does this tell you about the demand for very small rubies?

18. *Relative Time Problem* Time seems to pass faster when you are old than it did when you were very young. Assume that the length that a particular period of time *seems* to be is inversely proportional to your age. At your present age, a day seems like a day, a week seems like a week, and so forth.
   a. How long will a week seem to be when you are *twice* as old as you are now?
   b. How long did a week seem to be when you were a *tenth* as old as you are now?
   c. A mother 36 years old says to her 3-year-old child, "Don't get those toys out. You have only 5 minutes to play." Based on your model, and in terms of the mother's time scale, how long does that 5 minutes seem to be to the child? Does this result suggest a reason for some types of parent-child conflicts?

19. *Stopping Distance Problem* Your car's stopping distance is the *sum* of the braking distance (the distance you go after you get your foot on the brake pedal) and the reaction distance (the distance you go between the time you realize you need to stop and the time you put your foot on the brake pedal). The braking distance varies directly with the *square* of the car's speed, and the reaction distance varies directly (with the *first* power) with the car's speed.
   a. At 30 kph, your reaction distance is 7 meters and your braking distance is 6 meters. Calculate the reaction and braking distances for speeds of 60, 90, 120, 150, and 180 kph.
   b. By adding the reaction and braking distances, calculate the total stopping distances for the speeds in part a.
   c. Plot the graph of total stopping distance versus speed for speeds in the domain from 0 through 180 kph.
   d. Use the given information in part a to write particular equations expressing reaction distance and braking distance in terms of speed.
   e. Use the two equations from part d to predict the total stopping distance if you drive 100 kph. Show that this point lies on the graph of part c.
   f. If you drive 200 kph, how many football field lengths will it take you to stop your car after you realize that you need to stop?
   g. Consult a driver's manual or another source to find out just how accurate your mathematical model is

20. *Weight Above and Below the Earth* Sometimes a function is defined by *different* equations in different parts of its domain. For example, the weight of an object varies directly with its distance from the center of the Earth when the object is below the Earth's surface, but is inversely proportional to the square of its distance from the center when it is above the surface. (Note that an object *in orbit* is

"weightless" only because its weight is exactly counterbalanced by the upward force due to its motion.)

a. Phoebe Small weighs 81 pounds at the Earth's surface. Write particular equations expressing her weight as a function of distance from the center (*two* equations) assuming that the radius of the Earth is 4000 miles.

b. Predict Phoebe's weight 3000, 8000, and 12,000 miles from the center.

c. Draw a graph of this function in the domain from 0 through 12,000 miles.

21. *Egg Problem*   According to an ad for South African Airways in an old issue of *Time Magazine,* ostrich eggs are served at bush country "braaivleis" (barbecues). Each ostrich egg is claimed to be equivalent to two dozen chicken eggs!

a. If an ostrich egg really is equivalent to two dozen chicken eggs, and a chicken egg is about 6 centimeters long, about how long is an ostrich egg (to the nearest centimeter)? Justify your answer.

b. If a robin's egg is 1 cm long, how many of them would you have to scramble to get the equivalent of one chicken egg?

22. *Grapefruit Problem*   Suppose that you are shopping at a supermarket and find that the Texas grapefruits have *twice* the diameter of the Florida ones, but cost *seven* times as much. Recalling that the volumes of similarly shaped solids vary directly with the *cube* of a linear dimension such as a diameter, you instantly determine which kind of grapefruit gives you more for your money. Which one does, and why?

23. *Large and Small People Problem*   Two people of different size have the same "build" if they have the same proportions.

a. Write general equations expressing the following quantities in terms of height for people of the same build:

  i.   mass,
  ii. skin area,
  iii. belt length.

b. In *Gulliver's Travels,* Gulliver traveled to Brobdingnag, where people are 10 times as tall as normal people, and to Lilliput, where people are $\frac{1}{10}$ as tall as normal people. Les Moore, a normal person of average build, is 70 kg, has 25,000 square centimeters of skin, and wears a belt 90 cm long. Estimate the mass, skin area, and belt size of

  i.   a Brobdingnagian,
  ii. a Lilliputian.

c. How does the mass of a Lilliputian compare with that of a MacDonald's hamburger patty?

d. The mass a person's legs will support varies directly with the *square* of his or her height because the strength of the legs depends on their cross-sectional *area*. Les Moore's legs can support a total of 200 kg (including his own 70 kg). Based on this information, would a Brobdingnagian's legs be able to support his own mass? Justify your answer.

e. See the article, "On Being the Right Size," by J. B. S. Haldane in *The World of Mathematics*, Volume II, page 952, for more reasons why people cannot be excessively large or excessively small!

24. *Airplane Wing Problem*   John Garfinkle is Chief Mathematician for the Fly-By-Night Aircraft Corporation. His company is designing the Sopwith Hippopotamus, a larger version of the famous Sopwith Camel and John is called upon to answer the following questions:

a. The weight of an airplane varies directly with the *cube* of the plane's length. Write an equation expressing the weight of an airplane in terms of its length. Evaluate the proportionality constant if a Sopwith Camel is 40 feet long and weighs 3000 pounds.

b. The number of pounds a plane's wings can lift varies directly with the *square* of the plane's length. Write another equation expressing the number of pounds of lift in terms of the plane's length. Evaluate the proportionality constant if a Sopwith Camel's wings can lift 5000 pounds.

c. The Sopwith Hippopotamus is to be 60 feet long. Based on your model, will a Hippopotamus be able to fly? Explain.

d. What is the longest such airplane that would be able to fly?

25. *Shark Problem*   The photograph shows a great white shark caught off Catalina Island. The shark was 15 feet long, and weighed 2000 pounds.

    a. Assuming that all great white sharks have similar proportions, how should the weight of a great white shark vary with its length?

    b. Write the particular equation expressing weight in terms of length.

    c. Predict the weight of
        i. a baby shark, 2 feet long,
        ii. the shark in the novel *Jaws*, 25 feet long.

    d. If you caught a shark weighing 250 pounds, how long would you expect it to be?

    e. Fossilized teeth have been found in Florida that resemble those of a great white shark. If this creature had the same proportions as present-day sharks, it would have been 100 feet long. How much would such a shark have weighed?

26.   **Height-Mass Problem**   Professor Snarff, who considers himself to be of average build, is 91 kg and 194 cm tall.

    a. Write the particular equation expressing mass in terms of height for people of Professor Snarff's proportions.

    b. Use the equation of part a to calculate *your* mass. What can you conclude if your actual mass is significantly different from what you predicted?

    c. Show that a baby is significantly *fatter* in proportion to its height than an adult. You can do this by using the mathematical model to show that the predicted mass of a 50 cm baby is much smaller than its actual 3 to 4 kg.

    d. According to *Guinness Book of World Records,* the tallest man who ever lived was Robert P. Wadlow. When he died in 1940 at the age of 22, he was 272 cm tall and had a mass of 196 kg. Was Wadlow fatter or thinner in proportion to his height than Professor Snarff? Justify your answer. (Look at Wadlow's picture in *Guinness* to see if your conclusion is reasonable!)

27.   **Medication Problem**   The safe dosage of a new medicine is determined by testing it on animals. To predict the safe dosage for humans from the results of animal experiments, scientists assume that the safe dosage is directly proportional to the patient's skin area. This area is, of course, directly proportional to the *square* of the person's height (assuming that patients have the same proportions).

    a. Write general equations for safe dosage in terms of skin area, and for skin area in terms of height. Use *different* letters for the two proportionality constants.

    b. Combine the two equations in part a to get a general equation expressing safe dosage in terms of height. You can simplify the equation by realizing that the product of two constants is just another constant.

    c. Tell in words how safe dosage depends on height.

d. Suppose that a new cold remedy is tested on monkeys 30 cm tall, and that the safe dosage for the monkeys is found to be 1.2 milligrams (mg). Write the particular equation expressing safe dosage in terms of height.

e. Assuming that humans have roughly the same proportions as monkeys, predict the safe dosage of the cold remedy for
   i. a child, 90 cm tall
   ii. an average adult, 170 cm tall
   iii. a very tall adult, 2 meters tall.

28. *Pizza Problem*   The price you pay for a pizza may be assumed to be composed of two different terms. One term varies directly with the square of the diameter. It represents the amount you pay for the ingredients in the pizza, and is reasonable because the area (and thus the amount of ingredients) varies directly with the square of the diameter. The other term is a *constant*. It represents the fixed costs such as cooking and serving the pizza, washing the dishes, and making the mortgage payments on the building. The total price you pay is the *sum* of these two terms. Therefore, the general equation would be

$$p = ad^2 + c,$$

where p is the number of cents the pizza costs, d is the number of inches diameter, and a and c are constants. Answer the following questions:

a. A recent Pizza Hut menu lists the following prices for Supreme pizzas:

Kind	Diam. (in.)	Price ($)
Individual	(Not listed)	2.19
Small	9	6.55
Medium	13	11.20
Large	15	13.90

Use the prices and diameters for Small and Large pizzas to determine the values of the constants a and c. Then write the particular equation expressing price in terms of diameter.

b. According to your mathematical model, is the Medium pizza overpriced, underpriced, or about right? Justify your answer.

c. According to your mathematical model, what is the approximate diameter of the Individual pizza?

d. Obtain a menu from a pizzeria in your area. For each type of pizza listed, find the particular equation as in part a, using the largest and smallest size to determine the constants. Then predict the prices for other sizes of pizza of the same kind. The pizzeria manager might be interested in learning about any pizzas that seem to be particularly overpriced or underpriced!

29. *Epidemic Data Analysis Problem*   Suppose that you are working at the Center for Disease Control. You get reports that a new disease has been detected. Three days after the first report, there are 100 cases of the disease. Six days after the first report, the number of cases has risen to 200. The chart shows the number of cases (C) and days (D):

D	C
3	100
6	200
9	400
12	800

a.   Based on this data, which is the most appropriate mathematical model, a linear function, an exponential function, or a variation function? Justify your answer.

b.   Find the particular equation for C in terms of D using the function you assumed and the points (3, 100) and (6, 200).

c.   Show that your mathematical model is reasonable by showing that it gives the right results for 9 and 12 days.

d.   If nothing happens to stop it, when will 10,000 people have the disease?

30. *Pressure-Temperature Data Analysis Problem*   According to Charles' Law, the air pressure in a closed container should vary linearly with the Celsius temperature. However, due to experimental error the data points do not always lie in quite a straight line. Suppose that the following pressures (P pounds per square inch) and temperature (T degrees Celsius) are measured for a particular container:

T (°C)	P (psi)
100	20.3
200	28.4
300	33.9
400	40.2
500	48.0
600	52.8
700	62.1
800	68.2
900	72.1
1000	79.8

a.   Plot the data accurately on graph paper. Then line up a ruler so that the line you would draw using it will "fit" the data as closely as possible. Draw the line.

b.   Find the slope and P-intercept of your line by reading the graph. Use these to write the particular equation expressing P in terms of T.

c. Based on your equation, what Celsius temperature corresponds to "absolute zero," where the pressure of the gas will be zero?

7-12 | CHAPTER REVIEW AND TEST

In this chapter you have studied another major kind of function, the rational algebraic function. You have learned that the graphs may have vertical asymptotes and removable discontinuities, as well as horizontal asymptotes. You acquired skill in factoring polynomials so that you could operate with and simplify the rational expressions that appear in equations for these functions. A special kind of rational function, the inverse variation function, was used as mathematical model, as well as direct variation functions. The multiply-multiply property of variation functions helps you tell whether this kind of function is more reasonable than a linear or exponential function.

The Review Problems below parallel the sections in this chapter. The Concepts Problems let you try your hand at applying what you know to analyze a new situation. The Chapter Test is similar to one your instructor might give to see how well you understand rational algebraic functions.

REVIEW PROBLEMS

R1. For the function $f(x) = \dfrac{x - 3}{x^2 - 5x + 6}$,
  a. Explain why there are no values of $f(2)$ and $f(3)$.
  b. Find $f(2.1)$ and $f(3.1)$.
  c. What happens to the graph of $f(x)$ at $x = 2$? At $x = 3$?

R2. Draw the graph of the function in Problem R1.

R3. a. Multiply: $(3x + 7y)(3x - 7y)$
  b. Multiply: $(x + 3)(x^2 - 5x + 2)$
  c. Do the squaring: $(r - 4t)^2$
  d. Factor completely: $6ax + 15bx$
  e. Factor completely: $36r^2 - 81s^2$
  f. Factor completely: $2x^2 - 21xy - 36y^2$

R4. a. Factor completely: $x^3 - 8y^3$
  b. Factor completely: $12x^2 + 35x + 8$
  c. Use the discriminant to prove that $3x^2 - 2x + 11$ is prime.
  d. Factor completely: $9 - p^2 + 8p - 16$
  e. Factor completely: $x^4 - 10x^2 + 9$

R5. Write in mixed-number form: $\dfrac{x^3 + x^2 - 13x + 10}{x - 2}$

R6. a. Factor completely: $2x^3 - 13x^2 - 48x + 27$
     b. Factor completely: $32x^5 + y^5$

R7. a. State the multiplication property of fractions.
     b. State the definition of division.
     c. Divide and simplify: $\dfrac{x^2 - 2x - 15}{x^2 - 9x + 20} \div \dfrac{x^2 + 2x - 3}{x^2 - 3x - 4}$
     d. Do the operations and simplify:
         $$\dfrac{x^2 + 4x + 4}{x^2 - 8x + 15} \div \dfrac{3 + x}{3 - x} \cdot \dfrac{x^3 - x^2 - 17x - 15}{x^2 - 4}$$
     e. Simplify the complex fraction: $\dfrac{3 - \dfrac{7}{x + 1}}{1 + \dfrac{2x}{x - 4}}$

R8. a. Explain why fractions must have a common denominator to be added.
     b. Add and simplify: $\dfrac{3t + 7}{t - 11} - \dfrac{2t + 6}{11 - t}$
     c. Subtract and simplify: $\dfrac{7}{x^2 - x - 12} - \dfrac{2}{x^2 - 6x + 8}$
     d. Do the operations and simplify:
         $$\dfrac{2(2x + 1)}{x^2 + x - 6} - \dfrac{2}{x + 3} - \dfrac{x}{2 - x}$$
     e. Resolve into two partial fractions: $\dfrac{7x - 5}{x^2 - x - 2}$

R9. Plot the graph of: $f(x) = \dfrac{x^2 - 1}{(x - 3)^2(x + 1)}$.

R10. Solve the equations: The four fractional equations below all look somewhat alike. Yet each illustrates a different example of what might happen when you solve a fractional equation. By solving the equations, show what happens.
     a. $\dfrac{x}{x - 2} - \dfrac{2}{x + 4} = \dfrac{12}{x^2 + 2x - 8}$
     b. $\dfrac{x}{x - 2} - \dfrac{2}{x + 4} = \dfrac{19}{x^2 + 2x - 8}$
     c. $\dfrac{x}{x - 2} + \dfrac{1}{x + 4} = \dfrac{12}{x^2 + 2x - 8}$
     d. $\dfrac{1}{x - 2} + \dfrac{2}{x + 4} = \dfrac{3x}{x^2 + 2x - 8}$

R11. Suppose that y varies inversely with the cube of x.
     a. Write the general equation for this function.
     b. Write the particular equation if the function contains the ordered pair (4, 448).
     c. Calculate y when x is 0.7.
     d. *Without* using your equation, find y when x is 8.

CONCEPTS PROBLEMS

The following problems require you to combine several concepts of this chapter or to use the concepts to do things you have never done before. Work each problem and tell by number(s), 1 through 5, which one or ones of the objectives of this chapter were used in working each part of each problem.

C1. **One-Question Test on Rational Functions**   Suppose that

$$f(x) = \frac{2x^2 - 2x - 4}{x^3 - 4x^2 + x + 6} - \frac{\frac{x}{9} + \frac{1}{3} + \frac{1}{x}}{\frac{x^2}{9} - \frac{3}{x}} + \frac{2 - x}{x^2 - 4}.$$

   a.   Simplify each of the three fractions as much as possible.
   b.   Carry out the indicated addition and subtraction. Simplify the result as much as possible.
   c.   Plot the graph of f.
   d.   Find the value(s) of x for which $f(x) = \dfrac{-5}{4}$.
   e.   Find the value(s) of x for which $f(x) = 2$.

C2. **System of Rational Equations**   You have learned how to solve systems of equations with two variables when both equations were *linear*. The following system has one equation that is *rational*.

$$y = \frac{x^3 - 4x^2 + x + 6}{x - 2},$$

$$x - y = 5.$$

   a.   Combine the two equations so that y is eliminated. (There are at least two ways you can do this.)
   b.   Solve the resulting fractional equation to find the value(s) of x.
   c.   Find the value(s) of y corresponding to each value of x, and write the solution set.

C3. **Intensity Problem**   The *intensity* of light at a certain point is the amount of light that passes through a unit area in a given time. Suppose that Q units of light comes from a light bulb in a given time, and spreads out uniformly in all directions. If you imagine a sphere drawn around the bulb (Figure 7-12a), all the light must pass through this sphere. Thus, the intensity of light on the surface of the sphere is Q *divided by* the area of the sphere.
   a.   Show that the intensity of light at a distance r from the bulb varies *inversely* with the *square* of r. (Recall that the area of a sphere of radius r is $4\pi r^2$.)
   b.   What is the proportionality constant for the intensity function?
   c.   What intensity of light does your hand receive if you hold it 10 centimeters away from a light bulb for which $Q = 200$ watts?

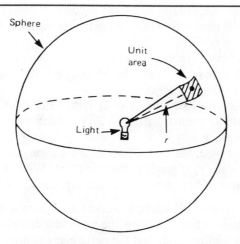

Figure 7-12a _____

    d.   If an intensity of 0.005 watts per square centimeter or more
        will cause damage to your eyes, how far must you stay from a
        600 watt bulb to avoid such damage?

C4.   *Slope of a Tangent Line* In the mathematical models problems of
      Section 7-11 you found meanings for asymptotes to graphs. In this
      problem you will find a meaning for a removable discontinuity in a
      graph.
    a.   A *secant* line is a line that cuts a graph in *two* places (Figure
        7-12b). Suppose that various secant lines are drawn through
        the *fixed* point $(2, f(2))$ and the *variable* point $(x, f(x))$. Since
        the graph of f is *curved,* the slope of the secant line will de-
        pend on the value of x. Recalling that slope equals $\frac{\text{rise}}{\text{run}}$, write
        an equation expressing the slope, $m(x)$, in terms of $x, f(x), 2,$
        and $f(2)$.

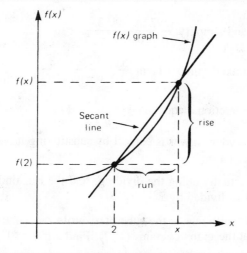

Figure 7-12b _____

b. Suppose that $f(x) = x^3 - 4x^2 + 5x + 3$. Find $f(2)$. Then use this information to write the particular equation for $m(x)$ in terms of x.

c. If you have been successful so far, the numerator for $m(x)$ should have $(x - 2)$ as a factor. Simplify the fraction.

d. Plot the graph of $m(x)$.

e. $m(x)$ is *undefined* when $x = 2$. What value does $m(x)$ seem to be close to when x is close to 2? What feature does the graph of m have at $x = 2$?

f. When $x = 2$, the secant line becomes a *tangent* line. That is, it touches the $f(x)$ graph at just *one* point. What is the slope of this tangent line? Justify your answer.

C5. You know how to tell where a vertical asymptote is on a rational function graph when you know the particular equation. Use this knowledge backwards to find the particular equation of a rational function that has a vertical asymptote at $x = 3$, and contains the point $(4, 1)$.

CHAPTER TEST

T1. Factor: $8x^3 + 1$

T2. Factor: $x^7 + y^7$

T3. Factor: $bx + 7x - 2by - 14y$

T4. Factor: $x^3 - 6x^2 + 5x + 12$

T5. Divide and simplify: $\dfrac{x^2 - 25}{x^2 - 5x + 6} \div \dfrac{5 + x}{x - 2}$

T6. Subtract and simplify: $\dfrac{7}{x + 6} - \dfrac{3}{x - 5}$

T7. Write in mixed-number form: $\dfrac{5x^2 - 3x + 8}{x - 2}$

T8. Solve the fractional equation $\dfrac{3x + 4}{5x - 7} = \dfrac{2}{3}$

Show that your answer is correct by substituting it back into the original equation.

T9. Without actually doing the dividing, find the remainder when $x^{99} + 13$ is divided by $x - 1$.

T10. If y varies inversely as the cube of x, write the particular equation, given that the graph contains $(4, 7)$. Find x if $y = 10$.

T11.   Show that the graph of $f(x) = \dfrac{x^3 - 10x^2 + 31x - 28}{x - 4}$ is a

parabola with a removable discontinuity at $x = 4$. Find the vertex. It is *not* necessary for you to draw the graph.

T12.   Draw the graph of $g(x) = \dfrac{(x - 2)(x + 3)}{(x + 3)(x + 1)(x - 4)}$

8

Irrational Algebraic Functions

*In this chapter you will study the fifth operation of algebra, **taking n^{th} roots**. By plotting graphs of irrational functions you will get a better insight into the nature of extraneous solutions. You will also prove that there really are real numbers which cannot be expressed as ratios of two integers. The operations with radical expressions should be easy for you since you already know how to deal with fractional exponents. Applications of radical functions will lead you to some startling conclusions, such as why mammals are the way they are, and where is the safest place to hide during a tornado!*

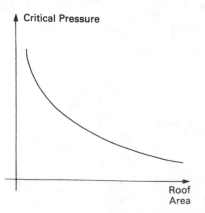

8-1 | INTRODUCTION TO IRRATIONAL ALGEBRAIC FUNCTIONS

A function such as

$$f(x) = 3 + \sqrt{x + 2}$$

is called an irrational algebraic function. The name is given to any function in which the independent variable appears under a radical sign. Since taking roots is equivalent to raising numbers to fractional powers, functions such as

$$g(x) = x^{\frac{1}{3}}$$

are also called irrational functions.

DEFINITION

> **IRRATIONAL ALGEBRAIC FUNCTION**
> An **irrational algebraic function** is a function in which the independent variable appears under a radical sign or in a power with a rational number for its exponent.

The most interesting thing about irrational functions is what happens when the value of x you pick makes the radicand a *negative* number. As you recall, square roots, fourth roots, etc., of negative numbers are imaginary numbers.

Objective:
Learn things about an irrational algebraic function by pointwise plotting of its graph and other algebraic techniques.

By correctly working the following exercise you will accomplish this objective.

EXERCISE 8-1

Given: $f(x) = 3 + \sqrt{x + 2}$

1. Find $f(-2), f(-1), f(0), f(2)$, and $f(14)$. Recall that the symbol $\sqrt{}$ is used only for the *positive* square root.

2. Try to find $f(-3)$ and $f(-6)$. What do you notice?

3. What numbers must be *excluded* from the domain of function f?

4. Plot the graph of f.

5. Find x if $f(x) = 6$. You can do this by isolating the radical on one side of the equation, then squaring both sides. Show on the graph that your answer is reasonable.

6. Find x if $f(x) = 1$. Show on the graph that the answer you get could not possibly be right.

7. See if you can figure out a reason why you get the result in Problem 6.

8-2   GRAPHS OF IRRATIONAL FUNCTIONS

In the last section you explored the function

$$f(x) = 3 + \sqrt{x + 2}.$$

Its graph is shown in Figure 8-2a.

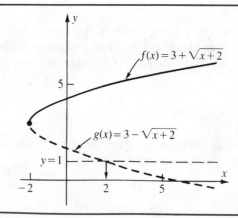

Figure 8-2a

Two interesting things happen when you evaluate this function. First, if you pick a value of x less than -2, the radicand $x + 2$ becomes *negative*. So $f(x)$ will be an imaginary number and will not show up on the graph.

Second, if you substitute a number such as 1 for $f(x)$ and try to solve for x you get

$$1 = 3 + \sqrt{x + 2}$$
$$-2 = \sqrt{x + 2}$$
$$(-2)^2 = (\sqrt{x + 2})^2$$
$$4 = x + 2$$
$$2 = x$$

From the figure, it is clear that there is *no* value of x for which $f(x) = 1$. The number 2 is an *extraneous* solution. From the second line above,

$$-2 = \sqrt{x + 2},$$

you can tell what went wrong. A *positive* square root, $\sqrt{x + 2}$, could not possibly equal -2. But when you square in the third line, both members of the equation become positive. The solution $x = 2$ is what you would get from the *conjugate* function,

$$g(x) = 3 - \sqrt{x + 2},$$

by substituting 1 for $g(x)$.

Squaring both members of an equation is called an *irreversible step*. The statement, "If $a = b$, then $a^2 = b^2$" is a true statement. But reversing the operation and saying, "If $a^2 = b^2$, then $a = b$" is *not* true. It is also possible that a could equal $-b$. Anytime you take an irreversible step in solving an equation, you might get an extraneous solution.

Objective:
Given the equation of an irrational algebraic function, find $f(x)$ when x is given, find x when $f(x)$ is given, and plot the graph.

The work above is an example of what you are expected to do. In the following exercise you will graph and analyze more functions.

EXERCISE 8-2

Do These Quickly

The following problems are intended to refresh your skills. You should be able to do all 10 in less than 5 minutes.

Q1. Find a number that is 40% of 300.

Q2. Write the general equation of an exponential function.

Q3. Write the equation for the definition of subtraction.

Q4. Solve: $12 - 2(x + 3) = 47$

Q5. Solve: $x^2 - 5x + 6 = 0$

Q6. Simplify: $23 - 3(4x - 5)$

Q7. Find two consecutive integers whose product is 72.

Q8. What axiom is illustrated? $(3)(4x + 5) = (4x + 5)(3)$

Q9. Find the slope of the line connecting $(2, 13)$ and $(6, 41)$.

Q10. What is the sum of the degree measures of supplementary angles?

For Problems 1 through 4, plot the graph of the function for the domain shown.

1. $f(x) = \sqrt{x}, 0 \le x \le 1$ (Plot $f(0), f(0.1), \ldots, f(1)$.)

2. $f(x) = \sqrt[3]{x}, -1 \le x \le 1$ (Include $f(-0.2), f(-0.1), f(0.1)$, and $f(0.2)$.)

3. $f(x) = \sqrt[10]{x}, 0 \le x \le 1$ (Plot $f(0), f(0.1), \ldots, f(1)$.)

4. $f(x) = x^{\frac{2}{3}}, -1 \le x \le 1$ (There is an easy way to get values of $f(x)$ from the results of Problem 2.)

5. Given $f(x) = x - 3\sqrt{x + 4}$:
    a. What is the least value of x for which there is a real-number value of $f(x)$?
    b. Plot the graph of function f using a suitable domain.
    c. What does the $f(x)$-intercept equal?
    d. What does the x-intercept equal?
    e. Find the *two* values of x for which $f(x) = -5$.
    f. Find the *one* value of x for which $f(x) = -3$.
    g. Show that there are *no* values of x for which $f(x) = -8$.
    h. $f(x)$ reaches a minimum value somewhere between $x = -4$ and $x = 0$. Approximately what is this value of x? Approximately what is the minimum value?

8-3 | ## RADICALS, AND SIMPLE RADICAL FORM

In Section 6-4 you learned the relationship between radicals and powers with fractional exponents. For example,

$$\sqrt[3]{128} = 128^{\frac{1}{3}}.$$

Since the operation of taking roots is really just a form of exponentiation, the properties of exponentiation you learned before automatically apply to radicals. Two of these properties are restated here to refresh your memory.

	Radical Form	*Exponential Form*
Root of a product	$\sqrt[n]{ab} = \sqrt[n]{a} \; \sqrt[n]{b}$	$(ab)^{\frac{1}{n}} = a^{\frac{1}{n}} \, b^{\frac{1}{n}}$
Root of a quotient	$\sqrt[n]{\dfrac{a}{b}} = \dfrac{\sqrt[n]{a}}{\sqrt[n]{b}}$	$\left(\dfrac{a}{b}\right)^{\frac{1}{n}} = \dfrac{a^{\frac{1}{n}}}{b^{\frac{1}{n}}}$

These properties can be used to *simplify* radicals. Note that these properties apply only to *non-negative* values of a and b, and that $b \neq 0$ in the second property.

Objective:
Given an expression containing radicals, be able to write it in as simple a form as possible without actually evaluating it.

The first three examples show you exactly what is meant by simple form.

EXAMPLE 1

Simplify $\sqrt{288}$. Check by calculator.

Solution:
288 is not a perfect square, but it has factors that *are* perfect squares. To find these factors you can use the "upside down short division" process you have learned before.

$$
\left.\begin{array}{r} \text{Divide by} \\ \text{perfect} \\ \text{squares} \end{array}\right\}
\begin{array}{r} 4\,\underline{|\,288} \\ 4\,\underline{|\,72} \\ 9\,\underline{|\,18} \\ 2 \end{array}
\left.\begin{array}{l} \text{Stop when the quotient} \\ \text{has no more square} \\ \text{factors.} \end{array}\right.
$$

So you can write

$$
\begin{aligned}
\sqrt{288} &= \sqrt{4 \cdot 4 \cdot 9 \cdot 2} \\
&= \sqrt{4 \cdot 4 \cdot 9} \; \sqrt{2} \quad \text{Root of a product} \\
&= 2 \cdot 2 \cdot 3 \cdot \sqrt{2} \quad \text{Root of a product} \\
&= \underline{12\sqrt{2}}
\end{aligned}
$$

Check: $\sqrt{288} = 16.9705 \ldots$

$\qquad\; 12\sqrt{2} = 16.9705 \ldots$ ∎

The expression $12\sqrt{2}$ in Example 1 is considered to be simpler than $\sqrt{288}$ because the *radicand* is *smaller*.

EXAMPLE 2

Simplify $\dfrac{1}{\sqrt[3]{2}}$. Check by calculator.

Solution:
At first glance this expression seems to be as simple as possible. However, there is a radical in the *denominator*. Radical denominators sometimes cause difficulty in operations such as adding fractions. By multiplying this expression by a clever form of 1 you can *rationalize* the denominator.

$$\frac{1}{\sqrt[3]{2}} = \frac{1}{\sqrt[3]{2}} \cdot \frac{\sqrt[3]{4}}{\sqrt[3]{4}}$$ Multiply by something that makes the denominator radicand a perfect cube.

$$= \frac{\sqrt[3]{4}}{\sqrt[3]{8}}$$ Multiplication property of fractions, and $\sqrt[n]{a}\ \sqrt[n]{b} = \sqrt[n]{ab}$

$$= \frac{\sqrt[3]{4}}{2}$$

Check: $\dfrac{1}{\sqrt[3]{2}} = 0.79370\ldots$

$\dfrac{\sqrt[3]{4}}{2} = 0.79370\ldots$ ✔

Note that although the radicand in the answer to Example 2 is larger (4 instead of 2), the expression is considered to be "simpler" because *there are no radicals in the denominator*.

EXAMPLE 3

Simplify $\sqrt[8]{64}$. Check by calculator.

Solution:
This radical seems to be as simple as possible. 64 is equal to 2^6, and thus has no factors that are perfect 8th powers. However, if you write the radical in *exponential* form, a simplification shows up.

$$\sqrt[8]{64} = 64^{\frac{1}{8}}$$ Definition of fractional exponents

$$= (2^6)^{\frac{1}{8}}$$ $64 = 2^6$

$$= 2^{\frac{6}{8}}$$ Power of a power

$$= 2^{\frac{3}{4}}$$

$$= \sqrt[4]{2^3}$$ Definition of fractional exponents

$$= \sqrt[4]{8}$$

Check: $\sqrt[8]{64} = 1.6817\ldots$

$\sqrt[4]{8} = 1.6817\ldots$ ✔

The answer to Example 3 is simpler than $\sqrt[8]{64}$ for two reasons. First, the radicand is smaller and second, *the root index is as small as possible.*

From these three examples, the definition of "simple radical form" can be extracted.

DEFINITION

> **SIMPLE RADICAL FORM**
> An expression is in **simple radical form** if
>
> 1. the radicand of an nth root contains no n^{th} powers as factors,
> 2. the root index is as low as possible, and
> 3. there are no radicals in the denominator.

Note that the third requirement, "rationalizing the denominator", also makes finding decimal approximations easier if you have no calculator, as you will see if you work Problem 55 in the following exercise. Historically, this is the most important reason for rationalizing denominators. Sometimes a problem is simpler if you rationalize the *numerator,* as you will see if you work Problem 56, below.

The third requirement, rationalizing the denominator, is tricky if the denominator contains two or more terms. For example, if the denominator were $5 + \sqrt{3}$, and you multiplied it by another $5 + \sqrt{3}$, you would get $25 + 2\sqrt{3} + 3$. (The denominator would still contain $\sqrt{3}$). A clever way around this difficulty is shown in Example 4.

EXAMPLE 4

Simplify $\dfrac{2}{5 + \sqrt{3}}$. Check by calculator.

Solution:

$$\frac{2}{5 + \sqrt{3}} = \frac{2}{5 + \sqrt{3}} \cdot \frac{5 - \sqrt{3}}{5 - \sqrt{3}}$$ Multiplicative identity. $5 - \sqrt{3}$ is the *conjugate* of $5 + \sqrt{3}$.

$$= \frac{2(5 - \sqrt{3})}{5^2 - (\sqrt{3})^2}$$ Multiply the conjugate binomials.

$$= \frac{2(5 - \sqrt{3})}{25 - 3}$$ Arithmetic

$$= \frac{2(5 - \sqrt{3})}{22}$$ More arithmetic

$$= \frac{5 - \sqrt{3}}{11} \qquad \text{Canceling}$$

Check: $\dfrac{2}{5 + \sqrt{3}} = 0.29708 \ldots$ $\dfrac{5 - \sqrt{3}}{11} = 0.29708 \ldots$

The procedure is to multiply by the *conjugate* of the denominator.   ■

The exercise which follows is designed to give you practice in transforming irrational algebraic expressions to simple radical form. Some challenging problems come at the end.

EXERCISE 8-3

Do These Quickly

The following problems are intended to refresh your skills. You should be able to do all 10 in less than 5 minutes.

Q1.   Why does $\sqrt{x} = -4$ have no real solutions?

Q2.   Evalute $\sqrt{121}$.

Q3.   For what values of x is $\sqrt{3 - x}$ a real number?

Q4.   What is 30% of 82?

Q5.   Sketch the graph of a function that has a vertical asymptote where $x = 3$.

Q6.   Sketch the graph of an increasing exponential function.

Q7.   Sketch the graph of $y = x^2$.

Q8.   Sketch the graph of $x = y^2$. Be clever!

Q9.   Subtract the complex numbers: $(5 - 4i) - (3 + 2i)$

Q10. Add and simplify: $\dfrac{13}{3} + \dfrac{23}{3}$

For Problems 1 through 38, transform the given expression to simple radical form. You can check your answer by evaluating it and the original expression by calculator.

1. $\sqrt{12} + 2\sqrt{48} + 5\sqrt{147} - 4\sqrt{3}$

2. $3\sqrt{125} - 2\sqrt{80} + \sqrt{405}$

3. $\sqrt[3]{2187} - 2\sqrt[3]{24}$ 4. $\sqrt[3]{108} + 10\sqrt[3]{32} + \sqrt[3]{500}$

5. $\dfrac{3}{2\sqrt{2}} + \dfrac{5\sqrt{2}}{4}$

6. $\dfrac{7}{5\sqrt{3}} - \dfrac{8\sqrt{3}}{15}$

7. $\dfrac{12}{\sqrt{6}} + \sqrt{6}$

8. $4\sqrt{5} - \dfrac{15}{\sqrt{5}}$

9. $7\sqrt{3} - \dfrac{12}{\sqrt{3}} + \sqrt{75}$

10. $4\sqrt{5} + \dfrac{35}{\sqrt{5}} - \sqrt{125}$

11. $(\sqrt{7} + \sqrt{2})^2$

12. $(\sqrt{5} - \sqrt{3})^2$

13. $(2\sqrt{5} - 3)^2$

14. $(4 + 3\sqrt{6})^2$

15. $(\sqrt{5} - \sqrt{3})(\sqrt{5} + \sqrt{3})$

16. $(\sqrt{7} - 2)(\sqrt{7} + 2)$

17. $(2\sqrt{3} - \sqrt{2})(2\sqrt{3} + \sqrt{2})$

18. $(3\sqrt{5} + \sqrt{7})(3\sqrt{5} - \sqrt{7})$

19. $(6\sqrt{7} + \sqrt{15})(\sqrt{7} - \sqrt{3})$

20. $(\sqrt{12} - \sqrt{6})(\sqrt{3} + \sqrt{27})$

21. $\dfrac{2}{\sqrt[3]{9}}$

22. $\dfrac{4}{\sqrt[3]{25}}$

23. $\dfrac{4}{\sqrt[4]{32}}$

24. $\dfrac{7}{\sqrt[5]{128}}$

25. $\dfrac{5}{\sqrt[6]{1024}}$

26. $\dfrac{9}{\sqrt[4]{25}}$

27. $\dfrac{7}{\sqrt[4]{49}}$

28. $\dfrac{12}{\sqrt[6]{512}}$

29. $\dfrac{1}{\sqrt{5} - 1}$

30. $\dfrac{4}{3 - 2\sqrt{2}}$

31. $\dfrac{4}{\sqrt{7} + \sqrt{3}}$

32. $\dfrac{57}{5\sqrt{3} - 3\sqrt{2}}$

33. $\dfrac{\sqrt{3} - 1}{\sqrt{2} - 1}$

34. $\dfrac{3\sqrt{3} - 1}{3\sqrt{2} - 1}$

35. $\dfrac{7\sqrt{2} + 3}{7\sqrt{2} - 3}$

36. $\dfrac{4\sqrt{7} + 3\sqrt{2}}{5\sqrt{2} + 2\sqrt{7}}$

37. $\dfrac{1 + \dfrac{1}{\sqrt{3}}}{1 - \dfrac{1}{\sqrt{3}}}$

38. $\dfrac{1 - \dfrac{1}{\sqrt{5}}}{1 + \dfrac{1}{\sqrt{5}}}$

For Problems 39 through 42, the denominator is a *tri*nomial. Associating *two* of the three terms gives a *bi*nomial, which can be simplified by multiplying by the conjugate. For example,

$$\frac{1}{2 + \sqrt{5} - \sqrt{3}} = \frac{1}{(2 + \sqrt{5}) - \sqrt{3}}$$

Associating, and multiplying by 1
$$\cdot \frac{(2 + \sqrt{5}) + \sqrt{3}}{(2 + \sqrt{5}) + \sqrt{3}}$$

$$= \frac{2 + \sqrt{5} + \sqrt{3}}{(2 + \sqrt{5})^2 - 3}$$

Carrying out the multiplication

$$= \frac{2 + \sqrt{5} + \sqrt{3}}{6 + 4\sqrt{5}}$$

Simplify the denominator.

This expression can be simplified as before. Simplify the following:

39. $\dfrac{12}{2 + \sqrt{3} - \sqrt{7}}$

40. $\dfrac{\sqrt{3} + \sqrt{2}}{\sqrt{3} + \sqrt{2} - 1}$

41. $\dfrac{1}{\sqrt{3} + \sqrt{2} - \sqrt{5}}$

42. $\dfrac{1}{\sqrt{5} + \sqrt{3} + 2\sqrt{2}}$

For Problems 43 through 46, the denominator looks like one factor of a sum or difference of two cubes. You recall, for example, that

$$a^3 + b^3 = (a + b)(a^2 - ab + b^2).$$

Using fractional exponents, you can write $a + b$ as

$$a + b = (a^{\frac{1}{3}} + b^{\frac{1}{3}})(a^{\frac{2}{3}} - a^{\frac{1}{3}} b^{\frac{1}{3}} + b^{\frac{2}{3}}).$$

Use this fact to find a clever form of 1 by which to multiply each of the following expressions, and thus rationalize the denominator.

43. $\dfrac{1}{\sqrt[3]{2} - \sqrt[3]{3}}$

44. $\dfrac{1}{\sqrt[3]{4} + \sqrt[3]{5}}$

45. $\dfrac{1}{\sqrt[3]{4} + \sqrt[3]{10} + \sqrt[3]{25}}$

46. $\dfrac{1}{\sqrt[3]{16} - \sqrt[3]{4} + 1}$

For Problems 47 through 54, the expression has the form $\sqrt{a \pm \sqrt{b}}$. Expressions like this can be transformed to $\sqrt{x} \pm \sqrt{y}$. For example, letting

$$\sqrt{10 + 2\sqrt{21}} = \sqrt{x} + \sqrt{y},$$

and squaring each member gives

$$10 + 2\sqrt{21} = x + 2\sqrt{xy} + y.$$

Setting $x + y = 10$ and $2\sqrt{xy} = 2\sqrt{21}$ (from which $xy = 21$), you get a *system* of two equations with two variables. From the first equation, $y = 10 - x$. Substituting this into the second gives

$$x(10 - x) = 21.$$

Distributing the x and getting 0 on the right side gives

$$x^2 - 10x + 21 = 0.$$

Factoring gives $(x - 3)(x - 7) = 0$, from which $x = 3$ or 7. Substituting these gives $y = 7$ or 3, so that

$$\sqrt{10 + 2\sqrt{21}} = \underline{\underline{\sqrt{3} + \sqrt{7}}}.$$

Use this technique to express the following as $\sqrt{x} \pm \sqrt{y}$:

47. $\sqrt{4 + 2\sqrt{3}}$ 48. $\sqrt{7 + 2\sqrt{6}}$

49. $\sqrt{12 - 6\sqrt{3}}$ 50. $\sqrt{17 - 12\sqrt{2}}$

51. $\sqrt{11 + 6\sqrt{2}}$ 52. $\sqrt{12 + 2\sqrt{35}}$

53. $\sqrt{32 - 8\sqrt{15}}$ 54. $\sqrt{101 - 28\sqrt{13}}$

55. a. Find a decimal approximation for $\frac{3}{\sqrt{2}}$ by using $\sqrt{2} \approx 1.414$ and carrying out the long division.
    b. Rationalize the denominator of $\frac{3}{\sqrt{2}}$. Then use $\sqrt{2} \approx 1.414$ to get a decimal approximation.
    c. Why do you suppose that rationalizing the denominator was so important in the days before calculators?

56. a. Solve $x^2 - 1,000,000x + 1 = 0$ using the quadratic formula.
    b. Show that $\sqrt{b^2 - 4ac}$ is so close to b that the numerator of one solution rounds off to 0.
    c. Rationalize the *numerator* of the solution in part b, and thus get a non-zero decimal approximation of the solution.

57. ***Existence of Irrational Numbers Problem***   As you recall from Chapter 1, an irrational number is a real number that cannot be written as a ratio of two integers. That such a number could exist was incomprehensible to even as great mathematicians as the Pythagorans. But you are now equipped to prove rather easily that numbers such as $\sqrt{2}$ are, indeed, irrational. It is easy to show that a particular rational number such as 1.414 is not exactly equal to $\sqrt{2}$ by squaring it. You get

$$(1.414)^2 = 1.999396,$$

which is close to 2, but not equal. A more instructive way to do the proof is as follows:

$$1.414 = \frac{1414}{1000} \qquad \text{Write 1.414 as a ratio of two integers.}$$

$$1.414 = \frac{707}{500}$$ Cancel all common factors.

$$1.414 = \frac{7 \times 101}{2^2 \times 5^3}$$ Factor numerator and denominator into primes. There are no common factors in the numerator and denominator.

$$1.414^2 = \left(\frac{7 \times 101}{2^2 \times 5^3}\right)^2$$ Square each member of the equation.

$$1.414^2 = \frac{7^2 \times 101^2}{2^4 \times 5^6}$$ Distribute the exponentiation. There are *still* no common factors in the numerator and denominator.

Since no canceling can be done on the right, the fraction could not possibly be an integer. So it could not equal 2. No matter *what* rational number you start with as an approximation for $\sqrt{2}$, if it is not an integer before you square it, it will not be an integer afterward, either. Squaring a fraction introduces no new factors that could cancel. The square root of a perfect square such as 64 is, of course, an integer. But the square root of any integer that comes out *between* two integers is an *irrational* number.

CONCLUSION

> **IRRATIONAL RADICALS**
> If x is a positive integer, then $\sqrt[n]{x}$ is either:
>
> a. an integer, or
> b. an irrational number if it is between two integers.

Do the following.
a. Show that each decimal approximation is close to the given radical by squaring or cubing it. Then write the decimal approximation as a ratio of two integers, as earlier in this problem, factor the numerator and denominator, and conclude that the rational number could not be equal to the radical.
    i. $\sqrt{5} \approx 2.236$ ii. $\sqrt{22} \approx 4.690$
    iii. $\sqrt[3]{84} \approx 4.380$ iv. $\sqrt[3]{4} \approx 1.587$
b. Show that the radical is a rational number because it is an integer, or is an irrational number because it is between two integers.
    i. $\sqrt[3]{100}$ ii. $\sqrt[5]{53}$ iii. $\sqrt{3}$
    iv. $\sqrt[4]{625}$ v. $\sqrt[3]{1332}$

8-4 | RADICAL EQUATIONS

As the name suggests, a radical equation is an equation with a radical in it. For example,

$$3 = x + \sqrt{x - 1}$$

is a radical equation. However, there are equations such as $x + \sqrt{2} = 13$ that have radicals but are *not* radical equations. Radical equations have a *variable* under a radical sign.

DEFINITION

RADICAL EQUATION
A **radical equation** is an equation in which a variable appears under a radical sign.

Objective:
Given a radical equation, be able to find its solution set, discarding any extraneous solutions.

Radical equations can arise in the study of functions when you must find x for a given value of y. For example, if $y = x + \sqrt{x - 1}$, then solutions of the radical equation on the preceding page would be values of x for which $y = 3$.

However, radical equations arise in other places too, as you will see in Chapter 9. So it is worth spending time studying them as a background for future work as well as a technique for finding x when you know y.

EXAMPLE 1

Solve $3 = x + \sqrt{x - 1}$.

Solution:
As with any new problem, the technique is to transform it into an old problem which you already know how to work. In this case, the technique is to transform the equation into a polynomial equation by squaring each member. A preliminary step is necessary in order to *isolate* the radical on one side of the equation.

$$3 - x = \sqrt{x - 1}$$

$$9 - 6x + x^2 = x - 1 \quad \text{Square each member.}$$

$$x^2 - 7x + 10 = 0$$

$$(x - 2)(x - 5) = 0$$

$$x = 2 \text{ or } x = 5$$

Substituting these values for x in the original equation gives you a surprise!

$$\begin{array}{ll} x = 2: & x = 5: \\ 3 = 2 + \sqrt{2 - 1} & 3 = 5 + \sqrt{5 - 1} \\ 3 = 2 + 1 & 3 = 5 + 2 \\ 3 = 3 & 3 \neq 7 \end{array}$$

So 2 is a solution, but 5 is not! The reason is because squaring each member is an *irreversible* step which leads to an extraneous solution sometimes. The extraneous solution occurred this time because there are two distinct equations,

$$3 - x = \sqrt{x - 1} \text{ and } 3 - x = -\sqrt{x - 1},$$

for which squaring produces the same polynomial equation,

$$9 - 6x + x^2 = x - 1.$$

The 2 is the solution of the equation on the left and the 5 is the solution of the equation on the right. So whenever you square each member of an equation, you must check the solutions and discard any which are extraneous. In this case you would mark 5 as extraneous, and write

$$\text{extraneous}$$

$$x = 2 \text{ or } x = 5$$

$$S = \{2\}. \qquad \blacksquare$$

In Problem 51 in the following exercise you will see by graph some reasons you get extraneous solutions.

EXAMPLE 2

Solve $\sqrt{x^2 + 5x - 6} + \sqrt{x^2 + 3x - 3} = 1$.

In this case the equation contains *two* radicals. So you isolate *one* of them, getting

$$\sqrt{x^2 + 5x - 6} = 1 - \sqrt{x^2 + 3x - 3}.$$

Squaring each member produces

$$x^2 + 5x - 6 = 1 - 2\sqrt{x^2 + 3x - 3} + x^2 + 3x - 3$$

which can be transformed to

$$2x - 4 = -2\sqrt{x^2 + 3x - 3}$$
$$2 - x = \sqrt{x^2 + 3x - 3}$$

with the radical isolated on the right side. Squaring again gives

$$4 - 4x + x^2 = x^2 + 3x - 3$$
$$7 = 7x$$
$$1 = x.$$

Checking by substitution into the original equation shows that 1 is a valid solution.

$$x = 1:$$
$$\sqrt{1^2 + 5 - 6} + \sqrt{1^2 + 3 - 3} = 1$$
$$\sqrt{0} + \sqrt{1} = 1$$
$$0 + 1 = 1$$
$$1 = 1.$$

Therefore,

$$S = \{1\}.$$

The steps in transforming and solving radical equations are summarized in the following flow chart.

The exercise which follows is designed to give you practice solving radical equations.

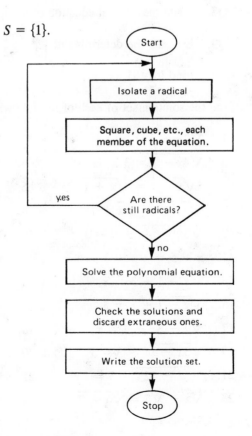

EXERCISE 8-4

Do These Quickly

The following problems are intended to refresh your skills. You should be able to do all 10 in less than 5 minutes.

Q1. Evaluate: $\sqrt[3]{64}$

Q2. Solve: $\sqrt{x} = 9$

Q3. Write in terms of i: $\sqrt{-25}$

Q4. Evaluate: $|-49|$

Q5. Sketch the graph: $y = 2x$

Q6. How many feet in a mile?

Q7. If each seed in a package of 1000 seeds has an 80% probability of germinating, what number of plants would you expect if the whole package is planted?

Q8. Write the general equation of an inverse square variation function.

Q9. Evaluate the determinant: $\begin{vmatrix} 7 & 1 \\ 3 & -2 \end{vmatrix}$

Q10. Find $\log_3 81$.

Find the solution set of each of the following equations:

1. $\sqrt{2x + 3} = 5$

2. $\sqrt{3x - 5} = 4$

3. $\sqrt[3]{4x - 1} = 3$

4. $\sqrt[3]{x - 2} = 2$

5. $5\sqrt{x - 1} = \sqrt{x + 1}$

6. $\sqrt{x + 14} - \sqrt{3x - 10} = 0$

7. $\sqrt{x - 7} = \sqrt{x} - 7$

8. $\sqrt{x + 5} - 1 = \sqrt{x}$

9. $\sqrt{3x^2 - 4x + 9} = 3$

10. $\sqrt{x^2 - 9} = 4$

11. $x + 5 = \sqrt{x + 5} + 6$

12. $x - 2 = \sqrt{x - 2} + 12$

13. $\sqrt{x - 1} + 3 = x$

14. $\sqrt{-3x - 14} - x = 4$

15. $\sqrt{x - 1} + x = 3$

16. $\sqrt{x + 6} - x = 4$

17. $\sqrt{7 - 3x} + 3 = x$

18. $x - \sqrt{6 - x} = 4$

19. $\sqrt{3x - 11} + 3 = x$

20. $\sqrt{3x + 10} - 4 = x$

21. $\sqrt{22 - 12x} + 5 = 2x$

22. $\sqrt{7 - 6x} + 3x = 2$

23. $\sqrt{x} - \sqrt{7} = \sqrt{x + 7}$

24. $\sqrt{x} + \sqrt{7} = \sqrt{x + 7}$

25. $\sqrt{x + 3} + \sqrt{x - 3} = 3$ 26. $\sqrt{x + 4} + \sqrt{x - 4} = 4$

27. $\sqrt{2x + 5} + 2\sqrt{x + 6} = 5$

28. $\sqrt{2x + 25} - 2\sqrt{x + 4} = 1$

29. $x^2 = 21 - \sqrt{x^2 - 9}$ 30. $x^2 = 3 - \sqrt{2x^2 - 3}$

31. $\sqrt{x^2 + 3x + 6} - \sqrt{x^2 + 3x - 1} = 1$

32. $\sqrt{x^2 - 4x - 12} - \sqrt{x^2 - 4x - 5} = 1$

33. $\sqrt{x} + \sqrt{x - 7} = \dfrac{21}{\sqrt{x - 7}}$

34. $2\sqrt{x} - \sqrt{4x - 3} = \dfrac{1}{\sqrt{4x - 3}}$

35. $\dfrac{1}{1 - x} + \dfrac{1}{1 + \sqrt{x}} = \dfrac{1}{1 - \sqrt{x}}$

36. $\dfrac{2}{\sqrt{x} + 2} - \dfrac{\sqrt{x}}{2 - \sqrt{x}} = \dfrac{x + 4}{x - 4}$

37. $\dfrac{\sqrt{x}}{\sqrt{x} - 1} + 3 = \dfrac{1}{\sqrt{x} - 1} - 1$

38. $\dfrac{1}{1 - \sqrt{x}} = 1 - \dfrac{\sqrt{x}}{\sqrt{x} - 1}$

39. $\sqrt[3]{2x^2 - 11x + 14} = 2 - x$ (Remember the Factor Theorem!)

40. $1 - x = \sqrt[3]{(x - 1)(x - 13)}$ (Remember the Factor Theorem!)

41. $x^2 + \sqrt{x^2 - 5x + 1} = 5x + 1$

42. $x^2 + \sqrt{x^2 + 3x + 5} = 7 - 3x$

For Problems 43 through 48 the transformed equation is a quadratic that does *not* factor. Use the Quadratic Formula to solve the transformed equation. You can check for extraneous solutions by finding the decimal approximations for the radicals using a calculator. You can also check the answers *exactly* by simplifying radicals such as $\sqrt{2 + \sqrt{3}}$ using the technique of Problems 47 through 54 in Exercise 8-2.

43. $x = 3 + \sqrt{20 - 4x}$ 44. $x - \sqrt{15 - 4x} = 4$

45. $2\sqrt{2x + 1} = \sqrt{4x + 9}$ 46. $\sqrt{6x - 1} = \sqrt{4x + 5}$

47. $\sqrt{2x} - \sqrt{x - 3} = \dfrac{2}{\sqrt{x - 3}}$

48. $\sqrt{-2x} - \sqrt{5 - x} = \dfrac{-3}{\sqrt{5 - x}}$

49. **Continued Radicals**   Under certain conditions, radicals such as

$$\sqrt{2 + \sqrt{2 + \sqrt{2 + \sqrt{2 + \ldots}}}}$$

that continue forever, can represent *rational* numbers. To find out what number such a radical represents, you can let it equal x and solve the resulting equation.

The key to the solution is realizing that x also appears *under the radical sign*.

$$x = \sqrt{2 + \underbrace{\left(\sqrt{2 + \sqrt{2 + \sqrt{2 + \ldots}}}\right)}_{}} \quad \leftarrow \text{This also equals } x.$$

So the equation is equivalent to $x = \sqrt{2 + x}$. Evaluate the following radicals by solving the appropriate radical equation.

a. $\sqrt{2 + \sqrt{2 + \sqrt{2 + \sqrt{2 + \ldots}}}}$

b. $\sqrt{6 + \sqrt{6 + \sqrt{6 + \sqrt{6 + \ldots}}}}$

c. $\sqrt{20 - \sqrt{20 - \sqrt{20 - \sqrt{20 - \ldots}}}}$

d. $\sqrt{42 - \sqrt{42 - \sqrt{42 - \sqrt{42 - \ldots}}}}$

e.   For what values of n does $\sqrt{n + \sqrt{n + \sqrt{n + \sqrt{n + \ldots}}}}$ stand for an *integer*?

50. **Computer Program for Continued Radicals**   Write a computer program to evaluate radicals of the form in Problem 49, above. The program should begin with inputting the constant that appears under the radical sign. Then the computer should calculate and print successive approximations such as

$$\sqrt{2}$$
$$\sqrt{2 + \sqrt{2}}$$

$$\sqrt{2 + \sqrt{2 + \sqrt{2}}},$$

and so forth. Use your program to evaluate the radicals in Problem 49 parts a, b, c, and d. When you are sure it is working correctly, use it to test the correctness of your conclusion in Problem 49, part e.

51. ***Extraneous Solutions and Computer Graphics Problem***   Figure 8-4a shows graphs of the two functions

$$f(x) = x + 3\sqrt{x + 4} \qquad \text{and}$$

$$g(x) = x - 3\sqrt{x + 4}$$

as plotted by the program PLOT TWO from the accompanying disk. (You may run the program yourself, if you wish.) Horizontal lines are drawn at $y = 4$, -5, and -8. The line at $y = 4$, for instance, crosses the f-graph at about -1, and the g-graph at about 18. By answering the following questions you will see how these graphs relate to valid and extraneous solutions.

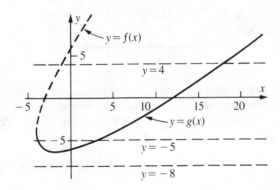

Figure 8-4a

a. Set $f(x) = 4$, thus getting a radical equation. Isolate the radical, square each member, and solve the equation. From the graph, tell which solution is valid and which is extraneous.

b. How does the extraneous solution in part (a) seem to relate to the graph of function g?

c. Set $g(x) = 4$, thus getting a different radical equation. Isolate the radical and square each member. What remarkable result do you notice? What is the valid solution of this radical equation, and what is the extraneous solution?

d. Get two radical equations by setting $f(x) = -5$ and $g(x) = -5$. Show that when the radicals are eliminated by squaring, both produce the same quadratic equation.

e. Solve the quadratic equation in part (d). Both solutions are valid for the equation from one function, and both are extraneous for the equation from the other function. Which is which?

f. Get two more radical equations by setting $f(x) = -8$ and $g(x) = -8$. Square to eliminate the radicals, and show that both produce the same quadratic equation.

g. Show that the quadratic equation in part (f) has no real solutions. How is this fact confirmed by the graph in Figure 8-4a?

52. *Extraneous Solutions Problem Number 2*

a. Transform the equation $3 = 8 + \sqrt{x - 7}$ by isolating the radical, then squaring each member.

b. Solve the transformed equation in part (a). Show that the value you get is extraneous.

c. What *other* equation could you square each member of and get the *same* equation you did in part (a)?

d. Show that the answer you got in part (b) is a solution of the equation in part (c).

e. Explain why *reversing* the process of squaring each member of an equation does not necessarily lead to the original equation.

8-5 VARIATION FUNCTIONS WITH NON-INTEGER EXPONENTS

In Chapter 7 you studied problems in which one variable was proportional to an integer power of another variable. In this section you will study variation problems in which the exponent is a *constant*, but *not* necessarily an integer.

Objective:
Given a real-world situation in which one variable is proportional to a non-integer power of another variable, determine the proportionality constant, and use the resulting variation function as a mathematical model.

As an example, the area of an egg's shell is directly proportional to the $\frac{2}{3}$ power of the mass of the egg. Suppose that a normal 60 gram chicken egg has a shell area of 28 square centimeters.

Let S = number of square centimeters.
Let M = number of grams.

So the general equation is

$$S = k M^{\frac{2}{3}}.$$

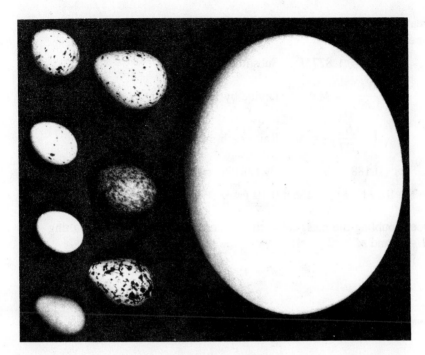

To find the particular equation, you must calculate k by substituting the known ordered pair, $(M, S) = (60, 28)$.

$$28 = k\,(60^{\frac{2}{3}})$$

Dividing each member by $60^{\frac{2}{3}}$ gives

$$\frac{28}{60^{\frac{2}{3}}} = k.$$

$$1.8269\ldots = k$$

So the particular equation is

$$\underline{\underline{S = 1.8269\ldots M^{\frac{2}{3}}}}$$

The value of k should be stored in the calculator's memory for use in the rest of the problem.

The model is now ready to use. For example, to predict the surface area of a 1600 gram ostrich egg, you simply substitute 1600 for M and do the indicated operations.

$$S = 1.827\left(1600^{\frac{2}{3}}\right)$$

$$S = 249.92\ldots$$

So the ostrich egg has about $\underline{\underline{250}}$ square centimeters of shell.

The model can also be used "backwards" to predict the mass of an egg when you know the surface area. Suppose that a lizard's egg has a surface area of 0.6 square centimeters. To find the mass, you would substitute 0.6 for S and solve for M.

$$0.6 = 1.827 M^{\frac{2}{3}} \quad \text{Substitution}$$

$$\frac{0.6}{1.827} = M^{\frac{2}{3}} \quad \text{Divide by 1.827.}$$

$$\left(\frac{0.6}{1.827}\right)^{\frac{3}{2}} = M \quad \text{Raise each member to the } \tfrac{3}{2} \text{ power.}$$

$$0.188 \ldots = M \quad \text{By calculator}$$

So the lizard's egg is about 0.19 grams.

Does doubling the mass cause the surface area to double? Substituting $M = 1$ and $M = 2$ gives:

$$M = 1:$$
$$S = 1.8269 \ldots \left(1^{\frac{2}{3}}\right)$$
$$S \approx 1.83$$
$$M = 2:$$
$$S = 1.8269 \ldots \left(2^{\frac{2}{3}}\right)$$
$$S \approx 2.90$$

Since twice 1.83 is 3.66 and S is only 2.90, doubling the mass does *not* double the area. This fact can be anticipated because M is raised to a power *less* than 1. If S equaled kM^1, then doubling M would double S.

In the exercise which follows, you are to use variation functions with appropriate integer or non-integer exponents as mathematical models for the given situations.

EXERCISE 8-5

Do These Quickly

The following problems are intended to refresh your skills. You should be able to do all 10 in less than 5 minutes.

Q1. What kind of function has a graph like Figure 8-5a?

Q2. If $f(x) = 2x + 5$, then $f^{-1}(x)$ equals what?

Q3. Sketch the graph of a system of two linear equations with two variables.

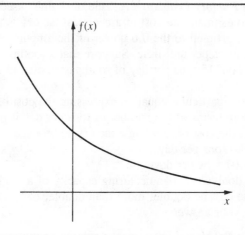

Figure 8-5a

Q4. Evaluate: $12 - 2 \times 5$

Q5. A 27° angle is ____% of a right angle. What number goes in the blank?

Q6. For whom was the Cartesian coordinate system named?

Q7. How many seconds in an hour?

Q8. Solve for x: $2 - 3x > -10$

Q9. Sketch a parabola with vertex $(1, 3)$, and y-intercept 7.

Q10. Divide 50 by $\frac{1}{2}$ and add 3.

Work the following problems.

1. *Ship Power Problem*   When a ship is travelling at high speed through the water, most of the power generated by the engines goes into formation of the wake (the waves that trail out behind the ship). At these speeds the speed of the ship is proportional to the seventh root of the power being generated by the engines. Suppose that you are on a ship going 30 knots (30 nautical miles per hour) and the engines are generating 45,000 horsepower.
    a. Write the particular equation expressing speed in terms of power.
    b. The engines are capable of producing 90,000 horsepower. How fast would you expect the ship to go if the Captain gives the order, "Full speed ahead!"?
    c. Does doubling the power cause the speed to double?
    d. Why do you suppose that ships do not go much faster than 30 knots?

2. **Toothpaste Factory Problem**   A "rule of thumb" used by chemical engineers to estimate the cost of a chemical factory is that the cost is directly proportional to the 0.6 power of the amount of chemical the factory produces per unit time. Suppose that a toothpaste factory which turns out 15 tons per day of toothpaste costs 43 million dollars to build.
    a. Write the particular equation expressing the cost of a toothpaste factory in terms of the number of tons per day it produces.
    b. Predict the cost of building a factory to produce
        i.   500 tons per day,
        ii. 0.07 tons per day.
    c. If you double the manufacturing capacity of a toothpaste factory will the cost be double, more than double, or less than double? Justify your answer.

3. **River Basin Problem**   From measurements on many rivers, geographers find that the length of a river that drains a particular "basin" of land is approximately proportional to the 0.6 power of the area of the basin. The Rio Grande is 3034 kilometers long, and drains a basin of about 500,000 square kilometers (see sketch).

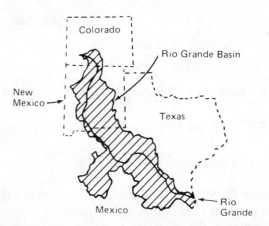

    a. Write the particular equation expressing river length in terms of basin area.
    b. The Suwannee River (made famous by Stephen Foster) flows from the Okefenokee Swamp (made famous by Pogo) to the Gulf of Mexico. It drains an area of about 15,000 square kilometers. According to your model, how long is the Suwannee River? (Check an atlas or encyclopedia to find out how close your prediction is!)
    c. The longest river in the world is the 6700 kilometer Nile. Approximately what area of land does the Nile drain?

4. **Home Range Problem**   According to information on Page 200 of J. M. Emlen's *Ecology: An Evolutionary Approach,* the number of

acres to which an animal confines its movements is directly proportional to the 1.41 power of its body mass.

a.   Find the particular equation for this function if an 80 kilogram deer confines itself to a range of 2000 acres.

b.   Predict the home range of
   i.   a 6000 kilogram African elephant,
   ii.   a 0.002 kilogram shrew.

c.   Suppose that you find evidence of a Tasmanian devil spread over a range of 300 acres. What would you predict the mass of a Tasmanian devil to be?

5.   *Tree Trunk Problem*   Thomas A. McMahon reports in the July, 1975, issue of *Scientific American* that the base diameter of a tree's trunk (cm) varies directly with the $\frac{3}{2}$ power of its height (m).

a. Suppose that you find a young sequoia tree 5 meters tall that has a base diameter of 14.5 centimeters. Write the particular equation expressing the base diameter of a sequoia in terms of its height.

b. What would you expect this tree's diameter to be when it has grown to a height of 50 meters? Does making the height 10 times as big make the diameter *more* than 10 times as big or *less* than 10 times as big?

c. It is difficult to measure the height of a tall tree, especially when it is in a dense forest. But it is relatively easy to measure its base diameter. The largest known sequoia, the General Sherman in California, has a base diameter of 985 centimeters (about the size of a small house). Approximately how tall is the General Sherman?

6. *Tire Pump Problem*   If you compress a gas quickly, such as by pushing down the handle of the tire pump on the sketch, the heat generated by compression does not have time to escape, and the gas warms up. In this case, the pressure varies inversely with the 1.4 power of the volume. (In problem 7 of Section 7-11, Boyle's Law said that the pressure varied inversely with the *first* power of the volume, but that was because the temperature remained *constant*.)

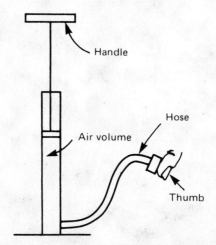

a. Suppose that when the pump handle is fully extended, the volume is 40 cubic inches, and the pressure is 15 pounds per square inch (psi), the normal atmospheric pressure. Write the particular equation expressing pressure in terms of volume.

b. You hold your thumb over the end of the hose, then push down on the handle, reducing the volume to 20 cubic inches. Predict the pressure.

c. Suppose that you connect the hose to a tire containing air at 50 psi. When you push down the handle, the pressure in the pump will increase until it just equals the pressure in the tire. What will the volume of air in the pump be when its pressure just reaches 50 psi?

d. Draw the graph of pressure versus volume in the domain $0 < \text{volume} \leq 40$ cubic inches with the pump connected to the tire. Take into account the fact that when the pressure reaches 50 psi, the air flows into the tire rather than being compressed to a higher pressure.

7. *Pendulum Problem*   The period of a pendulum (the length of time it takes to make one complete swing) varies directly with the square root of the length of the pendulum. By experiment, you find that a pendulum 0.3 meters long swings with a period of 0.55 seconds.

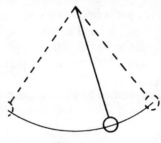

Pendulum

a. Write the particular equation expressing period in terms of length.

b. Grandfather clocks have pendulums that swing with a period of 1 second. How long is the pendulum?

c. Some hotels are constructed with rooms around the outside and empty space above the lobby in the middle. Suppose that a chandelier is suspended by a chain from the top story and hangs all the way down to the lobby. You observe the chandelier swinging with a period of 10 seconds. How tall is the hotel?

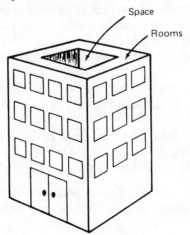

Space

Rooms

8. **Planetary Period Problem**   According to Keppler's Third Law, the period of a planet (the length of time it takes to make one revolution about the Sun) varies directly with the $\frac{3}{2}$ power of the planet's average distance from the Sun. The Earth is 150 million kilometers from the Sun, and has a period of 1 year.

    a. Write the particular equation expressing period in terms of distance.

    b. Predict the periods of the following planets:

Planet	Million km
Mercury	58
Mars	227.7
Pluto	5913

    (Check an encyclopedia or other source to see if you are correct.)

    c. The "Asteroid Belt," located about 400 million kilometers from the Sun, is thought to be the path of a planet that disintegrated many centuries ago. What would the period of that planet have been?

    d. Suppose that you wanted to build a space station orbiting the Sun every $\frac{1}{8}$ of a year. How close to the Sun would it have to be?

9. **Microwave Oven Problem**   The number of minutes it takes to cook bacon in a microwave oven depends on how many slices you put in at once. A popular brand of oven specifies 1.75 minutes for 2 slices, and 2.5 minutes for 4 slices.

    a. Explain why the number of minutes does *not* vary *directly* with the number of slices.

    b. Assume that the number of minutes varies directly with some *power* of the number of slices (not necessarily an integer power). Use the two given ordered pairs to derive the particular equation expressing the number of minutes in terms of the number of slices. (The system of equations you get after substituting the ordered pairs can be solved for the two unknown constants. You must be clever enough to figure out a way!)

    c. Where would you set the timer to cook 8 slices? 6 slices? 1 slice?

    d. The timer on this oven can be set for as much as 30 minutes. What is the maximum number of slices that could be cooked at once?

    e. What are the domain and range of this function?

    f. What things in the real world might make the domain even smaller than the domain you wrote in part e?

10. **Height-Mass Problem, Second Model**   The masses of similarly shaped people vary directly with the cube of their height (see Prob-

lem 26 of Exercise 7-11). However, tall people tend to be thinner in proportion to their height than short people. Assume that the masses of people of average build vary with some power of their height, close to 3 but not quite equal to 3. The following average heights and masses are published for boys and girls:

Height	Boys	Girls
150 cm	45 kg	41 kg
180 cm	74 kg	67 kg

a. Write the particular equation for boys expressing mass in terms of height. Since there are *two* unknown constants (the exponent and the proportionality constant), you must substitute *both* ordered pairs into the equation and solve the resulting system for the constants. You can make the equations *linear* by taking the logs of both members first.
b. Write another equation for girls, as in part a, above.
c. Predict Sally Forth's mass. She is 173 cm tall. Show that your answer is reasonable by showing that it is *between* 41 and 67 kg.
d. Use the equation for boys to predict Professor Snarff's mass. He is 193 cm tall.
e. Professor Snarff is actually 91 kilograms. A person's mass is considered to be "normal" if it is within 5% of that predicted by the model. Is the Professor normal, overweight, or underweight? Justify your answer.
f. Use the appropriate equation to predict *your* mass. Are you within 5% of the predicted mass???
g. What does your model predict for the mass of a newborn baby girl 50 centimeters long? Is this reasonable?

11. ***Water Hyacinth Data Analysis Problem***   The water hyacinth is a plant that grows while floating on the surface of the water in a lake or waterway. Although the purple flowers are attractive, the plants are a nuisance because they can completely cover the waterway and prevent boats from passing. Assume that the number of square feet covered by plants in a particular lake are as in the following chart:

Day Number	Square Feet
3	120
6	156
9	203
12	264

a. What kind of function is most reasonable for this data, linear, exponential, or variation? Justify your answer.
b. Use the ordered pairs for days 3 and 12 to get the particular equation.

c. Show that your equation gives, approximately, the right values for days 6 and 9.

d. The lake has an area of 10,000 square feet. If the plants keep growing according to the model, on what day will they first completely cover the lake?

12. ***Faucet Data Analysis Problem***   The rate at which water flows out of a faucet depends on how far open the faucet is. Assume that the following flow rates have been measured:

Percent Open	Gallons per Minute
5	4.86
10	5.99
15	6.76
20	7.37

a. Which kind of function, linear, exponential, or variation, best fits these data? Justify your answer.

b. Write the particular equation expressing flow rate in terms of percent open.

c. How many gallons per minute would you expect to flow from the faucet when it is wide open? Is this more or less than five times the flow rate at 20% open?

8-6 | ## FUNCTIONS OF MORE THAN ONE INDEPENDENT VARIABLE

In most real-world situations there are many variable quantities. So far you have considered only two at a time, one independent and one dependent variable, with the tacit assumption that the values of the others remain *constant*. If you consider more than two variables, there are several ways they can be interrelated. For example, if there are three variables, then

1. y and z might *both* depend on x,
2. z might depend on *both* x and y,
3. z might depend on y, and y might depend on x.

In this section you will study the second and third kinds, because functions of the first kind are really just *two* functions of the kind you have already studied.

Objective:
Given a real-world situation involving more than two variables, find general and particular equations relating the variables, and use these as mathematical models.

Functions with Several Independent Variables—If you studied linear programming in Section 4-11, you encountered linear functions that had two independent variables. For example, the profit made by an automobile manufacturer depends on both the number of large cars and on the number of small cars that are sold.

Another type of function with more than one independent variable is called a *combined variation function*. For example, the statement, "w varies directly with the square of x, and inversely with the cube of y," means that w is related to x and y by the general equation

$$w = \frac{kx^2}{y^3},$$

where k is, as usual, the constant of proportionality.

The reason for these words can be seen if you hold one independent variable constant. If x is constant, then $w = \frac{(\text{constant})}{y^3}$. Thus, w varies inversely with the cube of y. If y is held constant, then $w = \frac{kx^2}{(\text{constant})}$, which can be written $w = (\text{another constant})(x^2)$. Thus, w varies directly with the square of x.

To find the particular equation for a given situation, you must know one set of corresponding values of the variables. With these values, you can find the proportionality constant. For example, suppose that $w = 12$ when $x = 2$ and $y = 5$. Solving first for k, then substituting,

$$\frac{wy^3}{x^2} = k \qquad \text{Multiplying by } y^3 \text{ and dividing by } x^2$$

$$\frac{(12)(5^3)}{2^2} = k \quad \text{Substituting the given values}$$

$$375 = k$$

$$\therefore \text{The particular equation is } w = \frac{375x^2}{y^3}.$$

The equation can then be used for predicting and interpreting, as you have done in past mathematical models problems.

Composite Functions—Functions in which *one* variable depends on a *second* variable, and the second variable depends on a *third* variable are called "composite functions." For example, the statement, "w varies directly with the square of x, and x varies inversely with the cube of y," can be translated into *two* equations

$$w = k_1 x^2 \text{ and } x = \frac{k_2}{y^3},$$

where k_1 and k_2 are proportionality constants, *not* necessarily equal to each other. Often it is desirable to express the first variable, w, in terms of the third variable, y. This may be accomplished simply by substituting $\frac{k_2}{y^3}$ for x in the first equation.

$$w = k_1 x^2 \qquad \text{First equation}$$

$$w = k_1 \left(\frac{k_2}{y^3}\right)^2 \qquad \text{Substitution}$$

$$w = \frac{k_1 k_2^2}{y^6} \qquad \text{Properties of exponentiation and fractions}$$

Since k_1 and k_2 are constants, the quantity $k_1 k_2^2$ is also a constant. Calling this third constant k_3, you get

$$w = \frac{k_3}{y^6}.$$

In words, "w varies inversely with the sixth power of y."

Notes:

1. $f(x)$ terminology is sometimes convenient for writing about composite functions. If $w = f(x)$ and $x = g(y)$, then $w = f(g(y))$. You may recall having seen some examples of this terminology in Exercise 4-4.
2. A statement such as, "w depends on x *and* y *and* z," means that there is *one* equation which expresses w in terms of x, y, and z. A statement such as, "w depends on x, x depends on y, and y depends on z," means that there are *several* equations relating *pairs* of variables. You must be able to distinguish between these *combined* variation functions and *composite* functions to interpret the following problems.

EXERCISE 8-6

Do These Quickly

The follow problems are intended to refresh your skills. You should be able to do all 10 in less than 5 minutes.

Q1. Write the general equation for y is inversely proportional to the 0.7 power of x.

Q2. Write the general equation for y varies quadratically with x.

Q3. Evaluate $64^{-\frac{2}{3}}$.

Q4.   Evaluate $\sqrt[5]{32}$.

Q5.   Solve: $\sqrt[3]{x} = 8$

Q6.   Solve: $\sqrt{x} = -25$ if x can be a complex number.

Q7.   Write an irrational number between 1 and 2.

Q8.   How many cubic inches in a cubic foot?

Q9.   Find the slope of $4x + 7y = 112$

Q10.   Multiply and simplify: $\left(\dfrac{3}{8}\right)\left(\dfrac{2}{5}\right)$

Work the following problems.

1.   *Beam Strength Problem*   The safe load for a horizontal beam, such
as those that hold up the floor in a house, varies directly as the
breadth, directly as the square of the depth, and inversely as the
length between supports (see Figure 8-6a).

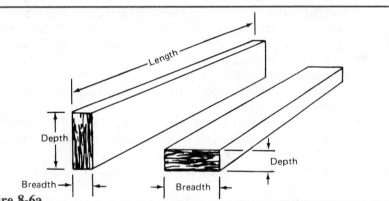

Figure 8-6a

a.   Write an equation expressing safe load in terms of these independent variables if a $2'' \times 8''$ beam 16 feet long, turned "on
edge" so that its breadth is $2''$ and its depth is $8''$, can support a
load of 1000 pounds.

b.   If the beam in part a is laid "flat" so that the breadth is $8''$ and
the depth is $2''$, how many pounds can it support?

c.   Why are houses built with the floor beams as in part a rather
than as in part b?

d.   What is the safe load for a beam 8 inches broad, 12 inches deep,
and 12 feet long?

e.   By what factor is the safe load changed if
   i.   the breadth is doubled?
   ii.   the depth is doubled?
   iii.   the length is doubled?

2. *Blood Pressure Problem*   In 1844 the French scientist J. L.
    Poiseuille found that the rate at which a fluid such as blood flows
    through small tubes such as arteries and veins varies directly with
    the product of the pressure acting on the fluid and the fourth power
    of the radius of the tube. Assume that you have an artery 0.2 cen-
    timeters in radius through which blood flows at 400 cubic millimeters
    per second when acted upon by the normal pressure of 100 units.
    a.   Write the particular equation expressing flow rate in terms of
         pressure and radius.
    b.   If the radius of the artery were reduced by 20% (to 0.16 cm)
         due to the build-up of cholesterol, what flow rate would be pro-
         duced by the normal blood pressure of 100 units?
    c.   If the heart pumped hard enough to restore the flow rate of 400
         cubic millimeters per second for the 0.16 cm artery, what would
         the blood pressure be?
    d.   Describe the effects on circulation rate and blood pressure of a
         relatively small build-up of cholesterol in the arteries.

3. *Spike Heel Problem*   The pressure exerted on the floor by a per-
    son's shoe heel is directly proportional to his or her weight and in-
    versely proportional to the square of the width of his or her heel.
    Professor Snarff weighs 200 pounds, wears a shoe with a 3 inch
    wide heel, and exerts a pressure of 24 pounds per square inch (psi)
    on the floor.
    a.   Write the particular equation expressing pressure in terms of
         weight and heel width.
    b.   Phoebe Small weighs 100 pounds. Plot a graph of the pressure
         she exerts versus her heel width for heels one inch to 4 inches
         wide.
    c.   On the same set of axes, plot two other graphs, one for John
         Garfinkle who weighs 150 pounds, and one for Professor Snarff
         who weighs 200 pounds. (The resulting three graphs form a *fam-
         ily* of curves, and the variable which characterizes each curve
         (weight, in this case) is often called a *parameter*.)
    d.   From time to time it is fashionable for ladies to wear "spike"
         heels which are very narrow. How much pressure would Phoebe
         Small's heel exert if it were $\frac{1}{4}$ inch wide? Surprising??
    e.   Why do you suppose that commercial airlines do not allow their
         stewardesses to wear spike heels?

4. *10-Speed Bike Problem*   A 10-speed bike changes gears by moving
    the chain to different size sprockets on the front and back (see Fig-
    ure 8-6b). The speed at which the bike goes varies directly with the
    number of revolutions per minute (rpm) you turn the pedals, directly
    with the number of teeth on the front sprocket, and inversely with
    the number of teeth on the back sprocket. A standard bike with 70
    cm. diameter wheels will go about 7.4 kilometers per hour (km/h) if

you pedal 40 rpm in the lowest gear (39-tooth front sprocket, 28-tooth back one.)

a. Write an equation expressing km/h in terms of the three independent variables.

b. The fastest you can turn the pedals is about 180 rpm. Calculate your top speed in each of the 10 gears.

c. Rank the gears, from "highest" to "lowest."

d. Suppose that you are most comfortable when you pedal 60 rpm. If you want to go 20 km/h, which gear should you use to get closest to your most comfortable speed? Justify your answer.

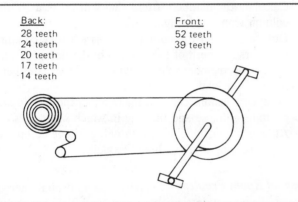

Back:
28 teeth
24 teeth
20 teeth
17 teeth
14 teeth

Front:
52 teeth
39 teeth

Figure 8-6b

5. *Bridge Column Problem*   A bridge is held up by columns 20 inches in diameter and of varying lengths (see Figure 8-6c) . From a Strength of Materials text you find that as you put more and more weight on a column, it can collapse either by *buckling* or by *crushing* (see sketch). The load which will buckle a column is directly proportional to the fourth power of its diameter, and inversely proportional to the square of its length. The load which will crush a column varies directly with the square of its diameter, and is *independent* of its length (i.e., length does *not* appear in the equation for the crushing load).

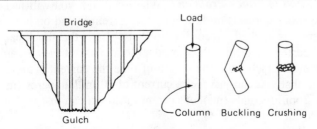

Bridge

Gulch

Load

Column Buckling Crushing

Figure 8-6c

a.   Write an equation expressing the number of tons which will *buckle* a column in terms of the length and diameter of the column. Evaluate the proportionality constant, using your laboratory findings that a 2″ diameter column 3 feet long will buckle under a load of 4 tons.

b.   Write another equation expressing the number of tons that will *crush* a column in terms of the diameter of the column, using the fact that the 2″ diameter laboratory column in part a is crushed by a load of 5 tons.

c.   Calculate the number of tons load needed to *buckle* 20″ diameter bridge columns which are 20 feet, 30 feet, and 50 feet long.

d.   Calculate the number of tons that will *crush* a 20″ diameter column from the bridge.

e.   Draw a graph of the number of tons a bridge column will support versus length of the column in the domain from 0 through 50 feet. Remember that the number of tons is either the *buckling* or *crushing* load, whichever is *less*.

f.   What conclusions can you make about the way in which *long* columns collapse and the way in which *short* ones collapse?

g.   At approximately what length will a bridge column collapse by both buckling *and* crushing? Explain.

6.   ***Hospital Room Problem***   Suppose that a hospital charges you $220 per day if you stay in a private room, and $166 per day if you stay in a room for 4 people. Assume that the amount you pay is the sum of a *constant* amount (for the services you receive) and an amount which *varies inversely* with the number of people the room will hold (to pay for your share of the room).

a.   Calculate the constant amount you pay for services, and the proportionality constant in the variation function.

b.   What does the hospital charge for a room, exclusive of the services to the patient?

c.   How much would you expect to pay per day if you stayed in
     i.   a semi-private room holding 2 people?
     ii. a ward holding 20 people?

7.   ***Reaction to Shock Problem***   Whether or not you will feel an electric shock depends on how high the current is and on how long the current is applied. According to Weiss' Law, the shock can be felt if the current is greater than or equal to a constant *plus* an amount that varies inversely with the length of time the current is applied. Suppose that you can just feel a current of 30 milliamperes (ma) applied for 2 milliseconds (ms). A current of 20 ma can just be felt when applied for 4 ms.

a.   Write the particular *inequality* expressing current that can be felt in terms of time.

b. How many milliamperes can be felt if the current is applied for 10 ms?

c. What is the minimum length of time a current of 100 ma could be applied and still be felt?

d. How low a current could be felt if it were applied for a long period of time?

e. Plot the graph of the inequality in part a.

8. *Airplane Flight Speed Problem* The weights of airplanes of similar shape are directly proportional to the cube of their lengths. In order for the airplane to fly, this weight must be directly proportional to the product of the wing area and the flight speed. The wing area varies directly as the square of the length of the airplane.

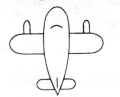

a. Write the general equation for each of the three variation functions above, using different symbols for each proportionality constant.

b. From these equations, derive another equation expressing the speed of an airplane in terms of its length.

c. How does flight speed vary with plane length?

d. How much faster would the plane have to fly if you doubled its length?

9. *Gas Consumption Problem* Assume that the wind resistance acting against a car traveling at high speed is directly proportional to the square of the speed. Assume also that the number of kilometers per liter of gasoline (km/l) is inversely proportional to the wind resistance.

a. Write general equations expressing each of the above relationships. Then use the two equations to get a third equation expressing km/l in terms of speed.

b. How does the number of km/l vary with speed?

c. If you get 8 km/l when you drive 100 kilometers per hour (km/h), find the proportionality constant and write the particular equation expressing km/l in terms of km/h.

d. Predict the number of kml for speeds of 120, 140, 160, 180, and 200 kmh. Use the results to plot the graph of km/h versus km/l.

e. Can you think of a reason other than safety for not driving 200 km/h?

f. Do you suppose that your mathematical model would give reasonable answers for km/l at very low speeds? Justify your answer.

10. *Electric Light Problem*   There are four variables concerned with the operation of an electric light:

power (watts),   current (amps), and
voltage (volts),   resistance (ohms).

The power is proportional to the product of the voltage and the current. The resistance varies directly with the voltage and inversely with the current.

a. Write general equations for each of the two variations above.
b. By appropriate substitutions, derive an equation expressing power as a function of resistance and current.
c. Evaluate the proportionality constant for the equation in part b if a 400 watt light bulb with a resistance of 100 ohms draws a current of 2 amps.
d. Why do you suppose the sizes of the various units of electrical measurement were chosen the way they were? (Clue: See your answer to part c.)
e. By what factor would the power change if the current were tripled?

11. *Why Mammals Are The Way They Are*   Some physical and behavioral characteristics of mammals can be explained by comparing the way their surface area and mass are related. Assume that,

i.   the mass of an animal is directly proportional to the *cube* of its length.
ii. the area of its skin is directly proportional to the *square* of its length,
iii. the rate at which it loses heat to its surroundings is directly proportional to its skin area, and
iv. the amount of food it must eat per day is directly proportional to the rate of heat loss.

a. Write general equations for each of the four functions above.
b. By appropriate substitutions, derive a general equation expressing amount of food per day in terms of the animal's mass. Tell how the food consumption varies with mass.
c. Divide both members of the equation in part b by the animal's mass to get an equation for the *fraction* of its mass an animal consumes per day. Tell how this fraction varies with mass.
d. The smallest mammal, the shrew, eats 3 times its mass each day. A shrew has a mass of about 2 grams (about that of a penny!). Find the proportionality constant for the equation in part c.
e. What fraction of its mass would a 6000 *kilogram* elephant eat each day?
f. As the size of the animal decreases, what seems to happen to the food-to-mass ratio? Based upon this result, why do you suppose that there are no mammals smaller than a shrew? What

makes a shrew so *mean*? Why do small mammals like shrews have fur, but large ones like elephants do *not*? Apart from the fact that whales have no legs, why is the sea a favorable environment for such large mammals?

g. See Haldane's article, "On Being the Right Size," in James R. Newman's *World of Mathematics,* page 952. Also, see *On Size and Life,* by Thomas McMahon and John Bonner, published by Scientific American Books in 1983.

12. *Tornado Problem* When a tornado moves over a house, the sudden decrease in air pressure creates a force that can lift off the roof.

a. The force exerted on the roof equals the pressure times the area of the roof. Write an equation expressing this fact.

b. If the joint between the roof and the walls is strong enough, the roof will not be lifted off. The force a roof will withstand varies directly with the length of the roof-to-walls joint (that is, the perimeter of the room). Write an equation expressing this fact.

c. Write an equation stating that the area of the roof varies directly with the square of the perimeter of the room.

d. Use the equation in parts b and c to show that the force a roof will withstand is directly proportional to the $\frac{1}{2}$ power of the roof's area.

e. The "critical pressure" for a room is the pressure at which the force exerted by the tornado just equals the force the roof will withstand. Combine the equations in parts a and d to show that the critical pressure varies *inversely* with the *square root* of the roof's area.

f. If one roof has an area 9 times that of another roof, how does the critical pressure for the first roof compare with the critical pressure of the second?

g. Based on your answer to part f, where is the safest place to hide if a tornado threatens your house?

13. *Car Trade-In Data Analysis Problem* The trade-in value of a car "depreciates" with time. The trade-in value of any particular make and model of car can be found in the "blue book" (which is often orange!) which is published each month. Suppose you own a car that is presently 20 months old, and whose trade-in value is $8000. Five months ago, the trade-in value was $9000.

a. Let t be the number of months old the car is. Let $f(t)$ be the predicted trade-in value if a *linear* function is assumed. Let $g(t)$ and $h(t)$ be the predicted trade-in value if exponential and inverse (fractional power) variation functions are assumed, respectively. Write particular equations for $f(t)$, $g(t)$, and $h(t)$.

b. Use each of the three functions to predict the trade-in value when the car is 60 months old. (There may be surprises!)

c. Use each of the three functions to predict the trade-in value when the car was new. (There may be other surprises!!)

d.   Based on your answers to parts (b) and (c), which of the three kinds of function is most reasonable for predicting the trade-in value over a long period of time?

14.   *Quadratic Function Second Differences Data Analysis Problem*   In this problem you will review quadratic functions. You will also learn something new about them that will help you decide whether or not a quadratic function is a reasonable mathematical model.

    a.   Let f be the general quadratic function $f(x) = ax^2 + bx + c$. Find values for $f(3), f(4), f(5), f(6)$, and $f(7)$ in terms of a, b, and c.

    b.   Find the *first* differences between these function values. That is, find $f(4) - f(3), f(5) - f(4), f(6) - f(5)$, and $f(7) - f(6)$.

    c.   Find the *second* differences between these function values. That is, find the differences between each pair of first differences.

    d.   What remarkable conclusion do you observe in the second differences?

    e.   The following are values of a function g:

x	$g(x)$
1	6
2	11
3	22
4	39

       Show that this data has the same second-difference property as the general quadratic function.

    f.   Find the particular equation for $g(x)$. Use the first three points in the table.

    g.   Confirm that your equation from part (f) gives the correct answer for $g(4)$.

8-7   CHAPTER REVIEW AND TEST

In this chapter you have studied functions with the last of the five algebraic operations, nth roots. You have graphed a few of these irrational algebraic functions, and used the graphs to learn something about extraneous solutions of radical equations. A special kind of irrational function, the variation function with non-integer exponents, was used as a mathematical model. You also examined functions relating more than two variables.

The Review Problems below parallel the sections in this chapter. The Concepts Problems let you try your hand at applying what you know to analyze new situations. The Chapter Test is similar to one your instructor might give to see how well you understand irrational algebraic functions.

REVIEW PROBLEMS

R1. Let $f(x) = 7 - \sqrt{x - 3}$.
   a. Tell the domain of x if $f(x)$ is to be a real number.
   b. Find $f(28)$.
   c. Find x if $f(x) = 1$.

R2. Plot the graph of $f(x) = 7 - \sqrt{x - 3}$ from Problem R1 in the domain $3 \leq x \leq 7$.

R3. Transform to simple radical form:
   a. $\sqrt{75} - \sqrt{27}$ b. $2\sqrt{7} + \dfrac{35}{\sqrt{7}}$

   c. $\dfrac{\sqrt{75}}{\sqrt{3} + \sqrt{8}}$ d. $\dfrac{3}{\sqrt[5]{3}}$

R4. Solve the following radical equations:
   a. $\sqrt{x + 6} + 6 = x$
   b. $\sqrt{3x + 1} - \sqrt{2x - 10} = 4$
   c. $\sqrt{3x} + \sqrt{2x - 1} = \dfrac{5}{\sqrt{2x - 1}}$

R5. *Defended Region Problem*   An animal will defend the region around its home by attacking intruders that come into the region. According to statistical studies reported in J. M. Emlen's *Ecology: An Evolutionary Approach,* the defended region's area varies directly with the 1.31 power of the animal's body mass.
   a. Suppose that a normal 20 kilogram beaver will defend a region of area 300 square meters. Write the particular equation for this function.
   b. Skeletons show that thousands of years ago North American beavers were up to 3.5 meters long (including the tail) and had masses of 200 kilograms (about the size of an Alaskan brown bear!). How many square meters would such a beaver have defended?
   c. What mass beaver would defend a region of area 50 square meters?

R6. *Composite Function Problem*   Suppose that y varies inversely with the cube of x, and that x varies directly with the square of z and inversely with w.
   a. Write general equations expressing y and x in terms of their independent variables.
   b. Write a general equation expressing y in terms of z and w.

c. Tell in words how y varies with z and w.
d. Write the particular equation expressing y in terms of z and w if $y = 40$ when $z = 3$ and $w = 6$.

CONCEPTS PROBLEMS

C1. In this problem you are to plot the graph of the irrational algebraic function

$$f(x) = \frac{1}{3 - \sqrt{x + 5}} - 2.$$

In doing so, you will have to use most of the techniques of this chapter, plus some that you have learned before.

a. Prove that the radical $\sqrt{x + 5}$ represents a *rational* number when $x = -1$, but an *irrational* number when $x = 1$.
b. What kind of number does $\sqrt{x + 5}$ represent when $x < -5$?
c. For what value(s) of x is the denominator of the fraction equal to zero? What do you suppose happens to the graph of f at these values?
d. Write the domain of f.
e. Rationalize the denominator of the fraction in $f(x)$.
f. Write $f(x)$ as a *single* fraction in simple radical form.
g. Find out whether or not there are any x-intercepts by setting the numerator of the fraction in part f equal to zero and solving the resulting radical equation. Remember that to be an x-intercept, the value of x must be in the domain of f.
h. Find decimal approximations for $f(3)$, $f(5)$, and $f(11)$.
i. Find a decimal approximation for the $f(x)$-intercept.
j. Plot the graph of f. Use the information you already know, and calculate any additional points you feel you need. Put dots at any places where the graph ends, and arrows to show places where the graph continues beyond your graph paper.

C2. Suppose that $g(x)$ varies inversely with the cube root of x^2.
a. Write the general equation for $g(x)$.
b. Write the particular equation if $g(8) = 25$.
c. Write the value of $g(5)$ in simple radical form.
d. Find, approximately, the value of x for which $g(x) = 3.47$.

CHAPTER TEST

Evaluate:

T1. $\sqrt{358}$ T2. $\sqrt[5]{-1988}$ T3. $\sqrt[8]{-1066}$

Write in simple radical form:

T4. $\sqrt{28} - 5\sqrt{63} + 10\sqrt{7}$ T5. $13\sqrt{5} + \dfrac{35}{\sqrt{5}}$

T6. $\dfrac{30}{\sqrt{11} - \sqrt{5}}$

T7. Rationalize the denominator of $\dfrac{10}{\sqrt[3]{25}}$. In order to do this, you must multiply by a form of 1 that makes the radicand in the denominator a perfect *cube*.

Solve the equations, discarding any extraneous solutions.

T8. $x + \sqrt{x - 7} = 3$ T9. $\sqrt{3x - 11} + 3 = x$

T10. If y varies inversely as the cube of x, write the particular equation, given that the graph contains $(4, 7)$. Find x if $y = 10$.

T11. Suppose that z varies directly with the cube of y, and that y varies inversely with the square of x. Write the general equation expressing z in terms of x. If z is 13 when x is 5, write the particular equation. Then use the equation to predict the value of x for which z is 100.

T12. Let $f(x) = \sqrt[13]{x}$.
   a. What is the domain of function f?
   b. How far out in the x-direction would you have to go before $f(x)$ reaches 2?
   c. Plot the graph of f on graph paper. Use values of x between -1 and 1, inclusive. Plot enough points to show the shape of the graph.

8-8 | CUMULATIVE REVIEW, CHAPTERS 6, 7, AND 8

The following exercise may be considered to be a "final exam" covering your work on exponential, rational, and irrational functions. If you are thoroughly familiar with the materials in Chapters 6, 7, and 8, you should be able to work all of these problems in 2 to 3 hours.

EXERCISE 8-8

1. For each of the following graphs, tell what kind of function it could be, and write the general equation for that kind of function.

a.

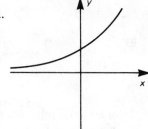

b.

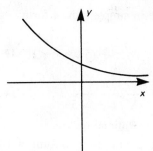

c.

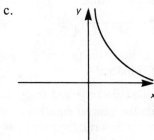

d.

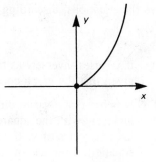

e.

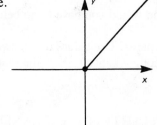

f.

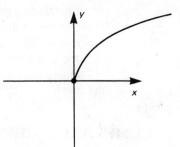

g.

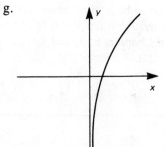

h.

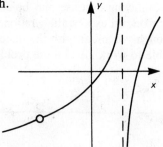

i.

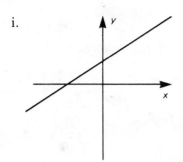

2. Write the general equation for a function that has the indicated property.
    a. Doubling x doubles y.
    b. Doubling x makes y half as big.
    c. Doubling x makes y $\frac{1}{8}$ as big.
    d. Doubling x makes y 16 times as big.
    e. Adding 7 to x makes y three times as big.

3. Multiply the following and simplify:
    a. $(\sqrt{15} + \sqrt{3})(\sqrt{12} - \sqrt{5})$
    b. $(\sqrt{2} - \sqrt{7})^2$
    c. $(\sqrt{2} - \sqrt{7})(\sqrt{2} + \sqrt{7})$
    d. $(\sqrt{x} + 5)(\sqrt{x} - 7)$
    e. $(x + 5)(x - 7)$
    f. $(x^2 - 5x + 4)(x^2 + 3x - 9)$

4. Factor the following polynomials:
    a. $r^7 + s^7$ b. $6x^2 - 71x - 120$
    c. $x^3 + x^2 - 10x + 8$

5. Carry out the indicated operations and simplify:
    a. $\dfrac{8}{x^2 - 16} - \dfrac{5}{x^2 + 3x - 4}$

    b. $\dfrac{x^2 - 4}{x^2 + 2x - 3} \div \dfrac{x^2 - 7x + 10}{(1 - x)(x - 3)}$

6. Simplify the following expressions (*no* decimal approximations!).
    a. $3x^{-\frac{1}{2}} \times 4x^{\frac{2}{3}}$ b. $\sqrt{27} \div \sqrt[3]{81}$

    c. $\dfrac{6}{\sqrt{19} - 4}$ d. $\dfrac{12}{\sqrt[5]{27}}$

    e. $\sqrt[4]{25}$ f. $3\sqrt{28} + \dfrac{21}{\sqrt{7}}$

    g. $\log_{27} 81$ h. $\log_3 15 + \log_3 6 - \log_3 10$

i. $\dfrac{\dfrac{2}{x-1}+3}{\dfrac{13}{x+4}-3}$

j. $\left((16a^{-4})\div(9a^{-2})\right)^{-\frac{1}{2}}$

7. Solve the following equations:

   a. $1-\sqrt{7-x}=x$

   b. $x+\dfrac{2}{x-1}=\dfrac{x-3}{1-x}$

8. Consider the expressisons $\frac{5}{0}$, $\frac{0}{0}$, and $\frac{0}{5}$.

   a. Two of these are *undefined*. Which two? What special words are used to distinguish between these two?

   b. The other expression *is* defined. Which one? What does it equal?

9. For the function $f(x)=\frac{x^3+x^2-10x+8}{x^2-1}$:

   a. Evaluate $f(-10),f(-4),f(-1),f(0),f(1),f(2)$, and $f(10)$.

   b. Plot a graph of f showing any removable discontinuities or asymptotes.

10. Prove that the graph of $f(x)=\frac{x-2}{x^2-x+2}$ has *no* removable discontinuities and *no* vertical asymptotes.

11. ***Iodine Problem***   A radioactive atom "decays" by shooting out something from its nucleus. Once the "thing" is shot out, the atom is no longer radioactive. Radioactive iodine, used to examine people's thyroid glands, decays with a "half-life" of 8.1 days. This means that when 8.1 days is *added* to the time, the amount of iodine remaining is *multiplied* by $\frac{1}{2}$.

    a. What kind of function would be an appropriate mathematical model relating the amount of iodine remaining to the time that has passed?

    b. A hospital receives a shipment of 23.7 millicuries of radioactive iodine. Write the particular equation expressing the amount of iodine remaining as a function of the number of days since they received the iodine.

    c. Assume that the hospital uses none of the iodine on patients. Use your equation to predict

       i. the amount of iodine remaining after 1 week,

       ii. the number of days until the amount of iodine has dropped to 0.8 millicuries.

    d. Show that your answers to part c are *reasonable* by using the fact that the *half*-life is 8.1 days.

    e. The iodine was produced in a nuclear reactor 3.7 days before it was received at the hospital. How many millicuries were there when it was produced?

12. *Heat Radiation Problem*   The rate at which you receive heat radiated from a hot sphere such as the Sun varies directly with the fourth power of its absolute temperature, directly with its surface area, and inversely with the square of your distance from the sphere.

   a. Write the general equation for this function.

   b. The surface area of a sphere varies directly with the square of its radius, and its volume varies directly with the cube of its radius. Write general equations for these two functions.

   c. Combine the equations in parts a and b to get an equation expressing the rate at which you receive heat in terms of the sphere's temperature and volume, and the distance between you and the sphere.

13. *Diesel Engine Problem*   You recall that when you compress air in a tire pump, the air warms up. A diesel engine works on the same principle. Air in the cylinders is compressed until it is hot enough to ignite the diesel fuel. As the air is compressed, its absolute temperature varies inversely with 0.4 power of its volume.

   a. As the air starts being compressed, it is at "room temperature" of 300°K, and occupies 60 cu. cm. volume. Write an equation expressing absolute temperature in terms of volume.

   b. What is the temperature when the air is compressed to 4 cu. cm.?

   c. The minimum temperature needed to make diesel fuel ignite is 750°K. To what volume must the air be compressed to reach this temperature?

9

Quadratic Relations and Systems

The quadratic functions of Chapter 5 have general equations of the form $y = ax^2 + bx + c$. If the equation also has a y^2-term or an xy-term, the relation is still quadratic, but may not be a function. In this chapter you will find out what the graphs of these relations look like, and how they are related to slices of a cone. These "conic sections" are good mathematical models of the paths of planets, spacecraft, and other objects traveling under the influence of gravity.

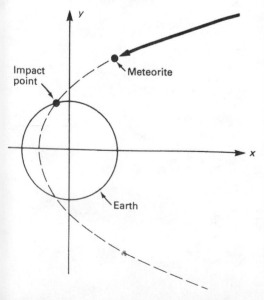

| 9-1 | INTRODUCTION TO QUADRATIC RELATIONS |

DEFINITION

> **QUADRATIC RELATION**
> A **quadratic relation** is a relation specified by an equation or inequality of the form
>
> $$Ax^2 + Bxy + Cy^2 + Dx + Ey + F = 0,$$
>
> where A, B, C, D, E, and F stand for constants, and where the "=" sign may be replaced by an inequality sign.

It will be your objective in the next few sections to determine what the graph of such a relation might look like and how the six constants affect the graph.

To begin this objective, you will plot the graphs of several such relations pointwise, and attempt to discover what geometrical figure each one is.

| EXERCISE 9-1 |

Plot a graph of each relation. Select values of x and calculate the corresponding values of y until you have enough points to draw a smooth curve. Use a calculator or square root tables to approximate any radicals. When you have finished, see if you can come to any conclusions about the *shape*, *size*, and *location* of each graph.

1. $\{(x, y): x^2 + y^2 = 25\}$

2. $\{(x, y): x^2 + y^2 + 6x = 16\}$

3. $\{(x, y): x^2 + y^2 - 4y = 21\}$

4. $\{(x, y): x^2 + y^2 + 6x - 4y = 12\}$

9-2   CIRCLES

In Exercise 9-1 you discovered that the graphs of some quadratic relations look like circles. In this section you will learn *why* this is true, and use the results to sketch the graphs *rapidly*.

Objective:
Give the equation or inequality of a circle or circular region, be able to draw the graph *quickly*.

To accomplish this objective, you will start with the geometric definition of a circle, and use the definition to find out what the equation of a circle looks like.

DEFINITION

GEOMETRICAL DEFINITION OF CIRCLE
A **circle** is a set of points in a plane, each of which is equidistant from a *fixed* point called the *center*.

Suppose that a circle of radius r units has its center at the fixed point (h, k) in a Cartesian coordinate system, as shown in Figure 9-2a. If (x, y)

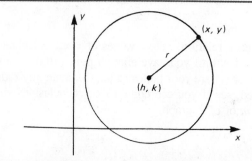

Figure 9-2a

is a point on the circle, then the distance between (x, y) and (h, k) is r units, the radius of the circle. This distance can be expressed in terms of the coordinates of the two points using the Distance Formula.

Background: *The Distance Formula*

Objective:
Express the distance between two points in a Cartesian coordinate system in terms of the coordinates of the two points.

You recall from your work with slopes of linear functions that the rise and run, Δy and Δx, for the line between the points (x_1, y_1) and (x_2, y_2) are

$$\Delta y = y_2 - y_1$$
$$\Delta x = x_2 - x_1.$$

Figure 9-2b shows that Δy, Δx, and the distance d between the two points are the measures of the sides of a right triangle. By Pythagoras, then,

$$d^2 = (\Delta x)^2 + (\Delta y)^2 \qquad \text{———} \qquad ①.$$

By substitution,

$$d^2 = (x_2 - x_1)^2 + (y_2 - y_1)^2 \qquad \text{———} \qquad ②.$$

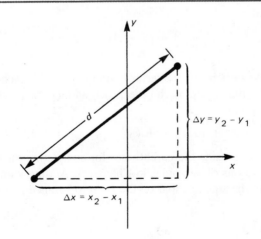

The Distance Formula

Figure 9-2b

Taking the positive square root of both members gives

$$d = \sqrt{(x_2 - x_1)^2 + (y_2 - y_1)^2} \qquad \text{———} \qquad ③.$$

Equations ①, ②, and ③ are different forms of the *distance formula*. Each form has certain advantages for different applications. The formula is, of course, just a fancy form of the Pythagorean Theorem.

Returning to the problem of finding the equation of a circle, the distance r between the points (x, y) and (h, k) in Figure 9-2a can be expressed using form ② of the distance formula as:

$$(x - h)^2 + (y - k)^2 = r^2$$

where the center is at (h, k), and the radius is r. This is called the *general equation* of a circle.

If the center is at the origin, then $(h, k) = (0, 0)$. In this case the equation reduces to

$$x^2 + y^2 = r^2$$

To show that an equation such as in Problem 4 of Exercise 9-1 is really that of a circle, it is sufficient to transform the equation into the general form, above. This transformation may be accomplished by completing the square.

EXAMPLE

Graph the relation

$$x^2 + y^2 + 6x - 4y - 12 = 0.$$

Solution:

Commuting and associating the terms containing x with each other, and the terms containing y with each other, then adding the constant 12 to both members gives

$$(x^2 + 6x \quad) + (y^2 - 4y \quad) = 12.$$

The spaces are left inside the parentheses for completing the square, as you did for equations of parabolas in Chapter 5. Adding 9 and 4 on the left to complete the squares, and on the right to balance the equation, gives

$$(x^2 + 6x + 9) + (y^2 - 4y + 4) = 12 + 9 + 4,$$

from which

$$(x + 3)^2 + (y - 2)^2 = 25.$$

Therefore, the graph will be a *circle* of radius 5 units, centered at $(h, k) = (-3, 2)$, as shown in Figure 9-2c. The graph you drew for Problem 4 of Exercise 9-1 should have looked something like this figure. The

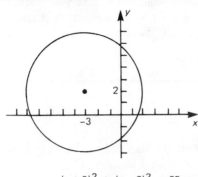

$$(x + 3)^2 + (y - 2)^2 = 25$$

Figure 9-2c

prior knowledge that the graph is a circle of known center and radius, however, will allow you to plot the graph much more quickly, in accordance with your objective for this section. ∎

If the open sentence is an *inequality,* then the graph will be the region *inside* the circle if the symbol is "<," as indicated in Figure 9-2d, or *outside* the circle if the symbol is ">."

An objective stated in Section 9-1 is to determine the effects of the constants A, B, C, D, E, and F on the graph of

$$Ax^2 + Bxy + Cy^2 + Dx + Ey + F = 0.$$

The above leads to a conclusion about the relative sizes of A and C.

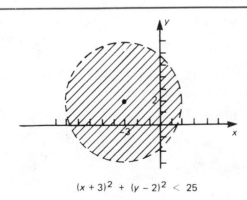

$$(x + 3)^2 + (y - 2)^2 < 25$$

Figure 9-2d

The graph of a quadratic relation will be a *circle* if the coefficients of the x^2 term and the y^2 term are *equal* (and the xy term is zero).

The following exercise is designed to give you practice drawing graphs of circles and circular regions given the equation or inequality.

EXERCISE 9-2

Do These Quickly

The following problems are intended to refresh your skills. You should be able to do all 10 in less than 5 minutes.

Sketch the graph of:

Q1. A linear function.

Q2. A quadratic function.

Q3. A decreasing exponential function.

Q4. An inconsistent linear system.

Q5. A linear inequality.

Q6. A function with a removable discontinuity at $x = 3$.

Q7. A function with a vertical asymptote at $x = 2$.

Write the general equation of:

Q8. A linear function.

Q9. A quadratic function.

Q10. An exponential function.

For Problems 1 through 12, complete the square (if necessary) to find the center and radius. Then draw the graph.

1. $x^2 + y^2 - 10x + 8y + 5 = 0$

2. $x^2 + y^2 + 12x - 2y + 21 = 0$

3. $x^2 + y^2 - 6x - 4y - 12 > 0$

4. $x^2 + y^2 + 16x + 10y - 11 < 0$

5. $x^2 + y^2 - 8x + 6y - 56 \leq 0$

6. $x^2 + y^2 + 4x - 18y + 69 \geq 0$

7. $x^2 + y^2 + 4x - 5 = 0$

8. $x^2 + y^2 - 14y + 48 = 0$

9. $x^2 + y^2 = 49$

10. $x^2 + y^2 = 4$

11. $x^2 + y^2 = 0$ (Watch for a surprise!)

12. $x^2 + y^2 + 16 = 0$ (Watch for a different surprise!)

For Problems 13 through 18, write an equation of the circle described.

13. Center at $(7, 5)$, containing $(3, -2)$

14. Center at $(-4, 6)$, containing $(-2, -3)$

15. Center at $(-9, -2)$, containing the origin

16. Center at $(5, -4)$, containing $(0, 3)$

17. Center at the origin, containing $(-6, -8)$

18. Center at the origin, containing $(-5, 1)$

19. Write a general equation for a circle
    a. of radius r, centered at a point on the x-axis,
    b. of radius r, centered at a point on the y-axis,
    c. of radius r, centered at the origin.

20. What do you suppose is meant by a "point circle?" How can you tell from the equation that a circle will be a point circle?

21. Sometimes the graph of a quadratic relation such as you have been plotting turns out to have no points at all! How can you tell from the equation whether or not this will happen?

22. *Introduction to Ellipses*   In this section you have found that the graph of a quadratic relation is a circle if x^2 and y^2 have *equal* coefficients. In this problem you will find out what the graph looks like if the coefficients are *not* equal, but have the same sign. Do the following things for the relation whose equation is

$$9x^2 + 25y^2 = 225.$$

    a. Solve the equation for y in terms of x.
    b. Explain why there are *two* values of y for each value of x between -5 and 5.
    c. Explain why there are *no* real values of y for $x > 5$ and for $x < -5$.
    d. Calculate values of y for each integer value of x from -5 to 5, inclusive. Use a calculator or square root tables to approximate any radicals which do not come out integers. Round off to one decimal place.
    e. Plot the graph. If you have been successful, you should have a *closed* figure called an *ellipse*.

9-3 | ELLIPSES

In Section 9-2 you learned that the graph of a quadratic relation is a circle if x^2 and y^2 have the *same* coefficient. If x^2 and y^2 have *different* coefficients, but the *same sign,* then the graph is called an "ellipse." If you worked Problem 22 of Exercise 9-2 you found by pointwise plotting that the graph of

$$9x^2 + 25y^2 = 225$$

is as shown in Figure 9-3a. In this section you will learn properties of ellipses that will allow you to sketch their graphs *quickly.* You will also use computer graphics to confirm that your sketches are correct.

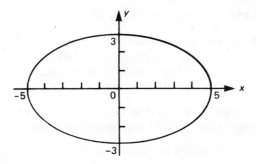

$$9x^2 + 25y^2 = 225$$

Figure 9-3a _____

Various parts of the ellipse are given special names, as shown in Figure 9-3b. All ellipses look rather like flattened circles. Thus, if you know where the center is, and how long the major and minor axes are, you can sketch the graph *quickly.* The trick is to transform the equation so that these lengths show up in it. Starting with

$$9x^2 + 25y^2 = 225,$$

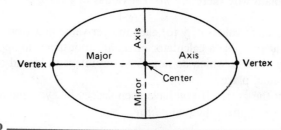

Figure 9-3b _____

you divide by 225 to make the right member equal 1.

$$\frac{9x^2}{225} + \frac{25y^2}{225} = 1$$

$$\frac{x^2}{25} + \frac{y^2}{9} = 1$$

$$\left(\frac{x}{5}\right)^2 + \left(\frac{y}{3}\right)^2 = 1$$

The "5" under the x is the distance from the center to the graph in the x-direction. The "3" under the y is the distance from the center to the graph in the y-direction. In this text these distances will be called the x-radius and the y-radius (see Figure 9-3c).

DEFINITION

> **X-RADIUS AND Y-RADIUS**
> If an ellipse has its major and minor axes parallel to the coordinate axes, then:
>
> the **x-radius** is the distance from the center to the ellipse in the x-direction, and
>
> the **y-radius** is the distance from the center to the ellipse in the y-direction.

By comparing the graphs in Figures 9-3b and 9-3c, you can tell that the x- and y-radii are each half of either the major or minor axis. Half the major

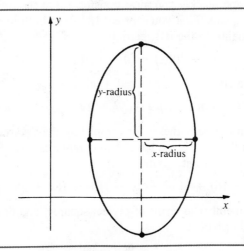

Figure 9-3c

axis is called the *semi-major axis*. Half the minor axis is called the *semi-minor axis*. Since the ellipse can be oriented with the major axis vertical as in Figure 9-3c, or horizontal as in Figure 9-3a, the semi-major axis is either the y-radius or the x-radius, whichever is larger.

Letting r_x and r_y stand for the x- and y-radii, respectively, the general equation of an ellipse centered at the origin is

$$\left(\frac{x}{r_x}\right)^2 + \left(\frac{y}{r_y}\right)^2 = 1$$

If the center is at (h, k) instead of at the origin, $(0, 0)$, then x and y in the above equation will be replaced by $(x - h)$ and $(y - k)$, as they were for the circle.

CONCLUSION

The graph of

$$\left(\frac{x - h}{r_x}\right)^2 + \left(\frac{y - k}{r_y}\right)^2 = 1$$

is an *ellipse*, centered at (h, k), having points r_x units from the center in the positive and negative x-direction, and r_y units from the center in the positive and negative y-direction.

EXAMPLE 1

Sketch the graph of

$$25x^2 + 9y^2 - 200x + 18y + 184 = 0.$$

Solution:

To sketch the graph quickly you must transform it to the form above by completing the square. First you subtract 184 from both members and associate what remains on the left, getting

$$(25x^2 - 200x) + (9y^2 + 18y) = -184.$$

Factoring out the coefficients of x^2 and y^2 gives

$$25(x^2 - 8x\quad) + 9(y^2 + 2y\quad) = -184.$$

Spaces are left in the parentheses for completing the square. Adding 16 and 1 completes the squares on the left, and requires that $25 \cdot 16$ and $9 \cdot 1$ be added on the right, giving

$$25(x^2 - 8x + 16) + 9(y^2 + 2y + 1) = -184 + 25 \cdot 16 + 9 \cdot 1.$$

Writing the left member in terms of perfect squares, and doing the arithmetic on the right gives

$$25(x - 4)^2 + 9(y + 1)^2 = 225.$$

Dividing both members by 225 produces the desired form of the equation,

$$\frac{(x - 4)^2}{9} + \frac{(y + 1)^2}{25} = 1$$

or

$$\left(\frac{x - 4}{3}\right)^2 + \left(\frac{y + 1}{5}\right)^2 = 1.$$

So the graph will be an *ellipse;* centered at $(4, -1)$, with x-radius 3 units and y-radius 5 units.

The graph may now be drawn quickly by plotting the four critical points, then sketching the ellipse, as shown in Figure 9-3d.

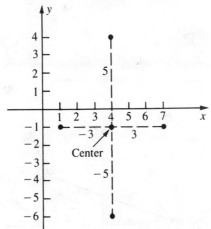

Plot the center and
x- and y- radii

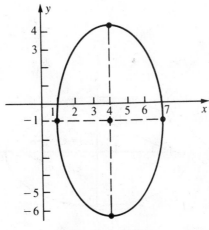

Sketch the ellipse

Figure 9-3d

If the "=" sign is replaced by one of the inequalities "<" or ">," then the graph will be the region inside the ellipse or outside the ellipse, respectively.

There is a pair of points associated with an ellipse that has an important geometrical property. Suppose that you tie two pins to a piece of string in such a way that there are 10 cm of string between them. Then you stick the pins at the points $F_1 = (4, 0)$ and $F_2 = (-4, 0)$ in a Cartesian coordinate system that has 1-cm squares (see Figure 9-3e). Placing a pencil as shown in the figure, and keeping the string tight, you can draw a curve. The curve turns out to be an *ellipse*, the same one as in Figure 9-3a!

This construction leads to a *geometrical* definition of the ellipse.

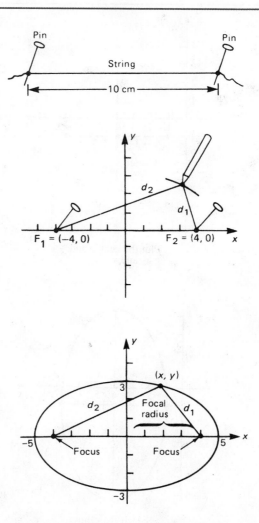

Figure 9-3e

DEFINITION

> **GEOMETRICAL DEFINITION OF ELLIPSE**
> An **ellipse** is a set of points in a plane. For each point, the *sum* of its distances, $d_1 + d_2$, from two fixed points F_1 and F_2, is *constant*.

Each point, F_1 and F_2, is called a *focus*. The name is chosen because sound or light emitted from one focus will be "focused" toward the other one by bouncing off the ellipse. (The plural of focus is "foci," the "c" being pronounced like an "s.")

The distance from the center to a focus is called the *focal radius*. By placing the pencil at two strategic positions, you can find out how to *calculate* the focal radius. Placing it on the *x*-axis as in Figure 9-3f, you can see that the length of the major axis is equal to the length of the string. That is, the constant sum of the distances, $d_1 + d_2$, equals the length of the major axis.

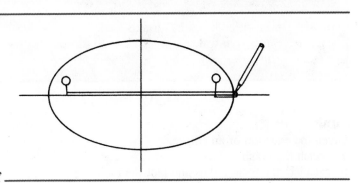

Figure 9-3f

By placing the pencil on the *y*-axis as in Figure 9-3g, a right triangle is formed by the two axes and the string. The hypotenuse is equal to *half* the length of the string.

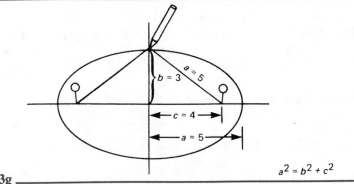

Figure 9-3g

If the *x*- and *y*-radii are known, then the semi-major axis is the larger one and the semi-minor axis is the smaller. Letting *a* stand for the semi-major axis, *b* stand for the semi-minor axis, and *c* stand for the focal radius, then the following conclusion is true:

CONCLUSION

In an ellipse,

If:

a is the length of semi-major axis,
b is the length of semi-minor axis,
c is the focal radius, and
d_1 and d_2 are the distances from a point (x, y) on the ellipse to the two foci,

Then:

$d_1 + d_2 = 2a$ = length of major axis,
$a^2 = b^2 + c^2$, from which
$c^2 = a^2 - b^2$.

Objective:
Given the equation of an ellipse,
a. sketch the graph,
b. calculate the focal radius and plot the foci,
c. check the sketch by computer graphics.

EXAMPLE 2

Find the foci of

$$25x^2 + 9y^2 - 200x + 18y + 184 = 0.$$

Solution:
This is the ellipse in Example 1. Completing the square gives

$$\left(\frac{x - 4}{3}\right)^2 + \left(\frac{y + 1}{5}\right)^2 = 1.$$

So $a = 5$ and $b = 3$. Using the fact that $c^2 = a^2 - b^2$

$$c^2 = 5^2 - 3^2$$

$$= 16$$

$$\therefore c = 4.$$

Since the major axis is in the *y*-direction, the foci will be located *vertically,* ±4 units from the center (Figure 9-3h).

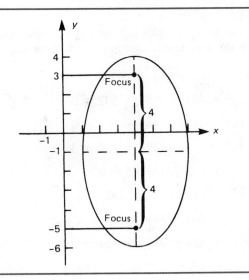

Figure 9-3h ———————————————————————— ∎

The exercise that follows is designed to give you practice in sketching graphs of ellipses and finding their foci.

EXERCISE 9-3

Do These Quickly

The following problems are intended to refresh your skills. You should be able to do all 10 in less than 5 minutes.

Q1.   What is the radius of the circle $(x - 5)^2 + (y - 2)^2 = 49$?

Q2.   Where is the center of the circle $(x + 3)^2 + (y - 4)^2 = 25$?

Q3.   Complete the square: $x^2 + 20x + $ ____ .

Q4.   Write as the square of a binomial: $x^2 - 8x + 16$

Q5.   Find k if $(3, 4)$ is on the graph of $y = kx^2$.

Q6.   Solve: $\sqrt{x} + 3 = 7$

Q7.   Solve: $|x - 11| = 2$

Q8.   Simplify: $7 + 3(x - 5)$

Q9.   Find 90% of 90.

Q10.   Solve: $-3x < 12$

For Problems 1 through 16,
a.   Sketch the graph of the relation,
b.   Calculate the focal radius and plot the two foci,
c.   Confirm your sketch by plotting the *original* equation, using PLOT CONIC on the accompanying computer disk, or similar program.

1. $4x^2 + 9y^2 - 16x + 90y + 205 = 0$

2. $4x^2 + 36y^2 + 40x - 288y + 532 = 0$

3. $49x^2 + 16y^2 + 98x - 64y - 671 = 0$

4. $25x^2 + 4y^2 - 150x + 32y + 189 = 0$

5. $x^2 + 4y^2 + 10x + 24y + 45 = 0$

6. $16x^2 + y^2 - 128x - 20y + 292 = 0$

7. $25x^2 + 9y^2 + 50x - 36y - 164 < 0$

8. $4x^2 + 36y^2 + 48x + 216y + 324 \geq 0$

9. $16x^2 + 25y^2 - 300y + 500 = 0$

10. $36x^2 + 9y^2 - 216x = 0$

11. $100x^2 + 36y^2 > 3600$

12. $25x^2 + 49y^2 \leq 1225$

13. $12x^2 + y^2 = 48$ 14. $x^2 + 6y^2 = 25$

15. $5x^2 + 8y^2 = 77$ 16. $11x^2 + 5y^2 = 224$

17.   ***Stadium Problem***   Suppose that you are Chief Mathematician for Ornery & Sly Construction Company. Your company has a contract to build a football stadium in the form of two concentric ellipses, with the field inside the inner ellipse, and the seats between the two ellipses. The seats are in the intersection of the graphs of

$$x^2 + 4y^2 \geq 100 \quad \text{and} \quad 25x^2 + 36y^2 \leq 3600,$$

where each unit on the graph represents 10 meters.
a.   Draw a graph of the seating area.
b.   From a handbook, you find that the area of an elliptical region is πab, where a and b are the semi-axes, and $\pi \approx 3.14159$. The Engineering Department estimates that each seat occupies 0.8 square meter. What is the seating capacity of the stadium?

18.   Show that the equation for an ellipse,

$$\left(\frac{x - h}{r_x}\right)^2 + \left(\frac{y - k}{r_y}\right)^2 = 1,$$

reduces to the equation of a *circle* if $r_x = r_y$.

19. *Introduction to Hyperbolas*   The ellipses you have plotted in this section have equations in which the x^2 and y^2 terms have the same sign. In this problem you will find out what the graph looks like if they have *opposite* signs. Do the following things for the relation whose equation is

$$9x^2 - 16y^2 = 144,$$

a. Solve the equation for y in terms of x.
b. Explain why there will be *no* real values of y for $-4 < x < 4$.
c. Explain why there will be *two* values of y for each value of x when $x > 4$ or $x < -4$.
d. Make a table of values of y for each integer value of x from 4 to 8, inclusive, finding decimal approximations from square root tables or by calculator, where necessary.
e. Explain why you can use the *same* table of values of y for values of x between -4 and -8.
f. Plot a graph of the relation from $x = -4$ to $x = -8$, and from $x = 4$ to $x = 8$.
g. On the same Cartesian coordinate system, plot graphs of the lines

$$y = \frac{3}{4}x \quad \text{and} \quad y = -\frac{3}{4}x.$$

If your graph in part f is correct, then it should have these two lines as diagonal asymptotes. The graph is called a *hyperbola,* and is a non-closed curve with *two* "branches."

9-4 | HYPERBOLAS

In the last section you learned that an ellipse has an equation in which the x^2 and y^2 coefficients are unequal, but have the same sign. If x^2 and y^2 have *opposite* signs, such as

$$9x^2 - 16y^2 = 144,$$

then the graph looks like that in Figure 9-4a, and is called a *hyperbola.* You may have discovered this fact already if you worked Problem 19 in Exercise 9-3.

Objective:
Given the equation of a hyperbola, be able to sketch its graph *quickly*.

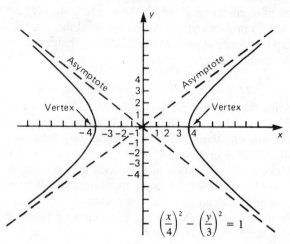

$$\left(\frac{x}{4}\right)^2 - \left(\frac{y}{3}\right)^2 = 1$$

Figure 9-4a _____

Hyperbolas have two disconnected branches. Each branch approaches diagonal asymptotes. You can see *why* by transforming the equation so that y is by itself on the left side.

$-16y^2 = -9x^2 + 144$ Subtract $9x^2$.

$16y^2 = 9(x^2 - 16)$ Multiply by -1 and
                            factor out 9.

$y = \pm\frac{3}{4}\sqrt{x^2 - 16}$ Divide by 16, then take
                            the square root.

Two observations about the graph may be made from this equation:

1. There are *no* real values of y when x is between -4 and 4 because the radicand, $x^2 - 16$, would be *negative*. This fact explains why the graph is split into two branches.
2. As x becomes larger, the difference between $\sqrt{x^2 - 16}$ and $\sqrt{x^2}$ gets close to zero. For example, if $x = 100$, then

$$\sqrt{x^2 - 16} = \sqrt{10000 - 16}$$
$$= \sqrt{9984}$$
$$\approx 99.92,$$

while $\sqrt{x^2} = \sqrt{10000} = 100$. Consequently, the larger x gets, the closer y gets to $\pm\frac{3}{4}\sqrt{x^2}$, or $y \approx \pm\frac{3}{4}x$. The lines $y = \pm\frac{3}{4}x$ are thus *asymptotes* of the graph. Their slopes are $\frac{3}{4}$ and $-\frac{3}{4}$.

The 4 and 3 in the slopes of the asymptotes can be made to show up in the equation by making the right member equal 1.

$$9x^2 - 16y^2 = 144 \quad \text{Given equation}$$

$$\frac{x^2}{16} - \frac{y^2}{9} = 1 \qquad \text{Divide by 144.}$$

$$\left(\frac{x}{4}\right)^2 - \left(\frac{y}{3}\right)^2 = 1$$

In this form, the 4 under the x is in the same position as the x-radius for an ellipse. The 3 under the y is in the same position as the y-radius. As shown in Figure 9-4b, the x-radius is, in this case, the distance from the center to the vertex of the hyperbola in the x-direction. The y-radius does not show up directly on the graph. It is the distance from the vertex to the *asymptote*, either upward or downward.

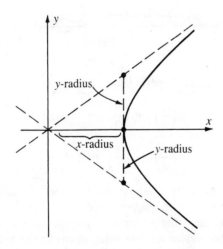

Figure 9-4b

If the signs had been reversed, like this,

$$-\left(\frac{x}{4}\right)^2 + \left(\frac{y}{3}\right)^2 = 1,$$

then the graph would have two branches opening in the y-direction. The asymptotes would still have slopes $\frac{3}{4}$ and $-\frac{3}{4}$. But the vertices would be 3 units in from the center in the y-direction since the y-radius is 3. The x-radius would tell how far to go in the x-direction to get from the vertex to the asymptotes. The graph of this hyperbola is shown in Figure 9-4c.

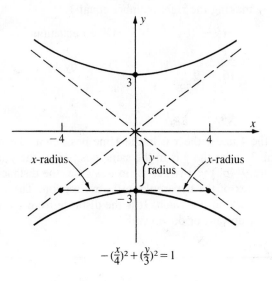

$$-\left(\tfrac{x}{4}\right)^2 + \left(\tfrac{y}{3}\right)^2 = 1$$

Figure 9-4c _____

The equations for the two hyperbolas,

$$-\left(\frac{x}{4}\right)^2 + \left(\frac{y}{3}\right)^2 = 1 \quad \text{and}$$

$$\left(\frac{x}{4}\right)^2 - \left(\frac{y}{3}\right)^2 = 1$$

are alike except that the signs are reversed on the left side. The two result-ing hyperbolas are said to be *conjugates* of each other. As shown in Fig-ure 9-4d, they have the same asymptotes and the same *x*- and *y*-radii. But one opens in the *y*-direction and the other opens in the *x*-direction. When the equation is written in the form above, with 1 on the right side, the hyperbola opens in the direction of the squared term that has the *positive* sign.

The axis that goes across the hyperbola, from vertex to vertex, is called the *transverse* axis. The other one is called the *conjugate axis* because it is the axis of the conjugate hyperbola.

There is a geometrical definition of hyperbola similar to that of ellipse. For any given point on an ellipse, the sum of its distances from the two foci is a constant. Hyperbolas also have two foci. In this case, the *difference* be-tween the two distances is constant.

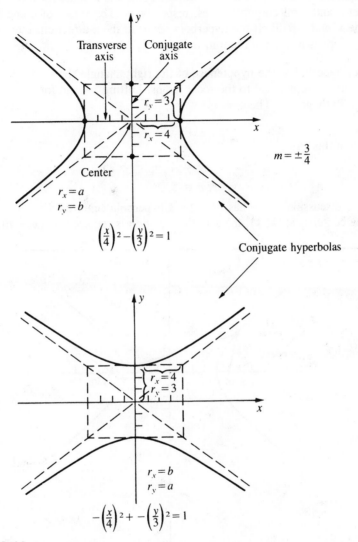

Figure 9-4d

DEFINITION

GEOMETRICAL DEFINITION OF HYPERBOLA
A **hyperbola** is a set of points in a plane. For each point (x, y) on the hyperbola, the *difference* between its distances from two fixed foci is a constant.

Figure 9-4e illustrates this definition. Let a and b stand for the semi-transverse and semi-conjugate axes, respectively. The values of a and b will be the x- and y-radii. If the hyperbola opens in the x-direction, then $a = r_x$. If it opens in the y-direction, then $a = r_y$.

For hyperbolas, the hypotenuse of the right triangle shown on the right in Figure 9-4e is equal to the focal radius. Letting c stand for focal radius, the Pythagorean Theorem gives

$$c^2 = a^2 + b^2.$$

So in this case,

$$c^2 = 4^2 + 3^2 = 25$$
$$\therefore c = 5.$$

The discussion above has been for a hyperbola centered at the origin. If the center is at (h, k), the x in the equation is replaced by $(x - h)$, and the

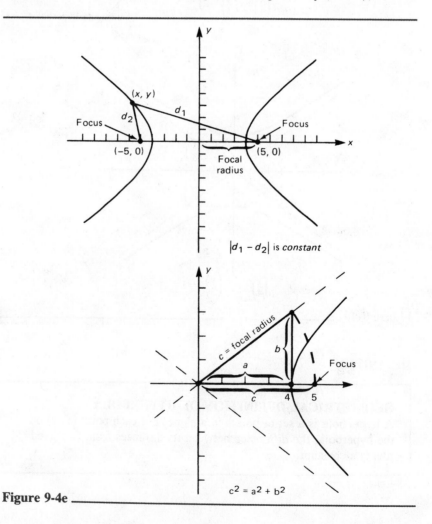

Figure 9-4e

y is replaced by $(y - k)$, as for the circle and ellipse. The following is a summary of the above information.

CONCLUSIONS

The general equation of a hyperbola is

$$\left(\frac{x - h}{r_x}\right)^2 - \left(\frac{y - k}{r_y}\right)^2 = 1$$

or

$$-\left(\frac{x - h}{r_x}\right)^2 + \left(\frac{y - k}{r_y}\right)^2 = 1.$$

The hyperbola opens in the x-direction if the sign in front of the term containing x is plus.
The hyperbola opens in the y-direction if the sign in front of the term containing y is plus.
The slope of the asymptotes is always $\pm \dfrac{(y\text{-radius})}{(x\text{-radius})}$.

If:

a is the length of semi-major axis,
b is the length of semi-minor axis,
c is the focal radius, and
d_1 and d_2 are the distances from a point (x, y) on the hyperbola to the two foci,

Then:

$|d_1 - d_2| = 2a =$ length of transverse axis.
$c^2 = a^2 + b^2$

If the center is at the origin, then $(h, k) = (0, 0)$, and these equations reduce to

$$\left(\frac{x}{r_x}\right)^2 - \left(\frac{y}{r_y}\right)^2 = 1 \quad \text{or} \quad -\left(\frac{x}{r_x}\right)^2 + \left(\frac{y}{r_y}\right)^2 = 1$$

EXAMPLE 1

Sketch a graph of

$$9x^2 - 4y^2 + 90x + 32y + 197 = 0.$$

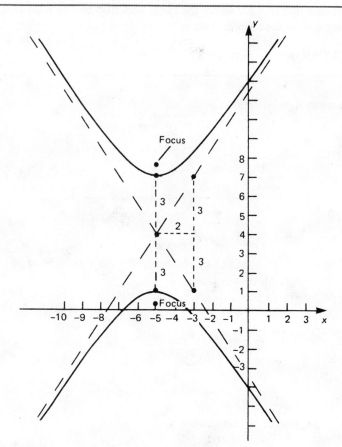

Figure 9-4f

Solution:

First transform the equation by completing the square.

$$9(x^2 + 10x \quad) - 4(y^2 - 8y \quad) = -197$$

$$9(x^2 + 10x + 25) - 4(y^2 - 8y + 16) = -197 + 9 \cdot 25 - 4 \cdot 16$$

$$9(x + 5)^2 - 4(y - 4)^2 = -36$$

To make the right member equal to +1, divide each member by −36, getting

$$-\frac{(x + 5)^2}{2^2} + \frac{(y - 4)^2}{3^2} = 1$$

after simplification.

The graph is a *hyperbola*, opening in the y-direction, centered at (−5, 4). The x-radius is asymptotes of slopes $\pm\frac{3}{2}$, and vertices which are ±3 units from the center in the y-direction.

Using this information, you should first locate the center, then draw in the asymptotes with the proper slope. The only actual points you need plot are the two vertices. With this information, you can sketch a remarkably good hyperbola, as shown in Figure 9-4f.   ■

EXAMPLE 2

Find and plot the foci of the hyperbola in Example 1.

Solution:
Since the focal radius, c, is given by $c^2 = a^2 + b^2$, you can locate the foci.

$$c^2 = 2^2 + 3^2$$
$$= 13$$
$$\therefore c = \sqrt{13} \approx 3.61$$

The foci are ± 3.61 units from the center, as shown in Figure 9-4f.   ■

The following exercise is designed to give you practice in sketching hyperbolas rapidly.

EXERCISE 9-4

Do These Quickly

The following problems are intended to refresh your skills. You should be able to do all 10 in less than 5 minutes.

Tell what figure the graph will be.

Q1. $3x^2 + 4y^2 = 17$

Q2. $3x^2 - 4y^2 = 17$

Q3. $3x^2 + 3y^2 = 17$

Q4. $3x + 3y = 17$

Q5. $y = 3x^2 + 17$

Answer the questions.

Q6. Evaluate $\sqrt[5]{32}$.

Q7. Simplify: $-3x(x + 5) - 17$

Q8. Multiply: $(3x + 4y)(3x - 4y)$

Q9.   Factor: $(x + 3)^2 - 16$

Q10.   What kind of function has the general equation $y = a \cdot b^x$?

For Problems 1 through 18,
a.   Complete the square (if necessary), find the center, draw the asymptotes, plot the vertices, then sketch the graph.
b.   Calculate the focal radius, and plot the foci.
c.   Confirm your sketch by plotting the original equation, using PLOT CONIC on the accompanying disk, or similar program.

1. $25x^2 - 16y^2 - 100x - 96y - 444 = 0$

2. $4x^2 - 9y^2 + 16x + 108y - 344 = 0$

3. $25x^2 - 9y^2 + 300x - 126y + 684 = 0$

4. $4x^2 - 36y^2 - 40x + 216y - 80 = 0$

5. $x^2 - y^2 + 4x + 16y - 69 = 0$

6. $x^2 - y^2 - 14x - 8y + 37 = 0$

7. $9x^2 - 4y^2 - 54x - 16y - 79 = 0$

8. $x^2 - 4y^2 + 4x + 32y - 96 = 0$

9. $9x^2 - y^2 - 90x + 4y + 302 = 0$

10. $25x^2 - 4y^2 + 200x - 8y + 796 = 0$

11. $16x^2 - 9y^2 + 144 = 0$

12. $25x^2 - 144y^2 - 3600 = 0$

13. $4x^2 - 5y^2 = 16$ 14. $27x^2 - 4y^2 = -36$

15. $16x^2 - 3y^2 = -11$ 16. $5x^2 - 7y^2 = 17$

17. $9x^2 - y^2 = 0$ 18. $4x^2 - y^2 = 0$

9-5   PARABOLAS

You recall that a quadratic equation has the general equation

$$y = ax^2 + bx + c.$$

The graph is a parabola with its axis of symmetry vertical, as shown in the left of Figure 9-5a. If the x and y are reversed,

$$x = ay^2 + by + c,$$

the parabola has a *horizontal* axis of symmetry. The right part of Figure 9-5a shows how the graph might look.

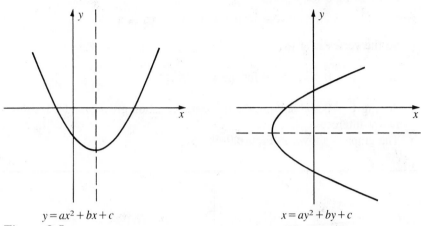

$$y = ax^2 + bx + c \qquad\qquad x = ay^2 + by + c$$

Figure 9-5a

All the graphing techniques you learned in Chapter 5 apply, but the roles of x and y are switched. Vertex form looks like this:

$$x - h = a(y - k)^2$$

The equation can be transformed to this form by completing the square. The quick way of finding the vertex applies, but to y instead of x. The y-coordinate, k, of the vertex is given by

$$k = -\frac{b}{2a}.$$

In this section you will refresh your memory about graphs of parabolas by sketching some that open in the x-direction, as well as the more familiar y-direction.

Objective:

Given the equation of a parabola, find the vertex and intercepts, sketch the graph, and check by computer graphics.

EXAMPLE

For $x = -2y^2 + 12y - 10$
a. Find the vertex and intercepts.
b. Sketch the graph.
c. Confirm your results by computer graphics.

Solution:
a. The y-coordinate of the vertex is

$$k = -\frac{12}{2(-2)} = 3.$$

Substituting 3 for y gives

$$x = -2(9) + 12(3) - 10 = 8$$

So the vertex is at (8, 3).

Setting $y = 0$ gives -10 for the x-intercept.

Setting $x = 0$ and solving the quadratic equation gives 5 and 1 for the two y-intercepts.

b. The graph is shown in Figure 9-5b.

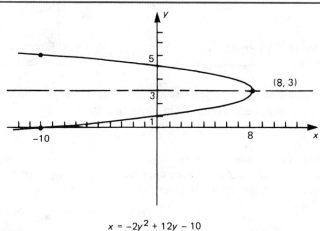

$$x = -2y^2 + 12y - 10$$

Figure 9-5b

c. To use the computer program PLOT CONIC on the accompanying disk, you must first have all terms on the left side and 0 on the right.

$$x = -2y^2 + 12y - 10$$

$$2y^2 + x - 12y + 10 = 0$$

When the program calls for the coefficients, you enter

$$0, 0, 2, 1, -12, 10$$

because the x^2 and xy terms have coefficients of 0. The graph looks similar to Figure 9-5b, thus confirming the sketch.   ■

You can tell just by looking at the equation if the graph is a parabola. The equation will have only *one* squared term. If the x^2 term is missing, the graph opens in the x-direction. If the y^2 term is missing, it opens in the y-direction.

In the next section you will learn how to tell what the graph of *any* quadratic relation is, just by looking at its equation. You will also learn that parabolas, too, have a geometrical definition involving a focus.

EXERCISE 9-5

Do These Quickly

The following problems are intended to refresh your skills. You should be able to do all 10 in less than 5 minutes.

What will the graph be?

Q1. $x^2 + y^2 = 25$

Q2. $x^2 - y^2 = 25$

Q3. $x^2 - y^2 = -25$

Q4. $x^2 + y^2 = -25$

Q5. $x + y = 25$

Q6. $x - y = 25$

Answer the questions.

Q7.   What percent of 200 is 30?

Q8.   If you go 50 miles in $2\frac{1}{2}$ hours, what is your average speed?

Q9.   Divide 90 by $\frac{1}{3}$.

Q10.   Evaluate the complex number i^7.

For Problems 1 through 10,
a.   Find the vertex and intercepts.
b.   Sketch the graph.
c.   Confirm your sketch using PLOT CONIC from the accompanying disk, or another suitable graphing program.

Find the vertex and intercepts of the following parabolas, and sketch the graph. Find decimal approximations for any radicals you encounter.

1. $x = y^2 - 4y + 3$ 2. $x = y^2 + 2y - 3$

3. $x = -3y^2 - 12y - 5$ 4. $x = -5y^2 + 30y + 11$

5. $x = \frac{1}{2}y^2 + 3y + 4$ 6. $x = \frac{1}{3}y^2 - 2y - 9$

7. $y = -4x^2 + 20x - 16$ 8. $y = \frac{1}{5}x^2 + 2x - \frac{11}{5}$

9. $x = \dfrac{1}{4}y^2$ 10. $x = -\dfrac{1}{10}y^2$

For Problems 11 through 14, sketch the graph quickly.

11. $y = x^2$ 12. $y = -x^2$

13. $x = -y^2$ 14. $x = y^2$

15. *Parabola Conclusions Problem*   From the graphs in Problems 11 through 14, what feature of the equation of a parabola tells you that it opens
    a.   in the positive y-direction?
    b.   in the positive x-direction?
    c.   in the negative y-direction?
    d.   in the negative x-direction?

9-6 | EQUATIONS FROM GEOMETRICAL DEFINITIONS

You have learned geometrical definitions for circles, ellipses, and hyperbolas in Sections 9-2, 9-3, and 9-4. In this section you will learn a geometrical definition for a parabola. You will also learn that there are *other* geometrical definitions for all four kinds of graphs. Using these definitions, you will derive equations for the graphs.

Objective:
Given the geometrical definition of a set of points, derive an equation relating x and y. If the equation is *quadratic*, tell whether the graph is a circle, ellipse, hyperbola, or parabola.

Circles, ellipses, hyperbolas, and parabolas have a *family* name that comes from their relationship to slices ("sections") of a cone. As shown in Figure 9-6a, a complete cone has two halves, called "nappes." If a plane cuts the cone *parallel* to one of its elements, the section is a *parabola*. If the plane exceeds the parallel position, it will cut *both* nappes, forming a *hyperbola* (from the Greek work "hyperbole," meaning "to exceed"). If the plane does not tilt far enough, one of the nappes will be left out, and the graph will be an ellipse (from the Greek word "ellipsis," meaning "to leave out"). A circle is formed by a cutting plane perpendicular to the axis of the cone.

Because of the properties stated above, circles, ellipses, hyperbolas, and parabolas are given the name *conic sections*. Perhaps you have seen vari-

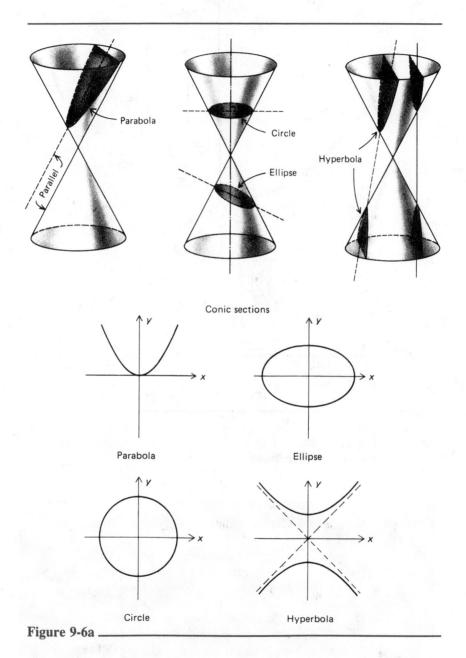

Conic sections

Parabola

Ellipse

Circle

Hyperbola

Figure 9-6a

ous conic sections when the cone of light from a lamp is cut by the plane of a wall or ceiling (Figure 9-6b).

The second part of the objective may now be stated, "If the equation is quadratic, tell which *conic section* the graph is." In order to do this, you should pull together what you have learned about the coefficients of the

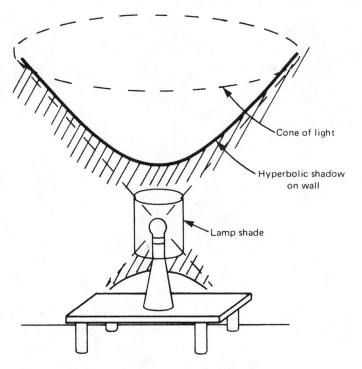

Cone of light

Hyperbolic shadow
on wall

Lamp shade

Figure 9-6b

squared terms in the equation of a quadratic relation. The following table should help refresh your memory.

RECOGNITION OF CONIC SECTIONS FROM THEIR EQUATIONS

Circle: x^2 and y^2 terms have *equal* coefficients.

Ellipse: x^2 and y^2 terms have *unequal* coefficients, but the *same* sign.

Hyperbola: x^2 and y^2 terms have *opposite* signs.

Parabola: Equation has only *one* squared term. If the x^2 term is missing, the parabola opens in the x-direction. If the y^2 term is missing, the parabola opens in the y-direction (a quadratic *function*).

Note: All of the above conclusions assume that there is *no* xy-term. If there *is* an xy-term, you must use the discriminant to identify the conic section, as explained in Exercise 9-7, Problem 5.

EXAMPLE

A *parabola* is defined to be a set of coplanar points, each of which is the *same* distance from a fixed focus as it is from a fixed straight line (called the "directrix"). Find the equation of the parabola whose focus is $(2, 3)$ and whose directrix is the line $y = -7$. Show that the equation has the form $y = ax^2 + bx + c$.

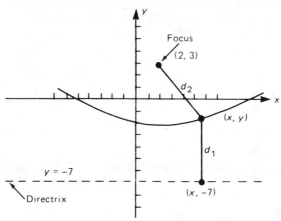

Figure 9-6c

The first step is to draw a picture showing the given focus and directrix (Figure 9-6c). Then pick a point (*any* point!) that could be on the graph, and label it (x, y). By the definition of parabola, above,

$$d_1 = d_2.$$

The point where the segment labeled d_1 meets the line $y = -7$ has coordinates $(x, -7)$. So d_1 and d_2 can be found using the Distance Formula. Substituting the appropriate coordinates into the equation $d_1 = d_2$ gives

$$\sqrt{(x - x)^2 + (y + 7)^2} = \sqrt{(x - 2)^2 + (y - 3)^2},$$

which reduces to

$$|y + 7| = \sqrt{(x - 2)^2 + (y - 3)^2}.$$

Squaring both members transforms this to a *polynomial* equation,

$$y^2 + 14y + 49 = (x - 2)^2 + (y - 3)^2.$$

Expanding the binomial squares on the right gives

$$y^2 + 14y + 49 = x^2 - 4x + 4 + y^2 - 6y + 9.$$

Note that the y^2 terms will cancel, leaving only *one* squared term. The equation can be transformed to

$$20y = x^2 - 4x - 36,$$

or

$$y = \frac{1}{20}x^2 - \frac{1}{5}x - \frac{9}{5}.$$

Since this last equation has the form $y = ax^2 + bx + c$, you can see that this set of points described geometrically fits your old definition of a parabola as the graph of a quadratic function. ■

The exercise which follows is designed to give you practice finding equations and identifying graphs from given geometrical definitions.

EXERCISE 9-6

For Problems 1 through 12, find a *polynomial* equation with *integer* coefficients for the set of coplanar points described. Tell whether or not the graph is a conic section and, if it is, tell *which* conic section.

1. For each point, its distance from the fixed point $(-3, 0)$ is *twice* its distance from the fixed point $(3, 0)$.

2. For each point, its distance from the fixed point $(0, -5)$ is $\frac{1}{3}$ of its distance from the fixed point $(0, 5)$.

3. For each point, its distance from the fixed point $(4, 3)$ is 3 times its distance from the fixed point $(-1, 2)$.

4. For each point, its distance from the fixed point $(-1, -3)$ is $\frac{1}{2}$ of its distance from the fixed point $(5, -8)$.

5. Each point is *twice* as far from the line $x = 3$ as it is from the line $y = -2$.

6. Each point is *three times* as far from the line $y = 5$ as it is from the line $x = 1$.

7. Each point is *equidistant* from the point $(3, -4)$ and the line $y = 2$.

8. Each point is *equidistant* from the point $(2, 5)$ and the line $x = -3$.

9. For each point, its distance from the point $(-3, 1)$ is *half* its distance from the line $y = 4$.

10. For each point, its distance from the point $(-4, -1)$ is $\frac{2}{3}$ times its distance from the line $x = -5$.

11. For each point, its distance from the point $(0, 3)$ is $\frac{3}{2}$ times its distance from the line $y = -3$.

12. For each point, its distance from the point $(4, 0)$ is *twice* its distance from the line $x = -4$.

13. Use the geometric definition of an ellipse (Section 9-3) to show that the ellipse with foci $(4, 0)$ and $(-4, 0)$ and major axis 10 units long is

$$9x^2 + 25y^2 = 225.$$

14. Use the geometric definition of hyperbola (Section 9-4) to show that the hyperbola with foci $(5, 0)$ and $(-5, 0)$ and transverse axis (i.e., the distance between vertices) 8 units long is

$$9x^2 - 16y^2 = 144.$$

15. Show that another definition of a circle is a set of points for each of which its distance from the fixed point $(f, 0)$ is c times its distance from the fixed point $(-f, 0)$.

16. Find a polynomial equation of a set of points for each of which the distance from the fixed point $(f, 0)$ is e times its distance from the vertical line $x = -f$, where e stands for a constant. Show that the graph will be an *ellipse* if $0 < e < 1$; a *parabola* if $e = 1$; and a *hyperbola* if $e > 1$.

17. The geometrical definitions in Problem 16 are called the "focus-directrix" definitions of the conic sections. The straight line is called the "directrix," the fixed point is called the "focus," and the constant e is called the "eccentricity." What would be the eccentricity for a *circle*? Where would the directrix be for a circle?

18. A parabola may be thought of as having a *second* focus, just like ellipses and hyperbolas do. Where do you suppose this second focus would be? (Remember the cones and the lamp shade of Figures 9-6a and 9-6b.)

9-7   QUADRATIC RELATIONS—xy-TERM

In your investigation of quadratic relations, you have not yet encountered one for which the equation had a non-zero xy-term. In this section you will find out that the graphs are still conic sections, but the xy-term *rotates* the graph and affects its *shape*.

Objective:
Determine by actual plotting what effects the xy-term in the equation of a quadratic relation has on the graph.

The following exercise is designed to accomplish this objective.

EXERCISE 9-7

1. Plot a graph of $x^2 + y^2 = 9$.

2. The following equations differ from the one in Problem 1 only by the addition of increasingly larger xy-terms:
   i. $x^2 + xy + y^2 = 9$.
   ii. $x^2 + 4xy + y^2 = 9$.
   a. For each relation, select values of x, calculate the corresponding values of y, and plot the graph.
   b. For each graph, tell which of the conic sections is plotted.
   c. Does the xy-term affect the x and y-intercepts? Explain.

3. *Computer Graphics for xy-Term Problem*   Use the program PLOT CONIC from the accompanying disk to draw the graphs of:
   a. $x^2 + y^2 - 10x - 8y + 16 = 0$
   b. $x^2 + xy + y^2 - 10x - 8y + 16 = 0$
   c. $x^2 + 2xy + y^2 - 10x - 8y + 16 = 0$
   d. $x^2 + 4xy + y^2 - 10x - 8y + 16 = 0$

4. *Identification Problem*   Tell which conic section each graph in Problem 3 will be.

5. *Discriminant Problem*   Use your graphs from Problems 1, 2, and 3 to answer the following questions:
   a. When there is an xy-term in the equation, can you still tell by looking at the coefficients of x^2 and y^2 just which of the conic sections the graph will be?
   b. The equation $Ax^2 + Bxy + Cy^2 + Dx + Ey + F = 0$ has a *discriminant*, which equals

   $$B^2 - 4AC.$$

   For each of the equations in Problems 1 and 3, calculate the discriminant.
   c. Show that the *sign* of the discriminant tells the following about the kind of conic section:

   > Circle or Ellipse—discriminant < 0.
   > Parabola—discriminant $= 0$.
   > Hyperbola—discriminant > 0.

6. Prove that the graph of an inverse variation function is a hyperbola.

9-8 | SYSTEMS OF QUADRATICS

In Chapter 4 you learned how to solve systems of two linear equations
with two variables. The answer tells the point where the two straight-line
graphs cross. There are situations in the real world where it is important
to know where the graphs of *quadratic* relations cross. For example, the
paths of spaceships, planets, comets, and so forth, which travel under the
action of gravity, turn out to be circles, ellipses, hyperbolas, or parabolas.
Finding the point where a spaceship crosses the path of the planet it is approaching is of fundamental importance! Ships at sea use the LORAN system (for *LO*ng *RA*nge *N*avigation) to find their location by receiving radio
signals which locate them on several hyperbolas. The intersection point of
the hyperbolas tells the ship's position (See Figure 9-8b).

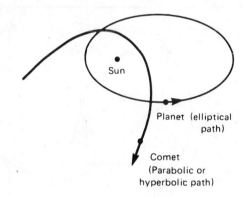

Sun

Planet (elliptical
path)

Comet
(Parabolic or
hyperbolic path)

Figure 9-8a _____

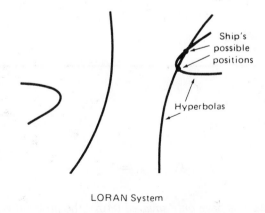

Ship's
possible
positions

Hyperbolas

LORAN System

Figure 9-8b _____

Objective:

Given a system of two equations in two variables, where at least one equation is quadratic (and none are higher degree), be able to:

a. Calculate the solution set of the system.
b. Show that your answer is reasonable by graphing.

As shown in Figure 9-8c, the graphs of a linear and a quadratic equation may cross in *two* places and the graphs of two quadratics may cross in *four* places. The technique for finding the solutions is the same as for systems of linears—eliminate one variable, solve the resulting equation for the other, then substitute back to find the corresponding value of the first variable. However, the algebraic operations get much more complicated. At worst, solving these systems may take just about every algebraic skill you have ever learned!

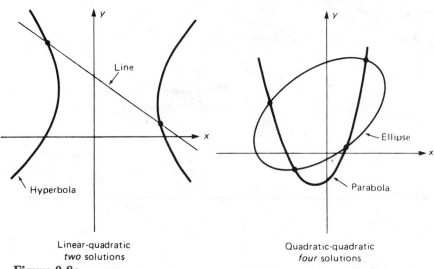

Linear-quadratic
two solutions

Quadratic-quadratic
four solutions

Figure 9-8c

EXAMPLE 1

Solve the system

$$9x^2 + 32y^2 = 324 \qquad \underline{\qquad} \quad ①,$$
$$3x^2 - y^2 = 3 \qquad \underline{\qquad} \quad ②.$$

Solution:

Since both equations have *only squared* terms, the problem is almost as easy as solving a system of two linears. You would multiply both members of Equation ② by -3 and add the resulting equation to Equation ①:

$$-9x^2 + 3y^2 = -9$$
$$\underline{9x^2 + 32y^2 = 324}$$
$$35y^2 = 315$$
$$y^2 = 9$$
$$y = \pm3.$$

These values of y may be substituted into either of the equations one at a time. Substituting into Equation ② gives

If $y = 3$,	If $y = -3$,
$3x^2 - 9 = 3$	$3x^2 - 9 = 3$
$3x^2 = 12$	$3x^2 = 12$
$x^2 = 4$	$x^2 = 4$
$x = \pm2$	$x = \pm2$

$$\therefore S = \{(2, 3), (2, -3), (-2, 3), (-2, -3)\}.$$

The solution set can be checked graphically. By sketching or computer graphics, you find that Equation ① gives an ellipse, centered at the origin, with x-radius $= \sqrt{\frac{324}{9}} = 6$, and y-radius $= \sqrt{\frac{324}{32}} \approx \sqrt{10} \approx 3.2$. Equation ② gives a hyperbola, centered at the origin, opening in the x-direction, with asymptotes of slope $\pm\sqrt{3} \approx \pm1.7$, and vertices 1 unit from the center. The graphs are shown in Figure 9-8d. You can see that the four points you have calculated are actually the points of intersection.

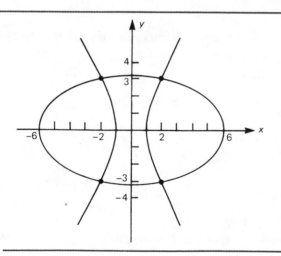

Figure 9-8d

EXAMPLE 2

Solve the system using the "substitution" technique.

$$7x^2 - 5y^2 + 20y = 3$$
$$21x^2 + 5y^2 = 209$$

Solution:

The linear combination technique used in Example 1 works only in special cases. A more general technique of eliminating a variable, called "substitution," works for any system of quadratics no matter how complicated. Starting with

$$7x^2 - 5y^2 + 20y = 3 \quad\text{——}\quad ①,$$
$$21x^2 + 5y^2 + \quad\;\; = 209 \quad\text{——}\quad ②,$$

you could solve Equation ② for x in terms of y, getting

$$21x^2 = 209 - 5y^2$$
$$x^2 = \frac{1}{21}(209 - 5y^2) \quad\text{——}\quad ③.$$

Substituting $\frac{1}{21}(209 - 5y^2)$ for x^2 in Equation ① gives

$$7 \cdot \frac{1}{21}(209 - 5y^2) - 5y^2 + 20y = 3,$$

which reduces to

$$y^2 - 3y - 10 = 0.$$

Factoring and solving for y gives

$$(y - 5)(y + 2) = 0,$$
$$y = 5 \quad\text{or}\quad y = -2.$$

These values of y may now be substituted, one at a time, into Equation ③ to find x.

If $y = 5$,	If $y = -2$,
$x^2 = \frac{1}{21}(209 - 125)$	$x^2 = \frac{1}{21}(209 - 20)$
$x^2 = 4$	$x^2 = 9$
$x = \pm 2$	$x = \pm 3$

$$\therefore S = \{(2, 5), (-2, 5), (3, -2), (-3, -2)\}. \qquad \blacksquare$$

EXAMPLE 3

Check the answer to Example 2 by graphing.

Solution:

The check is most easily done by computer graphics. Otherwise, by completing the square, Equation ① can be transformed into

$$-\frac{x^2}{\left(\dfrac{17}{7}\right)} + \frac{(y - 2)^2}{\left(\dfrac{17}{5}\right)} = 1.$$

This is a hyperbola, centered at $(0, 2)$, opening vertically, with asymptotes of slope $\pm \dfrac{\sqrt{\frac{17}{5}}}{\sqrt{\frac{17}{7}}} = \pm\sqrt{\frac{7}{5}} \approx \pm 1.2$.

Equation ② can be transformed to

$$\frac{x^2}{\left(\dfrac{209}{21}\right)} + \frac{y^2}{\left(\dfrac{209}{5}\right)} = 1.$$

This graph is an ellipse with y-radius of $\sqrt{\frac{209}{5}} \approx \sqrt{42} \approx 6.5$, and x-radius of $\sqrt{\frac{209}{21}} \approx \sqrt{10} \approx 3.2$.

The graphs are shown in Figure 9-8e. As you can see, the intersection points are $(2, 5)$, $(-2, 5)$, $(3, -2)$, and $(-3, -2)$.

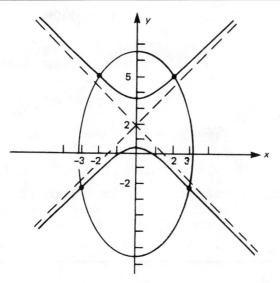

Figure 9-8e

EXAMPLE 4

Solve the system

$$x^2 + y^2 - 4x + 2y = 20,$$
$$4x + 3y = 5.$$

Solution:
If one of the two equations is linear, then the linear combination technique seldom works and you must use substitution.

$$x^2 + y^2 - 4x + 2y = 20 \quad \underline{\qquad} \quad ①$$
$$4x + 3y = 5 \quad \underline{\qquad} \quad ②$$

Solving ② for y in terms of x gives

$$y = \frac{1}{3}(5 - 4x) \underline{\quad\quad} \quad ③$$

Substituting $\frac{1}{3}(5 - 4x)$ for y in Equation ① gives

$$x^2 + \left[\frac{1}{3}(5 - 4x)\right]^2 - 4x + 2\left[\frac{1}{3}(5 - 4x)\right] = 20.$$

Simplifying and multiplying each member by 9 to eliminate the fractions gives

$$9x^2 + 25 - 40x + 16x^2 - 36x + 30 - 24x = 180$$
$$25x^2 - 100x - 125 = 0$$
$$x^2 - 4x - 5 = 0$$
$$(x - 5)(x + 1) = 0$$
$$x = 5 \quad \text{or} \quad x = -1.$$

Substituting these answers one at a time into the *linear* equation, or better still, into Equation ③, gives

$$\text{If } x = 5, \qquad\qquad \text{If } x = -1,$$
$$y = \frac{1}{3}(5 - 20) = -5 \qquad y = \frac{1}{3}(5 + 4) = 3$$
$$\therefore S = \{(5, -5), (-1, 3)\}.$$

By completing the square, you can find that the graph of Equation ① is a circle of radius 5, centered at $(2, -1)$. The second graph is a straight line of slope $-\frac{4}{3}$ and y-intercept $\frac{5}{3}$. The graphs are shown in Figure 9-8f.

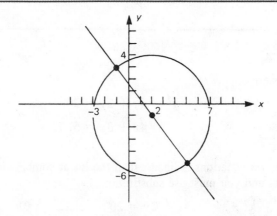

Figure 9-8f

If both equations have squared and also linear terms, or xy-terms, the job of solving the system becomes much more complicated. Solving one equation for y in terms of x involves a clever use of the quadratic formula. The resulting equation will be *fourth* degree in x, and will have four solutions. Problem 30 in the following exercise leads you stepwise through the solution of one such system. ∎

EXERCISE 9-8

Do These Quickly

The following problems are intended to refresh your skills. You should be able to do all 10 in less than 5 minutes.

What will the graph be?

Q1. $x^2 + y^2 = 100$

Q2. $x^2 + 9y^2 = 100$

Q3. $x^2 + 5xy + 9y^2 = 100$

Q4. $x^2 + 6xy + 9y^2 = 100$

Q5. $x^2 + 7xy + 9y^2 = 100$

Q6. $x^2 + 5xy - 9y^2 = 100$

Sketch the graph:

Q7. A system of independent linear equations

Q8. A system of inconsistent linear equations

Q9. An increasing exponential function

Q10. $x = y^2$

For Problems 1 through 26,
a. calculate the solution set, and
b. demonstrate that your solutions are right by drawing the graphs, preferably by computer.

1. $2x^2 + 5y^2 = 98$
    $2x^2 - y^2 = 2$

2. $x^2 - y^2 = -16$
    $8x^2 - 3y^2 = -3$

3. $x^2 + y^2 = 25$
    $y - x^2 = -5$

4. $4x^2 + y^2 = 100$
    $4x - y^2 = -20$

5. $3x^2 + 7y^2 = 187$
   $3x^2 - 7y = 47$

6. $9x^2 + y^2 = 85$
   $2x^2 - 3y^2 = 6$

7. $x^2 + 2y^2 = 33$
   $x^2 + y^2 + 2x = 19$

8. $5x^2 - 3y^2 = -22$
   $5x^2 - 6y^2 + 12y = -85$

9. $3x^2 - 5y^2 = 22$
   $3x^2 - y^2 - 6x = 8$

10. $x^2 + y^2 + 6x = 16$
    $2x^2 - 3y^2 = 24$

11. $x^2 + y^2 = 64$
    $x^2 + 10y = 100$

12. $x^2 + y^2 = 100$
    $8x^2 + 13y^2 = 1405$

13. $x^2 + y^2 + 8x = -15$
    $9x^2 + 25y^2 = 225$

14. $x^2 - 6y = 34$
    $x^2 + y^2 = 25$

15. $5x^2 + 9y^2 = 161$
    $x^2 - 4y = 4$

16. $20x^2 - 3y^2 + 12y = -16$
    $20x^2 + 3y^2 = 128$

17. $x^2 - 5y^2 = -44$
    $xy = -24$

18. $x^2 + 4y^2 = 68$
    $xy = 8$

19. $16x^2 - 3y^2 = -11$
    $8x - y = -11$

20. $7x^2 + y^2 = 64$
    $x + y = 4$

21. $x^2 + 2y^2 = 33$
    $3x + 2y = -11$

22. $2x^2 - y^2 = 7$
    $2x - 3y = -7$

23. $y = x^2 + 8x + 9$
    $x - y = -3$

24. $y = -2x^2 + 8x + 27$
    $2x + y = 15$

25. $x^2 + 9y^2 - 10x + 36y = 20$
    $x - 3y = 2$

26. $3x^2 - y^2 + 30x + 6y = -63$
    $x - y = -7$

27. Given the equations

$$x^2 - y^2 - 2y = 17 \qquad \underline{} \quad ①$$

$$7x^2 + 3y^2 - 24y = 139 \qquad \underline{} \quad ②$$

$$x - y = 9 \qquad \underline{} \quad ③ ,$$

   a. solve the system of ① and ②,
   b. solve the system of ① and ③,
   c. solve the system of ② and ③,
   d. graph all three equations on the same Cartesian coordinate system, showing that your answers for a, b, and c are reasonable.

28. Repeat Problem 27 for the equations

$$8x^2 - 3y^2 + 30y = 80 \qquad \underline{} \quad ①$$

$$32x^2 + 3y^2 = 140 \qquad \underline{} \quad ②$$

$$8x - 3y = 10 \qquad \underline{} \quad ③$$

29. **Meteorite Tracking Problem** Suppose that you have been hired by the Palomar Observatory near San Diego. Your assignment is to track incoming meteorites to find out whether or not they will strike the Earth. Since the Earth has a circular cross-section, you decide to set up a Cartesian coordinate system with its origin at the center of the Earth. The equation of the Earth's surface is

$$x^2 + y^2 = 40,$$

where x and y are distances in *thousands* of kilometers.

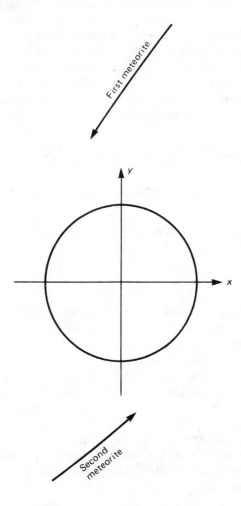

a. The first meteorite you observe is moving along the parabola whose equation is

$$18x - y^2 = -144.$$

Will this meteorite strike the Earth's surface? If so, *where*? If not, how do you tell?

b. The second meteorite is coming in from the lower left along one
branch of the hyperbola

$$4x^2 - y^2 - 80x = -340,$$

(see sketch). Will it strike the Earth's surface? If so, *where*? If
not, how do you tell?

c. To the nearest 100 kilometers, what is the radius of the Earth?

30. *General Quadratic—Quadratic System*   The solution of a *general*
system of quadratics is extremely complicated. It involves just about
all of the algebraic techniques you know! This problem leads you
stepwise through the solution of a system which is general except that
the equations contain no *xy*-terms. You must be able to use substitution, the Quadratic Formula, solving a radical equation, squaring a
trinomial, factoring a quartic polynomial by the Factor Theorem,
getting decimal approximations of radicals, and discarding extraneous solutions by drawing a graph.

Given the system

$$5x^2 + y^2 + 30x - 6y = -9 \quad \underline{} \quad \text{①}$$
$$x^2 + 3y^2 + 4x - 6y = 21 \quad \underline{} \quad \text{②},$$

do the following:

a. By considering x to be a "constant," write Equation ① as a
quadratic equation in y. Then use the Quadratic Formula to show
that

$$y = 3 \pm \sqrt{-5x^2 - 30x}.$$

b. Substitute this value of y into Equation ② and carry out the indicated operations. (Be careful squaring the value of y!) Then collect like terms and simplify as much as possible. You should find
that 2 is a common factor of each term.

c. Isolate the remaining radical on one side of the equation, then
square both members; all terms should now be polynomial.
(Don't worry if some of the coefficients are in the thousands!)

d. Transform the equation so that all terms are on the left and 0 is
on the right. You should have a quadratic (fourth degree) polynomial on the left, beginning with $49x^4$ and ending with 36.

e. Use the Factor Theorem to show that $(x + 1)$ and $(x + 6)$ are
factors of this polynomial. Then find the other polynomial by division.

f. Show that the remaining quadratic factor is *prime*.

g. Solve the equation in part d. Use the Quadratic Formula, where
needed, and get decimal approximations for the radicals.

h. Find the values of y corresponding to each value of x from part
g (4 values!).

i.   Sketch the graphs of the two equations. Then discard the *y*-values from part h which do not correspond to crossing points.

j.   Write the solution set of the system.

9-9 | CHAPTER REVIEW AND TEST

In this chapter you have extended your knowledge of quadratics to relations that have a y^2 term in the equation. You have found that the graph could be a circle, ellipse, or hyperbola, as well as the familiar parabola. For each of these conic sections you learned properties that allowed you to sketch the graph quickly. By analysis of geometric properties ("analytic geometry") you were able to derive equations of relations from geometric definitions. Finally, you extended the system-solving of Chapter 4 to systems of quadratic equations.

The Review Problems, below, give you a chance to try accomplishing these objectives one at a time. The Concepts Problems are designed to see if you are familiar enough with the concepts of the chapter to be able to use them in problems you have never seen before! This Chapter Test is more like a normal classroom test.

REVIEW PROBLEMS

The following problems are numbered according to the three objectives above.

R1. a.   Tell which conic section the graph or the boundary of the region will be.

    i. $x^2 + y^2 = 36$ ii. $x^2 + y^2 < 36$

    iii. $x^2 + y^2 \geq 36$ iv. $x^2 - y^2 = 36$

    v. $x^2 - y^2 = -36$ vi. $x^2 + y^2 = -36$

    vii. $x^2 + 4y^2 = 36$ viii. $4x^2 + y^2 = 36$

    ix. $4x^2 + y = 36$ x. $4x + y^2 = 36$

    xi. $x^2 - 9y^2 + 10x + 54y - 47 = 0$

    xii. $x^2 + y^2 + 16x - 22y + 85 = 0$

    xiii. $9x^2 + 4y^2 - 54x + 16y - 479 = 0$

    xiv. $x - y^2 + 6y - 3 = 0$

b.   Transform each equation in part a to a standard form (if necessary), and sketch the graph.

c.   Find the focal radius for Equations xi and xiii.

R2. a.   Write the geometric definition of

    i.   a circle,

    ii.   an ellipse,

iii. a hyperbola,

      iv. a parabola.

  b. From the geometric definition, derive a polynomial equation of the ellipse with foci $(3, 0)$ and $(-3, 0)$, and major axis 10 units long.

R3. a. Solve the following systems:

      i. $9x^2 + y^2 - 2y = 80$
         $x^2 + y^2 - 10y = 0$

      ii. $9x^2 - 16y^2 + 36x - 32y = -195$
         $3x + 4y = 15$

  b. Show by graphing that your solutions for part a are correct.

CONCEPTS PROBLEMS

C1. Sketch graphs that illustrate how a system of two quadratic equations with two variables can have

  a. exactly four solutions,

  b. exactly three solutions,

  c. exactly two solutions,

  d. exactly one solution,

  e. no solutions.

C2. You have learned how to find graphs of quadratic relations from their equations. Using the same properties, *reverse* the process and write equations or inequalities for the following graphs:

a.

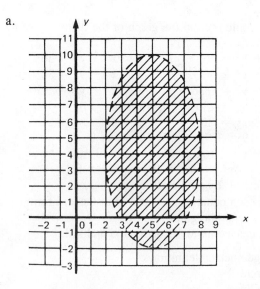

b.

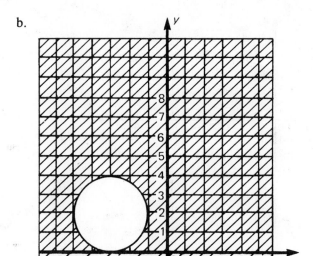

c.

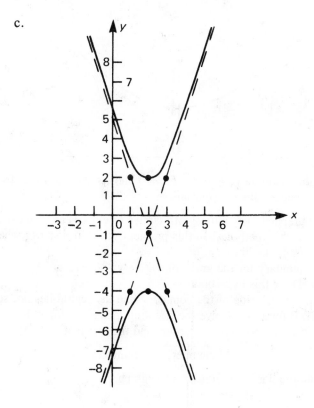

d.

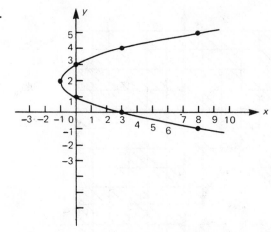

C3. It is possible to write the equation of a parabola in terms of the distance, p, between the focus and the directrix (see sketch).

a. Draw x- and y-axes so that the vertex is at the origin. Then use the definition of a parabola to show that the equation is

$$y = \frac{1}{2p}x^2.$$

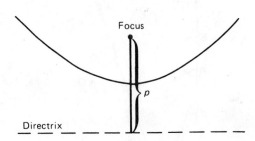

b. For the parabola $y = 3x^2 + 5x - 7$, how far is the focus from the directrix? Justify your answer.

C4. You have graphed inequalities with circles or ellipses as boundaries, but never with hyperbolas. In this problem you will discover what such a graph looks like.

a. The boundary for the graph of $4x^2 - y^2 \leq -16$ is a hyperbola. Draw this hyperbola.

b. To find which side of the boundary line the region lies on, substitute 0 for x, and solve the resulting inequality for y. Remember the properties of order, and the fact that

$$\sqrt{(\text{number})^2} = |\text{number}|.$$

c. Shade the correct region on your graph.

C5. Recalling the definitions of x-intercept and y-intercept, find the intercepts of

$$x^2 + y^2 + 16x - 22y + 85 = 0.$$

C6. Suppose that you are aboard a spaceship. The Earth is at the origin of a Cartesian coordinate system, and the path of your spaceship is the graph of

$$9x^2 + 25y^2 - 72x = 81.$$

a. Which conic section is this path, and how do you tell?
b. Sketch the graph of this path.
c. Show that the Earth is at the focus of this conic section.
d. To determine your position at a particular time, you tune in to the LORAN station and find that you are also on the graph of

$$9x^2 - 15y^2 = 9.$$

Which conic section is this graph, and how do you tell?
e. By solving the system formed by the equations of the two conic sections above, find the *three* possible points at which your spaceship could be located.
f. Draw the graph of the conic section in part d on the same Cartesian coordinate system as in part b, and thus show that your answer to part e is correct.
g. To ascertain at *which* one of the three points you are located, you find that you are also on the graph of

$$3x - 5y = 27.$$

At which of the points are you located? (There is a *clever* way to do this, as well as the longer way.)

CHAPTER TEST

For Problems T1 through T5, transform the equation by completing the square. Then sketch the graph.

T1. $4x^2 + y^2 - 40x + 6y + 93 = 0$

T2. $x^2 - 4y^2 - 8x + 16y - 36 = 0$

T3. $9x^2 - 16y^2 + 90x + 32y + 353 = 0$

T4. $x^2 + y^2 + 6x - 16y + 48 \le 0$

T5. $x = 0.2y^2 - 2y - 3$

For Problems T6 through T8, solve the system.

T6. $7x^2 - 9y^2 = 31$
      $5x^2 + 9y^2 = 161$

T7. $x^2 + y^2 - 4x = 21$
      $x^2 + 5y^2 = 49$

T8. $x^2 - 3y^2 = -11$
      $x - y = -1$

T9.   Sketch graphs that illustrate the following:
      a. A circle and an ellipse that intersect at four points.
      b. A parabola and an ellipse that intersect at exactly three distinct points.
      c. A hyperbola and a circle that intersect at exactly two distinct points.
      d. An ellipse and a hyperbola that intersect at only one point.
      e. Two parabolas that intersect at no points.

10

Higher Degree Functions and Complex Numbers

*In this chapter you will study functions in which the independent variable, **x**, is **cubed**, or raised to a higher power. The most significant mathematical concept concerns values of **x** that make **y** = 0. To make sense out of this concept, you will make use of imaginary numbers, to which you were introduced in Chapters 1 and 5. You will use higher degree functions as mathematical models for such things as the bending of beams and the payload carried by airplanes.*

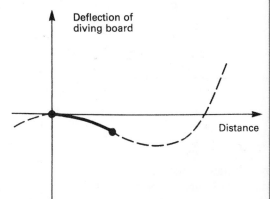

Deflection of diving board

Distance

10-1 | # INTRODUCTION TO HIGHER DEGREE FUNCTIONS

You recall that a polynomial function is a function with a general equation of the form

$$y = \text{a polynomial in } x.$$

You studied linear (first degree) and quadratic (second degree) functions in Chapters 3 and 5. In this section you will explore the graph of a cubic function.

Objective:
Discover by pointwise plotting what the graph of a cubic function looks like.

The exercise which follows is designed to allow you to accomplish this objective.

| ## EXERCISE 10-1

1.   Plot a graph of the cubic function

$$f(x) = x^3 - 4x^2 - 3x + 2$$

in the domain $-3 \le x \le 6$. Do this by calculating the value of $f(x)$ for each integer value of x in the domain. For example, $f(6) = 56$. Then plot the resulting points, and connect them with a smooth curve. You may wish to use different scales for the two axes so that the graph fits conveniently onto the graph paper. Be careful with the arithmetic, since even *one* point out of place can make the graph look completely different!

2. From your graph, you should be able to answer the following questions:
    a. How many x-intercepts does a cubic function seem to have?
    b. How many vertices does a cubic function graph seem to have?
    c. A quadratic function graph (a parabola) has two x-intercepts and one vertex. How many x-intercepts and vertices would you expect in the graph of a *quartic* (*fourth* degree) function?

3. Plot graphs of

$$g(x) = x^3 - 4x^2 - 3x + 18, \quad \text{and}$$

$$h(x) = x^3 - 4x^2 - 3x + 34.$$

This is easy if you observe that $g(x) = f(x) + 16$, and $h(x) = f(x) + 32$, where $f(x)$ is defined in Problem 1, above.
    a. How do the graphs of g and h compare with the graph of f?
    b. How many x-intercepts do the graphs of g and h have?
    c. What conclusion can you reach about the number of x-intercepts a cubic function can have?

10-2 | COMPLEX NUMBER REVIEW

In the last section you explored the functions

$$f(x) = x^3 - 4x^2 - 3x + 2,$$

$$g(x) = x^3 - 4x^2 - 3x + 18, \quad \text{and}$$

$$h(x) = x^3 - 4x^2 - 3x + 34.$$

Each is a cubic function, and each equation differs only in the constant term. The graphs, as drawn by the program PLOT CUBIC on the accompanying disk, are shown in Figure 10-2a. Each has the same shape, but is displaced 16 units from each other in the y-direction. This fact is reasonable because

$$g(x) = f(x) + 16, \quad \text{and}$$

$$h(x) = g(x) + 16.$$

The graph of function f has three distinct x-intercepts. The graph of function g is raised just enough so that the two intercepts on the right merge into one. When the graph is raised still higher, as for function h, these two intercepts vanish! You will find that they have disappeared into the set of complex numbers!

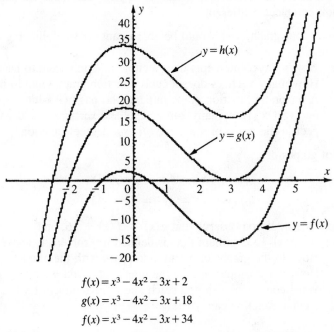

$$f(x) = x^3 - 4x^2 - 3x + 2$$
$$g(x) = x^3 - 4x^2 - 3x + 18$$
$$f(x) = x^3 - 4x^2 - 3x + 34$$

Figure 10-2a

In this section you will refresh your memory about complex numbers, to which you were exposed in Chapter 5. After you explore complex solutions of quadratic equations in the next section, you will be ready to find out some general conclusions about the x-intercepts of cubic and higher degree functions.

Objective:
Be able to add, subtract, multiply, and divide complex numbers.

An imaginary number is defined to be a square root of a negative real number. For instance,

$$\sqrt{-17}, \quad \sqrt{-100}, \quad -\sqrt{-3}, \quad \text{and} \quad \sqrt{-\pi}$$

are imaginary numbers. To make these numbers fit into what you already know, it is customary to give a name to $\sqrt{-1}$. The name is i (for "imaginary"). With this name, any imaginary number can be expressed in terms of i.

$$\sqrt{-17} = \sqrt{(-1)(17)} = \sqrt{-1}\sqrt{17} = i\sqrt{17} = 4.1231\ldots i$$

Similarly,

$$\sqrt{-100} = 10i, \quad -\sqrt{-3} = -i\sqrt{3}, \quad \text{and} \quad \sqrt{-\pi} = i\sqrt{\pi}.$$

Since the symbol "$\sqrt{n}$" means, "a number you can square and get n for the answer," the symbol i means "a number you can square and get -1 for the answer." The number i is not a real number. If you square any real number, the answer is non-negative. However, i is just as "real" as any other number. Like fractions and negative numbers, it was invented by *people* to give answers to certain kinds of problem. The name "imaginary" was picked a long time ago when some people started using these numbers, because other people found it hard to imagine such numbers.

The above discussion leads to the definitions that were first mentioned in Chapter 5.

DEFINITIONS

IMAGINARY AND COMPLEX NUMBERS
1. **Unit Imaginary Number**
   i is a number whose square is -1. That is,

$$i^2 = -1$$

   or equivalently,

$$i = \sqrt{-1}$$

2. **Imaginary Numbers in terms of i**
   If x is a non-negative real number, then

$$\sqrt{-x} = i\sqrt{x}$$

3. **Complex Number**
   A *complex number* is a number of the form a + bi, where the real number a is called the *real part* of a + bi, the real number b is called the *imaginary part* of a + bi, and i is $\sqrt{-1}$.
4. **Complex Conjugates**
   The complex numbers $a + bi$ and $a - bi$ are called *complex conjugates* of each other.

Complex numbers can be plotted on a complex number *plane*. Figure 10-2b shows the complex number $4 + 3i$. The real part, 4, is plotted as the abscissa. The imaginary part, 3 (a *real* number!), is plotted as the ordinate.

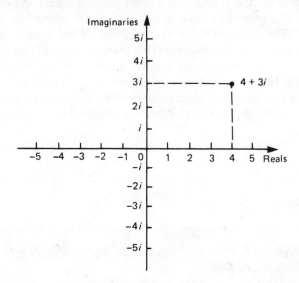

Figure 10-2b ——————————————————————————————

Since the real-number line and the imaginary-number line both lie in the complex plane, you can conclude that the set of real numbers and the set of imaginary numbers are both subsets of the set of complex numbers. Since 0 lies on both the real-number line and on the imaginary-number line, you can also conclude that 0 is both a real number and an imaginary number!!

With these definitions and conclusions in mind, you are ready to accomplish the objective of this section.

1. *Powers of i:*

By definition, $i^2 = -1$. To evaluate other integer powers of i, it is necessary only to use the definition of exponentiation with integer exponents:

$$i^3 = i^2 \cdot i = -1 \cdot i = -i \qquad \therefore i^3 = -i.$$

$$i^4 = i^2 \cdot i^2 = (-1)(-1) = 1 \qquad \therefore i^4 = 1.$$

$$i^5 = i \cdot i^4 = i \cdot 1 = i \qquad \therefore i^5 = i.$$

$$i^6 = i^2 \cdot i^4 = -1 \qquad \therefore i^6 = -1.$$

$$i^7 = i^3 \cdot i^4 = -i \qquad \therefore i^7 = -i.$$

$$i^8 = i^4 \cdot i^4 = 1 \qquad \therefore i^8 = 1.$$

$$\vdots \qquad\qquad\qquad\qquad \vdots$$

Note that any time the exponent is a multiple of 4, the power equals 1. Thus

$$i^{76} = 1,$$

because 76 is a multiple of 4.

Suppose that you wish to evaluate i^{39}. Since $39 = 36 + 3$, and 36 is a multiple of 4,

$$i^{39} = i^{36+3} = i^{36} \cdot i^3 = 1 \cdot i^3 = i^3 = -i.$$

A faster technique is to divide the exponent by 4, getting 9 with a remainder of 3. Throw away the quotient, 9, and keep the remainder, 3. So $i^{39} = i^3$, which equals $-i$.

EXAMPLE 1

Evaluate i^{1066}.

Solution:
Divide 1066 by 4. The quotient is 266 (which is irrelevant!) and the remainder is 2. So

$$i^{1066} = i^2 = \underline{\underline{-1}}. \qquad \blacksquare$$

2. *Sums and Differences of Complex Numbers*

Complex numbers behave just like linear binomials when they are added or subtracted.

EXAMPLE 2

If $z_1 = 7 - 8i$ and $z_2 = 2 + 11i$, find
a. $z_1 + z_2$.
b. $z_1 - z_2$.

Solution:
a. $z_1 + z_2$

$= (7 - 8i) + (2 + 11i)$

$= 7 - 8i + 2 + 11i$

$= \underline{\underline{9 + 3i}}$

b. $z_1 - z_2$

$= (7 - 8i) - (2 + 11i)$

$= 7 - 8i - 2 - 11i$

$= \underline{\underline{5 - 19i}} \qquad \blacksquare$

3. *Products of Complex Numbers*

Complex numbers also behave like linear binomials when you multiply them. The only extra thing to remember is that $i^2 = -1$.

EXAMPLE 3

Multiply: $(7 - 8i)(2 + 11i)$

Solution:

$(7 - 8i)(2 + 11i)$

$= 14 + 61i - 88i^2$ Multiply each term in one binomial by each term in the other.

$= 14 + 61i + 88$

$= \underline{\underline{102 + 61i}}$ ∎

EXAMPLE 4

Multiply: $(4 + 9i)(4 - 9i)$

Solution:

$(4 + 9i)(4 - 9i)$

$= 16 - 81i^2$ Middle term is zero

$= 16 + 81$

$= \underline{\underline{97}}$ ∎

Note that the complex numbers $4 + 9i$ and $4 - 9i$ are complex conjugates of each other. Their product is a *real* number. This fact has application in dividing by a complex number.

CONCLUSION

> **PRODUCT OF COMPLEX CONJUGATES**
> The product of two complex conjugates is a *real* number.
>
> $$(a + bi)(a - bi) = a^2 + b^2$$

4. *Quotients of Complex Numbers*

Dividing one complex number by another is a special case of transforming to simple radical form. You rationalize the denominator by multiplying by 1 in the form (conjugate of denominator)/(conjugate of denominator).

EXAMPLE 5

Divide: $\dfrac{4 + 3i}{5 - 2i}$

Solution:

$\dfrac{4 + 3i}{5 - 2i}$

$= \dfrac{4 + 3i}{5 - 2i} \cdot \dfrac{5 + 2i}{5 + 2i}$ Multiply by a clever form of 1 to rationalize the denominator.

$= \dfrac{20 + 23i + 6i^2}{25 - 4i^2}$

$= \dfrac{20 + 23i - 6}{25 + 4}$

$= \dfrac{14 + 23i}{29}$

$= \dfrac{14}{29} + \dfrac{23}{29}i$ ■

The exercise that follows is designed to make you comfortable operating with imaginary and complex numbers.

EXERCISE 10-2

Do These Quickly

The following problems are intended to refresh your skills. You should be able to do all 10 in less than 5 minutes.

Q1.   Write the coefficient of each term: $7x^3 - 4x^2 - x + 8$

Q2.   What does i^2 equal?

Q3.   Write a quartic monomial.

Q4.   Which conic section is the graph of $7x^2 - 7y^2 = 53$?

Q5.   Write the next prime number after 7.

Q6.   Find the slope of the line between (3, 7) and (11, 2).

Q7.   Which way does the parabola $x = -3y^2 + 5y + 8$ open?

Q8. What is the greatest possible number of intersection points of an ellipse and a hyperbola?

Q9. Sketch the graph of a decreasing exponential function.

Q10. Evaluate $64^{-\frac{3}{2}}$.

For Problems 1 through 20, simplify and write in terms of i.

1. i^5 2. i^7 3. i^{55} 4. i^{25}

5. i^{62} 6. i^{74} 7. i^{300} 8. i^{180}

9. i^0 10. i^{-2} 11. i^{-7} 12. i^{-25}

13. i^{-38} 14. i^{-54} 15. $\sqrt{-16}$ 16. $\sqrt{-25}$

17. $\sqrt{-18}$ 18. $\sqrt{-48}$ 19. $\sqrt{-7}$ 20. $\sqrt{-3}$

For Problems 21 through 28, plot graphs of the given numbers on a complex number plane.

21. $5 + 7i$ 22. $6 + 3i$ 23. $3 - 2i$ 24. $7 - 4i$

25. $-4 + 6i$ 26. $-2 + i$ 27. $-1 - 8i$ 28. $-5 - 2i$

For Problems 29 through 32, find (a) $z_1 + z_2$, (b) $z_1 - z_2$, (c) $z_1 z_2$, and (d) $\dfrac{z_1}{z_2}$.

29. $z_1 = 2 + 3i$ 30. $z_1 = 6 + 2i$
    $z_2 = 4 - 5i$ $z_2 = 5 - 7i$

31. $z_1 = -1 + 2i$ 32. $z_1 = -3 - i$
    $z_2 = 6 + 7i$ $z_2 = 4 + 8i$

33. Find the product of the complex number $a + bi$ and its complex conjugate, and explain why the answer is a *real* number.

34. Use the results of Problem 33 to factor the *sum* of two squares, $x^2 + y^2$.

For Problems 35 through 38, suppose that the *absolute value* of z, $|z|$, is defined to be the distance from the origin to the graph of z on the complex number plane (just the way the absolute value of a real number is its distance from the origin on a real number line). For each problem, plot z on a complex number plane, connect the graph of z to the origin, then find $|z|$ by appropriate use of the Pythagorean Theorem.

35. $z = 4 + 3i$ 36. $z = 2 - 3i$

37. $z = -5 + 12i$ 38. $z = -8 - 15i$

39. Suppose that $z_1 = 3 + 5i$ and $z_2 = 7 + 2i$.

a.   Plot the points z_1, z_2, and $z_1 + z_2$ on a complex number plane. Then connect each point to the origin. What do the lengths of these lines represent?

b.   Connect z_1 to $z_1 + z_2$. What does the length of this line equal?

c.   Explain why the inequality $|z_1 + z_2| \leq |z_1| + |z_2|$ is true for any two complex numbers z_1 and z_2. (Clue: This is called the "Triangle Inequality.")

40.   Suppose that $z_1 = 1 + i$ and $z_2 = 2 + 5i$.

a.   Find the product $z_1 z_2$.

b.   Find $|z_1|$, $|z_2|$, and $|z_1 z_2|$, then try to arrive at some conclusion about how these three absolute values are related to each other.

c.   Plot the points z_1, z_2, and $z_1 z_2$ on a complex number plane, then connect each point to the origin. How do the *angles* between the positive real axis and these three lines seem to be related to one another?

41.   Draw graphs of i, i^2, i^3, and i^4 on the same complex number plane. What seems to be happening to the graph each time the power of i is increased by one?

42.   Suppose that $z = 3 + 4i$.

a.   What does iz equal?

b.   Plot the points z and iz on a complex number plane, then connect each point to the origin.

c.   Show that multiplying z by i has *not* changed its absolute value.

d.   Show that multiplying z by i has *rotated* its graph through an angle of 90°.

43.   Show that

$$z = \frac{\sqrt{2}}{2}(1 + i)$$

is a *square root* of i by squaring $\frac{\sqrt{2}}{2}(1 + i)$ and showing that you get i for an answer. Also, show that $|z| = 1$.

44.   Suppose that $z = -1 + i\sqrt{3}$.

a.   Show that $|z| = 2$.

b.   Show that z is a *cube root* of 8 by cubing $-1 + i\sqrt{3}$ and showing that you get 8 for an answer.

| 10-3 | QUADRATIC EQUATIONS FROM THEIR SOLUTIONS—COMPLEX NUMBER FACTORS |

In Chapter 5 you learned how to solve quadratic equations such as
$$x^2 - 2x + 13 = 0$$
using the Quadratic Formula. You get

$$x = \frac{2 \pm \sqrt{4 - 4(1)(13)}}{2(1)} = \frac{2 \pm \sqrt{-48}}{2} = \frac{2 \pm 4i\sqrt{3}}{2}$$

$$x = 1 \pm 2i\sqrt{3}$$

$$\therefore S = \{1 + 2i\sqrt{3}, \quad 1 - 2i\sqrt{3}\}.$$

Observe that the solutions are *complex conjugates* of each other. This will always happen if the coefficients in the equation are *real* numbers. The imaginary parts of the solutions come from

$$\sqrt{b^2 - 4ac}.$$

You have learned how to solve quadratic equations such as

$$x^2 - 5x + 6 = 0$$

by factoring. You would write

$$(x - 3)(x - 2) = 0$$

$$x - 3 = 0 \quad \text{or} \quad x - 2 = 0$$

$$x = 3 \quad \text{or} \quad x = 2$$

$$S = \{3, 2\}$$

The process can be reversed to find a quadratic equation if you are given the two solutions. For instance, a quadratic equation whose solutions are 5 and 7 is

$$(x - 5)(x - 7) = 0$$

$$x^2 - 12x + 35 = 0.$$

In general, a quadratic equation whose solutions are s_1 and s_2 is

$$(x - s_1)(x - s_2) = 0.$$

This process can be done if the two solutions are fractions, decimals, radicals, or even complex numbers. But the algebra in transforming to the $ax^2 + bx + c = 0$ form is rather tedious. Fortunately, there are relationships between s_1 and s_2 and the coefficients a, b, and c, which make the job easier. To see what the relationships are, carry out the multiplication in $(x - s_1)(x - s_2) = 0$. You get

$$x_2 - s_1x - s_2x + s_1s_2 = 0$$

$$x^2 - (s_1 + s_2)x + s_1s_2 = 0 \quad \underline{} \quad ①$$

Dividing each member of $ax^2 + bx + c = 0$ by a gives

$$x^2 + \frac{b}{a}x + \frac{c}{a} = 0 \quad \underline{} \quad ②$$

By comparing Equations ① and ②, you should be able to see that

$$s_1 s_2 = \frac{c}{a} \quad \text{and} \quad -(s_1 + s_2) = \frac{b}{a}$$

Examples 1 and 2, below, show how to write a quadratic equation if you know its solutions. Examples 3 and 4 show you how you can use the concepts of this section to factor *any* quadratic trinomial, as long as you are willing to pay the price of using fractions, radicals, and complex numbers.

Objectives:

1. Given two numbers, write a quadratic equation having these numbers as its solutions.
2. Given a quadratic trinomial, factor it over the set of complex numbers.

EXAMPLE 1

Find a quadratic equation with $\frac{5}{3}$ and -2 as its solutions.

$$\frac{b}{a} = -(s_1 + s_2) = -\left(\frac{5}{3} - 2\right) = -\left(-\frac{1}{3}\right) = \frac{1}{3}$$

$$\frac{c}{a} = s_1 s_2 = \left(\frac{5}{3}\right)(-2) = -\frac{10}{3}$$

$\therefore$ the equation is $x^2 + \frac{1}{3}x - \frac{10}{3} = 0$.

If you want the equation to have integer coefficients, you can multiply both members by 3, getting

$$3x^2 + x - 10 = 0. \qquad \blacksquare$$

Note that the solutions of an equation are sometimes called *roots*. The name is reasonable based on what you have just learned. You have just made a quadratic equation "grow up out of its roots!" You should be familiar with this term so that you will recognize it on contests and standardized tests.

DEFINITION

ROOTS OF AN EQUATION
A **root** of an equation is a solution of that equation.

If a quadratic equation has complex solutions, and the coefficients in the equation are real numbers, then the solutions are complex conjugates of each other. The reason for this shows up in the quadratic formula. For instance, if you solve

$$x^2 - 10x + 34 = 0$$

you get

$$x = \frac{-(-10) \pm \sqrt{100 - 4(1)(34)}}{2(1)}$$

$$x = \frac{10 \pm \sqrt{-36}}{2}$$

$$x = 5 + 3i \quad \text{or} \quad 5 - 3i.$$

The real part is the same in both solutions. The imaginary part carries the "+" in one solution and the "−" in the other. So the solutions are conjugates of each other. This conclusion is true as long as the three coefficients in the equation are real numbers. In Problem 64 of the following exercise you will see that it might not be true if the coefficients involve imaginary numbers.

CONCLUSION

> **COMPLEX CONJUGATE SOLUTIONS OF QUADRATICS**
> If a quadratic equation with real coefficients has a negative discriminant, then the two solutions are complex conjugates of each other.

EXAMPLE 2

Find a quadratic equation with real-number coefficients if one solution is $2 + 3i$.

Solution:
Since complex solutions come in *conjugate pairs* when the coefficients are real numbers, the other solution will be $2 - 3i$.

$$\frac{b}{a} = -(s_1 + s_2) = -(2 + 3i + 2 - 3i) = -4$$

$$\frac{c}{a} = s_1 s_2 = (2 + 3i)(2 - 3i) = 4 - 9i^2 = 13.$$

∴ the equation is $\underline{x^2 - 4x + 13 = 0}$. ∎

Factoring Quadratics—Since factoring can be used to solve quadratic equations, solving quadratic equations can be used to help you factor. You use the fact that if s_1 and s_2 are solutions of the equation, then the equation is

$$(x - s_1)(x - s_2) = 0.$$

EXAMPLE 3

Factor $x^2 - 2x + 13$.

Solution:
First you set the polynomial equal to zero, and solve the resulting equation.

$$x^2 - 2x + 13 = 0$$

By the Quadratic Formula, the two solutions of this equation are

$$s_1 = 1 + 2i\sqrt{3} \quad \text{and} \quad s_2 = 1 - 2i\sqrt{3}.$$

Thus, the equation is equivalent to

$$[x - (1 + 2i\sqrt{3})][x - (1 - 2i\sqrt{3})] = 0.$$

Simplifying each factor gives

$$(x - 1 - 2i\sqrt{3})(x - 1 + 2i\sqrt{3}) = 0.$$

By the Transitive Property,

$$x^2 - 2x + 13 = \underline{(x - 1 - 2i\sqrt{3})(x - 1 + 2i\sqrt{3})}. \qquad \blacksquare$$

EXAMPLE 4

Factor $5x^2 + 3x - 7$.

Solution:
In this case, the leading coefficient is not equal to 1. Therefore, you must first factor it out, getting

$$5\left(x^2 + \frac{3}{5}x - \frac{7}{5}\right).$$

The polynomial inside the parentheses will factor into $(x - s_1)(x - s_2)$. Solving the equation $5x^2 + 3x - 7 = 0$, you find

$$x = \frac{-3 \pm \sqrt{9 - 4(5)(-7)}}{2(5)}$$

$$= \frac{-3 \pm \sqrt{149}}{10}$$

$$\therefore 5x^2 + 3x - 7 = 5\left(x - \frac{-3 + \sqrt{149}}{10}\right)\left(x - \frac{-3 - \sqrt{149}}{10}\right).$$

If desired, you can also find decimal approximations for these solutions:

$$\frac{-3 \pm \sqrt{149}}{10} \approx 0.92 \text{ or } -1.52.$$

$$\therefore 5x^2 + 3x - 7 \approx \underline{5(x - 0.92)(x + 1.52)}. \qquad \blacksquare$$

EXAMPLE 5

Factor $4x^2 + 9$.

Solution:
This is a *sum* of two squares, previously not factorable. You can factor it by the technique used in Example 4. An easier way is to turn it into an *old* problem by writing it as a *difference* of two squares.

$$4x^2 + 9$$
$$= 4x^2 - 9i^2 \qquad \text{Because } i^2 = -1$$
$$= \underline{(2x + 3i)(2x - 3i)}. \qquad \blacksquare$$

The exercise that follows is designed to give you practice in finding equations for given solutions and factoring quadratics into linear factors. There is a warm-up in which you will solve some quadratics first.

EXERCISE 10-3

Do These Quickly

The following problems are intended to refresh your skills. You should be able to do all 10 in less than 5 minutes.

Q1. Evaluate 9^2.

Q2. Evaluate $\sqrt{9}$.

Q3. Evaluate $-\sqrt{9}$.

Q4. Evaluate $\sqrt{-9}$.

Q5. Evaluate $-\sqrt{-9}$.

Q6. Sketch the graph of a function with a removable discontinuity where x is 2 and y is 5.

Q7. Write $\log 36 + \log 15 - \log 27$ as a single logarithm.

Q8. Evaluate $\log (10^{2.63})$.

Q9. Solve: $(2x + 5) = 49$

Q10.   Evaluate: $|2.3 - 11|$

For Problems 1 through 24, find the solution set of the given equation over the set of complex numbers (i.e., assume that the domain of x is the set of complex numbers).

1. $x^2 - 2x + 2 = 0$ 2. $x^2 + 2x + 2 = 0$

3. $x^2 - 4x + 5 = 0$ 4. $x^2 - 2x + 5 = 0$

5. $x^2 + 2x + 10 = 0$ 6. $x^2 - 6x + 10 = 0$

7. $x^2 - 4x + 29 = 0$ 8. $x^2 + 10x + 29 = 0$

9. $x^2 + 4x + 7 = 0$ 10. $x^2 - 6x + 11 = 0$

11. $x^2 - 10x + 27 = 0$ 12. $x^2 + 4x + 9 = 0$

13. $3x^2 - 4x + 10 = 0$ 14. $5x^2 + 2x + 7 = 0$

15. $25x^2 + 10x + 101 = 0$ 16. $9x^2 - 12x + 229 = 0$

17. $x^2 + 8x + 7 = 0$ 18. $x^2 + 8x + 15 = 0$

19. $x^2 - 6x + 4 = 0$ 20. $x^2 - 10x + 22 = 0$

21. $x^2 + 9 = 0$ 22. $x^2 + 16 = 0$

23. $4x^2 + 49 = 0$ 24. $9x^2 + 25 = 0$

For Problems 25 through 38, find a quadratic equation with the two given numbers as solutions.

25. 2 and -5 26. 4 and -3

27. -3 and -6 28. -5 and -2

29. $2 + i$ and $2 - i$ 30. $1 + 2i$ and $1 - 2i$

31. $-3 + 4i$ and $-3 - 4i$ 32. $-5 + i$ and $-5 - i$

33. $1 + i\sqrt{5}$ and $1 - i\sqrt{5}$ 34. $3 + i\sqrt{2}$ and $3 - i\sqrt{2}$

35. $-5 + 2i\sqrt{3}$ and $-5 - 2i\sqrt{3}$

36. $-6 + 3i\sqrt{5}$ and $-6 - 3i\sqrt{5}$

37. $4 + \sqrt{7}$ and $4 - \sqrt{7}$

38. $5 + \sqrt{3}$ and $5 - \sqrt{3}$

For Problems 39 through 52, factor the given polynomial into *linear* factors.

39. $x^2 - 2x + 5$ 40. $x^2 - 4x + 5$

41. $x^2 + 10x + 29$ 42. $x^2 + 2x + 10$

43. $x^2 - 6x + 11$ 44. $x^2 + 4x + 7$

45. $x^2 - 10x + 22$ 46. $x^2 - 6x + 4$

47. $x^2 + 16$ 48. $4x^2 + 25$

49. $9x^2 + 121$ 50. $36x^2 + 49$

51. $49x^2 + 1$ 52. $x^2 + 1$

53. $3x^2 - 4x + 10$ 54. $5x^2 + 2x + 7$

55. $25x^2 + 10x + 101$ 56. $9x^2 - 12x + 229$

57. Substitute each solution for the equation in Problem 1 into the equation, and thus show that these numbers actually *do* satisfy the equation.

58. Repeat Problem 57 for the equation in Problem 3.

59. Solve the equation you got as the answer to Problem 29, and thus show that the solutions really *are* $2 + i$ and $2 - i$.

60. Repeat Problem 59 for the equation from Problem 31.

61. Multiply together the factors for $x^2 - 2x + 5$ (Problem 39), and thus show that the product actually *is* $x^2 - 2x + 5$.

62. Repeat Problem 57 for $x^2 + 10x + 29$ (Problem 41).

63. **Sum and Product of the Solutions**   Prove directly from the Quadratic Formula that if s_1 and s_2 are the solutions of the equation $ax^2 + bx + c = 0$, then

$$s_1 + s_2 = -\frac{b}{a} \quad \text{and} \quad s_1 s_2 = \frac{c}{a}.$$

64. **Equations with Imaginary-Number Coefficients**
     a. Use the quadratic formula to solve
         i. $x^2 + 3ix - 2 = 0$,
         ii. $ix^2 - 2x - 3i = 0$.
     b. Are complex solutions of quadratic equations *always* conjugates of each other? Explain why your answer does *not* contradict the conclusion of this section concerning complex solutions of quadratic equations.

10-4   GRAPHS OF HIGHER DEGREE FUNCTIONS—
        SYNTHETIC SUBSTITUTION

You are now ready to return to the problem of graphing higher degree functions. The first thing you need is a rapid way to evaluate polynomials so that you can get plotting data quickly. A clever factoring scheme shows how this can be done. For example,

$$P(x) = 3x^4 - 19x^3 - 21x^2 + 51x - 14 \qquad \text{Given polynomial}$$

$$= (3x - 19)x^3 - 21x^2 + 51x - 14 \qquad \text{Factoring out } x^3$$

$$= ((3x - 19)x - 21)x^2 + 51x - 14 \qquad \text{Factoring out } x^2$$

$$= (((3x - 19)x - 21)x + 51)x - 14 \qquad \text{Factoring out } x$$

The polynomial is said to be in "nested form" since sets of parentheses are nested inside other parentheses.

Suppose, now, that you want to find $P(2)$. Starting with the innermost parentheses, you can use the following sequence of steps:

Start with 3   Start with the highest-degree coefficient.

$\begin{cases} 3 \times 2 = 6 \\ 6 - 19 = -13 \end{cases}$ Multiply by x.
Add the next coefficient, -19.

$\begin{cases} -13 \times 2 = -26 \\ -26 - 21 = -47 \end{cases}$ Multiply the answer by x.
Add the next coefficient, -21.

$\begin{cases} -47 \times 2 = -94 \\ -94 + 51 = -43 \end{cases}$ Multiply the answer by x.
Add the next coefficient, 51.

$\begin{cases} -43 \times 2 = -86 \\ -86 - 14 = -100 \end{cases}$ Multiply the answer by x.
Add the next coefficient, -14.

The answer is $P(2) = -100$. The virtue of this method is that the same pair of steps, "Multiply by x, then add the next coefficient," is done repeatedly. Such repetitive steps are easy to do on a calculator or to program into a computer, as you will see in Problems 54 and 55 of the following exercise.

There is a convenient way to arrange the steps for pencil-and-paper calculation, too. First, you write the coefficients of $P(x)$, and the value of x to be substituted.

Value substituted for x

$\underline{2|}$ 3   −19   −21   51   −14   ⟵   coefficients of P(x)

_____   ⟵   space for computation

You bring down the first coefficient, 3, multiply it by x, 2, write the answer, 6, under the −19 and *add*. The process is hard to *say* but easy *to do*!

$$\begin{array}{r|rrrrr} 2 & 3 & -19 & -21 & 51 & -14 \\ & \downarrow & 6 & & \text{Add} \\ \hline & 3 & -13 \end{array}$$

Multiply

The other steps are done in the same way. The completed computation
looks like this:

$$\begin{array}{r|rrrrr} 2 & 3 & -19 & -21 & 51 & -14 \\ & & 6 & -26 & -94 & -86 \\ \hline & 3 & -13 & -47 & -43 & -100 \end{array}$$ ← *x* times previous answer

$P(2)$

This process is called *synthetic substitution*.

The synthetic substitution process is essentially the same as the long division process. Dividing $P(x)$ by $(x - 2)$ gives:

$$\text{Quotient: } 3x^3 - 13x^2 - 47x - 43,$$

$$\text{Remainder: } -100.$$

The remainder and the coefficients of the quotient show up in the synthetic
substitution process.

$$\begin{array}{r|rrrrr} 2 & 3 & -19 & -21 & 51 & -14 \\ & & 6 & -26 & -94 & -86 \\ \hline & 3 & -13 & -47 & -43 & -100 \end{array}$$

Coefficients of   Remainder
Quotient

For this reason, synthetic substitution is sometimes called "synthetic division." The relationship between the two processes leads to the following
major theorem:

THE REMAINDER THEOREM

If $P(x)$ is a polynomial, then $P(b)$ is equal to the *remainder* when
$P(x)$ is divided by $x - b$.

To see *why* this is true, suppose that $P(x)$ is divided by $(x - b)$, giving a
quotient $Q(x)$ and a remainder R. Then

$$P(x) = (x - b) \cdot Q(x) + R.$$

Substituting b for x gives

$$P(b) = (b - b) \cdot Q(b) + R$$

$$P(b) = 0 \cdot Q(b) + R$$

$$P(b) = R.$$

The Remainder Theorem can be used as a lemma to prove the Factor Theorem of Section 7-6, as you will see in Problem 53 in the following exercise.

Armed with the synthetic substitution technique, you are ready to tackle the job of graphing and analyzing higher degree functions.

Objectives:

1. Plot the graph of a given higher degree function by using synthetic substitution to calculate plotting, data or by using computer graphics.
2. Find all values of x that make a polynomial $P(x)$ equal zero.

EXAMPLE 1

Plot the graph of $P(x) = x^3 - 4x^2 - 5x + 14$, and find all values of x that make $P(x) = 0$.

Solution:
To draw the graph, you must calculate many points. The table below shows a compact way to do many substitutions into the same polynomial. See if you can figure out how it works! The graph is shown in Figure 10-4a.

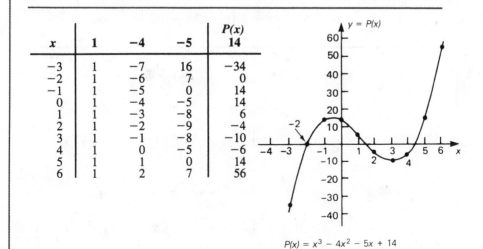

x	1	−4	−5	$P(x)$ 14
−3	1	−7	16	−34
−2	1	−6	7	0
−1	1	−5	0	14
0	1	−4	−5	14
1	1	−3	−8	6
2	1	−2	−9	−4
3	1	−1	−8	−10
4	1	0	−5	−6
5	1	1	0	14
6	1	2	7	56

$P(x) = x^3 - 4x^2 - 5x + 14$
Three x-intercepts

Figure 10-4a

To find the values of x that make $P(x) = 0$ (that is, the x-intercepts), you have already found that $P(-2) = 0$. By the Factor Theorem, you know that $(x + 2)$ is a factor of $P(x)$. The coefficients of the quotient appear in the synthetic substitution process. Therefore,

$$P(x) = (x + 2)(x^2 - 6x + 7).$$

Setting $P(x) = 0$ gives

$(x + 2)(x^2 - 6x + 7) = 0$

$x + 2 = 0$ or $x^2 - 6x + 7 = 0$ Multiplication Property of 0

$x = -2$ or $x = \dfrac{6 \pm \sqrt{36 - 4(1)(7)}}{2}$

$x = -2$ or $x = 3 \pm \sqrt{2}$

$x = \underline{\underline{-2}}$ or $x \approx \underline{4.414, 1.586}$ ■

You can see from Figure 10-4a that the graph actually does cross the x-axis at these three points.

EXAMPLE 2

Plot the graph of $P(x) = x^3 - 4x^2 - 5x + 48$, and find all values of x that make $P(x) = 0$.

Solution:
Repeating the procedure of Example 1, you will get a table of values which can be plotted as shown in Figure 10-4b. It turns out that $P(-3) = 0$, so that $(x + 3)$ is a factor of $P(x)$. The coefficients of the quotient can again be found in the table, and

$$P(x) = (x + 3)(x^2 - 7x + 16).$$

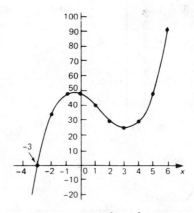

$$P(x) = x^3 - 4x^2 - 5x + 48$$
One x-intercept

Figure 10-4b

One x-intercept would be -3. To find the others you let

$$x^2 - 7x + 16 = 0.$$

By the Quadratic Formula,

$$x = \frac{7 \pm \sqrt{49 - 4(1)(16)}}{2} = \frac{7}{2} \pm \frac{i\sqrt{15}}{2}.$$

These values of x are *complex* numbers, so there are *no* other x-intercepts. Figure 10-4b shows this feature. However, these numbers *do* make $P(x)$ equal zero, and this fact leads to a more general name. ■

DEFINITION

ZERO OF A FUNCTION
A **zero** of a polynomial $P(x)$ is a value of x, real or complex, which makes $P(x) = 0$.

The process of finding zeros is illustrated above. As with quadratics, complex zeros of a polynomial with real coefficients always come in conjugate pairs. Thus, if you know that $5 + 7i$ is a zero of a polynomial with real coefficients, then you know that $5 - 7i$ is also a zero of the polynomial.

Once you know the zeros of a polynomial, you can factor it into linear factors. For Example 2, $P(-3) = 0$. Thus,

$$P(x) = (x + 3)(x^2 - 7x + 16)$$

$$= (x + 3)\left(x - \frac{7}{2} - i\sqrt{15}\right)\left(x - \frac{7}{2} + i\sqrt{15}\right).$$

Note that $P(x)$ is a *cubic* polynomial, and that it has exactly *three* linear factors. This is an example of an important algebraic theorem.

THEOREM

If $P(x)$ is an nth degree polynomial, then $P(x)$ has exactly n linear factors.

This means that $P(x)$ has exactly n zeros, although polynomials such as

$$P(x) = (x - 7)^3(x - 4)^2$$

would have the zeros 7 and 4 counted 3 and 2 times, respectively. This theorem is a corollary of the Fundamental Theorem of Algebra.

THEOREM

> **FUNDAMENTAL THEOREM OF ALGEBRA**
> A polynomial $P(x)$ has at least *one* zero, if you allow zeros to be complex numbers.

EXAMPLE 3

For the three functions

$$f(x) = x^3 - 4x^2 + 2x + 7$$

$$g(x) = x^3 - 6x^2 + 13x - 8$$

$$h(x) = -x^3 + 2x^2 + 3x + 5$$

a. Plot the graphs using PLOT CUBIC from the accompanying disk, or similar plotting program.
b. Do cubic function graphs always have two vertices?
c. Tell the major difference in the graphs when the x^3-coefficient is negative instead of positive.
d. Cubic function graphs always have a *point of inflection,* where the graph stops being curved one way and starts being curved the other way. If $y = ax^3 + bx^2 + cx + d$, the x-coordinate of the point of inflection is:

$$x = -\frac{b}{3a}.$$

Calculate this quantity for functions f, g, and h, above, draw a vertical line on each graph at these values of x, and thus show that the point of inflection really *is* at that location.

Solutions:
a. Figure 10-4c shows the three graphs as plotted by PLOT CUBIC.
b. No. Functions f and h have two vertices. In function g the graph curves one way for awhile as though it were going to roll over and form a vertex. But it starts curving back the other way before the vertex is formed.
c. If the x^3-coefficient is negative, the graph comes down from the upper left of the coordinate plane, and goes off to the lower right. For large values of x, the x^3-term is so much bigger than the other terms that the graph looks like $y = ax^3$. If x is a large negative number and a is negative, then y will be positive, and the graph will be in the second quadrant. Similarly, if x is a large positive number and a is negative, then y will be negative and the graph will be in the fourth quadrant.
d. f: $-\dfrac{b}{(3a)} = -\dfrac{(-4)}{[(3)(1)]} = \dfrac{4}{3}$

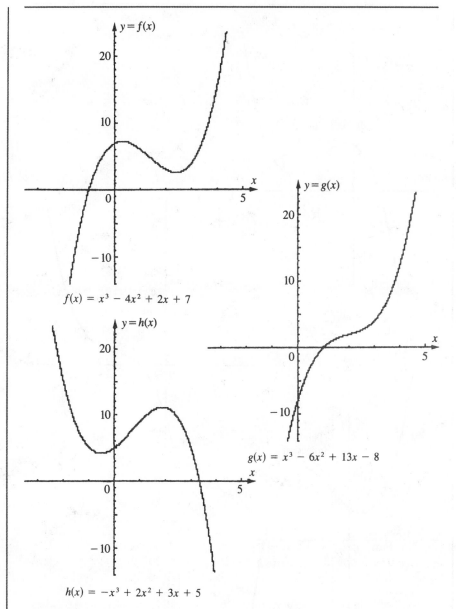

$f(x) = x^3 - 4x^2 + 2x + 7$

$g(x) = x^3 - 6x^2 + 13x - 8$

$h(x) = -x^3 + 2x^2 + 3x + 5$

Figure 10-4c

$$g: \quad -\frac{b}{(3a)} = -\frac{(-6)}{[(3)(1)]} = 2$$

$$h: \quad -\frac{b}{(3a)} = -\frac{(2)}{[(3)(-1)]} = \frac{2}{3}$$

The vertical lines are shown in Figure 10-4d. Each passes through the point of inflection.

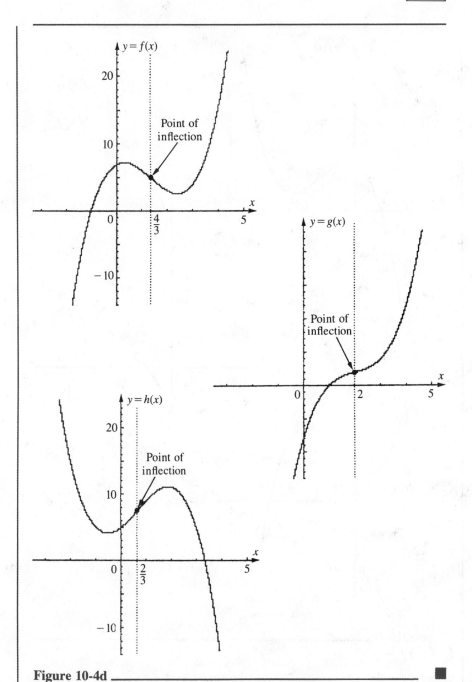

Figure 10-4d _____

The exercise which follows is designed to give you practice in analyzing higher degree polynomial functions by finding zeros and intercepts and plotting graphs.

EXERCISE 10-4

Do These Quickly

The following problems are intended to refresh your skills. You should be able to do all 10 in less than 5 minutes.

Q1.   Sketch the graph of $y = x^3$ (quickly!).

Q2.   Sketch the graph of $y = 3x$ (quickly!!).

Q3.   Sketch the graph of $y = 3^x$ (quickly!!!).

Q4.   Multiply: (9)(8)

Q5.   Find 2% of $378.

Q6.   Factor: $x^2 + 3x - 18$

Q7.   Simplify: $5 - 3x + 1$

Q8.   Evaluate: $\sqrt[4]{81}$

Q9.   How far do you go in 90 minutes at 50 miles per hour?

Q10.   Name the degree of $3x^5$.

For Problems 1 through 10, find the indicated function value by synthetic substitution.

1. $f(x) = x^3 + 7x^2 - 11x + 4$: Find $f(2)$.

2. $g(x) = x^3 - 4x^2 + 5x - 13$: Find $g(3)$.

3. $h(x) = 5x^3 - 3x^2 - 8x + 20$: Find $h(4)$.

4. $m(x) = 4x^3 + 2x^2 + 3x - 30$: Find $m(5)$.

5. $P(x) = -2x^3 + 4x^2 - 9x + 40$: Find $P(3)$.

6. $Q(x) = -3x^3 - 5x^2 + 7x - 9$: Find $Q(2)$.

7. $r(x) = x^3 + 6x^2 - 4x + 11$: Find $r(-5)$.

8. $c(x) = x^3 - x^2 + 10x + 15$: Find $c(-4)$.

9. $u(x) = 2x^4 - 5x^3 + 4x^2 - 10x - 90$: Find $u(2)$.

10. $v(x) = x^5 + x^4 - x^3 - 3x^2 + 4x + 21$: Find $v(-3)$.

For Problems 11 through 28,
      a.   Plot the graph on the given domain. You may use PLOT CUBIC or PLOT FUNCTION from the accompanying disk (or similar

plotting program), or calculate plotting data by synthetic substitution, either by pencil and paper or by the computer program of
Problem 54, below.

b. Find all zeros, real and complex. Those not found in part (a)
may be found by factoring $P(x)$ or by successive approximations
using the computer program of Problem 56, below.

11. $P(x) = x^3 - 4x^2 + x + 6$, $-3 \le x \le 5$

12. $P(x) = x^3 - x^2 - 4x + 4$, $-4 \le x \le 4$

13. $P(x) = x^3 - 7x^2 + 11x + 3$, $-2 \le x \le 6$

14. $P(x) = x^3 - x^2 - 10x + 10$, $-4 \le x \le 5$

15. $P(x) = x^3 + x^2 - 4x + 6$, $-4 \le x \le 3$

16. $P(x) = x^3 + x^2 - 7x - 15$, $-4 \le x \le 4$

17. $P(x) = x^3 + 2x^2 - 4x - 8$, $-4 \le x \le 3$

18. $P(x) = x^3 - 9x^2 + 24x - 16$, $-1 \le x \le 7$

19. $P(x) = x^3 - 6x^2 + 12x + 19$, $-2 \le x \le 5$

20. $P(x) = x^3 - 6x^2 + 12x - 7$, $-2 \le x \le 5$

21. $P(x) = -2x^3 - 3x^2 + 8x + 12$, $-4 \le x \le 3$

22. $P(x) = 3x^3 - x^2 - 40x + 48$, $-5 \le x \le 4$

23. $P(x) = 2x^3 + 4x^2 - 17x - 39$, $-4 \le x \le 4$

24. $P(x) = -2x^3 + 2x^2 + 7x - 10$, $-3 \le x \le 4$

25. $P(x) = x^4 - x^3 - 11x^2 + 9x + 18$, $-4 \le x \le 4$

26. $P(x) = x^4 + x^3 - 5x^2 + x - 6$, $-4 \le x \le 3$

27. $P(x) = x^4 - 5x^3 + 2x^2 + 22x - 20$, $-3 \le x \le 5$

28. $P(x) = -x^4 - 4x^3 + 12x^2 + 44x - 51$, $-5 \le x \le 4$

For Problems 29 through 40, find all zeros of the given polynomial.

29. $x^3 + x^2 - x + 15$ 30. $x^3 - 6x^2 + 13x - 10$

31. $x^3 + 3x^2 - 6x - 8$ 32. $x^3 + 4x^2 + x - 6$

33. $x^3 - 4x^2 + 2x + 4$ 34. $x^3 - 5x^2 + 5x + 3$

35. $x^4 + x^3 - 6x^2 - 14x - 12$

36. $x^4 - 8x^2 - 8x + 15$

37. $x^4 + x^3 - 7x^2 - x + 6$

38. $x^4 + 4x^3 - 3x^2 - 14x - 8$

39. $x^4 - 8x^3 + 27x^2 - 38x + 26$

Clues: One of the zeros is $3 + 2i$.
Complex zeros come in conjugate pairs.
It is possible to divide a *quadratic* into a quartic.

40. $x^4 - 12x^3 + 56x^2 - 120x + 100$
Clue: $3 + i$ is one zero.

For Problems 41 through 46, use the Remainder Theorem to find the remainder *quickly* when the polynomial on the left is divided by the linear binomial on the right. You may use synthetic substitution or *direct* substitution, whichever seems more efficient.

41. $2x^3 - 5x^2 + 11x + 6$ by $x - 4$

42. $3x^3 + 7x^2 - 12x + 1$ by $x + 3$

43. $x^5 - 3x^2 + 14$ by $x + 2$

44. $x^4 - 10x^2 + 9$ by $x - 3$

45. $x^{51} + 51$ by $x + 1$

46. $x^{2000} + 2000$ by $x - 1$.

For Problems 47 through 52, use what you have observed about the graphs of higher degree functions and what you know about the Fundamental Theorem of Algebra and its corollary, to sketch graphs of the functions described.

47. Quintic function with exactly 3 real zeros

48. Sixth degree function with exactly 4 real zeros

49. Cubic function with exactly two distinct real zeros

50. Quartic function with no real zeros

51. Cubic function with no real zeros

52. Quartic function with exactly five real zeros

53. *Proof of the Factor Theorem*   Use the Remainder Theorem to prove the Factor Theorem. That is, prove that a polynomial $P(x)$ has a linear factor of the form $(x - b)$ if, and only if, $P(b) = 0$. Remember that there are *two* parts to the proof, an "if" part and an "only if" part!

54. *Synthetic Substitution by Computer*   Write a computer program to carry out repeatedly the steps

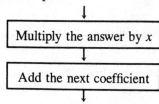

which appear in the synthetic substitution process. The input should be the value of x to be substituted, and the output should be the value of $P(x)$. The coefficients may be stored in a DATA statement and read one at a time as they are needed, using a READ statement. You should also read the *degree* of the polynomial, and use a counter to stop the process when the last coefficient has been read.

55. **Synthetic Division by Computer** Modify the program in Problem 54 so that the computer prints out the coefficients of the *quotient* polynomial as well as the values of x and $P(x)$.

56. **Zeros by Computer** If none of the zeros of a higher degree function is rational, it is quite complicated to find the exact values of the zeros. There is a "cubic formula" and a "quartic formula" which you can look up in handbooks such as *CRC Tables*. But they are too cumbersome to be practical. For fifth or higher degree functions, it can be shown that there is *no* general formula for finding zeros, so you seek a technique for finding *decimal approximations* of irrational zeros.

    a. Write a computer program which searches for zeros of a function. The program should begin with inputting the coefficients of $P(x)$. Then x should be started at some low value, L, and increased by 1 until a high value, H, is reached. At each step, the computer should see if there is a zero between x and $x + 1$ by checking to see if $P(x)$ and $P(x + 1)$ have *opposite* signs. You can do this by checking to see whether $P(x) * P(x + 1)$ is *negative*. When a zero has been located, the computer should explore the interval between x and $x + 1$ by increments of 0.1, looking for a sign change. Then it should proceed by increments of 0.01, and so forth, until the zero has been determined with the desired amount of accuracy.

    b. Test your program on the polynomial of Example 1,
    $$P(x) = x^3 - 4x^2 - 5x + 14,$$
    which has zeros of -2, 1.586, and 4.414. Your program should be able to handle the *integer* zeros as well as the irrational ones!

    c. For the following functions, find all real zeros that lie between -10 and 10.
        i. $P(x) = x^3 - 4x^2 + x + 5$
        ii. $P(x) = x^3 - 7x^2 + 11x + 3$
        iii. $P(x) = x^3 - 9x^2 + 24x - 29$
        iv. $P(x) = x^4 - x^3 - 11x^2 + 9x + 10$
        v. $P(x) = x^4 + x^3 - 5x^2 + x - 10$
        vi. $P(x) = x^4 + 17x^2 + 2x + 30$

    d. Explain why your program might *miss* some zeros if they are too close together.

57. **Cubic Function Zeros Problem**
    a. Sketch the graph of a cubic function that has 3 distinct real zeros.

b.   Sketch the graph of a cubic function that has only one real zero because it has no vertices.

c.   Sketch the graph of a cubic function that has only one real zero in spite of the fact that it has two vertices.

58.   **Computer Graphics Exploration Problem**   Figure 10-4e shows three cubic functions, f, g, and h, drawn by the program PLOT CUBIC from the accompanying disk. Function f has a *plateau* at (2, 5)

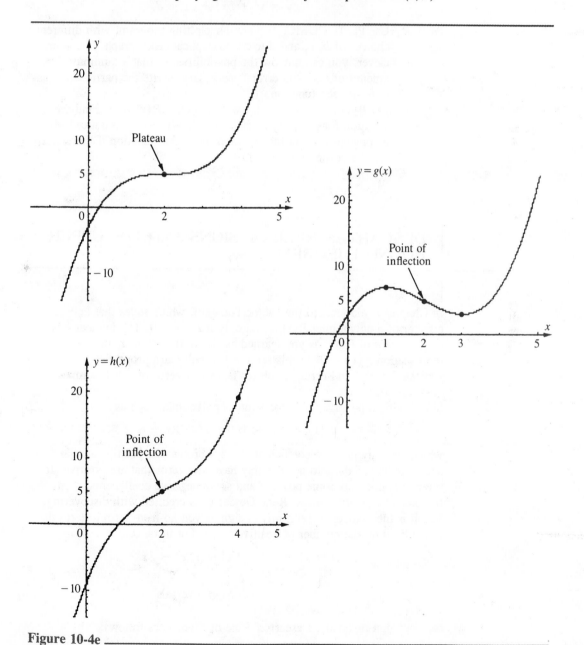

Figure 10-4e

where the graph levels off as though it were going to form two vertices, but it goes back up again before forming the vertices. Function
g actually has a high point at $(1, 7)$, a low point at $(3, 3)$, and a
point of inflection at $(2, 5)$. Function h has no vertices and no
plateau, but has a point of inflection at $(2, 5)$, and passes through
$(4, 19)$. The y-intercept for each function can be read from the
graph. Each function has an equation of the form

$$y = x^3 + bx^2 + cx + d.$$

a. Use PLOT CUBIC, or a similar plotting program, with different
    choices of b, c, and d to try to duplicate each graph. If you are
    clever, you can narrow the possibilities so that a minimum
    amount of trial and error is necessary. Write the particular equa-
    tion for each function.
b. Let $P(x)$ be a function for which $f(x) = P(x) + 5$. Find the
    equation for $P(x)$. Then factor $P(x)$. What do you notice? Make
    a conjecture about the equation of a cubic function if there is a
    plateau at the point (h, k).

| 10-5 | DESCARTES' RULE OF SIGNS AND THE UPPER BOUND THEOREM |

In Chapter 7 you learned the Factor Theorem, which states that $(x - c)$ is
a factor of a polynomial $P(x)$ if and only if $P(c) = 0$. The number c is
called a *zero* of $P(x)$, as you learned earlier in this chapter, or a *root* of
the equation $P(x) = 0$. In this section you will learn properties that
shorten the trial-and-error search for factors or zeros of a polynomial.

Substituting a positive value for x into a polynomial such as

$$P(x) = 3x^4 + 5x^3 + x^2 + 8x + 6$$

which has only positive coefficients always produces a positive answer. So
such a polynomial could not possibly have any zeros that are positive. If
the polynomial has some positive and some negative coefficients, then
there can be positive zeros. Rene Descartes is credited with discovering
that it is the number of *reversals* of sign as you go from term to term that
sets a limit on the number of positive zeros. For instance,

$$P(x) = x^5 - 7x^4 - 5x^3 + 11x^2 - 2x + 5$$

Sign reversals

has four sign reversals. Descartes' Rule of Signs is as follows:

DESCARTES' RULE OF SIGNS
The number of positive zeros of a polynomial is less than or equal to the number of sign reversals in $P(x)$. The number of negative zeros is less than or equal to the number of sign reversals in $P(-x)$. In both cases, the number of zeros has the same parity (odd or even) as the number of reversals.

So the polynomial above could have 4, 2, or 0 positive zeros. Since

$$P(-x) = -x^5 - 7x^4 + 5x^3 + 11x^2 + 2x + 5$$

One sign reversal

there is exactly *one* negative zero. By the corollary of the Fundamental Theorem of Algebra in Section 10-4, $P(x)$ has exactly 5 zeros. So there are three possible combinations of zeros for this polynomial.

positive	negative	non-real complex
4	1	0
2	1	2
0	1	4

Recall that complex zeros of polynomials with real coefficients always come in conjugate pairs.

A proof of Descartes' Rule can be found in texts such as L. E. Dickson; *New First Course in the Theory of Equations;* John Wiley & Sons, Inc.; 1939.

A related theorem concerns the maximum and minimum possible values of real zeros. If you divide a polynomial by $(x - c)$, and the signs of the quotient coefficients and the remainder are all the same, then no real zeros are greater than c.

THEOREM

UPPER BOUND THEOREM
For a positive number c, if $P(x)$ is divided by $(x - c)$ and the resulting quotient and remainder have no sign reversals, then $P(x)$ has no real zeros greater than c.

A lower bound can be found by determining an upper bound for the zeros of $P(-x)$, or equivalently, by finding a number c such that the signs of the quotient and remainder *alternate*.

The bounds are most easily found by synthetic substitution. In Example 1 of Section 10-4 you plotted $P(x) = x^3 - 4x^2 - 5x + 14$. This graph is shown again in Figure 10-5a.

From the graph you can see that there are two positive zeros (x-intercepts), and one negative zero, thus confirming Descartes' Rule of Signs.

$$P(x) = x^3 - 4x^2 - 5x + 14 \qquad \text{Two reversals}$$

$$P(-x) = -x^3 - 4x^2 + 5x + 14 \quad \text{One reversal}$$

x	1	-4	-5	$P(x)$ 14	
-3	1	-7	16	-34	↑
-2	1	-6	7	0	Signs alternate.
-1	1	-5	0	14	-3 is a lower
0	1	-4	-5	14	bound.
1	1	-3	-8	6	
2	1	-2	-9	-4	No sign reversals
3	1	-1	-8	-10	5 is an upper
4	1	0	-5	-6	bound.
5	1	1	0	14	↓
6	1	2	7	56	

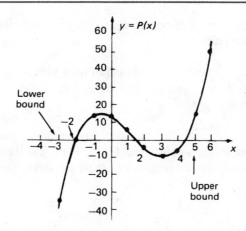

$$P(x) = x^3 - 4x^2 - 5x + 14$$

Three real zeros

Figure 10-5a

From the table you can see that if x is 5 or more, the signs of the quotient and remainder are all $+$. So 5 is an upper bound for the zeros. If x is -3 or less, the signs of the quotient and remainder alternate. So -3 is a lower bound for the zeros. These facts are confirmed by the x-intercepts of the graph.

In the following exercise you will learn what Descartes' Rule of Signs and the Upper Bound Theorem say, and something about why they work.

EXERCISE 10-5

Do These Quickly

The following problems are intended to refresh your skills. You should be able to do all 10 in less than 5 minutes.

Q1.   Sketch the graph of a cubic function with a plateau at $(3, 1)$.

Q2.   Sketch the graph of $y = 3 \times 2^x$.

Q3.   If $P(-5) = 0$, then polynomial $P(x)$ has what linear factor?

Q4.   If $P\left(\dfrac{2}{3}\right) = 0$, then polynomial $P(x)$ has what linear factor?

Q5.   If $P(x) = x^2 + 5x + 7$, find the quotient when $P(x)$ is divided by $(x - 1)$.

Q6.   What is the remainder when $x^{17} + 13$ is divided by $(x - 1)$?

Q7.   Solve for x: $3x + 4y = 8$
$\ 2x - 4y = 13$

Q8.   What is the difference between a *root* of an equation and a *solution* of an equation?

Q9.   Is -13 an integer?

Q10.   Is $\sqrt{25}$ a rational number?

For Problems 1 through 10, find the possible numbers of positive, negative, and non-real complex zeros.

1. $P(x) = x^3 - 5x^2 + 3x + 7$

2. $P(x) = x^3 + 4x^2 - 7x + 2$

3. $P(x) = x^3 - 5x^2 + 3x - 1$

4. $P(x) = x^3 - x^2 + 4x - 6$

5. $P(x) = x^4 - 2x^3 - x + 1$

6. $P(x) = x^4 + 5x^2 + 2x - 11$

7. $P(x) = x^4 + x^3 - 5x^2 + x - 6$

8. $P(x) = x^4 - x^3 - 11x^2 + 9x + 8$

9. $P(x) = x^8 + 3x^6 + 4x^2 + 5$

10. $P(x) = x^5 + 4x^3 + 2x$ (Think!)

For Problems 11 through 14, find the least integer that is an upper bound for the zeros and the greatest integer that is a lower bound. Plot the part of the graph for values of x between these two integers, inclusive.

11. $P(x) = x^3 - 2x^2 - 5x + 3$

12. $P(x) = x^3 + 2x^2 + 4x - 5$

13. $P(x) = 3x^3 - 5x^2 + 7x + 4$

14. $P(x) = 2x^3 + x^2 - 8x - 3$

15. The trinomial $x^2 + 2x + 8$ has no positive zeros because there are no sign reversals. If this trinomial is multiplied by $(x - c)$, then the resulting polynomial, $P(x) = (x - c)(x^2 + 2x + 8)$, has exactly one positive zero, namely c (provided c is a positive number).
    a. Find a value of c for which $P(x)$, when multiplied out, has exactly one sign reversal.
    b. Find a value of c for which $P(x)$ has exactly three sign reversals.
    c. Explain why $P(x)$ could not have exactly two sign reversals.

16. The trinomial $x^2 - 3x + 15$ has two sign reversals.
    a. According to Descartes' rule, how many positive zeros could it have?
    b. How many positive zeros does it actually have? Justify your answer.
    c. Use Descartes' rule to show that the trinomial has no negative zeros.
    d. If c is a positive number, then the polynomial $P(x) = (x + c)$ $(x^2 - 3x + 15)$ has exactly one negative zero, namely $-c$. Find a value of c for which $P(-x)$, when multiplied out, has exactly three sign reversals.
    e. Explain why $P(-x)$ in part (d) could not possibly have exactly two sign reversals.

17. According to Descartes' Rule, what can be said about the number of zeros of polynomials that begin and end as follows?
    a. $x^{14} \ldots + 8$ b. $x^{15} \ldots + 8$
    c. $x^9 \ldots -4$ d. $x^8 \ldots -4$

18. Based on the answers to Problem 17, write a conclusion concerning the parity (odd or even) of the number of sign reversals in a polynomial whose first term is positive.

19. Find the real zeros of the following. Then use Descartes' rule to prove that there are no other real zeros.
    a. $P(x) = x^5 - 32$ b. $P(x) = x^5 + 32$

c. $P(x) = x^6 - 64$ d. $P(x) = x^{10} + 1$

20. The polynomial $P(x) = 2x^3 - 8x^2 + 2x + 13$ has two sign rever-
     sals, and thus could have 0 or 2 positive zeros.
     a. Show that although $P(2)$ and $P(3)$ are positive, there is a zero
         between $x = 2$ and $x = 3$. Draw a graph.
     b. Use the Upper Bound Theorem to show that 4 is an upper bound
         for the zeros of $P(x)$.
     c. Explain why 3 is also an upper bound for the zeros, even though
         the quotient $\frac{P(x)}{(x - 3)}$ does have sign reversals. How is this fact
         consistent with the Upper Bound Theorem?

21. Write a computer program to find an upper bound for the zeros of a
     polynomial up to 5th degree using the Upper Bound Theorem. The
     program should allow you to input the six coefficients. Then the
     computer should divide by $(x - 1)$, $(x - 2)$, . . . , until all signs of
     the quotient and remainder are alike. The output of the program
     should be the quotient coefficients and the remainder at each pass
     through the loop. When the upper bound is reached, the computer
     should print its value along with an appropriate message. Test your
     program by showing that 9 is the least integer upper bound for the
     zeros of $P(x) = x^5 - 7x^4 - 9x^3 + x^2 - 99x - 11$.

10-6 | HIGHER DEGREE FUNCTIONS
     | AS MATHEMATICAL MODELS

Higher degree functions are used as models in two basically different
ways. A function may turn out to be polynomial based on theoretical considerations. For example, the shape into which a loaded beam bends is the
graph of a polynomial function. The degree of the function is determined
by the way the weight is distributed along the beam and the manner in
which the beam is supported.

The second way polynomial functions are applied is to *start out* by assuming that a polynomial function is a reasonable model, and then fit the polynomial graph to measured experimental data points. A model created in
this way is called an "empirical" model. For example, if you assume a *cubic* function, then you have assumed an equation of the form

$$y = ax^3 + bx^2 + cx + d,$$

where a, b, c, and d stand for constants. Fitting the model to the data requires finding values of these constants by substituting the values of (x, y)
and solving the resulting system of linear equations for a, b, c, and d. This
is the same procedure you used for quadratic functions in Chapter 5.

Objective:

Given a real-world situation in which one variable depends on another by a cubic or higher degree function, find the particular equation and use it as a mathematical model.

Since the technique of finding the particular equation is a familiar one, no specific examples are presented here. If you need a refresher on how to do it, see Sections 5-6 and 5-7.

The exercise which follows contains problems of each of the above types. There are also problems in which polynomial functions are used as mathematical models of the *mathematical* world.

EXERCISE 10-6

1. **Beam Deflection Problem**   A horizontal beam 10 meters long has its left end built into a wall, and its right end resting on a support, as shown in Figure 10-6a. The beam is loaded with weight uniformly distributed along its length. As a result, the beam sags downward according to the equation

$$y = -x^4 + 25x^3 - 150x^2$$

where x is the number of meters from the wall to a point on the beam, and y is the number of hundredths of a millimeter from the x-axis to the beam.

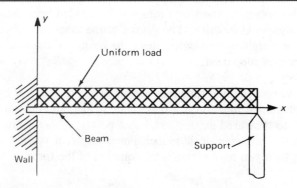

Figure 10-6a

a. What is an appropriate domain for x?
b. Find the zeros of this function and tell what they represent in the real world.

c. Using all integer values of x in the domain, plot a graph of this function.

2. *Diving Board Problem*   When you stand on a diving board (see Figure 10-6b), the amount the board bends, y, below its rest position is a cubic function of x, the distance from the built-in end to the point on the board. Suppose that you measure the following deflections:

x (ft.)	y (thousandth of an inch)
0	0
1	116
2	448
3	972

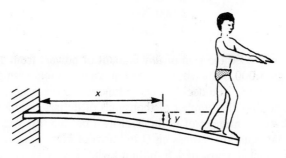

Figure 10-6b _____

a. Derive the particular equation expressing y in terms of x.
b. The board is 10 feet long. How far does its tip sag below the horizontal?

3. *Oil Viscosity Problem*   The viscosity, or "stickiness" of normal motor oil you use in your car decreases as its temperature increases. The "all-weather" motor oils, however, retain a relatively constant viscosity throughout their range of operating temperatures. Suppose that a chemical lab has found the following viscosities for an all-weather motor oil:

Temperature, °F	Viscosity
100	54
200	50
300	52
400	54

Let V be the number of units of viscosity, and T be the number of *hundreds* of degrees (i.e., $T = 1$ means temperature is 100°). Assume that a *cubic* function is a reasonable model of how V varies with T.

a.   Find the particular equation expressing V in terms of T.
b.   Predict the viscosity at 0°, 500°, and 600°.
c.   Plot a graph of V versus T in the domain $0 \le T \le 6$.
d.   Does $V = 0$ for any value of T in this domain? Justify your answer.

4.   ***Electric Power Cost Problem***   Suppose that you have a summer job
with a company that designs pollution control equipment. Your part
of the project is to estimate the monthly cost of electricity to operate
the smokestack scrubbers for a new cement plant. From the Power
Company, you find that the monthly bills for various amounts of
electricity would be

Kilowatt hours (kwh)	Dollars
1,000,000	$20,000
2,000,000	29,000
3,000,000	34,000
4,000,000	41,000

Since you need the cost of *any* amount of power, from 1,000,000
through 4,000,000 kwh, you need an equation expressing cost in
terms of kwh. You decide a *cubic* function is reasonable.
a.   Let D = the number of thousands of dollars per month, and let
k = the number of millions of kwh per month. Write the particular equation expressing D in terms of k.
b.   Predict the cost of 1.5 million kwh.
c.   According to your model, how much would you pay if you used
no electricity in a given month? Is this reasonable? Explain.
d.   Your boss wants to know how much electricity could be used
without exceeding $35,000 per month. Draw a graph of D versus
k, and use the graph to estimate this number.
e.   Use the computer program of Problem 53, Exercise 10-4, to get
a better answer to part d, above.

5.   ***Lumber Problem***   Woody Forester has the job of figuring out how
much lumber can be obtained from various sizes of monkeypuzzle
trees. From sawmill records he finds the following numbers of
board-feet of lumber can be cut from trees of the given diameters:

Diameter (feet)	Lumber (board-feet)
1	10
2	99
3	324
4	745

He figures that since board-feet is a cubic measure, a *cubic* function
would be a reasonable mathematical model.

a. Find the particular equation expressing board-feet in terms of diameter.

b. How much lumber can be obtained from a tree with a trunk five feet in diameter?

c. Woody finds that the function in part a has *one* integer zero. What is that zero? Find all other zeros.

d. Draw the graph of this function.

e. According to this mathematical model, what is the smallest diameter tree that will produce usable lumber?

f. Woody's boss tells him not to cut down any tree that would give less than 200 board-feet of lumber. Approximately what diameter trees can Woody cut down? There is a way to answer this question with almost *no* more work!

6. *Payload Problem*   The number of kilograms of "payload" an airplane can carry equals the number of kilograms the wings can lift *minus* the mass of the airplane itself and the mass of the flight crew and their equipment. The lift is directly proportional to the *square* of the plane's length since lift depends on wing *area*. The plane's mass varies directly with the *cube* of its length, since mass depends on *volume*. The mass of the crew and their equipment is *constant*, and does *not* depend on the plane's length.

a. Let L = number of meters long the plane is. Let $P(L)$ = number of kilograms of payload the plane can carry. Write the general equation expressing $P(L)$ in terms of L.

b. Find the particular equation if a plane 20 meters long can lift 2000 kilograms and has a mass of 800 kilograms. The mass of the flight crew and their equipment is 400 kilograms.

c. Calculate $P(L)$ for each 5 meters from $L = 10$ through $L = 50$.

d. Since P is a *cubic* function, it has *three* zeros. Find the zeros, then tell what each one represents in the real world.

e. Use the results of parts c and d to plot the graph of P in a suitable domain.

7. *Sum of the Squares Problem*   Let $S(n)$ be the *sum* of the *squares* of the integers from 0 through n. That is,

$$S(n) = 0^2 + 1^2 + 2^2 + 3^2 + \ldots + n^2.$$

a. Find $S(0)$, $S(1)$, $S(2)$, and $S(3)$.

b. $S(n)$ is a *cubic* function of n. Find the particular equation expressing $S(n)$ in terms of n using the ordered pairs from part a.

c. The coefficients in the particular equation are fractions. Factor out the appropriate fraction leaving a polynomial with *integer* coefficients inside the parentheses, then factor this polynomial. (This is the formula for the sum of the squares that you will find in handbooks such as *CRC Tables*.)

    d.   Use the equation of part d to find $S(4)$ and $S(5)$. Then show that your answers are correct by actually adding the squares of the integers.

    e.   Find $S(1000)$.

    f.   If you have studied mathematical induction (Appendix B), prove that your formula gives the right answer for $S(n)$ for *all* integers $n \geq 0$.

8.   *Sum of the Cubes Problem*   Let $S(n)$ be the *sum* of the *cubes* of the integers from 0 through n. That is,

$$S(n) = 0^3 + 1^3 + 2^3 + 3^3 + \ldots + n^3.$$

    a.   Find $S(0)$, $S(1)$, $S(2)$, $S(3)$, and $S(4)$. You should find that all of these numbers are perfect squares!

    b. $S(n)$ is a *quartic* function of n. Find the particular equation expressing $S(n)$ in terms of n, using the ordered pairs of part a.

    c.   The coefficients in the particular equation are fractions. Factor out the appropriate fraction, thus leaving a polynomial with *integer* coefficients inside the parentheses.

    d.   Factor the polynomial inside the parentheses from part c. From your answer, how can you conclude that $S(n)$ is *always* a perfect square, no matter what positive integer n is?

    e.   Find $S(1000)$. Which is quicker for this calculation—using the formula you have derived, or simply adding up all the cubes of the integers?

    f.   If you have studied mathematical induction (Appendix B), prove that your formula works for *all* integers $n \geq 0$.

10-7 | CHAPTER REVIEW AND TEST

In this chapter you have investigated higher degree polynomial functions. Synthetic substitution allowed you to calculate plotting data quickly. The Fundamental Theorem of Algebra and its corollary let you conclude that an nth degree function always has exactly n zeros, if you are willing to use complex numbers. You also learned that the familiar Factor Theorem is really just a corollary of the more general Remainder Theorem. Finally, you saw several examples in which higher degree functions are reasonable mathematical models.

The Review Problems below parallel the sections in this chapter. The Concepts Problems let you try your hand at applying what you know to analyze a new situation. The Chapter Test is similar to one your instructor might give to see how well you understand higher degree functions.

REVIEW PROBLEMS

R1. If $f(x) = -x^3 + 5x^2 + 4x - 11$, find $f(3)$ by direct substitution and evaluation of the function.

R2. a. Evaluate i^{59}.
     b. Evaluate i^{-15}.
     c. Evaluate i^{500}.
     d. Write in terms of i and simplify: $\sqrt{-63}$
     e. Plot $-5 + 3i$ on the complex plane.
     f. Write the complex conjugate of $-17 + 13i$.
     g. Subtract: $(8 - 2i) - (3 - 11i)$
     h. Multiply: $(5 - 7i)(2 + 8i)$
     i. Multiply: $(12 + i)(12 - i)$
     j. Do the squaring: $(12 + i)^2$
     k. Divide: $\dfrac{12 + 9i}{3 - 4i}$
     l. Find the absolute value of $11 + 4i$.

R3. a. Solve: $3x^2 + 4x + 10 = 0$
     b. Write a quadratic equation with real-number coefficients if one of the solutions is $3 + 4i$.
     c. Factor over the set of complex numbers: $x^2 - 4x + 5$
     d. Factor over the set of complex numbers: $25x^2 + 1$
     e. Without actually solving the equation, find the *sum* of the solutions and the *product* of the solutions: $5x^2 + 13x + 79 = 0$

R4. a. If $P(x) = 5x^3 - 11x^2 + 8x + 9$, find $P(2)$ by synthetic substitution.
     b. Plot the graph of $P(x) = -2x^3 - x^2 + 6x + 8$ in the domain $-3 \le x \le 3$.
     c. Find all zeros of the function in part (b).
     d. Find the remainder if $P(x) = x^3 + 17$ is divided by $(x + 2)$.
     e. Sketch the graph of a quartic function with two distinct positive zeros, two distinct negative zeros, and a negative y-intercept.

R5. a. Use Descartes' Rule of Signs to write the possible numbers of zeros, positive, negative, and non-real complex, for $P(x) = 8x^7 - 13x^5 + 11x^4 - 16x^2 - x + 3$.
     b. When you factor $x^5 - 1$ you get

$$x^5 - 1 = (x - 1)(x^4 + x^3 + x^2 + x + 1).$$

   Prove that the second factor is not zero for any positive value of x.
     c. Based in the Upper Bound Theorem, show that $P(x) = x^4 - 7x^3 - 8x^2 + 2x - 5$ has no zeros greater than 8, but may have a zero between -2 and 8.

R6.   A cubic function $P(x)$ contains the ordered pairs $(-1, -10)$,
$(2, -7)$, $(3, 2)$ and $(4, 45)$.
a.   Find the particular equation.
b.   Find $P(-2)$.
c.   Find one integer zero of $P(x)$.

CONCEPTS PROBLEMS

C1.   Sketch the graph of
a.   a seventh degree function,
b.   a quartic function with two distinct real zeros and two non-real complex zeros,
c.   a polynomial function with two real zeros at the same point.

C2.   Prove that

$$\frac{a - bi}{b + ai} = -i.$$

C3.   You have learned that if s_1 and s_2 are solutions of a quadratic equation $ax^2 + bx + c = 0$, then $s_1 + s_2 = -\dfrac{b}{a}$. If s_1, s_2, and s_3 are
solutions of a *cubic* equation $ax^3 + bx^2 + cx + d = 0$, prove that

$$s_1 + s_2 + s_3 = -\frac{b}{a}.$$

Then find the sum of the solutions of the equation

$$5x^3 + 11x^2 - 13x + 47 = 0.$$

C4.   *Catastrophe Theory Problem*   According to "catastrophe theory"
(see for example *Scientific American*, April, 1976), when a person
is under certain kinds of stress, the amount of food eaten is *not* a
simple function of how hungry he or she is (see Figure 10-7). As
hunger increases, food consumption increases slightly, but not
enough to satisfy the hunger. Then at a certain point a
"catastrophe" happens, and the person starts "gorging" himself or
herself. The hunger decreases, but remains high until a "reverse
catastrophe" happens, and the person starts "fasting" again. Suppose that Juanita Lott is under this kind of stress. When her hunger
is 16 units, she eats only 1000 Calories per day. At the catastrophe
point, 20 hunger units, she jumps from 2000 to 5000 Calories per
day. The point $(0, 0)$ is also on the graph.

Let x be the number of units of hunger.
Let y be the number of *thousands* of Calories per day.

a.   Write the given information as *four* ordered pairs, (x, y).

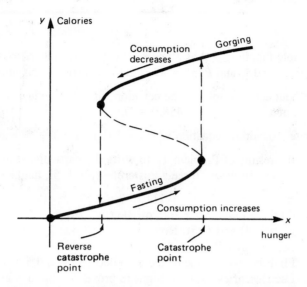

Figure 10-7

b. The graph looks like the *inverse* of a cubic function. That is, the general equation would be

$$x = ay^3 + by^2 + cy + d.$$

Based on this assumption, find the particular equation.

c. Explain why this relation is *not* a function.

d. Plot an accurate graph of this function by picking values of y and calculating the corresponding values of x. Use values of y from 0 through 6. You can check the accuracy of your equation by making sure that the given ordered pairs satisfy it.

e. Based on your graph, where does the reverse catastrophe seem to happen? Demonstrate that you are right by showing that there are *exactly two* distinct values of y for this value of x.

f. What is the *range* of this relation?

g. Find the two values of y in the range for which $x = 18$.

h. Show that there is only *one* real value of y when $x = 0$.

i. Juanita's doctor prescribes therapy that relieves the stress. Thereafter, her hunger and food consumption are related by the equation

$$x = y^3 - 6y^2 + 20y - 15.$$

Plot the graph of this relation. Use values of y from 0 through 4. Does there seem to be a catastrophe under these conditions?

CHAPTER TEST

T1. A cubic function, P, has $P(x)$-intercept equal to 8. Also, $P(1) =$ 7, $P(2) = 14$, and $P(3) = 47$. Find the particular equation.

T2. Without actually solving the equation, find the product of the solutions of $x^2 + 37.92x - 458.9 = 0$.

T3. Write a quadratic equation whose solutions are $3 + 5i$ and $3 - 5i$.

T4. Use the results of Problem T3 to write the particular equation of a cubic function whose three zeros are -1, $3 + 5i$, and $3 - 5i$.

T5. Given $P(x) = x^3 - 7x^2 + 11x + 3$:
  a. Find the *one* integer zero of $P(x)$.
  b. Find $P(4)$ and $P(5)$. How can you tell that $P(x)$ has a zero between 4 and 5?
  c. Find the exact value of the zero between 4 and 5.
  d. Use Descartes' Rule of Signs to prove that there is another positive zero of $P(x)$.
  e. Based on the Upper Bound Theorem, can you be sure that there is no zero of $P(x)$ greater than 5? Justify your answer.

T6. Sketch the graph of a cubic function that has a negative x^3-coefficient, a negative y-intercept, and just one real zero.

11

Sequences and Series

In this chapter you will study **sequences**, in which the independent variable jumps from integer to integer, with no values in between. The same kind of sequence can be used to model things ranging from the money in a savings account to the notes on a piano.

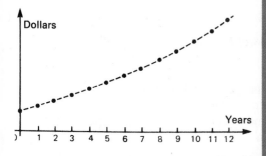

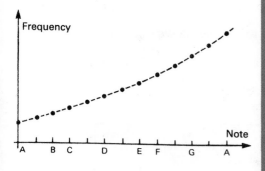

| 11-1 | INTRODUCTION TO SEQUENCES |

The numbers 3, 5, 7, . . . , seem to follow a pattern. Such a set of numbers is commonly called a "sequence," and each of the numbers in the set is called a "term" of the sequence. If you know what the pattern is, you can replace the ellipsis (the ". . ." punctuation mark) with other terms of the sequence. For example, you might write

$$3, 5, 7, 9, 11, 13, 15, 17, 19, 21, \ldots,$$

assuming that this is the sequence of odd integers beginning with 3. However, it could also be

$$3, 5, 7, 11, 13, 17, 19, 23, \ldots,$$

which is the sequence of odd primes. So you will be asked to discover "a" pattern rather than "the" pattern.

Sequences can be fit into the framework of what you have learned so far by considering them to be *functions*. Each term in a sequence has a *position* or *term number* (1st, 5th, 976th, etc.), and a *value* (3, 11, 1953, etc.). The sequence of odd integers above can be written

term *value*:   3 5 7 9 11 13 15 . . . ,

term *number*:   1 2 3 4   5   6   7 . . . .

For each term *number* there is a unique term *value*. Thus, a sequence can be thought of as a *function*.

DEFINITION

A **sequence** is a function whose domain is the set of natural numbers (the term numbers), and whose range is the set of term values.

Notes:

1. This definition implies that a sequence has an *infinite* number of terms.
2. The letter n will usually be used for the term number, and the letter t_n for the term value. Normal function notation such as $t(n)$ makes formulas awkward to read and write. The symbol t_n is pronounced "t sub-n," or simply "term number n."

Objective:
Given the first few terms of a sequence,

a. discover a pattern,
b. write a few more terms of the sequence,
c. get a formula for t_n,
d. use the formula to calculate other terms values, and
e. draw a graph of the sequence.

EXAMPLE

Do the above five things for the sequence 3, 5, 7, 9, 11, 13, 15, ...

a. An obvious pattern is that the terms increase by 2 each time.
b. Using this pattern, the next few terms are 17, 19, 21, 23, ...
c. Discovering a formula is tricky and will test your ingenuity. What you must do is find some link between the term *number, n,* and the term *value*, t_n. It helps to write the two sets of numbers close to each other.

$$3, 5, 7, 9, 11, 13, 15, \ldots \text{ Term } values$$

$$①②③④⑤ \quad ⑥ \quad ⑦ \ldots \text{ Term } numbers$$

In this case the term values seem to be increasing *twice* as fast as the term numbers. If you write the values of $2n$ by the values of t_n, a pattern shows up.

$$3, 5, 7, 9, 11, 13, 15, \ldots \leftarrow t_n$$
$$1 \; 2 \; 3 \; 4 \;\; 5 \;\; 6 \;\; 7 \qquad \leftarrow n$$
$$2 \; 4 \; 6 \; 8 \; 10 \; 12 \; 14 \qquad \leftarrow 2n$$

The value of t_n is always *one more than* the value of $2n$. So a formula would be

$$t_n = 2n + 1.$$

d. If you must calculate t_n for a *large* value of n, you would use the formula rather than continuing the pattern. For example, if n were 256, then

$$t_{256} = 2 \cdot 256 + 1$$

$$= 513.$$

e. The graph may be plotted pointwise, as shown in Figure 11-1a. The dots should *not* be connected with a solid line since the domain contains only *integers*.

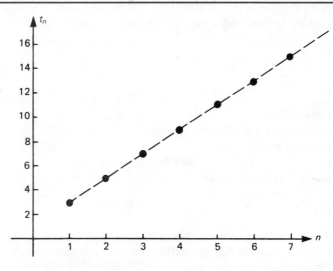

Figure 11-1a _____

Not all sequence graphs are linear. For example, the graph of 24, 12, 6, 3, $1\frac{1}{2}$, . . . , is shown in Figure 11-1b.

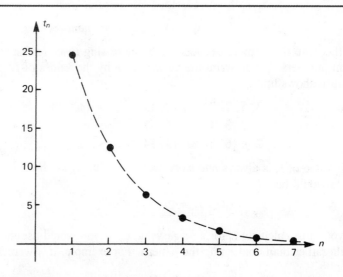

Figure 11-1b _____

The exercise which follows is designed to give you practice in accomplishing the objectives of this section.

EXERCISE 11-1

In Problems 1 through 12, t_1 through t_6 of a sequence are listed. For each sequence, do the following:
a. Draw the graph.
b. Find t_7 and t_8.
c. Figure out a formula for t_n.
d. Calculate t_{100}.

1. $1, \dfrac{1}{2}, \dfrac{1}{3}, \dfrac{1}{4}, \dfrac{1}{5}, \dfrac{1}{6}, \ldots$

2. $1, 4, 9, 16, 25, 36, \ldots$

3. $\dfrac{1}{3}, \dfrac{1}{5}, \dfrac{1}{7}, \dfrac{1}{9}, \dfrac{1}{11}, \dfrac{1}{13}, \ldots$

4. $\dfrac{1}{2}, \dfrac{3}{4}, \dfrac{7}{8}, \dfrac{15}{16}, \dfrac{31}{32}, \dfrac{63}{64}, \ldots$

5. $3, 4, 5, 6, 7, 8, \ldots$

6. $3, 6, 9, 12, 15, 18, \ldots$

7. $3, 6, 12, 24, 48, 96, \ldots$

8. $2, 6, 18, 54, 162, 486, \ldots$

9. $32, -16, 8, -4, 2, -1, \ldots$

10. $1, -1, 1, -1, 1, -1, \ldots$

11. $1, \dfrac{3}{2}, \dfrac{5}{4}, \dfrac{7}{8}, \dfrac{9}{16}, \dfrac{11}{32}, \ldots$

12. $0, \dfrac{13}{8}, \dfrac{26}{27}, \dfrac{39}{64}, \dfrac{52}{125}, \dfrac{65}{216}, \ldots$

For Problems 13 through 20, write the next two terms of the sequence, and tell what pattern you used.

13. $1, 2, 4, 7, 11, 16, \ldots$

14. $1, 11, 20, 28, 35, 41, \ldots$

15. $1, 1, 2, 3, 5, 8, 13, \ldots$ (A *Fibonacci* sequence)

16. $1, 2, 6, 24, 120, 720, \ldots$ (The sequence of *factorials*)

17. $1, 3, 6, 10, 15, \ldots$ (The sequence of *triangular* numbers)

18. $\dfrac{1}{12}, \dfrac{1}{19}, \dfrac{1}{26}, \dfrac{1}{33}, \ldots$ (A *harmonic* sequence)

19. 1, 1, 2, 2, 3, 4, 4, 8, 5, 16, 6, 32, . . .

20. 100, 100, 75, 50, 50, 25, 25, . . .

21. The sequence of letters $o, t, t, f, f, s, s, . . .$, has a mathematical pattern. Demonstrate that you have figured out this pattern by writing the next four letters in the sequence.

11-2 | ARITHMETIC AND GEOMETRIC SEQUENCES

Two types of sequences are of special interest mathematically because the formulas are easily derived, and of special interest practically because they fit the real world as mathematical models in many situations. Examples are

$$3, 10, 17, 24, 31, 38, . . . , \text{ and}$$

$$3, 6, 12, 24, 48, 96, ...$$

In the first sequence the next term is formed by *adding* a constant, 7, to the previous term. In the other, the next term is formed by *multiplying* the previous term by a constant, 2.

DEFINITION

> An **arithmetic** sequence is a sequence in which one term equals a constant *added* to the preceding term.

The constant for an arithmetic sequence is called the *common difference, d,* because the difference between any two adjacent terms equals this constant. In the sequence above,

$$10 - 3 = 7, \quad 17 - 10 = 7, \quad 24 - 17 = 7,$$

and so forth. The word "arithmetic" is used as an adjective here rather than as a noun, and is pronounced with the stress on the "-met-" syllable instead of the "-ith-" syllable.

DEFINITION

> A **geometric** sequence is a sequence in which each term equals a constant *multiplied* by the preceding term.

The constant for a geometric sequence is called the *common ratio, r,* because the ratio of one term to the preceding term is equal to this constant.

In the sequence above,

$$\frac{6}{3} = 2, \frac{12}{6} = 2, \frac{24}{12} = 2,$$

and so forth.

Arithmetic and geometric sequences are sometimes called "progressions" because the terms "progress" from one to the next in a regular manner. The word "progression" is often used when there is a *finite* number of terms. Sequences have infinite numbers of terms.

Objectives:

1. Given the first few terms of a sequence, tell whether it is arithmetic, geometric, or neither.
2. Given a value of n for a specified arithmetic or geometric sequence, find the value of t_n.
3. Given a value of t_n for a specified arithmetic or geometric sequence, find the value of n.

EXAMPLE 1

Is the sequence 4, 7, 10, . . . arithmetic, geometric, or neither?

Solution:
The first objective may be accomplished by seeing if adjacent terms have either a common difference or a common ratio. For the sequence

$$4, 7, 10, \ldots ,$$

the differences between adjacent terms are

$$t_2 - t_1 = 7 - 4 = 3, \text{ and}$$

$$t_3 - t_2 = 10 - 7 = 3.$$

Since these terms have a *common* difference, the sequence is *arithmetic*. Each term is formed by *adding* 3 to the preceding term. The terms do *not* have a common ratio, since $\frac{10}{7} \neq \frac{7}{4}$, so the sequence is *not* geometric.   ■

EXAMPLE 2

Is the sequence 3, 6, 12, . . . arithmetic, geometric, or neither?

Solution:
For this sequence the differences are

$$t_2 - t_1 = 6 - 3 = 3, \text{ and}$$

$$t_3 - t_2 = 12 - 6 = 6,$$

so the sequence is *not* arithmetic. But the ratios are

$$\frac{t_2}{t_1} = \frac{6}{3} = 2, \text{ and}$$

$$\frac{t_3}{t_2} = \frac{12}{6} = 2.$$

Thus, the sequence is <u>geometric</u> because adjacent terms have a common *ratio*. Each term is formed by *multiplying* the preceding term by 2. ■

EXAMPLE 3

Is the sequence 2, 6, 24, . . . arithmetic, geometric, or neither?

Solution:
For this sequence the differences are

$$t_2 - t_1 = 6 - 2 = 4, \text{ and}$$

$$t_3 - t_2 = 24 - 6 = 18,$$

and the ratios are

$$\frac{t_2}{t_1} = \frac{6}{2} = 3 \text{ and}$$

$$\frac{t_3}{t_2} = \frac{24}{6} = 4,$$

so the sequence is <u>neither</u> arithmetic nor geometric. (This turns out to be a "factorial" sequence where the next term is formed by multiplying the preceding term by a larger number each time.) ■

Formulas for calculating t_n for arithmetic and geometric sequences can be found by linking the term number to the term value, as you did in the previous section. The arithmetic sequence

$$3, 10, 17, 24, 31, \ldots ,$$

has as a first term $t_1 = 3$, and common difference $d = 7$. The first few terms can be constructed by adding 7 to the preceding term.

$$t_1 = 3$$

$$t_2 = 3 + 7$$

$$t_3 = 3 + 7 + 7 = 3 + (2)(7)$$

$$t_4 = 3 + 7 + 7 + 7 = 3 + (3)(7)$$

$$t_5 = 3 + 7 + 7 + 7 + 7 = 3 + (4)(7).$$

So the pattern consists of adding $(n - 1)$ common differences to the first term, t_1. Thus, the formula is as follows.

CONCLUSION

> **TERM- VALUE OF AN ARITHMETIC SEQUENCE**
> The nth term of an arithmetic sequence equals the first term plus $(n - 1)$ common differences. That is,
>
> $$t_n = t_1 + (n - 1)d$$

Examination of this formula should reveal to you that an arithmetic sequence is nothing more than a cleverly-disguised *linear* function, because the independent variable n appears to the *first* power. The slope of the function is the common difference d, and the y-intercept would be t_0, which equals $t_1 - d$, if zero were in the domain of the function.

The same procedure gives a formula for t_n for a geometric sequence. The sequence

$$3, 6, 12, 24, 48, \ldots ,$$

has $t_1 = 3$ and common ratio $r = 2$. The first few terms can be constructed by multiplying the preceding term by 2.

$$t_1 = 3$$
$$t_2 = 3 \cdot 2$$
$$t_3 = 3 \cdot 2 \cdot 2 = 3 \cdot 2^2$$
$$t_4 = 3 \cdot 2 \cdot 2 \cdot 2 = 3 \cdot 2^3$$
$$t_5 = 3 \cdot 2 \cdot 2 \cdot 2 \cdot 2 = 3 \cdot 2^4$$

So the pattern consists of multiplying the first term, t_1, by the common ratio, r, $(n - 1)$ times.

CONCLUSION

> **TERM VALUE OF A GEOMETRIC SEQUENCE**
> The nth term of a geometric sequence equals the first term multiplied by $(n - 1)$ common ratios. That is,
>
> $$t_n = t_1 \cdot r^{n-1}$$

Notes:

1. Since the independent variable n appears as an exponent, a geometric sequence is actually just an example of *exponential* function, which you

studied in Chapter 6. The only difference is that the domain of a geometric sequence is positive integers rather than all real numbers.
2. The formulas for arithmetic and geometric sequences are exactly alike. The only difference is the *operation* that is performed. For arithmetic sequences, $(n - 1)$ common differences are *added* to t_1. For geometric sequences, $(n - 1)$ common ratios are *multiplied* by t_1.

With the aid of these two conclusions, the second and third objectives of this section can be accomplished.

EXAMPLE 4

Calculate t_{100} for the arithmetic sequence

$$17, 22, 27, 32, \ldots .$$

Solution:
By subtracting adjacent terms, you find that the common difference, d, equals 5. Adding $(100 - 1)$ times 5 to the first term gives

$$t_{100} = 17 + (100 - 1)(5)$$

$$= 17 + 495$$

$$= \underline{\underline{512}}. \qquad \blacksquare$$

EXAMPLE 5

Calculate t_{100} for the geometric sequence with first term $t_1 = 35$ and common ratio $r = 1.05$.

Solution:
Since you know t_1, r, and n, you can multiply the first term by $(100 - 1)$ common ratios.

$$t_{100} = 35 \times 1.05^{100-1}$$

$$= 35 \times 1.05^{99}$$

$$\approx \underline{\underline{4383.375262}} \qquad \blacksquare$$

EXAMPLE 6

The number 68 is a term in the arithmetic sequence with $t_1 = 5$ and $d = 3$. *Which* term is it?

Solution:
In this case you know that $t_n = 68$, and you must find the term number, n. Using the formula,

$$t_n = t_1 + (n - 1)d$$

$$68 = 5 + (n - 1)(3) \quad \text{Substituting into the formula}$$

$$63 = (n - 1)(3)$$

$$21 = n - 1$$

$$\therefore n = \underline{\underline{22}}$$ ∎

EXAMPLE 7

A geometric sequence has $t_1 = 17$ and $r = 2$. If $t_n = 34816$, find n.

Solution:
Substituting in the formula gives

$$t_n = t_1 \cdot r^{n-1}$$

$$34816 = 17 \times 2^{n-1}$$

$$2048 = 2^{n-1}$$

Taking the log of each member,

$$\log 2048 = \log 2^{n-1}$$

$$\log 2048 = (n - 1) \log 2 \quad \text{Log of a power}$$

$$\frac{\log 2048}{\log 2} = n - 1$$

$$11 = n - 1$$

$$\underline{\underline{12}} = n$$ ∎

The exercise which follows is designed to give you practice identifying arithmetic and geometric sequences and finding term values or term number for such sequences.

EXERCISE 11-2

Do These Quickly

The following problems are intended to refresh your skills. You should be able to do all 10 in less than 5 minutes.

Q1.   Write the next two terms in the sequence of primes, 2, 3, 5, 7, 11, 13, 17, 19, ____, ____.

Q2.   Sketch an ellipse with center at (5, 2).

Q3.   Factor over the set of complex numbers: $25 + x^2$.

Q4.   Find the discriminant: $7x^2 - 11x + 3 = 0$

Q5.   Sketch the graph of a cubic function with three real zeros.

Q6.   What is the remainder when $x^7 - 8$ is divided by $x - 1$?

Q7.   Find the slope of the line through $(-2, 6)$ and $(3, 8)$.

Q8.   Write the general equation of an exponential function.

Q9.   What one word means the same as a *root* of an equation?

Q10.   If $f(x) = \dfrac{3}{x}$, find $f^{-1}(x)$.

In Problems 1 through 16 tell whether the sequence can be arithmetic or geometric, or if it is neither. If it is arithmetic, find the common difference; if it is geometric, find the common ratio.

1.   7, 12, 17, . . .   2.   3, 6, 12, . . .

3.   5, 10, 12, . . .   4. $-1, 0, 1, \ldots$

5. $-1, 1, -1, \ldots$ 6. $-1, 2, -3, \ldots$

7.   25, 50, 100, . . .   8.   25, 50, 75, . . .

9.   25, 75, 100, . . .   10. $2, -4, 8, \ldots$

11. $2, -4, 6, \ldots$ 12. $\dfrac{1}{2}, \dfrac{1}{3}, \dfrac{1}{4}, \ldots$

13. $\dfrac{1}{2}, \dfrac{1}{4}, \dfrac{1}{8}, \ldots$ 14. $\dfrac{1}{2}, \dfrac{1}{4}, 0, \ldots$

15. $\sqrt{5}, \sqrt[3]{5}, \sqrt[6]{5}, \ldots$ 16. $\sqrt{5}, \sqrt[3]{5}, \sqrt[4]{5}, \ldots$

For Problems 17 through 24, find the specified terms of the indicated arithmetic sequence.

17. 45th term of 2, 5, 8, . . .

18. 29th term of 7, 11, 15, . . .

19. 51st term of 18, 14, 10, . . .

20. 68th term of 95, 92, 89, . . .

21.   Thirtieth term of $\frac{1}{3}, 1, 1\frac{2}{3}, \ldots$

22.   Seventeenth term of $3\sqrt{2}, 7\sqrt{2}, 11\sqrt{2}, \ldots$

23. $t_{64}, t_{65},$ and t_{66} for 8, 11, 14, . . .

24. $t_{95}, t_{96},$ and t_{97} for 136, 131, 126, . . .

For Problems 25 through 36, find the specified terms of the indicated geometric sequence. Use logarithms if you do not have access to a calculator.

25.   Seventh term of 2, 6, 18, . . .

26.   Ninth term of 1, 2, 4, . . .

27.   Tenth term of 12, 6, 3, . . .

28.   Eighth term of 54, 18, 6, . . .

29.   Tenth term of 1, -2, 4, . . .

30.   Sixth term of 1, $-\frac{3}{2}$, $\frac{9}{4}$, . . .

31. 51st term of the sequence for which $t_1 = 7$ and $r = 1.02$

32. 43rd term of the sequence for which $t_1 = 100$ and $r = 1.04$

33. 37th term of the sequence for which $t_1 = 29$ and $r = 0.92$

34. 31st term of the sequence for which $t_1 = 1000$ and $r = 0.95$

35. 28th term of the sequence for which $t_1 = 0.01$ and $r = -3$

36. 64th term of the sequence for which $t_1 = 1$ and $r = -2$

For Problems 37 through 46, find out which term the given number is in the indicated sequence.

37.   101 in the arithmetic sequence with $t_1 = 5$ and $d = 3$

38.   111 in the arithmetic sequence with $t_1 = 7$ and $d = 4$

39.   13 in the arithmetic sequence with $t_1 = 88$ and $d = -5$

40.   0 in the arithmetic sequence with $t_1 = 57$ and $d = -3$

41.   1536 in the geometric sequence with $t_1 = 3$ and $r = 2$

42.   4374 in the geometric sequence with $t_1 = 2$ and $r = 3$

43.   1 in the geometric sequence with $t_1 = 729$ and $r = \frac{1}{3}$

44.   27 in the geometric sequence with $t_1 = 1728$ and $r = \frac{1}{2}$

45. -1215 in the geometric sequence with $t_1 = 5$ and $r = -3$

46. $-170\frac{2}{3}$ in the geometric sequence with $t_1 = \frac{1}{3}$ and $r = -2$

47.   ***Arithmetic Sequence Computer Problem***   Write a computer program to calculate and print terms of an arithmetic sequence. The input should be the first term, the common difference, and the number of terms. The output should be the term number and term value for each term. Test your program using $t_1 = 7\frac{2}{3}$ and $d = \frac{1}{3}$. This is the sequence of men's shoe sizes, where n is the size and t_n is the foot length in inches.

48. *Geometric Sequence Computer Problem*   Modify the computer pro-
    gram from Problem 47 so that it calculates and prints terms of a *geo-
    metric* sequence. Use the modified program to print the first 20 terms
    of the geometric sequence with $t_1 = 1050$ and $r = 1.05$. (Terms of
    this sequence represent the number of dollars you would have in a
    savings account after n years if you invested $1000 at 5% interest,
    compounded once a year.)

49. *Sequences by Computer Graphics*   Write a computer program to
    plot the graph of a geometric sequence on the computer's screen.
    The computer should let you input the first term and the common ra-
    tio. Then it should calculate and plot successive terms. You will
    have to read your computer's instruction manual to find out how to
    make it do graphics. The resulting program should produce a graph
    similar to that below for $t_1 = 9$ and $r = -0.95$.

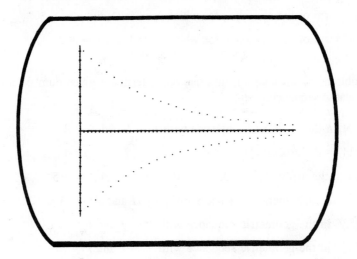

50. What is the difference between a geometric *sequence* and a geomet-
    ric *progression*?

11-3 | ARITHMETIC AND GEOMETRIC MEANS

Suppose that you are asked to find the *average* of two numbers, say 4 and
16. Adding the numbers and dividing by 2 gives 10. The numbers

$$4, 10, 16, \ldots$$

form an arithmetic sequence, since each pair of adjacent terms has a common difference of 6. The number 10 is called the *arithmetic mean* of 4
and 16, the word "mean" being just another word for "average" or "in between."

There are other ways of inserting numbers between 4 and 16 to form sequences which are either arithmetic or geometric. For example, putting 8 and 12 in between forms

$$4, 8, 12, 16, \ldots,$$

which is an arithmetic sequence with a common difference of 4. The numbers 8 and 12 are called the *two* arithmetic means between 4 and 16. Inserting just the number 8 between 4 and 16 forms

$$4, 8, 16, \ldots,$$

which is a *geometric* sequence with a common ratio of 2. So 8 is called a *geometric* mean of 4 and 16. The indefinite article "a" is used here because there is another geometric mean of 4 and 16, namely -8. This is because the sequence

$$4, -8, 16, \ldots,$$

is geometric with common ratio -2. In this section you will learn how to find specified numbers of means between two given numbers.

DEFINITION

> Arithmetic or geometric **means** between two numbers are numbers which form arithmetic or geometric sequences with the two given numbers.

Objective:
Given two numbers, be able to find a specified number of arithmetic or geometric means between them.

The key to accomplishing this objective is finding the common difference or common ratio. With this number known, you can use the *definition* of an arithmetic or geometric sequence to write the desired means.

EXAMPLE 1

Find four arithmetic means between 37 and 54

Solution:
The safest way to find these means is to write 37 and 54 with four spaces between them, into which you can write the means.

$$37, \underline{\quad}, \underline{\quad}, \underline{\quad}, \underline{\quad}, 54$$

These will be the first *six* terms of the sequence. So $n = 6$, $t_6 = 54$, and $t_1 = 37$. You can find d by recalling that t_6 equals t_1 plus *five* common differences.

$$t_6 = t_1 + (6 - 1)d$$

$$54 = 37 + 5d$$

$$17 = 5d$$

$$3\tfrac{2}{5} = d$$

With d known, the means can be written by successively adding d to form next terms.

$$37, \underline{40\tfrac{2}{5}}, \underline{43\tfrac{4}{5}}, \underline{47\tfrac{1}{5}}, \underline{50\tfrac{3}{5}}, 54$$

As a check on your work, you can make sure that you actually *get* the second given term, 54, when you add the common difference, $3\tfrac{2}{5}$, to the last mean, $50\tfrac{3}{5}$. ∎

EXAMPLE 2

Find three geometric means between 3 and 48.

Solution:
The process above works for geometric means, too. Only the computational details are different. By writing

$$3, \underline{\quad}, \underline{\quad}, \underline{\quad}, 48,$$

you realize that there are *five* terms. So $t_5 = 48$, $t_1 = 3$, and $n = 5$. Recalling that t_5 equals t_1 times *four* common ratios,

$$t_5 = t_1 \cdot r^{5-1}$$

$$48 = 3 \cdot r^4$$

$$16 = r^4.$$

By taking the *square* root of both members, you get

$$r^2 = 4 \quad \text{or} \quad r^2 = -4.$$

The first clause of the equation has solutions $r = 2$ or $r = -2$. Therefore, two possible sets of means are

$$3, \underline{6, 12, 24,} 48 \text{ and } 3, \underline{-6, 12, -24,} 48.$$

The second clause of the equation for r has no real solutions. However, it does have solutions in the set of *imaginary* numbers,

$$r = 2i \text{ or } r = -2i,$$

where $i = \sqrt{-1}$. So two other sets of means are

$$3, \underline{6i, -12, -24i,} 48 \text{ and } 3, \underline{-6i, -12, 24i,} 48. \quad ∎$$

The following exercise is designed to give you practice in finding arithmetic and geometric means. You will also discover some properties of arithmetic and geometric means.

EXERCISE 11-3

Do These Quickly

The following problems are intended to refresh your skills. You should be able to do all 10 in less than 5 minutes.

Q1.   Find the next term of the arithmetic sequence 3, 12, ...

Q2.   Find the next term of the geometric sequence 3, 12, ...

Q3.   Find $f(3)$ if $f(x) = 5 \cdot 2^x$.

Q4.   What kind of function has the graph sketched?

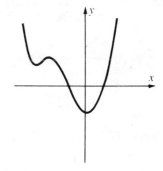

Q5.   If 20% of your $240 paycheck is withheld for taxes, how much do you get to take home?

Q6.   How many degrees in the sum of the measures of two supplementary angles?

Q7.   Evaluate: $9 - |4 - 7|$

Q8.   How many days in a leap-year?

Q9.   Solve for x: $\dfrac{3}{x} = \dfrac{5}{7}$

Q10. Factor: $3x^2 + 5x$

For Problems 1 through 12, find the specified number of *arithmetic* means between the given numbers.

1.   Three, between 42 and 70

2.   Four, between 55 and 85

3.   Six, between -107 and -86

4. Five, between −91 and −67

5. Five, between 23 and −31

6. Six, between 17 and −60

7. Two, between −143 and −215

8. Three, between −257 and −397

9. Three, between 53 and 75

10. Two, between 67 and 90

11. Four, between 123 and 55

12. Five, between 47 and −11

For Problems 13 through 24, find the specified number of *real* geometric means between the given numbers. (There may be *more* than one set of real means!)

13. Two, between 5 and 135

14. Three, between 7 and 112

15. Three, between 81 and 16

16. Two, between 128 and 54

17. Four, between $\frac{1}{32}$ and 32

18. Three, between $\frac{1}{525}$ and $\frac{25}{21}$

19. Two, between 13 and −4459

20. Four, between −7 and 1701

21. Five, between x^5 and x^{17}

22. Two, between x^5 and x^{17}

23. Two, between 13 and 26

24. Three, between 5 and 45

For Problems 25 through 28, find the specified number of geometric means, allowing the common ratio to be a *complex* number.

25. Three, between 2 and 162

26. Three, between 5 and 80

27. Three, between 1 and 16

28. Three, between 2 and 32

29. You know that the formula for the *arithmetic* mean (i.e., the average) of two numbers a and b is $\frac{1}{2}(a + b)$. Prove that the *geometric* mean of a and b is $\sqrt{ab}$.

30. Prove that the geometric mean, m, of two numbers a and b is the *mean proportional* of a and b. That is, show that $\frac{a}{m} = \frac{m}{b}$.

For Problems 31 through 34, find the arithmetic mean and the geometric mean of the given numbers.

31. 2 and 18

32. 3 and 108

33. $\frac{2}{3}$ and 24

34. $\frac{3}{5}$ and 15

35. From the answers to Problems 31 through 34, you can observe that the arithmetic mean is *larger* than the geometric mean. Prove that this is *always* true for the arithmetic and geometric means of two distinct, positive numbers. The formulas given in Problem 29 should help.

36. Prove that if $a, b, c, d, \ldots$, is a geometric sequence, then $a^2, b^2, c^2, d^2, \ldots$ is also a geometric sequence.

11-4 | INTRODUCTION TO SERIES

If you *add* the terms of a sequence, the result is called a *series*. For example, the series which comes from $3, 5, 7, 9, 11, \ldots$, is

$$3 + 5 + 7 + 9 + 11 + \ldots.$$

DEFINITION

SERIES

A **series** is the indicated sum of the terms of a sequence.

Since a sequence has an infinite number of terms, a series can be thought of as a *sum* of an *infinite* number of terms. The sum of *all* of the terms of a series will, therefore, usually be infinite. For this reason it is convenient to study sums of only a *finite* number of terms of a series. For example, the sum of the first four terms of the above series is

$$3 + 5 + 7 + 9,$$

which equals 24. The sum of part of a series is called a *partial sum*.

$3 + 5 + 7 + 9$ is called the "fourth partial sum" of the above series because it is the sum of the first four terms.

DEFINITION

> ### n^{th} PARTIAL SUM
>
> The nth **partial sum** of a series is the sum of the first n terms of that series.

The symbol S_n will be used to stand for the nth partial sum of a series. The value of the partial sum is clearly the dependent variable in a function whose independent variable is n. For the above series,

$$S_1 = 3$$

$$S_2 = 3 + 5 = 8$$

$$S_3 = 3 + 5 + 7 = 15$$

$$S_4 = 3 + 5 + 7 + 9 = 24,$$

and so forth. Note that the partial sums themselves form a sequence,

$$3, 8, 15, 24, \ldots.$$

So series can be dealt with by considering sequences of partial sums.

Unfortunately, there are not many series for which there is a convenient formula for calculating S_n. So mathematicians simply invented a symbol telling how to construct the partial sum. The symbol uses the Greek letter Σ ("sigma") for "sum," and is written

$$S_n = \sum_{k=1}^{n} t_k.$$

The symbol is read, "The sum from $k = 1$ to $k = n$ of t_k," and means $t_1 + t_2 + t_3 + \ldots + t_n$. The variable k is called the *index*. It does the same thing as the "counter" in a loop of a computer program. For example, if $t_k = 2 \cdot 3^k$, then

$$S_4 = \sum_{k=1}^{4} 2 \cdot 3^k = 2 \cdot 3^1 + 2 \cdot 3^2 + 2 \cdot 3^3 + 2 \cdot 3^4$$

$$= 6 + 18 + 54 + 162$$

$$= 240.$$

Objectives:

1. Given a partial sum in Σ notation, *evaluate* it by writing all the terms, then adding them.
2. Given the first few terms of a series, write S_n using Σ notation.

The following exercise is designed to give you practice accomplishing these objectives.

EXERCISE 11-4

Do These Quickly

The following problems are intended to refresh your skills. You should be able to do all 10 in less than 5 minutes.

Q1.   Write the next two terms of the arithmetic sequence 4, 11, ...

Q2.   Write the next two terms of the geometric sequence 4, 12, ...

Q3.   Multiply: $5 \cdot 4 \cdot 3 \cdot 2 \cdot 1$

Q4.   Is 80, 70, 60, ... part of a geometric sequence?

Q5.   What kind of function has this kind of graph?

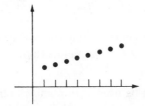

Q6.   Find x if $3^x = 4$.

Q7.   Find the x-coordinate of the vertex: $y = 10x^2 - 6x + 13$

Q8.   Solve: $-5x > 20$

Q9.   Evaluate $|13 - 20|$

Q10.   Find 60% of 80.

For Problems 1 through 20, evaluate the expression by writing the terms and adding them up.

1. $\displaystyle\sum_{k=1}^{5} 2k + 7$

2. $\displaystyle\sum_{k=1}^{6} 3k - 4$

3. $\displaystyle\sum_{k=1}^{10} k$

4. $\displaystyle\sum_{k=1}^{12} k$

5. $\displaystyle\sum_{k=1}^{4} \frac{1}{k}$

6. $\displaystyle\sum_{k=1}^{4} \frac{2}{k}$

7. $\displaystyle\sum_{k=1}^{6} k^2 + 1$

8. $\displaystyle\sum_{k=1}^{5} k^3 - 4$

9. $\displaystyle\sum_{k=1}^{5} (-1)^k(2k + 3)$

10. $\displaystyle\sum_{k=1}^{6} (-1)^k(3k - 2)$

11. $\displaystyle\sum_{k=1}^{5} 2^k$

12. $\displaystyle\sum_{k=1}^{4} 3^k$

13. $\displaystyle\sum_{k=1}^{3} 1.02^k$

14. $\displaystyle\sum_{k=1}^{3} 1.04^k$

15. $\displaystyle\sum_{k=1}^{5} (-1)^{k-1}(2)(3^{k-1})$

16. $\displaystyle\sum_{k=1}^{5} (-1)^{k-1}(3)(2^{k-1})$

17. $\displaystyle\sum_{k=1}^{4} 5 \cdot 3^k$

18. $\displaystyle\sum_{k=1}^{4} 3 \cdot 5^k$

19. $5 \cdot \displaystyle\sum_{k=1}^{4} 3^k$

20. $3 \cdot \displaystyle\sum_{k=1}^{4} 5^k$

21. The answers to Problems 17 and 19 are equal and so are the answers to Problems 18 and 20. What field axiom explains *why* these answers are equal?

22. The Σ notation can be used with numbers other than 1 for the lower value of the index k, and with other variables besides k in the argument. Write down what the following would equal:

   a. $\displaystyle\sum_{k=3}^{5} 4k - 7$

   b. $\displaystyle\sum_{j=0}^{10} (-1)^j x^j$

For Problems 23 through 34, write S_n using sigma notation.

23. S_{10} for $1 + 4 + 9 + 16 + 25 + \ldots$

24. S_{30} for $1 + 8 + 27 + 64 + 125 + \ldots$

25. S_{100} for $\dfrac{1}{3} + \dfrac{1}{4} + \dfrac{1}{5} + \dfrac{1}{6} + \dfrac{1}{7} + \ldots$

26. S_{100} for $\dfrac{1}{3} + \dfrac{1}{5} + \dfrac{1}{7} + \dfrac{1}{9} + \dfrac{1}{11} + \ldots$

27. S_{40} for $2 + 6 + 18 + 54 + 162 + \ldots$

28. S_{50} for $3 + 6 + 12 + 24 + 48 + \ldots$

29. S_{90} for $2 + 6 + 10 + 14 + 18 + \ldots$

30. S_{80} for $5 + 8 + 11 + 14 + 17 + \ldots$

31. S_{20} for $0 - 10 + 20 - 30 + 40 - \ldots$

32. S_{60} for $1 - \dfrac{1}{2} + \dfrac{1}{4} - \dfrac{1}{8} + \dfrac{1}{16} - \ldots$

33. S_{55} for $1 \cdot 2 + 2 \cdot 3 + 3 \cdot 4 + 4 \cdot 5 + \ldots$

34. S_{47} for $1 \cdot \frac{2}{3} + 2 \cdot \frac{3}{4} + 3 \cdot \frac{4}{5} + 4 \cdot \frac{5}{6} + \ldots$

35. Suppose that $S_n = \displaystyle\sum_{k=1}^{n} (2k - 1)$. Find S_n for each value of $n \in \{1, 2, 3, 4, 5, 6, 7\}$. What would you guess might be a *formula* for S_n?

36. Suppose that $S_n = \displaystyle\sum_{k=1}^{n} \dfrac{k}{2}(k + 1)$.
    a. Write the first five terms of the series.
    b. These terms are called *triangular* numbers. Show that each value of t_k is the number of balls that can be arranged in a triangle with k balls on a side.
    c. Find the first five partial sums of the series.
    d. These partial sums are called *pyramidal* numbers. Show that each value of S_n is the number of balls that can be arranged in a triangular pyramid with n balls on each side of the base.

37. Suppose that $S_n = \displaystyle\sum_{k=1}^{n} (\frac{1}{2})^k$. Find S_n for each value of $n \in \{1, 2, 3, 4, 5\}$. From what you observe about the sequence of partial sums, what do you suppose happens to S_n as n becomes very large?

38. **Computer for Series Problem**   Write a computer program to evaluate and print partial sums of a series. You may use a DEF FNY(X) . . . statement in the beginning to record the formula for calculating the next term. As terms are calculated, they should be added to a variable S (for sum) that accumulates their values. At each step, the computer should print the term number, the term value, and the value of the partial sum.

11-5   ARITHMETIC AND GEOMETRIC SERIES

You have learned that a series is what results from adding the terms of a sequence. In this section you will study series which come from adding terms of arithmetic or geometric sequences.

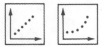

DEFINITION

> An **arithmetic** or **geometric** series is a series which results from adding the terms of an arithmetic or geometric *sequence*, respectively.

In Exercise 11-4 you calculated partial sums of series by writing down each term then adding them up. To find partial sums *quickly*, it is desirable to have a *formula* for S_n.

Objective:

Given an arithmetic or geometric series, be able to calculate S_n, the nth partial sum, *quickly*, and vice versa.

Suppose that you must find the sum of the first 100 terms of the arithmetic series

$$7 + 13 + 19 + 25 + 31 + \ldots$$

The 100th *term* of the series can be calculated by the pattern you already know.

$$t_{100} = t_1 + (100 - 1)d$$

Since $d = 6$ for this series, the formula gives

$$t_{100} = 7 + (99)(6)$$

$$= 601.$$

So the *last* few terms of the partial sum are 601, 595, 589, 583, and so forth. The partial sum is

$$S_{100} = 7 + 13 + 19 + 25 + 31 + \ldots$$

$$+ 583 + 589 + 595 + 601.$$

An interesting pattern shows up if you add the *first* and *last* terms, the *second* and *next-to-last* terms, and so on.

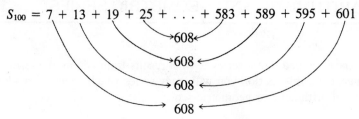

Each pair of terms adds up to 608. And there will be $\frac{100}{2}$, or 50 such pairs. Thus, the partial sum is

$$S_{100} = 608 + 608 + 608 + 608 + \ldots \text{(50 terms)}$$

$$= 50(608)$$

$$= 30400.$$

From this work you can find a *formula* for S_n. The 50 is equal to $\frac{1}{2}$ the number of terms, or $\frac{n}{2}$ and the 608 is equal to $t_1 + t_n$. So the formula is as follows.

CONCLUSION

PARTIAL SUM OF AN ARITHMETIC SERIES
The nth partial sum of an arithmetic series is:

a. the sum of the first and last term, multiplied by half the number of terms, or
b. n times the average of the first and last terms.
That is,

$$S_n = \frac{n}{2}(t_1 + t_n) = n\left(\frac{t_1 + t_n}{2}\right)$$

The formula was derived with an *even* value of n but it works for odd values of n, too. In this case there would be $\frac{(n-1)}{2}$ pairs, each equal to $t_1 + t_n$, plus the *middle* term. But the middle term is just the *average* of t_1 and t_n, which equals $\frac{1}{2}(t_1 + t_n)$. Adding this middle term to the sum of the $\frac{(n-1)}{2}$ pairs gives the same formula.

Carl Friederich Gauss, who lived from 1777 to 1855, is reputed to have discovered this formula at the age of 10. For an interesting account of how he amazed his school master, see James R. Newman's *The World of Mathematics*, Volume I, page 295.

An alternate form of this formula can be found by substituting the quantity $t_1 + (n - 1)d$ for t_n.

$$S_n = \frac{n}{2}(t_1 + t_n) \qquad \text{Previous formula}$$

$$S_n = \frac{n}{2}(t_1 + t_1 + (n - 1)d) \qquad \text{Substitution}$$

$$S_n = \frac{n}{2}(2t_1 + (n-1)d) \quad \longleftarrow \text{For } \textit{arithmetic} \text{ series}$$

This formula is more convenient if you know d, but *not* t_n, or if you want to *calculate* n when you know S_n, t_1 and d.

Another clever algebraic trick gives an S_n formula for *geometric* series. Suppose that you must find S_{100} for the geometric series

$$7 + 21 + 63 + \ldots.$$

In this case, $t_1 = 7$ and the common ratio is $r = 3$. It helps to write the terms in *factored* form.

$$S_{100} = 7 + 7 \cdot 3 + 7 \cdot 3^2 + 7 \cdot 3^3 + \ldots + 7 \cdot 3^{98} + 7 \cdot 3^{99}$$

If you multiply both members of this equation by -3, the *opposite* of the common ratio, then *add* the two equations (as you did with linear systems), you get

$$S_{100} = 7 + 7 \cdot 3 + 7 \cdot 3^2 + 7 \cdot 3^3 + \ldots + 7 \cdot 3^{99}$$
$$-3 \cdot S_{100} = \quad - 7 \cdot 3 - 7 \cdot 3^2 - 7 \cdot 3^3 - \ldots - 7 \cdot 3^{99} - 7 \cdot 3^{100}$$

$$\overline{S_{100} - 3 \cdot S_{100} = 7 + \quad 0 + \quad 0 + \quad 0 + \ldots + \quad 0 \quad - 7 \cdot 3^{100}}$$

All but one term in the top equation has its *opposite* in the bottom equation. So all of the terms "telescope" except for the 7 and the $-7 \cdot 3^{100}$. The result is

$$S_{100} - 3 \cdot S_{100} = 7 - 7 \cdot 3^{100}.$$

Factoring out 7 on the right and S_{100} on the left gives

$$(1 - 3) \cdot S_{100} = 7(1 - 3^{100}).$$

Dividing by $(1 - 3)$ gives

$$S_{100} = 7 \cdot \frac{1 - 3^{100}}{1 - 3}.$$

From this result you can extract a *formula* for S_n. The 7 is equal to t_1. The 3 is the common ratio, r, and the 100 is the number of terms, n. So the formula is as follows.

CONCLUSION

PARTIAL SUM OF A GEOMETRIC SERIES
The nth partial sum of a geometric series equals the first term times a *fraction*. The fraction is $\frac{(1 - r^n)}{1 - r}$.
That is,

$$S_n = t_1 \cdot \frac{1 - r^n}{1 - r}$$

The objective, rapid calculation of S_n, can be accomplished using these formulas.

EXAMPLE 1

Find the 127th partial sum of the arithmetic series with $t_1 = 17$ and $d = 4$.

Solution:
From the second form of the arithmetic series formula, you get

$$S_{127} = \frac{127}{2}(2 \cdot 17 + (127 - 1)(4))$$

$$= \frac{127}{2}(34 + 504)$$

$$= \frac{127}{2}(538)$$

$$= \underline{\underline{34163}}.$$

This calculation is certainly quicker than calculating all 127 terms, then adding them up! ■

EXAMPLE 2

Find S_{34} for the geometric series with $t_1 = 7$ and $r = 1.03$.

Solution:
From the formula for geometric series you get

$$S_{34} = 7 \cdot \frac{1 - 1.03^{34}}{1 - 1.03}.$$

By calculator, $1.03^{34} \approx 2.731905296$. Thus,

$$S_{34} \approx 7 \cdot \frac{1 - 2.731905296}{1 - 1.03}$$

$$= 7 \cdot \frac{-1.731905296}{-0.03}$$

$$\approx \underline{\underline{404.1112356}}. \quad ■$$

EXAMPLE 3

30705 is a partial sum in the arithmetic series with first term 17 and common difference 3. Which partial sum is it?

Solution:
Finding the number of terms requires going backwards with the pattern you have learned. Since t_1 and d are known,

$$S_n = \frac{n}{2}(2t_1 + (n - 1)d)$$

is the most appropriate.

$$30705 = \frac{n}{2}(34 + (n - 1)(3))$$

$$61410 = n(34 + 3n - 3)$$

$$61410 = 3n^2 + 31n$$

$$0 = 3n^2 + 31n - 61410$$

Using the quadratic formula,

$$n = \frac{-31 \pm \sqrt{961 - 4(3)(-61410)}}{2(3)}$$

$$n = \frac{-31 \pm \sqrt{737881}}{6}$$

$$n = \frac{-31 \pm 859}{6}$$

$$n = 138 \text{ or } -148\tfrac{1}{3}$$

The only possible answer is $\underline{\underline{n = 138}}$.   ■

EXAMPLE 4

50238.14 is the approximate value of a partial sum in the geometric series with $t_1 = 150$ and $r = 1.04$. Which term is it?

Solution:
Substituting into the formula for S_n gives

$$50238.14 = 150 \cdot \frac{1 - 1.04^n}{1 - 1.04}$$

$$\frac{(50238.14)(-0.04)}{150} = 1 - 1.04^n$$

$$-13.39683\ldots = 1 - 1.04^n$$

$$1.04^n = 14.39683\ldots$$

Taking the log of each member gets the n out of the exponent.

$$n \log 1.04 = \log 14.39683\ldots$$

$$n = \frac{\log 14.39683\ldots}{\log 1.04}$$

$$n = 68.000001\ldots$$

So $\underline{\underline{n = 68}}$ ■

The exercise which follows is designed to give you practice finding partial sums of arithmetic and geometric series.

EXERCISE 11-5

Do These Quickly

The following problems are intended to refresh your skills. You should be able to do all 10 in less than 5 minutes.

Q1.   Evaluate: $\displaystyle\sum_{k=1}^{4} 2k$

Q2.   Find the 5th term of geometric sequence 6, 12, ...

Q3.   Find the 7th term of the arithmetic sequence 10, 19, ...

Q4.   What is the term number of 40 in the arithmetic sequence 8, 16, . . . ?

Q5.   Find the arithmetic mean of 5 and 10.

Q6.   Find the geometric mean of 10 and 40.

Q7.   Find x if 40% of x is 80.

Q8.   Solve in the set of complex numbers: $x^2 = -81$

Q9.   Evaluate the complex number i^3.

Q10. Factor $2x^2 + 5x + 2$.

For Problems 1 through 10, find S_n for the indicated *arithmetic* series by either calculating the terms and adding them up, or by using the formula, whichever you think is quicker.

1. S_{10} for $4 + 7 + 10 + \ldots$

2. S_{13} for $9 + 20 + 31 + \ldots$

3. S_{20} for the series with $t_1 = 15$ and $d = 10$

4. S_{30} for the series with $t_1 = 17$ and $d = 10$

5. S_{15} for the series with $t_1 = 14$ and $d = -2$

6. S_{18} for the series with $t_1 = 29$ and $d = -3$

7. S_{40} for the series with $t_1 = 8$ and $t_6 = 38$

8. S_{50} for the series with $t_1 = 7$ and $t_9 = 47$

9. $\displaystyle\sum_{k=1}^{60} 3 + 2(k - 1)$ 10. $\displaystyle\sum_{k=1}^{70} 4 + 3(k - 1)$

For Problems 11 through 24, find S_n for the indicated *geometric* series by either calculating the terms and adding them up, or by using the formula, whichever you think is quicker.

11. S_5 for $1 + 2 + 4 + \dots$

12. S_6 for $2 + 6 + 18 + \dots$

13. S_6 for $1 - 3 + 9 - \dots$

14. S_5 for $3 - 6 + 12 - \dots$

15. S_{10} for the series with $t_1 = 5$ and $r = 3$

16. S_{10} for the series with $t_1 = 7$ and $r = 2$

17. S_9 for the series with $t_1 = 6$ and $r = -2$

18. S_9 for the series with $t_1 = 5$ and $r = -3$

19. S_{20} for the series with $t_1 = 11$ and $r = 1.3$

20. S_{30} for the series with $t_1 = 13$ and $r = 1.1$

21. S_{15} for the series with $t_1 = 10$ and $t_2 = 9$

22. S_{18} for the series with $t_1 = 20$ and $t_2 = 19$

23. $\displaystyle\sum_{k=1}^{6} 2 \cdot 3^{k-1}$ 24. $\displaystyle\sum_{k=1}^{7} 3 \cdot 2^{k-1}$

For Problems 25 through 32, a partial sum of a series is given, along with other information. Find the number of terms in the partial sum.

25.   Arithmetic series, $S_n = 3219$, $t_1 = 15$, $d = 4$. Find n.

26.   Arithmetic series, $S_n = 4859$, $t_1 = 8$, $d = 5$. Find n.

27.   Arithmetic series, $S_n = 25477.9$, $t_1 = 1.7$, $t_2 = 5.3$. Find n.

28.   Arithmetic series, $S_n = 19149.6$, $t_1 = 2.8$, $t_3 = 3.6$. Find n.

29.   Geometric series, $S_n \approx 23180.58$, $t_1 = 85$, $r = 1.05$. Find n.

      ies, $S_n \approx 6817.748$, $t_1 = 47$, $r = 1.06$. Find n.

      ies, $S_n \approx 109135.19$, $t_1 = 1000$, $t_2 = 998$. Find n.

32.   Geometric series, $S_n \approx 1856.42$, $t_1 = 200$, $t_3 = 162$. Find n.

33.   *Partial Sums by Computer*   Write a program to calculate and print partial sums of a series. The computer should let you input the number of terms. Then it should enter a loop in which the term value is calculated and added to the sum of the previous terms. At each pass

through the loop the computer should print the term number, the term value, and the partial sum.

34. For the geometric series $3 + \frac{3}{2} + \frac{3}{4} + \frac{3}{8} + \ldots$, find S_5, S_{10}, and S_{20}. What do you notice is happening to S_n as n becomes very large?

11-6   CONVERGENT GEOMETRIC SERIES

The series $5 + 8 + 11 + 14 + \ldots$ has partial sums that keep getting bigger and bigger as n increases. Consider what happens to the geometric series

$$5 + \frac{5}{2} + \frac{5}{4} + \frac{5}{8} + \frac{5}{16} + \frac{5}{32} + \ldots$$

The first few partial sums are

$$S_1 = 5$$

$$S_2 = 5 + \frac{5}{2} = 7\frac{1}{2}$$

$$S_3 = 5 + \frac{5}{2} + \frac{5}{4} = 8\frac{3}{4}$$

$$S_4 = 5 + \frac{5}{2} + \frac{5}{4} + \frac{5}{8} = 9\frac{3}{8}$$

$$S_5 = 5 + \frac{5}{2} + \frac{5}{4} + \frac{5}{8} + \frac{5}{16} = 9\frac{11}{16}.$$

The partial sums are getting larger, but seem to be less than 10. To see what happens when n is large, you can use the formula. For example, the 20th partial sum is

$$S_{20} = 5 \cdot \frac{1 - \left(\frac{1}{2}\right)^{20}}{1 - \frac{1}{2}}.$$

By calculator, you can find that $\left(\frac{1}{2}\right)^{20} \approx 0.0000009537$. Also, $1 - \frac{1}{2} = \frac{1}{2}$. So

$$S_{20} \approx 5 \cdot \frac{1 - 0.0000009537}{\frac{1}{2}}.$$

Dividing 5 by $\frac{1}{2}$ (getting 10) and doing the subtraction,

$$S_{20} \approx 10(0.9999990463)$$

$$= 9.999990463.$$

This number is *very* close to 10. A graph of the partial sums is shown in Figure 11-6a.

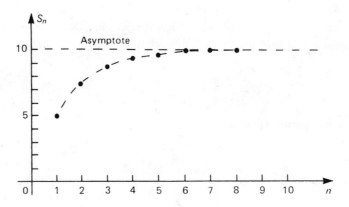

Figure 11-6a

The horizontal line at 10 is an *asymptote* to the graph. You can see that S_n will never be larger than 10, because it will always equal 10 multiplied by a number slightly *smaller* than 1. Since the points get closer and closer to 10, the series is said to "converge to 10."

DEFINITION

> A series **converges** to a number S if the partial sums, S_n, stay arbitrarily close to S as n gets very large.

Two questions now arise:

1. Under what conditions will a geometric series converge?
2. How do you find the number to which it converges?

The above series converges because the term $(\frac{1}{2})^n$ in the formula for S_n is very close to *zero* when n is large. This will happen as long as the common ratio is a *proper fraction*. That is, r must be between -1 and 1. So the series will converge if $|r| < 1$.

To find the *number* to which the series converges, you simply replace the r^n term with 0 in the formula for S_n, getting

$$t_1 \cdot \frac{1 - r^n}{1 - r} \rightarrow t_1 \cdot \frac{1 - 0}{1 - r}$$

$$= t_1 \cdot \frac{1}{1 - r}$$

This number is called the *limit* of the series as n approaches infinity. It is abbreviated this way: $S = \lim_{n \to \infty} S_n$.

CONCLUSION

CONVERGENT GEOMETRIC SERIES
A geometric series *converges* if $|r| < 1$. The limit, S, to which it converges is given by

$$S = \lim_{n \to \infty} S_n = t_1 \cdot \frac{1}{1 - r} = \frac{t_1}{1 - r}.$$

Note: Although there is an *infinite* number of terms in the series, you now have a reasonable definition for the sum of *all* the terms. In the above example, if you add any *finite* number of terms, the answer is less than 10. But you could define the sum of *all* the terms to be *equal* to 10. This definition allows you to find *exact* values of repeating decimals, as you will see below.

Objectives:

1. Given a geometric series, tell whether or not it converges. If it does converge, find the limit to which it converges.
2. Given a repeating decimal, write it as a convergent geometric series, and find a *rational* number equal to the decimal.

EXAMPLE 1

Does the geometric series $15 - 4.5 + 1.35 - \ldots$ converge? If so, to what number does it converge?

Solution:
The common ratio is

$$r = \frac{-4.5}{15} = -0.3.$$

Since $|r|$ is *less* than 1, the series *does* converge. By the formula,

$$S = \frac{15}{1 - (-0.3)}$$

$$= \frac{15}{1.3}$$

$$= \underline{\underline{11\tfrac{7}{13}}}.$$

EXAMPLE 2

Does the geometric series $2 - 3 + 4.5 - \ldots$ converge? If so, to what number does it converge?

Solution:
The common ratio is

$$r = \frac{-3}{2} = -1.5.$$

Since $|r|$ is *not* less than 1, the series *does not* converge. Figure 11-6b shows what happens to the partial sums of this series. If a series does not converge, you can say that it "diverges."

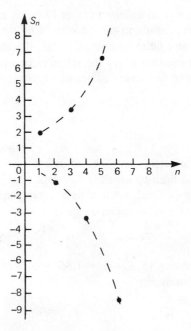

Figure 11-6b.

Figure 11-6b

EXAMPLE 3

Express 0.324324324. . . as the ratio of two integers, and simplify.

Solution:
Let $x = 0.324324324. . . .$

Since the decimal repeats every *three* digits, you can write

$$x = 0.324 + 0.000324 + 0.000000324 + ...$$

This is a *geometric series*, with $t_1 = 0.324$ and common ratio $r = 0.001$. So x is the sum of *all* the terms of the series. It is reasonable to define this sum to be the number to which the series *converges*. So you can write

$$x = \frac{0.324}{1 - 0.001}$$

$$= \frac{0.324}{0.999}$$

$$= \frac{324}{999}$$

$$x = \frac{12}{37}. \qquad \blacksquare$$

EXAMPLE 4

Express 0.26717171. . . as the ratio of two relatively prime integers.

Solution:
In this case the decimal does not start repeating until after the first few places. So you break off the non-repeating part and express the rest as a convergent geometric series. Letting $x = 0.26717171. . . ,$ you can write

$$x = 0.26 + 0.0071 + 0.000071 + 0.00000071 + . . .$$

$$= 0.26 + \frac{0.0071}{1 - 0.01}$$

$$= 0.26 + \frac{0.0071}{0.99}$$

$$= \frac{26}{100} + \frac{71}{9900}$$

$$= \frac{2645}{9900}$$

$$= \frac{529}{1980}. \qquad \blacksquare$$

The calculations above should reveal to you that a repeating decimal can always be written as a ratio of two integers. This observation leads to the following conclusion.

CONCLUSION

> If x is a repeating decimal, then x is a rational number.

The *converse* of this theorem is also true. Its proof uses the long division algorithm rather than geometric series, and so will not be presented here.

The exercise which follows is designed to give you practice in accomplishing the two objectives of this section.

EXERCISE 11-6

Do These Quickly

The following problems are intended to refresh your skills. You should be able to do all 10 in less than 5 minutes.

Q1.   Evaluate $\sum_{k=1}^{6} 3.4 + 0.1k$.

Q2.   If $f(x) = x - 3$, find $f^{-1}(5)$.

Q3.   Find S_3 for $89 + 23 + 71 + 42 + 55 + 102 + \ldots$.

Q4.   If a geometric sequence has $t_3 = 15$ and $t_4 = 30$, find t_2.

Q5.   Evaluate: $4 \cdot 3 \cdot 2 \cdot 1$

Q6.   Simplify: $13 - 3(x + 4)$

Q7.   Multiply the complex numbers: $(5i)(3i)$

Q8.   Do the squaring: $(x + 5)^2$

Q9.   Sketch the graph of a cubic function with three distinct real zeros.

Q10.   35 is what percent of 20?

For Problems 1 through 10, determine whether or not the indicated geometric series converges. If so, find the value to which it converges.

1. $t_1 = 3$ and $r = \dfrac{1}{5}$ 2. $t_1 = 5$ and $r = \dfrac{1}{3}$

3. $t_1 = 42$ and $r = -\dfrac{3}{4}$ 4. $t_1 = 42$ and $r = -\dfrac{4}{3}$

5. $t_1 = 18$ and $r = -\dfrac{7}{5}$ 6. $t_1 = 18$ and $r = -\dfrac{5}{7}$

7. $t_1 = 10$ and $r = 0.1$

8. $t_1 = 100$ and $r = 0.001$

9. $t_1 = 100$ and $t_3 = 1$ (*Two* answers!)

10. $t_1 = 81$ and $t_5 = 1$ (*Two* answers!)

For Problems 11 through 22, write the repeating decimal as a ratio of two integers, and simplify.

11. 0.636363. . .   12. 0.848484. . .

13. 0.567567567. . .   14. 00.990990990. . .

15. 1.060606. . .   16. 2.363636. . .

17. 1.4272727. . .   18. 1.6454545. . .

19. 0.4999999. . .   20. 0.9999999. . . (Surprising?)

21. 0.012345679012345679012345679. . . (Clue: Simplifying the fraction is difficult, but obvious.)

22. 0.987654320987654320987654320. . . (Clue: Use the answers to Problems 20 and 21.)

23. The sequence $\frac{1}{2}, \frac{1}{3}, \frac{1}{4}, \frac{1}{5}, \ldots$ is called the *harmonic* sequence. Clearly, t_n gets closer and closer to zero as n becomes very large. Yet the harmonic *series* $\frac{1}{2} + \frac{1}{3} + \frac{1}{4} + \frac{1}{5} + \ldots$ does *not* converge! It just keeps getting larger and larger as n increases. By associating terms, show that

$$\frac{1}{2} + \frac{1}{3} + \frac{1}{4} + \frac{1}{5} + \frac{1}{6} + \frac{1}{7} + \frac{1}{8} + \ldots$$

$$> \frac{1}{2} + \frac{1}{2} + \frac{1}{2} + \ldots,$$

and use the result to show that the series "diverges."

24. The *alternating* harmonic series,

$$S = \frac{1}{2} - \frac{1}{3} + \frac{1}{4} - \frac{1}{5} + \ldots,$$

does converge.

a. By associating the first and second terms, the third and fourth terms, and so on, show that $S > 0$.

b. By associating the second and third terms, the fourth and fifth terms, and so on, show that $S < \frac{1}{2}$.

c. Use the computer program of Exercise 11-4, Problem 38, to calculate the sum of the first 1000 terms of this series.

25. a. By long division, show that the fraction $\frac{1}{1-x}$ equals

$$1 + x + x^2 + x^3 + x^4 + \ldots$$

b. The series $1 + x + x^2 + x^3 + x^4 + \ldots$ is geometric with common ratio $r = x$. For what values of x will the series *converge*? For what values of x will the series *diverge*?

c. Using what you know about convergent geometric series, show that the partial sums of the series in part b really *do* approach $\frac{1}{(1-x)}$ when the series is convergent.

26. Calvin Butterball is taking a test on geometric series. He realizes that the series $1 - 1 + 1 - 1 + 1 - 1 + \ldots$ is geometric, with $t_1 = 1$ and common ratio $r = -1$. So he finds the number the sequence converges to, using the formula

$$S = \frac{t_1}{1 - r} = \frac{1}{1 - (-1)} = \frac{1}{2}.$$

a. Write the first few partial sums of this series.

b. Draw a graph of the sequence of partial sums, and thus show Calvin that his answer is not reasonable.

c. Explain to Calvin what error he made.

27. Using the techniques of convergent geometric series, it is possible to show that the series

$$1 + 2\left(\frac{1}{3}\right) + 3\left(\frac{1}{3}\right)^2 + 4\left(\frac{1}{3}\right)^3 + 5\left(\frac{1}{3}\right)^4 + \ldots$$

converges to a finite number. Find out what this number equals.

28. *Convergence by Computer Problem*   The program CONVERGENCE on the accompanying disk calculates and prints the first 1000 partial sums of a given geometric series. The input is the first term and the common ratio.

a. To what limit will the geometric series converge if $t_1 = 100$ and $r = 0.95$?

b. Run CONVERGENCE with $t_1 = 100$ and $r = 0.95$. Does the sequence seem to converge to the number you predicted in part (a)? How do you tell from what the computer prints on the screen that the sequence is "converging?"

c. To what limit will the geometric series converge if $t_1 = 360$ and $r = -0.8$?

  d. Run CONVERGENCE for the series in part (c). Does the series
      converge to the number you predicted? In what way does the pat-
      tern of the partial sums differ from that in part (b)? What fea-
      ture of this particular series causes that difference?
  e. Miss Take uses convergence formula for the series with first
      term 150 and common ratio 2. What limit does she get? Run
      CONVERGENCE with this series, and use the results to explain
      to her what really happens to the partial sums as the number of
      terms gets very large.

11-7 | ## SEQUENCES AND SERIES AS MATHEMATICAL MODELS

Since a sequence is a function whose domain is a set of integers, the graph
of a sequence changes by "jumps" rather than in a smooth, continuous
curve. Therefore, sequences are appropriate as mathematical models for
real-world phenomena in which the dependent variable changes stepwise
rather than continuously. For instance, when you hammer a nail into a
board, the distance the nail has gone into the board is a stepwise function
of the number of times you hit it with the hammer.

Objective:
Given a situation from the real world in which the dependent variable
changes stepwise, use an arithmetic or geometric sequence or series as a
mathematical model.

EXAMPLE 1

Suppose you start pounding a nail into a board. With the first impact the
nail moves 20 millimeters (mm); with the second impact it moves 18 mm
more. Predict the distance it moves and the total distance it has gone into
the board assuming that the distances it moves form

a. an arithmetic sequence,
b. a geometric sequence.

Solution:
  Let n = number of impacts.
  Let t_n = number of mm the nail moves on the nth impact. (See Figure
        11-7a.)
  Let S_n = total number of mm the nail has gone after n impacts.

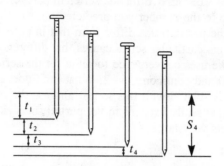

Figure 11-7a

a. Assuming an *arithmetic* sequence, $d = 18 - 20 = -2$. Therefore,

$$t_n = 20 + (n - 1)(-2).$$

On the fourth impact, the nail moves

$$t_4 = 20 + (4 - 1)(-2) = 20 - 6 = \underline{\underline{14 \text{ mm}}}.$$

The total distance the nail has gone after four impacts will be the *fourth partial sum* of the corresponding arithmetic series. Since $t_4 = 14$,

$$S_4 = \frac{4}{2}(20 + 14) = \underline{\underline{68 \text{ mm}}}.$$

b. If you assume a *geometric* sequence rather than an arithmetic one, the common ratio would be $r = \frac{18}{20} = 0.9$. On the fourth impact, the nail would go

$$t_4 = 20 \times 0.9^{4-1} = \underline{\underline{14.58 \text{ mm}}}.$$

After four impacts, the nail would have gone a total of

$$S_4 = \frac{20(1 - 0.9^4)}{1 - 0.9} = \underline{\underline{68.78 \text{ mm}}}.$$

Since the common ratio has an absolute value less than 1, the partial sums *converge* to some number as n gets very large. After many impacts, the total distance the nail has gone into the board will approach

$$S = \frac{t_1}{1 - r} = \frac{20}{1 - 0.9} = \frac{20}{0.1} = \underline{\underline{200 \text{ mm}}}.$$

Based on this model, if the nail were more than 200 mm long, it would remain sticking out of the board no matter how many times you hit it. If it were less than 200 mm long, it would eventually be driven all the way into the board. ■

EXAMPLE 2

Most banks "compound" the interest they pay you on savings accounts. This means that at regular intervals (daily, quarterly, yearly, etc.) they add the interest you have earned for that interval to the "principal" which you already had invested. During the next interval, you earn interest on the interest as well as on the original principal. Suppose that a bank pays 5% per year interest, compounded annually (once a year). If you invest a principal of $100, then at the end of one year the bank pays you 5% of 100, or

$$0.05 \times 100 = 5$$

dollars. So the new principal for the next compounding period is $100 + 5$, or $105. At the end of the second year, the bank pays you 5% of $105, or

$$0.05 \times 105 = 5.25$$

dollars, making the new principal $105 + 5.25 = 110.25$, and so forth. The amount of money you have in the bank at any time is a term in the sequence

$$100, 105, 110.25, \ldots .$$

The sequence is geometric, with a comon ratio of 1.05, as you could discover by dividing adjacent terms. Some clever factoring shows the same thing more instructively.

Let n = number of years the money has been in the bank.
Let t_n = number of dollars you have in the bank.

When you make the first deposit, time equals zero. Therefore, it is convenient to start n at 0 rather than 1 as you have been doing up to now. Therefore,

$$t_0 = 100.$$

At the end of one year, when $n = 1$, the interest is added to get the next term. Therefore,

$$t_1 = 100 + 0.05 \times 100 \quad \text{Adding 5\% interest}$$
$$= 100(1 + 0.05) \quad \text{Factoring out 100}$$
$$= 100(1.05) \quad \text{Adding 1 to 0.05}$$

To see the pattern more clearly, you should *not* carry out the multiplication yet.

To find t_2, you add the interest for the second year to t_1 (the principal for the first year) getting

$$t_2 = 100(1.05) + 0.05 \times 100(1.05) \quad \text{Adding 5\% interest}$$
$$= 100(1.05)(1 + 0.05) \quad \text{Factoring out } 100(1.05)$$

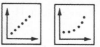

$$= 100(1.05)(1.05)$$

$$= 100(1.05)^2$$

Similarly, $t_3 = 100(1.05)^3$, $t_4 = 100(1.05)^4$, and so on. Since the exponent is always equal to the term number,

$$t_n = 100(1.05)^n.$$

This is the formula for the nth term of a geometric sequence with $r = 1.05$ and first term $= 100$. The exponent is n rather than $n - 1$ because the sequence started with term 0 instead of term 1.

To find the amount of money you would have after 7 years, you would substitute 7 for n and do the calculations.

$$t_7 = 100(1.05)^7$$

$$\approx \underline{140.71}$$

Finding the time at which the amount is $400 involves finding the exponent, n.

$$400 = 100(1.05)^n \qquad \text{Substituting 400 for } t_n$$

$$4 = 1.05^n$$

$$\log 4 = \log 1.05^n$$

$$\log 4 = n \log 1.05 \qquad \text{Log of a power}$$

$$\frac{\log 4}{\log 1.05} = n$$

$$28.413 \ldots = n$$

$$\underline{\text{After 29 years}}$$

The answer must be rounded *upward* since the amount is still below $400 at the end of 28 years. ■

EXAMPLE 3

Suppose you invest $100 in a savings account that pays 5% per year interest, as in Example 2, but the interest is compounded *quarterly* (every 3 months). How much would you have at the end of 7 years?

Solution:

Let $n =$ number of *quarters* the money has been in the bank.
Let $t_n =$ number of dollars you have in the bank.

The bank will pay only $\frac{1}{4}$ of the 5% interest after each compounding period, or 1.25% (0.0125). Using the same reasoning as in Example 2,

$$t_0 = 100$$

$$t_1 = 100(1.0125)$$

$$t_2 = 100(1.0125)^2$$

$$t_3 = 100(1.0125)^3.$$

Again, the term number equals the exponent, so

$$t_n = 100(1.0125)^n.$$

The amount of money you would have after 7 years would be t_{28} because there are 28 quarters in 7 years. Therefore,

$$t_{28} = 100(1.0125)^{28}$$

$$\approx \underline{141.60}. \qquad \blacksquare$$

Comparing this answer with Example 2, you make only 89 cents more in 7 years if the interest is compounded quarterly instead of yearly. If you work Problem 24 in the following exercise, you will discover the *real* advantage of compounding interest more frequently.

The exercise which follows is designed to give you practice using sequences and series as mathematical models.

EXERCISE 11-7

Do These Slowly!

The following problems are intended to tie together your skills with sequences and series before you work the mathematical models problems that follow. They are *not* meant to be done quickly.

S1.   A geometric series has first term 34 and common ratio 1.7. Find the twentieth term and the twentieth partial sum.

S2.   An arithmetic series has first term 78 and common difference 3.2. Find the thirtieth term and the thirtieth partial sum.

S3.   An arithmetic series has $t_1 = 44$ and $t_3 = 66$. Find t_2. Find S_{100}.

S4.   A geometric series has $t_1 = 100$ and $t_2 = 80$. Find t_3, t_4, and t_5. Find S_{20}. Find the limit to which the partial sums converge.

S5.   A sequence has the property that each term is 95% of the term before. The first term is 800. What is the tenth term? What kind of a sequence is it?

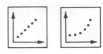

S6. A sequence has the property that each term is 7 less than the preceding term. The first term is 900. What is the tenth term? What is the term number of the first negative term?

S7. A geometric series has first term 12 and tenth term 120. What is the common ratio? 1200 is a term in this series; what is its term number?

S8. An arithmetic series has first term 17 and tenth term 27. What is the twentieth term?

S9. What are the next two terms of the sequence $\frac{1}{2}, \frac{2}{3}, \frac{3}{4}, \frac{4}{5}, \ldots$? Is the sequence arithmetic or geometric?

S10. A *factorial* is a partial *product* of the terms of a sequence. Find the tenth partial product of the sequence of counting numbers.

Work the following problems.

1. *Muscle-Building Problem*   Suppose that you start an exercise program to build up your biceps. On the first day, your biceps increase by 3 millimeters. The amount of increase on each following day is 0.95 times the amount of increase the day before.
    a. Your biceps increase by how much on the tenth day?
    b. By how many millimeters, total, have your biceps increased after 10 days?
    c. If you continue the exercise program for many days, what number does the total increase in bicep measurement approach?

2. *Chewing Gum Problem*   Anne X. Kewse gets caught chewing gum in algebra class. Quickly, she explains to her instructor that she is conducting a practical experiment in geometric sequences and series, since with each chew she gets 0.9 times as much flavor as she did with the preceding chew.
    a. If she gets 40 squirts of flavor with the first chew, how many squirts will she get with the tenth chew?
    b. What total amount of flavor will she get in the first 10 chews?
    c. Her punishment is to chew the gum *forever*. What total amount of flavor will she recieve?

3. *Blue Jeans Problem*   Assume that whenever you wash a pair of blue jeans, they lose 4% of the color they had just before they were washed.
    a. Explain why the percent of the original color *left* in the blue jeans varies geometrically with the number of washings. What is the common ratio?
    b. How much of the original color would be left after 10 washings?
    c. Suppose that you buy a new pair of blue jeans, and decide to wash them enough times so that only 25% of the original color remains. How many times must you wash them?

d. Explain why an arithmetic sequence would *not* be a reasonable mathematical model for the amount of color left after many washings.

4. ***Bouncing Ball Problem***   Suppose that you drop a superball from a window 20 meters above the ground. The ball bounces to 90% of its previous altitude with each bounce.

a. How far does the ball travel, up and down, between the first and the second bounce?
b. Show that the numbers of meters the ball travels up and down between bounces are terms of a geometric sequence.
c. Find the number of meters the ball travels up and down between the sixth and seventh bounce.
d. Find the total number of meters the ball travels between the first bounce and the seventh bounce.
e. If the ball continues to bounce in this manner until it comes to rest, how far will it have traveled, up and down, from the time it was dropped from the window?

5. ***George Washington Problem***   Recently, Anna Ward found she is a distant relative of George Washington. When he died in 1799, he left $1000 in his will, which now belongs to her. The money has been in a savings account at the Old Dominion Bank, where it has been earning interest at 5% per year, compounded annually (once a year). How much does Anna have *this* year? Why do you suppose that there are laws limiting a bank's liability for paying interest on dormant savings accounts?

6. ***Little Brother Problem***   Your little brother is hard up for cash, and asks you to lend him 10 cents. You get him to agree to pay 5% per day interest, compounded daily. You lend him the money, but you both forget the deal until exactly one year later. Being an expert at geometric sequences, you perform some calculations which show he is deeply in debt.
a. How much does he owe you for a 365-day year?
b. How much *more* would he owe you for a 366-day leap year?

7. *Manhattan Problem*   In 1626, Peter Minuit, Governor of the Dutch West India Company, purchased Manhattan Island from the Indians for $24 worth of beads, cloth, and trinkets. Suppose that the Indians had sold the stuff and invested the $24 in a savings account paying 6% per year interest compounded annually. How much would they have on deposit *this* year? Surprising??

8. *Louisiana Purchase Problem*   In 1803, when Thomas Jefferson was President, the United States purchased about 500,000,000 acres of land from the French for about $15,000,000.
    a. If Napoleon had invested this money in a savings account paying 7% per year interest, compounded annually, how much money would he have *now*? How does this amount compare with the current U. S. National Debt?
    b. How much per acre did the French get for the land? How much per acre could they afford to pay to buy it back if they had actually kept the money in such a savings account?

9. *Straight-Line Depreciation Problem*   The Internal Revenue Service (IRS) assumes that the value of an item which can wear out decreases by a *constant* number of dollars each year. For example, a house "depreciates" by $\frac{1}{40}$ of its original value each year.
    a. If your house were worth $84,000 originally, by how many dollars does it depreciate each year?
    b. What is your house worth after 0, 1, 2, and 3 years?
    c. Do these values form an arithmetic or a geometric sequence? What is the common difference or common ratio?
    d. Calculate the value of your house at the end of 27 years.
    e. According to this model, is your house ever worth *nothing*? Explain.
    f. Plot a graph of this sequence using the results of parts b, d, and e. Why do you suppose the IRS calls this model "straight-line" depreciation?

10. *Piggy Bank Problem*   Suppose that you put $.50 into an empty piggy bank. One week later you put in $.75. At the end of the next week, you put in $1.00, and so on.
    a. What kind of sequence do the individual deposits form?
    b. At the end of 76 weeks, how many deposits have you made?
    c. What amount do you deposit at the end of the 76th week?
    d. What total amount do you have in the piggy bank at the end of 76 weeks?

11. *Pile Driver Problem*   A pile driver (see Figure 11-7b) starts driving a piling into the ground. On the first impact, the piling goes 100 cm into the ground. On the second impact, it moves 96 cm more.
    a. Assuming the distances it moves form an *arithmetic* sequence,
        i.   how far will it move on the tenth impact?
        ii. how far into the ground will it be after ten impacts?

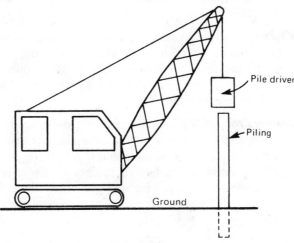

Figure 11-7b _____

b. If you assume that the distances the piling moves with each impact form a *geometric* sequence,
    i.   how far will it move on the tenth impact?
    ii. how far into the ground will it be after 10 impacts?
    iii. what is the farthest it can be driven into the ground?

12. *Calvin and Phoebe Problem*   Calvin Butterball and Phoebe Small start walking at the same time from the same point and in the same direction. Phoebe starts with a 12 inch step, and increases her stride by $\frac{1}{2}$ inch each step. She goes 21 steps, then stops. Calvin starts with a 36 inch step, and each subsequent step is 90% as long as the preceding one.
    a. What kind of sequence do Phoebe's steps follow?
    b. What kind of sequence do Calvin's steps follow?
    c. How long is Phoebe's last step?
    d. How long is Calvin's 21st step?
    e. After each has taken 21 steps, who is ahead? Justify your answer.
    f. If Calvin keeps on walking in the same manner, will he ever get to where Phoebe stopped? Explain.

13. *Ancestors Problem*   Your ancestors in the first, second, and third generation back are your natural parents, grandparents, and great grandparents, respectively.
    a. Write the numbers of ancestors you have (living or dead) in the first, second, and third generations back.
    b. Do the numbers of ancestors form a *geometric* sequence or an *arithmetic* sequence? What is the common ratio or the common difference?
    c. How many ancestors do you have in the 20th generation back?

d. What *total* number of ancestors do you have in the first 20 generations back?

14. ***Month's Pay Problem***   Your parents want you to do some work around the house on a regular basis. You get them to agree to pay you $0.01 the first day, $0.02 the second, $0.04 the third, $0.08 the fourth, and so on. At the end of 30 days, how much will they have paid you, total? Surprising?!

15. ***Tree Branch Problem***   Pine tree branches grow in layers (see sketch). As sunlight hits the top layer, a certain fraction of the light is absorbed by those branches, and the rest goes through to the next layer. 100% of the incoming sunlight reaches the top layer. Suppose you find that 45% of the incoming sunlight reaches the ground after passing through all 5 layers of branches on a particular tree.

a. What fraction of the light reaching one layer makes it through to the next layer?
b. Find the percent of the *original* light that reaches the second, third, fourth, and fifth layers.
c. If a layer of branches gets less than 20% of the original sunlight, the branches in that layer will die and drop off. What is the maximum number of layers of branches you would expect to find on such a tree?

16. ***Musical Scale Problem***   The musical scale on a piano has 12 notes (counting black keys) from A through G#, then starts over again with A (see sketch). The frequency at which the piano strings vibrate is 220 cycles per second (cps) for the A below middle C, and 440 cps for the A above. Each note has a frequency which is one of the 11 positive geometric means between 220 and 440.

a. Find the common ratio.
b. Calculate to one decimal place the frequency of each note between the two A's (220 cps and 440 cps).
c. What is the frequency of the highest note on the piano, the C which is 51 notes above the 220 cps A?
d. What is the frequency of the lowest note on the piano, the A which is 36 notes below the 220 cps A?

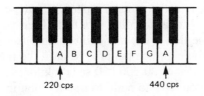

17. ***Pineapple Plantation Problem***   Suppose that you obtain a single pineapple plant of a new and unusual variety. You decide to go into the pineapple-growing business, propagating new plants from this one. You find the following:

   i.   New pineapple plants are started from cuttings of an old one as follows:

      1 from the crown (see sketch),
      4 from "slips" at the base of the fruit, 3 from "suckers" that grow from the roots, and 3 from sections of the stump.

   ii.   It takes 2 years for a pineapple to mature, which means that each generation takes 2 years.

   iii. You can plant 4000 plants per acre.

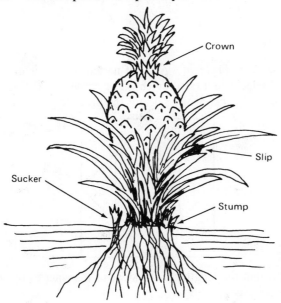

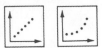

Answer the following questions.

a. Write the number of plants you would have after 0, 1, 2, and 3 generations, assuming that all possible plants live.

b. You have 1000 acres available for planting. How long would it take before all 1000 acres would be covered with pineapple plants?

18. *Lion Hunting in Africa*   When asked how to go about catching a lion in Africa, a mathematician replied, "That's easy. You just build a fence across Africa, dividing it in half. Then you find which side of the fence the lion is on, and build another fence, dividing that half in half. You continue the process until the lion is in a corral." Africa has an area of 30,300,000 square kilometers. How many fences would you have to build to trap the lion in a corral less than 10 square meters in area?

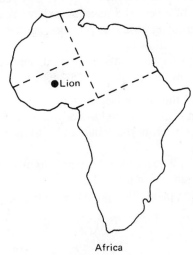

Africa

19. *Nested Squares Problem*   A set of nested squares is drawn inside a square of edge 1 unit (see sketch). The corners of the next square are at the midpoints of the sides of the preceding square.

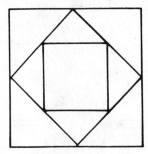

a. Show that the lengths of the sides of the squares form a geometric sequence.

b. Show that the perimeters of the squares form a geometric sequence.

c. Show that the areas of the squares form a geometric sequence.

d. Find the area of the tenth square.

e. Find the perimeter of the tenth square.

f. Find the *sum* of the areas of the first 10 squares.

g. Find the sum of the perimeters of the first 10 squares.

h. Show that the sum of the areas of the squares approaches a finite number, and tell what that number is.

i. Does the sum of the perimeters approach a finite number? Explain.

20. *Snowflake Curve Problem*   A "snowflake curve" is constructed as shown in the sketch. An equilateral triangle with sides of 1 unit length has each side trisected. The middle sections of each side serve as bases for smaller equilateral triangles. These triangles in turn have their sides trisected, and still smaller equilateral triangles are constructed. The process is carried on "infinitely."

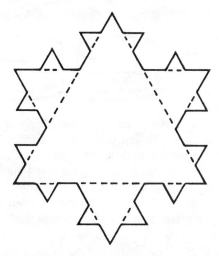

a. Show that as each set of smaller triangles is constructed,

  i. the total area enclosed by the curve is a partial sum of a geometric series, and

  ii. the perimeter of the figure (i.e., the length of the curve) is a term in a geometric sequence.

b. Show that the area enclosed by the snowflake curve approaches a *finite* number, and tell what that number equals.

c. Show that the perimeter of the snowflake curve becomes *infinite* as the number of sides increases. Surprising?

d. See Martin Gardner's article in the December, 1976, issue of *Scientific American* for further information about snowflakes, "flowsnakes," and other "pathological monster" curves.

21. When you clean a paint brush, the amount of paint remaining in the brush depends on the number of times you rinse it with turpentine, and on the volume of turpentine you use for each rinse. Assume that a brush retains 2 cubic centimeters (cc) of fluid after it has been shaken out.

a. Before the first rinse, the 2 cc retained in the brush is pure paint. If 8 cc of turpentine is used for the rinse, the total volume of paint and turpentine you are mixing around is $2 + 8 = 10$ cc. What is the percent of paint in this mixture?

b. When you shake out the brush, only 2 cc of the mixture is left in it. What percent of the original paint is left in the brush?

c. If you rinse again with 8 cc of turpentine, what percent of paint still remains in the brush after the second rinse? After the third rinse?

d. What percent of the paint would remain if you use *one* 24 cc rinse instead of three 8 cc rinses?

e. Which is the more economical way to use 24 cc of turpentine?

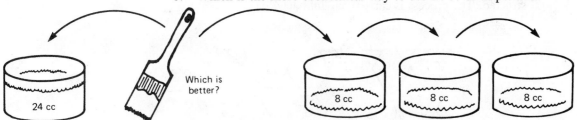

22. Many years ago, the people in Euclid, Ohio, planted a geoma tree. The first year it grew a trunk 2 meters long. The next year it grew two branches at right angles to each other, each 1 meter long. The third year it grew four $\frac{1}{2}$-meter branches, two from each tip of last year's branches, at right angles to each other. Unlike non-Euclidean geoma trees, all the branches and the trunk grew in the same plane (this is a plane geoma tree).

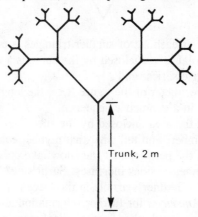

A Fine Geoma Tree

a.   Show that the lengths of the branches form a geometric sequence. What is the common ratio?

b.   How high will the tree be after 2 years? 3 years? 4 years?

c.   Show that the height of the tree is the sum of *two* geometric series. What are the common ratios?

d.   If the tree keeps on growing this way forever,
    i.   what height will it approach?
    ii. what width will it approach?
    iii. what will the length of a new branch approach?
    iv. what total length of branches will grow each year?
    v. what will the total length of all branches approach?
    vi. how close to the ground will the lowest branches come?

23.   *Middleman Problem*   When you purchase food, clothing, etc., in a retail store, the item has passed through many hands before reaching you. For example, the farmer might sell to a trucker, who sells to a wholesaler, who sells to a packager, who sells to a distributor, who sells to a retailer, who sells to you. Each person between you and the farmer is called a "middleman." Suppose that a farmer spends $.50 raising one pound of beef.

a.   If the farmer and the 5 middlemen each make a profit of 30% on what they spent for the pound of beef, how much will you, the consumer, have to pay for the beef?

b.   How many cents profit does the farmer make? How many cents profit do the five middlemen make, combined? Surprising?!

c.   The farmer and each middleman insist that their profit should be increased to 40%, arguing that the extra 10% increase in price will not hurt the consumer that much. How much would you *actually* pay for the pound of beef under this condition? Does the price really increase by only 10%?

24.   *Interest Compounding Problem*   Suppose that one bank pays $6\frac{1}{4}$% per year interest, compounded *annually,* and another bank pays 6% per year interest, compounded *monthly*. You have $1000 to invest, and wish to know which is the better deal.

a.   How much could you withdraw from each account at the end of 10 full years? On this basis, which seems better, a higher interest rate or more frequent compounding?

b.   How much could you withdraw from each account at the end of 9 years, 11 months? Remember, if you withdraw before the end of a compounding period, you get *no* interest for that period. Which type of account would be better if you are likely to have to withdraw your money on short notice?

c.   What annual interest rate, compounded annually, would you need in order to make the same amount of money at the end of 10 years as you would with 6% compounded monthly?

25.   *Rich Uncle Problem*   Claire Voyance has a rich uncle who wishes to give Claire $1000 on her 21st birthday. But there is a string at-

tached. Claire must calculate how much her uncle must invest *now* in a savings account in order to have $1000 on the 21st birthday. Claire is 16 years 7 months old now. The savings account pays 6.2% per year interest, compounded quarterly. Since Claire has studied geometric sequences she realizes that the value of the $1000 if left in the savings account *after* her 21st birthday would be a term in a geometric sequence, with independent variable p being the number of quarters the money has been left. The value of the $1000 *before* her 21st birthday, therefore, will be given by the *same* sequence, but with the appropriate *negative* value substituted for p. How much should Claire tell her uncle to invest? (Businessmen call this amount the "present value" of the $1000.)

26. *Sweepstakes Problem* Suppose that you have just won the Readers Digest Sweepstakes. You have a choice of accepting a lump sum of $20,000 now, or taking $100 per month for the rest of your life. In either case, you will put the money into a savings account paying 4% per year interest, compounded monthly, and let the interest accumulate. Assume that the Internal Revenue Service charges you no income tax (unlikely, but assume it anyway!).

   a. If you accept the $20,000, the amount you will have after n months is the nth term of a geometric sequence. How much will you have after 10 years? After 50 years?

   b. If you accept the $100 per month, the amount you will have after n months is the nth partial sum of a geometric series. How much will you have after 10 years? After 50 years?

   c. How long would it be before the amount you would have from the $100 per month plan would *exceed* the amount you would have from the $20,000 lump sum plan?

   d. Show that if you can get an annual interest rate of 7%, compounded monthly, the $100 per month plan will *never* give you as much money as the $20,000 lump sum plan.

   e. Ask your Economics instructor how income tax considerations might make the $20,000 lump sum plan *less* desirable than your calculations above indicate.

27. *General Formula for Arithmetic Sequences Problem* Prove that the nth term of an arithmetic sequence is equal to the kth term plus $(n - k)$ common differences. That is, prove

$$t_n = t_k + (n - k)d.$$

11-8   FACTORIALS

In the next section and in Chapter 12 you will study series and other expressions which contain products of many consecutive integers. In this section you will study a convenient way of writing these products.

DEFINITION

> The expression $n!$ (read "n factorial") means the product of the first n consecutive positive integers.

For example, $4! = 4 \cdot 3 \cdot 2 \cdot 1 = 24$, and $6! = 6 \cdot 5 \cdot 4 \cdot 3 \cdot 2 \cdot 1 = 720$.

There is one important property of factorials that follows directly from the definition. For example,

$$5! = 5 \cdot 4 \cdot 3 \cdot 2 \cdot 1$$
$$= 5 \cdot (4 \cdot 3 \cdot 2 \cdot 1)$$
$$= 5 \cdot 4!$$

So in general,

$$\boxed{n! = n \cdot (n - 1)!}$$

In plain English, this property says that you can get the next factorial by multiplying the previous factorial by n. Reversing this pattern, you can get the previous factorial by *dividing*.

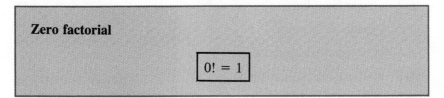

If the pattern continues backwards, 0! must equal $1 \div 1$, which equals 1. This fact leads to a reasonable *definition* of 0!.

DEFINITION

> **Zero factorial**
>
> $$\boxed{0! = 1}$$

Objective:
Be able to use the definition of factorials to simplify expressions containing factorials, or to express in factorial form expressions containing products of consecutive integers.

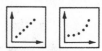

Fractions which have factorials in the numerator and denominator offer great possibilities for canceling. For example,

$$\frac{10!}{7!} = \frac{10 \cdot 9 \cdot 8 \cdot 7 \cdot 6 \cdot 5 \cdot 4 \cdot 3 \cdot 2 \cdot 1}{7 \cdot 6 \cdot 5 \cdot 4 \cdot 3 \cdot 2 \cdot 1} \qquad \text{Definition of factorials}$$

$$= 10 \cdot 9 \cdot 8 \qquad\qquad\qquad \text{Canceling}$$

$$= 720. \qquad\qquad\qquad\quad \text{Arithmetic}$$

Conversely, a product of consecutive integers can be expressed in compact form using factorial notation. For example,

$$9 \cdot 8 \cdot 7 \cdot 6 = 9 \cdot 8 \cdot 7 \cdot 6 \cdot \frac{5 \cdot 4 \cdot 3 \cdot 2 \cdot 1}{5 \cdot 4 \cdot 3 \cdot 2 \cdot 1} \qquad \begin{array}{l}\text{Multiplication} \\ \text{property of 1}\end{array}$$

$$= \frac{9 \cdot 8 \cdot 7 \cdot 6 \cdot 5 \cdot 4 \cdot 3 \cdot 2 \cdot 1}{5 \cdot 4 \cdot 3 \cdot 2 \cdot 1} \qquad \begin{array}{l}\text{Multiplication} \\ \text{property of fractions}\end{array}$$

$$= \frac{9!}{5!} \qquad\qquad\qquad\qquad \begin{array}{l}\text{Definition of} \\ \text{factorials}\end{array}$$

Once you understand this process, it can be done in *one* step in your head.

The exercise which follows is designed to give you practice working with factorials so that you will be familiar with them when you encounter them in the next section and in the next chapter.

EXERCISE 11-8

Do These Quickly

The following problems are intended to refresh your skills. You should be able to do all 10 in less than 5 minutes.

Write the general equation for:

Q1.   a linear function,

Q2.   a quadratic function,

Q3.   an exponential function,

Q4.   a rational algebraic function,

Q5.   a cubic function,

Q6.   the nth term of an arithmetic sequence,

Q7.   the nth term of a geometric sequence,

Q8.   the limit to which a convergent geometric series converges.

Answer the questions:

Q9.   What kind of function is a geometric sequence?

Q10.   What kind of function is an arithmetic sequence?

For Problems 1 through 16, simplify the given expression:

1. $3! \, 4!$ (i.e., $3! \cdot 4!$)   2. $3! \, 5!$ (i.e., $3! \cdot 5!$)

3. $\dfrac{8!}{4!}$ 4. $\dfrac{8!}{5!}$

5. $\dfrac{7!}{0!}$ 6. $\dfrac{8! \, 3!}{6!}$

7. $\dfrac{10!}{5! \, 3!}$ 8. $\dfrac{6!}{2! \, 4!}$

9. $\dfrac{5!}{2! \, 3!}$ 10. $\dfrac{10!}{7! \, 3!}$

11. $(3!)!$ 12. $(2!)!$

13. $\dfrac{(n - 1)!}{n!}$ 14. $\dfrac{(n + 1)!}{n!}$

15. $\dfrac{(n + 1)!}{(n - 1)!}$ 16. $\dfrac{(n + 2)!}{n!}$

For Problems 17 through 24, write the given expression as a ratio of factorials.

17. $7 \cdot 6 \cdot 5 \cdot 4$ 18. $9 \cdot 8 \cdot 7 \cdot 6$

19. $20 \cdot 19 \cdot 18 \cdot 17 \cdot 16 \cdot 15$ 20. $35 \cdot 34 \cdot 33 \cdot 32$

21. $20 \cdot 19 \cdot 18 \cdot 12 \cdot 11 \cdot 10$ 22. $100 \cdot 99 \cdot 98 \cdot 50 \cdot 49 \cdot 48$

23. $\dfrac{30 \cdot 29 \cdot 28 \cdot 27 \cdot 26 \cdot 25}{6!}$ 24. $\dfrac{43 \cdot 42 \cdot 41 \cdot 40}{4!}$

25.   For what values of n will $n!$ be evenly divisible by 9?

26.   For what values of n will $n!$ end in zero, when multiplied out?

27.   100! ends with a string of zeros. How many zeros are there at the end of 100!?

28.   a.   Write a computer program for calculating values of $n!$ for given values of n. The program should begin with inputting a value of n. You can start a variable P (for "product") at 1, then set up a loop in which P is multiplied by successive integers, 2, 3, 4, . . . , up through n. The output should be the value of n and the value of $n!$ at each pass through the loop.

b. Modify the program so that it *adds* the *logs* of the integers, then takes the antilog, thus allowing you to calculate numbers like 100!.

For Problems 29 through 32, evaluate the given sum.

29. $\displaystyle\sum_{k=0}^{4} k!$

30. $\displaystyle\sum_{k=0}^{4} \frac{(k+1)!}{k!}$

31. $\displaystyle\sum_{k=1}^{4} \frac{(k-1)!}{k!}$

32. $\displaystyle\sum_{k=1}^{5} \frac{(k+1)!}{(k-1)!}$

33. You have studied quadratic functions, exponential functions, and now factorials, each of which gets much bigger as the independent variable increases. Make a table of n^2, 2^n, and $n!$ for the integers $n = 0$ through 10. Tell which one of these functions grows the *fastest*.

34. In the sequence for which $t_n = (n-1)! + 1$, certain ones of the terms are divisible by n and others are not. For example, $t_5 = 25$, and 25 is divisible by 5. But $t_6 = 121$, and 121 is *not* divisible by 6. Write the values of t_1 through t_{11}. Then try to determine what kind of number n is when t_n is divisible by n. (This property is known as Wilson's Theorem.)

35. The series specified by $S_n = \displaystyle\sum_{k=0}^{n} \frac{1}{k!}$ has partial sums which get closer and closer to an interesting number as n gets very large.

a. Show that the ninth term of the series (i.e., $k = 8$) is so small that it contributes nothing to the first four decimal places.

b. Find a four decimal place approximation for S_7. (This number is called "e," and is used as the base for "natural" logarithms.)

36. The function specified by the series

$$f(x) = 1 - \frac{x^2}{2!} + \frac{x^4}{4!} - \frac{x^6}{6!} + \ldots,$$

converges to a *rational* number when x is certain multiples of the irrational number π.

a. Using a calculator or computer, find values of the first, second, third, . . . , tenth partial sum of $f(\pi)$. Use the decimal approximation 3.141592654 for π. To what number does the series seem to be converging?

b. Find an approximation for $f(\frac{\pi}{2})$. Use enough terms to find the rational number to which the series converges.

c. To what rational number does $f(\frac{\pi}{3})$ converge?

11-9 | INTRODUCTION TO BINOMIAL SERIES

You recall how to square a binomial. For example,

$$(a + b)^2 = a^2 + 2ab + b^2.$$

You can *cube* a binomial by using the above results. You get

$$(a + b)^3 = (a + b)^2(a + b)$$
$$= (a^2 + 2ab + b^2)(a + b)$$
$$= a^3 + 2a^2b + ab^2 + a^2b + 2ab^2 + b^3$$
$$= a^3 + 3a^2b + 3ab^2 + b^3.$$

The answer is a *series* of terms. It is called a *binomial* series because it comes from expanding a binomial raised to a power. There are several patterns which show up in this series. If you know the patterns, you will eventually be able to raise a binomial to a power *mentally*, in one step. In this section you will try to discover some of these patterns.

Objective:
Discover patterns followed by the signs, exponents, and coefficients in a binomial series.

The following exercise is designed to lead you to some of these discoveries.

EXERCISE 11-9

1. Expand the binomial power $(a + b)^4$ into a binomial series. This is most easily done by observing that $(a + b)^4 = (a + b)^3(a + b)$, and using the series for $(a + b)^3$ from above.

2. Expand $(a + b)^5$ as a binomial series using the results of Problem 1, above.

3. If you expand $(a + b)^6$, you will get

$$(a + b)^6 = a^6 + 6a^5b + 15a^4b^2 + 20a^3b^3 + 15a^2b^4$$
$$+ 6ab^5 + b^6.$$

By observing the patterns in this binomial series and in your answers to Problems 1 and 2, tell
a. the pattern followed by the powers of a,
b. the pattern followed by the powers of b,
c. the degree of each term,
d. the number of terms that will be in the series, and
e. any pattern you see in the coefficients as you look at the series from both ends.

4.   The pattern followed by the powers of a and b is easy to see. The pattern of the coefficients is more difficult. By arranging the coefficients for the various powers of $(a + b)$ in a *triangle*, one pattern shows up.

$$(a + b)^0\dots\dots\dots\dots\dots\quad 1$$
$$(a + b)^1\dots\dots\dots\dots\quad 1\quad 1$$
$$(a + b)^2\dots\dots\dots\dots\quad 1\quad 2\quad 1$$
$$(a + b)^3\dots\dots\dots\quad 1\quad 3\quad 3\quad 1$$
$$(a + b)^4\dots\dots\dots\quad 1\quad 4\quad 6\quad 4\quad 1$$
$$(a + b)^5\dots\dots\quad 1\quad 5\quad 10\quad 10\quad 5\quad 1$$
$$(a + b)^6\dots\dots\quad 1\quad 6\quad 15\quad 20\quad 15\quad 6\quad 1$$

This triangular array of numbers is called Pascal's Triangle after the French mathematician Blaise Pascal, who lived from 1623 to 1662. Tell what pattern relates the numbers in one row of Pascal's Triangle to the numbers in the *preceding* row. Then demonstrate that you *understand* the pattern by finding the coefficients which will be in the row for $(a + b)^7$.

5.   Suppose someone tells you that the coefficients of $(a + b)^9$ are 1 9 36 84 126 126 84 36 9 1. Use what you have discovered to expand $(a + b)^{10}$ as a binomial series in *one* step.

6.   Suppose you wish to expand a binomial with a "$-$" sign between the terms, such as $(x - y)^6$. Observe that $(x - y)^6$ equals $[x + (-y)]^6$. Then use the pattern for the binomial series for $(a + b)^6$ from Problem 3, above, to expand $(x - y)^6$ as a binomial series. What is the *only* difference in the series when the sign of the binomial is "$-$" instead of "$+$"?

7.   You have defined a "series" to be a sum of an *infinite* number of terms. Yet the binomial series of this section appears to have only a finite number of terms. What do you suppose all the rest of the terms of a binomial series must equal?

11-10 | THE BINOMIAL FORMULA

In Exercise 11-9 you raised binomials to powers. For example,

$$(a + b)^6 = a^6 + 6a^5b + 15a^4b^2 + 20a^3b^3 + 15a^2b^4 + 6ab^5 + b^6.$$

By examining such "binomial series," you can find several patterns. For the series from expanding $(a + b)^n$:

1. There are $n + 1$ terms.
2. Each term is n^{th} degree.
3. The powers of a start at a^n, and the exponent *decreases* by 1 each term; the powers of b start at b^0 and *increase* by 1 each term.
4. The coefficients are *symmetrical* with respect to the ends.
5. The coefficients can be calculated from the *previous row* of Pascal's Triangle by *adding* pairs of adjacent coefficients in that previous row (see Exercise 11-9, Problem 4).

In this section you will learn how to calculate *any* coefficient in *any* binomial series *without* having to know the previous row in Pascal's Triangle.

Objectives:

1. Given a binomial power, expand it as a binomial series in *one* step.
2. Given a binomial power of the form $(a + b)^n$, find term number k, or find the term which contains b^r, where k and r are integers from 0 through n.

There is a pattern to the coefficients which is difficult to discover, but is easy to remember and use once you have learned it. Consider the binomial series

$$(a + b)^8 = a^8 + 8a^7b + 28a^6b^2 + 56a^5b^3 + 70a^4b^4$$
$$\textcircled{1} \qquad \textcircled{2} \qquad \textcircled{3} \qquad \textcircled{4} \qquad \textcircled{5}$$
$$+ 56a^3b^5 + 28a^2b^6 + 8ab^7 + b^8.$$
$$\textcircled{6} \qquad \textcircled{7} \qquad \textcircled{8} \quad \textcircled{9}$$

The numbers in circles are the term numbers. If you multiply the coefficient of a term by the exponent of a over the term number, you get the coefficient of the *next* term! For example,

$$8 \cdot \frac{7}{2} = 28,$$

$$28 \cdot \frac{6}{3} = 56,$$

$$56 \cdot \frac{5}{4} = 70,$$

Exponent of *a*

Next coefficient

Term number

Coefficient

In general,

$$\frac{(\text{coefficient})(a\text{-exponent})}{\text{term number}} = \text{next coefficient}.$$

A still more interesting pattern shows up if you do *not* simplify the coefficients as you calculate them. For example, the first term of $(a + b)^8$ is

① a^8.

Using the pattern, the second term is

② $\frac{8}{1}a^7b$.

Multiplying the coefficient, $\frac{8}{1}$, by the exponent of *a* over the term number, $\frac{7}{2}$, allows you to write term 3.

③ $\frac{8}{1} \cdot \frac{7}{2}a^6b^2$

The fourth and fifth terms may be calculated in the same way.

④ $\frac{8}{1} \cdot \frac{7}{2} \cdot \frac{6}{3}a^5b^3$ ⑤ $\frac{8}{1} \cdot \frac{7}{2} \cdot \frac{6}{3} \cdot \frac{5}{4}a^4b^4$.

By now you should be able to see the pattern. The coefficients can be written as *factorials*. For example, the coefficient of the fourth term is

$$\frac{8}{1} \cdot \frac{7}{2} \cdot \frac{6}{3} = \frac{8 \cdot 7 \cdot 6}{1 \cdot 2 \cdot 3}$$ Multiplication property of fractions

$$= \frac{8 \cdot 7 \cdot 6}{1 \cdot 2 \cdot 3} \cdot \frac{5!}{5!}$$ Multiplicative identity

$$= \frac{8!}{3!\,5!} \qquad \text{Multiplication property of fractions,}$$
$$\text{and definition of factorials}$$

The three numbers 8, 3, and 5 show up as exponents at various places, as shown below.

$$(a + b)^8 = \ldots + \frac{8!}{3!\,5!}a^5b^3 + \ldots$$

The 8 in the numerator is the exponent n, to which $(a + b)$ is raised. The 3 and 5 in the denominator are the exponents of a and b in the term you are looking for.

With this knowledge, you can now accomplish the objective of this section.

EXAMPLE 1

Find the term in $(a - b)^{17}$ which contains b^{11}.

Your reasoning should be as follows:

1. The power of a must be a^6, since the exponents of a and b must add up to 17.
2. Therefore, the term is $\frac{17!}{11!\,6!}a^6(-b)^{11}$, which equals

$$-\frac{17!}{11!\,6!}a^6b^{11} \quad \text{since } -b \text{ is raised to an } odd \text{ power.}$$

3. If asked to, you can do the arithmetic, getting

$$\frac{17!}{11!\,6!} = \frac{17 \cdot 16 \cdot 15 \cdot 14 \cdot 13 \cdot 12 \cdot 11!}{11! \cdot 6 \cdot 5 \cdot 4 \cdot 3 \cdot 2}$$

$$= 12376, \text{ so the term is } -12376a^6b^{11}. \quad \blacksquare$$

EXAMPLE 2

Find the 8th term of $(a + b)^{12}$.

Your reasoning should be as follows:

1. The 8th term is the one that has b^7, since the 1st term has b^0.
2. Therefore, the 8th term has a^5b^7, since the exponents must add up to 12.
3. The term is thus $\frac{12!}{7!\,5!}a^5b^7$, which equals $792a^5b^7$. $\quad \blacksquare$

EXAMPLE 3

Find the 5th term of $(r^3 - 2s)^{10}$.

Your reasoning should be as follows:

1. Instead of a and b, the terms of the binomial are r^3 and $-2s$.
2. The 5th term will have $(-2s)^4$.
3. The power of r^3 will be $(r^3)^6$, since the exponents of r^3 and $-2s$ must add up to 10.
4. The term is therefore $\frac{10!}{4!\ 6!}(r^3)^6(-2s)^4$.
5. This can be simplified to $210r^{18}(16s^4)$ which equals $\underline{3360r^{18}s^4}$.

Note that the exponents no longer add up to 10 after the simplification is done. ∎

EXAMPLE 4

Find the term containing b^r in $(a + b)^n$.

Using the same reasoning you used in the previous examples, you can immediately write the answer:

$$\text{term} = \frac{n!}{r!\ (n - r)!}a^{n-r}b^r$$

This formula is called the *Binomial Formula* since it is used to calculate terms in a binomial series. ∎

EXAMPLE 5

Expand $(r^2 - 3s)^7$ as a binomial series.

This is most easily accomplished by using the "pattern" to find the coefficients. The first term is

$$(r^2)^7.$$
①

Multiplying the coefficient, 1, by the r^2 exponent, 7, and dividing by the term number, 1, gives 7. Thus the series begins

$$(r^2)^7 + 7(r^2)^6(-3s) + \ldots.$$
①   ②

Working with the second term, you multiply the coefficient 7 by $\frac{6}{2}$ (the r^2 exponent over the term number), getting 21. So the series continues

$$(r^2)^7 + 7(r^2)^6(-3s) + 21(r^2)^5(-3s)^2 + \ldots$$
$$\quad\quad\quad ① \quad\quad\quad ② \quad\quad\quad\quad ③$$

Using the same reasoning for following terms gives the complete series,

$$(r^2 - 3s)^7 = (r^2)^7 + 7(r^2)^6(-3s) + 21(r^2)^5(-3s)^2$$
$$+ 35(r^2)^4(-3s)^3 + 35(r^2)^3(-3s)^4$$
$$+ 21(r^2)^2(-3s)^5 + 7(r^2)(-3s)^6$$
$$+ (-3s)^7.$$

The objective, writing the binomial series in one step, has thus been accomplished. If you must do the arithmetic and simplify, you get

$$(r^2 - 3s)^7 = \underline{r^{14} - 21r^{12}s + 189r^{10}s^2 - 945r^8s^3 + 2835r^6s^4}$$
$$\underline{- 5103r^4s^5 + 5103r^2s^6 - 2187s^7}.$$

Note that the symmetrical pattern of the coefficients and the constant degree of the terms may disappear after you have done the simplifying. ∎

EXERCISE 11-10

Do These Quickly

The following problems are intended to refresh your skills. You should be able to do all 10 in less than 5 minutes.

Q1.   Multiply: $(x - 5)(x + 3)$

Q2.   Factor: $x^2 - 10x + 16$

Q3.   Multiply: $(x - 2y)(x - 7y)$

Q4.   Factor: $x^2 - 6xy + 9y^2$

Q5.   Multiply: $(3x + 5)^2$

Q6.   Factor: $16x^2 - 8xy + y^2$

Q7.   Evaluate: $6 \cdot 5 \cdot 4 \cdot 3 \cdot 2 \cdot 1$

Q8.   Evaluate: $6!$

Q9.   Evaluate: $\dfrac{10!}{9!}$

Q10. Sketch the graph of a cubic function with just one real zero, but with two vertices.

For Problems 1 through 20:
a. Expand the given binomial power as a binomial series.
b. Simplify the resulting series as much as possible.

1. $(x + y)^5$ 2. $(a + b)^8$

3. $(p - m)^7$ 4. $(z - w)^9$

5. $(a + 2)^4$ 6. $(x - 2)^6$

7. $(2x - 3)^5$ 8. $(3a + 2)^4$

9. $(x^2 + y^3)^6$ 10. $(a^3 - b^2)^5$

11. $(2a - b^4)^3$ 12. $(4r + s^2)^3$

13. $(x + x^{-1})^8$ 14. $(x^2 - x^{-2})^{10}$

15. $(x^{\frac{1}{2}} - x^{-\frac{1}{2}})^4$ 16. $(x^{\frac{1}{4}} + x^{-\frac{1}{4}})^8$

17. $(1 + i)^6$ 18. $(1 - i)^4$

19. $(1 - i)^5$ 20. $(1 + i)^7$

Note: $i = \sqrt{-1}$.

For Problems 21 through 40, find the term with the specified power in the expansion of the given binomial power. You may leave the coefficient in factorial form unless instructed otherwise.

21. $(x + y)^8$, y^5 22. $(p + j)^{11}$, j^4

23. $(r + s)^{13}$, s^7 24. $(m + q)^{10}$, q^5

25. $(p - j)^{15}$, j^{11} 26. $(c - d)^{19}$, d^{15}

27. $(a - b)^{21}$, b^{16} 28. $(x - y)^{25}$, y^{20}

29. $(e - f)^{58}$, f^{23} 30. $(g - h)^{64}$, h^{39}

31. $(x + y)^{73}$, x^{48} 32. $(a + b)^{81}$, a^{19}

33. $(x^3 + y^2)^{15}$, y^{12} 34. $(x^3 + y^2)^{29}$, y^{10}

35. $(x^3 - y^2)^{13}$, x^{18} 36. $(x^3 - y^2)^{24}$, x^{30}

37. $(x^3 + y^2)^{42}$, y^{15} 38. $(x^3 + y^2)^{107}$, y^{77}

39. $(3x + 2y)^8$, y^5 40. $(3x + 2y)^7$, y^4

For Problems 41 through 50, find the specified term in the expansion of the given binomial power. You may leave the coefficient in factorial form unless instructed otherwise.

41. $(j + k)^{34}$, 17th term

42. $(p + k)^{51}$, 19th term

43. $(r - q)^{15}$, 12th term

44. $(a - b)^{17}$, 8th term

45. $(a - b)^{12}$, 13th term

46. $(x - y)^{19}$, 20th term

47. $(3x^2 - 2y^3)^7$, 4th term

48. $(3x^2 - 2y^3)^8$, 6th term

49. $(x^3 - 5)^6$, 3rd term (Simplify the answer.)

50. $(r^4 - 7)^5$, 3rd term (Simplify the answer.)

51.   Suppose that $(r + s)$ is raised to some positive integer power, and one term in the binomial series is $27132r^{13}s^6$.
   a.   *Which* term is it?
   b.   To what *power* was $(r + s)$ raised?
   c.   What is the *next* term? (Simplify the coefficient.)
   d.   How *many* terms are there in this series?

52.   Suppose you are told that $3274r^{17}s^{66}$ is a term in a binomial series, and you are asked to find the *next* term. Can you do it? If so, *how*? If not, *why* not?

53.   Find a decimal approximation for 1.02^{10} by writing it as $(1 + 0.02)^{10}$ and calculating the first five terms of the resulting binomial series.

54.   The pattern of multiplying the coefficient by the exponent and then dividing by the term number works for *non-integer* exponents, too. Use this fact to expand

$$(a + b)^{\frac{3}{2}}$$

   as a binomial series. Tell how many terms there will be in this binomial series. Then tell why a binomial series has a *finite* number of terms when the exponent is an integer.

55.   Expand the binomial $(1 + 1)^5$ as a binomial series, simplify each term, then add up the terms. Next, show how you could have gotten the answer in a much easier way. Demonstrate that you understand the significance of what you have done by finding the *sum* of the *coefficients* of the binomial series for $(a + b)^{57}$ in *one* step.

11-11 | CHAPTER REVIEW AND TEST

In this chapter you have studied functions whose domain is a set of integers rather than the set of all real numbers. Sometimes you can figure out a formula for such sequences of numbers just by observing a pattern. In particular, you were able to derive general formulas for arithmetic and geometric sequences, and for partial sums of their corresponding series. You used sequences and series as mathematical models for things in the real world that change by "steps" rather than changing "continuously." Finally, you learned about factorials and binomial series, mainly as background for work with probability in the next chapter.

The Review Problems below parallel the sections in this chapter. The Concepts Problems let you try your hand at applying what you know to analyze a new situation. The Chapter Test is similar to one your instructor might give to see how well you understand sequences and series.

REVIEW PROBLEMS

R1. For the sequence, 2, 6, 12, 20, 30, 42, 56, . . . ;
   a. Write the next two terms, telling what pattern you used.
   b. Draw the graph of the first six terms of the series.
   c. Write an equation expressing t_n in terms of n.
   d. Use the equation to calculate t_{700}.

R2. Answer the following questions.
   a. Is the sequence in Problem R1 arithmetic, geometric, or neither?
   b. Find t_{56} for the arithmetic sequence with $t_1 = 237$ and common difference -7.
   c. An arithmetic sequence has $t_1 = 164$ and common difference -9. If $t_n = -484$, find n.
   d. Find t_{31} for the geometric sequence with $t_1 = 17$ and common ratio 1.2.
   e. A geometric sequence has $t_1 = 11$ and common ratio 3. If $t_n = 24057$, find n.

R3. Answer the following questions.
   a. Insert five arithmetic means between 17 and 63.
   b. Insert three geometric means between 4 and 100 if complex numbers are allowed.
   c. What is *the* geometric mean of 25 and 100 (two possible answers!)?

R4. Do the following:
   a. Evaluate $\sum_{k=1}^{5} k!$.
   b. Write using sigma notation: $\frac{1}{4} + \frac{1}{8} + \frac{1}{16} + \frac{1}{32} + \frac{1}{64} + \ldots$.

R5. Do the following:
   a. Find S_{200} for the arithmetic series $6 + 13 + 20 + \ldots$.
   b. 31161 is a partial sum of the series in part (a). What is its term number?

    c. Find S_{20} for the geometric series $100 + 96 + 92.16 + \ldots$.

    d. One of the partial sums of the series in part (c) is approximately 1850. Which partial sum is it?

R6. Do the following:

    a. Find the limit to which the series in part (c) of Problem R5, above, converges.

    b. Explain why the geometric series $5 + 10 + 20 + 40 + \ldots$ does *not* converge.

    c. Write the repeating decimal $0.279279\ldots$ as a ratio of relatively prime integers.

R7. ***Swinging Problem*** When a person is swinging, the "amplitude" of the swing increases with each pump (see sketch). According to *Scientific American* magazine (April, 1977, page 60), the amplitude increases by *adding* a constant when the person pumps sitting down, and by *multiplying* by a constant when the person pumps standing up. Suppose that when you get on a swing, it has an amplitude of 3 centimeters (i.e., $t_0 = 3$). Assume that the amplitude increases by adding 2 centimeters each pump when you are sitting, and by multiplying by 1.2 each pump when you are standing.

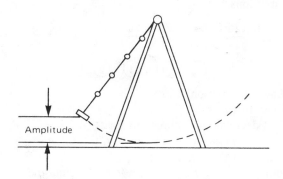

Amplitude

    a. If you are sitting, what is your amplitude after 10 pumps? After 20 pumps?

    b. If you are standing, what is your amplitude after 10 pumps? After 20 pumps?

    c. What is the minimum number of pumps it takes to make the amplitude equal 25 centimeters when you are sitting? Standing?

    d. What is the minimum number of pumps it takes to make the amplitude equal 75 centimeters when you are sitting? Standing?

    e. On the same Cartesian coordinate system, draw graphs of amplitude versus number of pumps for sitting and for standing. You should have enough plotting data from the above information and calculations.

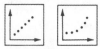

   f.   According to your mathematical model, what would happen if you started with an amplitude of 0 and tried to swing standing up?

   g.   Which way of pumping increases your amplitude faster, sitting or standing? Justify your answer.

R8.   Do the following:

   a.   Evaluate: $\frac{3! \, 6!}{9!}$

   b.   Write $24 \cdot 23 \cdot 22 \cdot 21$ as a ratio of two factorials.

R9.   Expand $(x - y)^4$ as a binomial series.

R10.   Do the following:

   a.   Expand as a binomial series and simplify: $(r^3 - 2p)^6$

   b.   Expand as a binomial series of complex numbers and simplify: $(3 + i)^8$

   c.   Find the term with d^5 in the binomial series from $(d + 2p)^7$.

   d.   Find the twelfth term of $(t - y^2)^{16}$. Simplify.

CONCEPTS PROBLEMS

C1.   The following is a geometric sequence that extends infinitely far in *both* directions.

$$\ldots, \; \frac{128}{243}, \; \frac{64}{81}, \; \frac{32}{27}, \; \frac{16}{9}, \; \frac{8}{3}, \; 4, \ldots \quad \longleftarrow \; t(n)$$

$$(-2) \quad (-1) \quad (0) \quad (1) \quad (2) \quad (3) \qquad \longleftarrow \; n$$

   a.   Find the common ratio r.

   b.   Show that $t_n = t_0 \cdot r^n$.

   c.   Find decimal approximations for t_{20} and t_{-10}.

   d.   Find the *sum* of the terms from t_1 through t_{20}.

   e.   Show that the sum $t_0 + t_1 + t_2 + \ldots$ *diverges*, but that the sum $t_0 + t_{-1} + t_{-2} + \ldots$ *converges*. Find the number to which this second sum converges.

   f.   Plot the graph of the above terms, t_{-2} through t_3.

   g.   If n could be *any* real number, rather than just an integer, what kind of function would t_n be called?

C2.   *Bode's Law Problem*   In 1776, Johann Titus discovered that the distances of the planets from the Sun are proportional to the terms of a rather simple sequence:

4	7	10	16	28	52	100
Mercury	Venus	Earth	Mars	Ceres (asteroid)	Jupiter	Saturn
①	②	③	④	⑤	⑥	⑦

   a.   Describe the pattern followed by the terms of this sequence.

(Planet 1, Mercury, does *not* fit this pattern.) Then use this pattern to find the term for Uranus, planet number 8.

b. Planets 9 and 10, Neptune and Pluto, have distances corresponding to the numbers 305 and 388. Are these numbers terms of the sequence? Justify your answer.

c. Find a formula for t_n, the term value, in terms of n, the planet number. For what values of n is the formula valid?

d. See *Scientific American* magazine, July, 1977, page 128, to see why this is called "Bode's" law.

C3. *Office Building Problem*   Suppose that you are responsible for predicting the cost of constructing a new multi-story office building. The cost per square meter of floor space for constructing the higher stories increases because it is more difficult to build them.

a. You find that the first story costs $400 per square meter, and the fifth story costs $500 per square meter. Assuming that the costs per square meter form an arithmetic sequence, find the common difference.

b. What is the cost per square meter for the second, third, and fourth stories?

c. The building is to be 48 stories high. How much per square meter will the top story cost?

d. What is the total cost per square meter for building all 48 stories?

e. If each story is to have 1000 square meters of floor space, what is the total cost of the building?

C4. Let $_nC_r$ be the *coefficient* of the b^r term in the binomial series from expanding $(a + b)^n$. For example, in $(a + b)^5$, the term with b^2 is $10a^3b^2$. So $_5C_2 = 10$.

a. Write $_{17}C_9$ in terms of factorials.

b. Find $_3C_0$, $_3C_1$, $_3C_2$, and $_3C_3$, then *add* these four numbers.

c. Find $\sum\limits_{r=0}^{4} {_4C_r}$.

d. Based on your answers to parts b and c, what is a formula for the *sum* of the coefficients in the binomial series that comes from expanding $(a + b)^n$? Show that your formula gives the correct answers for $(a + b)^2$, $(a + b)^1$, and $(a + b)^0$.

C5. Prove that the partial sum, S_n, of a geometric series is equal to a *constant* plus a term in a *different* geometric sequence.

CHAPTER TEST

(Note: This set is somewhat longer than a normal 1-hour test.)

T1.   Demonstrate that you know the difference between a sequence and a series by writing the first few terms of:
   a.   The arithmetic series with first term 100 and common difference 1.3.
   b.   The geometric sequence with first term 13 and common ratio 5.

T2.   For the arithmetic sequence 37, 43, 49, . . .
   a.   Find term number 4.
   b.   Find term number 1000, 1001, and 1002.
   c.   985 is one of the terms in this sequence. *Which* term is it?

T3.   For the geometric sequence with first term 2000 and common ratio 0.9,
   a.   Find the second and third terms.
   b.   Find the 79th term.
   c.   14.139301 is the approximate value of one of the terms in this sequence. *Which* term is it?

T4.   Find the 70th partial sum of the arithmetic series 37 + 49 + 61 + . . .

T5.   Find the 100th partial sum of the geometric series with first term 400 and common ratio 1.05.

T6.   Find the limit to which the geometric series 30 + 27 + . . . converges.

T7.   An arithmetic series has first term 444 and common difference −3. Is 231 a term in this series? If so, *which* term is it? If not, how do you tell?

T8.   Insert 2 geometric means between 38.9 and 98.6.

T9.   241.17248 is the fifth term in a geometric series with common ratio 1.6. What is the first term?

T10.   The sequence 6, 12, 20, 30, 42, 56, 72, . . . is neither arithmetic nor geometric. Find a pattern, and use it to figure out values of the next two terms.

T11.   *Tree Height Problem*   Assume that the number of inches a tree grows (up) each year is a term in a geometric series. Suppose that you plant a tree that grows 40 inches the first year and 38 inches the next year.
   a.   Predict how much it will grow the 5th year.
   b.   Predict how tall it will be after 10 years.
   c.   Predict the ultimate height it will reach.

T12.   Expand as a binomial series and simplify: $(x + 3)^7$

T13.   Find the tenth term of the binomial series $(a^7 - b^3)^{13}$. Simplify.

12

Probability, Data Analysis, and Functions of a Random Variable

16 to 21 days

*An occurrence is said to happen "at random" if there is **no** way of telling for sure what the outcome will be on any particular occasion. In this chapter you will make a precise definition of the **probability** that a random occurrence comes out a certain way. You will explore problems ranging from genetics and insurance to the reliability of power plants and rocket engines. Such problems will tie together much of the mathematics you have learned so far!*

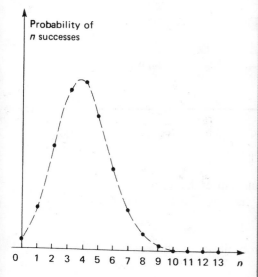

Probability of
n successes

0 1 2 3 4 5 6 7 8 9 10 11 12 13   *n*

12-1 | INTRODUCTION TO PROBABILITY

You have used statements such as, "I shall probably be home by 10:00 o'clock." Mathematicians attempt to make the word "probably" have a more precise meaning by attaching *numbers* to it. For example, the probability of rain may be 30%. The idea for doing this arose from the analysis of gambling games several hundred years ago.

Suppose that two dice are rolled, a black one and a white one. The possible outcomes are shown in Figure 12-1.

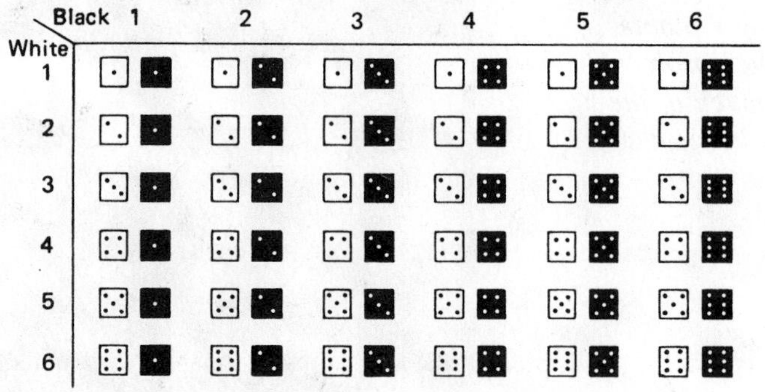

Black	1	2	3	4	5	6
White 1	⚀⚀	⚀⚁	⚀⚂	⚀⚃	⚀⚄	⚀⚅
2	⚁⚀	⚁⚁	⚁⚂	⚁⚃	⚁⚄	⚁⚅
3	⚂⚀	⚂⚁	⚂⚂	⚂⚃	⚂⚄	⚂⚅
4	⚃⚀	⚃⚁	⚃⚂	⚃⚃	⚃⚄	⚃⚅
5	⚄⚀	⚄⚁	⚄⚂	⚄⚃	⚄⚄	⚄⚅
6	⚅⚀	⚅⚁	⚅⚂	⚅⚃	⚅⚄	⚅⚅

Figure 12-1

There are *five* ways the total on the dice could equal 6.

⚀⚄   ⚁⚃   ⚂⚂   ⚃⚁   ⚄⚀

Since each outcome is *equally likely*, you would expect that in many rolls of the dice, the total would be 6 roughly $\frac{5}{36}$ of the time. This number, $\frac{5}{36}$, is called the *probability* of rolling a total of 6.

In the following exercise, you will find the probabilities of other such events.

EXERCISE 12-1

A pair of dice is rolled, one black and one white. Find the probability of each of the following events:

1.   The total is 10.

2.   The total is at least 10.

3.   The total is less than 10.

4.   The total is at most 10.

5.   The total is 7.

6.   The total is 2.

7.   The total is between 3 and 7, inclusive.

8.   The total is between 3 and 7.

9.   The total is between 2 and 12, inclusive.

10.   The total is 13.

11.   The numbers are 2 and 5.

12.   The black die has 2 and the white die has 5.

13.   The black die has 2 or the white die has 5.

12-2 | WORDS ASSOCIATED WITH PROBABILITY

So that people may talk more efficiently about probability, various things are assigned *names,* with precise meanings. For the dice-rolling example in Section 12-1, the names would be as follows:

The act of rolling the dice is called a *random experiment.* The word "random" lets you know that there is *no* way of telling beforehand just how any one roll is going to come out.

Each way in which the dice can come up, such as

,

is called an *outcome.* Outcomes are *equally likely* results of a random experiment.

An *event* is a *set* of outcomes. For example, the event "The total on the two dice is 6," is the five-element set

$$\left\{ \boxed{\cdot}\,\boxed{::}\;\;\; \boxed{\cdot\cdot}\,\boxed{::}, \;\;\; \boxed{\cdot\cdot}\,\boxed{:\cdot}, \;\;\; \boxed{::}\,\boxed{:\cdot}, \;\;\; \boxed{\cdot\cdot}\,\boxed{\cdot} \right\}.$$

Two events are usually *not* equally likely. The only condition under which they would be equally likely is if they contained the same number of outcomes.

The set of *all* outcomes is called the *sample space*. The sample space for the dice roll is the set of all 36 outcomes in the table of Section 12-1.

The *probability* of an event may now be defined more precisely.

DEFINITION

> The **probability** of an event is
>
> $$\text{Probability} = \frac{\text{Number of outcomes in the event}}{\text{Number of outcomes in the sample space}}.$$

Since the probability of an event depends on the number of outcomes in that event, a form of "$f(x)$" terminology can be used. Letting P stand for "probability," you can write

$$P(\text{The total is } 6) = \frac{5}{36}.$$

Note that the argument inside the parentheses may be a *set* rather than simply a number. The "$f(x)$" terminology can be used for the numbers of elements in the event and in the sample space. Letting n stand for "number," the numbers of elements in Event E and in the sample space, S, would be $n(E)$ and $n(S)$, respectively.

In general, therefore, the probability of Event E is

$$P(E) = \frac{n(E)}{n(S)}.$$

Note: All probabilities are numbers between 0 and 1. An event that is *certain* to occur has a probability of 1, since $n(E) = n(S)$. An event that cannot possibly occur has a probability of 0 since $n(E) = 0$.

Objective:
Be able to distinguish among the various words used to describe probability.

The following exercise has problems that use the words, "outcome," "event," "sample space," and so forth. By working the problems correctly, you will demonstrate that you know the meanings of these words.

EXERCISE 12-2

Do These Quickly

The following problems are intended to refresh your skills. You should be able to do all 10 in less than 5 minutes.

Q1. Find the probability of drawing a black club from a normal deck of cards.

Q2. Evaluate 5!.

Q3. If $f(x) = x^2 + 3x - 5$, find $f(4)$.

Q4. Find the third term in the binomial series from $(a + b)^{11}$.

Q5. Evaluate $5(0.4)^3(0.6)^2$.

Q6. If you select a marble at random from a bag containing 10 blue marbles and 5 black marbles, what is the probability that the marble is blue?

Q7. Sketch the graph of a decreasing exponential function.

Q8. Factor $x^2 + 7x + 10$.

Q9. Find 40% of $(35x + 45y)$.

Q10. Draw a 30°, 60° right triangle.

Work the following problems.

1. A card is drawn at random from a normal 52-card deck.
    a. What name is given to the act of drawing the card?
    b. How many outcomes are there in the sample space?
    c. How many outcomes are there in the event, "The card is a face card?"
    d. Calculate P(The card is a face card).
    e. Calculate P(The card is black).

f. Calculate P(The card is an Ace).
  g. Calculate P(The card is between 3 and 7, inclusive).
  h. Calculate P(The card is the 8 of clubs).
  i. Calculate P(The card belongs to the deck).
  j. Calculate P(The card is a Joker).

2. A penny, a nickel, and a dime are flipped at the same time. Each coin can come out either heads (H) or tails (T).
  a. What name is given to the act of flipping the coins?
  b. There are eight elements in the sample space (for example, *HHH*, *THT*, and so forth). List all eight outcomes.
  c. How many outcomes are there in the event, "Exactly two of the coins are heads?"
  d. Calculate P(*HHT*).
  e. Calculate P(Exactly two heads).
  f. Calculate P(At least two heads).
  g. Calculate P(Penny and nickel are tails).
  h. Calculate P(Penny or nickel are tails).
  i. Calculate P(None is tails).
  j. Calculate P(Zero, one, two or three heads).
  k. Calculate P(Four heads).

12-3 | TWO COUNTING PRINCIPLES

The difficulty with calculating probabilities is counting up the number of elements in an event or in the sample space. For example, if ten people line up at random, and you want to find the probability that you will be next to your best friend, the sample space contains over three *million* outcomes! Obviously, it is impractical to list all of the outcomes and count them as you did in Exercise 12-1 and 12-2.

Objective:
Be able to determine the number of outcomes in an event or sample space *without* listing and counting them.

There are two principles of counting which form the basis for accomplishing this objective. One applies when Event A and Event B are *both* performed. The other applies when *either* Event A *or* Event B is performed, but not both.

Suppose that a mouse is placed in Room X of a maze (See Figure 12-3a). There are four ways it can get to Room Y, and three ways it can get from

Y to Z. For each *one* way of getting to Y, there are *three* ways of getting to Z. So there is a total of

$$4 \times 3 \text{ ways}$$

or 12 ways it could go to Y *and then* to Z.

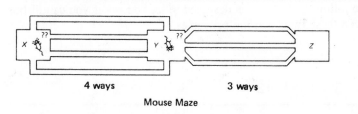

4 ways   **3 ways**

Mouse Maze

Figure 12-3a _____

If the mouse were placed in Room Y, it could go *either* to X *or* to Z. Since there are 4 ways of getting to x and 3 ways of getting to Z, there is a total of

$$4 + 3 \text{ ways}$$

or seven ways it could go to X *or* to Z.

These examples illustrate the two counting principles.

Principle 1: If $n(A)$ and $n(B)$ are the numbers of ways that Events A and B can occur, respectively, then

$$\boxed{n(A \text{ and then } B) = n(A) \times n(B)} \;.$$

Principle 2: If $n(A)$ and $n(B)$ are the numbers of ways that Events A and B can occur, respectively, then

$$\boxed{n(A \text{ or } B) = n(A) + n(B)} \;.$$

Notes:

1. An easy way to remember these two principles is that you *multiply* the numbers of ways when you do one *and then* the other. You *add* the numbers of ways when you do one *or* the other. If you ever forget, you can think of the mouse in the maze!
2. In the first principle, $n(B)$ must be the number of ways B can occur *after* A has already occurred. For example, if you are picking two people from a group of 5, the first person could be picked in 5 different ways. But the second person could be picked in only 4 different ways, since one person has already been picked.

3. In the second principle, it is assumed that A and B *cannot both* occur. For instance, the mouse cannot go to both rooms X and Z at the same time if it starts at Room Y. Such events are said to be "mutually exclusive." In Problem 17 of the following exercise, you will see what has to be done if Events A and B *could* both occur.

The following exercise is designed to let you see if you can distinguish between these two counting principles.

EXERCISE 12-3

Do These Quickly

The following problems are intended to refresh your skills. You should be able to do all 10 in less than 5 minutes.

Q1.   What is the difference between an *outcome* and an *event*?

Q2.   How many outcomes are there in the sample space?

Q3.   If the probability $P(A)$ is 20%, and the sample space has 50 outcomes in it, how many outcomes does Event A have?

Q4.   Write the 100th term of the arithmetic sequence 47, 46.4, ...

Q5.   Evaluate 2^x if x is 3.

Q6.   Solve: $(x + 7)(2x - 5) = 0$

Q7.   Evaluate $\dfrac{12!}{8!}$.

Q8.   What kind of function has a graph like this?

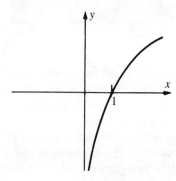

Q9.   What possible numbers of non-real complex zeros can a quintic function have?

Q10.   Sketch an ellipse with major axis 4 units long and minor axis 2 units.

Work the following problems.

1.   Ward Robe has 15 pairs of slacks and 23 shirts. In how many different ways could he select a slacks-and-shirt combination?

2.   Natalie Attired has 20 dresses and 17 pants outfits. In how many different ways could she select a dress or a pants outfit to wear?

3.   A salesman has 7 customers in Denver and 13 customers in Reno. In how many different ways could he telephone
   a.   a customer in Denver and then a customer in Reno?
   b.   a customer in Denver or a customer in Reno?

4.   Sally visits the pet store. There are 37 dogs and 15 cats. In how many ways could she select
   a.   a dog or a cat?
   b.   a dog and a cat?

5.   A pizza establishment offers 12 kinds of meat topping (pepperoni, sausage, etc.) and 5 kinds of vegetable topping (onions, green peppers, etc.). In how many different ways could you select
   a.   a meat topping or a vegetable topping?
   b.   a meat topping and a vegetable topping?

6.   A first grade class has 13 girls and 11 boys. In how many different ways could the teacher select
   a.   a boy and a girl to go to the office?
   b.   a boy or a girl to go to the office?

7.   A reading list contains 11 novels and 5 mysteries. In how many different ways could a student select
   a.   a novel or a mystery?
   b.   a novel and then a mystery?
   c.   a mystery and then another mystery?

8.   A submarine practices attacking a convoy that has 20 cargo ships and 5 escort vessels. In how many different ways could it attack
   a.   a cargo ship and then an escort vessel?
   b.   a cargo ship or an escort vessel?
   c.   a cargo ship and then another cargo ship?

9.   The menu at Valerio's lists seven kinds of salad, eleven entrees, and nine kinds of dessert. How many different salad-entree-dessert meals could you select? (Meals are considered to be *different* if any *one* thing is different.)

10.   Admiral Motors manufactures cars with five different body styles, uses eleven different colors of paint, and has six different interior

colors. Suppose that the Admiral Motors dealer for whom you work
wants to order one of each possible variety of car to display in the
showroom. Show your boss that the plan would be impractical because so many cars would have to be ordered.

11. Using only the letters in LOGARITHM:
    a. In how many ways could you pick a vowel or a consonant?
    b. In how many ways could you pick a vowel and a consonant?
    c. How many different three-letter "words" (such as "ORL,"
        "HLG," "AOI," etc.) could you make, using each letter no more
        than once in any given word? (There are *three* events; A,
        "Select the first letter;" B, "Select the second letter;" and C,
        "Select the third letter;" Find $n(A)$, $n(B)$, and $n(C)$, then figure
        out what to do with these three numbers.)

12. Using only the letters in SEQUOIA:
    a. In how many ways could you select a vowel and a consonant?
    b. In how many ways could you select a vowel or a consonant?
    c. How many different four-letter "words" could you form using
        no letter more than once in any given word? (See Problem 11,
        above, for a hint!)

13. There are 10 students in a class, and 10 chairs numbered 1 through
     10.
    a. In how many different ways could a student be selected to oc-
        cupy Chair Number 1?
    b. After somebody has been seated in Chair Number 1, how many
        different ways are there of seating someone in Chair Number 2?
    c. In how many different ways could Chairs 1 and 2 be filled?
    d. If Chairs 1 and 2 are already occupied with two of the students,
        in how many ways could Chair 3 be filled?
    e. In how many different ways could Chairs 1, 2, and 3 be filled?
    f. In how many different ways could all ten chairs be filled?

14. Nine people on a baseball team are trying to decide who will play
     which position.
    a. In how many different ways could they select a person to be
        pitcher?
    b. After someone has already been selected as pitcher, how many
        different ways could they select someone else to be catcher?
    c. In how many different ways could they select a pitcher and a
        catcher?
    d. After the pitcher and catcher have been selected, in how many
        ways could they select a first baseman?
    e. In how many different ways could they select a pitcher, a
        catcher, and a first baseman?
    f. In how many different ways could all nine positions be filled?
        Surprising?!

15. Many states use car license plates that have six characters. Some of these states use 2 letters and a number from 1 through 9999. Others use 3 letters and a number from 1 through 999.
    a. Which of these two plans allows there to be *more* possible license plates? How *many* more?
    b. How many license plates could there be using *either* 2 letters and 4 digits *or* 3 letters and 3 digits?
    c. There are about 100,000,000 motor vehicles in the United States. Would it be possible to have a *national* license plate program using the scheme of part b? Explain.

16. Telephone numbers in the United States and Canada have three groups of digits which must meet certain requirements:
    i. Area Code—3 digits, the first of which is *not* 0 or 1, and the second of which *must* be 0 or 1.
    ii. Exchange—3 digits, first and second cannot be 0 or 1.
    iii. Line Number—4 digits, not all zeros.
    a. How many possible area codes are there?
    b. How many possible exchanges are there?
    c. How many possible line numbers are there?
    d. How many valid 10-digit phone numbers can there be?
    e. What is the probability that a 10-digit number dialed *at random* is a valid phone number?

17. *Overlapping Events*   Suppose you draw one card from a normal 52-card deck, and ask, "In how many ways could it be a Heart *or* a Face Card?" As shown in Figure 12-3b, n(Heart) = 13 and n(Face) = 12. But simply adding 13 and 12 gives the *wrong* answer. The cards in the *intersection* (those that are Hearts *and* Faces) have been counted *twice*. An easy way to get the right answer is to *subtract* the number that are Hearts and Faces from the 13 + 12. That is,

$$n(\text{Heart } or \text{ Face}) = n(\text{Heart}) + n(\text{Face}) - n(\text{Heart } and \text{ Face}).$$

In general, the number of ways Events *A or B* could occur when they are *not* mutually exclusive is

$$n(A \ or \ B) = n(A) + n(B) - n(A \cap B)$$

Show that you understand this principle by working the following problems:
    a. 20 girls are on the basketball team. 17 are over 16 years old, 12 are over 170 centimeters tall, and 9 are both over 16 years old and over 170 centimeters tall. How many of the girls are over 16 years old or over 170 centimeters tall?
    b. Researchers discover 37 techniques used in working mathematics problems, and 29 techniques used in working physics problems.

21 of the techniques are used in both fields. If Wanda Learnit studies both physics and mathematics, how many different techniques must Wanda learn?

c. The library has 463 books dealing with science and 592 fiction books. Of these, 37 are science fiction books. How many books do they have that are science or fiction?

d. A jewelry store has 544 necklaces and 215 pieces containing puka shells. 129 of the pieces are puka shell necklaces. How many of the pieces are necklaces *or* contain puka shells?

e. The Senior Class has 367 girls, and 425 students with brown hair. 296 of the girls have brown hair. In how many different ways could you select a girl or a brownhaired student from the Senior Class?

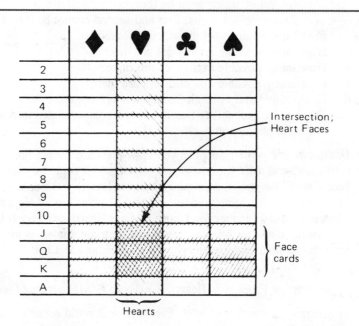

Figure 12-3b

12-4 | PROBABILITIES OF VARIOUS PERMUTATIONS

One of the more tedious counting problems is counting the number of different ways of *arranging* things. For example, the three letters "ABC" can be arranged in six different ways:

ABC   ACB   BAC   BCA   CAB   CBA.

But the ten letters "ABCDEFGHIJ" can be arranged in more than three *million* different ways!

An arrangement of letters, objects, or any elements from a given set is called a *permutation*. In this section you will learn how to calculate the probability that certain kinds of permutations will occur if you select elements at random from a set.

DEFINITION

> A **permutation** is an **arrangement** of some or all of the elements from a given set in a definite order.

Objective:
Given a description of a desired permutation, find the probability of getting that permutation if an arrangement is selected at random.

The first step toward accomplishing this objective is developing an efficient method of counting numbers of permutations.

EXAMPLE 1

In how many different ways could you arrange 3 books on a shelf if you have 7 books to choose from?

The process of selecting an arrangement of three books can be divided into three acts.

 A—Select a book to go in the first position (Figure 12-4a).
 B—Then select another book to go in the second position.
 C—Finally, select another book to go in the third position.

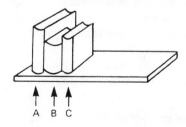

Figure 12-4a

The numbers of ways of doing each act are

$n(A) = 7$, since any of the 7 books can occupy the first position.
$n(B) = 6$, since only 6 books remain to choose from for the second position.
$n(C) = 5$, since only 5 books remain to choose from for the third position.

A convenient way to organize the calculations is to write three spaces representing the positions of the three books. You can pick a variable such as n to represent the number of ways of selecting all three books. You would write

$$n = \underline{\ }\ \underline{\ }\ \underline{\ }\ .$$

Then you would fill in the number of ways of selecting each book.

$$n = \underline{7}\ \underline{6}\ \underline{5}\ .$$

Finally, you would *multiply* the number of ways since all three acts are performed *in succession*.

$$n = \underline{7} \cdot \underline{6} \cdot \underline{5}$$
$$= \underline{\underline{210}}\ .$$

Once you understand the technique for calculating numbers of permutations, you can use it to find numbers of permutations in a given event of a random experiment, and in the sample space. As you recall from Section 12-2, the probability of Event E is

$$P(E) = \frac{n(E)}{n(S)}$$

where $n(S)$ is the number of outcomes in the sample space.   ■

EXAMPLE 2

A permutation is selected at random from the letters SEQUOIA. What is the probability that it has Q in the fourth position, and ends with a vowel?

To answer this question, you need to know the number of outcomes in the sample space, and the number of outcomes in the event, "The fourth letter is Q and the last letter is a vowel." Since the event is hard to analyze all at once, you break it down into three smaller events.

Event A—Select Q for the fourth position.
Event B—Select a vowel for the last position.
Event C—Select the five other letters.

Let $n(E)$ stand for the number of outcomes in the event, "The fourth letter is Q and the last letter is a vowel." You would write spaces for each letter, as you did in Example 1, above.

$n(E) = \underline{\ }\ \underline{\ }\ \underline{\ }\ \underline{1}\ \underline{\ }\ \underline{\ }\ \underline{\ }$ Write 1 in the fourth position, since only Q can go there.

$n(E) = \underline{\ }\ \underline{\ }\ \underline{\ }\ \underline{1}\ \underline{\ }\ \underline{\ }\ \underline{5}$ Write 5 in the last position since any of the 5 vowels can go there.

$n(E) = \underline{5}\ \underline{4}\ \underline{3}\ \underline{1}\ \underline{2}\ \underline{1}\ \underline{5}$ Fill in the remaining 5 letters in the remaining 5 spaces.

$n(E) = \underline{5} \cdot \underline{4} \cdot \underline{3} \cdot \underline{1} \cdot \underline{2} \cdot \underline{1} \cdot \underline{5}$ Multiply, since the events are done *in sequence*.

$= 600$ Do the arithmetic.

Therefore, there are 600 permutations that have Q in the fourth position and end in a vowel.

The fourth position is said to be a *fixed* position, since there is only *one* letter that can go there. The last position is said to be a *restricted* position because more than one letter can go there, but not all of the letters.

To calculate $n(S)$, the number of permutations in the sample space, you again write seven spaces. Then you write the number of ways to fill each space, as you did above.

$$n(S) = \underline{7} \cdot \underline{6} \cdot \underline{5} \cdot \underline{4} \cdot \underline{3} \cdot \underline{2} \cdot \underline{1}$$
$$= 5040$$

So there are 5040 possible permutations if *none* of the spaces is fixed or restricted.

To calculate the *probability* that the fourth letter is Q and the last is a vowel, you simply recall the definition of probability.

$$P(E) = \frac{n(E)}{n(S)}$$ Definition of probability

$$= \frac{600}{5040}$$ Substitution

$$= \frac{5}{42}$$ Canceling

If desired, this fraction can be expressed as a *percent*. You do the division, and multiply by 100.

$$P(E) \approx \underline{\underline{12\%}}$$ ■

The following problems are designed to give you practice in finding numbers of permutations, and in calculating probabilities of various permutations.

EXERCISE 12-4

Do These Quickly

The following problems are intended to refresh your skills. You should be able to do all 10 in less than 5 minutes.

Q1. If A and B are independent events, and $P(A) = 0.6$ and $P(B) = 0.8$, what is $P(A$ and $B)$?

Q2. If A and B are independent events as in question Q1, what is $P(A$ or $B)$?

Q3. If C and D are mutually exclusive events, and $P(C) = 0.3$ and $P(D) = 0.4$, what is $P(C$ or $D)$?

Q4. If C and D are mutually exclusive events as in Question Q3, what is $P(C$ and $D)$?

Q5. Evaluate: $\dfrac{8!}{3! \, 5!}$

Q6. Write as a ratio of two factorials: $20 \cdot 19 \cdot 18 \cdot 17 \cdot 16$

Q7. Sketch the graph of $y = x^2$.

Q8. Find the 100th term of the geometric sequence 40, 50, ...

Q9. Write in terms of i: $\sqrt{-36}$

Q10. Multiply: $(x + 5y)(x - 5y)$

Problems 1 through 10 involve calculating numbers of permutations.

1. In how many ways could you arrange the following numbers of books on a shelf?
    a.   4 books from a set of 9 books?
    b.   3 books from a set of 12 books?
    c.   5 books from a set of 8 books?
    d.   All 7 books from a set of 7 books?

2. Fran Tick takes a 10-problem algebra test. The problems may be worked in any order.
    a.   In how many orders could she work all 10 problems?
    b.   In how many orders could she work any 7 of the 10 problems?

3. The Hawaiian alphabet has twelve letters. How many permutations could be made using
    a.   2 different letters?
    b.   4 different letters?
    c.   all 12 letters, once each?

4. How many permutations of the 26 letters in the English alphabet could be made using
   a. 2 different letters?
   b. 3 different letters?
   c. 4 different letters?

5. Suppose that prestige license plates are made using exactly 4 of the 26 letters in the alphabet. How many different prestige plates could be made if all 4 letters are different?

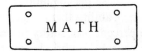

6. Triangles are usually named by placing a different letter at each vertex. In how many different ways could a given triangle be named?

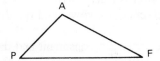

7. Fifteen people try out for a baseball team. In how many different ways could they select
   a. the pitcher and the catcher?
   b. the three outfielders, *after* the pitcher and catcher have been selected?
   c. the First, Second, and Third Basemen and the Shortstop, *after* the pitcher, catcher, and three outfielders have been selected?

8. Tom, Dick, and Harry each draw two cards from a normal deck of 52 cards, and do not replace them. Tom goes first.
   a. In how many orders could Tom draw his two cards?
   b. In how many orders could Dick draw his two cards, *after* Tom has drawn his?
   c. In how many orders could Harry draw his two cards, *after* Tom and Dick have drawn theirs?

9. The parking lot at Gypsum Bank has three spaces labeled "Vice-President." However, there are seven vice-presidents. In how many ways could these spaces be occupied by the vice-presidents' cars?

10. Professor Snarff says, "You may work these six problems in any order you choose." There are 100 students in the class. Is it possible for all 100 students to work the problems in a different order? Explain.

Problems 11 through 20 involve finding the probability of getting a certain kind of permutation if a permutation is selected at random.

11. A 6-letter permutation is selected at random from the letters NIMBLE.

a. How many permutations are possible?
b. How many of these permutations begin with M?
c. What is the probability that the permutation begins with *M*?
d. What is the percent probability in part c?
e. What is the probability that the word is "NIMBLE?"

12. A 5-letter permutation is selected at random from the letters GRATE.
a. How many permutations are possible?
b. How many of these permutations begin with *G*?
c. What is the probability that the permutation begins with *G*?
d. What is the percent probability in part c?
e. What is the probability that the permutation is GREAT?

13. A 6-letter permutation is selected at random from the letters NIMBLE, as in Problem 11. What is the probability that
a. the third letter is *I* and the last letter is *B*?
b. the second letter is a vowel and the third is a consonant?
c. the second and third letters are both vowels?
d. the second letter is a consonant and the last letter is *E*?
e. the second letter is a consonant and the last letter is *L*?

14. A 5-letter permutation is selected at random from the letters GRATE, as in Problem 12. What is the probability that
a. the second letter is *T* and the last letter is *G*?
b. the second letter is a vowel and the third is a consonant?
c. the second and third letters are both consonants?
d. the second letter is a consonant and the last letter is *E*?
e. the second letter is a consonant and the last letter is *R*?

15. Nine people try out for the nine positions on a baseball team.
a. In how many ways could the positions be filled if there are no restrictions on who plays which position?
b. In how many ways could the positions be filled if Fred must be the pitcher, but the other eight can take any positions?
c. If the positions are selected at random, what is the probability that Fred will be the pitcher?
d. What is the percent probability in part c?

16. Eleven girls try out for the eleven positions on the varsity soccer team.
a. In how many ways could the eleven positions be filled if there are no restrictions on who plays which position?
b. In how many ways could the positions be filled if Mabel must be the goal keeper?
c. If the positions are selected at random, what is the probability that Mabel will be goal keeper?
d. What is the percent probability in part c?

17. Nine people try out for the nine positions on the baseball team, as in Problem 15. If the players are selected at random for the positions, what is the probability that
   a. Fred, Mike, or Joe is pitcher?
   b. Fred, Mike, or Joe is pitcher, and Sam or Paul is first baseman?
   c. Fred, Mike, or Joe is pitcher, Sam or Paul plays first base, and Bob is catcher?

18. Eleven girls try out for the eleven positions on the varsity soccer team, as in Problem 16. If the players are selected at random for the positions, what is the probability that
   a. Mabel, Sue, or Diedra is goal keeper?
   b. Mabel, Sue, or Diedra is goal keeper, and Alice or Phyllis is center forward?
   c. Mabel, Sue, or Diedra is goal keeper, Alice or Phyllis is center forward, and Bea is left fullback?

19. Ten first-graders line up for a fire drill.
   a. How many possible arrangements are there?
   b. How many of these arrangements have Calvin and Phoebe next to each other? (Clue: Arrange *nine* things, the Calvin-Phoebe pair and the eight other children. Then arrange Calvin and Phoebe.)
   c. If they line up at random, what is the probability that Calvin and Phoebe will be next to each other?

20. The ten digits, 0, 1, 2, 3, . . . , 9, are arranged at random with no repeats. What is the probability that the numeral thus formed represents
   a. a number greater than 6 billion?
   b. an *even* number greater than 6 billion? (Clue: There are *two* cases to consider, "first digit odd" or "first digit even.")

21. *Permutations with Repeated Elements*   The word "TRUSSES" has 7 letters. But there are *less* than 7! permutations since rearranging the 3 S's does *not* produce a different permutation. Since there are 3! ways of arranging the 3 S's, only $\frac{1}{3!}$ or $\frac{1}{6}$, of the 7! permutations are actually different. So the number of permutations is

$$\frac{7!}{3!} = 840.$$

If several letters are repeated, such as in MISSISSIPPI, then the number of permutations would be

$$\frac{11!}{4!\ 4!\ 2!} = 34650,$$

because there are 4 identical I's, 4 identical S's, and 2 identical P's.

Answer the following questions:

a. Find the number of different permutations of the letters in:
    i.   FREELY.
    ii. BUBBLES.
    iii. LILLY.
    iv. MISSISSAUGA.
    v.   HONOLULU.
    vi. HAWAIIAN.

b. In how many different ways could seven first-graders line up if April, Mae, June, and Julie are quadruplets, and are considered to be identical?

c. Nine pennies are lying on a table. Five are "heads" and four are "tails." In how many ways such as "HHTHTTHHT" could the coins be lined up, considering only "heads" and "tails?"

22. ***Circular Permutations*** In Figure 12-4b, the letters ABCD are arranged in a circle. Though these may appear to be different permutations, they are considered to be the *same* since each of the four letters has the same position *with respect to the others*. An easy way to calculate the number of different "circular permutations" of n elements is to *fix* the position of one of them, and then arrange the other $(n - 1)$ elements with respect to it (Figure 12-4c). Thus, for the letters ABCD, the number of circular permutations would be

$$1 \cdot 3 \cdot 2 \cdot 1 = 6.$$

Figure 12-4b

a. How many different circular permutations could be made from
    i.   ABCDE,
    ii. QLMTXN,
    iii. LOGARITHM?

b. In how many different ways could King Arthur's twelve knights be seated around the Round Table?

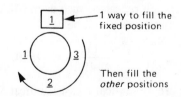

Figure 12-4c

c. Four boys and four girls sit around the merry-go-round.

  i. In how many different ways could they be arranged if boys and girls come alternately?

  ii. If they seat themselves at random, what is the probability that boys and girls alternate?

d. If you are concerned only with which elements come *between* other elements, then two different circular permutations would be "the same," a clockwise one and a counterclockwise one (Figure 12-4d). So there would be only *half* as many permutations as calculated above.

  i. In how many different ways could 7 people hold hands around a circle considering only who is *between* whom?

  ii. In how many different ways could 5 keys be arranged on a key ring considering only which key is *between* which?

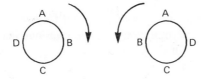

The same "betweenness" property

Figure 12-4d _____

12-5 | PROBABILITIES OF VARIOUS COMBINATIONS

There are 24 different 3-letter "words" that can be made from the 4 letters ABCD. These are listed below.

ABC	ACB	BAC	BCA	CAB	CBA
ABD	ADB	BAD	BDA	DAB	DBA
ACD	ADC	CAD	CDA	DAC	DCA
BCD	BDC	CBD	CDB	DBC	DCB

Only *four* different combinations

Since these "words" are *arrangements* of letters in a definite order, each one is a *permutation* of four elements taken three at a time.

Suppose that you are concerned only with *which* letters appear in the "word," not with the order in which they appear. For instance, ADC and

DAC would be considered to be the same, since they have the same three letters. Each different group is called a three-letter *combination* of the letters ABCD.

DEFINITION

> A **combination** of elements of a set is a **subset** of those elements, without regard to how the elements are arranged.

Objective:
Be able to calculate the number of combinations containing *r* elements that can be made from a set that has *n* elements.

From the table above, you can see that for every *one* combination, there are *six* possible permutations. So the total number of combinations equals the total number of permutations *divided by 6*. That is,

$$\text{number of combinations} = \frac{24}{6} = 4.$$

The "6" in the denominator is the number of permuations that can be made of each 3-letter combination.

CONCLUSION:

> $$\text{Number of combinations} = \frac{\text{total number of permutations}}{\text{number of permutations of each } one \text{ combination}}$$

The conclusion stated above can be used to accomplish the objective of this section. It helps to define symbols for numbers of combinations and permutations, and derive some formulas.

Let $_nC_r$ stand for the number of *combinations* that can be made by using *r* elements from a set of *n* elements.

Let $_nP_r$ stand for the number of *permutations* that can be made by using *r* elements from a set of *n* elements.

Notes:

1. $_nC_r$ and $_nP_r$ are pronounced, "n, C, r" and "n, P, r," respectively. Words such as "number of combinations of n elements taken r at a time" are often used.
2. In the example, above, $_4C_3 = 4$ and $_4P_3 = 24$.
3. The symbols C_r^n, $C(n, r)$ and $\binom{n}{r}$ are sometimes used for $_nC_r$.
4. The symbols P_r^n and $P(n, r)$ are sometimes used for $_nP_r$.

The conclusion above can now be written in symbols.

$$_nC_r = \frac{_nP_r}{_rP_r}$$

For example,

$$_4C_3 = \frac{_4P_3}{_3P_3} = \frac{24}{6} = 4.$$

It is possible to write $_nP_r$ in terms of *factorials*. For example, by the technique of Section 12-4, you can write

$$_9P_4 = \underline{9} \cdot \underline{8} \cdot \underline{7} \cdot \underline{6}.$$

Multiplying by a "clever" form of 1 gives

$$_9P_4 = 9 \cdot 8 \cdot 7 \cdot 6 \cdot \frac{5 \cdot 4 \cdot 3 \cdot 2 \cdot 1}{5 \cdot 4 \cdot 3 \cdot 2 \cdot 1}$$

$$= \frac{9!}{5!}.$$

The "9" in the numerator is the total number of elements in the set, n. The "5" in the denominator is the number of elements *not* used in the permutation, that is, $(n - r)$. In general,

$$\boxed{_nP_r = \frac{n!}{(n - r)!}} \qquad \text{Example:} \qquad \boxed{_9P_4 = \frac{9!}{5!}}$$

As a special case, $_nP_n$ is given by

$$_nP_n = \frac{n!}{(n - n)!} = \frac{n!}{0!} = \frac{n!}{1} = n!.$$

$$\boxed{_nP_n = n!} \qquad \text{Example:} \qquad \boxed{_3P_3 = 3!}$$

Using this information, $_nC_r$ can also be written in terms of factorials.

$$_nC_r = \frac{_nP_r}{_rP_r}$$

$$_nC_r = \frac{\dfrac{n!}{(n-r)!}}{r!}$$

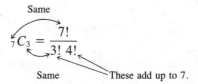

$$_nC_r = \frac{n!}{r!\,(n-r)!} \qquad \text{Example:} \qquad _7C_3 = \frac{7!}{3!\,4!}$$

The formula is easier to remember by the example than by using n and r, as shown below.

$$\overset{\text{Same}}{_7C_3} = \frac{7!}{3!\,4!}$$

Same   These add up to 7.

Note: You should recognize the expression for $_7C_3$ as being equal to a coefficient in a *binomial series* (see Section 11-10). If $(a + b)$ is raised to the 7th power, then $_7C_3$ is the coefficient of the term that has b^3. That is,

$$(a + b)^7 = \ldots + {}_7C_3\, a^4b^3 + \ldots$$

With this background you are now equipped to calculate numbers of combinations.

EXAMPLE 1

Evaluate $_9C_6$.

By the combinations formula,

$$_9C_6 = \frac{9!}{6!\,3!}.$$

If you have a calculator with a factorial key, the computation is straightforward, and the answer is 84. If not, the computations are still not too difficult.

$$_9C_6 = \frac{9 \cdot 8 \cdot 7 \cdot 6!}{6! \cdot 3 \cdot 2 \cdot 1} \qquad \text{Properties of factorials}$$

$$= \frac{9 \cdot 8 \cdot 7}{3 \cdot 2 \cdot 1} \qquad \text{Canceling the 6!'s}$$

$$= 3 \cdot 4 \cdot 7 \qquad \text{Further canceling}$$

$$= \underline{\underline{84}} \qquad \text{Arithmetic} \qquad ■$$

EXAMPLE 2

Evaluate $_9P_6$.

By the permutations formula,

$$_9P_6 = \frac{9!}{3!} \qquad \text{The "3" is } 9 - 6$$

$$= \frac{9 \cdot 8 \cdot 7 \cdot 6 \cdot 5 \cdot 4 \cdot 3!}{3!} \qquad \text{Properties of factorials}$$

$$= \underline{\underline{60480}} \qquad \text{Arithmetic} \qquad ■$$

EXAMPLE 3

In how many different ways can you form a committee of 5 people from a group of 9 people?

Committees are "different" only if different people are on the committee. It does not matter how the people are arranged. So the answer is a number of *combinations* rather than a number of permutations. Letting $n(5 \text{ people})$ be the number of committees

$$n(5 \text{ people}) = {}_9C_5$$

$$= \frac{9!}{5! \; 4!}$$

$$= \underline{\underline{126}} . \qquad ■$$

EXAMPLE 4

If a committee of five is selected at random from a group of 9 people (6 women and 3 men), what is the probability that it will have:

a. Eileen and Ben (two of the 9 people)?
b. Exactly 3 women and 2 men?
c. At least 3 women?

By the definition of probability,

$$P(\text{Event}) = \frac{n(\text{Event})}{n(\text{Sample Space})} .$$

For this problem, the sample space is the set of all possible 5-member committees. In Example 3 you found that the number of possible 5-member committees is $_9C_5$, which equals 126.

$$\therefore n(\text{Sample Space}) = 126.$$

To answer the three questions, you need to know the numbers of outcomes in each of the 3 events described.

a. To find $n(E \text{ and } B)$, you can divide the act of selecting a committee into two simple acts:

1.   Select Eileen and Ben..................................... 1 possible way.
2.   Select the other 3 people from the remaining
     7 people .... $_7C_3$ possible ways.

Since these two acts are performed *in succession,* the total number of ways is found by *multiplying.*

$$n(E \text{ and } B) = 1 \cdot {_7C_3}$$

$$= 1 \cdot \frac{7!}{3! \, 4!}$$

$$= 35$$

$$\therefore P(E \text{ and } B) = \frac{35}{126}, \qquad \text{or about } 28\%$$

b. To find the number of 3-woman, 2-man committees, you must realize that people are being selected from two different groups. So you should divide the act of selecting a committee into two simpler acts.

1.   Select the 3 women .... $_6C_3$ possible ways.
2.   Select the 2 men .... $_3C_2$ possible ways.

Since the acts must *both* be performed, *in succession,* the total number of ways, $n(3W, 2M)$, is found by *multiplying.*

$$n(3W, 2M) = {_6C_3} \cdot {_3C_2}$$

$$= \frac{6!}{3! \, 3!} \cdot \frac{3!}{2! \, 1!}$$

$$= 20 \cdot 3$$

$$= 60$$

$$\therefore P(3W, 2M) = \frac{60}{126}, \text{ or about } 48\%$$

c. If the committee has *at least* 3 women, then it could have 3 women *or* 4 women *or* 5 women. In each case, the remainder of the committee consists of *men*. The act of selecting a committee can be divided into 3 simpler acts:

1.   Select a 3-woman, 2-man committee .... $n(3W, 2M)$ ways.
2.   Select a 4-woman, 1-man committee .... $n(4W, 1M)$ ways.
3.   Select a 5-woman, 0-man committee .... $n(5W, 0M)$ ways.

Since these are "either-or" acts, the total number of ways is found by *adding*.

$$n(\text{at least } 3W) = n(3W, 2M) + n(4W, 1M) + n(5W, 0M)$$

Each of the numbers on the right may be calculated as in part b, above.

$$n(\text{at least } 3W) = {}_6C_3 \cdot {}_3C_2 + {}_6C_4 \cdot {}_3C_1 + {}_6C_5 \cdot {}_3C_0$$

$$= 20 \cdot 3 + 15 \cdot 3 + 6 \cdot 1$$

$$= 111$$

$$\therefore P(\text{at least } 3W) = \frac{111}{126}, \text{ or about } 88\%$$ ■

The following exercise is designed to give you practice finding numbers of combinations and permutations by using the formulas, and calculating the probability that a certain event will occur if a combination or permutation is selected at random.

EXERCISE 12-5

Do These Quickly

The following problems are intended to refresh your skills. You should be able to do all 10 in less than 5 minutes.

Q1.   Find $_4P_4$.

Q2.   Find the probability of rolling a sum of 3 on two dice.

Q3.   Find the 100th partial sum of the arithmetic series
      $3 + 3.2 + \ldots$.

Q4.   Evaluate: $3! \, 4!$

Q5.   Evaluate $\displaystyle\sum_{k=1}^{4} 3k$

Q6.   Evaluate: 3^2

Q7.   Solve: $x! = 24$

Q8.   Sketch a hyperbola opening in the y-direction.

Q9.   Simplify: $\dfrac{(x - 5)}{(5 - x)}$

Q10. Simplify: $\dfrac{x^{20}}{x^5}$

For Problems 1 through 12, calculate the indicated number of combinations.

1. $_5C_3$	2. $_6C_4$	3. $_8C_5$	4. $_9C_3$
5. $_6C_5$	6. $_{10}C_4$	7. $_{11}C_4$	8. $_{11}C_5$
9. $_{10}C_{10}$	10. $_{100}C_{100}$	11. $_{10}C_0$	12. $_{100}C_0$

For Problems 13 through 16, calculate the indicated number of permutations.

13. $_6P_4$	14. $_9P_3$	15. $_{11}P_5$	16. $_{15}P_8$

Problems 17 through 28 involve finding various numbers of combinations.

17.   A committee of five is to be selected from the 30 students in a Freshman English class. In how many ways could the committee be composed?

18.   Twelve people apply to go on a biology field trip but there is room in the car for only five of them. In how many different ways could the group making the trip be composed?

19.   Seven people come to an evening bridge party. Since only four people can play bridge at any one time, they decide to play as many games as it takes to use every possible foursome *once*. How many games would have to be played? Could all of these games be played in *one* evening?

20.   A well-known donut dealer has 34 varieties of donuts. Suppose that they decide to make sample boxes containing six different donuts each. How many different sample boxes could they make? Would it be practical to stock one of each kind?

21.   Ann Jellik goes to the toy store, where her mother will let her buy any three different toys. There are 1000 toys to choose from. How many different selections could Ann make?

22.   The Supreme Court justices have a hand-shaking ritual that they conduct just before each session. Each of the justices shakes hands

with every other justice. How many hand-shakes will there be in this ritual?

23. Horace Holmsley has a breakfast of scrambled eggs, bacon, sausage, grits, hash browns, and toast. How many different combinations of these foods could he put on his fork if he uses
   a.   three ingredients?
   b.   four ingredients?
   c.   three ingredients or four ingredients?
   d.   all six ingredients?

24. A well-known chain of pizza parlors has eleven different kinds of topping they can put on their pizzas. How many different kinds of pizza could they make using
   a.   three of the toppings?
   b.   five of the toppings?
   c.   three of the toppings or five of the toppings?
   d.   all eleven of the toppings?

25. A normal deck of cards has 52 cards.
   a.   How many different 5-card poker hands could be formed?
   b.   How many different 13-card bridge hands could be formed?

26. The diagonals of a convex polygon are made by combining the vertices two at a time. However, some of the combinations are *sides* rather than diagonals. How many diagonals are there in a convex
   a.   pentagon (5 sides)?
   b.   decagon (10 sides)?
   c.   n-gon (*n* sides)? Simplify your answer as much as possible.

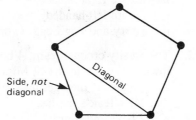

27. A set has 10 elements. How many subsets are there that contain
   a.   2 of the elements?
   b.   5 of the elements?
   c.   8 of the elements? Explain the relationship between this answer and the answer in part a.

28. A set has five elements.
   a.   How many subsets of this set are there that contain
      i.   1 element?
      ii.   2 elements?
      iii. 3 elements?
      iv.   4 elements?
      v.   5 elements?
      vi.   no elements?

How many subsets?

b. How many subsets are there altogether? What relationship does this number have to the number 5?

Problems 29 through 36 involve finding the probability that a certain event will occur if a combination is selected at random.

29. Ten first-graders, 6 boys and 4 girls, are playing on the playground. Miss Twiddle selects a group of 5 at random. What is the probability that the group has
a. 3 boys and 2 girls?
b. 2 boys and 3 girls?
c. 3 boys and 2 girls, or 2 boys and 3 girls?
d. Ella Quence, one of the girls?

30. Charlie Brown has 13 socks in his drawer, 7 blue and 6 green. He selects 5 socks at random. What is the probability that he gets
a. 2 blue and 3 green?
b. 3 blue and 2 green?
c. 2 blue and 3 green, or 3 blue and 2 green?
d. the one sock that has a hole in it?

31. In a group of 15 people, 6 are left-handed and the rest are right-handed. If 7 people are selected at random from this group, what is the probability that
a. 3 are left-handed and 4 are right-handed?
b. all are right-handed?
c. all are left-handed?
d. Harry and Peg Legg, two of the left-handers, are selected?

32. The varsity croquet team, 4 boys and 8 girls, travels to an out-of-town game. Their coach, Miss Teak, will take 7 of them in her station wagon. If they get into cars at random, what is the probability that Miss Teak's car has
a. 2 boys and 5 girls?
b. all girls?
c. all boys?
d. Peter Doubt and Manuel Dexterity, two of the boys?

33. Three cards are selected at random from a group of 7. Two of the cards have been marked with winning numbers.
a. What is the probability that exactly 1 of the 3 cards has a winning number?
b. What is the probability that at least 1 of the 3 cards has a winning number?
c. What is the probability that *none* of the 3 cards has a winning number?
d. What relationship is there between the answers to parts b and c?

34. Kay Paso, who is 3 years old, tears the labels off all 10 of the soup
     cans on her mother's shelf. Her mother knows that there were 2 cans
     of tomato soup and 8 cans of vegetable. She selects 4 cans at ran-
     dom.
     a. What is the probability that exactly 1 of the 4 cans
         is tomato?
     b. What is the probability that at least 1 of the 4 cans
         is tomato?
     c. What is the probability that *none* of the 4 cans
         is tomato?
     d. What relationship exists between the answers to
         parts b and c?

     Tomato?
     Vegetable?

35. Sata Light Company tests a sample of 5 of every 100 light bulbs pro-
     duced to make sure they work.
     a. How many different ways could a 5-bulb sample be taken from
         the 100 bulbs?
     b. To check on the Quality Control Department, the Chief Engi-
         neer puts 2 defective bulbs in with 98 good ones. How many
         ways could a sample of 5 of these 100 bulbs have *at least* one
         defective bulb?
     c. What is the probability that Quality Control will discover at
         least 1 of the defective bulbs?
     d. Do you think Sata Light Company has an adequate sampling
         program? Explain.

36. An ordinary deck of playing cards has 4 suits, with 13 cards of each
     suit. In many games, each of 4 players is dealt 13 cards at random.
     a. What is the probability that such a hand has
         i.   exactly 5 spades?
         ii.   exactly 3 clubs?
         iii. exactly 5 spades and 3 clubs?
         iv.   exactly 5 spades, 3 clubs, and 2 diamonds?
     b. Which is more probable, getting all 4 aces or getting all 13
         cards of the same suit? Justify your answer.

12-6 PROPERTIES OF PROBABILITY

In the preceding sections you have learned how to use the definition of
probability,

$$P(\text{Event}) = \frac{n(\text{Event})}{n(\text{Sample Space})},$$

to calculate probabilities. You simply counted the numbers of elements in the event and in the sample space, then divided. In this section you will learn some properties that will allow you to calculate probabilities *without* having to go all the way back to the definition.

Objective:
Given $P(A)$ and $P(B)$, the probabilities of Events A and B, be able to calculate
a. $P(A \text{ and then } B)$,
b. $P(A \text{ or } B)$,
c. $P(\text{not } A)$ and $P(\text{not } B)$.

Suppose that you draw two cards in succession from a normal 52-card deck, without replacing the first card before you draw the second. What is the probability that both cards are black?

There are 52 ways to choose the first card, and 51 ways to choose the second card *after* the first has been chosen. So the sample space contains

$$n(S) = 52 \cdot 51 = 2652$$

outcomes. There are 26 ways the first card could be black. After the first black has been drawn, there are only 25 ways that the second could be black. So

$$n(\text{both black}) = 26 \cdot 25 = 650.$$

Therefore,

$$P(\text{both black}) = \frac{650}{2652} = \frac{25}{102}.$$

It is more instructive, however, *not* to simplify. That is,

$$P(\text{both black}) = \frac{26 \cdot 25}{52 \cdot 51}$$

$$= \frac{26}{52} \cdot \frac{25}{51} \quad \text{Multiplication property of fractions}$$

The $\frac{26}{52}$ is the probability that the first card is black, and the $\frac{25}{51}$ is the probability that the second card is black, *after* you have already drawn one black card. From this example, you can extract the following property of probability:

$$P(A \text{ and then } B) = P(A) \cdot P(B)$$

Notes:

1. $P(B)$ must be the probability that B occurs *after* A has already occurred. If $P(B)$ does *not* depend on whether or not A has occurred, then A and B are said to be *independent* events.
2. This property corresponds exactly to the first counting principle, $n(A$ and then $B) = n(A) \cdot n(B)$.

The second part of the objective can be illustrated by the act of drawing a single marble at random from a bag containing 13 red ones, 17 black ones, and 11 green ones. What is the probability that the marble is *either* red *or* black?

The sample space contains 41 outcomes since there are 41 marbles in the bag. The event "red or black" contains

$$n(\text{red or black}) = n(\text{red}) + n(\text{black})$$
$$= 13 + 17$$
$$= 30$$

outcomes. The numbers of ways are *added* since these are "either-or" events. Therefore,

$$P(\text{red or black}) = \frac{30}{41}.$$

Again, it is more instructive *not* to simplify.

$$P(\text{red or black}) = \frac{13 + 17}{41} \quad \text{Definition of probability}$$

$$= \frac{13}{41} + \frac{17}{41} \quad \text{Division distributes over addition.}$$

$$= P(\text{red}) + P(\text{black})$$

In general,

$$\boxed{P(A \text{ or } B) = P(A) + P(B)}$$

Notes:

1. Events A and B must be "mutually exclusive" for this property to be true. That is, it must be impossible for A and B *both* to occur. If they *can* both occur, then $P(A \text{ or } B) = P(A) + P(B) - P(A \cap B)$, where $P(A \cap B)$ is the probability that A and B *both* occur.
2. Again, this property of probability corresponds exactly to the second counting principle, $n(A \text{ or } B) = n(A) + n(B)$.

The third part of the objective can be accomplished using the "either-or" property above.

Let $P(A)$ = the probability that Event A occurs.
Let $P(\text{not } A)$ = the probability that Event A does *not* occur.

Then

$$P(A \text{ or not } A) = P(A) + P(\text{not } A).$$

But $P(A \text{ or not } A) = 1$, because one of the two events, A or not A, is *certain* to happen. And the probability of an event that is certain to happen equals 1. Therefore,

$$P(A) + P(\text{not } A) = 1,$$

from which

$$\boxed{P(\text{not } A) = 1 - P(A)}\ .$$

These three properties can be used to calculate probabilities *without* having to go all the way back to the definition.

EXAMPLE

Calvin and Phoebe visit the Children's Ward at the hospital. The probability that Calvin will catch mumps as a result of the visit is $P(C) = 0.13$, and the probability that Phoebe will catch mumps is $P(Ph) = 0.07$. Find the probability that
a. both catch mumps,
b. Calvin does not catch mumps,
c. Phoebe does not catch mumps,
d. Calvin and Phoebe both do not catch mumps,
e. at least one of them catches mumps.

a. $P(C \text{ and } Ph) = P(C) \cdot P(Ph)$ Property of probability

   $= 0.13 \times 0.07$ Substitution

   $= \underline{0.0091}$ Arithmetic

b. $P(\text{not } C) = 1 - P(C)$ Property of probability

   $= 1 - 0.13$ Substitution

   $= \underline{\underline{0.87}}$ Arithmetic

c. $P(\text{not } Ph) = 1 - P(Ph)$ Property of probability

   $= 1 - 0.07$ Substitution

   $= \underline{\underline{0.93}}$ Arithmetic

d. P(not C and not Ph)

$$= P(\text{not } C) \cdot P(\text{not } Ph) \quad \text{Property of probability}$$

$$= 0.87 \times 0.93 \quad\quad\quad \text{From parts b and c}$$

$$= \underline{\underline{0.8091}} \quad\quad\quad\quad\quad \text{Arithmetic}$$

e.   If Event A is "neither one catches mumps," then "not A" is the event, "at least one *does* catch mumps." You have already calculated P(neither one) in part d. Therefore,

$$P(\text{at least 1}) = 1 - P(\text{not } C \text{ and not } Ph) \quad \text{Property of probability}$$

$$= 1 - 0.8091 \quad\quad\quad\quad\quad\quad\quad\quad \text{From part d}$$

$$= \underline{\underline{0.1909}} \quad\quad\quad\quad\quad\quad\quad\quad\quad\quad \text{Arithmetic}$$

■

The following exercise is designed to give you practice using these three properties of probability. In the next section you will use the properties to come to some rather startling conclusions about how probability relates to binomial series.

EXERCISE 12-6

Do These Quickly

The following problems are intended to refresh your skills. You should be able to do all 10 in less than 5 minutes.

Q1.   Find $_5C_3$.

Q2.   Find $_5P_3$.

Q3.   In which quantity are arrangements considered, permutations or combinations?

Q4.   Find the probability that a card drawn at random from a normal deck is black or a face card.

Q5.   How many different 3-letter permutations can be made from the letters GLMTX?

Q6.   How many different 3-letter combinations can be made from the letters TAXIS?

Q7.   Which conic section is this? $x^2 - y^2 + 4x - 7y = 100$

Q8.   Solve for y: $3x + 5y = 17$
$\quad\quad\quad\quad\quad\quad 3x + 7y = 9$

Q9.   Solve for x: $1 - 3x < 7$

Q10.   Sketch the graph of a cubic function with negative x^3-coefficient.

1.   *Calculator Components Problem*   The "heart" of a pocket calculator is one or more "chips," each of which contains several thousand components. These chips are mass produced, and have a fairly high probability of being defective. Suppose that a particular kind of calculator uses two chips. Chip A has a probability of 70% (0.7) of being defective, and Chip B has a probability of 80% of being defective. If one chip of each kind is selected at random, what is the probability that

     a.   both are defective?
     b. A is not defective?
     c. B is not defective?
     d.   neither chip is defective?
     e.   at least one chip is defective?

2.   *Grade Problem*   Kara Vann is a good student. She figures that her probability of making A is 0.92 for algebra and 0.88 for history. What is her probability of making
     a. A in algebra and history?
     b.   no A in algebra?
     c.   no A in history?
     d. A in neither algebra nor history?
     e.   at least one A?

3. ***Car Breakdown Problem***   You drive on a long vacation trip. The probability you will have a flat tire is 0.1, and the probability of engine trouble is 0.05. What is the probability you will have
   a.   no flat tire?
   b.   no engine trouble?
   c.   no flat tire and no engine trouble?
   d.   both a flat tire and engine trouble?
   e.   at least one, either a flat tire or engine trouble?

4. ***Menu Problem***   Doc Worker is a regular customer at the Waterfront Coffee Shop. The manager has figured that Doc's probability of ordering ham is 0.8; and eggs, 0.65. What is the probability that
   a.   he does not order ham?
   b.   he does not order eggs?
   c.   he orders neither ham nor eggs?
   d.   he orders ham and eggs?
   e.   he orders at least one, either ham or eggs?

   Eggs? Ham?

5. ***Traffic Light Problem***   Two traffic lights on Broadway operate independently. Your probability of being stopped at the first one is 0.4 and your probability of being stopped at the second one is 0.7. What is your probability of being stopped at
   a.   both lights?
   b.   neither light?
   c.   the first but not the second?
   d.   the second but not the first?
   e.   exactly one of the lights?

6. ***Visiting Problem***   The Dover children, Eileen and Ben, are away at college. They visit home on random weekends, Eileen with a probability of 0.2 and Ben with a probability of 0.25. On any given weekend, what is the probability that
   a.   both will visit?
   b.   neither will visit?
   c.   Eileen will visit but Ben will not?
   d.   Ben will visit but Eileen will not?
   e.   exactly one will visit?

7. ***Back-Up System Problem***   Vital systems such as electric power distribution systems have "back-up" components in case one component fails. Suppose that two generators each have a probability of 98% (0.98) of working. The system will continue to work as long as *at least one* of the generators works. What is the probability that the system will continue to operate?

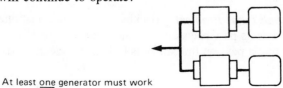

At least <u>one</u> generator must work

8. **Hide-and-Seek Problem**   The Katz brothers, Bob and Tom, are hiding in the cellar. If either one sneezes, they will reveal their hiding place and be found. Bob's probability of sneezing is 0.6 and Tom's probability is 0.7. What is the probability that at least one sneezes?

9. **Basketball Problem**   The three basketball teams from Lowe High each play on Friday night. The probabilities that they will win are: varsity, 0.7; junior varsity, 0.6; and freshman, 0.8. What is the probability that
   a. all three win?
   b. all three lose?
   c. at least one team wins?
   d. the varsity wins and the other two lose?

10. **Another Grade Problem**   Terry Torrey has the following probabilities of passing various courses: Humanities, 90%; Speech, 80%; and Latin, 95%. What is his probability of
   a. passing all 3?
   b. failing all 3?
   c. passing at least 1?
   d. passing exactly 1?

11. **Spaceship Problem**   Fly-By-Night Spaceship Company produces a booster rocket that has 1000 vital parts. If any *one* of these parts fails, the booster will crash, so they design each part with a reliability of 99.9%, meaning that the probability of an individual part working is 0.999.
   a. What is the probability that all 1000 parts work, and the booster does not crash? Surprising?
   b. What is the minimum reliability needed for each part to insure that there is a 90% probability of all 1000 parts working?

12. **Silversword Problem**   The silversword is a rare plant that grows only atop the 10,000 foot high Haleakela volcano in Maui, Hawaii. The seeds have only a small probability of germinating, but if enough are planted, there is a fairly good chance of getting a new plant. Suppose that the probability of any one seed germinating is 0.004.
   a. What is the probability that a seed will *not* germinate?
   b. If 100 seeds are planted, what is the probability that
      i.   none will germinate?
      ii. at least one will germinate?
   c. If 1000 seeds are planted, what is the probability that at least one will germinate?

13. **Football Plays Problem**   Backbay Polytechnic Institute's quarterback selects pass plays and run plays randomly. His probability of selecting a pass on first down is 0.4. If he selects a pass on first

down, his probability of selecting another pass on second down is
0.3. Otherwise, his probability of passing on second down is 0.8.
What is his probability of passing on

a.   first down and second down?
b.   first down but not second down?
c.   second down but not first down?
d.   neither first down nor second down?

14.   ***Operation Problem***   Ann Teak must undergo two operations. The
first has a 70% probability of success. If it succeeds, the second operation has a 90% probability of success; if not, the second operation
has only a 40% probability of success. What is the probability that

a.   both succeed?
b.   both fail?
c.   the first succeeds and the second fails?
d.   the first fails and the second succeeds?

15. ***Measles and Chicken Pox Problem***   Suppose that a child has a
    probability of 0.12 of catching measles and a probability of 0.2 of
    catching chicken pox in any one given year.
    a. If these events are *independent* of each other, what is the proba-
        bility that he or she will get *both* diseases in a given year?
    b. Suppose that statistics show the following probabilities for get-
        ting both diseases in the same year:

    $$P(\text{measles, then chicken pox}) = 0.006.$$

    $$P(\text{chicken pox, then measles}) = 0.18.$$

    Calculate the probability of getting.
    i.   chicken pox *after* measles,
    ii. measles *after* chicken pox.
    c. Based on the answers to part b, what could you conclude about
        the effects of the two diseases on each other?

16. ***Airplane Engine Problem***   Wing and Prayer Aircraft Corporation
    manufactures a twin-engine plane. Laboratory tests indicate that the
    probability of any one engine failing during a particular flight is
    0.03.
    a. If the engines operate independently, what is the probability that
        both fail?
    b. Flight records reveal that the probability of both engines failing
        during a particular flight is actually 0.006. What is the probabil-
        ity that the second engine will fail *after* the first has already
        failed?
    c. Based on your answer to part b, do the engines actually seem to
        operate independently? Explain.

17. ***Combinations and Binomial Series Problem***   A group of five stu-
    dents compete for National Merit Scholarships.
    a. Calculate the numbers of ways that 0, 1, 2, 3, 4, or 5 of them
        could win a scholarship.
    b. Add the answers to part a, and thus show that there are 32
        ways, total, for 0 through 5 of them to win scholarships.
    c. Expand $(1 + 1)^5$ as a binomial series. Simplify each term, but
        do not carry out the addition. How does this series relate to
        parts a and b, above?
    d. Show a very easy way to answer part b directly, without using
        the results of part a.
    e. Demonstrate that you understand the significance of part d by
        calculating *quickly* the number of ways 0 through 10 students
        could win a scholarship.

18. ***Combinations and Powers of 2 Problem***   In Problem 17, above,
    you found that

    $$_5C_0 + {_5C_1} + {_5C_2} + {_5C_3} + {_5C_4} + {_5C_5} = 2^5.$$

In general,

$$\boxed{\sum_{r=0}^{n} {}_nC_r = 2^n} \ .$$

a.   Show that this property works for $n = 3$ and $n = 4$.
b.   Use this property to find *quickly*
   i.   the number of combinations of 0 or 1 or 2 or . . . or 10 people that could be made from a set of 10 people,
   ii.   the number of subsets of a 12-element set,
   iii.   the number of combinations of 10 people taken at least one at a time; at least two at a time.

12-7	FUNCTIONS OF A RANDOM VARIABLE

Suppose that you conduct the random experiment of flipping a coin. The coin is bent, so that the probability of "heads" on any one flip is only 0.4. If you flip the coin 5 times, what is $P(3T, 2H)$, the probability that exactly two of the outcomes are "heads" and the other three are "tails?"

To answer this question, it helps to look at the simpler event $P(TTTHH)$, the probability of 3 tails and 2 heads *in that order*.

$$P(TTTHH) = P(T) \cdot P(T) \cdot P(T) \cdot P(H) \cdot P(H).$$

You are told that $P(H) = 0.4$. Since T is the only other possible outcome on any one flip,

$$P(T) = 1 - 0.4$$
$$= 0.6.$$

Therefore,

$$P(TTTHH) = 0.6^3 \times 0.4^2.$$

There are 10 possible outcomes that have exactly 2 heads. They are

$$HHTTT, \quad HTHTT, \quad HTTHT, \quad HTTTH, \quad THHTT,$$
$$THTHT, \quad THTTH, \quad TTHHT, \quad TTHTH, \quad TTTHH.$$

The 10 equals the number of ways of selecting a *group* of 2 of the 5 flips to be "heads." But this is just the number of *combinations* of 5 elements taken 2 at a time, ${}_5C_2$. So

$$P(3T, 2H) = {}_5C_2 \times 0.6^3 \times 0.4^2$$

$$= \frac{5!}{2! \ 3!} \times 0.6^3 \times 0.4^2.$$

You should recognize this as a term in the *binomial series* that comes from expanding

$$(0.6 + 0.4)^5.$$

In general,

If b is the probability that Event B happens, and a is the probability that Event B does *not* happen, then

$$P(B \text{ happens } x \text{ times out of } n) = {}_nC_x \cdot a^{n-x}b^x$$

$$= \frac{n!}{(n-x)!\,x!}a^{n-x}b^x$$

$$= \text{term with } b^x \text{ in the binomial series}$$
$$(a + b)^n.$$

Once you see the pattern, you can quickly write the probabilities of other events.

　　　Let x = number of times the coin is "heads" in 5 flips.
　　　Let $P(x)$ = probability that it is "heads" x times.

Therefore,

$$P(0) = {}_5C_0 \times 0.6^5 \times 0.4^0 = 1 \times 0.6^5 \times 0.4^0 = 0.07776$$

$$P(1) = {}_5C_1 \times 0.6^4 \times 0.4^1 = 5 \times 0.6^4 \times 0.4^1 = 0.2592$$

$$P(2) = {}_5C_2 \times 0.6^3 \times 0.4^2 = 10 \times 0.6^3 \times 0.4^2 = 0.3456$$

$$P(3) = {}_5C_3 \times 0.6^2 \times 0.4^3 = 10 \times 0.6^2 \times 0.4^3 = 0.2304$$

$$P(4) = {}_5C_4 \times 0.6^1 \times 0.4^4 = 5 \times 0.6^1 \times 0.4^4 = 0.0768$$

$$P(5) = {}_5C_5 \times 0.6^0 \times 0.4^5 = 1 \times 0.6^0 \times 0.4^5 = 0.01024$$

A calculator is helpful for the last step.

As a check on the answers, you should realize that x is *certain* to take on one of the values 0 through 5. So $P(0$ or 1 or 2 or 3 or 4 or 5) must equal 1, or 100%. Adding the probabilities,

$$P(0) + P(1) + P(2) + P(3) + P(4) + P(5)$$

$$= 0.07776 + 0.2592 + 0.3456 + 0.2304 + 0.0768 + 0.01204$$

$$= 1.00000,$$

which shows that the answers are reasonable.

The independent variable x is called a *random* variable since you cannot be sure what value x will have on any one run of the random experiment. The dependent variable $P(x)$ is the *probability* that the value is x. So P is a *function* of a random variable. The graph of this function is shown in Figure 12-7.

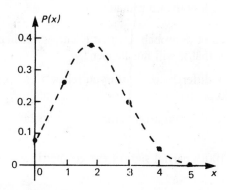

Figure 12-7

The function P shows how the total probability, 1.00000, is "distributed" among the possible values of x. This function of a random variable is often called a *probability distribution*. Since this particular distribution has probabilities that are terms of a binomial series, it is called a *binomial* distribution.

Binomial distributions occur when you perform a random experiment repeatedly, and each time there are only *two* possible outcomes (e.g., heads or tails, boy or girl, win or lose, yes or no).

Once you have found the probability distribution, you can use the properties of probability to calculate the probabilities of related events. For example, if the bent coin is flipped 5 times, as above, then the probability of getting *at least two* heads is

$$P(x \geq 2) = P(2) + P(3) + P(4) + P(5)$$

$$= 0.3456 + 0.2304 + 0.0768 + 0.01024$$

$$= \underline{\underline{0.66304}},$$

which is about $\frac{2}{3}$, or 66%.

The following exercise starts with some binomial distribution problems. The later problems let you analyze some probability distributions that are *not* binomial.

EXERCISE 12-7

Do These Quickly

The following problems are intended to refresh your skills. You should be able to do all 10 in less than 5 minutes.

Q1.   If there is a 60% probability that Event A will happen, what is the probability that it will not happen?

Q2.   How many different ways can you select a group of 3 people from a set of 10 people?

Q3.   How many different arrangements are possible for the letters LYNX?

Q4.   Find the 100th partial sum of the geometric series $0.1 + 0.12 +$ . . . .

Q5.   Write in sigma notation: $2^3 + 3^3 + 4^3 + 5^3 + 6^3$.

Q6.   Simplify: $\dfrac{x^2 + 18x - 40}{x - 2}$

Q7.   Which conic section is this? $4x + y^2 - 2y - 5 = 0$

Q8.   Write a quadratic equation with $2 + 7i$ and $2 - 7i$ as its solutions.

Q9.   What possible numbers of positive roots does this equation have?
$x^6 + 8x^5 - 3x^4 - x^3 - 7x^2 + 8x + 13 = 0$

Q10.   Find 30% of $_7P_3$.

Work the following problems.

Note: You may want to write the computer program of Problem 19 *before* you work Problems 1 through 11.

1.   *Heredity Problem*   If a dark-haired mother and father have a particular type of genes, they have a $\frac{1}{4}$ probability of having a light-haired baby.
   a.   What is their probability of having a dark-haired baby?
   b.   If they have 3 babies, calculate $P(0)$, $P(1)$, $P(2)$, and $P(3)$, the probabilities of having exactly 0, 1, 2, and 3 *dark*-haired babies, respectively.
   c.   Show that your answers to part b are reasonable by finding their sum.
   d.   Plot the graph of the probability distribution, P.

2. **Multiple Choice Test Problem**   A short multiple choice test has 4 questions. Each question has 5 choices, exactly *one* of which is right. Willie Makitt has not studied for the test, so he guesses at random.
   a.   What is his probability of guessing any one answer right? Wrong?
   b.   Calculate his probabilities of guessing 0, 1, 2, 3, and 4 answers right.
   c.   Perform a calculation that shows your answer to part b is reasonable.
   d.   Plot the graph of the probability distribution in part b.
   e.   Willie passes the test if he gets at least 3 answers right. What is his probability of passing?

3. **Thumbtack Problem**   If you flip a thumbtack, it can come out either "up" or "down" (see sketch). Suppose that the probability of "up" on any one flip is 0.7.

   "up"   "down"

   a.   If the tack is flipped 4 times, find the probabilities that it is "up" exactly 0, 1, 2, 3, and 4 times.
   b.   Plot the graph of this probability distribution.
   c.   Which is more probable, more than 2 "ups" or at most 2 "ups?" Justify your answer.

4. **Traffic Light Problem**   Three widely-separated traffic lights on U.S. 1 operate independently of each other. The probability that you will be stopped at any one of them is 40%.
   a.   Calculate the probability that you will make all 3 lights "green."
   b.   Calculate the probabilities that you will be stopped at exactly *one*, exactly *two*, and *all three* lights.
   c.   Plot the graph of this probability distribution.
   d.   Which is more probable, being stopped at more than one light or at one or less lights? Justify your answer.

5. **Bull's-Eye Problem**   Mark Wright can hit the bull's-eye with his 22 rifle 30% of the time. He fires 5 shots.
   a.   Calculate his probabilities of making 0, 1, 2, 3, 4, and 5 bull's-eyes.
   b.   Plot the graph of this probability distribution.
   c.   Calculate the probability that he will make at least 2 bull's-eyes.

6. **Dice Problem**   You roll a die 6 times. Let x be the number of times the die comes up 1 or 2, and let $P(x)$ be the probability it comes out that way x times.
   a.   On any one roll, what is the probability that the die *will* come up 1 or 2? Will *not* come up 1 or 2?
   b.   Calculate $P(x)$ for each value of x in the domain.

c. Plot the graph of P.

d. You win the game if the die comes up 1 or 2 at least twice. What is your probability of winning?

e. Since the probability of getting a 1 or 2 is $\frac{1}{3}$, you might assume that the probability of getting a 1 or 2 on *two* of the six rolls is also $\frac{1}{3}$. Is this assumption true or false? Justify your answer.

7. *Color-Blindness Problem*   Statistics show that about 5% of all males are color-blind. Suppose that 20 males are selected at random. Let x be the number who are color-blind, and let $P(x)$ be the probability that x of them are color-blind.

a. Calculate $P(0)$, $P(1)$, $P(2)$, and $P(3)$.

b. Plot a graph of this probability distribution.

c. What is the probability that at least 4 of the 20 people are color-blind?

8. *Operation Problem*   Suppose that for a certain kind of surgery, the probability that an individual will survive is 98%. If 100 people have the operation:

a. Calculate the probabilities of 0, 1, 2, 3, and 4 people dying.

b. Plot the graph of this probability distribution. Show how the graph would look for larger values of the random variable.

c. What is the probability that at least one of the 100 people dies?

9. *Eighteen-Wheeler Problem*   Large tractor-trailer trucks usually have 18 tires. Suppose that the probability of any one tire blowing out on a cross-country trip is 0.03.

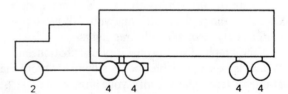

a. What is the probability that any one tire does *not* blow out?

b. What is the probability that
   i.   none of the 18 tires blows out?
   ii. exactly one tire blows out?
   iii. exactly two tires blow out?
   iv. more than two tires blow out?

c. If the trucker wants to have a 95% probability of making the trip without a blowout, what must the reliability of each tire be? That is, what is the probability that any one tire will blow out?

10. *Perfect Solo Problem*   Clara Nett plays a musical solo. She is quite good, and figures that her probability of playing any one note right is 99%. The solo has 60 notes.

a. What is her probability of
   i.   getting every note right?
   ii. making exactly one mistake?
   iii. making exactly two mistakes?
   iv. making at least two mistakes?
   v.   making more than two mistakes?
b. What must be Clara's probability of getting any one note right if she wants to have a 95% probability of getting all 60 notes right?

11. *Airplane Engine Problem*   A Boeing 707 has 4 jet engines. Assume that the probability of any one engine failing during flight is 0.1. (It is not nearly that high, but assume it anyway!)

Which is
safer?

a. What is the probability that a given engine does *not* fail?
b. Calculate the probabilities that 0, 1, 2, 3, and 4 of the engines fail during a given flight.
c. Show that the probabilities in part b add up to 1.
d. If the plane will keep flying as long as *no more than one* engine fails, what is the probability that the plane keeps flying?
e. A Boeing 727 has only 3 jet engines. If the plane will keep flying with no more than 1 engine out, and the probability of any one engine failing is the same as in part a, above, what is the probability that a 727 keeps flying?
f. Based on these calculations, which is safer, a 3-engine plane or a 4-engine plane?

12. *World Series Problem*   Suppose that the Dodgers and Yankees are in the World Series of baseball. From their season's records, you predict that the Dodgers have a probability of 0.6 of beating the Yankees in any particular game. In order to win the *Series*, a team must win *four* games.
a. What is the probability that the Yankees beat the Dodgers in any particular game?
b. What is the probability that
   i.   the Dodgers win all the first four games?
   ii. the Yankees win all the first four games?
c. For the Dodgers to win the Series in exactly 5 games, they must win exactly three of the first four games, then win the fifth game. What is the probability that the Series goes exactly 5 games, and
   i.   the Dodgers win?
   ii. the Yankees win?

d. What is the probability that the Series lasts
    i.   exactly 4 games?
    ii.   exactly 5 games?
e. Recalling, as in part c, that the winner of the Series must win
    the *last* game, calculate the probability that
    i.   the Dodgers win in 6 games.
    ii.   the Dodgers win in 7 games.
    iii. the Yankees win in 6 games.
    iv.   the Yankees win in 7 games.
f. What is the most probable length of the Series, 4, 5, 6, or 7
    games?

Problems 13 through 18 involve probability distributions *other* than binomial distributions.

13. **Another Dice Problem**   Suppose that a random experiment consists
     of rolling two dice, a black one and a white one, as in the example
     of Section 12-1.
     a. Plot graphs of the probability distributions for the following ran-
         dom variables. You may count outcomes from Figure 12-1.
         i. x is the *sum* of the numbers on the two dice.
         ii. x is the *difference,* black die minus white die.
         iii. x is the *absolute value* of the difference between the num-
               bers on the two dice.
     b. For each of the probability distributions in part a, find the most
         probable value of x.

14. **Proper Divisors Problem**   An integer from 1 through 10 is selected
     at random. Let x be the number of proper divisors the integer has.
     (A "proper divisor" of a number is an integer *less* than the number
     that divides *exactly* into the number. For example, 12 has five proper
     divisors, 1, 2, 3, 4, and 6.)
     a. List the proper divisors and the *number* of proper divisors for
         each integer from 1 through 10.
     b. For each possible value of x, tell how many of the integers from
         1 through 10 *have* that number of proper divisors.
     c. Let $P(x)$ be the probability that the integer selected at random
         has x proper divisors. Calculate $P(x)$ for each value of x in the
         domain.
     d. Plot the graph of the probability distribution P. You may wish to
         leave the points *un*connected.

15. **First Girl Problem**   Eva and Paul Lution decide to keep having ba-
     bies until they have a girl. They know that the probability of having
     a girl on any single birth is 0.5.
     a. Let x be the number of babies they have, and let $P(x)$ be the
         probability that the xth baby is the *first* girl. $P(1)$ will be 0.5.

$P(2)$ is the probability that the first is *not* a girl, and the second *is* a girl. Calculate $P(2)$, $P(3)$, and $P(4)$.

b.   Plot the graph of P. Show what happens as x becomes very large.

c.   Besides being called a probability distribution, what other special kind of function is P?

d.   Show that the *sum* of the values of $P(x)$ approaches 1 as x becomes very large.

16.   *Target Practice Problem*   A single bullet is loaded into one of the six chambers in a revolver, and the cylinder is spun around so that the bullet is in a random position. The revolver is aimed at a target and the trigger is pulled. Let x be a random variable equal to the number of times the trigger is pulled before the revolver goes off. Let $P(x)$ be the probability that it goes off on the xth pull.

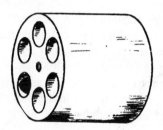

a.   Find $P(1)$.

b. $P(2)$ is the probability the gun does *not* go off on the first pull, then *does* go off on the second pull. Find $P(2)$.

c.   Find $P(3)$, $P(4)$, $P(5)$, and $P(6)$.

d.   What is the significance of the fact that the sum of $P(1)$ through $P(6)$ equals 1?

e.   Find $P(1)$ through $P(6)$ if the cylinder is spun each time before the trigger is pulled.

f.   Plot a graph of $P(x)$ versus x using the values from part e.

g.   Show that the sum of the probabilities calculated in part e approaches 1 as x becomes very large.

17.   *Lucky Card Problem*   An index card is marked with a lucky number, then shuffled with 9 other blank index cards. Three people play a game in which each, in turn, draws a card at random. If it is not the marked card, it is replaced, the cards are shuffled again, and the next player draws at random. The winner is the first player to draw the marked card. Let $P(x, y)$ be the probability that the xth player (1, 2 or 3) wins on his y^{th} turn.

a.   What is $P(1, 1)$?

b. $P(2, 1)$ is the probability that Player 1 does *not* win on his first turn, and Player 2 *does* win on his first turn. Find $P(2, 1)$ and $P(3, 1)$.

c. Show that $P(1, 1)$, $P(1, 2)$, $P(1, 3)$, . . . is a geometric sequence.

d. The probability that Player 1 wins is the sum of *all* the terms of the corresponding geometric series. Find his probability of winning.

e. Find the second and third players' probabilities of winning.

f. Show that your answers to parts d and e are reasonable based on their relative sizes and their sum.

18. ***Same Birthday Problem*** A group of students compare their birthdays.

a. What is the probability that John's birthday is *not* the same as Mark's?

b. If John and Mark have different birthdays, what is the probability that Fred's birthday is not the same as John's and not the same as Mark's?

c. What is the probability that John and Mark have different birthdays, *and* that Fred has one different from both?

d. Using the pattern you observe in part c, predict the probability that a group of 10 students will all have different birthdays. Get a decimal approximation for this answer.

e. What is the probability that in a group of 10 students, at least two have the same birthday (i.e., *not* all of them have different birthdays)?

f. Write a computer program to print a table showing the probability that at least two people in a group have the same birthday as a function of the number of people in the group. Run the program for groups from 2 through 60 people.

g. Plot the graph of the probability of at least two people with the same birthday versus the number of people in the group. You may use the output of the computer program in part f for plotting data.

h. From your graph or computer output, find how many people must be in the group to make the probability of at least two birthdays the same equal

    i. 50%, and

    ii. 99%.

    Surprising?

19. ***Computer Program for Binomial Distribution*** Write a computer program to calculate $P(x)$ for each value of x in a binomial distribution. The input should be n, the number of times the experiment is run, and b, the probability of success on any one run. The appropriate binomial is $(a + b)^n$, where $a = 1 - b$. Note that x will equal the exponent of b in the series. The output should be a table of values such as

x	$P(x)$
0	0.216
1	0.432
2	0.288
3	0.064

You should find that the coefficients are most easily calculated using the pattern

$$\frac{(\text{coefficient})(\text{exponent of } a)}{\text{term number}} = \text{next coefficient},$$

which you recall from Section 11-10. Also, since the powers of *a drop* one each time, and the powers of *b increase* one, you can simply divide the previous term by *a* and multiply it by *b*. Debug your program by using $n = 3$ and $b = 0.4$, and showing that the output is the above table of values.

12-8 | MATHEMATICAL EXPECTATION

Suppose that you play a dice game for money. You pay 50 cents, then roll a die. The payoffs are

Roll a 6: Win $1.00 (and get the 50 cents back).
Roll a 2 or 4: Win 10 cents (and get the 50 cents back).
Roll an odd number: Win nothing (and lose the 50 cents).

Since each outcome, 1, 2, 3, 4, 5, and 6, is equally likely, you would "expect" to get number *once* in 6 rolls. (You probably *won't*, but that is what you would "expect" on the average, if you rolled *many* times.) If this did happen, your winnings would be

Number	Cents Won
1	-50
2	10
3	-50
4	10
5	-50
6	100
Total:	-30

Since there were 6 rolls, and you *lost* a total of 30 cents, you would expect your average winnings per roll to be

$$\frac{-30}{6} = -5 \text{ cents per roll.}$$

The number "−5 cents per roll" is called your *mathematical expectation,*
or the *expected value* of your winnings. If you play the game many times
(thousands!), you would expect to lose about 5 cents per roll, on the
average.

Objective:
Be able to calculate the mathematical expectation of a given random experiment.

An important pattern shows up if you do *not* carry on the addition of the
payoffs in the above experiment. Letting E stand for mathematical expectation.

$$E = \frac{-50 + 10 - 50 + 10 - 50 + 100}{6} \quad \text{Adding the 6 payoffs and dividing by 6}$$

$$= \frac{3(-50) + 2(10) + 1(100)}{6} \quad \text{Commuting, associating, and factoring}$$

$$= \frac{3(-50)}{6} + \frac{2(10)}{6} + \frac{1(100)}{6} \quad \text{Division distributes over addition.}$$

$$= \frac{3}{6}(-50) + \frac{2}{6}(10) + \frac{1}{6}(100) \quad \text{Properties of fractions}$$

The $\frac{3}{6}$ is the probability of getting an odd number, and the -50 is the
payoff for getting an odd number. The $\frac{2}{6}$ and $\frac{1}{6}$ are the probabilities of
getting a 2 or 4, and of getting a 6, respectively, and the 10 and 100 are
the respective payoffs. So the mathematical expectation can be calculated
by multiplying *probability* $\times$ *payoff* for each event, then *adding* the
results.

DEFINITION

The **mathematical expectation** of a random experiment is

$$E = (\text{probability})(\text{payoff}) + (\text{probability})(\text{payoff})$$
$$+ \dots + (\text{probability})(\text{payoff}),$$

for all possible mutually exclusive events in the experiment.

Note: This definition can be stated compactly using Σ terminology (see
Section 11-4):

$$E = \sum_{k=1}^{n} \text{Probability}(k) \times \text{Payoff}(k)$$

for the n mutually exclusive events in the experiment.

EXAMPLE

The basketball toss at Playland costs you 50 cents to play. You shoot three balls. If you make no baskets, you win nothing (and lose your 50 cents, of course!). If you make just one basket, you win a paper hat worth 5 cents. For two baskets you win a stuffed animal worth 60 cents. Making all three baskets wins you a doll worth 2.50. The basket hoop is small, so your probability of making any one shot is only 0.3. What is your mathematical expectation for this game?

Let $P(x)$ be your probability of making x baskets. Your probability of *missing* on any one shot is $1 - 0.3 = 0.7$. Therefore,

$$P(0) = {}_3C_0 \times (0.7)^3(0.3)^0 = 1 \times 0.343 = 0.343$$
$$P(1) = {}_3C_1 \times (0.7)^2(0.3)^1 = 3 \times 0.147 = 0.441$$
$$P(2) = {}_3C_2 \times (0.7)^1(0.3)^2 = 3 \times 0.063 = 0.189$$
$$P(3) = {}_3C_3 \times (0.7)^0(0.3)^3 = 1 \times 0.027 = \underline{0.027}$$

Total probability $\quad\quad\quad\quad\quad\quad \overline{1.000}$

The payoffs for each event are found by subtracting the 50 cent "admission fee" from the amount you win.

x	Payoff
0	$0 - 50 = -50$
1	$5 - 50 = -45$
2	$60 - 50 = 10$
3	$250 - 50 = 200$

By the definition of mathematical expectation,

$$E = (0.343)(-50) + (0.441)(-45) + (0.189)(10) + (0.027)(200)$$
$$= -17.15 - 19.845 + 1.89 + 5.4$$
$$= -29.705.$$

So on the average, you would expect to *lose* about 30 cents per game. (This is the way amusement parks make money!)

Once you understand the computations, you can arrange the work compactly in table form. The table for the above example would look like this:

x	$P(x)$	Payoff	$P(x) \times$ Payoff
0	0.343	-50	-17.15
1	0.441	-45	-19.845
2	0.189	10	1.89
3	0.027	200	5.4
Totals:	1.000		-29.705

$$\therefore E = \underline{\underline{-29.705}}.$$

Adding up the values of $P(x)$ and seeing that you get exactly 1 gives you a
check against possible errors.   ∎

The following problems are designed to give you practice finding the
mathematical expectation of various random experiments. The ability to
estimate expected payoffs is the major reason people are interested in calculating probabilities.

EXERCISE 12-8

Do These Quickly

The following problems are intended to refresh your skills. You should be
able to do all 10 in less than 5 minutes.

Q1. Is $4 + 4 + 4 + 4 + \ldots$ a geometric series or an arithmetic
     series?

Q2. Sketch the graph of a binomial probability distribution.

Q3. Subtract: $\dfrac{3}{x+1} - \dfrac{2}{x-2}$

Q4. Find $\dfrac{3}{8}$ of 200.

Q5. Draw an isosceles right triangle.

Q6. What kind of function has a graph like this?

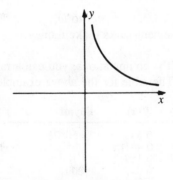

Q7. Find $_9C_2$.

Q8. To what limit does the geometric series $30 + 20 + \ldots$ converge?

Q9. Find 70% of 2^5.

Q10.   Write the solution of the linear system whose augmented matrix is shown.

$$\begin{bmatrix} 1 & 0 & | & 3 \\ 0 & 1 & | & 5 \end{bmatrix}$$

Work the following problems.

1. *Card Draw Problem*   You pay 26 cents, and draw a card at random from a normal 52-card deck. The payoffs are as follows:

    Ace: Get $1.56.
    Face card: Get 65 cents.
    Any other card: Get nothing.

    a.   What is your mathematical expectation for this game?
    b.   In the long run, would you expect to gain money or lose money playing this game? How much money?

2. *Uranium Fission Problem*   When a uranium atom splits ("fissions"), it releases 0, 1, 2, 3, or 4 neutrons. Assume that the probabilities of these various numbers are:

Number	P(Number)
0	0.05
1	0.2
2	0.25
3	0.4
4	0.1

    a.   What is the mathematically expected number of neutrons released per fission?
    b.   The number of neutrons released in a fission must be an *integer*. How do you explain the fact that the mathematically expected number is *not* an integer?

3. *Archery Problem*   An expert marksman at archery has the following probabilities of hitting various rings on the target (see sketch):

Color C	Probability	Points
Gold	0.20	9
Red	0.36	7
Blue	0.23	5
Black	0.14	3
White	0.07	1

    a.   What is her mathematical expectation on any one shot?
    b.   In a National Round, she shoots 48 arrows. What would you expect her score to be?

4. *Calvin's Grade Problem*   Calvin Butterball's father offers to pay
him $90 if he makes all A's, or to pay him $10 for each A he makes.
However, he must decide in advance which offer to accept. Calvin is
a good student, and estimates his probabilities of making A's to be

Algebra—0.9
English—0.7
Chemistry—0.8
Spanish—0.6

a. Calculate his mathematical expectation if he chooses $10 per A.
b. Calculate his probability of making all A's.
c. Calculate his mathematical expectation if he chooses $90 for
making all A's.
d. Which offer should Calvin choose?

5. *Seed Germination Problem*   A package of seeds for an exotic tropi-
cal plant states that the probability of any one seed germinating is
80%. You plant 4 of the seeds.
a. Find the probabilities that exactly 0, 1, 2, 3, and 4 of the seeds
germinate.
b. Find the mathematically expected number of seeds that will germinate.

6. *Batting Average Problem*   Milt Famey has a baseball batting average of 300, which means that his probability of getting a hit at any
one time at bat is 0.3. Suppose that Milt comes to bat 5 times during
a game.
a. Calculate the probabilities that he gets exactly 0, 1, 2, 3, 4, and
5 hits.
b. What is Milt's mathematically expected number of hits in these
5 at-bats?

7. *Expectation of a Binomial Experiment*   Suppose that you conduct a
random experiment that has a binomial probability distribution. Suppose that the probability of success on any one trial is 0.4. Let $P(x)$
be the probability of x successes in 5 trials.
a. Calculate $P(x)$ for all values of x in the domain.
b. Find the mathematically expected value of x.
c. Show that the mathematical expectation of x is equal to 0.4 (the
probability of success on any *one* trial) times 5 (the total number
of trials).
d. If the probability of success on one trial is b, and the probability
of failure on one trial is a, prove that in 5 trials, the expected
value of x is $5b$.
e. From what you have observed above, what do you suppose the
mathematically expected value of x would be in n trials, if the
probability of success on any one trial is b?

f.   If you plant 100 seeds, each of which has a probability of 0.71 of germinating, how many seeds would you expect to germinate?

8.   *Dollar Bill Problem*   You play a game in which a dollar bill is selected at random. You win the bill if all 8 digits in its serial number are different. What is your mathematical expectation, if you pay 5 cents each time to play the game?

9.   *Dice Game Problem*   You pay a dollar and roll a die 3 times. If the outcome is "Ace" (that is, 1) at least two of the three times, you get back $10.00. Otherwise you get back nothing. What is your mathematical expectation for this game?

10.   *Multiple Choice Test Problem*   Suppose that you are taking your College Board tests. You answer all the questions you can, and have some time left over, so you decide to guess at the answers to the rest of the questions.
   a.   Each question is multiple choice with 5 choices. If you guess at random, what is the probability of getting an answer right?
   b.   What is the probability of getting an answer wrong?
   c.   When Educational Testing Service grades your paper, they give you 1 point if the answer is right, and subtract $\frac{1}{4}$ point if the answer is wrong. What is your mathematically expected score on any question for which you guess at random?
   d.   Suppose you can eliminate two of the choices you know are wrong, and you randomly guess among the other three. What is your mathematically expected score on the question?
   e.   If you can eliminate three choices, and randomly guess between the other two, what is your mathematically expected score?
   f.   Based on your answers, is it really worthwhile guessing answers on a multiple choice test?

11.   *Bad Egg Problem*   An egg salesman has 5 dozen eggs that he will sell for $1.00 per dozen. Before they can be sold, they must pass an inspection. Three eggs are selected at random. If all three are good, the inspection is passed. If exactly one is bad, the 5 dozen are rejected, and the salesman loses his cost of $.60 per dozen. If two or more are bad, he loses his $.60 per dozen, and must pay a fine of $100 for trying to sell such inferior products. Suppose that exactly two eggs *are* bad. What is the salesman's mathematically expected profit?

12.   *Accident/Illness Insurance Problem*   Ripov's Insurance Company has an accident/illness policy that pays $500 if you get ill during the year, $1000 if you have an accident, and $6000 if you both get ill and have an accident. For this policy, you pay $100 per year premium. One of your friends who has studied actuarial science tells

you that your probability of becoming ill in any one year is 0.05,
and your probability of having an accident is 0.03.
a.   What is your probability of
   i.   becoming ill and having an accident?
   ii. becoming ill and not having an accident?
   iii. not becoming ill, but having an accident?
   iv. not becoming ill and not having an accident?
b.   What is your mathematical expectation for this policy?

13. *Nuclear Reactor Problem*   When a uranium atom inside the reactor
of a nuclear power plant is hit by a neutron, it splits, or "fissions,"
releasing energy. It also releases 1, 2, 3, or 4 new neutrons. The
mathematically expected number of new neutrons is about 2.3 per
fission.

Neutron hits
uranium atom.   Atom   New neutrons

a.   Suppose that there are 100 neutrons in the reactor initially. If all
of these neutrons cause fissions, how many neutrons would you
expect there to be after this first generation of fissions?
b.   If all of the new neutrons from the first generation of fissions
strike other uranium atoms and cause them to fission, what is the
mathematically expected number of neutrons after 2 generations?
3 generations? 4 generations?
c.   If each generation takes $\frac{1}{1000}$ of a second, how many neutrons
would you expect there to be after 1 second? Surprising? This is
what makes atomic bombs *explode*!
d.   Not all of the neutrons from one generation actually do cause
fissions in the next generation. Some leak out of the reactor,
some are captured by atoms other than uranium, and some that
are captured by uranium do not cause fissions. Assume that

$$P(\text{leaking}) = 0.36$$
$$P(\text{other atom capture}) = 0.2$$
$$P(\text{non-fission capture}) = 0.15.$$

Calculate the probability that *none* of these things happens, and
thus the neutron *does* cause a fission in the next generation.
e.   Use the probability of part c and the payoff of 2.3 new neutrons
per fission to calculate the expected number of neutrons in the
second generation produced by 1 neutron in the first generation.
f.   If you start with one neutron in the reactor as in parts d and e,
and each generation takes $\frac{1}{1000}$ second, as in part c, how many
neutrons would you expect to have at the end of one second?
Would this reactor explode like a bomb?

g.   Why can you say that the number of neutrons in the reactor is "increasing exponentially" with time?

14.   *Life Insurance Problem*   Functions of random variables are useful as mathematical models in the insurance business. Some of the highest-paid mathematicians are the actuaries, who figure out what rates you should pay for various types of insurance policies. The following is a portion of a mortality table used by insurance companies. The table shows the probability, $P(x)$, that a person alive on his x^{th} birthday will die before he reaches age $x + 1$.

Age, x	$P(x)$
15	0.00146
16	0.00154
17	0.00162
18	0.00169
19	0.00174
20	0.00179

A group of 10,000 fifteen-year-olds gets together to form their own life insurance company. For a premium (i.e., a payment) of $2.00 per year, they agree to pay $1000 to the family of anyone in the group who dies while he is 15 through 20 years old.

a.   Calculate $D(15)$, the number expected to die while they are 15. This should be rounded off to an integer, for obvious reasons!

b.   Calculate $A(16)$, the number expected to be alive on their sixteenth birthday. (Subtract the number who die from 10,000).

c.   Calculate $D(16)$. Use the answer to part b, and round off to an integer.

d.   Calculate $A(x)$ and $D(x)$ for ages 17 through 20. Present the results in table form by adding more columns to the above mortality table.

e.   For each x, calculate $I(x)$ and $O(x)$, the income from the $2.00 premiums and the outgo from the $1000 death payments, respectively. You realize of course, that if a person dies, he no longer pays the $2.00 per year premium! Present the results as additional columns in the table.

f.   Calculate $NI(x)$, the net income per year, for each year by subtracting the total paid out from the total premiums taken in. Why does $NI(x)$ *decrease* each year? (2 reasons!)

g.   On the average, how much does the company expect to earn per year? Would this be enough to pay a person full time to operate the company?

15.   *Another Life Insurance Problem*   A group of 10,000 people, each now 55 years old, is to be insured as in Problem 14, above. Upon the death of the insured person, his survivors receive $1000, at any age 55 through 59. You are to calculate the annual premium which

should be charged for each policy. Another portion of the mortality
table, as in Problem 14, is:

Age, x	$P(x)$
55	0.01300
56	0.01421
57	0.01554
58	0.01700
59	0.01859

a. Calculate $D(x)$ and $A(x)$ for $x = 55$ through 59, as in Problem
    14.
b. Calculate $O(x)$ for each year, the amounts to be paid out for
    $1000 death benefits.
c. A part-time administrator is to be paid $5000 per year to operate
    the insurance program. Calculate the *total* expenses (death
    benefits plus administration costs) for the five-year period.
d. Calculate the *number* of premiums which will be paid during the
    five years. This will be 10,000 the first year, and will decrease
    each subsequent year.
e. Divide the total number of premiums into the total expenses to
    find the annual premium which should be charged.
f. Why is the premium for this insurance program so much higher
    than the $2.00 per year for the program in Problem 14?

12-9   STATISTICS AND DATA ANALYSIS

So far in this chapter you have been finding probabilities of various outcomes of a random experiment. In each case you have *known* what the
population is. For example, there may have been five boys and five girls.
Statistics is concerned with the **converse.** If you know the *outcome* of a
random experiment, find out what the *population* is. For instance, if a
sample of 100 people from a given city is asked who they plan to vote for,
how well does the information predict the preference of all 200,000 voters
in that city?

In this section you will learn a bit about sampling, how to find the **mean**
and **standard deviation** of a sample, and what the **normal distribution**
is. In courses in statistics you will learn how to use these results to tell
how sure you can be that the population has the same composition as the
sample.

MEAN AND STANDARD DEVIATION

Suppose Alice and Beth compare their latest five algebra test scores.

Alice: 97, 63, 85, 90, 72
Beth: 86, 79, 84, 78, 80

To find each one's average, you add the scores and divide by 5.

Alice: Score	Beth: Score
97	86
63	79
85	84
90	78
72	80
407	407

$$\frac{407}{5} = 81.4 \qquad \frac{407}{5} = 81.4$$

Each one has the same average, 81.4. This average is called the *mean* (as in "arithmetic means"). But Alice's scores range from 63 to 97, while Beth's range only from 78 to 86.

To measure how much the individual scores deviate from the mean, statisticians use a quantity called the *standard deviation*. The *deviation* of any one test grade is just the difference between that grade and the mean.

Deviation = (one data value) − (mean of the data values)

Figure 12-9a shows the deviations of each girl's scores from the mean.

To combine the deviations into a single number, each deviation is *squared*, and then added together. The table below is a continuation of the one above.

Alice: Score	Deviation	Dev^2	Beth: Score	Deviation	Dev^2
97	15.6	243.36	86	4.6	21.16
63	−18.4	338.56	79	−2.4	5.76
85	3.6	12.96	84	2.6	6.76
90	8.6	73.96	78	−3.4	11.56
72	−9.4	88.36	80	−1.4	1.96
407		757.2	407		47.2

$$\frac{407}{5} = 81.4 \qquad\qquad \frac{407}{5} = 81.4$$

For Alice, the sum of the squares of the deviations is 757.2. For Beth, it is only 47.2.

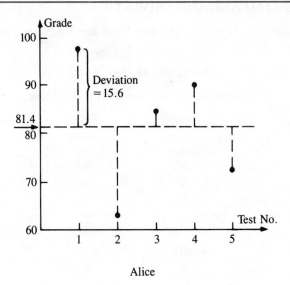

Alice

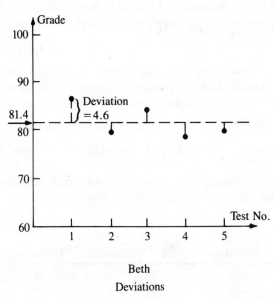

Beth

Deviations

Figure 12-9a

To be able to compare these numbers to the test grades themselves, a kind
of average is taken. You divide by the number of *degrees of freedom,*
which is defined to be one less than the number of data points.

Alice: $\dfrac{757.2}{(5-1)}$ Beth: $\dfrac{47.2}{(5-1)}$

= 189.3   = 11.8

Since these numbers have the units (grade)^2, you take the square root. The result is called the standard deviation.

Alice: $\sqrt{189.3} = 13.758\ldots$ Beth: $\sqrt{11.8} = 3.435\ldots$

You can interpret the result as meaning that Alice's grades are usually within about 13.8 points of her average, while Beth's are usually within about 3.4.

NORMAL DISTRIBUTION

If you measure many values of a quantity, such as lengths of fish in a lake or scores on an IQ test, most of the values normally lie close to the average. Fewer lie farther away, and very few are very far away. Figure 12-9b shows a graph of 500 numbers in the neighborhood of 25, selected at random by a computer. There is a dot in the column for each time that particular number appeared. The majority of the dots are between 20 and 30. Very few are over 40 or under 10.

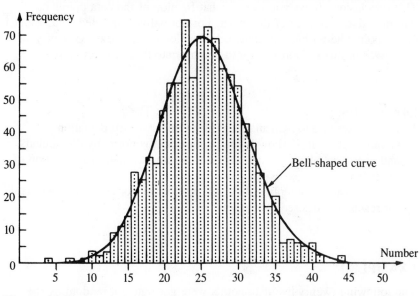

Figure 12-9b

The graph itself is called a **frequency distribution.** It tells how frequently each data value occurred. The actual outline of the columns is quite jagged. But you can draw a smooth curve around the border in such a way that there are just as many dots above the curve as there are missing spaces below the curve. When the curve is "bell-shaped" as it is in Figure 12-9b, the numbers are said to be *normally distributed* about the mean. The bell-shaped curve is called the *normal distribution curve*.

Each column is 1 unit wide. The altitude of each column is the number of data points in that column. So the *area* of the column equals the *number* of data points. If you add the areas of the columns, the sum equals the total number of data points. But there are as many data points above the curve as there are gaps below it. So you can conclude that the area of the region under the normal distribution curve is equal to the total number of data points.

CONCLUSION

> **AREA UNDER THE NORMAL CURVE**
>
> The *area* of the region under the normal distribution curve equals the *number of data points* in the distribution.

This conclusion allows you to find what fraction of the data points lie within a given distance of the mean. For normally-distributed data, about $\frac{2}{3}$ of the points lie within one standard deviation of the mean. One of your objectives in this section will be to demonstrate that this fact is true.

Objectives:
1. Given a set of data, calculate the mean and standard deviation.
2. Given a set of data, show by graphing that it is normally distributed, and show that about $\frac{2}{3}$ of the data lies within one standard deviation of the mean.
3. Given a plan for sampling data, tell whether or not it will be reasonable for reaching a desired conclusion.

EXAMPLE 1

The following twenty-five data points were generated at random by the computer program RANDOM NORMAL INTEGERS on the accompanying disk.

$$82\ 84\ 83\ 82\ 83\ 81\ 85\ 84\ 80\ 85\ 85\ 85\ 87$$

$$83\ 82\ 83\ 84\ 83\ 80\ 81\ 83\ 85\ 84\ 80\ 79$$

a. Plot a frequency distribution as in Figure 12-9b.
b. Find the mean and the standard deviation of the data.
c. Sketch a normal distribution curve on your graph in part (a). Make the high point of the curve come at the mean you calculated in part (b).

Draw the curve so that there are about as many points above the curve as there are spaces left out below.

d. Draw a vertical line one standard deviation to the left of the mean, and another vertical line one standard deviation to the right. Count the number of data points that are between the two vertical lines. Does roughly $\frac{2}{3}$ of the data lie within one standard deviation of the mean?

Solutions:

a. The graph is shown in Figure 12-9c. The easiest way to plot the graph is to start at the beginning of the data, and put a dot in the box on your graph paper for the 82, a dot for the 84, a dot for the 83, and so on. The next time you come to a particular number, put the dot in the next available square. This way you can get the entire graph with just one pass through the data.

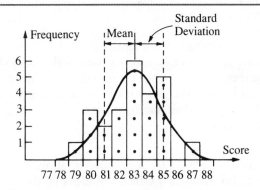

Figure 12-9c

b. Once you have made the frequency distribution in Figure 12-9c, you can use the results to simplify the process of finding the mean and standard deviation. In one column, list each value of the data that appears. In a second column, write the frequency with which that value appears. Then you can calculate the mean and the squares of the deviation for each value just *once*, and multiply the result by the frequency before adding. The table is as follows:

Value	Frequency	(Val) (Freq)	Dev.	Dev.^{2}	(Dev.^{2}) (Freq)
79	1	79	−3.92	15.3664	15.3664
80	3	240	−2.92	8.5264	25.5792
81	2	162	−1.92	3.6864	7.3728
82	3	246	−0.92	0.8464	2.5392
83	6	498	0.08	0.0064	0.0384
84	4	336	1.08	1.1664	4.6656
85	5	425	2.08	4.3264	21.6320
86	0	0	3.08	9.4864	0.
87	1	87	4.08	16.6464	16.6464
Sums.	25	2073			93.8400

$$\text{Mean} = \frac{2073}{25} = 82.92$$

The number 93.8400 at the lower right is what you need. The number of degrees of freedom is $25 - 1$, or 24. The standard deviation is:

$$\text{Std. Dev} = \sqrt{\frac{(93.8400)}{(24)}} = \underline{1.97737 \ldots}$$

c. See graph in Figure 12-9c.
d. The mean is about 83, and the standard deviation is about 2. The vertical lines in Figure 12-9c are drawn 2 units either side of the *middle* of the 83 column. So all the 82s, 83s and 84s, and half of the 81s and 85s are within 2 units of the mean. The number of data points is thus

$$\left(\frac{1}{2}\right)(2) + 3 + 6 + 4 + \left(\frac{1}{2}\right)(5) = 16.5.$$

Two thirds of 25 is $16\frac{2}{3}$. So roughly $\frac{2}{3}$ of the data is within one standard deviation of the mean.   ■

The computations in Example 1 are ideally suited for computer spreadsheets. If you have access to the software, you might like to try this example and see if you can reproduce the results. Once the spreadsheet is set up, you can use it to work the problems in the following exercise. All you have to do is change the values and frequencies.

EXAMPLE 2

Artie Facts wants to determine the total value of all the houses in his city. So he goes to the Tax Assessor's Office and looks up the values of all 26 houses on his block. He finds that the average for these houses is about $87,300, with a standard deviation of $5,400. From the tax rolls he finds that there are 7468 houses within the city limits. So he concludes that the total value of the houses is about 652 million dollars (7468)(87,300), and that he could be off by as much as $40 million dollars (7468)(5,400).
a. In what way(s) might Artie's sampling plan lead to inaccurate results?
b. Would doubling his sample size by including all 26 houses on the next block help very much in improving the accuracy? Explain.
c. What conclusion of Artie's would be incorrect even if his average value and standard deviation *were* accurate?

Solutions:
a. Artie is assuming that the 26 houses on his block are representative of *all* houses in the city. He would do much better to select 26 houses *at random* from the tax rolls so that he is likely to get houses from many areas of town.
b. Doubling his sample size by including the next block would do very little to improve the accuracy. He must sample from all areas of town.
c. In determining his margin of error, Artie is erroneously assuming that no house has a value more than one standard deviation away from the

mean. If the values are normally distributed, about $\frac{1}{3}$ of the houses *will* have values above or below. So it is possible that he is off by more than \$40 million, even if his sampling plan had been o.k.   ■

In the following exercise you will explore more problems involving sampling to predict the composition of a population.

EXERCISE 12-9

Do These Quickly

The following problems are intended to refresh your skills. You should be able to do all 10 in less than 5 minutes.

Q1.   Find $_7C_5$.

Q2.   Find $_8P_3$.

Q3.   Write the first three terms of the binomial series: $(x - y)^{17}$

Q4.   What kind of function has a graph like this?

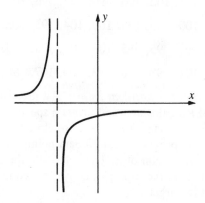

Q5.   If $P(A) = 0.7$ and $P(B) = 0.9$, and if $P(A \text{ and } B) = 0.63$, find $P(A \text{ or } B)$.

Q6.   How many different permutations of the letters ARABIA are possible?

Q7.   Find the approximate value of $\log_3 7$.

Q8.   Sketch a graph that has a vertical asymptote where $x = 3$.

Q9.   Factor: $3p^2 + 4p - 4$

Q10.   If $P(A) = 0.3$, what is $P(\text{not } A)$ as a percent?

Work the following problems.

1. Find the mean and standard deviation of 85, 79, 84, and 75.

2. Find the mean and standard deviation of 30, 34, 36, 37, 39, and 40.

3. For the following data:

$$93, 89, 89, 89, 90, 86, 88, 84, 91, 92,$$

$$88, 87, 88, 90, 95, 94, 86, 87, 96, 89,$$

$$93, 94, 91, 90, 87, 90, 91, 92, 90, 94;$$

a. Plot a frequency distribution.
b. Find the mean and the standard deviation.
c. Sketch a normal distribution curve around the frequency distribution graph in part (a). Put the high point at the mean, and
make the number of data points above the curve approximately
equal to the number of spaces left out below the curve.
d. Show that roughly $\frac{2}{3}$ of the data points lie within one standard
deviation of the mean.

4. Repeat Problem 3 for the following data:

$$103, 101, 102, 100,\ \ 96,\ \ 99,\ \ 96, 101, 100,\ \ 99,$$

$$103, 100, 100, 103, 100, 104,\ \ 95, 103,\ \ 98, 105,$$

$$97,\ \ 97,\ \ 95,\ \ 95, 103,\ \ 94, 100,\ \ 99, 105, 101,$$

$$100, 101,\ \ 98,\ \ 98,\ \ 98, 100, 107,\ \ 98, 106, 104.$$

5. *Computer-Generated Random Data*   The program RANDOM NOR-
MAL INTEGERS calculates and prints a specified number of integers which (as its name suggests!) are close to normally distributed. Run the program with 20 data points, using a mean of 50
and a standard deviation of 3. Then compute the mean and the standard deviation as in the example, above, to see how close the computer came to its target.

6. *Computer-Generated Normal Distribution Graph*   The program
PLOT NORM AND BELL plots a frequency distribution for random
numbers it selects. You tell the computer the number of data points,
and what you want the mean and standard deviation to be. The computer then plots a frequency distribution using the numbers it selects.
When it has finished it draws a normal curve through the end points.
Run the program with $n = 300$ data points, mean $= 25$, and standard deviation 5. Show that there are approximately as many data
points above the curve as there are empty spaces below. What does
the area of the region under the curve represent?

7. *Sampling Problem #1*   An algebra class has the assignment of estimating how many people in the community work for a living. The class decides to conduct a telephone survey next Wednesday afternoon. They select people at random from the phone book, and call up until 100 have answered the phone and responded to their question, "Do you work for a living?" The result showed that 73 of the 100 people did *not* work for a living. So they concluded that of the 200,000 people who live in the community, there are $(\frac{73}{100})(200,000)$, or 146,000 who do not work for a living.

   a. In what way(s) might the sampling procedure lead to an inaccurate conclusion?

   b. Do you think the sampling procedure would err on the high side (suggesting that there are more people who do not work for a living than there really are), or on the low side? Explain.

   c. Write at least one way the sampling procedure could be changed to produce a more accurate conclusion.

8. *Sampling Problem #2*   Sam Pullman is in charge of quality control at an automobile assembly plant. To insure that workers are doing a good job putting together the engines, he has every 20th engine taken off the assembly line and given a thorough testing. Sam is pleased to find that the engines that are tested have virtually nothing wrong with them. However, automobile dealers complain that most of the cars reaching their showrooms have something wrong with the engine. Explain how Sam's sampling procedure may account for these seemingly contradictory results. What could Sam do to improve the procedure, without having to test more engines?

9. *Normal Curve by Computer Graphics Problem*   The normal distribution curve has an equation of the form

$$y = k \cdot b^{(x-m)^2},$$

where *m* is the mean of the data, and *k* and *b* are constants that depend on how many data points there are, and what the standard deviation is.

   a. Plot the graph of this function on the computer screen using $k = 10$, $b = 0.9$, and $m = 13$. If you use PLOT FUNCTION from the accompanying disk, it is convenient to define the function like this:

   1 DEF FN Y(X) = K * B $^\wedge$ ((X-M)*(X-M))

   Then add line 206 in the program:

   206 INPUT "TYPE K,B,M ";K,B,M

   b. Does the graph look like the normal curve? Is the high point really where *x* equals the mean?

c. Plot the graph of this function if $k = 10$, $b = 0.8$, and $m = 13$. Do this without erasing the graph in part (a). In what way is the graph different from the one in part (a)? What property of the distribution seems to affect constant b?

d. Show by actual graphing that the equation above does not give the normal curve when $b > 1$.

12-10 | CHAPTER REVIEW AND TEST

In this chapter you have analyzed functions in which the independent variable takes on *random* values. The dependent variable is the *probability* that a certain value occurs. For this purpose you made a precise definition of "probability" as the ratio of favorable outcomes to total outcomes. At first you calculated probabilities from this definition by calculating numbers of combinations or permutations and dividing. Then you found properties that would let you calculate probabilities using other known probabilities. You found that some probability distributions are closely related to binomial series. You concluded by using probability distributions to calculate mathematically expected "payoffs" of random experiments. Finally, you were introduced to statistics, the converse of probability.

REVIEW PROBLEMS

The Review Problems below parallel the sections in this chapter. The Concepts Problems let you try your hand at applying what you know to analyze a new situation. The Chapter Test is similar to one your instructor might give to see how well you understand random variables.

R1. Two fair dice are rolled, a blue one and a green one. Find the probability that the blue one has a 4 or the green one has a 3.

R2. A penny, a nickel, a dime, and a quarter are tossed.
a. Write the 16 elements in the sample space (HHHH, HHHT, etc.).
b. Find the probability that the quarter is heads.
c. Find the probability that exactly two of the coins are tails.

R3. Baskin Robbins has 20 flavors of ice cream and 11 flavors of sherbet. In how many ways could you select
a. a scoop of ice cream and then a scoop of sherbet?
b. a scoop of ice cream or a scoop of sherbet?

R4. Using the letters SARDINE,
  a. How many different linear arrangements could be made using all the letters?
  b. How many of these arrangements have D first and a consonant second?
  c. If an arrangement is selected at random, what is the probability that D comes first and a consonant is second?
  d. In how many different ways could the seven letters be arranged in a circle?
  e. If the letters were changed to AMANDAS, how many different linear arrangements could be made?

R5. a. Five marbles are selected from a bag, without replacement. The bag originally contained 7 red marbles and 9 blue ones. What is the probability that
    i. exactly 3 are red?
    ii. at least 3 are red?
  b. Mr. Rhee's car has a probability of 70% of starting, and Ms. Rhee's car has an 80% probability of starting. What is the probability that
    i. neither car will start?
    ii. both cars will start?
    iii. either both cars or neither car will start?
    iv. exactly one of the cars will start?

R6. Flicka Bick's cigarette lighter has a 60% probability of lighting on any one flick. She flicks it 4 times. Let $P(x)$ be the probability that it lights exactly x of those times.
  a. Find $P(x)$ for each value of x in the domain.
  b. Plot the graph of P.
  c. Find the probability that it lights at least half of the times.

R7. Professor Snarff determines his students' averages by "weighting" each test a different amount. Test 1 counts 10% of the grade. Tests 2, 3, and 4 count 20% each. The Final Exam counts 30%.
  a. Suppose that Nita B. Topaz makes grades of 72, 86, 93, 77, and 98 on the five tests, in that order. What is her average?
  b. The average in part a is called a "weighted" average. Explain why the process of finding a weighted average is exactly the same as finding the mathematical expectation of a probability distribution.

R8. a. Find the mean and standard deviation of 37, 48, 43, 52, and 50.
  b. Sketch the normal distribution curve.
  c. Dee Student is given the project of finding out how many students in a high school are taking or plan to take four years of math. So Dee samples 50 students at random from math

classes, finding that 74% do plan four years of math. Tell Dee
why it is not valid to conclude from the sample that 74% of the
student body plans four years of math.

CONCEPTS PROBLEMS

The following questions concern the game of BINGO. Each player receives
a card as shown in the sketch. The *B*-column contains exactly 5 of the integers 1 – 15, arranged in any order. The *I, N, G,* and *O* columns contain
the integers from 16 – 30, 31 – 45, 46 – 60, and 61 – 75, respectively,
the *N*-column having only 4 integers. Answer the following questions. For
each part of each question, tell by number(s) which one(s) of the three objectives of this chapter you used on that part.

B	I	N	G	O
3	19	45	52	67
11	22	37	53	75
7	16	✕	49	66
2	30	38	60	68
13	18	41	47	72

C1. These questions concern the BINGO card itself.
  a. How many different groups of 4 integers could there be for the
      N-column?
  b. How many different groups of 5 integers could there be for the
      B-column?
  c. How many different arrangements of 5 of the 15 integers could
      there be for the *B*-column?
  d. After 5 integers have been selected for the *B*-column, in how
      many different ways could these 5 be arranged?
  e. If integers are selected at random for the *B*-column, what is
      the probability that all are *even*? All are *odd*?
  f. To avoid the possibility of two different people winning a game
      with the same 5 numbers, no two cards have the same group
      of numbers in the same column. What is the maximum possi-
      ble number of cards that satisfy this requirement? (The answer
      is obvious, but requires careful thought.)

C2. The game is played by selecting integers at random, without re-
     placement, and seeing if they are on your card. What is the proba-
     bility that
  a. the first 4 numbers selected for the *N*-column are all on your
      card?
  b. the first 5 numbers selected for the *B*-column are all on your
      card?

c. the first 10 numbers selected for the *B*-column include the 5 on your card?

C3. Suppose that you are one of 5 people playing BINGO.
  a. Since each person is equally likely to win any one given game, what is the probability that you win? That you lose?
  b. If the 5 people play 4 games, find the probabilities that you win 0, 1, 2, 3, and all 4 of these games.
  c. Plot the graph of the probability distribution in part b.
  d. Which is more likely, that you win no games or that you win at least 2 games? Justify your answer.
  e. Use the definition of mathematical expectation and the probability distribution of part b to find the expected number of games you will win. Show that this number equals the number of games played, multiplied by your probability of winning any one game.
  f. The five of you decide on the following payoffs:

  > Win 0 games, pay $2.00.
  > Win 1 game, break even. (Pay nothing, win nothing.)
  > Win 2 games, win $3.00.
  > With 3 games, win $5.00.
  > Win all 4 games, win $100.00.

  What is *your* mathemathically expected number of dollars for playing the 4 games?

CHAPTER TEST

(Note: This test is somewhat longer than a normal classroom test.)

For Problems T1 through T5, eight first-graders, 4 boys and 4 girls, are playing on the playground. Since you have studied probability, they consult *you* for answers to the following questions.

T1. In how many ways can they arrange themselves?
  a. all 8 in a line?
  b. all 8 in a line with boys and girls alternating?
  c. in a line of 5?
  d. in a line of 5 consisting of 3 boys and 2 girls?
  e. around the merry-go-round?
  f. with one turning the merry-go-round, and the other 7 sitting around it?

T2. If a group of 5 is selected at random, what is the probability that it contains

a. 3 boys and 2 girls?

    b. exactly 1 boy?

    c. at least 2 boys?

T3. The kids have a mud-slinging contest. Each kid has a probability of 0.3 of getting a muddy shirt. What is the probability that

    a. all 8 get muddy shirts?

    b. nobody gets a muddy shirt?

    c. exactly 5 get muddy shirts?

T4. Suppose that each kid has a probability of 0.2 of getting a muddy face in the mud fight. What is the probability that Polly Nomail gets

    a. *no* muddy face?

    b. *no* muddy shirt?

    c. no muddy face *and* no muddy shirt?

    d. no muddy face *or* no muddy shirt?

    e. a muddy face *and* a muddy shirt?

T5. Let x be the number of kids who get muddy shirts, and $P(x)$ be the probability that exactly x kids get muddy shirts. Since it is *certain* that either 0 or 1 or 2 or . . . or 8 of them will get muddy shirts, $P(0$ or 1 or 2 or . . . or 8) must equal 1. By using an appropriate binomial series, explain how you can tell *quickly* that $P(0) + P(1) + P(2) + . . . + P(8)$ *will* equal 1.

T6. Records from Buzz Sawmill show that workers have a 0.02 probability of losing an arm, and a 0.03 probability of losing a leg in any one year.

    a. What is the probability that a worker

       i. does *not* lose an arm?

      ii. does *not* lose a leg?

     iii. loses neither an arm nor a leg?

     iv. loses both an arm and a leg?

    b. Armand Legg Casualty Insurance Co. plans to offer insurance policies for the workers. The company will pay the worker $300 if he loses an arm, $400 if he loses a leg, and $7000 if he loses both an arm and a leg. On the average, how much will the company expect to pay out per policy?

    c. Armand Legg wants to make a profit of $5 per policy. How much should the premium be? That is, how much should Armand Legg charge each worker for the policy?

T7. Phoebe Small takes a 5-question true-false test. She hasn't studied, so she guesses answers at random. By using her ESP, she figures she has a 60% probability of getting any one answer right.

    a. What is her probability of getting any one answer wrong?

    b. Let $P(x)$ be her probability of getting exactly x of the 5 answers right. Calculate $P(0)$ through $P(5)$.

    c. What is her probability of getting at least 3 answers right?

   d. Show that your answers to part (b) are reasonable by finding
       $P(0$ or 1 or 2 or 3 or 4 or 5$)$.
   e. What special name is given to this kind of probability distribu-
       tion, and why is it given that name?
   f. Plot the graph of this probability distribution.

T8. The high temperature in Scorpion Gulch on five successive July
     4ths was 100, 105, 103, 101, and 108.
   a. Find the mean and standard deviation.
   b. Assuming that the high temperatures are normally distributed
       about the mean of the sample, approximately what is the prob-
       ability that the temperature will be within one standard devia-
       tion of the mean on next July 4th?

12-11 | CUMULATIVE REVIEW, CHAPTERS 9
        THROUGH 12

The following exercise may be considered to be a "final exam" covering
quadratic relations, higher degree functions, complex numbers, sequences
and series, and probability. If you are thoroughly familiar with these concepts, as presented in Chapters 9 through 12, you should be able to work
all of the problems in about 2 hours.

   EXERCISE 12-11

1. Write an equation in the form $Ax^2 + Bxy + Cy^2 + Dx + Ey +$
    $F = 0$ for each of the quadratic relations whose graph is sketched in
    Figure 12-11.

a. 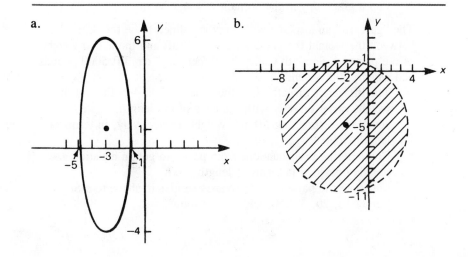 b.

c.

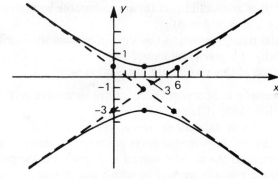

d.

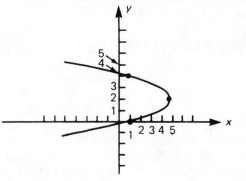

Figure 12-10 _____

2. Solve the system:

$$x^2 + 2y^2 = 33$$

$$x^2 + y^2 + 2x = 19$$

3. For the cubic function $f(x) = x^3 - 7x^2 + 11x + 3$:
    a. Show that 3 is a real zero of $f(x)$.
    b. Find all the other zeros of $f(x)$, real and complex.
    c. Plot a graph of f in the domain $-2 \le x \le 6$.

4. The "payload" an airplane will carry is defined to be the difference
    between the weight the plane's wings will lift and the actual weight
    of the plane. A Sopwith Camel is 40 feet long, can lift 5000 pounds,
    and weighs 3000 pounds.
    a. The lift varies directly with the square of the length, and the
        weight varies directly with the cube of the length. Write two
        equations, expressing lift and weight, respectively, in terms of
        length.
    b. Combine the two equations from part a to get an equation ex-
        pressing payload in terms of length.
    c. Calculate the payload for airplanes similar in shape to a Sopwith
        Camel 10, 20, 30, 50, and 60 feet long.

    d. Find the zeros of the function in part b, and tell what each of them represents in the real word.

    e. Plot the graph of payload versus length, using a suitable domain.

    f. Approximately what length plane shaped like a Sopwith Camel can carry the *maximum* payload?

5. Simplify the following expressions:

    a. i^{55}

    b. $\dfrac{6}{\sqrt{-24}}$

    c. $\dfrac{10}{1 - 2i}$

6. Find a quadratic equation with one variable and real-number coefficients if one of the solutions is $3 + 4i$.

7. An arithmetic sequence has terms $t_1 = 3$, and $t_9 = 7$.

    a. Find the common difference.

    b. Write the seven arithmetic means between 3 and 7.

    c. Find t_{101}, the 101st term.

    d. Find S_{101}, the 101st partial sum.

8. A geometric series has first term $t_1 = 8$ and common ratio $r = -\frac{1}{2}$.

    a. Find S_4, the fourth partial sum.

    b. Find the sum of *all* the terms. That is, find the number which S_n approaches as n becomes very large.

9. Find the term that contains b^3 in the binomial series that comes from expanding $(a - b)^7$.

10. Annie Moore invests $500 in a savings account that pays 8% per year interest, compounded quarterly (4 times a year). She knows that the amount of money she has after n quarters is a term in a geometric sequence. How much will she have after 5 years?

11. Using the 9 letters ABCDEFGHI:

    a. In how many different ways can an arrangement be made using

       i. any 5 of these letters?

      ii. all 9 of these letters?

     iii. all 9 of these letters, with a consonant first and G last?

    b. In how many different ways can a group of 5 of these letters be made if

       i. F must be one of the letters?

      ii. any 5 of the letters can be used?

     iii. exactly 3 of the 5 must be consonants?

12. Kay Oss and Hezzy Tate are competing for the title of top mathematics student. Each has tied on all tests, and the Mathematics Club

Sponsor, Miss Fortune, must break the tie. She flips a thumbtack
five times. The winner is the one who correctly guesses the number
of times the tack will land point-up. Kay selects 3 and Hezzy selects
4. If the probability of "point-up" on any one flip is 0.6, who is
more likely to win, Kay or Hezzy? Justify your answer.

13.   Plutonium is used as a fuel in some nuclear power plants. When a
       plutonium atom fissions ("splits"), it emits 0, 1, 2, 3, or 4 new neu-
       trons. Assume that the probabilities are

Number	P(Number)
1	0.1
2	0.15
3	0.5
4	0.25

a.   Calculate $P(0)$.
b.   What is the expected number of neutrons per fission?
c.   Neutrons come only in integer quantities. How do you explain
      the fact that the expected number is *not* an integer?

13

Trigonometric and Circular Functions

*The position of the pedal on a bicycle is a **periodic** function of how far the cyclist has traveled. This means that the dependent variable takes on the same set of values over and over again as the independent variable increases. In this chapter you will invent "trigonometric" and "circular" functions whose graphs are periodic. Your ultimate objective will be to write the particular equation of such a function from information about its graph. This way you can use the function as a mathematical model of periodic phenomena.*

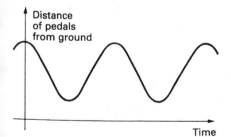

13-1 | INTRODUCTION TO PERIODIC FUNCTIONS

A function is said to be "periodic" if the dependent variable takes on the
same set of values over and over again as the independent variable
changes. In this section you will sketch reasonable graphs of real-world situations, as you did in Section 2-3. Some will be periodic and others will
not.

Objective:
Given a situation from the real world with two related variables,
a. sketch a reasonable graph showing how those two variables are related,
b. tell whether or not the function is periodic.

The following exercise is designed to see if you can accomplish this objective. If you have difficulty, reread Section 2-3.

EXERCISE 13-1

For each of the following,
a. sketch a reasonable graph,
b. tell whether or not the function graphed is periodic.

1. The depth of the water at the beach depends on the time of day due to
   the motion of the tides.

2. The distance required to stop your car depends on how fast you were
   going when you applied the brakes.

3. The temperature of a cup of coffee depends on how long it has been
   since the coffee was poured.

4. As you breathe, the volume of air in your lungs depends on time.

5. A gymnast is jumping up and down on a trampoline. Her distance from the floor depends on time.

6. The distance you go depends on how long you have been going (at a constant speed).

7. As you ride the Ferris wheel at the amusement park, your distance from the ground depends on how long you have been riding.

8. The average temperature for any particular day (averaged over many years) depends on the day of the year.

9. A pendulum swings back and forth in a grandfather clock. The distance from the end of the pendulum to the left side of the clock depends on time.

10. A straight line starts along the positive x-axis and rotates counterclockwise around and around the origin of a Cartesian coordinate system. The *slope* of the line depends on the number of degrees through which the line has been rotated.

13-2 | MEASUREMENT OF ARCS AND ROTATION

In the last section you sketched graphs of "periodic" functions which repeat themselves at regular intervals. One of the simplest examples of a periodic phenomenon is rotation. In this section you will invent ways to specify how far an object has rotated and in which direction.

Suppose that an object is going around a circular path. For simplicity, suppose that the circle has a radius of 1 unit (a "unit circle"), as in Figure 13-2a. If the object starts at the point $(u, v) = (1, 0)$, then its position may be specified in one of two different ways:

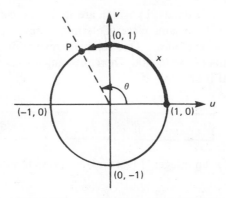

Figure 13-2a

1. The distance, x, the point has traveled around the curved path.
2. The number of degrees, θ, through which the point has rotated.

Since the point could travel many times around the circle, the angle θ could be more than 360°.

Objective:
Given the angle measure, θ, or the arc length, x, sketch the position of the point P on the unit circle.

Notes:

1. The letters u and v are used for the coordinate system since x and y will be used later for independent and dependent variables.
2. The symbol θ is the Greek letter "theta." Greek letters are often used for angles. Some more frequently used ones are:

    α alpha θ theta
    β beta ϕ phi
    γ gamma ω omega

3. The letter θ may be used for the angle *itself* rather than the measure of the angle. In this case the measure of θ in degrees would be written

$$m°(\theta).$$

For the sake of brevity, the symbol θ is often used interchangeably for the angle or for its measure, provided no confusion will result.

A directed angle or arc beginning at the positive u-axis and measured *counterclockwise* is said to be in *standard position*. Thus, if θ or x is *negative*, the angle or arc would be measured in the *clockwise* direction. Several arcs and angles in standard position are shown in Figure 13-2b.

Two angles or arcs in standard position are said to be *coterminal* if they terminate ("end") at the same place. Coterminal arcs or angles differ by an integral number of revolutions. One complete revolution corresponds to 360° or to 2π units of arc length. Therefore, angles θ and ϕ, or arcs x and w, are coterminal if and only if

$$\phi = \theta + 360n° \quad \text{and} \quad w = x + 2\pi n$$

where n stands for an integer. Figure 13-2c shows three coterminal angles.

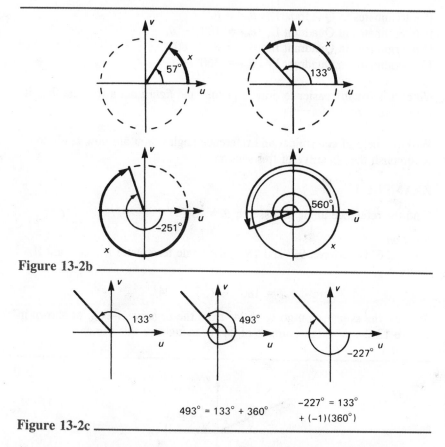

Figure 13-2b _____

Figure 13-2c _____

$$493° = 133° + 360°$$

$$-227° = 133° + (-1)(360°)$$

In order to draw an angle or arc in standard position, it helps to find the measure of the acute angle between the terminal side and the u-axis. This angle is called the *reference angle*. Figure 13-2d shows reference angles for various values of θ.

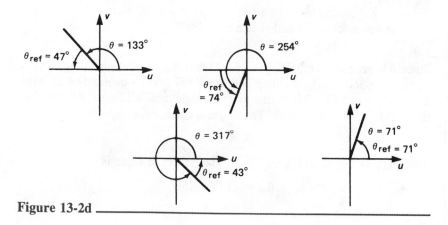

Figure 13-2d _____

If θ terminates in Quadrant I, $\theta_{ref} = \theta$.
If θ terminates in Quadrant II, $\theta_{ref} = 180° - \theta$.
If θ terminates in Quadrant III, $\theta_{ref} = \theta - 180°$.
If θ terminates in Quadrant IV, $\theta_{ref} = 360° - \theta$.

Note: It is usually easier to draw a picture and *figure out* a formula than it is to memorize the formula.

With the help of coterminal and reference angles, you are now ready to accomplish the objective of this section.

EXAMPLE 1

Find the reference angle and sketch $\theta = 156°$.

Solution:
Since 156° is between 90° and 180°, the angle terminates in Quadrant II. Therefore,

$$\theta_{ref} = 180° - 156° = 24°.$$

To draw the sketch, you go *back* 24° from the negative u-axis, as shown in Figure 13-2e. A rough estimate of 24° is enough for this sketch.

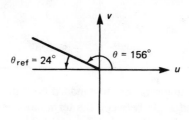

Figure 13-2e ———————————————————— ■

EXAMPLE 2

Find the reference angle and sketch $\theta = 4897°$.

Solution:
Since θ is greater than 360°, you should first find a coterminal angle that is *less* than 360°. Long dividing 360 into 4897 gives a quotient of 13 with a remainder of 217. This means that the angle makes 13 complete revolutions, then goes 217° farther. Therefore, a coterminal angle is

$$\theta_c = 217°.$$

This angle is shown in Figure 13-2f. The reference angle is

$$\theta_{ref} = 217° - 180°$$

$$= 37°.$$

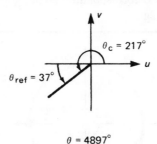

$\theta_c = 217°$

$\theta_{ref} = 37°$

$\theta = 4897°$

Figure 13-2f _____

So θ terminates in the third quadrant, 37° beyond the negative u-axis. ■

EXAMPLE 3

Sketch an arc of a unit circle measuring $x = \frac{5\pi}{3}$ in standard position on a unit circle.

Solution:
You already know how to draw angles in standard position. You can draw this arc by first finding the measure of the corresponding central angle, θ. Since the circumference of a unit circle is 2π, and a complete revolution is 360°, you can conclude that

$$\theta = \frac{360}{2\pi}x,$$

or, after canceling,

$$\theta = \frac{180}{\pi}x$$

Similarly,

$$x = \frac{\pi}{180}\theta$$

Therefore, for this example,

$$\theta = \frac{180}{\pi} \cdot \frac{5\pi}{3}$$

$$= 300°.$$

Since θ terminates in Quadrant IV, the reference angle is

$$\theta_{ref} = 360° - 300°$$

$$= 60°.$$

After you have drawn the corresponding angle, you simply sketch an arc as shown in Figure 13-2g.

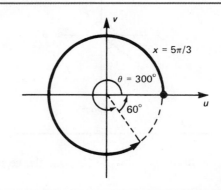

Figure 13-2g ———————————————————————— ■

The following exercise is designed to give you practice with sketching arcs and angles in standard position.

EXERCISE 13-2

Do These Quickly

The following problems are intended to refresh your skills. You should be able to do all 10 in less than 5 minutes.

Q1. Draw a 30°, 60° right triangle.

Q2. If the hypotenuse in Problem Q1 is 14 cm, how long is the shorter leg?

Q3. If the shorter leg in Problem Q1 is 20 cm, how long is the longer leg?

Q4. Draw an isosceles right triangle.

Q5. If the one leg in Problem Q4 is 100 cm, how long is the hypotenuse?

Q6. If two legs of a right triangle are 7 and 9, how long is the hypotenuse?

Q7. What is the complement of 29°?

Q8. What is the supplement of 34°?

Q9. Sketch the graph of a periodic function.

Q10. Write π to 3 decimal places.

For Problems 1 through 12, find the measure of the reference angle, then draw the angle in standard position. Mark the reference angle on your sketch.

1. 137°	2. 259°	3. 342°
4. 54°	5. 412°	6. 591°
7. −186°	8. −303°	9. 5481°
10. 7321°	11. −2746°	12. −3814°

For Problems 13 through 24, sketch the indicated arc of a unit circle in standard position.

13. $\dfrac{\pi}{3}$	14. $\dfrac{2\pi}{5}$	15. π
16. $\dfrac{3\pi}{2}$	17. $\dfrac{7\pi}{6}$	18. 0.8π
19. $-\dfrac{\pi}{4}$	20. $-\dfrac{2\pi}{3}$	21. $\dfrac{7\pi}{2}$
22. 4.7π	23. -9.8π	24. $-\dfrac{11\pi}{3}$

13-3   DEFINITIONS OF TRIGONOMETRIC AND CIRCULAR FUNCTIONS

In the previous section you drew arcs and angles in standard position around a unit circle. The relationships among the angle measure, θ, the arc length, x, and the coordinates u and v are shown in Figure 13-3a. Since there is one and only one ordered pair (u, v) for each angle or arc, u and v are *functions* of θ or x. These functions are given special names.

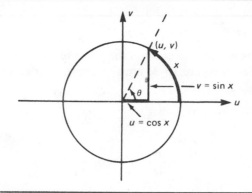

Figure 13-3a

DEFINITION

> **Sine Function:** $v = \sin\theta = \sin x$.
>
> **Cosine Function:** $u = \cos\theta = \cos x$.

Notes:

1. The symbols cos x and sin x are forms of "$f(x)$" terminology. The letters "cos" and "sin" are the *names* of the functions, and the independent variable θ or x is called the *argument*. As was true with log x, the parentheses around the argument are usually omitted unless they are needed for clarity.
2. These functions are called *circular* functions if the argument is an arc length, and *trigonometric* functions if the argument is an angle measure. The latter name comes from "trigon" meaning triangle, and "metry" meaning measurement.
3. The name "sine" comes from the Latin word "sinus," which is a mistranslation of an Arabic word meaning "bowstring." The v-distance to the terminal point resembles half of a bowstring! The prefix "co-" in cosine comes from the word "complement," as you will see later.

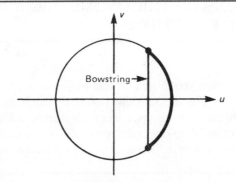

Figure 13-3b

The sine and cosine are also equal to the *ratios* of sides of a right triangle. The two triangles in Figure 13-3c are similar, so their corresponding sides are proportional. Therefore,

$$\frac{v_1}{r} = \frac{v}{1} = v = \sin\theta, \text{ and}$$

$$\frac{u_1}{r} = \frac{u}{1} = u = \cos\theta$$

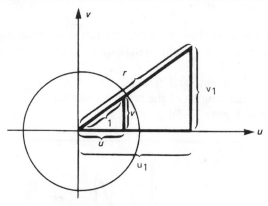

Figure 13-3c _____

In general, if $P(u, v)$ is *any* point on the terminal side of θ, and r is the distance from the origin to P, then

$$\sin \theta = \frac{v}{r} \quad \text{and} \quad \cos \theta = \frac{u}{r}.$$

There are six possible ratios that can be formed using any two of the numbers u, v, and r. The other four ratios are defined to be other trigonometric or circular functions.

DEFINITION

tangent: $\tan \theta = \tan x = \dfrac{v}{u}.$ **secant:** $\sec \theta = \sec x = \dfrac{r}{u}.$

cotangent: $\cot \theta = \cot x = \dfrac{u}{v}.$ **cosecant:** $\csc \theta = \csc x = \dfrac{r}{v}.$

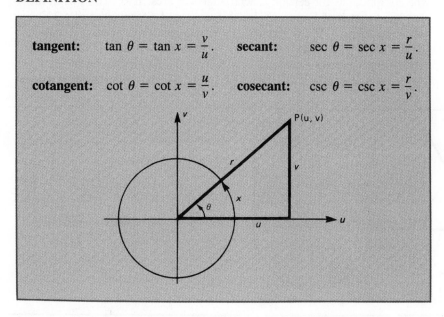

Notes:

1. Again, these are called *trigonometric* functions if the argument is an angle measure, and *circular* functions if the argument is an arc length.
2. The names "tangent" and "secant" come from the facts that tan x and sec x equal the lengths of the tangent and secant lines, respectively, as shown in Figure 13-3d.

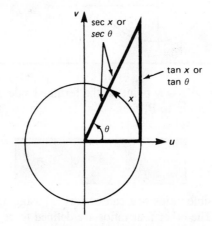

Figure 13-3d

These trigonometric ratios provide an easy way to figure out the values of the six functions for certain special angles or arcs. If $\theta = 60°$, as in the left hand sketch of Figure 13-3e, then u, v, and r form sides of a 30° − 60° right triangle. From geometry, you will recall that the hypotenuse of such a triangle is *twice* the shorter leg. Therefore, if $u = 1$, then $r = 2$. By the Pythagorean Theorem, $v = \sqrt{3}$. In the middle sketch of Figure 13-3e, $\theta = 45°$. If $u = 1$, then $v = 1$ also, because the triangle is isosce-

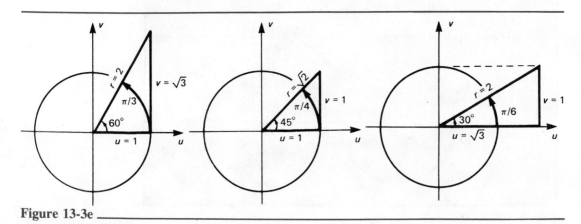

Figure 13-3e

les. By Pythagoras, $r = \sqrt{2}$. In the right sketch of Figure 13-3e, $\theta = 30°$. Reversing the triangle in the left sketch, $u = \sqrt{3}$, $v = 1$, and $r = 2$. From these three sketches, you can use the ratios to write the function values.

FUNCTIONS OF SPECIAL ARGUMENTS

Function	Ratio	$\theta = 30°$ $x = \dfrac{\pi}{6}$	$\theta = 45°$ $x = \dfrac{\pi}{4}$	$\theta = 60°$ $x = \dfrac{\pi}{3}$
$\sin \theta$ $\sin x$	$\dfrac{v}{r}$	$\dfrac{1}{2}$	$\dfrac{1}{\sqrt{2}} = \dfrac{\sqrt{2}}{2}$	$\dfrac{\sqrt{3}}{2}$
$\cos \theta$ $\cos x$	$\dfrac{u}{r}$	$\dfrac{\sqrt{3}}{2}$	$\dfrac{1}{\sqrt{2}} = \dfrac{\sqrt{2}}{2}$	$\dfrac{1}{2}$
$\tan \theta$ $\tan x$	$\dfrac{v}{u}$	$\dfrac{1}{\sqrt{3}} = \dfrac{\sqrt{3}}{3}$	1	$\sqrt{3}$
$\cot \theta$ $\cot x$	$\dfrac{u}{v}$	$\sqrt{3}$	1	$\dfrac{1}{\sqrt{3}} = \dfrac{\sqrt{3}}{3}$
$\sec \theta$ $\sec x$	$\dfrac{r}{u}$	$\dfrac{2}{\sqrt{3}} = \dfrac{2\sqrt{3}}{3}$	$\sqrt{2}$	2
$\csc \theta$ $\csc x$	$\dfrac{r}{v}$	2	$\sqrt{2}$	$\dfrac{2}{\sqrt{3}} = \dfrac{2\sqrt{3}}{3}$

If the angle or arc terminates at a quadrant boundary, the function values are even easier to find. For example, if $\theta = 90°$, then the point to pick is $(u, v) = (0, 1)$. If $\theta = 0°$, then the point to pick is $(u, v) = (1, 0)$. In both cases, $r = 1$. The arcs and angles are shown in Figure 13-3f, and the function values are given in the following table.

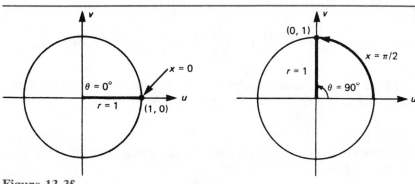

Figure 13-3f

MORE FUNCTIONS OF SPECIAL ARGUMENTS

Function	Ratio	$\theta = 0°$ $x = 0°$	$\theta = 90°$ $x = \frac{\pi}{2}$
$\sin \theta$ $\sin x$	$\dfrac{v}{r}$	0	1
$\cos \theta$ $\cos x$	$\dfrac{u}{r}$	1	0
$\tan \theta$ $\tan x$	$\dfrac{v}{u}$	0	Undefined
$\cot \theta$ $\cot x$	$\dfrac{u}{v}$	Undefined	0
$\sec \theta$ $\sec x$	$\dfrac{r}{u}$	1	Undefined
$\csc \theta$ $\csc x$	$\dfrac{r}{v}$	Undefined	1

Notes:

1. The function value is *undefined* whenever the denominator of the ratio equals zero. For example, tan 90° would be $\frac{1}{0}$, and division by zero is undefined.
2. There is a clever way to remember the function values by writing them in *radical* form.

$$
\begin{array}{cccccc}
\theta & 0° & 30° & 45° & 60° & 90° \\[4pt]
\sin \theta & \dfrac{\sqrt{0}}{2} & \dfrac{\sqrt{1}}{2} & \dfrac{\sqrt{2}}{2} & \dfrac{\sqrt{3}}{2} & \dfrac{\sqrt{4}}{2} \\[10pt]
\cos \theta & \dfrac{\sqrt{4}}{2} & \dfrac{\sqrt{3}}{2} & \dfrac{\sqrt{2}}{2} & \dfrac{\sqrt{1}}{2} & \dfrac{\sqrt{0}}{2} \\[10pt]
\tan \theta & \sqrt{\dfrac{0}{4}} & \sqrt{\dfrac{1}{3}} & \sqrt{\dfrac{2}{2}} & \sqrt{\dfrac{3}{1}} & \sqrt{\dfrac{4}{0}} \;\; \text{(undefined)}
\end{array}
$$

With the help of reference angles, you can find the functions of *any* size angle or arc, provided the angle is a multiple of 30° or 45°.

Objective:
Find *exact* values of the six trigonometric or circular functions if the angle measure is a multiple of 30° or 45°.

EXAMPLE 1

Find the six trigonometric functions of 315°.

Solution:

Since 315° terminates in Quadrant IV, its reference angle is

$$\theta_{\text{ref}} = 360° - 315°$$

$$= 45°.$$

Therefore, an isosceles right triangle can be drawn as shown in Figure 13-3g for which $u = 1$, $v = -1$, and $r = \sqrt{2}$. The value of v is *negative* in Quadrant IV. Using the ratios,

$$\sin 315° = \frac{v}{r} = \frac{-1}{\sqrt{2}} = \underline{\underline{-\frac{\sqrt{2}}{2}}} \qquad \cot 315° = \frac{u}{v} = \frac{1}{-1} = \underline{\underline{-1}}$$

$$\cos 315° = \frac{u}{r} = \frac{1}{\sqrt{2}} = \underline{\underline{\frac{\sqrt{2}}{2}}} \qquad \sec 315° = \frac{r}{u} = \frac{\sqrt{2}}{1} = \underline{\underline{\sqrt{2}}}$$

$$\tan 315° = \frac{v}{u} = \frac{-1}{1} = \underline{\underline{-1}} \qquad \csc 315° = \frac{r}{v} = \frac{\sqrt{2}}{-1} = \underline{\underline{-\sqrt{2}}}$$

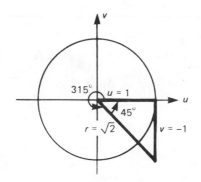

Figure 13-3g

EXAMPLE 2

Find the six circular functions of $\frac{4\pi}{3}$.

Solution:

If $x = \dfrac{4\pi}{3}$, then

$$\theta = \frac{180}{\pi} \cdot \frac{4\pi}{3}$$

$$= 240°.$$

Therefore,

$$\theta_{ref} = 240° - 180°$$

$$= 60°.$$

So you can draw a right triangle for which $u = -1$, $v = -\sqrt{3}$, and $r = 2$, as shown in Figure 13-3h. Using the ratios,

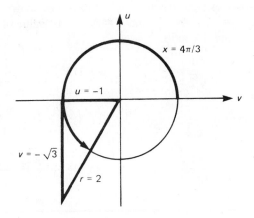

Figure 13-3h

$$\sin \frac{4\pi}{3} = \frac{v}{r} = -\frac{\sqrt{3}}{2} \qquad \cot \frac{4\pi}{3} = \frac{u}{v} = \frac{-1}{-\sqrt{3}} = \frac{\sqrt{3}}{3}$$

$$\cos \frac{4\pi}{3} = \frac{u}{r} = -\frac{1}{2} \qquad \sec \frac{4\pi}{3} = \frac{r}{u} = -2$$

$$\tan \frac{4\pi}{3} = \frac{v}{u} = \frac{-\sqrt{3}}{-1} = \sqrt{3} \qquad \csc \frac{4\pi}{3} = \frac{r}{v} = \frac{2}{-\sqrt{3}} = -\frac{2\sqrt{3}}{3} \qquad ■$$

From the above examples you should be able to see that the *absolute value* of a function is equal to the same function of its *reference angle*. For example,

$$|\sin \theta| = \sin \theta_{ref},$$

or

$$\sin \theta = \pm \sin \theta_{ref}.$$

The proper sign to pick depends on the signs of u and v in the quadrant where θ terminates. As shown in Figure 13-3i, *all* the functions are positive in the *first* quadrant. The *tangent* and its reciprocal are positive in the *third* quadrant. The *cosine* and its reciprocal are positive in the *fourth* quadrant.

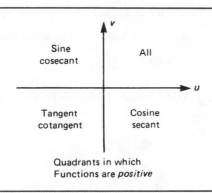

Figure 13-3i ————————————————————————————

The following exercise has two purposes: First, you are to demonstrate your knowledge of the *definitions* of the trigonometric and circular functions and second, you are to get practice in finding *special* values of these functions. These special values will come up frequently throughout your future mathematical career, and you should be comfortable using them.

EXERCISE 13-3

Do These Quickly

The following problems are intended to refresh your skills. You should be able to do all 10 in less than 5 minutes.

Q1. What is the reference angle for 260°?

Q2. Sketch a negative, fourth-quadrant angle.

Q3. Sketch an angle of 30° in standard position.

Q4. Sketch an arc of $\frac{\pi}{3}$ in standard position on a unit circle.

Q5. How many degrees correspond to a unit circle arc of $\frac{\pi}{2}$?

Q6. How long a unit circle arc corresponds to 120°?

Q7. What kind of function has a graph like this?

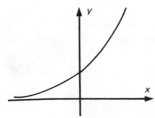

Q8.   What kind of function has a constant slope?

Q9.   What kind of function may have vertical asymptotes?

Q10.   Divide $x^2 + 5x - 6$ by $x - 1$.

For Problems 1 through 6, find exact values of the six trigonometric functions of the given angle.

1. 60°	2. 135°	3. −315°
4. 330°	5. 180°	6. −270°

For Problems 7 through 12, find exact values of the six circular functions of the given argument.

7. $\dfrac{5\pi}{4}$	8. $\dfrac{2\pi}{3}$	9. $\dfrac{5\pi}{6}$
10. $\dfrac{-7\pi}{4}$	11. $\dfrac{-5\pi}{2}$	12. $-\pi$

For Problems 13 through 36, find the exact value of the given trigonometric or circular function. You should try doing this *quickly*, either from memory or by visualizing the diagram in your head.

13. sin 180°	14. sin 225°	15. cos 240°
16. cos 120°	17. tan 315°	18. tan 270°
19. cot 0°	20. cot 300°	21. sec 150°
22. sec 0°	23. csc 45°	24. csc 330°
25. $\sin \dfrac{\pi}{3}$	26. $\sin \dfrac{11\pi}{6}$	27. $\cos \dfrac{3\pi}{4}$
28. $\cos \dfrac{\pi}{4}$	29. $\tan \pi$	30. $\tan \dfrac{3\pi}{4}$
31. $\cot \dfrac{7\pi}{6}$	32. $\cot \pi$	33. $\sec 2\pi$
34. $\sec \dfrac{\pi}{2}$	35. $\csc \dfrac{4\pi}{3}$	36. $\csc \dfrac{2\pi}{3}$

For Problems 37 through 76, evaluate the given expression, leaving the answer in simple radical form. Note that the expression $\sin^2 \theta$ means $(\sin \theta)^2$.

37. sin 30° + cos 60°	38. tan 120° + cot (−30°)
39. tan 300° sec 300°	40. sin 300° csc 300°

41. $12 \sin 45° \cos 45°$

42. $20 \sin 60° \cos 240°$

43. $\cos 45° \sin 210° - \sin 30° \cos 135°$

44. $\cos 180° \cos 45° - \sin 180° \sin 45°$

45. $\tan 30° \cot 30° + \tan 60° \cot 60°$

46. $\sec 60° \tan 135° - \cot 60° \sin 60°$

47. $\cos^2 60° + \sin^2 60°$

48. $\cos^2 150° + \sin^2 150°$

49. $\cot^2 330° - \csc^2 330°$

50. $\tan^2 240° - \sec^2 240°$

51. $\cos^2 45° - \sin^2 135°$

52. $\sin^2 150° + \cos^2 30°$

53. $\dfrac{\sec 30°}{\cos 30°}$

54. $\dfrac{\sin 120°}{\cos 120°}$

55. $\sin^2 30° + \cos^2 30° + \tan^2 30° - \sec^2 30°$

56. $\sin^2 30° + \cos^2 150° + \tan^2 60°$

57. $\sin \dfrac{\pi}{2} + 6 \cos \dfrac{\pi}{3}$

58. $\sin \dfrac{\pi}{3} + 6 \cos \dfrac{\pi}{4}$

59. $\csc \dfrac{\pi}{2} \sin \dfrac{\pi}{2}$

60. $4 \sin \dfrac{4\pi}{3} \cos \dfrac{4\pi}{3}$

61. $4 \sin \dfrac{\pi}{3} \cos \dfrac{\pi}{3}$

62. $\sin \dfrac{\pi}{6} \csc \dfrac{\pi}{6}$

63. $\sin \dfrac{2\pi}{3} \cos \dfrac{5\pi}{6} - \cos \dfrac{2\pi}{3} \sin \dfrac{5\pi}{6}$

64. $\sin \dfrac{2\pi}{3} \cos \dfrac{\pi}{6} + \cos \dfrac{2\pi}{3} \sin \dfrac{\pi}{6}$

65. $\sec \dfrac{\pi}{4} \sin \dfrac{\pi}{4} - \tan \dfrac{3\pi}{4} \csc \dfrac{\pi}{3}$

66. $\sec \dfrac{\pi}{3} \cos \dfrac{\pi}{3} + \tan \dfrac{\pi}{3} \cot \dfrac{\pi}{3}$

67. $\cos^2 \pi + \sin^2 \pi$

68. $\cos^2 \dfrac{2\pi}{3} + \sin^2 \dfrac{2\pi}{3}$

69. $\tan^2 \dfrac{\pi}{6} - \csc^2 \dfrac{\pi}{6}$

70. $\csc^2 \pi - \tan^2 \pi$

71. $\cos^2 \dfrac{3\pi}{4} - \sin^2 \dfrac{\pi}{3}$

72. $\sin^2 \dfrac{7\pi}{6} + \cos^2 \dfrac{\pi}{4}$

73. $\dfrac{\cos \dfrac{5\pi}{3}}{\sin \dfrac{5\pi}{3}}$

74. $\dfrac{\cos \dfrac{\pi}{4}}{\sec \dfrac{\pi}{4}}$

75. $\tan \dfrac{\pi}{6} \cot \dfrac{\pi}{3} + \tan \dfrac{\pi}{4}$

76. $\tan^2 \dfrac{2\pi}{3} \left(1 - \tan^2 \dfrac{7\pi}{6}\right)$

77. Find all values of θ from 0° through 360° for which
     a. $\sin \theta = 0$ b. $\cos \theta = 0$ c. $\tan \theta = 0$
     d. $\cot \theta = 0$ e. $\sec \theta = 0$ f. $\csc \theta = 0$

78. Find all values of θ from 0° through 360° for which
     a. $\sin \theta = 1$ b. $\cos \theta = 1$ c. $\tan \theta = 1$
     d. $\cot \theta = 1$ e. $\sec \theta = 1$ f. $\csc \theta = 1$

79. Find all values of x from 0 through 2π for which
     a. $\sin x = 1$ b. $\cos x = 1$ c. $\tan x = 1$
     d. $\cot x = 1$ e. $\sec x = 1$ f. $\csc x = 1$

80. Find all values of x from 0 through 2π for which
     a. $\sin x = 0$ b. $\cos x = 0$ c. $\tan x = 0$
     d. $\cot x = 0$ e. $\sec x = 0$ f. $\csc x = 0$

81. *Radians*   Dividing a complete revolution into 360° was done be-
     cause there are approximately 360 days in a year. A more natural
     unit of angular measure is called the "radian." The radian measure of
     an angle is defined to be equal to the length of the corresponding arc
     of a unit circle. Using $m° (\theta)$ for the degree and radian measures of
     angle θ, respectively, if $m° (\theta) = 120$, then

$$x = \frac{\pi}{180} \cdot 120$$

$$= \frac{2\pi}{3}$$

$$\therefore m^R (\theta) = \frac{2\pi}{3}.$$

As you can see from Figure 13-3j, the *radian* measure of an angle is equal
to the *arc length*, x, of the unit circle.

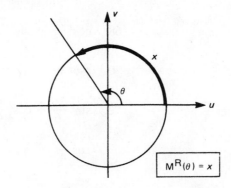

Figure 13-3j

Find the radian measure of each of the following angles.

a. 30°   b. 45°   c. 60°   d. 90°   e. 150°
f. 180°   g. 300°   h. −270°   i. 3000°   j. −1080°

13-4 | APPROXIMATE VALUES OF TRIGONOMETRIC AND CIRCULAR FUNCTIONS

Exact values of the trigonometric and circular functions can be found for certain special arguments such as 30° or $\frac{\pi}{4}$. In this section you will learn how to use a calculator to find decimal approximations for functions of *any* argument. Internally, the calculator uses infinite series, similar to convergent geometric series you studied in Chapter 11, to find these values. The exact values are transcendental numbers, and thus cannot be expressed in terms of a finite number of operations of algebra.

Objectives:
1. Given the degree measure of an angle or length of an arc, find any of the six trigonometric or circular function values.
2. Given a trigonometric or circular function value, find the approximate degree measure of the angle or length of the arc.

EXAMPLE 1

Find the six trigonometric functions of 58.6°.

Solution:
Most calculators have sine, cosine, and tangent built in. To get the other three functions, you must use the fact that they are reciprocals of the values of the first three.

$$\cot \theta = \frac{u}{v} = \frac{1}{\tan \theta}$$

$$\sec \theta = \frac{r}{u} = \frac{1}{\cos \theta}$$

$$\csc \theta = \frac{r}{v} = \frac{1}{\sin \theta}$$

The technique for the first three is to enter the angle, and then press the function key. Make sure *you* can get these answers!

$$\sin 58.6° = \underline{0.853550 \ldots}$$

$$\cos 58.6° = \underline{0.521009 \ldots}$$

$$\tan 58.6° = \underline{1.638262 \ldots}$$

For cotangent press 58.6, tan, reciprocal. The other two are done similarly. Be sure you can get these answers!!

$$\cot 58.6° = \frac{1}{(\tan 58.6°)} = \underline{0.610402 \ldots}$$

$$\sec 58.6° = \frac{1}{(\cos 58.6°)} = \underline{1.919350 \ldots}$$

$$\csc 58.6° = \frac{1}{(\sin 58.6°)} = \underline{1.171576 \ldots}$$ ■

EXAMPLE 2

Find cos 39° 47′.

Solution:
Some calculators allow you to enter an angle in degrees and minutes. If yours does not, then first convert 47′ to decimal degrees by dividing by 60.

$$\cos 39° 47′ = \cos 39.78333 \ldots = \underline{0.768469 \ldots}$$

Note that 4-place decimal approximations for functions in degrees and minutes can also be found in Table III at the back of the book.   ■

EXAMPLE 3

Find sec 4.68.

Solution:
Since the argument has no "degree" sign, this is a *circular* function value. The arc length is the same as the number of *radians* in the corresponding angle. So you first put your calculator in the *radians mode*. Then you proceed just as in Example 1. Make sure you can press the right keys to get the following answer on *your* calculator.

$$\sec. 4.68 = \frac{1}{(\cos 4.68)} = \underline{-30.88009 \ldots}$$

The answer may also be found with the aid of Table IV at the back of the book. You will first have to find the reference *arc* by subtracting π from 4.68. You must then supply the "−" sign in the answer. The arc 4.68 terminates in Quadrant III, and the secant is negative there.   ■

Accomplishing the second objective, finding the angle measure from the function value, involves pressing the *inverse* function keys on the calculator. These are usually marked $\sin^{-1}$, $\cos^{-1}$, and $\tan^{-1}$, and are read, "sine inverse," "cosine inverse," and "tangent inverse," respectively. Their meanings are:

> $\sin^{-1} x$ means, "An angle whose sine is x."
>
> $\cos^{-1} x$ means, "An angle whose cosine is x."
>
> $\tan^{-1} x$ means, "An angle whose tangent is x."
>
> $\cot^{-1} x$ means, "An angle whose cotangent is x."
>
> $\sec^{-1} x$ means, "An angle whose secant is x."
>
> $\csc^{-1} x$ means, "An angle whose cosecant is x."

Note: Do not confuse the expression $\sin^{-1} x$ with the *reciprocal* of $\sin x$. The "-1" exponent here is used to mean the function inverse, not the multiplicative inverse.

EXAMPLE 4

Find the acute angle $\theta = \sin^{-1} 0.3684$ correct to 2 decimal places.

Pressing 0.3684 and then $\sin^{-1}$ gives

$$\theta = \sin^{-1} 0.3684 = 21.61697\ldots^{\circ} \approx \underline{21.62^{\circ}}$$

If desired, the 0.61697 . . . can be converted to minutes by multiplying it by 60, giving

$$\theta = 21°37.018\ldots' \approx \underline{21°37'} \qquad\blacksquare$$

EXAMPLE 5

Find the acute angle $\theta = \sec^{-1} 1.273$ correct to 2 decimal places.

Since there is no $\cot^{-1}$, $\sec^{-1}$, or $\csc^{-1}$ key on most calculators, you must take advantage of the reciprocal properties listed above. If $\sec \theta = 1.273$, then $\cos \theta = \frac{1}{1.273}$. So you take the *reciprocal* of 1.273 first, then press the $\cos^{-1}$ key.

$$\theta = \sec^{-1} 1.273 = \cos^{-1}\left(\frac{1}{1.273}\right)$$

$$= 38.2287\ldots^{\circ} \approx \underline{38.23^{\circ}}$$

Again, if degrees and minutes are desired, multiply the 0.2287 . . . by 60, getting

$$\theta \approx \underline{38°14'}. \qquad\blacksquare$$

EXAMPLE 6

Find the first-quadrant arc $x = \cot^{-1} 1.386$.

Solution:

The computation for a circular function is the same as for the corresponding trig function. You just need to have your calculator in the "radians mode." Since the 1.386 is a value of cotangent, its reciprocal, $\frac{1}{1.386}$, is a value of tangent. Make sure you can get this answer.

$$\cot^{-1} 1.386 = \tan^{-1} \left(\frac{1}{1.386} \right) = \underline{0.625010 \ldots}$$

The sequence of keystrokes is 1.386, reciprocal, inverse tangent.   ■

The following exercise gives you practice finding function values from given arguments, and vice versa.

EXERCISE 13-4

Do These Quickly

The following problems are intended to refresh your skills. You should be able to do all 10 in less than 5 minutes.

Sketch the graph of:

Q1.   A periodic function.

Q2.   A decreasing linear function.

Q3.   An increasing exponential function.

Answer the questions:

Q4.   Which parabola opens in the negative x-direction, $y = -x^2$ or $x = -y^2$?

Q5.   If adding a constant to x multiplies y by a constant, what kind of function is it?

Find the *exact* value of:

Q6. $\cos 180°$

Q7. $\sin \dfrac{\pi}{3}$

Q8.   tan 135°

Q9.   sec $\left(\dfrac{-\pi}{4}\right)$

Q10.   csc 0

For Problems 1 through 20, find the indicated function value. Round to four significant digits.

1.   sin 27.4°

2.   cos 77.9°

3.   tan 48.6°

4.   cot 85.2°

5.   sec 12.3°

6.   csc 4.9°

7.   cos 21° 46′

8.   sin 75° 23′

9.   csc 2° 52′

10.   sec 52° 37′

11.   cot 17° 4′

12.   tan 85° 18′

13.   sin 0.74

14.   cos 1.17

15.   tan 5.3

16.   cot 7.8

17.   sec(−2.5)

18.   csc 5

19.   sin 1

20.   cos 2

For Problems 21 through 32, find the measure of the acute angle θ. Round to two decimal places or to the nearest minute.

21. $\theta = \sin^{-1} 0.4791$

22. $\theta = \sin^{-1} 0.9353$

23. $\theta = \cos^{-1} 0.9125$

24. $\theta = \cos^{-1} 0.5271$

25. $\theta = \tan^{-1} 1.074$

26. $\theta = \tan^{-1} 4.613$

27. $\theta = \cot^{-1} 0.5234$

28. $\theta = \cot^{-1} 1.452$

29. $\theta = \sec^{-1} 2.581$

30. $\theta = \sec^{-1} 3.000$

31. $\theta = \csc^{-1} 1.062$

32. $\theta = \csc^{-1} 1.234$

For Problems 33 through 40, find the argument x (between 0 and $\frac{\pi}{2}$). Round to 4 decimal places.

33. $x = \sin^{-1} 0.6210$

34. $x = \cos^{-1} 0.2092$

35. $x = \cot^{-1} 1.345$

36. $x = \tan^{-1} 3.482$

37. $x = \sec^{-1} 3.7$

38. $x = \csc^{-1} 10$

39. $x = \cos^{-1} 0.8458$

40. $x = \sin^{-1} 0.3651$

41.   On a computer screen or a piece of graph paper using a large scale, plot a circle of radius 1 unit. Then plot an angle of measure 26° in standard position. Do the following:

a.   Measure the u- and v-coordinates of the point where the terminal side of the angle crosses the circle. Confirm that these values are, approximately, the cosine and sine of 26°.

b. Divide the coordinates of the point in part (a), vertical over hori-
    zontal. Confirm that the answer is, approximately, tan 26°.

42. Repeat Problem 41 for an angle of 107°.

43. *The Wrapping Function*   Figure 13-4a shows an *x*-axis wrapped
    around the unit circle $u^2 + v^2 = 1$ in the *uv*-coordinate system. For
    each number *x* on the number line, there is a unique point (u, v) on
    the circle. Thus, the point on the circle is a *function* of *x*. This func-
    tion is called the *wrapping function, W,* defined by

$$W(x) = (u, v)$$

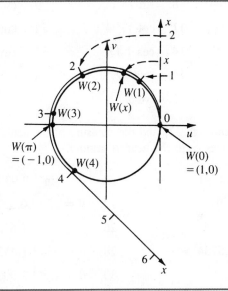

Figure 13-4a _____

As shown in Figure 13-4a,

$$W(0) = (1, 0)$$

$$W(\pi) = (-1, 0)$$

and so forth. Answer the following questions.

a. Find $W\left(\frac{\pi}{2}\right)$, $W\left(\frac{3\pi}{2}\right)$, $W\left(-\frac{\pi}{2}\right)$, and $W(2\pi)$.
b. True or false: For each point on the unit circle, there is a unique
    value of *x*. Explain.
c. Explain why $W(x) = (\cos x, \sin x)$.
d. Find exact values of $W\left(\frac{\pi}{3}\right)$, $W\left(\frac{5\pi}{6}\right)$, and $W\left(-\frac{3\pi}{4}\right)$.
e. Find decimal approximations for $W(5)$ and $W(-2.37)$.
f. Explain why $(0.6, 0.8)$ *can* be a value of $W(x)$, but $(0.3, 0.9)$
    cannot.

g.   Find three possible values of x for which $W(x) = (0.6, 0.8)$.
h.   Given $W(x) = (0.28, 0.96)$, find $W(x + \pi)$, $W(-x)$, and $W(2\pi + x)$.

| 13-5 | GRAPHS OF TRIGONOMETRIC AND CIRCULAR FUNCTIONS |

You have defined six new functions and know how to find their values. The next step in the study of a new kind of function is to see what the graphs look like.

As you have done with other functions, you will first draw the graphs accurately by pointwise plotting. Then you will identify features that will allow you to *sketch* the graphs *quickly*.

Objective:
Be able to draw graphs of the six trigonometric or circular functions

a.   *accurately,* by pointwise plotting, and
b.   *quickly,* by finding certain "critical points."

Start by drawing the graphs of $y = \cos x$ and $y = \sin x$. Since the values of $\cos x$ repeat themselves each 2π units of x, it is convenient to mark off the x-axis in multiples of π. For both graphs, y will range from -1 to 1. The easiest values to plot are those for x equals multiples of $\frac{\pi}{2}$. These "critical" values will be either 1, 0, or -1. You can recall them quickly by thinking of the unit circle. The points are plotted in Figure 13-5a. In that graph, one space in the x-direction represents $\frac{\pi}{6}$ units of x.

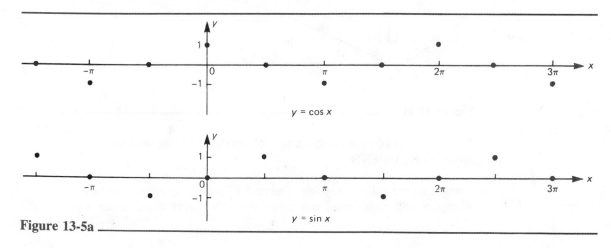

Figure 13-5a

To see what the graph looks like *between* these points, recall the *special* values

$$\cos \frac{\pi}{6} = \frac{\sqrt{3}}{2} \approx 0.87 \qquad \sin \frac{\pi}{6} = \frac{1}{2} = 0.5$$

$$\cos \frac{\pi}{4} = \frac{\sqrt{2}}{2} \approx 0.71 \qquad \sin \frac{\pi}{4} = \frac{\sqrt{2}}{2} \approx 0.71$$

$$\cos \frac{\pi}{3} = \frac{1}{2} = 0.5 \qquad \sin \frac{\pi}{3} = \frac{\sqrt{3}}{2} \approx 0.87$$

Figure 13-5b shows these values plotted on an expanded portion of Figure 13-5a.

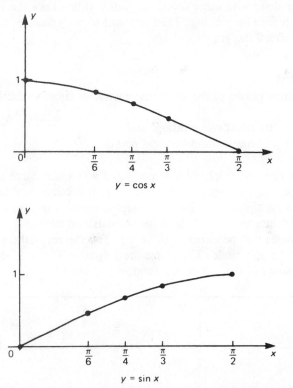

$y = \cos x$

$y = \sin x$

Figure 13-5b

The remainder of each graph consists of repetitions of these curves, as shown in Figure 13-5c.

The graphs are called *sinusoids*. The prefix "sinus-" is pronounced like what gets stopped up when you have a cold. The suffix "-oid" means "like."

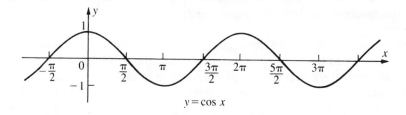

$$y = \cos x$$

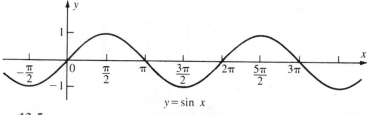

$$y = \sin x$$

Figure 13-5c ─────────────────────────────────

Certain features of these graphs are given special names, as shown in Figure 13-5d.

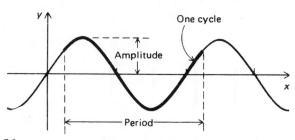

Figure 13-5d ─────────────────────────────────

DEFINITIONS

A **cycle** of a periodic function is a portion of the graph from one point to the point at which the graph starts repeating itself.

The **period,** p, of a periodic function is the change in x corresponding to one cycle. That is, $f(x + p) = f(x)$ for all values of x.

The **amplitude** of a sinusoid is the distance from its axis to a high point or a low point.

For both sine and cosine, the amplitude is 1 and the period is 2π (for circular functions) or $360°$ (for trigonometric functions).

The graphs of the other four functions can also be drawn by pointwise plotting. Since the function is *undefined* when the denominator of the ratio equals zero, there will be a *vertical asymptote* at each such value of x or θ. The graphs of the four circular functions are shown in Figure 13-5e. The graphs of the trigonometric functions are similar, except that the horizontal axis is marked in *degrees* instead of units of arc length.

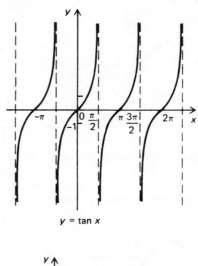

$y = \tan x$

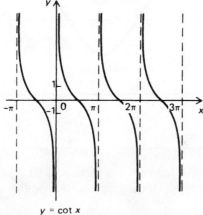

$y = \cot x$

Figure 13-5e

The period of secant and cosecant is 2π or $360°$, as it was for the sine and cosine. However, the period of the tangent and cotangent is only π or $180°$. None of these functions has an amplitude.

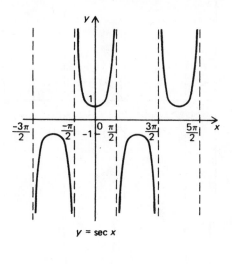

$y = \sec x$

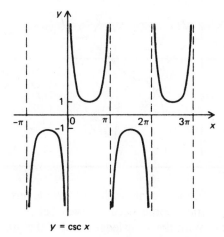

$y = \csc x$

Figure 13-5f _____

Once you know the shapes of the graphs, you can sketch them by finding asymptotes and critical points.

EXAMPLE

Sketch two cycles of the graph of $y = \sec \theta$.

Sec θ is the *reciprocal* of cos θ since sec $\theta = \frac{r}{u}$ and cos $\theta = \frac{u}{r}$. It helps to sketch lightly the graph of $y = \cos \theta$ first, as in the left side of Figure 13-5g.

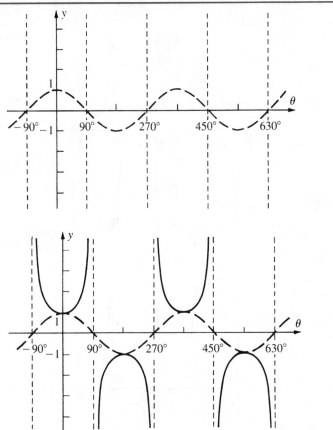

Figure 13-5g

Each place cos $\theta = 0$, the secant graph will have a vertical asymptote, so
you sketch these. Critical points occur halfway between each asymptote,
where sec $\theta = \pm 1$. With the knowledge of what the graph looks like, you
can sketch it as shown in the right side of Figure 13-5g. ■

The following exercise is designed to let you find out the exact shapes of
the graphs of the six functions by pointwise plotting. Then you will use
critical features to sketch these graphs quickly.

EXERCISE 13-5

Do These Quickly

The following problems are intended to refresh your skills. You should be
able to do all 10 in less than 5 minutes.

Find the exact value of:

Q1.   tan 120°

Q2.   sec $\dfrac{\pi}{2}$

Q3.   sin 270°

Find the acute angle:

Q4. $\sin^{-1} 0.5$

Q5. $\cot^{-1} \sqrt{3}$

Find the arc length between 0 and $\dfrac{\pi}{2}$:

Q6. $\cos^{-1} 0.5$

Q7. $\tan^{-1} 1$

Sketch the graph:

Q8. $y = x$

Q9. $y = x^2$

Q10. $y = 2^x$

Work the following problems.

1.   Carefully plot the graphs of the six trigonometric functions for each
     10° from $\theta = 0°$ to $\theta = 90°$. You should choose scales so that the
     graphs are fairly *large*. It is *not* necessary to use the same scale for
     both the y-axis and the θ-axis. Connect the points with smooth
     curves.

2.   Carefully plot the graphs of the six circular functions for each 0.2
     units from $x = 0$ to $x = \frac{\pi}{2}$. Choose as large a scale as possible, and
     use the *same* scale for both axes. Connect the points with smooth
     curves.

For Problems 3 through 14, sketch *quickly* two complete cycles of the
trigonometric or circular function graph. Do this by locating critical features such as high or low points and asymptotes. After you have sketched
the graph, look back at this section to make sure you are correct. If not,
then redraw your graphs.

3. $y = \sin \theta$ 4. $y = \cos \theta$

5. $y = \tan \theta$ 6. $y = \cot \theta$

7. $y = \sec \theta$ 8. $y = \csc \theta$

9. $y = \cos x$ 10. $y = \sin x$

11. $y = \cot x$ 12. $y = \tan x$

13. $y = \csc x$ 14. $y = \sec x$

In Problems 15 through 19, you will try to discover what happens to the period and amplitude of a sinusoid when *constants* are introduced at various places in the equation. Plot each graph using the *same* scales, but four *different* sets of axes.

15. $y = \sin x$

16. $y = 3 \sin x$ (Find sin x *first*, then multiply by 3.)

17. $y = \sin 2x$ (Multiply x by 2 *first*, then find the sine of the resulting argument.)

18. $y = 3 \sin 2x$

19. For the equation $y = A \sin Bx$, describe the effects of the multiplicative constants A and B on the graph.

13-6   GENERAL SINUSOIDAL GRAPHS

Many periodic phenomena have graphs that look like sinusoids. For example, the time of sunrise as a function of the day of the year has a graph that looks like Figure 13-6a.

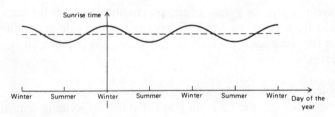

Figure 13-6a

In order to use sinusoidal functions as mathematical models for these phenomena, you must be able to graph sinusoids that have periods other than 2π or 360° and amplitudes other than 1. You must also be able to position the graph away from the horizontal axis.

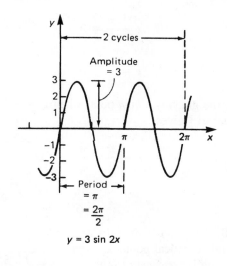

$$y = 3 \sin 2x$$

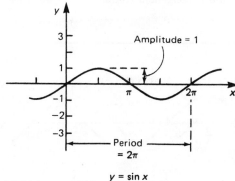

$$y = \sin x$$

Figure 13-6b _____

Figure 13-6b shows the graph of $y = 3 \sin 2x$. The graph of $y = \sin x$ is also drawn for comparison. The coefficient of 3 has the effect of "stretching out" the graph in the vertical direction. Thus, the amplitude of $y = 3 \sin 2x$ is 3. The factor of 2 in the argument tells the number of cycles the graph makes in 2π units of x. Thus, the period of $y = 3 \sin 2x$ is $p = \frac{2\pi}{2}$, or π units.

Suppose that you are to graph

$$y = \cos\left(x - \frac{\pi}{3}\right).$$

To find critical points on the graph, you need to find values of x that make the argument $(x - \frac{\pi}{3})$ equal to 0, $\frac{\pi}{2}$, π, $\frac{3\pi}{2}$, 2π, and so forth. Setting the

argument equal to 0,

$$x - \frac{\pi}{3} = 0$$

$$x = \frac{\pi}{3}.$$

Since cos 0 = 1, the graph is a *high* point when $x = \frac{\pi}{3}$. Similarly, setting the argument equal to $\frac{\pi}{2}$ gives

$$x - \frac{\pi}{3} = \frac{\pi}{2}$$

$$x = \frac{5\pi}{6}.$$

Since cos $\left(\frac{\pi}{2}\right) = 0$, the graph crosses the axis at $x = \frac{5\pi}{6}$. By similar reasoning, you can get other critical points and draw the graph as shown in Figure 13-6c. The graph is *congruent* to that of $y = \cos x$, but is *displaced* $\frac{\pi}{3}$ units to the right.

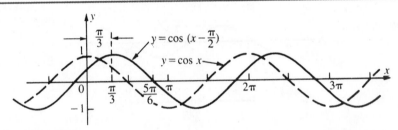

Figure 13-6c

CONCLUSION

If $y = \cos (x - D)$, then the graph is congruent to that of $y = \cos x$, but is *displaced D* units in the x-direction.

The constant D is called the *phase displacement*.

Now, suppose that you must graph

$$y = 3 + \cos x.$$

Each point will be 3 units *higher* than the corresponding point on the graph of $y = \cos x$, as shown in Figure 13-6d.

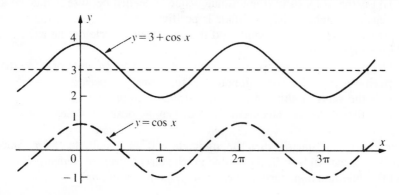

Figure 13-6d

CONCLUSION

If $y = C + \cos x$, then the *sinusoidal axis* (see Figure 13-6d) is C units above the x-axis.

Drawing together the above conclusions, the *general* sinusoidal equation is

$$y = C + A \cos B (x - D).$$

A graph of this equation is shown in Figure 13-6e.

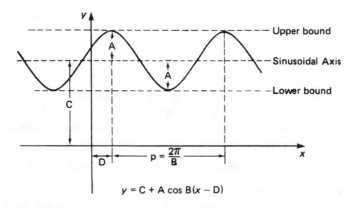

Figure 13-6e

The effects of the four constants A, B, C, and D are shown on the graph. The names are summarized as follows.

1. $|A|$ is the **amplitude** (the absolute value is needed because A may be a negative number, and amplitude is positive). If A is negative, the cosine starts a cycle at a *low* point, and the sine starts a cycle on the axis, but going *downward*.
2. $|B|$ is the number of cycles the sinusoid makes in 2π units of x, so the **period** is $p = \frac{2\pi}{|B|}$. For trigonometric functions, the period is $p = \frac{360°}{|B|}$.
3. C is the **vertical shift**. It may be positive or negative.
4. D is the **phase displacement**. It, too, may be positive or negative.

Note: A cycle "starts" when the argument is 0, or a multiple of 2π. Since $\cos 0 = 1$ and $\sin 0 = 0$, the cosine graph starts a cycle at a *high* point and the sine function starts a cycle at a *midpoint*, going *up*.

These conclusions allow you to accomplish the following objective.

Objective:
Given the equation of a particular sinusoid, sketch the graph *quickly*.

EXAMPLE 1

Sketch the graph of

$$y = 5 + 3 \cos \frac{1}{4}(x + \pi).$$

Solution:
An efficient stepwise procedure for drawing the graph is:

1. Draw the sinusoidal axis at $y = 5$.
2. Draw upper and lower bounds by going 3 units above and below the sinusoidal axis, since the amplitude is 3.
3. Find the starting point of a cycle at $x = -\pi$, the phase displacement. Cosine starts a cycle at a *high* point.
4. The period is $\frac{2\pi}{\left(\frac{1}{4}\right)}$, which equals 8π. So the cycle will end 8π units down the x-axis, at $x = 7\pi$.
5. Halfway between these two high points there is a low point. Halfway between each high and low point the graph crosses the sinusoidal axis.
6. Sketch the graph going through these critical points.

The graph is shown in Figure 13-6f.

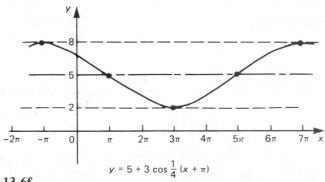

$$y = 5 + 3 \cos \frac{1}{4}(x + \pi)$$

Figure 13-6f _____ ∎

EXAMPLE 2

Sketch the graph of

$$y = -2 + 4 \sin \frac{\pi}{5}(x - 3).$$

Solution:
The period is

$$p = \frac{2\pi}{\frac{\pi}{5}} = 10.$$

Notice that when B is a multiple of π, the π's will cancel, and the period will *not* be a multiple of π. In this case, the x-axis can be marked in more familiar units.

The sinusoidal axis is at $y = -2$. The upper and lower bounds are 4 units above and below this sinusoidal axis. A cycle starts at $x = 3$, the phase displacement. Since this is the *sine* function, the graph starts at a *mid-point*, going *up*. The end of this cycle is at $x = (3 + 10) = 13$. Again, there are critical points each $\frac{1}{4}$-cycle. The graph is shown in Figure 13-6g.

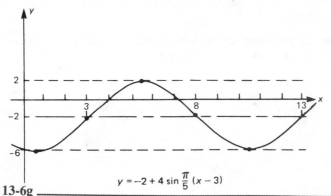

Figure 13-6g _____ $y = -2 + 4 \sin \frac{\pi}{5}(x - 3)$ _____ ∎

EXAMPLE 3

Sketch the graph of the trigonometric function $y = -5 + 7 \cos 30(\theta + 4°)$.

Solution:

The only way the trigonometric function graphs differ from the circular functions is that the horizontal axis is labeled in degrees. The period is

$$p = \frac{360°}{30} = 12°.$$

Since the phase displacement is $-4°$, the graph starts with a high point at $\theta = -4°$, and has its next high point at $\theta = (-4 + 12)° = 8°$. The sinusoidal axis is at $y = -5$, and the amplitude is 7. The graph is shown in Figure 13-6h.

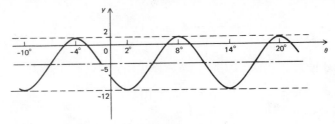

$$y = -5 + 7 \cos 30(\theta + 4°)$$

Figure 13-6h

The exercise that follows is designed to give you practice in sketching the graphs of sinusoids.

EXERCISE 13-6

Do These Quickly

The following problems are intended to refresh your skills. You should be able to do all 10 in less than 5 minutes.

Sketch the graph:

Q1. $y = \sin x$

Q2. $y = \tan x$

Q3. $y = \sec x$

Q4. $y = 0.5x$

Find the exact value:

Q5. $\sec \dfrac{3\pi}{4}$

Q6. $\csc 30°$

Q7. $\tan 2\pi$

Q8. $\theta = \cos^{-1} \dfrac{\sqrt{3}}{2}$

Q9. $x = \cot^{-1} 1$

Q10.   Find the approximate value: $\cot 35°$

For Problems 1 through 14, sketch the graph of the indicated trigonometric or circular function. You may use different scales on the horizontal and vertical axes, if necessary, to make the graphs have reasonable proportions.

1. $y = 5 + 2 \cos 3(\theta - 20°)$

2. $y = 3 + 4 \cos 5(\theta - 10°)$

3. $y = -3 + 4 \sin 10(\theta + 5°)$

4. $y = -1 + 3 \sin 12(\theta + 6°)$

5. $y = 3 + 2 \cos \dfrac{1}{5}(x - \pi)$

6. $y = 7 + 3 \cos \dfrac{1}{4}(x - 3\pi)$

7. $y = -4 + 5 \sin \dfrac{2}{3}\left(x + \dfrac{\pi}{2}\right)$

8. $y = -5 + 4 \sin \dfrac{1}{3}\left(x + \dfrac{\pi}{2}\right)$

9. $y = -10 + 20 \cos \dfrac{\pi}{3}(x - 1)$

10. $y = 2 + 6 \cos \dfrac{\pi}{4}(x - 3)$

11. $y = 3 + 5 \sin \dfrac{\pi}{4}(x - 3)$

12. $y = -6 + 7 \sin \dfrac{\pi}{4}(x - 2)$

13. $y = 100 + 150 \cos \pi(x + 0.7)$

14. $y = 1 + \cos \pi(x + 0.3)$

15. By *reversing* the graphing process you did above, you should be able to find the particular equation of a sinusoid from a given graph. Demonstrate that you can do this by writing the particular equation of the following sinusoid:

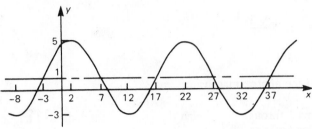

Figure 13-6i _____

13-7 | **EQUATIONS OF SINUSOIDS FROM THEIR GRAPHS**

Now that you know the effects of the four constants A, B, C, and D on the graph of the general equation $y = C + A \cos B(x - D)$, you are ready to use such sinusoidal functions as mathematical models. In order to do this, you must be able to write the *particular* equation that has the right period, amplitude, phase, and vertical placement.

Objective:
Given the graph of a sinusoidal function or information about the graph, write the particular equation.

EXAMPLE

Write the particular equation of the sinusoid in Figure 13-7a.

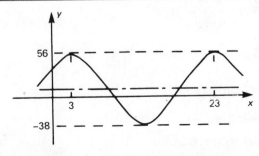

Figure 13-7a _____

Solution:
Your reasoning should be as follows:

1. It is easier to use the *cosine* function since a cycle starts at a *high* point. So the general equation is

$$y = C + A \cos B(x - D).$$

2. One cycle starts at $x = 3$ and ends at $x = 23$. So the period is $p = 23 - 3 = 20$. Therefore,

$$B = \frac{2\pi}{p} = \frac{2\pi}{20} = \frac{\pi}{10}.$$

3. The sinusoidal axis is halfway between the upper bound, 56, and the lower bound, -38. So the vertical shift is the *average* of 56 and -38. Therefore,

$$C = \frac{1}{2}(56 + (-38)) = \frac{1}{2}(18) = 9.$$

4. The amplitude is the distance between the sinusoidal axis and the upper bound. Therefore,

$$A = 56 - 9 = 47.$$

5. Using the cosine function, the phase displacement is 3. Therefore, $D = 3$.

6. Having found the four constants, you can write the equation:

$$y = 9 + 47 \cos \frac{\pi}{10}(x - 3).$$

If the horizontal axis had been labeled in *degrees,* the function would be *trigonometric,* and the variable would (probably) have been θ. In this case, the period would be $20°$, and the value of B would be

$$B = \frac{360°}{20°} = 18.$$

The equation would be $y = 9 + 47 \cos 18(\theta - 3°)$. ■

The exercise that follows is designed to give you practice finding particular equations from the graph or from information about the graph.

EXERCISE 13-7

Do These Quickly

The following problems are intended to refresh your skills. You should be able to do all 10 in less than 5 minutes.

For $y = 2 + 3 \cos 4(x - 5)$, what is the:

Q1.   period?

Q2.   amplitude?

Q3.   sinusoidal axis location?

Q4.   phase displacement?

Answer the following:

Q5.   Sketch the graph of $y = \cos x$.

Q6.   Find the exact value of $\sin \dfrac{2\pi}{3}$.

Q7.   Find the approximate value of $\cot 0.3°$.

Q8.   Find the reference angle of $253°$.

Q9.   Find the x-coordinate of the vertex of $y = x^2 + 7$.

Q10.   Find the prime factors of 51.

For Problems 1 through 14, write the particular equation of the sinusoid sketched.

1.

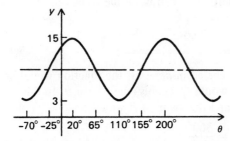

2.

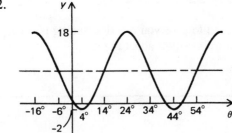

3.

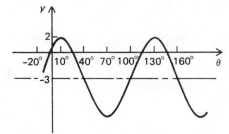

4.

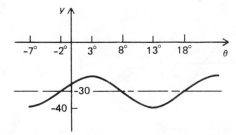

5.

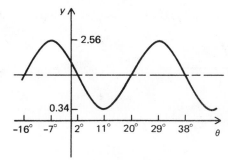

6.

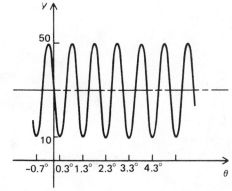

7.

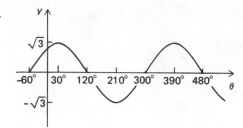

8.

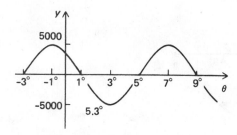

9.

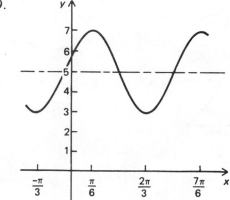

10.

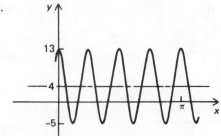

11.

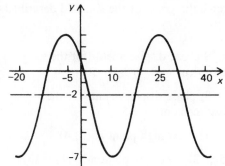

12.

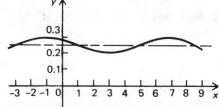

13.

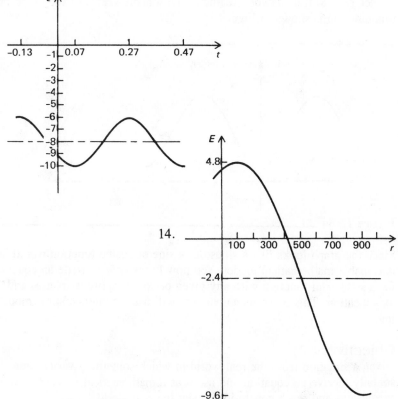

14.

For Problems 15 through 18, sketch the graph of the sinusoid described. Then write the particular equation.

15. Period = 12, amplitude = 7, phase displacement (for the cosine) = 5, vertical displacement = 3.

16. Period = 0.1, amplitude = 8, phase displacement (for the cosine) = 0.02, vertical displacement = −5.

17. Low point at $(x, y) = (2, -1)$, next high point at $(5, 4)$.

18. High point at $(r, s) = (-5, -3)$, next low point at $(-1, -13)$.

13-8 | SINUSOIDAL FUNCTIONS AS MATHEMATICAL MODELS

In Section 13-1 you found several real-world situations in which a dependent variable repeated its values at regular intervals as the independent variable changed. For example, the volume of air in your lungs varies periodically with time as you breathe. A reasonable sketch of the graph of this function is shown in Figure 13-8a.

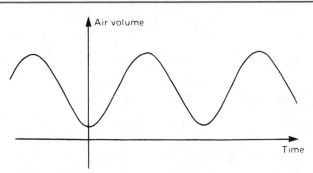

Figure 13-8a _____

Since the graph looks like a sinusoid, a sine or cosine function would be a reasonable mathematical model. You now know how to write an equation for a sinusoidal function with any given period, amplitude, phase, and axis location. This is the technique you will use for mathematical modeling.

Objective:
Given a situation from the real world in which something varies sinusoidally, derive an equation and use it as a mathematical model to make predictions and reach conclusions about the real world.

EXAMPLE

Suppose that the waterwheel in Figure 13-8b rotates at 6 revolutions per minute (rpm). You start your stopwatch. Two seconds later, point P on the rim of the wheel is at its greatest height. You are to model the distance d of point P from the surface of the water in terms of the number of seconds t the stopwatch reads.

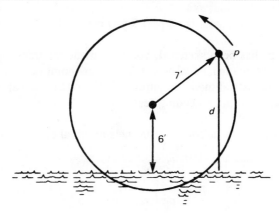

Figure 13-8b _____

Solution:
Assuming that d varies sinusoidally with t, you can sketch a graph as in Figure 13-8c. Your thought process should be:

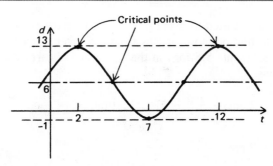

Figure 13-8c _____

1. The sinusoidal axis is 6 units above the t-axis, because the center of the waterwheel is 6 feet above the surface of the water.
2. The amplitude is 7 units, since the point P goes 7 feet above and 7 feet below the center of the wheel.
3. Therefore, the upper and lower bounds of the graph are $6 + 7 = 13$, and $6 - 7 = -1$.

4. The point P was at its highest when the stopwatch read 2 seconds. Thus, the phase displacement (for the cosine) is 2 units.
5. The period is 10 seconds, since the waterwheel makes 6 complete revolutions every 60 seconds (1 minute).
6. Therefore, the sinusoid reaches its next high point at $2 + 10 = 12$ units on the t-axis.
7. Halfway between two high points there is a low point at $t = \frac{1}{2}(2 + 12) = 7$; halfway between each high and low point the graph crosses the sinusoidal axis.
8. With the critical points from part 7 you can sketch the graph.

Once the graph has been sketched, you have made the transition from the real world to the mathematical world. From this point on, completing and using the mathematical model requires only the mathematical techniques you have learned in the preceding sections.

From the graph, the four constants in the sinusoidal equation are

$$A = 7,$$

$$B = \frac{2\pi}{\text{period}} = \frac{2\pi}{10} = \frac{\pi}{5},$$

$$C = 6,$$

$$D = 2.$$

The equation is therefore

$$d = 6 + 7 \cos \frac{\pi}{5} (t - 2).$$

The equation can be used to make predictions of d for given values of t. For example, to find out how far P is from the water when $t = 5.5$, you would simply substitute 5.5 for t in the equation and carry out the indicated operations.

$d = 6 + 7 \cos \dfrac{\pi}{5} (5.5 - 2)$ Substitution

$ = 6 + 7 \cos \dfrac{3.5\pi}{5}$ Arithmetic

$ = 6 + 7 \cos 0.7\pi$ More arithmetic

$ \approx 6 + 7(-0.5878)$ By calculator or by the methods of Section 13-4

$ = 1.8854$

So the point is <u>about 1.9 feet</u> above the water when $t = 5.5$.   ■

The exercise that follows is designed to give you practice using sinusoidal functions as mathematical models. In doing so, you will use most of the trigonometric techniques you have learned so far, as well as a lot of algebraic techniques you have learned in the past.

EXERCISE 13-8

Do These Quickly

The following problems are intended to refresh your skills. You should be able to do all 10 in less than 5 minutes.

For the sinusoid shown, what is:

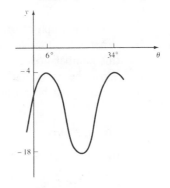

Q1.   the period?

Q2.   the amplitude?

Q3.   the phase displacement for the cosine?

Q4.   the phase displacement for the sine?

Q5.   the sinusoidal axis location?

Answer the questions:

Q6.   Find a *second* quadrant angle whose sine is 0.3.

Q7.   How long is the shorter leg of a 30°, 60° right triangle if the hypotenuse is $2\sqrt{3}$ cm?

Q8.   What function is the reciprocal of the cosine function?

Q9.   Evalaute $\sin^2 47° + \cos^2 47°$.

Q10.   Evaluate $\theta = \sin^{-1} 2\pi$.

Work the following problems.

1.   *Ferris Wheel Problem* As you ride the Ferris wheel, your distance from the ground varies sinusoidally with time. When the last seat is filled and the Ferris wheel starts, your seat is at the position shown in Figure 13-8d. Let t be the number of seconds that have elapsed since the Ferris wheel started. You find that it takes you 3 seconds to reach the top, 43 feet above the ground, and that the wheel makes a revolution once every 8 seconds. The diameter of the wheel is 40 feet.

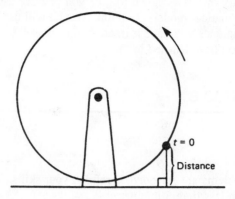

Figure 13-8d _____

    a.   Sketch a graph of this sinusoid.

    b.   What is the lowest you go as the Ferris wheel turns, and why is this number greater than zero?

    c.   Write the particular equation of this sinusoid.

    d.   Predict your height above the ground when

        i. $t = 6$,

       ii. $t = 4\frac{1}{3}$,

      iii. $t = 9$,

      iv. $t = 0$.

2.   ***Bouncing Spring Problem***   A weight attached to the end of a long spring is bouncing up and down (Figure 13-8e). As it bounces, its distance from the floor varies sinusoidally with time. You start a

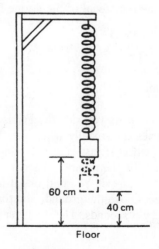

Figure 13-8e _____

stopwatch. When the stopwatch reads 0.3 second, the weight first reaches a high point 60 centimeters above the floor. The next low point, 40 centimeters above the floor, occurs at 1.8 seconds.

a. Sketch a graph of this sinusoidal function.

b. Write the particular equation expressing distance from the floor in terms of the number of seconds the stopwatch reads.

c. Predict the distance from the floor when the stopwatch reads 17.2 seconds.

d. What was the distance from the floor when you started the stopwatch?

3. **Tidal Wave Problem** A tsunami (commonly called a "tidal wave" because its effect is like a rapid change in tide) is a fast-moving ocean wave caused by an underwater earthquake. The water first goes down from its normal level, then rises an equal distance above its normal level, and finally returns to its normal level. The period is about 15 minutes.

Suppose that a tsunami with an amplitude of 10 meters approaches the pier at Honolulu, where the normal depth of the water is 9 meters.

a. Assuming that the depth of the water varies sinusoidally with time as the tsunami passes, predict the depth of the water at the following times after the tsunami first reaches the pier:

   i. 2 minutes.

   ii. 4 minutes.

   iii. 12 minutes.

b. According to your model, what will the *minimum* depth of the water be? How do you interpret this answer in terms of what will happen in the real world?

c. The "wavelength" of a wave is the distance a crest of the wave travels in one period. It is also equal to the distance between two adjacent crests. If a tsunami travels at 1200 kilometers per hour, what is its wavelength?

d. If you were far from land on a ship at sea and a tsunami was approaching your ship, what would you *see*? Explain.

4. **Tarzan Problem** Tarzan is swinging back and forth on his grapevine. As he swings, he goes back and forth across the river bank, going alternately over land and water (Figure 13-8f.) Jane decides to mathematically model his motion and starts her stopwatch. Let t be the number of meters Tarzan is from the river bank. Assume that y varies sinusoidally with t, and that y is positive when Tarzan is over water and negative when he is over land.

Jane finds that when $t = 2$, Tarzan is at one end of his swing, where $y = -23$. She finds that when $t = 5$ he reaches the other end of his swing and $y = 17$.

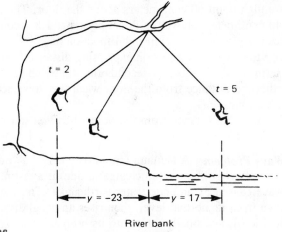

Figure 13-8f _____

a. Sketch a graph of this sinusoidal function.
b. Write the particular equation expressing Tarzan's distance from the river bank in terms of t.
c. Predict y when
    i. $t = 2.8$,
    ii. $t = 6.3$,
    iii. $t = 15$.
d. Where was Tarzan when Jane started the stopwatch?

5. *Pebble-in-the-Tire Problem*   As you stop your car at a traffic light, a pebble becomes wedged between the tire treads. When you start off, the distance of the pebble from the pavement varies sinusoidally with the distance you have traveled. The period is, of course, the circumference of the wheel. Assume that the diameter of the wheel is 24 inches.
a. Sketch a graph of this function.
b. Write the particular equation of this function. Be sure to use a *circular* function. It is possible to get a form of the equation that has *zero* phase displacement.
c. Predict the distance from the pavement when you have gone 15 inches.

6. *Spaceship Problem*   When a spaceship is fired into orbit from a site such as Cape Canaveral, which is not on the equator, it goes into an orbit that takes it alternately north and south of the equator. Its distance from the equator is approximately sinusoidal function of time.

Suppose that a spaceship is fired into orbit from Cape Canaveral. Ten minutes after it leaves the Cape, it reaches its farthest distance *north* of the equator, 4000 kilometers. Half a cycle later it reaches its farthest distance *south* of the equator (on the other side of the Earth, of course!), also 4000 kilometers. The spaceship completes an orbit once every 90 minutes.

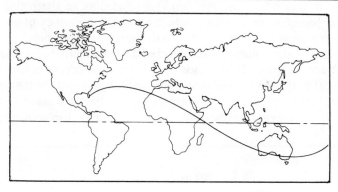

Figure 13-8g ───────────────────────────────

Let y be the number of kilometers the spaceship is *north* of the equator (you may consider distances south of the equator to be negative). Let t be the number of minutes that have elapsed since liftoff.

a.   Sketch a complete cycle of the graph of y versus t.
b.   Write the particular equation expressing y in terms of t.
c.   Use your equation to predict the distance of the spaceship from the equator when
  i. $t = 25$,
  ii. $t = 41$,
  iii. $t = 163$.
d.   Calculate the distance of Cape Canaveral from the equator by calculating y when $t = 0$.
e.   See if you can find how far Cape Canaveral *really* is from the equator to see if the model gives reasonably accurate answers.

7. *Electric Current Problem*   The electricity supplied to your house is called "alternating current" because the current varies sinusoidally with time (Figure 13-8h.). The frequency of the sinusoid is 60 cycles per second. Suppose that at time $t = 0$ seconds the current is at its maximum, $i = 5$ amperes.

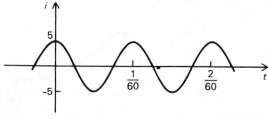

Figure 13-8h ───────────────────────────────

a. Write an equation expressing current in terms of time.
b. What is the current when $t = 0.01$?

8. ***Electrical Voltage Problem***   The alternating electrical current sup-
    plied to your house (see Problem 7) is created by an alternating elec-
    trical potential, or "voltage," which also has a frequency of 60 cy-
    cles per second. For reasons you will learn when you study
    electricity, the voltage usually reaches a peak slightly before the cur-
    rent does (Figure 13-8i). Since the voltage peak occurs *before* the
    current peak, the voltage is said to "lead" the current, or the current
    "lags" the voltage. Leading corresponds to a *negative* phase displace-
    ment, and lagging corresponds to a *positive* phase displacement.

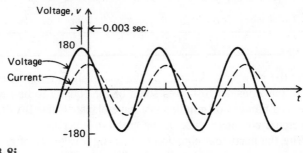

Figure 13-8i

a. Suppose that the peak voltage is 180 volts and that the voltage
    leads the current by 0.003 seconds. Write an equation expressing
    voltage in terms of time. (Note that the "115 volts" supplied to
    your house is an *average* value, whereas the 180 volts is the
    peak value.)
b. Predict the voltage when the current is a maximum.

9. ***Roller Coaster Problem***   A portion of a roller coaster track is to be
    built in the shape of a sinusoid (Figure 13-8j). You have been hired
    to calculate the lengths of the vertical timber supports to be used.

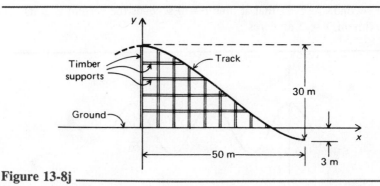

Figure 13-8j

a. The high and low points on the track are separated by 50 meters horizontally and by 30 meters vertically. The low point is 3 meters below the ground. Letting y be the number of meters the track is above the ground and x be the number of meters horizontally from the high point, write the particular equation expressing y in terms of x.

b. How long is the vertical timber at the high point? At $x = 4$ meters? At $x = 32$ meters?

c. The vertical timbers are spaced every 2 meters, starting at $x = 0$ and ending where the track goes below the ground. Write a computer program which prints out the length of each timber. The program should also print the total length of all the vertical timbers, so that you will know how much to purchase.

10. **Rock Formation Problem** An old rock formation is warped into the shape of a sinusoid. Over the centuries, the top has eroded away, leaving the ground with a flat surface from which various layers of rock are cropping out (Figure 13-8k).

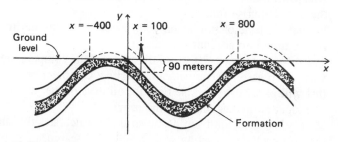

Figure 13-8k

Since you have studied sinusoids, the geologists call upon you to predict the depth of a particular formation at various points. You construct an x-axis along the ground and a y-axis at the edge of an outcropping, as shown. A hole drilled at $x = 100$ meters shows that the top of the formation is 90 meters deep at that point.

a. Write the particular equation expressing the y-coordinate of the formation in terms of x.

b. If a hole were drilled to the top of the formation at $x = 510$, how deep would it be?

c. What is the maximum depth of the top of the formation, and what is the value of x where it reaches this depth?

d. How high above the present ground level did the formation go before it eroded away?

e. The geologists decide to drill holes to the top of the formation every 50 meters from $x = 50$ through $x = 750$, searching for valuable minerals. Write a computer program to print the depth and the cost of each hole if drilling costs $75 per meter of depth. The program should also print the total cost of drilling the holes.

11. *Sunrise Problem*   Assume that the time of sunrise varies sinusoidally with the day of the year. Let t be the time of day that the Sun rises, and let d be the number of the day of the year, starting with $d = 1$ on January 1. To calculate the constants in the equation, recall that the period is 365 days. The amplitude and axis location can be calculated from the times of sunrise on the longest and shortest days of the year (i.e., June 21 and December 21). You may find these times for various cities in an almanac (they are 5:34 a.m. and 7:24 a.m. CST for San Antonio). The phase displacement will, of course, be related to the day number on which the sinusoid reaches its maximum, if you use cosine.

a.   Sketch a graph of this sinusoid. You may neglect daylight-saving time.

b.   Write an equation for this function.

c.   Calculate the time of sunrise for your city *today*. Check your answer with today's newspaper to see how close your model is to the actual sunrise time.

d.   Predict the time of sunrise on your birthday, taking daylight-saving time into account if necessary.

e.   The difficulty with parts c and d is the tedious computations involved. To ease the computations, write a computer program that will predict the sunrise time for all days of the year which you input at the beginning of the program.

f.   Modify the program from part e so that it calculates the sunrise time for each day, starting with $d = 1$, and searches for the first day on which the sun rises at 6:07 a.m. (or earlier).

g.   If you plot a graph of predicted and actual sunrise time versus d, you will find something like Figure 13-81, where the maximum occurs *after* the predicted maximum, but the minimum occurs *before* the predicted minimum. From what you have learned about how the Earth orbits the Sun, think of a reason why the actual sunrise times differ from the predicted ones in this manner.

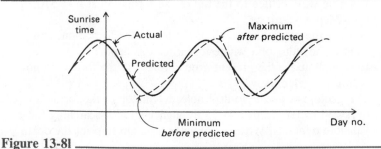

Figure 13-81

12. **Rotating Beacon Problem**   A police car pulls up alongside a long brick wall. While the police are away from the car, the red beacon light continues to rotate, shining a spot of red light that moves along the wall (Figure 13-8m). As you watch, you decide to make a mathematical model of the position of the light spot as a function of time.

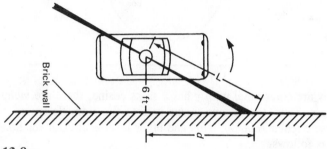

Figure 13-8m

a.   You start your stopwatch when the beam of light is perpendicular to the wall. You find that the light makes one complete revolution in exactly 2 seconds. The perpendicular distance from the light to the wall is 6 feet. Write equations expressing the distances d and L in terms of the number of seconds t, that the stopwatch reads.

b.   Calculate d and L when t equals
  i.   0.1,
  ii. 0.3,
  iii. 0.5,
  iv. 0.8.

c.   Sketch graphs of d and L versus time t.

13-9 | INVERSE CIRCULAR FUNCTIONS

You have been using the sinusoidal function

$$y = C + A \cos B(x - D)$$

to find values of y when x is known. By generalizing the concept of inverse circular functions such as $\cos^{-1}$ from Section 13-4, you can find values of x when y is known.

The geometrical meaning of $\cos^{-1}$ can be seen by drawing a unit circle, as in Figure 13-9a. If $x = \cos y$, then y is the *arc* whose *cosine* is x. Because of this fact, $\cos^{-1} x$ is often written

$$\cos^{-1} x = \arccos x.$$

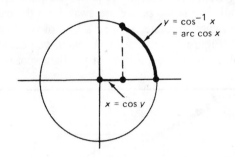

Figure 13-9a _____

Since *any* arc coterminal with y has x as its cosine, there are *many* values of arccos x. Thus, the inverse cosine is *not* a function. So arccos is called an inverse circular *relation*. This and other inverse circular relations are defined as follows.

DEFINITIONS

$$y = \arcsin x = \sin^{-1} x \quad \text{means } x = \sin y.$$
$$y = \arccos x = \cos^{-1} x \quad \text{means } x = \cos y.$$
$$y = \arctan x = \tan^{-1} x \quad \text{means } x = \tan y.$$
$$y = \text{arccot } x = \cot^{-1} x \quad \text{means } x = \cot y.$$
$$y = \text{arcsec } x = \sec^{-1} x \quad \text{means } x = \sec y.$$
$$y = \text{arccsc } x = \csc^{-1} x \quad \text{means } x = \csc y.$$

The next thing you do after inventing a new kind of relation is draw the graphs. To draw

$$y = \arcsin x,$$

for example, you would simply plot

$$x = \sin y.$$

This is most easily done by picking values of y and finding x. The graph is shown in Figure 13-9b. Since x and y are *reversed* for the inverse relation, everything that happened along the x-axis for $y = \sin x$ will happen along the y-axis for $y = \arcsin x$.

Figure 13-9b makes it clear that $y = \arcsin x$ is *not* a function. There are *many* values of y for each value of x. By picking only *part* of the graph in Figure 13-9b, it is possible to get a function graph. Several attempts are shown in Figure 13-9c with comments below. The first one is still not a function. The second one is a function but does not use the entire domain

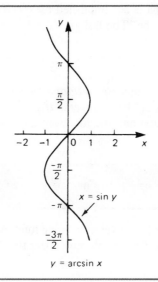

Figure 13-9b _____

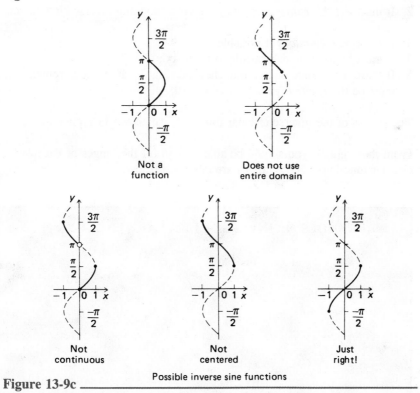

Figure 13-9c _____

$-1 \leq x \leq 1$. The third sketch uses the entire domain but is not in one continuous piece. The fourth one is continuous and uses the entire domain, but is located away from the origin. The last sketch is the most desirable.

Picking part of the graph is accomplished by specifying what you want the *range* of the function to be. The last graph in Figure 13-9c is specified by

$$y = \arcsin x \text{ and } -\frac{\pi}{2} \le y \le \frac{\pi}{2}.$$

This function is called an *inverse circular function.* If the range were $-90° \le y \le 90°$, it would be an *inverse trigonometric function.* To distinguish between the relation and the function, a *capital* letter is usually used for the function.

> $$y = \text{Arcsin } x = \text{Sin}^{-1} x \text{ means } x = \sin y \text{ and } -\frac{\pi}{2} \le y \le \frac{\pi}{2}.$$

The ranges of the other five inverse circular functions are found by the same reasoning process. The graph must meet the following requirements:

1. It must be a *function* graph.
2. It must use the *entire domain* of the corresponding inverse circular relation.
3. It must be *continuous* if possible.
4. It must be as close as possible to the *x*-axis.
5. If there is a choice of two branches meeting the above requirements, it must be the *positive* branch (i.e., $y \ge 0$).

The graphs of the inverse circular functions are shown in Figure 13-9d.

From these graphs you should be able to read off the ranges of the inverse circular functions. These ranges are tabulated below.

> **RANGES OF INVERSE CIRCULAR FUNCTIONS**
>
> $$y = \text{Arcsin } x = \text{Sin}^{-1} x, \quad -\frac{\pi}{2} \le y \le \frac{\pi}{2}$$
>
> $$y = \text{Arccos } x = \text{Cos}^{-1} x, \quad 0 \le y \le \pi$$
>
> $$y = \text{Arctan } x = \text{Tan}^{-1} x, \quad -\frac{\pi}{2} < y < \frac{\pi}{2}$$
>
> $$y = \text{Arccot } x = \text{Cot}^{-1} x, \quad 0 < y < \pi$$
>
> $$y = \text{Arcsec } x = \text{Sec}^{-1} x, \quad 0 \le y \le \pi \text{ and } y \ne \frac{\pi}{2}$$
>
> $$y = \text{Arccsc } x = \text{Csc}^{-1} x, \quad -\frac{\pi}{2} \le y \le \frac{\pi}{2} \text{ and } y \ne 0$$

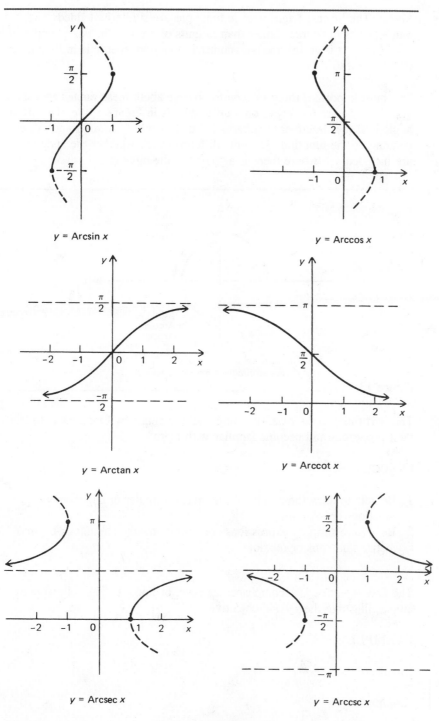

y = Arcsin x

y = Arccos x

y = Arctan x

y = Arccot x

y = Arcsec x

y = Arccsc x

Inverse circular functions

Figure 13-9d

Note: The inverse *trigonometric* functions are similarly defined. The range of y is in degrees rather than in units of arc length. For example, if $y = \text{Arccos } x$ is an inverse trigonometric function, then y is in the range $0° \le y \le 180°$.

The most important thing for you to observe about these ranges appears if you draw the arc (or angle) on a uv-graph, as in Figure 13-9e. The arc or angle is always in either Quadrants I and II or in Quadrants I and IV, depending on the function. The only differences are whether the endpoints are included and where there is a "hole" in the middle.

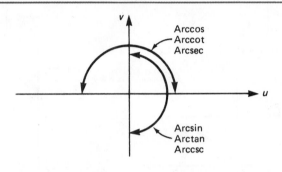

Inverse circular function ranges

Figure 13-9e

The next thing to do after inventing and graphing new functions is to learn their properties and become familiar with them.

Objectives:

1. Be able to draw the graphs of the inverse circular or trigonometric functions or relations.
2. Be able to simplify expressions containing inverse circular or trigonometric functions or relations.

The first objective is accomplished as described above. The following examples illustrate the second objective.

EXAMPLE 1

Evaluate $\text{Cos}^{-1}\left(\dfrac{\sqrt{3}}{2}\right)$.

Solution:

Let $x = \text{Cos}^{-1}\left(\dfrac{\sqrt{3}}{2}\right)$.

By the definition of Cos^{-1},

$$\cos x = \frac{\sqrt{3}}{2}, \text{ and } 0 \leq x \leq \pi.$$

From the functions of special arguments which you learned in Section 13-3, you should recognize that $\cos \frac{\pi}{6} = \frac{\sqrt{3}}{2}$. Therefore,

$$x = \underline{\underline{\frac{\pi}{6}}}.$$

For an inverse trigonometric function,

$$x = \underline{\underline{30°}}.$$

These answers are illustrated in Figure 13-9f.

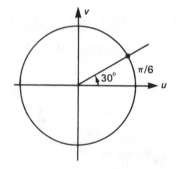

Figure 13-9f ———————————————————————————— ■

EXAMPLE 2

Evaluate $\cos^{-1}\left(\frac{\sqrt{3}}{2}\right)$.

Solution:
This example is the same as Example 1 except that the inverse *relation* is asked for rather than the inverse function. So x is no longer restricted to Quadrants I or II. As shown in Figure 13-9g, there are two arcs whose cosines are $\frac{\sqrt{3}}{2}$. So

$$x = \frac{\pi}{6} \text{ or } -\frac{\pi}{6}.$$

But x could also be any arc *coterminal* with $\frac{\pi}{6}$ or $-\frac{\pi}{6}$. Coterminal arcs differ by multiples of 2π. Letting n stand for an integer, any multiple of 2π

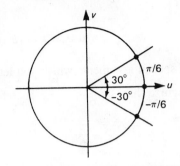

Figure 13-9g _____

has the form $2\pi n$. So in general,

$$x = \frac{\pi}{6} + 2\pi n \text{ or } -\frac{\pi}{6} + 2\pi n.$$

For an inverse *trigonometric* relation, x would be

$$x = 30° + 360n° \text{ or } -30° + 360n°.$$

This general solution can be used to find particular values of x. For example, if $n = 3$, then

$$x = \frac{\pi}{6} + 6\pi \text{ or } -\frac{\pi}{6} + 6\pi$$

$$= \frac{37\pi}{6} \text{ or } \frac{35\pi}{6}.$$

If $n = -1$, then

$$x = \frac{\pi}{6} - 2\pi \text{ or } -\frac{\pi}{6} - 2\pi$$

$$= -\frac{11\pi}{6} \text{ or } -\frac{13\pi}{6}. \qquad ∎$$

EXAMPLE 3

Evaluate $\tan\left(\text{Sin}^{-1}\frac{3}{5}\right)$.

Solution:
A picture helps. Since $\text{Sin}^{-1}\frac{3}{5}$ means "the angle whose sine is $\frac{3}{5}$," you can draw that angle in standard position. Figure 13-9h shows the angle with $v = 3$ and $r = 5$. By Pythagoras, $u = 4$. Therefore,

$$\tan\left(\text{Sin}^{-1}\frac{3}{5}\right) = \frac{3}{4},$$

$$\text{because } \tan x = \frac{v}{u}.$$

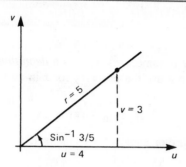

Figure 13-9h

EXAMPLE 4

Evaluate $\sin\left(\text{Sin}^{-1}\frac{5}{7}\right)$.

Solution:
The uv-graph for $\text{Sin}^{-1}\frac{5}{7}$ is shown in Figure 13-9i. Here, $v = 5$ and $r = 7$. Since you are looking for the *sine* of this angle,

$$\sin\left(\text{Sin}^{-1}\frac{5}{7}\right) = \frac{5}{7}$$

$$\text{because } \sin x = \frac{v}{r}.$$

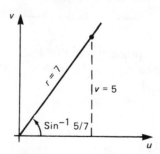

Figure 13-9i

The result of Example 4 is really not surprising. Translated into words, the problem says, "Find the sine of the angle whose sine is $\frac{5}{7}$." It is important because it illustrates a property that applies to inverses of *any* kind of function.

PROPERTY

$f(f^{-1}(x)) = x$ for all x in the appropriate domain.

In fact, this property is sometimes used as a *definition* of inverse functions. Beware that you do not use the property for x in an inappropriate domain. For example,

$$\sin(\text{Sin}^{-1} 15) \neq 15,$$

because there is no arc or angle whose sine is 15.

EXAMPLE 5

Evaluate $\text{Cos}^{-1}(\cos 60°)$.

$$\text{Cos}^{-1}(\cos 60°) = \text{Cos}^{-1}\left(\frac{1}{2}\right) \quad \text{because } \cos 60° = \frac{1}{2}.$$

$$= 60° \quad \text{because } \cos 60° = \frac{1}{2}.$$

Here again the answer is the number you started with. This will work for all appropriate values. But beware of such things as $\text{Cos}^{-1}(\cos 315°)$, which equals $\text{Cos}^{-1}\left(\frac{\sqrt{2}}{2}\right)$, which equals 45° and *not* 315°.

PROPERTY

$f^{-1}(f(x)) = x$ for all x in the appropriate domain.

You will prove these two properties in Problems 97 and 98 of the following exercise. You will also get practice working with inverse trigonometric and circular functions and relations.

EXERCISE 13-9

Do These Quickly

The following problems are intended to refresh your skills. You should be able to do all 10 in less than 5 minutes.

Q1.   What name is given to functions whose graphs repeat themselves at regular intervals?

Q2.   Is $|y| = x$ the equation of a *function*?

Q3.   Find the amplitude: $y = \sin 2x$

Q4.   Find the period: $y = 3 \cos x$

Q5.   Find the phase displacement: $y = 3 + 2 \cos 4(x - 7)$

Q6.   Find the sinusoidal axis location: $y = 7 + \cos (x + 4)$

Q7.   Does $\cos (2 \cdot 30°)$ equal $2 \cdot \cos 30°$?

Q8.   How many radians in $180°$?

Q9.   What is the hypotenuse of a right triangle whose legs are 8 cm and 6 cm?

Q10.   Find the reference angle for $-176°$.

For Problems 1 through 6, sketch the graph of the inverse circular relation *without* looking at Figure 13-9d. After you have drawn the graph, check the figure to make sure you are correct.

1. $y = \arcsin x$
2. $y = \arccos x$
3. $y = \arctan x$
4. $y = \text{arccot } x$
5. $y = \text{arcsec } x$
6. $y = \text{arccsc } x$

For Problems 7 through 12, sketch the graph of the inverse circular function *without* looking at Figure 13-9d. After you have drawn the graph, check the figure to make sure you are correct.

7. $y = \text{Arccos } x$
8. $y = \text{Arcsin } x$
9. $y = \text{Arccot } x$
10. $y = \text{Arctan } x$
11. $y = \text{Arccsc } x$
12. $y = \text{Arcsec } x$

For Problems 13 through 36, find *exact* values of the inverse *circular* functions or relations.

13. $\arctan 1$
14. $\tan^{-1} 1$
15. $\text{Tan}^{-1} 1$
16. $\text{Arctan } 1$
17. $\arcsin \left(-\dfrac{1}{2} \right)$
18. $\text{Arccos } (-1)$
19. $\text{Sec}^{-1} 2$
20. $\cot^{-1} \sqrt{3}$
21. $\text{arccsc } 2$
22. $\cos^{-1} 0$

23. Arccos 2

24. Arcsec 0

25. arccot $\sqrt{3}$

26. Arcsin (-1)

27. $\text{Sin}^{-1} \dfrac{\sqrt{2}}{2}$

28. $\sin^{-1}\left(-\dfrac{\sqrt{2}}{2}\right)$

29. $\cos^{-1}(-1)$

30. $\text{Csc}^{-1}\ 1$

31. Arccot 0

32. $\text{Sec}^{-1}\ 1$

33. $\text{arcsec}\left(-\dfrac{2}{\sqrt{3}}\right)$

34. $\text{arccot}\left(-\dfrac{\sqrt{3}}{3}\right)$

35. $\text{Csc}^{-1}(-\sqrt{2})$

36. $\text{arccsc}\ \dfrac{2}{\sqrt{3}}$

For Problems 37 through 60, find *exact* values of the inverse *trigonometric* functions or relations.

37. $\cos^{-1}\dfrac{\sqrt{2}}{2}$

38. $\text{Cot}^{-1}\ 1$

39. Arcsin (-1)

40. $\text{Cos}^{-1}\ 1$

41. arccot (-1)

42. $\text{Sin}^{-1}\ 1$

43. $\text{Csc}^{-1}\ \sqrt{2}$

44. Arcsec 2

45. $\text{arcsec}\ \dfrac{1}{2}$

46. Arcsin 2

47. $\text{arcsin}\ \dfrac{1}{2}$

48. $\tan^{-1}\ \sqrt{3}$

49. $\cos^{-1}\ 1$

50. arccsc (-1)

51. Arctan $(-\sqrt{3})$

52. $\text{Csc}^{-1}\left(-\dfrac{2}{\sqrt{3}}\right)$

53. $\text{csc}^{-1}\left(-\dfrac{2}{\sqrt{3}}\right)$

54. Arcsec (-1)

55. Arcsec (-2)

56. $\cot^{-1}(-\sqrt{3})$

57. Arccos $\left(-\dfrac{1}{2}\right)$

58. Arctan (-1)

59. $\tan^{-1}\dfrac{\sqrt{3}}{3}$

60. $\text{arccos}\left(-\dfrac{\sqrt{2}}{2}\right)$

For Problems 61 through 72, use tables or a calculator to find the following inverse circular functions correct to 3 decimal places.

61. Arccos 0.4531

62. Sin^{-1} 0.7753

63. Sec^{-1} 1.233

64. Arccsc 2.647

65. Arccot 2.331

66. Arctan 1.872

67. Tan^{-1} (−0.4375)

68. Cot^{-1} (−4.011)

69. Arcsin (−0.9692)

70. Cos^{-1} (−0.7573)

71. Csc^{-1} (−1.873)

72. Arcsec (−4.502)

For Problems 73 through 96, find the *exact* value of the expression.

73. $\tan \left(\text{Cos}^{-1} \dfrac{4}{5} \right)$

74. $\cos \left(\text{Arctan} \dfrac{4}{3} \right)$

75. $\sin \left(\text{Tan}^{-1} \dfrac{5}{12} \right)$

76. $\sec \left(\text{Arcsin} \dfrac{15}{17} \right)$

77. $\cos \left(\text{Arcsin} \left(-\dfrac{8}{17} \right) \right)$

78. $\cot \left(\text{Csc}^{-1} \left(-\dfrac{13}{12} \right) \right)$

79. $\sec \left(\text{Arccos} \dfrac{2}{3} \right)$

80. $\sin (\text{Cot}^{-1} 4)$

81. $\cot \left(\text{Sin}^{-1} \left(-\dfrac{\sqrt{2}}{2} \right) \right)$

82. $\tan (\text{Arcsec} (-\sqrt{2}))$

83. $\csc (\text{Arccot } 3)$

84. $\csc \left(\text{Tan}^{-1} \dfrac{1}{2} \right)$

85. $\csc (\text{Arccsc } 5)$

86. $\sin \left(\text{Sin}^{-1} \dfrac{2}{3} \right)$

87. $\cos (\text{Sin}^{-1} 2)$

88. $\tan (\text{Arcsec } 0)$

89. $\text{Arctan} \left(\tan \dfrac{\pi}{6} \right)$

90. $\text{Cos}^{-1} (\cos 30°)$

91. $\text{Sin}^{-1} (\sin (-17°))$

92. $\text{Arcsec} (\sec (-1.5))$

93. $\text{Sec}^{-1} (\sec 210°)$

94. $\text{Arccsc} \left(\csc \dfrac{2\pi}{3} \right)$

95. $\text{Arccot} (\tan 79°)$

96. $\text{Sin}^{-1} (\cos 17°)$

97. Prove that $f^{-1}(f(x)) = x$ by letting $y = f(x)$, using the definition of f^{-1} and using a clever substitution.

98. Prove that $f(f^{-1}(x)) = x$ by letting $y = f^{-1}(x)$, using the definition of f^{-1} and using a clever substitution.

99. Suppose that you have been hired by I.M.F. Computer Corporation
     to do some programming using inverse circular functions. Since
     many computer languages such as BASIC and FORTRAN have only
     the Arctan function available, I.M.F. calls upon you to find other in-
     verse circular functions in terms of Arctangents.

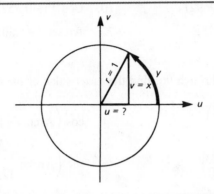

Figure 13-9j

a. Let $y = \text{Arcsin } x$. Write an equation expressing x in terms of y.
b. Figure 13-9j is a uv-graph showing an arc of length y in stan-
    dard position on a unit circle. The coordinate v equals the x of
    part a, above. What does u equal in terms of x?
c. With the help of the sketch, write an equation expressing $\tan y$
    in terms of x.
d. Transform the equation from part c so that y is expressed as an
    Arctangent. Explain why you can use the Arctangent *function*
    here instead of the arctangent relation.
e. Demonstrate that your equation in part d gives correct answers
    by using it to calculate Arcsin 0.5 and by comparing the answer
    with the actual value of Arcsin 0.5.

100. Repeat Problem 99 to get an equation for Arccos x as an Arctangent.
     Explain what you must do to get the right value of Arccos x if
     $x < 0$.

101. Show that there is a very easy way to find Arccsc x in terms of an
     Arcsine. Then use the results of Problem 99 to write an equation ex-
     pressing Arcsec x as an Arctangent function.

102. Use the techniques of Problems 100 and 101 to derive equations ex-
     pressing Arccot x and Arcsec x in terms of Arctangents.

103. Write a computer program and use it to print a short table of values
     of Arcsin x, Arccos x, Arctan x, and Arccot x for each 0.1 unit from
     $x = -1$ through $x = 1$. The formulas of Problems 99 through 102
     should help you if your computer has only the Arctangent function
     available.

104. a.   Draw graphs of $y = \tan x$, for $-\frac{\pi}{2} < x < \frac{\pi}{2}$, $y = \text{Tan}^{-1} x$ on the same set of axes, using the same scale for both axes.
   b.   Draw the line $y = x$ on this set of axes and tell what the relationship is among this line and the graphs of part a.
   c.   Explain why the relationship in part b would *not* be true for the *trigonometric* tangent function $y = \tan \theta$, for $-90° < \theta < 90°$.

105. a.   Carefully plot the portions of $y = \sin x$ and $y = \text{Sin}^{-1} x$ for each 0.1 unit from $x = 0$ through $x = 0.8$. You may find values by calculator or from Table IV. Use the same scales on both axes, and make the scale large enough to show the separation between the two graphs.
   b.   Draw the line $y = x$ on the same set of axes. Does this line intersect either of the graphs at any points besides the origin?
   c.   What is the slope of the line *tangent* to each graph at $x = 0$?
   d.   Plot another graph of the *trigonometric* sine function $y = \sin x$ for values of x from $0°$ through $0.8°$, using the *same* scale for both axes. Does the line $y = x$ seem to have the same relationship to the trigonometric sine function as it does to the circular sine function? Explain.

| 13-10 | EVALUATION OF INVERSE RELATIONS |

In Section 13-8 you used sinusoidal functions with the general equation

$$y = C + A \cos B(x - D)$$

as mathematical models. You derived the particular equation from information about the real world, then used the equation to find values of y for given values of x.

It is just as important to be able to find x when you know y. The difficulty is that there are *many* values of x for the *same* value of y. In this section you will learn how inverse circular or trigonometric relations can be used to help out.

Objective:
Given a circular function with equation

$$y = C + A \cos B(x - D) \text{ or } y = C + A \sin B(x - D),$$

or a trigonometric function with equation

$$y = C + A \cos B(\theta - D) \text{ or } y = C + A \sin B(\theta - D),$$

find the values of x or θ for a given value of y.

EXAMPLE 1

For the trigonometric function

$$y = 2 + 3\cos 4(\theta + 31°),$$

find the first three positive values of θ for which $y = 1.5$.

Solution:
Substituting 1.5 for y gives

$1.5 = 2 + 3 \cos 4(\theta + 31°)$	Substitution
$-0.5 = 3 \cos 4(\theta + 31°)$	Subtracting 2
$-0.1667 = \cos 4(\theta + 31°)$	Dividing by 3
$\arccos(-0.1667) = 4(\theta + 31°)$	Taking arccos of each member

By calculator, the value of Arccos (-0.1667) is about 99° 36'. The same thing can be found by using Table III to get the reference angle, 80° 24', then subtracting this number from 180°. So the values of the arccosine relation are

$$\pm 99°36' + 360n°,$$

as indicated in Figure 13-10a.

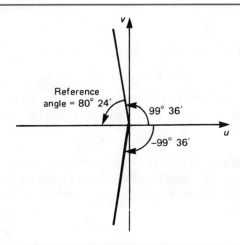

Figure 13-10a

Substituting these values for the left member of the equation gives

$\pm 99° 36' + 360n° = 4(\theta + 31°)$	
$\pm 24° 54' + 90n° = \theta + 31°$	Dividing by 4
$-7° 54' + 90n°$ or $-55° 54' + 90n° = \theta$	Subtracting 31°
$\theta = -7° 54', 82° 6', 172° 6', \ldots$ or	Substituting
$\qquad -55° 54', 34° 6', 124° 6', \ldots$	$n = 0, 1, 2, \ldots$

So the first three positive values of θ are

$$\theta = 34°\ 6',\ 82°\ 6',\ \text{and}\ 124°\ 6'\,.$$ ■

EXAMPLE 2

For the circular function

$$y = 2 + 3 \sin 4(x + 0.5),$$

find the least positive value of x for which $y = 4.1$.

Substituting 4.1 for y and using symmetry,

$2 + 3 \sin 4(x + 0.5) = 4.1$ Substitution

$3 \sin 4(x + 0.5) = 2.1$ Subtracting 2

$\sin 4(x + 0.5) = 0.7$ Dividing by 3

$4(x + 0.5) = \arcsin 0.7$ arcsin of each member

From Table IV or by calculator, Arcsin 0.7 is approximately 0.7754. But arcsin 0.7 could terminate in Quadrant I or Quadrant II since sine is positive in these quadrants. As shown in Figure 13-10b, another value of arcsin 0.7 is

$$\arcsin 0.7 \approx \pi - 0.7754$$

$$\approx 3.1416 - 0.7754$$

$$= 2.3662.$$

So in general,

$$\arcsin 0.7 \approx 0.7754 + 2\pi n \text{ or } 2.3662 + 2\pi n.$$

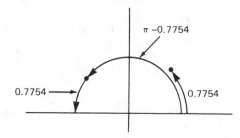

Figure 13-10b

Returning to the original problem,

$4(x + 0.5) \approx 0.7754 + 2\pi n \text{ or } 2.3662 + 2\pi n$ Substitution

$x + 0.5 \approx 0.1938 + \dfrac{\pi}{2}n \text{ or } 0.5915 + \dfrac{\pi}{2}n$ Dividing by 4

$$x \approx -0.3062 + \frac{\pi}{2}n \text{ or } 0.0915 + \frac{\pi}{2}n \qquad \text{Subtracting } 0.5$$

Substituting 0 for n gives

$$x \approx -0.3062 \text{ or } 0.0915.$$

So the least positive value of x is about $\underline{0.0915}$. ∎

EXAMPLE 3

For the circular function

$$y = 2 + 3 \cos \frac{\pi}{4}(x - 0.6),$$

a. Transform the equation so that x is expressed in terms of y.
b. Find the third positive value of x for which $y = -0.7$.

Solution:

a. $2 + 3 \cos \dfrac{\pi}{4}(x - 0.6) = y$ Symmetry

$\cos \dfrac{\pi}{4}(x - 0.6) = \dfrac{1}{3}(y - 2)$ Subtracting 2 and dividing by 3

$\dfrac{\pi}{4}(x - 0.6) = \arccos \dfrac{1}{3}(y - 2)$ arccos of each member

$x - 0.6 = \dfrac{4}{\pi} \arccos \dfrac{1}{3}(y - 2)$ Multiplying by $\frac{4}{\pi}$

$x = 0.6 + \dfrac{4}{\pi} \arccos \dfrac{1}{3}(y - 2)$ Adding 0.6

b. To find x when $y = -0.7$, you simply substitute -0.7 for y and carry
out the indicated operations. All of the algebra has already been done.

$x = 0.6 + \dfrac{4}{\pi} \arccos \dfrac{1}{3}(-0.7 - 2)$ Substitution

$= 0.6 + \dfrac{4}{\pi} \arccos(-0.9)$ Arithmetic

$\approx 0.6 + \dfrac{4}{\pi}(\pm 2.6906 + 2\pi n)$ Arccos 0.9 ≈ 0.4510

$\approx 0.6 \pm 3.4257 + 8n$ Arithmetic, and $\pi \approx 3.1416$

$= 4.0257 + 8n \text{ or } -2.8257 + 8n$ Arithmetic

Letting $n = 0$ and then $n = 1$ gives

$$x \approx 4.0257, -2.8257, 12.0257, \text{ or } 5.1743$$

So the third positive value of x is about $\underline{5.1743}$. ∎

In the following exercise you will get practice finding x or θ for given values of y. This technique will be used for real-world problems in the following section.

EXERCISE 13-10

Do These Quickly

The following problems are intended to refresh your skills. You should be able to do all 10 in less than 5 minutes.

Q1.   Sketch the graph of $y = \cos x$.

Q2.   Sketch the graph of $y = \sin x$.

Q3.   Sketch the graph of $y = \tan x$.

Q4.   Evaluate $x = \text{Arctan } \sqrt{3}$.

Q5.   Evaluate $\theta = \text{arcsec } 2$.

Q6.   Evaluate $\cos x$ if $\sec x = 2$.

Q7.   Does $\tan^{-1} x$ equal $\dfrac{1}{(\tan x)}$?

Q8.   Does $\dfrac{1}{(\tan x)}$ equal $\cot x$?

Q9.   Does $\dfrac{1}{(\sin x)}$ equal $\cos x$?

Q10.   How many degrees in a radian?

Work the following problems.

For Problems 1 through 10
a. Transform the equation so that θ or x is in terms of y.
b. Find the first three positive values of θ or x for which $y = 5$.
c. By sketching the graph of the *given* function, show that your answers are reasonable.

1. $y = 3 + 4 \cos 2(\theta + 10°)$

2. $y = -1 + 12 \cos 3(\theta - 10°)$

3. $y = 6 + 2 \cos \dfrac{1}{4}(x - 3\pi)$

4. $y = 7 + 4 \cos \dfrac{1}{3}(x - 5\pi)$

5. $y = -3 + 10 \cos 4(\theta - 40°)$

6. $y = 4 + 3 \cos 2(\theta + 20°)$

7. $y = 1 + 5 \sin \dfrac{\pi}{2}(x + 0.7)$

8. $y = -2 + 8 \sin \dfrac{2\pi}{3}(x - 1)$

9. $y = 1 + 3 \cos \pi(x + 0.2)$

10. $y = 2 + 2 \cos 2\pi(x - 0.1)$

For Problems 11 and 12, you must apply the techniques of this section to the inverse tangent and secant functions.

11. Suppose that $y = 2 + \frac{1}{2} \tan \frac{\pi}{4}(x - 0.6)$.
   a. Transform the equation so that x is expressed in terms of y.
   b. Find the smallest positive value of x for which
      i. $y = 2.5$,
      ii. $y = 0$.
   c. Show that your answers are right by sketching the graph.

12. Suppose that $y = 4 + 2 \sec 3(\theta + 20°)$.
   a. Transform the equation so that θ is expressed in terms of y.
   b. Find the least positive value of θ for which
      i. $y = 6$,
      ii. $y = 3$,
      iii. $y = 0$.
   c. Show that your answers are right by sketching the graph.

13-11 | INVERSE CIRCULAR RELATIONS AS MATHEMATICAL MODELS

In the previous section you learned how to find values of x for known values of y in the equation

$$y = C + A \cos B(x - D).$$

In this section you will apply the techniques you learned to problems from the real world.

Objective:
Given a situation from the real world in which y varies sinusoidally with x, derive the particular equation and use it to find x for a given value of y.

EXAMPLE

A water wheel 14 feet in diameter is rotating as shown in Figure 13-11a. You start a stopwatch and observe the motion of point P on the rim of the wheel. When the stopwatch reads 2 seconds, P is at its maximum distance from the surface of the water. When the stopwatch reads 7 seconds, P is at its maximum depth below the water.

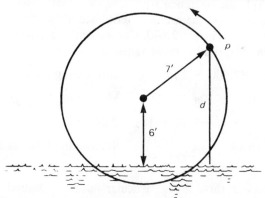

Figure 13-11a

a. Find the particular equation expressing the distance of P from the surface as a function of stopwatch reading.
b. Find the time at which P first *emerges* from the water.

a. The first part of this problem is similar to the example in Section 13-8. By sketching the graph (Figure 13-11b) you can derive the following equation:

$$d = 6 + 7 \cos \frac{\pi}{5} (t - 2),$$

where d is feet above the surface of the water, and t is the number of seconds the stopwatch reads.

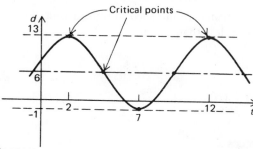

Figure 13-11b

b. Point P emerges from the water when $d = 0$. Setting $d = 0$ gives

$$6 + 7 \cos \frac{\pi}{5} (t - 2) = 0 \qquad \text{Substitution and symmetry}$$

$$\cos \frac{\pi}{5} (t - 2) = -\frac{6}{7} \qquad \text{Subtracting 6 and dividing by 7}$$

$$\frac{\pi}{5} (t - 2) = \arccos \left(-\frac{6}{7} \right) \qquad \text{arccos of both members}$$

Since $\frac{6}{7} \approx 0.8571$, the reference arc (Table IV or calculator) is 0.541. Since cosine is *negative*, the arc must terminate in Quadrant II or III. So Arccos $(-\frac{6}{7}) \approx \pi - 0.541 \approx 2.600$. Consequently, arccos $(-\frac{6}{7}) \approx \pm 2.600 + 2\pi n$. Substituting these values for arccos $(-\frac{6}{7})$ gives

$$\frac{\pi}{5}(t - 2) \approx \pm 2.600 + 2\pi n \qquad \text{Substituting for arrcos } (-\tfrac{6}{7})$$

$$t - 2 \approx \pm 4.14 + 10n \qquad \text{Multiplying by } \tfrac{5}{\pi}$$

$$t \approx 6.14 + 10n \text{ or } -2.14 + 10n \qquad \text{Adding 2}$$

$$t \approx 6.14, 16.14, \ldots , \qquad \text{Substituting integers for } n$$
$$\text{or } -2.14, 7.86, \ldots$$

To find out which of these is the particular value of t desired, you must return to the real world. From Figure 13-11b, you can see that *P emerges* from the water the *second* time $d = 0$. So the particular value of t required is $t = \underline{7.86}$. ∎

In the following exercise you will find values of the independent variable for given values of the dependent one. Some of the problems are continuations of those in Exercise 13-8.

EXERCISE 13-11

Do These Quickly

The following problems are intended to refresh your skills. You should be able to do all 10 in less than 5 minutes.

Sketch the graph:

Q1. $y = \text{Cos}^{-1} x$.

Q2. $y = \cos^{-1} x$.

Q3. $y = \text{Arccos } x$.

Evaluate:

Q4. $\sin 0.5$

Q5. $\sin 0.5°$

Q6. $\theta = \text{Sin}^{-1} 0.5$

Q7. $x = \text{Arcsin } 0.5$

Answer the question:

Q8. Find the reference angle of 359°.

Q9. How many radians in 60°?

Q10. In the word "trigonometry," what does "trigon" mean?

1. *Ferris Wheel Problem*   For Problem 1 in Exercise 13-8, find the second time your seat in the Ferris wheel is 18 feet above the ground.

2. *Bouncing Spring Problem*   For Problem 2 in Exercise 13-8, predict the first positive value of time at which the weight is 59 centimeters above the floor.

3. *Tidal Wave Problem*   For Problem 3 in Exercise 13-8, between what two times is there no water at the pier?

4. *Tarzan Problem*   For Problem 4 in Exercise 13-8, find the least positive value of time t for which Tarzan is directly over the river bank (i.e., $y = 0$).

5. *Pebble-in-the-Tire Problem*   For Problem 5 in Exercise 13-8, find the first two distances you have traveled when the pebble in the tire tread is 11 inches above the pavement.

6. *Spaceship Problem*   For Problem 6 in Exercise 13-8, find the first time at which the spaceship is 1600 kilometers *south* of the equator.

7. *Another Spaceship Problem*   A spacecraft is in an elliptical orbit around the Earth (Figure 13-11c). At time $t = 0$ hours, it is at its apogee (highest point) $d = 1000$ kilometers above the Earth's surface. Fifty minutes later, it is at its perigee $d = 100$ kilometers above the surface.

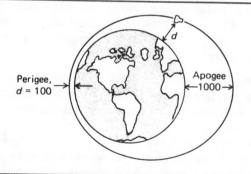

Perigee,
$d = 100$

Apogee
1000

Figure 13-11c

a.   Assuming that d varies sinusoidally with time, write the particular equation expressing d in terms of t.

b. Solve the equation for t in terms of d.
c. Predict the first three positive values of t for which the space-craft is 200 kilometers from the surface.
d. In order to transmit information back to Earth, the spacecraft must be within 700 kilometers of the surface. For how many consecutive minutes will the spacecraft be able to transmit?

8. *Tide Problem*   At a certain point on the beach, a post sticks out of the sand, its top being 76 centimeters above the beach (Figure 13-11d). The depth of the water at the post varies sinusoidally with time due to the motion of the tides. Using the techniques of Section 13-8, you find that the depth d in centimeters is

$$d = 40 + 60 \cos \frac{\pi}{6} (t - 2),$$

where t is the time in hours since midnight.

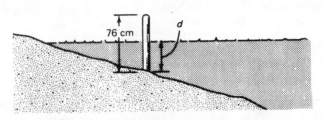

Figure 13-11d ———————————————————————

a. Sketch a graph of the sinusoid.
b. Solve the equation for t in terms of d.
c. What is the earliest time of day at which the water level is just at the top of the post?
d. At the time you calculated in part c, is the post just going under water or just emerging from the water? Explain.
e. When d is negative, the tide is completely out and there is no water at the post. Between what times will the entire post be out of the water?

9. *Tunnel Problem*   Scorpion Gulch & Western Railway is preparing to build a new line through Rolling Mountains. They have hired you to do some calculations for tunnels and bridges needed on the line (Figure 13-11e).

You set up a Cartesian coordinate system with its origin at the entrance to the tunnel through Bald Mountain. Your surveying crew finds that the mountain rises 250 meters above the level of the track and that the next valley goes down 50 meters below the level of the track. The cross section of the mountain and valley is roughly sinu-

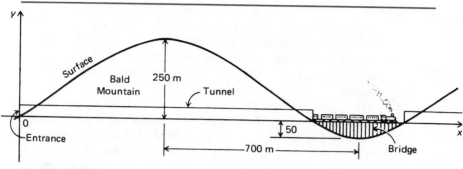

Figure 13-11e _____

soidal with a horizontal distance of 700 meters from the top of the mountain to the bottom of the valley.

a.   Write the particular equation expressing the vertical distance y from the track to the surface of the mountain or valley in terms of the horizontal distance x from the tunnel entrance. This can be done by finding the constants A, B, and C from the distances given. Finding D requires that you substitute the other constants and the ordered pair $(0, 0)$ into the equation and solve for D.

b.   Solve the equation from part a for x in terms of y.

c.   How long will the tunnel be?

d.   How long will the bridge be?

e.   The company thinks it might be cheaper to build the line if the entire project is raised by $y = 20$, thus making the tunnel shorter and the bridge longer. Find the new values of x at the ends of the tunnel and bridge. Then find the new lengths of each.

10.   *Roller Coaster Problem*   A sinusoidal roller coaster track is to be built with a high point $h = 27$ meters at a horizontal distance $d = 0$ meters. It has a low point $h = -3$ meters at $d = 50$ meters (Figure 13-11f).

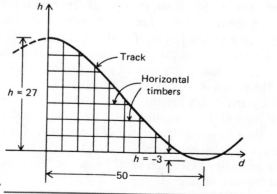

Figure 13-11f _____

a. Write the particular equation expressing h in terms of d.

b. Solve the equation of part a for d in terms of h.

c. The lengths of the horizontal timbers used to build the roller-coaster supporting structure are values of d. Calculate the length of the horizontal timber that is 4 meters above the ground.

d. Write a computer program to print the lengths of each of the horizontal timbers. The first one is 2 meters above the ground, and they are spaced 2 meters apart. The program should also find the *sum* of the lengths of the timbers, so that the builders will know how much material to order. If your computer has only the Arctangent function available, you can use the results of Problem 100 in Section 13-9 to express Arccosine as an Arctangent.

11. **Sun Elevation Problem**   The "angle of elevation" of an object above you is the angle between a horizontal line and the line of sight between you and the object, as shown in Figure 13-11g. After the Sun rises, its angle of elevation increases rapidly at first, then more slowly, reaching a maximum near noontime. Then the angle decreases until sunset. The next day the phenomenon repeats itself.

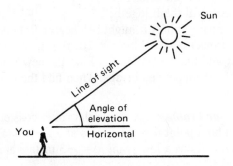

Figure 13-11g

Assume that when the Sun is up, its angle of elevation E varies sinusoidally with the time of day. Let t be the number of hours that has elapsed since midnight last night. Assume that the amplitude of this sinusoid is 60°, and the maximum angle of elevation occurs at 12:45 p.m. Assume that at this time of year the sinusoidal axis is at $E = -5°$. The period is, of course, 24 hours.

a. Sketch a graph of this function.

b. What is the real-world significance of the t-intercepts?

c. What is the real-world significance of the portion of the sinusoid which is *below* the t-axis?

d. Predict the angle of elevation at 9:27 a.m., at 2:30 p.m.

e. Predict the time of sunrise.

f.   As you know, the maximum angle of elevation increases and
decreases with the changes of season. Also, the times of sunrise and sunset change with the seasons. What *one* change
could you make in your mathematical model that would allow
you to use it for predicting the angle of elevation of the Sun at
any time on *any* day of the year?

13-12	CHAPTER REVIEW AND TEST

Time: 1 or 2 days

The Review Problems below parallel the sections in this chapter. The
Concepts Problems let you try your hand at applying what you know to
analyze a new situation. The Chapter Test is similar to one your instructor
might give to see how well you understand trigonometric and circular
functions.

REVIEW PROBLEMS

R1. As you jump up and down on a trampoline, your distance from the
ground depends on time. Sketch a reasonable graph.

R2. a. Find the reference angle and sketch in standard position:
    i. $163°$ ii. $283°$ iii. $-150°$
  b. Sketch the indicated arc of a unit circle in standard position:

    i. $\dfrac{\pi}{6}$ ii. $-\pi$ iii. 2

R3. Find the exact value:

  a. $\sin 60°$ b. $\cos \dfrac{\pi}{4}$ c. $\tan \dfrac{\pi}{6}$

  d. $\sec 180°$ e. $\csc 225°$ f. $\cot 0$

  g. $4 \sin^2 240°$ h. $\tan^2 \dfrac{\pi}{4} - \sec^2 \dfrac{\pi}{4}$

R4. Find decimal approximations for:
  a. $\sin 57.3°$ b. $\tan 49.1°$ c. $\sec 238°$

  d. $\cos 1.57$ e. $\cot (-3.05)$ f. $\csc \left(\dfrac{\pi}{5} \right)$

  g. $\theta = \mathrm{Sin}^{-1} 0.3$ h. $x = \mathrm{Cos}^{-1} 0.9$ i. $x = \mathrm{Tan}^{-1} 3.7$
  j. $\theta = \mathrm{Cot}^{-1} 0.02$ k. $\theta = \mathrm{Sec}^{-1} 13.2$ l. $x = \mathrm{Csc}^{-1} 1$

R5. Sketch the graph:
  a. $y = \cos x$ b. $y = \tan x$ c. $y = \sec x$

R6. Sketch two cycles of the graph:

  a. $y = 3 + 4 \cos 5(\theta - 7°)$ b. $y = 3 + 4 \cos \dfrac{\pi}{5}(x - 7)$

R7. Write the particular equation of each sinusoid sketched in Figure
     13-12a.

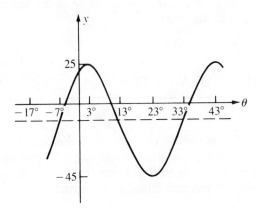

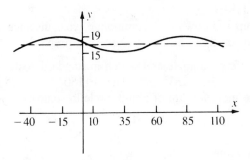

Figure 13-12a

R8. *Porpoising Problem:*
     Assume that you are aboard a submarine, submerged in the Pacific
     Ocean. At time $t = 0$, you make contact with an enemy destroyer.
     Immediately, you start "porpoising" (going deeper and shallower).
     At time $t = 4$ minutes, you are at your deepest, $y = -1000$ me-
     ters. At time $t = 9$ minutes, you next reach your shallowest,
     $y = -200$ meters. Assume that y varies sinusoidally with t for
     $t \geq 0$.
     a. Sketch the graph of y versus t.
     b. Write the particular equation expressing y in terms of t.
     c. Your submarine is "safe" when it is below $y = -300$ meters.
         At time $t = 0$, was your submarine safe? Justify your answer.

R9. a. Sketch the graph of:
         i. $y = \text{Arccot } x$.   ii. $y = \sin^{-1} x$.

b. Find the exact value, if possible. Otherwise, find a decimal approximation.

    i. $x = \text{Arcsin } 0.5$ ii. $\theta = \arccos(-1)$

    iii. $x = \text{Tan}^{-1} 0.3241$ iv. $\theta = \sec^{-1} \sqrt{2}$

    v. $x = \text{Csc}^{-1} 0.5$ vi. $\theta = \text{arccot}(-1)$

c. Evaluate $\tan\left(\text{Cos}^{-1} \frac{3}{8}\right)$.

d. Evaluate $\text{Arcsin}(\cos 23°)$.

R10. Transform the following equations so that x or θ is expressed in terms of y. Then find the first three positive values of x or θ for which $y = 1$.

a. $y = 5 + 4 \cos 3(\theta - 77°)$

b. $y = 6 + 2 \tan \frac{\pi}{4}(x - 3)$

R11. Between what two non-negative times is the submarine in Problem R8 first safe?

CONCEPTS PROBLEMS

You apply for a job with Y. O. Ming Mining Company. Since your work will involve using circular functions, Mr. Ming poses some problems for you to solve during your interview to see how useful you would be to his company.

C1. The first question concerns exact values. Find

a. $\sin \dfrac{5\pi}{3}$ b. $\cos 180°$

c. $\tan \dfrac{3\pi}{4}$ d. $\sec 120°$

e. $\csc 0$ f. $\text{Cos}^{-1}\left(-\dfrac{\sqrt{2}}{2}\right)$

g. $\text{Arccot}(-\sqrt{3})$ h. $\text{arcsec } 2$

i. $\text{arcsin } 2$ (Your résumé is *shredded* if you miss *this* one!)

j. $\tan\left(\text{Arccot} \dfrac{2}{5}\right)$

C2. Another question concerns the use of tables. There are other functions of angles called "versine" and "coversine." The abbreviations are "vers θ" and "covers θ," respectively. The tables are constructed just like Table III at the back of this book. Use the adjacent portion of the table to find

a. vers 66° 52′,

b. θ, if covers $\theta = 0.6045$.

c. By looking at Table III, see if you can figure out what vers θ and covers θ *really* are!

$m(\theta)$	covers θ	
23′ 00′	0.6093	67° 00′
10′	0.6066	50′
20′	0.6039	40′
30′	0.6013	30′
40′	0.5986	20′
50′	0.5959	10′
24° 00′	0.5933	66° 00′
10′	0.5906	50′
20′	0.5880	40′
30′	0.5853	30′
40′	0.5827	20′
50′	0.5800	10′
25° 00′	0.5774	65° 00′
	vers θ	$m(\theta)$

C3. The next question concerns graphs, and your ability to apply your present knowledge to an unfamiliar problem. Figure 13-12b shows graphs of $y = 4 \sin x$ and $y = \sin 4x$.
a. Tell which graph is which.
b. Copy the graphs. Then, on the same Cartesian coordinate system, draw the graph of

$$y = 4 \sin x + \sin 4x$$

by *adding* the ordinates of the other two graphs.

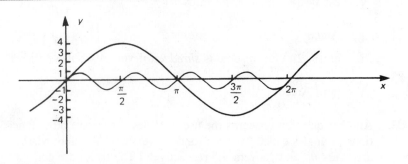

Figure 13-12b

For example, at a value of x for which the "small" graph has $y = 1$, the desired graph is 1 unit *above* the "big" graph.

C4.   The last question concerns your knowledge of graphs. Sketch:
  a. $y = \csc \theta$,
  b. $y = \text{Cos}^{-1} x$.

C5.   Mr. Ming is satisfied with your performance and assigns you to the Uranium Mining Project (UMP). A layer of ore beneath the ground has surfaces that are sinusoidal in cross section, as shown in Figure 13-12c. UMP plans to drill a vertical mine shaft through the ore layer and then dig a horizontal tunnel, again going through the ore layer. Your job is to find out how far this horizontal tunnel goes through the ore.

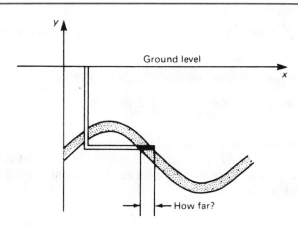

Figure 13-12c _____

You set up a Cartesian coordinate system with the x-axis at ground level and x and y in meters. You find that the top surface of the ore layer has a high point at $(x, y) = (80, -40)$, and that the graph next crosses the sinusoidal axis at $(x, y) = (205, -100)$. The bottom surface of the ore layer is 20 meters below the top surface for every value of x.
  a.   Write the particular equations of the top and bottom surfaces.
  b.   The vertical shaft is dug at $x = 50$. At what depth will it first reach the ore layer?
  c.   Transform the equations of the top and bottom surfaces so that x is expressed in terms of y.
  d.   How far will the horizontal shaft go through the formation if it is dug at a depth of
    i. $y = -90$?
    ii. $y = -170$?

CHAPTER TEST

T1. Find the exact value of:

   a. $\cos 30°$ b. $\tan \dfrac{5\pi}{6}$

   c. $\sec^{-1} 2$ d. $\mathrm{Cot}^{-1}\,(-\sqrt{3})$

   e. $\csc\theta$ if $(5, -7)$ is on the terminal side.

   f. the number of degrees in 3 radians.

T2. Find a decimal approximation for:

   a. $\sin 37°$ b. $\cot 1.9$

   c. $\theta = \mathrm{Arccsc}\,4.5$ d. $x = \arcsin 3$

T3. Sketch the graph of:

   a. $y = \sec \dfrac{\pi}{4}x$ b. $y = -3 + 5\cos 10(\theta - 4°)$

   c. $y = \mathrm{Arctan}\,x$

T4. Find and sketch the reference angle for $253°$.

T5. Solve the equation $y = -3 + 5\cos 10(\theta - 4°)$ for θ in terms of y.

T6. A sinusoidal function has a high point at $(x, y) = (2, 13)$. The next low point is at $(7, 1)$. Sketch the graph. Find the particular equation. Use the equation to predict the *third* positive value of x for which $y = 6$.

14

Properties of Trigonometric and Circular Functions

The angle of elevation of the Sun varies sinusoidally with the time of day. Predicting the time of sunrise involves finding x in an equation such as
$4 + 3 \cos \pi(x - 2) = 0$. In order to solve more complicated trigonometric equations such as

$$4 \sin (x + 75°) \cos(x - 75°) = 1,$$

you must learn some **properties** that will allow you to **transform** the left member to a simpler expression. Since the properties of trigonometric and circular functions are virtually the same, the word "trigonometric" function will be used for both kinds unless it is necessary to distinguish between them.

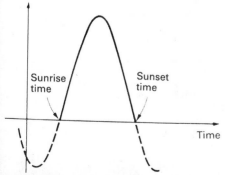

Angle of elevation

Sunrise time

Sunset time

Time

| **THREE PROPERTIES OF TRIGONOMETRIC
FUNCTIONS**

When you defined the six trigonometric functions, you probably observed that certain ones were *reciprocals* of others. For example, $\sec x = \dfrac{1}{\cos x}$.
In this section you will become familiar with this property and two other kinds that also come directly from the definitions. The variable x will be used for the argument whether the function is trigonometric or circular.

Objective:
Be able to use the three types of properties below to transform a given expression to a specified, equivalent form, possibly simplifying the expression.

1. *Reciprocal Properties:*   By the definitions of the trigonometric functions,

$$\tan x = \frac{v}{u} \quad \text{and} \quad \cot x = \frac{u}{v},$$

where u and v are the abscissa and ordinate, respectively, of a point on the terminal side of the angle or arc x (see Figure 14-1). Therefore, tan x and cot x are *reciprocals* of each other. Similarly, sin x and csc x are reciprocals of each other, and cos x and sec x are reciprocals of each other. In summary:

$$\cot x = \frac{1}{\tan x} \quad \csc x = \frac{1}{\sin x} \quad \sec x = \frac{1}{\cos x}$$

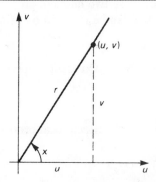

Figure 14-1 _____

These are known as the *reciprocal* properties. Since the product of a number and its reciprocal equals 1, these properties may also be written:

$$\tan x \cot x = 1 \quad \sin x \csc x = 1 \quad \cos x \sec x = 1$$

2. *Quotient Properties:*   The expression $\frac{\sin x}{\cos x}$ can be written using the definitions of the trigonometric functions as:

$$\frac{\sin x}{\cos x} = \frac{\dfrac{v}{r}}{\dfrac{u}{r}} \qquad \text{Definition of } \sin x \text{ and } \cos x$$

$$= \frac{v}{r} \cdot \frac{r}{u} \qquad \text{Definition of division}$$

$$= \frac{v}{u} \qquad \text{Multiplicaton property of fractions and canceling}$$

But $\frac{v}{u}$ is defined to be $\tan x$ (Figure 14-1). So by transitivity:

$$\tan x = \frac{\sin x}{\cos x}$$

This is called a *quotient* property because $\tan x$ is expressed as a quotient. Since $\cot x$ is the reciprocal of $\tan x$, the quotient can be inverted to give a second quotient property:

$$\cot x = \frac{\cos x}{\sin x}$$

There is another form of these two quotient properties that is sometimes useful. The $\sin x$ and $\cos x$ can be replaced by using the reciprocal properties to give:

$$\tan x = \frac{\sin x}{\cos x} \qquad \text{Quotient property}$$

$$= \frac{\dfrac{1}{\csc x}}{\dfrac{1}{\sec x}} \qquad \text{Reciprocal properties}$$

$$= \frac{1}{\csc x} \cdot \frac{\sec x}{1} \qquad \text{Definition of division}$$

$$= \frac{\sec x}{\csc x} \qquad \text{Multiplication property of fractions}$$

$$\therefore \quad \boxed{\tan x = \frac{\sec x}{\csc x}} \qquad \text{Transitivity}$$

Again using the reciprocal property, $\cot x = \frac{1}{\tan x}$:

$$\boxed{\cot x = \frac{\csc x}{\sec x}}$$

These two are usually not considered to be new properties, but rather to be alternate forms of the two quotient properties.

3. *Pythagorean Properties:*   The numbers u, v, and r in Figure 14-1 are the legs and hypotenuse of a right triangle. By the Pythagorean Theorem.

$$u^2 + v^2 = r^2.$$

Dividing both members by r^2 gives

$$\frac{u^2}{r^2} + \frac{v^2}{r^2} = 1.$$

Since $\frac{u}{r} = \cos x$ and $\frac{v}{r} = \sin x$, it follows that

$$(\cos x)^2 + (\sin x)^2 = 1.$$

It is customary to drop the parentheses and to write "$(\cos x)^2$ as "$\cos^2 x$." The exponent is placed in a position where it cannot possibly be mistaken for x^2. So this property is usually written:

$$\boxed{\cos^2 x + \sin^2 x = 1}$$

By dividing both members of $u^2 + v^2 = r^2$ by u^2, you get

$$1 + \tan^2 x = \sec^2 x$$

and by dividing both members by v^2, you get

$$\cot^2 x + 1 = \csc^2 x$$

These three properties are called the *Pythagorean* properties, since they come from the Pythagorean Theorem.

You are now prepared to accomplish the objective of transforming given expressions to equivalent, simpler forms.

EXAMPLE 1

Suppose you are asked to transform $\sin x \cot x$ to $\cos x$. The thought process you would go through is as follows:

1. Neither factor in $\sin x \cot x$ has $\cos x$ in it.
2. Therefore, either $\sin x$ or $\cot x$ should be *replaced* by something that *does* have $\cos x$ in it.
3. Sin x has no convenient forms that have $\cos x$ in them.
4. But by the quotient properties, $\cot x = \frac{\cos x}{\sin x}$.

The actual work would be done as follows:

$$\sin x \cot x = \sin x \cdot \frac{\cos x}{\sin x} \qquad \text{Quotient properties}$$

$$= \cos x \qquad \text{Multiplication property of fractions and canceling } \sin x$$

$$\therefore \sin x \cot x = \cos x \qquad \text{Transitivity} \qquad \blacksquare$$

EXAMPLE 2

Suppose that you are asked to transform the expression $\sin x \sec x \cot x$ into 1. The thought process is:

1. Since the answer is 1, there must be some canceling that can be done.
2. Canceling requires *fractions,* which can be obtained either from *reciprocal* properties or from *quotient* properties.
3. By the reciprocal properties, $\sec x = \frac{1}{\cos x}$. By the quotient properties, $\cot x = \frac{\cos x}{\sin x}$.

The actual work you would write down is as follows:

$\sin x \sec x \cot x$

$$= \sin x \cdot \frac{1}{\cos x} \cdot \frac{\cos x}{\sin x} \qquad \text{Reciprocal and quotient properties}$$

$$= \frac{\sin x \cos x}{\cos x \sin x} \qquad \text{Multiplication property of fractions}$$

$$= 1 \qquad \text{Canceling, or } \tfrac{n}{n} = 1$$

$\therefore \sin x \sec x \cot x \qquad \text{Transitivity}$
$= 1$

There are often several ways the transformation can be done. In the preceding example, you could have written

$\sin x \sec x \cot x$

$$= \sin x \cdot \frac{1}{\cos x} \cdot \cot x \qquad \text{Reciprocal properties}$$

$$= \frac{\sin x}{\cos x} \cdot \cot x \qquad \text{Multiplication property of fractions}$$

$$= \tan x \cot x \qquad \text{Quotient properties}$$

$$= 1 \qquad \text{Reciprocal properties}$$

$\therefore \sin x \sec x \cot x \qquad \text{Transitivity}$
$= 1$ ∎

EXAMPLE 3

Suppose you are asked to transform the expression $\cos^2 x - \sin^2 x$ into the equivalent expression $1 - 2\sin^2 x$. Your thought process would be:

1. The answer has no cosines in it. So you must get *rid* of the $\cos^2 x$.
2. Since the expression involves *squares* of functions, the Pythagorean properties should be helpful.
3. The Pythagorean property that has cosines in it is $\cos^2 x + \sin^2 x = 1$, from which $\cos^2 x = 1 - \sin^2 x$.

The actual steps in the transformation would be

$\cos^2 x - \sin^2 x$
$$= (1 - \sin^2 x) - \sin^2 x \qquad \text{Pythagorean properties}$$
$$= 1 - \sin^2 x - \sin^2 x \qquad \text{Associativity}$$
$$= 1 - 2\sin^2 x \qquad \text{Adding like terms}$$
$\therefore \cos^2 x - \sin^2 x \qquad \text{Transitivity}$
$= 1 - 2\sin^2 x$ ∎

In the exercise that follows, you will get practice using the reciprocal, quotient, and Pythagorean properties to transform expressions.

EXERCISE 14-1

Do These Quickly

The following problems are intended to refresh your skills. You should be able to do all 10 in less than 5 minutes.

Q1. Evaluate $\sin^2 60°$.

Q2. Evaluate $\cos^2 60°$.

Q3. Evaluate $\cos^2 60° + \sin^2 60°$.

Q4. If $y = \dfrac{2}{3}$, what does $\dfrac{1}{y}$ equal?

Using the letters in the diagram, write the definition of:

Q5. $\sin A$

Q6. $\cos A$

Q7. $\tan A$

Q8. $\cot A$

Q9. $\sec A$

Q10. $\csc A$

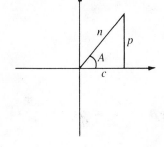

For Problems 1 through 26, transform the expression on the left to the one on the right.

1. $\cos x \tan x$ to $\sin x$

2. $\csc x \tan x$ to $\sec x$

3. $\sec x \cot x \sin x$ to 1

4. $\csc x \tan x \cos x$ to 1

5. $\sin^2 \theta \sec \theta \csc \theta$ to $\tan \theta$

6. $\cos^2 A \csc A \sec A$ to $\cot A$

7. $\tan A + \cot A$ to $\csc A \sec A$

8. $\sin \theta + \cot \theta \cos \theta$ to $\csc \theta$

9. $\csc x - \sin x$ to $\cot x \cos x$

10. $\sec \theta - \cos \theta$ to $\sin \theta \tan \theta$

11. $\tan x (\sin x + \cot x \cos x)$ to $\sec x$

12. $\cos x (\sec x + \cos x \csc^2 x)$ to $\csc^2 x$

13. $(1 + \sin B)(1 - \sin B)$ to $\cos^2 B$

14. $(\sec x - 1)(\sec x + 1)$ to $\tan^2 x$

15. $(\cos \phi - \sin \phi)^2$ to $1 - 2 \cos \phi \sin \phi$

16. $(1 - \tan \phi)^2$ to $\sec^2 \phi - 2 \tan \phi$

17. $(\tan n + \cot n)^2$ to $\sec^2 n + \csc^2 n$

18. $(\cos k - \sec k)^2$ to $\tan^2 k - \sin^2 k$

19. $\dfrac{\csc^2 x - 1}{\cos x}$ to $\cot x \csc x$

20. $\dfrac{1 - \cos^2 x}{\tan x}$ to $\sin x \cos x$

21. $\dfrac{\sec^2 \theta - 1}{\sin \theta}$ to $\tan \theta \sec \theta$

22. $\dfrac{1 + \cot^2 \theta}{\sec^2 \theta}$ to $\cot^2 \theta$

23. $\dfrac{\sec A}{\sin A} - \dfrac{\sin A}{\cos A}$ to $\cot A$

24. $\dfrac{\csc B}{\cos B} - \dfrac{\cos B}{\sin B}$ to $\tan B$

25. $\dfrac{1}{1 - \cos C} + \dfrac{1}{1 + \cos C}$ to $2 \csc^2 C$

26. $\dfrac{1}{\sec D - \tan D} + \dfrac{1}{\sec D + \tan D}$ to $2 \sec D$

27. There are quite a few properties in which the number 1 occurs. By appropriate algebra, if necessary, write *six* trigonometric expressions, each of which equals 1.

28. Use the Pythagorean properties to write expressions equivalent to:
    a. $\sin^2 x$ b. $\cos^2 x$ c. $\tan^2 x$
    d. $\cot^2 x$ e. $\sec^2 x$ f. $\csc^2 x$

29. Write equations expressing each of the six trigonometric functions in terms of $\sin x$.

30. Write equations expressing each of the six trigonometric functions in terms of cos x.

14-2 │ TRIGONOMETRIC IDENTITIES

A *trigonometric* open sentence is (obviously!) an open sentence that contains trigonometric functions.

For example,

$$\sin x = \frac{1}{2}$$

is a trigonometric equation. The solution set of such an open sentence is the set of all values of the argument x that makes the sentence true. If x is the degree measure of an angle, then the only solutions of the above open sentence are 30°, 150°, or any angle coterminal with these. Such an equation is called a *conditional* equation, because it is true only under certain conditions.

Some open sentences are true under *all* conditions. For example,

$$\cos^2 x = 1 - \sin^2 x$$

is true for *every* value of x. Such an equation is called an *identity*, because the two members are "identical" to each other. (Actually, the two members are *equivalent* expressions.)

Objective:
Given a trigonometric equation, prove that it is an *identity*.

There are two purposes for learning how to prove *identities*.

1. To learn the relationships among the functions.
2. To learn to transform one trigonometric expression to another equivalent form, usually simplifying it.

To accomplish the objective without defeating these purposes, the following agreeement will be made:

Agreement: To prove that an equation is an identity, start with one member and transform it into the other.

Note that this is exactly what you were doing in the previous section! The only thing that is new is that you are free to pick *either* member to start with.

EXAMPLE 1

Prove that $(1 + \cos x)(1 - \cos x) = \sin^2 x$.

Proof:

$(1 + \cos x)(1 - \cos x)$	Start with the more complicated member.
$= 1 - \cos^2 x$	Do the obvious algebra.
$= \sin^2 x$	Look for familiar expressions.
$\therefore (1 + \cos x)(1 - \cos x)$ $= \sin^2 x$, Q.E.D.	Transitivity

Notes:

1. It is tempting to *start* with the given equation and then work on *both* members until you have reduced the equation to an obviously true statement, such as "$\cos x = \cos x$." What this actually does is prove the *converse* of what you were asked to prove. That is, "*If* the identity is true, *then* the reflexive property is true." This is circular reasoning. It is dangerous because you might actually "prove" a *false* identity by taking an irreversible step, such as squaring both members.
2. The letters "Q.E.D." at the end stand for the Latin words *quod erat demonstrandum,* which means, "which was to be demonstrated." ■

EXAMPLE 2

Prove that $\cot x + \tan x = \csc x \sec x$.

Proof:

$\cot x + \tan x$	Pick a member to work on.
$= \dfrac{\cos x}{\sin x} + \dfrac{\sin x}{\cos x}$	Answer has only *one* term, so try adding fractions. The fractions must be *created first*.
$= \dfrac{\cos^2 x + \sin^2 x}{\sin x \cos x}$	Find common denominator and add the fractions.
$= \dfrac{1}{\sin x \cos x}$	Familiar Pythagorean property
$= \dfrac{1}{\sin x} \cdot \dfrac{1}{\cos x}$	Answer has *two* factors, so *make* two factors.

$$= \csc x \sec x \qquad \text{Familiar reciprocal properties}$$

$$\therefore \cot x + \tan x$$
$$= \csc x \sec x, \text{ Q.E.D.} \qquad \text{Transitivity}$$

EXAMPLE 3

Prove that $\dfrac{\sin x}{1 + \cos x} = \dfrac{1 - \cos x}{\sin x}$.

Proof:

$$\dfrac{\sin x}{1 + \cos x} \qquad \text{Pick a member to work on and multiply}$$
it by a clever form of 1.

$$= \dfrac{\sin x}{1 + \cos x} \cdot \dfrac{1 - \cos x}{1 - \cos x}$$

$$= \dfrac{\sin x \,(1 - \cos x)}{1 - \cos^2 x} \qquad \text{Do the obvious algebra, but } \textit{don't}$$
destroy the "$1 - \cos x$," because you
want it in the answer.

$$= \dfrac{\sin x \,(1 - \cos x)}{\sin^2 x} \qquad \text{Familiar Pythagorean property}$$

$$= \dfrac{1 - \cos x}{\sin x} \qquad \text{Do the obvious canceling.}$$

$$\therefore \dfrac{\sin x}{1 + \cos x}$$

$$= \dfrac{1 - \cos x}{\sin x}, \text{ Q.E.D.} \qquad \text{Transitivity}$$

Note that there could be *two* reasons for picking the form of "1" used in the first step. It has the *conjugate* of $1 + \cos x$ in its denominator. Or it has $1 - \cos x$ in its numerator, an expression you *want* in the answer. ■

EXAMPLE 4

Prove that $\csc \theta \cos^2 \theta + \sin \theta = \csc \theta$.

Proof:

$$\csc \theta \cos^2 \theta + \sin \theta \qquad \text{Pick the more complicated}$$
member.

$$= \csc \theta \left(\cos^2 \theta + \dfrac{\sin \theta}{\csc \theta} \right) \qquad \text{If you want } \csc \theta \text{ as a factor}$$
of the answer, then *factor it out!*

$$= \csc \theta \,(\cos^2 \theta + \sin \theta \qquad \text{Familiar reciprocal property}$$
$$\cdot \sin \theta)$$

$$= \csc \theta \,(\cos^2 \theta + \sin^2 \theta) \qquad \text{Obvious algebra}$$

$$= \csc \theta \qquad\qquad\qquad\quad \text{Familiar Pythagorean property}$$

$$\therefore \csc \theta \cos^2 \theta + \sin \theta \qquad \text{Transitivity}$$
$$= \csc \theta, \; Q.E.D.$$

Factoring out the csc θ in the second line of the proof is sometimes called "factoring out a rabbit," because you are reaching in and pulling out a common factor that wasn't there!   ■

Note that the reasons written for the steps in the above examples are reasons you *chose to do* the particular step, rather than mathematical reasons why the steps are true. From these examples, certain useful techniques emerge that help guide your thought process as you attempt to prove identities. These steps are summarized below for your convenience.

STEPS IN PROVING IDENTITIES

1. Pick the member you wish to work with and write it down. Usually it is easier to start with the more complicated member.
2. Look for *algebraic* things to do.
   a. If there are two terms and you want only one,
      i. add fractions,
      ii. factor something out.
   b. Multiply by a clever form of 1
      i. to multiply a numerator or denominator by its conjugate,
      ii. to get a desired expression in numerator or denominator.
   c. Do any obvious algebra such as distributing, squaring, or multiplying polynomials.
3. Look for *trigonometric* things to do.
   a. Look for familiar trigonometric expressions like

$$1 - \cos^2 x, \; \cos x \sec x, \; \text{or} \; \frac{\sin x}{\cos x}.$$

   b. If there are *squares* of functions, think of Pythagorean properties.
   c. Reduce the number of different functions, transforming them to the ones you want in the answer.
4. Keep looking at the answer to make sure you are headed in the right direction.

The exercise that follows is designed to give you practice proving identities, so that you may become more familiar with the properties of the trigonometric functions and may gain practice transforming one expression into another simpler form.

EXERCISE 14-2

Do These Quickly

The following problems are intended to refresh your skills. You should be able to do all 10 in less than 5 minutes.

Q1. State the Pythagorean property for cosine and sine.

Q2. State the quotient property for tangent.

Q3. State the reciprocal property for secant.

Q4. Sketch the graph of $y = \cos x$.

Q5. Evaluate $\tan \left(\dfrac{\pi}{3} \right)$.

Q6. Evaluate $\theta = \text{Cot}^{-1} 2$ (approximately).

For $y = 3 + 7 \cos 4(x - 1)$, what is the

Q7. phase displacement?

Q8. sinusoidal axis location?

Q9. period?

Q10. amplitude?

In Problems 1 through 34, prove that each equation is an identity.

1. $\sec x (\sec x - \cos x) = \tan^2 x$

2. $\tan x (\cot x + \tan x) = \sec^2 x$

3. $\sin x (\csc x - \sin x) = \cos^2 x$

4. $\cos x (\sec x - \cos x) = \sin^2 x$

5. $\csc^2 \theta - \cos^2 \theta \csc^2 \theta = 1$

6. $\cos^2 \theta + \tan^2 \theta \cos^2 \theta = 1$

7. $(\sec \theta + 1)(\sec \theta - 1) = \tan^2 \theta$

8. $(1 + \sin \theta)(1 - \sin \theta) = \cos^2 \theta$

9. $\sec^2 A + \tan^2 A \sec^2 A = \sec^4 A$

10. $\cot^2 A \csc^2 A - \cot^2 A = \cot^4 A$

11. $\cos^4 t - \sin^4 t = 1 - 2 \sin^2 t$

12. $\sec^4 t - \tan^4 t = 1 + 2\tan^2 t$

13. $\dfrac{1}{\sin x \cos x} - \dfrac{\cos x}{\sin x} = \tan x$

14. $\dfrac{\sec x}{\sin x} - \dfrac{\sin x}{\cos x} = \cot x$

15. $\dfrac{\sin x}{\csc x} + \dfrac{\cos x}{\sec x} = 1$

16. $\dfrac{1}{\sec^2 x} + \dfrac{1}{\csc^2 x} = 1$

17. $\dfrac{1}{1 + \cos s} = \csc^2 s - \csc s \cot s$

18. $\dfrac{1}{1 - \sin r} = \sec^2 r + \sec r \tan r$

19. $\dfrac{\cos x}{\sec x - 1} - \dfrac{\cos x}{\tan^2 x} = \cot^2 x$

20. $\dfrac{\sin x}{1 - \cos x} + \dfrac{1 - \cos x}{\sin x} = 2\csc x$

21. $\dfrac{\sec x}{\sec x - \tan x} = \sec^2 x + \sec x \tan x$

22. $\dfrac{1 + \sin x}{1 - \sin x} = 2\sec^2 x + 2\sec x \tan x - 1$

23. $\sin^3 z \cos^2 z = \sin^3 z - \sin^5 z$

24. $\sin^3 z \cos^2 z = \cos^2 z \sin z - \cos^4 z \sin z$

25. $\sec^2 \theta + \csc^2 \theta = \sec^2 \theta \csc^2 \theta$

26. $\sec \theta + \tan \theta = \dfrac{1}{\sec \theta - \tan \theta}$

27. $\dfrac{1 - 3\cos x - 4\cos^2 x}{\sin^2 x} = \dfrac{1 - 4\cos x}{1 - \cos x}$

28. $\dfrac{\sec^2 x - 6\tan x + 7}{\sec^2 x - 5} = \dfrac{\tan x - 4}{\tan x + 2}$

29. $\dfrac{\sin^3 A + \cos^3 A}{\sin A + \cos A} = 1 - \sin A \cos A$

30. $\dfrac{\sec^3 B - \cos^3 B}{\sec B - \cos B} = \sec^2 B + 1 + \cos^2 B$

31. $\csc^6 x - \cot^6 x = 1 + 3 \csc^2 x \cot^2 x$

32. $(2 \sin x + 3 \cos x)^2 + (3 \sin x - 2 \cos x)^2 = 13$

33. $\dfrac{1 + \sin x + \cos x}{1 + \sin x - \cos x} = \dfrac{1 + \cos x}{\sin x}$

34. $\dfrac{1 + \sin x + \cos x}{1 - \sin x + \cos x} = \dfrac{1 + \sin x}{\cos x}$

35.   *Graphs of 1 + tan² x and sec² x*   In this problem you will demonstrate by graphing that the identity

$$1 + \tan^2 x = \sec^2 x$$

is reasonable.
a.   Draw an auxiliary graph of $y = \tan x$.
b.   On the same Cartesian coordinate system, draw a graph of $y = \tan^2 x$ by *squaring* the ordinates of the graph from part a.
c.   Draw a graph of $y = \sec^2 x$ the same way.
d.   By comparing the two graphs, show that the graph of $y = \sec^2 x$ is always 1 unit above the graph of $y = \tan^2 x$.

36.   *Introduction to Odd and Even Functions*   In this problem you will learn a property possessed by some algebraic functions and all six trigonometric functions, namely, "oddness" and "evenness." Suppose that functions f_1, f_2, f_3, and f_4 are defined as follows:

$$f_1(x) = x, f_2(x) = x^2, f_3(x) = x^3, f_4(x) = x^4.$$

a.   For each function, find $f(-3), f(-2), f(2)$, and $f(3)$.
b.   A function is called an *even* function if $f(-x) = f(x)$ for all values of x. From your answers in part a, tell which of the above functions are even functions.
c.   A function is called an *odd* function if $f(-x) = -f(x)$ for all values of x. From your answers to part a, tell which of the above functions are odd functions.
d.   Why do you suppose the names "odd" and "even" were picked to describe the properties in parts b and c?
e.   Write down the values of the six trigonometric functions of $-30°$. Then decide which of the trigonometric functions satisfy the requirements of an *odd* function and which ones satisfy the requirements of an *even* function. Write your answers in a form such as

$$\sin(-x) = \sin x \quad \text{or} \quad \sin(-x) = -\sin x,$$

whichever is correct.

| # PROPERTIES INVOLVING FUNCTIONS OF MORE THAN ONE ARGUMENT

The Pythagorean, quotient, and reciprocal properties of Section 14-1 involve *one* argument only. In this section you will learn properties in which more than one argument appears. For example, the argument may be composed of a *sum* of two numbers, such as cos $(x - D)$, which you encountered when you worked with sinusoids.

The operation cos does *not* distribute over addition or subtraction. That is, cos $(x - D)$ does *not* equal cos x − cos D. You can prove this by substituting angles such as $x = 60°$ and $D = 90°$ and showing that the two expressions are not equal. In this section you will learn how to express functions of sums or differences of two angles in terms of functions of the angles themselves.

Objectives:

1. Be able to express functions of $-x$ in terms of functions of x.
2. Be able to express cos $(A - B)$, cos $(A + B)$, sin $(A - B)$, and sin $(A + B)$ in terms of sin A, cos A, sin B, and cos B.
3. Be able to express tan $(A - B)$ and tan $(A + B)$ in terms of tan A and tan B.

1. *Functions of $-x$:*   Suppose that $f(x) = x^5$. Then:

$$f(-x) = (-x)^5 \quad \text{Definition of } f$$

$$f(-x) = -x^5 \quad \text{Negative power raised to odd power}$$

$$f(-x) = -f(x) \quad \text{Substitution}$$

But if $f(x) = x^4$, then

$$f(-x) = (-x)^4 \quad \text{Definition of } f$$

$$f(-x) = x^4 \quad \text{Negative number raised to even power}$$

$$f(-x) = f(x) \quad \text{Definition of } f$$

So when the exponent is odd, $f(-x) = -f(x)$; when the exponent is even, $f(-x) = f(x)$. This property of odd and even exponents leads to a general definition of odd and even functions.

DEFINITION

If $f(-x) = f(x)$, then f is called an **even function.**
If $f(-x) = -f(x)$, then f is called an **odd function.**

The names "odd" and "even" carry over to functions that do not involve exponents. If you worked Problem 36 in the previous section, you discovered that the trigonometric functions possess these properties also.

Figure 14-3a shows two arcs on a unit circle, one with measure x, the other with measure $-x$. From the picture, you can see that if (u, v) is the endpoint of the arc x, then $(u, -v)$ is the endpoint of the arc $-x$. By the definition of circular functions, $\cos x = u$, and $\cos (-x) = u$ also. Therefore,

$$\cos (-x) = \cos x,$$

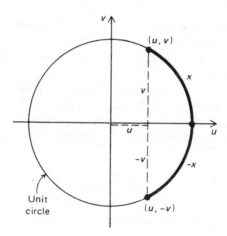

Figure 14-3a _____

which means that cosine is an *even* function. Similarly, $\sin x = v$ and $\sin (-x) = -v$, which implies that

$$\sin (-x) = -\sin x,$$

and sine is an *odd* function. Each function whose definition involves v will be an odd function, since the ordinate of $-x$ is $-v$. For example,

$$\tan (-x) = \frac{-v}{u} = -\frac{v}{u} = -\tan x.$$

The cosine and its reciprocal, the secant, which involve only u, are the only even functions. The properties are summarized below.

PROPERTIES

ODD AND EVEN FUNCTION PROPERTIES

$\cos(-x) = \cos x$	even function
$\sin(-x) = -\sin x$	odd function
$\tan(-x) = -\tan x$	odd function
$\cot(-x) = -\cot x$	odd function
$\sec(-x) = \sec x$	even function
$\csc(-x) = -\csc x$	odd function

Note that these properties also hold for the trigonometric functions. For example, $\sin(-\theta) = -\sin \theta$ and $\cos(-\theta) = \cos \theta$.

2. *Functions of Complementary Arcs:*   You recall from Section 13-4 that the *co*sine of an angle equals the *sine* of its *complement*. For example, the complement of 76° is 90° − 76°, or 14°. So cos 76° = sin 14°.

Using the definitions of the circular functions, it is easy to see why this property is true. Figure 14-3b shows an arc x with endpoint (u, v). The *complement* of x is $\frac{\pi}{2} - x$. If this arc is moved into standard position, as in the right-hand sketch, its endpoint will be (v, u).

Consequently,

$$\cos\left(\frac{\pi}{2} - x\right) = v,$$

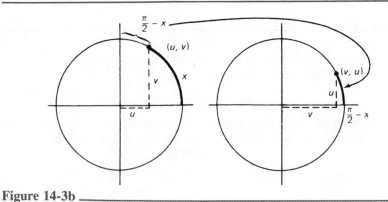

Figure 14-3b

the abscissa of the endpoint of $(\frac{\pi}{2} - x)$. But $v = \sin x$, as shown in the left-hand sketch of Figure 14-3b. Therefore,

$$\cos\left(\frac{\pi}{2} - x\right) = \sin x.$$

By similar reasoning,

$$\sin\left(\frac{\pi}{2} - x\right) = \cos x.$$

The cofunction properties for tangent and secant are similarly derived and are summarized below.

PROPERTIES

COFUNCTION PROPERTIES FOR CIRCULAR FUNCTIONS

$$\cos\left(\frac{\pi}{2} - x\right) = \sin x \quad \text{and} \quad \sin\left(\frac{\pi}{2} - x\right) = \cos x$$

$$\cot\left(\frac{\pi}{2} - x\right) = \tan x \quad \text{and} \quad \tan\left(\frac{\pi}{2} - x\right) = \cot x$$

$$\csc\left(\frac{\pi}{2} - x\right) = \sec x \quad \text{and} \quad \sec\left(\frac{\pi}{2} - x\right) = \csc x$$

The cofunction properties for the trigonometric functions are virtually the same. Since an arc of $\frac{\pi}{2}$ corresponds to an angle of 90°, the complement of θ is $(90° - \theta)$. The properties are summarized below.

PROPERTIES

COFUNCTION PROPERTIES FOR TRIGONOMETRIC FUNCTIONS

$$\cos(90° - \theta) = \sin \theta \quad \text{and} \quad \sin(90° - \theta) = \cos \theta$$

$$\cot(90° - \theta) = \tan \theta \quad \text{and} \quad \tan(90° - \theta) = \cot \theta$$

$$\csc(90° - \theta) = \sec \theta \quad \text{and} \quad \sec(90° - \theta) = \csc \theta$$

3. *Cos (A − B):*   From Section 9-2 you recall the Distance Formula for finding the distance between two points in a Cartesian coordinate system. It is really just a special case of the Pythagorean Theorem. The

distance between points (x_1, y_1) and (x_2, y_2) in Figure 14-3c is given by

$$d^2 = (\Delta x)^2 + (\Delta y)^2,$$

from which

$$d^2 = (x_2 - x_1)^2 + (y_2 - y_1)^2.$$

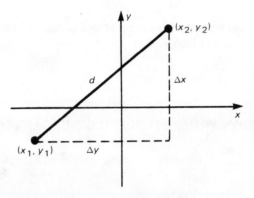

Figure 14-3c

With this piece of background information, you are now ready to derive a formula for cos $(A - B)$ in terms of sines and cosines of A and B. Figure 14-3d shows two arcs of measures A and B in standard position on a unit circle. Their terminal points have coordinates (cos A, sin A) and (cos B, sin B), respectively. The arc between these two terminal points has measure $(A - B)$. Figure 14-3e shows the arc of measure $(A - B)$ moved around the circle into standard position. In this position, the coordinates of its terminal point are (cos$(A - B)$, sin $(A - B)$).

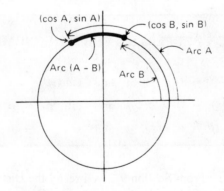

Arcs A, B, and (A − B) on a unit circle

Figure 14-3d

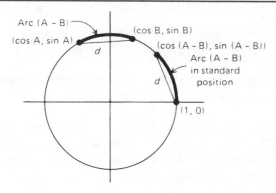

Arc (A – B) rotated into standard position

Figure 14-3e _____

The length d of the chord for this arc is simply the distance between two points in a Cartesian coordinate system. The Distance Formula can be used to calculate d in two different ways. When the arc $(A - B)$ is in its original position,

$$d^2 = (\cos A - \cos B)^2 + (\sin A - \sin B)^2.$$

Doing the indicated squaring gives

$$d^2 = \cos^2 A - 2\cos A \cos B + \cos^2 B$$
$$+ \sin^2 A - 2\sin A \sin B + \sin^2 B.$$

You have learned to think of Pythagorean properties whenever you see squares of functions. Commuting and associating $\cos^2 A + \sin^2 A$ and $\cos^2 B + \sin^2 B$ allows you to use the Pythagorean properties to replace each expression with the number 1. Therefore,

$$d^2 = 2 - 2\cos A \cos B - 2\sin A \sin B.$$

When the arc is rotated into standard position, the distance formula can be applied again, giving

$$d^2 = (\cos (A - B) - 1)^2 + (\sin (A - B) - 0)^2.$$

Upon carrying out the indicated squaring, this becomes

$$d^2 = \cos^2 (A - B) - 2\cos (A - B) + 1 + \sin^2 (A - B).$$

Associating the $\cos^2 (A - B) + \sin^2 (A - B)$ and using the Pythagorean properties gives

$$d^2 = 2 - 2\cos (A - B).$$

Note that this form of d^2 contains the desired $\cos (A - B)$. The other form of d^2 above contains sines and cosines of A and B. Using the transitive property to equate these expressions gives

$$2 - 2\cos (A - B) = 2 - 2\cos A \cos B - 2\sin A \sin B.$$

Subtracting 2 and then dividing by -2 gives

$$\cos (A - B) = \cos A \cos B + \sin A \sin B .$$

The property is called a "composite argument" property, because the argument is composed of measures of two arcs or angles.

4. *Composite Argument Properties for cos (A + B), sin (A − B), sin (A + B):*   The way to solve a new problem is to turn it into an old problem. To derive a formula for cos (A + B), you can first transform the argument into a *difference*, getting

$$\cos (A + B) = \cos (A - (-B)).$$

Using the composite argument property you have just derived, this becomes

$$\cos A \cos (-B) + \sin A \sin (-B).$$

Using the odd-even properties on this, you get

$$\cos A \cos B - \sin A \sin B.$$

$$\therefore \quad \boxed{\cos (A + B) = \cos A \cos B - \sin A \sin B} .$$

The expression sin (A − B) can be transformed to a cosine using the cofunction properties. Considering A and B to be angles,

$$\sin (A - B) = \cos (90° - (A - B)) \quad \text{Cofunction property}$$

$$= \cos ((90° - A) + B) \quad \text{Associativity}$$

The last expression is now a *cosine* of a *sum*. Using the above composite argument property gives

$$\sin (A - B) = \cos (90° - A) \cos B - \sin (90° - A) \sin B.$$

Applying the cofunction properties again gives:

$$\boxed{\sin (A - B) = \sin A \cos B - \cos A \sin B}$$

Similar reasoning gives:

$$\boxed{\sin (A + B) = \sin A \cos B + \cos A \sin B}$$

5. *Composite Argument Properties for tan (A + B) and tan (A − B):*   The expression tan (A + B) can be written in terms of functions of A and B

with the aid of the quotient properties:

$\tan (A + B)$

$$= \frac{\sin (A + B)}{\cos (A + B)} \qquad \text{Quotient property}$$

$$= \frac{\sin A \cos B + \cos A \sin B}{\cos A \cos B - \sin A \sin B} \qquad \text{Composite argument properties}$$

It is possible to transform this into terms of $\tan A$ and $\tan B$ *alone*. Since tangents have cosines for denominators, you seek a way to get $\cos A$ and $\cos B$ as denominators. A clever way to do this is simply to *factor out* $\cos A \cos B$ (i.e., "factor out a rabbit!").

$\tan (A + B) \qquad\qquad\qquad\qquad\qquad \text{Factoring}$

$$= \frac{\cos A \cos B \left(\dfrac{\sin A \cos B}{\cos A \cos B} + \dfrac{\cos A \sin B}{\cos A \cos B} \right)}{\cos A \cos B \left(\dfrac{\cos A \cos B}{\cos A \cos B} + \dfrac{\sin A \sin B}{\cos A \cos B} \right)}$$

$$= \frac{\dfrac{\sin A}{\cos A} + \dfrac{\sin B}{\cos B}}{1 - \dfrac{\sin A \sin B}{\cos A \cos B}} \qquad \text{Canceling}$$

$$= \frac{\tan A + \tan B}{1 - \tan A \tan B} \qquad \text{Quotient properties}$$

$$\therefore \quad \boxed{\tan (A + B) = \frac{\tan A + \tan B}{1 - \tan A \tan B}} \qquad \text{Transitivity}$$

Writing $\tan (A - B)$ as $\tan (A + (-B))$ and using the odd-even properties gives:

$$\boxed{\tan (A - B) = \frac{\tan A - \tan B}{1 + \tan A \tan B}}$$

Note: The composite argument properties are also called the "Addition Formulas."

The following exercise is designed to help you learn the odd-even, cofunction, and composite argument properties by using them.

EXERCISE 14-3

Do These Quickly

The following problems are intended to refresh your skills. You should be able to do all 10 in less than 5 minutes.

Q1.   Is $\cos^2 x - \sin^2 x = 1$ an identity?

Q2.   Is $\tan x = \dfrac{(\sec x)}{(\csc x)}$ an identity?

Q3.   Is $\sin y = \dfrac{1}{(\cos y)}$ an identity?

Q4.   Write $\cos^2 A$ in terms of $\sin A$.

Q5.   Evaluate $\sin \left(\dfrac{4\pi}{3} \right)$.

Q6.   Evaluate $\sec (-60°)$.

Q7.   Sketch the graph of $y = \arcsin x$.

Q8.   What does $(\sin x)(\csc x)$ equal?

Q9.   Write the general equation of an exponential function.

Q10.   Evaluate 4^{-2}.

For Problems 1 through 6, show by substituting 60° for A and 90° for B that:

1. $\cos (A + B) \neq \cos A + \cos B$

2. $\sin (A + B) \neq \sin A + \sin B$

3. $\tan (A - B) \neq \tan A - \tan B$

4. $\cot (A - B) \neq \cot A - \cot B$

5. $\sec (A + B) \neq \sec A + \sec B$

6. $\csc (A - B) \neq \csc A - \csc B$

For Problems 7 through 12, demonstrate that the given property really works by substituting:
a. $A = 60°,$ $B = 30°$
b. $A = \dfrac{2\pi}{3},$ $B = \dfrac{\pi}{6}$

7. $\cos (A - B) = \cos A \cos B + \sin A \sin B$

8. $\cos (A + B) = \cos A \cos B - \sin A \sin B$

9. $\sin (A - B) = \sin A \cos B - \cos A \sin B$

10. $\sin (A + B) = \sin A \cos B + \cos A \sin B$

11. $\tan (A - B) = \dfrac{\tan A - \tan B}{1 + \tan A \tan B}$

12. $\tan (A + B) = \dfrac{\tan A + \tan B}{1 - \tan A \tan B}$

For Problems 13 through 16, prove that the given equation is an identity.

13. $\cos (x - 90°) = \sin x$

14. $\sin \left(x - \dfrac{\pi}{2} \right) = -\cos x$

15. $\tan \left(x - \dfrac{\pi}{2} \right) = -\cot x$

16. $\sec (x - 90°) = \csc x$

17. Use what you recall about sinusoids and phase displacements from
     Section 13-6 to do the following:
     a.   Draw a graph of $y = \cos (x - 90°)$.
     b.   Draw a graph of $y = \sin x$.
     c.   Explain from your graphs why the equation in Problem 13 is
          reasonable.

18. Use what you recall about sinusoids and phase displacements from
     Section 13-6 to do the following:
     a.   Draw a graph of $y = \sin (x - \frac{\pi}{2})$.
     b.   Draw a graph of $y = \cos x$.
     c.   Explain how your graphs show that the equation in Problem 14
          is *reasonable*.

19. Show that giving a sinusoid a phase displacement of 180° has the
     same effect as turning it over. That is, show that $\cos (x - 180°) =$
     $-\cos x$.

20. Show that giving a sinusoid a phase displacement of $-180°$ has the
     same effect as giving it a phase displacement of $+180°$. That is,
     show that $\cos (x + 180°) = \cos(x - 180°)$.

For Problems 21 through 26, assume that A and B are in standard position
and that $\sin A = \frac{1}{2}$, $\cos A > 0$, $\tan B = \frac{3}{4}$, and $\sin B < 0$. Draw A and B
in standard position, then find the following:

21. $\cos (A - B)$

22. $\sin (A - B)$

23. $\sin (A + B)$

24. $\cos (A + B)$

25. $\tan (A - B)$

26. $\tan (A + B)$

The composite argument properties may be used to find *exact* values of functions of 15°. Use a clever choice of A and B, (such as 30°, 45°, 60°, 90°, etc.) and any of the properties you need to find exact values of the following. Express the answers in simple radical form.

27. $\cos 15°$

28. $\sin 15°$

29. $\tan 15°$

30. $\cot 15°$

31. $\sec 15°$

32. $\csc 15°$

Use the cofunction properties and the answers to Problems 27 through 32 to find *exact* values of the following, leaving the answers in simple radical form.

33. $\sin 75°$

34. $\cos 75°$

35. $\cot 75°$

36. $\tan 75°$

37. $\csc 75°$

38. $\sec 75°$

Use a calculator or square-root table and the answers to Problems 27 through 38 to find decimal approximations for the following. Then look in Table III or use a calculator to make sure you are right.

39. $\cos 15°$

40. $\sin 15°$

41. $\tan 15°$

42. $\tan 75°$

43. $\csc 75°$

44. $\sec 75°$

For Problems 45 through 50, prove that the given equation is an identity.

45. $\sin (x + 60°) - \cos (x + 30°) = \sin x$

46. $\sin (x + 30°) + \cos (x + 60°) = \cos x$

47. $\tan \left(x + \dfrac{\pi}{4}\right) + 1 = \sqrt{2} \cos x \sec \left(x + \dfrac{\pi}{4}\right)$

48. $\sqrt{2} \cos \left(x - \dfrac{\pi}{4}\right) = \cos x + \sin x$

49. $(\cos A \cos B - \sin A \sin B)^2 + (\sin A \cos B + \cos A \sin B)^2 = 1$

50. $\sin \left(\dfrac{3x}{7}\right) \cos \left(\dfrac{4x}{7}\right) + \cos \left(\dfrac{3x}{7}\right) \sin \left(\dfrac{4x}{7}\right) = \sin x$

The composite argument properties have sums of *two* angles or arcs. Similar properties for sums of *three* angles can be derived by first associating two of the angles. For Problems 51 and 52, write the given expression in terms of $\sin A$, $\sin B$, $\sin C$, $\cos A$, $\cos B$, and $\cos C$.

51. $\cos (A + B + C)$ 52. $\sin (A + B + C)$

Problems 53 through 56 let you discover for yourself some of the properties you will learn in the next section.

The composite argument properties can be used to express functions of *twice* an angle or arc in terms of functions of that angle or arc. For example, $\sin 2A = \sin (A + A)$, which is a function of a composite argument. Use this fact to derive "double argument" properties, expressing Problems 53 through 56 in terms of functions of A.

53. $\sin 2A$ 54. $\cos 2A$

55. $\tan 2A$ 56. $\cot 2A$

14-4 | ## MULTIPLE-ARGUMENT PROPERTIES

The composite argument properties can be used to derive properties expressing functions of *twice* an angle or arc in terms of functions of that angle or arc.

Objective:
Be able to express $\sin 2A$, $\cos 2A$, and $\tan 2A$ in terms of $\sin A$, $\cos A$, and $\tan A$.

1. *Double Argument Property for sin 2A:*   Recognizing that $\sin 2A = \sin (A + A)$, you can write:

$\sin 2A = \sin (A + A)$

$\qquad = \sin A \cos A + \cos A \sin A$ Composite argument properties

$\qquad = 2 \sin A \cos A$ Adding "like terms"

$\therefore$ $\boxed{\sin 2A = 2 \sin A \cos A}$ Transitivity

2. *Double Argument Property for cos 2A:*   Using the above reasoning:

$\cos 2A = \cos (A + A)$

$\qquad = \cos A \cos A - \sin A \sin A$ Composite argument properties

$\qquad = \cos^2 A - \sin^2 A$ Definition of exponentiation

∴ $\boxed{\cos 2A = \cos^2 A - \sin^2 A}$ Transitivity

Note that this property looks a lot like the Pythagorean property $\cos^2 A + \sin^2 A = 1$. In fact, the Pythagorean property can be used to transform the double argument property to two other forms.

$\cos 2A = \cos^2 A - \sin^2 A$ Double argument property

$\qquad = (1 - \sin^2 A) - \sin^2 A$ Pythagorean property

$\qquad = 1 - 2 \sin^2 A$ Associativity

∴ $\boxed{\cos 2A = 1 - 2 \sin^2 A}$ Transitivity

In this form, cos 2A is expressed in terms of sin A *alone*. Cos 2A can be expressed in terms of cos A alone.

$\cos 2A = \cos^2 A - \sin^2 A$ Double argument property

$\qquad = \cos^2 A - (1 - \cos^2 A)$ Pythagorean property

$\qquad = 2 \cos^2 A - 1$ Commutativity and associativity

∴ $\boxed{\cos 2A = 2 \cos^2 A - 1}$ Transitivity

3. *Doubling Argument Property for tan 2A:*   A double argument property for tan 2A may be derived the same way as for sin 2A and cos 2A.

$\tan 2A = \tan (A + A)$

$\qquad = \dfrac{\tan A + \tan A}{1 - \tan A \tan A}$ Composite argument properties

$\qquad = \dfrac{2 \tan A}{1 - \tan^2 A}$ Associativity and definition of exponentiation

∴ $\boxed{\tan 2A = \dfrac{2 \tan A}{1 - \tan^2 A}}$ Transitivity

The exercise that follows is intended to give you enough practice using these properties so that you will *learn* them. You will also use them to derive properties for *higher* multiples of angles. In the last problems you will derive properties of *inverse* circular functions.

EXERCISE 14-4

Do These Quickly

The following problems are intended to refresh your skills. You should be able to do all 10 in less than 5 minutes.

Q1.   Is $\cos (A + B) = \cos A + \cos B$ an identity?

Q2.   Is $1 - \sin^2 x = \cos^2 x$ an identity?

Q3.   Write $\tan x$ in terms of $\sin x$ and $\cos x$.

Q4.   Write $\sin (R + S)$ in terms of sines and cosines of R and S.

Q5.   If $\tan x = 3$, what *two* numbers could $\sin x$ equal?

Q6.   Sketch the graph of $y = \tan \theta$.

Q7.   Sketch the graph of $y = 2^x$.

Q8.   Find $\log_2 8$.

Q9.   Find the next term of the arithmetic sequence 17, 21, ...

Q10.   What is the probability of drawing a King from a normal 52-card deck?

Work the following problems.

1.   a.   Recalling what you have learned about graphing sinusoids in Section 13-6, draw a graph of $y = \cos 2x$.
   b.   Draw another graph of $y = 2 \cos x$ using the *same* scales as in part a.
   c.   Based on your graphs, explain why $\cos 2x$ is *not* equal to $2 \cos x$.

2.   Repeat Problem 1 using $y = \sin 2x$ and $y = 2 \sin x$.

For Problems 3 through 8, show that the double argument property really works by substituting the given measures of angles or arcs into the formula and showing that you get the right answer.

3. $\sin 2A, A = 30°$ 4. $\cos 2A, A = 30°$

5. $\cos 2A$, $A = \dfrac{\pi}{4}$

6. $\sin 2A$, $A = \dfrac{\pi}{4}$

7. $\tan 2A$, $A = 60°$

8. $\tan 2A$, $A = \dfrac{\pi}{4}$

For Problems 9 through 12, calculate $\sin 2A$, $\cos 2A$, and $\tan 2A$ for the angles or arc described.

9. $\sin A = \dfrac{3}{5}$, A terminates in Quadrant I

10. $\cos A = -\dfrac{3}{5}$, A terminates in Quadrant II

11. $\tan A = -\dfrac{3}{4}$, A terminates in Quadrant IV

12. $\tan A = \dfrac{4}{3}$, A terminates in Quadrant III

For Problems 13 through 22, prove that the given equation is an identity.

13. $\sin 2x = \dfrac{2 \tan x}{1 + \tan^2 x}$

14. $\sec 2x = \dfrac{\sec^2 x}{2 - \sec^2 x}$

15. $\cos 2\phi = \dfrac{1 - \tan^2 \phi}{1 + \tan^2 \phi}$

16. $\sin 2\phi = 2 \cot \phi \sin^2 \phi$

17. $\dfrac{\cos 2D}{\cos D - \sin D} = \cos D + \sin D$

18. $(1 + \tan x) \tan 2x = \dfrac{2 \tan x}{1 - \tan x}$

19. $\tan r = \dfrac{1 - \cos 2r}{\sin 2r}$

20. $\tan y = \dfrac{\sin 2y}{1 + \cos 2y}$

21. $\sin^2 \theta = \dfrac{1}{2}(1 - \cos 2\theta)$

22. $\cos^2 \theta = \dfrac{1}{2}(1 + \cos 2\theta)$

The composite argument properties can be combined with the double argument properties to derive triple, quadruple, etc., argument properties. For example, $\sin 3x = \sin (2x + x)$, which is a sine of a composite argument. For Problems 23 through 26, derive multiple argument properties for the given functions.

23. $\sin 3x$ in terms of $\sin x$ alone

24. $\cos 3x$ in terms of $\cos x$ alone

25. $\cos 4x$ in terms of $\cos x$ alone

26. $\sin 4x$ in terms of $\sin x$ and $\cos x$

The double argument properties work whenever one of the arguments is twice as large as the other. For Problems 27 through 34, write equations expressing:

27. $\tan 14x$ in terms of $\tan 7x$.

28. $\cot 14x$ in terms of $\cot 7x$.

29. $\cos 6x$ in terms of $\sin 3x$ and $\cos 3x$.

30. $\sin 6x$ in terms of $\sin 3x$ and $\cos 3x$.

31. $\cos 10x$ in terms of $\cos 5x$ *alone*.

32. $\cos 10x$ in terms of $\sin 5x$ *alone*.

33. $\cos x$ in terms of $\cos \frac{1}{2} x$ *alone*.

34. $\cos x$ in terms of $\sin \frac{1}{2} x$ *alone*.

Problems 35 and 36 allow you to discover something about the next section.

35.   Use the answer to Problem 33 to write an equation expressing $\cos \frac{1}{2} x$ in terms of $\cos x$.

36.   Use the answer to Problem 34 to write an equation expressing $\sin \frac{1}{2} x$ in terms of $\cos x$.

In Problems 37 through 40 you will learn some properties of *inverse* circular functions. For example, there is a *cofunction* property,

$$\text{Arccos } x = \frac{\pi}{2} - \text{Arcsin } x.$$

This equation states, "The arc whose cosine is x is the *complement* of the arc whose sine is x." The geometrical meaning can be seen in Figure 14-4. A proof is given below.

Let $y = \text{Arcsin } x$

$\therefore x = \sin y$, and $-\frac{\pi}{2} \le y \le \frac{\pi}{2}$ Definition of Arcsin

$\therefore x = \cos \left(\frac{\pi}{2} - y \right)$ Cofunction property

$\therefore \text{arccos } x = \frac{\pi}{2} - y$ arccos of both members.

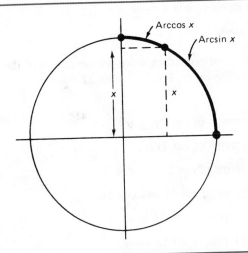

Figure 14-4

The arccos *relation* can be replaced with the Arccos *function* if $\frac{\pi}{2} - y$ is always in the range of Arccos. Operating with the inequality $-\frac{\pi}{2} \le y \le \frac{\pi}{2}$, you get

$$\frac{\pi}{2} \ge -y \ge -\frac{\pi}{2} \qquad \text{Multiplying by } -1$$

$$\pi \ge \left(\frac{\pi}{2} - y\right) \ge 0 \quad \text{Adding } \frac{\pi}{2}$$

Since the interval from 0 to π is the range of Arccos,

$$\text{Arccos } x = \frac{\pi}{2} - y \qquad \text{Definition of Arccos}$$

$$\therefore \text{Arccos } x = \frac{\pi}{2} - \text{Arcsin } x \quad \text{Substitution}$$

For Problems 37 through 40, use similar reasoning to derive the indicated property.

37. Prove the *cofunction* property $\text{Csc}^{-1} x = \frac{\pi}{2} - \text{Sec}^{-1} x$.

38. Prove the *cofunction* property $\text{Cot}^{-1} x = \frac{\pi}{2} - \text{Tan}^{-1} x$.

39. Prove the *reciprocal* property $\text{Arctan } x = \text{Arccot } \frac{1}{x}$, and tell for which values of x the property is true.

40. Prove the *reciprocal* property Arcsec x = Arccos $\dfrac{1}{x}$, and tell for which values of x the property is true.

For Problems 41 through 54, use the appropriate properties to find the *exact* value of the expression.

41. $\cos\left(2 \text{ Arctan } \dfrac{4}{3}\right)$

42. $\cos\left(2 \text{ Arcsin } \dfrac{1}{3}\right)$

43. $\sin$ (2 Arcsec 3)

44. $\tan\left(2 \text{ Arctan } \dfrac{1}{2}\right)$

45. $\tan$ (2 Arctan 5)

46. $\sin\left(2 \text{ Arccot } \dfrac{2}{3}\right)$

47. $\sin\left(\text{Tan}^{-1} \dfrac{1}{2} + \text{Tan}^{-1} \dfrac{1}{3}\right)$

48. $\cos\left(\text{Sec}^{-1} \dfrac{3}{2} - \text{Cos}^{-1} \dfrac{1}{5}\right)$

49. $\sin\left(\dfrac{\pi}{2} - \text{Arccos } \dfrac{11}{13}\right)$

50. $\csc$ (90° − Arcsec 19)

51. $\cos$ (Arcsec 1000)

52. $\csc\left(\dfrac{\pi}{2} - \text{Tan}^{-1} (-3)\right)$

53. $\tan$ (Cot^{-1} 4)

54. $\sin$ (Csc^{-1} (−5))

14-5 | HALF-ARGUMENT PROPERTIES

Objective:

Be able to express $\cos \dfrac{1}{2}x$, $\sin \dfrac{1}{2}x$, and $\tan \dfrac{1}{2}x$ in terms of functions of x.

The cosine double argument property in the forms

$$\cos 2A = 2 \cos^2 A - 1$$

and

$$\cos 2A = 1 - 2 \sin^2 A$$

is useful for deriving other properties. For example, starting with the first form, you can isolate $\cos^2 A$:

$$\cos 2A = 2\cos^2 A - 1 \qquad \text{Double argument property}$$

$$1 + \cos 2A = 2\cos^2 A \qquad \text{Adding 1 to both members}$$

$$\tfrac{1}{2}(1 + \cos 2A) = \cos^2 A \qquad \text{Dividing by 2}$$

$$\therefore \quad \boxed{\cos^2 A = \tfrac{1}{2}(1 + \cos 2A)} \qquad \text{Symmetry}$$

This equation expresses a *power* of a function in terms of a function of a *multiple* angle or arc. Solving $\cos 2A = 1 - 2\sin^2 A$ for $\sin^2 A$ gives:

$$\boxed{\sin^2 A = \tfrac{1}{2}(1 - \cos 2A)}$$

These two properties are also interesting because the argument A on the left is *half* the argument $2A$ on the right. Letting $A = \tfrac{1}{2}x$ and substituting gives

$$\cos^2 \tfrac{1}{2}x = \tfrac{1}{2}(1 + \cos x)$$

and

$$\sin^2 \tfrac{1}{2}x = \tfrac{1}{2}(1 - \cos x).$$

Taking the square root of both members of each equation gives:

$$\boxed{\begin{aligned} \cos \tfrac{1}{2}x &= \pm\sqrt{\tfrac{1}{2}(1 + \cos x)} \\ \sin \tfrac{1}{2}x &= \pm\sqrt{\tfrac{1}{2}(1 - \cos x)} \end{aligned}}$$

These are called *half-argument* properties for sine and cosine, because they express $\cos \tfrac{1}{2}x$ and $\sin \tfrac{1}{2}x$ in terms of $\cos x$. The ambiguous sign $\pm$ is determined by the quadrant in which $\tfrac{1}{2}x$ terminates (*not* by where x terminates!) For example, if $x = 120°$ then $\tfrac{1}{2}x = 60°$, which terminates in Quadrant I. So,

$$\sin \tfrac{1}{2}x = +\sqrt{\tfrac{1}{2}(1 - \cos x)}.$$

But if $x = 480°$, which is coterminal with $120°$ as shown in Figure 14-5, then $\tfrac{1}{2}x = 240°$. Since $240°$ terminates in Quadrant III,

$$\sin \tfrac{1}{2}x = -\sqrt{\tfrac{1}{2}(1 - \cos x)}.$$

The half-argument property for the tangent is obtained from the sine and cosine half-argument properties by using the quotient property.

$$\tan \tfrac{1}{2}x = \frac{\sin \tfrac{1}{2}x}{\cos \tfrac{1}{2}x} \qquad \text{Quotient property}$$

$$= \frac{\pm\sqrt{\tfrac{1}{2}(1 - \cos x)}}{\pm\sqrt{\tfrac{1}{2}(1 + \cos x)}} \qquad \text{Half-argument properties}$$

$$= \pm\sqrt{\frac{1 - \cos x}{1 + \cos x}}$$ Properties of radicals and fractions

$$\therefore \quad \boxed{\tan \frac{1}{2}x = \pm\sqrt{\frac{1 - \cos x}{1 + \cos x}}}$$ Transitivity

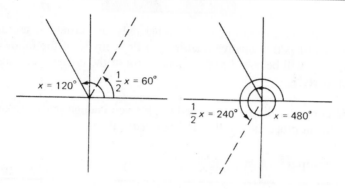

± sign in the half-argument properties

Figure 14-5

This tangent half-argument property can be simplified by rationalizing the denominator.

$$\tan \frac{1}{2}x$$

$$= \pm\sqrt{\frac{1 - \cos x}{1 + \cos x} \cdot \frac{1 + \cos x}{1 + \cos x}}$$ Multiplication property of 1

$$= \pm\sqrt{\frac{1 - \cos^2 x}{(1 + \cos x)^2}}$$ Multiplication property of fractions

$$= \pm\frac{\sqrt{1 - \cos^2 x}}{|1 + \cos x|}$$ $\sqrt{n^2} = |n|$

$$= \pm\frac{\sqrt{1 - \cos^2 x}}{1 + \cos x}$$ $1 + \cos x \geq 0$ for all x

An added benefit appears immediately, since the radicand $1 - \cos^2 x$ in the numerator is equal to $\sin^2 x$, a perfect square. So the tangent half-argument property may be written:

$$\boxed{\tan \frac{1}{2}x = \frac{\sin x}{1 + \cos x}}$$

In Problem 29 that follows, you will be asked to explain why the $\pm$ sign can be dropped.

A still more interesting form of the property can be obtained by rationalizing the *numerator* instead of the denominator.

$$\tan \frac{1}{2}x = \frac{1 - \cos x}{\sin x}$$

Since the denominator in this last form has only *one* term, it is useful for proving identities that involve fractions. In Problem 30 of the following exercise, you will be asked to prove this form of the tangent half-argument property.

The exercise that follows is designed to give you enough practice using the half-argument properties so that you will *learn* them.

EXERCISE 14-5

Do These Quickly

The following problems are intended to refresh your skills. You should be able to do all 10 in less than 5 minutes.

Q1. Write $\cos 2x$ in terms of $\cos x$.

Q2. Write $\sin 2x$ in terms of $\sin x$ and $\cos x$.

Q3. Is $\tan 2x = 2 \tan x$ an identity?

Q4. Is $\sin x = \dfrac{1}{\csc x}$ an identity?

Q5. Is $\cos^2 t + \sin^2 t = 1$ an identity?

Q6. Is $\cos (r - s) = \cos r \cos s + \sin r \sin s$ an identity?

Q7. What is the smallest positive value of θ for which $\sin \theta = -0.5$?

Q8. Evaluate $\cos 30°$.

Q9. Find the slope: $3x + 5y = 150$

Q10. What conic section is the graph of $3x^2 + 4y^2 = 36$?

Work the following problems.

1. Use what you recall about graphing sinusoids from Section 13-6 to:

 a. Draw a graph of $y = \cos \frac{1}{2}x$.

b. Draw a graph of $y = \frac{1}{2}\cos x$.

c. Explain from your graphs why $\cos \frac{1}{2}x \neq \frac{1}{2}\cos x$.

2. Repeat Problem 1 using $y = \sin \frac{1}{2}x$ and $y = \frac{1}{2}\sin x$.

3. a. Draw a graph of $y = \cos x$.

   b. Using this as an auxiliary graph, *square* ordinates to get a graph of $y = \cos^2 x$.

   c. The graph of $y = \cos^2 x$ is a *sinusoid*. From your sketch in part b, figure out its period, amplitude, and axis location. Then write an equation of the sinusoid in the form $y = C + A \cos Bx$.

   d. Use the properties of this section to demonstrate that your equation is correct.

4. Repeat Problem 3 using $y = \sin^2 x$. You must be clever enough to get an equation where the phase displacement is 0.

For Problems 5 through 14, verify that the half-argument properties actually work by substituting the given measure of the angle or arc into the formula and showing that you get the right answer.

5. $\cos \frac{1}{2}x$, $x = 60°$

6. $\sin \frac{1}{2}x$, $x = 60°$

7. $\sin \frac{1}{2}x$, $x = \frac{\pi}{2}$

8. $\cos \frac{1}{2}x$, $x = \frac{\pi}{2}$

9. $\tan \frac{1}{2}x$, $x = \frac{2\pi}{3}$

10. $\tan \frac{1}{2}x$, $x = \pi$

11. $\cos \frac{1}{2}x$, $x = 420°$

12. $\sin \frac{1}{2}x$, $x = 420°$

13. $\sin \frac{1}{2}x$, $x = -60°$

14. $\cos \frac{1}{2}x$, $x = -60°$

For Problems 15 through 20, calculate $\sin \frac{1}{2}x$, $\cos \frac{1}{2}x$, and $\tan \frac{1}{2}x$, for the angle described.

15. $\cos x = \frac{3}{5}$, $0° < x < 90°$

16. $\cos x = \frac{3}{5}$, $270° < x < 360°$

17. $\cos x = -\frac{3}{5}$, $180° < x < 270°$

18. $\cos x = -\frac{3}{5}$, $90° < x < 180°$

19. $\cos x = \frac{3}{5}$, $630° < x < 720°$

20. $\cos x = -\frac{3}{5}$, $450° < x < 540°$

For Problems 21 through 28, prove that the given equation is an identity.

21. $\tan \frac{1}{2}x + \cot \frac{1}{2}x = 2 \csc x$ 22. $\tan x \tan \frac{1}{2}x = \sec x - 1$

23. $\dfrac{2 \tan \frac{1}{2}x}{1 + \tan^2 \frac{1}{2}x} = \sin x$ 24. $\tan \frac{1}{2}x \left(2 \cot x + \tan \frac{1}{2}x \right) = 1$

25. $\dfrac{\cos \frac{1}{2}\theta - \sin \frac{1}{2}\theta}{\cos \frac{1}{2}\theta + \sin \frac{1}{2}\theta} = \dfrac{\cos \theta}{1 + \sin \theta}$

26. $\dfrac{\cos \frac{1}{2}\phi + \sin \frac{1}{2}\phi}{\cos \frac{1}{2}\phi - \sin \frac{1}{2}\phi} = \sec \phi + \tan \phi$

27. $\tan \frac{1}{2}A = \csc A - \cot A$ 28. $\tan \left(\dfrac{\pi}{4} + \dfrac{x}{2} \right) = \sec x + \tan x$

29. The property $\tan \dfrac{1}{2}x = \dfrac{\sin x}{1 + \cos x}$ comes from $\dfrac{\pm \sqrt{1 - \cos^2 x}}{1 + \cos x}$.

By considering the quadrants in which x and $\frac{1}{2}x$ may terminate, explain why the ambiguous sign $\pm$ disappears in this property.

30. Prove that

$$\tan \frac{1}{2}x = \pm \sqrt{\dfrac{1 - \cos x}{1 + \cos x}}$$

can be transformed to

$$\tan \frac{1}{2}x = \dfrac{1 - \cos x}{\sin x},$$

and explain what happens to the $\pm$ sign.

Problems 31 and 32 allow you to discover something about the next section.

31. The right-hand members of the composite argument properties for $\sin (A + B)$ and $\sin (A - B)$ are *conjugates* of each other. When you add or subtract conjugates, one of the two terms drops out, leaving twice the other term.
   a. Write an equation expressing $\sin (A + B) + \sin (A - B)$ in terms of functions of A and B.
   b. Write an equation expressing $\sin (A + B) - \sin (A - B)$ in terms of functions of A and B.

32. Repeat Problem 31 for $\cos (A + B)$ and $\cos (A - B)$.

Problem 33 is meant to challenge the most diligent students!

33. *Sin 18°, etc.:*   You have learned how to find exact values of func-

tions of multiples of 15°. It is possible to find exact values for functions of certain other angles, too. In this problem, you will combine trigonometric properties with algebraic techniques and a little ingenuity to find the exact value of sin 18°.

a. Use the double argument property for sine to write an equation expressing sin 72° in terms of sin 36° and cos 36°.

b. Transform the equation in part a so that sin 72° is expressed in terms of sin 18° and cos 18°. You should find that the *sine* form of the double argument property for cos 36° is best.

c. You recall by the cofunction property that sin 72° = cos 18°. Replace sin 72° in your equation from part b with cos 18°. Then simplify the resulting equation. If you have done everything correctly, the cos 18° should disappear from the equation, leaving a *cubic* (third degree) equation in sin 18°.

d. Solve the equation in part c for sin 18°. It may help to let $x = \sin 18°$ and solve for x. If you transform the equation so that the right member is 0, you should find that $(2x - 1)$ is a factor of the left member. The other factor may be found by long division. To solve the equation, recall the multiplication property of zero and the Quadratic Formula.

e. You should get *three* solutions for the equation in part d. Only *one* of these could possibly be sin 18°. *Which* one?

f. A pattern shows up for some exact values of sin θ:

$$\sin 15° = \frac{\sqrt{6} - \sqrt{2}}{4}$$

$$\sin 18° = \frac{\sqrt{5} - 1}{4} = \frac{\sqrt{5} - \sqrt{1}}{4}$$

$$\sin 30° = \frac{1}{2} = \frac{2}{4} = \frac{\sqrt{4} - \sqrt{0}}{4}$$

See if you can figure out what the pattern is!!

14-6 | SUM AND PRODUCT PROPERTIES

The composite argument properties for sine are

$$\sin (A + B) = \sin A \cos B + \cos A \sin B,$$

$$\sin (A - B) = \sin A \cos B - \cos A \sin B.$$

By *adding* respective members of the two equations you get:

$$\boxed{\sin (A + B) + \sin (A - B) = 2 \sin A \cos B}$$

This property is of interest because the left member is a *sum* of two sines, and the right member is a *product* of a sine and a cosine.

Objectives:

1. Be able to transform a *sum* (or difference) of two sines or two cosines into a *product* of sines and cosines.
2. Be able to transform a *product* of two sines, two cosines, or a sine and cosine into a *sum* (or difference) of two sines or cosines.

By subtracting respective members of the composite argument properties for sine, above, you get:

$$\sin (A + B) - \sin (A - B) = 2 \cos A \sin B$$

The other two "sum and product" properties needed to accomplish the objectives come from adding and subtracting the composite argument properties for the cosine:

$$\cos (A + B) = \cos A \cos B - \sin A \sin B$$

$$\cos (A - B) = \cos A \cos B + \sin A \sin B$$

$$\cos (A + B) + \cos (A - B) = 2 \cos A \cos B$$

By subtracting instead of adding:

$$\cos (A + B) - \cos (A - B) = -2 \sin A \sin B$$

EXAMPLE 1

Express $2 \sin 13° \cos 48°$ as a sum. Using the first form of the sum and product properties,

$2 \sin 13° \cos 48°$

$\qquad = \sin (13° + 48°) + \sin (13° - 48°)$ Sum and product properties

$\qquad = \sin 61° + \sin (-35°)$ Arithmetic

$\qquad = \underline{\sin 61° - \sin 35°}$ Sine is an *odd* function.

If you want $\sin 13° \cos 48°$ instead of $2 \sin 13° \cos 48°$, you can simply divide both members by 2, getting

$$\sin 13° \cos 48° = \frac{1}{2} \sin 61° - \frac{1}{2} \sin 35°.$$

∎

EXAMPLE 2

Express $\cos 47° + \cos 59°$ as a *product*.

The sum of two cosines property is

$$\cos (A + B) + \cos (A - B) = 2 \cos A \cos B.$$

So you let the arguments $A + B = 47°$ and $A - B = 59°$, and solve the resulting *system* of equations for A and B.

$$A + B = 47°$$

$$A - B = 59°$$

Adding the respective members of these equations gives

$$2A = 47° + 59° = 106°$$

$$A = \tfrac{1}{2}(106°) = 53°,$$

and subtracting the respective members gives

$$2B = 47° - 59° = -12°$$

$$B = \tfrac{1}{2}(-12°) = -6°.$$

$$\therefore \cos 47° + \cos 59°$$

$$= 2 \cos 53° \cos (-6°) \quad \text{Substitution}$$

$$= \underline{\underline{2 \cos 53° \cos 6°}} \qquad \text{Cosine is an } \textit{even } \text{function.}$$

The procedure of Example 2 can be done in *general*, letting

$$A + B = x,$$

$$A - B = y.$$

The solutions are $A = \tfrac{1}{2}(x + y)$ and $B = \tfrac{1}{2}(x - y)$. Substituting these values into the sum and product properties gives alternate forms in which a *sum* is expressed as a *product*.

$$\sin x + \sin y = 2 \sin \tfrac{1}{2}(x + y) \cos \tfrac{1}{2}(x - y)$$

$$\sin x - \sin y = 2 \cos \tfrac{1}{2}(x + y) \sin \tfrac{1}{2}(x - y)$$

$$\cos x + \cos y = 2 \cos \tfrac{1}{2}(x + y) \cos \tfrac{1}{2}(x - y)$$

$$\cos x - \cos y = -2 \sin \tfrac{1}{2}(x + y) \sin \tfrac{1}{2}(x - y)$$

These properties are difficult to remember correctly, since they are all so similar to one another. Therefore, it is usually more reliable for you to remember how you derived them from the composite argument properties (which you *should* remember by now!). Then you can *derive* the sum and product properties whenever you need them.

In the following exercise you will use these properties to transform sums to products, and vice versa.

EXERCISE 14-6

Do These Quickly

The following problems are intended to refresh your skills. You should be able to do all 10 in less than 5 minutes.

Q1.   Write $\sin 0.5x$ in terms of $\cos x$.

Q2.   Write $\tan 0.5x$ in terms of $\sin x$ and $\cos x$.

Q3.   Write $\cos 2x$ in terms of $\sin x$.

Q4.   Write $\sec 13x$ in terms of $\cos 13x$.

Q5.   Is $\tan (90° - \theta) = \cot \theta$ an identity?

Q6.   Is $\sin (-x) = -\sin x$ an identity?

Q7.   Is $\cot A = \dfrac{(\csc A)}{(\sec A)}$ an identity?

Q8.   Is $\sin^{-1} x = \dfrac{1}{(\sin x)}$ an identity?

Q9.   What is the amplitude? $y = 3 \cos 5x$

Q10.   What is the period? $y = 4 \sin 6\theta$

For Problems 1 through 12, transform the indicated product to a *sum* (or difference) of sines or cosines of *positive* arguments.

1. $2 \sin 41° \cos 24°$

2. $2 \cos 73° \sin 62°$

3. $2 \cos 53° \cos 49°$

4. $2 \sin 29° \sin 16°$

5. $2 \cos 3.8 \sin 4.1$

6. $2 \cos 2 \cos 3$

7. $2 \sin 4.6 \sin 7.2$

8. $2 \sin 1.8 \cos 6.2$

9. $2 \sin 3x \cos 5x$

10. $2 \sin 8x \sin 2x$

11. $2 \cos 4x \cos 7x$

12. $2 \cos 11x \sin 9x$

For Problems 13 through 24, transform the indicated sum (or difference) into a *product* of sines and cosines of *positive* arguments.

13. $\cos 46° + \cos 12°$

14. $\cos 56° - \cos 24°$

15. $\sin 54° + \sin 22°$

16. $\sin 29° - \sin 15°$

17. $\cos 2.4 - \cos 4.4$

18. $\sin 1.8 + \sin 6.4$

19. $\sin 2 - \sin 6$

20. $\cos 3.2 + \cos 4.8$

21. $\sin 3x + \sin 9x$

22. $\sin 9x - \sin 11x$

23. $\cos 8x - \cos 10x$

24. $\cos 5x + \cos 13x$

For Problems 25 through 36, prove that the given equation is an identity.

25. $\cos x - \cos 5x = 4 \sin 3x \sin x \cos x$

26. $\sin 5x + \sin 3x = 4 \sin 2x \cos 2x \cos x$

27. $\dfrac{\sin 3x + \sin x}{\sin 3x - \sin x} = \dfrac{2 \cos^2 x}{\cos 2x}$

28. $\dfrac{\sin 5x + \sin 7x}{\cos 5x + \cos 7x} = \tan 6x$

29. $\sin x + \sin 2x + \sin 3x = \sin 2x(1 + 2 \cos x)$

30. $\cos x + \cos 2x + \cos 3x = \cos 2x(1 + 2 \cos x)$

31. $1 + \cos x = \dfrac{1}{2} + \dfrac{\sin \frac{3}{2}x}{2 \sin \frac{1}{2}x}$

32. $1 + \cos x + \cos 2x = \dfrac{1}{2} + \dfrac{\sin \frac{5}{2}x}{2 \sin \frac{1}{2}x}$

33. $\sin (x + y) \sin (x - y) = \sin^2 x - \sin^2 y$

34. $\sin (x + y) \sin (x - y) = \cos^2 y - \cos^2 x$

35. $\cos (x + y) \cos (x - y) = \cos^2 x - \sin^2 y$

36. $\sin (x + y) \cos (x - y) = \dfrac{1}{2} \sin 2x + \dfrac{1}{2} \sin 2y$

14-7 | LINEAR COMBINATION OF COSINE AND
SINE WITH EQUAL ARGUMENTS

If r and s are variables, then an expression such as $3r - 5s$ is called a *linear combination* of r and s. In this section you will study expressions such as $7 \cos x + 2 \sin x$, which are linear combinations of a cosine and a sine with equal arguments. These expressions differ from those of the previous section because the sum involves both a sine and a cosine. The sum and product properties have sums of two cosines or two sines.

Objective:

Be able to express $A \cos x + B \sin x$ in the form $C \cos (x - D)$, where A, B, C, and D stand for constants.

Starting with the expression $C \cos (x - D)$ and using the composite argument properties, you can write

$$C \cos (x - D) = C(\cos x \cos D + \sin x \sin D).$$

Upon distributing, commuting, and associating, this equation becomes

$$C \cos (x - D) = (C \cos D) \cos x + (C \sin D) \sin x.$$

Since D is a constant, $\cos D$ and $\sin D$ are also constants. The objective may be accomplished by making

$$A = C \cos D,$$

$$B = C \sin D.$$

By a clever combination of algebra and trigonometry, C and D can be expressed in terms of A and B. Squaring and then adding gives

$$A^2 = C^2 \cos^2 D$$

$$\underline{B^2 = C^2 \sin^2 D}$$

$$A^2 + B^2 = C^2 \cos^2 D + C^2 \sin^2 D$$

$$= C^2 (\cos^2 D + \sin^2 D)$$

$$= C^2$$

$$\therefore C = \boxed{\sqrt{A^2 + B^2}}$$

The positive square root is used simply as a matter of convenience. Once C is known, D is the argument that satisfies:

$$\cos D = \frac{A}{C} \quad \text{and} \quad \sin D = \frac{B}{C}$$

EXAMPLE

Transform $3 \cos 2x - 4 \sin 2x$ to the form $C \cos (2x - D)$.

First, observe that the sine and cosine have the *same* argument, $2x$. Also, $A = 3$ and $B = -4$. Therefore,

$$C = \sqrt{3^2 + (-4)^2} = 5.$$

Consequently,

$$\cos D = \frac{3}{5} \quad \text{and} \quad \sin D = -\frac{4}{5}.$$

From Table III, the reference angle is approximately 53°. Since cos D is positive and sin D is negative, D must terminate in Quadrant IV. Therefore $D \approx 360° - 53° = 307°$. In summary,

$$3 \cos 2x - 4 \sin 2x = 5 \cos (2x - 307°).$$

Note that the two terms on the left have graphs that are sinusoids with the same period (180°) but different amplitudes (3 and 4). The expression on the right is another sinusoid with the *same* period (180°), but a *different* amplitude (5) and phase angle (307°/2). It is this property that explains why two sound waves of the same pitch will add together to form another sound wave of the same pitch. Only the amplitude and phase are changed. Note also that the amplitudes do not simply add together. This explains why a choir of 100 members all singing the same note is not 100 times as loud as only one member singing the note.   ■

In the following exercise you will get practice expressing linear combinations of sine and cosine in terms of a single cosine.

EXERCISE 14-7

Do These Quickly

The following problems are intended to refresh your skills. You should be able to do all 10 in less than 5 minutes.

Q1.   Expand and simplify: $\cos (\theta - 30°)$

Q2.   Expand and simplify: $\sin (\theta + 45°)$

Q3.   Is $\cos (r + t) = \cos r - \cos t$ an identity?

Q4.   Is $\cos (r + t) = \dfrac{1}{\sec (r + t)}$ an identity?

Q5.   Solve for θ: $\sin 2\theta = 0.5$

Q6.   Solve for x: $\cos x = \dfrac{\sqrt{2}}{2}$

Q7.   Solve the system: $x + y = 13$
$\qquad\qquad\qquad\quad x - y = 5$

Q8.   In what quadrant does θ terminate if $\cos \theta = -0.754 \ldots$ and
$\sin \theta = 0.656 \ldots$?

Q9.   In what quadrant does $\dfrac{\theta}{2}$ terminate if $450° \le \theta \le 540°$?

Q10.   Sketch the graph of $y = \dfrac{1}{x}$.

For Problems 1 through 10, transform the given expression to the form
$C \cos (x - D)$, assuming that the functions are:
a. trigonometric,
b. circular.

1. $\cos x + \sqrt{3} \sin x$ 2. $\sqrt{3} \cos x + \sin x$

3. $5 \cos x - 5 \sin x$ 4. $\sqrt{2} \cos x - \sqrt{2} \sin x$

5. $5 \sin x - 12 \cos x$ 6. $4 \sin x - 3 \cos x$

7. $-15 \cos 3x - 8 \sin 3x$ 8. $-12 \cos 7x - 5 \sin 7x$

9. $(\sqrt{6} + \sqrt{2}) \cos x + (\sqrt{6} - \sqrt{2}) \sin x$

10. $0.6561 \cos x + 0.7547 \sin x$

For Problems 11 through 14, sketch at least one cycle of the graph of the
given equation.

11. $y = 5 \sqrt{3} \cos 2x - 5 \sin 2x$ 12. $y = 6 \cos 3x + 6 \sin 3x$

13. $y = 4 \cos \pi x + 4 \sin \pi x$ 14. $y = -\cos \dfrac{\pi}{6} x + \sqrt{3} \sin \dfrac{\pi}{6} x$

For Problems 15 through 24, transform the expression to the form
$C \cos (x - D)$, where C and D are constants. Express D exactly as an
Arctangent function. If D terminates in Quadrant II or III, you should use
the *opposite* of the appropriate Arctangent.

15. $3 \cos x + 4 \sin x$ 16. $5 \cos x + 12 \sin x$

17. $5 \cos x + 6 \sin x$ 18. $3 \cos x + 8 \sin x$

19. $0.6 \cos x - 0.8 \sin x$ 20. $0.8 \cos x - 0.6 \sin x$

21. $-4 \cos x - 2 \sin x$ 22. $-8 \cos x - 15 \sin x$

23. $-2 \cos x + 7 \sin x$ 24. $-\cos x + 4 \sin x$

14-8 | SIMPLIFICATION OF TRIGONOMETRIC EXPRESSIONS

The ultimate objective of this chapter is for you to be able to solve trigonometric equations. Doing this requires that you be able to transform a trigonometric expression to an equivalent, specified form, possibly simplifying it. Unfortunately, merely stating "simplify" a given trigonometric expression is not enough. As with any mathematical expression, "simple" means "simpler to use in subsequent work." For example, if $\sin 3x + \sin 5x$ appears in an equation, the equation may be easier to solve if the expression is transformed to a product. But in more advanced mathematics such as calculus, it may be simpler to use if left as a sum. It is for this reason that the desired form of the answer will always be specified.

In this section you will be given the desired algebraic form (sum, product, etc.) or trigonometric form (sines, double arguments, etc.) but not the answer itself. The transformations will give you skills you must have for solving trigonometric equations in the next section. There, *you* must decide which form is most desirable.

Objective:

Given a trigonometric expression, transform it to a specified algebraic or trigonometric form.

For your convenience, the properties you have learned so far are summarized below. You should, of course, try to work the problems *without* reference to the table.

PROPERTIES

SUMMARY OF PROPERTIES OF TRIGONOMETRIC FUNCTIONS

1. *Reciprocal*

$$\cot x = \frac{1}{\tan x} \quad \text{or} \quad \tan x \cot x = 1$$

$$\sec x = \frac{1}{\cos x} \quad \text{or} \quad \cos x \sec x = 1$$

$$\csc x = \frac{1}{\sin x} \quad \text{or} \quad \sin x \csc x = 1$$

2. *Quotient*

$$\tan x = \frac{\sin x}{\cos x} = \frac{\sec x}{\csc x}$$

$$\cot x = \frac{\cos x}{\sin x} = \frac{\csc x}{\sec x}$$

3. *Pythagorean*

$$\cos^2 x + \sin^2 x = 1$$

$$1 + \tan^2 x = \sec^2 x$$

$$\cot^2 x + 1 = \csc^2 x$$

4. *Odd-Even*

$$\sin(-x) = -\sin x \quad \text{(odd)}$$

$$\cos(-x) = \cos x \quad \text{(even)}$$

$$\tan(-x) = -\tan x \quad \text{(odd)}$$

$$\cot(-x) = -\cot x \quad \text{(odd)}$$

$$\sec(-x) = \sec x \quad \text{(even)}$$

$$\csc(-x) = -\csc x \quad \text{(odd)}$$

5. *Cofunction*

$$\cos(90° - \theta) = \sin \theta; \cos\left(\frac{\pi}{2} - x\right) = \sin x$$

$$\cot(90° - \theta) = \tan \theta; \cot\left(\frac{\pi}{2} - x\right) = \tan x$$

$$\csc(90° - \theta) = \sec \theta; \csc\left(\frac{\pi}{2} - x\right) = \sec x$$

6. *Composite-Argument*

$$\cos(A - B) = \cos A \cos B + \sin A \sin B$$

$$\cos(A + B) = \cos A \cos B - \sin A \sin B$$

$$\sin(A - B) = \sin A \cos B - \cos A \sin B$$

$$\sin(A + B) = \sin A \cos B + \cos A \sin B$$

$$\tan(A - B) = \frac{\tan A - \tan B}{1 + \tan A \tan B}$$

$$\tan(A + B) = \frac{\tan A + \tan B}{1 - \tan A \tan B}$$

7. *Double-Argument*

$$\sin 2x = 2 \sin x \cos x$$

$$\cos 2x = \cos^2 x - \sin^2 x = 1 - 2 \sin^2 x = 2 \cos^2 x - 1$$

$$\tan 2x = \frac{2 \tan x}{1 - \tan^2 x}$$

$$\cos^2 x = \frac{1}{2}(1 + \cos 2x)$$

$$\sin^2 x = \frac{1}{2}(1 - \cos 2x)$$

8. *Half-Argument*

$$\sin \frac{1}{2}x = \pm \sqrt{\frac{1}{2}(1 - \cos x)}$$

$$\cos \frac{1}{2}x = \pm \sqrt{\frac{1}{2}(1 + \cos x)}$$

$$\tan \frac{1}{2}x = \pm \sqrt{\frac{1 - \cos x}{1 + \cos x}}$$

$$= \frac{\sin x}{1 + \cos x} = \frac{1 - \cos x}{\sin x}$$

9. *Sum and Product*

$$2 \cos A \cos B = \cos(A + B) + \cos(A - B)$$

$$2 \sin A \sin B = -\cos(A + B) + \cos(A - B)$$

$$2 \sin A \cos B = \sin(A + B) + \sin(A - B)$$

$$2 \cos A \sin B = \sin(A + B) - \sin(A - B)$$

$$\cos x + \cos y = 2 \cos \frac{1}{2}(x + y) \cos \frac{1}{2}(x - y)$$

$$\cos x - \cos y = -2 \sin \frac{1}{2}(x + y) \sin \frac{1}{2}(x - y)$$

$$\sin x + \sin y = 2 \sin \frac{1}{2}(x + y) \cos \frac{1}{2}(x - y)$$

$$\sin x - \sin y = 2 \cos \frac{1}{2}(x + y) \sin \frac{1}{2}(x - y)$$

10. *Linear Combination of Sine and Cosine*

$$A \cos x + B \sin x = C \cos(x - D); \text{ where}$$

$$C = \sqrt{A^2 + B^2}, \cos D = \frac{A}{C}, \text{ and } \sin D = \frac{B}{C}.$$

EXERCISE 14-8

Do These Quickly

The following problems are intended to refresh your skills. You should be able to do all 10 in less than 5 minutes.

Q1.   State the Pythagorean property for tangent and secant.

Q2.   State the reciprocal property for cosecant.

Q3.   State the quotient property for cotangent.

Q4.   State the odd-even property for tangent.

Q5.   State the cofunction property for sine.

Q6.   State the double argument property for $\sin 2x$.

Q7.   State the composite argument property for $\cos (p - z)$.

Q8.   Solve for θ: $\tan \theta = 1$

Q9.   Solve for x: $\sec x = 2$

Q10.   Evaluate $x = \text{Sin}^{-1} 1$.

For Problems 1 through 26, transform the expression on the left of the comma so that it involves *only* the trigonometric functions or algebraic form on the right. Note that you should work *all* these problems, rather than just the odd- or even-numbered ones.

1. $\sin 2x$, $\sin x$ *and* $\cos x$

2. $\sin^2 x$, $\cos 2x$

3. $\sin^2 x$, $\cos x$

4. $\cos^2 x$, $\sin x$

5. $\cos^2 x$, $\cos 2x$

6. $\cos 2x$, $\cos x$

7. $\cos 2x$, $\sin x$

8. $\cos 2x$, $\cos x$ *and* $\sin x$

9. $\tan 2x$, $\tan x$

10. $\sin \frac{1}{2}x$, $\cos x$

11. $\cos \frac{1}{2}x$, $\cos x$

12. $\tan \frac{1}{2}x$, $\cos x$

13. $\tan \frac{1}{2}x$, $\cos x$ *and* $\sin x$

14. $\sin 3x$, $\sin x$

15. $\cos 4x$, $\cos 2x$

16. $\cos 6x$, $\cos 3x$

17. $\sin x \cos x$, $\sin 2x$

18. $\sin x \cos y$,   sum of sines or cosines

19. $\cos x \cos y$,   sum of sines or cosines

20. $\cos x + \cos y$,   product of sines and/or cosines

21. $\sin x + \sin y$,   product of sines and/or cosines

22. $\sin x + \cos x$,   *single* cosine

23. $\sin 3x \sin 7x$,   sum of sines or cosines of positive multiples of x

24. $\sin 3x + \sin 7x$,   product of sines and/or cosines of positive multiples of x

25. $\sqrt{3} \cos x - \sin x$,   cosine with phase displacement

26. $-4 \cos x - 4 \sin x$,   cosine with phase displacement

For Problems 27 through 30, a definition of "simple form" is given. Use the definition to "simplify" the expressions.

27. Simple form involves no multiple or composite arguments. Simplify:
     a. $\cos (x - 37°)$
     b. $\cos (x + y + z)$
     c. $\cos 3x$

28. Simple form consists of *one* term, which may be composed of several factors. Simplify:
     a. $\cos 37° \cos x + \sin 37° \sin x$
     b. $\cos 37° + \cos x$
     c. $\cos x + \cos 2x + \cos 3x$

29. Simple form involves *no* products or powers of trigonometric functions, but may involve functions of multiple arguments. That is, the expression should be *linear* (first degree) in functions of multiple arguments. Simplify:
     a. $\sin x \cos x$ b. $\cos^2 x$
     c. $\cos^2 x \sin x$ d. $\sin^4 x$

30. Simple form involves a *single* cosine or sine term (no products, powers or sums of functions!), but may involve multiple or composite arguments. Simplify:
    a. $\cos x + \sin x$ b. $\cos x \sin x$
    c. $\cos x - \sin x$ d. $\sin x - \cos x$

Problem 31 is designed to let you discover how to solve a trigonometric equation.

31. Given the equation $\sin 3x - \sin x = 0$:
    a.   Use the sum and product properties to transform the left member to a product of sines and/or cosines.
    b.   Use the multiplication property of zero to set each factor on the left in part a, equal to zero.
    c.   Solve the equations in part b for all values of the arguments that make the equations true. Remember that if θ is such a value, then all angles coterminal with θ will also make the equation true (i.e., $\theta + 360n°$).
    d.   If the argument in part c is a multiple of x, solve for x.
    e.   Find all values of x in the domain $0° \le x < 360°$ that make the equation true. There should be *six*!

14-9 | TRIGONOMETRIC EQUATIONS

When you were working with sinusoids in Section 13-6, you had equations of the form

$$y = C + A \cos B(x - D),$$

where A, B, C, and D stand for constants. In Section 13-10, when you substituted a value of y and calculated the corresponding values of x, you were actually solving a trigonometric equation. In this section you will solve other types of trigonometric equations.

DEFINITION

> A **solution** of a trigonometric equation is a value of the variable in the argument that makes the equation true.
>
> That is, if an expression such as $\cos 3(x - 5)$ appears in the equation, a solution is a value of x and not a value of the entire argument $3(x - 5)$.

Objective:

Given a trigonometric equation and a domain of the variable, find all solutions of the equation in the domain.

EXAMPLE 1

Solve $2 \sin x - 1 = 0$ for $x \, \epsilon \, \{$real numbers of degrees$\}$.

$2 \sin x - 1 = 0$ Given equation

$2 \sin x = 1$ Adding 1 to both members

$\sin x = \dfrac{1}{2}$ Dividing by 2

Recalling functions of special angles, you know that $\sin 30°$ equals $\frac{1}{2}$. So does $\sin 150°$, since $150°$ has a reference angle of $30°$ and terminates in Quadrant II, where the sine is positive. Any angles coterminal with $30°$ and $150°$ are also solutions. Thus

$$x = 30° + 360n° \quad \text{or} \quad x = 150° + 360n°,$$

so that

$$S = \{30° + 360n°, \; 150° + 360n°\}.$$

This is known as the *general* solution of the equation. Particular solutions can be obtained by substituting *integers* for n. For instance, if the domain were $0° \le x < 360°$, then

$$S = \{30°, \; 150°\},$$

which you get by letting $n = 0$. If the function had been *circular* instead of trigonometric, the general solution would have been

$$S = \left\{ \frac{\pi}{6} + 2\pi n, \; \frac{5\pi}{6} + 2\pi n \right\}.$$

If the domain had been $0 \le x < 2\pi$, the particular solution would have been

$$S = \left\{ \frac{\pi}{6}, \; \frac{5\pi}{6} \right\}.$$

Finally, if the domain had been $180° \le x \le 360°$, then the particular solution would have been

$$S = \phi,$$

since there are *no* solutions in this interval.

From this example, you can see that the solution set depends on the domain. A compact way of writing a set of numbers such as $180° \le x \le 360°$ is $[180°, 360°]$. This is read, "the closed interval between $180°$ and $360°$."

Other interval notations are as follows:

INTERVAL NOTATION		
Written	Meaning	Name
$x \in [180°, 360°]$	$180° \leq x \leq 360°$	Closed interval
$x \in (180°, 360°)$	$180° < x < 360°$	Open interval
$x \in [180°, 360°)$	$180° \leq x < 360°$	Half-open interval
$x \in (180°, 360°]$	$180° < x \leq 360°$	Half-open interval

EXAMPLE 2

Solve $\sin 2x \cos x + \cos 2x \sin x = 1$ for $x \in [0, 2\pi)$.

$\sin 2x \cos x + \cos 2x \sin x = 1$	Given equation
$\sin (2x + x) = 1$	Composite argument properties
$\sin 3x = 1$	Adding "like" terms
$3x = \dfrac{\pi}{2} + 2\pi n$	$\sin \dfrac{\pi}{2} = 1$
$x = \dfrac{\pi}{6} + \left(\dfrac{2\pi}{3}\right) n$	Dividing by 3
$x = \dfrac{\pi}{6}, \dfrac{5\pi}{6}, \dfrac{3\pi}{2}$	Picking those integer values of n for which $x \in [0, 2\pi]$

$$\therefore S = \left\{ \dfrac{\pi}{6}, \dfrac{5\pi}{6}, \dfrac{3\pi}{2} \right\}$$

The most difficult part of solving an equation is getting started. The thing that gets you started this time is recognizing a familiar property, the composite argument property, that can be used on the left-hand member.

EXAMPLE 3

Solve $\cos 2\theta - \cos 4\theta = \sqrt{3} \sin 3\theta$ for $\theta \in [0°, 360°)$.

This problem is complicated because there are three different arguments, 2θ, 4θ, and 3θ. Luckily, the number of arguments can be reduced by applying the sum and product properties to the left member, getting

$$-2 \sin 3\theta \sin (-\theta) = \sqrt{3} \sin 3\theta.$$

This has the advantage of reducing the number of *functions*, too. Now everything is in terms of sines. Since sin is an *odd* function,

$$2 \sin 3\theta \sin \theta = \sqrt{3} \sin 3\theta.$$

At this point it is tempting to divide both members by sin 3θ. But you recall that dividing by a variable that can equal zero might *lose* solutions. So you resist the temptation and try something else.

$2 \sin 3\theta \sin \theta - \sqrt{3} \sin 3\theta = 0$ Subtracting $\sqrt{3} \sin 3\theta$

$\sin 3\theta (2 \sin \theta - \sqrt{3}) = 0$ Factoring

$\sin 3\theta = 0$ or $2 \sin \theta - \sqrt{3} = 0$ Multiplication property of 0

$\sin 3\theta = 0$ or $\sin \theta = \dfrac{\sqrt{3}}{2}$ Addition and multiplication properties

$\therefore 3\theta = 0° + 360n°, 180° + 360n°;$ or $\theta = 60° + 360n°, 120° + 360n°$

$\therefore \theta = 0° + 120n°, 60° + 120n°, 60° + 360n°,$ or $120° + 360n°$

$\therefore S = \{0°, 60°, 120°, 180°, 240°, 300°\}$

Again the solution set is determined by picking all values of *n* that give solutions in the domain. ■

EXAMPLE 4

Solve cos $(x - 57°) = -1$ for $x \in (-180°, 180°)$.

The composite argument $(x - 57°)$ suggests use of the composite argument properties. However, the equation is already in the form of *one* function of *one* argument equal to a *constant*. Thus, the composite argument properties would take you in the wrong direction! So you simply write

$x - 57° = 180° + 360n°$ cos $180° = -1$

$x = 237° + 360n$ Adding 57° to both members

$x = -123°$ Letting $n = -1$

This is the only solution in the domain.

$$\therefore S = \{-123°\}$$ ■

EXAMPLE 5

Solve cos$^2 x + \sin x + 1 = 0$ for $x \in [-90°, 270°)$.

These are two different functions, sine and cosine. Cos$^2 x$ is easily transformed to sines using the Pythagorean properties. This transformation will *reduce* the number of functions and thus simplify the equation.

$1 - \sin^2 x + \sin x + 1 = 0$ Pythagorean properties

$\sin^2 x - \sin x - 2 = 0$ Commutativity, associativity and multiplication by -1

$(\sin x - 2)(\sin x + 1) = 0$ Factoring

$\therefore \sin x = 2$ or $\sin x = -1$ Multiplication property of zero

The equation $\sin x = 2$ has no real solutions.

$\therefore \sin x = -1$ Only other choice

$x = 270° + 360n°$ $\sin 270° = -1$

The only solution in the domain occurs when $n = -1$, for which $x = -90°$. The 270° you get when $n = 0$ is out of the domain, since the interval is *open* at the upper end.

$$\therefore S = \{-90°\}$$ ■

EXAMPLE 6

Solve $\dfrac{\sin x}{1 + \cos x} = 1$ for $x \in (0°, 360°)$.

There are two ways of approaching this problem. The first is to eliminate the fraction by multiplying both members by $1 + \cos x$.

$$\sin x = 1 + \cos x.$$

This equation contains two different functions. Since it is easier to transform *squares* of sines into cosines, you can square both members.

$\sin^2 x = 1 + 2 \cos x + \cos^2 x$ Squaring both members

$1 - \cos^2 x = 1 + 2 \cos x + \cos^2 x$ Pythagorean properties

$0 = 2 \cos x + 2 \cos^2 x$ Addition property of equality

$0 = \cos x (1 + \cos x)$ Division by 2, then factoring

$\cos x = 0$ or $1 + \cos x = 0$ Multiplication property of zero

$\cos x = 0$ or $\cos x = -1$ Subtracting 1

$x = 90° + 360n°,\ 270° + 360n°$ or $180° + 360n$

The solutions in the domain are 90°, 270°, and 180°. However, substituting these into the original equation reveals that only 90° works. The 180° is an *extraneous* solution introduced by multiplying both members by $1 + \cos x$, and the 270° is another extraneous solution introduced by squaring both members. Your next step should look something like this:

extraneous

$x = 90°,\ \cancel{270°},\ \cancel{180°}$

$\therefore S = \{90°\}.$

You should remember that whenever you square both members or multiply by a variable that can equal zero, you must check *all* the solutions. Any which do not satisfy the original equation should be marked "extraneous" and should not be put in the solution set.

A clever application of trigonometric properties can sometimes avoid steps that give extraneous solutions. In this example, $\frac{\sin x}{(1+\cos x)}$ is recognizable as the half-argument property for tangent. Therefore, the original equation becomes

$\tan \frac{1}{2}x = 1$ Half-argument properties

$\frac{1}{2}x = 45° + 180n°$ $\tan 45° = 1$, and period of tangent is $180°$

$x = 90° + 360n°$ Multiplying by 2

$\therefore S = \{90°\}$ ■

The preceding examples were selected to show you many of the useful techniques that exist for solving trigonometric equations and some of the pitfalls you might stumble into. The following table summarizes these techniques.

TECHNIQUES FOR SOLVING TRIGONOMETRIC EQUATIONS

1. Get an equation (or equations) in which *one* function of *one* argument equals a *constant*. Some ways are:
   a. Reduce the number of different arguments (Examples 2 and 3).
   b. Reduce the number of different functions (Examples 5 and 6).
   c. Do any obvious algebra (Example 1).
   d. *Do not divide* both members by a variable (Example 3).
   e. Use any obvious trigonometric properties (Examples 2, 6).
   f. Get a product equal to zero (Examples 3, 5, 6).
2. Get the *general* solution by finding the argument.
   a. If it is a *special* angle, write the *exact* value.
   b. If it is *not* a special angle, use a calculator.
3. Do whatever algebra you need to find the *variable* in the argument (Examples 2, 3, 4, and 6).
4. Write the solution set.
   a. Find all solutions in the domain by picking integer values of n in the general solution.
   b. Check for extraneous solutions if you have multiplied by a variable.

The following exercise will give you practice solving trigonometric equations.

EXERCISE 14-9

Do These Quickly

The following problems are intended to refresh your skills. You should be able to do all 10 in less than 5 minutes.

Write the exact value:

Q1. $\cos 60°$

Q2. $\sin \dfrac{3\pi}{4}$

Q3. $\tan \dfrac{3\pi}{2}$

Q4. $\cot 90°$

Q5. $\sec (-45°)$

Q6. $\csc 0$

Q7. $\theta = \text{Sin}^{-1} \dfrac{\sqrt{3}}{2}$

Q8. $x = \text{Arctan} (-1)$

Q9. $x = \text{Cos}^{-1} 0$

Q10. $\theta = \text{Arccsc } 2$

For Problems 1 through 40, solve the equation in the indicated domain.

1. $\tan x + \sqrt{3} = 0,$ $x \in [0°, 360°)$

2. $2 \cos x + \sqrt{3} = 0,$ $x \in [0°, 360°)$

3. $2 \sin (x + 47°) = 1,$ $x \in [0°, 360°)$

4. $\sec (x + 81°) = 2,$ $x \in [0°, 360°)$

5. $4 \cos^2 x = 1,$ $x \in [-180°, 180°]$

6. $4 \sin^2 x = 3,$ $x \in [-180°, 180°]$

7. $2 \sin x \cos x = \sqrt{2} \cos x,$ $x \in \{\text{real numbers of degrees}\}$

8. $\tan x \sec x = \tan x,$ $x \in \{\text{real numbers of degrees}\}$

9. $\tan x - \sqrt{3} = 2 \tan x$, $x \in \{\text{real numbers}\}$

10. $\cos x + 2 = 3 \cos x$, $x \in \{\text{real numbers}\}$

11. $2 \sin^2 x + \sin x = 0$, $x \in (-180°, 180°)$

12. $\tan^2 x + \tan x = 0$, $x \in [-90°, 90°)$

13. $2 \cos^2 x - 5 \cos x + 2 = 0$, $x \in [0, 2\pi)$

14. $2 \sec^2 x - 3 \sec x - 2 = 0$, $x \in [0, 2\pi)$

15. $\sin^2 x + 5 \sin x + 6 = 0$, $x \in [0°, 360°)$

16. $4 \csc^2 x + 4 \csc x + 1 = 0$, $x \in [0°, 360°)$

17. $\tan^2 x - \sec x - 1 = 0$ $x \in [-\pi, \pi)$

18. $3 - 3 \sin x - 2 \cos^2 x = 0$, $x \in [-\pi, \pi]$

19. $1 - \cos x = -\sin x$, $x \in [-180°, 180°)$

20. $\dfrac{1 + \cos x}{\sin x} = -1$, $x \in [-180°, 180°)$

21. $4 \sin x \cos x = \sqrt{3}$, $x \in [0, 2\pi)$

22. $\sin x = \sin 2x$, $x \in [0, 2\pi)$

23. $\dfrac{\sin (90° - x)}{\sin x} = -\sqrt{3}$, $x \in (-270°, 270°)$

24. $\tan (90° - x) = -1$, $x \in [-180°, 180°)$

25. $\sin 2x \cos 64°$
    $+ \cos 2x \sin 64° = \dfrac{\sqrt{3}}{2}$, $x \in [0°, 360°)$

26. $\cos 3x \cos 12°$
    $- \sin 3x \sin 12° = \dfrac{1}{2}$, $x \in [-120°, 120°)$

27. $\cos 4x - \sin 2x = 0$, $x \in (-90°, 90°)$

28. $\cos 4x - \sin 2x = 1$, $x \in [-90°, 90°)$

29. $\cos 3x + \cos 5x = 0$, $x \in (-90°, 90°)$

30. $\sin 5x + \sin 7x = 0$, $x \in [-90°, 90°)$

31. $\cos x - \sqrt{3} \sin x = 1$, $x \in (0, 2\pi]$

32. $\sin x - \sqrt{3} \cos x = 1$, $x \in [-\pi, \pi]$

33. $\dfrac{\tan 10x + \tan 50°}{1 - \tan 10x \tan 50°} = \dfrac{\sqrt{3}}{3}$, $x \in (0°, 90°)$

34. $\tan x - \tan 10°$
    $= 1 + \tan x \tan 10°$, $x \in [-180°, 180°]$

35. $\tan \dfrac{1}{2} x + 1 = \cos x$, $x \in [0, 4\pi]$

36. $2 \cos^2 \frac{1}{2}x - 2 = 2 \cos x,$ $x \in [-\pi, \pi)$

37. $2 \cos (x + 30°) \cos (x - 30°) = 1,$ $x \in [-180°, 180°]$

38. $4 \sin (x + 75°) \cos (x - 75°) = 1,$ $x \in [-180°, 180°)$

39. $\cos^2 \frac{1}{2}x - \frac{1}{2} \cos x = \frac{1}{2},$ $x \in \{$real numbers$\}$

40. $\sin x \tan \frac{1}{2}x = 1 - \cos x,$ $x \in \{$real numbers$\}$

For Problems 41 through 50, solve the equation in the domain $\theta \in [0,$ $360°)$ or $x \in [0, 2\pi)$, obtaining approximate values by calculator or from Tables III or IV.

41. $5 \sec^2 \theta + 2 \tan \theta - 8 = 0$ 42. $3 \tan^2 \theta - 5 \sec \theta - 9 = 0$

43. $3 \cos \theta - 4 \sin \theta = 1$ 44. $5 \cos \theta + 12 \sin \theta = 13$

45. $3 \sin^2 x - \sin x = 0$ 46. $4 \cos^2 x + \cos x = 0$

47. $\sin^2 x + \sin x - 1 = 0$ 48. $\cos^2 x - 2 \cos x - 2 = 0$

49. $4 \sin (-x) = 3$ 50. $5 \cos (-x) = 2$

For Problems 51 through 53, solve the equation for the indicated values of x. Note that this is what you did with sinusoids in Section 13-10.

51. $3 + 4 \cos 2(x - 10°) = 5,$ $x \in [0°, 360°)$

52. $4 + 3 \cos 2(x - 10°) = 5,$ $x \in [0°, 360°)$

53. $4 + 3 \cos 2(x - 1) = 2,$ x is the smallest positive real number satisfying the equation.

14-10 | CHAPTER REVIEW AND TEST

In this chapter you have learned properties with which you can *transform* trigonometric expressions to forms that look simpler or are simpler to use in a given problem. The properties are particularly useful for solving trigonometric equations.

The objectives of this chapter may be summarized as follows:

1. *Use the quotient, reciprocal, and Pythagorean properties to transform expressions containing functions with the **same** argument.*
2. *Use the odd-even properties to transform functions with **negative** arguments.*

3. Use the composite argument properties and cofunction properties to transform functions whose arguments contain a **sum**.
4. Use the double argument and half-argument properties to transform to functions of **half** or **twice** the argument.
5. Use the sum and product properties to express sums of sines or cosines as products of sines and cosines, and vice versa.
6. Use the linear combination of sinusoid properties to transform to a cosine with a phase displacement.
7. Transform a trigonometric expression using any combination of the above properties.
8. Solve trigonometric equations.

The Review Problems below parallel the sections in this chapter. The Concepts Problems let you try your hand at applying what you know to analyze a new situation. The Chapter Test is similar to one your instructor might give to see how well you understand properties of trigonometric and circular functions.

REVIEW PROBLEMS

R1. a. Transform $\sec x \cot x$ to $\csc x$.
  b. Transform $(1 + \tan A)^2$ to $2 \tan A + \sec^2 A$.
  c. Transform $\dfrac{1}{1 - \sin A} - \dfrac{1}{1 + \sin A}$ to $2 \sec A \tan A$.

R2. Prove that each of the following is an identity:
  a. $(\tan B + 1)(\tan B - 1) = \sec^2 B - 2$
  b. $\sin^4 p \sec^2 p + \sin^2 p = \tan^2 p$

R3. a. Write the composite argument property for $\tan (A + H)$.
  b. If $\sin (90° - \theta) = 0.631$, find $\cos \theta$.
  c. If A and B are first-quadrant angles, and $\sin A = 0.8$ and $\cos B = \frac{1}{3}$, find $\cos (A + B)$.
  d. Find the exact value of $\sin 15°$.
  e. Prove that this is an identity: $\sin (\theta - 30°) + \cos (\theta + 60°) = 0$
  f. Write the odd-even property for tangent.

R4. a. If $\cos x = \frac{3}{4}$, find $\cos 2x$.
  b. If $\sin x = 0.8$, find $\tan 2x$.
  c. Prove that $2 \cos^2 A = 1 + \cos 2A$ is an identity.
  d. Express $\sin 6x$ in terms of $\sin 3x$ and $\cos 3x$.

R5. a. If $\cos B = -0.8$, and $180° \le B \le 270°$, find $\cos (0.5B)$.
  b. If $\sin C = \frac{2}{3}$, and C is an acute angle, find $\tan (0.5C)$.
  c. Sketch the graphs of $y = \sin (0.5x)$ and $y = \sin x$ on the same set of axes.

R6. a. Write as a sum or difference of sines or cosines of positive arguments: $2 \cos 37° \sin 17°$.

  b. Write as a product of sines and cosines of positive arguments: $\sin 5x - \sin 9x$.

  c. Prove that $\cos 3x + \cos x = 4 \cos^3 x - 2 \cos x$ is an identity.

R7. a. Express in the form $C \cos (\theta - D)$: $7 \sin \theta - 24 \cos \theta$

  b. Sketch the graph of $y = \sqrt{3} \cos \theta + \sin \theta$.

R8. a. Express $\tan x$ in terms of $\sec x$ and $\csc x$.

  b. Express $\sin^2 x$ in terms of $\cos x$.

  c. Express $\sec (-x)$ in terms of $\sec x$.

  d. Express $\tan (h + v)$ in terms of $\tan h$ and $\tan v$.

  e. Express $\sin 2u$ in terms of $\sin u$ and $\cos u$.

  f. Express $\cos \left(\frac{u}{2}\right)$ in terms of $\cos u$.

  g. Express as a sum: $\cos x \sin y$

  h. Express as a product: $\cos A - \cos B$

  i. Express $5 \cos x - 7 \sin x$ as a cosine with a phase displacement.

R9. Solve the equation.

  a. $\sin 2x = \cos x$, $x \in \left[\frac{\pi}{4}, \frac{3\pi}{4}\right]$

  b. $\tan 2(x + 41°) = 1$, $x \in \{\text{real numbers of degrees}\}$

  c. $\sqrt{3} \sin x - \cos x = 1$, $x \in \{\text{real numbers}\}$

CONCEPTS PROBLEMS

C1. Assuming that none of the composite argument properties are known, derive the equation expressing $\cos (A - B)$ in terms of sines and cosines of A and B.

C2. Explain how you determine whether to use the "+" sign or the "−" sign outside the radical in the half-argument property for sine.

C3. The half-argument properties for sine and cosine differ only by the sign between the terms under the radical. Show by clever choice of the argument how you can remember which sign goes with which property.

C4. Let $i = \sqrt{-1}$. Expand the binomial $(\cos x + i \sin x)^2$. Show that the *real* part of the answer is the double argument property for cosine, and the imaginary part is the double argument property for sine.

CHAPTER TEST

T1. Solve the equation.
  a. $\csc x \tan x \cos x = 1$, $\quad x \in [-\pi, \pi]$
  b. $\sin x + \sin 3x + \sin 5x = 0$, $\quad x \in [0°, 360°]$
  c. $\sin x \cos 37° = \cos x \sin 37°$, $\quad x \in (-180°, 180°)$

T2. Prove that the following are identities.
  a. $\sin (x + y) \sin (x - y) = \sin^2 x - \sin^2 y$
  b. $\cot^2 x - \cos^2 x = \cot^2 x \cos^2 x$
  c. $\dfrac{\sin x + \sin y}{\cos x + \cos y} = \tan \dfrac{1}{2} (x + y)$

T3. Find *exact* values of:
  a. $\cos 15°$
  b. $\sin \dfrac{\pi}{8}$

T4. a. Transform $\cos 2(x + y)$ to functions of x and y.
  b. Transform $\sin 58° + \sin 33°$ to a *single* term.
  c. Transform $\sin^2 x \cos x$ to a *sum* of functions of *multiples* of x which involves *no* products of functions.
  d. Transform $\cos 38x$ to
  i. functions of $19x$,
  ii. functions of $76x$.
  e. Simplify $\sin 37° \cos 53° + \cos 37° \sin 53°$.
  f. Transform $\cos 23° + \sin 23°$ to a *multiple* of a *cosine* of a *positive* angle.

15

Triangle Problems

*The word "trigonometry" means "triangle measuring." In this chapter you will use the trigonometric functions for their original purpose. In the first section you will solve right triangle problems using just the **definitions** of the six functions. Then you will learn properties that will allow you to find unknown sides, angles, and the area of **any** triangle. The techniques you will develop are used, for example, by surveyors to measure irregularly-shaped tracts of land, or for finding the slope of a hill.*

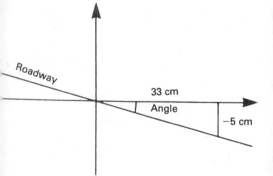

15-1 | RIGHT TRIANGLE PROBLEMS

You will recall from your previous studies that the six trigonometric functions are defined in terms of the coordinates (u, v) of a point on the terminal side of an angle in standard position (Figure 15-1a). Together with the distance r from the origin to (u, v), the numbers u and v can be thought of as lengths of the sides of a right triangle. If the angle measure and one side are known, the other two sides can be found. Similarly, the lengths of any two sides can be used to find the measures of the acute angles.

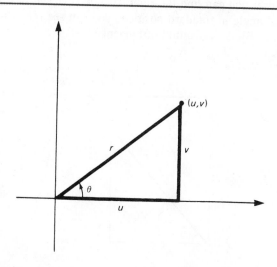

Figure 15-1a

Objective:
Given two sides or a side and an angle of a right triangle, find measures of the other sides and angles.

EXAMPLE 1

Suppose you have been assigned the job of measuring the height of the local water tower.

Climbing makes you dizzy, so you decide to do the whole job at ground level. From a point 47.3 meters from the base of the tower, you find that you must look up at an angle of 53° to see the top of the tower (Figure 15-1b.). How high is the tower?

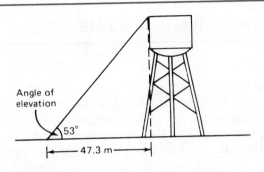

Angle of elevation

53°

47.3 m

Figure 15-1b _____

From the picture, you can find the right triangle sketched in Figure 15-1c. Placing the 53° angle in standard position, you can see that $u = 47.3$, and you must find v. By the definition of tangent,

$$\frac{v}{47.3} = \tan 53°.$$

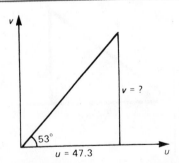

v

$v = ?$

53°

$u = 47.3$

u

Figure 15-1c _____

Multiplying by 47.3 then doing the indicated operations, you get

$$v = 47.3 \tan 53°$$

$$= 62.769 \ldots$$

So the tower is approximately <u>62.8 meters</u> high.

Notes:

1. It would have been possible to start with $\frac{47.3}{v} = \cot 53°$. However, the algebra would be easier if you start with the side to be calculated in the *numerator* of the trigonometric ratio, rather than in the denominator.
2. The 47.3 is assumed to be a *measured* length known to only three significant digits. The 62.769. . . is a decimal approximation with 6 to 10 significant digits. Whenever two decimal approximations are *multiplied* together, the answer should be rounded off to the number of significant digits in the *least* accurately known factor.

It is possible to use the definitions of the trigonometric functions *without* placing the angle in standard position. For this purpose, it helps to observe where the sides u, v, and r are with respect to the angle.   ■

Figure 15-1d shows $\triangle HDJ$ (triangle *HDJ*) with acute angle H placed in standard position and right angle D on the u-axis. By the definitions of the six trigonometric functions:

$$\sin H = \frac{v}{r} \qquad \sec H = \frac{r}{u} \qquad \cot H = \frac{u}{v}$$

$$\tan H = \frac{v}{u} \qquad \cos H = \frac{u}{r} \qquad \csc H = \frac{r}{v}.$$

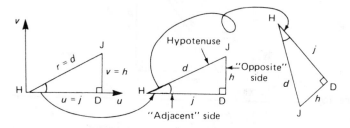

Figure 15-1d _____

It is customary to name the length of the side *opposite* an angle with the same *lower* case letter as the name of the angle. So the side opposite Angle H has measure h, and so forth. Using this lettering scheme, $\sin H = \frac{h}{d}$, since $h = v$ and $d = r$. But d and h are properties of the triangle itself, not the coordinate system. So it is possible to write the trigonometric functions of the angles of a right triangle *without* reference to the coordinates u, v, and r. The *hypotenuse* is one of the sides that includes Angle H. The other side is called the *adjacent* side, the word "adjacent" meaning "next to." Using these words, the definitions of the six trigonometric functions for Angle H of a right triangle become:

$$\sin H = \frac{\text{opposite}}{\text{hypotenuse}} \qquad \cos H = \frac{\text{adjacent}}{\text{hypotenuse}}$$

$$\tan H = \frac{\text{opposite}}{\text{adjacent}} \qquad \cot H = \frac{\text{adjacent}}{\text{opposite}}$$

$$\sec H = \frac{\text{hypotenuse}}{\text{adjacent}} \qquad \csc H = \frac{\text{hypotenuse}}{\text{opposite}}$$

These definitions allow you to write the trigonometric functions of H even if the triangle is flipped over and rotated, as in Figure 15-1d.

EXAMPLE 2

In $\triangle PQR$, Q is the right angle, $q = 147.6$, and $r = 72.15$. Find:

i. $m\angle P$ ii. $m\angle R$ iii. p

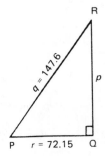

Figure 15-1e

i. $\cos P = \dfrac{r}{q}$ $\cos P = \dfrac{\text{adjacent}}{\text{hypotenuse}}$

$\qquad\quad = \dfrac{72.15}{147.6}$ Substitution

$\qquad\quad = 0.4888\ldots$ By calculator

$\therefore m\angle P = 60.7368\ldots^{\circ}$ By calculator

$\qquad\quad \approx 60°\ 44'$ Converting to minutes

Note: Save $60.7368\ldots$ in memory, without round-off, for use in the next part of the problem.

ii. $m \angle R = 180° - 90° - 60° 44' = \underline{\underline{29° 16'}}$

iii. $\dfrac{p}{r} = \tan P$ $\tan P = \dfrac{\text{opposite}}{\text{adjacent}}$

   $p = r \tan P$ Multiplication by r

   $= 72.15 \tan P$ Substitution

   $= 128.763 \ldots$ Recalling P from memory

   $\underline{\underline{= 128.8}}$ Rounding off to four significant digits   ■

The exercise that follows is designed to give you practice finding unknown side and angle measures of right triangles.

EXERCISE 15-1

Do These Quickly

The following problems are intended to refresh your skills. You should be able to do all 10 in less than 5 minutes.

In the right triangle shown, what is

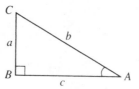

Q1.   The leg opposite angle A?

Q2.   The leg adjacent to angle A?

Q3.   The hypotenuse?

Q4. $\sin A$?

Q5. $\cos A$?

Q6. $\tan A$?

Find the following.

Q7.   If $\tan x = 0.3$, find $\tan 2x$.

Q8.   Find $\cos 30°$.

Q9.   Find $\sin \left(\dfrac{4\pi}{3} \right)$.

Q10. Find $\text{Sec}^{-1} (-2)$.

For Problems 1 through 8, find the other side and angle measures for the given right triangle:

	Name	Right angle	Given data
1.	ABC	A	$m\angle B = 34°, c = 14.7$
2.	ABC	B	$m\angle C = 71°, b = 36.8$
3.	LMN	M	$m\angle N = 47° 32', m = 3.465$
4.	HPJ	H	$m\angle J = 29° 51', j = 4651$
5.	XYZ	X	$x = 35, y = 27$
6.	KLM	L	$k = 5.2, m = 3.3$
7.	RST	T	$s = 9.85, t = 47.3$
8.	UVW	W	$u = 439.8, v = 641.2$

9. **Ladder Problem**   You lean a ladder 6.7 meters long against the wall. It makes an angle of 63° with the level ground. How high up is the top of the ladder?

10. **Flagpole Problem**   You must order a new rope for the flagpole. To find out what length of rope is needed, you observe that the pole casts a shadow 11.6 meters long on the ground. The angle of elevation of the sun is 36° 50' (Figure 15-1f). How tall is the pole?

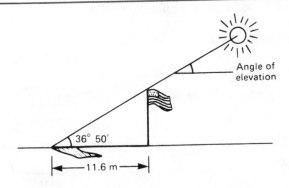

Angle of elevation

36° 50'

11.6 m

Figure 15-1f

11. **Cat Problem**   Your cat is trapped on a tree branch 6.5 meters above the ground. Your ladder is only 6.7 meters long. If you place the ladder's tip on the branch, what angle will the ladder make with the ground?

12. **Observation Tower Problem**   The tallest free-standing structure in the world is the 553-meter tall CN Tower in Toronto, Ontario. Suppose that at a certain time of day it casts a shadow 1100 meters long on the ground. What is the angle of elevation of the sun at that time of day?

13. ***Moon Crater Problem***   Scientists estimate the heights of features on the moon by measuring the lengths of the shadows they cast on the moon's surface. From a photograph, you find that the shadow cast on the inside of a crater by its rim is 325 meters long (Figure 15-1g). At the time the photograph was taken, the sun's angle of elevation from this place on the moon's surface was 23° 37′. How high does the rim rise above the inside of the crater?

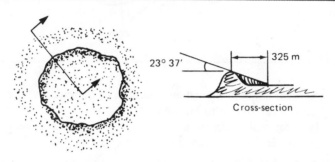

Figure 15-1g _____

14. ***Lighthouse Problem***   An observer 80 feet above the surface of the water measures an angle of depression of 0° 42′ to a distant ship (Figure 15-1h). How many miles is the ship from the base of the lighthouse? (A mile is 5280 feet.)

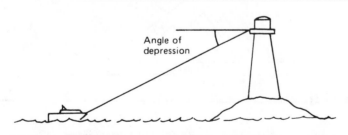

Figure 15-1h _____

15. ***Airplane Landing Problem***   Commercial airliners fly at an altitude of about 10 kilometers. They start descending toward the airport when they are still far away, so that they will not have to dive at a steep angle.
   a.   If the pilot wants the plane's path to make an angle of 3° with the ground, how far from the airport must he start descending?
   b.   If he starts descending 300 kilometers from the airport, what angle will the plane's path make with the horizontal?

16. ***Radiotherapy Problem***   A beam of gamma rays is to be used to treat a tumor known to be 5.7 centimeters beneath the patient's skin.

To avoid damaging a vital organ, the radiologist moves the source over 8.3 centimeters (Figure 15-1i).

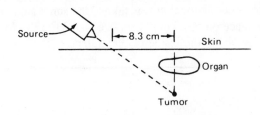

Figure 15-1i

a. At what angle to the patient's skin must the radiologist aim the gamma ray source to hit the tumor?
b. How far will the beam have to travel through the patient's body before reaching the tumor?

17. ***Triangular Block Problem***   A block bordering Market Street is a right triangle (Figure 15-1j). You start walking around the block, taking 125 paces on Market Street and 102 paces on Pine Street.

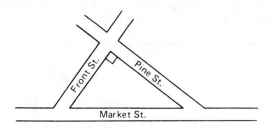

Figure 15-1j

a. At what angle do Pine and Market Streets intersect?
b. How many paces must you take on Front Street to complete the trip?

18. ***Cable Car Problem***   Wendy Uptmore is waiting for the cable car in the 600 block of Powell Street in San Francisco. Since the street seems to be so steep, she decides to find out what angle it makes with the horizontal. On the wall of a house, she measures horizontal and vertical distances of 33 centimeters and 5 centimeters, respectively (Figure 15-1k).

a. What angle does Powell Street make with the horizontal?

b.   While she waited, Wendy went up to the top of the block, counting 101 paces. She is tall and figures each pace is 1 meter long. How many meters did she go *vertically*?

c.   If Powell Street had been level instead of slanted, how many paces would Wendy have to go to walk the 600 block of Powell Street? Surprising?!

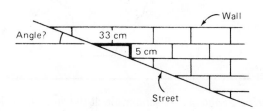

Figure 15-1k —————————————————————————

19.   **Surveying Problem**   When surveyors measure land that slopes significantly, the distance which is measured will be *longer* than the *horizontal* distance which must be drawn on the map. Suppose that the distance from the top edge of the Cibolo Creek bed to the edge of the water is 37.8 meters (Figure 15-1l). The land slopes downward at 27° 36′ to the horizontal.

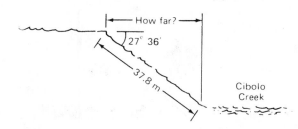

Figure 15-1l —————————————————————————

a.   What is the horizontal distance from the top of the bank to the edge of the creek?

b.   How far is the surface of the creek below the level of the surrounding land?

20.   **Grand Canyon Problem**   From a point on the North Rim of the Grand Canyon, a surveyor measures an angle of depression of 1° 18′ to a point on the South Rim (Figure 15-1m). From an aerial photograph, he determines that the horizontal distance between the two points is 10 miles. How many feet is the South Rim below the North Rim? (A mile is 5280 feet.)

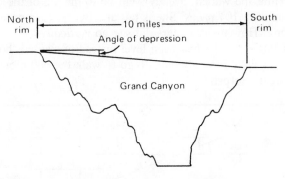

Figure 15-1m _____

21. *Submarine Problem*   A submarine at the surface of the ocean
    makes an emergency dive, its path making an angle of 21° with the
    surface.
    a.   If it goes for 300 meters along its downward path, how deep
         will it be? What horizontal distance is it from its starting point?
    b.   How many meters must it go along its downward path to reach a
         depth of 1000 meters?

22. *Missile Problem*   An observer 5.2 kilometers from the launch pad
    observes a missile ascending (Figure 15-1n).

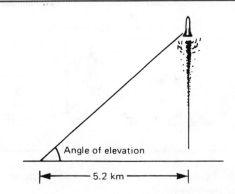

Figure 15-1n _____

    a.   At a particular time, the angle of elevation is 31° 27′. How high
         is the missile? How far is it from the observer?
    b.   What will the angle of elevation be when the missile reaches 30
         kilometers?

23. *The Grapevine Problem*   Interstate 5 in California enters the San
    Joaquin Valley through a mountain pass called the Grapevine. The
    road descends from an altitude of 3000 feet to 500 feet above sea
    level in a distance of 6 miles. (A mile is 5280 feet.)

    a.   Approximately what angle does the road make with the horizontal?

    b.   What assumption must you make about how the road slopes?

24.   *Pyramid Problem*   The Great Pyramid of Cheops in Egypt has a square base 230 meters on each side. The faces of the pyramid make an angle of 51° 50' with the horizontal (Figure 15-1o).

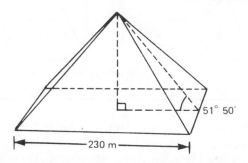

Figure 15-1o

    a.   How tall is the pyramid?

    b.   What is the shortest distance you would have to climb up a face to reach the top?

    c.   Suppose that you decide to make a model of the pyramid by cutting four triangles out of cardboard and gluing them together. What must the angles of the triangle be?

    d.   Show that the ratio of the answer from part b to half the length of the base is very close to the Golden Ratio, $\frac{\sqrt{5}+1}{2}$. (See Martin Garner's article in the June 1974 issue of *Scientific American* for other startling relationships among the dimensions of the pyramid.)

15-2   OBLIQUE TRIANGLES—LAW OF COSINES

You have learned to find unknown measures in right triangles. Now you must learn how to do the same things for *oblique* triangles, which do *not* have a right angle.

Objectives:

1. Given two sides and the included angle, find the length of the third side of the triangle.
2. Given three sides of a triangle, find the measure of a specified angle.

Suppose that the lengths of two sides, b and c, of △ABC are known, and also the measure of the included angle A (Figure 15-2a). The length of the third side, a, is to be found.

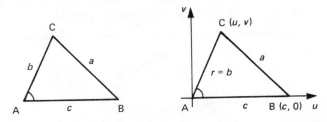

Figure 15-2a

If you construct a uv-coordinate system with Angle A in standard position, as in the second sketch of Figure 15-2a, then a becomes a distance between two points in a Cartesian coordinate system. These are the points $B(c, 0)$ and $C(u, v)$. By the Distance Formula,

$$a^2 = (u - c)^2 + (v - 0)^2.$$

In order to get a^2 in terms of b, c, and $m \angle A$, all you need to do is observe that A is the *angle* and b is the *radius* to point $C(u, v)$. By the definitions of cosine and sine,

$$\frac{u}{b} = \cos A \quad \text{and} \quad \frac{v}{b} = \sin A.$$

Multiplying both members of each equation by b gives

$$u = b \cos A \quad \text{and} \quad v = b \sin A.$$

Substituting these values for u and v into the Distance Formula above gives

$$a^2 = (b \cos A - c)^2 + (b \sin A - 0)^2.$$

Upon expanding the squares on the right, you get

$$a^2 = b^2 \cos^2 A - 2bc \cos A + c^2 + b^2 \sin^2 A.$$

Associating the $\sin^2 A$ and $\cos^2 A$ terms and then factoring out b^2 gives

$$a^2 = b^2 (\cos^2 A + \sin^2 A) - 2bc \cos A + c^2.$$

The Pythagorean properties may now be applied to give

$$a^2 = b^2 - 2bc \cos A + c^2,$$

which is usually written:

$$\boxed{a^2 = b^2 + c^2 - 2bc \cos A} \quad \longleftarrow \quad \text{Law of cosines}$$

This equation is called the Law of Cosines because the *cosine* of an angle appears in it. Note that if $m \angle A = 90°$, then $\cos A = 0$. The Law of Cosines thus reduces to

$$a^2 = b^2 + c^2,$$

which is, of course, the Pythagorean Theorem! In fact, the Law of Cosines simply says that $2bc \cos A$ is what you must *subtract* from the Pythagorean $a^2 = b^2 + c^2$ in order to get the proper value for a^2 when A is not a right angle. If A is obtuse then $\cos A$ is negative. So subtracting $2bc \cos A$ actually *adds* a number to $b^2 + c^2$. The situation is illustrated in Figure 15-2b.

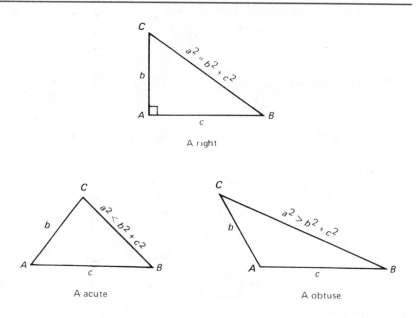

Law of Cosines and the Pythagorean Theorem

Figure 15-2b

You should not jump to the conclusion that the Law of Cosines gives an easy way to *prove* the Pythagorean Theorem. Doing so would involve circular reasoning, because Pythagoras was used to *derive* the Law of Cosines!

Accomplishing the first objective, finding the third side from two sides and the included angle, is illustrated in Examples 1 and 2. Accomplishing the second objective, finding an angle from three given sides, is illustrated in Examples 3 and 4.

EXAMPLE 1

In △ABC, if $b = 5$, $c = 7$, and $m\angle A = 39°$, find a (Figure 15-2c).

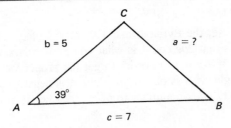

Figure 15-2c

By direct substitution into the Law of Cosines:

$$a^2 = 5^2 + 7^2 - 2(5)(7) \cos 39°$$

$$= 19.5997 \ldots \qquad \text{By calculator}$$

$$\therefore a = 4.42716 \ldots \qquad \text{Taking the square root}$$

$$\approx 4.427 \qquad \text{Rounding off}$$

The sequence of keystrokes is long, but straightforward.

Arithmetic logic:

$$5 \; \boxed{x^2} \; \boxed{+} \; 7 \; \boxed{x^2} \; \boxed{-} \; 2 \; \boxed{\times} \; 5 \; \boxed{\times} \; 7 \; \boxed{\times}$$
$$39 \; \boxed{\cos} \; \boxed{=} \; \boxed{\surd}$$

RPN:

$$5 \; \boxed{x^2} \; 7 \; \boxed{x^2} \; \boxed{+} \; 2 \; \boxed{\text{enter}} \; 5 \; \boxed{\times} \; 7 \; \boxed{\times}$$
$$39 \; \boxed{\cos} \; \boxed{\times} \; \boxed{-} \; \boxed{\surd}$$

EXAMPLE 2

In △KSD, $m\angle S = 127° \, 42'$, $k = 15.78$, and $d = 2.654$. Find s.

You should recognize that the Law of Cosines is *independent* of the letters you use to express it. All that matters is that you know two sides and the *included* angle. A picture such as Figures 15-2d will help.

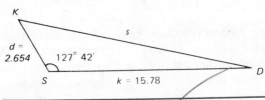

Figure 15-2d

Applying the Law of Cosines gives:

$$s^2 = k^2 + d^2 - 2kd \cos S$$

$\qquad = 15.78^2 + 2.654^2$

$\qquad\quad - 2(15.78)(2.654) \cos 127° 42'$ Substitution

$\qquad = 307.27 \ldots$ By calculator

$\therefore s = 17.5292 \ldots$ Taking the square root

$\qquad \approx \underline{\underline{17.53}}$ Rounding off to 4 significant digits

Note: A *product* of two decimal approximations is rounded off to the least number of *significant digits* in any factor. A *sum* of two decimal approximations is rounded off to the least number of *decimal places* in any term. You can see why if you will write each factor or term with an "x" for each digit beyond the last one you know. Wherever you add or multiply by an unknown digit, place another x. Where an x first appears in the answer is the place to which you must round off. ■

EXAMPLE 3

In $\triangle XYZ$, $x = 3$, $y = 7$, and $z = 9$. Find $m \angle Z$.

Again, drawing a picture will help you figure out how to set up the Law of Cosines (Figure 15-2e). Since Angle Z is to be measured, and Sides x and y *include* Angle Z, you use the Law of Cosines in the form

$$z^2 = x^2 + y^2 - 2xy \cos Z.$$

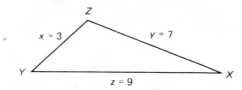

Figure 15-2e

Since x, y, and z are known and $m \angle Z$ is to be found, the equation can be solved for $\cos Z$, giving

$$\cos Z = \frac{x^2 + y^2 - z^2}{2xy}.$$

Substituting the given information yields

$$\cos Z = \frac{3^2 + 7^2 - 9^2}{2(3)(7)}$$

$$= \frac{-23}{42} \qquad \text{Arithmetic}$$

$$= -0.54761. . . \qquad \text{By calculator}$$

$$\therefore m \angle Z = 123.203. . .° \qquad \text{By calculator}$$

$$\approx 123° \, 12' \qquad \text{Converting to minutes} \qquad \blacksquare$$

EXAMPLE 4

In $\triangle XYZ$, $x = 3$, $y = 7$, and $z = 11$. Find $m \angle Z$.

At first glance, this problem seems equivalent to Example 3. Using the Law of Cosines as before gives:

$$\cos Z = \frac{3^2 + 7^2 - 11^2}{2(3)(7)}$$

$$= \frac{-63}{42} \qquad \text{Arithmetic}$$

$$= -1.5 \qquad \text{Arithmetic}$$

But there can be *no* such angle Z, because cosines must be between -1 and 1, inclusive. The reason is clear when you compare the lengths of the three sides (Figure 15-2f). Sides x and y add up to 10, which is *less* than the length 11 of the third side z, so there can be no such triangle! The Law of Cosines automatically detects this situation, if you have overlooked it at first, by giving a cosine *outside* the range $-1 \leq \cos \theta \leq 1$.

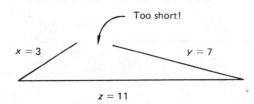

Figure 15-2f ⎯⎯⎯⎯⎯⎯⎯⎯⎯⎯⎯⎯⎯⎯⎯⎯⎯ ■

The exercise that follows is designed to give you practice using the Law of Cosines to find the third side given two sides and the included angle, or to find an angle given three sides.

EXERCISE 15-2

Do These Quickly

The following problems are intended to refresh your skills. You should be able to do all 10 in less than 5 minutes.

Q1. Draw a right triangle with acute angle B. Mark the leg *adjacent* to angle B.

Q2. Find the area of a right triangle with sides 3 cm, 4 cm, and 5 cm.

Q3. Sketch the graph of $y = 2 \cos \theta$.

Q4. Sketch the graph of $y = \text{Cos}^{-1} x$.

Q5. Sketch the graph of $y = (\cos x)^{-1}$.

Q6. What is the period of $y = 4 + 3 \sin 2(x - 1)$?

Q7. If $\sec x = 10$, find $\cos x$.

Q8. If $\sin \theta = 0.315$, find $\cos (90° - \theta)$.

Q9. Write the general solution: $\tan x = \sqrt{3}$.

Q10. Find the next term in the geometric series $13 + 26 + \cdots$.

For Problems 1 through 6, find the length of the side *opposite* the given angle.

1. In $\triangle ABC$, $b = 4$, $c = 5$, and $m \angle A = 51°$.

2. In $\triangle ABC$, $a = 7$, $c = 9$, and $m \angle B = 34°$.

3. In $\triangle PQR$, $p = 3$, $q = 2$, and $m \angle R = 138°$.

4. In $\triangle HJK$, $h = 8$, $j = 6$, and $m \angle K = 172°$.

5. In $\triangle DEF$, $d = 36.2$, $f = 49.8$, and $m \angle E = 67° \, 40'$.

6. In $\triangle BAD$, $a = 2.897$, $d = 5.921$, and $m \angle B = 119° \, 23'$.

For Problems 7 through 14, find the measure of the specified angle.

7. $m \angle A$ in $\triangle ABC$, if $a = 2$, $b = 3$, and $c = 4$.

8. $m \angle C$ in $\triangle ABC$, if $a = 5$, $b = 6$, and $c = 8$.

9. $m \angle T$ in $\triangle BAT$, if $b = 6$, $a = 7$, and $t = 12$.

10. $m \angle E$ in $\triangle PEG$, if $p = 12$, $e = 20$, and $g = 16$.

11. $m \angle Y$ in $\triangle GYP$, if $g = 7$, $y = 5$, and $p = 13$.

12. $m \angle N$ in $\triangle GON$, if $g = 8$, $o = 3$, and $n = 12$.

13. $m \angle O$ in $\triangle NOD$, if $n = 1475$, $o = 2053$, and $d = 1428$.

14. $m \angle Q$ in $\triangle SQR$, if $s = 1504$, $q = 2465$, and $r = 1953$.

15. **Accurate Drawing Problem No. 1**   Construct accurately $\triangle ABC$ from Problem 1. Measure $b = 4$ cm, and $c = 5$ cm with a ruler, and use a protractor to construct $\angle A = 51°$. Then measure side a. Your answer should agree with the calculated value to within ± 0.1 cm.

16. ***Accurate Drawing Problem No. 2*** Construct accurately $\triangle ABC$
from Problem 8. Draw side c, 8 cm, as the base. Use a compass to
mark off arcs of 5 cm and 6 cm from the two ends of side c. Where
the arcs intersect will be point C. Then measure angle C with a protractor. The measured value should agree with the calculated value
to within $\pm 1°$.

15-3 | AREA OF A TRIANGLE

Objective:
Given the measures of two sides and the included angle, find the area of
the triangle.

From geometry you recall that the area of a triangle is half the product of
the base and the altitude. For $\triangle ABC$ in Figure 15-3a,

$$\text{Area} = \frac{1}{2}\, bh.$$

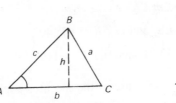

Figure 15-3a

If you know the lengths of b and c and the measure of Angle A, you can
calculate the altitude h in terms of these numbers. Constructing a uv-coor-
dinate system as in the second sketch of Figure 15-3a, $B(u, v)$ becomes a
point in a Cartesian coordinate system. By the definition of sine,

$$\frac{v}{r} = \sin A.$$

Multiplying both members of this equation by r gives

$$v = r \sin A.$$

Since $h = v$ and $c = r$, you can substitute these and get

$$h = c \sin A.$$

Substituting this value of h into the area equation gives:

$$\text{Area} = \frac{1}{2}\, bc \sin A$$

EXAMPLE 1

Find the area of $\triangle ABC$ if $b = 13$, $c = 15$, and $m\angle A = 71°$.

Using the above equation,

$$\text{Area} = \frac{1}{2}(13)(15) \sin 71°$$

$\qquad = 92.1880\ldots$ By calculator

$\qquad \approx \underline{\underline{92.19}}$ Assuming 13 and 15 are *exact* and rounding off to four significant digits   ∎

EXAMPLE 2

Find the area of $\triangle HPJ$ if $h = 5$, $p = 7$, and $j = 11$.

In order to use the area equation, you must first know one of the angles. Suppose you decide to calculate $m\angle J$. Drawing a picture as in Figure 15-3b and applying the Law of Cosines as you did in Section 15-2,

$$j^2 = h^2 + p^2 - 2hp \cos J.$$

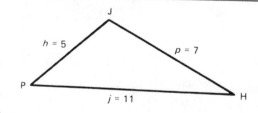

Figure 15-3b

Solving for $\cos J$ gives:

$$\cos J = \frac{h^2 + p^2 - j^2}{2hp}$$

$$\qquad = \frac{25 + 49 - 121}{2(5)(7)} \qquad \text{Substitution}$$

$$\qquad = -0.671428\ldots \qquad \text{By calculator}$$

$$\therefore m\angle J = 132.177\ldots° \qquad \text{By calculator}$$

This value should be saved in memory, without round-off, for use next. Applying the area equation gives:

$$\text{Area} = \frac{1}{2}\, hp \sin J$$

$$= \frac{1}{2}(5)(7) \sin J \quad \text{Substitution}$$

$$= 12.9687. . . \quad \text{Recalling } 132.177. . .° \text{ from memory}$$

$$\approx \underline{12.97} \quad \text{Rounding off to four significant digits} \quad \blacksquare$$

The following exercise is designed to give you practice finding areas of specified triangles.

EXERCISE 15-3

Do These Quickly

The following problems are intended to refresh your skills. You should be able to do all 10 in less than 5 minutes.

For right triangle *ABC*, find

Q1. *a.*

Q2. *b.*

Q3. angle *C.*

Q4. the area.

Answer the questions.

Q5. For triangle *DEF*, find *e.*

Q6. Find $\sin\left(\text{Arctan } \dfrac{3}{4}\right)$.

Q7. Show by sketch that 3, 4, and 8 cannot be side lengths in the same triangle.

Q8. Find tan 90°.

Q9. Find the third partial sum of $2 + 5 + 13 + 7 + 8 + 14 + \cdots$.

Q10. Sketch the graph of a cubic function.

Work the following problems.

Find the area of each triangle.

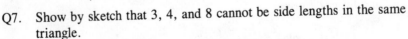

1. $\triangle ABC$, if $a = 5$, $b = 9$, and $m \angle C = 14°$.

2. $\triangle ABC$, if $b = 8$, $c = 4$, and $m \angle A = 67°$.

3. $\triangle RST$, if $r = 4.8$, $t = 3.7$, and $m \angle S = 43° \ 10'$.

4. $\triangle XYZ$, if $y = 34.19$, $z = 28.65$, and $m \angle X = 138° \ 27'$.

5. $\triangle MAP$, if $m = 6$, $a = 9$, and $p = 13$.

6. $\triangle ABX$, if $a = 5$, $b = 12$, and $x = 13$.

7. You may recall from geometry that Hero's Formula can be used to find the area in *one* computation. This formula is

$$\text{Area} = \sqrt{s(s - a)(s - b)(s - c)},$$

where s (for "semiperimeter") equals half the perimeter of the triangle. Use Hero's Formula to find the area of $\triangle MAP$ in Problem 5.

8. Use Hero's Formula to find the area of $\triangle ABX$ in Problem 6.

15-4   OBLIQUE TRIANGLES—LAW OF SINES

The Law of Cosines may be used directly when you know two sides and the included angle. If you know only *one* side length, the Law of Cosines cannot be used. In this section you will find out what can be done in this case to calculate other side measures.

Objective:
Given the measure of an angle, its opposite side, and one other angle measure, calculate the length of another side.

In the previous section you learned that the area of a triangle such as $\triangle ABC$ in Figure 15-4a is

$$\text{Area} = \frac{1}{2} bc \sin A.$$

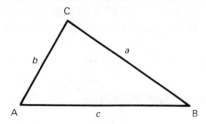

Figure 15-4a

The area is also equal to $\frac{1}{2}ac \sin B$ and to $\frac{1}{2}ab \sin C$, since the area is *constant* no matter which sides and angle you use to measure it. Setting these expressions equal to each other gives

$$\frac{1}{2} bc \sin A = \frac{1}{2} ac \sin B = \frac{1}{2} ab \sin C.$$

Multiplying all three members by 2 eliminates the fraction $\frac{1}{2}$ each time it occurs. Dividing all three members by abc produces a rather startling simplification.

$$\frac{bc \sin A}{abc} = \frac{ac \sin B}{abc} = \frac{ab \sin C}{abc}.$$

In each member, the coefficients of the sine cancel, giving:

$$\frac{\sin A}{a} = \frac{\sin B}{b} = \frac{\sin C}{c}$$ $\longleftarrow$ Law of Sines, first form

This relationship is called the Law of Sines for reasons that should be obvious! Since a is opposite Angle A, and so forth, the law actually says,

"Within any given triangle, the ratio of the sine of an angle to the length of its opposite side is *constant*."

Since you know that if two non-zero numbers are equal, then their reciprocals are equal, you can "flip over" the Law of Sines, getting:

$$\frac{a}{\sin A} = \frac{b}{\sin B} = \frac{c}{\sin C}$$ $\longleftarrow$ Law of Sines, second form

The following examples show you how the Law of Sines may be used to accomplish the objective of this section. Watch out for surprises!

Because of the different combinations of sides and angles that might be given in a triangle, it is convenient to revive some terminology that you may recall from geometry. The abbreviation "SAS" stands for "side, angle, side." This means that as you go around the perimeter of the triangle, you are given the length of a side, the measure of the next angle, and the length of the next side. Thus, "SAS" is equivalent to knowing two sides and the included angle. Similar meanings are attached to ASA, AAS, SSA, and SSS.

EXAMPLE 1

Given AAS, find the other sides.

In $\triangle ABC$, $m \angle B = 64°$, $m \angle C = 38°$ and $b = 9$. Find c and a.

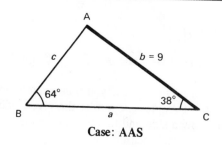

Case: AAS

Figure 15-4b

The first thing to do is draw a picture, as in Figure 15-4b. Using part of the Law of Sines,

$$\frac{c}{\sin C} = \frac{b}{\sin B}.$$

You pick two of the three members of the Law of Sines equation in such a way that the quantity you are looking for is in the *numerator* of the left member and the *known* side and opposite angle are in the *right* member. Multiplying each member by $\sin C$ isolates the quantity you seek on the left side, giving:

$$c = \frac{b \sin C}{\sin B}$$

$$= \frac{9 \sin 38°}{\sin 64°} \qquad \text{Substitution}$$

$$= 6.16487. . . \qquad \text{By calculator}$$

$$\approx \underline{6.165} \qquad \text{Rounding off to four significant digits}$$

To find a, you must first find the measure of its opposite angle A. Since the sum of the three angle measures is 180°,

$$m\angle A = 180° - 38° - 64° = 78°.$$

Using the appropriate form of the Law of Sines:

$$\frac{a}{\sin A} = \frac{b}{\sin B}$$

$$\therefore a = \frac{b \sin A}{\sin B} \qquad \text{Multiplication by } \sin A$$

$$= \frac{9 \sin 78°}{\sin 64°} \qquad \text{Substitution}$$

$$= 9.79460. . . \qquad \text{By calculator}$$

$$\approx \underline{9.795} \qquad \text{Correct to four significant digits}$$ ∎

EXAMPLE 2

Given ASA, find another side.

In $\triangle ABC$, $a = 8$, $m\angle B = 64°$, and $m\angle C = 38°$. Find c.

Drawing a picture as in Figure 15-4c, you immediately notice that you do *not* know the measure of Angle A, opposite the given side. To use the Law of Sines, you must know a side and the opposite angle. Again using the fact that the sum of the angle measures is 180°,

$$m\angle A = 180° - 64° - 38° = 78°.$$

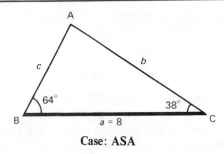

Case: ASA

Figure 15-4c

Using the appropriate part of the Law of Sines:

$$\frac{c}{\sin C} = \frac{a}{\sin A}$$

$$\therefore c = \frac{a \sin C}{\sin A} \qquad \text{Multiplication by } \sin C$$

$$= \frac{8 \sin 38°}{\sin 78°} \qquad \text{Substitution of known information}$$

$$= 5.03532. \ldots \qquad \text{By calculator}$$

$$\approx \underline{\underline{5.035}} \qquad \text{Correct to four significant digits} \qquad \blacksquare$$

The exercise that follows is designed to give you practice using the Law of Sines to find unknown side lengths when you know one side and its opposite angle.

EXERCISE 15-4

Do These Quickly

The following problems are intended to refresh your skills. You should be able to do all 10 in less than 5 minutes.

For Triangle *GHI*, find

Q1. side *h*.

Q2. the area.

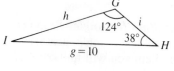

For right triangle *JKL*, find

Q3. sin *J*

Q4. sin *K*

Q5. sin *L*

Q6. the area.

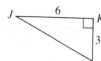

Answer the questions:

Q7. What number is 30% of cos 60°?

Q8. Find cos (cos (cos (cos 1))).

Q9. Find cos 2*A* if cos *A* = 0.4.

Q10. Sketch the graph of *y* = tan *x*.

Work the following problems.

1. In △*ABC*, *m∠A* = 52°, *m∠B* = 31°, and *a* = 8. Find:
    a. *b*
    b. *c*

2. In △*PQR*, *m∠P* = 13°, *m∠Q* = 133°, and *q* = 9. Find:
    a. *p*
    b. *r*

3. In △*AHS*, *m∠A* = 27°, *m∠H* = 109°, and *a* = 120. Find:
    a. *h*
    b. *s*

4. In △*BIG*, *m∠B* = 2°, *m∠I* = 79°, and *b* = 20. Find:
    a. *i*
    b. *g*

5. In △*PAF*, *m∠P* = 28°, *f* = 6, and *m∠A* = 117°. Find:
    a. *a*
    b. *p*

6. In △*JAW*, *m∠J* = 48°, *a* = 5, and *m∠W* = 73°. Find:
    a. *j*
    b. *w*

7. In △*ALP*, *m∠A* = 85°, *p* = 30, and *m∠L* = 87°. Find:
    a. *a*
    b. *l*

8. In $\triangle LOW$, $m \angle L = 2°$, $o = 500$, and $m \angle W = 3°$. Find:
    a. l
    b. w

9. *Law of Sines for Angles Problem*   The Law of Sines can be used to find an unknown *angle* measure. However, the technique is risky! In this problem you will find out *why*.

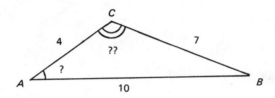

Figure 15-4d

Triangle *ABC* has sides of 4, 7, and 10 units, as shown in Figure 15-4d.

a. Use the Law of Cosines to find $m \angle A$, as you did in Section 15-2.
b. Use the answer to part (a) in the Law of *Sines* to find $m \angle C$.
c. Find $m \angle C$ again, directly from the side lengths, using the Law of Cosines.
d. Your answers to parts (b) and (c) probably do not agree! If not, and if you have made no computation errors, your error is in interpreting the results of the Law of Sines in part (b). Use the fact that there is also an *obtuse* angle whose sine is the same as in part (b) to correct your answer to part (b).
e. Explain why it is dangerous to use the Law of Sines to find an angle measure, but is *not* dangerous to use the Law of Cosines.

10. *Accurate Drawing Problem*   Using ruler, protractor, and a sharp pencil, draw a triangle with base 10.0 centimeters, and angles of 40° and 30° at the ends of the base. Measure the side opposite the 30° angle. Then calculate its length by the Law of Sines. Your measured value should be within ±0.1 centimeter of the calculated value.

15-5   THE AMBIGUOUS CASE

You may recall from geometry that a triangle is not necessarily determined uniquely by the measures of two sides and a non-included angle. This case is called SSA (side, side, angle), and is illustrated in Figure 15-5a.

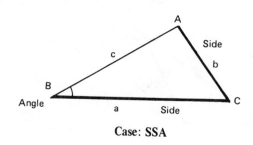

Case: SSA

Figure 15-5a _____

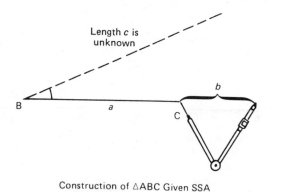

Construction of △ABC Given SSA

Figure 15-5b _____

There are *four* ways a triangle *ABC* would come out if you knew the lengths of *a* and *b* and the measure of Angle *B*. To see why, it is helpful to start *constructing* the triangle. Figure 15-5b shows *a* and Angle *B* constructed.

Since *c* is not given, you simply draw a long line in the correct direction, making an angle of $m \angle B$ with *a*. To complete the triangle, you place the point of a compass at Point *C*, open it to length *b*, which *is* given, and draw an arc. Wherever the compass arc cuts the dotted line in Figure 15-5b is the correct position for Point *A*. Figure 15-5c shows the four possible ways Point *A* might come out. There are either *two*, *one*, or *no* possible triangles when you are given SSA. For this reason, SSA is sometimes called the "ambiguous case." *Ambiguous* means "two or more possible meanings."

Objective:
Given SSA, determine whether or not there are possible triangles, and if so, find the other side length and angle measures.

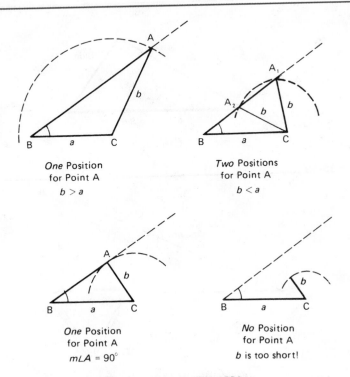

One Position
for Point A
$b > a$

Two Positions
for Point A
$b < a$

One Position
for Point A
$mLA = 90°$

No Position
for Point A
b is too short!

Possible Triangles Given SSA

Figure 15-5c

EXAMPLE 1

In $\triangle XYZ$, $x = 4$, $y = 5$, and $m \angle X = 27°$. Find the possible values of z.

Since $x < y$, there can be two possible triangles, as shown in Figure 15-5d. The Law of Sines cannot be used directly to find z, since $m \angle Z$ is unknown. The Law of Cosines can be used, however, because there are two side lengths known. The process is complicated by the fact that z is not opposite the known angle. You write:

$$4^2 = z^2 + 5^2 - 2(z)(5) \cos 27°$$

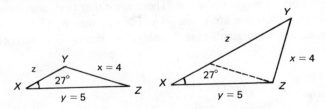

Figure 15-5d

This is a quadratic equation in the variable z. Making the left member equal 0, and using the Quadratic Formula gives

$$0 = z^2 - (10 \cos 27°)z + 25 - 16$$

$$0 = z^2 - (8.91 . . .)z + 9$$

$$z = \frac{8.91 . . . \pm \sqrt{(8.91 . . .)^2 - 4(1)(9)}}{2(1)}$$

$$z = \frac{8.91 . . . \pm 6.58 . . .}{2}$$

$$z \approx \underline{7.75 \text{ or } 1.16}$$

When you evaluate the Quadratic Formula, it helps to evaluate the radical first. Then save its value in memory for use when you calculate the second value of z. ■

EXAMPLE 2

In $\triangle XYZ$, $x = 6$, $y = 5$, and $m \angle X = 27°$. Find the possible values of z.

Since $x > y$, there will be only *one* possible triangle, as shown in the first sketch of Figure 15-5c. This triangle is shown in Figure 15-5e. By the Law of Cosines,

$$6^2 = z^2 + 5^2 - 2(z)(5) \cos 27°$$

$$0 = z^2 - (8.91 . . .)z - 11$$

$$z = \frac{8.91 . . . \pm \sqrt{(8.91 . . .)^2 - 4(1)(-11)}}{2}$$

$$z = 10.009 . . . \text{ or } -1.099 . . .$$

$$z \approx \underline{\underline{10.01}}$$

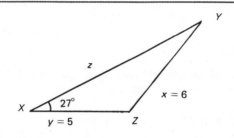

Figure 15-5e

The negative value of z confirms that there is only *one* possible triangle. ■

EXAMPLE 3

In $\triangle XYZ$, $x = 2$, $y = 5$, and $m \angle X = 27°$. Find the possible values of z.

This example is the same as Examples 1 and 2 except for the value of x. By the Law of Cosines,

$$2^2 = z^2 + 5^2 - 2(z)(5) \cos 27°$$

$$0 = z^2 - (8.91 \ldots)z + 21$$

$$z = \frac{8.91 \ldots \pm \sqrt{(8.91 \ldots)^2 - 4(1)(21)}}{2(1)}$$

$$z = \frac{8,91 \ldots \pm \sqrt{-4.61 \ldots}}{2}$$

No solutions because of the negative radicand

∴ There is <u>no triangle</u>.

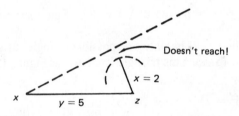

Doesn't reach!

$x = 2$

$y = 5$ z

x

Figure 15-5f

The radicand will be negative whenever the side opposite the given angle is too short to reach the other side, as shown in Figure 15-5f.   ■

In the following exercise you will analyze more triangles of the case SSA.

EXERCISE 15-5

Do These Quickly

The following problems are intended to refresh your skills. You should be able to do all 10 in less than 5 minutes.

In triangle *MNO*, find

Q1. side *m*.

Q2. angle *O*.

Q3. the area.

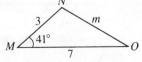

In right triangle PQR, find

Q4.   cos P.

Q5.   Angle P.

Q6.   side p.

Q7.   the area.

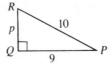

Answer the questions.

Q8.   Find the amplitude of the sinusoid $y = \sin x + \cos x$.

Q9.   If $\theta = \text{Tan}^{-1}\, 3$, find tan θ.

Q10.   Sketch the graph of a linear function with a positive y-intercept and a negative slope.

For Problems 1 through 8, find the possible lengths of the indicated side.

1.   In $\triangle ABC$, $m\angle B = 34°$, $a = 4$, and $b = 3$. Find c.

2.   In $\triangle XYZ$, $m\angle X = 13°$, $x = 12$, and $y = 5$. Find z.

3.   In $\triangle ABC$, $m\angle B = 34°$, $a = 4$, and $b = 5$. Find c.

4.   In $\triangle XYZ$, $m\angle X = 13°$, $x = 12$, and $y = 15$. Find z.

5.   In $\triangle ABC$, $m\angle B = 34°$, $a = 4$, and $b = 2$. Find c.

6.   In $\triangle XYZ$, $m\angle X = 13°$, $x = 12$, and $y = 60$. Find z.

7.   In $\triangle RST$, $m\angle R = 130°$, $r = 20$, and $t = 16$. Find s.

8.   In $\triangle OBT$, $m\angle O = 170°$, $o = 19$, and $t = 11$. Find b.

The Law of Sines can be used to find an angle in the SSA case. But you must be careful because there can be two different angles, one acute and the other obtuse, which have the same sine. For Problems 9 through 12, determine beforehand whether there can be two triangles or just one. Then find the possible values of the indicated angle measure.

9.   In $\triangle ABC$, $m\angle A = 19°$, $a = 25$, and $c = 30$. Find $m\angle C$.

10.   In $\triangle HDJ$, $m\angle H = 28°$, $h = 50$, and $d = 20$. Find $m\angle D$.

11.   In $\triangle XYZ$, $m\angle X = 58°$, $x = 9.3$, and $z = 7.5$. Find $m\angle Z$.

12.   In $\triangle BIG$, $m\angle B = 110°$, $b = 1000$, and $g = 900$. Find $m\angle G$.

13.   *Accurate Drawing Problem No. 1*   Triangles ABC in Problems 1, 3, and 5 differ only in the length of side b. Draw side a 4 centimeters long as the base. Then construct angle B of measure 34° at one end of the base.

a. Use a compass to mark off the two possible triangles if $b = 3$ centimeters, as in Problem 1. Measure the two possible values of c. Your answers should be within ± 0.1 centimeter of the calculated values.

b. Use a compass to mark off $b = 5$ centimeters, as in Problem 3. Measure the value of c, and confirm that it agrees with the calculated value. Then extend segment $\overline{AB}$ beyond angle B. Find the point on this segment where the 5 centimeter arc cuts it. Show that the distance between this point and B equals the *negative* value of c that is discarded in working Problem 3.

c. Use a compass to draw an arc of radius $b = 2$ centimeters, as in Problem 5. Show that this arc *misses* the other side of Angle B, and thus that there is *no* possible triangle.

14. ***Accurate Drawing Problem No. 2***   Repeat Problem 13 for triangles XYZ in Problems 2, 4, and 6.

15-6 | GENERAL SOLUTION OF TRIANGLES

You have learned the techniques necessary for analyzing oblique triangles when you are told which to use, the Law of Sines or the Law of Cosines. Before you tackle the real-world problems in Section 15-9, you must be sure that you can select the appropriate technique when you are *not* told which one to use.

Objective:
Given SSS, SAS, ASA, AAS, or SSA, be able to select the appropriate technique and to calculate the other side and angle measures and the area of the triangle.

Sometimes you can use either the Law of Cosines or the Law of Sines. You should recognize situations where a given technique does *not* work. Some guidelines are presented on the following page.

The following exercise requires you to select the appropriate technique and then work the problem. Your instructor may assign you only certain parts of each problem. Since working all parts of the problems requires much computation, you may wish to write and use a computer program as outlined in Problems 29 and 30.

> **TRIANGLE TECHNIQUES**
>
> 1. The Law of Cosines involves *three* sides. Therefore, it will *not* work for ASA or AAS, where there are *two unknown sides*.
> 2. The Law of Sines involves the ratio of the sine of an angle to the length of its *opposite* side. Therefore, it will *not* work where *no* angle is known (SSS) or where only *one* angle is known, but *not* its opposite side (SAS).
> 3. The Law of Sines should *not* be used to find *angle* measures unless you know in advance whether the angle is obtuse or acute.
> 4. The area formula requires you to know SAS. If you do not know two sides and the included angle, you must first find them. Hero's Formula (Exercise 15-3, Problem 7) will work if you know SSS.

EXERCISE 15-6

Do These Quickly

The following problems are intended to refresh your skills. You should be able to do all 10 in less than 5 minutes.

Q1.   In triangle ABC, $\dfrac{a}{\sin A} = 13$. If $\sin B = 0.2$, find b.

Q2.   In triangle DEF, $d = 3$, $f = 4$, and angle $E = \text{Arccos } 0.7$. Find side e.

Q3.   In triangle GHI, $g = 5$, $i = 6$, and angle $H = \text{Arcsin } 0.4$. Find the area.

Q4.   Copy triangle JRE onto your paper. If angle J and sides j and e are known, draw the *other* possible way the triangle could look.

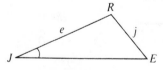

Q5.   Find the greatest value of y: $y = 7 + 5 \cos 19(x + 0.2)$

Q6.   Find the exact value of $\cot\left(\dfrac{\pi}{3}\right)$.

Q7.   Find $\log_3 81$.

Q8.   Draw an angle of 1 radian.

Q9.   If cos θ = 0.9, find cos 2θ.

Q10.   Is cos $(A + B)$ = cos A cos B + sin A sin B an identity?

Work the following problems. Unless your instructor tells you otherwise, find the measures of all three unspecified sides and angles as well as the area. If you are going to write a computer program to do this, go immediately to Problem 29 and then come back to Problems 1 through 28.

	Case	a	b	c	A	B	C
1.	SAS	3	4	——	—————	——	71° 40′
2.	SAS	8	5	——	—————	——	32° 10′
3.	SAS	30	60	——	—————	——	23° 50′
4.	SAS	18	40	——	—————	——	82° 30′
5.	SAS	100	210	——	—————	——	113° 20′
6.	SAS	2000	1700	——	—————	——	142° 00′
7.	SSS	8	9	7	—————	——	——
8.	SSS	4	3	2	—————	——	——
9.	SSS	3	6	4	—————	——	——
10.	SSS	18	10	9	—————	——	——
11.	SSS	3	9	4	—————	——	——
12.	SSS	18	8	9	—————	——	——
13.	ASA	——	——	400	143° 10′	8° 20′	——
14.	ASA	——	——	30	122° 50′	15° 00′	——
15.	ASA	——	——	50	11° 30′	27° 40′	——
16.	ASA	——	——	17	84° 20′	87° 30′	——
17.	AAS	6	——	——	56° 20′	64° 30′	——
18.	AAS	10	——	——	139° 10′	38° 40′	——
19.	SSA	7	5	——	25° 50′	——	——
20.	SSA	10	6	——	31° 10′	——	——
21.	SSA	5	7	——	25° 50′	——	——
22.	SSA	6	10	——	31° 10′	——	——
23.	SSA	5	7	——	126° 40′	——	——
24.	SSA	10	6	——	144° 50′	——	——

Case	a	b	c	A	B	C
25. SSA	7	5	____	126° 40′	_____	_____
26. SSA	3	10	____	31° 10′	_____	_____
27. SSA	3	5	____	36° 52.19386′	_____	_____
28. SSA	5	13	____	22° 37.19189′	_____	_____

29. **Computer Solution of Triangles**   In this problem you will write a computer program to find unspecified sides, angles, and area of a given triangle. Since there are five different ways the data might be given and a different sequence of computations for each case, the program is divided into blocks. Your class may wish to divide into seven groups, each group responsible for one of the tasks outlined below. By writing the program in this manner, you will get experience in the way really big programs are written, such as those used to get spacecraft to the Moon. The length of such programs makes them impossible for one person to write in a reasonable length of time.

Specific tasks are given below. (If you are using a language other than BASIC, you may need to modify some of the instructions.)

Task 1:   Write a "menu." This part of the program directs the activities of all other parts. It should first print on the screen a way for you to select the case, such as

```
ENTER CASE
1 FOR SSS
2 FOR SAS
3 FOR SSA
4 FOR AAS
5 FOR ASA
WHICH?
```

Depending on what the person using the program enters, the menu should direct the computer to the proper subroutine described below. Upon returning from the subroutine, this portion of the program should direct the computer to find the area, convert angles in radians (as the computer calculates them) to angles in degrees and minutes, and print the results in a form such as

```
CASE: SAS
S1 = 3
S2 = 4
S3 = 4.177
A1 = 42D, 59M
A2 = 65D, 21M
```

```
A3 = 71D, 40M
AREA = 5.695
```

Task 2:   Write a subroutine for the case SSS. It should begin with a statement letting the user input the three lengths. The screen should display a message such as

```
TYPE S1, S2, S3
```

The computer should then calculate the three angles, and return to the menu. The subroutine should also be able to detect when the three given sides are impossible for a triangle.

Task 3:   Write a subroutine for the case SAS. It should first print a message such as

```
TYPE S1, D3, M3 S2
```

where S1 and S2 are two side lengths, and D3 and M3 are the degrees and minutes in angle 3, included between sides 1 and 2. The subroutine should calculate the third side length and the measures of the other two angles, then return to the menu.

Task 4:   Write a subroutine for the case SSA. Since this is the ambiguous case, the subroutine should allow the computer to detect when there are two possible triangles, or no triangle, and return an appropriate message to the menu so that it will know what to do.

Task 5:   Write a subroutine for the case AAS, as above.

Task 6:   Write a subroutine for the case ASA, as above.

Task 7:   Write any special functions needed. If you use ordinary BASIC, you will have COS(X), SIN(X), and ATN(X) available. These are the *circular* cosine, sine, and Arctangent, respectively, where the argument of Arctangent is in *radians*. So you will need to define

a. FNR(X) for converting X degrees to radians.

b. FND(X) and FNM(X) for converting X radians to degrees and minutes, respectively.

c. FNC(X) and FNS(X) for finding arccos X and arcsin X, respectively, from ATN(X). The properties of Exercise 13-9, Problem 99 and 100, should be helpful.

30.   Debug the program from Problem 29 by using it to work the *odd-numbered* problems above. If your program can solve each triangle correctly, you may consider it to be completely debugged.

15-7   VECTORS

A *vector quantity* is something that has *direction* as well as magnitude (size). Velocity is an example. When you are traveling, it is important to know in what direction as well as how fast! A quantity that has *no* direction, such as volume, is called a *scalar* quantity. The *scalar* quantity "speed" and a direction combine to form the *vector* quantity "velocity."

In this section you will use directed line segments to represent vector quantities. The *length* of the line segment represents the *magnitude* (size) of the vector quantity, and the direction of the line segment represents the direction of the vector quantity. An arrowhead is used to distinguish the head of a vector from its tail (Figure 15-7a).

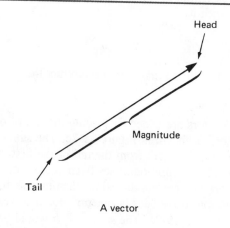

A vector

Figure 15-7a

If a variable is used to represent a vector, you put a small arrow over the top of it, such as $\vec{x}$, to distinguish it from a scalar. The three vectors in Figure 15-7b are considered to be *equal* since they have the same length and the same direction.

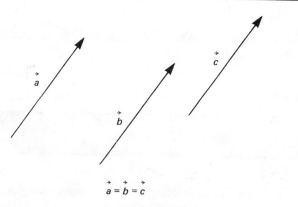

$$\vec{a} = \vec{b} = \vec{c}$$

Figure 15-7b

The above discussion leads to the following definitions.

DEFINITIONS

> 1. A **vector** is a directed line segment.
> 2. Two vectors are **equal** if and only if they have the same magnitude and the same direction.
> 3. The **absolute value** of a vector is its length or magnitude.

Having invented a new kind of mathematical quantity, you must now find out how to operate with it.

Objective
Given two vectors, be able to *add* them or *subtract* them.

Vector Addition: Vectors are added by placing the tail of one vector at the head of the other, as shown in Figure 15-7c. The *sum* of the vectors is defined to be the vector that goes from the tail of the first vector to the head of the last one. This definition arises from vectors in the real world. If you walk 20 meters in a certain direction, then turn and walk 13 meters more in a new direction, these "displacements" could be represented by Vectors $\vec{a}$ and $\vec{b}$ in Figure 15-7c. The sum $\vec{a} + \vec{b}$ would be a vector representing your net displacement from the starting point. A displacement of $\vec{a} + \vec{b}$ would produce the same result as a displacement of $\vec{a}$ followed by another displacement of $\vec{b}$. For this reason, the sum of two vectors is often called *resultant* vector. *Vector Subtraction:*   The opposite of a number x, $-x$, is the same distance from the origin as x, but in the opposite direction. Similarly, the opposite of vector $\vec{b}$, $-\vec{b}$, is defined to be a vector having the *same magnitude* as $\vec{b}$ but pointing in the *opposite direction* (Figure 15-7d).

The definition of vector subtraction follows directly from the definition of subtraction for real numbers.

DEFINITION

$$\vec{a} - \vec{b} = \vec{a} + (-\vec{b})$$

Since vector addition and subtraction involve forming triangles, the triangle techniques you have just learned will be useful.

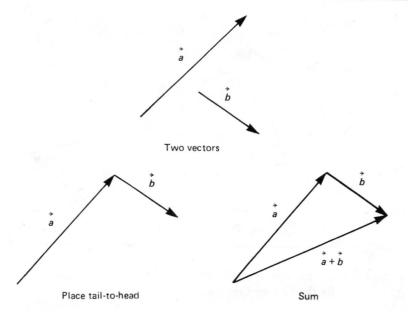

Two vectors

Place tail-to-head   Sum

Figure 15-7c _____

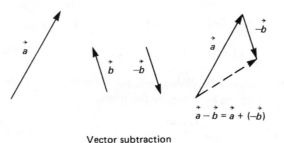

Vector subtraction

Figure 15-7d _____

EXAMPLE 1

Two vectors, $\vec{a}$ and $\vec{b}$, have magnitudes of 5 and 9, respectively. The angle between the vectors is 53°, as shown in the first sketch of Figure 15-7e. Find $|\vec{a} + \vec{b}|$, $|\vec{a} - \vec{b}|$, and the angles these sum and difference vectors make with $\vec{a}$.

A vector can be moved *parallel* to itself without changing its magnitude or direction. Moving $\vec{b}$ parallel to itself until its tail is at the head of $\vec{a}$ forms a triangle (Figure 15-7e). Since θ and the 53° angle are supplementary,

$$\theta = 180° - 53° = 127°.$$

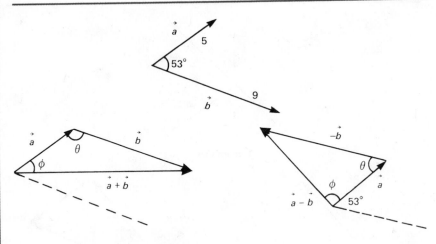

Figure 15-7e _____

Vectors $\vec{a}$ and $\vec{b}$ are two sides of a triangle with included angle θ and third side $\vec{a} + \vec{b}$. By the Law of Cosines,

$$|\vec{a} + \vec{b}|^2 = 5^2 + 9^2 - 2(5)(9)\cos 127°$$

$$= 160.163\ldots \qquad \text{By calculator}$$

$$\therefore |\vec{a} + \vec{b}| = 12.655\ldots \qquad \text{Taking the square root}$$

$$\approx \underline{12.66} \qquad \text{Rounding off}$$

The 12.655. . . should be stored, without rounding off, in the calculator's memory for use in the next part of the problem.

To find the angle ϕ that $\vec{a} + \vec{b}$ makes with $\vec{a}$, you may use the Law of Cosines as in Section 15-2.

$$\cos \phi = \frac{5^2 + (12.655\ldots)^2 - 9^2}{2(5)(12.655\ldots)}$$

$$= 0.8230\ldots \qquad \text{By calculator}$$

$$\therefore \phi = 34.607\ldots° \qquad \text{Taking inverse cosine}$$

$$\approx \underline{34° \, 36'} \qquad \text{Transforming to degrees and minutes}$$

To find $\vec{a} - \vec{b}$, you simply turn $\vec{b}$ around in the opposite direction and slide its tail to the head of $\vec{a}$, as shown in the third sketch of Figure 15-7e. Angle θ between $\vec{a}$ and $-\vec{b}$ is now an alternate interior angle of the 53° angle. So θ is also 53°. Applying the Law of Cosines:

$$|\vec{a} - \vec{b}|^2 = 5^2 + 9^2 - 2(5)(9)\cos 53°$$

$$= 51.836\ldots \qquad \text{By calculator}$$

$$\therefore |\vec{a} - \vec{b}| = 7.199\ldots \qquad \text{Taking the square root}$$

$$\approx \underline{\underline{7.200}} \qquad \text{Rounding off}$$

Using the Law of Cosines to find ϕ:

$$\cos \phi = \frac{5^2 + (7.199\ldots)^2 - 9^2}{2(5)(7.199\ldots)}$$

$$= 0.0578\ldots \qquad \text{By calculator}$$

$$\therefore \phi = 93.315\ldots^\circ \qquad \text{Taking inverse cosine}$$

$$\approx \underline{\underline{93^\circ\ 19'}} \qquad \text{Transforming to degrees and minutes}$$

Note: The Law of Sines could have been used to find ϕ.

$$\sin \phi = \frac{9 \sin 53^\circ}{7.119\ldots}$$

$$= 0.9983\ldots$$

Taking the inverse sine would give $86.684\ldots^\circ$, which is the *reference* angle for $93.315\ldots^\circ$. Since there is no easy way to tell whether ϕ is obtuse or acute, it is preferable to use the Law of Cosines technique. The sign of $\cos \phi$ tells that ϕ is obtuse.

Vectors can be used to find displacements of objects that move on the earth's surface. Navigators commonly measure angles clockwise from north as shown in Figure 15-7f, rather than counterclockwise from the positive x-axis. The direction thus determined is called a *bearing*. The figure shows a vector with a bearing of 250 degrees.

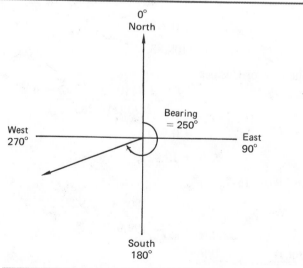

Figure 15-7f

EXAMPLE 2

An object moves 90 meters due south (bearing 180 degrees), then turns and moves 40 more meters along a bearing of 250 degrees (Figure 15-7g).

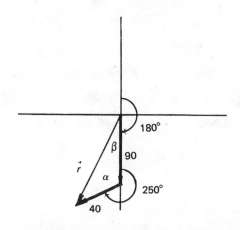

Figure 15-7g

a. Find the resultant of these two displacement vectors.
b. What is the bearing from the ending point back to the starting point?

a. The resultant, $\vec{r}$, goes from the tail of the first vector to the head of the last.

$$\text{Angle } \alpha = 360° - 250° = 110°.$$

By the Law of Cosines,

$$|\vec{r}|^2 = 90^2 + 40^2 - 2(90)(40) \cos 110°$$

$$= 12162.54. . .$$

$$\therefore |\vec{r}| = 110.283. . .$$

By the Law of Cosines,

$$\cos \beta = \frac{90^2 + (110.283. . .)2 - 40^2}{2(90)(110.283. . .)}$$

$$= 0.9401. . .$$

$$\therefore \beta = 19.927. . .°$$

From Figure 15-7g,

$$\text{Bearing} = 180° + 19.927. . .°$$

$$= 199.927. . .°$$

Vector is 110.3 at 199.9°

b. To find the bearing from the end point to the starting point, all you need realize is that it points the opposite direction.

$$\text{Bearing} = 199.9° + 180°$$

$$= 379.9°$$

Since this is greater than 360°, you subtract 360° (one full revolution) getting

$$\underline{\underline{\text{Bearing} = 19.9°}}$$ ■

The following exercise gives you practice adding and subtracting vectors.

EXERCISE 15-7

Do These Quickly

The following problems are intended to refresh you skills. You should be able to do all 10 in less than 5 minutes.

Q1.   Draw a parallelogram.

Q2.   Find the reference angle of 231°.

Q3.   Find the shorter leg of a right triangle with one angle 20° and hypotenuse 100.

Q4.   Find the third side of a triangle if two sides are 4 and 5, and the included angle is $\text{Cos}^{-1}(-0.8)$.

Q5.   Find the exact value of $\theta = \text{Csc}^{-1} 1$.

Q6.   Find the exact value of $\tan \pi$.

Q7.   If $\cos\left(\dfrac{\pi}{6}\right)x = 0.5$, find the smallest positive value of x.

Q8.   Sketch the graph of $y = \cot \theta$.

Q9.   What is the range of the (circular) inverse tangent function?

Q10. Sketch the graph of $y = 2^{-x}$.

For Problems 1 through 4, find $|\vec{a} + \vec{b}|$, $|\vec{a} - \vec{b}|$, and the angle that each of these resultant vectors makes with $\vec{a}$, (Figure 15-7h).

1. $|\vec{a}| = 7$, $|\vec{b}| = 11$, $\theta = 73°$

2. $|\vec{a}| = 8,$ $|\vec{b}| = 2,$ $\theta = 41°$

3. $|\vec{a}| = 9,$ $|\vec{b}| = 20,$ $\theta = 163°$

4. $|\vec{a}| = 10,$ $|\vec{b}| = 30,$ $\theta = 122°$

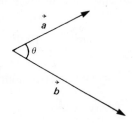

Figure 15-7h

For Problems 5 through 8, do the following:

   a. Find the resultant of the two given displacements. Express the answer as a distance and a bearing (clockwise from north) from the starting point to the end point.
   b. Tell the bearing from the ending point back to the starting point.
   c. Draw the vectors on graph paper, using ruler and protractor, and thus show that your answers are correct to 0.1 unit of length and 1 degree of angle.

5. 11 units north (0°) followed by 5 units along a bearing of 70°

6. 8 units east (90°) followed by 6 units along a bearing of 210°

7. 6 units west (270°) followed by 14 units along a bearing of 110°

8. 4 units south (180°) followed by 9 units along a bearing of 320°

15-8 | **VECTORS—RESOLUTION INTO COMPONENTS**

Sometimes it is important to reverse the addition process and express a single vector as the sum of two other vectors. For example, if a pilot knows the plane's air speed and angle of climb, the rate of climb and the ground velocity can be calculated (Figure 15-8a). For this purpose you must be able to resolve, or break up, a vector into components whose sum is the original vector. Two pieces of background information are helpful.

Vector times scalar: When you add a real number x to itself, you get

$$x + x = 2x.$$

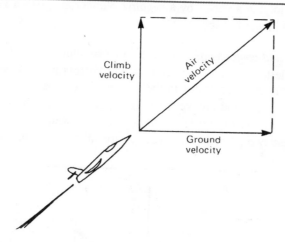

Figure 15-8a

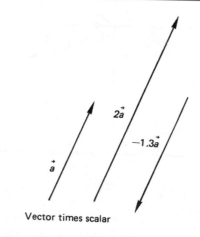

Vector times scalar

Figure 15-8b

It is reasonable to say that when you add a *vector* to itself, you get twice that vector. That is,

$$\vec{a} + \vec{a} = 2\vec{a}.$$

The answer $2\vec{a}$ is a vector in the *same* direction, but with 2 times the magnitude. The reasoning leads you to define what you mean by a scalar (i.e., a real number) times a vector.

DEFINITION

The **product** $x\vec{a}$ is a vector in the *same* direction as $\vec{a}$ but with a magnitude equal to x times the magnitude of $\vec{a}$.

Note: Multiplying a vector by a *negative* number, x, gives a vector of magnitude $|x|\,|\vec{a}|$, but *opposite* direction.

Unit vectors and components: A vector of magnitude 1 is called a *unit* vector. The letters $\vec{i}$ and $\vec{j}$ are used for unit vectors in the x- and y-directions, respectively. Any vector in the x-direction can be written as a scalar multiple of $\vec{i}$ and any vector in the y-direction can be written as a scalar multiple of $\vec{j}$. Figure 15-8c shows vector $\vec{v}$ which is the sum of $4\vec{i}$ and $3\vec{j}$. These two perpendicular vectors are called *components* of $\vec{v}$.

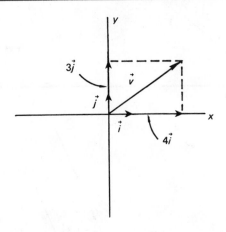

Figure 15-8c

Objective:
Given a vector in a Cartesian coordinate system, express it as the sum of two component vectors, one in the x-direction, the other in the y-direction.

EXAMPLE 1

Vector $\vec{a}$ has magnitude 3 and direction 143°, as shown in Figure 15-8d. Resolve $\vec{a}$ into horizontal and vertical components.

By definition of sine and cosine,

$$\frac{x}{3} = \cos 143° \text{ and } \frac{y}{3} = \sin 143°.$$

$$\therefore x = 3 \cos 143° = -2.3959. . .$$

$$y = 3 \sin 143° = 1.8054. . .$$

$$\therefore \vec{a} \approx -2.396\vec{i} + 1.8054\vec{j}$$

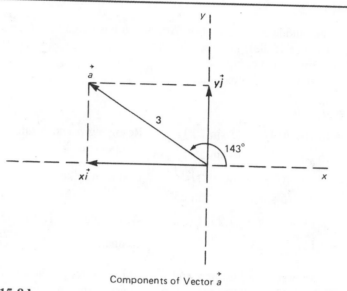

Components of Vector $\vec{a}$

Figure 15-8d _____

From Example 1 you can conclude that if θ is the angle in standard position for vector $\vec{v}$, then

$$\vec{v} = (|\vec{v}| \cos \theta)\vec{i} + (|\vec{v}| \sin \theta)\vec{j}$$

Components give an easy way to add two vectors. As shown in Figure 15-8e, if $\vec{r}$ is the resultant of $\vec{a}$ and $\vec{b}$, then the components of $\vec{r}$ are the sums of the components of $\vec{a}$ and $\vec{b}$. Since the two horizontal components have the same direction, they can be added simply by adding their magnitudes. The same is true for the vertical components.

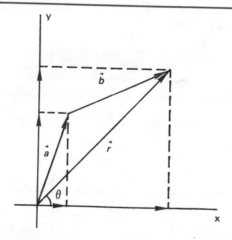

Figure 15-8e _____

EXAMPLE 2

If $\vec{a}$ has magnitude 5 and direction 70°, and $\vec{b}$ has magnitude 6 and direction 25° (Figure 15-8e), find the resultant, $\vec{r}$,

a. as the sum of two components,
b. as a magnitude and direction.

a. $\vec{r} = \vec{a} + \vec{b}$

$= (5 \cos 70°)\vec{i} + (5 \sin 70°)\vec{j}$ Resolving $\vec{a}$ and $\vec{b}$ into
$+ (6 \cos 25°)\vec{i} + (6 \sin 25°)\vec{j}$ components

$= (5 \cos 70° + 6 \cos 25°)\vec{i}$ Collecting like terms
$\qquad + (5 \sin 70° + 6 \sin 25°)\vec{j}$

$= 7.1479\ldots\,\vec{i} + 7.2341\ldots\,\vec{j}$ By calculator

$\approx \underline{7.15\vec{i} + 7.23\vec{j}}$ Rounding off

b. The more precise values of x and y should be stored in the calculator's memory or written down for use in this part of the problem.

$|\vec{r}| = \sqrt{(7.147\ldots)^2 + (7.234\ldots)^2}$ By the Pythagorean Theorem

$= 10.169\ldots$ By calculator

$\tan \theta = \dfrac{7.234\ldots}{7.147\ldots} = 1.012\ldots$ Definition of tangent

$\therefore \theta = 45.343\ldots°$ θ is in Quadrant I since $\sin \theta$
$\therefore \vec{r} \approx \underline{10.17 \text{ at } 45° \, 21'}$ and $\cos \theta$ are both positive. ∎

The component technique is useful for navigation problems. When neither vector is along a coordinate axis, the triangle technique of the last section can be difficult. You can first transform the bearing, β, into an angle in standard position. As shown in Figure 15-8f, the bearing β and the angle θ are complementary. Thus,

$$\boxed{\beta = 90° - \theta \text{ and } \theta = 90° - \beta}$$

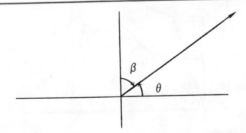

Figure 15-8f

If this relationship produces a negative value of θ or β, a positive coterminal angle can be found by adding 360°.

EXAMPLE 3

A ship sails for 20 miles on a bearing of 325°, then turns and sails on a bearing of 250° for 7 more miles. Find its displacement vector, $\vec{d}$, from the starting point (Figure 15-8g).

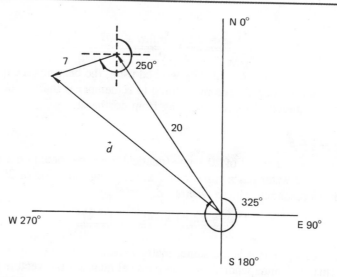

Figure 15-8g

The two angles are

$$\theta_1 = 90° - 325° = -235°$$

$$\theta_2 = 90° - 250° = -160°$$

Adding 360° to each gives coterminal angles of positive measure.

$\theta_1 = 125°$

$\theta_2 = 200°$

$\therefore \vec{d} = (20 \cos 125° + 7 \cos 200°)\, \vec{i}$ Adding the components
$\qquad + (20 \sin 125° + 7 \sin 200°)\, \vec{j}$

$\underline{\vec{d} = -18.049\ldots\, \vec{i} + 13.988\ldots\, \vec{j}}$

This vector can be transformed to a distance and bearing.

$$\vec{d} = \sqrt{(-18.049\ldots)^2 + (13.988\ldots)^2}$$

$$= 22.835\ldots$$

$$\tan \theta = \frac{13.988. \ldots}{-18.049. \ldots}$$

$$= -0.7750. \ldots$$

$$\therefore \theta = 142.223. \ldots °$$

$$\therefore \beta = 90° - 142.223. \ldots$$

$$= -52.223. \ldots °$$

Adding 360° gives

$$\beta = 307.776. \ldots °$$

$$\therefore \vec{d} \approx \underline{22.84 \text{ miles at } 307° \ 47'}$$

Note: This problem can also be worked using the bearings themselves, without first finding θ. The main thing to remember is that the quadrants will be numbered *clockwise*, starting from northeast.   ■

EXAMPLE 4

A ship sails at a speed of 20 knots (nautical miles per hour) on a bearing of 325°. The water has a current of 7 knots along a bearing of 250°. Find the ship's resultant velocity vector, $\vec{v}$.

$$\vec{v} \approx \underline{22.84 \text{ knots at } 307° \ 47'}$$

Note: This problem is the same, mathematically, as Example 3. The mathematics is independent of what physical quantity the vectors represent.   ■

The following exercise gives you practice resolving vectors into components, and adding vectors by adding their components.

EXERCISE 15-8

Do These Quickly

The following problems are intended to refresh your skills. You should be able to do all 10 in less than 5 minutes.

Q1.   Sketch a vector bearing 150°.

Q2.   Sketch the sum of two vectors.

Q3.   State the Law of Cosines.

Q4.   State the Law of Sines.

Q5.   If two sides of a triangle are 10 and 20, and the included angle is 150°, what is the area?

Q6.   In which quadrants is the secant function negative?

Q7.   How many radians in 3 revolutions?

Q8.   If $\sin 3x = 0.6$ and $\cos 3x = 0.8$, find $\sin 6x$.

Q9.   If $\cos x = 0.7$, what does $\cos(-x)$ equal?

Q10.   Sketch the graph of $y = \sin \theta$.

For Problems 1 through 4, resolve the vector into horizontal and vertical components.

1.

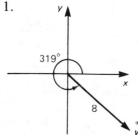

2.

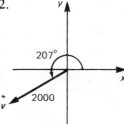

3.

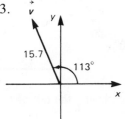

4.

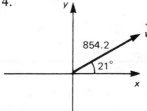

5.   If $\vec{r} = 21$ units at $\theta = 70°$ and $\vec{s} = 40$ units at $\theta = 120°$, find $\vec{r} + \vec{s}$
   a.   as a sum of two components,
   b.   as a magnitude and a direction.

6.   If $\vec{u} = 12$ units at $\theta = 160°$ and $\vec{v} = 8$ units at $310°$, find $\vec{u} + \vec{v}$
   a.   as a sum of two components,
   b.   as a magnitude and direction.

7.   A ship sails 50 miles on a bearing of $\beta = 20°$, then 30 miles further on a bearing of $\beta = 80°$. Find the resultant displacement vector as a distance and bearing.

8.   A plane flies 30 miles on a bearing of $\beta = 200°$, then turns and flies 40 miles on a bearing of $\beta = 10°$. Find the resultant displacement vector as a distance and bearing.

9. A plane flies 200 miles per hour (mph) along a bearing of 320°. The air is moving with a wind speed of 60 mph along a bearing of 190°. Find the plane's resultant velocity (speed and bearing) by adding these two velocity vectors.

10. A scuba diver swims 100 feet per minute along a bearing of 170°. The water is moving with a current of 30 feet per minute along a bearing of 115°. Find the diver's resultant velocity (speed and bearing) by adding these two velocity vectors.

Problems 11 through 13 refer to $\vec{a}$, $\vec{b}$, and $\vec{c}$, shown in Figure 15-8h.

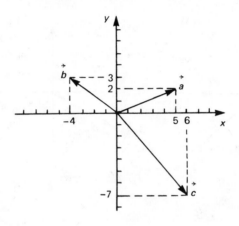

Figure 15-8h _____

11. a. On a piece of graph paper, draw $\vec{a} + \vec{b}$ by placing the tail of $\vec{b}$ at the head of $\vec{a}$.
    b. On the same Cartesian coordinate system, draw $\vec{b} + \vec{a}$ by placing the tail of $\vec{a}$ at the head of $\vec{b}$.
    c. How does your picture illustrate the fact that vector addition is *commutative*?

12. Illustrate that vector addition is *associative* by drawing $(\vec{a} + \vec{b}) + \vec{c}$ and $\vec{a} + (\vec{b} + \vec{c})$.

13. *Draw* $\vec{a} + (-\vec{a})$ on a Cartesian coordinate system. What is the *magnitude* of $\vec{a} + (-\vec{a})$? Does it make sense to assign a *direction* to the vector? Why do you suppose this vector is called the "zero vector"?

14. How can you conclude that {vectors} is *closed* under addition? Why is the zero vector necesary to insure closure?

15. How can you conclude that {vectors} is closed under multiplication by a scalar? Is the zero vector necessary to insure closure in this case? Explain.

15-9 | REAL-WORLD TRIANGLE PROBLEMS

Throughout this chapter you have been developing the computational skills you need to work real-world problems involving measurement of triangles. Each problem in the following exercise requires you to identify one or more triangles, right or oblique, and then apply the appropriate technique to find the side, angle, or area you seek. You may use the computer program of Section 15-6.

EXERCISE 15-9

Do These Quickly

The following problems are intended to refresh your skills. You should be able to do all 10 in less than 5 minutes.

Q1. A vector has horizontal component 8 cm and vertical component 15 cm. How long is the vector?

Q2. What angle does the vector make with the *x*-axis?

Q3. A vector 25 ft long makes an angle of 60° with the horizontal axis. What is its vertical component?

Q4. Find the vertical displacement of $y = 3 + 5 \cos 4(x - 7)$.

Q5. A triangle has sides 10 in. and 11 in., and Arccos of the included angle is 0.8. Find the third side.

Q6. Find the area of the triangle in Q5.

In right triangle *APB*, find

Q7. the length of the leg adjacent to angle *A*.

Q8. the measure of angle *B*.

Q9. the measure of the other acute angle.

Q10. the area.

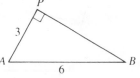

Work the following problems.

1. *Swimming Problem 1*   You swim at 3 km/h with your body perpendicular to a stream with a current of 5 km/h. Your actual velocity is the vector sum of the stream's velocity and your swimming velocity. Find your actual velocity.

2. *Swimming Problem 2*   You swim at 4 km/h with your body perpendicular to a stream. But because the water is moving, your actual velocity vector makes an angle of 34° with the direction you are heading.
   a. How fast is the current?
   b. What is the magnitude of your *actual* velocity?

3. *Mountain Height Problem*   A surveying crew is given the job of measuring the height of a mountain (Figure 15-9a). From a point on level ground, they measure an angle of elevation to the top of 21° 34'. They move 507 meters closer and find the angle is now 35° 41'. How high is the mountain? (You may need to calculate some other numbers first!)

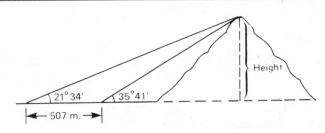

Figure 15-9a

4. *Harbor Problem*   As a ship sails into harbor, the navigator sights a buoy at an angle of 15° to the path of the ship (Figure 15-9b). The ship sails 1300 meters further and finds that the buoy now makes an angle of 29°.

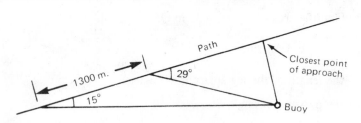

Figure 15-9b

   a. How far is the ship from the buoy at the second sighting?
   b. What is the closest the ship will come to the buoy?
   c. How far must the ship go from the second sighting point to this closest point of approach?
   d. When the ship has gone 7000 meters beyond the second sighting point, what will be the angle from the bow of the ship to the line-of-sight with the buoy?

5. *Missile Problem*   An observer 2 kilometers from the launching pad observes a vertically ascending missile at an angle of elevation of 21°. Five seconds later, the angle has increased to 35°.
    a.   How far did the missile travel during the 5-second interval?
    b.   What was its average speed during this interval?
    c.   If it keeps going vertically at the same average speed, what will its angle of elevation be 15 seconds after the *first* sighting?

6. *Oil Well Problem*   An oil well is to be located on a hillside that slopes at 10° (Figure 15-9c). The desired rock formation has a dip of 27° to the horizontal in the same direction as the hill slope. The well is located 3200 feet downhill from the nearest edge of the outcropping rock formation. How deep will the driller have to go to reach the top of the formation?

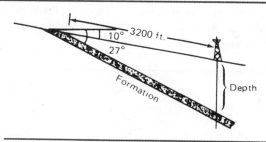

Figure 15-9c

7. *Visibility Problem*   Suppose you are aboard a jet destined for Hawaii. The pilot announces that your altitude is 10 kilometers. Since you have nothing to do but stare at the Pacific Ocean, you decide to calculate how far away the horizon is. You draw a sketch as in Figure 15-9d and realize that you must calculate an *arc length*. You recall that the radius of the Earth is about 6400 kilometers. How far away is the horizon along the Earth's curved surface? Surprising?

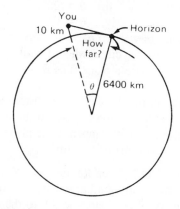

Figure 15-9d

8. **Airplane Velocity Problem**   An airplane is flying through the air at a speed of 500 km/h. At the same time, the air is moving with respect to the ground at an angle of 23° to the plane's path through the air with a speed of 40 km/h (i.e., the wind speed is 40 km/h). The plane's ground speed is the magnitude of the *vector sum* of the plane's air speed and the air's speed with respect to the ground. Find the plane's ground speed if it is flying
   a.   against the wind,
   b.   with the wind.

9. **Airplane Lift Problem**   When an airplane is in flight, the air pressure creates a force vector, called the "lift," perpendicular to the wings. When the plane banks for a turn, this lift vector may be resolved into horizontal and vertical components. The vertical component has magnitude equal to the plane's weight (this is what holds the plane up), and the horizontal component "pushes" the plane into its curved path. Suppose that a jet plane weighing 500,000 pounds banks at an angle θ (Figure 15-9e).

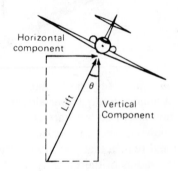

Figure 15-9e

   a.   Find the magnitude of the lift and the horizontal component if
        i. $\theta = 10°$,   ii. $\theta = 20°$,
        iii. $\theta = 30°$,   iv. $\theta = 0°$.
   b.   Based on your answers to part (a), why do you suppose a plane can turn in a *smaller* circle when it banks at a *greater* angle?
   c.   Why do you suppose a plane flies *straight* when it is *not* banking?
   d.   If the maximum lift the wings can sustain is 600,000 pounds, what is the maximum angle at which the plane can bank?
   e.   What *two* things might happen if the plane tried to bank at an angle *steeper* than this maximum?

10. **Canal Barge Problem**   Freda Pulliam and Yank Hardy are on opposite sides of a canal, pulling a barge with tow ropes (Figure 15-9f). Freda exerts a force of 50 pounds at 20° to the canal, and Yank pulls

at an angle of 15° with just enough force so that the resultant force vector is directly along the canal. Find the number of pounds with which Yank must pull and the magnitude of the resultant vector.

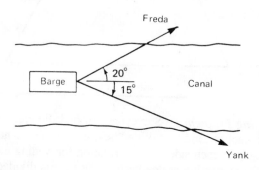

Figure 15-9f

11. **Detour Problem** Suppose that you are the pilot of a commercial airliner. You find it necessary to detour around a group of thunder-showers (Figure 15-9g). You turn at an angle of 21° to your original path, fly for a while, turn, and intercept your original path at an angle of 35°, 70 kilometers from where you left it.

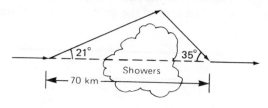

Figure 15-9g

a. How much further did you have to go because of the detour?
b. What area is enclosed by this triangle?

12. **Surveying Problem 1** A surveyor measures the three sides of a triangular field and gets 114, 165, and 257 meters.
a. What is the measure of the largest angle of the triangle?
b. What is the area of the field?

13. **Surveying Problem 2** A field has the shape of a quadrilateral that is *not* a rectangle. Three sides measure 50, 60, and 70 meters, and two angles measure 127° and 132° (Figure 15-9h).
a. By dividing the quadrilateral into two triangles, find its area. You may have to find some intermediate sides and angles first.
b. Find the length of the fourth side.
c. Find the measures of the other two angles.

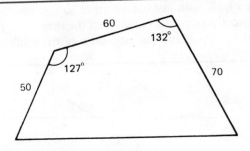

Figure 15-9h

14. *Surveying Problem 3* Surveyors can find the area of an irregularly shaped tract of land by taking "field notes." These notes consist of the length of each side and information for finding each angle measure. Then, starting at one vertex, the tract is divided into triangles. For the first triangle, two sides and the included angle are known (Figure 15-9i), so its area can be calculated. To calculate the area of the second triangle, you must recognize that one of its sides is also the *third* side of the *first* triangle, and one of its angles is an angle of the polygon (147° in Figure 15-9i) *minus* an angle of the first triangle, By calculating this side and angle and using the next side of the polygon (15 in Figure 15-7i), you can calculate the area of the second triangle. The areas of the remaining triangles are calculated in the same manner. The area of the tract is the *sum* of the areas of the triangles.

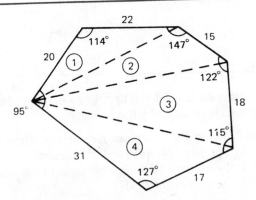

Figure 15-9i

   a. Write a computer program for calculating the area of a tract, using the technique described above. The input should be the sides and angles of the polygon, and the output should be the area of the tract. As a check on your program, you can have it print out the intermediate sides and angles.

b. Use your program to show that the area of the tract in Figure 15-9i is 1029.69 square units.

c. Show that the last side of the polygon is calculated to be 30.6817 units, which is close to the measured value of 31.

d. The polygon in Figure 15-9i is called a *convex polygon*, because none of its angles measure more than 180°. Explain why your program might give *wrong* answers if the polygon were *not* convex.

For Problems 15 through 18, suppose that the country of Parah has just launched two satellites. The government of Noya sends aloft its most self-reliant astronaut, Ivan Advantage, to observe the satellites.

15. ***Ivan Problem 1***   As Ivan approaches the two satellites, he finds that one of them is 8 kilometers from him and the other is 11 kilometers, and the angle between the two (with Ivan at the vertex) is 120°. How far apart are the satellites?

16. ***Ivan Problem 2***   Several orbits later as he is about to re-enter, only Satellite No. 1 is visible to Ivan, the other one being near the opposite side of the Earth (Figure 15-9j). He determines that Angle *A* measures 37° 43′, Angle *B* measures 113° 00′, and the distance between him and Satellite No. 1 is 4362 kilometers. Correct to the nearest kilometer, how far apart are Ivan and Satellite 2?

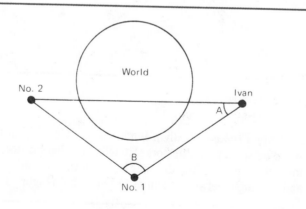

Figure 15-9j _____

17. ***Ivan Problem 3***   Three ships are assigned to rescue Ivan as his spacecraft plunges into the ocean. The ships are at the vertices of a triangle with sides of 5, 7, and 10 kilometers.

a. Find the measure of the largest angle of this triangle.

b. Find the area of ocean in the triangular region bounded by the three ships.

18. ***Ivan Problem 4***   To welcome their returning hero, the Noyans give Ivan a parade. The parade goes between the cities of Om, Mann, and Tra. These cities are at the vertices of an equilateral triangle. The roads connecting them are straight, level, and direct, and the parade goes at a constant speed with no stops. From Om to Mann takes 80 minutes, from Mann to Tra takes 80 minutes, but from Tra back to Om takes 1 hour and 20 minutes. How do you explain the discrepancy in times?

19. ***Torpedo Problem***   Suppose that you are Torpedo Officer aboard the U.S.S. Skipjack. Your submarine is conducting torpedo practice off the Florida coast. The target is 7200 meters from you on a bearing of 276° and is steaming on a course of 68° (Figure 15-9k). You have long-range torpedoes that will go 6400 meters and short-range torpedoes that will go 3200 meters. Between what two bearings can you fire torpedoes that will reach the target's path if you use

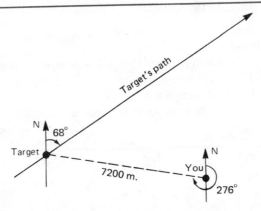

Figure 15-9k

    a. long-range torpedoes,
    b. short-range torpedoes?

20. ***Alligator Problem***   Calvin Butterball is swimming in Lake Rancid when he spots two alligators. He tells you that his distance to Alligator 1 is 30 meters, the distance between the alligators is 20 meters, and the angle between them at Calvin is 58° (Figure 15-9l).

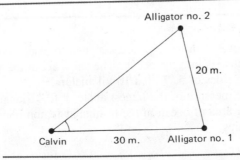

Figure 15-9l

a.   Show Calvin that he must have made a mistake in measurement, since there is no such triangle.

b.   Find the *two* possible distances between Calvin and Alligator 2 using the *correct* angle, 28°.

15-10 | CHAPTER REVIEW AND TEST

The objectives for this chapter may be summarized as follows:

1. Solve right triangle problems, given

   a. two sides
   b. one side and one acute angle.

2. Solve oblique triangle problems, given

   a. two sides and the included angle,
   b. three sides,
   c. one side, the opposite angle, and one other side or angle.

3. Find the area of a triangle, given two sides and the included angle measure.
4. Add and resolve vectors.
5. Solve real-world problems involving triangles.

The Review Problems below parallel the sections in this chapter. The Concepts Problems let you try your hand at applying what you know to analyze a new situation. The Chapter Test is similar to one your instructor might give to see how well you understand solution of triangle problems.

REVIEW PROBLEMS

R1. a.   Right triangle *XYZ* has hypotenuse of length $y = 14.7$ cm and one leg of length $z = 8.3$ cm. Find x and the measures of the acute angles.

    b.   Right triangle *BJF* has $m \angle B = 39° \, 54'$ and hypotenuse $f = 19$ km. Find b, j, and $m \angle J$.

R2. a.   Triangle *FUN* has $u = 14$, $n = 13$, and $m \angle F = 145° \, 20'$. Find f, $m \angle U$, and $m \angle N$.

    b.   Triangle *GYM* has $g = 7$, $y = 8$, and $m = 13$. Find the measures of the three angles.

R3. Find the area of Triangle *FUN* in Problem R2.a.

R4. Triangle *BAS* has $m \angle B = 123°$, $m \angle S = 56°$, and $a = 10$ mm. Find the lengths of the other two sides. Surprising?

R5.   Triangle *TWO* has o = 20 m, t = 12 m, and $m \angle T$ = 31°. Find the two possible values of w.

R6.   a.   What information must be known about a triangle to use the Law of Cosines to find:
         i.   a side length?
         ii. an angle measure?
      b.   What information must be known about a triangle to use the Law of Sines to find a side length?
      c.   Why is it risky to use the law of sines to find an angle measure?
      d.   How do you find the area of a triangle from the lengths of two sides and the measure of the included angle?
      e.   What information must you know about a triangle to find its area using Hero's formula?
      f.   What three pieces of information about a triangle lead to the ambiguous case?

R7.   Vectors $\vec{a}$ and $\vec{b}$, which have magnitudes 6 and 10, respectively, make an angle of 174° with each other, as shown in Figure 15-10a. Find the magnitude of $\vec{a} - \vec{b}$ and the angle that this difference vector makes with $\vec{a}$ when placed tail-to-tail.

Figure 15-10a

R8.   Vector $\vec{a}$, 15 units long, is directed at 37°. Vector $\vec{b}$, 11 units long, is directed at 168°. Find the horizontal and vertical components of each vector. Find the horizontal and vertical components of the resultant vector. Find the magnitude and direction of the resultant vector.

R9.   The rotor on a helicopter creates an upward force vector. To move forward, the pilot tilts the helicopter forward. The vertical component of the force vector (the "lift") holds the helicopter up, and the horizontal component (the "thrust") makes it move forward.

Suppose that a helicopter tilts forward at a sufficient angle to generate a thrust of 400 pounds. The helicopter weighs 3000 pounds, so the lift has a magnitude of 3000 pounds.
      a.   What angle does the helicopter make with the ground?
      b.   What total force must the rotor generate?

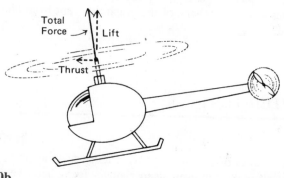

Figure 15-10b _____

CONCEPTS PROBLEMS

Figure 15-10c shows Earth and Mars in orbit around the Sun. Earth is about 93 million miles from the Sun and Mars is about 155 million miles from the Sun.

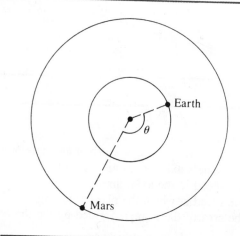

Figure 15-10c _____

C1.   Write the distance between Earth and Mars as a function of the angle θ at the Sun.

C2.   Earth makes a revolution about the Sun in about 365 Earth days. Mars makes a revolution about the Sun in about 687 Earth days. Earth and Mars were at their closest ($\theta = 0°$) on September 25, 1988. On what day is the next time they will be at their closest?

C3.   Write an equation for the distance between Earth and Mars as a function of t, the number of days that have elapsed since September 25, 1988.

C4. Plot a complete cycle of the graph of the function in Problem C3.
     In what way is the shape of the graph different from an ordinary si-
     nusoid?

CHAPTER TEST

As a jet plane takes off, its path makes a fairly steep angle to the ground.
The plane itself makes an even steeper angle. Its velocity vector may be
resolved into two components, as shown in Figure 15-10d. The axial
component (the one directed along the plane's axis) is the plane's velocity
ignoring the action of gravity. The vertical component is the velocity at
which the plane is "falling" under the influence of gravity.

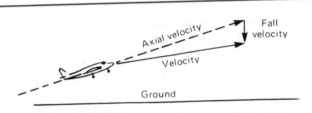

Figure 15-10d

T1. A plane's velocity vector is 250 km/h at an angle of 10° to the
     ground. The plane's axis makes an angle of 15° with the ground.
     a. Find the speed in the axial direction.
     b. Find the speed at which the plane is falling.
     c. Find the area of the triangle formed by the three vectors.

T2. If the plane maintains an angle of 15° with the ground, and the fall
     vector stays the same as in Problem T1:
     a. What is the minimum speed the plane can go without going
         downward? (That is, the velocity vector must be *horizontal*.)
     b. At this minimum speed, what will the axial velocity vector
         equal?

T3. The plane increases its speed to 700 km/h. The navigator determines
     the axial speed to be 702 km/h and the fall speed to be the same as
     in Problem T1. What angle does the plane's path make with the
     ground?

15-11 | CUMULATIVE REVIEW: CHAPTERS 13
      | THROUGH 15

The following exercise may be considered to be a final examination that
tests your ability to use all you have learned about trigonometric and circular functions. If you are thoroughly familiar with the concepts, you
should be able to work all of the problems in about two hours.

Suppose you have joined the Navy and are stationed aboard the nuclear
submarine Seawolf. Your boat has been assigned to conduct torpedo target
practice in the Gulf of Mexico. Answer the following questions.

1. As you approach the practice area, you travel a displacement vector of
    6 kilometers along a bearing of 22°. Then you turn and go a displace-
    ment vector of 15 kilometers along a bearing of 82°.

a. Add these two vectors to find your resultant displacement.
b. What is the area of ocean enclosed by these three vectors?

2. While you wait for the target ships to arrive, you steam submerged in
    a circle of diameter 100 kilometers, making a complete revolution ev-
    ery 20 hours. The closest you come to the coastline is 30 kilometers
    (see Figure 15-11).

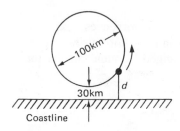

Figure 15-11 _____

a. Your distance, d, from the coastline varies sinusoidally with time, t.
    When $t = 2$ hours, you are at your maximum distance from the coast-
    line. Write an equation expressing d in terms of t.
b. Predict your distance from the coastline when $t = 9$.
c. Transform the equation from part c so that t is expressed in terms of
    d.
d. What are the first three positive values of t for which $d = 123$?

3. On the fourth day of your patrol, your electronic gear picks up four
   strange signals:

   i. $y_1 = \sec^2 x \sin^2 x + \tan^4 x$

   ii. $y_2 = \dfrac{\sin^2 x}{\cos^4 x}$

   iii. $y_3 = \cos^2 x$

   iv. $y_4 = \cos 3x \cos 5x$

   a. Prove that the expressions for y_1 and y_2 are identical.
   b. Before your computer can analyze signals iii and iv, number iii must
      be expressed in terms of $\cos 2x$ and number iv must be expressed as a
      sum of sines or cosines. Perform these two transformations.

4. The signals are coming from three unmanned target ships, the Hic,
   the Haec, and the Hoc. Your sonar detects a sound coming from
   Hoc's engines. The sound is described by the equation

   $$y = 5 + 3 \cos \frac{\pi}{4} (x - 1).$$

   Sketch one complete cycle of the graph of this function.

5. You can fire torpedos at any angle θ to the ship's axis in the interval
   $[-180°, 180°]$, but $\theta \neq 0$. (Firing them straight ahead might give
   away your position.) However, the best angles are those in the solution set of the trigonometric equation

   $$\cos 4\theta - \cos 2\theta = 0.$$

   Solve this equation in the given domain.

6. In preparation for firing torpedoes, you must evaluate the following.
   Leave the answer in *exact* form using π or radicals, if necessary, unless otherwise specified. Assume circular functions unless degrees or θ
   is specified.

   a. $\cos 150°$ b. $\sin \dfrac{5\pi}{4}$

   c. $\tan \theta$, if θ terminates in Quadrant IV, and $\cos \theta = \dfrac{7}{11}$
   d. $\csc 3$, to 5 decimal places

   e. $\theta = \text{Arcsin} \left(\dfrac{1}{2} \right)$ f. $x = \text{Arccos} (-1)$

   g. $x = \text{Tan}^{-1} (-\sqrt{3})$ h. $x = \text{Sec}^{-1} \left(-\dfrac{2}{\sqrt{3}} \right)$

   i. $\sin \left(\cos^{-1} \left(-\dfrac{2}{\sqrt{3}} \right) \right)$

   j. $\cos (\cos(\cos 2))$, to 5 decimal places

7. The last piece of information you need is sin 0.06 correct to *twelve* decimal places. Unfortunately, you have no calculator accurate enough. From a handbook of mathematical tables, you find that sin x is given by a "Taylor series," as follows:

$$\sin x = x - \frac{x^3}{3!} + \frac{x^5}{5!} - \frac{x^7}{7!} + \frac{x^9}{9!} - \frac{x^{11}}{11!} + \dots$$

Calculate sin 0.06 correct to 12 decimal places using as many terms as you need of the Taylor series for sin x. Show that your answer, when rounded off, agrees with the value of sin 0.06 on your calculator.

8. Your first torpedo sinks the Hic. The Haec and Hoc leave the practice area along a bearing of Arctan $(-\sqrt{3})$.

a. Find exactly the inverse *circular* Arctan $(-\sqrt{3})$.
b. Find exactly the inverse *trigonometric* Arctan $(-\sqrt{3})$.
c. What are the values of arctan $(-\sqrt{3})$? (Trig or circular.)
d. What is the value of sin (Arctan 2)?
e. Sketch a graph of $y = $ Arctan x.

9. On the trip home you dig out an old trigonometry text and see if you can apply your knowledge to a new situation.

You find stated, without proof, the *Law of Tangents*, which says that in any triangle ABC,

$$\frac{\tan \frac{1}{2}(A - B)}{\tan \frac{1}{2}(A + B)} = \frac{a - b}{a + b}.$$

You decide to prove the Law of Tangents.

a. Use the Law of Sines and the addition property of equality to show

$$\text{i.} \quad \frac{\sin A + \sin B}{\sin B} = \frac{a + b}{b}$$

and

$$\text{ii.} \quad \frac{\sin A - \sin B}{\sin B} = \frac{a - b}{b}.$$

b. Divide equation ii by equation i, left member by left member and right member by right member, and simplify. Then use the sum and product properties to express the numerator and denominator of the left member as *products*.
c. Use the quotient properties to arrive at the Law of Tangents from your work in part b.

Final Examination

In this book you have studied various kinds of algebraic and trigonometric functions and relations. For each kind, you have **defined** it, **graphed** it, found its **properties,** and used it as a **mathematical model.** The examination below tests your ability to do these four things with the functions you have studied. If you are thoroughly familiar with the concepts, you should be able to work the examination in about three hours.

I.	DEFINITIONS

1. Usually, a function is defined by a *general equation*. Write the general equation for each of the following:
   a. A linear function.
   b. A direct variation function.
   c. y is directly proportional to the 1.6 power of x.
   d. y varies directly with x and inversely with the square of z.
   e. A quadratic function.
   f. A quartic function.
   g. An exponential function.
   h. A rational algebraic function.
   i. A hyperbola opening in the y-direction.
   j. The probability of Event E.
   k. A sinusoidal function.
   l. The inverse secant function.

2. For sequences and series, the definition is usually a *pattern* followed by the terms. You had to *figure out* a general equation from the pattern.
   a. Write the definition of a *geometric* sequence.
   b. Write the definition of an *arithmetic* sequence.
   c. Write the general equation for t_n, the nth term, of a
      i. geometric sequence,
      ii. arithmetic sequence.
   d. Figure out a general equation for t_n in terms of n for the sequence 0, 3, 8, 15, 24, 35, ...

II. | GRAPHS

3. For each of the following graphs, tell what kind of function or relation it could be.

a.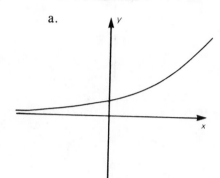

b.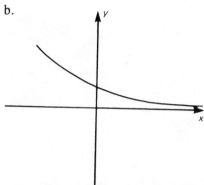

c.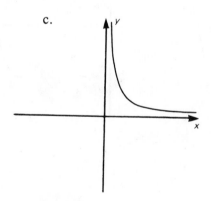

d.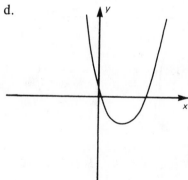

e.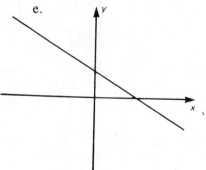

f.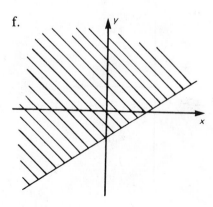

g.

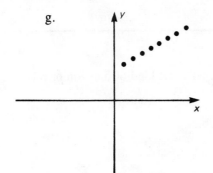

h.

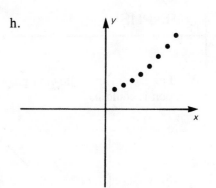

i.

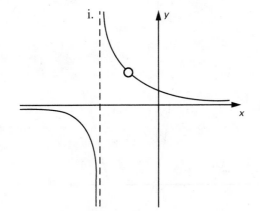

j.

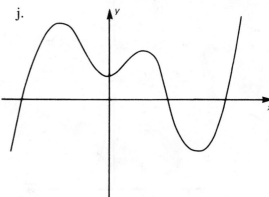

k.

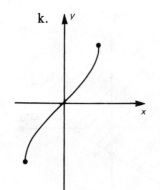

l.

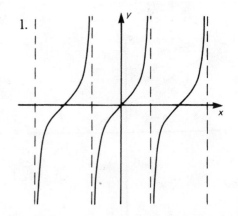

III. | PROPERTIES

4. At the beginning of the course you learned fundamental properties, called *axioms*, on which all of algebra and trigonometry is based. Tell which axiom is illustrated by each equation. No abbreviations, please! Write out the *full* name.

   a. $x \cdot (y \cdot z) = (x \cdot y) \cdot z$
   b. $x \cdot (y \cdot z) = x \cdot (y \cdot z)$
   c. $x \cdot (y + z) = xy + xz$
   d. If $x < y$ and $y < z$, then $x < z$.
   e. $x < y$, $x = y$, or $x > y$.
   f. $x \cdot \dfrac{1}{x} = 1$
   g. $x \cdot 1 = x$

5. From the axioms and definitions, you have proved other properties that allow you to write expressions in different forms. Complete each equation below. Do not write in the book unless you own it.

   a. $x^{\frac{3}{4}} = $ _____

   b. $(x^3)^4 = $ _____

   c. $(xy)^4 = $ _____

   d. $(x + y)^3 = $ _____

   e. $x^3 + y^3 = $ _____

   f. $\log (xy) = $ _____

   g. $\log (x^y) = $ _____

   h. If $r = \log_s t$, then $t = $ _____

   i. $n(A \text{ or } B) = $ _____

   j. $\sqrt{x^2} = $ _____

   k. If $rx^2 + sx + t = 0$, then $x = $ _____

   l. $\cos 2x = $ _____ (in terms of $\sin x$)

   m. $\tan (x + y) = $ _____ (in terms of $\tan x$ and $\tan y$)

   n. $\sin^2 x = $ _____ (in terms of $\cos x$)

IV.	MATHEMATICAL MODELS

A. SELECTING A FUNCTION

6. Often you can tell what kind of function to use as a mathematical model by looking at the real-world graph. For instance, the distance you are standing from the fireplace and how hot you feel are related.
   a. Sketch a reasonable graph showing how these two variables are related.
   b. Based on your graph, what kind of function would make a reasonable mathematical model?

7. Sometimes a kind of function can be selected based on known properties of the real-world variables. For example, when a taxi driver first turns on the meter, it reads a certain number of cents. Each time the meter clicks, you owe an additional number of cents. The total you owe depends on the number of clicks.
   a. Sketch a reasonable graph of this function.
   b. What kind of function would be a reasonable mathematical model? Tell why this kind of function would be reasonable.

B. GETTING THE PARTICULAR EQUATION

8. Once you have selected a kind of function, you must get the particular equation that fits the given ordered pairs. For each of the following, find the particular equation.
   a. y varies inversely with the cube of x, and $(3, 50)$ is on the graph.
   b. y varies exponentially with x, and $(0, 73)$ and $(3, 146)$ are on the graph.
   c. y varies quadratically with x, and $(1, 8)$, $(4, 5)$, and $(-3, -16)$ are on the graph.
   d. y varies sinusoidally with x. The ordered pair $(-3, 2)$ is a low point, and $(5, 11)$ is the next high point.

C. USING THE MATHEMATICAL MODEL

The following problems test your ability to use various techniques associated with functions and relations.

9. For the system of inequalities
   $$4x + 9y \geq 13$$
   $$3x - 6y > -20$$
   a. Use determinants to find the intersection of the boundary lines.
   b. Plot the graph of the solution set of the system of inequalities.

10. If $f(x) = \dfrac{x - 9}{\sqrt{x} + 3}$,

    a. Express $f(x)$ in simple radical form.
    b. Find $f(45)$, and express the answer in simple radical form.
    c. Set $f(x) = -5$, and solve the resulting radical equation. Show that the solution you get is *extraneous*.

11. a. Tell which conic section the graph of each of the following will be:

        i. $4x^2 + 4y^2 - 40x + 6y = -93$
        ii. $4x^2 - 4y^2 - 40x + 6y = -93$
        iii. $4x^2 + 4y - 40x + 6y = -93$
        iv. $4x^2 + y^2 - 40x + 6y = -93$

    b. For the equation in iv, complete the square, find the center, and sketch the graph.

12. a. If $P(x)$ is a quintic polynomial with real-number coefficients, and if $3 + 2i$ is a complex zero of $P(x)$, what is another complex zero of $P(x)$?
    b. If $f(x) = 3x^4 - 5x^3 + 7x^2 - 4x + 9$, use synthetic substitution to find $f(2)$.
    c. If $3x^4 - 5x^3 + 7x^2 - 4x + 9$ is divided by $x - 2$, what is
        i. the quotient?
        ii. the remainder?
    d. Name the theorem that allows you to get the answer to part c. ii. *quickly*.

13. The following is a computer program in BASIC:

```
10 INPUT N, R
20 LET U = N-R+1
30 LET P = 1
40 FOR F = U TO N
50 LET P = P*F
60 NEXT F
70 PRINT N; "P";R;"=";P
80 END
```

    a. Show the simulated computer memory and the output if 10 and 3 are put in for N and R, respectively, in Step 10.
    b. What kind of problem would the program be used for?

14. a. For the arithmetic series $7 + 10 + 13 + \ldots$, find t_{1000} and S_{1000}.
    b. For the geometric series with first term 300 and common ratio 1.03, find t_{100} and S_{100}.

15. a. Expand $(x - 2i)^5$ as a binomial series, and simplify. Assume that $i = \sqrt{-1}$.

b. Find the term of the binomial series from $(r - s)^{37}$ that has s^{15}. You may leave the coefficient in factorial form.

c. Find two geometric means between 5 and 50. Get a decimal approximation for the common ratio and for each mean.

16. A triangular tract of land has sides of 10 meters and 15 meters, and an included angle of 120°. Find *exact* values of

a. the length of the third side,   b. the area of the triangle.

D. PUTTING IT ALL TOGETHER

The following problems require you to use many of the things you have learned in the *same* problem.

17. *Skin Diving Problem* When you skin dive, nitrogen from the air you breathe dissolves in your blood. According to Henry's Law, the concentration of nitrogen in your blood varies linearly with the depth at which you are swimming. At 20 feet, the concentration is about 190 milligrams of nitrogen per liter of blood. At 30 feet, the concentration is about 225 milligrams per liter.

a. Write the particular equation expressing nitrogen concentration in terms of depth.

b. Predict the nitrogen concentration at 100 feet.

c. If too much nitrogen dissolves in your blood, you will get "nitrogen narcosis," the rapture of the depths. Assume that nitrogen narcosis starts to set in when the nitrogen concentration reaches 680 milligrams per liter. How deep can you safely dive?

d. According to your mathematical model, how much nitrogen is normally dissolved in your blood when you are *out* of the water? What part of the model tells you this?

18. *Probability Distribution Problem* A group of four people is to be selected at random from a class containing 5 girls and 4 boys. Answer the following questions.

a. In how many different ways could such a group be selected?

b. In how many different ways could the group have

   i.   all girls?

   ii. 3 girls and 1 boy?   iv. 1 girl and 3 boys?

   iii. 2 girls and 2 boys?   v.   all boys?

c. Find the probability for each event in part b.

d. Show that the sum of the probabilities in part c equals 1, and tell the significance of this fact.

e. Let x be the number of girls in the group. Let $P(x)$ be the probability that the group has x girls. Plot the graph of $P(x)$ versus x.

f. In how many different ways could a line be formed having exactly 2 boys and 2 girls?

g. In how many different ways could all 9 people line up if boys and girls must come alternately?

APPENDICES

There are several topics which are sometimes made a part of advanced algebra, but which would interrupt the mainstream of the text. Of these topics, operations with matrices and mathematical induction are presented in this appendix for those instructors who choose to present them.

APPENDIX A
OPERATIONS WITH MATRICES

In Sections 4-3, 4-7, and 4-8 you were introduced to determinants and matrices. A matrix is a rectangular array of numbers such as those below.

$$\begin{bmatrix} 2 & 5 & 3 \\ -1 & 4 & -2 \end{bmatrix} \quad \begin{bmatrix} 5 & 1 \\ 7 & 3 \\ 2 & -4 \end{bmatrix} \quad \begin{bmatrix} 9 & 7 & 1 & 3 \end{bmatrix} \quad \begin{bmatrix} 2 \\ -5 \end{bmatrix}$$

2×3 3×2 1×4 2×1
matrix   matrix   matrix   matrix

The first matrix above has an *order* of "2 by 3" since it has 2 *rows* and 3 *columns*. The number of rows is written first and the number of columns second. Each number in a matrix is called an *element*. Two matrices (the plural of matrix) are equal if and only if they are the same order and have their corresponding elements equal.

A determinant is a number produced by doing operations on the elements of a square matrix, as explained in Chapter 4. So a determinant is a number whereas a matrix is an array of numbers.

ADDITION AND SUBTRACTION

Two matrices of the same order can be added or subtracted by adding or subtracting the corresponding elements. For instance,

$$\begin{bmatrix} 5 & 2 & 7 \\ 1 & 3 & 9 \end{bmatrix} + \begin{bmatrix} 4 & 6 & 8 \\ 5 & 1 & 3 \end{bmatrix} = \begin{bmatrix} 9 & 8 & 15 \\ 6 & 4 & 12 \end{bmatrix}$$

$$\begin{bmatrix} 6 & 5 \\ 2 & 3 \end{bmatrix} - \begin{bmatrix} 4 & 7 \\ 5 & 2 \end{bmatrix} = \begin{bmatrix} 2 & -2 \\ -3 & 1 \end{bmatrix}$$

MULTIPLICATION BY A SCALAR

A matrix can be multiplied by a scalar (a number) by multiplying each element of the matrix by that scalar. For instance,

$$5\begin{bmatrix} 2 & 3 & 4 \\ 6 & 1 & 7 \end{bmatrix} = \begin{bmatrix} 10 & 15 & 20 \\ 30 & 5 & 35 \end{bmatrix}$$

MULTIPLICATION OF TWO MATRICES

Multiplying a matrix by another matrix is complicated to explain, but easy to do once you learn the pattern. The order in which you write the two factors is important. The number of *columns* in the *left* matrix must equal the number of *rows* in the *right* one, as shown below. You begin by multiplying the elements in the first row of the left matrix by the corresponding elements in the first column of the right matrix.

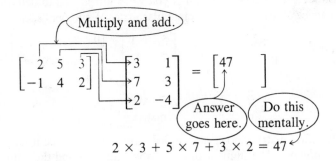

$$2 \times 3 + 5 \times 7 + 3 \times 2 = 47$$

An efficient way to do this is to slide your left index finger across the row and your right index finger down the column, multiplying and adding mentally. The answer goes in the first row, first column of the product matrix.

The procedure is repeated for each possible pairing of rows in the left matrix and columns in the right one. The result goes in the product matrix at the row you used from the left matrix and the column you used from the right matrix. The completed product is shown.

$$\begin{bmatrix} 2 & 5 & 3 \\ -1 & 4 & 2 \end{bmatrix}\begin{bmatrix} 3 & 1 \\ 7 & 3 \\ 2 & -4 \end{bmatrix} = \begin{bmatrix} 47 & 5 \\ 29 & 3 \end{bmatrix}$$

You should try doing the above multiplication to make sure you understand the process.

IDENTITIES AND INVERSES

The matrix

$$\begin{bmatrix} 1 & 0 & 0 \\ 0 & 1 & 0 \\ 0 & 0 & 1 \end{bmatrix}$$

is the *multiplicative identity* for 3×3 matrices. The identity for a square matrix has 1's along the *main diagonal* and 0's everywhere else. Multiplying a square matrix by the identity matrix leaves the matrix unchanged.

If the product of two square matrices is the identity matrix, then those two matrices are *inverses* of each other. For instance,

$$\begin{bmatrix} 3 & 2 \\ 8 & 7 \end{bmatrix}\begin{bmatrix} 7/5 & -2/5 \\ -8/5 & 3/5 \end{bmatrix} = \begin{bmatrix} 1 & 0 \\ 0 & 1 \end{bmatrix}$$

as you can readily see by doing the multiplication. The numerators in the second matrix are the elements of the first matrix, rearranged or changed in sign. The denominators, 5, are equal to the *determinant* of the first matrix.

$$\det \begin{bmatrix} 3 & 2 \\ 8 & 7 \end{bmatrix} = \begin{bmatrix} 3 & 2 \\ 8 & 7 \end{bmatrix} = 3 \cdot 7 - 2 \cdot 8 = 5$$

An easy way to write the inverse of a 2×2 matrix is to interchange the top left and bottom right elements, reverse the signs of the other two elements, and multiply the resulting matrix by the reciprocal of the determinant. That is,

$$\text{If } M = \begin{bmatrix} a & b \\ c & d \end{bmatrix}, \text{ then } M^{-1} = \frac{1}{\det M}\begin{bmatrix} d & -b \\ -c & a \end{bmatrix}$$

Adjoint of M, adj M

The last matrix is called the *adjoint* of matrix M, abbreviated adj M. The inverse of M, as indicated above, is abbreviated M^{-1}.

Finding the inverse of a higher-order square matrix is explained at the end of this section.

MATRIX SOLUTION OF A LINEAR SYSTEM

A system of linear equations such as

$$ax + by = c$$
$$dx + ey = f$$

can be written as a product of matrices,

$$\begin{bmatrix} a & b \\ d & e \end{bmatrix} \begin{bmatrix} x \\ y \end{bmatrix} = \begin{bmatrix} c \\ f \end{bmatrix}$$

or more briefly,

$$CV = A,$$

where C is the coefficient matrix, V is the variables matrix, and A is the answers matrix. The variables matrix can be isolated by multiplying each member of the equation by the inverse of C.

$$C^{-1}CV = C^{-1}A$$
$$V = C^{-1}A$$

For example, to solve

$$5x - y = 7$$
$$2x + 3y = -1$$

you would write

$$\begin{bmatrix} 5 & -1 \\ 2 & 3 \end{bmatrix} \begin{bmatrix} x \\ y \end{bmatrix} = \begin{bmatrix} 7 \\ -1 \end{bmatrix}$$

$$\begin{bmatrix} x \\ y \end{bmatrix} = \frac{1}{17} \begin{bmatrix} 3 & 1 \\ -2 & 5 \end{bmatrix} \begin{bmatrix} 7 \\ -1 \end{bmatrix}$$

$$\begin{bmatrix} x \\ y \end{bmatrix} = \frac{1}{17} \begin{bmatrix} 20 \\ -19 \end{bmatrix}$$

$$\therefore x = \frac{20}{17} \text{ and } y = -\frac{19}{17}$$

$$S = \left\{ \left(\frac{20}{17}, -\frac{19}{17} \right) \right\}$$

INVERSE OF A HIGHER ORDER MATRIX

As for 2×2 matrices, the inverse of a higher-order square matrix is given by

$$M^{-1} = \frac{1}{\det M} \cdot \text{adj } M$$

For higher-order matrices the adjoint matrix must be found by a more general procedure. For example, let

$$M = \begin{bmatrix} 2 & 3 & 4 \\ 5 & 1 & 2 \\ 6 & 8 & 7 \end{bmatrix}$$

First, find the *transpose* of M, written M^T, which is the matrix formed by interchanging the rows and the columns of M.

$$M^T = \begin{bmatrix} 2 & 5 & 6 \\ 3 & 1 & 8 \\ 4 & 2 & 7 \end{bmatrix}$$

The elements of the adjoint matrix are found by evaluating the *minor* determinant for each element of M^T. For instance, the minor of the 2 in the upper left corner is the determinant

$$\begin{vmatrix} 1 & 8 \\ 2 & 7 \end{vmatrix} \quad \text{which equals } -9.$$

Each of these minor determinants is given a sign according to the following pattern:

$$\begin{matrix} + & - & + \\ - & + & - \\ + & - & + \end{matrix}$$

Since the sign in the upper left corner is $+$, the -9 remains -9. Had the sign been $-$, the -9 would have changed to $+9$. The minor determinants along with their signs shown above are called *cofactors* of the elements in the matrix. Evaluating the other eight cofactors produces the answer,

$$\text{adj } M = \begin{bmatrix} -9 & 11 & 2 \\ -23 & -10 & 16 \\ 34 & 2 & -13 \end{bmatrix}$$

You should try evaluating a few of the cofactors above to make sure you know the pattern. In general, the adjoint of a square matrix is the *matrix of cofactors of the transpose* of that matrix. The pattern for a 2×2 matrix is a special case of this more general pattern.

Evaluating the determinant of M as in Section 4-9 gives det $M = 49$. Therefore, the inverse of M is

$$M^{-1} = \frac{1}{49} \begin{bmatrix} -9 & 11 & 2 \\ -23 & -10 & 16 \\ 34 & 2 & -13 \end{bmatrix}$$

The $\frac{1}{49}$ can be distributed to each element in the matrix or can be left factored out, whichever is more convenient.

The following exercise has problems to make you familiar with matrix operations.

942   Appendices

EXERCISE A

For Problems 1 through 16 perform the indicated operations.

1. $\begin{bmatrix} 3 & 5 \\ -2 & 4 \\ 7 & 1 \end{bmatrix} + \begin{bmatrix} -5 & 8 \\ 2 & 6 \\ -7 & 10 \end{bmatrix}$

2. $\begin{bmatrix} -4 & 7 & 11 \\ 13 & 5 & -2 \end{bmatrix} + \begin{bmatrix} -9 & 3 & 7 \\ 1 & 0 & 14 \end{bmatrix}$

3. $[7 \quad 9 \quad 2 \quad 5] - [4 \quad 8 \quad 2 \quad 3]$

4. $\begin{bmatrix} 5 & 7 & -4 \\ 10 & 0 & -2 \\ 11 & -3 & 12 \end{bmatrix} - \begin{bmatrix} 4 & 5 & -7 \\ 6 & -5 & -8 \\ 4 & -11 & 3 \end{bmatrix}$

5. $7\begin{bmatrix} 2 & 8 \\ -4 & 1 \end{bmatrix} + 3\begin{bmatrix} -5 & 1 \\ 2 & -6 \end{bmatrix}$

6. $4[-8 \quad 5 \quad 3] - 2[-5 \quad -1 \quad 7]$

7. $\begin{bmatrix} 5 & 2 & 1 \\ 4 & -3 & 8 \end{bmatrix}\begin{bmatrix} 2 & -3 \\ 5 & -1 \\ 4 & -1 \end{bmatrix}$

8. $\begin{bmatrix} 5 & -8 \\ 7 & 1 \end{bmatrix}\begin{bmatrix} 4 & 7 \\ -3 & 9 \end{bmatrix}$

9. $\begin{bmatrix} 4 & 7 \\ 5 & 3 \\ 2 & -1 \end{bmatrix}\begin{bmatrix} 6 & 8 \\ 3 & -6 \end{bmatrix}$

10. $[-2 \quad 3 \quad 5]\begin{bmatrix} 1 & 4 \\ 7 & -3 \\ -1 & -5 \end{bmatrix}$

11. $\begin{bmatrix} 2 & 4 & -3 \\ 5 & 1 & 2 \\ -1 & 3 & 4 \end{bmatrix}\begin{bmatrix} -1 & 3 & 1 \\ 2 & 4 & 3 \\ 1 & 0 & 2 \end{bmatrix}$

12. $\begin{bmatrix} -1 & 3 & 1 \\ 2 & 4 & 3 \\ 1 & 0 & 2 \end{bmatrix}\begin{bmatrix} 2 & 4 & -3 \\ 5 & 1 & 2 \\ -1 & 3 & 4 \end{bmatrix}$

13. $\begin{bmatrix} 1 & 0 & 0 \\ 0 & 1 & 0 \\ 0 & 0 & 1 \end{bmatrix}\begin{bmatrix} 1 & 4 & 7 \\ 2 & 5 & 8 \\ 3 & 6 & 9 \end{bmatrix}$

14. $\begin{bmatrix} 10 & 20 \\ 30 & 40 \end{bmatrix} \begin{bmatrix} 1 & 0 \\ 0 & 1 \end{bmatrix}$

15. $\begin{bmatrix} 7 & 4 \\ 5 & 3 \end{bmatrix} \begin{bmatrix} 3 & -4 \\ -5 & 7 \end{bmatrix}$

16. $\begin{bmatrix} 2 & 3 & 4 \\ 5 & 1 & 2 \\ 6 & 5 & 7 \end{bmatrix} \begin{bmatrix} -3 & -1 & 2 \\ -23 & -10 & 16 \\ 19 & 8 & -13 \end{bmatrix}$

For Problems 17 through 22 find the inverse of the matrix, or show that it has no inverse because its determinant is zero.

17. $\begin{bmatrix} 5 & 7 \\ 3 & 2 \end{bmatrix}$

18. $\begin{bmatrix} 6 & -1 \\ -10 & 8 \end{bmatrix}$

19. $\begin{bmatrix} -2 & 1 \\ \dfrac{3}{2} & -\dfrac{1}{2} \end{bmatrix}$

20. $\begin{bmatrix} 0.2 & -0.3 \\ -0.4 & 1.1 \end{bmatrix}$

21. $\begin{bmatrix} 6 & 3 \\ 8 & 4 \end{bmatrix}$

22. $\begin{bmatrix} -10 & 5 \\ 6 & -3 \end{bmatrix}$

For Problems 23 and 24, find the adjoint matrix.

23. $\begin{bmatrix} 4 & -3 \\ 1 & 5 \end{bmatrix}$

24. $\begin{bmatrix} -2 & 8 \\ 5 & 6 \end{bmatrix}$

For Problems 25 through 30 solve the system by writing it in matrix form, then multiplying each member by the inverse of the coefficient matrix.

25. $5x + 2y = 11$
    $x + y = 4$

26. $x - y = -11$
    $7x + 4y = -22$

27. $6x - 7y = 47$
    $2x + 5y = -21$

28. $8x + 3y = 41$
    $6x + 5y = 39$

29. $4x - 3y = 11$
    $5x - 6y = 9$

30. $3x + 4y = 18$
    $9x + 6y = 17$

For Problems 31 through 34, find the inverse.

31. $\begin{bmatrix} 3 & 7 & -1 \\ 4 & 1 & -5 \\ -2 & 3 & 1 \end{bmatrix}$

32. $\begin{bmatrix} 2 & -6 & -3 \\ 1 & -3 & 5 \\ 0 & 4 & -2 \end{bmatrix}$

33. $\begin{bmatrix} 5 & -1 & 4 \\ 0 & 3 & -2 \\ 1 & 4 & 3 \end{bmatrix}$

34. $\begin{bmatrix} 5 & 7 & 2 \\ 1 & 4 & 3 \\ 2 & 8 & 6 \end{bmatrix}$

35. Show that matrix multiplication is *not* commutative by showing that

$$\begin{bmatrix} 2 & 3 \\ 4 & 5 \end{bmatrix}\begin{bmatrix} 6 & 7 \\ 8 & 9 \end{bmatrix} \neq \begin{bmatrix} 6 & 7 \\ 8 & 9 \end{bmatrix}\begin{bmatrix} 2 & 3 \\ 4 & 5 \end{bmatrix}$$

36. Show that the set of matrices is *not* closed under multiplication by showing two matrices whose product is not a matrix.

37. For real numbers, the converse of the multiplication property of zero states that a product can be zero only if one of the factors is zero. Show that the corresponding property for matrix multiplication is *false* by finding two 2×2 matrices whose product is the *zero matrix* (each element equals 0), but for which no element of either matrix is 0. (Clue: Find a matrix whose determinant is 0, and multiply it by its adjoint matrix.)

38. Prove that if the elements of a 3×3 matrix are consecutive integers, starting at the upper left corner, then the determinant of the matrix is 0.

APPENDIX B
MATHEMATICAL INDUCTION

You recall that the distributive axiom states that

$$a(x_1 + x_2) = ax_1 + ax_2.$$

In other words, multiplication distributes over a sum of *two* terms. You then simply assume that multiplication distributes over sums of three terms, four terms, etc. For example,

$$a(x_1 + x_2 + x_3 + x_4 + x_5) = ax_1 + ax_2 + ax_3 + ax_4 + ax_5.$$

Although it *seems* reasonable that this property should be true for any number of terms, mathematicians prefer to be able to *prove* properties based upon axioms. The technique used to prove such properties as the extended distributive property is called *mathematical induction*.

Objective:
Given a sequence of statements, $S_1, S_2, S_3, S_4, \ldots, S_n$, prove that each of the statements is true for *any* positive integer n.

In the above example, the statements would be

$$S_2: \quad a(x_1 + x_2) = ax_1 + ax_2$$

$$S_3: \quad a(x_1 + x_2 + x_3) = ax_1 + ax_2 + ax_3$$

$$S_4: \quad a(x_1 + x_2 + x_3 + x_4) = ax_1 + ax_2 + ax_3 + ax_4$$

$$\vdots$$

$$S_n: \quad a(x_1 + x_2 + \cdots + x_n) = ax_1 + ax_2 + \cdots + ax_n$$

(The statement $S_1: a(x_1) = ax_1$ is trivial, and so is omitted.)

Unfortunately, the extended distributive property cannot be proved using the Field Axioms alone. Another axiom must be introduced. Although there are several axioms which will do the job, the most easily understood is the Well-ordering Axiom.

Well-ordering Axiom: Any non-empty set of positive integers contains a *least* element.

The truth of the axiom should be obvious to you. The name comes from the fact that a set is said to be "well-ordered" if it has a least element. The reason for restricting the axiom to non-empty sets is that the empty set has no elements at all. Thus, it could not possibly have a least element.

Proof of the extended distributive property is possible with the aid of this axiom. It is done by assuming that the property is *false*, and showing that this leads you to a *contradiction* (an impossible conclusion).

EXAMPLE 1:   EXTENDED DISTRIBUTIVE PROPERTY OF MULTIPLICATION OVER ADDITION

Prove that $a(x_1 + x_2 + \cdots + x_n) = ax_1 + ax_2 + \cdots + ax_n$ for *any* positive integer n.

Proof:
By the Distributive Axiom, $a(x_1 + x_2) = ax_1 + ax_2$. So Statement S_2 is true.

Assume that there is an integer n for which the property is false. Let F be the set of integers n for which S_n is false. So F is a non-empty set of positive integers. By the Well-ordering Axiom, F has a least element. Let ℓ be the least element of F. ∎

Because S_ℓ is false, you know that

$$a(x_1 + x_2 + \cdots + x_{\ell-1} + x_\ell) \neq ax_1 + ax_2 + \cdots + ax_{\ell-1} + ax_\ell.$$

Because ℓ is the *least* element of F, $S_{\ell-1}$ must be *true*. That is,

$$a(x_1 + x_2 + \cdots + x_{\ell-1}) = ax_1 + ax_2 + \cdots + ax_{\ell-1}.$$

A contradiction can now be reached by starting with the expression

$$a(x_1 + x_2 + \cdots + x_{\ell-1} + x_\ell)$$

and *associating* terms to get

$$a[(x_1 + x_2 + \cdots + x_{\ell-1}) + x_\ell].$$

The expression in brackets now has only *two* terms. The ordinary distributive axiom lets you distribute a to both terms, giving

$$a(x_1 + x_2 + \cdots + x_{\ell-1}) + ax_\ell.$$

By substituting the above for $a(x_1 + x_2 + \cdots + x_{\ell-1})$ you get

$$ax_1 + ax_2 + \cdots + ax_{\ell-1} + ax_\ell.$$

By the transitive property, the first expression equals the last, so

$$a(x_1 + x_2 + \cdots + x_{\ell-1} + x_\ell) = ax_1 + ax_2 + \cdots + ax_{\ell-1} + ax_\ell,$$

which directly contradicts the above *in*equality! The only thing that could have gone wrong was assuming at the beginning that the theorem was false. So the assumption was wrong, the theorem is *true*, and

$$a(x_1 + x_2 + \cdots + x_n) = ax_1 + ax_2 + \cdots + ax_n$$

for *any* integer value of $n \geq 2$. Q.E.D.

Once you understand the process, the proof may be shortened a great deal. All you need to do is to show that assuming one of the statements is true implies that the next statement is true, and that one of the statements actually is true. These two ideas combined are called the induction principle.

INDUCTION PRINCIPLE

If you can show that:

1. *Assuming* that one of the statements is true implies that the *next* statement is true, and
2. One of the statements actually *is* true,

then you can conclude that *all* of the statements are true, from the one that actually is true on up.

The proof of the extended distributive property can be condensed as follows. Proofs done in this manner are said to be done by *Mathematical Induction*.

EXAMPLE 1 (BY MATHEMATICAL INDUCTION):

Prove that $a(x_1 + x_2 + \cdots + x_n) = ax_1 + ax_2 + \cdots + ax_n$ for *any* positive integer n.

Proof:

Anchor: $a(x_1 + x_2) = ax_1 + ax_2$ by the Distributive Axiom, so the theorem is actually true when $n = 2$.

Induction Hypothesis: Assume the theorem is true for $n = k$. That is,

$$a(x_1 + x_2 + \cdots + x_k) = ax_1 + ax_2 + \cdots + ax_k.$$

Demonstration for $n = k + 1$: If $n = k + 1$, then

$$a(x_1 + x_2 + \cdots + x_k + x_{k+1}) = a[(x_1 + x_2 + \cdots + x_k) + x_{k+1}]$$

Associativity.

$$= a(x_1 + x_2 + \cdots + x_k) + ax_{k+1}$$

By the anchor.

$$= ax_1 + ax_2 + \cdots + ax_k + ax_{k+1}$$

By the Induction Hypothesis.

Conclusion: Since 1., assuming the property is true for $n = k$ implies that it is true for $n = k + 1$, and 2., it is actually true for $n = 2$, you can conclude that

$$a(x_1 + x_2 + \cdots + x_n) = ax_1 + ax_2 + \cdots + ax_n$$

for *all* integers $n \geq 2$. Q.E.D.   ■

If you have been very alert, you may have detected one weakness in the above proof. You are trying to extend one of the field axioms, distributivity, to sums of more than two terms. But without ever stating it, you have used in the proof an extended *associative* property and an extended *transitive* property!

The proof of the extended associative property is a bit tricky, and is presented below as Example 2. *You* will prove the extended transitive property in Exercise B. First, you must define just what it is you mean by a sum of n terms.

DEFINITION

$$x_1 + x_2 + x_3 + x_4 + \cdots + x_{n-1} + x_n$$
$$= (\ldots (((x_1 + x_2) + x_3) + x_4) + \cdots + x_{n-1}) + x_n.$$

In plain English, you associate the first two terms and get an answer. Then you add the third term to this answer to get another answer, and so on. The extended associative property which you will prove says that you get the same answer if you remove all of the *inner* parentheses. That is, you can associate the first $n - 1$ terms.

EXAMPLE 2:   EXTENDED ASSOCIATIVE PROPERTY OF ADDITION

Prove that $x_1 + x_2 + x_3 + \cdots + x_{n-1} + x_n$
$$= (x_1 + x_2 + x_3 + \cdots + x_{n-1}) + x_n$$
for all integers $n \geq 3$.

Proof:
Anchor: For $n = 3$, $x_1 + x_2 + x_3 = (x_1 + x_2) + x_3$ by definition.

Induction Hypothesis: Assume that for k terms, you can associate
$x_1 + x_2 + x_3 + \cdots + x_{k-1} + x_k$
$$= (x_1 + x_2 + x_3 + \cdots + x_{k-1}) + x_k.$$

Demonstration for $n = k + 1$:   If there are $k + 1$ terms, then

$x_1 + x_2 + x_3 + \cdots + x_{k-1} + x_k + x_{k+1}$
$$= ((\ldots ((x_1 + x_2) + x_3) + \cdots + x_{k-1}) + x_k) + x_{k+1}$$
definition of a sum of $k + 1$ terms
$$= ((x_1 + x_2 + x_3 + \cdots + x_{k-1}) + x_k) + x_{k+1}$$
definition of a sum of $k - 1$ terms
$$= (x_1 + x_2 + x_3 + \cdots + x_{k-1} + x_k) + x_{k+1}$$
by Induction Hypothesis.

Conclusion:

$\therefore x_1 + x_2 + x_3 + \cdots + x_{n-1} + x_n = (x_1 + x_2 + x_3 + \cdots + x_{n-1}) + x_n$

for *all* integers $n \geq 3$. Q.E.D.   ■

EXAMPLE 3

Induction is useful for proving that formulas for series (see Chapter 11) are true for *any* finite number of terms. For example, the sum of the first n terms in a geometric series
$$a + ar + ar^2 + ar^3 + \cdots + ar^{n-1}$$
is equal to $\dfrac{a(1 - r^n)}{1 - r}$, where $a = t_1$.

Proof:
Anchor: For $n = 1$, the series consists of just *one* term, a. The formula gives

$$\frac{a(1 - r^1)}{1 - r},$$

which is equal to a. So the formula is correct for $n = 1$.

Induction Hypothesis: Assume that the formula is true for $n = k$. That is,

$$a + ar + ar^2 \cdots + ar^{k-1} = \frac{a(1 - r^k)}{1 - r}.$$

Demonstration for $n = k + 1$: If there are $k + 1$ terms, then

$a + ar + ar^2 + \cdots + ar^{k-1} + ar^k$

$$= (a + ar + ar^2 + \cdots + ar^{k-1}) + ar^k \qquad \text{Associativity}$$

$$= \frac{a(1 - r^k)}{1 - r} + ar^k \qquad \text{Induction Hypothesis}$$

$$= \frac{a(1 - r^k) + ar^k(1 - r)}{1 - r} \qquad \text{Adding fractions}$$

$$= \frac{a - ar^k + ar^k - ar^{k+1}}{1 - r} \qquad \text{Distributivity}$$

$$= \frac{a - ar^{k+1}}{1 - r} \qquad \text{Adding like terms}$$

$$= \frac{a(1 - r^{k+1})}{1 - r} \qquad \text{Factoring out } a$$

$\therefore a + ar + ar^2 + \cdots + ar^k + ar^{k+1}$

$$= \frac{a(1 - r^{k+1})}{1 - r} \qquad \text{Transitivity}$$

Conclusion: Since assuming that the formula is true for $n = k$ implies that it is also true for $n = k + 1$, and since the formula actually *is* true for $n = 1$, you can conclude that

$$a + ar + ar^2 + \cdots + ar^{n-1} = \frac{a(1 - r^n)}{1 - r}$$

for *all* integers $n \geq 1$. Q.E.D. ∎

You should be careful not to read too much into the conclusion of an induction proof. The proof is good only for any *finite* value of n. For example, in Problem 4 you will prove the extended closure property for addition. This says that the sum of any finite number of terms equals a real number.

If there is an *infinite* number of terms, the sum may or may not equal a real number. For example,

$$1 + \frac{1}{2} + \frac{1}{4} + \frac{1}{8} + \cdots + \frac{1}{2^n} + \cdots$$

is equal to 2, which *is* a real number. But

$$1 + \frac{1}{2} + \frac{1}{3} + \frac{1}{4} + \cdots + \frac{1}{n} + \cdots$$

is *larger* than any real number. When you study analysis or calculus, you will learn about the concepts of limits, which will allow you to prove things about sums of infinite numbers of terms.

In the exercise which follows, you will use mathematical induction to prove other extended field, equality, and order axioms; properties of exponentiation and logarithms; formulas for sequences and series; and some interesting properties of numbers.

EXERCISE B

Prove the following theorems either
a.   directly from the Well-Ordering Axiom, or
b.   by Mathematical Induction.

You may use the conclusions of the examples or of any *prior* problem in the exercise to help you prove the one you are working on.

1.   *Extended Associativity for Multiplication*—The product $a_1 a_2 a_3 \ldots$ $a_{n-1} a_n$ is defined in the same way as the *sum* of n terms (see the above text material). Prove that for $n \geq 3$,

$$a_1 a_2 a_3 \ldots a_{n-1} a_n = (a_1 a_2 a_3 \ldots a_{n-1}) a_n .$$

2.   *Extended Commutativity for Multiplication*—Prove that you can commute a factor in a product past *any* number of other factors. That is, prove for any $n \geq 2$,

$$a_1 a_2 a_3 \ldots a_{n-1} a_n = a_n a_1 a_2 a_3 \ldots a_{n-1} .$$

3.   *Extended Closure under Multiplication*—Prove that the product of *any* finite number of real numbers is a real number. That is, if a_1, a_2, a_3, . . . , a_n are real numbers, then $a_1 a_2 a_3 \ldots a_n$ is a real number, for *any* integer $n \geq 2$.

4.   *Extended Closure under Addition*—Prove that the sum of *any* finite number of real numbers is a real number. That is, if a_1, a_2, a_3, . . . , a_n are real numbers, then $a_1 + a_2 + a_3 + \cdots + a_n$ is a real number, for *any* integer $n \geq 2$.

5.   *Extended Transitivity for Equality*—Prove that in a chain of equalities, the first number equals the last number, no matter how many

"=" signs come between. That is, if $a_1 = a_2 = a_3 = \cdots = a_n$, then $a_1 = a_n$, for any integer $n \geq 3$.

6. *Extended Transitivity for Order*—Prove that in a chain of inequalities with "<," the first number is less than the last number, no matter how many "<" signs come between. That is, if $a_1 < a_2 < a_3 < \cdots < a_n$, then $a_1 < a_n$ for any integer $n \geq 3$.

7. *Exponentiation Distributes over Multiplication*—Exponentiation with positive integer exponents may be defined as follows:

$$x^1 = x$$

$$x^n = x^{n-1} \cdot x, \quad \text{for} \quad n > 1.$$

Use this definition to prove inductively that $(ab)^n = a^n b^n$ for all integers $n \geq 1$.

8. *Exponentiation Distributes over Division*—Prove that

$$\left(\frac{a}{b}\right)^n = \frac{a^n}{b^n} \quad \text{for } any \text{ integer } n \geq 1.$$

9. *Product of Two Powers with the Same Base*—Prove that a product of two powers with the same base may be evaluated by *adding* the exponents. That is, prove that

$$a^r a^n = a^{r+n}$$

for all integers $n \geq 1$.

10. *Power of a Power*—Prove that a power of a power may be evaluated by *multiplying* the exponents. That is, prove that

$$(a^r)^n = a^{rn}$$

for *any* integer $n \geq 1$.

11. *nth power of a Number Larger than 1*—Prove that if $x > 1$, then $x^n > x^{n-1}$ for all integers $n \geq 1$.

12. *nth Power of a Number Between 0 and 1*—Prove that if $0 < x < 1$, then $x^n < x^{n-1}$ for all integers $n \geq 1$.

13. *Logarithm of a Product of n Factors*—Prove that the log of a product is the sum of the logs of the factors, no matter how many factors there are. That is, for any $n \geq 2$, prove that

$$\log (x_1 x_2 x_3 \ldots x_n) = \log x_1 + \log x_2 + \log x_3 + \cdots + \log x_n.$$

14. *Logarithm of a Power*—Prove that the log of a number raised to a power is the exponent times the log of the number. That is,

$$\log (x^n) = n \log x$$

for *any* integer $n \geq 1$. The property of the log of a product should be helpful as a lemma.

15. *Absolute Value of a Product*—Prove that the absolute value of a product equals the product of the absolute values of the factors. That is, for all integers $n \geq 2$,

$$|a_1 a_2 a_3 \ldots a_n| = |a_1||a_2||a_3| \ldots |a_n|.$$

The anchor, $|a_1 a_2| = |a_1||a_2|$, can be proved by recalling that $|x| = \sqrt{x^2}$, and using the properties of products of square roots.

16. *Absolute Value of a Sum (Polygonal Inequality)*—Prove that the absolute value of a sum is less than or equal to the sum of the absolute values of the terms. That is, for all integers $n \geq 2$,

$$|a_1 + a_2 + a_3 + \cdots + a_n| \leq |a_1| + |a_2| + |a_3| + \cdots + |a_n|$$

The anchor, $|a_1 + a_2| \leq |a_1| + |a_2|$, is called the Triangle Inequality. It is quite tricky to prove. You may find that the inequality $-|x| \leq x \leq |x|$, and the fact that if $-r \leq s \leq r$, then $|s| \leq r$, are helpful.

17. *Upper Bound for the nth Prime*—Let p_n be the nth prime number. That is, $p_1 = 2$, $p_2 = 3$, $p_3 = 5$, $p_4 = 7$, $p_5 = 11$, and so forth. Bertrand's Postulate (actually a proven theorem) states that there is at least one prime between p_n and $2p_n$. For example, $p_4 = 7$, so $2p_4 = 14$. The prime 11 (and also the prime 13) is between 7 and 14. Use Bertrand's Postulate to prove that

$$p_n < 2^n$$

for all integers $n \geq 2$.

18. *Formula for Triangular Numbers*—The numbers 1, 3, 6, 10, 15, 21, ... , are called "triangular numbers" because these are the numbers of balls that can be arranged in various sized equilateral triangles (see sketch). As you can see from the sketch, the nth triangular number is formed by adding n to the previous triangular number. Prove by induction that the nth triangular number, T_n, is given by

$$T_n = \frac{n}{2}(n + 1).$$

19. *Formula for Pyramidal Numbers*—In the "olden days" when armies and navies used cannon balls, the balls were often stacked in triangular pyramids. Each layer in the stack was an equilateral triangle, with one less cannon ball per side than the layer below. It was important

to be able to determine the number of cannon balls in a stack *quickly*. You realize that this number is just the *sum* of the first n triangular numbers if the stack has n cannon balls in the side of the bottom layer. Prove by induction that the nth "pyramidal number," P_n, is

$$P_n = \frac{n}{6}(n + 1)(n + 2).$$

20. *Formula for Pentagonal Numbers*—The numbers 1, 5, 12, 22, 35, 51, 70, 92, . . . , are called "pentagonal numbers" because these are the numbers of balls that can be arranged in regular pentagons (see sketch).

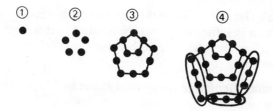

As you can see from the sketch, the fourth pentagonal number is formed from the third one by adding three rows of dots, one containing 4 dots, and the other two containing 3 dots each. In general, if P_n is the nth pentagonal number, then

$$P_{n+1} = P_n + (n + 1) + 2n = P_n + (3n + 1).$$

Prove by induction that for all integers $n \geq 1$,

$$P_n = \frac{n}{2}(3n - 1).$$

21. *Sum of the First* n *Positive Integers*—Prove that the sum of the first n positive integers is

$$1 + 2 + 3 + \cdots + n = \frac{n}{2}(n + 1).$$

22. *Sum of the Squares of the First* n *Positive Integers*—Prove that the sum of the squares of the first n positive integers is

$$1^2 + 2^2 + 3^2 + \cdots + n^2 = \frac{1}{6}(n)(n + 1)(2n + 1).$$

23. *Sum of the Cubes of the First* n *Positive Integers*—Prove that the *sum* of the *cubes* of the first n positive integers is equal to the *square* of the *sum* of the first n positive integers. That is,

$$1^3 + 2^2 + 3^3 + \cdots + n^3 = (1 + 2 + 3 + \cdots + n)^2.$$

The results of Problem 21 should be helpful!

24. *Sum of the First* n *Odd Positive Integers is a Perfect Square*—Prove that for all $n \geq 1$,

$$1 + 3 + 5 + \cdots + (2n - 1) = n^2.$$

25. *Sum of Reciprocals of Pairwise Products*—Prove for all $n \geq 1$,

$$\frac{1}{1 \cdot 2} + \frac{1}{2 \cdot 3} + \frac{1}{3 \cdot 4} + \cdots + \frac{1}{n(n + 1)} = \frac{n}{n + 1}.$$

26. *Sum of Reciprocals of Powers of 2*—Prove for all $n \geq 1$ that

$$\frac{1}{2^1} + \frac{1}{2^2} + \frac{1}{2^3} + \cdots + \frac{1}{2^n} = 1 - \frac{1}{2^n}.$$

27. *Factorials Get Large Faster than Exponentials*—Prove that $n! > 3^n$ whenever n is sufficiently large. Note that to get an anchor, you may have to try several values of n, because the conclusion is *false* when n is close to 1.

28. *Exponentials Get Large Faster than Powers*—Prove that $2^n > n^2$ whenever n is sufficiently large. As in Problem 27, you will have to search for the lowest value of n for which the theorem is true. The algebra in the demonstration for $n = k + 1$ is rather difficult. You may need to know that $2^k > 2k + 1$ in order to arrive at the desired conclusion.

29. n*th Term of an Arithmetic Sequence*—You recall that the nth term of an arithmetic sequence is formed by adding a constant, d, to the preceding term. If t_n is the nth term of an arithmetic sequence, prove that

$$t_n = t_1 + (n - 1)d$$

for all integer values of $n \geq 1$.

30. n*th Term of a Geometric Sequence*—You recall that the nth term of a geometric sequence is formed by multiplying the preceding term by a constant, r. If t_n is the nth term of a geometric sequence, prove that

$$t_n = t_1 \cdot r^{n-1}$$

for all integer values of $n \geq 1$.

31. n*th Partial Sum of an Arithmetic Series*—You recall that the nth partial sum of a series is the sum of the first n terms. You also recall that an arithmetic series has as its $n + 1^{st}$ term

$$t_{n+1} = t_n + d$$

where d is a constant called the common difference. Prove by induction that S_n, the nth partial sum, of an arithmetic series, is equal to

$$S_n = \frac{n}{2}(2t_1 + (n - 1)d)$$

for all integer values of $n \geq 1$.

32. *Term of a Binomial Series*—Prove that the term containing b^r in the expansion of the binomial $(a + b)^n$ is

$$\frac{n!}{r! \, (n - r)!} a^{n-r} b^r$$

for all integers $n \geq 2$. Note that after assuming it is true for $n = k$, you will use the fact that $(a + b)^{k+1} = (a + b)^k(a + b)$. The term with b^r in $(a + b)^{k+1}$ comes from only *two* terms in the expansion of $(a + b)^k$; the one with b^r, which gets multiplied by a, and the one with b^{r-1}, which gets multiplied by b. You will need to be very clever in finding the common denominator when you add the two fractions!!

33. *Sum of Cosines of Odd Multiples of* x—Prove that

$$\cos x + \cos 3x + \cos 5x + \cdots + \cos (2n - 1)x = \frac{\sin 2nx}{2 \sin x}$$

for all integers $n \geq 1$.

34. *Every Positive Integer is both Odd and Even?*—Calvin Butterball supplies the following "proof" that every positive integer is both odd and even.

Proof:

Assume that it is true for $n = k$.

That is, k is both odd and even.

Since k is even, it can be written in the form $2r$, where r is an integer.

Since k is odd, it can be written in the form $2s + 1$, where s is an integer.

So $k = 2r = 2s + 1$ by transitivity.

If $n = k + 1$, then $k + 1 = 2r + 1 = 2s + 2$.

Since $k + 1 = 2r + 1$, $k + 1$ is *odd*.

Since $k + 1 = 2s + 2 = 2(s + 1)$, $k + 1$ is *even*.

$\therefore k + 1$ is both odd and even.

Therefore, *any* positive integer n is both odd and even. Q.E.D.

Where did Calvin go wrong in his proof?

35. *Primes from Polynomials??*—The polynomial $n^2 - n + 41$ is interesting because when you substitute numbers for n, you get *primes*.

n	$n^2 - n + 41$	
1	41	(prime)
2	43	(prime)
3	47	(prime)
4	53	(prime)
5	61	(prime)
6	71	(prime)

Either prove by induction that $n^2 - n + 41$ is prime for *all* integers $n \geq 1$, or find a counter-example in which it is *not* prime.

36. *Every Number Equals Every Other Number???*—Phoebe Small supplies the following "proof" that every number is equal to every other number:

Prove that if $a_1, a_2, a_3, \ldots, a_n$ are real numbers, then

$$a_1 = a_2 = a_3 = \cdots = a_n \text{ for } all \text{ integers } n \geq 1.$$

Proof:

Let S be a set containing n numbers.

Anchor: If $n = 1$, then S contains only *one* number, a_1. By the Reflexive Axiom, $a_1 = a_1$, which anchors the induction.

Induction Hypothesis: Suppose that whenever S contains k elements, $a_1 = a_2 = a_3 = \cdots = a_k$.

Demonstration for n = k + 1: Suppose that S contains $k + 1$ numbers. If a_1 is removed from the set, then S contains only k numbers, $a_2, a_3, a_4, \ldots, a_k$, and a_{k+1}.

By the Induction Hypothesis, $a_2 = a_3 = a_4 = \cdots = a_k = a_{k+1}$. If a_1 is put back, and a_{k+1} is removed from the set, S again contains only k numbers, and thus $a_1 = a_2 = a_3 = \cdots = a_k$.

Therefore, by the Extended Transitive Property (Problem 5),

$$a_1 = a_2 = a_3 = \cdots = a_k = a_{k+1}.$$

Conclusion: Therefore, $a_1 = a_2 = a_3 = \cdots a_n$ for *all* integers $n \geq 1$. Q.E.D.

What did Phoebe do wrong in her proof? (Note: This "proof" is sometimes used to show that all people in a room have the same sex!)

APPENDIX C
AN EXPLORATION OF FUNCTIONS

This appendix contains six activities designed to give you some hands-on work with different types of functions. While you are working on them, think about how your results relate to functions you are familiar with.

ACTIVITY 1: FUNCTIONS "CAN" BE FUN

Question: How does the circumference of a circle relate to its diameter?

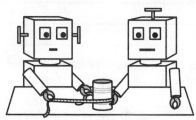

1. Make a table, like the one below, to record your results.

Cans	Diameter	Circumference
A		
B		
(Continue table.)		

2. Use the centimeter tape to measure the circumference of one of your group's cans. Record the result to the nearest millimeter in your table.

3. Carefully trace the base of the can onto a piece of scratch paper. Now, fold the circle you have traced in half. When you unfold the paper, the crease will represent the diameter of the circle. Measure this to the nearest millimeter and record the result.

4. Repeat steps 2 and 3 until you have measured all the cans.

5. On a piece of graph paper, plot the ordered pairs from the table, using the diameter as the independent (x) variable and circumference as the dependent (y) variable.

6. Draw a "line of best fit" through your points. Does it pass through the origin? Should it?

7. What type of function do you believe this is?

8. Determine the equation for this function. Express the slope as a decimal accurate to hundredths, if possible.

9. What is the significance of the slope of your line? Write a few sentences explaining why this experiment came out as it did.

ACTIVITY 2: U CAN PLOT THIS!

Question: How does the area of an open rectangle with a limited perimeter depend on the height you choose? Is there a maximum area?

1. Measure your pipe cleaner according to the scale on the sheet of graph paper provided. Record this answer on your paper.

2. Make a table with the headings shown below. Label it Table 1. You'll need to make it long enough for 10–15 entries.

Table 1

x = Height of U	Base of U	Area of U
1		
(Continue table.)		

3. Now hold one end of the pipe cleaner at 0 on the scale and bend it into the shape of a "U" of height 1 as shown:

1 └─────┘

Complete the first line of Table 1. "Area of U" refers to the rectangular area inside the U.

4. Form a U of height 2 and fill in the second line of Table 1. Repeat for U's of height 3, 4, and so on, until you run out of pipe cleaner.

5. Let $A(x)$ be the area of the rectangular region inside the U that results when the height is x. Copy Table 2 and fill it out as far as you can.

Table 2

x	$A(x)$

6. After you have finished Table 2, graph the function $A(x)$ on a sheet of graph paper. Then answer these questions on your paper:
   a. Does it make sense to connect your points with a smooth curve? Why or why not?
   b. What is the domain of function $A(x)$? What is its range?
   c. What type of function do you think it is?

7. Determine the equation for function $A(x)$ and write it on your paper. Be sure to use the form: $A(x) = $ _____

8. For what height (x-value) does the U have the greatest area?

9. Now ask some of your classmates for two pieces of information: (1) the length of their pipe cleaner and (2) the value of x that produced the greatest area. Make a table relating the length of the pipe cleaner to the height that produced the greatest area. Do you see a relationship in your table? Describe this relationship on your paper.

10. If the length of the pipe cleaner is n units, what value of x will give the U with the greatest area?

ACTIVITY 3: HALF A LIFE IS BETTER THAN NO LIFE AT ALL

Question: If you begin with a given quantity of radioactive material, how does the amount that is still radioactive decrease over time?

1. In your bag are a number of atoms of radioactive plutonium. They look amazingly like dice! Count the number of "atoms" in your bag and record it. This is your "initial quantity," and it represents the value of a in the equation $y = a \cdot 10^{kx}$.

2. Plutonium and other radioactive elements "decay" over time into less harmful ones. To simulate this, roll all your atoms. The dice that have the marked side up have "decayed." Remove these and record your results in a table like the one below. Continue rolling the dice until all have decayed. Repeat this experiment three times.

Number of rolls	Radioactive atoms left
1	
2	
(Continue until first trial finished, then continue the table for two more trials.)	

3. Plot the results of all your trials on the same grid. Use "number of rolls" as your independent (x) variable and "radioactive atoms left" as your dependent (y) variable. Draw a smooth curve that fits the points best.

4. From the graph, determine the approximate *half-life* for your atoms. (The half-life of a radioactive substance is the time it takes for half of the particles to decay. So, if you began with 22 particles, see how many rolls it took for 11 to remain.)

5. Pick out and record three points that your curve seems to pass through or close to. Do not use your "initial quantity" point as one of these.

6. Working with $y = a \cdot 10^{kx}$, calculate the value of k for each of the three points. Show your work. (See problem 1 for the value of a.)

7. Compute the average of the three values of k and use this to write your specific "decay" formula.

8. a. Calculate the half-life of your atoms.
   b. Does this calculated half-life seem to agree with your answer to problem 4?
   c. Did the other groups of students get similar half-life values?

9. Plutonium, an extremely toxic substance, has a half-life of 24,000 years. If 8 ounces of plutonium are produced by a nuclear power plant:
   a. How many years will it take to decay to 4 ounces? 1 ounce?
   b. What special problems does this cause in developing nuclear power?

ACTIVITY 4: A SWINGING TIME

Question: How does the time it takes a pendulum to swing relate to the length of the pendulum?

1. Your teacher will provide a string with a weight on it. The string should be marked at 10 cm intervals, measured from the end with the weight.

2. Make a table with the headings shown below. Label it Table 1.

Table 1

Length of string	Time (30 periods)	Time (1 period)
10 cm		
20 cm		
30 cm		
40 cm		
50 cm		
60 cm		
70 cm		

3. Hold the string at the mark that is 10 cm from the weight. Pull the weight to the side with your other hand and let it swing freely. The time it takes for the weight to make one complete swing (across and back) is the *period* of the pendulum. To measure the period, let the weight swing through 30 periods, record the time, and then divide the time by 30 to find the time for *one* period.

4. Repeat this procedure for each length of the string in Table 1. Record your results.

5. Let L represent the length of the pendulum, and let T be the time period that results from swinging that pendulum. Copy and fill out Table 2 below, expressing T as a function of L.

Table 2

L	$T = f(L)$
10 cm	
20 cm	
30 cm	

(Continue table to $L = 70$ cm.)

6. Plot the points in Table 2 on graph paper.
   a. Should you connect them on a smooth curve?
   b. What period T would correspond to a string length of 0? (Include this point on your graph.)
   c. What is the domain of this function? The range?

7. Describe the shape of the curve in your graph. Try to classify it by its shape—what type of function does it remind you of?

8. Did you conclude that the shape of the graph suggests a function of the type $y = \sqrt{x}$?
   Let's suppose that our points fit a function of the type $y = a\sqrt{x}$ where a is a constant to be determined. So, $T = a\sqrt{L}$. For each ordered pair listed in problem 5, compute a and record its value. Then calculate the mean (average) of these values of a. Record your estimate for a.

9. The behavior of pendulums is studied in physics. A physics student can tell you that $T = 2\pi\sqrt{L/g}$. g is a constant related to the force of gravity at the Earth's surface, and it is approximately equal to 980 cm/sec². Knowing this and an approximate value for π will allow you to rewrite $T = 2\pi\sqrt{L/g}$ in the form $T = a\sqrt{L}$. Does this theoretical value for a seem close to the experimental value you found in problem 8?

10. Make a table with the headings shown below. Label it Table 3. Use the theoretical value for a that you found in problem 9 to predict the theoretical period for each length L. Next to that, write the actual period you found. Compare the results. Are they close?

Table 3

L	Theoretical period	Actual period (Table 2)
10 cm		
(Continue table to 70 cm.)		

11. What reasons can you think of to explain any difference there might be between your results and the theoretical ones?

12. If you were making a pendulum-driven clock and you needed the period of the pendulum to double, what should you do to its length?

ACTIVITY 5: BOXES WITHOUT TOPSES

Question: How does the volume of an open box made by folding up a rectangular sheet depend on the height you choose for the box?

1. Make a table with the headings shown below. Label it Table 1.

Table 1

Side	Length of box	Width of box	Height of box	Volume
1 cm				
2 cm				
(Continue table.)				

2. Take a piece of centimeter graph paper and cut out a 1 cm square from each corner. Fold up the edges to make a shallow box without a lid.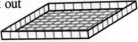

3. Calculate the volume of this box. (Remember, the volume of a rectangular solid = length · width · height.) Record your results in Table 1.

4. Now cut out a 2 cm square from each corner, fold up the paper again, and calculate the volume of the box. Record your results. Continue the process for 3 cm squares, 4 cm squares, and so on, until you run out of graph paper.

5. Let x equal the side length of a cut-out (corner) square, and let $V(x)$ be the volume of the resulting box. Copy and fill out Table 2 for this function, using your values from Table 1.

Table 2

x	$V(x)$
1	
2	
3	

(Continue table.)

6. Graph the function on a piece of graph paper, using your Table 2 data. Then answer the following questions:
   a. What would happen if you "cut out" a square of side 0 from each corner? What would the resulting volume be?
   b. Is there another value of x that produces this volume? Include these data pairs in Tables 1 and 2 and on your graph.
   c. Does it make sense to connect your points with a smooth curve?
   d. What is the domain for this function? Would this change if you had started with a different size sheet of graph paper?
   e. What type of function do you think this is?

7. Write an equation for this function. Be sure to use the form:
   $V(x) = $ _____

8. a. What x-value gives the *maximum* volume for the box? (Determine this to the nearest tenth of a centimeter.)
   b. What x-value(s) gives the *minimum* volume for the box?
   c. What is the range of this function?

ACTIVITY 6: ABSOLUTELY FLIPPED!

Question: What is the probability of any particular sum coming up when two dice are rolled, and what do the graph and the equation of this proba-bility distribution function look like?

1. Make a table with the headings shown below. Label it Table 1. List the *possible* sums, in consecutive order, for your pair of dice in the first column.

Table 1

Sums	Tally marks	Your total	Class total	Rel. frequency (class)
2				
3				
(Continue table.)				

2. Toss the dice 20 times and record each sum with a tally mark in Table 1. Write the total of tally marks for each sum in the next column.

3. Find the total for each sum for the whole class. Write these totals in the next column.

4. Calculate the "relative frequency" for each sum, using the class totals. The relative frequency of each sum is equal to:

$$\frac{\text{How many times that sum came up (whole class)}}{\text{Total number of rolls (whole class)}}$$

For instance, if the class had 68 rolls of 4 out of a total of 200 rolls, the relative frequency for 4 would be 68/200 = .340.
Write these frequencies as decimals, rounded to the nearest thousandth, in the last column.

5. Draw a graph representing the class results. Use "relative frequencies" on the vertical (y) axis and "possible sums" on the horizontal (x) axis. When you've plotted these points, should you connect them? What type of function does this remind you of?

You now have the graph of a function. Its equation may be difficult to obtain, although its shape may remind you of a type of function that you've seen before. To help us find an equation for the function, we're going to relate "theoretical probabilities" to possible sums— in other words, find out what mathematics says "should happen." It ought to resemble the function you just graphed.

6. Draw up and complete Table 2 to show the sums that can result from tossing the two dice. Then answer the questions below the table.

Table 2

Die 2 \ Die 1	1	2	3	4	(Continue if necessary.)
1					
2					
3					
4					
(Continue if necessary.)					

    a. How many possible sums are there?
    b. Which sum is most likely to occur?
    c. What is the probability of getting that sum?
    d. Find the probability of getting each possible sum.

7. Draw a graph representing this theoretical probability function, showing "probabilities" on the vertical axis and "possible sums" on the horizontal axis.
    a. Should you connect the plotted points?
    b. What is the domain of the function?
    c. What type of function do the plotted points suggest?
    d. Name the vertex of the function.
    e. What is the slope of the ray that has its endpoint at the vertex and goes along the right side of the graph?
    f. Write the equation for the function. Be sure to include the correct domain.

8. Complete problems 6 and 7 for another pair of dice.

9. CHALLENGE: Find the equation of the theoretical probability function for tossing two m-sided dice.

Tables

TABLE I. SQUARES AND SQUARE ROOTS, CUBES AND CUBE ROOTS

N	N^2	$\sqrt{N}$	$\sqrt{10N}$	N	N^2	$\sqrt{N}$	$\sqrt{10N}$
1.0	1.00	1.000	3.162	5.5	30.25	2.345	7.416
1.1	1.21	1.049	3.317	5.6	31.36	2.366	7.483
1.2	1.44	1.095	3.464	5.7	32.49	2.387	7.550
1.3	1.69	1.140	3.606	5.8	33.64	2.408	7.616
1.4	1.96	1.183	3.742	5.9	34.81	2.429	7.681
1.5	2.25	1.225	3.873	6.0	36.00	2.449	7.746
1.6	2.56	1.265	4.000	6.1	37.21	2.470	7.810
1.7	2.89	1.304	4.123	6.2	38.44	2.490	7.874
1.8	3.24	1.342	4.243	6.3	39.69	2.510	7.937
1.9	3.61	1.378	4.359	6.4	40.96	2.530	8.000
2.0	4.00	1.414	4.472	6.5	42.25	2.550	8.062
2.1	4.41	1.449	4.583	6.6	43.56	2.569	8.124
2.2	4.84	1.483	4.690	6.7	44.89	2.588	8.185
2.3	5.29	1.517	4.796	6.8	46.24	2.608	8.246
2.4	5.76	1.549	4.899	6.9	47.61	2.627	8.307
2.5	6.25	1.581	5.000	7.0	49.00	2.646	8.367
2.6	6.76	1.612	5.099	7.1	50.41	2.665	8.426
2.7	7.29	1.643	5.196	7.2	51.84	2.683	8.485
2.8	7.84	1.673	5.292	7.3	53.29	2.702	8.544
2.9	8.41	1.703	5.385	7.4	54.76	2.720	8.602
3.0	9.00	1.732	5.477	7.5	56.25	2.739	8.660
3.1	9.61	1.761	5.568	7.6	57.76	2.757	8.718
3.2	10.24	1.789	5.657	7.7	59.29	2.775	8.775
3.3	10.89	1.817	5.745	7.8	60.84	2.793	8.832
3.4	11.56	1.844	5.831	7.9	62.41	2.811	8.888
3.5	12.25	1.871	5.916	8.0	64.00	2.828	8.944
3.6	12.96	1.897	6.000	8.1	65.61	2.846	9.000
3.7	13.69	1.924	6.083	8.2	67.24	2.864	9.055
3.8	14.44	1.949	6.164	8.3	68.89	2.881	9.110
3.9	15.21	1.975	6.245	8.4	70.56	2.898	9.165
4.0	16.00	2.000	6.325	8.5	72.25	2.915	9.220
4.1	16.81	2.025	6.403	8.6	73.96	2.933	9.274
4.2	17.64	2.049	6.481	8.7	75.69	2.950	9.327
4.3	18.49	2.074	6.557	8.8	77.44	2.966	9.381
4.4	19.36	2.098	6.633	8.9	79.21	2.983	9.434
4.5	20.25	2.121	6.708	9.0	81.00	3.000	9.487
4.6	21.16	2.145	6.782	9.1	82.81	3.017	9.539
4.7	22.09	2.168	6.856	9.2	84.64	3.033	9.592
4.8	23.04	2.191	6.928	9.3	86.49	3.050	9.644
4.9	24.01	2.214	7.000	9.4	88.36	3.066	9.695
5.0	25.00	2.236	7.071	9.5	90.25	3.082	9.747
5.1	26.01	2.258	7.141	9.6	92.16	3.098	9.798
5.2	27.04	2.280	7.211	9.7	94.09	3.114	9.849
5.3	28.09	2.302	7.280	9.8	96.04	3.130	9.899
5.4	29.16	2.324	7.348	9.9	98.01	3.146	9.950
5.5	30.25	2.345	7.416	10	100.00	3.162	10.000

TABLE I (CONCLUDED)

N	N^3	$\sqrt[3]{N}$	$\sqrt[3]{10N}$	$\sqrt[3]{100N}$	N	N^3	$\sqrt[3]{N}$	$\sqrt[3]{10N}$	$\sqrt[3]{100N}$
1.0	1.000	1.000	2.154	4.642	5.5	166.375	1.765	3.803	8.193
1.1	1.331	1.032	2.224	4.791	5.6	175.616	1.776	3.826	8.243
1.2	1.728	1.063	2.289	4.932	5.7	185.193	1.786	3.849	8.291
1.3	2.197	1.091	2.351	5.066	5.8	195.112	1.797	3.871	8.340
1.4	2.744	1.119	2.410	5.192	5.9	205.379	1.807	3.893	8.387
1.5	3.375	1.145	2.466	5.313	6.0	216.000	1.817	3.915	8.434
1.6	4.096	1.170	2.520	5.429	6.1	226.981	1.827	3.936	8.481
1.7	4.913	1.193	2.571	5.540	6.2	238.328	1.837	3.958	8.527
1.8	5.832	1.216	2.621	5.646	6.3	250.047	1.847	3.979	8.573
1.9	6.859	1.239	2.668	5.749	6.4	262.144	1.857	4.000	8.618
2.0	8.000	1.260	2.714	5.848	6.5	274.625	1.866	4.021	8.662
2.1	9.261	1.281	2.759	5.944	6.6	287.496	1.876	4.041	8.707
2.2	10.648	1.301	2.802	6.037	6.7	300.763	1.885	4.062	8.750
2.3	12.167	1.320	2.844	6.127	6.8	314.432	1.895	4.082	8.794
2.4	13.824	1.339	2.884	6.214	6.9	328.509	1.904	4.102	8.837
2.5	15.625	1.357	2.924	6.300	7.0	343.000	1.913	4.121	8.879
2.6	17.576	1.375	2.962	6.383	7.1	357.911	1.922	4.141	8.921
2.7	19.683	1.392	3.000	6.463	7.2	373.248	1.931	4.160	8.963
2.8	21.952	1.409	3.037	6.542	7.3	389.017	1.940	4.179	9.004
2.9	24.389	1.426	3.072	6.619	7.4	405.224	1.949	4.198	9.045
3.0	27.000	1.442	3.107	6.694	7.5	421.875	1.957	4.217	9.086
3.1	29.791	1.458	3.141	6.768	7.6	438.976	1.966	4.236	9.126
3.2	32.768	1.474	3.175	6.840	7.7	456.533	1.975	4.254	9.166
3.3	35.937	1.489	3.208	6.910	7.8	474.552	1.983	4.273	9.205
3.4	39.304	1.504	3.240	6.980	7.9	493.039	1.992	4.291	9.244
3.5	42.875	1.518	3.271	7.047	8.0	512.000	2.000	4.309	9.283
3.6	46.656	1.533	3.302	7.114	8.1	531.441	2.008	4.327	9.322
3.7	50.653	1.547	3.332	7.179	8.2	551.368	2.017	4.344	9.360
3.8	54.872	1.560	3.362	7.243	8.3	571.787	2.025	4.362	9.398
3.9	59.319	1.574	3.391	7.306	8.4	592.704	2.033	4.380	9.435
4.0	64.000	1.587	3.420	7.368	8.5	614.125	2.041	4.397	9.473
4.1	68.921	1.601	3.448	7.429	8.6	636.056	2.049	4.414	9.510
4.2	74.088	1.613	3.476	7.489	8.7	658.503	2.057	4.431	9.546
4.3	79.507	1.626	3.503	7.548	8.8	681.472	2.065	4.448	9.583
4.4	85.184	1.639	3.530	7.606	8.9	704.969	2.072	4.465	9.619
4.5	91.125	1.651	3.557	7.663	9.0	729.000	2.080	4.481	9.655
4.6	97.336	1.663	3.583	7.719	9.1	753.571	2.088	4.498	9.691
4.7	103.823	1.675	3.609	7.775	9.2	778.688	2.095	4.514	9.726
4.8	110.592	1.687	3.634	7.830	9.3	804.357	2.103	4.531	9.761
4.9	117.649	1.698	3.659	7.884	9.4	830.584	2.110	4.547	9.796
5.0	125.000	1.710	3.684	7.937	9.5	857.375	2.118	4.563	9.830
5.1	132.651	1.721	3.708	7.990	9.6	884.736	2.125	4.579	9.865
5.2	140.608	1.732	3.733	8.041	9.7	912.673	2.133	4.595	9.899
5.3	148.877	1.744	3.756	8.093	9.8	941.192	2.140	4.610	9.933
5.4	157.464	1.754	3.780	8.143	9.9	970.299	2.147	4.626	9.967
5.5	166.375	1.765	3.803	8.193	10	1000.000	2.154	4.642	10.000

TABLE II. FOUR-PLACE LOGARITHMS OF NUMBERS

n	00	10	20	30	40	50	60	70	80	90
1.0	0000	0043	0086	0128	0170	0212	0253	0294	0334	0374
1.1	0414	0453	0492	0531	0569	0607	0645	0682	0719	0755
1.2	0792	0828	0864	0899	0934	0969	1004	1038	1072	1106
1.3	1139	1173	1206	1239	1271	1303	1335	1367	1399	1430
1.4	1461	1492	1523	1553	1584	1614	1644	1673	1703	1732
1.5	1761	1790	1818	1847	1875	1903	1931	1959	1987	2014
1.6	2041	2068	2095	2122	2148	2175	2201	2227	2253	2279
1.7	2304	2330	2355	2380	2405	2430	2455	2480	2504	2529
1.8	2553	2577	2601	2625	2648	2672	2695	2718	2742	2765
1.9	2788	2810	2833	2856	2878	2900	2923	2945	2967	2989
2.0	3010	3032	3054	3075	3096	3118	3139	3160	3181	3201
2.1	3222	3243	3263	3284	3304	3324	3345	3365	3385	3404
2.2	3424	3444	3464	3483	3502	3522	3541	3560	3579	3598
2.3	3617	3636	3655	3674	3692	3711	3729	3747	3766	3784
2.4	3802	3820	3838	3856	3874	3892	3909	3927	3945	3962
2.5	3979	3997	4014	4031	4048	4065	4082	4099	4116	4133
2.6	4150	4166	4183	4200	4216	4232	4249	4265	4281	4298
2.7	4314	4330	4346	4362	4378	4393	4409	4424	4440	4456
2.8	4472	4487	4502	4518	4533	4548	4564	4579	4594	4609
2.9	4624	4639	4654	4669	4683	4698	4713	4728	4742	4757
3.0	4771	4786	4800	4814	4829	4843	4857	4871	4886	4900
3.1	4914	4928	4942	4955	4969	4983	4997	5011	5024	5038
3.2	5051	5065	5079	5092	5105	5119	5132	5145	5159	5172
3.3	5185	5198	5211	5224	5237	5250	5263	5276	5289	5302
3.4	5315	5328	5340	5353	5366	5378	5391	5403	5416	5428
3.5	5441	5453	5465	5478	5490	5502	5514	5527	5539	5551
3.6	5563	5575	5587	5599	5611	5623	5635	5647	5658	5670
3.7	5682	5694	5705	5717	5729	5740	5752	5763	5775	5786
3.8	5798	5809	5821	5832	5843	5855	5866	5877	5888	5899
3.9	5911	5922	5933	5944	5955	5966	5977	5988	5999	6010
4.0	6021	6031	6042	6053	6064	6075	6085	6096	6107	6117
4.1	6128	6138	6149	6160	6170	6180	6191	6201	6212	6222
4.2	6232	6243	6253	6263	6274	6284	6294	6304	6314	6325
4.3	6335	6345	6355	6365	6375	6385	6395	6405	6415	6425
4.4	6435	6444	6454	6464	6474	6484	6493	6503	6513	6522
4.5	6532	6542	6551	6561	6571	6580	6590	6599	6609	6618
4.6	6628	6637	6646	6656	6665	6675	6684	6693	6702	6712
4.7	6721	6730	6739	6749	6758	6767	6776	6785	6794	6803
4.8	6812	6821	6830	6839	6848	6857	6866	6875	6884	6893
4.9	6902	6911	6920	6928	6937	6946	6955	6964	6972	6981
5.0	6990	6998	7007	7016	7024	7033	7042	7050	7059	7067
5.1	7076	7084	7093	7101	7110	7118	7126	7135	7143	7152
5.2	7160	7168	7177	7185	7193	7202	7210	7218	7226	7235
5.3	7243	7251	7259	7267	7275	7284	7292	7300	7308	7316
5.4	7324	7332	7340	7348	7356	7364	7372	7380	7388	7396

TABLE II (CONCLUDED)

n	00	10	20	30	40	50	60	70	80	90
5.5	7404	7412	7419	7427	7435	7443	7451	7459	7466	7474
5.6	7482	7490	7497	7505	7513	7520	7528	7536	7543	7551
5.7	7559	7566	7574	7582	7589	7597	7604	7612	7619	7627
5.8	7634	7642	7649	7657	7664	7672	7679	7686	7694	7701
5.9	7709	7716	7723	7731	7738	7745	7752	7760	7767	7774
6.0	7782	7789	7796	7803	7810	7818	7825	7832	7839	7846
6.1	7853	7860	7868	7875	7882	7889	7896	7903	7910	7917
6.2	7924	7931	7938	7945	7952	7959	7966	7973	7980	7987
6.3	7993	8000	8007	8014	8021	8028	8035	8041	8048	8055
6.4	8062	8069	8075	8082	8089	8096	8102	8109	8116	8122
6.5	8129	8136	8142	8149	8156	8162	8169	8176	8182	8189
6.6	8195	8202	8209	8215	8222	8228	8235	8241	8248	8254
6.7	8261	8267	8274	8280	8287	8293	8299	8306	8312	8319
6.8	8325	8331	8338	8344	8351	8357	8363	8370	8376	8382
6.9	8388	8395	8401	8407	8414	8420	8426	8432	8439	8445
7.0	8451	8457	8463	8470	8476	8482	8488	8494	8500	8506
7.1	8513	8519	8525	8531	8537	8543	8549	8555	8561	8567
7.2	8573	8579	8585	8591	8597	8603	8609	8615	8621	8627
7.3	8633	8639	8645	8651	8657	8663	8669	8675	8681	8686
7.4	8692	8698	8704	8710	8716	8722	8727	8733	8739	8745
7.5	8751	8756	8762	8768	8774	8779	8785	8791	8797	8802
7.6	8808	8814	8820	8825	8831	8837	8842	8848	8854	8859
7.7	8865	8871	8876	8882	8887	8893	8899	8904	8910	8915
7.8	8921	8927	8932	8938	8943	8949	8954	8960	8965	8971
7.9	8976	8982	8987	8993	8998	9004	9009	9015	9020	9025
8.0	9031	9036	9042	9047	9053	9058	9063	9069	9074	9079
8.1	9085	9090	9096	9101	9106	9112	9117	9122	9128	9133
8.2	9138	9143	9149	9154	9159	9165	9170	9175	9180	9186
8.3	9191	9196	9201	9206	9212	9217	9222	9227	9232	9238
8.4	9243	9248	9253	9258	9263	9269	9274	9279	9284	9289
8.5	9294	9299	9304	9309	9315	9320	9325	9330	9335	9340
8.6	9345	9350	9355	9360	9365	9370	9375	9380	9385	9390
8.7	9395	9400	9405	9410	9415	9420	9425	9430	9435	9440
8.8	9445	9450	9455	9460	9465	9469	9474	9479	9484	9489
8.9	9494	9499	9504	9509	9513	9518	9523	9528	9533	9538
9.0	9542	9547	9552	9557	9562	9566	9571	9576	9581	9586
9.1	9590	9595	9600	9605	9609	9614	9619	9624	9628	9633
9.2	9638	9643	9647	9652	9657	9661	9666	9671	9675	9680
9.3	9685	9689	9694	9699	9703	9708	9713	9717	9722	9727
9.4	9731	9736	9741	9745	9750	9754	9759	9763	9768	9773
9.5	9777	9782	9786	9791	9795	9800	9805	9809	9814	9818
9.6	9823	9827	9832	9836	9841	9845	9850	9854	9859	9863
9.7	9868	9872	9877	9881	9886	9890	9894	9899	9903	9908
9.8	9912	9917	9921	9926	9930	9934	9939	9943	9948	9952
9.9	9956	9961	9965	9969	9974	9978	9983	9987	9991	9996

INSTRUCTIONS FOR TABLE III

TABLE III. TRIGONOMETRIC FUNCTIONS AND DEGREES-TO-RADIANS

Degrees	Radians	sin θ	csc θ	tan θ	cot θ	sec θ	cos θ		
36° 00′	.6283	.5878	1.701	.7265	1.376	1.236	.8090	.9425	54° 00′
10′	.6312	.5901	1.695	.7310	1.368	1.239	.8073	.9396	50′
20′	.6341	.5925	1.688	.7355	1.360	1.241	.8056	.9367	40′
30′	.6370	.5948	1.681	.7400	1.351	1.244	.8039	.9338	30′
40′	.6400	.5972	1.675	.7445	1.343	1.247	.8021	.9308	20′
50′	.6429	.5995	1.668	.7490	1.335	1.249	.8004	.9279	10′
37° 00′	.6458	.6018	1.662	.7536	1.327	1.252	.7986	.9250	53° 00′
10′	.6487	.6041	1.655	.7581	1.319	1.255	.7969	.9221	50′
20′	.6516	.6065	1.649	.7627	1.311	1.258	.7951	.9192	40′
30′	.6545	.6088	1.643	.7673	1.303	1.260	.7934	.9163	30′
40′	.6574	.6111	1.636	.7720	1.295	1.263	.7916	.9134	20′
50′	.6603	.6134	1.630	.7766	1.288	1.266	.7898	.9105	10′
38° 00′	.6632	.6157	1.624	.7813	1.280	1.269	.7880	.9076	52° 00′
10′	.6661	.6180	1.618	.7860	1.272	1.272	.7862	.9047	50′
20′	.6690	.6202	1.612	.7907	1.265	1.275	.7844	.9018	40′
30′	.6720	.6225	1.606	.7954	1.257	1.278	.7826	.8988	30′
40′	.6749	.6248	1.601	.8002	1.250	1.281	.7808	.8959	20′
50′	.6778	.6271	1.595	.8050	1.242	1.284	.7790	.8930	10′
39° 00′	.6807	.6293	1.589	.8098	1.235	1.287	.7771	.8901	51° 00′
10′	.6836	.6316	1.583	.8146	1.228	1.290	.7753	.8872	50′
	.6865	.6338			1.220	1.293	.7735		40′
40			1.423	.9884					
50′	.7825	.7050	1.418	.9942	1.006	1.410	.7092	.7883	10′
45° 00′	.7854	.7071	1.414	1.000	1.000	1.414	.7071	.7854	45° 00′
		cos θ	sec θ	cot θ	tan θ	csc θ	sin θ	Radians	Degrees

Column heading at top: m(θ) over Degrees / Radians. Bottom: m(θ) under Radians / Degrees.

Example 3 → 50′ (36° row area)
Example 5 → 40′/30′
Example 4 → 53° 50′/40′
Example 1 → 37° 40′
Example 2 → 20′ (38° area)

EXAMPLE 1

tan 37°40′ ≈ 0.7720

Find 37°40′ in the column headed $m(\theta)$ on the left. The answer is in the column headed tan θ at the top of the page.

EXAMPLE 2

cos 51°20′ ≈ 0.6248

Find 51°10′ by reading *up* the *righthand* column headed $m(\theta)$. The answer is in the column that is headed cos θ at the *bottom* of the page.

EXAMPLE 3

sec 126° 10′ ≈ −1.695

Find the reference angle, 180° − 126°10′ = 53°50′. Look up 53°50′ in the righthand column and use the column labeled sec θ at the bottom of the page. The "−" sign is needed because sec θ is negative in Quadrant II.

EXAMPLE 4

cos 52°43′ ≈ <u>0.6058</u>

Find cos 52°40′ = 0.6065 and cos 52°50′ = 0.6041. Since 43′ is 0.3 of the way from 40′ to 50′, assume that cos 52°43′ is 0.3 of the way from 0.6065 to 0.6041. The total difference between the numbers, ignoring the decimal point, is −24. (0.3)(−24) is about −7. Adding −7 to 6065 gives 6058, which gives the answer above. This process is called *interpolation*.

EXAMPLE 5

If tan θ = 1.356, then θ ≈ <u>53°36′</u>

Find the two values in the tan θ column, 1.351 and 1.360, which 1.356 is between. The corresponding angles are 53°30′ and 53°40′. Since 1.356 is $\frac{5}{9}$ of the way from 1.351 to 1.360, assume that the number of minutes is $\frac{5}{9}$ of the way from 30′ to 40′. ($\frac{5}{9}$)(10) is about 6. Adding 6′ to 30′ gives 36′, which gives the above answer. This process is also called interpolation.

TABLE III. TRIGONOMETRIC FUNCTIONS AND DEGREES-TO-RADIANS

Degrees	Radians	$\sin \theta$	$\csc \theta$	$\tan \theta$	$\cot \theta$	$\sec \theta$	$\cos \theta$		
0° 00′	.0000	.0000	Undef.	.0000	Undef.	1.000	1.0000	1.5708	90° 00′
10′	.0029	.0029	343.8	.0029	343.8	1.000	1.0000	1.5679	50′
20′	.0058	.0058	171.9	.0058	171.9	1.000	1.0000	1.5650	40′
30′	.0087	.0087	114.6	.0087	114.6	1.000	1.0000	1.5621	30′
40′	.0116	.0116	85.95	.0116	85.94	1.000	.9999	1.5592	20′
50′	.0145	.0145	68.76	.0145	68.75	1.000	.9999	1.5563	10′
1° 00′	.0175	.0175	57.30	.0175	57.29	1.000	.9998	1.5533	89° 00′
10′	.0204	.0204	49.11	.0204	49.10	1.000	.9998	1.5504	50′
20′	.0233	.0233	42.98	.0233	42.96	1.000	.9997	1.5475	40′
30′	.0262	.0262	38.20	.0262	38.19	1.000	.9997	1.5446	30′
40′	.0291	.0291	34.38	.0291	34.37	1.000	.9996	1.5417	20′
50′	.0320	.0320	31.26	.0320	31.24	1.001	.9995	1.5388	10′
2° 00′	.0349	.0349	28.65	.0349	28.64	1.001	.9994	1.5359	88° 00′
10′	.0378	.0378	26.45	.0378	26.43	1.001	.9993	1.5330	50′
20′	.0407	.0407	24.56	.0407	24.54	1.001	.9992	1.5301	40′
30′	.0436	.0436	22.93	.0437	22.90	1.001	.9990	1.5272	30′
40′	.0465	.0465	21.49	.0466	21.47	1.001	.9989	1.5243	20′
50′	.0495	.0494	20.23	.0495	20.21	1.001	.9988	1.5213	10′
3° 00′	.0524	.0523	19.11	.0524	19.08	1.001	.9986	1.5184	87° 00′
10′	.0553	.0552	18.10	.0553	18.07	1.002	.9985	1.5155	50′
20′	.0582	.0581	17.20	.0582	17.17	1.002	.9983	1.5126	40′
30′	.0611	.0610	16.38	.0612	16.35	1.002	.9981	1.5097	30′
40′	.0640	.0640	15.64	.0641	15.60	1.002	.9980	1.5068	20′
50′	.0669	.0669	14.96	.0670	14.92	1.002	.9978	1.5039	10′
4° 00′	.0698	.0698	14.34	.0699	14.30	1.002	.9976	1.5010	86° 00′
10′	.0727	.0727	13.76	.0729	13.73	1.003	.9974	1.4981	50′
20′	.0756	.0756	13.23	.0758	13.20	1.003	.9971	1.4952	40′
30′	.0785	.0785	12.75	.0787	12.71	1.003	.9969	1.4923	30′
40′	.0814	.0814	12.29	.0816	12.25	1.003	.9967	1.4893	20′
50.	.0844	.0843	11.87	.0846	11.83	1.004	.9964	1.4864	10′
5° 00′	.0873	.0872	11.47	.0874	11.43	1.004	.9962	1.4835	85° 00′
10′	.0902	.0901	11.10	.0904	11.06	1.004	.9959	1.4806	50′
20′	.0931	.0929	10.76	.0934	10.71	1.004	.9957	1.4777	40′
30′	.0960	.0958	10.43	.0963	10.39	1.005	.9954	1.4748	30′
40′	.0989	.0987	10.13	.0992	10.08	1.005	.9951	1.4719	20′
50′	.1018	.1016	9.839	.1022	9.788	1.005	.9948	1.4690	10′
6° 00′	.1047	.1045	9.567	.1051	9.514	1.006	.9945	1.4661	84° 00′
10′	.1076	.1074	9.309	.1080	9.255	1.006	.9942	1.4632	50′
20′	.1105	.1103	9.065	.1110	9.010	1.006	.9939	1.4603	40′
30′	.1134	.1132	8.834	.1139	8.777	1.006	.9936	1.4573	30′
40′	.1164	.1161	8.614	.1169	8.556	1.007	.9932	1.4544	20′
50′	.1193	.1190	8.405	.1198	8.345	1.007	.9929	1.4515	10′
7° 00′	.1222	.1219	8.206	.1228	8.144	1.008	.9925	1.4486	83° 00′
10′	.1251	.1248	8.016	.1257	7.953	1.008	.9922	1.4457	50′
20′	.1280	.1276	7.834	.1287	7.770	1.008	.9918	1.4428	40′
30′	.1309	.1305	7.661	.1317	7.596	1.009	.9914	1.4399	30′
40′	.1338	.1334	7.496	.1346	7.429	1.009	.9911	1.4370	20′
50′	.1367	.1363	7.337	.1376	7.269	1.009	.9907	1.4341	10′
8° 00′	.1396	.1392	7.185	.1405	7.115	1.010	.9903	1.4312	82° 00′
10′	.1425	.1421	7.040	.1435	6.968	1.010	.9899	1.4283	50′
20′	.1454	.1449	6.900	.1465	6.827	1.011	.9894	1.4254	40′
30′	.1484	.1478	6.765	.1495	6.691	1.011	.9890	1.4224	30′
40′	.1513	.1507	6.636	.1524	6.561	1.012	.9886	1.4195	20′
50′	.1542	.1536	6.512	.1554	6.435	1.012	.9881	1.4166	10
9° 00′	.1571	.1564	6.392	.1584	6.314	1.012	.9877	1.4137	81° 00′
		$\cos \theta$	$\sec \theta$	$\cot \theta$	$\tan \theta$	$\csc \theta$	$\sin \theta$	Radians	Degrees
								$m(\theta)$	

TABLE III (CONTINUED)

$m(\theta)$ Degrees	$m(\theta)$ Radians	$\sin \theta$	$\csc \theta$	$\tan \theta$	$\cot \theta$	$\sec \theta$	$\cos \theta$		
9° 00′	.1571	.1564	6.392	.1584	6.314	1.012	.9877	1.4137	81° 00′
10′	.1600	.1593	6.277	.1614	6.197	1.013	.9872	1.4108	50′
20′	.1629	.1622	6.166	.1644	6.084	1.013	.9868	1.4079	40′
30′	.1658	.1650	6.059	.1673	5.976	1.014	.9863	1.4050	30′
40′	.1687	.1679	5.955	.1703	5.871	1.014	.9858	1.4021	20′
50′	.1716	.1708	5.855	.1733	5.769	1.015	.9853	1.3992	10′
10° 00′	.1745	.1736	5.759	.1763	5.671	1.015	.9848	1.3963	80° 00′
10′	.1774	.1765	5.665	.1793	5.576	1.016	.9843	1.3934	50′
20′	.1804	.1794	5.575	.1823	5.485	1.016	.9838	1.3904	40′
30′	.1833	.1822	5.487	.1853	5.396	1.017	.9833	1.3875	30′
40′	.1862	.1851	5.403	.1883	5.309	1.018	.9827	1.3846	20′
50′	.1891	.1880	5.320	.1914	5.226	1.018	.9822	1.3817	10′
11° 00′	.1920	.1908	5.241	.1944	5.145	1.019	.9816	1.3788	79° 00′
10′	.1949	.1937	5.164	.1974	5.066	1.019	.9811	1.3759	50′
20′	.1978	.1965	5.089	.2004	4.989	1.020	.9805	1.3730	40′
30′	.2007	.1994	5.016	.2035	4.915	1.020	.9799	1.3701	30′
40′	.2036	.2022	4.945	.2065	4.843	1.021	.9793	1.3672	20′
50′	.2065	.2051	4.876	.2095	4.773	1.022	.9787	1.3643	10′
12° 00′	.2094	.2079	4.810	.2126	4.705	1.022	.9781	1.3614	78° 00′
10′	.2123	.2108	4.745	.2156	4.638	1.023	.9775	1.3584	50′
20′	.2153	.2136	4.682	.2186	4.574	1.024	.9769	1.3555	40′
30′	.2182	.2164	4.620	.2217	4.511	1.024	.9763	1.3526	30′
40′	.2211	.2193	4.560	.2247	4.449	1.025	.9757	1.3497	20′
50′	.2240	.2221	4.502	.2278	4.390	1.026	.9750	1.3468	10′
13° 00′	.2269	.2250	4.445	.2309	4.331	1.026	.9744	1.3439	77° 00′
10′	.2298	.2278	4.390	.2339	4.275	1.027	.9737	1.3410	50′
20′	.2327	.2306	4.336	.2370	4.219	1.028	.9730	1.3381	40′
30′	.2356	.2334	4.284	.2401	4.165	1.028	.9724	1.3352	30′
40′	.2385	.2363	4.232	.2432	4.113	1.029	.9717	1.3323	20′
50′	.2414	.2391	4.182	.2462	4.061	1.030	.9710	1.3294	10′
14° 00′	.2443	.2419	4.134	.2493	4.011	1.031	.9703	1.3265	76° 00′
10′	.2473	.2447	4.086	.2524	3.962	1.031	.9696	1.3235	50′
20′	.2502	.2476	4.039	.2555	3.914	1.032	.9689	1.3206	40′
30′	.2531	.2504	3.994	.2586	3.867	1.033	.9681	1.3177	30′
40′	.2560	.2532	3.950	.2617	3.821	1.034	.9674	1.3148	20′
50′	.2589	.2560	3.906	.2648	3.776	1.034	.9667	1.3119	10′
15° 00′	.2618	.2588	3.864	.2679	3.732	1.035	.9659	1.3090	75° 00′
10′	.2647	.2616	3.822	.2711	3.689	1.036	.9652	1.3061	50′
20′	.2676	.2644	3.782	.2742	3.647	1.037	.9644	1.3032	40′
30′	.2705	.2672	3.742	.2773	3.606	1.038	.9636	1.3003	30′
40′	.2734	.2700	3.703	.2805	3.566	1.039	.9628	1.2974	20′
50′	.2763	.2728	3.665	.2836	3.526	1.039	.9621	1.2945	10′
16° 00′	.2793	.2756	3.628	.2867	3.487	1.040	.9613	1.2915	74° 00′
10′	.2822	.2784	3.592	.2899	3.450	1.041	.9605	1.2886	50′
20′	.2851	.2812	3.556	.2931	3.412	1.042	.9596	1.2857	40′
30′	.2880	.2840	3.521	.2962	3.376	1.043	.9588	1.2828	30′
40′	.2909	.2868	3.487	.2994	3.340	1.044	.9580	1.2799	20′
50′	.2938	.2896	3.453	.3026	3.305	1.045	.9572	1.2770	10′
17° 00′	.2967	.2924	3.420	.3057	3.271	1.046	.9563	1.2741	73° 00′
10′	.2996	.2952	3.388	.3089	3.237	1.047	.9555	1.2712	50′
20′	.3025	.2979	3.356	.3121	3.204	1.048	.9546	1.2683	40′
30′	.3054	.3007	3.326	.3153	3.172	1.049	.9537	1.2654	30′
40′	.3083	.3035	3.295	.3185	3.140	1.049	.9528	1.2625	20′
50′	.3113	.3062	3.265	.3217	3.108	1.050	.9520	1.2595	10′
18° 00′	.3142	.3090	3.236	.3249	3.078	1.051	.9511	1.2566	72° 00′
		$\cos \theta$	$\sec \theta$	$\cot \theta$	$\tan \theta$	$\csc \theta$	$\sin \theta$	Radians	Degrees
								$m(\theta)$	

TABLE III (CONTINUED)

Degrees	Radians	sin θ	csc θ	tan θ	cot θ	sec θ	cos θ		
18° 00′	.3142	.3090	3.236	.3249	3.078	1.051	.9511	1.2566	72° 00′
10′	.3171	.3118	3.207	.3281	3.047	1.052	.9502	1.2537	50′
20′	.3200	.3145	3.179	.3314	3.018	1.053	.9492	1.2508	40′
30′	.3229	.3173	3.152	.3346	2.989	1.054	.9483	1.2479	30′
40′	.3258	.3201	3.124	.3378	2.960	1.056	.9474	1.2450	20′
50′	.3287	.3228	3.098	.3411	2.932	1.057	.9465	1.2421	10′
19° 00′	.3316	.3256	3.072	.3443	2.904	1.058	.9455	1.2392	71° 00′
10′	.3345	.3283	3.046	.3476	2.877	1.059	.9446	1.2363	50′
20′	.3374	.3311	3.021	.3508	2.850	1.060	.9436	1.2334	40′
30′	.3403	.3338	2.996	.3541	2.824	1.061	.9426	1.2305	30′
40′	.3432	.3365	2.971	.3574	2.798	1.062	.9417	1.2275	20′
50′	.3462	.3393	2.947	.3607	2.773	1.063	.9407	1.2246	10′
20° 00′	.3491	.3420	2.924	.3640	2.747	1.064	.9397	1.2217	70° 00′
10′	.3520	.3448	2.901	.3673	2.723	1.065	.9387	1.2188	50′
20′	.3549	.3475	2.878	.3706	2.699	1.066	.9377	1.2159	40′
30′	.3578	.3502	2.855	.3739	2.675	1.068	.9367	1.2130	30′
40′	.3607	.3529	2.833	.3772	2.651	1.069	.9356	1.2101	20′
50′	.3636	.3557	2.812	.3805	2.628	1.070	.9346	1.2072	10′
21° 00′	.3665	.3584	2.790	.3839	2.605	1.071	.9336	1.2043	69° 00′
10′	.3694	.3611	2.769	.3872	2.583	1.072	.9325	1.2014	50′
20′	.3723	.3638	2.749	.3906	2.560	1.074	.9315	1.1985	40′
30′	.3752	.3665	2.729	.3939	2.539	1.075	.9304	1.1956	30′
40′	.3782	.3692	2.709	.3973	2.517	1.076	.9293	1.1926	20′
50′	.3811	.3719	2.689	.4006	2.496	1.077	.9283	1.1897	10′
22° 00′	.3840	.3746	2.669	.4040	2.475	1.079	.9272	1.1868	68° 00′
10′	.3869	.3773	2.650	.4074	2.455	1.080	.9261	1.1839	50′
20′	.3898	.3800	2.632	.4108	2.434	1.081	.9250	1.1810	40′
30′	.3927	.3827	2.613	.4142	2.414	1.082	.9239	1.1781	30′
40′	.3956	.3854	2.595	.4176	2.394	1.084	.9228	1.1752	20′
50′	.3985	.3881	2.577	.4210	2.375	1.085	.9216	1.1723	10′
23° 00′	.4014	.3907	2.559	.4245	2.356	1.086	.9205	1.1694	67° 00′
10′	.4043	.3934	2.542	.4279	2.337	1.088	.9194	1.1665	50′
20′	.4072	.3961	2.525	.4314	2.318	1.089	.9182	1.1636	40′
30′	.4102	.3987	2.508	.4348	2.300	1.090	.9171	1.1606	30′
40′	.4131	.4014	2.491	.4383	2.282	1.092	.9159	1.1577	20′
50′	.4160	.4041	2.475	.4417	2.264	1.093	.9147	1.1548	10′
24° 00′	.4189	.4067	2.459	.4452	2.246	1.095	.9135	1.1519	66° 00′
10′	.4218	.4094	2.443	.4487	2.229	1.096	.9124	1.1490	50′
20′	.4247	.4120	2.427	.4522	2.211	1.097	.9112	1.1461	40′
30′	.4276	.4147	2.411	.4557	2.194	1.099	.9100	1.1432	30′
40′	.4305	.4173	2.396	.4592	2.177	1.100	.9088	1.1403	20′
50′	.4334	.4200	2.381	.4628	2.161	1.102	.9075	1.1374	10′
25° 00′	.4363	.4226	2.366	.4663	2.145	1.103	.9063	1.1345	65° 00′
10′	.4392	.4253	2.352	.4699	2.128	1.105	.9051	1.1316	50′
20′	.4422	.4279	2.337	.4734	2.112	1.106	.9038	1.1286	40′
30′	.4451	.4305	2.323	.4770	2.097	1.108	.9026	1.1257	30′
40′	.4480	.4331	2.309	.4806	2.081	1.109	.9013	1.1228	20′
50′	.4509	.4358	2.295	.4841	2.066	1.111	.9001	1.1199	10′
26° 00′	.4538	.4384	2.281	.4877	2.050	1.113	.8988	1.1170	64° 00′
10′	.4567	.4410	2.268	.4913	2.035	1.114	.8975	1.1141	50′
20′	.4596	.4436	2.254	.4950	2.020	1.116	.8962	1.1112	40′
30′	.4625	.4462	2.241	.4986	2.006	1.117	.8949	1.1083	30′
40′	.4654	.4488	2.228	.5022	1.991	1.119	.8936	1.1054	20′
50′	.4683	.4514	2.215	.5059	1.977	1.121	.8923	1.1025	10′
27° 00′	.4712	.4540	2.203	.5095	1.963	1.122	.8910	1.0996	63° 00′
		cos θ	sec θ	cot θ	tan θ	csc θ	sin θ	Radians	Degrees
								m(θ)	

TABLE III (CONTINUED)

$m(\theta)$ Degrees	Radians	$\sin \theta$	$\csc \theta$	$\tan \theta$	$\cot \theta$	$\sec \theta$	$\cos \theta$		
27° 00'	.4712	.4540	2.203	.5095	1.963	1.122	.8910	1.0996	63° 00'
10'	.4741	.4566	2.190	.5132	1.949	1.124	.8897	1.0966	50'
20'	.4771	.4592	2.178	.5169	1.935	1.126	.8884	1.0937	40'
30'	.4800	.4617	2.166	.5206	1.921	1.127	.8870	1.0908	30'
40'	.4829	.4643	2.154	.5243	1.907	1.129	.8857	1.0879	20'
50'	.4858	.4669	2.142	.5280	1.894	1.131	.8843	1.0850	10'
28° 00'	.4887	.4695	2.130	.5317	1.881	1.133	.8829	1.0821	62° 00'
10'	.4916	.4720	2.118	.5354	1.868	1.134	.8816	1.0792	50'
20'	.4945	.4746	2.107	.5392	1.855	1.136	.8802	1.0763	40'
30'	.4974	.4772	2.096	.5430	1.842	1.138	.8788	1.0734	30'
40'	.5003	.4797	2.085	.5467	1.829	1.140	.8774	1.0705	20'
50'	.5032	.4823	2.074	.5505	1.816	1.142	.8760	1.0676	10'
29° 00'	.5061	.4848	2.063	.5543	1.804	1.143	.8746	1.0647	61° 00'
10'	.5091	.4874	2.052	.5581	1.792	1.145	.8732	1.0617	50'
20'	.5120	.4899	2.041	.5619	1.780	1.147	.8718	1.0588	40'
30'	.5149	.4924	2.031	.5658	1.767	1.149	.8704	1.0559	30'
40'	.5178	.4950	2.020	.5696	1.756	1.151	.8689	1.0530	20'
50'	.5207	.4975	2.010	.5735	1.744	1.153	.8675	1.0501	10'
30° 00'	.5236	.5000	2.000	.5774	1.732	1.155	.8660	1.0472	60° 00'
10'	.5265	.5025	1.990	.5812	1.720	1.157	.8646	1.0443	50'
20'	.5294	.5050	1.980	.5851	1.709	1.159	.8631	1.0414	40'
30'	.5323	.5075	1.970	.5890	1.698	1.161	.8616	1.0385	30'
40'	.5352	.5100	1.961	.5930	1.686	1.163	.8601	1.0356	20'
50'	.5381	.5125	1.951	.5969	1.675	1.165	.8587	1.0327	10'
31° 00'	.5411	.5150	1.942	.6009	1.664	1.167	.8572	1.0297	59° 00'
10'	.5440	.5175	1.932	.6048	1.653	1.169	.8557	1.0268	50'
20'	.5469	.5200	1.923	.6038	1.643	1.171	.8542	1.0239	40'
30'	.5498	.5225	1.914	.6128	1.632	1.173	.8526	1.0210	30'
40'	.5527	.5250	1.905	.6168	1.621	1.175	.8511	1.0181	20'
50'	.5556	.5275	1.896	.6208	1.611	1.177	.8496	1.0152	10'
32° 00'	.5585	.5299	1.887	.6249	1.600	1.179	.8480	1.0123	58° 00'
10'	.5614	.5324	1.878	.6289	1.590	1.181	.8465	1.0094	50'
20'	.5643	.5348	1.870	.6330	1.580	1.184	.8450	1.0065	40'
30'	.5672	.5373	1.861	.6371	1.570	1.186	.8434	1.0036	30'
40'	.5701	.5398	1.853	.6412	1.560	1.188	.8418	1.0007	20'
50'	.5730	.5422	1.844	.6453	1.550	1.190	.8403	.9977	10'
33° 00'	.5760	.5446	1.836	.6494	1.540	1.192	.8387	.9948	57° 00'
10'	.5789	.5471	1.828	.6536	1.530	1.195	.8371	.9919	50'
20'	.5818	.5495	1.820	.6577	1.520	1.197	.8355	.9890	40'
30'	.5847	.5519	1.812	.6619	1.511	1.199	.8339	.9861	30'
40'	.5876	.5544	1.804	.6661	1.501	1.202	.8323	.9832	20'
50'	.5905	.5568	1.796	.6703	1.492	1.204	.8307	.9803	10'
34° 00'	.5934	.5592	1.788	.6745	1.483	1.206	.8290	.9774	56° 00'
10'	.5963	.5616	1.781	.6787	1.473	1.209	.8274	.9745	50'
20'	.5992	.5640	1.773	.6830	1.464	1.211	.8258	.9716	40'
30'	.6021	.5664	1.766	.6873	1.455	1.213	.8241	.9687	30'
40'	.6050	.5688	1.758	.6916	1.446	1.216	.8225	.9657	20'
50'	.6080	.5712	1.751	.6959	1.437	1.218	.8208	.9628	10'
35° 00'	.6109	.5736	1.743	.7002	1.428	1.221	.8192	.9599	55° 00'
10'	.6138	.5760	1.736	.7046	1.419	1.223	.8175	.9570	50'
20'	.6167	.5783	1.729	.7089	1.411	1.226	.8158	.9541	40'
30'	.6196	.5807	1.722	.7133	1.402	1.228	.8141	.9512	30'
40'	.6225	.5831	1.715	.7177	1.393	1.231	.8124	.9483	20'
50'	.6254	.5854	1.708	.7221	1.385	1.233	.8107	.9454	10'
36° 00'	.6283	.5878	1.701	.7265	1.376	1.236	.8090	.9425	54° 00'
		$\cos \theta$	$\sec \theta$	$\cot \theta$	$\tan \theta$	$\csc \theta$	$\sin \theta$	Radians	Degrees
								$m(\theta)$	

TABLE III (CONCLUDED)

m(θ) Degrees	m(θ) Radians	sin θ	csc θ	tan θ	cot θ	sec θ	cos θ		
36° 00′	.6283	.5878	1.701	.7265	1.376	1.236	.8090	.9425	54° 00′
10′	.6312	.5901	1.695	.7310	1.368	1.239	.8073	.9396	50′
20′	.6341	.5925	1.688	.7355	1.360	1.241	.8056	.9367	40′
30′	.6370	.5948	1.681	.7400	1.351	1.244	.8039	.9338	30′
40′	.6400	.5972	1.675	.7445	1.343	1.247	.8021	.9308	20′
50′	.6429	.5995	1.668	.7490	1.335	1.249	.8004	.9279	10′
37° 00′	.6458	.6018	1.662	.7536	1.327	1.252	.7986	.9250	53° 00′
10′	.6487	.6041	1.655	.7581	1.319	1.255	.7969	.9221	50′
20′	.6516	.6065	1.649	.7627	1.311	1.258	.7951	.9192	40′
30′	.6545	.6088	1.643	.7673	1.303	1.260	.7934	.9163	30′
40′	.6574	.6111	1.636	.7720	1.295	1.263	.7916	.9134	20′
50′	.6603	.6134	1.630	.7766	1.288	1.266	.7898	.9105	10′
38° 00′	.6632	.6157	1.624	.7813	1.280	1.269	.7880	.9076	52° 00′
10′	.6661	.6180	1.618	.7860	1.272	1.272	.7862	.9047	50′
20′	.6690	.6202	1.612	.7907	1.265	1.275	.7844	.9018	40′
30′	.6720	.6225	1.606	.7954	1.257	1.278	.7826	.8988	30′
40′	.6749	.6248	1.601	.8002	1.250	1.281	.7808	.8959	20′
50′	.6778	.6271	1.595	.8050	1.242	1.284	.7790	.8930	10′
39° 00′	.6807	.6293	1.589	.8098	1.235	1.287	.7771	.8901	51° 00′
10′	.6836	.6316	1.583	.8146	1.228	1.290	.7753	.8872	50′
20′	.6865	.6338	1.578	.8195	1.220	1.293	.7735	.8843	40′
30′	.6894	.6361	1.572	.8243	1.213	1.296	.7716	.8814	30′
40′	.6923	.6383	1.567	.8292	1.206	1.299	.7698	.8785	20′
50′	.6952	.6406	1.561	.8342	1.199	1.302	.7679	.8756	10′
40° 00′	.6981	.6428	1.556	.8391	1.192	1.305	.7660	.8727	50° 00′
10′	.7010	.6450	1.550	.8441	1.185	1.309	.7642	.8698	50′
20′	.7039	.6472	1.545	.8491	1.178	1.312	.7623	.8668	40′
30′	.7069	.6494	1.540	.8541	1.171	1.315	.7604	.8639	30′
40′	.7098	.6517	1.535	.8591	1.164	1.318	.7585	.8610	20′
50′	.7127	.6539	1.529	.8642	1.157	1.322	.7566	.8581	10′
41° 00′	.7156	.6561	1.524	.8693	1.150	1.325	.7547	.8552	49° 00′
10′	.7185	.6583	1.519	.8744	1.144	1.328	.7528	.8523	50′
20′	.7214	.6604	1.514	.8796	1.137	1.332	.7509	.8494	40′
30′	.7243	.6626	1.509	.8847	1.130	1.335	.7490	.8465	30′
40′	.7272	.6648	1.504	.8899	1.124	1.339	.7470	.8436	20′
50′	.7301	.6670	1.499	.8952	1.117	1.342	.7451	.8407	10′
42° 00′	.7330	.6691	1.494	.9004	1.111	1.346	.7431	.8378	48° 00′
10′	.7359	.6713	1.490	.9057	1.104	1.349	.7412	.8348	50′
20′	.7389	.6734	1.485	.9110	1.098	1.353	.7392	.8319	40′
30′	.7418	.6756	1.480	.9163	1.091	1.356	.7373	.8290	30′
40′	.7447	.6777	1.476	.9217	1.085	1.360	.7353	.8261	20′
50′	.7476	.6799	1.471	.9271	1.079	1.364	.7333	.8232	10′
43° 00′	.7505	.6820	1.466	.9325	1.072	1.367	.7314	.8203	47° 00′
10′	.7534	.6841	1.462	.9380	1.066	1.371	.7294	.8174	50′
20′	.7563	.6862	1.457	.9435	1.060	1.375	.7274	.8145	40′
30′	.7592	.6884	1.453	.9490	1.054	1.379	.7254	.8116	30′
40′	.7621	.6905	1.448	.9545	1.048	1.382	.7234	.8087	20′
50′	.7650	.6926	1.444	.9601	1.042	1.386	.7214	.8058	10′
44° 00′	.7679	.6947	1.440	.9657	1.036	1.390	.7193	.8029	46° 00′
10′	.7709	.6967	1.435	.9713	1.030	1.394	.7173	.7999	50′
20′	.7738	.6988	1.431	.9770	1.024	1.398	.7153	.7970	40′
30′	.7767	.7009	1.427	.9827	1.018	1.402	.7133	.7941	30′
40′	.7796	.7030	1.423	.9884	1.012	1.406	.7112	.7912	20′
50′	.7825	.7050	1.418	.9942	1.006	1.410	.7092	.7883	10′
45° 00′	.7854	.7071	1.414	1.000	1.000	1.414	.7071	.7854	45° 00′
		cos θ	sec θ	cot θ	tan θ	csc θ	sin θ	Radians m(θ)	Degrees m(θ)

TABLE IV. CIRCULAR FUNCTIONS AND RADIANS-TO-DEGREES

Real Number x or $m^R(\theta)$	$m^o(\theta)$	sin x or sin θ	csc x or csc θ	tan x or tan θ	cot x or cot θ	sec x or sec θ	cos x or cos θ
0	0°	0	Undef.	0	Undef.	1	1
0.01	0° 34′	0.0100	100.0	0.0100	100.0	1.000	1.000
.02	1° 09′	.0200	50.00	.0200	49.99	1.000	0.9998
.03	1° 43′	.0300	33.34	.0300	33.32	1.000	0.9996
.04	2° 18′	.0400	25.01	.0400	24.99	1.001	0.9992
0.05	2° 52′	0.0500	20.01	0.0500	19.98	1.001	0.9988
.06	3° 26′	.0600	16.68	.0601	16.65	1.002	.9982
.07	4° 01′	.0699	14.30	.0701	14.26	1.002	.9976
.08	4° 35′	.0799	12.51	.0802	12.47	1.003	.9968
.09	5° 09′	.0899	11.13	.0902	11.08	1.004	.9960
0.10	5° 44′	0.0998	10.02	0.1003	9.967	1.005	0.9950
.11	6° 18′	.1098	9.109	.1104	9.054	1.006	.9940
.12	6° 53′	.1197	8.353	.1206	8.293	1.007	.9928
.13	7° 27′	.1296	7.714	.1307	7.649	1.009	.9916
.14	8° 01′	.1395	7.166	.1409	7.096	1.010	.9902
0.15	8° 36′	0.1494	6.692	0.1511	6.617	1.011	0.9888
.16	9° 10′	.1593	6.277	.1614	6.197	1.013	.9872
.17	9° 44′	.1692	5.911	.1717	5.826	1.015	.9856
.18	10° 19′	.1790	5.586	.1820	5.495	1.016	.9838
.19	10° 53′	.1889	5.295	.1923	5.200	1.018	.9820
0.20	11° 28′	0.1987	5.033	0.2027	4.933	1.020	0.9801
.21	12° 02′	.2085	4.797	.2131	4.692	1.022	.9780
.22	12° 36′	.2182	4.582	.2236	4.472	1.025	.9759
.23	13° 11′	.2280	4.386	.2341	4.271	1.027	.9737
.24	13° 45′	.2377	4.207	.2447	4.086	1.030	.9713
0.25	14° 19′	0.2474	4.042	0.2553	3.916	1.032	0.9689
.26	14° 54′	.2571	3.890	.2660	3.759	1.035	.9664
.27	15° 28′	.2667	3.749	.2768	3.613	1.038	.9638
.28	16° 03′	.2764	3.619	.2876	3.478	1.041	.9611
.29	16° 37′	.2860	3.497	.2984	3.351	1.044	.9582
0.30	17° 11′	0.2955	3.384	0.3093	3.233	1.047	0.9553
.31	17° 46′	.3051	3.278	.3203	3.122	1.050	.9523
.32	18° 20′	.3146	3.179	.3314	3.018	1.053	.9492
.33	18° 54′	.3240	3.086	.3425	2.919	1.057	.9460
.34	19° 29′	.3335	2.999	.3537	2.827	1.061	.9428
0.35	20° 03′	0.3429	2.916	0.3650	2.740	1.065	0.9394
.36	20° 38′	.3523	2.839	.3764	2.657	1.068	.9359
.37	21° 12′	.3616	2.765	.3879	2.578	1.073	.9323
.38	21° 46′	.3709	2.696	.3994	2.504	1.077	.9287
.39	22° 21′	.3802	2.630	.4111	2.433	1.081	.9249
0.40	22° 55′	0.3894	2.568	0.4228	2.365	1.086	0.9211
.41	23° 29′	.3986	2.509	.4346	2.301	1.090	.9171
.42	24° 04′	.4078	2.452	.4466	2.239	1.095	.9131
.43	24° 38′	.4169	2.399	.4586	2.180	1.100	.9090
.44	25° 13′	.4259	2.348	.4708	2.124	1.105	.9048
0.45	25° 47′	0.4350	2.299	0.4831	2.070	1.111	0.9004
.46	26° 21′	.4439	2.253	.4954	2.018	1.116	.8961
.47	26° 56′	.4529	2.208	.5080	1.969	1.122	.8916
.48	27° 30′	.4618	2.166	.5206	1.921	1.127	.8870
.49	28° 04′	.4706	2.125	.5334	1.875	1.133	.8823

TABLE IV (CONTINUED)

Real Number or $m^R(\theta)$	$m^o(\theta)$	sin x or sin θ	csc x or csc θ	tan x or tan θ	cot x or cot θ	sec x or sec θ	cos x or cos θ
0.50	28°39′	0.4794	2.086	0.5463	1.830	1.139	0.8776
.51	29°13′	.4882	2.048	.5594	1.788	1.146	.8727
.52	29°48′	.4969	2.013	.5726	1.747	1.152	.8678
.53	30°22′	.5055	1.978	.5859	1.707	1.159	.8628
.54	30°56′	.5141	1.945	.5994	1.668	1.166	.8577
0.55	31°31′	0.5227	1.913	0.6131	1.631	1.173	0.8525
.56	32°05′	.5312	1.883	.6269	1.595	1.180	.8473
.57	32°40′	.5396	1.853	.6410	1.560	1.188	.8419
.58	33°14′	.5480	1.825	.6552	1.526	1.196	.8365
.59	33°48′	.5564	1.797	.6696	1.494	1.203	.8309
0.60	34°23′	0.5646	1.771	0.6841	1.462	1.212	0.8253
.61	34°57′	.5729	1.746	.6989	1.431	1.220	.8196
.62	35°31′	.5810	1.721	.7139	1.401	1.229	.8139
.63	36°06′	.5891	1.697	.7291	1.372	1.238	.8080
.64	36°40′	.5972	1.674	.7445	1.343	1.247	.8021
0.65	37°15′	0.6052	1.652	0.7602	1.315	1.256	0.7961
.66	37°49′	.6131	1.631	.7761	1.288	1.266	.7900
.67	38°23′	.6210	1.610	.7923	1.262	1.276	.7838
.68	38°58′	.6288	1.590	.8087	1.237	1.286	.7776
.69	39°32′	.6365	1.571	.8253	1.212	1.297	.7712
0.70	40°06′	0.6442	1.552	0.8423	1.187	1.307	0.7648
.71	40°41′	.6518	1.534	.8595	1.163	1.319	.7584
.72	41°15′	.6594	1.517	.8771	1.140	1.330	.7518
.73	41°50′	.6669	1.500	.8949	1.117	1.342	.7452
.74	42°24′	.6743	1.483	.9131	1.095	1.354	.7385
0.75	42°58′	0.6816	1.467	0.9316	1.073	1.367	0.7317
.76	43°33′	.6889	1.452	.9505	1.052	1.380	.7248
.77	44°07′	.6961	1.437	.9697	1.031	1.393	.7179
.78	44°41′	.7033	1.422	.9893	1.011	1.407	.7109
.79	45°16′	.7104	1.408	1.009	.9908	1.421	.7038
0.80	45°50′	0.7174	1.394	1.030	0.9712	1.435	0.6967
.81	46°25′	.7243	1.381	1.050	.9520	1.450	.6895
.82	46°59′	.7311	1.368	1.072	.9331	1.466	.6822
.83	47°33′	.7379	1.355	1.093	.9146	1.482	.6749
.84	48°08′	.7446	1.343	1.116	.8964	1.498	.6675
0.85	48°42′	0.7513	1.331	1.138	0.8785	1.515	0.6600
.86	49°16′	.7578	1.320	1.162	.8609	1.533	.6524
.87	49°51′	.7643	1.308	1.185	.8437	1.551	.6448
.88	50°25′	.7707	1.297	1.210	.8267	1.569	.6372
.89	51°00′	.7771	1.287	1.235	.8100	1.589	.6294
0.90	51°34′	0.7833	1.277	1.260	0.7936	1.609	0.6216
.91	52°08′	.7895	1.267	1.286	.7774	1.629	.6137
.92	52°43′	.7956	1.257	1.313	.7615	1.651	.6058
.93	53°17′	.8016	1.247	1.341	.7458	1.673	.5978
.94	53°51′	.8076	1.238	1.369	.7303	1.696	.5898
0.95	54°26′	0.8134	1.229	1.398	0.7151	1.719	0.5817
.96	55°00′	.8192	1.221	1.428	.7001	1.744	.5735
.97	55°35′	.8249	1.212	1.459	.6853	1.769	.5653
.98	56°09′	.8305	1.204	1.491	.6707	1.795	.5570
.99	56°43′	.8360	1.196	1.524	.6563	1.823	.5487
1.00	57°18′	0.8415	1.188	1.557	0.6421	1.851	0.5403
1.01	57°52′	.8468	1.181	1.592	.6281	1.880	.5319
1.02	58°27′	.8521	1.174	1.628	.6142	1.911	.5234
1.03	59°01′	.8573	1.166	1.665	.6005	1.942	.5148
1.04	59°35′	.8624	1.160	1.704	.5870	1.975	.5062

TABLE IV (CONCLUDED)

Real Number x or $m^R(\theta)$	$m^o(\theta)$	sin x or sin θ	csc x or csc θ	tan x or tan θ	cot x or cot θ	sec x or sec θ	cos x or cos θ
1.05	60°10′	0.8674	1.153	1.743	0.5736	2.010	0.4976
1.06	60°44′	.8724	1.146	1.784	.5604	2.046	.4889
1.07	61°18′	.8772	1.140	1.827	.5473	2.083	.4801
1.08	61°53′	.8820	1.134	1.871	.5344	2.122	.4713
1.09	62°27′	.8866	1.128	1.917	.5216	2.162	.4625
1.10	63°02′	0.8912	1.122	1.965	0.5090	2.205	0.4536
1.11	63°36′	.8957	1.116	2.014	.4964	2.249	.4447
1.12	64°10′	.9001	1.111	2.066	.4840	2.295	.4357
1.13	64°45′	.9044	1.106	2.120	.4718	2.344	.4267
1.14	65°19′	.9086	1.101	2.176	.4596	2.395	.4176
1.15	65°53′	0.9128	1.096	2.234	0.4475	2.448	0.4085
1.16	66°28′	.9168	1.091	2.296	.4356	2.504	.3993
1.17	67°02′	.9208	1.086	2.360	.4237	2.563	.3902
1.18	67°37′	.9246	1.082	2.427	.4120	2.625	.3809
1.19	68°11′	.9284	1.077	2.498	.4003	2.691	.3717
1.20	68°45′	0.9320	1.073	2.572	0.3888	2.760	0.3624
1.21	69°20′	.9356	1.069	2.650	.3773	2.833	.3530
1.22	69°54′	.9391	1.065	2.733	.3659	2.910	.3436
1.23	70°28′	.9425	1.061	2.820	.3546	2.992	.3342
1.24	71°03′	.9458	1.057	2.912	.3434	3.079	.3248
1.25	71°37′	0.9490	1.054	3.010	0.3323	3.171	0.3153
1.26	72°12′	.9521	1.050	3.113	.3212	3.270	.3058
1.27	72°46′	.9551	1.047	3.224	.3102	3.375	.2963
1.28	73°20′	.9580	1.044	3.341	.2993	3.488	.2867
1.29	73°55′	.9608	1.041	3.467	.2884	3.609	.2771
1.30	74°29′	0.9636	1.038	3.602	0.2776	3.738	0.2675
1.31	75°03′	.9662	1.035	3.747	.2669	3.878	.2579
1.32	75°38′	.9687	1.032	3.903	.2562	4.029	.2482
1.33	76°12′	.9711	1.030	4.072	.2456	4.193	.2385
1.34	76°47′	.9735	1.027	4.256	.2350	4.372	.2288
1.35	77°21′	0.9757	1.025	4.455	0.2245	4.566	0.2190
1.36	77°55′	.9779	1.023	4.673	.2140	4.779	.2092
1.37	78°30′	.9799	1.021	4.913	.2035	5.014	.1994
1.38	79°04′	.9819	1.018	5.177	.1931	5.273	.1896
1.39	79°38′	.9837	1.017	5.471	.1828	5.561	.1798
1.40	80°13′	0.9854	1.015	5.798	0.1725	5.883	0.1700
1.41	80°47′	.9871	1.013	6.165	.1622	6.246	.1601
1.42	81°22′	.9887	1.011	6.581	.1519	6.657	.1502
1.43	81°56′	.9901	1.010	7.055	.1417	7.126	.1403
1.44	82°30′	.9915	1.009	7.602	.1315	7.667	.1304
1.45	83°05′	0.9927	1.007	8.238	0.1214	8.299	0.1205
1.46	83°39′	.9939	1.006	8.989	.1113	9.044	.1106
1.47	84°13′	.9949	1.005	9.887	.1011	9.938	.1006
1.48	84°48′	.9959	1.004	10.98	.0910	11.03	.0907
1.49	85°22′	.9967	1.003	12.35	.0810	12.39	.0807
1.50	85°57′	0.9975	1.003	14.10	0.0709	14.14	0.0707
1.51	86°31′	.9982	1.002	16.43	.0609	16.46	.0608
1.52	87°05′	.9987	1.001	19.67	.0508	19.70	.0508
1.53	87°40′	.9992	1.001	24.50	.0408	24.52	.0408
1.54	88°14′	.9995	1.000	32.46	.0308	32.48	.0308
1.55	88°49′	0.9998	1.000	48.08	0.0208	48.09	0.0208
1.56	89°23′	.9999	1.000	92.62	.0108	92.63	.0108
1.57	89°57′	1.000	1.000	1256	.0008	1256	.0008
$\frac{\pi}{2}$	90°	1	1	Undef.	0	Undef.	0

Glossary

Algebraic expression: An expression containing no operations on variables other than $+$, $-$, $\times$, $\div$, or $\sqrt{}$.

Amplitude: The distance from the axis of a periodic function to a high or low point.

Antilogarithm: The argument of a logarithm.

Argument: The variable or expression on which a function operates. For $\log (3x + 5)$, the expression $(3x + 5)$ is the argument.

Asymptote: A line which a graph gets closer and closer to, but never touches, as x or y become very large.

Axiom: A property accepted without proof, used as a starting point for a mathematical system.

Axis of symmetry If the graph of a parabola is folded so that its two sides coincide, the line on which the fold occurs is the axis of symmetry.

Base Face of a geometric figure upon which the altitude is constructed.

BASIC: Acronym for "Beginners All-purpose Symbolic Instruction Code," an easily-learned computer language.

Binomial A polynomial of two terms.

Cancellation in fractions: Dividing the numerator and the denominator by the same common factor.

Characteristic: The integer part of a base-10 logarithm, or exponent of 10 for a number in scientific notation.

Circular function: A function (sin, cos, tan, cot, sec, csc) whose independent variable, x, is a real number representing the length of an arc of a unit circle.

Combination: A subset of the elements in a given set, without regard to the order in which these elements are arranged.

Complex number Number of the form $a + bi$ where a and b are real numbers and $i^2 = -1$.

Conic sections: Circles, ellipses, parabolas, and hyperbolas (and occasionally lines or points) formed by the intersection of a plane and a cone.

Conjugate binomials: Binomials of the form $a + b$ and $a - b$, where the only difference is the sign of the second term.

Constant function: A function whose general equation is $y =$ a constant.

Converge: To get closer and closer to, without necessarily reaching.

Converse Theorem resulting from exchanging conclusion and hypothesis.

Cubic function: A function whose general equation is $y = ax^3 + bx^2 + cx + d$, where a, b, c, and d stand for constants, and $a \neq 0$.

Degree of a polynomial: The maximum number of variables that are multiplied together in any one term of the polynomial.

Dependent variable: The variable appearing *second* in an ordered pair.

Descartes' Rule of Signs: The number of positive zeros of a polynomial is less than or equal to the number of sign reversals in $P(x)$. The number of negative zeros is less than or equal to the number of sign reversals in $P(-x)$. In both cases, the number of zeros has the same parity (odd or even) as the number of reversals.

Determinant: A square array of numbers evaluated according to specific rules explained in the text.

Discontinuity A point in the domain of a function for which there is no corresponding point in the range.

Discriminant: The quantity $b^2 - 4ac$, where a, b, and c are coefficients of the quadratic equation $ax^2 + bx + c = 0$.

Division The inverse operation to multiplication.

Domain of a function: The set of permissible values of the independent variable.

Ellipse: A set of points in a plane, for each of which the *sum* of its distances from two fixed points (foci) is equal to a constant.

Equivalent equations: Equations that have the same solution set.

Equivalent expressions: Expressions that stand for equal numbers, no matter what permissible value is substituted for the variable(s).

Evaluating an expression: Substituting numbers for the variables, and thus finding the *value* of the expression.

Exponent Number placed at the upper right of a symbol to denote degree or power of the symbol.

Exponential function: A function whose general equation is $y = a \times b^x$ or $y = a \times 10^{kx}$, where a, b, and k stand for constants.

Extraneous solution: A number that satisfies an equation which has been transformed, but does not satisfy the original equation.

Function: A relation in which each value of the independent variable takes on a *unique* value of the dependent variable.

General equation: An equation such as $y = ax^2 + bx + c$, in which letters (a, b, c) are used to stand for the constants.

Greatest common factor, GCF: The GCF of integers x and y is the product of the numbers in the *intersection* of the sets of prime factors of x and y.

Higher degree function: A function whose general equation is $y = P(x)$, where $P(x)$ is a cubic or higher degree polynomial.

Hyperbola: A set of points in a plane, for each of which the *difference* of its distances from two fixed points (foci) is constant.

Imaginary number Square root of a negative real number.

Independent variable: The variable appearing *first* in an ordered pair.

Indeterminate expression: An expression such as $0/0$ or $0°$, which could take on *any* value, depending on what expression gives the "0."

Infinitely large: Larger than any real number.

Intercept: A value of a variable when all other variables in the equation equal zero.

Intersection: The intersection of sets A and B, written $A \cap B$, is the set of elements that are in both A and B.

Interval: A set of all the real numbers between (and sometimes including) two given numbers.

Irrational algebraic function: A function whose general equation is $y = f(x)$, where $f(x)$ is an expression containing a root of a variable, and perhaps the operations $+$, $-$, $\times$, and $\div$, but no other operations on a variable.

Irreversible step: A transformation of an equation, such as multiplying both sides by an expression that can equal 0, which when reversed may not produce the original equation uniquely.

Least common multiple, LCM: The LCM of integers x and y is the product of the numbers in the *union* of the sets of prime factors of x and y.

Linear: First degree.

Linear combination: A linear combination of two functions f and g is an expression of the form $af(x) + bg(x)$, where a and b stand for constants.

Linear function: A function whose general equation is $y = mx + b$, where m and b stand for constants, and $m \neq 0$.

Logarithm The power to which it is necessary to raise a base number to produce a desired number.

Mantissa: The decimal part of a base-10 logarithm, or factor multiplied by the power of 10 for numbers in scientific notation.

Mathematical model: A representation in the mathematical world of some phenomenon in the real world. In this text, a mathematical model consists of a *function* or *relation* specifying how two or more variables are related.

Matrix: A rectangular array of numbers representing such things as the coefficients in a system of equations.

Mean The average; the sum of a set of numbers divided by the number of members in the set.

Open sentence: An equation or inequality containing at least one variable.

Parabola: A set of points in a plane for each of which its distance from a fixed line (the directrix) is equal to its distance from a fixed point (the focus) not on the line.

Partial sum: The sum of the first n terms of a series.

Particular equation: An equation such as $y = 3x + 7$, where particular numbers (3 and 7 in this case) appear as the constants.

Permutation: An arrangement of some or all of the elements from a given set.

Phase displacement: The value of the independent variable of a function when the argument of the function is equal to zero.

Polynomial: An expression containing no operations other than $+$, $-$, or $\times$ performed on the variable(s).

Polynomial function: A function whose general equation is $y = P(x)$, where $P(x)$ is a polynomial in x.

Power Degree to which a symbol is to be multiplied by itself, denoted by its exponent.

Prime number: One of the numbers 2, 3, 5, 7, 11, . . . , which have no integer factors besides 1 and itself.

Quadratic equation: An equation (with one variable) of the form $ax^2 + bx + c = 0$, where a, b, and c stand for constants, and $a \neq 0$.

Quadratic Formula: If $ax^2 + bx + c = 0$, then $\dfrac{-b \pm \sqrt{b^2 - 4ac}}{2a}$.

Quadratic function: A function whose general equation is $y = ax^2 + bx + c$, where a, b, and c stand for constants, and $a \neq 0$.

Quartic function: A function whose general equation is $y = ax^4 + bx^3 + cx^2 + dx + e$, where a, b, c, d, and e stand for constants, and $a \neq 0$.

Quintic function: A function whose general equation is $y = ax^5 + bx^4 + cx^3 + dx^2 + ex + f$, where a, b, c, d, e, and f stand for constants and $a \neq 0$.

Radian: A unit of angular measure equal to $1/(2\pi)$ of a complete revolution.

Radical The symbol $\sqrt{}$.

Range of a function: The set of numbers that are actually used as values of the dependent variable.

Rational algebraic expression: An expression that can be written as the ratio of two polynomials.

Rational Root Theorem: $(ax - b)$ is a factor of $P(x)$ if and only if $P(b/a) = 0$.

Reciprocal Two expressions are reciprocals if their product is 1. Multiplicative inverse.

Reference angle: The smallest postive angle between the terminal side of an angle in standard position and the x-axis.

Relation: A set of ordered pairs, triples, etc.

Relatively prime: Two integers are relatively prime if they have no common prime factors.

Scientific notation A number expressed as the product of a power of 10 and a number ≥ 1 but < 10.

Sequence: A function whose independent variable is the term number, and whose dependent variable is the term value.

Series: The indicated sum of the terms of a sequence.

Significant digit The digits of a number beginning with the first nonzero digit on the left and ending with the last nonzero digit on the right.

Sinusoidal function: A function whose general equation is $y = C + A \cos B(x - D)$, or $y = C + A \sin B(x - D)$, where A, B, C, and D stand for constants.

Slope: The constant m in the linear function equation $y = mx + b$. Also equal to rise/run.

Solution set: A set of equations or inequalities containing the same variables.

Standard deviation The positive square root of the sum of the squares of a set of mean deviations.

Subtraction The process of finding a quantity which when added to one of the given quantities will give the other.

System: A set of equations or inequalities containing the same variables.

Terms: Parts of an expression separated by "$+$" or "$-$" signs.

Trace Point at which a line intersects a coordinate plane.

Transcendental number: A number that cannot be expressed exactly by performing a finite number of algebraic operations ($+$, $-$, $\times$, $\div$, and $\sqrt[n]{}$) on integers.

Trichotomy: The Comparison Axiom; For any two real numbers x and y, exactly *one* of the following is true: $x < y$, $x = y$, or $x > y$.

Trigonometric function: A function (sin, cos, tan, cot, sec, csc) whose independent variable is an *angle measure*, usually in degrees or radians.

Union: The union of sets A and B, written A∪B, is the set of elements that are in at least one of sets A or B.

Unique: "There is a unique number . . . ," means both that there *is* a number and that there is only *one* number of the kind described.

Upper Bound Theorem: For a positive number c, if $P(x)$ is divided by $(x - c)$ and the resulting quotient and remainder have no sign reversals, then $P(x)$ has no zeros greater than c.

Variable: A letter used to stand for an unspecified number in a given set of numbers (the domain).

Variation function: A function whose general equation is $y = kx^n$, where k and n stand for constants.

Vector (quantity): A directed line segment used to represent a quantity that has both magnitude (size) and direction, such as force or velocity.

Vertex The maximum or minimum point of a graph.

Vinculum Bar over two or more symbols indicating they are to be treated as a single term.

Zero of a function: A value of x (real or complex) that makes $y = 0$.

Answers to
Selected Problems

CHAPTER 1
PRELIMINARY INFORMATION

Exercise 1-1, Sets of Numbers

1. a. whole numbers, positive, negative, and 0 **b.** 0, 1, 2, 3, 4, 5, 6, 7, 8, 9 **c.** integers divisible by 2 **d.** numbers greater than 0 **e.** numbers less than 0 **f.** numbers expressible as a ratio of two integers **g.** numbers not expressible as a ratio of two integers **h.** square roots of negative numbers **i.** numbers on the number line **j.** positive integers **k.** positive integers **l.** numbers not expressible using only a finite number of the operations $+$, $-$, $\times$, $\div$, or $\sqrt[n]{}$ on integers
3. See Chapter 1 Opener.
5. {natural numbers} counting was probably the first thing done with numbers
7. rational **9.** 0

Exercise 1-2, The Field Axioms

1. a. 0 **b.** 1
3. Examples may vary.
Closure:
$x + y \in \mathcal{R} \quad xy \in \mathcal{R}$
Commutativity:
$x + y = y + x \quad xy = yx$
Associativity:
$(x + y) + z = x + (y + z)$
$(xy)z = x(yz)$
Distributivity:
$x(y + z) = xy + xz$
Identity elements:
$x + 0 = x \quad x \cdot 1 = x$
Inverses:
$x + (-x) = 0 \quad x \cdot \dfrac{1}{x} = 1$
5. The answer always comes out the *same*.
7. Calvin is right. Phoebe distributed multiplication over multiplication. **9. a.** Associativity for addition **b.** Closure under multiplication **c.** Commutativity for addition **d.** Commutativity for multiplication **e.** Distributivity of multiplication over addition **f.** Additive identity **g.** Additive inverses **h.** Multiplicative identity **i.** Multiplicative inverses

Exercise 1-3, Variables and Expressions

1. 47 **3.** 10 **5.** 8 **7.** 7 **9.** 16
11. a. 7 **b.** -13 **13. a.** 1 **b.** 14
15. a. -17 **b.** 18 **17. a.** 0 **b.** 21
19. a. 2 **b.** 27 **21. a.** -5 **b.** 40
23. a. 1 **b.** 11 **25.** $4 - x$
27. $21x - 42$ **29.** $4x + 17$
31. 5 **33.** $32 - 6x$ **35.** $3x + 3$
37. $2y^2 - 2xy$ **39.** x **41.** Phoebe

Exercise 1-4, Polynomials

1. yes, quartic trinomial **3.** yes, quadratic binomial **5.** no, division by a variable **7.** yes, linear binomial **9.** no, division by a variable **11.** yes, constant monomial **13.** yes, four-term cubic **15.** yes, quintic binomial **17.** no, square root of a variable **19.** yes, linear binomial **21.** yes, 10th degree binomial **23.** yes, monomial, no degree **25.** $x^2 + 4x - 21$ **27.** $2x^2 + 7x - 4$ **29.** $6x^2 - 37x + 56$ **31.** $4x^2 - 20x + 25$ **33.** $4x^2 - 20x + 25$

Exercise 1-5, Equations

Note: Solutions in parentheses are not in domain.

1. $\{-5\}$ **3.** $\emptyset$ (-4) **5.** $\{0\}$
7. a. $\left\{-\dfrac{11}{3}\right\}$ **b.** $\emptyset\left(-\dfrac{11}{3}\right)$ **9. a.** $\{-4\}$ (4)
b. $\{4, -4\}$ **11. a.** $\left\{\dfrac{1}{3}, -\dfrac{1}{3}\right\}$
b. $\emptyset\left(\dfrac{1}{3}, -\dfrac{1}{3}\right)$ **13.** $\left\{-3, \dfrac{2}{3}\right\}$
15. $\{-1,\}\left(\dfrac{5}{2}\right)$ **17.** $\left\{\dfrac{2}{3}\right\}$ (-3)
19. $\left\{-\dfrac{3}{2}, 5, -1\right\}$ **21.** $\left\{0, \dfrac{1}{2}, -4\right\}$
23. $\{7, -7\}$ **25.** $\emptyset$ **27.** $\{2, -8\}$
29. $\left\{3, -\dfrac{5}{2}\right\}$ **31.** $\left\{2, \dfrac{16}{9}\right\}$
33. a. $S = \left\{-7, \dfrac{5}{3}\right\}$ for both equations.
b. equivalent **35. a.** true **b.** true **c.** if $a < b$, then $a + c < b + c$, and if $a > b$, then $a + c > b + c$

Exercise 1-6, Inequalities

1. (Graph) $x < 3$ **3.** (Graph) $x \geq -1$
5. (Graph) $x \geq 4$ where $x \in J$, the set of integers   **7.** (Graph) $-1 < x \leq 7$
9. (Graph) $x < -10$ or $x \geq -1$
11. (Graph) $0 < x < 3$ or $x \geq 5$
13. (Graph) $\varnothing$ **15. a.** (Graph) $-5 < x < 5$ **b.** (Graph) $-4 \leq x \leq 4$ where $x \in J$ **c.** (Graph) $0 < x < 5$
17. a. (Graph) $x \leq -2$ or $x \geq 2$
b. (Graph) the same as **a** except that $x \in J$
c. (Graph) $x \geq 2$ **19. a.** (Graph) $-5 \leq x \leq 1$ **b.** (Graph) same as **a** except that $x \in J$ **c.** (Graph) $0 < x \leq 1$
21. a. (Graph) $x < -7$ or $x > 2$
b. (Graph) same as **a** except that $x \in J$
c. (Graph) $x > 2$ **23. a.** (Graph) $-2 \leq x \leq 4.4$ **b.** (Graph) same as **a** except that $x \in J$ **c.** (Graph) $0 < x \leq 4.4$
25. a. (Graph) $x \leq -7$ or $x \geq 14$
b. (Graph) same as **a** except that $x \in J$
c. (Graph) $x \geq 14$ **27. a.** (Graph) $-2\frac{3}{4} < x < 1\frac{3}{4}$ **b.** (Graph) same as **a** except that $x \in J$ **c.** $0 < x < 1\frac{3}{4}$
29. a. (Graph) $\varnothing$ **b.** (Graph) $\varnothing$ **c.** (Graph) $\varnothing$ **31. a.** (Graph) $-3 < x \leq -1$ or $5 \leq x < 7$ **b.** (Graph) same as **a** except that $x \in J$ **c.** $5 \leq x < 7$

Exercise 1-7, Properties Provable from Axioms

1. a. If $x = y$ and $y = z$, then $x = z$. **b.** If $x < y$ and $y < z$, then $x < z$. **c.** If $x = y$, then $y = x$. **d.** If $x \in \mathcal{R}$, then $x = x$. **e.** If $x, y \in \mathcal{R}$, then exactly one of the following is true: **i.** $x > y$ **ii.** $x = y$ **iii.** $x < y$
3. An axiom is assumed to be true without proof. Other properties are provable from the axioms.   **5.** Reflexive Axiom
7. $xz = xz$ Reflexive Axiom
   $x = y$ Given (hypothesis)
   $\therefore xz = yz$, QED   Substitution into a product
9. If $xz = yz$ and $z \neq 0$, then $x = y$. Cancellation Property of Equality for Multiplication
11. $-(-x) + (-x) = 0$ Additive inverses
   $x + (-x) = 0$ Additive inverses
   $0 = x + (-x)$ Symmetry
   $\therefore -(-x) + (-x)$

   $= x + (-x)$ Transitivity
   $\therefore -(-x) = x$, QED   Converse of the Addition Property of Equality

13. a. Multiplicative Inverses **b.** Multiplication Property of Equality **c.** Associativity **d.** Multiplicative Inverses **e.** Multiplicative Identity **f.** Multiplication Property of Equality **g.** Associativity **h.** Multiplicative Inverses **i.** Multiplicative Identity **j.** Commutativity   **15. a.** Trichotomy ($y \neq 0$ is equivalent to $y > 0$ or $y < 0$.) **c.** Multiplicative Inverses **d.** Hypothesis (given) **e.** Multiplication Property of Equality **f.** Multiplication Property of Zero **g.** Associativity **h.** Multiplicative Inverses **i.** Multiplicative Identity (Case II proved)
17. a. Multiplicative Identity **b.** Distributivity **c.** Additive Inverses **d.** Multiplication Property of Zero **e.** Additive Inverses **f.** Transitivity **g.** Converse of the Addition Property of Equality
19. a. If $x = y$, then $-x = -y$.
b. $x = y$ Hypothesis
   $-1 \cdot x = -1 \cdot y$ *Multiplication Property for Equality*
   $\therefore -1 \cdot x = -y$, QED   Multiplication Property of -1
21. Prove that if $x \in \mathcal{R}$, then $x^2 \geq 0$.
Proof: $x > 0$, $x < 0$, or $x = 0$ Trichotomy
   Case I: $x > 0$
      $x \cdot x > 0 \cdot x$ Mult. Prop. of Order
      $x \cdot x > 0$ Mult. Prop. of Zero
      $x^2 > 0$ Defn. of x^2
   Case II: $x < 0$
      $x \cdot x > 0 \cdot x$ Mult. Prop. of Order
      $x \cdot x > 0$ Mult. Prop. of Zero
      $x^2 \geq 0$ Defn. of x^2
   Case III: $x = 0$
      $x \cdot x = 0 \cdot x$ Mult. Prop. of Equality
      $x \cdot x > 0$ Mult. Prop. of Zero
      $x^2 = 0$ Defn. of x^2
      $x^2 \geq 0$ Summarizing Cases I, II, and III

23. Prove that $\dfrac{x + y}{z} = \dfrac{x}{z} + \dfrac{y}{z}$.

Proof: $\dfrac{x + y}{z} = (x + y) \cdot \dfrac{1}{z}$ Defn. of division

   $= x \cdot \dfrac{1}{z} + y \cdot \dfrac{1}{z}$ Distributivity

$$= \frac{x}{z} + \frac{y}{z} \qquad \text{Defn. of division}$$

$$\frac{x + y}{z} = \frac{x}{z} + \frac{y}{z}, \text{ QED} \qquad \text{Transitivity}$$

25. Prove that $\frac{x - y}{z} = \frac{x}{z} - \frac{y}{z}$.

Proof: $\frac{x - y}{z} = (x - y) \cdot \frac{1}{z} \qquad \text{Defn. of division}$

$$= x \cdot \frac{1}{z} - y \cdot \frac{1}{z} \qquad \text{Distributivity}$$

$$= \frac{x}{z} - \frac{y}{z} \qquad \text{Defn. of division}$$

$$\frac{x - y}{z} = \frac{x}{z} - \frac{y}{z}, \text{ QED} \qquad \text{Transitivity}$$

27. Prove that $\frac{1}{1} = 1$.

Proof: $\frac{n}{n} = 1 \qquad \text{Exercise 26}$

$$\frac{1}{1} = 1, \text{ QED} \qquad \text{Substitution}$$

29. Prove that $\frac{-x}{y} = -\frac{x}{y}$.

Proof: $\frac{-x}{y} = (-x) \cdot \frac{1}{y} \qquad \text{Defn. of division}$

$$= [-1 \cdot x] \cdot \frac{1}{y} \qquad \text{Mult. Prop. of } -1$$

$$= -1 \cdot \left(x \cdot \frac{1}{y}\right) \qquad \text{Associativity}$$

$$= -1 \cdot \frac{x}{y} \qquad \text{Defn. of division}$$

$$= -\frac{x}{y} \qquad \text{Mult. Prop. of } -1$$

$$\frac{-x}{y} = -\frac{x}{y}, \text{ QED} \qquad \text{Transitivity}$$

31. Prove that $-(x + y) = -x + (-y)$.
Proof: $-(x + y) = -1 \cdot (x + y)$

$$\text{Mult. Prop. of } -1$$

$$= -1 \cdot x + (-1) \cdot y$$

$$\text{Distributivity}$$

$$= -x + (-y)$$

$$\text{Mult. Prop. of } -1$$

Exercise 1-8, Chapter Review

R1. Examples may vary. **a. i.** $\frac{11}{3}$ **ii.** $-\sqrt{7}$
iii. $\sqrt{-7}$ **iv.** π **v.** -24 **vi.** 1275 **vii.** 37
viii. 37.2 **ix.** 0 (*only* correct ans.) **x.** No
such number **b. i.** 2: Integer, digit, even,
positive, rational, real, natural, counting.
ii. -3: Integer, negative, rational, real, odd.

iii. $\sqrt{3}$: Positive, irrational, real, radical.
iv. $\sqrt{-3}$: Imaginary. **v.** 2.3: Positive,
rational, real, non-integer.
R2. a. i. Axiom: Property accepted without proof. **ii.** Lemma: Property used to
prove another property. **iii.** Corollary: Property easily proved using another property.
iv. Hypothesis: The "if" part (*given* part) of
a property. **b. i.** $x - y = x + (-y)$; Not
an Axiom **ii.** $x \cdot \frac{1}{x} = 1$; Field Axiom **iii.** If
x and y are real numbers then exactly *one* of
the following is true: $x < y$, $x = y$, $x > y$;
Axiom **iv.** If x and y are real numbers, then
$x + y$ is a unique, real number; Field Axiom **v.** $x + 0 = x$; Field Axiom **vi.** If
$x > y$, then: $xz > yz$ for $z > 0$, $xz < yz$
for $z < 0$, $xz = yz$ for $z = 0$; Not an Axiom **c. i.** Defn. of division. **ii.** Mult. Prop.
of -1 **iii.** Reciprocal of a Product **iv.** -1 is
its own reciprocal because $(-1)(-1) = 1$.
v. Associativity for multiplication
vi. Commutativity for multiplication
vii. Associativity for multiplication
viii. Defn. of division **ix.** Multiplication Property of -1 **x.** Transitivity for
equality **d.** Prove that $a(b + c + d) = ab + ac + ad$.

Proof: $a(b + c + d) = a(b + (c + d))$
$$\text{Associativity for addition}$$
$$= ab + a(c + d))$$
$$\text{Distributivity}$$
$$= ab + ac + ad$$
$$\text{Distributivity}$$
$a(b + c + d) = ab + ac + ad$, QED
$$\text{Transitivity}$$

R3. a. i. Cubic binomial **ii.** Not a polynomial. Division by a variable. **iii.** Not a polynomial. Square root of a variable.
iv. Quartic binomial **v.** Quintic monomial
vi. Quadratic trinomial **b. i.** 9 **ii.** 8 **iii.** 21
iv. $3x^2 - 17x - 56$ **v.** $39x - 121$

c.

	$x = 5$	$x = -4$
i.	7	-20
ii.	0	18
iii.	76	67

R4. a. i. $\{-6\}$ **ii.** $\emptyset$ $\left(\frac{11}{5}\text{ is not an integer.}\right)$
iii. $\left\{-3, \frac{2}{3}\right\}$ **iv.** $\left\{\frac{3}{2}\right\}$ (-3 is not positive)
v. $\{9, -9\}$ **b. i.** $x < 2.5$ **ii.** $x \geq -3$
iii. $x > 7$ or $x < -3$
iv. $x \leq 3$ and $x \geq -\frac{3}{2}$

CHAPTER 2 FUNCTIONS AND RELATIONS

Exercise 2-1, Graphs of Equations with Two Variables

1. $2x - 3 = 15$
$2(9) - 3(1) = 15$
        $15 = 15$ is a true statement.
(9, 1) satisfies the equation.
(1, 9) does not satisfy the equation.
3. $2(6) - 3y = 15$
        $-3y = 3$
         $y = -1$
See (6, -1) on graph.
5. (Graph) The points (6, -1), (3, -3), (0, -5), and (-3, -7) all lie on a straight line.

Exercise 2-2, Graphs of Functions

1. (Graph) $R = \{y : y \geq 0\}$ **3.** (Graph) $R = \{y : y > 2$ and y is an integer$\}$ **5.** (Graph) $R = \{y : y < 0\}$ **7.** (Graph) $R = \{y : 2 < y < 10\}$ **9.** (Graph) $R = \{y : 0 \leq y \leq 4\}$ **11.** (Graph) $R = \{y : y = 1, 3, 7, 13\}$ **13.** $D = \{x : -4 < x < 6\}$ $R = \{y : -2 < y < 7\}$ **15.** $D = \{x : -3 \leq x \leq 4\}$ $R = \{y : -5 \leq y \leq 5\}$ **17.** (Graph) **19.** (Graph) Answers may vary.

Exercise 2-3, Functions in the Real World

1-43. (Graphs) Answers may vary.

Exercise 2-4, Graphs of Functions and Relations

1. (Graph) not a function   **3.** (Graph) function   **5.** (Graph) function   **7.** (Graph) not a function   **9.** (Graph) not a function   **11.** function   **13.** function   **15.** not a function   **17.** function   **19.** not a function   **21.** function   **23.** not a function   **25.** function

2-5, Chapter Review

R1. a. $R = \{y : -1 \leq y \leq 3\}$ function
b. $R = \{-2, 1, 2\}$ function
c. $R = \{-2, -1, 0, 1, 2\}$ not a function
d. $R = \{y : -4 \leq y \leq 4\}$ not a function

R2. a. function **b.** not a function **c.** function **d.** not a function **e.** not a function **f.** function   **R3. a-d.** (Graphs) Answers may vary.

CHAPTER 3 LINEAR FUNCTIONS

Exercise 3-1, Introduction to Linear Functions

1. (Graphs)   **3.** The equation $y = b$ is a constant function rather than a linear function.

Exercise 3-2, Properties of Linear Function Graphs

1. (Graph) $m = \dfrac{3}{5}$; $b = 3$ **3.** (Graph) $m = -\dfrac{3}{2}$; $b = -4$ **5.** (Graph) $m = 2$; $b = -5$ **7.** (Graph) $m = -3$; $b = 1$ **9.** (Graph) $m = -\dfrac{7}{2}$; $b = 5$ **11.** (Graph) $m = \dfrac{1}{4}$; $b = -3$ **13.** (Graph) $m = 3$; $b = 0$ **15.** (Graph) $m = 0$; $b = 3$ **17.** (Graph) vertical line   **19.** (Graph) $m = 0$; $b = 0$ **21.** Problems 15, 16, and 19 are constant, not linear, functions. Problems 17, 18, and 20 are not functions.   **23.** $\dfrac{1}{0.1} = 10$; $\dfrac{1}{0.01} = 100$; $\dfrac{1}{0.001} = 1000$; $\dfrac{1}{0.0001} = 10{,}000$. The size of the fraction increases as its denominator gets close to zero. For any real number $x \neq 0$, $x = \dfrac{1}{\frac{1}{x}}$, so $\dfrac{1}{0}$ would be larger than $\dfrac{1}{\frac{1}{x}}$. $\therefore \dfrac{1}{0}$ would be larger than any real number. A quantity larger than any real number is infinitely large.

Exercise 3-3, Other Forms of the Linear Function Equation

1. a. (Graph) **b.** $y = \dfrac{3}{5}x + \dfrac{7}{5}$ **c.** $3x - 5y = -7$ **3. a.** (Graph) **b.** $y = \dfrac{7}{2}x - \dfrac{29}{2}$ **c.** $7x - 2y = 29$

5. a. (Graph) **b.** $y = -\dfrac{1}{4}x + \dfrac{11}{2}$

c. $x + 4y = 22$ **7. a.** (Graph)
b. $y = -2x - 9$ **c.** $2x + y = -9$

9. a. (Graph) **b.** $y = \dfrac{1}{3}x - 4$

c. $x - 3y = 12$ **11.** $y - 7 = -3(x - 5)$

13. $y - 5 = \dfrac{9}{13}(x + 2)$

Exercise 3-4, Equations of Linear Functions from Their Graphs

1. a. $y = -5x + 21$ **b.** $y = -5x + 21$
c. $5x + y = 21$ **3. a.** $y - 7 = 11(x - 3)$
b. $y = 11x - 26$ **c.** $11x - y = 26$
5. a. $y + 5 = -6(x - 4)$
b. $y = -6x + 19$ **c.** $6x + y = 19$

7. a. $y - 7 = \dfrac{3}{2}(x - 1)$

b. $y = \dfrac{3}{2}x + \dfrac{11}{2}$ **c.** $3x - 2y = -11$

9. a. $y + 4 = \dfrac{6}{7}(x - 2)$ **b.** $y = \dfrac{6}{7}x - \dfrac{40}{7}$

c. $6x - 7y = 40$
11. a. $y - 8 = 7(x - 5)$
b. $y = 7x - 27$ **c.** $7x - y = 27$
13. a. $y - 6 = -2.5(x + 4)$
b. $y = -2.5x - 4$ **c.** $5x + 2y = -8$

15. a. $y - 8 = -\dfrac{2}{3}(x - 5)$

b. $y = -\dfrac{2}{3}x + \dfrac{34}{3}$ **c.** $2x + 3y = 34$

17. a. $y - 1 = -\dfrac{7}{5}(x - 4)$

b. $y = -\dfrac{7}{5}x + \dfrac{33}{5}$ **c.** $7x + 5y = 33$

19. a. $y - 0 = -\dfrac{2}{3}(x - 5)$

b. $y = -\dfrac{2}{3}x + \dfrac{10}{3}$ **c.** $2x + 3y = 10$

21. a. $y = 0.315x$ **b.** $y = 0.315x + 0$
c. $315x - 1000y = 0$ $(63x - 200y = 0)$
23. a. $y = 9$ **b.** $y = 0x + 9$ **c.** $0x - y = 9$ **25. a.** $x = -8$ **b.** Can't be done!
c. $x + 0y = -8$ **27.** All slopes equal -1, so the particular equation is $x + y = 8$.

29. All slopes equal $\dfrac{3}{2}$, so the particular

equation is $3x - 2y = -5$.   **31.** *Intercept*

Form **a.** If $x = 0$, then $\dfrac{0}{a} + \dfrac{y}{b} = 1$.

So $y = b$. If $y = 0$, then $\dfrac{x}{a} + \dfrac{0}{b} = 1$. So
$x = a$. $\therefore$ a and b are the x- and y-inter-

cepts, respectively. **b. i.** $\dfrac{x}{3} + \dfrac{y}{5} = 1 \rightarrow$

$5x + 3y = 15$ **ii.** $y = -\dfrac{5}{3}x + 5$ **c.** $y =$

$4x - 12 \rightarrow 4x - y = 12 \rightarrow \dfrac{x}{3} - \dfrac{y}{12} = 1$

x-intercept is 3, y-intercept is -12.
33. *Computer Graphics Problem* **a.** Find its slope. If the slope is positive, the graph will go up; if negative, it will go down. The

slope is $-\dfrac{3}{5}$, so the graph should go down.

b. Answers may vary. **c.** The two graphs should be parallel. **d.** Answers may vary.

e. $m = \dfrac{5}{3}$; $y + 4 = \dfrac{5}{3}x$. **f.** Answers may

vary.

Exercise 3-5, Linear Functions as Mathematical Models

1. *Computer Diskette Problem* (Graph),
$D = 1.25d + 2.5$ $127.50   **3.** *Milk Problem* **a.** $c = 72q + 21$ **b.** $8.85 **c.** The actual price per pint, 57¢, equals the predicted price. The actual price per quart, 99¢, is more than the predicted price, 93¢.
d. 4.48111 . . . or about 4.5 quarts.
e. (Graph) **f.** A fixed cost of production independent of the size of the carton.
g. Cents/quart represents the amount of increase in price for each quart added.
5. *Cricket Problem* **a.** $c = 4t - 160$
b. 200 chirps/min **c.** 70°F **d.** 40°F
e. (Graph) **f.** no significance, zero is out of domain   **7.** *Speed on a Hill Problem*
a. $s = -7a + 90$ **b.** 139 mph **c.** 1° up, because $a > 0$. **d.** $a = 0$, $s = 90$; speed is

90 mph on the level **e.** $s = 0$, $a = 12\dfrac{6}{7}$,

steepest hill is 13° **f.** (Graph)   **9.** *Calorie Consumption Problem* **a.** constant rate,
$m = -30$, $C = -30T + 3630$
b. i 2130 cal **ii** 5130 cal **c.** 121°C
d. (Graph)   **11.** *Terminal Velocity Problem*
a. Velocity is constant. **b.** $d = -60t + 4500$
c. 75 sec **d.** 4500 m **e.** Terminal velocity not reached for 15 s; average velocity is slower. **f.** (Graph) **g.** 60 m/s, 216 km/h
13. *Shoe Size Problem* **a.** $s = 3L - 22$

b. 14 **c.** $14\frac{2}{3}$ in. **d.** (Graph) **15.** *Celsius-to-Fahrenheit Temperature Conversion*

a. $F = 1.8C + 32$ **b.** $C = \frac{5}{9}(F - 32)$

c. $2948°F$ **d.** $37°C$ **e.** hot **f.** $-459.4°F$
g. $C = -40$ **h.** (Graph) **17.** *Elevator Problem* **a.** $c = 20s + 35$ is of the linear form $y = mx + b$. **b.** 615 ft **c.** 17 stories **d.** feet of cable per story **e.** $s = 0, c = 35$. Fixed length of cable independent of the number of stories. **f.** $D = \{2, 3, 4, \ldots, 170\}$ Maximum may vary. **g.** (Graph)
19. *Income Tax Problem*
a. $9761.50 + 0.33(x - 43150)$
b. $9761.50, $25076.80 **c.** 25076.80
d. (Graph) **e.** $33,600 **f.** (Graph)

3-6, Chapter Review

R1. a. $x = -1$ $y = -10$
    $x = 2$ $y = -1$
    $x = 5$ $y = 8$
b. (Graph) $m = 3; b = -7$
R2. a. (Graph) $m = \frac{2}{5}; b = -3$ **b.** (Graph)

$m = -\frac{7}{3}; 7$ **c.** (Graph)   **d.** (Graph)

R3. a. point-slope **b.** $(4, -3)$ **d.** $y =$
$-\frac{5}{2}x + 7$ **e.** $5x + 2y = 14$ **R5. a.** $t =$
$0.06n + 2$ **b.** 3.8 s, 602 s **c.** 350 times
d. t-intercept tells you it takes 2 seconds.
e. m is in seconds per loop, so it takes 0.06
seconds for one loop. **f.** (Graph) $m = 0.06;$
$b = 2$

CHAPTER 4 SYSTEMS OF LINEAR EQUATIONS AND INEQUALITIES

Exercise 4-1, Introduction to Linear Systems

1. $6x - 3y = 30 \dashv (3)$ **3.** $x = 3$
5. $(3, -4)$

Exercise 4-2, Solution of Systems of Linear Equations

1. $\{(1, 3)\}$ **3.** $\{(2, -5)\}$ **5.** $\{(-3, 0)\}$
7. $\left\{\left(\frac{1}{2}, \frac{1}{3}\right)\right\}$ **9.** $\{(-1, -2)\}$
11. $\{(4, -2)\}$ **13.** $\{(1, -2)\}$ **15.** $\{(3, 2)\}$

17. $\{(1, -3)\}$ **19.** $\{(-2, 0)\}$
21. $\left\{\left(\frac{13}{3}, \frac{19}{9}\right)\right\}$ **23.** $\left\{\left(\frac{22}{7}, -\frac{5}{14}\right)\right\}$
25. $\left\{\left(\frac{139}{33}, \frac{173}{33}\right)\right\}$ **27.** $\left\{\left(\frac{1}{4}, \frac{5}{3}\right)\right\}$
29. $\left\{\left(\frac{2}{3}, \frac{5}{7}\right)\right\}$ **31.** Inconsistent
33. Independent **35.** Dependent
37. Inconsistent **39.** (Graph)
41. (Graph) **43.** $\{(-4, 3)\}$ **45.** $\{(7, 0)\}$
47. $\{(2.5, -3.5)\}$ **49.** $\{245.45, 109.09)\}$
51. a. Additional Property of Equality: Eq 1 (left) + Eq 2 (right) = Eq 1 (right) + Eq 2 (right). Substitution into sums: Eq 1 (left) + Eq 2 (left) = Eq1 (right) + Eq 2 (right)

b. $p = q$ Hypothesis
   $p + r = q + r$ Addition Property
                            of Equality
   $p + r = q + s$, QED Substitution into
                            Sums

Exercise 4-3, Second-Order Determinants

1. $\{(1, 3)\}$ **3.** $\{(2, -5)\}$ **5.** $\{(-3, 0)\}$
7. $\left\{\left(\frac{1}{2}, \frac{1}{3}\right)\right\}$ **9.** $\{(-1, -2)\}$
11. $\left\{\left(\frac{13}{3}, \frac{19}{9}\right)\right\}$ **13.** $\left\{\left(\frac{22}{7}, -\frac{5}{14}\right)\right\}$
15. $\left\{\left(\frac{139}{33}, \frac{173}{3}\right)\right\}$ **17. b.** $S =$
$\left\{\left(1\frac{39}{41}, 2\frac{36}{41}\right)\right\}$ **c.** The solutions looked like integers on the graph, but were not integers in fact. **19. a. i.** (Graph) **b. i.** inconsistent **ii.** dependent **c.** 0 **d.** If $x = \frac{\text{non-zero}}{\text{zero}}$, then equations are inconsistent. If $x = \frac{\text{zero}}{\text{zero}}$, then equations are dependent.
i. 12 **ii.** 0 **e. i.** inconsistent **ii.** independent
$S = \left\{\left(\frac{11}{12}, \frac{23}{48}\right)\right\}$ **iii.** dependent
ii. inconsistent **21. a.** $\{(-1, -2)\}$
b. $\{(7.5, -7.3)\}$
23. $adx + bdy = cd$ Equation 1
                            multiplied by d
   $adx + aey = af$ Equation 2
                            multiplied by a
   $(bd - ae)y = cd - af$ Subtract
   $y = \dfrac{cd - af}{bd - ae}$
   $= \dfrac{af - cd}{ae - bd}$ Mult. by $\dfrac{-1}{-1}$.

Exercise 4-4, $f(x)$ Terminology, and Systems as Models

1. 32   **3.** 7   **5.** 11   **7.** $1\frac{4}{9}$ **9.** $\frac{26}{31}$
11. 3   **13.** 32   **15.** 3   **17.** $3r + 11$
19. $k^2 + k = 1$ **21.** $3s + 3t + 11$
23. $9x^2 + 69x + 133$ **25.** $9x + 44$
27. *Cops and Robbers Problem* **a.** 9, 3, −6
b. 4, 20 **c.** 8 min, 6 km **d.** 5 min
e. (Graph) **f.** Robin, 45 km/h; Willie,
120 km/h   **29.** *Efficient Car Problem*
a. $f(d) = 0.22d + 11,000$ **b.** 11,220;
13,200; 33,000 **c.** $g(d) = 0.20d + 11,300$
d. 11,500; 13,300; 31,300 **e.** 15,000 miles

Exercise 4-5, Linear Equations with Three or More Variables

1. (Graphs)   **3. a.** w-intercept = 6 x-inter-
cept = 14 y-intercept = −10.5 z-inter-
cept = 7 **b.** xyz trace: $3x − 4y + 6z = 42$
5. a. The intersection is a line, representing
all ordered triples that satisfy both equations. There are an infinite number of such
ordered triples. **b.** Three planes can intersect at a unique point.
c. (Graphs)   **d.** (Graphs) **e.** No

Exercise 4-6, Systems of Linear Equations with Three or More Variables

1. $\{(-4, 1, 3)\}$ **3.** $\{(1, 2, -3)\}$
5. $\left\{\left(2, -1, \frac{1}{3}\right)\right\}$ **7.** $\{(-1, 1, -5)\}$
9. $\left\{\left(3, 2\frac{1}{2}, 1\right)\right\}$ **11.** inconsistent
13. $\{(-1, 1, -2, 3)\}$ **15.** $\{(12, 24, 36)\}$
17. Wat1000 12 mph, UB41 0 mph (can't
run!), Pi314 18 mph

Exercise 4-7, Solution of Second-Order Systems by Augmented Matrices

1. $\{(2, 6)\}$ **3.** $\{(8, -1)\}$ **5.** $\{(1, 4)\}$
7. $\{(-5, 1)\}$ **9.** $\{(-2, 0)\}$
11. $\left\{\left(\frac{185}{11}, -\frac{226}{11}\right)\right\}$
13. $\left\{\left(-\frac{6044}{455}, \frac{13967}{455}\right)\right\}$ **15.** inconsistent   **17.** dependent

Exercise 4-8, Solution of Higher-Order Systems by Augmented Matrices

1. $\{(-4, 1, 3)\}$ **3.** $\{(1, 2, -3)\}$
5. $\left\{\left(2, -1, \frac{1}{3}\right)\right\}$ **7.** $\{-1, 1, -5)\}$
9. $\left\{\left(3, 2\frac{1}{2}, 1\right)\right\}$ **11.** inconsistent
13. $\{(-1, 1, -2, 3)\}$ **15.** $\{(1.525423,$
$0.135593, -1.13559)\}$
17. $\{(4, -2, 1, 3, -1)\}$

Exercise 4-9, Higher-Order Determinants

1. $\{(-4, 1, 3)\}$ **3.** $\{(1, 2, -3)\}$

Exercise 4-10, Systems of Linear Inequalities

1-15. (Graphs)

Exercise 4-11, Linear Programming

1. *Music Shop Problem* **a.** $C = 900B +$
$750G$ **b. i.** $B + G \le 50$ **ii.** $G \ge 2B$
iii. $G \ge 17; B \ge 5$ **c.** (Graph)
d. $C \ge 36,000 : 900B + 750G \ge$
$36,000 \to B \ge -\frac{5}{6}G + 40$ **e.** 34 guitars
and 16 basses for $39,900   **3.** *Park Clean-
up Problem* **a.** Let $x = $ number of old
members who work. Let $y = $ number of
new members who work. Let $D = $ number
of dollars earned. $D = 10x + 8y$
b. i. $x \ge 0, y \ge 0$ **ii.** $x \le 9, y \le 8$
iii. $6 \le x + y \le 15$ **iv.** $y \ge 3$
v. $\frac{x}{2} \le y < 3x$ **c.** (Graph) **d.** no
e. (Graph) **f.** (Graph); no **g.** $138 **h.** $52
i. $166   **5.** *Aircraft Problem* **a.** Let
$H = $ number of Hippos/day. Let
$C = $ number of Camels/day. **i.** $H \le 7$.
$C \le 11$ **ii.** $H + C \le 12$ **iii.** $H \le 2C$
iv. $H > 5 - \frac{C}{2}$ **c.** 11 Camels and 1 Hippo
for profit of $3500   **7.** *Feedlot Problem*
a. i. $y \ge -\frac{5}{2}x + 25$ **ii.** $y \ge -\frac{6}{5}x + 20$
iii. $y \ge -\frac{5}{8}x + 16$ **iv.** $y \ge -\frac{1}{4}x + 10$
v. $y \ge -x + 30$ **b.** Corn only is feasible.
Pellets only is not feasible. **c.** $d = 16x +$
$8y$ **d.** (Graph) **e.** $192/day **f.** $8/day
g. $7.39/day   **9.** *Cookie Problem* $37\frac{1}{2}$

dozen oatmeal brownie and 12.5 dozen chocolate chip for $68.75.   **11.** *Coal Problem* **a.** Pikkitt $7 - x$; Weedies $5 - y$; Treadwell $4 - z$ **b.** $x + y + z = 10$; $z = 10 - x - y$ **c.** $4 - (10 - x - y)$ $= x + y - 6$ **d. i.** $x \geq 0$ **ii.** $y \geq 0$ **iii.** $x \leq 7$ **iv.** $y \leq 5$ **v.** $x + y \geq 6$ **vi.** $x + y \leq 10$ **f.** $d = 6x - 3y + 186$ **g.** $y > 2x - 2$; (Graph) **h.** min $177 max $228

4-12, Chapter Review

R1. a. $\{(3, -4)\}$ **b.** $\left\{ \left(\dfrac{7}{29}, -\dfrac{39}{29} \right) \right\}$

R2. 1. $w(t) = 16 + 0.7t$; $c(t) = 24 + 0.3t$ **b.** $w(5) = 19.5$; $c(5) = 25.5$ **c.** $20.00 **d.** (Graph)   **R3.** $\{(-3, 1, 2)\}$ **R4.** (Graph)   **R5. a.** 10 each **b.** 120 **c.** 29

CHAPTER 5 QUADRATIC FUNCTIONS AND COMPLEX NUMBERS

Exercise 5-1, Introduction to Quadratic Functions

1.

x	y	(Graph)
-2	18	
-1	9	
0	2	
1	-3	
2	-6	
3	-7	
4	-6	
5	-3	
6	2	
7	9	
8	18	

3. (Graph) **5.** 0.4, 5.6 **7.** For real coefficients and domain, each term is real and unique by closure under multiplication. The value of the function, which is the sum of these real terms, is real and unique by closure under addition. Because a unique value is assigned each member of the domain, the quadratic relation is a function.

Exercise 5-2, Graphs of Quadratic Functions

1. $x^2 - 16x + 64$ **3.** $25x^2 + 60x + 36$

5. 100 **7.** $\dfrac{169}{4}$

9.

x	y
-2	15
-1	9
0	5
1	3
2	3
3	5
4	9
5	15

11.

x	y
-3	-52
-2	-32
-1	-18
0	-10
1	-8
2	-12
3	-22
4	-38

13. (Graph) **15.** (Graph) **17.** (Graph) **19.** (Graph) V: $(-3, 2)$; y-int: $(0, 11)$; sym. pt: $(-6, 11)$ **21.** (Graph) V: $(4, -31)$; y-int: $(0, 17)$; sym pt: $(8, 17)$ **23.** (Graph) V: $-1\dfrac{1}{2}, -20$; y-int: $(0, -11)$; sym pt: $(-3, -11)$ **25.** (Graph) V: $\left(2\dfrac{3}{4}, -27\dfrac{1}{8} \right)$; y-int: $(0, -12)$; sym pt: $\left(5\dfrac{1}{2}, -12 \right)$ **27.** (Graph) V: $(-3, 96)$; y-int: $(0, 51)$; sym pt: $(-6, 51)$ **29.** (Graph) V: $\left(\dfrac{1}{2}, 1\dfrac{1}{4} \right)$ y-int: $(0, 1)$; sym pt: $(1, 1)$ **31. a.** up **b.** wider **c.** graph opens downward, same proportions **d.** same proportions, shifted 3 units downward. **e.** no effect on proportions, shift in location. **f. i.** downward, negative coefficient of x^2 **ii.** wide, magnitude of x^2 coefficient less than 1 **iii.** somewhere else, non-zero x coefficient **iv.** below, y-intercept $= -4$ **g.** (Graphs)

33. a. $y - \left(c - \dfrac{b^2}{4a} \right) = a\left(x + \dfrac{b}{2a} \right)^2$

b. $-\dfrac{b}{2a}$ **c.** $c - \dfrac{b^2}{4a}$ **d.** a in $y = ax^2 + bx + c$ corresponds in position to the a in $y - k = a(x - h)^2$.

Exercise 5-3, x-Intercepts, and the Quadratic Formula

1. $\{2, 1\}$ **3.** $\{-3, -4\}$ **5.** $\{4, -2\}$ **7.** $\{-2 + \sqrt{7}, -2 - \sqrt{7}$ **9.** $\left\{ \dfrac{1}{2}, -5 \right\}$ **11.** $\left\{ \dfrac{7}{3}, 0 \right\}$ **13.** $\left\{ \dfrac{3}{2} \right\}$ **15.** $\{-1 \pm 2i\sqrt{3}\}$ **17.** $\left\{ \dfrac{2}{3}, -1 \right\}$ **19.** $\{2 + \sqrt{2}, 2 - \sqrt{2}\}$ **21.** -47 imaginary **23.** 49 real, rational, unequal **25.** 81 real, rational, unequal **27.** 1 real, rational, unequal **29.** 0 real, rational, equal **31.** (Graph) V: $(3, -1)$; x-int: $(2, 0)$ and $(4, 0)$; y-int: $(0, 8)$; sym pt: $(6, 8)$ **33.** (Graph) V: $(1, -16)$; x-int: $(-3, 0)$ and $(5, 0)$; y-int: $(0, -15)$; and sym pt: $(2, 15)$ **35.** (Graph) V: $(-1, 4)$; x-int: $(1, 0)$ and $(-3, 0)$; y-int: $(0, 3)$; sym pt:

$(-2, 3)$ **37.** (Graph) V: $\left(-1\frac{3}{4}, -3\frac{1}{8}\right)$;
x-int: $\left(-\frac{1}{2}, 0\right)$ and $(-3, 0)$; y-int: $(0, 3)$;
sym pt: $\left(-3\frac{1}{2}, 3\right)$ **39.** (Graph) V: $\left(\frac{1}{2}, 0\right)$;
x-int: $\left(\frac{1}{2}, 0\right)$; y-int: $(0, -1)$; sym pt:
$(1, -1)$
41. (Graph) V: $(-1, 4)$; x-int: none; y-int:
$(0, 5)$; sym pt: $(-2, 5)$ **43.** (Graph) V:
$(-1, -6)$; x-int: $(-1 + \sqrt{6}, 0)$ and
$(-1 - \sqrt{6}, 0)$; y-int: $(0, -5)$; sym pt: $(-2, -5)$ **45. a.** $\{-3 + \sqrt{5}, -3 - \sqrt{5}\}$
b. $\{3, 7\}$ **c.** $\left\{\frac{-7 + 2\sqrt{7}}{7}, \frac{-7 - 2\sqrt{7}}{7}\right\}$ **d.** $\{7.531 \ldots , -0.531 \ldots\}$
e. $\{3.366 \ldots , 1.633 \ldots\}$ **47.** $x = \frac{-b \pm \sqrt{b^2 - 4ac}}{2a}$ is the form of the
quadratic equation.

Exercise 5-4, Imaginary and Complex Numbers

1. a. $\{7 + 3i, 7 - 3i\}$ **b.** Answers may vary. **3. a.** $\{5 + i, 5 - i\}$ **b.** Answers may vary. **5. a.** $\left\{\frac{-2 + 8i}{3}, \frac{-2 - 8i}{3}\right\}$ **b.** Answers may vary.
7. a. $\{2.5, -1\}$ **b.** Answers may vary.
9. a. $\{2 + 5i, 2 - 5i\}$
b. Answers may vary.
11. a. $\left\{\frac{-7 + i\sqrt{171}}{10}, \frac{-7 - i\sqrt{171}}{10}\right\}$
b. Answers may vary. **13-19.** (Graph complex numbers on a single complex-number plane) **21.** *Quadratic Function Intercepts Problem* **a.** $\{5, 1\}$; $\{3\}$; $\{3 + 2i, 3 - 2i\}$ **c.** If the x-intercepts are both real and distinct (as for $f(x)$), the graph will intersect the x-axis at 2 distinct points. If the x-intercepts are real and equal (as for $g(x)$), the graph will be tangent to the x-axis. If the x-intercepts are non-real complex, the graph will not cross the x-axis.
23. *Complex Conjugates Problem* **a.** $4 - 7i$
b. $3 + 8i$ **c.** 58; the product is real. **d.** 22; the sum is real. **e.** $20i$; the difference is imaginary.
f. $(a + bi)(a - bi)$
$= a^2 + abi - abi$ Distributive axiom
    $- b^2 i^2$ applied twice

$= a^2 - b^2 i^2$ Combine like terms
$= a^2 + b^2$ Definition of i
$a^2 + b^2$ is real   Closure of reals un-
Q.E.D.   der addition and
                 multiplication
$(a + bi) - (a - bi)$
$= a + bi - a + bi$ Distributive axiom
$= 2bi$ Combine like terms
$2b$ is real   Closure of reals un-
                 der multiplication
$2bi$ is pure   Definition of imagi-
imaginary Q.E.D. nary number
25. *Powers of i Problem*
a. $i^4 = 1$ **b.** For an integer n:
$i^5 = i$ $i^{4n} = 1$
$i^6 = -1$ $i^{4n+1} = i$
$i^7 = -i$ $i^{4n+2} = -1$
$i^8 = 1$ $i^{4n+3} = -i$
$i^9 = i$
$i^{10} = -1$
c. $i = i^{4(0)+1} = i$
$i^0 = i^{4(0)} = 1$
The zero power of any number except zero is 1.
d. 1
e. $i^{2001} = i$
$i^{137} = i$
$i^{50} = -1$

Exercise 5-5, Evaluating Quadratic Functions

1. a. 14 **b.** 0.4, -2 **c.** $\approx 0.628, -2.228$
3. a. -199 **b.** 1, 0.5 **c.** no real values
5. a. $-2, -6$ **b.** $-4 \pm \sqrt{3}$ **c.** $-3, -5$
d. -4 **e.** no real values **f.** 0, -8 **7.** yes;
no **9.** no; no **11.** no; yes **13.** yes; yes
15. a. $0 = x^2 - 6x + 34$
$$x = \frac{6 \pm \sqrt{36 - 4(1)(34)}}{2(1)}$$
$$= \frac{6 \pm \sqrt{-100}}{2}$$
$$= 3 \pm 5i$$
b. $f(3 + 5i) = (3 + 5i)^2 - 6(3 + 5i)$
                $+ 34$
            $= 9 + 30i - 25 - 18$
                $- 30i + 34$
            $= 0$
c. $f(3 + 2i) = (3 + 2i)^2 - 6(3 + 2i)$
                $+ 34$
            $= 9 + 12i - 4 - 18$
                $- 12i + 34$
$12i - 12i = 0$
imaginary part disappears $\therefore$ real.

d. $f(7 + 4i) = (7 + 4i)^2 - 6(7 + 4i)$
$+ 34$
$= 49 + 56i - 16 - 42$
$- 24i + 34$
$56i - 24i = 32i$
result has an imaginary part $\therefore$ not real.

e. If $f(a + bi)$ is real, then $a = 3$. The imaginary part of the first term of the expansion of $f(a + bi)$ is $2abi$. The imaginary part of the 2nd term in the expansion is $-6bi$. For $2abi - 6bi$ to disappear for all real b, a must be 3.

f. $f(a + bi) = (a + bi)^2 - 6(a + bi)$
$+ 34$
$= a^2 + 2abi + b^2i^2 - 6a$
$- 6bi + 34$
Distributive axiom applied 3 times
$= a^2 + 2abi - b^2 - 6a$
$- 6bi + 34$
Definition of i
$= (a^2 - b^2 - 6a + 34)$
$+ (2abi - 6bi)$
Associative and commutative axioms of addition
$= (a^2 - b^2 - 6a + 34)$
$+ 2bi(a - 3)$
Distributive axiom
$a^2 - b^2 - 6a + 34$
is real
Closure of reals under addition and multiplication
$2bi(a - 3)$ is real iff $2b(a - 3)$ is 0
Definition of imaginary number
Since b can be any real, $a - 3 = 0$
Zero product property
$\therefore a = 3$ Additive identity

Exercise 5-6, Equations of Quadratic Functions from Their Graphs

1. $y = 3x^2 - 2x + 5$ **3.** $y = -4x^2 + 11x - 3$ **5.** $y = 0.2x^2 + 0.7x + 1.3$

7. $y = 0.4x^2$ **9.** $y = -\frac{1}{2}x^2 + 7x - 1$

11. $y = 2x^2 - 5x$

13. $y = 2x^2 + 16x + 35$

15. inconsistent; $(5, 2)$ and $(5, -7)$ give y not unique for each x, not a function

Exercise 5-7, Quadratic and Linear Functions as Mathematical Models

1. *Phoebe Small's Rocket Problem* **a.** $d = 3t^2 - 78t + 500$ **b.** 500; distance from surface in km when motor fires **c.** $t = 15$, $d = 5$ $t = 16$, $d = 20$ pulling away **d.** vertex $(13, -7)$ Phoebe crashed before $t = 13$. **f.** $\{t: 0 \leq t \leq 11.5\}$ **3.** *Car Insurance Problem* **a.** $A = 0.4t^2 - 36t + 1000$ **b.** 680 accidents/100 million km **c.** 70-year-olds appear to be safer **d.** 45-year-olds appear to be safest. **e.** $\{t: 16 \leq t \leq 85\}$ **5.** *Artillery Problem* **a.** $y = -80x^2 + 120x + 610$ **b. i.** 530 m **ii.** 610 m **c.** $x \approx -1.81$ km **d.** no danger; maximum ordinate 655 m **7.** *Rectangular Field Problem* **a.** length = $500 - 2x$; width = $300 - 2x$; linear functions **b.** $A = 4x^2 - 1600x + 150{,}000$ quadratic function

c.

x	A
5	142,100
10	134,400
15	126,900

d. 34.168 . . . or about 34 yards wide
f. 54.226 . . . or about 54 yds. wide
9. *Loan Problem* **a.** $D(w) = 765 - 17w$ **b.** constant rate of payment **c.** \$45 **d.** week 40 **e.** 765, the original loan amount. **f.** 45, the week of final payment   **11.** *Dee Side's Pig Problem* **a.** \$280 **b.** $W(t) = 200 + 5t$ linear **c.** $P(t) = 1.40 - 0.02t$ linear **d.** $T(t) = -0.1t^2 + 3t + 280$ quadratic

e.

t	T(t)
8	\$297.60
16	302.40
24	294.40

f. 15 weeks   **13.** *Quadratic or Linear Problem Number 1* The function is not linear because the slope is not constant. $y = 0.16x^2 + 5.16x + 264$ **15.** *Color TV Problem* **b.** $p = \frac{8}{3}s^2 - 60\frac{2}{3}s + 760$

c. \$840

d.

s	p
5	$523\frac{1}{3}$
12	416
17	$499\frac{1}{3}$
21	662

f. reasonable, except at $s = 5$ **g.** higher costs, smaller demand   **17.** *Spaceship Problem* **a.** $y = 0.03x^2 - 7$ **b.** midcourse

maneuver necessary   **19.** *Barley Problem*
a. $(0, 0)$ $(2, 22)$ $(4, 40)$ **b.** $B = -0.5s^2 +$
$12s$ **c.** 64 **d.** 70 bushels/acre for 10 or 14
million seeds **e.** 12 million seeds **f.** yes,
$s \geq 24$

5-8, Chapter Review and Test

R1. 121 quadratic function   **R2. a.** $9x^2 -$
$24x + 16$ **b.** $y + 12.8 = 5(x + 1.4)^2$
c. (Graph) **d.** $2.198 . . .$ and $-0.531 . . .$
R3. a. $\{2.397 . . . , -1.772 . . .\}$ **b.** -347
c. i. 2 rational solutions **ii.** 2 irrational solutions **iii.** 2 equal rational solutions **iv.** 2
complex solutions **d.** $(-1.7, 76.55)$
R4. a. $8i$ **b.** (Graph) **c.** $\{1 + 7i, 1 - 7i\}$
R5. a. 22 **b.** $10.588 . . .$ or $-3.588 . . .$
c. no   **R6. a.** $y = 2x^2 - 4x + 1$ **b.** $y =$
$5x - 31$ **R7. a.** $d = -5t^2 + 9t + 20$
b. 20 m from surface Set $t = 0$. **c.** 24.05
meters **d.** about 3.1 sec

5-9, Cumulative Review: Chapters 1 Through 5

1. a. C **b.** P **c.** C **d.** B **e.** B **f.** P **g.** C
h. N **i.** C **j.** N **k.** N **l.** P **m.** P **n.** C
3. a. $A\frac{2}{3}$; $B -\frac{2}{3}$; $C\frac{2}{3}$; $D -\frac{3}{2}$
b. $A \parallel C$; $A \perp D$; $C \perp D$ **c.** See Additional Answers.
5. definition of division   not an axiom
  multiplicative inverse   field axiom
  transitivity   axiom
7. a. $H = 4A + 19$ **b.** 83 in. **c.** 19 (inches
at birth) **d.** constant rate of growth,
4 inches/year **e.** cessation of growth in teen
years   **9. a.** $V = -t^2 + 120t + 1300$
b. Yes: there are real values of t for which
$V = 4500$. **c.** after 130 min
e. $\{t: 0 \leq t \leq 130\}$ $\{V: 0 \leq V \leq 4900\}$

CHAPTER 6 EXPONENTIAL AND LOGARITHMIC FUNCTIONS

Exercise 6-1; Introduction to Exponential Functions

1. 16; 8; 4; 2 (Graph)
3. asymptote
5. $2^0 = 1$
  $2^{-1} = 0.5$
  $2^{-2} = 0.25$
  $2^{-3} = 0.125$
  $2^{2.5} = 5.656 . . .$

Exercise 6-2, Exponentiation for Positive Integer Exponents

1. a. 1296 **b.** 162 **c.** 162   **3. a.** 625
b. 19 **c.** 19   **5. a.** -27 **b.** -339 **c.** -339
7. a. -162 **b.** 1296 **c.** -162 **d.** -162
9. 32   **11.** 2187   **13.** 32,768   **15.** *Product of Two Powers Problem* **a.** $x^3 \cdot x^5 =$
$x \cdot x \cdot x \cdot x \cdot x \cdot x \cdot x \cdot x = x^8$ 8 x's
b. $3 + 5 = 8$ **17.** *Power of a Power
Problem* **a.** $(x \cdot x \cdot x \cdot x \cdot x)(x \cdot x \cdot x \cdot x)$
$(x \cdot x \cdot x \cdot x \cdot x) = x^{15}$ **b.** $5 \cdot 3 = 15$
19. *Power of a Quotient Problem*
a. $\left(\frac{x}{y}\right)\left(\frac{x}{y}\right)\left(\frac{x}{y}\right)\left(\frac{x}{y}\right) = \frac{x \cdot x \cdot x \cdot x}{y \cdot y \cdot y \cdot y} = \frac{x^4}{y^4}$
b. distribute   **21.** *Computer Graphics Prob-
lem* **a.** 1; 1 **b.** increase; decrease **c.** (Graph)

Exercise 6-3, Properties of Exponentiation

1. 36   **3.** 80   **5.** -150 **7.** -81
9. 64   **11.** $625x^{28}$ **13.** $392y^3$ **15.** $\frac{9x}{2}$
17. $\frac{x^{26}}{y^2}$ **19.** $\frac{243k^{10}m^5}{32}$ **21.** $4{,}084{,}101 =$
$243 \cdot 16{,}807$ **23.** $9^{10} = 3^{20}$ **25.** $2^{(25-5)} =$
2^{20} **27.** 9   **29.** 896   **31.** 9
33-39. Answers may vary. Possible answers
are given.   **33.** $(2^3)^2 = 8^2 = 64$; $2^{(3 \cdot 2)} =$
$2^6 = 64$; $\therefore (2^3)^2 = 2^{(3 \cdot 2)}$ **35.** $5^2 \cdot 5^3$
$= 25 \cdot 125 = 3125$; $5^{(2+3)} = 5^5 = 3125$;
$\therefore 5^5 = 5^{(2+3)}$
37. $\left(\frac{3}{4}\right)^3 = \left(\frac{3}{4}\right)\left(\frac{3}{4}\right)\left(\frac{3}{4}\right) = \frac{27}{64}$; $\frac{3^3}{4^3} = \frac{27}{64}$;
$\therefore \left(\frac{3}{4}\right)^3 = \frac{3^3}{4^3}$ **39.** Assume exponentiation
distributes over addition. Then
$(a + b)^n = a^n + b^n$ for all real a and b. Let
$a = 1$, $b = 2$, $n = 2$. $(1 + 2)^2 = 3^2 = 9$;
$1^2 + 2^2 = 1 + 4 = 5$; $9 \neq 5$, so $(1 + 2)^2$
$\neq 1^2 + 2^2$. Because a counter-example has
been shown, exponentiation does not distribute over addition for all reals.   **41.** *Exponential Function Graphing Problem*
a. 5.0625 3.375 2.25 1.5 **b.** 1.0 $0.\overline{6}$
0.4 $0.\overline{296}$ **c.** 0.2962963 **e.** about 1.7
$1.5^{1.7} = 1.9923 . . . \approx 2$ **43.** *Ancestors
Problem* $A(n) = 2^n$; exponential; 1,048,567

Exercise 6-4, Exponentiation for Rational Exponents

1. $\frac{1}{3^2} = \frac{1}{9} = 0.1111111 . . .$

3. $3.8485011 . . .$ is reasonable
because it is between 3 and 4;
$(3.8485011 . . .)(3.8485011 . . .)$

$(3.8485011 \ldots) = 57$; $57^{\frac{1}{3}}$ gives 57 when it is cubed **5.** $(2^6)^{\frac{1}{3}} = 2^{\frac{6}{3}} = 2^2 = 4$

7. $\dfrac{7^3}{7^3} = 7^{3-3} = 7^0 = 1$

$\dfrac{7^3}{7^3} = \dfrac{343}{343} = 1$ **9.** $8^{-\frac{1}{3}} = (8^{\frac{1}{3}})^{-1} = \dfrac{1}{8^{\frac{1}{3}}}$

11. $437^{\frac{1}{5}} = 3.373 \ldots$ **13.** $99735^{\frac{1}{4}} = 17.771 \ldots$ **15.** $279936^{\frac{1}{7}} = 6$

17. $73157^{\frac{1}{2}} = 270.475 \ldots$ **19.** $18x^3$

21. $10x^{-7}$ **23.** $51a^{-6}$ **25.** $-648x^2y^8$

27. $648x^{-4}y^3$ **29.** $\dfrac{1}{3}a^{-9}b^8$

31. $5a^2 - 3a$ **33.** $xy^{-5}z^4$ **35.** $\dfrac{1}{3}x^4yz^{-2}$

37. 1 **39.** $12x^{\frac{1}{6}}$ **41.** $1728x^{-1}$ **43.** $u^{6.6}p^3$

45. $x^3y^{\frac{7}{4}}$ **47.** *Increasing and Decreasing Exponential Functions Problem* **b.** $f(x)$ increases, $g(x)$ decreases on this domain; $f(0) = g(0) = 1$. Both are "concave" upward. **c.** $f(x)$ **d.** $0 < b < 1 \rightarrow$ decreasing $b > 1 \rightarrow$ increasing

Exercise 6-5, Powers of Radicals without Calculators

1. *Table of Powers Problem*

base exp	2	3	4	5	6	7	8	9	10	11	12
2	4	9	16	25	36	49	64	81	100	121	144
3	8	27	64	125	216	343	512	729	1000	1331	1728
4	16	81	256	625							
5	32	243	1024								
6	64	729									
7	128										
8	256										
9	512										
10	1024										

3. 4 **5.** 5 **7.** 6 **9.** 2 **11.** 32

13. 16 **15.** 32 **17.** $\dfrac{1}{512}$ **19.** 16

21. -16 **23.** $\dfrac{1}{64}$ **25.** 4 **27.** $\dfrac{1}{729}$

29. 49 **31.** $-\dfrac{1}{1000}$ **33.** $\dfrac{343}{27}$ **35.** $\dfrac{16}{81}$

37. 12 **39.** $\sqrt{3}$ **41.** $2^{\frac{1}{4}}$ **43.** $2^{\frac{29}{6}}$

45. $2^{0.8}$ **47.** $10^{1.24}$ **49.** $\sqrt[3]{2}$ or $2^{\frac{1}{3}}$

51. $\sqrt[3]{6}$ or $6^{\frac{1}{3}}$ **53.** $\dfrac{1}{3}$ **55.** $\dfrac{3}{2}$ **57.** 10

59. 0 **61.** *Areas and Volumes Problem* **a.** 1728 **b.** 27 **c.** 144 **d.** 9 **e.** 10,000 **f.** 1,000,000 **g.** 10^9 **63.** *Negative Bases Problem* **a.** -2 **b.** 2 **c.** Even roots of negative numbers are not defined in the real numbers. **d.** Real numbers are not closed under nth root operations.

Exercise 6-6, Scientific Notation

1. 3.72×10^5 **3.** 2.61×10^{-3}
5. 2.001×10^3 **7.** 2.024×10^{-1}
9. 2.47×10^7 **11.** 6×10^{15}
13. 3.5×10^{16} **15.** 4.2×10^{-4}
17. 5.4×10^1 **19.** 5.6×10^{-23}
21. 4×10^{11} **23.** 2×10^{-7}
25. 3.5×10^8 **27.** 2×10^9
29. 1.2×10^{-16} **31.** 6.6×10^{12}
33. 1.7×10^{-12} **35.** 6.1×10^{-14}
37. 1.308×10^4 **39.** 6×10^{13}
41. 4×10^7 **43.** 3×10^{17}
45. 4×10^{13} **47.** 8×10^{-15}
49. 3×10^{-7} **51.** 4×10^7
53. 1×10^{-7} **55.** 3×10^{-13}
57. 9×10^5 **59.** 3×10^8
61. 1.70×10^{-5} **63.** 6.17×10^6
65. 5.48×10^{10} **67.** 1.66×10^{-9}
69. 7.22×10^{14} **71.** *Brain Cell Problem* 2×10^{18} **73.** *Rain-fall Problem* 1.4×10^7 about 14 million pounds

Exercise 6-7, Exponential Equations Solved by Brute Force

1. *Iterative Solution Problem* **b.** 7.203 $\ldots$ **c.** 2.6 **d.** 3.973 **e.** 2.6126 **f.** -1.3063
3. $\{2.73\}$ **5.** $\{-0.569\}$ **7.** $\emptyset$
9. *Computer Program for Evaluating Functions* 2.28309 **11.** $\{3.299956\}$
13. $\{-2.570195\}$ **15.** $\{155.796915\}$
17. *Compound Interest Problem*
a. \$1790.84 interest = \$790.84
b. \$5743.49 false **c.** \$339,302.08
d. 12 years

Exercise 6-8, Exponential Equations Solved by Logarithms

1. $\{2.598 \ldots\}$ **3.** $\{1.607 \ldots\}$ **5.** $\emptyset$
7. $\{0.386 \ldots\}$ **9.** $\{0.212 \ldots\}$
11. $\{2.271 \ldots\}$

13. $x = \dfrac{\log 3}{\log 2}$; $\{1.584 \ldots\}$

15. $x = \dfrac{\log 17.2}{\log 54.3}$; $\{0.712 \ldots\}$

17. $x = \dfrac{\log 987}{2 \log 4.13}$; $\{2.430 \ldots\}$

19. $x = \dfrac{\log\left(\dfrac{4}{7}\right)}{\log 5}$; $\{-0.347 \ldots\}$

21. $x = \dfrac{\log 1000}{5 \log 13} = \dfrac{3}{5 \log 13}$; $\{0.538 \ldots\}$

23. $x = \dfrac{5 \log \left(\dfrac{371}{4}\right)}{\log 23}$; $\{7.223 \ldots\}$

25. *Exponential Equation Shortcut Problem*

a. $x = \dfrac{\log c}{\log b}$ **b.** $\{-0.041 \ldots\}$

c. $29^{-0.041 \ldots} = 0.87$

27. *Exact Power Problem* $\dfrac{1}{27}$

Exercise 6-9, Logarithms with Other Bases

1. 8   **3.** 27   **5.** $\dfrac{1}{81}$ **7.** 81   **9.** $\dfrac{1}{16}$

11. $\dfrac{1}{2}$ **13.** 2   **15.** -2 **17.** 10   **19.** -5

21. 3   **23.** no number   **25.** 0   **27.** 9

29. 9   **31.** 2   **33.** 4   **35.** $\dfrac{1}{8}$ **37.** 27

39. $\dfrac{1}{36}$ **41.** no number   **43.** *Logarithm*

Base Restrictions Problem **a.** Let $b = -1$ and $y = 0.5$ $(-1)^{0.5} = \sqrt{-1} = i$
b. There are no x satisfying $1^x = 5$ or $0^x = 5$. **c.** For a positive number x, $b^y > 0$ for all real numbers y. **d.** error message
45. *Exponential Properties Problem*

$x^a \cdot x^b = x^{(a+b)}$

$\dfrac{x^a}{x^b} = x^{(a-b)}$

$(x^a)^b = x^{ab}$

$x^{-a} = \dfrac{1}{x^a}$

$x^{a/b} = \left(\sqrt[b]{x}\right)^a$

Exercise 6-10, Properties of Logarithms

1. 1.3222193   **3.** 0.9542425
5. 2.5352941   **7.** 0.602   **9.** 0.903
11. -0.176 **13.** 1.000   **15.** 1.176
17. 2.862   **19.** 2.000   **21.** 0.477
23. 1.477   **25.** 2.477   **27.** 3.477
29. 12.477   **31.** The value to the left of the decimal varies; the value to the right is constant.   **33.** $\log_3 35$ **35.** $\log_2 3$
37. $\log_7 30$ **39.** $\log_5 16$ **41.** $\log_{12} 32$
43. $\log_6 135$ **45.** 0.5462217
47. 11.118056   **49.** -1.8231641
51. *Log Property Statement Problem*

$\log_b (xy) = \log_b x + \log_b y$

$\log_b \left(\dfrac{x}{y}\right) = \log_b x - \log_b y$

$\log_b (x^n) = n \log_b x$

53. *Powers too Large for Calculators Problem* **a.** 1.6614×10^{172} **b.** 1.6633×10^{320}
c. 5.43618×10^{-227} **d.** 678 **e.** 698
55. *Decibel Problem* **a.** 0 db **b.** 36 db
c. 88 db **d.** 124 db **e.** 130 db

Exercise 6-11, Proofs of Properties of Logarithms

1. 1.7124   **3.** -0.4958 **5.** 7
7. -3.3725 **9.** no number
11. *Log Properties Review Problem*

$\log_b (xy) = \log_b x + \log_b y$

$\log_b \left(\dfrac{x}{y}\right) = \log_b x - \log_b y$

$\log_b (x^n) = n \log_b x$

13. 8   **15.** -2 **17.** 7   **19.** 9   **21.** *Natural Logarithm Problem* **a.** 0.6931472
1.0986123 **b.** 2.718 **c.** 2.718281   **23.** *Log and Exponential Function Graph Problem*
a. (Graph) **b.** (Graph) **c.** The graphs are mirror images through the line $x = y$
25. *Log Proof Problem 1*

Let $r = \log_b x$, $s = \log_b y$

Then $b^r = x$, $b^s = y$ Definition of logarithm

$\dfrac{b^r}{b^s} = \dfrac{x}{y}$ Divide and substitute

$b^{r-s} = \dfrac{x}{y}$ Division of powers of the same base

$\log_b \dfrac{x}{y} = r - s$ Definition of logarithm

$\therefore \log_b \dfrac{x}{y} =$
$\quad \log_b x - \log_b y$ Substitution

27. *Change of Base*

Let $y = \log_a x$.

Then $a^y = x$ Definition of logarithm.

$\log_b a^y = \log_b x$ Take $\log_b$ of both sides.

$y \cdot \log_b a = \log_b x$ Log of a power.

$y = \dfrac{\log_b x}{\log_b a}$, QED   Divide by $\log_b a$.

29. *Reciprocal*

$\log_a b = \dfrac{\log_b b}{\log_b a}$ Change-of-Base Property.

$\quad = \dfrac{1}{\log_b a}$, QED $\log_b b = 1$.

31. *Product of Three Logs Property*
$(\log_a b)(\log_b c)(\log_c d)$
$\qquad = \log_a c \, (\log_c d)$ Associativity and
$\qquad\qquad\qquad$ Product of Two
$\qquad\qquad\qquad$ Logs Property
$\qquad = \log_a d$ QED $\qquad$ Product of Two
$\qquad\qquad\qquad$ Logs Property

33. *Base and Argument are Like Powers*
$\log_{(b^n)} (x^n)$

$\qquad = \dfrac{1}{n} \log_b (x^n)$ $\quad$ From Problem 32

$\qquad = \dfrac{1}{n} (n \cdot \log_b x)$ $\quad$ Log of a power

$\qquad = \log_b x$, QED $\quad$ Associativity and
$\qquad\qquad\qquad$ Mult. Inverses.

35. *Base-2 Logs Quickly* **a.** 3.321928096
b. i. 3.7004397 **ii.** −0.6665763
iii. 10.794416 **iv.** 12 **v.** 19.931569
37. *Introduction to the Inverse of a Function*

a. $x = \dfrac{3}{2}y - \dfrac{21}{2}$ **b.** $x = \pm\sqrt{\dfrac{y}{3}}$

c. $x = \log_7 y$ **39.** no real number
41. 6.559 **43.** no real number **45.** 4

47. $\dfrac{1}{3}$ **49.** 0 **51.** {(27, 64), (3, 4)}

53. 3 **55.** 3 **57.** $\dfrac{46}{45}$ **59.** 25

Exercise 6-12, Inverses of Functions—The Logarithmic Function

1. a. $f^{-1}(x) = \dfrac{1}{3}x - \dfrac{5}{3}$ **c.** function
3. a. $f^{-1}(x) = 2.5x + 15$ **c.** function
5. a. $f^{-1}(x) = \pm\sqrt{10x}$ **c.** not a function
7. a. $f^{-1}(x) = \sqrt[3]{x} - 2$ **c.** function
9. a. $f^{-1}(x) = x - 3$ **c.** function
11. a. $f^{-1}(x) = x^2 + 4$ for $x \geq 0$
c. function **13. a.** $f^{-1}(x) = \log_{1.4} x$
for $x \geq 0$ **c.** not a function
15. a. $f^{-1}(x) = 0.5(5^x)$ for $x > 0$
c. function **17.** no **19.** yes **21.** inverses **23.** not inverses **25.** inverses
27. k must be restricted to $k \neq 0$
$\qquad f(x) = kx$

$\qquad x = \dfrac{f(x)}{k}$ $\quad$ Divide both sides by k
$\qquad\qquad\qquad$ and symmetry.

$\qquad f^{-1}(x) = \dfrac{x}{k}$ $\quad$ Switch roles of independent and dependent variables.

29. No. The inverse would be the mirror image of a horizontal line through the line $y = x$, which would be a vertical line,

which is not a function. **31.** *Inverse of a Linear Function Problem* $f^{-1}(x) = \dfrac{x - b}{m}$ for $m \neq 0$ **33.** *Inverse of an Exponential Function Problem* $f^{-1}(x) = \dfrac{1}{a} \log_b x$ for a, x, $b > 0$ and $b \neq 1$.

35. *Misconception Problem*
$\qquad f(x) = mx + b$

$\qquad x = \dfrac{1}{m} f(x) + \dfrac{b}{m}$

$\qquad \therefore f^{-1}(x) = \dfrac{1}{m}x + \dfrac{b}{m}$ $\quad$ for $m \neq 0$

$\qquad \dfrac{1}{f(x)} = \dfrac{1}{mx + b}$

$\qquad$ But $\dfrac{1}{m}x + \dfrac{b}{m}$

$\qquad \neq \dfrac{1}{mx + b}$ $\qquad$ for some values
$\qquad\qquad\qquad\qquad$ of m, b, x

$\qquad \therefore f^{-1}(x) \neq \dfrac{1}{f(x)}$

Exercise 6-13, The Add-Multiply Property of Exponential Functions

1.

x	$f(x)$
−4	16
−1	24
2	36
5	54
8	81
11	121.5

3.

x	$f(x)$
0	204.1
2	142.9
4	100
6	70
8	49
10	34.3

5.

x	$f(x)$
−12	0.25
−7	0.5
−2	1
3	2
8	4
13	8

7.

x	$f(x)$
2	60.1
5	39.3
8	25.7
11	16.8
14	11.0
17	7.2

9. yes **11.** no **13.** yes **15.** 12.167
17. *Particular Equation Problem* **a.** $a = 7$

b. $b = \left(\dfrac{19}{7}\right)^{1/3}$ **c.** $f(x) = 7 \cdot \left(\dfrac{19}{7}\right)^{x/3}$

d. $f(6) = 51.571 \ldots$

$f(3) \cdot \dfrac{19}{7} = 19\left(\dfrac{19}{7}\right) = 51.571 \ldots$

Exercise 6-14, Exponential and Other Functions as Mathematical Models

1. *Population Problem* **a.** 1.1133005
1990: 251.6 million; 2000: 280.1 million;
2010: 311.8 million **c.** $P = 203 \times$
$1.01079 \ldots^t$ **d.** Answers may vary.
e. 2033 **f.** prediction: about 25 million;
actual: about 4 million. Population grew
more rapidly before 1960 than since.
3. *Car-Stopping Problem* **a.** $s = 64 \times$
$0.97164 \ldots^t$ **b.** about 31 km/h **c.** about 65
sec **f.** According to the model, he never
completely stops. **5.** *Phoebe's Next Rocket
Problem* **a.** $s > 17{,}500$ at $t = 30$. She will
orbit **b.** $29.46s$ **c.** $36.9s$

7. *Car Trade-In Problem*
a. year 0   2350
   year 1   1645
   year 2   1151.50
   year 3   806.05
b. Adding 1 to years multiplies value by
0.7. **c.** $V = 2350 \times 0.70000 \ldots^t$
d. about 3.8 years **e.** about $6156 **f.** mostly
dealer profit **9.** *Carbon-14 Dating Problem* **a.** $P = 100 \times 0.99987 \ldots^t$
b. about 78.58% **c.** about 61.74% **d.** yes,
about 4045 B.C. **e.** $P = 10^{-5233}$, undetect-
able **11.** *Corn Flakes Problem* **a.** $c =$
$7w + 23$ **c.** overpriced by 4¢ **d.** 51 oz
13. *Studying Problem* **a.** 85 points; 2 h
b. 65 p-intercept **c.** about 6.1 h; it is reasonable to expect a poor grade after 6 hours
of study because she will be tired the next
day . . . and may oversleep and miss the
test! **15.** *Coffee Cup Problem* **a.** (0, 65)
(5, 52) **b.** $D = 65 \times 0.95635 \ldots^t$
c. about 94.3°C **d.** about 16.87 min
17. *Car Acceleration Problem* **a.** $D =$
$160 \times 0.94408 \ldots^t$ **b.** about 103.2 km/h
c. about 48 sec **e.** $S = 160 - D =$
$160 - 160 \times 0.94408 \ldots^t =$
$160(1 - 0.94408 \ldots^t)$
19. *Sunlight Below the Water Problem*
a. $I = 1000 \times 0.24494 \ldots^d$

b. *d*

d	I	$\log I$
0	1000	3
2	60	1.78
4	3.6	0.56
6	0.216	−0.67
8	0.01296	−1.89
10	0.0007776	−3.11

c. 9.8 m **d.** (Graph) **e.** straight line, $\log I$
varies linearly with d
21. *Deep Oil Well Cost Problem*
a. $P = 10 \times 1.04137 \ldots^d$
b. *d*

d	P
0	20
10	30
20	45
30	67.5
40	101.25
50	151.875

c. (Graph) **d.** Answers will vary.
e. Answers will vary. **f.** $3,252,000
23. *Radioactive Brain Tracer Problem*
a. $P = a_1 b_1^t$
   $B = a_2 b_2^t$
   $F = PB = (a_1 b_1^t)(a_2 b_2^t)$
   $F = (a_1 a_2)(b_1 b_2)^t$
   $F = a_3 b_3^t$
b. $F = 1 \times 0.84440 \ldots^t$ **c.** $B = 1 \times$
$0.94780 \ldots^t$ **d.** about 12.9 h

6-15, Chapter Review

R1. $f(4) = 81$ $f(3) = 27$ $f(2) = 9$
$f(1) = 3$

$\dfrac{1}{3}f(4) = \dfrac{1}{3}(81) = 27 = f(3)$

$\dfrac{1}{3}f(3) = \dfrac{1}{3}(27) = 9 = f(2)$

$\dfrac{1}{3}f(2) = \dfrac{1}{3}(9) = 3 = f(1)$

In general $f(x - 1) = \dfrac{1}{3}f(x)$

$3^0 = f(0) = \dfrac{1}{3}f(1) = 1$

$3^{-1} = f(-1) = \dfrac{1}{3}f(0) = \dfrac{1}{3}$

$3^{-2} = f(-2) = \dfrac{1}{3}f(-1) = \dfrac{1}{9}$

R2. a. 75 **b.** −25 **c.** 0
R3. a. Product of Powers
   of the same base: $x^a x^b = x^{a+b}$
   Quotient of Powers
   of the Same Base: $\dfrac{x^a}{x^b} = x^{a-b}$

   Power of a Power: $(x^a)^b = x^{ab}$
   Power with a
   Negative Exponent $x^{-a} = \dfrac{1}{x^a}$

Power with a
Fractional Exponent $x^{a/b} = (\sqrt[b]{x^a})$
b. i. -16 **ii.** -125 **iii.** 16 **c. i.** $32x^{35}$
ii. $4x^{24}y^{40}$ **iii.** $3r^9p^6$ **d.** 625 **R4. a.** $x^{-a} =$
$\dfrac{1}{x^a}, x \neq 0$ **b.** $x^0 = 1, x \neq 0$ **c.** $x^{\frac{1}{t}} = \sqrt[t]{x}$,
where defined **d. i.** $100x^{-11}$ **ii.** $\dfrac{1}{27}x^3y^{12}$
iii. $720x^{-\frac{1}{4}}$ **e i.** 16 **ii.** 8 **iii.** $4.14105\ldots$
iv. $0.05766\ldots$ **v.** $71.91856\ldots$ **f.** (Graphs)

R5. a. i. 16 **ii.** $\dfrac{1}{4}$ **iii.** 12 **b.** $\dfrac{\sqrt[5]{5^2}}{5}$ **c.** $\left\{\dfrac{2}{3}\right\}$

d. 100 **R6. a.** $5.4(10^{61})$ **b.** $2.4(10^{23})$
c. $1.018(10^{-38})$ **d.** (Graph) **R7.** $\{3.600\}$
R8. a. $\{-0.657\ldots\}$ **b.** (Graph)
R9. a. $j = 9$ **b.** $m = 4$ **c.** $p = 7$
R10. a. 1.653 **b.** 169 **c.** $\log_{13} 20$
R11. $2.057\ldots$ **R12. a.** $f^{-1}(x)$
$= \dfrac{1}{7}x - 6$ **b.** $g^{-1}(x) = \dfrac{1}{3}(5^x)$

c. $h^{-1}(x) = \pm\sqrt{x}$ **d.** not a function; for
some x, $a(x)$ has more than one value:
$x - 3$ and $-x - 3$.
R13. 21.4375 **R14.** *Fog Problem* **a.** 32
units **b.** $f(x) = 128(0.5^{\frac{x}{43}})$ **c.** about 233 ft
d. by a factor of 2 in each case **e.** At 30
mph (45 ft/s) the intensity doubles each second, which is very rapid.

CHAPTER 7 RATIONAL ALGEBRAIC FUNCTIONS

Exercise 7-1, Introduction to Rational Algebraic Functions

1. $f(0) = -\dfrac{1}{3}; f(1) = -\dfrac{1}{2}; f(2) = -1;$

$f(4) = 1; f(5) = \dfrac{1}{2}; f(-1) = -\dfrac{1}{4};$

$f(-3) = -\dfrac{1}{6}$

3. Domain excludes $x = 3$ and $x = -2$.
5. The graph might have a *vertical asymptote* or a "hole." The hole is called a
"removable discontinuity."

Exercise 7-2, Rational Function Graphs—Discontinuities and Asymptotes

1. *Graphing Problem No. 1*
(Graph)

x	$f(x)$
-10	-0.1
-8	-0.125
-5	-0.2
-2	-0.5
-1	-1

x	$f(x)$
0.1	10
0.2	5
0.5	2
2	0.5
5	0.2
8	0.125
10	0.1

3. *Graphing Problem No. 3*

a. $\dfrac{(x - 4)}{(x - 4)(x - 1)}$ discontinuous at $x = 4$

and $x = 1$ **b.** $\dfrac{1}{x - 1}$ vertical asymptote at

$x = 1$, removable discontinuity at $\left(4, \dfrac{1}{3}\right)$

c. See Additional Answers. **5.** *Canceling
Problem* **a.** associativity **b.** definition of
division and multiplicative inverse
c. multiplicative identity **d.** transitivity

Exercise 7-3, Special Products and Factoring

1. *Graphing Problem* $f(x) = \dfrac{1}{x - 2}$ for

$x \neq 2, -3$; vertical asymptote at $x = 2$;

removable discontinuity at $\left(-3, -\dfrac{1}{5}\right)$

3. $x^2 - 2x - 15$ **5.** $3x^2 - 19xy + 28y^2$
7. $x^2 - 64$ **9.** $9x^2 - 49$ **11.** $4p^2 -$
$121f^2$ **13.** $x^6 - 36$ **15.** $16 - 9x^{10}$
17. $9a^2 + 6ab + b^2$ **19.** $36x^2 - 60x +$
25 **21.** $x^3 + 5x^2 + 2x - 8$ **23.** $x^3 -$
$13x^2 + 30x - 88$ **25.** $x^3 - y^3$
27. $2x^3 - 11x^2 + 19x - 7$ **29.** $x^4 -$
$6x^3 + x^2 - 6x - 35$ **31.** $x^5 +$
$3x^4 - 12x^3 + 9x^2 + x - 2$ **33.** $x^5 +$
$7x^4 + 4x^3 - 27x^2 + 21x - 10$
35. $x^3 + 6x^2 + 3x - 10$ **37.** $2x^3 -$
$5x^2 - x + 6$ **39.** $x^3 - 3x^2 + 3x - 1$
41. $x^3 + 3x^2y + 3xy^2 + y^3$
43. $(x + 7)(x - 2)$ **45.** $3(x + 5)(x - 2)$
47. $(4x + y)(2x + y)$ **49.** $(3r - 5s) \cdot$
$(r + 2s)$ **51.** $(3x + 1)(2x + 3)$
53. $(x + 4)(6x - 5)$
55. $(2x - 3)(5x - 7)$
57. $(2x - 7)(5x + 3)$ **59.** $(2x - 3)^2$
61. $(x + 8)^2$ **63.** $(x + 3)(x - 3) \cdot$
65. $(2x + 5)(2x - 5)$
67. $(7 + 3x)(7 - 3x)$ **69.** $(y + 1) \cdot$
$(y - 1)$ **71.** $36(a + 2)(a - 2)$
73. $5(4y + z)(4y - z)$ **75.** $(x^2 + y^2) \cdot$
$(x + y)(x - y)$ **77.** $(x^3 + y^2)(x^3 - y^2)$
79. $a^3(a + 1)(a - 1)$ **81.** $x^2y^2(x + y) \cdot$
$(x - y)$ **83.** $(x + 10)(x + 4)$
85. $(x + 1)(11 - x)$

87. *Product of a Binomial Proof*

$(a + b)(c + d)$

$= (a + b)c + (a + b)d$ Distributive axiom

$= ac + bc + ad + bd$ Distributive axiom

$= ac + ad + bc + bd$ Commutativity of
                       addition

$\therefore (a + b)(c + d)$

$= ac + ad + bc + bd$ Transitivity

89. 2001 **91.** 5096 **93.** 13,986
95. 280,973

Exercise 7-4, More Factoring and Graphing

1. (Graph)

x	$f(x)$
0	-0.2
4	-1
4.5	-2
5.5	2
6	1
10	0.2

3. a. $\dfrac{24}{x^2 + 2x + 4}$ for $x \neq 2$ **b.** discriminant $= -12$ no real solution of $0 = x^2 + 2x + 4$ **c.** removable discontinuity at $(2, 2)$ **d.** false **5.** $(a - b)(a^2 + ab + b^2)$
7. $(y + 4) \cdot (y^2 - 4y + 16)$
9. $(d^2 + h) \cdot (d^4 - d^2h + h^2)$
11. $3c(c - 3) \cdot (c^2 + 3c + 9)$
13. $x(x + 1)(x - 1)$ **15.** difference of squares first: $(x^3 + y^3) \cdot$
$(x^3 - y^3) = (x + y)(x^2 - xy + y^2) \cdot$
$(x - y)(x^2 + xy + y^2)$ 4 factors
difference of cubes first: $(x^2 - y^2) \cdot$
$(x^4 + x^2y^2 + y^4) = (x + y)(x - y) \cdot$
$(x^4 + x^2y^2 + y^4)$ 3 factors **17.** $(4x + 3) \cdot$
$(3x + 4)$ **19.** $(x - 5)(24x - 1)$
21. $(15x - 2)(2x + 3)$ **23.** prime
25. $(3x - 4)(12x - 5)$ **27.** -16; does not factor **29.** 169; perfect square; $(x - 17) \cdot$
$(x - 4)$ **31.** 81; perfect square; $(3x - 2) \cdot$
$(6x - 1)$ **33.** -47; does not factor
35. 656; perfect square; $(8x + 1)(x - 10)$
37. $4(x + 2y)(x - 2y)$ **39.** $(2x - 3y)^2$
41. $(a + 11)(a - 8)$ **43.** $5(3x + 2) \cdot$
$(2x + 5)$ **45.** $x(x^3 + 5x^2 - 2x + 10)$
47. $(x^2 + 3)(x + 2)(x - 2)$
49. $4(15x - 2)(x - 1)$ **51.** $(x - 2) \cdot$
$(16x - 3)$ **53.** $(5x + 6)(x + 3)(x - 3)$
55. Prime. **57.** $(10 + x - y) \cdot$
$(10 - x + y)$ **59.** $(7a + b)(5a + 6b)$
61. $(a + b + c)(a - b - c)(a + b - c) \cdot$
$(a - b + c)$ **63.** $(x + 3 + y)(x + 3 - y)$
65. $(a - (b - 1))(a + (b - 1))$
67. $(p - 7 + 3k)(p - 7 - 3k)$

69. $(x - 2y + 1)(x + 2y - 1)$
71. $(x^2 + 3x + 4)(x^2 - 3x + 4)$
73. $(x^2 + 6 - x)(x^2 + 6 + x)$
75. $(x^2 + 5x + 3)(x^2 - 5x + 3)$
77. $(x^2 + 6x + 5)(x^2 - 6x + 5)$
79. $(x^2 + 2x + 2)(x^2 - 2x + 2)$
81. $x + y$ and $x - y$: conjugates; $x - y$ and $y - x$: additive inverses
83. *Factoring Into Radicals Problem*

$x - y = (x^{\frac{1}{2}})^2 - (y^{\frac{1}{2}})^2$

$= (x^{\frac{1}{2}} - y^{\frac{1}{2}})(x^{\frac{1}{2}} - y^{\frac{1}{2}})$ [2 factors]

$= (x^{\frac{1}{2}} + y^{\frac{1}{2}})[(x^{\frac{1}{4}})^2 - (y^{\frac{1}{4}})^2]$

$= (x^{\frac{1}{2}} + y^{\frac{1}{2}})(x^{\frac{1}{4}} + y^{\frac{1}{4}})(x^{\frac{1}{4}} - y^{\frac{1}{4}})$

                         [3 factors]

$= (x^{\frac{1}{2}} + y^{\frac{1}{2}})(x^{\frac{1}{4}} + y^{\frac{1}{4}})(x^{\frac{1}{8}} + y^{\frac{1}{8}})$

$(x^{\frac{1}{8}} - y^{\frac{1}{8}})$ [4 factors]

The pattern of treating the factor containing a difference as a difference of squares can go on endlessly, so that any number of factors is possible. This method violates the agreement of completely factored form because the exponents of the variables are not integers. **85.** $(5)(3)(1)$
87. $(257)(17)(5)(3)(1)$

Exercise 7-5, Long Division of Polynomials

1. $x^2 - 4x + 5 + \dfrac{2}{x + 2}$ **3.** $4x^2 - x - 5 - \dfrac{5}{2x + 3}$ **5.** $x^2 - x + 3$ **7.** $x^2 - 3x + 2$ **9.** $x^2 + 2x - 10 + \dfrac{1}{x + 5}$
11. $4x^2 + 28x - 4$ **13.** $x + 1$
15. $x^2 - x + 1$ **17.** $x^3 + x^2 - x - 2 - \dfrac{2}{x + 6}$ **19.** $x^3 + x^2 + x + 1$

21. b. $x + 3 + \dfrac{1}{x - 2}$ **d.** Graphs are the same. The farther x is from 2, the closer $\dfrac{1}{x - 2}$ is to zero, so the linear expression $x + 3$ dominates.

Exercise 7-6, Factoring Higher Degree Polynomials—The Factor Theorem

1. $(x + 2)(x - 4)(x + 5)$ **3.** $(x - 2) \cdot$
$(x + 3)(x - 11)$ **5.** $(x + 2) \cdot$
$(x^2 - 3x + 1)$ **7.** Prime. **9.** $(x - 1) \cdot$
$(x + 2)(x - 3)(x + 4)$ **11.** $(x + 1)^2 \cdot$
$(x - 2)^2$ **13.** $(x + 1)^5$ **15.** $(2x - 1) \cdot$
$(x + 2)(x + 1)$ **17.** $(2x + 1) \cdot$
$(x^2 + x - 1)$ **19.** $(2x + 1)(3x + 1) \cdot$
$(2x - 1)$ **21.** $(2x + 3)(2x - 5)(3x - 2)$

23. $(x + y)(x^6 - x^5y + x^4y^2 - x^3y^3 + x^2y^4 - xy^5 + y^6)$ **25.** $(x - 1)(x^{10} + x^9 + x^8 + x^7 + x^6 + x^5 + x^4 + x^3 + x^2 + x + 1)$ **27.** $(x + 2)(x^4 - 2x^3 + 4x^2 - 8x + 16)$ **29.** $(a - b)(a^{12} + a^{11}b + a^{10}b^2 + a^9b^3 + a^8b^4 + a^7b^5 + a^6b^6 + a^5b^7 + a^4b^8 + a^3b^9 + a^2b^{10} + ab^{11} + b^{12})$ **31.** $(a + 2b^2)(a^4 - 2a^3b^2 + 4a^2b^4 - 8ab^6 + 16b^8)$ **33.** $(x - y)(x^2 + xy + y^2)$ **35.** $(x + 2)(x^2 - 2x + 4)$ **37.** $(r - s^2)(r^2 + rs^2 + s^4)$ **39.** $(x + y) \cdot (x^2 - xy + y^2)(x - y)(x^2 + xy + y^2)$ **41.** $8(x - 2b)(a^2 + 2ab + 4b^2)$ **43.** $xy(x + y)(x^2 - xy + y^2)$ **45.** $-2b(3a^2 + b^2)$ **47.** *Sum of Two Squares*

$P(x) = x^2 + c^2$
$P(1) = 1 + c^2 \neq 0$
$P(c) = c^2 + c^2 \neq 0$
$P(c^2) = c^4 + c^2 \neq 0$
$P(-1) = 1 + c^2 \neq 0$
$P(-c) = c^2 + c^2 \neq 0$
$P(-c^2) = c^4 + c^2 \neq 0$

$\therefore P(x)$ has *no* linear factors. Since the only possible polynomial factors of a quadratic are linear factors, $P(x)$ is *prime*.

Exercise 7-7, Products and Quotients of Rational Expressions

1. See Exercise 1-7, Problem 13.

3. a. -1 **b.** 1 **c.** $\dfrac{x - 5}{x + 5}$ **d.** 1 **5.** $\dfrac{x + 2}{2}$

7. $\dfrac{x^2 + 8x + 15}{5x}$ **9.** $\dfrac{x^2 + 6}{6x}$ **11.** -1

13. $-\dfrac{x + 7}{7}$ **15.** -1 **17.** $-\dfrac{x + 1}{4 + x}$

19. $\dfrac{(x - 5y)^2}{xy(x + 5y)}$ **21.** $\dfrac{x + 1}{x - 1}$ **23.** $\dfrac{x - 1}{x + 4}$

25. $x + 2$ **27.** $\dfrac{x + 5}{5 - x}$ **29.** $x^2 - 1$ **31.** x

33. $\dfrac{1}{x + y}$ **35.** $\dfrac{x^2 - x - 6}{x - 2}$

37. $\dfrac{x^2 + 6x + 5}{x - 5}$ **39.** $\dfrac{x^2 + 10x + 25}{x^2 - 14x + 49}$

41. 1 **43.** $\dfrac{(x + 2)^2(x + 3)}{(x - 4)^3}$ **45.** $x^4 -$

$2x^2y^2 + y^4$ **47.** $\dfrac{x - 1}{x}$ **49.** $\dfrac{x^2 + x}{x - 2}$

51. $-\dfrac{x + 1}{(3 + x)(x^2)}$ **53.** $\dfrac{1}{x}$ **55.** $\dfrac{x + 3}{x - 2}$

57. $\dfrac{y^2 - x^2}{xy}$ **59.** $\dfrac{x - 1}{x + 1}$ **61.** $\dfrac{6}{x^2}$

Exercise 7-8, Sums and Differences of Rational Expressions

1. See Exercise 1-7, Problem 23. **3.** $\dfrac{x}{12}$

5. $\dfrac{2x}{x^2 - 1}$ **7.** $\dfrac{9}{2x - 3y}$ **9.** $\dfrac{2 - 4x}{x^2 - 1}$

11. 0 **13.** $\dfrac{3x}{x^2 - y^2}$ **15.** $\dfrac{y}{(x - y)^2}$

17. $-\dfrac{1}{1 + 2x}$ **19.** $\dfrac{7 - 3x}{(1 - x)^2}$ **21.** $\dfrac{1}{x + 4}$

23. $\dfrac{3x + 4y}{(x + y)(2x + 3y)}$ **25.** $\dfrac{2xy}{x^3 - 8y^3}$

27. $-\dfrac{2x}{x - 3}$ **29.** $-\dfrac{x}{a}$ **31.** $-\dfrac{1}{x^2 - 1}$

33. $\dfrac{4x^2 - 16x + 14}{(x - 1)(x - 2)(x - 3)}$ **35.** $\dfrac{2}{x + y}$

37. $-\dfrac{2}{(x - 1)(x - 3)}$ **39.** $\dfrac{3x + 9}{(x + 2)(x - 1)}$

41. $\dfrac{2x}{x^2 - 1}$ **43.** $\dfrac{2}{x + 1} + \dfrac{3}{x - 2}$

45. $\dfrac{5}{x + 1} - \dfrac{2}{x + 4}$ **47.** $\dfrac{2}{x + 1} + \dfrac{3}{x - 2} - \dfrac{1}{x + 3}$ **49.** *Partial Fractions and Computer Graphics Problem*

a. (Graph) x-intercept $= -\dfrac{1}{3}$. This is reasonable because the numerator of the fraction, $3x + 1$, is zero for $x = -\dfrac{1}{3}$.

b. $\dfrac{2}{x - 3} + \dfrac{1}{x + 2}$

c. (Graph) **d.** yes

e. At $x = -\dfrac{1}{3}$, the sum of the partial fractions is zero.

Exercise 7-9, Graphs of Rational Algebraic Functions, Again

1. a. $\dfrac{7}{0}$ and $\dfrac{0}{0}$ **b.** $\dfrac{7}{0}$ is infinite. $\dfrac{0}{0}$ is indeterminate. **c.** $\dfrac{0}{7} = 0$

	a.	b.
3.	5	asymptote
5.	-2	asymptote
	3	removable discontinuity at $\dfrac{2}{5}$
7.	-5	asymptote
	2	asymptote
9.	-4	asymptote
	1	removable discontinuity at $\dfrac{1}{5}$

11. 3   removable discontinuity at 8
13. 2   removable discontinuity at 12
15. −2   removable discontinuity at 15
17. none
19. −5   removable discontinuity at $\frac{1}{9}$

    −2   asymptote
21. −2   asymptote
    3   asymptote

    4   removable discontinuity at $\frac{1}{2}$

23. 1   removable discontinuity at 3
    2   asymptote
25. 1   removable discontinuity at −1
    2   asymptote
27. −2   asymptote

    1   removable discontinuity at $-3\frac{1}{2}$

    5   asymptote
29. −1   removable discontinuity at −1
    0   asymptote

Exercise 7-10, Fractional Equations and Extraneous Solutions

1. *Extraneous Solutions Problem*
  a. $x(x − 4) = 3(x − 4)$
  b. Both members of transformed equation equal 0 when $x = 4$.
  c. Extraneous
  d. Cannot divide by zero.

3. $\{3, −1\}$ **5.** $\{12, −2\}$ **7.** $\{-\frac{5}{2}, −1\}$

9. $\{\frac{2}{3}, 1\}$ **11.** $\{0, −3\}$ **13.** $\{0, 2\}$

15. $\{7, −2\}$ **17.** $\{−1, 2, −3\}$ **19.** $\{1,$
$−1 + \sqrt{5}, −1−\sqrt{5}$ **21.** $x \ne 2$ $\{−1\}$
23. $x \ne 3, −5$ $\{−1\}$ **25.** $x \ne −4, 3$ $\emptyset$
27. $x \ne 3, 4$ $\{7\}$ **29.** $x \ne 3, 6$ $\left\{\frac{14}{3}\right\}$
31. $x \ne −2, 2$ $\emptyset$ **33.** $x \ne 1$ {real nos.,
$x \ne 1\}$ **35.** $x \ne 3/2, −3/2$ $\{3\}$
37. $x \ne 3, −3$ $\{5\}$ **39.** $x \ne 2, −3$ $\emptyset$
41. $x \ne 0, 3$ $\{−2\}$ **43.** $1 + \sqrt{2}$

Exercise 7-11, Variation Functions

1. *Kilograms-to-Pounds Problem*
  a. $p = 2.2k$
  b. i. 220 lb
   ii. 55 lb
   iii. 330 lb
  c. 75 kg
  d. Answers may vary.
  f. 2.2 lb/kg

3. *Wrench Problem*
  a. inversely, $F = \frac{k}{L}$
  b. $F = \frac{1890}{L}$
  c. inch-pounds
  d.

L	F
3	630
10	189
15	126
30	63
60	31.5

  e. 6.3 in
  f. 37.8 in

5. *Water Main Problem*
  a. $h = 0.5\,d^2$
  b.

d	h
30	450
43	924
100	5000

  c. 55 cm

7. *Gas Law Problem*
  a. $V = \frac{16{,}560}{P}$
  c. 60 psi
  d. $\frac{16{,}560}{P} \ne 0$
  e. $PV = k$
  f. $P_1V_1 = k$
   $P_2V_2 = k$
   $P_1V_1 = P_2V_2$

9. *Radio Transmitter Problem*
  a. $s = \frac{4000}{d^2}$
  b. 40 units
  c. 400,000 units
  d. Strong signal overwhelms more distant sources.

11. *Lightning Problem*
  a. Answers may vary. Time is dependent; distance is independent.
  b. $t = 3d$
  c. 3 s/km
  d.

d	t
1	3
2.5	7.5
10	30

  f. $9\frac{2}{3}$ km
  g. Lightning hit you.

13. *Friction Problem*
  a. directly
  b. $F = 0.6W$
  c. 78 lb
  d. 108 lb

15. *Radiant Heat Problem*
  a. 1280 cal/min
  b. fourth power
  c. $H = (6.1728 \times 10^{-10})T^4$
  d. i. about 253 cal/min
     ii. about 617 cal/min
17. *Ruby Problem*
  a. $2,000,000, very rare
  b. 2¢, little demand
19. *Stopping Distance Problem*
  d. $r = \dfrac{7}{30}s \qquad b = \dfrac{1}{150}s^2$
  e. 90 m
  f. about 3 football fields
  g. Answers may vary.
21. *Egg Problem*
  a. 18 cm
  b. 216
23. *Large and Small People Problem*
  c. 70 g is 60% of a quarter-pounder
  d. His legs support 20,000 kg, but his mass is 70,000 kg
  e. Answers may vary.
25. *Shark Problem*
  a. directly with the cube
  b. $W = 0.5926L^3$
  c. i. about 5 lb
     ii. about 9259 lb
  d. 7.5 ft
  e. about 592,600 lb
27. *Medication Problem*
  a. $d = k_1 A$
     $A = k_2 h^2$
  b. $d = k_3 h^2$
  c. It varies directly with the square of the height.
  d. $d = 0.001333h^2$
  e. i. 10.8 mg
     ii. 38.5 mg
     iii. 53.3 mg
29. *Epidemic Data Analysis Problem*
  a. Cases double every three days; exponential
  b. $C = 50(2)^{D/3}$
  c. $50(2)^{9/3} = 400$ for 9 days
     $50(2)^{12/3} = 800$ for 12 days
  d. after 23 days

7-12, Chapter Review

R1. a. undefined
  b. $f(2.1) = 10$
     $f(3.1) = 0.909...$
  c. vertical asymptote at $x = 2$.
     removable discontinuity at $(3, 1)$

R2. (Graph)

x	$f(x)$
-2	-0.25
0	-0.5
1	-1
1.5	-2
2.5	2
3	1
4	0.5
6	0.25

R3. a. $9x^2 - 49y^2$
  b. $x^3 - 2x^2 - 13x + 6$
  c. $r^2 - 8rt + 16t^2$
  d. $3x(2a + 5b)$
  e. $9(2r + 3s)(2r - 3s)$
  f. $(2x + 3y)(x - 12y)$
R4. a. $(x - 2y)(x^2 + 2xy + 4y^2)$
  b. $(4x + 1)(3x + 8)$
  c. discriminant $= -128$, not a perfect square
  d. $(-1 + p)(7 - p)$
  e. $(x + 3)(x - 3)(x + 1)(x - 1)$
R5. $x^2 + 3x - 7 - \dfrac{4}{x - 2}$
R6. a. $(2x - 1)(x - 9)(x + 3)$
  b. $(2x + y)(16x^4 - 8x^3y + 4x^2y^2 - 2xy^3 + y^4)$
R7. a. $\dfrac{a}{b} \cdot \dfrac{c}{d} = \dfrac{ac}{bd}$ **b.** $\dfrac{a}{b} = a \cdot \dfrac{1}{b}$
  c. $\dfrac{x + 1}{x - 1}$ **d.** $-\dfrac{(x + 2)(x + 1)}{x - 2}$
  e. $\dfrac{x - 4}{x + 1}$
R8. a. Division (common denominator) distributes over addition.
  b. $\dfrac{5t + 13}{t - 11}$ **c.** $\dfrac{5}{x^2 + x - 6}$
  d. $\dfrac{x + 2}{x - 2}$ **e.** $\dfrac{3}{x - 2} + \dfrac{4}{x + 1}$
R9. $f(x) = \dfrac{x - 1}{(x - 3)^2}, x \neq -1, 3$ (Graph)

(x)	$f(x)$
-3	$-\dfrac{1}{9}$
-2	$-\dfrac{3}{25}$
-1	Hole at $-\dfrac{1}{8}$
0	$-\dfrac{1}{9}$
1	0
2	1
3	Asymptote
4	3
5	1
6	$\dfrac{5}{9}$

R10. a. $\emptyset$ (-4 and 2 are extraneous)
b. $\{-5, 3\}$ **c.** $\{-7\}$ (2 is extraneous)
d. {all real numbers except 2 and -4}
R11. a. $y = \dfrac{k}{x^3}$ **b.** $y = \dfrac{28{,}672}{x^3}$

c. about 83,592 **d.** 56

CHAPTER 8 IRRATIONAL ALGEBRAIC FUNCTIONS

Exercise 8-1, Introduction to Irrational Algebraic Functions

1. $f(-2) = 3; f(-1) = 4;$
$f(0) = 3 + \sqrt{2}; f(2) = 5; f(14) = 7$
3. $x < -2$ **5.** 7 **7.** extraneous solution

Exercise 8-2, Graphs of Irrational Functions

1. (Graph)

x	$f(x)$
0.0	0.00000
0.1	0.31623
0.2	0.44721
0.3	0.54772
0.4	0.63246
0.5	0.70711
0.6	0.77460
0.7	0.83666
0.8	0.89443
0.9	0.94868
1.0	1.00000

3. (Graph)

x	$f(x)$
0.0	0.00000
0.1	0.79433
0.2	0.85134
0.3	0.88657
0.4	0.91244
0.5	0.93303
0.6	0.95020
0.7	0.96496
0.8	0.97793
0.9	0.98952
1.0	1.00000

5. a. -4
b. (Graph)

x	$f(x)$
-4	-4.00000
-3	-6.00000
-2	-6.24264
-1	-6.19615
0	-6.00000
1	-5.70820
2	-5.34847

x	$f(x)$
3	-4.93725
4	-4.48528
5	-4.00000
8	-2.39230

c. -6 **d.** 12 **e.** $-3.854\ldots$ and $2.854\ldots$
f. $6.908\ldots$ **g.** discriminant $= -63$, no real solutions **h.** $(-1.75, -6.25)$

Exercise 8-3, Radicals, and Simple Radical Form

1. $41\sqrt{3}$ **3.** $5\sqrt[3]{3}$ **5.** $2\sqrt{2}$ **7.** $3\sqrt{6}$
9. $8\sqrt{3}$ **11.** $9 + 2\sqrt{14}$ **13.** $29 - 12\sqrt{5}$ **15.** 2 **17.** 10 **19.** $42 -$
$6\sqrt{21} + \sqrt{105} - 3\sqrt{5}$ **21.** $\dfrac{2\sqrt[3]{3}}{3}$
23. $\sqrt[4]{8}$ **25.** $\dfrac{5\sqrt[3]{2}}{4}$ **27.** $\sqrt{7}$
29. $\dfrac{(\sqrt{5} + 1)}{4}$ **31.** $\sqrt{7} - \sqrt{3}$
33. $\sqrt{6} + \sqrt{3} - \sqrt{2} - 1$
35. $\dfrac{(107 + 42\sqrt{2})}{89}$ **37.** $2 + \sqrt{3}$
39. $2\sqrt{3} + 3 + \sqrt{21}$
41. $\dfrac{(3\sqrt{2} + 2\sqrt{3} + \sqrt{30})}{12}$
43. $-(\sqrt[3]{4} + \sqrt[3]{6} + \sqrt[3]{9})$
45. $\dfrac{(\sqrt[3]{5} - \sqrt[3]{2})}{3}$ **47.** $\sqrt{3} + 1$
49. $3 - \sqrt{3}$ **51.** $3 + \sqrt{2}$ **53.** $2\sqrt{5} - 2\sqrt{3}$ **55. a.** 2.1216 **b.** 2.121 **c.** Short division is easier than long division.
57. a. i. 4.999696 **ii.** 21.9961
iii. 84.027672 **iv.** 3.996969003
b. i. $4 < r < 5$, irrational **ii.** $2 < r < 3$, irrational **iii.** $1 < r < 2$, irrational **iv.** 5, rational **v.** $11 < r < 12$, irrational

Exercise 8-4, Radical Equations

1. $\{11\}$ **3.** $\{7\}$ **5.** $\left\{\dfrac{13}{12}\right\}$ **7.** $\emptyset$ (16 is
extraneous) **9.** $\left\{0, \dfrac{4}{3}\right\}$ **11.** $\{4\}$ **13.** $\{5\}$
15. $\{2\}$ **17.** $\emptyset$ **19.** $\{4, 5\}$ **21.** $\emptyset$ **23.** $\emptyset$
25. $\left\{\dfrac{13}{4}\right\}$ **27.** $\{-2\}$ **29.** $\{3\sqrt{2}, -3\sqrt{2}\}$
31. $\{2, -5\}$ **33.** $\{16\}$ **35.** $\left\{\dfrac{1}{4}\right\}$ **37.** $\emptyset$
39. $\{-1, 2, 3\}$ **41.** $\{0, 5\}$ **43.** $\{1 + 2\sqrt{3}\}$
45. $\{3 - \sqrt{5}\}$ **47.** $\{2 + \sqrt{5}\}$
49. a. 2 **b.** 3 **c.** 4 **d.** 6 **e.** product of consecutive integers **51. a.** $\{-1.104\ldots\}$

18.104 is extraneous **b.** 18.104... is the value of x for which $g(x)$ equals 4. **c.** Same solutions, but 18.104... is valid, and $-1.104...$ is extraneous. **d.** Both produce $0 = x^2 + x - 11$. **e.** Valid for $g(x) = -5$, extraneous for $f(x) = -5$. **f.** $0 = x^2 + 7x + 28$. **g.** discriminant $= -63$, no real solutions. Line $y = -8$ does not cross either graph.

Exercise 8-5, Variation Functions with Non-Integer Exponents

1. *Ship Power Problem* **a.** $s = 6.492p^{\frac{1}{7}}$ **b.** 33.12 knots **c.** no **d.** power requirement prohibitive **3.** *River Basin Problem* **a.** $L = 1.155A^{0.6}$ **b.** about 370 km **c.** about 1,870,000 km² **5.** *Tree Trunk Problem* **a.** $d = 1.30h^{\frac{3}{2}}$ **b.** 459 cm, 32 times as big **c.** 83.2 m **7.** *Pendulum Problem* **a.** $p = 1.004\sqrt{L}$ **b.** 0.992 m **c.** 99.2 m **9.** **a.** Doubling slices less than doubles time. **b.** $t = 1.225s^{0.5146}$ **c.** 3.57 sec, 3.08 sec, 1.225 sec **d.** about 500 slices **e.** domain: $0 \le s \le 500$ range: $0 \le t \le 30$ **f.** Ovens don't hold 500 slices of bacon. **11.** *Water Hyancinth Data Analysis Problem* **a.** exponential; Data has the "Add-Multiply" property **b.** $y = (92.265...) \cdot (1.091)^x$ **c.** $(92.265...)(1.091...)^6 = 156.070...$; $(92.265...)(1.091...)^9 = 202.984...$ **d.** day 54

Exercise 8-6, Functions of More than One Independent Variable

1. *Beam Strength Problem* **a.** $w = \dfrac{125bd^2}{L}$ **b.** 250 lb **c.** Beams support more weight on edge. **d.** 12,000 lb **e. i.** twice **ii.** 4 times **iii.** half **3.** *Spike Heel Problem* **a.** $p = \dfrac{1.08w}{d^2}$ **d.** 1728 psi **e.** High pressure dents the aluminum floors. **5.** *Bridge Column Problem* **a.** $b = \dfrac{9d^4}{4L^2}$ **b.** $c = \dfrac{5}{4}d^2$ **c.** 900 tons, 400 tons, 144 tons **d.** 500 tons **f.** Long columns buckle, short columns crush. **g.** about 26.8 ft **7.** *Reaction to Shock Problem* **a.** $C \ge 10 + \dfrac{40}{t}$ **b.** $C \ge 14$ ma **c.** $\dfrac{4}{9}$ ms **d.** 10 ma **9.** *Gas Consumption Problem* **a.** $g = \dfrac{k_3}{s^2}$ **b.** inverse square **c.** $g = \dfrac{80,000}{s^2}$ **e.** poor fuel efficiency

f. No: at very low speeds, friction and heat predominate over wind. **11.** *Why Mammals Are the Way They Are* **a. i.** $m = k_1L^3$ **ii.** $A = k_2L^2$ **iii.** $H = k_3A$ **iv.** $F = k_4H$ **b.** $F = k_5m^{\frac{2}{3}}$; F varies directly with the $\dfrac{2}{3}$ power of m. **c.** $\dfrac{F}{m} = k_5m^{-\frac{1}{3}}\dfrac{F}{m}$ varies inversely with the $\dfrac{1}{3}$ power of m.

d. $\dfrac{F}{m} = 3.78m^{-\frac{1}{3}}$ **e.** 2% **f.** $\dfrac{F}{m}$ increases as m decreases. Answers may vary. **13.** *Car Trade-In Data Analysis Problem* **a.** $f(t) = -200t + 12,000$
$g(t) = (12,814.453...)(0.976...)^t$
$h(t) = \dfrac{27,274.624}{t^{0.409...}}$
b. $f(60) = \$0$ $g(60) = \$3117.95$ $h(60) = \$5102.07$ **c.** $f(0) = \$12,000$ $g(0) = \$12,814.45$ $h(0)$ approaches infinity **d.** exponential $g(t)$

8-7, Chapter Review

R1. a. domain $= \{x: x \ge 3\}$ **b.** 2 **c.** 39
R2.

x	$f(x)$
3	7
4	6
5	5.58579
6	5.26795
7	5

R3. a. $2\sqrt{3}$ **b.** $7\sqrt{7}$ **c.** $2\sqrt{6} - 3$ **d.** $\sqrt[5]{81}$ **R4. a.** $\{10\}$ **b.** $\{5, 133\}$ **c.** $\left\{\dfrac{3}{2}\right\}$ **R5. a.** $A = 5.926m^{1.31}$ **b.** 6125 m² **c.** about 5 kg **R6. a.** $y = \dfrac{k_1}{x^3}$; $x = \dfrac{k_2z^2}{w}$; **b.** $y = \dfrac{k_3w^3}{z^6}$ **c.** Varies directly with the cube of w and inversely with the sixth power of z. **d.** $y = \dfrac{135x^3}{z^6}$

8-8, Cumulative Review: Chapters 6 Through 8

1. a. Exponential, $y = ab^x$ $(b > 1)$ **b.** Exponential, $y = ab^x$ $(0 < b < 1)$ **c.** Inverse variation, $y = k/x^n$ **d.** Direct n^{th} power variation, $y = kx^n$ $(n > 1)$ **e.** Direct variation, $y = kx$ **f.** Direct n^{th} power variation, $y = kx^n$ $(0 < n < 1)$ **g.** Logarithmic, $y = \log_b x$ (or rational algebraic) **h.** Rational algebraic, $y = \dfrac{P(x)}{Q(x)}$, where $P(x)$ and $Q(x)$ are polynomials. **i.** Linear,

$y = mx + b$ **2. a.** $y = kx$ **b.** $y = \dfrac{k}{x}$

c. $y = \dfrac{k}{x^3}$ **d.** $y = kx^4$ **e.** $y = a \times 10^{kx}$

3. a. $6\sqrt{5} + 6 - 5\sqrt{3} - \sqrt{15}$
b. $9 - 2\sqrt{14}$ **c.** -5 **d.** $x - 2\sqrt{x} - 35$
e. $x^2 - 2x - 35$ **f.** $x^4 - 2x^3 -$
$20x^2 + 57x - 36$ **4. a.** $(r + s)$
$(r^6 - r^5s + r^4s^2 - r^3s^3 + r^2s^4 - rs^5 + s^6)$
b. $(2x + 3)(3x - 40)$ **c.** $(x - 1)(x - 2)(x + 4)$ **5. a.** $\dfrac{3}{(x - 4)(x - 1)}$

b. $-\dfrac{(x + 2)(x - 3)}{(x + 3)(x - 5)}$ or $-\dfrac{x^2 - x - 6}{x^2 - 2x - 15}$
6. a. $12x^{\frac{1}{6}}$ **b.** $3^{\frac{5}{6}}$ **c.** $2\sqrt{19} + 8$ **d.** $4\sqrt[5]{9}$

e. $5^{\frac{1}{2}}$ or $\sqrt{5}$ **f.** $9\sqrt{7}$ **g.** $\dfrac{4}{3}$ **h.** 2 **i.** $-\dfrac{x + 4}{x - 1}$

j. $\dfrac{3}{4}|a|$ **7. a.** $S = \{-2\}$ (3 is extr.)

b. $S = \{-1\}$ (1 is extr.) **8.** $\dfrac{5}{0}$ is infinite. $\dfrac{0}{0}$

is indeterminate. **b.** 0
9. a. $f(-10) = -8; f(-4) = 0; f(-1)$:
Asymptote; $f(0) = -8; f(1)$: Hole at -2.5;
$f(2) = 0$ **b.** $f(10) = 10.2$ **10.** If the denominator is 0, then $x^2 - x + 2 = 0$.
$b^2 - 4ac = 1^2 - 4(1)(2) = -7$. Since the discriminant is negative, there are no real solutions. So the fraction never has a zero denominator.
11. *Iodine Problem* **a.** *Exponential* function, because when you *add* a constant to the number of days, you *multiply* the amount of iodine by a constant. **b.** Let $m = $ no. of millicuries.   Let $d = $ no. of days since they received it. $m = 23.7 \times 10^{-0.037164\ldots d}$ **c. i.** 13.02 millicuries **ii.** 39.6 days **d.** 11.85 **e.** 32.53 millicuries

12. *Heat Radiation Problem* **a.** $h = \dfrac{k_1 T^4 S}{d^2}$

b. $S = k_2 r^2$ $V = k_3 r^3$ **c.** $h = \dfrac{k_4 T^4 V^{\frac{2}{3}}}{d^2}$

13. *Diesel Engine Problem* **a.** Let T = no. of degrees K Let V = no. of cubic

centimeters volume. $T = \dfrac{1543.0562\ldots}{V^{0.4}}$

b. 886.3° K **c.** 6.07 cm³

CHAPTER 9   QUADRATIC RELATIONS AND SYSTEMS

Exercise 9-1, Introduction to Quadratic Relations

1. (Graph)   **3.** (Graph)

Exercise 9-2, Circles

1. (Graph)   **3.** (Graph)   **5.** (Graph)
7. (Graph)   **9.** (Graph)   **11.** (Graph)
13. $(x - 7)^2 + (y - 5)^2 = 65$
15. $(x + 9)^2 + (y + 2)^2 = 85$
17. $x^2 + y^2 = 100$
19. a. $(x - h)^2 + y^2 = r^2$
b. $x^2 + (y - k)^2 = r^2$
c. $x^2 + y^2 = r^2$ **21.** If r^2 is less than 0, r will be an imaginary number, and there will be no circle.

Exercise 9-3, Ellipses

1. **a.** $\dfrac{(x - 2)^2}{3^2} + \dfrac{(y + 5)^2}{2^2} = 1$ **b.** $c = \sqrt{5} \approx 2.24$ **c.** (Graph) Ellipse with center at $(2, -5)$. **3.** **a.** $\dfrac{(x + 1)^2}{4^2} + \dfrac{(y - 2)^2}{7^2} = 1$

b. $c = \sqrt{33} \approx 5.7$ **c.** (Graph) Ellipse with center at $(-1, 2)$.

5. **a.** $\dfrac{(x + 5)^2}{4^2} + \dfrac{(y + 3)^2}{2^2} = 1$ **b.** $c = \sqrt{12} \approx$
3.5 **c.** (Graph) Ellipse with center at
$(-5, -3)$ **7.** **a.** $\dfrac{(x + 1)^2}{3^2} + \dfrac{(y - 2)^2}{5^2} < 1$
b. $c = 4$ **c.** (Graph) All points inside the ellipse with center at $(-1, 2)$. **9.** **a.** $\dfrac{x^2}{5^2} +$
$\dfrac{(y - 6)^2}{4^2} = 1$ **b.** $c = 3$ **c.** (Graph)
Ellipse with center at $(0, 6)$. **11.** **a.** $\dfrac{x^2}{6^2} +$
$\dfrac{y^2}{10^2} > 1$ **b.** $c = 8$ **c.** (Graph) All points outside of the ellipse with center at $(0, 0)$.
13. **a.** $\dfrac{x^2}{4} + \dfrac{y^2}{48} = 1$ **b.** $c = \sqrt{44} \approx 6.6$
c. (Graph) Ellipse with center at $(0, 0)$.
Graph contains $(\pm 1, \pm 6)$ **15.** **a.** $\dfrac{x^2}{\frac{77}{5}} + \dfrac{y^2}{\frac{77}{8}}$
$= 1$ **b.** $c = \sqrt{\dfrac{231}{40}}$ **c.** (Graph) Ellipse with
center at $(0, 0)$. Graph contains $(\pm 1, \pm 3)$, $(\pm 3, \pm 2)$.   **17.** **b.** 27,489 seats

19. **a.** $y = \pm \dfrac{3}{4}\sqrt{x^2 - 16}$ **b.** y is an

imaginary number **c.** The ambiguous sgn, $\pm$, shows that there are two values of y for each value of x.

d.

x	y
± 4	0
± 5	± 2.25
± 6	± 3.35
± 7	± 4.31
± 8	± 5.20

e. $(-x)^2 = x^2$

Exercise 9-4, Hyperbolas

1. a. $\dfrac{(x-2)^2}{4^2} - \dfrac{(y+3)^2}{5^2} = 1$ **b.** $c =$

$\sqrt{41} \approx 6.4$ **c.** (Graph) **3. a.** $-\dfrac{(x+6)^2}{3^2}$

$+ \dfrac{(y+7)^2}{5^2} = 1$ **b.** $c = \sqrt{34} \approx 5.8$

c. (Graph)

5. a. $\dfrac{(x+2)^2}{3^2} - \dfrac{(y-8)^2}{3^2} = 1$

b. $c = \sqrt{18} \approx 4.2$ **c.** (Graph)

7. a. $\dfrac{(x-3)^2}{4^2} - \dfrac{(y+2)^2}{6^2} = 1$

b. $c = \sqrt{52} \approx 7.2$ **c.** (Graph)

9. a. $-\dfrac{(x-5)^2}{3^2} + \dfrac{(y-2)^2}{9^2} = 1$

b. $c = \sqrt{90} \approx 9.5$ **c.** (Graph)

11. a. $-\dfrac{x^2}{3^2} + \dfrac{y^2}{4^2} = 1$ **b.** $c = 5$ **c.** (Graph)

13. a. $\dfrac{x^2}{4} - \dfrac{y^2}{\frac{16}{5}} = 1$; $m \approx \pm 0.9$; graph

contains $(\pm 3, \pm 2)$. **b.** $c \approx 2.7$ **c.** (Graph)

15. a. $-\dfrac{x^2}{\frac{11}{16}} + \dfrac{y^2}{\frac{11}{3}} = 1$; $b \approx 1.91$, $m =$

± 2.3; (graph) **b.** $c \approx 2.1$ **c.** (Graph)
17. a. $9x^2 - y^2 = 0$; $a = b = c = 0$;
$m = \pm 3$ **b.** (Graph)

Exercise 9-5, Parabolas

1. a. $x + 1 = ((y-2)^2$; V: $(-1, 2)$; y-int:
$(0, 1)$, $(0, 3)$; x-int: $(3, 0)$ **b.** (Graph)
3. a. $x - 7 = -3(y+2)^2$; V: $(7, -2)$;
y-int: $(0, \approx -0.5)$, $(0, \approx -3.5)$; x-int $(-5, 0)$

b. (Graph) **5. a.** $x + \dfrac{1}{2} = \dfrac{1}{2}(y+3)^2$; V:
$\left(-\dfrac{1}{2}, -3\right)$; y-int: $(0, -2)$, $(0, -4)$; x-int:
$(4, 0)$ **b.** (Graph) **7. a.** $y - 9$
$= -4(x - 2.5)^2$; V: $(2.5, 9)$; y-int:
$(0, -16)$; x-int: $(1, 0)$, $(4, 0)$ **b.** (Graph)

9. a. $x = \dfrac{1}{4}y^2$; V: $(0, 0)$; y-int $=$ x-int:

$(0, 0)$; **b.** (Graph) **11.** (Graph)
13. (Graph)

15. *Parabola Conclusions Problems*
a. positive second-degree x-term
b. positive second-degree y-term
c. negative second-degree x-term
d. negative second-degree x-term

Exercise 9-6, Equations from Geometrical Definitions

1. $x^2 + y^2 - 10x + 9 = 0$ *circle*
3. $4x^2 + 4y^2 + 13x - 15y + 10 = 0$
circle
5. $x^2 - 4y^2 - 6x - 16y - 27 = 0$
hyperbola (degenerate)
7. $x^2 - 6x + 12y + 21 = 0$ *parabola*

9. $4x^2 + 3y^2 + 24x + 24 = 0$ *ellipse*

11. $4y^2 - 5y^2 - 78y - 45 = 0$ *hyperbola*
13. $\sqrt{(x-4)^2 + (y-0)^2} +$
$\quad \sqrt{(x+4)^2 + (y-0)^2} = 10$
$(x - 4)^2 + y^2$
$\quad = 100 - 20\sqrt{(x+4)^2 + y^2}$
$\quad + (x+4)^2 + y^2$
$4x + 25 = 5\sqrt{(x+4)^2 + y^2}$
$16x^2 + 200x + 625 = 25[(x+4)^2 + y^2]$
$9x^2 + 25y^2 = 225$, QED
15. $\sqrt{(x-f)^2 + y^2} = c\sqrt{(x+f)^2 + y^2}$
$(1 - c^2)x^2 + (1 - c^2)y^2 -$
$\quad 2f(1 + c^2)x + (1 - c^2)f^2 = 0$
x^2 and y^2 both have the coefficient,
$(1 - c^2)$. **17.** For a circle, $e = 0$. But
the radius is also 0 unless the directrix is
infinitely far away.

Exercise 9-7, Quadratic Relations—xy-Term

1. (Graph) Circle with center $(0, 0)$ and radius 3. **3. a.** (Graph) Circle with center
$(5, 4)$ and radius 5 **b.** (Graph) Ellipse with
center $(4, 2)$ and diagonally oriented.
c. (Graph) Parabola containing $(2, 0)$, $(8, 0)$
d. (Graph) Hyperbola.
5. a. no **b.** Problem 1, -4, Circle
Problem 2.i., -3, Ellipse
Problem 2.ii., 12, Hyperbola
Problem 3.a., -4, Circle
Problem 3.b., -3, Ellipse
Problem 3.c., 0, Parabola
Problem 3.d., 12, Hyperbola
c. circles and ellipses: $B^2 - 4AC < 0$
$\quad$ parabola: $B^2 - 4AC = 0$
$\quad$ hyperbola: $B^2 - 4AC > 0$

Exercise 9-8, Systems of Quadratics

1. a. $\{(3, 4), (3, -4), (-3, 4), (-3, -4)\}$
b. (Graph) An ellipse and hyperbola intersecting at the points listed in (a). **3. a.** $\{(3, 4),$

$(-3, 4)$, $(0, -5)\}$ **b.** (Graph) A circle and parabola intersecting at the points listed in (a).   **5. a.** $\{(5, 4), (-5, 4), (2, -5),$ $(-2, -5)\}$ **b.** (Graph) A circle and parabola intersecting at the points listed in (a).   **7. a.** $\{(1, 4), (1, -4), (-5, 2), (-5, -2)\}$ **b.** (Graph) A circle and parabola intersecting at the points listed in (a).   **9. a.** $\{(3, 1),$ $(3, -1)\}$ **b.** (Graph) A parabola and hyperbola intersecting at the points listed in (a).   **11. a.** $\emptyset$ **b.** (Graph) A circle and parabola that do not intersect.   **13. a.** $\{(-5, 0)\}$ **b.** An ellipse and circle that intersect at the point listed in (a).   **15. a.** $\{(4, 3), (-4, 3)\}$ **b.** (Graph) An ellipse and parabola that intersect at the points listed in (a).   **17. a.** $\{(-6, 4), (6, -4)\}$ **b.** (Graph) Two hyperbolas that intersect at the points listed in (a).   **19. a.** $\{(-1, 3), (-2, 5)\}$ **b.** A straight line and a hyperbola intersecting at the points listed in (a).   **21. a.** $\{(-5, 2),$ $(-1, -4)\}$ **b.** An ellipse and straight line intersecting at the points listed in (a).   **23. a.** $\{(-1, 2), (-6, -3)\}$ **b.** A straight line and parabola intersecting at the points listed in (a).   **25. a.** $\{(5, 1), (-4, -2)\}$ **b.** (Graph) An ellipse and straight line intersecting at the points listed (a).   **27. a.** $\{(5, 2), (-5, 2), (4, -1), (-4, -1)\}$ **b.** $\{(5, -4)$ **c.** $\emptyset$ **29.** *Meteorite Tracking Problem* **a.** No, $x^2 + y^2 = 40$ and $18x - y^2 = -144$ do not intersect. **b.** Meteorite strikes the Earth at $(6, -2)$. **c.** about 6300 km

9-9, Chapter Review

R1. a. i. circle **ii.** circle **iii.** circle **iv.** hyperbola **v.** hyperbola **vi.** $\emptyset$ **vii.** ellipse **viii.** ellipse **ix.** parabola **x.** parabola **xi.** hyperbola **xii.** circle **xiii.** ellipse **xiv.** parabola   **c. xi.** $c = \sqrt{10}$ **xiii.** $c = \sqrt{80}$ **R2. a. i.** A circle is a set of points each of which is equidistant from a fixed point (the center). **ii.** An ellipse is a set of points with a constant sum of distances from each point to two other fixed points (foci). **iii.** A hyperbola is a set of points with a constant difference between distances from each point and two other fixed points (foci). **iv. a.** A parabola is a set of points each of which is equidistant from a fixed point (focus) and a fixed straight line (directrix). **b.** $16x^2 + 25y^2 = 400$ **R3. a. i.** $\{(0, 10)(3, 1) \cdot (-3, 1)\}$ **ii.** $\{(1, 3)\}$

CHAPTER 10   HIGHER-DEGREE FUNCTIONS AND COMPLEX NUMBERS

Exercise 10-1, Introduction to Higher Degree Functions

1.

x	$f(x)$	x	$f(x)$
-3	-52	2	-12
-2	-16	3	-16
-1	0	4	-10
0	2	5	12
1	-4	6	56

3. See Figure 10-2a. **a.** The graphs of g and h have the same shape as f, but are raised up by 16 units and 32 units respectively. **b.** g: 2 x-intercepts h: 1 x-intercept **c.** A cubic function can have 1, 2, or 3 intercepts.

Exercise 10-2, Complex Number Review

1. $i^5 = i$.   **3.** $i^{55} = -i$.   **5.** $i^{62} = -1$. **7.** $i^{300} = 1$.   **9.** $i^0 = 1$.   **11.** $i^{-7} = i$. **13.** $i^{-38} = -1$.   **15.** $\sqrt{-16} = 4i$. **17.** $\sqrt{-18} = 3i\sqrt{2}$ **19.** $\sqrt{-7} = i\sqrt{7}$. **21.-27.** (Graphs)   **29. a.** $6 - 2i$ **b.** $-2 + 8i$ **c.** $23 + 2i$ **d.** $\dfrac{-7}{41} + \dfrac{22}{41}i$ **31. a.** $5 + 9i$ **b.** $-7 - 5i$ **c.** $-20 + 5i$ **d.** $\dfrac{8}{85} + \dfrac{19}{85}i$ **33.** $(a + bi)(a - bi) = a^2 - b^2i^2 = a^2 + b^2$ Since a and b are real numbers, and the set of real numbers is *closed* under multiplication and addition, $a^2 + b^2$ is also a real number. **35.** $|z| = 5$

37. $|z| = 13$

Exercise 10-3, Quadratic Equations from Their Solutions—Complex Number Factors

1. $\{1 + i, 1 - i\}$ **3.** $\{2 + i, 2 - i\}$ **5.** $\{-1 + 3i, -1 - 3i\}$ **7.** $\{2 + 5i, 2 - 5i\}$ **9.** $\{-2 + i\sqrt{3}, -2 - i\sqrt{3}\}$ **11.** $\{5 + i\sqrt{2}, 5 - i\sqrt{2}\}$ **13.** $\left\{\dfrac{2 + i\sqrt{26}}{3}, \dfrac{2 - i\sqrt{26}}{3}\right\}$

15. $\left\{-\dfrac{1}{5} + 2i, -\dfrac{1}{5} - 2i\right\}$ 17. $\{-1, -7\}$

19. $\{3 + \sqrt{5}, 3 - \sqrt{5}\}$ 21. $\{3i, -3i\}$

23. $\left\{\dfrac{7i}{2}, -\dfrac{7i}{2}\right\}$ 25. $x^2 + 3x - 10 = 0$

27. $x^2 + 9x + 18 = 0$ 29. $x^2 - 4x + 5$
$= 0$ 31. $x^2 + 6x + 25 = 0$ 33. $x^2 -$
$2x + 6 = 0$ 35. $x^2 + 10x + 37 = 0$

27. $x^2 + 9x + 18 = 0$ 29. $x^2 - 4x + 5$
$= 0$ 31. $x^2 + 6x + 25 = 0$ 33. $x^2 -$
$2x + 6 = 0$ 35. $x^2 + 10x + 37 = 0$

37. $x^2 - 8x + 9 = 0$ 39. $(x - 1 - 2i)(x$
$- 1 + 2i)$ 41. $(x + 5 - 2i)(x + 5 + 2i)$

43. $(x - 3 - i\sqrt{2})(x - 3 + i\sqrt{2})$

45. $(x - 5 - \sqrt{3})(x - 5 + \sqrt{3})$

47. $(x + 4i)(x - 4i)$

49. $(3x + 11i)(3x - 11i)$

51. $(7x + i)(7x - i)$

53. $3\left(x - \dfrac{2 + i\sqrt{26}}{3}\right)\left(x - \dfrac{2 - i\sqrt{26}}{3}\right)$

55. $(5x + 1 + 10i)(5x + 1 - 10i)$

57. $(1 + i)^2 - 2(1 + i) + 2 = 1 + 2i - 1$
$- 2 - 2i + 2 = 0;\ (1 - i)^2 - 2(1 - i)$
$+ 2 = 1 - 2i - 1 - 2 + 2i + 2 = 0$

59. $\dfrac{4 \pm \sqrt{16 - 4(1)(5)}}{2} = 2 \pm i$

61. $(x - 1 - 2i)(x - 1 + 2i) =$
$x^2 - 2x + 5$ 63. $s_1 + s_2 =$

$\dfrac{-b + \sqrt{b^2 - 4ac}}{2a} + \dfrac{-b - \sqrt{b^2 - 4ac}}{2a}$

$= -\dfrac{b}{a};\ s_1 s_2 = \left(\dfrac{-b + \sqrt{b^2 - 4ac}}{2a}\right) \cdot$

$\left(\dfrac{-b - \sqrt{b^2 - 4ac}}{2a}\right) = \dfrac{c}{a}$

Exercise 10-4, Graphs of Higher Degree Functions—Synthetic Substitution

1. 18   3. 260   5. −5   7. 56   9. −102

11. a. (Graph)

x	$P(x)$
−3	−60
−2	−20
−1	0
0	6
1	4
2	0
3	0
4	10
5	36

b. Zeros: −1, 2, 3

13. a. (Graph)

x	$P(x)$
−2	−55
−1	−16
0	3
1	8
2	5
3	0
4	−1
5	8
6	33

b. Zeros: $P(x) = (x - 3)(x^2 - 4x - 1)$;
Zeros: 3, $2 + \sqrt{5}$, $2 - \sqrt{5}$

15. a. (Graph)

x	$P(x)$
−4	−26
−3	0
−2	10
−1	10
0	6
1	4
2	10
3	30

b. $P(x) = (x + 3)(x^2 - 2x + 2)$;
Zeros: −3, $1 + i$, $1 - i$

17. a. (Graph)

x	$P(x)$
−4	−24
−3	−5
−2	0
−1	−3
0	−8
1	−9
2	0
3	25

b. $P(x) = (x + 2)(x + 2)(x - 2)$;
Zeros: −2, −2, 2

19. a. (Graph)

x	$P(x)$
−2	−37
−1	0
0	19
1	26
2	27
3	28
4	35
5	54

b. $P(x) = (x + 1)(x^2 - 7x + 19)$;
Zeros: $-1, \dfrac{7 + 3i\sqrt{3}}{2}, \dfrac{7 - 3i\sqrt{3}}{2}$

21. a. (Graph)

x	$P(x)$
−4	60
−3	15
−2	0
−1	3
0	12
1	15
2	0
3	−45

b. Zeros: $-2, 2, -\dfrac{3}{2}$

23. a. (Graph)

x	$P(x)$
-4	-35
-3	-6
-2	-5
-1	-20
0	-39
1	-50
2	-41
3	0
4	85

b. $P(x) = (x - 3)(2x^2 + 10x + 13)$;

Zeros: $3, \dfrac{-5 + i}{2}, \dfrac{-5 - i}{2}$

25. a. (Graph)

x	$P(x)$
-4	126
-3	0
-2	-20
-1	0
0	18
1	16
2	0
3	0
4	70

b. Zeros: $-3, -1, 2, 3$

27. a. (Graph)

x	$P(x)$
-3	148
-2	0
-1	-34
0	-20
1	0
2	8
3	10
4	36
5	140

b. $P(x) = (x + 2)(x - 1)(x^2 - 6x + 10)$; Zeros: $-2, 1, 3 + i, 3 - i$
29. $-3, 1 + 2i, 1 - 2i$ **31.** $2, -1, -4$
33. $2, 1 + \sqrt{3}, 1 - \sqrt{3}$ **35.** $-2, 3, -1 + i, -1 - i$ **37.** $1, -1, 2, -3$
39. $3 + 2i, 3 - 2i, 1 + i, 1 - i$ **41.** 98
43. -30 **45.** 50 **47-51.** (Graphs) Answers may vary.
53. Prove that $P(x)$ has a linear factor of the form $(x - b)$ if and only if $P(b) = 0$.
If part of proof:
If $P(x)$ has $(x - b)$ as a factor, then
$$P(x) = (x - b) \text{ (another polynomial factor)}$$
$\therefore P(b) = (b - b)$ (real number)
$$= 0 \cdot \text{(real number)}$$
$$= 0$$

Only if part of proof:
Suppose that $P(b) = 0$. By the Fundamental Theorem of Algebra and its corollary, $P(x)$ can be factored completely into linear factors. By the converse of the Multiplication Property of Zero, one of these factors must be zero when $x = b$, because $P(b) = 0$. Linear factors have the form $(ax - c)$.
$\quad \therefore ax - c = 0$ when $x = b$
$\quad \therefore ab - c = 0$
$\qquad c = ab$
$\quad \therefore$ the factor is $(ax - ab)$, which equals
$$a(x - b).$$
$\therefore (x - b)$ is a factor of $P(x)$, QED.

55.
```
10   PRINT"WHAT VALUE OF X";
20   INPUT X
*25  PRINT"DIVISOR: X _";X
30   READ D
40   DATA 3, 1, -4, -5, 14
50   FOR I=0 TO D
60   READ C
*65  IF I>0 THEN 70
66   PRINT"QUOTIENT COEFF.;";
70   LET P=P*X+C
*72  IF I=D THEN 85
*75  PRINT P;
80   NEXT I
*85  PRINT
*90  PRINT"REMAINDER:";P
100  END
```

57. a. (Graph) **b.** (Graph) **c.** (Graph)

Exercise 10-5, Descartes' Rule of Signs, and the Upper Bound Theorem

	pos.	neg.	comp.
1.	2	1	0
	0	1	2
3.	3	0	0
	1	0	2
5.	2	0	2
	0	0	4
7.	3	1	0
	1	1	2
9.	0	0	8

15. a. 1 **b.** 3 **c.** Since the trinomial is being multiplied by by $(x - c)$ and c is positive, the last sign will be negative. Since the first sign is positive, there must be an odd number of sign reversals. **17.a.** pos. zeros even, neg. zeros even **b.** pos. zeros even, neg. zeros odd **c.** pos. zeros odd, neg. zeros even **d.** pos. zeros odd, neg. zeros odd **19. a.** 2 **b.** -2 **c.** 2 or -2 **d.** no real zeros

Exercise 10-6, Higher Degree Functions as Mathematical Models

1. *Beam Deflection Problem* **a.** $0 \leq x \leq 10$
b. 0, 0, 10, 15   The zeros at 0 and 10 indicate the beam is not deflected at the supports. The zero at 15 is out of the domain and meaningless.
3. *Oil Viscosity Problem* **a.** $V = -T^3 + 9T^2 - 24T + 70$ **b.** 70, 50, 34
5. *Lumber Problem* **a.** $B(D) = 10D^3 + 8D^2 - 5D - 3$ **b.** 1422 board-ft **c.** -1, $0.1 \pm \sqrt{0.31}$ **e.** about 8 in. **f.** at least 2.5 ft   **7.** *Sum of the Squares Problem* **a.** 0, 1,

5, 14 **b.** $S(n) = \frac{1}{3}n^3 + \frac{1}{2}n^2 + \frac{1}{6}n$

c. $\frac{n}{6}(2n + 1)(n + 1)$ **d.** 30, 55

e. 333,833,500

10-7, Chapter Review

R1. 19
R2. a. $-i$ **b.** i **c.** 1 **d.** $3i\sqrt{7}$ **e.** (Graph)
f. $-17 - 13i$ **g.** $5 + 9i$ **h.** $66 + 26i$
i. 145 **j.** $143 + 24i$ **k.** $3i$ **l.** $\sqrt{137}$

R3. a. $\left\{ \dfrac{-2 + i\sqrt{26}}{3}, \dfrac{-2 - i\sqrt{26}}{3} \right\}$

b. $f(x) = x^2 - 6x + 25$ **c.** $(x - 2 - i)(x - 2 + i)$ **d.** $(5x + i)(5x - i)$

e. $r_1 + r_2 = -\dfrac{13}{5}$ $r_1 r_2 = \dfrac{79}{5}$

R4. a. 21 **b.** (Graph) There is a zero at

$x = 2$. **c.** $\left\{ 2, -\dfrac{5 + i\sqrt{7}}{4}, -\dfrac{5 - i\sqrt{7}}{4} \right\}$

d. 9 **e.** (Graph) A quartic function with 2 positive and 2 negative zeros; the y-intercept is negative.

R5. a.

pos.	neg.	comp.
4	3	0
4	1	2
2	3	2
2	1	4
0	3	4
0	1	6

b. There are no sign changes, so there are

no positive zeros. **c.** $\dfrac{P(x)}{x - 8} = x^3 + x^2 +$

$2 + \dfrac{11}{x - 8}$. There are no sign reversals in

the quotient and the remainder, so there are no zeros of P which are greater than 8.

$\dfrac{P(x)}{x + 2} = x^3 - 9x^2 + 10x - 18 + \dfrac{31}{x + 2}$

The signs of the quotient and remainder alternate, so there are no zeros less than -2. There are 2 sign reversals in $P(x)$, so there may be 2 or zero positive solutions. $P(-x)$ has one sign reversal, so there must be a negative solution. Thus there are 1 or 3 real solutions, which must lie between -2 and 8.
R6. a. $P(x) = 3x^3 - 10x^2 + 2x + 5$
b. -63 **c.** 1

CHAPTER 11 SEQUENCES AND SERIES

Exercise 11-1, Introduction to Sequences

1. a. (Graph) **b.** $t_7 = \dfrac{1}{7}$; $t_8 = \dfrac{1}{8}$ **c.** $t_n = \dfrac{1}{n}$

d. $t_{100} = \dfrac{1}{100}$ **3. a.** (Graph) **b.** $t_7 = \dfrac{1}{15}$;

$t_8 = \dfrac{1}{17}$ **c.** $t_n = \dfrac{1}{2n + 1}$ **d.** $t_{100} = \dfrac{1}{201}$

5. a. (Graph) **b.** $t_7 = 9$; $t_8 = 10$
c. $t_n = 2 + n$ **d.** $t_{100} = 102$
13. 22, 29. Add 1 more each time to get next term.   **15.** 21, 34. Add preceding 2 terms to get next term.   **17.** 21, 28. Starting with 1, add 2, then 3, then 4, and so forth. (See Exercise 11-4, Problem 36.)
19. 7, 64. There are *two* sequences put together, 1, 2, 3, 4, 5, 6, 7, . . . , and 1, 2, 4, 8, 16, 32, 64, ...   **21.** e, n, t, e. These are the first letters of the natural numbers' names!!

Exercise 11-2, Arithmetic and Geometric Sequences

1. Arithmetic. $d = 5$ **3.** Neither.
5. Geometric. $r = -1$ **7.** Geometric. $r = 2$ **9.** Neither.   **11.** Neither.
13. Geometric $r = \frac{1}{2}$ **15.** Geometric. $r = 5^{-\frac{1}{6}}$ **17.** 134   **19.** -182 **21.** $19\frac{2}{3}$

23. 197, 200, 203   **25.** 1458   **27.** $\dfrac{3}{128}$

29. -512 **31.** 18.84   **33.** 1.44
35. -7.626×10^{10} **37.** 33   **39.** 16
41. 10   **43.** 7   **45.** 6

Exercise 11-3, Arithmetic and Geometric Means

1. 49, 56, 63   **3.** $-104, -101, -98,$
$-95, -92, -89$ **5.** $14, 5, -4, -13, -22$
7. $-167, -191$ **9.** $58\frac{1}{2}, 64, 69\frac{1}{2},$
11. $109\frac{2}{5}, 95\frac{4}{5}, 82\frac{1}{5}, 68\frac{3}{5}$ **13.** 15, 45
15. $54, 36, 24; -54, 36, -24$
17. $\frac{1}{8}, \frac{1}{2}, 2, 8$ **19.** $-91, 637$
21. $x^7, x^9, x^{11}, x^{13}, x^{15}$
$\quad -x^7, x^9, -x^{11}, x^{13}, -x^{15}$
23. $13\sqrt[3]{2}, 13\sqrt[3]{4}$ or 16.38, 20.64
25. 6, 18, 54
$\quad -6, 18, -54$
$\quad 6i, -18, -54i$
$\quad -6i, -18, 54i$
27. 2, 4, 8
$\quad -2, 4, -8$
$\quad 2i, -4, -8i$
$\quad -2i, -4, 8i$
29. The sequence is $a, m, b, \ldots$.
Since the adjacent terms have a
common ratio,
$$\frac{b}{m} = \frac{m}{a}$$
Multiplying by am gives
$$ab = m^2$$
from which
$$m = \sqrt{ab}, \text{ QED}$$
Note: $m = -\sqrt{ab}$, also.
31. $AM = 10, GM = 6$ or -6
33. $AM = 12\frac{1}{3}, GM = 4$ or -4
35. Prove that for any two unequal numbers
a and b, both positive, that $AM > GM$.
Proof: Since $AM = \frac{1}{2}(a + b)$, and
$GM = \sqrt{ab}$, it is sufficient to prove
that $\frac{1}{2}(a + b) > \sqrt{ab}$.
Since $a \neq b$, the quantity $(a - b)^2$ is
positive.

$\therefore a^2 - 2ab - b^2 > 0$	Squaring
$a^2 + 2ab - b^2 > 4ab$	$a - b$
$(a + b)^2 > 4ab$	Adding $4ab$
$\frac{1}{2}(a + b) > \sqrt{ab}$	Factoring
	Multiplying
	by $\frac{1}{4}$, then
	taking posi-
$\therefore AM > GM$, QED.	tive sq. root

Exercise 11-4, Introduction to Series

1. 65   **3.** 55   **5.** $\frac{25}{12}$ **7.** 97   **9.** -9
11. 62   **13.** 3.121608   **15.** 122   **17.** 600

19. 600   **21.** Distributivity   **23.** $\sum\limits_{k=1}^{10} k^2$

25. $\sum\limits_{k=1}^{100} \dfrac{1}{k+2}$ **27.** $\sum\limits_{k=1}^{40} 2(3^{k-1})$

29. $\sum\limits_{k=1}^{90} 2 + (k-1)(4)$

31. $\sum\limits_{k=1}^{20} (-1)^{k-1}(k-1)(10)$

33. $\sum\limits_{k=1}^{55} (k)(k+1)$

35. $S_n = n^2$
37. S_n approaches but never equals 1.

Exercise 11-5, Arithmetic and Geometric Series

1. 175   **3.** 2200   **5.** 0   **7.** 5000   **9.** 3720
11. 31   **13.** -182 **15.** 147,620   **17.** 1026
19. about 6931.82   **21.** about 79.4109
23. 728   **25.** 37   **27.** 119   **29.** 55   **31.** 123
33. (Type formula for t_k on line 10.)

```
10   DEF FN T(K)=3*0.8 ^ (K-1)
20   INPUT "NO. OF TERMS:";N
30   S=0
40   FOR K=1 TO N
50   T=FN T(K)
60   S=S+T
70   PRINT K; TAB(5)T; TAB (20)S
80   NEXT K
90   END
```

Exercise 11-6, Convergent Geometric Series

1. $3\frac{3}{4}$ **3.** 24   **5.** diverges   **7.** $11\frac{1}{9}$
9. $111\frac{1}{9}, 90\frac{10}{11}$ **11.** $\frac{7}{11}$ **13.** $\frac{21}{37}$ **15.** $\frac{35}{33}$
17. $\frac{157}{110}$ **19.** $\frac{1}{2}$ **21.** $\frac{1}{81}$
23. $S = \frac{1}{2} + \frac{1}{3} + \frac{1}{4} + \frac{1}{5} + \frac{1}{6} + \frac{1}{7} + \frac{1}{8} + \frac{1}{9} +$
$\frac{1}{10} + \frac{1}{11} + \frac{1}{12} + \frac{1}{13} + \frac{1}{14} + \frac{1}{15} + \frac{1}{16} + \ldots =$
$\frac{1}{2} + (\frac{1}{3} + \frac{1}{4}) + (\frac{1}{5} + \frac{1}{6} + \frac{1}{7} + \frac{1}{8}) +$
$(\frac{1}{9} + \frac{1}{10} + \frac{1}{11} + \frac{1}{12} + \frac{1}{13} + \frac{1}{14} + \frac{1}{15} +$
$\frac{1}{16}) + \ldots >$
$\frac{1}{2} + (\frac{1}{4} + \frac{1}{4}) + (\frac{1}{8} + \frac{1}{8} + \frac{1}{8} + \frac{1}{8}) +$
$(\frac{1}{16} + \frac{1}{16} + \frac{1}{16} + \frac{1}{16} + \frac{1}{16} + \frac{1}{16} + \frac{1}{16} + \frac{1}{16})$
$= \frac{1}{2} + \frac{1}{2} + \frac{1}{2} + \frac{1}{2} + \ldots$
$\therefore S > \frac{1}{2} + \frac{1}{2} + \frac{1}{2} + \frac{1}{2} + \ldots$, which
clearly diverges.
25. b. converges for $-1 \leq x < 1$
$\quad$ diverges for $x \geq 1$ or $x < -1$
$\quad$ **c.** $S = \dfrac{t(1)}{1 - r} = \dfrac{t(1)}{1 - x}$
27. $\dfrac{9}{4}$

Exercise 11-7, Sequences and Series as Mathematical Models

1. a. 1.89 mm **b.** about 24 mm **c.** 60 mm
3. a. geometric **b.** about 66.48% **c.** about 34 times **d.** It would predict negative color eventually.   **5.** $m = 1000(1.05)^t$; over $11 million in 1990; banks could go broke if there were no limit to their liability.
7. *Manhattan Problem:* $m = 24(1.06)^t$ over $39 billion in 1990 **9. a.** $2100
b. $84,000; $81,900; $79,800; $77,700
c. arithmetic, $d = -2100$ **d.** $27,300
e. 40 years **11. a. i.** 64 cm **ii.** 820 cm
b. i. about 69.25 cm **ii.** 837.92 cm
iii. 2500 cm **13. a.** 2, 4, 8 **b.** geometric, $r = 2$ **c.** 1,048,576 **d.** 2,097,150
15. a. about 0.8524 **b.** 85.24%, 72.66%, 61.93%, 52.79% **c.** 11   **17. a.** 1, 11, 121, 1331

b. 14 years   **19. a.** $t_1 = 1; r = \dfrac{\sqrt{2}}{2}$

b. $t_1 = 4; r = \dfrac{\sqrt{2}}{2}$ **c.** $t_1 = 1; r = \dfrac{1}{2}$

d. $\dfrac{1}{512}$ **e.** $\dfrac{\sqrt{2}}{8}$ **f.** $1\dfrac{511}{512}$ **g.** about 13.23008
h. 2 **i.** $8 + 4\sqrt{2}$ **21. a.** 20% **b.** 20%
c. 4%, 0.8% **d.** 7.69% **e.** three 8-cc rinses
23.   a. $2.41 **b.** $0.15/lb, $1.76/lb
c. $3.76/lb, 56%   **25.** $769.91
27. $t_n = t_1 + (n - 1)d$ Definition of
         arithmetic sequence
    $= t_1 + (n + 0 - 1)d$ Additive
                        identity
    $= t_1 + (n - k + k - 1)d$ Additive
                            inverse
    $= t_1 + (n - k)d + (k - 1)d$ Distribu-
                                tivity
    $= t_1 + (k - 1)d + (n - k)d$ Commu-
                            tativity of addition
    $= t_k + (n - k)d$ Definition of
                    arithmetic sequence
    $\therefore t_n = t_k + (n - k)d$ Transitivity

Exercise 11-8, Factorials

1. 144 **3.** 1680 **5.** 5040 **7.** 5040 **9.** 10
11. 720 **13.** $\dfrac{1}{n}$ **15.** $(n + 1)(n)$ **17.** $\dfrac{7!}{3!}$
19. $\dfrac{20!}{14!}$ **21.** $\dfrac{20! \, 12!}{17! \, 9!}$ **23.** $\dfrac{30!}{6! \, 24!}$
25. $n \geq 6$ **27.** 24 zeros **29.** 34
31. $\dfrac{25}{12}$

33.

n	n^2	2^n	$n!$
0	0	1	1
1	1	2	1
2	4	4	2
3	9	8	6
4	16	16	24
5	25	32	120
6	36	64	720
7	49	128	5040
8	64	256	40320
9	81	512	362880
10	100	1024	3628800

35. a. 0.0000248
b. 2.7183

Exercise 11-9, Introduction to Binomial Series

1. $a^4 + 4a^3b + 6a^2b^2 + 4ab^3 + b^4$
3. a. decrease by 1 each term
   b. increase by 1 each term
   c. nth degree **d.** $n + 1$ terms
   e. symmetrical
5. $a^{10} + 10a^9b + 45a^8b^2 + 120a^7b^3 + 210a^6b^4 + 252a^5b^5 + 210a^4b^6 + 120a^3b^7 + 45a^2b^8 + 10ab^9 + b^{10}$
7. 0

Exercise 11-10, The Binomial Formula

1. $x^5 + 5x^4y + 10x^3y^2 + 10x^2y^3 + 5xy^4 + y^5$
3. $p^7 - 7p^6m + 21p^5m^2 - 35p^4m^3 + 35p^3m^4 - 21p^2m^5 + 7pm^6 - m^7$
5. $a^4 + 8a^3 + 24a^2 + 32a + 16$
7. $32x^5 - 240x^4 + 720x^3 - 1080x^2 + 810x - 243$
9. $x^{12} + 6x^{10}y^3 + 15x^8y^6 + 20x^6y^9 + 15x^4y^{12} + 6x^2y^{15} + y^{18}$
11. $8a^3 - 12a^2b^4 + 6ab^8 - b^{12}$
13. $x^8 + 8x^6 + 28x^4 + 56x^2 + 70 + 56x^{-2} + 28x^{-4} + 8x^{-6} + x^{-8}$
15. $x^2 - 4x + 6 - 4x^{-1} + x^{-2}$
17. $-8i$ **19.** $-4 + 4i$ **21.** $56x^3y^5$
23. $1716r^6s^7$ **25.** $-1365p^4j^{11}$
27. $20349 \, a^5b^{16}$ **29.** $-\dfrac{58!}{35! \, 23!} e^{35}f^{23}$
31. $\dfrac{73!}{48! \, 25!} x^{48}y^{25}$ **33.** $5005x^{27}y^{12}$
35. $-1716x^{18}y^{14}$ **37.** No such term.
39. $48384x^3y^5$ **41.** $2,203,961,430 \, j^{18}k^{16}$
43. $-1365r^4q^{11}$ **45.** b^{12}
47. $-22680x^8y^9$ **49.** $375x^{12}$
51. a. 7th term. **b.** 19th power.
   c. $50388r^{12}s^7$ **d.** 20 terms.

53. 1.2189936

55. $(1 + 1)^5 = 32$. For $(a + b)^{57}$, sum of coefficients is 2^{57}.

11-11, Chapter Review

R1. a. 72, 90 **b.** (Graph) **c.** $t_n = n^2 + n$
d. 490,700 **R2. a.** neither **b.** -148 **c.** 73
d. 4035.397 . . . **e.** 8

R3. a. $24\frac{2}{3}, 32\frac{1}{3}, 40, 47\frac{2}{3}, 55\frac{1}{3}$

    b. $(4\sqrt{5}, 20, 20\sqrt{5})$
       $(-4\sqrt{5}, 20, -20\sqrt{5})$
       $(4i\sqrt{5}, -20, -20i\sqrt{5})$
       $(-4i\sqrt{5}, -20, -20i\sqrt{5})$
    c. ± 50

R4. a. 153 **b.** $S_n = \sum_{k=1}^{\infty} \frac{1}{2^{k+1}}$

R5. a. 140,500 **b.** 94 **c.** about 1394.99
d. 33

R6. a. 2500 **b.** $r = 2$. Geometric series converge only for r such that
    $|r| < 1$. **c.** $\frac{31}{111}$

R7. a. 23 cm, 43 cm
    b. 18.58 cm, 115.01 cm
    c. 11 pumps, 12 pumps
    d. 36 pumps, 18 pumps
    e. (Graph)
    f. never start
    g. Sitting increases amplitude faster going low; standing increases amplitude faster going high.

R8. a. $\frac{1}{84}$ **b.** $\frac{24!}{20!}$

R9. $x^4 - 4x^3y + 6x^2y^2 - 4xy^3 + y^4$

R10. a. $r^{18} - 12r^{15}p + 60r^{12}p^2$
      $- 160r^9p^3 + 240r^6p^4 - 192r^3p^5$
      $+ 64p^6$
    b. $-8432 + 5376i$
    c. $84d^5p^2$
    d. $-4368t^5y^{22}$

CHAPTER 12 PROBABILITY, DATA ANALYSIS, AND FUNCTIONS OF A RANDOM VARIABLE

Exercise 12-1, Introduction to Probability

1. $\frac{1}{12}$ **3.** $\frac{5}{6}$ **5.** $\frac{1}{6}$ **7.** $\frac{5}{9}$ **9.** 1 **11.** $\frac{1}{18}$

13. $\frac{11}{36}$

Exercise 12-2, Words Associated with Probability

1. a. random experiment **b.** 52 **c.** 12
d. $\frac{3}{13}$ **e.** $\frac{1}{2}$ **f.** $\frac{1}{13}$ **g.** $\frac{5}{13}$ **h.** $\frac{1}{52}$ **i.** 1 **j.** 0

Exercise 12-3, Two Counting Principles

1. 345 **3. a.** 91 **b.** 20 **5. a.** 17 **b.** 60
7. a. 16 **b.** 55 **c.** 20 (Only 4 are left for the 2nd selection.) **9.** 693 **11. a.** 9
b. 18 **c.** 504 **13. a.** 10 ways. **b.** 9 ways.
c. 90 ways. **d.** 8 ways. **e.** 720 ways
f. 3,628,800 ways.
15. a. 2 letters: 6,759,324;
3 letters: 17,558,424;
$\therefore$ 10,799,100 more with 3 letters
b. 24,317,748 **c.** A national license plate program would *not* be possible using this scheme since there are more cars than there are possible plates.
17. *Overlapping Events* **a.** 20 **b.** 45
c. 1018 **d.** 630 **e.** 496

Exercise 12-4, Probabilities of Various Permutations

1. a. 3024 **b.** 1320 **c.** 6720 **d.** 5040
3. a. 132 **b.** 11880 **c.** 479,001,600
5. 358,800 **7. a.** 210 **b.** 1716 **c.** 5040
9. 210 **11. a.** 720 **b.** 120 **c.** $\frac{1}{6}$

d. $P \approx 17\%$ **e.** $P(NIMBLE) = \frac{1}{720}$

13. a. $n = 24$; $P = \frac{24}{720} = \frac{1}{30}$

b. $n = 192$; $P = \frac{192}{720} = \frac{4}{15}$

c. $n = 48$; $P = \frac{48}{720} = \frac{1}{15}$

d. $n = 96$; $P = \frac{96}{720} = \frac{2}{15}$

e. $n = 72$; $P = \frac{72}{720} = \frac{1}{10}$

15. a. $n(S) = 362880$ **b.** $n(E) = 40320$

c. $\frac{1}{9}$ **d.** $P \approx 11\%$ **17. a.** $\frac{1}{3}$ **b.** $\frac{1}{12}$

c. $\frac{1}{84}$ **19. a.** 3628800 **b.** 725760 **c.** $\frac{1}{5}$

21. *Permutations with Repeated Elements*
a. i. 360 **ii.** 840 **iii.** 20 **iv.** 415,800
v. 5040 **vi.** 3360 **b.** 210 **c.** 126

Exercise 12-5, Probabilities of Various Combinations

1. 10 **3.** 56 **5.** 6 **7.** 330 **9.** 1
11. 1 **13.** 360 **15.** 55,440
17. 142,506 committees
19. 35 games (too many for one evening!)
21. 166,167,000 sel. **23. a.** 20 **b.** 15
c. 35 **d.** 1 **25. a.** 2,598,960 hands
b. $\approx 6.35 \times 10^{11}$ hands **27. a.** 45
b. 252 **c.** 45 Selecting 8 to *take* is equivalent to selecting 2 *not* to take.
29. a. $\approx 48\%$ **b.** $\approx 24\%$
c. $\approx 71\%$ **d.** 50% **31. a.** $\approx 39\%$
b. $\approx 0.56\%$ **c.** 0 **d.** 20% **33. a.** $\approx 57.1\%$
b. $\approx 71.4\%$ **c.** $\approx 28.6\%$
d. $P(\text{none}) = 1 - P(\geq 1)$
35. a. 75,287,520 **b.** 7,376,656
c. $\approx 9.8\%$ **d.** The sampling plan is inadequate. The probability of finding bad bulbs is too low.

Exercise 12-6, Properties of Probability

1. *Calculator Components Problem*
a. 56% **b.** 30% **c.** 20% **d.** 6% **e.** 94%
3. *Car Breakdown Problem*
a. 90% **b.** 95% **c.** 85.5% **d.** 0.5%
e. 14.5%
5. *Traffic Light Problem*
a. 28% **b.** 18% **c.** 12% **d.** 42% **e.** 54%
7. *Back-Up Systems Problem*
99.96%
9. *Basketball Problem*
a. 33.6% **b.** 2.4% **c.** 97.6% **d.** 5.6%
11. *Spaceship Problem*
a. 36.8% Surprisingly low probability!
b. 99.9895%
13. *Football Plays Problem*
a. 12% **b.** 28% **c.** 48% **d.** 12%
(Note: The sum of the probabilities equals 1, indicating that these four are the only possible events.
15. *Measles and Chicken Pox Problem*
a. 2.4% **b. i.** 5% **ii.** 90%
c. Since $P(C \text{ after } M) < P(C)$, measles seems to give *immunity* to chicken pox. Since $P(M \text{ after } C) > P(M)$, chicken pox seems to *increase* susceptibility to measles. (Note: These numbers are *hypothetical*, and do not necessarily represent correct biology.)
17. *Combinations and Binomial Series Problem*
a. $n(0) = {}_5C_0 = 1$; $n(1) = {}_5C_1 = 5$;
$n(2) = {}_5C_2 = 10$; $n(3) = {}_5C_3 = 10$;
$n(4) = {}_5C_4 = 5$; $n(5) = {}_5C_5 = 1$

b. $1 + 5 + 10 + 10 + 5 + 1 = 32$
c. $(1 + 1)^5 = 1 + 5 + 10 + 10 + 5 + 1$, which is the same as the sum in part (b).
d. $(1 + 1)^5 = 2^5 = 32$ **e.** ${}_{10}C_0 - {}_{10}C_1 + \cdots + {}_{10}C_{10} = 2^{10} = 1024$

Exercise 12-7, page 0; Functions of a Random Variable

1. *Heredity Problem*
a. $P(\text{dark}) = 1 - \frac{1}{4} = 0.75$
b.

x	$P(x)$
0	0.015625
1	0.140625
2	0.421875
3	0.421875

c. Sum = 1.000000 $\therefore$ Ans. is reasonable.
d. (Graph)
3. *Thumbtack Problem*
a.

x(up)	$P(x)$
0	0.0081
1	0.0756
2	0.2646
3	0.4116
4	0.2401
Sum =	1.0000

b. (Graph) **c.** $P(>2 \text{ up}) = 0.4116 + 0.2401 = 0.6517 = 65.17\%$
$P(\leq 2 \text{ up}) = 0.0081 + 0.0756 + 0.2646 = 0.3483 = 34.83\%$ $\therefore$ *More than 2 up* is more probable.

5. *Bull's Eye Problem*
a.

x	$P(x)$
0	0.16807
1	0.36015
2	0.30870
3	0.13230
4	0.02835
5	0.00243
Sum =	1.00000

b. (Graph)
c. $P(\text{at least 2}) = 0.3087 + 0.1323 + 0.02835 = 0.47088 \approx 47\%$
7. *Color Blindness Problem*
a.

x	$P(x)$
0	0.35848592
1	0.37735360
2	0.18867680
3	0.05958215

b. (Graph)
c. $P(\text{at least 4}) = 1 - P(<4) = 1 - (P(0) + P(1) + P(2) + P(3)) = 1 - 0.9840985 = 0.0159015 \approx 1.6\%$
9. *Eighteen-Wheeler Problem*
a. $P(\text{not}) = 1 - 0.03 = 0.97 = 97\%$

b.

x	P(x)
0	0.57795126
1	0.32174606
2	0.08458273
3	0.01395179
4	0.00161812
5	0.00014013

i. $P(0) \approx 58\%$ **ii.** $P(1) \approx 32\%$
iii. $P(2) \approx 8\%$ **iv.** $P(>2) = 1 - P(0) -$
$P(1) - P(2) \approx 0.0150 \approx 1.6\%$
c. If $P(0) = 0.95$, and the probability that
any one tire blows is P, then: $p^{18} = 0.95$
$P = 0.95^{1/18} \approx 0.9972 \approx 99.7\%$

11. *Airplane Engine Problem*
a. $P(\text{not fail}) = 1. - 0.1 = 0.9$
b.

x	P(x)
0	0.6561
1	0.2916
2	0.0486
3	0.0036
4	0.0001

c. Sum $= 1.0000$, so the answers are reasonable.
d. $P(\geq 1) = P(0) + P(1) = 0.9477 \approx 95\%$
e.

x	P(x)
0	0.729
1	0.243
2	0.027
3	0.001

Sum $= 1.000$ $\therefore P(1) = P(0) +$
$P(1) = 0.972 = 97\%$
f.   The 3-engine plane appears to be safer.
The assumed engine reliability is so low
(only 90%) that adding more engines just
gives more things that can go wrong! For
engines of higher reliability, the 4-engine
plane is safer.

13. *Another Dice Game*
a. i.

x	n(x)	P(x)
2	1	$\frac{1}{36}$
3	2	$\frac{1}{18}$
4	3	$\frac{1}{12}$
5	4	$\frac{1}{9}$
6	5	$\frac{5}{36}$
7	6	$\frac{1}{6}$
8	5	$\frac{5}{36}$
9	4	$\frac{1}{9}$
10	3	$\frac{1}{12}$
11	2	$\frac{1}{18}$
12	1	$\frac{1}{36}$

ii.

x	n(x)	P(x)
-5	1	$\frac{1}{36}$
-4	2	$\frac{1}{18}$
-3	3	$\frac{1}{12}$
-2	4	$\frac{1}{9}$
-1	5	$\frac{5}{36}$
0	6	$\frac{1}{6}$
1	5	$\frac{5}{36}$
0	6	$\frac{1}{6}$
1	5	$\frac{5}{36}$
2	4	$\frac{1}{9}$
3	3	$\frac{1}{12}$
4	2	$\frac{1}{18}$
5	1	$\frac{1}{36}$

iii.

x	n(x)	P(x)
0	6	$\frac{1}{6}$
1	10	$\frac{5}{18}$
2	18	$\frac{2}{9}$
3	6	$\frac{1}{6}$
4	4	$\frac{1}{9}$
5	2	$\frac{1}{18}$

b. Most probable is $x = 7$.
Most probable is $x = 0$.
Most probable is $x = 1$.

15. *First Girl Problem*
a.

x	P(x)
1	0.5
2	0.25
3	0.125
4	0.0625

b. (Graph). The x-axis is an asymptote.
c. Geometric sequence, or exponential func-

tion. **d.** Sum $= \dfrac{t(1)}{1-r} = \dfrac{0.5}{1-0.5} = 1$,

QED.   **17.** *Lucky Card Problem*
a. $P(1, 1) = 0.1$ **b.** $P(2, 1) = (0.9)$
$(0.1) = 0.09$
$P(3, 1) = (0.9)(0.9)(0.1) = .081$
c. $P(1, 2) = (0.9)(0.9)(0.9)$
$(0.1) = 0.0729 \therefore = 0.1, 0.1(0.9)^3$,
$0.1(0.9)^6, \ldots$, which is a geometric sequence with $t(1) = 0.1$ and $r = (0.9)^3 = 0.729$. **d.** $P(1) = \dfrac{0.1}{1-0.729} \approx 0.369 \approx$
37% **e.** *Second player's probability is a geometric series with* $t(1) = 0.09$ *and* $r = 0.729$. *Third player's probability is a geometric series with* $t(1) = 0.081$ *and* $r = 0.729$.
$\therefore P(2) = \dfrac{0.09}{1-0.729} \approx 0.0332 \approx 33\%$
$P(3) = \dfrac{0.081}{1-0.729} \approx 0.299 \approx 30\%$
f. The answers are reasonable since: **i.** First player has greatest probability, etc. **ii.**
$P(1) + P(2) + P(3) \approx .369 + .332 + .299 = 1.000$.   **19.** *Computer Program for Binomial Distributions* In the following program, PRINT generates output on the screen, and PRINT=4 generates output on the printer.

```
10 PRINT "TYPE PROBABILITY OF
   SUCCESS ON 1 TRIAL."
20 INPUT B
30 PRINT "TYPE NUMBER OF
   TRIALS"
40 INPUT N
50 PRINT "TYPE HIGHEST VALUE
   OF X TO BE PRINTED."
60 INPUT H
70 PRINT#4, "P(SUCCESS) =
   #.######",B
80 PRINT#4,USING "NO. OF
   TRIALS = ####",N
90 PRINT#4
100 A=1-B
110 PRINT#4," X       P(X)"
120 FOR X=0 TO H
130 IF X=0 THEN P=ATN;GO TO
    150
140 P=P*(N-X+1)/X*B/A
150 PRINT#4, "### ###.
    ########",X,P
160 NEXT X
170 PRINT#4,LF,LF,LF
180 GO TO 10
190 END
```

Output:

P(SUCCESS) = .400000 NO. OF
TRIALS = 3

X	P(X)
0	.21600000
1	.43200000
2	.28800000
3	.06400000

Exercise 12-8, Mathematical Expectation

1. *Card Draw Problem*
a.

Event	P(Event)	payoff	$P \times p$
A	4/52	$1.56 - .26 = 1.30$	0.10
F	12/52	$.65 - .26 = 0.39$	0.09
Other	36/52	$- .26$	−0.18
			E = 0.01

b. You would expect to *gain* about 1 cent per game.
3. *Archery Problem*
a.

Color	P(color)	points	$P \times p$
Gold	0.20	9	1.80
Red	0.36	7	2.52
Blue	0.23	5	1.15
Black	0.14	3	0.42
White	0.07	1	0.07
			E = 5.96

b. Expected score = (no. of shots)(avg. per shot) = $(48)(5.96) = 286.08$, or about 286
5. *Seed Germination Problem*
a.

x	$P(x)$	$x \cdot P(x)$
0	0.0016	0
1	0.0256	0.0256
2	0.1536	0.3072
3	0.4096	1.2288
4	0.4096	1.6384

b.   E = 3.2 seeds
7. *Expectation of a Binomial Experiment*
a.

x	$P(x)$	$x \cdot P(x)$
0	0.07776	0
1	0.2592	0.2592
2	0.3456	0.6912
3	0.2304	0.6912
4	0.0768	0.3072
5	0.01024	0.0512

b. E = 2
c. $(0.4)(5) = 2$, which equals the expected value. **d.** $E = {}_5C_0 \cdot a^5 \cdot 0 + {}_5C_1 \cdot a^4b \cdot 1 + {}_5C_2 \cdot a^3b^2 \cdot 2 + {}_5C_3 \cdot a^2b^3 \cdot 3 + {}_5C_4 \cdot ab^4 \cdot 4 + {}_5C_5 \cdot b^5 \cdot 5 = 0a^5 + 5(1-b)^4b + 20(1-b)^3b^2 + 30(1-b)^2b^3 + 20(1-b)b^4 - 5b^5$
Upon expanding and simplifying, this equals $5b$. **e.** $E = nb$ **f.** $E = nb = (100)(0.71) = 71$ seeds.

9. *Dice Game Problem*

$P(A) = \dfrac{1}{6}$ on any one roll.

$P(2A) = {}_3C_2\left(\dfrac{1}{6}\right)^2\left(\dfrac{5}{6}\right) = \dfrac{5}{72};$

$P(3A) = {}_3C_3\left(\dfrac{1}{6}\right)^3 = \dfrac{1}{216};$

$\therefore P(\geq 2A) = \dfrac{5}{72} + \dfrac{1}{216} = \dfrac{16}{216} = \dfrac{2}{27}.$

Event	$P(E)$	payoff	$p \cdot P(E)$
$\geq 2A$	$\dfrac{2}{27}$	$10 - 1$	$\dfrac{18}{27}$
$<2A$	$\dfrac{25}{27}$	-1	$-\dfrac{25}{27}$

$$E = -\dfrac{7}{27}$$

You lose about 26 cents per time!

11. *Bad Egg Problem*
about $1.34 profit.

13. *Nuclear Reactor Problem*
a. $E(1) = 100(2.3) = 230$
b. $E(2) = 230(2.3) = 529;$
$E(3) = 529(2.3) = 1216.7;$
$E(4) = 1216.7(2.3) = 2798.41$
c. $E(1 \text{ second}) = 100(2.3^{1000}) \approx 5.3 \times 10^{363}$
d. $P(\text{none}) = (0.64)(0.8)(0.85) = 0.4352$
e. $E = 100(2.3)(0.4352) = 100.096$
f. $E(1 \text{ second}) = 100(1.00096^{1000}) \approx 261.05$
This reactor would *not* explode like a bomb since the neutron level rises relatively slowly.
g. $E(x) = 100 \times 1.00096^x$, which has the form of the general exponential function equation. Therefore, $E(x)$ increases exponentially with time, QED.

15. *Another Life Insurance Problem*

x	$P(x)$	$D(x)$	$A(x)$	$O(x)$
55	0.01300	130	10,000	130,000
56	0.01421	140	9,870	140,000
57	0.01554	151	9,730	151,000
58	0.01700	163	9,579	163,000
59	0.01859	175	9,416	175,000
		759	48,295	759,000

c. Number of dollars paid out = (no. of deaths)(1000) = 759,000, which is the same as the sum of the $O(x)$ values. Administrative expenses = 5(5,000) = 25,000
∴ total expenses for the 5-year period = 759,000 + 25,000 = $784,000
d. Total number of premiums paid is the sum of the $A(x)$ values, 48,295.
e. Premium = 784,000/48,295 ≈ $16.23 per year. **f.** The premium is higher because older people have a higher death probability.

Exercise 12-9, Statistics and Data Analysis

1. Mean = 80.75   S. Dev. = 4.64 . . .
3. a. (Graph)
b. Mean = 90.1   S. Dev. = 2.92845
c. (Graph)
d. 90.1 − 3 = 87.1   90.1 + 3 = 93.1
Thus all of the 88–92 columns and half of the 87 and 93 columns are within 2 units of the mean. Summing: 0.5(3) + 3 + 4 + 5 + 3 + 2 + 0.5(2) = 19.5 which is close to $\dfrac{2}{3}$(30) = 20.

5. *Computer-Generated Random Data*
Answers will vary.
7. *Sampling Problem #1*
a. The phone book contains predominantly home phones. Most people who work are away from home working on a Wednesday afternoon, and so will not be able to respond. A disproportionate nuimber of the people responding will be unemployed, so the sample is not random enough.
b. The error would most likely be on the high side because a large number of the employed population would not be able to respond as described in part (a).
c. Make the calls at a time when both employed and unemployed people would be equally likely to be able to respond, perhaps 7:00–8:00 PM on a Monday.
9. *Normal Curve by Computer Graphics Problem*
a. (Graph)
b. The graph does look like the normal curve with the high point at the mean.
c. The graph is "thinner", that is more concentrated close to the mean. For $b = 0.8$, the standard deviation is smaller.
d. Let $b = 1.1$.

12-10, Chapter Review

R1. $\dfrac{11}{36}$

R2. a.
HHHH	HHHT	HHTH	HHTT
HTHH	HTHT	HTTH	HTTT
THHH	THHT	THTH	THTT
TTHH	TTHT	TTTH	TTTT

b. 0,5 **c.** 0.375
R3. a. 220 **b.** 31   **R4. a.** 5040 **b.** 360
c. about 0.071 **d.** 720 **e.** 840
R5. a. i. ≈28.8% **ii.** ≈36.5% **b. i.** 0.06
ii. 0.56 **iii.** 0.62 **iv.** 0.38

R6. This is a binomial distribution, since the lighter either lights or does not light, and the experiment is done repeatedly.

a.

x	$P(x)$
0	0.0256
1	0.1536
2	0.3456
3	0.3456
4	0.2296

b. (Graph) **c.** $P(\geq 2) = P(2) + P(3) + P(4) = \underline{0.8208} \approx 82\%$

R7. a.

Test	Grade	Weight	$w \times g$
1	72	0.1	7.2
2	86	0.2	17.2
3	93	0.2	18.6
4	77	0.2	15.4
5	98	0.3	$\underline{29.4}$
		Average =	$\underline{87.8}$

b. Each weight is a fraction of the total, 1, and is thus analogous to a *probability*. Each grade is a "payoff." So the weighted average is the sum of fraction × payoff, which is equivalent to a mathematical expectation. **R8. a.** 46; 6.041... **b.** Check student work. **c.** Math students are not representative of the student body as a whole.

12-11, Cumulative Review: Chapters 9 Through 12

1. a. $25x^2 + 4y^2 + 150x - 8y + 129 = 0$
b. $x^2 + y^2 + 4x + 10y - 7 = 0$
c. $4x^2 - 9y^2 - 24x - 36y + 63 = 0$
d. $y^2 + x - 4y - 1 = 0$
3. a. The following is synthetic substitution in table form, searching for zeros and generating plotting data.

x	1	-7	11	3 $\quad f(x)$
-2	1	-9	29	-54
-1	1	-8	19	-16
0	1	-7	11	3
1	1	-6	5	8
2	1	-5	1	5
3	1	-4	-1	0
4	1	-3	-1	-1
5	1	-2	1	9
6	1	-1	5	33

$\therefore$ 3 is a zero of $f(x)$.
b. $f(x) = (x - 3)(x^2 - 4x - 1)$
If $x^2 - 4x - 1 = 0$, then $x = 2 \pm \sqrt{5}$
Zeros are 3, $2 + \sqrt{5}$, $2 - \sqrt{5}$
c. (Graph)

5. a. $-i$ **b.** $-\dfrac{i\sqrt{6}}{2}$ **c.** $2 + 4i$

7. a. $d = \frac{1}{2}$. **b.** $3\frac{1}{2}$, 4, $4\frac{1}{2}$, 5, $5\frac{1}{2}$, 6, $6\frac{1}{2}$, **c.** 53 **d.** 2828

9. $-\dfrac{7!}{3! \, 4!} a^4 b^3 = -35a^4 b^3$

11. a. i. 15,120 **ii.** 362,880 **iii.** 25,200
b. i. 70 **ii.** 126 **iii.** 60 **13. a.** 0.0

b.

n	$P(n)$	$n \cdot P(n)$
0	0	0
1	0.1	0.1
2	0.15	0.3
3	0.5	1.5
4	0.25	$\underline{1.0}$
	$E = $	$\overline{2.9}$

c. The number 2.9 is an *average* number of neutrons per fission, over *many* fissions.

CHAPTER 13 TRIGONOMETRIC AND CIRCULAR FUNCTIONS

Exericse 13-1, Introduction to Periodic Functions

1. a. (Graph) Time, x-axis; depth, y-axis
b. periodic
3. a. (Graph) Time, x-axis; temp, y-axis
b. not periodic
5. a. (Graph) Time, x-axis; distance, y-axis
b. periodic
7. a. (Graph) Time, x-axis; distance, y-axis
b. periodic
9. a. (Graph) Time, x-axis; distance, y-axis
b. periodic

Exercise 13-3, Definitions of Trigonometric and Circular Functions

	θ	$\sin \theta$	$\cos \theta$	$\tan \theta$
1.	60°	$\dfrac{\sqrt{3}}{2}$	$\dfrac{1}{2}$	$\sqrt{3}$
3.	$-315°$	$\dfrac{\sqrt{2}}{2}$	$\dfrac{\sqrt{2}}{2}$	1
5.	180°	0	-1	0

	θ	$\cot \theta$	$\sec \theta$	$\csc \theta$
1.	60°	$\dfrac{\sqrt{3}}{3}$	2	$\dfrac{2\sqrt{3}}{3}$
3.	$-315°$	1	$\sqrt{2}$	$\sqrt{2}$
5.	180°	und.	-1	und.

x	sin x	cos x	tan x
7. $\frac{5\pi}{4}$	$-\frac{\sqrt{2}}{2}$	$-\frac{\sqrt{2}}{2}$	1
9. $\frac{5\pi}{6}$	$\frac{1}{2}$	$-\frac{\sqrt{3}}{2}$	$-\frac{\sqrt{3}}{3}$
11. $-\frac{5\pi}{2}$	-1	0	und.

x	cot x	sec x	csc x
7. $\frac{5\pi}{4}$	1	$-\sqrt{2}$	$-\sqrt{2}$
9. $\frac{5\pi}{6}$	$-\sqrt{3}$	$-\frac{2\sqrt{3}}{3}$	2
11. $-\frac{5\pi}{2}$	0	und.	-1

13. 0 **15.** $-\frac{1}{2}$ **17.** -1 **19.** undefined

21. $-\frac{2\sqrt{3}}{3}$ **23.** $\sqrt{2}$ **25.** $\frac{\sqrt{3}}{2}$

27. $-\frac{\sqrt{2}}{2}$ **29.** 0 **31.** $\sqrt{3}$ **33.** 1

35. $-\frac{2\sqrt{3}}{3}$ **37.** 1 **39.** $-2\sqrt{3}$ **41.** 6

43. 0 **45.** 2 **47.** 1 **49.** -1 **51.** 0

53. $\frac{4}{3}$ **55.** 0 **57.** 4 **59.** 1 **61.** $\sqrt{3}$

63. $-\frac{1}{2}$ **65.** $1 + \frac{2\sqrt{3}}{3}$ **67.** 1

69. $-\frac{11}{3}$ **71.** $-\frac{1}{4}$ **73.** $-\frac{\sqrt{3}}{3}$ **75.** $\frac{4}{3}$

77. a. 0°, 180°, 360° **b.** 90°, 270° **c.** 0°, 180°, 360° **d.** 90°, 270° **e.** no values of θ
f. no values of θ **79. a.** $\frac{\pi}{2}$ **b.** 0, 2π **c.** $\frac{\pi}{4}$, $\frac{5\pi}{4}$ **d.** $\frac{\pi}{4}$, $\frac{5\pi}{4}$ **e.** 0, 2π **f.** $\frac{\pi}{2}$ **81.** *Radians*

a. $\frac{\pi}{6}$ radians **b.** $\frac{\pi}{4}$ radians

c. $\frac{\pi}{3}$ radians **d.** $\frac{\pi}{2}$ radians **e.** $\frac{5\pi}{6}$ radians

f. π radians **g.** $\frac{5\pi}{3}$ radians **h.** $-\frac{3\pi}{2}$ radians

i. $\frac{50\pi}{3}$ radians **j.** -6π radians

Exercise 13-4, Approximate Values of Trigonometric and Circular Functions

1. $\sin 27.4° \approx 0.4602$ **3.** $\tan 48.6° \approx 1.134$ **5.** $\sec 12.3° \approx 1.023$ **7.** 0.9287
9. 20.01 **11.** 3.257 **13.** 0.6743

15. -1.5013 **17.** -1.2482 **19.** 0.8415
21. 28.63° **23.** 24.15° **25.** 47.04°
27. 62.37° **29.** 67.20° **31.** 70.33°
33. 0.6700 **35.** 0.6393 **37.** 1.2971
39. 0.5627
41.

	θ	u	v	$\sin \theta$	$\cos \theta$
a.	26°	.90	.44	0.44	0.90

b. $\frac{.44}{.90} \approx 0.4889 \approx \tan 26°$

	$\tan \theta$	$\cot \theta$	$\sec \theta$	$\csc \theta$
a.	0.49	2.0	1.1	2.3
	0.4877	2.0503	1.1126	2.2812
b.	-3.4	-0.28	-3.6	1.0
	-3.2709	-3.05733	-3.4203	1.0457
c.	1.2	0.83	-1.6	-1.3
	1.1918	0.8391	-1.5557	-1.3054
d.	-0.73	-1.4	1.25	-1.7
	-0.7536	-1.3270	1.2521	-1.6616

43. (a) $W\!\left(\frac{\pi}{2}\right) = (0, 1)$

$W\!\left(\frac{3\pi}{2}\right) = (0, -1)$

$W\!\left(\frac{-\pi}{2}\right) = (0, -1)$

$W(2\pi) = (1, 0)$

(b) False. There is an infinite number of values of x for each point. The values are spaced 2π units apart. **(c)** Since the circle is a unit circle, $u = \frac{u}{r} = \cos x$, and $v = v/r = \sin x$. $\therefore W(x) = (\cos x, \sin x)$.

(d) $W(\pi/3) = \left(1/2, \sqrt{\frac{3}{2}}\right)$

$W(5\pi/6) = \left(-\sqrt{\frac{3}{2}}, 1/2\right)$

$W(-3\pi/4) = \left(-\sqrt{\frac{2}{2}}, -\sqrt{\frac{2}{2}}\right)$

(e) $W(5) = (0.2836 \ldots, -0.9589 \ldots)$
$W(-2.37) = (-0.7168 \ldots, -0.6972 \ldots)$
(f) $0.6^2 + 0.8^2 = 1$ $\therefore$ $(0.6, 0.8)$ *can* be a value of $W(x)$. $0.3^2 + 0.9^2 = 0.9 \neq 1$ $\therefore$ $(0.3, 0.9)$ *cannot* be a value of $W(x)$.
(g) $W(x) = (0.6, 0.8)$ $\therefore \cos x = 0.6$ and $\sin x = 0.8$
$\therefore x = 0.9279 \ldots + 2\pi n = 0.9279 \ldots$, $7.2104 \ldots$, $13.4936 \ldots$, etc.
(h) $W(x) = (0.28, 0.96)$
$W(x + \pi) = (-0.28, -0.96)$
$W(-x) = (0.28, -0.96)$
$W(2\pi + x) = (0.28, 0.96)$

Exercise 13-5, Graphs of Trigonometric and Circular Functions

1–17. (Graphs) **19.** If $y = A \sin Bx$ then: A tells how far the graph goes up or down from its axis; B tells how many "cycles" the graph makes in every 2π units of x.

Exercise 13-6, General Sinusoidal Graphs

1. (Graph) $y = 5 + 2 \cos 3(\theta - 20°)$; per $= 120°$
3. (Graph) $y = -3 + 4 \sin 10(\theta + 5°)$; per $= 36°$
5. (Graph) $y = 3 + 2 \cos \dfrac{1}{5}(x - \pi)$; per $= 10\pi$
7. (Graph) $y = -4 + 5 \sin \dfrac{2}{3}\left(x + \dfrac{\pi}{2}\right)$; per $= 3\pi$
9. (Graph) $y = -10 + 20 \cos \dfrac{\pi}{3}(x - 1)$; per $= 6$
11. (Graph) $y = 3 + 5 \sin \dfrac{\pi}{4}(x - 3)$; per $= 8$
13. (Graph) $y = 100 + 150 \cos \pi(x + 0.7)$; per $= 2$
15. $y = 1 + 4 \cos \dfrac{\pi}{10}(x - 2)$

Exercise 13-7, Equations of Sinusoids from Their Graphs

1. $y = 9 + 6 \cos 2\,(\theta - 20°)$
3. $y = -3 + 5 \cos 3\,(\theta - 10°)$
5. $y = 1.45 + 1.11 \cos 10\,(\theta + 7°)$
7. $y = \sqrt{3} \cos (\theta - 30°)$
9. $y = 5 + 2 \cos 2\,(x - \dfrac{\pi}{6})$
11. $y = -2 + 5 \cos \dfrac{\pi}{15}(x + 5)$
13. $y = -8 + 2 \cos 5\pi(x + 0.13)$
15. (Graph) $y = 3 + 7 \cos \dfrac{\pi}{6}(x - 5)$
17. (Graph) $y = 1.5 + 2.5 \cos \dfrac{\pi}{3}(x - 5)$

Exercise 13-8, Sinusoidal Functions as Mathematical Models

1. *Ferris Wheel Problem* **a.** (Graph)
b. The lowest you go is 3 feet above the ground, because seats in a Ferris wheel do not scrape the ground.

c. Let y = no. of feet above ground.
$y = C + A \cos B(t - D)$
$C = 23$, $A = 43 - 23 = 20$,
$B = 2\pi/(11 - 3) = x/4$, $D = 3$.
$\therefore y = 23 + 20 \cos \dfrac{\pi}{4}(t - 3)$

d. i. $y = 23 + 20 \cos \dfrac{\pi}{4}(6 - 3) \approx 8.86$ ft.
ii. $y = 23 + 20 \cos \dfrac{\pi}{4}\left(4\dfrac{1}{3} - 3\right) = 33$ ft.
iii. $y = 23 + 20 \cos \dfrac{\pi}{4}(9 - 3) = 23$ ft.
iv. $y = 23 + 20 \cos \dfrac{\pi}{4}(0 - 3) \approx 8.86$ ft.

3. *Tidal Wave Problem*
Let y = no. of meters deep.
Let t = no. of min. since tsunami first reached pier.
Using the *negative* of the *sine* function makes the phase displacement equal zero. So
$y = C - A \sin Bt$?
$C = 9$; $A = 10$; Per. $= 15$, $B = 2\pi/15$.
$\therefore$ equation is $y = 9 - 10 \sin \dfrac{2\pi}{15}t$

a. i. $y = 9 - 10 \sin \dfrac{2\pi}{15}(2) \approx 1.57$ m
ii. $y = 9 - 10 \sin \dfrac{2\pi}{15}(4) \approx -0.95$ m.
Since $y < 0$, the water has receded beyond the point at which the depth is being measured, meaning that the depth at that point is zero. **iii.** $y = 9 - 10 \sin \dfrac{2\pi}{15}(12) \approx$
18.51 m **b.** According to the model, the minimum depth is -1 meter. So there is a time interval, represented by the dotted part of the graph above, during which the water is all gone. **c.** Distance = rate $\times$ time, so
wave length $= 1200 \times \dfrac{1}{4} = 300$ km.

d. Since the wave length is so long compared to the amplitude, a person on a ship at sea would not even notice that a tsunami had passed. Note that the motion of the water is up-and-down. It is only the location of the crest of the disturbance which moves horizontally at 1200 km per hour.

5. a. (Graph) **b.** $y = 12 - 12 \cos \dfrac{1}{12}x$
c. 8.22 in. **7. a.** $i = 5 \cos 120\pi t$
b. -4.045 amperes
9. a. $y = 12 + 15 \cos \dfrac{\pi}{50}x$ **b. i.** 27 m

ii. 26.53 m iii. 5.61 m   **11. a. b.** $t = 6$:

$29 + 55 \cos \dfrac{2\pi}{365}(d + 10)$ **c.** 7:11 a.m.

d. 5:36 a.m.

Exercise 13-9, Inverse Circular Functions

1–6. (Graphs)

7–12. See Figure 13-9d   **13.** $\dfrac{\pi}{4} + \pi n$

15. $\dfrac{\pi}{4}$ **17.** $-\dfrac{\pi}{6} + 2\pi n,\ -\dfrac{5\pi}{6} + 2\pi n$

19. $\dfrac{\pi}{3}$ **21.** $\dfrac{\pi}{6} + 2\pi n, \dfrac{5\pi}{6} + 2\pi n$

23. Undefined.   **25.** $\dfrac{\pi}{6} + \pi n$ **27.** $\dfrac{\pi}{4}$

29. $\pi + 2\pi n$ **31.** $\dfrac{\pi}{2}$ **33.** $\pm\dfrac{5\pi}{6} + 2\pi n$

35. $-\dfrac{\pi}{4}$ **37.** $\pm 45° + 360n°$ **39.** $-90°$

41. $-45° + 180n°$ **43.** $45°$ **45.** Undefined.   **47.** $30° + 360n°,\ 150° + 360n°$
49. $0° + 360n°$ **51.** $-60°$ **53.** $-60° + 360n°,\ -120° + 360n°$ **55.** $120°$
57. $120°$ **59.** $30° + 180n°$ **61.** 1.101
63. 0.625 **65.** 0.405 **67.** -0.412

69. -1.322 **71.** -0.563 **73.** $\dfrac{3}{4}$ **75.** $\dfrac{5}{13}$

77. $\dfrac{15}{17}$ **79.** $\dfrac{3}{2}$ **81.** -1 **83.** $\sqrt{10}$

85. 5 **87.** Undefined. **89.** $\dfrac{\pi}{6}$ **91.** $-17°$

93. $150°$ ($210°$ is not in the range of Sec^{-1}.)
95. $11°$
97. Let $y = f(x)$.

Then $x = f^{-1}(y)$ by the definition of f^{-1}

$= f^{-1}(f(x))$ substituting $f(x)$ for y

$\therefore f^{-1}(f(x)) = x$ by transitivity and symmetry

99. a. $x = \sin y$, and $y \in \left[-\dfrac{\pi}{2}, \dfrac{\pi}{2}\right]$.

b. (Graph) **c.** $\tan y = \dfrac{x}{\sqrt{1 - x^2}}$ **d.** $y =$

Arctan $\dfrac{x}{\sqrt{1 - x^2}}$ The Arctan function can be used since the ranges of both Arctan and Arcsin are Quadrants I and IV. **e.** Arcsin

$0.5 = $ Arctan $\dfrac{0.5}{\sqrt{1 - 0.25}} = $ Arctan $\dfrac{0.5}{\sqrt{3/4}} =$

Arctan $\dfrac{2(0.5)}{\sqrt{3}} = $ Arctan $1/\sqrt{3} = \dfrac{\pi}{6}$, which

is the correct value of Arcsin 0.5.

101. Arccsc $x = $ Arcsin $\dfrac{1}{x} =$

Arctan $\dfrac{\frac{1}{x}}{\sqrt{1 - (\frac{1}{x})^2}} = $ Arctan $\dfrac{1}{\sqrt{x^2 - 1}}$

103.

```
10    PRINT ''X          ARCSIN D ARCCOS ARCTAN''
20    FOR X = 0.9 TO -0.09 STEP 0.1
30    LET S=ATN(X/SQR(1-X↑2))
40    LET C=ATN(SQR(1-X↑2)/X)
50    IF C>0 THEN 70
60    LET C=C+3.141592654
70    LET ↑=ATN(X)
80    PRINT X;S;C;T
90    NEXT X
100   END
```

X	ARCSIN	ARCCOS	ARCTAN
-.9	-1.11977	2.69057	-.732815
-.8	-.927295	2.49809	-.674741
-.7	-.775397	2.34619	-.610726
-.6	-.643501	2.2143	-.54042
-.5	-.523599	2.0944	-.463648
-.4	-.411517	1.98231	-.380506
-.3	-.304693	1.87549	-.291457
-.2	-.201358	1.77215	-.197396
-.1	-.100167	1.67096	-9.96687E-2
.1	.100167	1.47063	9.96687E-2
.2	.201358	1.36944	.197396
.3	.304693	1.2661	.291457
.4	.411517	1.15928	.380506
.5	.523599	1.0472	.463648
.6	.643501	.927295	.54042
.7	.775397	.795399	.610726
.8	.927295	.643501	.674741
.9	1.11977	.451027	.732815

To avoid division by 0 and undefined values, the program was run only from -0.9 through -0.1, then from 0.1 through 0.9. Line 20 in the program was changed as shown below for the second run of the program. The upper limits were made -0.09 and 0.91 instead of -0.1 and 0.9, respectively, to prevent round-off errors from stopping the program before the last sets of values were calculated.

```
10   PRINT ''X          ARCSIN D  ARCCOS     ARCTAN
20   FOR X = 0.1 TO -0.91 STEP 0.1
30   LET S=ATN(X/SQR(1-X↑2)
40   LET C=ATN(SQR(1-X↑2)/X)
50   IF C>0 THEN 70
60   LET C=C+3.141592654
70   LET ↑=ATN(X)
80   PRINT X;S;C;T
90   NEXT X
100  END
```

105. a. (Graph) **b.** The line $y = x$ intersects the two graphs only at the origin, although near the origin, the graphs are so close together it is hard to distinguish them. **c.** The line $y = x$ is tangent to both graphs at the origin, so the slope of the tangent line to each graph there equals 1. This property makes the circular functions more desirable in calculus than the trigonometric functions. **d.** The line $y = x$ is not tangent to the graph of $y = \sin x$ for x in degrees.

Exercise 13-10, Evaluation of Inverse Relations

1. a. $\theta = -10° + \dfrac{1}{2} \arccos \dfrac{1}{4}(y - 3)$

 b. $\theta = 20°, 140°, 200°$
 c. (Graph)

3. a. $x = 3\pi + 4 \arccos \dfrac{1}{2}(y - 6)$

 b. $x \approx 1.047, 17.802, 26,180$
 c. (Graph)

5. a. $\theta = 40° + \dfrac{1}{4} \arccos \dfrac{1}{10}(y + 3)$

 b. $= 30°47', 49°13', 120°47'$ **c.** (Graph)

7. a. $x = -0.7 + \dfrac{2}{\pi} \arcsin \dfrac{1}{5}(y - 1)$

 b. $x = 0.710, 3.890, 4.710$ **c.** (Graph)

9. a. $x = -0.2 + \dfrac{1}{\pi} \arccos \dfrac{1}{3}(y - 1)$

 b. $\emptyset$ **c.** (Graph) **11. a.** $x = 0.6 +$

$\dfrac{4}{\pi} \arctan 2(y - 2)$ **b. i.** $x = 1.6$

 ii. $x \approx 2.912$ **c.** (Graph)

Exercise 13-11, Inverse Circular Relations as Mathematical Models

1. $t \approx 5.32$ sec.   **3.** between about 2.7 and 4.8 minutes   **5.** 17.85 in. and

55.55 in.   **7. a.** $d = 550 + 450 \cos \dfrac{\pi}{50}t$

b. $t = \dfrac{50}{\pi} \arccos \dfrac{d - 550}{450}$ **c.** 39.18, 60.82, and 139.18 minutes. **d.** 60.82 min.

9. a. $y = 100 + 150 \cos \dfrac{\pi}{700}(x - 512.6)$

b. $x = 512.6 + \dfrac{700}{\pi} \arccos \dfrac{y - 100}{150}$

c. 1025.2 meters long **d.** 374.8 meters long. **e.** Tunnel length = 950.6 m Bridge length = 449.4 m   **11. a. b.** The t-intercepts are the times of sunrise and sunset. **c.** The portion of the graph below the t-axis indicates *negative* angles of elevation (sometimes called "angles of depression") at which you could "look" *down* through the earth to see the sun on the other side of the world when it is nighttime where you are.

d. $\therefore E = -5 + 60 \cos \dfrac{\pi}{12}(t - 12.75)$

i. 34° **ii.** 49° **e.** At $t = 18.42$, the sun is setting. At t = 7.08, the sun is rising. 7.08 hr. = 7 hr., 5 min. ∴ Time of sunrise is 7:05 a.m. (7.04 by calculator) **f.** Instead of C being a constant in $E = C + A \cos B(t - D)$, make C vary sinusoidally with time. The period would be 365 days (or 365.24 days), amplitude 23°27' (the tilt of the earth to the ecliptic plane), and the phase displacement 172 days (to June 21).

13-12, Chapter Review

R1. (Graphs) **R2.** (Graphs) **R3. a.** $\dfrac{\sqrt{3}}{2}$

b. $\dfrac{\sqrt{2}}{2}$ **c.** $\dfrac{\sqrt{3}}{3}$ **d.** -1 **e.** $-\sqrt{2}$

f. undefined **g.** 3 **h.** -1 **R4. a.** 0.8415 **b.** 1.154 **c.** -1.887 **d.** 0.0008 **e.** 10.89 **f.** 1.701 **g.** 17.46° **h.** 0.4510 **i.** 1.307 **j.** 88.85° **k.** 85.66° **l.** 1.571 **R5.** (Graphs) **R6.** (Graphs) **R7. a.** $\therefore y = -10 + 35 \cos 9(\theta - 3°)$

b. $\therefore y = 17 + 2 \cos \dfrac{\pi}{50}(x + 15)$

R8. a. (Graph)

b. $y = -600 + 400 \cos \dfrac{\pi}{5}(t - 9)$

c. $y = -276.4$ m at $t = 0$, not safe

R9. a. (Graph) **b. i.** $\dfrac{\pi}{6}$ **ii.** $\{180° + 360°n\}$

iii. 0.3134 **iv.** $\{\pm45° + 360°n\}$ **v.** x does not exist **vi.** $\{135° + 180°n\}$ **c.** 2.472 **d.** $67°$

R10. a. $\theta = \dfrac{\cos^{-1}\left(\dfrac{y - 5}{4}\right)}{3} + 77;$

$\theta = \{17°, 137°, 257°\}$

b. $x = \dfrac{4\tan^{-1}\left(\dfrac{y - 6}{2}\right)}{\pi} + 3; x = \{1.484,$

$9.484, 17.484\}$ **R11.** $t = 0.1503$ and $t = 7.850$

CHAPTER 14 PROPERTIES OF TRIGONOMETRIC AND CIRCULAR FUNCTIONS

Exercise 14-1, Three Properties of Trigonometric Functions

1. $\cos x \dfrac{\sin x}{\cos x}$ **3.** $\sec x \dfrac{\cos x}{\sin x} \sin x =$

$\sec x \cos x$ **7.** $\dfrac{\sin A}{\cos A} + \dfrac{\cos A}{\sin A} =$

$\dfrac{\sin^2 A + \cos^2 A}{\cos A \sin A} = \dfrac{1}{\cos A \sin A} =$

$\sec A \csc A$ **9.** $\dfrac{1}{\sin x} - \sin x =$

$\dfrac{1 - \sin^2 x}{\sin x} = \dfrac{\cos^2 x}{\sin x} = \dfrac{\cos x}{\sin x} \cos x$

11. $\tan x \sin x + \tan x \cot x \cos x =$

$\dfrac{\sin x}{\cos x} \sin x + 1 \cdot \cos x = \dfrac{\sin^2 x}{\cos x} + \cos x =$

$\dfrac{\sin^2 x + \cos^2 x}{\cos x} = \dfrac{1}{\cos x}$ **13.** $1 - \sin^2 B$

15. $\cos^2 \theta - 2 \cos \theta \sin \theta + \sin^2 \theta$

17. $\tan^2 n + 2 \tan n \cot n + \cot^2 n =$

$\sec^2 n - 1 + 2 + \csc^2 n - 1$

19. $\dfrac{\cot^2 x}{\cos x} = \cot x \cot x \dfrac{1}{\cos x} =$

$\cot x \dfrac{\cos x}{\sin x \cos x} = \cot x \dfrac{1}{\sin x}$

21. $\dfrac{\tan^2 \theta}{\sin \theta} = \tan \theta \tan \theta \dfrac{1}{\sin \theta} =$

$\tan \theta \dfrac{\sin \theta}{\cos \theta \sin \theta} \dfrac{1}{}$

23. $\dfrac{\sec A \cos A - \sin^2 A}{\sin A \cos A} =$

$\dfrac{1 - \sin^2 A}{\sin A \cos A} = \dfrac{\cos^2 A}{\sin A \cos A} = \dfrac{\cos A}{\sin A}$

25. $\dfrac{1 + \cos C + 1 - \cos C}{(1 - \cos C)(1 + \cos C)} =$

$\dfrac{2}{1 - \cos^2 C} = \dfrac{2}{\sin^2 C}$

27. $\sin x \csc x, \cos x \sec x, \tan x \cot x,$

$\cos^2 x + \sin^2 x, \csc^2 x - \cot^2 x,$ and

$\sec^2 x - \tan^2 x.$

29. $\sin x = \sin x$

$\cos x = \pm\sqrt{1 - \sin^2 x}$

$\tan x = \pm\dfrac{\sin x}{\sqrt{1 - \sin^2 x}}$

$\cot x = \pm\dfrac{\sqrt{1 - \sin^2 x}}{\sin x}$

$\sec x = \pm\dfrac{1}{\sqrt{1 - \sin^2 x}}$

$\csc x = \dfrac{1}{\sin x}$

Exercise 14-2, Trigonometric Identities

1. $\sec^2 x - \sec x \cos x = \sec^2 x - 1$

3. $\sin x \csc x - \sin^2 x = 1 - \sin^2 x$

5. $\csc^2 \theta(1 - \cos^2 \theta) = \csc^2 \theta \sin^2 \theta$

7. $\sec^2 \theta - 1$ **9.** $\sec^2 A(1 + \tan^2 A) =$

$\sec^2 A(\sec^2 A)$ **11.** $(\cos^2 t + \sin^2 t) \cdot$

$(\cos^2 t - \sin^2 t) = 1 \cdot (1 - \sin^2 t - \sin^2 t)$

13. $\dfrac{1 - \cos^2 x}{\sin x \cos x} = \dfrac{\sin^2 x}{\sin x \cos x} = \dfrac{\sin x}{\cos x}$

15. $\sin^2 x + \cos^2 x$ **17.** $\dfrac{1}{1 + \cos s} \cdot$

$\dfrac{1 - \cos s}{1 - \cos s} = \dfrac{1 - \cos s}{1 - \cos^2 s} = \dfrac{1 - \cos s}{\sin^2 s} =$

$\csc^2 s(1 - \cos s) = \csc^2 s - \csc^2 s \cos s =$

$\csc^2 s - \csc s \dfrac{1}{\sin s} \cos s$ **19.** $\dfrac{\cos x}{\sec x - 1} \cdot$

$\dfrac{\sec x + 1}{\sec x + 1} = \dfrac{\cos x}{\tan^2 x} = \dfrac{1 + \cos x}{\tan^2 x} - \dfrac{\cos x}{\tan^2 x}$

21. $\dfrac{\sec x}{\sec x - \tan x} \cdot \dfrac{\sec x + \tan x}{\sec x + \tan x} =$

$\dfrac{\sec^2 x + \sec x \tan x}{\sec^2 x - \tan^2 x} = \dfrac{\sec^2 x + \sec x \tan x}{1}$

23. $\sin^3 z(1 - \sin^2 z)$ **25.** $\dfrac{1}{\cos^2 \theta} + \dfrac{1}{\sin^2 \theta} =$

$\dfrac{\sin^2 \theta + \cos^2 \theta}{\cos^2 \theta \sin^2 \theta} = \dfrac{1}{\cos^2 \theta \sin^2 \theta}$

27. $\dfrac{(1 + \cos x)(1 - 4 \cos x)}{1 - \cos^2 x} =$

$\dfrac{(1 + \cos x)(1 - 4 \cos x)}{(1 + \cos x)(1 - \cos x)}$

29. $\dfrac{(\sin A + \cos A)(\sin^2 A - \sin A \cos A + \cos^2 A)}{\sin A + \cos A}$

31. $(\csc^2 x - \cot^2 x)(\csc^4 x + \csc^2 x \cot^2 x + \cot^4 x) = 1(\csc^2 x (1 + \cot^2 x) + \csc^2 x \cot^2 + \cot^2 x (\csc^2 x - 1)) = \csc^2 x + \csc^2 x \cot^2 x + \csc^2 x \cot^2 x + \cot^2 x \csc^2 x - \cot^2 x = (\csc^2 x - \cot^2 x) + 3 \csc^2 x \cot^2 x$

33. $\dfrac{1 + \sin x + \cos x}{1 + \sin x - \cos x} \cdot \dfrac{\sin x}{\sin x}$

$= \dfrac{\sin x + \sin^2 x + \sin x \cos x}{(1 + \sin x - \cos x) \sin x}$

$= \dfrac{\sin x + 1 - \cos^2 x + \sin x \cos x}{(1 + \sin x - \cos x) \sin x}$

$= \dfrac{\sin x(1 + \cos x) + (1 + \cos x)(+ 1 - \cos x)}{(1 + \sin x - \cos x) \sin x}$

$= \dfrac{(1 + \cos x)(\sin x + 1 - \cos x)}{(1 + \sin x - \cos x) \sin x}$

35. a–c. (Graphs)
d. Observe that the graph of $y = \sec^2 x$ is the same as that of $y = \tan^2 x$, but raised up by 1 unit.

Exercise 14-3, Properties Involving Functions of More Than One Argument

1. $\dfrac{1}{2} \neq -\dfrac{\sqrt{3}}{2}$.   **3.** $-\dfrac{\sqrt{3}}{3} \neq$ undefined

5. $-\dfrac{2}{\sqrt{3}} \neq$ undefined   **7. a.** $\dfrac{\sqrt{3}}{2}$.   **b.** 0.

9. a. $\dfrac{1}{2}$ **b.** 1   **11. a.** $\dfrac{\sqrt{3}}{3}$ **b.** undefined

13. $\cos x \cos 90° + \sin x \sin 90° =$

$\cos x \cdot 0 + \sin x \cdot 1$ **15.** $\dfrac{\sin\left(x - \dfrac{\pi}{2}\right)}{\cos\left(x - \dfrac{\pi}{2}\right)} =$

$\dfrac{-\cos x}{\sin x}$

17. a–b. (Graphs) **c.** Graphs are the same.   **19.** $\cos(x - 180°) = \cos x \cos 180° + \sin x \sin 180° = \cos x(-1) + \sin x(0) = -\cos x$.

21. $\dfrac{-4\sqrt{3} - 3}{10}$ **23.** $\dfrac{-4 - 3\sqrt{3}}{10}$

25. $\dfrac{25\sqrt{3} - 48}{39}$ **27.** $\dfrac{\sqrt{6} + \sqrt{2}}{4}$

29. $2 - \sqrt{3}$ **31.** $\sqrt{6} - \sqrt{2}$

33. $\dfrac{1}{4}(\sqrt{6} + \sqrt{2})$.   **35.** $2 - \sqrt{3}$

37. $\sqrt{6} - \sqrt{2}$.   **39.** ≈ 0.9659258263

41. ≈ 0.2679491924 **43.** 1.035276180

45. $\sin x \cos 60° + \cos x \sin 60° - \cos x$

$\cos 30° + \sin x \sin 30° = \dfrac{1}{2} \sin x +$

$\dfrac{\sqrt{3}}{2} \cos x - \dfrac{\sqrt{3}}{2} \cos x + \dfrac{1}{2} \sin x$

47. $\dfrac{\sin(x + \pi/4)}{\cos(x + \pi/4)} + 1 = \left(\sin x \cos \dfrac{\pi}{4} + \right.$

$\left. \cos x \sin \dfrac{\pi}{4} + \cos x \cos \dfrac{\pi}{4} - \sin x \sin \dfrac{\pi}{4}\right)$.

$= \left(\dfrac{\sqrt{2}}{2} \sin x + \dfrac{\sqrt{2}}{2} \cos x + \dfrac{\sqrt{2}}{2} \cos \right.$

$\left. x - \dfrac{\sqrt{2}}{2} \sin x\right) \cdot \sec \left(x + \dfrac{\pi}{4}\right)$

49. $\cos^2(A + B) + \sin^2(A + B)$
51. $\cos A \cos B \cos C - \sin A \sin B \cos C - \sin A \cos B \sin C - \cos A \sin B \sin C$.

53. $2 \sin A \cos A$.   **55.** $\dfrac{2 \tan A}{1 - \tan^2 A}$

Exercise 14-4, Multiple Argument Properties

1. a–b. (Graphs) **c.** In cos 2x, the "2" affects the *period*. In 2 cos x, the "2" is the *amplitude*. **3.** $2 \sin 30° \cos 30° = 2 \cdot \dfrac{1}{2} \cdot \dfrac{\sqrt{3}}{2} = \dfrac{\sqrt{3}}{2}$ **5.** $\cos^2 \dfrac{\pi}{4} - \sin^2 \dfrac{\pi}{4} = \dfrac{1}{2} - \dfrac{1}{2} = 0$ **7.** $\dfrac{2 \tan 60°}{1 - \tan^2 60°} = \dfrac{2\sqrt{3}}{1 - 3} = -\sqrt{3}$

9. $\sin 2A = \dfrac{24}{25}$.

$\cos 2A = \dfrac{7}{25}$.

$\tan 2A = \dfrac{24}{7}$.

11. $\sin 2A = \dfrac{-24}{25}$.

$\cos 2A = \dfrac{7}{25}$.

$\tan 2A = \dfrac{-24}{7}$.

13. $2 \sin x \cos x = 2 \sin x \cos x$
$\dfrac{\cos x}{\cos x} = 2 \tan x \cos^2 x = \dfrac{2 \tan x}{\sec^2 x}$
15. $\dfrac{1 - \tan^2 \theta}{\sec^2 \theta} = \dfrac{1}{\sec^2 \theta} - \dfrac{\tan^2 \theta}{\sec^2 \theta} = \cos^2 \theta - \sin^2 \theta$ **17.** $\dfrac{\cos^2 D - \sin^2 D}{\cos D - \sin D} = \dfrac{(\cos D + \sin D)(\cos D - \sin D)}{\cos D - \sin D}$
19. $\dfrac{1 - (1 - 2 \sin^2 r)}{2 \sin r \cos r} = \dfrac{2 \sin^2 r}{2 \sin r \cos r} = \dfrac{\sin r}{\cos r}$ **21.** $\frac{1}{2}(1 - (1 - 2 \sin^2 \theta)) = \frac{1}{2}(2 \sin^2 \theta)$ **23.** $3 \sin x - 4 \sin^3 x$ **25.** $8 \cos^4 x - 8 \cos^2 x + 1$. **27.** $\dfrac{2 \tan 7x}{1 - \tan^2 7x}$
29. $\cos^2 3x - \sin^2 3x$ **31.** $2 \cos^2 5x - 1$
33. $2 \cos^2 \frac{1}{2}x - 1$ **35.** $\cos \frac{1}{2}x = \pm \sqrt{\frac{1}{2}(1 + \cos x)}$ **37.** Let $y = \text{Csc}^{-1} x$. Then $x = \csc y$ and $y \in [\frac{-\pi}{2}, \frac{\pi}{2}] - \{0\}$ $x = \sec (\frac{\pi}{2} - y)$ by the cofunction property. $\therefore \frac{\pi}{2} - y = \sec^{-1} x$ by the definition of $\sec^{-1}$. Since $-\frac{\pi}{2} \le y \le \frac{\pi}{2}$, it follows that $0 \le \frac{\pi}{2} - y \le \frac{\pi}{2}$, which is the range of the Sec^{-1} *function*. $\therefore \frac{\pi}{2} - y = \text{Sec}^{-1} x$, from which $y = \frac{\pi}{2} - \text{Sec}^{-1} x$, Q.E.D **39.** Let

$y = \text{Arctan } x$. Then $x = \tan y$ and $y \in (-\frac{\pi}{2}, \frac{\pi}{2})$. $\therefore \frac{1}{x} = \cot y$ by the reciprocal properties. $\therefore y = \text{arccot } \frac{1}{x}$ by the definition of arccot. But the range of the Arccot function is $(0, \pi)$. $\therefore \text{Arctan } x = \text{Arccot } \frac{1}{x}$ in the interval $(-\frac{\pi}{2}, \frac{\pi}{2}) \cap (0, \pi)$, which equals $(0, \frac{\pi}{2})$. This interval corresponds to *positive* values of x only. **41.** $\dfrac{-7}{25}$ **43.** $\dfrac{4\sqrt{2}}{9}$ **45.** $\dfrac{-5}{12}$ **47.** $\dfrac{\sqrt{2}}{2}$ **49.** $\dfrac{11}{13}$ **51.** $\dfrac{1}{1000}$ **53.** $\dfrac{1}{4}$

Exercise 14-5, Half-Argument Properties

1. a–b. (Graphs) **c.** In $\cos \frac{1}{2}x$, the "$\frac{1}{2}$" affects the *period*. In $\frac{1}{2} \cos x$, the "$\frac{1}{2}$" is the *amplitude*.

3. a–b. (Graphs) **c.** $y = \frac{1}{2} + \frac{1}{2} \cos 2x$ **d.** $\cos^2 x = \frac{1}{2}(1 + \cos 2x)$ **5.** $\dfrac{\sqrt{3}}{2}$ **7.** $\dfrac{\sqrt{2}}{2}$ **9.** $\sqrt{3}$ **11.** $-\dfrac{\sqrt{3}}{2}$ **13.** $-\dfrac{1}{2}$

15. $\sin \frac{1}{2}x = \dfrac{\sqrt{5}}{5}$; $\cos \frac{1}{2}x = \dfrac{2\sqrt{5}}{5}$ $\tan \frac{1}{2}x = \dfrac{1}{2}$ **17.** $\sin \frac{1}{2}x = \dfrac{2\sqrt{5}}{5}$; $\cos \frac{1}{2}x = \dfrac{-\sqrt{5}}{5}$; $\tan \frac{1}{2}x = -2$

19. $\sin \frac{1}{2}x = \dfrac{-\sqrt{5}}{5}$; $\cos \frac{1}{2}x = \dfrac{2\sqrt{5}}{5}$; $\tan \frac{1}{2}x = -\dfrac{1}{2}$ **21.** $\dfrac{1 - \cos x}{\sin x} + \dfrac{1 + \cos x}{\sin x} = \dfrac{2}{\sin x}$ **23.** $\dfrac{2 \tan \frac{1}{2}x}{\sec^2 \frac{1}{2}x} = 2 \cdot \dfrac{\sec \frac{1}{2}x}{\csc \frac{1}{2}x} \cdot \dfrac{1}{\sec^2 \frac{1}{2}x} = 2 \sin \frac{1}{2}x \cos \frac{1}{2}x$

25. $\dfrac{\cos \frac{1}{2}\theta - \sin \frac{1}{2}\theta}{\cos \frac{1}{2}\theta + \sin \frac{1}{2}\theta} \cdot \dfrac{\cos \frac{1}{2}\theta + \sin \frac{1}{2}\theta}{\cos \frac{1}{2}\theta + \sin \frac{1}{2}\theta} = \dfrac{\cos^2 \frac{1}{2}\theta - \sin^2 \frac{1}{2}\theta}{\cos^2 \frac{1}{2}\theta + 2 \cos \frac{1}{2}\theta \sin \frac{1}{2}\theta + \sin^2 \frac{1}{2}\theta}$

27. $\dfrac{1 - \cos A}{\sin A} = \dfrac{1}{\sin A} - \dfrac{\cos A}{\sin A}$ **29.** tan

$\dfrac{1}{2}x = \dfrac{\pm \sin x}{1 + \cos x}$. For $x \in (0, \pi)$, $\dfrac{1}{2}x \in$

$(0, \pi/2)$, so $\tan \dfrac{1}{2}x$ and $\sin x$ are both *positive*, and "+" should be used. For $x \in$

$(\pi, 2\pi)$, $\dfrac{1}{2}x \in (\dfrac{\pi}{2}, \pi)$, and so $\tan \dfrac{1}{2}x$ and

$\sin x$ are both *negative*. Since $\tan \dfrac{1}{2}x$ and $\sin$

x have the *same* sign, the "+" must be used again to avoid a double negative. Similarly, for $x \in (2\pi, 3\pi)$ and for $x \in (3\pi, 4\pi)$, $\sin x$

and $\tan \dfrac{1}{2}x$ have the *same* sign. So the "+"

must always be used. Note that $1 + \cos x$ is

never negative, so the sign of $\tan \dfrac{1}{2}x$ will

come out the same as that of $\sin x$.
31. a. $\sin (A + B) + \sin (A - B) = 2 \sin$
$A \cos B$. **b.** $\sin (A + B) - \sin (A - B) =$
$2 \cos A \sin B$.   **33. a.** $\sin 72° = 2 \sin 36°$
$\cos 36°$. **b.** $\sin 72° = 2(2 \sin 18° \cos 18°)$
$(1 - 2 \sin^2 18°)$. **c.** $8 \sin^3 18° - 4 \sin$

$18° + 1 = 0$. **d.** $x = \dfrac{-1 \pm \sqrt{5}}{4}$.

e. $\dfrac{\sqrt{5} - 1}{4}$. The pattern *cannot* be general-

ized to $\sin (\pi/d) = (\sqrt{n} - \sqrt{n - 4})/4$.

Exercise 14-6, Sum and Product Properties

1. $\sin 65° + \sin 17°$ **3.** $\cos 102° + \cos 4°$
5. $\sin 7.9 + \sin 0.3$ **7.** $-\cos 11.8 + \cos$
2.6 **9.** $\sin 8x - \sin 2x$ **11.** $\cos$
$11x + \cos 3x$ **13.** $2 \cos 29° \cos 17°$
15. $2 \sin 38° \cos 16°$ **17.** $2 \sin 3.4 \sin 1.0$
19. $-2 \cos 4 \cos 2$ **21.** $2 \sin 6x \cos 3x$
23. $2 \sin 9x \sin x$ **25.** $-2 \sin 3x \sin$
$(-2x) = 2 \sin 3x \sin 2x = 2 \sin 3x (2 \sin x$

$\cos x)$ **27.** $\dfrac{2 \sin 2x \cos x}{2 \cos 2x \sin x} =$

$\dfrac{4 \sin x \cos^2 x}{2 \cos 2x \sin x}$ **29.** $\sin 2x + (\sin x + \sin 3x)$

$= \sin 2x + 2 \sin 2x \cos x$

31. $\dfrac{\sin \dfrac{1}{2}x + \sin \dfrac{3}{2}x}{2 \sin \dfrac{1}{2}x} = \dfrac{2 \sin x \cos \dfrac{1}{2}x}{2 \sin \dfrac{1}{2}x}$

$= \sin x \cot \dfrac{1}{2}x = \sin x \dfrac{1 + \cos x}{\sin x}$

33. $\dfrac{1}{2}[-\cos (x + y + x - y) + \cos (x + y -$

$x + y)] = \dfrac{1}{2}(-\cos 2x + \cos 2y) =$

$\dfrac{1}{2}(-1 + 2 \sin^2 x + 1 - 2 \sin^2 y)$

35. $\dfrac{1}{2}(\cos 2x + \cos 2y) = \dfrac{1}{2}(2 \cos^2 x - 1 +$

$1 - 2 \sin^2 y)$

Exercise 14-7, Linear Combination of Cosine and Sine with Equal Arguments

1. a. $2 \cos (x - 60°)$ **b.** $2 \cos (x - \dfrac{\pi}{3})$
3. a. $5\sqrt{2} \cos (x + 45°)$ **b.** $5\sqrt{2} \cos$
$(x + \pi/4)$ **5. a.** $13 \cos (x - 157° 23')$
b. $13 \cos (x - 2.747)$ **7. a.** $17 \cos$
$(3x - 208° 04')$ **b.** $17 \cos (3x - 3.632)$
9. a. $4 \cos (x - 15°)$ **b.** $4 \cos$
$(x - 0.2618)$

15. $5 \cos\left(x - \text{Arctan } \dfrac{4}{3}\right)$

17. $\sqrt{61} \cos\left(x - \text{Arctan } \dfrac{6}{5}\right)$

19. $\cos\left(x + \text{Arctan } \dfrac{4}{3}\right)$

21. $-2\sqrt{5} \cos\left(x - \text{Arctan } \dfrac{1}{2}\right)$

23. $-\sqrt{53} \cos\left(x + \text{Arctan } \dfrac{7}{2}\right)$

Exercise 14-8, Simplification of Trigonometric Expressions

1. $2 \sin x \cos x$ **3.** $1 - \cos^2 x$

5. $\dfrac{1}{2}(1 + \cos 2x)$ **7.** $1 - 2 \sin^2 x$

9. $\dfrac{2 \tan x}{1 - \tan^2 x}$ **11.** $\pm\sqrt{\dfrac{1}{2}(1 + \cos x)}$

13. $\dfrac{\sin x}{1 + \cos x}$ **15.** $2 \cos^2 2x - 1$

17. $\dfrac{1}{2} \sin 2x$ **19.** $\dfrac{1}{2} \cos (x + y) + \dfrac{1}{2} \cos$

$(x - y)$ **21.** $2 \sin \dfrac{1}{2}(x + y) \cos \dfrac{1}{2}(x - y)$

23. $-\dfrac{1}{2} \cos 10x + \dfrac{1}{2} \cos 4x$ **25.** $2 \cos$

$(x + 30°)$ **27. a.** $\cos x \cos 37° + \sin x$
$\sin 37°$ **b.** $\cos x \cos y \cos z - \sin x \sin y$

$\cos z - \sin x \cos y \sin z - \cos x \sin y \sin z$

c. $\cos 3x = 4 \cos^3 x - 3 \cos x$

29. a. $\frac{1}{2} \sin 2x$ **b.** $\frac{1}{2}(1 + \cos 2x)$

c. $\frac{1}{4} \sin 3x + \frac{1}{4} \sin x$ **d.** $\frac{3}{8} - \frac{1}{2} \cos 2x + \frac{1}{8}$

$\cos 4x$. **31. a.** $2 \cos 2x \sin x$ **b.** $\cos$

$2x = 0$ or $\sin x = 0$. **c.** $x = 0° + 360n°$,

$180° + 360n°$. **d.** $x = 0° + 360n°$,

$180° + 360n°$. **e.** $[45°, 135°, 225°, 315°,$

$0°, 180°]$

Exercise 14-9, Trigonometric Equations

1. $\{120°, 300°\}$ **3.** $\{103°, 343°\}$ **5.** $\{60°,$

$-60°, 120°, -120°\}$ **7.** $\{90° + 180n°,$

$45° + 360n°, 135° + 360n°\}$ **9.** $\left\{\frac{2\pi}{3} + \pi n\right\}$

11. $\{0°, -30°, -150°\}$ **13.** $\left\{\frac{\pi}{3}, \frac{5\pi}{3}\right\}$

15. $\emptyset$ **17.** $\left\{\frac{\pi}{3}, -\frac{\pi}{3}, -\pi\right\}$ **19.** $\{-90°,$

$0°\}$ **21.** $\left\{\frac{\pi}{6}, \frac{7\pi}{6}, \frac{\pi}{3}, \frac{4\pi}{3}\right\}$ **23.** $\{150°,$

$-30°, -210°\}$ **25.** $\{178°, 358°, 28°, 208°\}$

27. $\{15°, 75°, -45°\}$ **29.** $\left\{22\frac{1}{2}°, -67\frac{1}{2}°,\right.$

$\left.-22\frac{1}{2}°, 67\frac{1}{2}°\right\}$ **31.** $\left\{2\pi, \frac{4\pi}{3}\right\}$ **33.** $\{16°,$

$34°, 52°, 70°, 88°\}$ **35.** $\left\{0, 2\pi, 4\pi, \frac{3\pi}{2},\right.$

$\left.\frac{7\pi}{2}\right\}$ **37.** $\{30°, -150°, -30°, 150°\}$

39. $\{$real numbers$\}$ **41.** $\{30° 58', 210°$

$58', 135°, 315°\}$ **43.** $\{25° 20', 228° 24'\}$

45. $\{0, 3.1416, 0.3398, 2.8018\}$

47. $\{0.6662, 2.475\}$ **49.** $\{5.435, 3.990\}$

51. $\{40°, 220°, 160°, 340°\}$ **53.** $\{2.150\}$

14-10, page 0, Chapter Review

R1. a. $\frac{1}{\cos x}\left(\frac{\cos x}{\sin x}\right) = \frac{1}{\sin x} = \csc x$

b. $1 + 2\tan A + \tan^2 A = 2\tan A +$

$1 + \tan^2 A = 2\tan A + \sec^2 A$

c. $\frac{1 + \sin A - (1 - \sin A)}{(1 - \sin A)(1 + \sin A)} = \frac{2\sin A}{1 - \sin^2 A} =$

$\frac{2\sin A}{\cos^2 A} = 2\frac{1}{\cos A}\left(\frac{\sin A}{\cos A}\right) = 2\sec A \tan A$

R2. a. $(\tan B + 1)(\tan B - 1)$

$= \tan^2 B - 1$ Distributive axiom (twice)

$= \sec^2 B - 1 - 1$ Pythagorean property

$= \sec^2 B - 2$ Additive identity and definition of subtraction

b. $\sin^4 p \sec^2 p + \sin^2 p$

$= \sin^2 p (\sin^2 p \sec^2 p + 1)$ Distributivity

$= \sin^2 p \left(\frac{\sin^2 p}{\cos^2 p} + 1\right)$ Reciprocal property

$= \sin^2 p (\sec^2 p)$ Pythagorean property

$= \frac{\sin^2 p}{\cos^2 p}$ Reciprocal property

$= \tan^2 p$ Quotient property

$\therefore \sin^4 p \sec^2 p + \sin^2 p$

$= \tan^2 p$ Transitivity

R3. a. $\tan(A + H) = \frac{\tan A + \tan H}{1 - \tan A \tan H}$

b. 0.631 **c.** -0.5542 **d.** $\frac{\sqrt{2 - \sqrt{3}}}{2}$

e. $\sin(\theta - 30) + \cos(\theta + 60) =$

$\sin \theta \cos 30 + \sin 30 \cos \theta +$

$\cos \theta \cos 60 - \sin \theta \sin 60$

Composite Argument prop

$= \frac{\sqrt{3}}{2} \sin \theta - \frac{1}{2} \cos \theta + \frac{1}{2} \cos \theta -$

$\frac{\sqrt{3}}{2} \sin \theta$ Substitution

$= 0$ Combine like terms

$\therefore \sin(\theta - 30) + \cos(\theta + 60) =$

0 Transitivity

f. $\tan(-x) = -\tan x$

R4. a. $\frac{1}{8}$ or 0.125 **b.** -3.429

c. $2 \cos^2 A = 2\left[\frac{1}{2}(1 + \cos 2A)\right]$

   Double argument prop.

$= 1 + \cos 2A$ Assoc and mult inverse

$\therefore 2 \cos^2 A = 1 + \cos 2A$ Transitivity

d. $\sin 6x = 2 \sin 3x \cos 3x$

R5. a. -0.3162 **b.** 0.3820 **c.** (Graph)

R6. a. $\sin 54° - \sin 20°$ **b.** $-2 \cos 7x \sin 2x$

c. $\cos x + \cos 3x$

$= 2 \cos 2x \cos(-x)$ Sum and product prop

$= 2 \cos 2x \cos x$ Odd-even prop

$= 2(\cos^2 x - \sin^2 x)\cos x$ Double angle prop

$= 2(2 \cos^2 x - 1) \cos x$ Pythagorean prop

$= 4 \cos^3 x - 2 \cos x$ Distributivity

$\therefore \cos x + \cos 3x$

$= 4 \cos^3 x - 2 \cos x$ Transitivity

R7. a. $25 \cos (\theta - 163.7°)$ **b.** (Graph)

R8. a. $\dfrac{\sec x}{\csc x}$ **b.** $1 - \cos^2 x$ **c.** $\sec x$

d. $\dfrac{\tan h + \tan v}{1 - \tan h \tan v}$ **e.** $2 \sin u \cos u$

f. $\pm \sqrt{\dfrac{1}{2}(1 + \cos u)}$ **g.** $\dfrac{1}{2} \sin (x + y) -$

$\dfrac{1}{2} \sin (x - y)$ **h.** $-2 \sin \dfrac{1}{2}(A + B)$

$\sin \dfrac{1}{2}(A - B)$ **i.** $\sqrt{74} \cos (x + 54.46°)$

R9. a. $\left\{ \dfrac{\pi}{2} \right\}$ **b.** $\{-18.5° + 90°n\}$

c. $\left\{ \pi + 2\pi n, \dfrac{\pi}{3} + 2\pi n \right\}$

CHAPTER 15 TRIANGLE PROBLEMS

Exercise 15-1, Right Triangle Problems

1. $a \approx 17.7$; $b \approx 9.92$; $m\angle C = 56°$
3. $l \approx 2.339$; $n \approx 2.556$; $m\angle L = 42°28'$
5. $m\angle Y \approx 50°29'$; $m\angle Z \approx 39°31'$;
$z \approx 22.27$ **7.** $m\angle R \approx 77°59'$;
$m\angle S \approx 12°01'$; $r \approx 46.3$ **9.** 6.0 m
11. 76° **13.** 142 m **15. a.** ≈ 191 km
b. 1°55' **17. a.** 35°20' **b.** 72 paces
19. a. 33.5 m **b.** 17.5 m **21. a.** 108 m,
280 m **b.** 2790 m **23. a.** 4°32' **b.** Slope
is assumed to be constant.

Exercise 15-2, Oblique Triangles—Law of Cosines

1. 3.978 **3.** 4.682 **5.** 49.20 **7.** 28°57'
9. 134°37' **11.** no such triangle **13.** 90°
15. (Graph)

Exercise 15-3, Area of a Triangle

1. 5.443 **3.** 6.1 **5.** 23.66 **7.** 23.66

Exercise 15-4, Oblique Triangles—Law of Sines

1. a. 5.229 **b.** 10.08 **3. a.** 249.9
b. 183.6 **5. a.** 9.321 **b.** 4.911
7. a. 214.7 **b.** 215.3 **9. a.** $33.122\ldots°$
b. $51.317\ldots°$ (apparently)
c. $128.682\ldots°$ (actually) **d.** $128.682\ldots°$
e. Knowing $\sin C = 0.78062\ldots$ does not
tell whether C is acute or obtuse. Knowing
$\cos C = -0.625$, a *negative* number, tells
that C is *obtuse*.

Exercise 15-5, The Ambiguous Case

1. 5.315 or 1.317 **3.** 7.79 **5.** no values
7. 5.52 **9.** 23.00° or 157.00°
11. 38.15° **13. a–c.** (Graphs)

Exercise 15-6, General Solution of Triangles

Note: The solutions presented here were obtained by the computer program of Problem 29. Answers to the selected exercises are underlined.

Case	a	b	c	A
1. SAS	3	4	4.177	42°59'
3. SAS	30	60	34.74	20°25'
5. SAS	100	210	266.0	20°12'
7. SSS	8	9	7	58°25'
9. SSS	3	6	4	26°23'
11. SSS	3	94		No such triangle
13. ASA	502.5	121.5	400	143°10'
15. ASA	15.78	36.76	50	11°30'
17. AAS	6	6.507	6.190	56°20'
19. SSA	7	5	11.15	25°50'
21. SSA	5	7	10.26	25°50'
or:	5	7	2.339	25°50'
23. SSA	5	7		126°40'
25. SSA	7	5	2.751	126°40'
27. SSA	3	5	4.000	36°52.19386'

	B	C	Area
1.	65°21'	71°40'	5.695
3.	135°45'	23°50'	363.7
5.	46°28'	113°20'	9641
7.	73°24'	48°11'	26.83
9.	117°17'	36°20'	5.333
13.	8°20'	28°30'	14567
15.	27°40'	140°50'	183.2
17.	64°30'	59°10'	16.76
19.	18°08'	136°02'	12.15
21.	37°36'	116°34'	15.65
	142°24'	11°45'	3.567

Problem Title Index